CHINA
GUIDE

BE A TRAVELER - NOT A TOURIST!

CRITICAL ACCLAIM FOR RUTH LOR MALLOY'S *CHINA GUIDE*
– *New, revised, 10th edition* –

"The most comprehensive and practical of the many recent books I've seen. An up-to-date, informative guide to China travel."

Loren Fessler, author of *China* and *Chinese in America*

"This hefty book is packed with facts, maps, and terrific tips on everything from accidents to earthquakes, toilets to tipping. (A) first-rate history of the awakening giant, Malloy answers most questions a novice traveler might have."

Paul King, *The Toronto Star*

"This guide may be the best once-over-lightly look at China ... it not only covers destinations, restaurants, hotels and shopping, but also gives you a passing acquaintance with useful aspects of Chinese culture."

Keith Graham, *The Atlanta Journal/The Atlanta Constitution*

"For my money, this is the best book on the market. "

Lorraine Williams, *The Budget Traveler*

"I use your guidebook as my sole reference when planning all different aspects of my tours to China (I lead several tours there each year). Your book has been a tremendous help to me and is the most readable and useful one out there, as far as I'm concerned."

Wendy Abraham, *Jewish Historical Tours of China*

ABOUT THE AUTHOR

Ruth Lor Malloy is a Canadian of Chinese ancestry. She has been a travel writer, conference organizer, social worker, freelance photographer, wife and mother, and author of guide books to China since 1975. Her guides have included *Fielding's People's Republic of China*, now an Open Road travel guide. She travels frequently to China for fun, and has lectured on Yangtze River cruise ships and to tour groups in China (IST and Concepts East).

She has also published a novel and, with her daughter Linda, is the author of Open Road Publishing's *Hong Kong & Macau Guide*. Her home is in Toronto, but she has recently been living in Kazakhstan and India.

She will be updating the information when available on her website: *http://webhome.idirect.com/~mmalloy*. There she can answer your questions, inform you of new bargains, and share reports of recent travelers. She will also tell you how you can get autographed copies of Open Road's *China Guide* and dates of tours she will be escorting to China.

BE A TRAVELER, NOT A TOURIST - WITH OPEN ROAD TRAVEL GUIDES!

Open Road Publishing has guide books to exciting, fun destinations on four continents. As veteran travelers, our goal is to bring you the best travel guides available anywhere!

No small task, but here's what we offer:

•All Open Road travel guides are written by authors with a distinct, opinionated point of view – not some sterile committee or team of writers. Our authors are experts in the areas covered and are polished writers.

•Our guides are geared to people who want to make their own travel choices. We'll show you how to discover the real destination – not just see some place from a tour bus window.

•We're strong on the basics, but we also provide terrific choices for those looking to get off the beaten path and experience the country or city – not just see it or pass through it.

•We give you the best, but we also tell you about the worst and what to avoid. Nobody should waste their time and money on their hard-earned vacation because of bad or inadequate travel advice.

•Our guides assume nothing. We tell you everything you need to know to have the trip of a lifetime – presented in a fun, literate, no-nonsense style.

•And, above all, we welcome your input, ideas, and suggestions to help us put out the best travel guides possible.

CHINA

GUIDE

BE A TRAVELER - NOT A TOURIST!

Ruth Lor Malloy

OPEN ROAD PUBLISHING

10th Edition

TABLE OF CONTENTS

CONTENTS

CONTENTS

CONTENTS

CONTENTS

CONTENTS

CONTENTS

MAPS

SIDEBARS

CONTENTS

CONTENTS

ACKNOWLEDGMENTS

Many people are responsible for this book: travelers who took the time to share their experiences and impressions, hotel managers who talked not just of their work but of the problems and joys of living in China, business travelers on airplanes, and fellow tourists in hotel elevators, Yangtze cruise ships, and trains.

I am particularly grateful to those who traveled with me on Concepts East and IST tours, whose reactions I could get immediately, and who helped decide by their comments, the restaurants to include and the warnings to make. Particularly valuable was the companionship of Joan Ahrens on a trip we did together. Her knowledge of gems, antiques and curios kept opening my eyes to the bargains and the scams. Then there was Joan Annis with another equally helpful perspective, the visitor with roots in the country. Extremely valuable were the comments of national guides Ai Bin, Sun Shu-er, Sun Ying, Norman Zhang, and Tony Wang, and that of many other guides who volunteered information and advice.

A special thank-you goes to the China National Tourism Administration especially Wu Bo, the China Tourist Office in Toronto, the Hong Kong Tourist Association, provincial and local tourism bureaus and administrations. The hospitality of these organizations made gathering information such a pleasure in Beijing, Guangdong, Guizhou, Hainan, Heilongjiang, Hong Kong, Jiangsu, Jilin, Liaoning, Shandong (especially Xu Fei), Sichuan, and Shanghai.

Officials and travel agents were also generous with their hospitality, time and information in Changchun, Chengdu, Chongqing, Dalian, Fuzhou, Guangzhou, Guiyang, Haikou, Harbin, Huangguoshu Falls, Jilin, Jinan, Kaili, Nanjing, Qingdao, Qufu, Sanya, Shenzhen, Suzhou, Tai'an, Taishan, Weifang, Wuyi, Wuxi, Xiamen, Yangzhou, Zhuhai, and Zibo. Many others wrote long letters, and endured hours of questioning at the China International Travel Mart in Shanghai, and in their home turfs. You will see the names of their companies later in the book. I chose to mention them because they were helpful to me and I expect they will be useful to you.

For their help in making arrangements, I would like to thank Bonnie Chu of Bass Hotels & Resorts, Rita Goh and Annie Shum of Gloria International, Jerome de la Fuente of Hilton International, Karisa Lui of the Hong Kong Tourist Association, Daniella Wu of Hyatt International, Ricky Lam of Marriott, Ellen Levy and Marion Darby of Shangri-La International, John O'Shea of the Wuxi Sheraton, Lauren Kaufman of Spring O'Brien, and Stella Chan of Zenith Hotels. Thanks also to Guo Yimei of China Travel Service (Hong Kong), Steve Powers, the incomparable Michael Sun of the Guangzhou Tourist Corporation, John Ma of

Shandong Tourism Corporation, and many, many others. Among the travelers who have contributed much have been Margaret Duda, Kristin Fein, Norman Sklarewitz, Ted Stannard Jr., and Steve Steinberg. There was also Mialana Mak. Especially generous were the Orient Royal Cruises (East King), Victoria Cruises, and Regal China Cruises. Hotels whose help made the research possible were in **Beijing**: China World, Gloria Plaza, Great Wall Sheraton, Holiday Inn Lido, Holiday Inn Downtown, Jianguo, Movenpick, SAS Radisson, Shangri-La, Sheraton International Club, and Xiyuan; **Chengdu**: Holiday Inn Crowne Plaza, Yinhe Dynasty; **Chongqing**: Holiday Inn, Harbour Plaza, Dazu; **Dalian**: Gloria Plaza, Shangri-La; **Guangzhou**: Garden, China; **Guilin**: Royal Garden; **Harbin**: Shangri-La, Flamingo Hotel; **Hangzhou**: Shangri-La; **Hong Kong**: Century Hong Kong, Grand Hyatt, Great Eagle, Island Shangri-La, Kowloon Shangri-La, Renaissance Harbour View, The Peninsula, The Salisbury YMCA; **Macau**: Hyatt Regency; **Nanjing**: Holiday Inn, Hilton, Sheraton; **Qingdao**: Huiquan Dynasty Hotel; **Shanghai**: Crowne Plaza, Hilton, Holiday Inn Pudong, Novotel, Portman Ritz-Carlton, Pudong Shangri-La, Westin Tai Ping Yang, Yangtze New World; **Shenyang**: Gloria Plaza Hotel, Traders; **Shenzhen**: Shangri-La; **Suzhou**: Gloria Plaza, Sheraton; **Taishan**: Garden; **Tianjin**: Hyatt; **Wuhan**: Holiday Inns Tian An and Riverside; **Wuxi**: Milido, Courtyard by Marriott, Pan Pacific, and Sheraton; **Xi'an**: Bell Tower, Golden Flower, Grand New World, and Hyatt; **Zhuhai**: Grand Bay View Hotel and Guangdong Regency.

Thanks to travelers and China residents: Seona Baillie, S.J. Chan, Margaret Duda, Alison and Saul Lockhart, Hilda Looi, Laine and Ralph Loveland, Steve Takaos and Roz Gillund, Alison and Richard Wong, and Godfrey Wong.

My appreciation also goes to my editor Jonathan Stein for his guidance, patience, and support, and to Yue Chi of Concepts East for the opportunities she provided, her insights, and encouragement.

Most of all, this book would not have been possible without the cooperation of my family, especially my husband Michael Malloy and my daughter Linda, who along with Caroline Walker edited and proofread parts. Last and certainly not least, a note should be made of the contribution of Northwest Airlines, which provided complimentary transportation between Canada and China for me on two occasions so I could research this edition. They also gave me the information for the sidebar on page 93. To all go my thanks, and the thanks of our readers.

1. INTRODUCTION

China is a fascinating place, a historically and culturally rich country. A visit is an enrichening experience. In this 10th edition, I've updated this book to bring you the real China once again. I'll take you to all the great destinations you've heard so much about, plus hundreds more you may not know. I'll show you terrific hotels and guest houses, restaurants and temples, and recommend hundreds of fun and exciting things to do.

I'll take you along the length of the Great Wall, steer you to a fun camel ride along the romantic Silk Road, show you where to bicycle among the beautiful mountains of Guilin, guide you along China's great rivers and dramatic gorges. I'll take you strolling through the backstreets and alleys of Beijing, Shanghai, and Kunming, and steer you to my favorite birdwatching spots. For sheer beauty, China is hard to beat. It has some of the world's most spectacular and little known natural scenery.

In Beijing, wander the Forbidden City and marvel at the majestic Summer Palace and the intriguing Temple of Heaven. What did it all mean? In Shanghai, stroll along the Bund and ride the ancient stand-up ferry to Pudong. In Xi'an, take in the incredible terracotta army (nearly 2,200 years old) and the magnificent city wall. And sleep in world-class hotels and dine on China's famous banquet food – where else can you get culinary delights shaped like phoenixes, swans, and rabbits?

You'll also find hundreds of pages of travel advice, trip planning ideas, and local customs and food. You'll get frank information about hotels and guides, detailed descriptions of where to go and what to do. There's special advice for business people and Overseas Chinese. You'll get important place names and food in both Chinese and English throughout this book and in our special glossary. I've even given leads on finding a job.

So go west – across the Pacific to China for the trip of a lifetime!

2. OVERVIEW

Yes, you must visit China. You've got to see what it has to offer. It's too big a country to ignore. It has the world's largest population and one of the oldest civilizations. It has had thousands of years to develop a variety of multi-splendored cultures, some so different you won't associate them with China.

For the sightseer, China has fantastic international-class attractions. There's something here for the history nut, the archaeology freak, and the nature lover. It has scenes of great beauty for the photographer, challenges for the adventurer, and places for the vacationer to relax. I hope you have the time and means.

Visit its ancient monuments, palaces, and tombs and temples. Raft its river gorges and climb its mountains. Hike through primitive forests, past varieties of trees once eaten by dinosaurs. Enjoy festivals of sweet and juicy *lichis* and dancing dragons; worship at smoky temples with burning incense and prostrating pilgrims. Meet China's different peoples, many of whose ornate embroidered hand-made costumes differ from village to village within the same tribe. Take photos of curved temple roofs silhouetted against golden red sunsets. Capture on film the misty look of mountain paintings seen on aged scrolls.

Shop or just enjoy looking at antiques, carved gilded beds, inlaid chests, porcelain, jades, cloisonne, carpets, cashmere and silk. Consider everything from up-to-date stainless steel cutlery to suitcases to gowns covered with beads and sequins. I'll show you how you can save half or more of the price you'd pay at home.

Sample China's great food with its endless variety and styles of cooking. It ranges from bland to fiery hot, chicken and prawns, camel humps and scorpions! I'll take away the mystery and teach you how to order - and how to eat the Chinese way.

See where people lived 6000 years ago, where they made pottery and buried their dead. Puff your way up the Great Wall that 2200 years ago was linked together for over 6000 kilometers, or meditate in China's classical gardens. Search for traces of foreign influence – Marco Polo, Jesuit missionaries, Jewish refugees, Muslim traders and Mongol invaders. I'll show you the development of Buddhist art.

Say "Wow!" at the camels, sand dunes, Siberian tigers, and the Chinese people who write in Arabic. Feel wonder at the functioning mountain-top monasteries, fighting *kung fu* monks, cities full of 19th-century European architecture, creepy tombs, and eerie caves. Get a tan on a beach or be pampered by China's growing number of international class resorts. Get treated with some Chinese herbal medicines, acupuncture or *qigong*. They just might work for you.

Discover terraced mountains, gothic cathedrals, pagodas, and 100 scarlet and gold-robed "monks" marching as one with lighted lanterns on their heads. Look for the world's highest mountains, jeep through the desert, hot-air balloon over the Yellow River. Gallop horses on China's prairies. Make friends with the hospitable natives.

Find out about one of the world's fastest growing economies, China's rite of passage as she resists yet tries to join the world community, as she moves from feudal thinking beyond communist quotas to free-market capitalism. See how the current Asian recession is affecting it. Look for surviving pockets of the primitive and exotic. Look for the soul of the great cities with their new modern buildings, palatial hotels, subways and superhighways. Relax at nightclubs, discos, karaoke bars and in jacuzzis, and enjoy the convenience of international direct-dial telephones, credit cards, cellular-phones, and fiber optics.

In **East China**, look for traces of the old maritime trade, the hybrid temples with fancy eaves, and the great adventurers who sailed to Africa, saved Taiwan from the Dutch, and fought the pirates. Look for the schools and hospitals, monuments built by successful migrants to Southeast Asia, and evidence of the Muslim traders and their mosques. Go to the silk cities with their museums, to the tranquil beauty of West Lake, and discover the legacy of the Song dynasty. Plan your trip to include a re-enactment of an emperor's ritual worship at the temple of Confucius.

Marvel at the huge kites in the kite museum or take in the annual kite festival in Weifang. And enjoy bustling Shanghai with its European architecture, its shopping and one of the best museums in the country.

Search for traces of Chiang Kai-shek and first president Sun Yat-sen in the Nationalist capital of Nanjing. Consider charming Yangzhou where Marco Polo was an official. Enjoy the old garden cities and Huangshan, the favorite of landscape mountain painters. Find the China of American author Pearl S. Buck and read her beautifully-written novels.

In **North China**, explore Beijing, the national capital, and marvel at the magnificence of the 15th-century Forbidden City palace. Walk where emperors and their families rode bicycles and played badminton. Go to

PEOPLE'S REPUBLIC OF CHINA

KAZAKHSTAN

MON

● Karamay

● Yining

Shihezi ●

KYRGYZSTAN

Urumqi ●

Turpan ●

● Kashi

X I N J I A N G

NORTHWEST CHINA

Dunhuang ●
Jiuquan ●

G A

AFG.

Q I N G H A I

PAK.

Golmud ●

Yello

T I B E T

Yangtze River

S I C H

○ New Delhi

Lhasa ●

NEPAL

Tingri ●

Xigaze ● ● Qonggyai

Mo

Kathmandu ○

BHUTAN

Dali ●

INDIA

Xiaguqn ●

BANGLADESH

○
Dacca

Y U N N A

MYANMAR
(BURMA)

Jinghong ●

Bay of Bengal

THAILAND

the Ming and Qing imperial tombs, summer palaces, and fly a kite in Tiananmen Square. Further north, see the great Yungang Cave Temple and the incredible Hanging Temple. Hike around the temples of Wutai Mountain and Chengde.

Follow the Great Wall by road from Badaling to the Bohai Sea and relax on the beach in Beidaihe. Hike or ride through the Mongolian grasslands with their vast vistas and horse herds.

If you can, visit the Great Wall at both ends and also in between for a better conception of its immense length and the centuries it still spans.

In **Northwest China**, follow Marco Polo from oasis to oasis along the Silk Road, thrill at the vibrant Sunday market and question the veiled women in the Uygur city of Kashi. Admire the Buddhist murals in Dunhuang's famous caves where the oldest existing printed book in the world was found. In Central China, bask in the refined culture of the Song dynasty in old Kaifeng, gasp at a martial arts display at the Shaolin Temple, and applaud the giant buddhas in the Longmen caves. Try to conceive of life in the Shang dynasty (16th to 11th century B.C.) when they made those incredible bronzes and sacrificed humans to the gods. And don't miss the Terracotta Warriors, the Tang and Han tombs, the temples, dance shows, and museums of Xi'an.

In **Northeast China**, ride behind one of the endangered steam locomotives and look for signs of Japanese and Russian occupation. Spy on great flocks of red-crested cranes and thrill at the sparkling ice sculpture festival. Follow in the footsteps of Puyi, the last emperor, his Manchurian palace and Communist prison.

In **South China**, pay your respects to a 2000-year old noblewoman and her beautiful lacquerware and silks, and inspect the ancestral home-land of many Chinese migrants to North America, Britain and Australia. Visit the hyper-active trading port of Guangzhou with its museums, pagodas, and family temples. Enjoy the miniatures of China's main tourist attractions and the theme park of China's minorities in Shenzhen. Cruise the lovely mountain-lined Li River in Guilin, visit minority villages, and botanical gardens.

In **Southwest China**, join a tour to visit Miao, Bouyei, Bai, Dong and Tibetan villages. Get water-splashed in the traditional way and look for former headhunters. Relax as dramatic scenery floats by on a Yangtze River cruise, and race a dragon boat in the hometown of its inspiration. Examine the fine sculptures of Buddha and ancient life in Dazu, trek in the forests of Jiuzhaigou, and look for endangered pandas in or outside of Chengdu. Climb sacred Emei Mountain or make a less stenuous visit to the great Buddha at Leshan. Find the dinosaurs and the equally giant lanterns. Go south and up to Tibet for one of the world's unique, isolated, and thriving cultures.

THE BEST OF CHINA

The Best...

Beach: *Yalong Bay, Hainan*
City walls: *Xi'an and Nanjing*
Cleanest cities: *Dalian, Xiamen, Weihai*
Confucian experience: *Qufu*
Cruises: *Yangtze Gorges and the Li River, Guilin*
Gardens *(Classical): Beijing, Suzhou, Hangzhou, Yangzhou*
Imperial palaces: *Forbidden City; Summer Palace (Beijing); Shenyang*
Imperial tombs: *Ming (Beijing), Qing (Zunhua) and Tang (Xi'an)*
Mosques: *Xi'an and Kashi*
Mountain for scenery: *Huangshan*
Mountain for climbing: *Qomolangma (Everest, in Tibet)*
Museums: *Beijing, Chengdu, Shanghai, Xi'an, Zhengzhou*
Museum *(dinosaurs): Zigong (Chengdu)*
Museum *(neolithic): Xi'an*
Museum *(kite): Weifang*
Nature Reserves: *Jiuzhaigou (Chengdu) and Zhangjiajie (see Changsha) for wilderness; Wolong near Chengdu for pandas; Bird Island near Xining, Poyang Lake near Jiujiang, and Qiqihar near Harbin for birds; Jing Hong for wild elephants; Wuhan for dolphins; Yichang for sturgeon; Hefei for alligators*
Panda-watching: Chengdu and Beijing
Shopping *(general, arts and crafts): Shanghai and Beijing*
Street markets for antiques: *Tianjin, Shanghai and Beijing; for silks in Hangzhou.*
Shopping for minority crafts: *Chengdu, Tibet, Yunnan, Guizhou.*
Temples *(Buddhist): Tibet, Suzhou, Hangzhou, Chengde, Beijing*
Temples *(caves): Dunhuang, Datong, Luoyang and then Dazu.*
Temple *(kung fu): Shaolin (Zhengzhou)*
Tomb figures: *Xi'an*

The Largest ...

Monument: *the Great Wall*
Statues: *Hong Kong (new), Macau (new), Wuxi (new), Leshan (ancient)*

The Most ...

Romantic cities: *Hangzhou, Suzhou, and Guilin*
Exotic experience: *Lhasa in March, minority festivals in Guizhou, Yunnan, Xinjiang.*
Important Buddhist sights: *Xi'an, Luoyang, and Dunhuang; the Sacred Mountains with many temples: Putuo Shan (Ningbo), Jiuhua Shan (Hefei), Wutai Shan (Datong), and Emei Shan*
Interesting small cities: *Chengde, Dali, Guilin, Kaifeng, Kashi, Lhasa, Lijiang, Quanzhou, Qufu, Suzhou, Taishan, Turfan, Xigaze, Yangzhou, Zhaoqing*
Last Emperor sites: *Puyi lived in Beijing, Changchun, Fushun, and Tianjin. Manchu dynasty palace and tombs in Shenyang*
Steam locomotives locations: *Northeast China*

In **Hong Kong**, now returned to China, walk around the Peak at dusk, and take a ferry ride in its famous harbor. In **Macau**, returned to China in 1999, enjoy this relic of old Portugal, and the fusion of European, African, and Chinese food.

Keep reading and I'll help get you to all of these and more!

HOW TO USE THIS BOOK

More than 1,000 destinations are open to foreign visitors. Listed here are the most important. Mentioned under these headings, especially those of the provincial capitals, are minor destinations that you might also like. The list here is grouped by regions along traditional Chinese lines so you will know what else is close by to see.

Where the Chinese characters for tourist sites have been available, they are listed in the *Glossary of Chinese Characters* at the end of this book. You can point to the characters or attempt to say the *pinyin* or romanization.

Don't jump to the conclusion that a temple founded in 1250 A.D. means the buildings are over 700 years old. The buildings may have been rebuilt recently. In a country that has had many upheavals, air raids, and revolutions, it's amazing that so many great monuments have survived to this day.

For shoppers, listed are items produced locally which tend to be cheaper than elsewhere. Hours given for stores and tourist sites are approximate and subject to change. Those in summer are about an hour later than those in winter. Telephone first if in doubt. Schools, villages, and factories are basically the same in the whole of China, and these are not mentioned in every destination unless there is something special about them. Please visit schools, villages, and factories wherever possible to give your trip more depth about the people.

China is now producing a great deal of travel literature of its own. I encourage you to supplement the information here with what is available in China, especially more detailed maps. Get help and maps from your hotel. Ask the concierge to write your destination in Chinese characters for taxi and bus drivers. Do not consider any guidebook as your only source of information. A guidebook should stimulate your interest, give you good background, and give you leads. So ask many questions while you are in China.

Some of the tours mentioned, especially those away from the main cities, are available only to tour groups booking in advance, not to individuals on the spot.

As anyone who has been to China knows, you get seven different answers to the same question if you ask seven different people. Getting solid information has been difficult, even to the number of rooms in a hotel. Finding hotel prices is almost impossible as they fluctuate according to demand and request.

Names

There is some redundancy in names, such as Lu Shan Mountain, (*shan* means mountain). This is for people who don't know Chinese, and such names are commonly used in English. It may appear cumbersome to put in the *pinyin*, the English, and the Chinese characters for place names, but in China some people will use the Chinese name and others will use the English. You might think they are talking of two different places. The multiple names listed are to help avoid confusion.

Sources differ frequently as to historical dates and events, and English translations of site names. Names like Han, Song, Ming, and Qing refer to dynasty, as 'in the Ming,' with Mongol the same as Yuan, and Manchu the same as Qing. These are usually accurate. It would help if you learned the names and general dates of the dynasties.

The words "Guest House" and "Hotel" are interchangeable and do not imply quality. The words "monastery" and "temple" are also interchangeable.

Spellings

In 1979, China adopted the *pinyin* system of romanizing its language based on the Beijing pronunciation. Thus "Peking" became Beijing. The old spellings can still be found in old books and are still used occasionally in China. I have tried to use the *pinyin* spelling but on some occasions the old Wade-Giles for historical people. The old and new names of major cities and dynasties are in Chapter 7, and pages 62 and 138.

Another confusing area has been whether words like Hong Qiao should be together as one or separated into two words. The tendency now is to combine place names into one word even though they can be very long. Shijiazhuang, for example, would be easier to pronounce if separated into Shi Jia Zhuang, but is found written both ways.

Avoid confusing the provinces Hunan and Henan, Jiangxi and Jiangsu, Shaanxi and Shanxi, Hubei and Hebei, and the cities Jilin and Jinan.

There is still no standard translation for important place names; for example, Lingyan Si in Jinan has been translated Magic Cliff or Intelligent Rock Temple in different pieces of Jinan tourist literature.

Sometimes correct telephone numbers have been difficult to obtain. In some places more than one is listed because sources differed. Try both. Failing that, ask an English-speaker from CITS (China International Travel Service), your hotel telephone operator, business center, or an embassy for an up-to-date telephone number.

Miscellaneous

I have tried to make the information in this book as accurate as possible at press time. The situation in China is so fluid that changes will have taken place by the time you visit. When in doubt, ask. And should you find things different, please let me know so I can make changes for future editions.

The travel agencies, hotels, restaurants, and other enterprises listed here should be able to help you. As far as I can see they are reliable, but a mention in this book is not necessarily a recommendation. I have given several options.

Finally, to avoid having to carry a book as heavy as this, you might want to cut out the pages you think you'll need in China, and staple each section. Carrying 'Beijing' is a lot easier than carrying the whole book around Beijing.

Have a great trip!

3. SUGGESTED ITINERARIES

I recommend concentrating on one area of China. It's a big country with much to offer! You can spend at least five days sightseeing in Beijing alone – and you'll see in the Beijing and Shanghai chapters extensive day-to-day itineraries.

However, if you think you'll never see China again and want to cover the highlights in 18 days, try Beijing, Xi'an, Shanghai, Suzhou or Hangzhou, the Yangtze River cruise, Kunming or Guiyang, Guilin, and exit via Hong Kong. You should include Shanghai, China's most cosmopolitan city, to balance out the rural impressions of the Yangtze valley. You have to include Chongqing, and Wuhan or Yichang, because that's where you get the Yangtze River cruise boat.

This itinerary is an enlightening introduction with a wide variety of sights to see and includes the Terracotta Warriors, classical gardens, big cities, quiet towns, the Grand Canal, good temples, ancient mummies, and an introduction to China's minorities. It also includes the Great Wall, Forbidden City, and Summer Palace. But you go at a hectic pace and fly a lot. Many travel agents offer this kind of tour.

I'm all for tours by road because China's countryside is so interesting. In five days from Shanghai, you can drive to Hangzhou, then see Shaoxing, 1000 Island Lake, and onward to Huangshan, one of the most gorgeous mountains in the country. In between are charming villages and farms, as yet relatively untouched by modern skyscrapers.

Shandong province is interesting and some visitors do a tour that covers the tiny hometown of Confucius, a medium-sized city, a sacred and unique mountain under UNESCO protection, the capital, the largest sea port and former foreign colonized city. In eight days, seven nights, you can do Beijing, Jinan, Tai'an, Qufu, Suzhou, Shanghai.

Henan province also has variety: the Shang dynasty relics at Anyang, the Song dynasty capital of Kaifeng, the Song tombs, the cave-temple statues at Luoyang, the *kung fu* Shaolin Temple and a lot of pleasant countryside in between. This can be done by car in a week. For more details, see Zhengzhou.

People fly on long weekends out of Hong Kong for a relaxing holiday in Guilin, or shopping in Shanghai, Tianjin or Beijing. From Shanghai, you can visit the temples of Ningbo, or do a pilgrimage to Putuoshan in three days. From Beijing, you can take the train and spend a weekend visiting Buddhist temples and the summer palace in Chengde.

In the cooler weather, I would also head out of Macau or Hong Kong for Guangdong province, nothing spectacular but interesting and enlightening: Zhongshan for the delta countryside and Dr. Sun Yat-sen's home, Taishan because it's the home of early Chinese-American immigrants, Foshan for the Ancestral Temple, Zhaoqing for charming mountain scenery, Guangzhou for the Cantonese food, and Shenzhen for the theme parks. China Travel Service offers four-day tours to some of these destinations, and you can stay longer in Shenzhen and do the theme parks on your own before returning to Hong Kong.

You could also head for Yalong Bay for a few days of sun and beach.

Most of the above suggestions tend to concentrate on South, East and North China. One of my favorite tours especially for people interested in textiles, China's minorities, and great scenery is in the Southwest: from Shanghai and Suzhou or Hangzhou, you fly to Guiyang, for Kaili, and Huangguoshu. The hotels in the Southwest are not as nice but you can visit minority villages and meet real weavers and embroiderers. Suzhou has a good silk museum. An itinerary like this can take ten days. If you want to see Tibet, an ancient culture clinging to the roof of the world, that's another four to six days at least.

For the adventurous and more minorities, there's the Burma Road of World War II fame and Dali, Lijiang, and Zhongdian, and then south to the Burmese (Myanmar) border. You need a week to ten days for this.

And don't forget the Silk Road, especially for people who have already done classical China. You can spend more time in imperial Xi'an. Don't miss Jiayuguan with its fortress at the western end of the Great Wall, the best of the cave temples in Dunhuang, the earthen ruins in Turpan and the Sunday market in Kashi. Forget Urumqi except to go in and out, and to enjoy the lovely Holiday Inn. In 12 to 14 days you can see Beijing, Urumqi, Kashi, Turpan, Dunhuang, Jiayuguan, Xi'an and Shanghai.

If you're into nature hiking, there's Wuyi (Fuzhou), Zhangjiajie (Changsha), and Jiuzhaigou (Chengdu).

A PROPOSED BEIJING ITINERARY

To help you plan your time in **Beijing** so you can cover the most important sights, these groupings are suggested. The days can be interchangeable, depending on weather, train schedules, upset stomachs, traffic jams, and the hours an attraction is open. Your own interests and needs, of course decide your schedule here. For full details, see Seeing the Sights in Chapter 14, *Beijing & The Great Wall*.

Day One

Spend at least an hour at the **Museum of Chinese History**. You must see **Tiananmen Square**, **the Forbidden City**, and **Jing Hill**. You can have a snack lunch inside the palace, or dine in one of the neighborhood restaurants. Today you will see some of China's finest relics. And do not miss the **Temple of Heaven**. You might want to shop after your visit to the Temple of Heaven in nearby Hongqiao Market or the Yuan Long Silk Store. If you love museums and palaces, you might want to spread all of these into two days instead, seeing "everything." There's a lot of walking here.

Day Two

Take the **hutong** or back-lane tour in bicycle rickshaws and have lunch in a home. Afterward, take a walk through historic Beihai Park. You could also do some antique and window shopping at Liulichang or the Hongqiao market or shop for bargains at Silk Alley if time.

Day Three

Go to the northwest of the city to the **Summer Palace, temples of the Western Hills**, **Fragrant Hill** and **Yuanmingyuan Palace Ruins**.

Day Four

Visit the **Great Wall** and **Ming Tombs**, but not on a weekend because of heavy traffic. Avoid these also in bad weather. Most tourists visit the Great Wall at Badaling. If you want a more remote part of the Wall with less people, ask for Mutianyu or drive a little further to an even more remote section like Simatai or Jinshanling. See *The Great Wall* section Chapter 14 for more details.

Day Five

Go back to the northwest but only to the Shangri-La Hotel. The **Beijing Art Museum** is here. You can also visit the **Great Bell Temple**, **Beijing University**, the pandas in the **Beijing Zoo**, and the **Blue Zoo**. Except for the zoo, these can all be done indoors in case of rain. Lunch at the Friendship, Shangri-La, Xiyuan or New Century Hotel.

Day Six

Visit the **Lama Temple**, my favorite. Nearby is the **Confucius Temple/ Capital Museum** and **Victory Gate**. For the remainder of the day, there's a choice of arts and crafts factories, or visits to places missed earlier.

A PROPOSED SHANGHAI ITINERARY

Four days in Shanghai is sufficient to cover what you should see, but you have to make choices. This is a suggested itinerary.

Day One

In the morning, **Huangpu Park**, and a walk along the **Bund** (preferably between 6 and 7am to see the *taiji* people), a look at the **Friendship Store**, a tour of the **Peace Hotel**, and lunch at the Peace or Hyland Sofitel hotels. Then consider the **Nanjing Road shops** and **Jewish ghetto**.

Day Two

The **Jade Buddha Temple**, **Children's Palace**, any of the modern history sites if only to see the inside of some old buildings, and a visit to **Yuyuan Garden** for shopping and sightseeing. Lunch at the Mongolian barbecue restaurant.

Day Three

The **Shanghai Museum** is for as long as your legs will let you. There's good shopping in the area. In the afternoon, Pudong and the television tower don't require much walking. Dine at the Hyatt or Shangri-La and watch the lights come on from Pudong.

Day Four

Zhouzhuang village and **She Shan Catholic Basilica** or **Suzhou**. You can't do all of these unless you stay longer.

One evening, try to see the **Shanghai Acrobats** or a performance at the **Grand Theatre**.

4. LAND & PEOPLE

THE LAND

China extends from Mongolia and Siberia on the north and to Central Asia, Afghanistan, Pakistan, India and Nepal on the west. On the south it borders Bhutan, Bangladesh, Myanmar, Laos and Vietnam. And on the east, it touches only North Korea and the Special Administrative Zones of Hong Kong and Macau. Its east coast is washed by the Yellow Sea, the East China Sea and the South China Sea. It also considers Taiwan and the Paracel Islands part of China. It is 9.6 million square kilometers, the world's third largest country.

China has 23 provinces, five autonomous regions, four administrative municipalities, and in 1999, two Special Administrative Regions.

If you keep in mind that Beijing is the same latitude as Philadelphia, Guangzhou the same as Havana, and Urumqi in the far west is a four-hour flight to Beijing in the east, you get a feeling for the vastness of the country. Its northernmost tip is as far north as James Bay in Canada.

China extends upwards too, with the highest mountains in the world, and downwards to the second lowest body of water. It has vast deserts and fertile valleys, great prairies, evergreen forests and rubber plantations. It is big and varied.

THE PEOPLE

China has 1.2 billion people, 22% of the earth's population living on 7% of the earth's arable land. That she has done so much with so little is a credit to Chinese pragmatism and ingenuity. The official language is **Mandarin Chinese** or *putonghua*. This is taught in the schools. You will also hear the distinctive Shanghai, Fujian, and Guangdong (Cantonese) languages, and hundreds of minor languages and dialects. Most people, however, use a common written language.

China has 56 different ethnic groups. The majority are Han. Eight percent of the population are members of 55 other nationalities. These 91 million people live in areas totaling half of China, including strategic areas near its borders. Yunnan province for example has 26 different nationalities. Although they are usually less educated and poorer, the varied cultures of these minorities are rich, meaningful, and fascinating.

A nationality doesn't necessarily settle in one location. Often sub-branches are spread over several provinces, with different costumes and dialects; for example, the Miao are found in Guizhou, Hunan, Yunnan, Guangdong, Guangxi, and Sichuan. Miao women in Guizhou wear pleated shirts and in Hunan wear trousers. The color and designs of their headdress also varies.

During festivals and market days, most minorities, especially women, wear their distinctive costumes, which many decorate with fine embroidery, and, sometimes, heavy silver jewelry. Hairstyles could indicate marital status and have historical meaning.

The festivals of the nationalities are worth experiencing. The **Dai** celebrate a water-splashing festival similar to that in neighboring Thailand and Burma. The **Kazakhs** have a horse racing festival, the **Yi** a torch festival, the **Tibetans** celebrate the Great Prayer Festival, and so on. Mongolians have colorful sporting meets, with distinctive wrestling, horses, and archery. Facilities for tourists in minority areas are still modest but not impossible.

The Chinese Psyche

China is a country that has infuriated yet tantalized the world for centuries. China's arrogant indifference, the wealth and 'divine right' of its emperors have intrigued generations of curious people everywhere.

In recent years, its fanatical adherence to communism has continued to mystify. People around the world are asking, 'Is it becoming capitalist?' Before the terrible 1989 events at Tiananmen Square, people asked: 'Is it becoming democratic?'

Before 1949

China became a nation over 2200 years ago. Thousands of years of relative isolation allowed the Chinese to develop their unique Confucian-based culture until the 19th century. At that time, more advanced technology and greed led many European countries and Japan to grab power and territory in China. The Chinese reacted with bewilderment, anti-foreign rebellions, and in 1911 with a republican revolution. After a period of embarrassing national disintegration, first under the warlords and then during the civil war and the Japanese invasion, the country was finally reunited in 1949 under the Communists.

The Chinese people, until very recently, have been 80% agricultural. Attachment to land has colored their behavior. Their religion, loyalties, and efforts have always been based on pragmatism, family, and ancestral lineage. They subordinated the wishes of the individual to the system and in most cases still do. This is changing, unless one considers 'getting rich' a part of the system too. After all, the acquisition of money is now another government-approved campaign.

Before 1950, China's economy stemmed primarily from a feudal system, land rented to peasants in return for a percentage of the crops. Landlords ideally had responsibility for the welfare of their serfs, on whom they were largely dependent for their wealth.

After 1949

After taking over China, the Communist leaders embarked on a series of programs following religiously the theories of Mao Zedong (Mao Tse-tung), the man who had led them to power. But the Chinese leaders were pragmatists first. When one approach didn't work, they tried another.

The Communists started out with a land-to-the-peasants program, then collectivization, communes, and finally private plots. The upheavals of the Cultural Revolution cost millions their lives. This troubled period ended with Mao's death in 1976.

During the Cultural Revolution, begun in earnest in 1966, they abolished private plots, then reinstated and encouraged them later. In the 1970s, it was apparent that even that system was not meeting the needs of the people.

The New Economic Policies

In the early 1980s, an economy largely based on the family replaced the communes. Most counties adopted the **Responsibility System**, whereby rural inhabitants rent land or machines. The government receives an agreed share of the produce while villagers keep or sell the surplus. Anybody can also work on projects such as handicrafts, livestock, and vegetables for their own gain. These you will see in 'free markets.' Families and collectives have opened hotels, restaurants, and factories. It would seem that China has almost come around full circle, with the government replacing the feudal landlords. But has it?

Under the new economic system, the government no longer determines all that is grown or produced, nor does it mandate quantities; the market affects most production directly. Many peasants have been working furiously and are making more money then ever before. China is undergoing another revolution. For the first time, rural China is earning less than 50% of its income from agriculture and many rural inhabitants are making more than salaried city dwellers.

The revolutionary slogans of nationalistic self-sufficiency and personal sacrifice of the nineteen fifties and sixties have given way to international cooperation and modernization and some people are getting richer faster than others. The new economic policies also include opening to foreign investment. The leadership has successfully attracted foreign capital, especially to its coastal areas, with a series of regional development zones extending from Dalian in the north to Beihai city in the south, and especially in Shenzhen, Guangzhou, Shanghai, Dalian, and Tianjin. Other areas are following: parts of Guangdong, Fujian, the Yangtze valley (from Pudong in Shanghai to Chongqing), and Hainan Island.

In these zones, the government has given tax breaks and has built harbors, roads, and improved telecommunications. Factories, office blocks and hotels have spread everywhere. Many areas have or will soon have IDD telephones and international airports. Beijing, Hangzhou, and Shanghai have video telephone services. In early 1993, China had over 200,000 mobile telephone subscribers. By mid-decade, it had four million pagers. The progress is uneven; some previously booming cities have lost their steam because of poor leadership – but Pudong has just built the tallest building in the world.

New Freedoms & Affluence?

The effects of the new economic policies are apparent everywhere, as you can see by the many construction cranes, satellite dishes, and traffic jams. Groups of former peasants have built hotels, roads, libraries, and schools in their own villages. In many areas, you can see a great deal of new peasant housing, most of luxury size. You can find American clothing like Victoria's Secret and North Face in fashionable street markets and hotel stores. China in some ways has become a fashion leader. High thick soles on women's shoes were common in 1998.

You can see the relaxing of the puritanical Maoist ethic in the freedom to enjoy life. People are eating out in restaurants and families are ordering more elaborate wedding feasts. People are buying video machines, color televisions, washing machines, refrigerators, and mopeds. Many private citizens can afford cars and trucks, and rooms in fancy hotels.

In many ways, life is much easier and more fun. Check out the dancing and exercises at six in the morning and the outdoor evening dance parties in every city. Women are adding glamour to their lives with permanent waves, lipstick, and colorful dresses. Notice the billiard halls, discos, and state lotteries. Chinese tourists flock everywhere, especially on their two-day weekends. Many even travel outside the country. None of this was permitted ten years ago.

Ten years ago, anything foreign was considered counterrevolutionary. Now, Paul Simon, Jose Carreras, foreign orchestras, dance groups, and artists like Robert Rauschenberg have performed or lectured in China. The country is becoming more permissive and you find nude statues in hotel lobbies as well as art galleries. New also is the more mature approach to history. The mainlanders are giving credit to the Nationalists for their help in fighting the Japanese invaders.

After decades of drabness, China is looking more cheerful and prosperous. It is a nice change.

The Flip Side

But the new economic policies have had other results. People became aware of what was going on in the outside world. Students and government officials traveled abroad and many of its best brains stayed. Thousands of foreign teachers spread democracy along with new languages. Young people working in tourism or selling in free markets make more money than their parents, especially if the parents worked for the government.

The importation of luxury goods like television sets, video machines, and Mercedes Benzes depleted foreign exchange. The attitude that nothing Chinese was good and everything foreign was desirable began to permeate people's thinking.

New classes of wealthy farmers and merchants, and on the other extreme, large numbers of poor people have developed. A 'floating population,' tied by registration to rural communities, has moved to the cities hoping for lucrative work. Beijing's floating population is about three million, and *The Wall Street Journal* estimated 100 million nationwide, with an annual increase of seven million. The children of these floaters are not getting adequate schooling or immunization. Nor are they being overseen by work units and villages for birth control and criminal behavior. Municipal governments are now trying to regulate them.

China's Economy Today

In the early 1990s, China's industrial output grew 20% annually, investment over 40%, foreign trade over 22%, and the GNP more than 12%. The gross domestic product, about one-tenth of the United States, was expected to increase to about two-thirds of that of the United States in the next ten years. The Asian recession changed that, but China has so far kept to its promise not to devaluate its currency. In the mid-1990s, the government slowed down the inflation. China also tried to cut down on government subsidies and eliminate the many unprofitable government enterprises that were taking up one-third of the national budget. You will see many of these unemployed people peddling wares in street markets, and operating bicycle rickshaw taxis.

Guanxi, which is business based on who you know, not who has the best deal, is still important, and bribery exists on all levels.

China has been developing its infrastructure. In 1998 and 1999, it increased the speed of many of its trains, completed many expressways worked on the trans-China superhighways, new nuclear power plants, airports, and ship ports. It is going ahead full steam with the controversial Three Gorges Dam across the Yangtze River, and a new Yellow River dam.

The growing middle and upper classes have an increasing appetite for consumer goods from abroad. There are opportunities to sell foreign-made products to the Chinese. And foreign travel agencies, department stores, as well as restaurants have opened in China.

China is attempting to develop better relations with all its neighbors: both Koreas, Vietnam, India, Laos, the new Central Asian nations, and especially Russia. It has rebuilt the train and trade links with Hanoi, for example.

China's Government

First and foremost, the government is Communist. Sometimes it's easy to forget that in today's apparently free atmosphere. **Jiang Zemin** is President of China and General Secretary of the Communist Party. The Prime Minister is **Zhu Rongji**, and Chairman of the National People's Congress is **Li Peng**. Officially at the top of the government is the **National People's Congress**.

The State Council is the executive organ accountable to this congress and is similar to a cabinet. The Communist Party now is trying to re-enter almost every facet of life, after pulling back in the mid-to-late 1980s. It blamed the 1989 student demonstrations on the lack of political education of the people. But many Communist Party members seem to be afflicted now with money fever too – at least until the next campaign against corruption. At press time, people seemed very casual about politics.

Current Atmosphere & Questions

Now is a crucial time to visit because what happens in the coming years will determine China's future direction. The 1990 census revealed that China has 1,160,017,381 people, a lot more than it had expected and planned for. Many intellectuals are afraid of another suppression and are trying to leave the country. Young people with little faith in their government still dream of making a fortune in richer countries abroad. Conversely, a growing number of North Americans are setting up businesses, getting jobs and establishing homes in China.

Many people speak freely with foreigners now. I suggest you use discretion in talking politics, human rights, and the western point of view, unless you want to be booted out of the country. Be careful what you send out over e-mail.

With care, there are many questions for you to ask: What about social security? Free health care? What is being done about AIDS, and illegal drugs? Legal rights? What is the effect of satellite television? E-mail and the internet? Fax machines? How is the government regulating these sources of foreign information?

What is it doing about pollution? What do the Chinese feel about the fall of Communism and the disintegration of the Soviet Union? Is China really killing baby girls? Is China ready for democracy? Is there any possibility of direct flights between Taiwan and the mainland? What is the problem there? Perhaps you can find the answers.

Religion

At first, the Communists discouraged religion and the Cultural Revolution destroyed many religious buildings and symbols. Since the late 1970s the government again has allowed religion to openly exist and has been helping reconstruct religious buildings. Today you will see worshippers in most temples, mosques and churches. There has been a revival of religions and superstitions. Although the Chinese constitution says that all Chinese citizens have freedom of belief, implementation remains uneven. Today, in some provinces, there is interference in Christian church affairs by 'leftist cadres.' Generally, however, religion is flourishing, as you can see.

China's great traditional religions are Taoism, Buddhism, and Confucianism, although in some sense, Confucianism is more of an ideology or philosophy. Taoism and Confucianism are uniquely Chinese. Buddhism came later. Islam and Christianity are more recent imports. Ancestor worship and animism are ancient folk religions.

Chinese people are pragmatic, worshipping whatever gods might answer their prayers. They want to cover all the bases. If a friend prayed successfully to one god for a baby boy, then other barren women would try that god too. It is not unusual for the same person to have his children baptized as Christians, burn incense to a deceased grandfather, and then retire to contemplate in a Taoist or Buddhist monastery. The same person may support several different temples and churches at the same time and worship his or her ancestors.

Religions have been encouraged, tolerated, and persecuted. In the early Tang, some emperors ordered the killing of Buddhists, while other emperors encouraged Buddhism. Additionally, emperors financed many religious buildings.

Ancestor Worship

Ancestor Worship involves praying to departed ancestors as you would pray to Buddha or a saint. You take care of them with incense and offerings and they take care of you. You worship your ancestors in gratitude for your life.

There used to be at least one ancestral temple, or **miao**, for every village, since each village was comprised of people with a common ancestor. Some temples were very elaborate and were used as the village school. If people moved away from the village, they might set up shrines in their homes where they informed the ancestors of important family events like births and marriages. Many families kept a family history book. The Red Guards destroyed many of these books and family tablets during the Cultural Revolution. When you go to a village, ask about the ancestral temple. In ancestral temples, tablets with the names of the ancestors were kept in neat rows and worshipped with burning incense, gifts of food, and ceremonial bowing at least twice a year.

Animism & Other Religions

There are temples to city gods. Fishermen worship the Goddess of Heaven, **Tian Hou** or **Mazu**, who bears some resemblance to the goddess Guanyin. (See Quanzhou.) In villages, you will see incense burned at the foot of sacred trees and in tiny shrines. See Quanzhou for **Manicheanism**, and Xi'an and Quanzhou for **Nestorianism**.

Buddhism

Buddhism arrived in China from India. **Gautama**, the founder, was an Indian prince, born in the sixth century B.C., who was brought up confined to a palace. When he was 29, he saw the suffering of the outside world for the first time and forsook his wealth and family. For six years, he traveled in search of life's meaning. He found it, became known as Buddha (the awakened or enlightened one) and then preached his ideas for 45 years: the **Four Noble Truths** and the **Noble Eightfold Path** to nirvana. The circles on top of Buddhist stupas and pagodas are in the same numbers: four and eight.

Buddha taught that the source of all suffering is selfish desire, and one must stop all desire. Some sects believe in asceticism. The Chinese, Mongolians, and Tibetans generally follow the **Mahayana** school of faith and good works, and believe Buddha is divine and can answer prayers – even though Buddha never asked people to petition or worship him.

You will see people in temples, smoking incense in hand, nodding to the statues or *kowtowing* on the floor, asking for favors, without regard for the extinction of all desire. Achieving **nirvana** is the aim of all forms of Buddhism, accomplished by ending the continuous cycle of reincarnation through the extinction of the self. Today, China has more than 3,600 Buddhist temples open for worship with over 30,000 monks and nuns.

Buddhist temples come in two basic varieties, of which there are infinite variations. First are **Chinese Buddhist temples**, surrounded by windowless walls, which frequently have four fierce-looking, larger than life-size, human-type guardians after the first gate. Each temple might have different names for these. Inside the first hall, visitors are greeted by the fat, laughing Buddha, **Maitreya**, or in Chinese, *Mi Lo Fu*. He is the Buddha still-to-come. Behind him is **Wei Tou**, the military *bodhisattva*, the armed warrior who guards the Buddhist scriptures. Wei Tou is probably comparable to the Indian god Indra.

Central in the main hall is the **Buddha** (known also as the **Enlightened One**, **Sakyamuni**, or **Prince Siddhartha Gautama**). Also in this hall are usually statues or paintings of *bodhisattvas,* known in Chinese as *pusas*. These are saints who have gained enlightenment but have come back to the world to help other people attain it too. A favorite *bodhisattva* is *Avalokita*, known in China as **Guanyin** (Kwan Yin, Kuan Yin), or the **Goddess of Mercy**. Guanyin may have several heads and arms and may be carrying a vase or a child. She is usually behind Sakyamuni, facing north.

BODHISATTVA

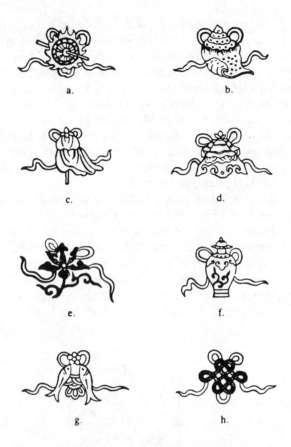

THE EIGHT BUDDHIST EMBLEMS OF HAPPY AUGURY

a. The wheel of the law   e. The lotus flower
b. The conch shell   f. The covered vase
c. The state umbrella   g. The pair of fishes
d. The canopy   h. The endless knot

Guanyin started out as a male god in China until about the 12th century, when his followers preferred to worship him as a woman. He is still sometimes depicted as male. Said one guide, 'Men believe he is male and women believe she is female.'

Other *bodhisattvas* are **Amitabha**, in charge of the souls of the dead, **Manjusri**, in charge of Wisdom, usually with a sword in his right hand and a lotus in his left, and the *bodhisattvas* of Pharmacy, Universal Benevolence, and the Earth.

Arhats, known in Chinese as *lohan*, are people who have achieved nirvana. They are usually depicted in groupings of 16, 18, or 500, and are based on real Indian holy men. These are frequently seen in paintings or as statues. Devout Buddhists should know each of them by name.

The swastika is a Buddhist symbol of good luck, of Indian origin, later inverted and used by the Nazis. Most temples have live fish and turtles. Full-time Buddhists are vegetarians. Some Buddhist monks had pieces of incense burned into their skulls at their initiation, but this is no longer required.

An interesting study to make as you sightsee is of the clothing carved on buddhas. Some wear the plain, draped robes of Indian holy men, others the fancy, feminine Chinese court dress with jewelry. Buddhism arrived in China from India, but Buddhist art in China became distinctly Chinese. Can you date a statue from its clothes? The fatness of its face?

You will probably see many more Buddhist temples than Taoist and Confucian. You might also see the robed monks chanting prayers if your timing is right. Do you find the rituals mechanical or mystical?

The second kind of Buddhist temple you'll see are called **Lama Temples** by the Chinese, and are different from other Chinese Buddhist temples not only in their statues, but also in their architecture. Usually built on mountainsides, they have tall, narrow windows, flatter less ornate roofs, and are usually decorated over the main door with a gilded wheel of Buddhist doctrine and two deer. Statues inside are frequently decorated with turquoise and coral, and many of the statues wear pointed caps, or are of couples copulating. The best known of these temples are in **Tibet**, but important examples are also in Beijing, Chengde, Qinghai, and Inner Mongolia.

Lama temples are expressions of the Tibetan and Mongolian form of Buddhism, into which have been injected elements of the early Tibetan religion called **Bon**.

Many Tibetan Buddhists believe that the Dalai Lama, who is considered both the temporal and religious head of Tibetan Buddhism, is a reincarnation of Avalokita or Guanyin, or the god Chenrezi. The religion's peaceful and wrathful aspects are reflected in the murals and statues of these temples. Tibetan Buddhism is also divided into sects, the main ones being the meditative **Yellow Hats** and the sensual **Red Hats**.

Note: The Chinese government refers to Tibetan Buddhism as 'Lamaism' and their temples as 'Lama' temples or 'lamaseries,' but the Tibetans themselves do not. See also *Lhasa* and *Chengde*.

Cave Temples with frescoes and Buddhist statues were first built in India and spread with the Silk Road into China. Caves have always been conducive to meditation. One gets a feeling of security, like being back in a mother's womb. **Dunhuang** is the greatest for its paintings. The two at **Lanzhou** are noted for their strikingly dramatic sites and the richness of their sculpture. Important for carvings are also **Datong** and **Luoyang**.

Other cave temples listed as protected historical monuments by the State Council are at Anxi and Linxia in Gansu; Handan in Hebei; Turpan, Baichen, and Kuqu in Xinjiang; Guangyuan, Leshan, and Dazu in Sichuan; Jianchuan in Yunnan; Gongxian in Henan; Guyuan in Ningxia; and Hangzhou in Zhejiang.

Christianity

Christianity arrived in full force with Christian missionaries in the latter part of the 19th century. The treaties after the **Opium War** in 1842 forced China to accept missionaries. Because of backing by foreign powers, Chinese Christians tended to be an elite group, at times successfully appealing to their foreign protectors if they got in trouble with Chinese law. This caused much resentment. Christian Churches were most frequently built in western architecture with gothic windows, and many Roman Catholic churches look like transplants from Europe.

Some foreign missionaries closed their eyes to ancestor worship to make converts. Many Chinese questioned the exclusivity of Christianity.

Dr. Sun Yat-sen, the father of the Chinese republic, was a Christian, but as a Chinese nationalist he criticized missionaries as lackeys of foreign imperialists. Many Chinese misunderstood the missionaries' motives. Some of these fears led to such incidents as the **Tientsin Massacre** (see Tianjin). The Chinese attacked missionaries more because of nationalism than religious hostility.

Missionary schools influenced some Chinese Communist leaders. Mao Zedong once edited the Christian-sponsored *Yale-in-China Review*. Zhou Enlai admired the ideals and the work of the YMCA and YWCA.

In 1950, the hysteria of the Korean War led the Chinese to consider westerners, including many missionaries, as 'enemy aliens.' They accused them of spying and sabatoge and jailed some. After all, Americans and Canadians were killing Chinese soldiers in Korea. (This hysteria was similiar to the incarceration of Japanese people on our west coasts during World War II.)

The Communists felt that foreign imperialism was linked to the Chinese Christian dependence on foreign missionaries. After 1949, the Communists encouraged Christian churches to cut their ties with their foreign mentors and Protestants set up the **Three-Self Patriotic Movement**. The Catholic Church, however, officially opposed the rulers of new China. Most of the bishops not jailed fled. When those Catholic leaders who remained nominated new bishops to meet the pastorial needs of more than 100 vacant dioceses, the Vatican ignored these nominations. When Chinese leaders went ahead with consecrations, Rome regarded them as irregular.

The situation has improved now. Having missed Vatican II, some priests still celebrate the Mass in Latin for older Catholics, but young priests are being trained to celebrate in Chinese. Many consecrations are now recognized (unofficially) by Rome.

During the **Cultural Revolution**, the Red Guards destroyed and closed churches and temples as part of the movement against the 'Four Olds.' Many church buildings became apartments, factories and warehouses. The Catholic Cathedral in Guangzhou was used for storage.

In 1978-79 after the Cultural Revolution, the government encouraged the rebuilding of temples and churches, returned deeds to congregations and paid overdue rents. It had to relocate the people and factories who had taken over the buildings. Some Christians had actually continued to tithe even while the churches were closed and later brought these treasures to their newly-opened gathering places.

Over 8000 Protestant churches and over 20,000 meeting points across China are flourishing with over 12 million Protestant Christians and 15 to 25 million enquirers. Thirteen seminaries and Bible Schools are open. A few churches have to open Saturdays as well as Sundays to accommodate worshippers. Some Christians worship corporately in their homes.

While some foreigners have questioned the authenticity of the 'state-recognized' versus the 'house' Christian, most Chinese believers do not think they are different. It may be a matter of convenience. Some Christians attend both the small family fellowships and the large general congregations. Leadership training is the major challenge for the burgeoning congregations of often semi-literate Christians in the countryside. In 1988, two Protestant bishops were installed. It was the first such event since 1955.

Foreigners wanting to contact Protestant groups should ask for the **China Christian Council** or **Three-Self Patriotic Movement**. Catholics should ask for the **Chinese Catholic Patriotic Association**. Don't let the word Patriotic bother you. It doesn't sound as chauvinistic in Chinese. You should also consult your own church or national church organizations. When you get to China, worship with the Chinese and please do not disturb the service with a camera, or by being late or leaving early.

Chinese Christians, particularly those in isolated places, will probably be delighted to have you join them. Please don't be overly generous. The Chinese want to be self-reliant. Donations with no strings attached can be made to the **Amity Foundation**, a Christian-inspired people's organization devoted to health, education, and welfare projects for all Chinese, not just Christians.

Recently, a group of foreigners was arrested and deported for proselytizing. You can ask Christians in China if they want missionaries.

As for smuggling in Bibles, those days are over. The United Bible Society has given a modern press to the Amity Foundation, which is helping the Protestant churches publish their own literature. Since 1981, the China Christian Council has printed over 10 million Bibles.

There are also about 4.5 million **Catholic Christians**, 1,000 large Catholic churches, and 10,000 chapels. Between 1980 and 1985, about 130,000 adults were baptized. Eleven seminaries are now open and about 12 convents with 200 women under formation. In 1990, several Roman Catholic clergymen with ties to the Vatican were arrested.

Confucianism

Confucian temples used to be in every sizable community in China, at one time about 2,680 of them, now dwindled in number down to about 300. For a history and description of Confucianism, see *Qufu*.

Confucius was worshipped because his teachings supported the stratification of society, with the emperor and elder males on top. He was officially worshipped during the spring and autumn equinoxes. Try to imagine the burning incense and the muffled clang of gongs, as slow, rhythmic processions of officials in long red gowns and caps arrived, each man to *kowtow*, head to the ground, in deepest reverence. They left offerings of food and wine on the altar. Musicians played ritual bells. Such ceremonies still take place in Qufu and in Taiwan.

Confucian temples did not usually have statues, but simply tablets with the names of ancestors written on them. The walls were red. The south gate was usually left unbuilt until a son from the town passed the difficult examinations and became a Senior Scholar. Only a Senior Scholar and the Emperor could enter by the south gate. No women were considered for the examinations, but if Chinese opera plots are to be believed, some did successfully take them disguised as men.

Was Confucianism a religion or a philosophy? This question is frequently debated. While Confucius himself skeptically rejected the supernatural, Chinese people did and, in some cases, still do consider him a god. He is among the Taoist deities too. But he was primarily a teacher of ethics, of 'right conduct,' and good, stable government. Many Confucian temples now are only museums because Confucianism no longer has imperial patronage. The largest temples are in Beijing and Qufu.

Taoism

Taoism (Daoism) was founded 1800 years ago by a sage named **Lao Zi** (Lao Tzu), whose message was conveyed to the world by a disciple named Mencius. It preaches that everything exists through the interplay of two opposite forces: male-female; positive-negative; hot-cold; light-dark; heaven-earth; yang-yin, etc.

Taoists try to achieve harmony out of the conflict of these forces through the Tao or the Way. Taoism is closer to nature than other religions, its saints have found enlightenment by spending years meditating in caves. Over the years, it has been diluted by superstitions like charms, spells, ghosts, nature spirits, and supernatural beings. Taoism was most popular in the Tang and Song, but declined in the Ming. Its most famous monasteries are in Beijing, Chengdu, Shenyang, and Suzhou.

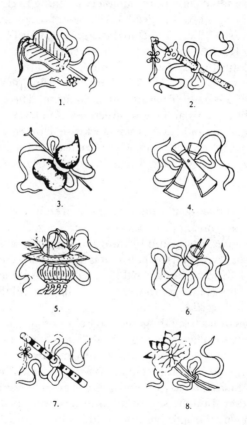

THE ATTRIBUTES OF THE EIGHT TAOIST GENII

1. The fan
2. The sword
3. The pilgrims' staff & gourd
4. The castanets
5. The flower baskets
6. The tube and rods
7. The flute
8. The lotus flower

Taoist temples are identified by Taoist gods, among whom are **Guanyin** and **Confucius**. You can identify other gods and saints by the symbols they carry.

The **Eight Taoist Genii** (Immortals or Fairies) were originally eight humans who discovered the secrets of nature. They lived alone in remote mountains (one of them in a cave at Lushan), had magic powers and could revive the dead. They are usually found together on a vase or in one painting, or as a set of eight porcelain pieces. Chung Li-chuan carries the fan to revive the spirits of the dead, Lu Tung-in the supernatural sword, Li Tieh-kuai the staff, Tsao Kuo-chiu the castanets, Lan Tsai-ho the flower basket, Chang Kuo the bamboo tube, Han Hsiangtzu the flute, and Ho Hsien-ku the lotus flower. Two are women.

In the center of the dual **Yin-Yang**, the principles of being are surrounded by the eight **Trigrams of Divination**. The Eight Trigrams represent eight animals and eight directions. At eleven o'clock are the three unbroken lines of heaven; then clockwise, clouds, thunder, mountains, water, fire, earth, and wind. These are used in fortune telling. You may have heard of the **I Ching**, which uses these trigrams.

Feng Shui

Geomancy is making a comeback, influenced by its success in Hong Kong. *Feng* means wind and *shui* means water. It is geomancy, the placing of graves, dwellings, doors and furniture in harmony with the forces of nature. **Feng shui** is related to Taoism. It is more an art or pseudo-science than a religion. In some cases it makes practical sense since its teachings advise that dwellings face south with mountains behind them to protect people from cold northern winds.

Good luck comes from dragons who live in mountains, and it is best to site a structure or village so that good luck goes down into it. If you don't have mountains, you plant trees where the dragons can reside.

Spirits only travel in straight lines, so windows and doors should not be in line with each other as the good luck will go in one side of a building and out the other. Buildings must not interfere with the flow of *chi*, the cosmic breath which brings harmony and health.

It is preferable for a structure to be surrounded on three sides by running water. If it isn't, the geomancer may suggest a fountain. He might tell you to hinge a door in another direction or to get gold fish for good luck with one black one to absorb the bad luck.

One Chinese-Canadian attributes his success to moving his brother's grave to a site with better *feng shui*. He smuggled the bones out of Hong Kong to the ancestral home in China on the advice of a fortune teller, and was careful to consult a geomancer.

Islam

Moslems are followers of the Prophet Mohammed, who was born in 570 A.D. This religion gives a different emphasis to the god of Judaism and Christianity. Old Testament prophets and Jesus Christ are considered honored prophets, but Mohammed was the last and the greatest. The holy book is the Koran, which teaches a strict code of behavior (no pork, alcohol, idols, etc.), and the universal brotherhood of all believers. During the holy month of Ramadan, they fast during the day.

Islam arrived in China in 652 A.D. during the Tang Dynasty, with Arab and Persian traders who settled in Guangzhou, Quanzhou, Hangzhou, and Yangzhou. During the 13th century, Kublai Khan brought Moslem soldiers, artisans, and officials to China to work for him. Approximately 10 million Chinese Moslems are known today as **Hui**, but **Uygurs**, **Kazaks**, **Kirgiz**, **Uzbeks**, etc., are also Moslems, a total of about 17 million followers of Mohammed. Mosques are always open afternoons on Friday, the holy day.

Islamic mosques are architecturally of two varieties. Those with rounded, onion-like domes and minarets, are mainly in northwest China. Other mosques look like Chinese temples, with curved roofs and ornate dragons and phoenixes (in spite of the prophet's teachings against making images).

In either style, visitors always remove their shoes inside the great halls. There is a place for washing hands and feet before prayers. The main building is the Great Hall, which is decorated with Arabic writing, arches, and flower motifs. Moslems pray five times a day, facing the holy city of Mecca in Saudi Arabia.

Moslems can pray anywhere, but the devout usually pray in a mosque if they can. Note the prayer rugs with designs woven into them indicating the direction in which to kneel. Carpets made in Moslem areas deliberately do not have images of animals or objects on them. Note also the disproportionate number of women worshippers, and in some mosques, separate sections for women.

5. A SHORT HISTORY

EARLIEST TIMES

The ancestors of human beings have lived in China 8,000,000 years ago. Archaeologists found the remains of Ramapithecus man in Lufeng in Yunnan province. Yuanmou Man lived 1,000,000 years ago and Lantian Man, 600,000 to 700,000 years ago.

The famous **Peking Man** is a mere youngster. He's only 400,000 to 500,000 years old. About 20,000 to 30,000 years ago, Liuchiang Man lived in Guangxi, near Guilin. Hotao Man lived in Inner Mongolia, and Upper Cave Man back in Zhoukoudian. Other milestones are the **Lungshan Culture** and **Yangshao Culture** in Henan of 5,000 to 7,000 years ago. (See Xi'an's Banpo Museum.)

Dynasties date from about 2000 B.C. and overlap because different dynasties controlled different parts of China at the same time. Eastern and Western usually refer to periods of the same dynasty with different capitals.

The **Xia** dynasty usually dates from about the 21st to 16th centuries B.C. and marks the beginning of the slave system. It is known for irrigation and flood control work, a rudimentary calendar, the earliest form of writing (about 2300 B.C.) and the earliest bronzes. Some archaeologists place its capital in Henan province.

The **Shang** (16th to 11th centuries B.C.) had the earliest glazes, wine, and silk. It developed ritual bronze casting to a high art and even had carved jade handles on swords and spears. A famous Shang relic is an ivory cup inlaid with jade. It had iron and used cowry shells for money. This culture traded outside of China and developed writing and ancestor worship. They communicated with the gods by cracking tortoise shells and began the first cities: Zhengzhou and Anyang.

The **Western Zhou** (11th century to 771 B.C.) and the **Eastern Zhou** (770 to 249 B.C.) welded bronze and produced the first lacquer. They used copper coins and crossbows and lived in walled cities, developed elaborate rituals and music using jade instruments, and further developed ritual bronze vessels in profusion.

Confucius lived in the **Spring And Autumn Period** (770 to 476 B.C.). Warring states fought for power. Confucius preached a return to the Zhou rituals and tried to stabilize society by insisting on obedience to emperors, fathers, husbands, and older brothers. This was the beginning of feudalism. This period had cylindrical tile sewer pipes, iron implements and oxen for plowing, and a form of steel. They used metal spade-shaped coins, chopsticks, and had a knowledge of mathematics, astronomy and medicine.

The **Warring States** (47 to 221 B.C.) was a transitional period to feudalism. Master Sun produced his famous book *The Art of War*, praised as recently as a few years ago by General Norman Schwartzkof. During this period, **Mencius** promoted Taoism. The silent Mohists flourished. The first large scale irrigation and dams included erosion control. People used iron farm tools and manure for fertilizer. They mined and produced salt. Doctors first diagnosed diseases through feeling the pulse. Scientists wrote the first books on astronomy, and used magnets.

Emperor Qin (221 to 206 B.C.) unified China for the first time, and started building the Great Wall and the Terracotta Army. He standardized weights, measures, writing, and currency. He developed a strict legal code. His dynasty had the first clay burial figures, highly developed medicine and agriculture. But he is infamous for burning most historical records and for executing scholars.

The **Eastern and Western Han** (206 B.C. to 220 A.D.) had the water wheel, windmill and the first seismograph. They produced the first plant-fiber paper and a water-powered bellows for smelting and the first important Chinese medical text, and used general anesthesia in surgical operations, acupuncture and moxibustion. Its astrologers produced the first armillary sphere and discovered that moonlight comes from the sun. During its reign, **Szuma Chien** wrote China's first history book. And burying rich people in jade suits was fashionable. **Emperor Han Ming-ti** ordered the first Buddhist temple built in Luoyang in 68 A.D.

The **Silk Road** (2nd century B.C. to 14th century A.D.) connected China to India, Western Asia, and even Rome with trade routes along which the Chinese exported silk, tea, iron and steel, peach and pear trees, and the knowledge of paper making and deep-well digging. They received grapes, pomegranate and walnut trees, sesame, coriander, spinach, the Fergana horse, alfalfa, Buddhism, Nestorianism, and Islam. The main stops in China west from Xi'an were Lanzhou, Wuwei, Dunhuang, then north through Turpan or south through Ruoqiang. Arab and Persian traders settled in Xi'an and Yangzhou.

During the **Three Kingdoms** (220 to 265) people managed to develop a water pump, celadon, and ships big enough to carry 3000 men, in spite of the fighting.

The **Western and Eastern Jin** (265 to 420) followed, then the **Southern and Northern Dynasties** (420 to 589). During these periods the Chinese developed the first arched stone bridge, the widespread use of celadon, and two crops a year. The **Northern Wei dynasty** started the construction of the Buddhist cave statues at Luoyang and Datong.

The **Sui** (581 to 618) built the 2,000 kilometer-long Grand Canal, built ships up to 70 meters long, and an arched stone bridge still in use today in Zhaoxian county, Hebei.

CHINESE CIVILIZATION FLOURISHES

The **Tang** (618 to 907) was one of China's most prosperous and culturally developed dynasties. From this era we have three-color and snow-white porcelains, inlaid mother-of-pearl, gold and silver, wood-block printing, fine silk, and woven feathers. They used an adjustable curved-shaft plow and made an attempt at land reform. The Tang was the most prosperous period of the Silk Road era, but they also traded by sea. They opened a special office for foreign trade in Guangzhou, where Arab traders built a mosque.

Buddhism entered Tibet during this dynasty from Nepal and China. Later, Chinese monks took Buddhism to Japan and Korea. (Kyoto is modeled on Xi'an). The Chinese monk **Hsuan Tsang** went to India (629-645) to obtain the Buddhist sutras. Chinese travelers also went to Persia, Arabia, and Byzantium. Tang poets are still the most respected. Look for fat faces in paintings and sculptures. They are most likely Tang.

The **Five Dynasties** (907 to 960) was a transitional warring period. The **Liao** (916 to 1125) controlled Inner Mongolia and part of southern Manchuria. It invaded China and occupied Beijing and built an extant 66.6-meter wooden pagoda in Ying Xian, Shaanxi.

The **Northern and Southern Song** (960 to 1279) was a prosperous and culturally-developed period. It had the first paper money, moveable type, compass, gunpowder, and rocket-propelled spears. It made fine porcelains and red lacquer and improved on the use of acupuncture and moxibustion. It made progress in mining and metallurgy. Hangzhou, then known as Qinsai, was the largest, richest city in the world according to Marco Polo.

The **Western Xia** (1038-1277) controlled today's Gansu and western Inner Mongolia. During the **Jin** (1115 to 1234) the first western missionaries were recorded. Franciscan friars arrived in Inner Mongolia. The Jin captured Beijing and controlled Kaifeng, the Wei River valley, Inner Mongolia, and northwestern China.

The **Yuan or Mongols** (1271 to 1368) had a water clock and improved cotton spinning and weaving. They gave us the famous blue-and-white, the underglaze red porcelain, and cloisonne. They controlled all of today's China and areas north and east including Moscow, Kiev, Damascus, Baghdad, and Afghanistan. From 1275-92, **Marco Polo** visited and served in the court of Kublai Khan.

The **Ming** (1368 to 1644) imported corn, potato, tobacco, peanuts, sunflower, and tomatoes from America. They refined the blue-and-white porcelain and added colors and had sea links with Malacca, Java, Ceylon, and East Africa. The Chinese lent Macau to the Portuguese, and the first Christian missionary, **Matteo Ricci** of the Society of Jesus, lived in Macau and then in Beijing. The Dutch colonized Formosa (Taiwan) until 1662.

The **Qing** (1644 to 1911) is noted for some of the best porcelains. It had to cope with foreign incursions. Cheng Chengkung, or **Koxinga**, drove the Dutch from Taiwan. Qing forces expanded into Russia, Korea, Vietnam, Burma, and Sikkim, but later lost a great deal of territory. The British introduced most of the opium as a narcotic. During this dynasty, the first U.S. trading ship, *Empress of China*, arrived in Guangzhou, the first British mission met the emperor (at Chengde), and the first Protestant missionary, Robert Morrison of Britain, arrived. American missionary work started in 1830.

In 1839, China attempted to stop the opium trade. It burned 20,000 chests near Guangzhou, more than half a year's trade. This resulted in the **Opium War** (1840 to 1842). Britain needed to sell China opium to balance trade. British forces with French help seized a few cities along the coast and threatened Nanjing. The Chinese gave in, ceding Hong Kong island to Britain and opening to foreign trade Guangzhou, Xiamen, Fuzhou, Ningbo, and Shanghai. This was the beginning of the foreign exploitation of China, and the establishment of "foreign concessions" in Shanghai. Countries with concessions in China included Germany, Italy, Japan, Belgium, Russia and the United States. About this time, in 1848, Chinese emigration to America and Australia started.

THE DECLINE OF THE DYNASTIES

The **Taiping Heavenly Kingdom** (1851 to 1864) was a rebellion against the Manchus led by a Christianity-inspired Cantonese who believed himself the younger brother of Jesus Christ. Starting in 1851 in Guangxi, this became the largest peasant movement in Chinese history. At one time the rebels occupied most of China. They established a capital at Nanjing for eleven years and were defeated in part by a foreign mercenary army led by British officer **Charles Gordon**, known as Chinese Gordon, who was later killed in the Sudan.

The **Second Anglo-Chinese War** (1856 to 1860) was also known as the Arrow War. It ended after the sacking of Beijing, the burning down of the Summer Palace, and more unequal treaties for China, including the ceding of Kowloon to the British. In 1870, China started to send thirty students a year to the United States to study. Students also went to Britain and France.

During the latter half of the 19th century, the French took Vietnam (then a tributary state of China) and Japan seized Taiwan, the Pescadores, and the Liaoning peninsula from China. In 1898, Britain leased the area north of Kowloon and about 235 islands around Hong Kong for 99 years. The Chinese reacted with unhappy incidents like the Tientsin Massacre of French missionaries. It was during this turn-of-the century period that the **Empress Dowager Tzu Hsi** kept the **Kuang Hsu Emperor** under house arrest for defying her (he passed various reforms to modernize China).

In 1899, the United States declared that foreign powers should not cut up China into colonies and all nations should be free to trade with China. Only Britain bothered to reply, but for a while China looked to the United States as its only foreign friend. Then in 1900 came the **Boxer Rebellion**, also known as the Rebellion of the Society of the Righteous and Harmonious Fists, a reaction, at times encouraged by the Empress Dowager, against increasing foreign domination. The Boxers attacked foreigners and Chinese Christians.

Foreign powers, including the Americans, responded by capturing Beijing, sacking it, and forcing another humiliating treaty on China. Then the Japanese invaded southern Manchuria. The Empress Dowager died in 1908 and was succeeded by two-year-old **Pu-yi**, the last emperor of China.

THE REPUBLIC

On October 10, 1911, the first victory of **Dr. Sun Yat-sen**'s republican revolutionaries followed an accidental explosion in one of their bomb factories in Hankou. Dr. Sun became president of the Chinese republic with its capital at Nanjing. But the new country suffered a lot of growing pains and external problems. Outer Mongolia, with Russian help, declared independence from China. In 1913, **Yuan Shih-kai** was elected president. Then Japanese troops took over the naval base at Qingdao and won its infamous Twenty-one Demands. Many Chinese protested. They protested more after Yuan proclaimed himself emperor.

The republic was saved when Yuan died of a heart attack, but warlords gained control of the country. World War I ended with the Japanese keeping its gains in China and western powers retaining their pre-war concessions.

The May 4, 1919, student demonstrations against the Versailles Treaty marked the beginning of the nationalistic and cultural upsurge known as the **May Fourth Movement**, the training ground for many Communist revolutionaries.

On July 1, 1921, the Chinese Communist Party was founded in Shanghai with Russian Communist help, although the Soviets preferred to support Sun Yat-sen. Dr. Sun agreed to cooperate with Russian and Chinese Communists and sent **Chiang Kai-shek** to Moscow for military training. Mikhail Borodin and General Vassily Blucher arrived as advisers. Dr. Sun could not be sure of help from Britain and America. On March 12, 1925, he died of cancer in Beijing.

In 1926, **Generalissimo Chiang Kai-shek** and officers with Soviet supplies led the **Northern Expedition** in a successful attempt to unify China, wrest control from the warlords, and fight the unequal treaties. In 1927, the Northern Expedition took Nanjing and Chiang tried to purge Communists in Shanghai. **Chou En-lai** escaped and went on to found the Chinese Red Army which attempted to take Changsha. Ill-prepared, it withdrew to Jiangxi where the Communists established the first Chinese soviet, distributing land to the peasants in the area. The next year the Nationalists took Beijing and renamed it **Peiping** (Northern Peace).

In 1931, the Japanese invaded Manchuria and set up a puppet government under Pu-yi called Manchukuo. Chiang accepted a humiliating truce in 1933 while continuing to attack the Communists on Jinggang Shan with a 'scorched earth' policy. On October 16, 1934, the Communists, aware they could no longer hold their base on Jinggang Shan, started out with 80,000 troops on the **Long March**. They arrived three months later in Xunyi, Guizhou. **Mao Tse-tung** took over as leader of the march and they decided on northern Shaanxi as their goal, the only Communist base big enough. In addition, they could fight the Japanese invaders in that area.

From Xunyi, the march continued in spite of Nationalist bombs and troops. The major battles were fought at Loushan Pass (February 1935) and Luting suspension bridge over the Tatu River. Edgar Snow gives a good account of the march in his book *Red Star Over China*. Some of the important battles have been immortalized in ivory or porcelain. The Long March was joined by other Communist armies and ended in northern Shaanxi in 1935, a journey of 12,500 kilometers. The original marchers were reduced to 8,000, including 30 women. The Communists moved to Yan'an in 1937.

The Communists fought against the Japanese while the Nationalists tried to eliminate the Communists. In 1936, Chiang was kidnapped by one of his own officers at Huaqing Hot Spring and forced into a wartime coalition with the Communists against the Japanese, in what is known as the **Xi'an Incident**.

THE JAPANESE WAR & CIVIL WAR

On July 7, 1937, the killing of Japanese soldiers near Beijing set off the 1937-45 war between Japan and China, during which Japan occupied most of urban China. Chiang moved his capital to Hankou and finally to Chongqing while the western powers remained neutral. Many warlords with their private armies rallied to fight the Japanese but were destroyed.

Although the Nationalists blocked supply routes, the Communist armies waged guerrilla warfare against the Japanese, engaged in political and economic work among peasants, and developed strategy, discipline, and plans for the takeover of the rest of China.

In 1938, the Canadian surgeon **Dr. Norman Bethune** joined the Communist Eighth Route Army and died the following year of blood poisoning while operating without antiseptics. Because of his skills at improvisation and selfless devotion to duty, Bethune later became a Chinese national hero. (See Shijiazhuang.)

The United States entered the war after Japan's attack on Pearl Harbor in 1941. It increased aid to Chiang and tried to reconcile Mao and Chiang against the Japanese.

The war ended in 1945. China got most of her territory back, including Taiwan and the Pescadores. Outer Mongolia and Manchuria were placed under the Russian sphere of influence. The **Chinese civil war** continued though, especially in Manchuria. US President Harry Truman ended aid to the Nationalists to avoid American involvement in the civil war.

The Communists advanced and eventually won because of severe inflation, Nationalist corruption, the breakdown of law and order, mass Nationalist troop defections, and the Communists' success in winning the hearts and minds of the peasants.

THE MAO YEARS

On October 1, 1949, known as **Liberation Day**, Chairman Mao proclaimed the birth of the **People's Republic of China** from the Gate of Heavenly Peace, Tiananmen, in Beijing. Later Chiang and loyal troops and officials fled to Taiwan. Refugees flooded Hong Kong. The Communists tried but failed to take the offshore islands of Matsu and Quemoy across from Taiwan.

For the next decade the Communists, with Russian help, tried to rebuild the nation and put their ideals into practice. They started trials by peasants of landlords and executed about two million people. They attempted to "remold" intellectuals. They divided the land among the peasants, 0.15 to 0.45 acres each.

In 1950, the **Korean War** began with North Korea invading South Korea. Chinese forces joined the North after the United Nations and

South Koreans counterattacked north of the 38th Parallel (the border between the two Koreas) and China felt threatened. The Chinese jailed and expelled many foreign missionaries, teachers, and scholars as imperialist spies. China accused the United States of using poison gas and germ warfare and circulated maps showing American bases surrounding China. The Americans began an embargo which ended many years after the war ended, in the 1970s.

China started to use Hong Kong and Macau as trading centers and sources of foreign exchange. In 1950, Britain recognized China. In 1949-50, China took **Tibet**. In 1955, the Chinese suppressed a rebellion there and in 1959, the **Dalai Lama** fled to India.

During 1956-57, Mao, in an effort to incorporate intellectuals into the revolution, began the **Hundred Flowers Movement**: "Let a hundred flowers bloom together, let the hundred schools of thought contend." Mao believed the overwhelming majority of intellectuals supported the revolution and communism, and encouraged intellectuals to speak freely about the bureaucracy. Intellectuals did not respond and about a year later the Communist Party began its own efforts to clean up the bureaucracy. Once started, the intellectuals participated fully. However, the attacks were so severe that within five weeks the Movement ended and the **Anti-Rightest Campaign** began, aimed at the intellectuals.

The **Great Leap Forward** (1958-60) was a failed economic plan that led to the death of millions of people. Mao was convinced that food production could be substantially increased by reorganizing people into communes. Unfortunately, the communes were reporting increases in production when production was actually decreasing. Initial efforts to report the bad news were not well received by Mao, and the devastating program continued until 1960.

In 1961, Mao accused the Russians of being revisionists, giving in to capitalism and to "nuclear blackmail." China rejected Russia's offer of nuclear weapons in exchange for bases in China. China and Russia divorced in 1960 when **Nikita Khrushchev** ordered the end of all Soviet aid. Russian advisers left and the Chinese insisted on repaying Russian military aid immediately.

These years, 1959 to 1962, were a difficult period for China. In addition to the repayments, the country endured 'natural calamities.' **Liu Shao-chi** became president while Mao continued as Communist Party Chairman. India asserted control of disputed border territory. China sent a punitive invasion force into India and then announced a ceasefire and withdrew.

In 1963, China started to supply Hong Kong with fresh water. In 1964, it exploded a nuclear bomb at the Lop Nor testing grounds in Xinjiang. That same year **Chiang Ching**, Mao's wife, started a campaign to make culture serve the revolution and abolished traditional Peking opera. Later she allowed only eight operas to be performed, all written by revolutionary committees. In 1965, an article instigated by Mao in a Shanghai newspaper introduced the **Great Proletarian Cultural Revolution** to the public for the first time. The next year, activists put up the first important 'Big Character Poster' at Beijing University, and Chairman Mao felt that people were forgetting the aims of the revolution. He swam the Yangtze River at Wuhan (nine miles) to show he was still powerful and in charge.

Mao taught that workers and peasants were the basis of the Chinese revolution. Many party cadres were re-educated in 'correct' political thinking by learning to respect and love physical labor. Doctors swept floors to help them identify with the masses and understand their problems. Corruption was punished harshly.

The first of many **Red Guard** rallies in Tiananmen Square in support of Chairman Mao was held August 18, 1966. Schools closed so that students, really Red Guards, could travel and learn to make revolution. Red Guards, riding free on trains and sleeping in school dormitories were fed by municipalities. They traveled the country taking part in revolutionary movements against the Four Olds: the elimination of old ideas, culture, customs, and habits. They destroyed religious statues, buildings and ancestral tablets. Many Tibetan and other monasteries were destroyed during this period.

They changed the names of streets and parks from old dynastic names to 'The East Is Red' (Dong Fang) and 'Liberation' (Jiefang), stripped some women of their tight western trousers and cut off long 'bourgeois' hair. They also attacked elements of foreign influence, and any obstacles to completing the course of the revolution.

They denounced **Deng Xiaoping** and in 1968 deposed President Liu, who died shortly afterward (but was officially rehabilitated in 1979). The Cultural Revolution became very violent and led to riots in Hong Kong and Macau. The schools re-opened in 1969. Fellow peasants and workers chose which student should study in university. They based eligibility on the completion of at least two years of manual labor, how well you knew Maoist theory, and how enthusiastic and selfless you were in serving the people.

The next year, China launched its first satellite. In 1971, the United States table tennis team and US Secretary of State **Henry Kissinger** visited China and paved the way for American recognition of China and the visit of **President Richard Nixon** in 1972. China took the United Nations seat occupied by Taiwan, and Canada resumed diplomatic relations.

Deng Xiaoping was rehabilitated in 1973, and became vice-premier in charge of planning. In 1974 China asserted control of the Paracel

Islands as one million Soviet troops ringed its northern border. In January 1976, **Premier Chou En-lai** died and Deng Xiao-Ping became acting premier. Chou supporters put wreaths in Tiananmen Square in his honor. Chiang Ching, Mao's wife, ordered the removal of the wreaths. A clash ensued and Mao blamed Deng, who once again fell into disfavor.

Not long after, a massive earthquake shook North China centering on the city of Tangshan and was believed by many to foretell the death of Mao Tse-tung a few months later. **Hua Guo-feng** succeeded him and arrested the **Gang of Four** who were blamed for many of the country's ills. The Four were Chiang Ching, Mao's widow, and three leaders from Shanghai. Deng was rehabilitated again and resumed his previous posts. The following year, posters advocating personal freedoms and democracy appeared on **Democracy Wall**, but this experiment didn't last very long at all.

In 1979, the U.S. and China resumed full diplomatic relations. Tensions between China and Vietnam were worsening in the late 1970s, and China went to war in 1979 owing to what Beijing termed Vietnamese 'armed incursions' into China.

THE DENG XIAO-PING ERA

In 1980, **Zhao Ziyang** became premier. Leaders tried to improve living standards and eliminate "left deviation, that is, the over-rigid and excess control of the economic system, the rejection of commodity production, and the mistaken attempt to transfer prematurely the ownership of all enterprises to the state."

Under the orders of Deng Xiao-ping, they began an economic reassessment and encouraged foreign investment. They banned Democracy Walls and sentenced **Wei Jingsheng**, one of the leaders of the movement, to 15 years in prison for subversion. (He was jailed again for another 14 years in 1995 but has since been released for medical reasons and exiled.)

By 1980, Chinese officials had stated that Mao's contribution to China outweighed his mistakes. China modified the commune system, making the family the basic economic unit and diminished the role of the Communist Party. They gave the Gang of Four suspended death sentences. **Hu Yao-bang** replaced Hua Guo-feng, Mao's chosen successor as Chairman of the Communist Party. China announced gradual price changes based on market forces. The following year US Defense Secretary Casper Weinberger visited, and permitted the sale of some U.S. military technology to China. The campaign against 'spiritual pollution' (immoral foreign influences) was vigorously pursued for a while but gradually declined.

The leadership denounced the Cultural Revolution and the Communist Party booted out thousands of leftists. They started encouraging intellectuals to contribute to modernization.

Record harvests and an increase in cash crops encouraged the new economic policies. The leadership ordered all state-owned companies to make a profit and pay taxes. Foreign exchange reserves hit a record high, and China went on an importing spree. Factories became independent and made their own production and marketing decisions. **President Ronald Reagan** visited, and US-China relations warmed. Britain and China agreed that Hong Kong would revert back to China in 1997. Deng proclaimed a one-country, two-systems policy in dealing with Taiwan and Hong Kong.

The Communist Party spelled out its plan for the next three to five years and explained 'socialism with Chinese characteristics.' In 1985 the leadership reduced two-hour lunch breaks to one hour for factory workers. Sweden became the first customer for China's satellite launching service in 1986. **Queen Elizabeth II** visited. China joined the Asian Development Bank. Some government-owned factories were allowed to issue stock. For the first time since Liberation (1949), a factory declared bankruptcy and a stock market opened (in Shanghai). The government announced that all new factory workers would be under limited instead of life-time assignments. The government also started a federal unemployment insurance and pension scheme.

In 1987, student demonstrations for more freedom led to the resignation of leaders advocating 'bourgeois liberalization.' This included the Communist Party general secretary. University students were forced to take courses in Marxist-Leninist theories, trips to the countryside and factories, and military training.

As a result of independence demonstrations by Tibetans in Lhasa, China closed Tibet to all foreign tourists except for prepaid tours. It expelled some foreigners from the region for "interfering." Taiwan permitted its citizens to visit the mainland. Many tearful reunions took place between family members who had not seen each other since 1949. Mail, telegram, and telephone service also resumed. China opened the rostrum on the Gate of Heavenly Peace to tourists in 1988. China's foreign debt grew to $35 billion. Ugly demonstrations against African students occurred, especially in Nanjing.

In the late 1980s, previously suppressed individualism surfaced. The press printed real news, not just government-approved news. For students, the new attitudes extended to politics and demonstrations. The leadership, once benevolent on many levels, became nepotistic and corrupt with lavish state spending on banquets, foreign cars, and overseas trips. If Mao were alive, he probably would have started another Cultural Revolution. Inflation started getting out of control.

In 1989, the **Panchen Lama**, the second highest Tibetan Buddhist leader, died and more demonstrations for independance took place in Lhasa. The **Dalai Lama** offered a compromise: China could oversee its foreign affairs and keep troops in Tibet in exchange for religious and cultural autonomy. He was awarded the Nobel Peace Prize.

In Beijing, the death of **Hu Yao-bang** set off student demonstrations and hunger strikes that continued relatively unopposed for a month and a half. The students asked for the end of government corruption and a say in student government. They shouted defiant foreign slogans. Demonstrations centered in Tiananmen Square in Beijing, but took place in other towns and cities as well. Plans for the historic visit of Soviet **President Mikhail Gorbachev** were thwarted because of the students. The leadership was divided on how to react.

What emerged was a reversion to old ways. Like a traditional, autocratic Chinese father who 'lost face' in front of a guest and realized his authority was disintegrating, the Chinese leadership regressed to brute force. An estimated 300 to 3000 people were killed in Tiananmen Square on **June 4**: innocent bystanders, unarmed demonstrators, civilians, soldiers and some rioters. Over 450 military, police, and public vehicles were alleged by the government to be destroyed. Student leaders were arrested.

The government said those killed were 'ruffians and criminal elements taking advantage of the turmoil.' It said the students needed political education and sent some to the army. It set students and workers to studying the government's version of the 'counter-revolutionary rebellion.' Shanghai and Beijing executed 'rioters.' It arrested a youth for trying to place a wreath in the square and jailed a number of people for 'counter-revolutionary crimes.'

Around the world, thousands of protesters marched, especially in Hong Kong. Some foreign governments imposed economic sanctions. Some of the student leaders took refuge in foreign missions. The most prominent was astrophysicist **Fang Lizhi**, who lived for almost a year in the US Embassy before being allowed to leave for the U.S.

Tourism almost stopped. The World Bank suspended all loans (it has since resumed them). Some foreign businesses withdrew. Countries abroad gave preferential treatment to Chinese refugees and made it easier for Chinese students to stay. Because of these actions and the awarding of the Nobel Peace Prize to the Dalai Lama, China accused foreign governments of interfering in its internal affairs. Amnesty International said at least 500 people were executed for offenses related to the demonstrations and for counter-revolutionary activities.

DEMOCRACY & HUMAN RIGHTS

Democracy movements are not new. Writing criticisms and complaints in public places has occurred in China for centuries and especially during the Cultural Revolution, when they were used to attack capitalist roaders (but not to criticize the government).

Late in 1978, the writing of big character posters on Democracy Walls flourished unhindered. Four months later, this right was restricted. Criticism of socialism, the dictatorship of the proletariat, party leadership, and the ideas of Marx, Lenin, and Mao were taboo.

In 1979, foreigners could visit Democracy Walls, talk with anyone and accept leaflets. But then some Chinese were arrested and charged with passing state secrets to foreigners. In December 1979, however, wall posters were curtailed. In September 1980, these rights were deleted from the constitution.

In 1989, a million people supported student demonstrations for democracy in Beijing, and more elsewhere in the country. They were brutally suppressed. If you want more information on this subject, and on political rights in general, contact Amnesty International, Asia Watch, and the US State Department.

By late 1990, China was relatively back to normal, the press dull and obedient. Foreign businesses came back. International sanctions were lifted. The economy continued to grow, especially in the countryside, and China soon had an international trade surplus. Martial law was lifted in Beijing and Lhasa. Inflation was held down to 2%, compared to 17% in 1989. Twelve Catholic bishops were arrested because of secret Vatican ties. Beijing's Asian Games was an organizational success, but did not attract the large numbers hoped for. Taiwan and other Asian tour groups helped to bring up 1990 tourism figures to about 95% of 1988 levels.

In 1991, China's first nuclear power plant started operating in Zhejiang province. China counted eight AIDS victims since 1985 and 607 HIV-positive people, mainly in Yunnan. China implemented a five-day work week and cut back on free health care and subsidies to state corporations.

The United States accused China of using forced prison labor for exports and demanded the protection of intellectual property rights. Still, China achieved an international trade surplus including a $10 billion surplus with the United States.

In 1992 the **Euro-Asia Railway Bridge** from Rotterdam to Lianyungang was completed. Hong Kong Governor Chris Patten and Chinese officials clashed over giving more political power to the Hong Kong people and the construction of the new Hong Kong airport. And the nation had a 12% economic growth rate.

TODAY

From about 1992 until 1997, the country was booming. China continued to buy airplanes and cars from the United States and its overheated economy triggered inflation and subsequent economic controls. The government announced a staff cutback of 25% within the next three years and kept trying to get rid of highly subsidized state enterprises.

The collapse of the Gouhou Dam in Xinjiang region killed 242 people and President Jiang Zemin ordered the Chinese press to print positive news. The government forbade officials from going into business or practicing nepotism. They were forbidden from trading in stocks or accepting gifts of money. But as they have for thousands of years, many officials bypassed the rules. The government announced that over 60% of China's 500 cities was short of water.

In the mid-1990s, China arrested, sentenced, and then released Chinese-American **Harry Wu**, a former prisoner who was determined to enlighten the world about conditions in China's prisons. The deportation instead of imprisonment permitted US First Lady **Hilary Clinton** to attend the United Nation's Women's Conference in Beijing along with about 30,000 other women.

China strongly protested visits of the Taiwan president to the United States, even though these were private. The government felt threatened by the Taiwan elections. The United States continued to object to the violation of intellectual property rights and human rights. A conflict between the government and the Dalai Lama about the reincarnation of the Panchen Lama threatened even more any reconciliation on Tibet.

Work on the controversial **Yangtze Gorges Dam** continued in earnest. China bought American cars, factories, electric generators, subway and railway cars and airplanes. Canadians were hired to design shopping malls.

In 1997, **Hong Kong** returned to Chinese rule, and Macau will revert on December 20, 1999. An economic recession in the rest of Asia stopped China's growth and started a price war in its hotels. China vowed not to devalue its currency. It started monitoring messages sent over electronic mail and arrested a server for giving mailing lists to democracy rights organizations abroad. In 1998, the worst floods in decades caused much damage along the Yangtze River. The government continued its efforts to close down factories that were not productive.

And in 1999, the People's Republic of China celebrates its 50th anniversary.

CHINA'S DYNASTIES

The names of the dynasties below are given two ways: the first word is spelled using *pinyin* transliteration; the word in parentheses is the old spelling.

Xia (Hsia)	c. 21st-16th century B.C.
Shang (Shang)	c. 16th-11th century B.C.
Western Zhou (Chou)	c. 11th century-771 B.C.
Spring & Autumn Period	770-476 B.C.
Warring States Period	475-221 B.C.
Qin (Chin)	221-206 B.C.
Western Han (Han)	206 B.C. - A.D. 24
Eastern Han (Han)	25-220
The Three Kingdoms	220-265
Wei (Wei)	220-265
Shu (Shu)	221-263
Wu (Wu)	222-280
Western Jin (Tsin)	265-316
Eastern Jin (Tsin)	317-420
Southern/Northern Dynasties	420-589
Southern Dynasties	420-589
Song (Sung)	420-479
Qi (Chi)	479-502
Liang (Liang)	502-557
Chen (Chen)	557-589
Northern Dynasties	386-581
Northern Wei (Wei)	386-534
Eastern Wei	534-550
Western Wei	535-556
Northern Qi (Chi)	550-577
Northern Zhou (Chou)	557-581
Su (Sui)	581-618
Tang (Tang)	618-907
Five Dynasties	907-960
Liao (Liao)	916-1125
Song (Sung)	960-1279
Northern Song (Sung)	960-1127
Southern Song (Sung)	1127-1279
Western Xia (Hsia)	1038-1227
Jin (Kin)	1115-1234
Yuan (Yuan)	1271-1368
Ming (Ming)	1368-1644
Hongwu (Hung Wu)	1368-1399

Jianwen (Chien Wen)	1399-1403
Yongle (Yung Lo)	1403-1425
Hongxi (Hung Hsi)	1425-1426
Xuande (Hsuan Teh)	1426-1436
Zhengtong (Cheng Tung)	1436-1450
Jingtai (Ching Tai)	1450-1457
Tianshun (Tien Shun)	1457-1465
Cheng Hua (Cheng Hua)	1465-1488
Hongzhi (Hung Chih)	1488-1506
Zhengde (Cheng Teh)	1506-1522
Jiajing (Chia Ching)	1522-1567
Longqing (Lung Ching)	1567-1573
Wanli (Wan Li)	1573-1620
Taichang (Tai Chang)	1620-1621
Tianqi (Tien Chi)	1621-1628
Chongzhen (Chung Chen)	1628-1644
Qing (Ching)	1644-1911
Shunzhi (Shun Chih)	1644-1662
Kangxi (Kang Hsi)	1662-1723
Yongzhen (Yung Cheng)	1723-1736
Qianlong (Chien Lung)	1736-1796
Jiaqing (Chia Ching)	1796-1821
Daoguang (Tao Kuang)	1821-1851
Xianfeng (Hsien Feng)	1851-1862
Tongzhi (Tung Chih)	1862-1875
Guangxu (Kuang Hsu)	1875-1908
Xuantong (Hsuan Tung)	1908-1911

6. PLANNING YOUR TRIP

BEFORE YOU GO

WHEN TO GO

The best time weather-wise is **May-June** or **September-October**, but you could run into crowds and delays. You could also try late April or early November and hope for good weather. In November, plan to go to Beijing first and then move south.

Definitely avoid the lunar new year (around late January or early February), especially in Guangzhou and Fujian, as hotels and trains are full of Overseas Chinese visitors, prices are at their highest, and some tourist attractions are closed. Avoid Guangzhou during the trade fairs and any other cities with big events. Go to Lhasa in March when the days are warm, the nomads are pilgrimaging, and few other tourists are around. Avoid Lhasa in the summer when tourists outnumber costumed Tibetans.

The **hottest time** of the year is usually July and early August. Almost all hotels, most tourist buses and some taxis are air-conditioned. Put mountain or seaside resorts at the end of a hot tour. During April-May and through the summer, rain and high humidity make **south China** (including Guangzhou and Guilin) quite oppressive, but the greenery is lush and beautiful. Inner Mongolia and the Silk Road have sandstorms in spring and autumn. Avoid mountain areas, the Yangtze Gorges and any other place with outdoor sights in the rainy season because of floods or landslides that could disrupt sightseeing and photography.

Again, China extends from the same latitudes as James Bay in Canada to Cuba. Beijing is at almost the same latitude as Philadelphia, and Guangzhou as Havana. Take altitude into account: the higher, the colder, especially at night.

Winter in **North China** begins in mid-November and extends to late February and the air is very dry. The Spring Festival/lunar new year is frequently the coldest time. Air pollution is particularly bad in winter as coal is used for fuel. But most tour agencies and hotels give discounts.

Wise tourists who are healthy and not afraid of the cold could plan trips in the winter even in the north. New-fallen snow transforms any city into a wonderland and makes red pavilions and curved gold roofs intensely beautiful. It also makes roads slippery and traffic slow-moving. Hotels are not crowded (except for conventions.)

It is important to remember that the Chinese do not heat their buildings (like museums and palaces) as warmly as we do even though it can be cold. South of the Yangtze these have no heat at all. But most tourist hotels three stars and up are heated. Some low-priced hotels are not. If the cold bothers you, go only to the tropics to Hainan and south Yunnan in winter. Even in Guangzhou, you might need a top coat and a sweater at that time of year.

MOVIES TO GET YOU READY FOR CHINA!

You can borrow videos of tourist attractions from Chinese missions, and film festivals do show Chinese films occasionally. Check your neighborhood video store. Look for Academy Award nominees Ju Dou and Raise the Red Lantern by director Zhang Yimou. Then there's Farewell My Concubine and Red Sorghum. The Horse Thief, set in Tibet, and The Ballad of the Yellow River are also tragic. Other good movies are The Day the Sun Turned Cold, The Puppetmaster, Good Men, Good Women, Yellow Earth, In the Heat of the Sun, To Live and The Blue Kite. If you want something funny there's Eat, Drink, Man, Woman, and the Wedding Banquet, both Taiwan-made and set in Taiwan.

Good foreign-made movies are The Sand Pebbles (although filmed in Taiwan), The Last Emperor (with great shots of The Forbidden City), A Great Wall, and Bethune, The Making of a Hero. The First Emperor (shown on the museum circuit), is short but excellent, especially if you're going to Xi'an. Even if you're not going to teach, or interested in kung fu, do see Iron and Silk.

Then there's the 1999 Oscar nominee for best documentary short, Sunrise Over Tiananmen Square, available from the National Film Board of Canada. This is an autobiographical movie about a young Chinese person's disillusionment with Chairman Mao.

Other Things to Consider When Planning
If you are interested in visiting schools, factories, and offices, avoid vacations, holidays and weekends. If you want to see a festival consider those dates.

Now that China has a five-day work week, business hotels are not full on Friday and Saturdays nights and prices are softer. Do not expect business appointments on weekends. Cheaper tourist hotels and popular tourist attractions however are busier on weekends with China's growing number of domestic tourists. Avoid the Forbidden City and Great Wall on weekends.

WHAT TO PACK

Clothing & Luggage
Sightseers should dress for comfort with good walking shoes. Sneakers are ideal. White is not practical in China's polluted air; besides, it is the color of mourning, so brighten it up. Bring sunscreen, and a sun hat or buy a cheap one there.

You might feel compelled to dress up for dinner in five-star hotels and for a captain's banquet on Yangtze cruise ships. But you don't have to. Chinese people are generally informal. While top class hotel restaurants would like men to wear jackets and ties, they will not send you away if you don't.

From mid-November to late March, **north China**, including Beijing, is bitterly cold. I even froze in Beijing one May; two sweaters and a top coat were barely enough. Many of the cheaper hotels are not well heated.

A jogging suit is ideal for lounging and sleeping on trains. Take along a coat, long underwear, heavy slacks, thermal socks, and warm boots. A hot water bottle will help keep you warm in cheaper hotels.

Do as the natives do: plan on layers of clothing and a windbreaker top. If you have to, you can buy a down coat (half US prices), windbreaker (Y30), and wool or silk long johns (Y95 for bottoms) in China. If you are also traveling to warmer climes or need room in your luggage for purchases, you could take clothes you can discard when no longer useful.

The **rainy season** is March to May in the **south**, with rain or drizzle almost every day. After it starts getting hot, a trench coat will feel like a sauna. You can buy cheap umbrellas there.

All of lowland China is hot in July and August, so bring cotton clothing. Shorts are common on women now, but tops should be more modest. Most Chinese women wear trousers and loose-fitting blouses, and, increasingly, skirts. Men wear slacks and white shirts even in offices. In winter, they wear layers of sweaters and western-style or Mao jackets. Everyone wears padded coats. Trench coats are in style for office workers.

The new, with-it generation has been dressing more colorfully. Jeans are in style. Modern young women wear tights and even miniskirts.

Women should dress conservatively. Chinese women don't dress elegantly except in the wealthiest levels of society. The Chinese like to see foreign women wearing Chinese dress, but try not to look like restaurant staff. They also like to see the latest styles from America.

If you are invited to dinner, you can ask your host if what you have on is all right. Should men wear ties? Women should not overdo makeup or you'll have other people wondering if your eyelashes and hair are real. Does everyone in Australia have blue eyelids? Younger Chinese women are into makeup. Sure, take your heels but go easy on the jewelry. The current style with the younger set is three inch soles.

At less formal banquets, many Chinese men and women wear loose-fitting shirts and trousers. Some might be coming from work or arriving by bicycle. Chinese officials do not usually bring their spouses to banquets, but this is changing slowly at the upper levels.

Wearing cosmetics, jewelry, and bright colors (except for children) was considered self-indulgent, bourgeois, and counter-revolutionary from 1949 until recently. Doing so led to assault, hours of interrogation and even imprisonment during the Cultural Revolution. It is understandable why the older generation hesitates about changes. For business, dress as you would in your own country to show respect.

Laundry is done in one day at most hotels if in by 8 am. All hotels three stars and up in big cities have dry cleaning. The Chinese do an adequate job, but if your dress is special, the average hotel could ruin it. It would be wise to wash delicate clothes like silk underwear yourself. Some hotels provide clothes lines in bathrooms.

Your **luggage** should have a **lock** and will probably have to endure a lot of punishment. Some bags have been left out in the rain and I sometimes take a large garbage bag to protect the contents. Your bags should have your name, telephone number, and address outside and inside, and something like a wide ribbon to identify it on an airport luggage belt.

Free luggage allowance: If you're going in a group tour, you're usually allowed one or two suitcases. You should also have a carry-on bag for overnight train rides (your big bag may not be accessible), and airplanes (in case your checked luggage is delayed or lost).

China's **domestic airlines** are sometimes strict about the limit on bags. For first class it's 40 kg for checked and carry-on, 30 kg for business class, and 20 kg for economy class. For discounted fares it's 20 kg first class and 15 kg economy. Economy class carry-on bags should not exceed 20 x 40 x 55 cm and five kg. I once argued that I had arrived on an international flight and showed my ticket, and didn't have to pay for overweight. On another occasion, in Xi'an which guides say is notorious about overweight luggage, we had to pay considerably for the extra.

Air China allows two pieces of luggage on **trans-Pacific flights**. Each bag should not exceed 32 kg and the sum of the height, width and length no more than 158 cm or 62" in first and executive class, and less in economy. Carry-on bags should fit under the seat. The sum of the width, height and depth should not exceed 45" or 115 cm.

A weight limit of 35 kg usually applies on trains; in 1998 we were caught twice and had to pay!

PEOPLE JUST LAUGHED AT US

Porters and trolleys are available in some but not all train stations and airports. Independent travelers should be prepared to carry their own bags in some train stations, perhaps up and down a flight of steps, to a taxi. We've had people laughing at us – two women struggling with bags – and no offer to help. Consider a set of luggage wheels.

In some places, notably the train from Luoyang to Xi'an, porters insist that luggage be locked. If you can't get a lock, they will sell you one – cheap. It might fall apart. It's best to take your own lock.

Toiletries

Four- and five-star hotels give away free shampoo, conditioner, and soap. Most hotels will probably give you toothbrushes, soap, and a few other goodies like combs. China has international brand soaps, toothpaste and shampoo. The lemon shampoo is acceptable. Handy-wipes for cleaning hands are good too. Take your favorite sanitary napkins or tampons.

Short-wave Transistor Radios

During the 1989 turmoil, in the days following June 4, *China Daily* mentioned nothing of the tanks and killings. And shortly afterwards, CNN and foreign newspapers were jammed. They have resumed, but one never knows. Many hotels have news in English and/or CNN. Hotels are supposed to do their own censoring. But as the government owns part of the satellite, in case of emergency, do take a short-wave radio.

Photography

You can buy Kodak and Fuji print film but usually only 100 ASA. Ektachrome is getting more common. It is best to bring your own. Be sure to take extra batteries, flash cubes, video tapes, and Polariod film. You don't want to spend time looking for it.

Personal video cameras are allowed. Use of commercial video cameras requires permission at tourist sites. Video cassettes might be erased by airport x-ray machines, so pack them in lead pouches. If declared, your cassettes could be seized and screened with a charge, but I haven't heard of this happening lately. Still, officials are looking for pornography and religious materials. If you don't have any, your tapes should be returned in hours or weeks.

To avoid x-rays at airport security, ask for a hand inspection. Multiple exposures to x-rays can adversely affect them.

Maps & Books

You can usually get a free detailed map in English at four and five star hotels. For wandering around on your own without a guide, take a Chinese-English phrase book.

Medicines, Vitamins, & Goodies

Take what you need. Exact equivalents may be hard to find. Chinese traditional medicines are frequently effective, so if you're adventurous, you might try them. Many hotels and cruise ships have doctors. With Chinese painkillers, you might experience strange mood changes. A few pharmacists in big cities can fill Western prescriptions, but don't count on it except in Beijing and Shanghai. Take two batches of essential medicines. Keep one on you, and one in your luggage in case one set gets lost.

Take Pepto-Bismol tablets (mild) and Immodium (serious) in case of diarrhea or upset stomach. Ask your doctor about Diamox for altitude sickness for Tibet. If you're bothered by pollution or dust, take a nose mask (or buy a cheap silk scarf in China).

Please consult a knowledgeable doctor about malaria. The danger is only in Hainan and the tropics close to the Laotian and Myanmar borders. For these infected areas, take long sleeves and trousers for after dark (when these mosquitoes bite), and a good repellent. If you have flu-like symptoms after being bitten, tell your doctor to check for malaria. It can be fatal.

Take a few snacks and if you need more, buy them in China. Some hotels and ships provide bottled water. All have free boiled water.

Gifts

Gifts are not essential, but you may want to give them to friends, or exceptional service people. Cash is becoming the norm. What are good gifts? Anything not made in China is usually acceptable. Some people give novelties like refrigerator magnets or unusual ball-point pens. You can give candy, postcards, Italian silk ties, cosmetics, souvenir playing cards, baseball caps, t-shirts, pins, or picture books with scenes of your country.

PHOTOCOPIES

Photocopies of the first important pages of your passport, your Chinese visa, and birth certificate (or certificate of citizenship) are essential. These are in case you lose your passport and should be kept separate from your passport. It is also helpful to have photocopies of plane tickets and credit cards. You should have the telephone numbers of your credit card companies so you can stop payment in case of loss. It is also good to have extra copies of passport photos. If your prescription medicines can be mistaken for illegal drugs, take a copy of your prescriptions.

Something for children like coloring books or books in English is great. For breaking the ice with children, take a bag of balloons or tiny cars.

You don't have to take gifts to schools, and certainly not to factories and communes. But schools do not usually receive any compensation for the disruption caused by visitors. If you want to leave a souvenir of your visit, give general gifts like books, frisbees, and pictures that everyone can enjoy. Giving to a few individuals may upset the others.

Since people everywhere are studying English and other foreign languages, books are a great idea. China is short of teaching materials in English. Guides, of course, would prefer cash, but you might also want to leave them magazines such as Vogue or People, your used guide book, music tapes, or cartons of cigarettes (Marlboro Lights is a favorite). If you are going to Lhasa, Tibetans appreciate photos of the Dalai Lama, but passing these out may be construed as interference in an internal dispute by the Chinese authorities. If you are visiting foreign residents in China, ask what gifts they would like. They can usually get everything there now.

Packing for Business

Business cards are essential for business people, preferably in Chinese on the back. It is good to take a one-page introduction in Chinese of your company (if possible). A few hotels print cards within 24 hours.

Officials dealing with Japan and Hong Kong have been accepting television sets and condos! Some have asked shamelessly for computers and 'Benzes.' There is no guarantee that an expensive gift will get you what you want. The danger is that from time to time, campaigns rage against corrupt officials who use their positions for personal gain. Chinese jails aren't nice. Chinese legal rights aren't the same. The government has executed people for accepting bribes.

Usually, inviting an official to a banquet to celebrate a deal, or to thank especially helpful people, is sufficient. Modest corporate gifts like agenda books and lighters are fine. Some Chinese appreciate hard liquor, like Chivas Regal, but the tendency is now for wine. People are more concerned about health.

Money & Travel Costs

First, it's a good idea to take a money belt and neck safe (a neck safe is a small purse worn under the clothes suspended by a cord around the neck) to hold valuables. Fanny packs worn on the outside of your clothes can be slashed. Take mainly travelers' checks as a precaution against theft.

If you're on a prepaid tour you only have to worry about incidentals like airport taxes (Y50 for domestic and Y90 for international), bicycle rentals, shopping, overweight luggage, a massage, barber or hairdresser, a round of drinks at a bar, postage stamps, long-distance telephone calls home, laundry, and unexpected emergencies. Then there are **tips**; some tour operators suggest US$6 or Y50 a day for guides and drivers.

If you're not on a prepaid trip, take your credit card (most hotels three stars and up accept Visa, MasterCard and American Express) and travelers checks. Some travel agents and Chinese airlines now accept credit cards.

CHINESE YUAN/US DOLLAR EXCHANGE RATE

*You'll note that prices in this book, as in China, are listed with a "Y" before the number, as in Y100. This tells you that the cost is 100 **yuan**. The 1999 rate of exchange is **8.3 yuan to one US dollar**, so divide the yuan price by 8.3 to get the dollar equivalent.*

Because of the fear that Chinese currency will be devalued, many Chinese are collecting US cash. Take this for shopping in small bills. You get better prices. The bills should not be old, worn nor torn.

Prices differ. Hotels in big, busy cities like Beijing and Shanghai are just as expensive as New York City. Hotels in smaller towns like Guilin and Suzhou are much cheaper. Food in restaurants outside of hotels is cheaper. In street markets you can eat well for less than Y10 a meal if you have to and want to.

Laundry prices and quality depend on the quality of the hotel but if you're watching your pennies, take wash and wear. This book lists sample prices. Telephone calls from hotels can add up. Take more than you need. It will cost you time and money if your bank has to send you more.

ESSENTIAL UP-TO-DATE INFORMATION

In addition to the information below, you can also find websites listed under individual cities throughout this book.

If you're worried about civil unrest, floods, whatever, phone the **U.S. State Department** in Washington, D.C., *Tel. 202/647-5225 or 202/647-3000*, or consult any American consulate abroad (American Citizens' Services). State Department travel information publications are available online at *http://travel.state.gov*.

For Canadians, phone the **Ministry of Foreign Affairs**, *Tel. 800/267-6788 or fax-back 800/575-2500 or online at http://www.dfait-maeci.gc.ca. (other numbers include Tel. 800/561-8868 and 800/267-8376)*. On working abroad, call *613/944-4000*. For immunization requirements look up Health Canada: *http:hwcweb.hwc.ca/hpb/lcdc/osh/travel/index.html*. The Canadian Commission Hong Kong website is *http://www.canada.org.hk*.

Note: some of the airline websites below sometimes have special discounts for web visitors only.

Other Helpful Websites

Some of these websites don't seem to be in operation, or are out-of-date. Hopefully they will be updated soon. They are all in English.

• **Air Couriers**: *http://www.aircourier.org*. You can only take carry-on luggage but you might be able to get a return fare to Hong Kong for $125.
• **Big China**: *http://www.bigchina.com/travel.htm*
• **China Hotels and Buyers' Guide**: *http://www.hotelschina.com/guide1.htm*
• **Chinese Business World's Air Travel Guide for China**: *http://www.cbw.com/tourism/airline/airguide.htm*
• **Chinese Embassy**, Ottawa. *http://www.chinaembassycanada.org/*
• **Chinese Embassy**, Washington. *http://www.china-embassy.org/EmbassyInfo.htm*.
• **China National Tourist Administration**: *http://www.cnta.com*. This site has a train map, cost of taxis, and general information.
• **Foreign Ministry of China**: *http://www.fmprc.gov.cn*
• **Canadian Airlines**: *http://www.cdnair.ca*
• **Cathay Pacific**: *http://www.cathay.ca*
• **Northwest Airlines**: *http://www.nwa.com*
• **United Airlines**: *http://www.ual.com*
• **Cultural Background**: *http://www.chinapage.org/china.html*. This site has a few maps, music, poetry, and history.
• **Prices and Discounts**: Travelocity at *http://www.travelocity.com*

- **Websites on China travel**, weather forecasts, hotel prices (for comparison), and some reservations. These tend to give lists, not evaluation: *http://www.buildlink.com/embassy/.* This site gives the address of China's Ottawa consulate, postal codes, and telephone codes in China. *http://www.chinavista.com* – Chinese culture. *http://www.nihao.com/travel.* See Beijing. *http://www.chinatour.com* *http://www.insidechina.com/cgi-bin/interact/china* *http://www.mapquest.com.* This site has a map of Beijing.

CHINA NATIONAL TOURIST OFFICES

You can get brochures and questions answered from the China National Tourist Offices. Their branches include:

- **Australia**: *19/F, 44 Market Street, Sydney NSW 2000, Tel. 61/2/2994057, Fax 2901958*
- **Canada**: *480 University Avenue, Suite 806, Toronto, Ontario, M5G 1V2, Tel. 416/599-6636, Fax 599-6382*
- **Israel**: *Post Office Box 3281, Tel Aviv, 610303, Tel. 972/3/ 5226272, 5240891, Fax 5226281*
- **Japan**: *8/F, Air China Building, 2-5-2 Toranomon, Minato-ku, Tokyo, Tel. and Fax 81/3/35918686*
- **Singapore**: *1 Shenton Way, #17-05, Robina House, 0106, Tel. 65/2218681, Fax 2219267*
- **United Kingdom**: *4 Glentworth Street, London NW1, Tel. 44/71/9359427, Fax 4875842*
- **United States**: *Empire State Building, 350 Fifth Avenue, Suite 6413, New York, NY 10118, Tel. 212/760-8218 (business), 760-9700 (information). Fax 212/760-8809; and 333 West Broadway, Suite 201, Glendale, CA 91204, Tel. 818/545-7505 (Information), 545-7507 (business), Fax 545-7506*

CUSTOMS

It is easier to get customs information before you leave the US than in China. Find out what you cannot take back. Customs have confiscated dried beef and pork. The US allows no fruit unless canned or dried, but Agriculture Canada allows tropical fruit like fresh mangoes, that are not grown in Canada. Dried medicinal herbs are okay. Certain animal products are forbidden or restricted. For example, both Canada and the US allow no ivory, crocodile, alligator, leopard, or tiger products, as these are endangered.

Many countries allow duty-free coin and stamp collections, antiques (over 100 years old), and 'works of art' (one of a kind-not factory-made copies). Be sure to get a certificate of proof when you buy. The red wax seal on an antique is China's proof that the item is allowed out of the country.

Before you leave, register valuable items you will be bringing back with your own Customs, especially if they look new. You will need serial numbers, or you could carry an appraisal report for jewelry with photo, bill of sale, or Customs receipt (if applicable). This is to avoid hassles on your return. You don't want to pay duty on possesions you've had for years.

In the **United States**, you can obtain the booklet *Know Before You Go* from the US Customs Service, Department of the Treasury, Washington, DC 20229. Americans are allowed a duty-free exemption of $400 on accompanied baggage every 30 days after a 48 hours absence. You pay 10% on the next $1000 worth of goods. This includes a maximum of 200 cigarettes (one carton) and one liter (33.8 fl.oz.) of alcohol. Tax rates vary. For example, the tax rate on carvings from Hong Kong is lower than on carvings from China. You can mail gifts worth US$50 or less, but the receiver cannot accept more than one duty-free parcel in one day. You should tell US Customs if you are carrying over $10,000 in cash.

Canada has a duty and tax-free personal exemption on CDN$50 worth of goods after 24 hours, $200 after 48 hours, and $500 after seven days absence. Over that, you pay about 15%. This limit might be extended soon so ask before you leave Canada. You may send duty-free gifts from abroad of no more than $60 in value each but they must have a gift card enclosed.

Certificates of Origin, obtained at some Friendship Stores and factories, could mean a much lower duty rate on silk, for example. For more detailed information, contact your local customs office or the **InfoCentre**, *Department of Foreign Affairs and International Trade, 125 Sussex Drive, Ottawa, K1A 0G2, Tel. 800/267-8376, or 613/944-4000.* Ask for the booklet *Bon Voyage But...* You can also call *800/461-9999* for automated information, or call *613/993-0534.*

HEALTH PRECAUTIONS

Consult a travel clinic for updating your **immunization** record especially tetanus. You are not required to have any immunizations as a requirement for entering China, unless you've been in an African **yellow fever** area six days prior to your arrival in China. Long-term travelers should ask about Encephalitis B and Hepatitis B.

Some North American travel doctors are recommending **immunization** against **typhoid**, **tetanus**, **polio**, and **Hepatitis A**, good protection if you are going to rural areas off the tourist track. A health certificate is required for people residing in China for over a year and includes an AIDS test. Get one before you leave home.

In south China, **malaria pills** are recommended for malarial areas. Most tourists do not have to worry about this, but those going off-the-beaten-track to Hainan Island or areas of China bordering Laos, Burma, and Vietnam should consider it. Consult US travel advisories before you get to China.

Be warned about the poisonous **lead level** in some glazes. Do not eat or drink regularly out of Chinese ceramics, especially yellows, until you have them checked.

Because of the heavy **air pollution** in Chinese cities, people who are susceptible to respiratory ailments such as asthma and allergies, should take air filtering masks to wear. They should also head for its marvelous countryside. See Adventure and Eco-tourism.

For more details, see Chapter 7, *Basic Information*.

PASSPORTS & VISAS

You will, of course, need a **valid passport** for the duration of your trip and possibly six months afterwards. My husband, whose passport was due to expire in four days, was allowed into Hong Kong and Macau but only after much arguing. It won't be so easy in China. Give yourself plenty of time to get a copy of your birth certificate, photos, and sponsors.

You can get a **tourist visa** from any Chinese consulate in five working days. If you're in a hurry, it can be done in less for more money. You can also get a visa in one working day (or in less if you pay more) at the Chinese visa office in **Hong Kong**. Your travel agent can also get a visa for you for a fee. A frequent traveler should think about a multiple-entry visa.

For a prepaid group tour of nine or more, travel agents can obtain one visa but you have to enter and leave China together. You should ask for a separate visa if you want to leave on your own.

Transit visas are not necessary if you stay less than 24 hours inside the transit lounge of the airport. You must have a visa for your next stop, and a confirmed plane reservation out. In an emergency, visas can be obtained at some ports in China.

Travelers to **Tibet** need to be on a prepaid tour even for one person, and travel agents can arrange this. If you want to book this in China after you get there (cheaper), do not mention Tibet on your visa application form. If you do, the consulate will insist that you get a permit for Tibet before you go.

See **Hong Kong** and **Macau** which also have different requirements.

A **Visa Application Form** requires one photo, the usual information, and the name of your host unit in China. The host can be CITS, the Chinese agency organizing your trip, the hotel where you have a confirmed reservation, or a friend in China who has invited you.

If you are visiting relatives or friends you will need their name(s), nationality, occupation, place of work, and relationship to you. In case of unexpected delays, ask for a few more days in China than you think you need.

Your visa will admit you to any international airport or seaport in China, and to any of the cities currently open to foreign visitors within the time limit mentioned. Your hotels will check the validity of your visa. If you're staying with friends, someone from the neighborhood will probably look at your passport.

A one-month visa for example is good for one month from the day you enter China, not from the day you get a visa. If need be, travel agents can help you extend your visa after you get to China.

Visas are good for most of China. You may need an *alien travel permit* later to go to some off-the-beaten track places even if just traveling by road between open cities. Some provinces like Fujian, Guangdong, and Shandong have no restrictions. Border areas may need permits.

You can apply directly yourself to a consulate, sending your passport by pre-paid return courier, or have a travel agent do it. Line-ups at consulates for visas can be long.

If you arrive in China **without a visa**, you will probably be sent back on the same plane to where you came from. Your carrier will be fined as it is supposed to check your passport before letting you on the plane. You might be fined as well. However, I have only seen this happen once, and I think our guide at the airport bribed the immigration officer who allowed the culprit entry. But please don't count on it.

You may need visas for other countries in which you will be traveling, such as train travel through Germany, Poland, Russia and Mongolia. All these have missions in Beijing. It can be difficult getting a Mongolian visa because its embassy keeps irregular hours. It is faster and cheaper to go to a country's mission yourself. It can be done by mail or courier; otherwise, consult your travel agent. Get as many visas as you can before you leave home.

WARNING FOR THOSE WITH CHINESE & HONG KONG PASSPORTS

If a foreign citizen of Chinese ethnic origin who is also a Chinese or Hong Kong citizen returns to these places, and uses a Hong Kong or Chinese passport, he or she is seen by the Chinese government as a Chinese national. The foreign government cannot help in event of trouble.

CHINESE MISSIONS

Canada

  Embassy of the People's Republic of China, *515 St. Patrick Street, Ottawa, Ontario, K1N 5H3, Tel. 613/789-3434.*

  Consulate Generals of the People's Republic of China, *240 St. George Street, Toronto, Ontario, M5R 2P4, Tel. 416/964-7260, Fax 324-6468; 3380 Granville Street, Vancouver, B.C., V6H 3K3, Tel. 604/734-7492, Fax 737-0154.*

US

  Embassy of the People's Republic of China, *2300 Connecticut Avenue, NW, Washington, DC 20008, Tel. 202/328-2500, Fax 202/588-0032. E-mail:webmaster@china-embassy.org.*

  Consulate Generals of the People's Republic of China:

• *100 West Erie Street, Chicago, IL 60610. Tel. 312/803-0098, Fax 312/803-0122*

• *3417 Montrose Blvd., Houston, TX 77066, Tel. 713/524-4311, Fax 713/524-7656*

• *443 Shatto Place, Los Angeles, CA 90020, Tel. 213/807-8088, Fax 213/380-1961*

• *520 12th Avenue, New York, NY 10036, Tel. 212/868-7752, Fax 212/502-0245*

• *1450 Laguna Street, San Francisco, CA 94115, Tel. 415/674-2900, Fax 415/563-0494.*

HOTEL RESERVATIONS

  Reservations are recommended during high tourist season, festivals, or trade fairs. Definitely have a hotel booked at least for your first night then. Your travel agent can reserve rooms or you can do it yourself. Phone your airline or the relevant hotel reservation system. For example, for the Sheraton Hotel in Beijing, phone Sheraton's toll-free number below or the Sheraton nearest you. You can also fax and e-mail hotels directly. Hotels should give you a confirmation if asked.

  You can also use hotel toll-free numbers to get an idea of prices and specials and then compare these with what travel agents have to offer. Cheaper hotels do not usually accept reservations. If you are traveling prepaid, make sure you are carrying the relevant vouchers and the telephone number of your travel agent in case something goes wrong.

  Some of the major cities like Beijing and Shanghai have direct hotel telephone connections at the international airport. You can try to make a reservation immediately upon arrival. Many hotels have representatives at airports, some of whom get commissions for snaring you.

Some travel agents in North America or China have booked blocks of rooms in many Chinese hotels at group rates. Book through them. Only about two per cent of guests pay the published hotel rates in China. Save your money for something else.

MEDICAL & TRAVEL INSURANCE

If you pay for your travel through some credit cards, you automatically get travel insurance. Do check the terms. Otherwise consider it. Your travel agent can sell it. Ask your travel agent about evacuation insurance if you are going off the well-beaten tourist track. **AEA/SOS International** has clinics and doctors in Beijing, *Tel. 800/523-8930 for enquiries or Tel. 215/245-4707 or fax 215/245-2466 for medical matters; http://www.intsos.com or e-mail:webmaster@intsos.com.*

Check prices and conditions also with **Access America**, *Tel. 800/244-9421. It's at P.O. Box 11188, Richmond, VA 23236-4949.*

HOW SHOULD YOU GO? PACKAGE TOUR OR SOLO?

A prepaid group tour is the most convenient, but individual travel has become easier, more popular, sometimes cheaper, and tailored to your own pace. Individual travel can be time-consuming and frustrating if you make your own bookings. Travel agents are in every good hotel so help is readily available.

Prepaid Tours

Just book with a good travel agent and most of your problems are solved. You can choose a set tour with other people (cheaper) or have one custom-made. The average size is 20 people or less. The fewer people you have, the more expensive the rate per person will be. It is probably cheaper to book a hotel through a travel agent well established with China than to book on the spot after arrival.

China prefers prepaid tours. They use scarce staff interpreters more efficiently and are given preference. Even groups of four pay-as-you-go individuals run the risk of being downgraded or having their reservations canceled in favor of a tour group.

If you just want to see China, a general-interest tour is ideal. Figure out what areas interest you and call a lot of travel agents. If you want to visit schools, factories, or hospitals, take a special-interest or Friendship Association tour. Or make sure schools, factories, or hospitals are included in your tour.

Prepaid tours are usually treated the same in China except for the quality of the hotel and food. You can choose between a standard or a more expensive 'deluxe' room. If the price of a tour differs from one agency to another, it could be because (1) all meals or better meals are included; (2) there is an orientation session, and perhaps a full-time, knowledgeable international guide; (3) one agent is getting a bigger commission; (4) the tour operator has better connections in China and gets better discounts.

Most group tours are flexible, so you can avoid most of the group activities or stay in another hotel (at your own expense). However, deviation means more money. If you get sick and spend another night in the same hotel, the hotel probably charges individual not group rates.

Tour groups can be fun if you have the right people. But a tendency does develop to regard the Chinese as 'them' as opposed to 'us.' As soon as group members start joking about the 'natives,' you've crossed the line and become a group tourist. If you are visiting China to meet the people and learn about the country, make an effort to break free. Venture out into the streets alone. Lounge in parks, especially on Sundays. A lot of students are waiting to practice their English on you. You might even be invited to someone's home.

Tour groups tend to get you up and out by 8:30am-9am daily and you won't see your hotel room until 9pm that night. You won't have a chance to relax before dinner. You usually eat breakfast in your hotel but other meals in different restaurants around town, usually close to the last museum or zoo of the day. Organizers try to save money by not driving you back and forth to your hotel.

Questions for Prepaid Tours with Set Itineraries

How many of your desired destinations are offered? How many days will you have in each place? How many people are in the group? How old? Sexes? Will you be asked for tips for guides and drivers in each city? Airport taxes? Do you have an international guide? National guide? What happens if your plane is canceled or your guide doesn't meet you? Ask about refunds if you are stuck in an airport for a day.

What is the price? Why is it different from another organizer with the same cities and number of days? Usually the price includes visa fee, group transportation (from your home airport or your first point in China?), hotel accommodation (double or single occupancy?), one, two or three meals a day, sightseeing, group transfers, and admission tickets to tourist attractions and cultural events. Does the price include taxes and service charges? Will you be traveling with a guide or interpreter? Are the hotel rooms 'standard' or 'deluxe'? Are the trains soft or hard class?

Price quotes do not usually include passport fees, excess baggage, medical, and other personal expenses. Nor do they include expenses for itinerary changes or prolonged tours 'due to unforeseen circumstances.' Ask about those 'unforeseen circumstances.' These could include plane cancellations, overbooking, arriving at the airport after the plane leaves, illness, or accident. Who pays for these inconveniences? Will you be expected to pay on the spot? Ask about health, evacuation, and cancellation insurance. What are the benefits? What language will the guide speak? What refund do you get if the tour is partly canceled? What hotels do you get? (Check the hotels in this book to see if those are what you want.) What happens if the tour operator goes out of business?

On the Yangtze cruise, are shore excursions included in the price?

All tours are subject to changes in itinerary by the Chinese, so don't blame your travel agent entirely. Prices, too, are subject to change.

Cruising to China

Cruise lines include Cunard, EuroLloyd, Pearl Cruises, Princess and Royal Viking. You usually pay extra if you want a guided tour at ports of call. See also Yangtze Gorges.

Minipackages

Travel agents offer packages that could include only travel tickets, hotel accommodations, and breakfast. You sightsee on your own or book sightseeing tours locally. It is an ideal compromise for business people and those who want to do their own thing. In some but not all cities, you can join a relatively inexpensive local tour, but times are not necessarily at your convenience.

Independent Traveling

Many foreigners have traveled in China happily and successfully on their own. Some backpackers have loved it, not minding dormitory accommodations and delays. Travelers with bigger budgets have an easier time. Your four or five-star hotel can meet your plane or train if requested. You can join a group tour or hire a taxi for sightseeing and hire a guide whenever you need one.

On-your-own traveling is not as easy in China as in Europe. If you can't speak Chinese, however, you can get around with this guide book. The Chinese are usually sympathetic and helpful to lost and bewildered foreigners.

Special Tours

Chinese travel agents are willing and eager to accommodate you, but they are not always able to. Put your special request to several travel agents at home and in China. Give them plenty of time. You can write an organization in China directly with a pretty good chance of getting a reply. The best way to communicate is by fax or e-mail. Letters can take up to three weeks from North America. They arrive faster if addressed in

Chinese with the postal number (code). They are answered more quickly if written in Chinese. If you telephone China, it helps to have a Mandarin-speaking person with you.

Scientists can contact the Foreign Affairs Department of the Chinese Academy of Sciences. Mountain climbers should contact the Chinese Mountaineering Association. School groups contact CYTS. Sports teams wanting to play Chinese teams, or individuals wanting a ski package or parachuting should try China International Sports Travel Service. For factory, farm and school visits as well as monuments, try China Friendship tours. For religious groups, consult your own organizations.

Travelers of Chinese Ancestry – The "Roots" Route

An **Overseas Chinese** is anyone with a Chinese surname, face, or the address of a relative and/or an ancestral village in China. There are no special discounts now for Overseas Chinese. CTS is the most experienced agency for Overseas Chinese. They can help find your relatives and tell you what gifts you can take them duty-free.

It is permissible to live with relatives in China or have relatives stay with you in your hotel. You can take part in special camps and seminars offered by the Overseas Chinese Association in some counties in Guangdong province. Xinhui county has been giving free or cheaper room, board, and travel in the county, and courses for two weeks, mostly for young people with roots in the county. Taishan gives courses, but it charges. These are great introductions to China and the area. Courses could be on language, painting, medicine, music, dance - and are in English.

You could write the Overseas Chinese Association or travel agent in your county for information, or try a Chinatown travel agent, a family association, or a county association. You can probably find these in any large Chinatown in America. A Chinese consulate or travel agent might have information.

Again, if you enter China on a Chinese passport, you are considered Chinese and subject to Chinese laws, not the laws of your country of citizenship.

Before you go, Overseas Chinese should start collecting the names of relatives, particularly of ancestors, born in China. The name of your ancestral village is essential if you want to visit it. Be aware that many villages have changed their names, but in China, you might find an older person who remembers it. Usually you refer only to your father's family. No one cares about maternal lines! The names should help people in your village place you. The welcome is better if they can establish a connection than if they can't. The names, of course, should be written in Chinese.

Take as much documentation as you can: a letter in Chinese from your family association, your father's or grandfather's old passport, and a map of where they lived in the village. If you don't have a Chinese name, get one. It doesn't have to be legal, but it will make things easier for you as you travel around China. Just be sure you know how it is pronounced in both your family dialect and *pu tong hua*.

China Friendship Associations

These associations the world over can give information on China and some sponsor their own study tours. Some entertain visiting Chinese delegations, teach English, collect books for China, show movies, and provide lecturers on China. They can give you an idea of organizations who send people to China.

The Cultural Affairs Office at a Chinese mission can usually give addresses:

In **China**, it's the Chinese People's Association for Friendship with Foreign Countries *(Youxie), No. 1 Taijichang Street, Beijing, 100740.*

In **Canada**, it's the Federation of Canada-China Friendship Associations, *1344 Hutchison Avenue, Prince George, B.C., V2M 5J8, Tel. and Fax 250/562-1655.*

In **England**, look up the Great Britain-China Centre, *15 Belgrave Square, London, SW1X 8PS, Tel. 0171/235 6696, Fax 245 6885. E-mail:contact@gbcc.org.uk. http://www.gbcc.org.uk.*

In the **US**, contact USCPFA, New York Chapter, *122 West 27th Street, 10th floor, New York, NY 10001-6227. Tel. 212/989-5852.* Sidney Gluck, Co-President, *Tel. 212/929-9850, Fax 929-9851.* Isidore Chevat, Co-President, *Tel. 212/321-2524. E-mail:sholom@worldnet.att.net.*

Traveling On Business

The usual procedure is to communicate with a trade or commercial office at a Chinese diplomatic mission, your mission in China, or your government's department of trade. These will all probably tell you to contact a Chinese trading corporation, some of whom have representatives in North America. If the Chinese are interested, they will send you an invitation that will give you a visa, or you could get a tourist visa and investigate business possibilities directly in China. No one has ever asked to see a business visa.

If you want to sell goods retail through Chinese stores, look for a Chinese joint-venture partner. Your hotel business center, trade council, sister-city offices, trade shows, and your country's trade office in China might be able to introduce you to potential partners.

If you have a host organization make your travel arrangements, you should tell your host the quality of the hotel you want because s/he might assume you want to save money. It may not be up to your standards. It is embarrassing for a host to make changes after you arrive since your host probably booked through an old school chum.

Don't forget the business cards, and some description of your company, preferably in Chinese. See also Business in the Basic Information chapter.

Study Tours & Language Learning

For **student exchanges**, in the United States contact the Council on International Exchange of Scholars. In Canada, contact the Chinese Embassy *(http://www.china-embassy.org/)*. Some universities, colleges, states, provinces, and cities organize exchanges. Ask around.

'Self-supporting' foreign students are accepted at some schools in China. You can apply directly to addresses from the Internet or from the Education office at a Chinese mission.

Academic credits may not be equivalent. Tuition depends on the school and has been about $1600 to $2500 for a Masters program, with living expenses $2.50 to $7 a day. Living conditions can be hard.

Some helpful contacts include:
- *http://www.study-in-China.com*
- **Academic Travel Abroad**, **Inc.**, *1000 16th Street NW, Suite 350, Washington, DC, 20036. Tel.800/556-789, Fax 202/342-0317. E-mail:Progdept@academic-travel.com.* This arranges tours to China for key clients like National Geographic and the Smithsonian Institution.
- **CET**, **Academic Programs**, *1000 16th Street NW, Suite 350, Washington, DC, 20036. Tel. 800/225-4262, Fax 202/342-0317. Email:cet@academic-travel.com. http://www.cetacademicprograms.com.* Since 1982 it has been operating programs at Beijing's Capital Normal University, College of Foreign Languages, and the Harbin Institute of Technology (HIT).

Visiting as a Foreign Expert

Specialists and professionals can give lectures or demonstrations to their Chinese counterparts if invited to do so. Don't expect anything more than a 'thank you' and maybe a tax write-off for part of your expenses.

Jobs

The China Educational Exchange wants physicians and agricultural specialists. Foreign commercial companies offer the highest salaries and usually the best living conditions. Get a list of North American companies with offices in China and contact them before you leave home. We have head-hunters listed in Tianjin and Dalian. Ask around. Guides know where English is taught. You can find advertisements for jobs in *China*

Daily and the *South China Morning Post* and websites listed here. If you're in Hong Kong on a Friday, the *Post* has 70 pages of job ads, and there's a giveaway distributed in the MTR.

The **Canadian Executive Service Organization** sends retired Canadian scholars (mainly scientists) and technical experts to China. It aims to transfer Canadian expertise to businesses, communities, and organizations to help them achieve their goals of economic self-sufficiency.

You can also contact the **Chinese Educational Association for International Exchange**, *37 Damucang Hutong, Beijing,* or the *Foreign Experts Bureau, Friendship Hotel Beijing, 100873 or P.O. Box 300, Beijing, 100086.* For job applications, it could be faster to write directly to the Office of the President or the Foreign Affairs Office of the school where you wish to teach; the Foreign Experts Bureau is primarily a central clearing house. The Bureau is looking for people to work in universities, newspapers, publishing houses, and other cultural institutes.

Traveling to China As a Job Hunter

Tourists can try to pick up jobs while traveling in China but don't count on it. If you are an experienced teacher, ask around, anyone who speaks English, even a travel agent, a hotel manager, or any college or university. If you speak English and have any idea about teaching, you could ask any about-to-be-opened hotel or a tourism school if it wants an English teacher or other staff.

Talk with business people about job possibilities. Good English-speaking secretaries are in short supply. But check out work regulations and income tax first. Local hires might be paid Chinese-level salaries, which isn't much.

Teaching in China

China hires foreign language teachers on one to two year contracts. The great need is for English language teachers and also teachers of middle-level technology and managerial skills. There have been more than 9000 foreign teachers a year working in China.

Long-term experts usually have at least a Masters and three years' teaching experience. They should receive a contract, transportation and home leave. The stipend ranges from Y1000 to Y1200 a month, not much. Be aware that 30% to 50% of your salary can be taken out of China in foreign currency. Some experts receive free accommodation, medical care, etc. Their salary is frequently ten times that of local teachers, so no complaints, please.

Foreign teachers (not experts) are usually locally hired and do not get the same benefits. Some money-strapped colleges have hired native English-speakers without any teaching qualifications who just drop by.

(See Fuzhou). They give only room and board and try to help find financing through North American organizations. Some foreigners teach and study part-time. In Guilin, one American student was teaching English in a hotel six hours a week for Y30 RMB an hour plus a meal.

Foreigners should know how to say 'no,' if the Chinese pile work on them. I would also suggest getting advice from someone who has taught in China and bring as many teaching materials as possible. Ask a China Friendship Association. A commitment about sufficient heat and hot water is essential. Some foreign experts have had a terrible time with the cold and one elderly man was billeted on the seventh floor without an elevator. Then they tried to give him a lower salary. Others however have been very happy with their experience.

If you'd like to teach in China, a helpful publication is *China Bound: A Guide to Academic Life and Work in the PRC* by Karen Turner-Gottschang.

Contact also the United Board for Christian Higher Education and the Amity Foundation if you want to teach. Amity is looking for native speakers. Some of the following are professional positions, others are volunteer in which you pay your expenses.

Amity Foundation, *Overseas Program Administration, Church World Service, 475 Riverside Drive, New York, NY 10115-0050, Tel. 212/870-2630, Fax 870-2055. E-mail:daveh@ncccusa.org.*

CESO International Services, *175 Bloor Street East, Suite 400, South Tower, Toronto, Ontario, M4W 3R8, Tel: 416/961-2376 or 800/268-9052, Fax 416/961-1096. E-mail: toronto@ceso-saco.com. http://www.ceso-saco.com.* This is for retired Canadian executives.

China Educational Exchange, *c/o Mennonite Central Committee, 134 Plaza Drive, Winnipeg, MB R3T 5K9. Tel. 204/261-6381.*

China Educational Exchange, *1251 Virginia Avenue, Harrisonburg, VA 22801. Tel. 540/432-6983. Fax 540/434-5556. E-mail: ChinaEdEx@aol.com*

China Teaching Program, *Western Washington University, Old Main 530, Bellingham, WA 98225-9047. Tel. 360/650-3753. Fax 360/650-2847. E-mail:ctp@cc.wwu.edu; website: http://www.wwu.edu/-ctp*

Global Volunteers teaching English, it's at *375 E. Little Canada Road, St. Paul, Minnesota 55117-1628, Tel. 314/239-7793 or Michele Gran at 800/ 487-1074.* Volunteers pay fees and airfare.

International Executive Service Corporation (IESC), *333 Ludlow Street, Stamford, Conn. 06902, Tel. 203/967-6000, Fax 203/3242531. http://www.iesc.org.* This not-for-profit business development organization sends US business experts to China to provide technical and management assistance in support of US-China business.

Peace Corps, *Room 8500, 1990 K Street, NW, Washington, DC, 20526, Tel. 800/424-8580 and press 1.*

United Board for Christian Higher Education, *475 Riverside Drive, New York, 10115 Tel. 212/870-2608.* The United Board is looking for PhDs in the humanities and social sciences, and Tesol-qualified.

United Nations Volunteer, *Postfach 260 111, D-53153 Bonn, Germany. Tel. 49/228/815 2000, fax 49/228/815 2001. E-mail:hq@unv.org. http://www.unv.org.*

VSO Canada, *151 Slater Street, Suite 806, Ottawa, Ontario, K1P 5H3, Canada. Tel. 613/234-1364, Fax 234-1444. E-mail:inquiry@vsocan.com; website: http://www.magi.com/~vsocan/.* They have teaching positions.

WorldTeach, *Harvard Institute for International Development, 14 Story Street, Cambridge, MA 02138, Tel. 800/4TEACH-0, 617/495-5527, Fax 495-1599. E-mail:info@worldteach.org. http://www.worldteach.org.* Six month contracts in Yantai, and a summer language camp in Beijing. You pay a fee and airfare. No teaching experience required.

Traveling As a Casual Student

Many provincial travel and tourism offices offer courses in cooking, martial arts, acupuncture, and other Chinese arts, but primarily for groups. Several colleges and universities offer six-to-eight-week Chinese language courses. It's best to start learning before you go to China, and expect polishing from a short course.

Traveling to China as a Guest

Lucky you. Do be aware that local residents and even government corporations may not know all the attractions you might want to see. One visitor to Shenyang desperately wanted to find the locomotive museum, but local friends had never heard of it. Another guest wasted hours waiting for the host's car. It would be more efficient to take a taxi.

Tell your hosts what you want to do in advance and what kind of accommodations you would like. Offer to pay. Give them plenty of time to make arrangements. And don't expect them to be as efficient as a travel agency. Expect delays and much time wasted with formalities.

Wheelchair-confined Travelers

Only a few hotels have been set up for people in wheelchairs, with wider bathroom doors and bars near toilets. A lot of helpful hands are available, however, and many hotels have ramps. Most of those are in top-of-the-line hotels. If these facilities are crucial to your visit, contact these hotels to make sure a room is available for you.

Among the hotels with lower sinks, bathtub bars, etc., for wheelchair-confined travelers: in Beijing, the Capital, China World, Guangdong Regency, Hilton, Holiday Inns, Kempinski, Shangri-La, Swissotel; in Chongqing, the Holiday Inn; in Dalian, the Holiday Inn; in

Fuzhou, the Lakeside; in Guangzhou, the Garden, Holiday Inn, and International; in Guilin, the Sheraton; in Kunming, the Green Lake Hotel and Holiday Inn; in Shanghai, the Garden, Hilton, Holiday Inn and Westin; in Shenzhen, the Forum and Shangri-La; in Tianjin, the Hyatt; in Xiamen, the Holiday Inn; in Xian, the Garden, Holiday Inn, Hyatt, Lee Garden, and Sheraton.

See also Yangtze Gorges

CHOOSING A TRAVEL AGENT

You should consult an agent experienced with China. In dealing with North American travel agents, consider the following. How long have they been sending people to China? How many people did they send last year? If the answer is more than three years, and in the hundreds, you should be okay. The Chinese do their best for people they know and trust.

It's best to book everything in advance in high tourist season. Many tours from North America are cheaper than flying to Hong Kong or China and booking tours from there. The cheapest flights are probably through Chinatown agencies.

Contact all convenient China-bound airlines, get a quote from its major consolidators, and see if your own travel agent can match it. These are agents who buy large groups of tickets at cheaper rates and sell them at cheaper rates. There may be restrictions of various sorts with them.

For individual travelers, can the agent advise you what to do if your guide doesn't meet you at the airport? Would the agent know the prices and quality of cheaper hotels? Does the city have tour groups you can join on the spot? The cost of taxis?

You can use any of the experienced agents below. And yes, you might save money organizing your own tour group but it's not easy. The more people you have, the cheaper it is. But there are also a lot of headaches as flight schedules, prices and the people you count on change their plans without warning.

GET IT IN WRITING!

If you are traveling without a guide, and your travel agent at home says you can pick up your plane ticket in China, or that your hotel room has been paid, just be sure you get it in writing. I have gone to CITS in China to pick up tickets and they never heard of me. The tickets were later found under the code number of the tour group I was leading, or my nationality. I have seen guests arguing in hotels because the hotels had no record of payment. The traveler has to pay and then collect refunds from travel agents at home.

Travel Agents & Tour Operators

The following agencies have all been in business a long time, especially China Travel Service in the United States and Canada, and China International Travel Service in the US. Most can book Chinese domestic flights, ferry, and train tickets. They can confirm and ticket charter flights between Hong Kong and China. They can confirm hotels with discounted rates in major cities.

These agencies and those listed below can book tours, mini-packages, join-in tours, and special interest tours for individuals or groups. A few can book the trans-Siberian train. All tour agents can probably book international tours like China and Vietnam, or China and Hong Kong. Phone them and compare services and prices.

Prepaid travelers booking through a travel agent usually have to pay the full price of the tour prior to their arrival in China. You may have to pay extra at the end of your trip. If there are to be additional expenses, you are usually consulted during the trip. For example, flights delayed by weather might mean an option of paying for an additional day or cutting out another part of the tour. Many travel agencies cover small additional costs themselves rather than antagonize their clients. On the other hand, you might get some money back.

The top of the line is **Abercrombie and Kent**. Among the big operators are **Pacific Delight**, which can do both individual travel and groups. Smaller travel agents might treat you with more care.

CET specializes in tours for academic groups. **Distant Horizons** has high quality tours with lecturers.

In the US:

Abercrombie & Kent International, **Inc.**, *1520 Kensington Road, Oak Brook, IL 60523-2141, Tel. 800/757-5884 (brochures), Tel. 800/323-7308. http://www.abercrombiekent.com.* This is among the top of the line.

American-International Homestays, **Inc.**, *Post Office Box 1754, Boulder, CO 80466. Tel. 303/642-3088, Fax 642-3365. E-mail:ash@igc.apc.org. http://www.commerce.com/homestays/.* They arrange a minimum of three nights per city with a family in Shanghai, Nanjing and Beijing.

Asian Pacific Adventures, *826 South Sierra Bonita Avenue, Los Angeles, CA 90036-4704. Tel. 323/935-3156, Fax 935-2691. E-mail: travelasia@earthlink.net.* They have had bicycle tours in south and southwest China and Inner Mongolia.

Avia Travel, *717 Market Street, Suite 514, San Francisco, CA, 94103, Tel. 415/536-4155, 800/950-2842. Fax 415/536-4158; http://www.avia.com.* Their specialty is cheaper airfares.

Backroads Bicycle Touring, *801 Cedar Avenue, Berkeley, CA 94710, Tel. 510/527-1555. Fax 510/527-1444; http://www.backroad.com.* Bicycle tours, of course.

China Focus, *875 Market Street 1215, San Francisco, CA 94102, Tel. 415/788-8660, 800/868-7244, 888/688-1898. E-mail:chinaft@pacbell.net.* Expect cheaper three- and four-star hotels – saves you money for shopping.

China and Asia Travel Service, *975E, Green Street, Suite 101, Pasadena, CA 91106, Tel. 818/568-8933, Fax 818/568-9207.* Mr. Zhang Jianhua. They are a branch of China International Travel Service.

Distant Horizons, *350 Elm Avenue, Long Beach, CA 90802, Tel. 562/983-8828, 800/333-1240, Fax 983-8833. Email: disthoriz@aol.com.* They offer high quality tours with lecturers.

Elderhostel, *75 Federal Street, Boston, MA 02110-1941. Tel. 617/426-7788, (toll-free) 877/426-8056, Fax 426-8351; http://www.elderhostel.org.* They provide educational opportunities for adults over 55 with longer stays in each city than most tours.

Indochina Services, *Booking Office Americas, 870 Market Street, Suite 923, San Francisco, CA 94102. Tel. 415/434-4015, Fax 415/434-4145; http://www.indochina-services.com.* They can help you plan an excursion to Myanmar, or enter China from Myanmar.

Hidden Treasure Tour, *Tel. 800/373 5151, Fax 516/889 6665. E-mail:HiddenTours@aol.com.* Contact Steve Powers, who specializes in customized arrangements for Tibet and Nepal.

Intourist USA, *12 South Dixie Highway, Lake Worth, Florida, 33460, Tel. 561/585-5305 or 800/556-5305, Fax 561/582-1353. E-mail:info@intourist-usa.com; http://www.intourist.ru/usa/usa.htm.* For trips to China via Russia.

Mountain Travel-Sobek, *6420 Fairmount Avenue, El Cerrito, CA 94530-3606. Tel. 888/mtsobek (687-6235), 510/527-8100, Fax 510/525-7710. E-mail:info@mtsobek.com. http://www.mtsobek.com.* They offer trips to Tibet and Pakistan and have branches in England and Australia.

Pacific Delight Tours, Inc., *205 East 42nd Street, Suite 1908, New York, 10017, Tel. 800/221-7179 or 212/818-1780, Fax 212/818-1781.* They have offices also in Los Angeles and Minneapolis.

TraveLearn, *P.O.Box 315, Lakeville, PA 18438, Tel. 800/235-9114, 717/226-9114, Fax 717/226-6912. E-mail:travelearn@aol.com; http://www.travelearn.com.*

US China Travel Service, *L/L, 575 Sutter Street, San Francisco, CA 94102, Tel. 415/398-6627, 800/332-2831, Fax 415/398-6669. E-mail:ctsusa@aol.com; also Suite 303, US CTS Building, 119 South Atlantic Blvd., Monterey Park, CA 91754, Tel. 626/457-8668, Fax 626/457-8955. E-mail:usctsla@sol.com.*

If the Canadian dollar is low, tours from Canada might be cheaper. Some experienced Canadian travel agencies are:

Sitara International, Inc., *No. 102 - 3540 West 41st Avenue, Vancouver, B.C., V6N 3E6. Tel. 604/264-8747, 800/888 7216. Fax 604/ 264-7774. E-*

mail:sitara@sitara.com; http://www.sitara.com. They specialize in travel between Pakistan, China, and Central Asia.

Concepts East Travel, *120 Eglinton Avenue East, Suite 904, Toronto, Ontario, M4P 1E2, Tel. 416/322-3387, Fax 416/322-3129. E-mail:chiyue@idirect.com; http:conceptseast.com.* They specialize in cultural, educational, and soft-adventure programs to China.

China Travel Service (Canada) Inc., *438 University Avenue, Suite 306, Box 28, Toronto, Ontario, M5G 2K8, Tel. 416/979-8993, 800/387-6622, Fax 416/979-8220. E-mail:ctsyyz@idirect.com; also 556 West Broadway, Vancouver, B.C., V5Z 1E9, Tel. 604/872-8787, 800/663-1126. Fax 604/873-2823. E-mail:chinatl@max-net.com.*

Chinapac International, *Suite 301, 1195 West Broadway, Vancouver, B.C., V6H 3X5, Tel. 604/731-1693, Canada, Tel. 800/661-8182, USA, Tel. 800/887-8382, Fax 604/731-1694. E-mail:chinapac_intl@bc.sympatico.ca; http://www.chinapac.com.*

Conference Travel and Tours, *4141 Yonge Street, Suite 402, Toronto, Ontario, M2P 2A8. Tel. 416/221-6411, 800/387-1488, Fax 225-7334. E-mail:conftour@interlog.com; http://conferencetours.com.* They are the agent for the fancy China Orient Express railway train.

Intours Corporation, *2150 Bloor Street West, Suite 308, Toronto, Ontario, M6S 1M8. Tel. 416/766-4720, 800/268-1785. Fax 416/7668507. E-mail:intours@pathcom.com.* They can book Trans-Russian trains to China.

Tour East Holidays, *1033 Bay Street, Suite 302, Toronto, M5S 3A5, Tel. 416/929-0888, 800/667-3951. Fax 416/929-8295. E-mail:tour@toureast.com. Also 101-1014 Homer Street, Vancouver, B.C., V6B 2W9, Tel. 604/683-2828, 800/818-1885, Fax 683-3682.* Good flight prices.

Knowledgeable travel agents in other countries:

Note: China Travel Service also has branches in Bangkok, Berlin, Frankfurt, Kuala Lumpur, London, Manila, Paris, Seoul, Singapore, and Tokyo.

Australia: China Travel Service, *G/F 757-759, George Street, Sydney, N.S.W. 2000, Tel. 61/2/92112633, Fax 92813595. E-mail:cts@all.com.au.*

Australia: Helen Wong's Tours, *Level 18, Town Hall House, 456 Kent Street, Sydney, N.S.W.2000, Tel. 2/92677833, 800/252760, Fax 2/92677717. E-mail:hwtaus@ozemail.com.au; http://www.helenwongstours.com.*

Australia: CITS Australia Pty Ltd., *99 King Street, Melbourne 3000, P.O. Box 115 Market Street, Tel. 61/3/9621-2198, Fax 61/3/9621-2919. Attention Mr. Wang Zhenbei.*

Kazakkstan: Central Asia Tourism Corporation, *537, Seyfullina Street, Almaty, 480012, Tel. 7-3272-501070, Fax 3272-501707. E-mail: catfvk@online.ru. Contact: Folke and Christina von Knobloch.*

Nepal: Great Escapes Trekking, *Post Office Box 9523, Baluwatar, Kathmandu, Nepal, Tel. 977-1-418951 or Fax 977-1-411533. E-mail: grt@greatpc.mos.com.np.* They can arrange trips to Tibet from Nepal.

Nepal: Nepal Ecology Treks, *GPO Box 12441, Kathmandu, Nepal, Tel. 997/1-430664, Fax 1-424198; http://www.pacwan.net/raw/trekking. E-mail:ecotrek@mos.com.np.* They can arrange trips to Tibet from Nepal.

Pakistan: Sitara Travel Consultants (Pvt) Ltd., *Waheed Plaza, 3/F, 52 West, Jinnah Avenue, Blue Area, P.O. Box 1662, Islamabad, Tel. 92/51/ 813372-75, Fax 92/51/111-SITARA. E-mail:sitarapk@ish.compol.com; http://www.sitara.com.* Tours from Pakistan into China.

Uzbekistan: Sitara International Limited, *Dom 45, Office 42, Usmon Nosyr Street, 700100, Tashkent, Tel. 998/712/553504, Fax 71/120 6500. E-mail:sitara@silk.org.*

Travel Agents in China

If you want to deal directly with China, Chinese travel agents are listed under the different cities. The head offices of the main competing travel agencies are listed in Beijing. All travel agencies in this book are legally qualified to deal with foreign travelers.

MAKING RESERVATIONS

Book as much of your itinerary as possible beforehand in high season, preferably two months or more in advance. Prices are cheaper in China for flights and trains but you can't always get the flight you want after you arrive. You pay nothing to make a reservation and can always cancel later. Flight schedules are difficult to obtain in China. They do exist in English but it is easier to get them from a Chinese airline abroad.

If you want one of the cheaper seats set aside on some flights for discounted prices (not Chinese airlines), you should book at least six months in advance. If you can't get the flight you want, you can always take a chance and try 'stand-by.' I was 16th in line for stand-by once out of Shanghai and managed to get on my desired flight, but you never know.

For big events like the United Nations Women's Conference, you should try to book six months to a year in advance, even if you're not attending these.

You can book bus tours from Pakistan, ferries from Japan and Korea, and trains from Europe. As for the trans-Siberian railway, it's easier to book now than before. See the Beijing chapter for Monkey Business Infocenter. You should start asking travel agents about these at least two months in advance.

GETTING TO CHINA

BY AIR

In some cases, you pay less through an agent because a good one should know about cheaper flights, excursion fares, off-season discounts, and charter airlines. But shop around and check both airlines and agents.

Airlines do not fly all routes daily; some fly once a week, so plan your schedule carefully. Give your agent a list of stops you want to make before and after China, and how long you want to spend in each place. Suggest several options.

You can fly direct, with one or two stops from many countries and to many cities in China. You can fly to Beijing and Shanghai from Brussels, Los Angeles, New York, Paris, San Francisco, Seattle, Tokyo, Vancouver, etc. There are flights to Beijing from Helsinki (Finnair only), Karachi, Kuwait, London, Pyongyang, Rome, Stockholm, Tel Aviv, Ulan Bator, Vientiane, Zurich, etc. You can fly to Guangzhou from Ho Chi Minh City, Los Angeles, Melbourne, Penang, Surabaya, etc. You can also enter at Urumqi, Harbin and Kunming.

Ask your agent if the international flights are nonstop. Is there an extra charge for stopovers? A day in Paris? You've always wanted to see Kyoto! Is going via Hong Kong or Macau really the cheapest? Maybe it's better via Karachi, Singapore, or Bangkok. How about going on to Australia? How about around-the-world fares? How long are the flights? Vancouver to Beijing is 10.5 hours.

Airlines

You have a lot of choices. **Northwest** is my first choice of a US carrier; see sidebar on next page for more information.

Finnair flies from New York to Helsinki in a little over seven hours, and then Helsinki to Beijing in about eight. You can break up a long plane trip with a stop there. Or you can take it in one big dose. Northwestern's Detroit-Beijing flight is 14 hours. **China Southern** flies non-stop Los Angeles to Guangzhou in 15 hours and back in 11 hours. All seats are big and have individual video monitors. **Cathay Pacific** has been offering free companion tickets if you pay full fare on first and business class between Los Angeles, New York or San Francisco, and Hong Kong. The flight must be paid for with an American Express card.

Airlines flying from North America into China also include Air China, Air France, Aeroflot, All Nippon Airways, CAIL, China Eastern, Dragonair, Japan Airlines, JAS, LOT, Lufthansa, Malaysia, Northwest

CONSIDER NORTHWEST AIRLINES

Northwest Airlines, the leading US airline to Asia, originally started flying to China in 1947. Northwest has an extensive route network with flights to Beijing, Shanghai and Hong Kong. Northwest's Detroit-Beijing service represents the only nonstop flight operated by a US airline to China. Northwest expanded the service from three to four weekly flights in 1998 and offers connections to the Detroit-Beijing flights from points throughout the Midwest, Eastern and Southeast regions of the US.

Northwest's Detroit-Beijing service saves travelers up to seven hours of travel time compared to connecting over the US West Coast to Beijing on another carrier. Northwest operates comfortable Boeing 747-400 aircraft on the route in a First Class, World Business Class and Coach Class configuration.

Northwest also operates two weekly flights from the US to Shanghai via Tokyo and three weekly flights from the US to Beijing via Tokyo. In addition, Northwest offers daily service from New York's Kennedy Airport to Hong Kong via Tokyo.

Northwest's WorldPerks frequent flyer program offers one of the quickest ways to earn free travel in the industry. Membership is complimentary and free travel can be earned for as little as 20,000 miles flown. As a bonus, free travel can be earned and redeemed on Northwest's other partner airlines, such as KLM Royal Dutch Airlines, Alaska Airlines, America West Airlines, and Air China. Northwest and Air China began a formal alliance in November 1998, which includes code-share service, flight connections, "seamless" airport service, and other travel benefits.

Airlines, Pakistan International Airlines, SAS, Silkair, Singapore Airlines, Swissair, Thai International and United.

Regular charter flights are organized by **China Travel Service** and **China International Travel Service** (see below). These are "charters" because of a technicality in aviation regulations. They fly regularly and are okay, but travel agents aside from CTS and CITS abroad cannot usually book them.

Together these companies fly from Hong Kong to Beihai, Beijing, Changchun, Changsha, Chengdu, Chongqing, Dalian, Fuzhou, Guangzhou, Guilin, Guiyang, Haikou, Hangzhou, Harbin, Hefei, Huangshan, Jinan, Kunming, Meixian, Nanchang, Nanjing, Nanning, Ningbo, Qingdao, Sanya, Shanghai, Shantou, Shenyang, Shijiazhuang, Tianjin, Urumqi, Wenzhou, Wuhan, Wuyishan, Xiamen, Xi'an, Yantai, Zhanjiang, and Zhengzhou. Airlines keep adding new cities so do ask.

BY LAND & SEA

Via Central Asia

Travel from Kazakhstan, Kyrgyzstan, and Uzbekistan into China is possible but the rules keep changing. The Chinese embassy in Almaty has refused for a while to give tourist visas, but tourists have managed to go with business visas through Central Asia Travel there. Sometimes the land border is closed for days. By air, the Kazair flights are not reliable. Chinese airlines fly between Almaty and Urumqi, Guangzhou and Beijing and they should be fine. When you get to Urumqi, officials might give you forms in Chinese and Russian. Just ask for one in English. Tashkent also has flights once a week with Urumqi.

Road travel has only been available to tour groups and hitchhiking is not advisable, especially through Kyrgyzstan where the border area is sparcely populated. Adventurers who have done it have gone for six hours in summer and only seen two vehicles and one horseman. If you disappeared, no one would know what happened.

That routing is Tashkent-Bishkek-Naryn-Kashgar. Don't count on public buses. From Bishkek it takes two days by land to the Chinese border at Torugart which closes by 4pm local time. You are also at the mercy of Kyrghyz border guards who have asked in the past for World Health Organization proof of cholera shots as a ploy to get a bribe.

In 1999, a new route should be Ferghana (Uzbekistan)-Osh (Kyrgyzstan)-Naryn-Kashgar. Contact Sitara in Vancouver and Central Asia Travel in Almaty above.

Trains from Almaty leave Kazakhstan at least once a week and arrive in Urumqi about 36 hours later of which 10 hours is spent at the border changing wheels. Intourist, Intours, and Sitara, can make train reservations before you leave home. They might be able to sell a train ticket alone without the preceding land (hotel) package in Russia and Kazakhstan. Central Asia Travel (Almaty) can usually book just about anything.

Via Europe

The **Euro-Asia Land Bridge** is a railway line that runs from Rotterdam to Lianyungang on China's east coast. You change trains in Moscow, Almaty and Urumqi. There are daily trains from Moscow to Almaty. You enter China from Almaty (Kazakstan) close to Urumqi. Contact Intourist (Florida) and Intours (Canada).

Via Hong Kong

Many travelers enter China through Hong Kong. The train from here to Beijing is highly recommended. Buses, ferries and trains go to many places in south China. Travel agents here have a high degree of expertise and many have direct connections with individual tourism officials in

China. Hong Kong is also loaded with professional China watchers, China-related banks, and experienced business people who can give advice. See Hong Kong.

Via Korea

There are flights but also ferries between South Korea or Japan and Qingdao, Weihai and Tianjin. Between Inchon and Tianjin it's a 758 km trip done in about 28 hours. Do not expect a fancy cruise ship. These are cargo/passenger ferries. You can fly from Pyongyong in North Korea to Dalian and Beijing, but you can also cross the Yalu River at Dandong in Liaoning province and then take a train to Beijing.

Via Macau

Macau has an international airport and flight connections with a growing number of Chinese cities among them Chongqing, Fuzhou, Guilin, Haikou, Kunming, Shanghai, Wuhan, Xiamen, and Xian. You can also cross the border on foot or bus. See Macau.

Via Mongolia

An international train arrives from Ulan Bator.

Via Myanmar (Burma)

Indochina Services (see US travel agents below) says that Myanmar has now opened border points at Mong La (87 km and five hours by land from Kengtung) and Muse (124 km and four hours drive from Lashio). You must have both Myanmar and China visas. Indochina Services can arrange a Myanmar car to the border, and a Chinese car to meet you on the other side. Be prepared to tip border officials. You can also fly to Kengtung.

Via Nepal

You can get Nepalese visas easily at the border or at the airport on arrival for about $15 for 15 days or $25 for one month. August is usually the busiest month and should be avoided if possible. You won't get the best guides or hotel rooms. The Chinese embassy is open Mondays, Wednesdays and Fridays only.

China Southwest Airlines flies new 757's between Kathmandu and Lhasa. Flights have been pretty reliable and are scheduled on Tuesdays and Saturdays from April first to the end of November. For views of Mt. Everest, sit on the left side from Kathmandu.

You can also go by road to Lhasa from Kathmandu, but because of rains between June 15 and September 15, there are treacherous land-slides. Most happen before Barabise at the 52-km and 54-km marks (from

Kathmandu), and the 100-km mark. On the China side, landslides are common 13 km from the border. Porters on the Nepal side can carry luggage over the slides for about US$10 each. They have been known to disappear around corners, so keep up with them. Be prepared to hike several hours yourself in rugged countryside.

From Kathmandu to the border is 114 km (four hours or more). From Zhangmu at the border, travelers switch to landcruisers and buses for a rugged 800 to 900 km to Lhasa. See Tibet and Lhasa.

The most expensive tours usually get the best buses. Although the two governments have signed an agreement allowing buses from each side to cross the border, no scheduled bus service has started yet so it is still necessary to switch to Chinese-owned vehicles. From here to Lhasa can take three days if you sightsee.

Travel agents like Great Escapes in Kathmandu can also arrange for you to enter northwest Tibet and drive to Lake Manasarvovar and Mt. Kailash.

Via Pakistan

Pakistan and Chinese airlines both have had flights between Beijing, Urumqi, Islamabad, and Karachi. You can also go by land. Sitara International is the expert on this spectacular route. You can usually get Chinese visas in Islamabad in three working days if all papers are in order.

The **Karakorum Highway** and border posts at Sust (Pakistan) and Tashkurgan (China) are usually open May 1 to October 31 but the rains in July and early August frequently set off landslides, and snow might block the pass early May and late October.

From Islamabad in Pakistan, you can try to fly to Gilgit (Pakistan). Be prepared for delays especially mid-May to July of one or two days because of weather. You can also try to fly from Islamabad to Skardu with less chance of delay. From here the drive to Gilgit is about five hours.

The alternative is road from Islamabad to Gilgit, a beautiful drive with overnight at Besham (six hours from Islamabad), or at Chilas (nine hours from Islamabad and three hours from Gilgit). It is amazing. Think Himalayas and Pamirs. If you can, you should fly one way and drive one way for the view. Sitara Travel in Pakistan (see above under Travel Agents & Tour Operators) can help arrange transportation. The weather is most reliable in September and October.

From Gilgit, a public bus leaves about 9am taking about six hours (189 miles) to the border. You can also get a car. There are two Government of Pakistan vehicles that take passengers between Sust (Pakistan checkpost) and Tashkurgan/Taxorgan where the Chinese immigration is done. Passengers then stay the night at the Pamir Hotel in Taxorgan. From there to Kashgar it takes six hours on a good 179 km road. (It used to take nine hours.) If you have the opportunity, stop at Karakuli Lake at the foot of the Muztaghata mountain. There are some yurts. If you want to pay more to be sure of transportation, CITS can meet you with a vehicle at the border.

Public mini-buses are available from Taxkorgan but don't budge until full. Individuals have successfully hitchhiked. Motion sickness might be a problem. Women have traveled alone on this route safely, though I wouldn't recommend it.

The altitude at Taxkorgan is about 3200 meters or over 9000 feet, almost the same as Lhasa so read up about altitude sickness. The highest point on the road is over 5000 meters at Khunjerab/Kunjirap Pass. The temperature ranges from -4 C to 30 C in summer. I suggest you read William Dalrymple's *In Xanadu, A Quest*, about his 1986 visit before the road was finished, and Diana Shipton's *The Antique Land* about her life in Kashgar in 1946-48.

Besides the scenery, the advantage of this route is its proximity to what used to be Gandhara, the area between today's Peshawar and Taxila, where Chinese pilgrims came in the Tang dynasty to learn about Buddhism. Here are ruins of great monasteries, the influence of Alexander the Great, and superb collections of Greco-Indo art in museums.

Via Southeast Asia

The Vietnam-China border is open and you can take a train right into China. You should take advantage of being in this remote area of Guangxi to see its ethnic minorities. Tours can be picked up at the border.

You can also go by passenger ship from Haiphong in Vietnam to Fangcheng in Guangxi province, 131 miles, and about 10 hours away. See Nanning.

The Lao and Myanmar borders are not generally open to foreigners by land. You can fly into Kunming from Bangkok and soon from Yangon (Rangoon) and Chiangmai. Consulates are in Beijing and Kunming. See Nanning and Kunming.

Via Russia

From Moscow, the Chinese train to Beijing has been leaving Tuesdays and goes through Irkutsk, Ulan Bator, Erlian and Datong, before arriving in Beijing on Mondays. The Russian train has been leaving Saturdays and goes through Irkutsk, Manzhouli, Harbin, Shenyang to Beijing. The routes are the same for both trains until Ulan-Ude near Lake Baikal, but the Russian one continues for 12 hours via Harbin to Beijing.

Moonsky Star Ltd. (Hong Kong, with a sister travel agency called Monkey Business Infocenter in Beijing) can give you detailed information and copies of *The Trans-Siberian Handbook* by Bryn Thomas. It says that there are four- and two-bed sleepers. The Chinese hard-class is very dirty. Take your own food, especially for the Mongolian sector.

You will need visas for most countries on the route. You can book through Moonsky Star (Hong Kong), Intourist (US), CITS, or Intours (Canada). See also Beijing chapter.

Russian Railways say that the Chinese train is 'irresponsibly' overbooked and 'does not allow any mid-trip interruptions or boardings during May-September... If you wish to stop enroute, you should plan your trip using local trains...'

It also says that the Chinese trains have downgraded confirmed reservations, allowed too many people into the compartments, and passengers pass the time drinking. Some cars do not have heat in winter. I have heard the same about the Russian trains. US sources say the Chinese soft-class train is better.

Via Taiwan

At press time, there were no ferry services between Taiwan and China. Travelers from Taiwan usually go to China via Hong Kong or Macau. This could change any day.

ARRIVING IN CHINA

BORDER FORMALITIES

Have your passport, Health Declaration, and entry forms ready for inspection. You get these from your plane or look for them upon arrival at Immigration. You have to present your passport, pick up your luggage, and pass through Customs in your first Chinese city. Give yourself plenty of time between planes. If you are taking in any large duty-free gifts to China necessitating a stamp on a receipt, have that and a completed Customs form ready too.

People with nothing to declare do not have to fill a Customs form (except in Urumqi). If you declare recorded videotapes upon entry, you may be delayed as Customs officials screen them. If you have any trouble, just say they're for personal use. Chances are, your bags will not be searched.

Keep your Baggage Declaration (if any) and your Departure Card in a safe place. You might need them on the way out.

You are allowed duty-free items for your own personal use. Forbidden are fire arms, ammunition and explosives, materials like books and video tapes "detrimental" to China's politics, economy, culture and ethics, poisonous drugs, narcotics and opium, morphia, heroin, etc., diseased animals, plants and their products, unsanitary foodstuffs and Chinese currency over Y6000.

CHANGING MONEY

Every arrival hall and every hotel three stars and higher and some two stars have a place to buy Chinese currency.

GETTING TO YOUR HOTEL

Top hotels have vehicles that can meet you upon arrival if you let them know when and on what you are arriving with train or flight number. In some cities, aggressive touts might compete for your fare and grab your bags. Usually there is a cheaper taxi stand outside. Insist on using the meter or settle on a price before you get in. Take down the odometer reading if there's no meter. No taxi should charge more than Y2 per kilometer. Consult the distance from the airport to the hotel as listed in this book. Most taxi drivers are honest, but you never know.

There is also an airport bus to the downtown office of the CAAC-affiliated airline from which you can get a taxi. It is cheap.

If you neglected to make hotel reservations, or otherwise need help, look first to see if there is a CITS branch or hotel representative in the arrival hall. If not, telephone the tourist hotline, CITS, CTS, or one of the hotels listed in this book.

NOW THAT YOU'VE ARRIVED, DON'T FORGET TO ...

Keep your passport handy for registering at hotels, buying travel tickets, checking in at most airports, applying for an alien travel permit, and changing money. Otherwise keep it locked up in a safe deposit box or in a pouch around your neck. You have to show some identification if you are involved in an automobile accident, for example. If you are staying in China a long time or there is reason for an evacuation or worried parents, register with your embassy or consulate. If you lose your passport after registering, it's easier to get a new one.

Adjust your watch. All of China is in the same time zone.

You can change money at the airport and in your hotel. Keep your receipts from changing money. You will need them if you want to buy back foreign currency.

MAKING CONNECTING FLIGHTS

Consult your cabin crew before you arrive, more than one person. At the terminal, look for the information desk. International passengers do have to go through immigration and customs formalities before boarding domestic flights. Usually the two terminals are close together, but Shanghai is getting a new one over an hour away.

LEAVING CHINA

Reconfirm your flight at least 72 hours before departure. You can telephone the airline yourself unless you are flying a Chinese airline. While Air China says you can reconfirm international flights by telephone, my own experience has been different. Some airlines do not require reconfirmations.

If you telephone, get a reservation number so you can locate your reservation later. Some hotels don't charge for reconfirmations.

Make sure your visa has not expired or you will be detained and fined. See Emergencies in the Basic Information chapter.

If your flight is early in the morning, book transport and breakfast the night before. Some airports have restaurants that open about 7am. Be prepared to pay the Y90 airport tax required for all international flights, including those to Hong Kong.

You can buy foreign currency back before or after Customs clearance if you have your foreign exchange receipts. You need your departure form completed for immigration when you leave China.

Your next big hurdle is Customs in your own country. Have your list of purchases and receipts handy. If you know the rate of duty, list the goods with the highest rate first on your declaration form. Report unaccompanied luggage so they will be exempted too. Show your Certificates of Origin if you have any. The onus of proof that an article is an 'antique' or 'work of art' and therefore free of duty, is on the owner of the goods. A Customs officer might not accept your certificate or receipts. Depending on the country, you probably have the right to appeal any decision.

7. BASIC INFORMATION

AIR POLLUTION

You might be affected by polluted air. Recently, the National Environment Protection Agency said the cities with the cleanest air were Shenzhen, Xiamen, Hefei, Zhuhai, Fuzhou, Nanning, Dalian, Chongqing, Wuhan, Hangzhou, Shanghai, Nanjing and Shenyang, in descending order with Shenzhen the cleanest. The cities with the dirtiest unacceptable air in order are Qingdao, Tianjin, Guangzhou, Zhengzhou and Beijing, with Beijing the worst. *China Daily*, the English-language newspaper which you'll see in China, publishes a weekly air index of 31 cities. On particularly bad days, Shanghai for one tells its elderly to stay indoors.

China is trying to doing something about its pollution: no-smoking areas, no coal-burning downtown, no polluting factories downtown, and compulsory car washing in some cities. Many cities are building expressways to eliminate congestion and fumes. Traffic from outside is restricted during the day.

For your own sake, make sure you use air-conditioned vehicles and don't be proud, wear a nose mask – even if you're the only one. You might have to start to tour early (like 8am) to avoid the rush hour. Some large tour groups (such as convoys of five tour buses all from ocean cruise ships), have moved around with police car escorts. You can visit small cities and the countryside instead, which are interesting and have much cleaner air.

Development means a lot of construction noises too, and you should avoid hotels in the process of renovating if you expect to spend time there during the day. You might also notice that some cities have banned the honking of horns.

BARBERS & HAIRDRESSERS

The best are in hotels and every hotel seems to have a beauty salon. The quality of work, even in a three-star is not bad but you might wonder about the hygiene at that level.

BEGGARS

Yes, there are a few. Use your own discretion. As I would in New York City and if I could, I would ask them why they have to beg, and then decide whether to give. Or take them to the closest restaurant and give them a meal. Or ignore them. Beggars in China are not in rags, nor do they look on the verge of starvation. Many are badly deformed.

BOOKSTORES

Stores with a selection of books in English are usually in major hotels (like Beijing's **Holiday Inn Lido** and Shanghai's **Jinjiang Hotel**), and Friendship Stores (like Beijing's and Shanghai's). Some department stores have them. The best selection is in **Foreign Languages Book Stores**. Good ones are in Shanghai on Fuzhou Street, and in Beijing on Wangfujing Avenue. Don't expect much in smaller cities. Bookstores in hotels should also have the *International Herald Tribune, Asian Wall Street Journal, Time,* and *Newsweek,* and Hong Kong's *South China Morning Post.*

BUSINESS

Trading with China is not like trading with other countries. As one trade official put it, "If you want to play in the Chinese sand pile, you have to play by Chinese rules."

These rules are much too complicated to put into a travel guide. There are lots of books, business guides, and experienced people to give advice. But to get you started: trading with China is done primarily through foreign trading corporations, a list of which you can obtain from a Chinese mission. Joint ventures are negotiated through the **Ministry of Foreign and Economic Cooperation** (MOFTEC). An increasing amount of business is now done with private companies.

Do not expect decisions to be made as quickly as elsewhere. You may need two or three visits as an introduction to show the sincerity of your interest. On the other hand, in one factory, the managers dawdled long enough to take me and several of their buddies to lunch at company expense, more a treat for themselves than for me.

Do take a pile of your business cards preferably with a Chinese translation on the flip side. It would also be helpful to take a one-page introduction of your company in Chinese. Exchanging cards with both hands is now part of the ritual when people meet for business. Talk to people in your embassy or government department of foreign trade and commerce. See also Commercial Disputes below.

BOOKS IN ENGLISH

*To help get immersed in old (and new) China, read **Romance of the Three Kingdoms** while sitting on a cliff at Zhenjiang, overlooking the Yangtze, at the place where the widow of Liu Pei pined for her husband. Read **A Dream of the Red Chamber** while relaxing in the courtyard of one of the reproductions of the setting. Read **Pilgrimage to the West** on a trip along the Silk Road. Translations of these books are cheaper in China, and if you have the time, will add immeasurably to your experiences there.*

*A **Dream of the Red Chamber** (also known as Dream of Red Mansions) is one of the most popular novels because it paints a vivid and convincing picture of how the rich (and their servants) lived during feudal times. Any Chinese over 35 years of age should know it. It is the story of a wealthy family, connected with the imperial court, who lived and declined during the Qing dynasty. The plot might move too slowly for Western readers, who probably will have trouble also remembering the Chinese names. (Make notes as you read it.) However, for details of lifestyles it is excellent, with descriptions of a funeral, impertinent bond servants, the visit home of daughter and imperial concubine Yuan-chun, etc. The sexual encounters are mentioned, and some are surprising, but they are not fully described.*

Attendants dressed as the characters inhabit the Red Chamber reproductions, known also as Daguan Yuan (Grand View Garden) in Beijing and Shanghai.

BUSINESS HOURS

Office hours are usually 8:30am-4:30 or 5:30pm with lunch 11:30 or 12-1:30 or 2pm. China has a five-day work week. Store hours vary with each city and are usually open Sundays and holidays.

CHILDREN - TAKING THE KIDS

I took my five-year-old for a five-week visit, my seven-year old to visit relatives, and my nine-year-old on a group tour. I even took a reluctant teenager on an eight-destination tour. I was glad I did, but then, this depends on the child. A year later, the teenager went back to China on her own with her school to work on a commune!

I did not use a baby-sitter because the children accompanied me to evening movies and theatrical performances. Chinese dance dramas are easy for a child to understand, and acrobats and puppets are fun for all ages. The younger children did find the traditional operas boring except for the amazing fighting scenes.

I would not take a child just to be left with a Chinese-speaking baby-sitter unless the child understood Chinese. On one trip, at communes and factories, many willing hands kept them amused while grown-ups talked. The children were interested in seeing how things were made. Guilin, with its caves, mountains, and boat trip was ideal. They would love the Shenzhen theme parks.

The Chinese love children and are intrigued by those different from their own. You do have to protect children with blond hair and blue eyes, for instance, from being overly fondled. Tour-bus drivers bought mine popsicles and pinched cheeks. In restaurants they disappeared with waiters to be shown off to the cooks.

Two of them became sick with bad colds, but doctors took care of them. They were well in a couple of days, missing only one day of the tour. Two lived with relatives. The seven-year-old had a ball learning how to bring up water from an open well, washing his own clothes by hand, and tending a wood fire. It took a while to adjust to the smelly outhouses, but he managed. The neighborhoods where we lived with family were full of other children, and in spite of initial shyness and the language barrier, they made friends. Strangers on the street and in buses would stop and try to talk to them. Barriers of formality melted right away, and I'm not the only one who has gotten a room in an overcrowded hotel because my child was very tired.

Food was a problem. The young ones lived only on scrambled eggs and *cha siu bow* (barbecued pork buns). Hamburgers and milk are now easier to find. Baby food in jars for infants and disposable diapers are in Friendship Stores. Most hotels do not charge for children sharing their parent's room. Most hotels can arrange for babysitters.

CIVIL DISTURBANCES

If there is any possibility of unrest in China, check with your country's mission for advice. You should send a copy of your itinerary to your mission so they will know where to contact you.

COMMERCIAL DISPUTES

In cases of commercial disputes, the authorities have seized the passports of the foreigners involved, especially those of Chinese origin, until the dispute is settled. A commercial dispute could be the non-payment of a hotel bill by your credit card company. Contact your embassy.

COMPLAINTS

The **China National Tourism Administration** is directly under the State Council, China's cabinet. It oversees tourism in China, regulating prices and quality of hotels, restaurants, guides, and some travel agencies. For complaints regarding travel agencies organizing tours from abroad, contact the Quality Supervisory Bureau addresses in the destination section of this book. You might get a refund if warranted. These bureaus have the power to punish or take away licenses. This authority may not work perfectly, but they should help you. Give as many details as you can: venue, date, people and amount of money involved.

CONTACTING YOU IN CHINA IN AN EMERGENCY

Your family has your itinerary. Your travel agent has given them the telephone numbers of your hotel. But no one at your hotel speaks English and your next scheduled trip to American Express' Client Mail isn't for a week.

The best way to contact you in China in an emergency is to phone the State Department in Washington or Foreign Affairs in Ottawa for help and advice. You can also telephone your country's mission in China. A Chinese-speaking officer can phone the hotel and ask you to phone. And go through your travel agent, the people who booked your itinerary. If you're on a boat on the Yangtze, and the cruise company has an office in the US, ask it to contact you. This book also has addresses for other ships too in Chongqing and Wuhan.

Your family could put an advertisement in *China Daily* too but this only reaches the main cities.

ELECTRICITY

Chinese appliances are 220 volts and have either two, or more commonly, three-pronged plugs (with straight or slanted prongs). Many hotel bathrooms have transformers for electric razors with North American two-prong plugs. Power outages are not common in hotels three stars and up, many of which have their own generators.

EMBASSIES & CONSULATES

Foreign embassies are in Beijing; some consulates are in Chengdu, Chongqing, Guangzhou, Kunming, Shanghai, and Shenyang.

EMERGENCIES

Chances are these things won't happen, but just in case, here are some things to do. In case of earthquakes, flood, plane crashes, and other such events reported by the media at home, do contact your friends and family at home to tell them you are all right, that the floods were a thousand km away. They could be bothering your embassy needlessly about your safety.

Credit cards: if lost, telephone your credit card company collect as soon as possible or you'll be charged for any purchases after date of loss. Hopefully, you will have made a photocopy of the number.

Deaths: someone should contact the relevant embassy, which in turn tries to get in touch with next-of-kin and take charge. The mission can make arrangements for the repatriation of remains. Goods belonging to the deceased and death certificates might be released to next-of-kin only after the bills are paid.

Demonstrations: Don't be afraid of them. They are usually orderly except in Tibet, where demonstrators and bystanders have been shot without warning by police. If a policeman asks you to move on and not take photos, please obey or accept the consequences. Recent demonstrations against African students should not discourage other black people from visiting. I have never heard of any other unpleasantness against blacks. Chinese people stare and occasionally titter at all foreigners. Please let me know if you find anything different. During the 1989 democracy demonstrations, foreigners were treated with respect by the students and caution by the military. I don't know of any foreigners hurt.

Earthquakes: The main danger is collapsing buildings. If you can't get outside into the open, away from falling debris, dive under a desk, table, bed, or take shelter in a doorway. As soon as the shaking stops, usually after a few seconds, rush outside by the stairway (not the elevator).

Expired visas: You can get an extension from the Foreign Affairs Department of the Security Police in five working days in any city. If you pay more, you can get it sooner. Travel agents can help you. See Passports below.

Hostile Crowds: The May 1985 soccer riot in Beijing proved that this could happen. Anyone looking like the victorious Hong Kong Chinese were threatened and abused. If you think you're surrounded by hostile people, try smiling. Chances are they're just curious or even jealous. Ignore them or try to make friends. Speak to individuals quietly, in English if you don't know Chinese. Someone may understand. Above all, act friendly and cool. Shouting obscenities is counterproductive. Call for the police. Apologize if you need to. If someone is drunk, just leave.

Law-breaking: if you are accused of breaking a Chinese law, contact your country's mission. Do not expect the rights that you would have in your own country, like bail, but you might see a lawyer. Minor violations could mean detention and deportation. An American once fell asleep while smoking and set fire to a hotel. Ten people died and he was sentenced to 18 months imprisonment and ordered to pay compensation. Some foreign travelers have wandered into *restricted areas* and detained by the police, questioned most impolitely, and put on the next bus out. You might be put in jail and deported or nothing might happen.

Someone in one of my tour groups took a cloth laundry bag from a hotel. The manager was very officious and accusative, not the least bit friendly.

Just don't do anything illegal! China has relations with Interpol. Illegal possession of drugs could mean seven years imprisonment. Journalists must get permits before interviewing students and reporting on activities in universities. If in doubt, ask.

MEDICAL EMERGENCIES

*Generally for medical emergencies, taxis are quicker to get than ambulances. In Beijing and some other large cities, however, if you **telephone 120** and inform the despatcher that the patient has had a heart attack, the ambulance should arrive with a defibrillator. 120 is also used for ambulances in many other cities.*

For a medical problem while in your hotel, try "Reception," "Assistant Manager," or the attendant on your floor. Some attendants sleep in a room close to the service desk. Many hotels have doctors during the day or on call. As a precaution, always get the room number of your guides.

Facilities for treating emergencies in China are not as sophisticated as in many other countries but Beijing and Shanghai have western doctors. Do not expect elaborate life-support equipment, or to be up walking the day after a broken hip.

The Chinese do not store O-negative blood in their blood banks because Chinese people do not have it. In case of very serious ailments, contact your country's mission for help and advice. A medical evacuation by air even from nearby Guangzhou to Hong Kong could cost about $25,000. Do consider evacuation insurance.

Money Problems: If you run out, ask your embassy to cable home for some, or telephone collect. It usually takes five banking days. **Western Union** can transfer US dollars brought to one of its outlets for a 0.5% fee. The sender has to have your passport number. Western Union is not available in every Chinese city yet. It is however in Beijing, Dalian, Hangzhou, Nanjing, Qingdao, Shanghai, Urumqi, and Xi'an. Its hotline in China is *Tel. 10/63184313.*

Borrow if you can from fellow travelers. Your credit card can get you cash advances with a 4% or so service charge, or some cards can get you free check cashing from the Bank of China or American Express. Away from big cities, cash advances might take hours to clear with questions like, "What is your mother-in-law's first name?" Some airlines take credit cards. You can ask your hotel for a cash advance to be paid for with your bill on your credit card. Embassies might give small emergency loans, but very reluctantly.

Any Visa card with a logo can access any of 1,700 ATMs in China. Shanghai alone has 700 for cash withdrawals. American Express offices are in Beijing, Guangzhou, Shanghai and other cities.

Passports: if lost or stolen, talk to your guide or hotel. Get a certificate from the Public Security Bureau saying it's been lost, and contact your country's mission. This certificate acts as a temporary identification that will get you to a city with your consulate. You should have a photocopy of your passport number. If you are staying in China a long time (US citizens over six months, Canadians over three months), it is always good to register with your country's mission. You will be able to get a new passport a lot easier if yours is lost. Missing passports are so common, CITS has a package that includes two trips to Public Security with a guide and car. You should be able to do it on your own however.

If you are traveling with a guide, your escort might have your passport number. You need a passport to travel in China, leave China, and get a hotel room.

For a new passport, you need evidence of citizenship, like a birth certificate, and photos. Your embassy could give you a temporary passport within one or two hours if you have the proper papers. With this document you can get a Chinese visa so you can leave China.

Losing a passport creates a lot of trouble and additional expense. It could mean staying a couple of extra days or leaving your tour group. Guard yours carefully.

Police: in most cities, the emergency number is **110**.

Safe deposit boxes: you'll find these in hotel rooms, and you should use them. You program them with a code you choose yourself. Just don't wait until the last minute to get your valuables in case you can't get them open. Usually one manager in the hotel has the ability to open them and it could take time to find him.

Theft: pickpockets operate even in daytime. Do not leave purses or brief cases unattended. Hotels have safe deposit boxes. Cheaper hotels have more chance of theft. Always use the peephole in your hotel room door before opening it to strangers. If in doubt, phone Reception. If something of yours is missing from your room, notify the management. If you need a police report so you can claim insurance, go to the Public Security Bureau. Recent travelers in Xian found it took them 3.5 hours to register the loss of a walkman. Did you declare it to Chinese Customs coming in?

Traffic Accidents: If your car accidentally injures anyone, do what you should in your own country. Attend to the injured. Otherwise, stay where you are. Do not get involved in arguments. Wait for the police to arrive. The police will take statements, and if you are found to be in any way responsible as the driver or even as a passenger (were you distracting the driver?), you may be liable for a fine or payment for damages. The fine would remunerate the family of the injured, or deceased for the rest of his productive years. There is a standard formula. If the accident is serious, contact your country's mission.

Travelers Checks: if lost, take your receipts to the Bank of China. For American Express, contact their offices in China. It has courier refunds.

Typhoons: This Cantonese word meaning big wind denotes a hurricane or tropical cyclone. These may hit China anywhere along its east coast from April to November. They usually last for a maximum of three days and you should stay inside substantial buildings on high ground with bottled water to drink and some food. The danger is falling debris, as well as strong winds, rain and floods. Airports will probably be closed. Typhoon Signal One is a warning, and Ten is a direct hit.

ENDANGERED SPECIES

China and many other countries are parties to the **Convention on International Trade in Endangered Species of Wild Fauna and Flora** (CITES). Any species or products of a species on its lists could be seized by the Customs Department of the signatories, unless you have a permit. Get details from your government wildlife service. The much-publicized **Save the Panda** campaign is an expression of this concern. It means that while you pass through any country, you risk confiscation of garments, ornaments and other products made of parts of certain animals, like some turtles.

Locally, however, Chinese officials are relaxed about restricting the sale and eating of some endangered or threatened species, like the giant salamander. Coats of spotted cats have been found for sale in Friendship Stores. But China has executed the killers of pandas.

The problem is knowing what is or is not on the list, and what is fake. When in doubt, don't eat or buy products made from any wild animals, especially spotted cats, alligators, and birds. But some deer, game, birds, bears, and snakes for example, are grown commercially and can be eaten.

Among the other Chinese species listed by the Convention are: Himalayan argali, Tibetan brown bear, golden cat, dhole (wild dog), gibbons, Przewalski's horse, langur, macaque, and wild yak. Among the birds are the relict gull, crested ibis, and some varieties of cranes, storks, pheasant, and egrets. Avoid parts of elephants, crocodiles, tortoises, and marine turtles. You will need a permit for live specimens of all parrots, monkeys, cats (except domestic), hawks, eagles, falcons, tortoises, boas, pythons, and iguanas, and some song birds, cobras, lizards, fish, butterflies, corals and mollusks. Also all orchids and all cacti and many other flora are protected.

There are rules about traveling with exotic pets, and permits must be obtained prior to departure. Contact the **U.S. Federal Wildlife Permit Office**, *Tel. 703/358-2104*, or the **Canadian Wildlife Service**, *Tel. 819/ 997-1840*, if you have any questions.

The authority allowed to issue CITES permits in China is: **The Peoples Republic of China Endangered Species of Wild Fauna and Flora Import and Export Administrative Office**, *Ministry of Forestry, Hepingli, P.O. Box 100714, Beijing, Tel. 64214180 or 64229944*. Branches are also in Chengdu, Fuzhou, Guangzhou, Shanghai, Tianjin. and Hong Kong.

GARDENS & PARKS

Relaxing in a Chinese garden is different from rushing through on a guided tour. Go back to one you especially like and just sit and absorb. A Chinese garden is not just a park or something attached to a building. It is an art form, the world in miniature, with mountains, water, plants, and buildings – a three-dimensional Chinese painting you can enter to try to experience infinity.

Gardens were built for a leisurely lifestyle in which poetry, philosophical contemplation, and the beauty of nature were of the utmost importance. Imagine living here! The ugly world of poverty and injustice was kept outside the high walls.

Take your time exploring. Look at the integration of the buildings with nature, the pinpointing of places of particular beauty by unusually-shaped windows and moon gates. Absorb the tranquillity of the water. Look at the reflections. Think of poetry. The meaning of life. A garden takes time – infinite time.

GAMBLING

Gambling has been illegal here, but it's gradually coming back. There have been state lotteries for decades. In the last few years, horseraces have started again, at first with prizes like cartons of cigarettes, but lately, with real cash. Casinos are planned.

Members of the Hong Kong Jockey Club have been able to place bets on Hong Kong horseraces in Beijing's Hong Kong-Macau Centre. But aside from Macau, China is not the place for gamblers.

GIFTS

Never give a pet dog as a gift. In Beijing, registering one costs Y5,000 for the first year, and Y2,000 each subsequent year. It might end up in the stew pot. See also Weddings below, and Hospitality, and What to Bring.

GLOSSARY OF TERMS & ABBREVIATIONS

An asterisk throughout this book (*) indicates that a site is genuine and under the protection of the national government.

arhats - Buddhists who have attained Nirvana.

bodhisattvas - Buddhist saints who attained Nirvana but returned to help others.

CAAC - formerly China's only airline. Now it oversees all Chinese airlines. It is used here collectively for former CAAC regional airlines.

cadre - in Chinese *kanpu*, meaning core element. Any person who plays a leadership role in the Party.

CITS - China International Travel Service.

CTS - China Travel Service

dagoba - similar to an Indian stupa, a bell-shaped tower under which is buried a Buddhist relic or the ashes of a monk.

feng-shui - also known as geomancy, it is the placing of graves, dwellings, doors and furniture in harmony with the forces of nature

Food Street - term usually used for Chinese fast food or snack restaurant.

guanxi - connections

HK - Hong Kong

JV - joint venture; a business arrangement involving several parties. This is most frequently used in international ventures.

lohan - the Chinese word for arhat, or Buddhist saint

Manchu - the group from northeast China who ruled China under the dynasty name Qing.

Mongol - the group from north China who ruled China under the dynasty name Yuan.

neolithic - pertaining to the Stone-Age period in which man developed pottery, weaving, and agriculture, and worked with polished stone and metal tools.

penjing - the art of growing miniature trees and plants. Similar to Japanese **bonsai**.

PLA - Peoples' Liberation Army.

pinyin - the official system of romanizing the Chinese language.

pusa - the Chinese word for bodhisattva or Buddhist saint, who is on a higher level than *lohan*.

qigong - Chinese yoga. Health and healing through breathing exercises, massage, and magnetism.

RMB - ren min bi - peoples' money, one of the terms used to refer to Chinese currency.

stele - a large stone tablet used to commemorate an event, a life, or an important piece of writing.

taiji or **taichi** - Chinese shadow boxing

Wade-Giles - The most commonly used of the old systems of romanizing the Chinese language.

WC - water closet. Toilet.

wok - a large, round pan for cooking.

work unit - Every salaried worker belongs to one of these.

X - telephone extension.

GUIDES

The people who escort foreign visitors are guide-interpreters, "guides" for short. Training is on the job, usually learned by accompanying an experienced guide for several months. But some agencies have been so short-handed that guides with little English and no training have been used. The Department of Education is responsible for staff training, and prospective guides should spend four years learning a language, Chinese history, geography, and art history. Guides must pass an exam before they can wear an official badge with their photo.

If you are on a group tour of several cities, you might get a **national guide** who stays with you during your whole stay and makes sure that you get your plane and your luggage, and all goes smoothly. At each city you also get a local guide and, at some attractions, an on-the-spot guide. If there is a shortage, you may not get a national guide.

For most visitors, your Chinese escorts will be the only Chinese people you can get to know well. Ask them lots of questions about life in China. Guides are open about discussing their salaries and training, especially if they like you. Some might tell you they get no salaries and depend on tips. It might not be true.

Please be patient when a guide is speaking English. If it is painful to listen to, keep it to yourself. It is better than nothing unless you think you can get a better one.

Confusion over numbers is a common translation problem. The Chinese think in terms of ten thousands rather than thousands. Do not mistake sixteen for sixty or seventeen for seventy. Ask your guide to write down important figures for you. When you are using an interpreter, speak slowly and simply, preferably one sentence at a time.

Remember that guides are not scholars. Their knowledge of traditional Chinese culture is frequently limited to memorizing a set spiel. Take this book with you for background information.

Guides do not usually eat with you. At mealtimes, you can find them at a staff table. Most also stay in your hotel overnight. It is good to know where they can be reached.

If any of them greets you with "It's my birthday today but I wanted to help you out so I came" or some such, don't believe it.

Do be aware that some guides have to take you shopping, even if you don't want to. China's travel agencies have been hit hard by competition. Because they tend to book tours six months to a year in advance, their profit margins get shrunk by inflation by the time the groups arrive with payment. In order to break even, they have been taking a share of the tips given to guides and drivers, making contracts with tourist stores, and taking a percentage of sales. They may have to downgrade the restaurants to which they take their groups. The competition between Chinese agencies is so severe that agencies try to keep prices down at the expense of quality. If you want better service, you have to pay for it. Talk it over with your travel agent at home or head for upmarket tours.

One guide broke into tears and said she would lose her job if she didn't take our group to a particular factory! Our group didn't want to go. This is such a shortsighted policy. Do raise your objections if this happens to you!

As a tour escort, I've even thought of paying money to the guide *not* to take us to a factory. But that solution is ridiculous. With one group, the national guide tried to explain the situation to the group, and offered us other goodies to entice us to go to the factory. We got unscheduled stops in return, and it worked out but members of the group complained. Other groups have gone to the factory and refused to leave the bus. Then they complained bitterly to the travel agency.

I hope something can be worked out before you go. See also Tourism Realities below.

HEALTH & MEDICAL CONCERNS

China is among the healthiest and cleanest countries in Asia but there have been reports of typhoid, malaria, plague, and rabies, usually in isolated rural areas far off the tourist routes. (A few cases of rabies have shown up in Shanghai however). Venereal diseases are back and like elsewhere HIV positives are growing in number. HIVs are still rare compared to other Asian countries. One hears occasionally of encephalitis, hepatitis, cholera, and intestinal parasites. Avoid wading in lakes and rivers in central China's Yangtze River area because of schistosomiasis.

You can find out about these and malaria areas from the World Health Organization or your travel clinic. Malaria only occurs in Hainan and the tropical parts of Yunnan province and you should ask about precautions. It is spread by mosquitos, usually after dark. If you are bothered by mosquitoes there, use the net above your bed, or ask for one. You should use mosquito repellents after dark, and wear long sleeves and pants when you go out at night. Check for malaria if you have flu-like symptoms within a year afterwards.

Chinese medical facilities are good for common ailments. Many Overseas Chinese go to China for acupuncture, *qigong*, and even western medical treatment. If you are sick, you will probably be given a choice of western or traditional Chinese medicine, or both. Chinese herbal medicines are frequently effective, but my son had to be bribed with lots of candy to drink his herbal tea, because it tasted so awful.

Outside of a few clinics in Beijing and Shanghai, Chinese medical facilities might look grubbier than those in the West. A consultation at a hotel clinic is usually cheap or free, medicines extra.

Chinese guides are usually concerned about the health of their guests. They frequently check whether you have enough clothing on. If you complain about your health too much, you might get a doctor even if you don't request one. Most tour organizers state emphatically that tours to China are rugged. They are not for invalids or people with respiratory or heart conditions because of the climbing, the dust and air pollution. The Chinese are especially nice to older people, but older or frail people should take precautions.

Some North American prescriptions can now be filled in China especially at western clinics in Beijing. Some Chinese pharmacies might have our patent medicines. But don't count on it.

If you are hospitalized, you might have to take your own mug, plate, towel, soap, and a friend. The staff and other patients may not speak English. Standards are not the same as in America. In one of the best hospitals in Beijing, beds were only changed once a week.

Remember, a prepaid group tour is usually strenuous with a packed schedule, unless the group agrees to a slower pace. Most hotels but not all restaurants have elevators. Things can be easier for pay-as-you-go individual travelers who can do things at their own speed. If you're not in good health, don't travel alone.

Chinese hospitals are adequate, and some doctors have western training and excellent western standards especially in Beijing and Shanghai. But most facilities are at least 30 years behind what you're used to.

HOLIDAYS, FAIRS, & FESTIVALS

These are the official Chinese holidays:

January 1	(offices closed)
Spring Festival/New Year	the date depends on the lunar calendar around the end of January or early February (offices closed for three days).
May 1	Labor Day
October 1- 2	National Day, celebrating the founding of the PRC in 1949

In addition, the following are celebrated with special programs, but offices and schools are open:

March 8	International Working Women's Day
March 12	Tree-planting day, South China
April (first Sunday)	Tree-planting day, North China
May 4	Youth Day (May 4th Movement)
June 1	Children's Day
July 1	Founding Day of The Communist Party of China
August 1	Founding Day of the Peoples' Liberation Army
September 10	Teachers Day
September 27	World Tourism Day; celebrated by different cities in turn.

The Chinese also celebrate several other traditional holidays. The **Lantern Festival** starts the last day of the **Spring Festival**. The **Dragon Boat races** commemorate the untimely death of an upright official. (See Zigui and Yueyang.) The **Mid-Autumn Festival** celebrates the most beautiful full moon of the year.

Check with travel agents about the dates of festivals around the time of your visit like Weifang (for the kite festival), Kunming (for the Water-splashing Festival and Third Moon Market), and Guiyang for festivals of the nationalities. Be aware that the dates for some festivals might not be decided until the last minute, especially in Tibet. On the other hand, festivals might be canceled without much warning.

Some festivals are just an excuse to sell something, but most are colorful and exotic. Bring lots of film. People dress in their best. Many festivals are punctuated with fireworks, dragon dances, competitions, courtship rituals, parades, pageants, thousands of dancing school children, and special banquets. Some are genuine folk festivals, religious celebrations, and horse and camel markets and, as such, are not organized for tourists. Arrangements for these should improve with experience and time but tourism might ruin the spontaneity.

Some festivals are so well organized, tourists travel with police escorts quickly from place to place, without a chance to stop and take photographs.

I suggest booking a tour for a festival with a travel agency because festivals attract tens of thousands of people. As one of the crowd, you won't see much unless you're well over six feet tall. If a travel agency has organized something, you should be able to get a good seat and at least a place to sleep.

INFORMATION FOR TOURISTS

Beijing and Shanghai have tourist handouts distributed in hotels, bars and restaurants frequented by foreigners. See Practical Information under those cities. In Shanghai, you should be able to get a free booklet from the Shanghai Information Booth in the east end of People's Square mass transit station, one floor down below ground level. Several cities and all provinces and regions have tourist offices and travel agents where free literature is available. Addresses are also in this book.

Consider your hotel your friend. The better quality the hotel, the more information it can give you. Hotels, four stars and up, are usually the best sources. Try assistant managers, concierges, business centers, or public relations. Some hotels organize their own tours. Hotel telephone operators and business centers can usually find telephone numbers for you. Many hotels give out free maps. Ask them to write destinations for you in Chinese so you can go where you want.

Contact travel agents at their local head offices, especially North American Sales Managers. Branches in hotels only want to sell tours and clerks might not even speak English.

China has been producing a large number of maps, guidebooks in English, and a twice-a-month tourism newspapers. The Cartographic Department maps are helpful if up to date. They are very detailed. Jinan's, for example, shows Taishan Mountain and diagrams of the Confucian Family Mansion and Confucian temple. These maps list major hotels, tourist attractions, restaurants, stores, and important telephone numbers. Check the date. Information desks have opened at some airports.

Many tourist attractions have inexpensive, knowledgeable on-site guides paid by the hour. A few speak English. Some tourist attractions also have unofficial freelance guides, who may know very little and speak poor English. Test their knowledge first and decide on a price beforehand. Try Y20 an hour for your group, not per person. You could also eavesdrop on someone else's guide.

Some diplomatic missions have libraries with books about China. The US consulates have current travel advisories with up-to-date information on travel risks. Consulates should also have important addresses like those of doctors and pharmacies.

Fellow travelers are great. Most love to share their experiences. They can tell you what was worthwhile to visit and what was not. Dont be shy about asking.

Foreign residents are also great. Foreign students and experts may look down on tourists, but if you invite them to dinner they should be able to give you a lot of good tips, such as where you can buy cheap name brands and a good tailor. Contact these people at the expat hangouts listed in major cities.

LANGUAGES OF CHINA

In Shanghai they speak Shanghainese; in Shantou, Hainan, and Taishan, they speak dialects of Cantonese; in Fujian, they speak Fukienese. Most of the 55 national minorities have their own distinctive languages or dialects. But the whole country knows **putonghua** or **Mandarin**, based on Beijing pronunciation. Many of the older officials speak Russian. Younger ones might speak English. A few people speak French.

Chinese is not all that hard to understand. Listen carefully as it is spoken because tones are very important and a wrong tone could change the meaning of a word. Some words recur frequently. Ask what these mean. You probably know some Chinese already. Shanghai means above the sea – *Shang* is above. When you get to Beijing, you will hear about Beihai Park, North Sea Park. *Hai* again is sea. As for *Bei*, also found in Beijing, it means north. Beijing is Northern Capital. *Jing* is the same *jing* as in Nanjing, Southern Capital.

Other words that you will probably encounter:

ang = nunnery
binguan = guesthouse
can guan = restaurant
si = temple
da lu = avenue
dong = east
fan dian = hotel or restaurant
ge = small pavilion
guan = pass
he = river
hu = lake
jiang = river
jie = street
ling = tomb
lou = multi-storied pavilion big enough for people to live in
lu = road
men = gate
miao = temple, usually ancestral or Confucian
quan = spring (of water)
sha = sand
shan = mountain
si = temple
ta = pagoda
tang = temple
ting = tiny pavilion
xi = west
xian = county

A PHONETIC GUIDE TO CHINESE

To pronounce Chinese letters, learn the following phonetic alphabet showing pronunciation with approximate English equivalents. Letters in the Wade-Giles system are in parentheses. The following is in **putonghua**:

a (a), a vowel, as in far;

b (p), a consonant, as in be;

c (ts), a consonant, as in ts in its; and

ch (ch), a consonant, as in ch in church, strongly aspirated;

d (t), a consonant, as in do;

e (e), a vowel, as er in her, the r being silent; but ie, a diphthong, as in yes and ei, a diphthong, as in way;

f (f), a consonant, as in foot;

g (k), a consonant, as in go;

h (h), a consonant, as in her, strongly aspirated;

i (i), a vowel, two pronunciations:

1) as in eat

2) as in sir in syllables with the consonants c, ch, r, s, sh, z and zh;

j (ch), a consonant, as in jeep;

k (k), a consonant, as in kind, strongly aspirated;

l (l), a consonant, as in land;

m (m), a consonant, as in me;

n (n), a consonant, as in no;

o (o), a vowel, as in aw in law;

p (p), a consonant, as in par, strongly aspirated;

q (ch), a consonant, as ch in cheek;

r (j), a consonant pronounced as r but not rolled, or like z in azure;

s (s, ss, sz), a consonant, as in sister; and sh (sh), a consonant, as sh in shore;

t (t), a consonant, as in top, strongly aspirated;

u (u), a vowel, as in too, also as in the French u in tu or the German umlauted u in Muenchen;

v (v), is used only to produce foreign and national minority words, and local dialects;

w (w), used as a semi-vowel in syllables beginning with u when not preceded by consonants, pronounced as in want;

x (hs), a consonant, as sh in she;

y used as a semi-vowel in syllables beginning with i or u when not preceded by consonants, pronounced as in yet;

z (ts, tz), a consonant, as in suds and zh (ch), a consonant, as j in jump.

yuan = garden
zhong = middle or central
zhou = city state (smaller than a province; larger than a city)

If you can, ask someone to teach you numbers because you need to hear the tones. Reading numbers will help in museums. You only have to learn ten; the rest are combinations. Learn the polite things first: good morning, please, thank you, and good-bye. When someone asks you to help with English, ask for help with your Chinese.

LAUNDRY

Most hotels three stars and above will do your laundry and dry cleaning if you get it to them by 8am. It should be done the same day by 6pm. Many also have express service.

LEARN ABOUT CHINA

To get the most out of your trip, read before you go. There is a dizzying list of good books on China. The more you know, the more you'll learn and enjoy. A statue may be striking, but it is more meaningful if you know it's the 'warrior woman,' made famous in American literature by Maxine Hong Kingston. A building in a park in Lhasa becomes the movie theater built by Heinrich Herrar where the German refugee showed the young Dalai Lama his first movies. Many books are listed with individual cities throughout this guide.

Lectures

China Friendship Associations and universities can recommend lecturers and some have copies of Chinese periodicals. Talk to old China hands, recently returned school teachers as well as travelers contacted through these groups. See addresses in the previous chapter.

LEARN SOME CHINESE

It is best to learn Mandarin which is understood all over China. But your friends or relatives could speak a local dialect in their home. They should however understand Mandarin.

The same Chinese characters are understood throughout China. The characters used today have been simplified since 1950. Make sure that your teacher gives you the new script and the *pinyin* romanization.

The level of English is improving daily, but is still poor. Take a phrase book. I don't speak much Chinese and sometimes travel alone and have a good time even without an interpreter. The Chinese try very hard to understand attempts to communicate. Draw pictures and try charades.

Make friends with potential interpreters. And remember the more you try to speak Chinese, the more friends you'll make, and the more you'll enjoy China.

Some key phrases are:

hello!	*ni hao?*
how are you?	*ni hao?*
goodbye	*zai jian*
thank you	*xie xie*
I'm sorry	*dui bu qi*
how much?	*duo shao qian?*
good	*hao*
no good	*bu hao*
restaurant	*canting, or fandian*
hotel	*binguan, fandian, or dajiudian*
toilet	*cesuo*
east	*dong*
south	*nan*
west	*xi*
north	*bei*
middle	*zhong*
street	*jie*
avenue	*dajie*
road	*lu*

LEFT LUGGAGE

How do you cope with purchases in China? Is there an alternative to lugging them around the country and paying excess baggage?

This is no problem if you are going to be in the same city twice. Leave purchases with friends, hotels, or airport baggage checkrooms (big cities only) to be picked up later. If you did a lot of shopping in Shanghai and are leaving from Guangzhou in a week, one possibility is sending a package EMS (Express Mail Service) from a post office or DHL courier to your hotel in Guangzhou. It should arrive on time. Just don't count on the regular mail service to get there on time but you can mail packages back home. It just takes a lot more time. See Postal Service below.

LOOKING UP SPECIFIC CHINESE CITIZENS

Yes, you can visit friends and relatives in China, even while on a group tour or business trip. Give yourself at least 30 days for an answer by mail. Ask for their telephone and fax numbers so you can contact them when you arrive. Chinese friends and relatives should also be able to take time off with pay to visit and even sightsee with you. Inform guides if you want to take time off from the planned schedule. Local Chinese can go to your hotel without any problem except after 11pm.

Some local people may feel uneasy about entering a hotel, particularly a fancy one. Many are glad to see inside and brag to their friends that they ate there or at least had a photograph taken inside. If they are reluctant, you could arrange to meet in a restaurant, a park, or their home. You could take them on sightseeing trips with your tour group (for a fee). This will give you time to visit without missing the attractions.

Your chances of going to the home of a friend will depend on the political climate at the time. It could also depend on how embarrassed some Chinese are about the modesty of their lodgings or whether they can afford a taxi or elaborate meal for you. So do not insist if local Chinese friends hesitate.

Overseas Chinese have a freer time talking with Chinese citizens. Chinese people generally are not open to discussing their deepest feelings, problems or sex life. It took six months of living together before one Chinese roommate confided to me how unhappy she was about her parents.

China does go through occasional xenophobic periods; your Chinese friends might get into difficulty if they meet you. Immediately after the 1989 Tiananmen troubles, many Chinese intellectuals were fearful of contacting foreign friends. And in 1999, e-mail was being monitored.

LUNAR CALENDAR

This is uniquely Chinese with the year consisting of 12 months of 29 or 30 days each. Every three or so years, an extra month is added. The year starts on the second new moon following the winter solstice, which could be any time between January 21 and February 20 on the western calendar. In 2000, New Year's is February 5; in 2001, it's January 24; in 2002, it's February 12; in 2003, it's February 1; and in 2004, it's January 22.

MARRIAGE

It could take about one month but it is possible for a foreigner to marry a Chinese citizen. Permission has to be given by the work unit of the Chinese spouse and in some cases compensation paid before permission is granted to leave the country. The government might want to be repaid for education in return for a contracted number of years of work. Consult your country's mission about the implications.

MONEY & BANKING

Major credit cards are accepted at top hotels, many of the medium-priced hotels in big cities, some top restaurants, and many tourist stores. American Express seems to be the most useful, with its free emergency check-cashing service and its ability to pay for Chinese airplane tickets. But Visa can access more ATMs and seems to be accepted in more places. You can buy airplane tickets with a credit card from only a few foreign airlines, like Dragonair, Canadian Airlines, Finnair, JAL, Northwest, United, and Lufthansa. With an American Express card, you can purchase travelers checks at the Bank of China.

Be aware that:

• **Counterfeit** bank notes have been circulating. Money exchanged at hotels and banks are not usually a problem, but money given as change has been. Counterfeits have been as small as Y10 notes. To detect them, hold bills up to the light. You should be able to see watermarks, pictures unseen when lighted from the top. Always carry lots of small change to avoid getting change.

• **Cash advances** cost about 4% and could take hours to get. You might be able to convince your hotel to charge a cash advance as well as your hotel expenses to your credit card.

• **Personal checks** are not generally accepted, but some can be cashed at the Bank of China with some credit cards. You could also try your embassy or hotel.

• It takes five banking days to **cable money** to China, assuming everyone knows his job and has your passport number.

• Payment can also be made with **Renminbi Travelers Letter of Credit** bought with foreign currencies and issued by Bank of China branches overseas.

• **Cash** brings a slightly lower foreign exchange rate than travelers checks.

• **Credit card fraud** is common. Always be aware of where your card is. Make sure only one impression is made. Never leave a card in the hotel lobby's safe deposit box. Always ask for the card's impression back, the one made when you checked into the hotel.

The Hong Kong Bank, Royal Bank of Canada, and Bank of America have branches in China but not always for retail business. This is changing, so check with your bank before you go. Most foreign bank branches are in Shanghai or Shenzhen.

Foreign Currencies & Exchanging Money

In early 1999, the US dollar was worth about 8.25 Chinese yuan, the Canadian 5.5 yuan, and the Hong Kong dollar 1.06 yean.

It is best to take US dollars. Among the foreign currencies also accepted are: Australian, Austrian, Belgian, British, Canadian, Danish, French, German, Hong Kong, Japanese, Malaysian, Dutch, Norwegian, Singaporean, Swedish, and Swiss.

You can change money at border points, government tourist stores, the Bank of China, and major hotels. You can buy back 50% of the foreign currency you originally sold if you can present your exchange receipts.

Before you go to isolated places like Xigaze, Jing Hong and Kaili, ask about money changing. Frequently, this is only done there in banks, not open on Sundays, early mornings, or evenings. Get enough changed before you go. Some four and five-star hotels can change money almost 24 hours a day. A small service charge is added every time you exchange money both in hotels and at the bank. There's no difference in rates between the two. You will probably need your passport number or hotel room number to change money at the hotels. Clerks sometimes accept a photocopy.

In Guangdong province near the Hong Kong border, Hong Kong cash has been accepted in stores and by street peddlers. However, using foreign currency is illegal. Local Chinese value Hong Kong and US dollars because of inflation and because some people are going abroad and need it. Peddlers everywhere, even in far-off Tibet, accept US dollars eagerly.

Remember, foreign exchange rates fluctuate. Please consult your bank, the Bank of China, hotel, or *China Daily*.

Local currency is called *renminbi* (RMB) – peoples' money. The Chinese dollar, known as the **yuan** (or **kuai**) equals 10 **ji'ao** or 100 **fen**. Yuan notes are in denominations of 100, 50, 20, 10, 5, 2, and 1. The smaller jiao notes are 5, 2, and 1. The coins are 5, 2, and 1 fen, and Y1.

Although prices are quoted in foreign currencies, you must pay for tourist hotels in *renminbi*.

MUSEUMS

China has recently opened some very exciting museums: you must not miss the Shanghai Museum. The lighting is good and the titles are in English. The displays are great. Provincial museums in Zhengzhou and Xi'an are also great. So is the Shu Museum in Chengdu. Most other museums however can be deadly dull if you don't do it right. I have seen people hurrying past pieces without batting an eyelash that set my heart pounding.

You will get much more out of a Chinese museum: (1) if you read something about Chinese history first (for a quick course see Chapter 4, *A Short History*); (2) if you take a knowledgeable guide; and (3) if you are eager to learn things like the date of the earliest pottery, weaving, writing, money, etc. It might excite you even more to compare these with the earliest in your civilization. Try to figure out how and why things were made. Trace their development.

China is so rich in archaeology that most cities have good collections. It's just the displays that are unimaginative. Museums are lessons in history, collections of exquisite art, and links with humans who came before you. The problem for foreigners is that most museums do not have titles in English. If you don't have a guide and have learned your Chinese numbers, at least you could look up the dates and get a general idea of the period and what the relic might be. Each gallery is usually labeled with a dynasty name and/or a date and is usually set up chronologically from primitive to revolutionary times.

Some museums have booklets in English. Some museums have been built over archaeological sites, a most intriguing idea. You stand where you know people stood 6,000 years ago and look at the remains of their children. The skeletons are still there, excavated and protected by glass. If you are at all psychic, you might feel some ancient vibes in a situation like this.

Bronzes are not as well known abroad as Chinese porcelains or paintings. The museums in China are full of these ceremonial vessels, easily dismissed as uninteresting. They are, in fact, very special, the product of a highly developed technology with no peer anywhere else in the world at that time. Where else over 3000 years ago has anyone cast 800 kilograms of molten bronze into a one-piece bell? Just think of the logistics of doing it. Did they use cranes? How many finished bells had to be melted again when they did not produce the correct tone? Did anyone get beheaded for the mistake?

And then to bury the result! The economy must have been pretty solid to support this kind of extravagance. Or did the masses have to suffer for it? Confucius, who seems to have been sensitive to the needs of common people, looked back to the Zhou dynasty as a golden age of order and prosperity. Something about the bronze era must have been right.

Bronzes are uncensored history books cast in metal. The earliest script was inscribed on them, like a family Bible, recording family names and important dates. Later, historical events were recorded on them.

The shapes of ritual bronzes were based originally on everyday utensils. From bronzes, archaeologists have concluded that weapons and agricultural tools were basically of the same designs. No one seems to know if the bronzes themselves were used in daily life. They were usually found in tombs buried with the dead for the use of the spirits.

The Chinese cast this alloy of tin and copper from molds. Emperor Yu of the Xia Dynasty (about 21st-16th century B.C.) is believed to have ordered some vessels made by vassal states as tribute. Unfortunately, these bronzes were lost by the end of the Zhou dynasty and have yet to surface.

The oldest surviving bronzes are from the Shang dynasty, and one can trace the development of the art in China's well-stocked museums; the shapes of the legs, the decorations, the type of script. Even if you can't read Chinese, at least you can see the differences in style from dynasty to dynasty.

As you study them, note that the early thin-walled Shang pieces were relatively crude, with two-dimensional patterns and stylized bogeyman figures. Look for ogres, serpents, dragons, and nipples (bosses) in bands. Later, the patterns covered the whole vessel in increasingly elaborate ways. Can you recognize cowrie shells, cicadas, birds, and braided rope motifs? Animal heads became three-dimensional and realistic. Animal statues like elephants and tigers started appearing. Bosses became coiled serpents. (Castings of human figures were rare except among the Ba people of the Yangtze.) Walls became thicker. The shapes of the legs developed from blades to dowels. Then gold or silver inlay was added. More and different shapes appeared. Can you look at an incense burner and guess its date now?

Bronzes were fashionable until the Han, after which the art died out. (See Provincial Museum under Wuhan.)

Some guides are steering tourists away from the revolutionary sections of museums, thinking they may not be interested. Do tell them if you are. It is good to see China's version of historic events. It may differ from what you have always heard. For this reason, Chinese history from 1840 on should be of tremendous interest. Did British soldiers really sack and rape in every city they captured? Was the British ship Amethyst acting cowardly or heroically? Did the missionaries deserve to be thrown out of China? Why do the Communists glorify the Christian-inspired Taipings and the fanatical Boxers? Was the Long March a cowardly or heroic act? Was the Great Leap Forward a mistake? Was the Cultural Revolution a mistake without any redeeming features?

MUSIC & CHINESE OPERA

Music lovers can find classical Western and contemporary Chinese and Western music. Among the best Chinese orchestras are the Shanghai Chinese Orchestra, Hong Kong Chinese Orchestra, Peking Central Folk Orchestra, Beijing Central Philharmonic Orchestra, and China Broadcasting Symphony Orchestra.

Among the most famous contemporary Chinese composers are Chou Wen-Chung (USA), Luo Jing-jing (Shanghai), Tan Dun (Beijing), Ma Sitson (USA), and Ju Hsiaosong (Beijing).

Also look for programs or cassettes that include popular compositions like the *erhu* concerto *Manjianghong*; *The Butterfly Lovers* for orchestra and violin; *Reflections of the Moon on Two Lakes*, an *erhu* concerto; *Lady General Mu Kweiying*, an orchestral work converted from Chinese opera.

The *erhu*, *banhu*, *gaohu*, and *zhonghu* are stringed instruments held upright and played with a bow. The *pipa* and *liuqin* look and sound like mandolins, the *ruan* more like a banjo. The *yangqin* is like a dulcimer played with bamboo mallets. Other Chinese instruments are the *guqin, sheng, bamboo flute,* and *zheng.*

Cui Jian is China's top pop singer.

Traditional **Chinese Opera** should be experienced at least once. It is very popular with older people and is sung in its own classical language. Your guide might not understand it without the subtitles in Chinese. The jabbering in the audience is usually a discussion of what is going on. Beijing has shorter performances for foreigners in comfortable theaters, with subtitles in English.

To the uninitiated, traditional Chinese opera can be dull, with its many long monologues, high-pitched singing, and sluggish action. The villain is always known at the beginning. The chairs are frequently hard, and there may not be heat or air-conditioning. The performance usually takes three hours, and the percussion instruments especially are loud, as if to elevate the audience to a higher level of consciousness – but not as high as at a rock concert.

Chinese opera dates from the Yuan and blossomed into one of the most popular entertainment forms during the Ming. For a largely illiterate population, operas were courses in history. They were performed at major festivals, weddings, funerals, birthdays and promotions for human and ghostly guests.

China has many forms of traditional opera. The most popular are Beijing and Qunqi. Qunqi has more dancing movements and more melodic, mellow tunes. During a performance, one sees either a whole story or excerpts from several operas.

In the old days, operas were social events. As some went on for weeks, people came and left as they pleased, chatted with friends, ate and drank. The crack of watermelon seeds and the sipping of tea blended with the music, which spectators also sang if the tune was familiar. In addition to shouting approval and clapping, one also growled and swore when actors were less than perfect. In the old days, performers were considered little better than beggars and prostitutes in spite of many years of training and practice. Today, performers are considered cultural workers and are respected as artists. You must see the Chinese movie *Farewell My Concubine* about opera performers.

The stories are usually ancient, so a knowledge of history helps. They are also based on classic literature, like *The Dream of the Red Chamber* or *Pilgrimage to the West.* Some are based on modern history. Two books, published in China, should be helpful: Latsch's *Peking Opera as a European Sees It* and Wu's *Peking Opera and Mei Lanfang.*

Mei Lanfang was the greatest female impersonator. It is common to have a man play a woman's role. (The Shaoxing opera company has only female players.) The makeup might bewilder you, but much goes into it: the temples taped to slant the eyes, paste-on hair pieces to reshape faces, and many colors to indicate character. A white face shows a treacherous but dignified person and a white patch on the nose indicates a villain. Red is for loyalty and sincerity, black, honesty and all-around goodness, yellow, impulsiveness, gold and silver for demons and gods.

It is always fun to watch the actresses in love scenes expressing themselves with delicate and reserved gestures. Note how they excitedly carry their tune to a higher and higher pitch within one breath.

Usually the staging, the costumes, and the acting are outstanding. The fighting scenes, if any, are breathtaking and graceful, like ballet. Cymbals and hollow wooden knockers punctuate the action. The audience frequently applauds a musician, especially the one playing the stringed *erhu*. Usually a good opera singer tries to keep his own *erhu* player for life. The costumes are handmade and artfully embroidered, depending on the character played.

The singing takes some getting used to. It can sound like screeching and whining. But it takes many years of training to achieve such perfection. Settings are usually simple and symbolic. The acting, too, is symbolic, and Chinese audiences know what every gesture, every move of the eyebrow means.

Among the symbols: an old man and a girl with an oar are on a boat; a man lifting up his foot as he exits is stepping over the high threshold of a door; crossed eyes mean anger; walking with hands extended in front means it's dark; a man holding a riding crop means he's riding a horse, or sometimes he is a horse. You should be able to tell the difference! A particularly well-executed swing of long hair (anguish) or prolonged trembling (fear) will elicit gasps of appreciation and applause.

Two bamboo poles with some cloth attached represent a city wall or gate. A chariot is two yellow flags with a wheel drawn on each. A couple of poles on either side of an actor is a sedan chair. A hat with two long, dangling pheasant or peacock feathers is worn by a high military officer, usually a marshal; a hat with wobbling wings out to the sides just above the ears belongs to a magistrate. Generals have flags matching their costumes and are mounted like wings on their backs. The flags are distributed to identify imperial messengers.

After the performance, you may want to go backstage to see everything up close, and makeup being removed.

NIGHTLIFE & RECREATION

Just about anything you might want to do can be found now in China. This runs the gamut from typical western activities, such as the symphony and discos, to more uniquely Asian activities like *karaoke* (you sing with a video), acrobats, and opera. Most movies are in Chinese. Look for historical dramas so you can see costumes and architecture, like *The Three Kingdoms* and *The Dream of the Red Chamber*. *China Daily* has notices about cultural events and on national television.

Chinese television consists primarily of documentaries, travelogues, *kung fu* action thrillers, and tearjerkers. It also has news, sports, boring political speeches, and educational broadcasts, such as language lessons.

Chinese acrobats are usually very entertaining. Also offered are song and dance shows and sports competitions. I highly recommend exhibitions of *wushu*, a traditional martial art, and variety shows like the Lao She Tea House in Beijing, where you can appreciate talent in spite of language differences.

Most tour groups will be taken to one or two cultural presentations. If you want to go to more, you can on your own. They are very cheap – usually Y10-Y60. Tickets should be booked in advance through your hotel or travel agent. You can also go to the theatre yourself, just like home.

Dance parties and discos are more fun if you get up and dance, and so are *karaoke* bars if you get up and sing. Dances are organized in public parks (7pm to whenever). Because people are shy, you will find men dancing with other men and women dancing with each other. But many couples dance too. The music is a melange of fox trots, waltzes, tangos, cha-cha, and rock. In some places, you can take your own cassettes.

Night markets are opening up all over where weather permits, for clothes and for some great cheap food.

Nightclubs and North American-type bars have opened, some with live entertainment in the big cities. The best bars are in hotels but many small decent bars have opened. Just be wary of bars where hostesses sit down and drink with you and then bill you excessively for their drinks. Many hotels now have gyms, bowling alleys, and lighted tennis courts. There are huge, magnificent swim worlds in unexpected places like Harbin and Shenyang. There are ice skating rinks in Tianjin and Chongqing.

Hotel coffee shops, bars, and many stores stay open late. Massages are great. By law, men massage men and women massage women, but it doesn't always work out that way. Beijing, Guilin, Wuhan, and Xi'an are among the cities with dinner theatres.

In Beijing and Shanghai, there's jazz, good theatre and a lot to do. Look for western performers too. In many cities, batches of seats are reserved for foreigners. You might be able to get some of these at your hotel service desk and travel agent.

With many foreigners now living and working in China, activities foreigners like to do have now been organized. Many cities now have a Hash House Harrier group, a drinking club with a running problem. Joining a weekend run is not just a good way to get exercise, but an opportunity to meet resident foreigners and English-speaking, western-ized Chinese. On Friday evenings, many local foreigners get together to celebrate TGIF (Thank God It's Friday). They are good sources of information though they tend to be cliquish. Foreigners have organized just about everything from Frisbee tournaments to alpine skiing and camping on the Great Wall.

The days of going to bed at 9pm because there's nothing to do are disappearing in the big cities.

To get information on these activities, look up the *Xianzai Beijing* website, in Beijing. Contact your consulate or foreigners working in hotels for locations and contacts.

NURSERY SCHOOLS

Many tours schedule visits to nursery schools or children's palaces, which are always entertaining and charming. Count on half a day. In some nursery schools, visitors are involved in some of the children's games. In all nursery schools you will have a performance of songs and dances, and get a briefing with an opportunity to ask questions.

Nursery-school songs are a good indicator of the current political atmosphere. At one time the children were singing songs about shooting down American planes. Recently, we found a five-year-old girl doing a sexy dance. Of course we voiced objections to her teachers! In more advanced schools, you may be expected to read an English lesson. Suggest that your reading be recorded so the children can hear your accent and inflections over and over again.

OVERSEAS CHINESE

Do not hesitate to look up relatives (if you have any) in China. You can learn more about China from your relatives than from any tour. It won't be the same but it will be a deeper kind of experience. I'm third generation Canadian. The first time I met my family in China, they pointed out a long-forgotten photograph on the wall of my Canadian family taken 20 years before. My aunt knew everyone by name. Until I started planning a trip to China, I didn't know she existed.

In her home, I saw how a six-course meal could be cooked in one wok in one hour. I learned how politeness smoothes over a multitude of sins, all ignoring my embarrassing encounter with a naked grown-up nephew who was bathing behind a screen in the kitchen; there was nowhere else to bathe. On the streets they pointed to the strange-looking foreigners, my fellow North Americans who had then just started to invade Xinhui. I didn't learn much about the history of the city, but I sure learned a lot about Chinese people and myself.

I think people of Chinese ancestry in particular should visit China. If you feel this bicultural conflict as many of us do, it would be good to explore the Chinese part of your roots. If nothing else, it will help you understand your parents, your grandparents, or your great-grandparents. It might even help you understand yourself.

In my father's village in Taishan, I was shocked to learn he had been born in a mud house. I found the watch towers where he used to look out for bandits, and imagined him riding the water buffalos. My grandfather's grave was a simple mound. I had expected something more elaborate, considering the money my father sent back to the village.

I highly recommend a visit to your ancestral village, if you can find it. Even if you have no relatives there, at least you can look around and see how you would have lived if your ancestors had not emigrated. If you do find relatives, you might find your name, if you're male, in a family history book.

Don't be concerned if you don't have money to take expensive presents. People outside China send back presents to family partly to show off. They also send them because they feel a strong family obligation. People in China ask for expensive luxury presents like Omega watches because they want to keep up with the Wongs. Remittances have supported a few idlers. If you don't want to contribute to idleness and foolish pride, don't give expensive gifts.

Sure they'll ask you to pay for schooling and to help your cousin emigrate to the US. If you can help them, do. If you can't, don't. Getting to know your relatives and learning about China are much more important than a few dollars. You might just want to treat them to dinner at a restaurant, a nice gesture, especially if you're staying with them.

PHOTOGRAPHY

China is now like most other countries regarding photographs. Over twenty years ago, I couldn't even take a photo of my five-year-old on a public boat. Today you can take pictures everywhere except inside police stations and prisons, military installations, and certain museums. Flash photography damages relics. Museums charge a fee or confiscate your film. Out of courtesy, please ask people if you can photograph them close up. Would you like someone to stick a camera in your face without permission? You might find in China people wanting to pose their children beside you for *their* cameras.

If your camera breaks down, look for a Kodak agent, who might be able to repair it for you. China has lots of camera stores. If you want to buy film in China, there's Kodak and Fuji. The Kodak boxes for 100 ASA print film are entirely in Chinese. Do not buy from peddlars who leave the film in the sun. Aim for air-conditioned stores. It is not easy to buy film with speeds higher than 100. Try the Beijing Friendship Stores or specialized photo stores.

POSTAL SERVICES

These are generally reliable and airmail takes seven to ten days to North America. Hotels can provide stamps but for mailing packages you need a real post office. Only international post offices can despatch parcels overseas. Some hotels can send packages for you but you have to pay a service charge and the taxi fare to and from the international post office. In addition, you probably have to have your package sewn up in white cloth or sealed in regulation boxes after Customs inspection. You have to fill out forms in triplicate. A few post offices provide boxes. Customs inspect all packages, even those sent inside China. Registration and insurance are cheap and recommended if you have someone in the city to follow up should packages get lost.

Surface mail to North America can take six weeks to three months. Airmail can take a week to 10 days. Letters mailed in China to Chinese addresses must have an envelope with red squares at the top for the postal code. It must also be a regulation size and addressed in Chinese. Consult your hotel's business center if you have a problem.

Stamps for an airmail postcard to North America costs about Y3.20, to Asia-Pacific Y2.70. A letter of up to 100 grams cost Y10.40; 100-250 grams cost Y20.80 to North America. Registration costs an additional Y6.50. Prices might have gone up lately, so ask.

Post offices are usually open 8:30am to 6pm on weekdays, and some are closed Saturday afternoons. All are closed on Sundays. Express Mail Service (EMS) from post offices takes three days to the United States and cost at least Y147 for up to 500 grams. You can book courier services through hotel business centers or directly with DHL, UPS, TNT, or OCS. These have very strict rules about sending goods abroad.

As for mailing letters to you from home, chances are you'll be home before mail can get to you. If you're in China a long time, you could schedule regular mail pick-ups at your embassy. American Express has client mail service in several cities like Beijing and Guangzhou.

If you expect to receive faxes in your hotel, give your room number as part of your address to correspondents. And keep asking for incoming messages at the front desk or business center.

Warning: many travelers have found that postcards left with money for hotel staff to mail don't arrive. This happens all over the world. It is best to glue the stamps on yourself. Do be aware that some stamps don't have glue on the back. If you want to save money, carry the cards back home and mail them from home. They will probably get there more quickly.

PUBLIC SAFETY

Chinese safety standards are casual except where a lot of foreigners are concerned. We urge you to avoid the average amusement park ride since these are primarily for locals. I have only heard of one cable car accident where foreigners go. A tourist at the Great Wall was in the car when it stopped for the night. Trying to attract attention, he fell out.

Yes, you can go out at night alone on the streets but not to places that are deserted. It's probably safe but one never knows. Recently there have been reports of people being drugged by "friends" and then robbed. Passports as well as cash are much in demand. Most people are fine but you do have to be suspicious, in China as well.

SAVING MONEY

Those who want to save money need more time, and shouldn't care about the highest available standards of cleanliness and comfort. The more expensive the hotel, the higher the cost of other services like laundry and food. Chinese-managed hotels with the same star ratings as joint ventures are usually cheaper. Spend time comparing prices and quality. Avoid services offered by hotels, especially tempting room mini-bars. But ask your hotel about reconfirming or booking flights. They just might do it for free.

All Holiday Inns discount 20% off the published rate for persons 65 years and over. It also gives 10% off food and beverages. Sheraton gives seniors' discounts, and cheaper room prices if booked in advance. Look into special hotel packages, especially in winter.

At each hotel ask to look at the cheaper rooms. They could be all right.

Reception clerks tend to think all foreigners want the top quality rooms. Rooms on the uppermost floors and with the best views are usually more expensive. Tell the clerk you're a student (if you have your card), or a foreign expert (even if you've just given one lecture). Ask if the hotel has CAA, AAA or seniors' discounts. Anything! Ask for the Sales Manager who is in a position to give the biggest discounts. Many hotels have dorms with up to 30 or 40 beds in a room for about Y35 a bed and up. Try hostels. Share rooms with friends, as most rooms cost the same for one or two guests.

Hotels in big cities are more expensive, so stay away from the center of the city. Find a room in small town hotels and commute. Or take anything you can get for the first night, and then look around.

On telephone calls home, ask your family to call you in your hotel room. Rates are cheaper from North America. Avoid hotel e-mail services. They usually charge over Y100 an hour. Look for cyber cafes, or China

Telecom offices where e-mail is cheaper. I've mentioned only the cheaper ones.

Book hard-class trains or take buses or ferries between cities. You might not mind it. Express buses are getting better – almost like home. Avoid travel agents. If you have to use them, use travel agents associated with hotels that cater to backpackers. Their services are usually cheaper.

Do not assume that the Chinese are giving you anything free. Always ask, "What is the charge?"

Eat in bun or noodle shops or at market stalls. These cost less than hotel restaurants and some are clean. One backpacker spent two and a half months eating cheaply at market stalls and never got sick. But others aren't so lucky, so stick to well-cooked food and avoid tap water and raw vegetables. China has a lot of food stores now with cheap, decent looking cooked foods on sale. I've taken paper bowls to China to be filled at street markets. No worries.

Travel with Chinese friends. Avoid tourist restaurants. Invite one of the young people trying to practice English on you to take you to a restaurant where ordinary people eat. Foreign hitchhikers have traveled around China successfully, sleeping in hostels for local Chinese (after much persistent pleading), sometimes for less than Y2 a night. (Take your own bedding and you won't be surprised by bedbugs.)

Some New World Hotels offer a "Hungry Hour" where for the price of one drink, you can eat all the snacks you want. It's a good deal.

Stay with friends or relatives. Courtesy demands you take them presents, but this could be anything from cookies to a refrigerator.

Travel during low tourist season. The south is pleasant in the wintertime.

Backpackers should be able to manage on $20-$25 a day for a bed in a dorm, food, and local transportation.

Take public transportation, or bicycle rickshaws for short trips instead of taxis. Rent a bicycle.

Ask your hotel service desk or CITS if there is a tour you can join. Try to round up other individual travelers to go with you on the same tour. This lowers the rate you have to pay. If you are one or two people, this may be cheaper than taking taxis. But four people sharing a taxi might be cheaper than taking a bus tour.

You might try to hitch free rides with tour groups. While you're at a tourist attraction or hotel, ask other foreigners if you can get a ride with them. They usually don't mind.

Do your own laundry or take it outside your hotel to be done. At the Holiday Inn Lido in Beijing, you don't pay a service charge if you leave your laundry at a store in the building. If laundry is too expensive, buy underwear and tee shirts, and dress shirts at street markets instead.

SAVE ON AIRFARE!

Save before you go to China: look for bargain airfares. Haggle with managers in travel agencies and airline offices (especially Air China, CAIL, KAL, SIA, and CAL). You have nothing to lose but your pride. Read the youth travel columns in newspapers. Talk to backpackers about cutting costs. Look up the web for last minute deals. Fly as a courier. Look at our helpful websites. Check out travel agents in local Chinatowns. What about the train from London to Beijing via Moscow? Check out Avia Travel (See Chapter 6, Planning Your Trip). If the Canadian dollar remains low, US-based travelers might consider buying plane tickets and tours from a Canadian travel agent. It's worth your while to investigate.

Let the Chinese pay your way, or at least part of it. Go as a teacher or foreign expert. Organize your own tour group. You could get free airfare and hotel rooms, but expect a lot of work. You need about 15 people.

SECURITY

Pilfering in hotel rooms is possible so lock your valuables away. Strong padlocks and fancy luggage tags have disappeared between hotels on flights, though usually nothing else is missing. You should watch your purse and wallet in crowded areas. Like elsewhere in the world, take the usual precautions.

Double lock doors at night. Memorize the fire escape map on the door. Do not allow strangers into your hotel room. Check with the front desk by telephone if the person at your door has no key and claims to be hotel maintenance. But generally, do not worry. You can go out safely at night.

China is safer than many places in the US. If political disturbances erupt again, please feel confident that in 1989, tour guides acted professionally. They avoided danger and got their guests out of China safely. No tourists were injured. Some hotels acted admirably, the Palace in particular, checking people out and in to make sure they were safe.

US Citizens Services in Guangzhou which covers southern China says there is very little crime, except for pickpocketing, mostly around the Guangzhou railway station, and in Yangshuo at the end of the Li River trip from Guilin.

SMOKING

There is more awareness of the hazards of cigarette smoking. A growing number of hotels have non-smoking areas in restaurants, elevators, and some floors. Smoking is forbidden in airport waiting rooms and on some trains and all domestic flights. But smoking is still very common. China has the most smokers in the world and 4.4 million Chinese die of smoking-related illnesses a year.

SOCIAL SITUATIONS

Does Yes Mean YES? Well, usually. Cultural differences do create misunderstandings. For example, a memorandum of understanding in trade means that negotiations can begin in earnest. It does not mean, as many foreigners have sadly discovered, that a contract has been signed.

If a Chinese nods and says yes, yes, he could be just trying to please you. He may not understand a word you are saying. So be wary. Ask a question that requires a full sentence in answer. For the same reason, a Chinese might give you dates and spellings and swear they are right. But what he means is that it is the best information he has and if you press him, he will check.

Chinese people are very polite in their personal relationships with friends or business acquaintances. They try not to hurt feelings. If you make a mistake, the very polite ones will not point it out to you. If you do something they do not like, they might ask someone senior to talk to you about it.

But Chinese people may not seem polite at times, especially in crowds, or clerks in government stores. But if someone introduces you properly, most Chinese will prove to be extremely hospitable and helpful. The shop girl who ignores you is probably afraid of you or is unfulfilled by her job. Don't take it personally.

Once I caught my knee in the door of a crowded bus and got a bad bruise. At the time, my cousins laughed while I felt like crying. It was their way of reacting to embarrassment. Just don't feel offended.

Does No Mean NO? Well, sometimes. You will have to judge for yourself when a negative decision can be challenged.

You might hear *mei you*. It means "there isn't any." It basically means please disappear, but when you don't, something has to be done. Some foreigners have challenged it at airline offices by standing firm, smiling, asking for the manager, and refusing to budge until they got a ticket.

By protesting to a hotel clerk who said there was no room, I did get a bed in a dorm. This does not mean you should try to argue every time you are told it is not possible, or that your safety cannot be guaranteed. It could mean: (1) language is a problem and they do not understand your request; (2) they don't want to be bothered trying; (3) they don't want too many people going there, but if you insist, they'll let you go; (4) there is genuine concern for your safety; (5) you really aren't allowed to go.

Arguing is an art too. Do not lose your temper or you've lost the battle. Suggest an alternative.

Note: Sometimes a 'no' answer is a 'no.' Sometimes 'no' should be answered with "How much will it cost?" or "Would Y10 help?"

Ask Questions: an official of the Overseas Chinese Travel Service once told me the only advice he had for visitors was, "ask questions." It is good advice. The Chinese do not volunteer much information. So when in doubt, ask!

Applause: you could be greeted by applause as a sign of welcome at institutions and cultural performances. It might even happen on the streets. Applaud back.

Criticisms and Suggestions: you may be asked for these. If you have any, do give them. It will help improve services. Mention that the bathroom floor is filthy. Ask the attendant to clean it. If an attendant has been particularly helpful, write it down. She may get a bonus.

Good Manners: while it may be fashionable to be late elsewhere in Asia, this is not so in China, where groups of children may be outside in the rain waiting for your car so they can applaud as you arrive. Traditionally, Chinese conversations, even business conversations, start out with something innocuous: a discussion of the weather or a painting on the wall. A friendly mood is set first. Then comes the business.

Chinese people may not be polite in crowds. They may surround your bus and stare at you. But it is their country. Also, when using an interpreter, don't forget to look at the person with whom you are actually conversing. When giving out business cards, use both hands and stand, with the writing facing the receiver. Do not put cards received immediately into your pocket. Read them carefully first and maybe make some comment about them.

Chinese Hospitality: this can be very lavish and people may go into debt to show how happy they are to see you. It is always appropriate to take a gift when you go to a Chinese home. Presents or money for the children are fine (about Y20 each) if you are a relative or a close friend. Otherwise, it is insulting. Wine, fruit or candy is acceptable. If you have time for a return banquet, that would be the easy way out.

If you are accompanied by Chinese friends or relatives, avoid buying anything in a store because they may want to pay for it. The salary range for most people is quite low. Chinese don't have to pay exorbitant medical bills when sick, most pay no income tax, and rent is low. But people have to save a long time to buy what you wouldn't think twice about buying. Hospitality may demand that you be given a gift. Suggest something inexpensive if you are asked.

I have visited many homes – of peasants, officials, workers, and professional people. By western standards, most are crowded. Poorer families might share a kitchen and bathroom with other families. In only rare cases will there be room for overnight guests, especially in the cities.

In rural areas, you might have to sightsee on foot or on the hard back ends of bicycles if your hosts cannot afford any other means of transportation. It is a real adventure!

If You're Invited to a Wedding: in old China, a gift of money in a red packet was the accepted thing to give. Money is still much appreciated. But gifts to help set up a new household are more frequently given now: porcelain tea sets, video players, and bed covers (preferably red, for happiness). In some places, giving a clock is bad luck. It implies a time limit on the marriage.

Wedding invitations usually mean a banquet, but do ask. You can say something like: "I've never been to a Chinese wedding before. Tell me what to expect." Budget Y200 for casual acquaintances, more for business colleagues.

Weddings have become big business. Wedding stores have sprung up renting out elaborate costumes for photographs with expensive make-up artists to help.

Names and Forms of Address: "attendant" is the best translation for all service personnel like waiters, room boys, and chambermaids. If you have to get their attention, you can call them *fu wu yuan*. Ask people what they want to be called. Some have names in English.

Relatives are referred to and called by their relationship to you, like Second Aunt Older Than My Father, or Fifth Maternal Uncle of My Grandfather's Generation, both one word in Chinese. Your relatives will tell you what to call them.

Chinese put surnames first. Chou En-lai would be Premier Chou. You rarely address a person by his given name, except children or relatives. Recently there's been talk of a return to 'tung chi' or 'comrade,' back to communist discipline.

Guanxi: this means relationships, influence, pull, or connections, and are an important part of Chinese life. Schoolmates, teachers, relatives, workmates - people who know each other well have a stronger and longer hold on each other than in the West. Guanxi is related to merit and to helping each other. Strangers are politely accepted, but with reservation, until they have proved themselves trustworthy, friendly, and useful. But this isn't fair to capable people without connections.

Flirting: you will probably embarrass older Chinese people if you indulge in too much display of affection in public, even with your own spouse. Older Chinese will be embarrassed. Friendly embraces are unusual even upon greeting a Chinese friend of long standing. The younger generation is more understanding. You will also embarrass Chinese people if you lose your temper with anyone.

Joking about Politics and Sex: many visitors are warned not to make fun of sex or politics, particularly Chinese politics. With the older generation, to joke about sex is embarrassing. Sex is very private. To joke about politics or even to argue about it is to show lack of sensitivity. Politics is taken very seriously in China. People are put into jail because of it, lose their jobs, and spend long hours in meetings discussing political implications. Some young people, however, might find such humor refreshing and I have heard some tell hilarious (and perhaps dangerous) political jokes in public.

Political Questions: don't be afraid. If it is done in the right spirit, both the Chinese and you can learn a lot. Political discussions can get heated. If you succeed in convincing them, it wont be because of shouting and red faces.

If they look uncomfortable with the question, don't pursue it. They may be under a lot of pressure to give the correct political answer and they may not know it. The better you know a person, the franker an answer you will get. And no answer is also an answer, if you know what I mean.

Warning: if a young Chinese woman is walking with a Caucasian man, many Chinese assume she is a prostitute. Prostitution is illegal and the police have been known to wait and watch so they can catch couples in bed. It is illegal to be a customer. It is illegal for a man to be in the same taxi cab as a Chinese woman after 11pm.

SPELLINGS: NAMES OF PEOPLE

Pinyin	Wade-Giles
Bainqen Lama	Panchen Lama
Cixi	Tzu Hsi (Tsu-hsi, Qing Empress Dowager)
Deng Xiaoping	Teng Hsiao-ping
Feng Yuxiang	Feng Yu-hsiang (general)
Guan Yu	Kuan Yu (Three Kingdoms)
Guo Moruo	Kuo Mo Ruo
Hua Kuofeng	Hua Guo-feng (former Party chairman)
Jiang Jieshi	Chiang Kai-shek
Jiang Qing	Chiang Ching (widow of Mao Tse-tung)
Lin Biao	Lin Piao
Liu Shaoqi	Liu Shao-chi (former president)
Mao Zedong	Mao Tse-tung
Sun Yixian	Sun Yat-sen (father of republican China)
Xuan Zhang	Hsuan-tsang (Tang dynasty monk)
Yuan Shikai	Yuan Shih-kai (2nd president of China)
Zhong Shan	Chung Shan (honorific name of Sun Yat-sen)
Zhou Enlai	Chou En-lai (former premier of China)
Zhu Yanzhang	Chu Yuan-chuan (first Ming Emperor)

SPITTING

Campaigns in some cities have taken place against the unhealthy and disgusting habit of spitting in public, a reflection of rural society. Fines in Beijing have averaged Y42 and have been successful in curtailing, but not eliminating it. The Chinese believe that swallowing phlegm is unhealthy.

SYMBOLS

You will see these everywhere; in palaces, temples, pagodas, museums, fancy restaurants, gardens, parks, on dishes, windows, and screens. Knowing what they are will help you recognize bits of Chinese culture even in North America in Chinese restaurants.

The Chinese **Dragon** is said to have the head of a camel, the horns of a deer, the eyes of a rabbit, the ears of a cow, the neck of a snake, the belly of a frog, the scales of a carp, the claws of a hawk, and the palm of a tiger. It has whiskers and a beard and is deaf. It is generally regarded as benevolent but is also the source of thunder and lightning. The five-clawed variation was once reserved exclusively for the emperor. The flaming ball represents thunder and lightning, the sun or the moon, or the pearl of potentiality. It is frequently surrounded by clouds.

THE DRAGON OF HEAVEN

The **cloud design** is most frequently blue and depicted in the lower border of a rich man's gown, in a traditional opera costume, or in an antique portrait.

The **scepter** is frequently about half a meter long and made of metal, stone, bone, or wood. It is like a magic wand and is given as a gift, a symbol of good wishes for the prosperity and longevity of the recipient. The larger ones are found in museums.

The **lion** is not native to China. The design is unique to China because the craftsmen never saw a real one. Lions are frequently seen in front of buildings as protectors either playing with a ball (male) or a kitten (female). They are considered benevolent. The **ball** is said by some to represent the imperial treasury or peace. Others say it is the sun, a precious stone, or the Yin-yang. Seen also on festive occasions as a costume for dancers, the lion is sometimes confused with the **Fo dog**, which is usually blue with longer ears.

The **phoenix** is said to resemble a swan in front, a unicorn behind, with the throat of a swallow, the bill of a fowl, the neck of a snake, the tail of a peacock, the forehead of a crane, the crown of a Mandarin duck, the stripes of a dragon, and the back of a tortoise. Its appearance is said to mean an era of peace and prosperity. It was the symbol used by the empresses of China and is often combined in designs with the dragon.

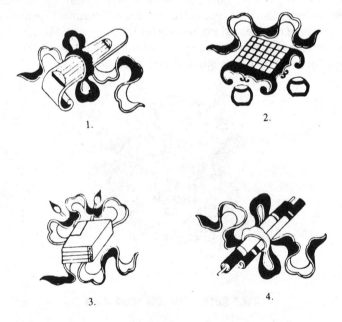

The intellectual elite was associated
with these four symbols in ancient times with:
1. The harp 2. The chess board 3. The books 4. The paintings.

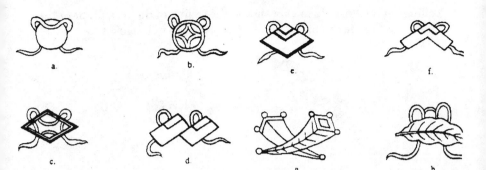

THE EIGHT PRECIOUS THINGS:
a. the pearl; b. the coin; c. the rhombus (victory); d. the books;
e. the paintings; f. the musical stone of jade (blessing);
g. the rhinoceros-horn cups; h. the artemisia leaf (dignity)

*These are only two of the many variations frequently seen.
There is even a teapot in the Shou design.*
1. the round *Shou* 2. the long *Shou*, both meaning long life

Below is one of the many variations of the character for happiness.
Sometimes it is circular and doubled, especially prominent at weddings.

THE FU (HAPPINESS)

The word for bat in Chinese is *fu*. So is the word for happiness. A bat
is thus a symbol of happiness. These are everywhere: on the walls and

ceilings of the Forbidden City and on the ceiling of the restaurant of the Peace Hotel in Shanghai. The peach is a symbol of longevity.

The bat

Bat and peach

FIVE BATS, SURROUNDING THE CHARACTER SHOU

When five bats are combined with the longevity character, they mean the five great blessings: happiness, wealth, peace, virtue, and longevity.

SCEPTER, WRITING BRUSH, & UNCOINED SILVER

Together, these are a symbol of success.

THE THREE FRUITS

The three fruits are fragrant fingers of Buddha, peach, and pomegranate. Together they mean happiness, longevity, and male children.

Prunus   Orchid

Bamboo   Peony

The prunus or plum blossom symbolizes beauty; the orchid, fragrance; bamboo is an emblem of longevity, and the peony means wealth and respectability.

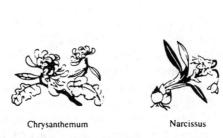

Peach blossom   Lotus flower

Chrysanthemum   Narcissus

These are featured singly or combined in a set of four: the peach blossom represents spring, the lotus flower is summer, chrysanthemum is autumn, and narcissus is winter. Frequently there are only one of each of these on a four-panel screen.

Other common symbols are the **crane** (longevity), the **stag** (longevity and prosperity), and the **lotus** (purity and perfection). The Buddha is usually seated on a lotus.

Among the many strange beings are the two at the top two corners of many temple roofs, tails pointing to the sky. This is a carp turning into a dragon, symbolic of a scholar turning into a magistrate. There is also the unicorn, known as *qi-lin*, with the body of the musk deer, the tail of an ox, the forehead of a wolf, and the hoofs of a horse. The male has a horn, the female does not. It is a good, gentle, and benevolent creature.

The **wooden fish**, a red object found in most Buddhist temples, is a clapper, used for beating time while the monks chant the sutras. Some say that monks dropped the sutras in water as the holy scriptures were being brought from India. A fish ate the sutras, so it was beaten to force it to regurgitate. Others say if you don't beat the fish, there will be an earthquake.

The tortoise, usually seen with a giant stele on its back, is one of the four supernatural animals, the others being the phoenix, the dragon, and the unicorn. Real ones are frequently kept at Buddhist temples, for they are sacred, an emblem of longevity, strength, and endurance.

TELEPHONE, TELECOMMUNICATIONS, & E-MAIL

You should be aware that telephone, fax, and e-mail communications could be government-monitored. E-mail providers have had to sign agreements stating they are not sending anything illegal.

Not all mail gets answered, so if you're booking a room in a hotel, you could say that if you don't hear from the the hotel, you are going to assume that there's no room.

Most local **telephone** calls from hotels have been free, but top hotels in the big cities, are charging Y1 to Y2 a call. A few hotels, like the JC Mandarin (Shanghai) have a complimentary telephone just off the lobby. These telephones are also in most restaurants or on the assistant manager's desk. Most hotels prefer you use their business center and charge Y2 a call. Public telephones range from Y0.05 to Y2.00.

Many local Chinese now have private telephones. Those that don't might share a telephone with everyone else in their building. You need a Chinese-speaker to reach them. Each village has at least one telephone in the village office. You can leave a message asking your friends to telephone you at your hotel. Be sure to give your room number.

Over 500 cities have **International Direct Dial** (IDD). Direct dial is much faster (20 seconds) than operator-assisted calls, which might take from three minutes to a couple of days (in remote towns). Dialing direct from your hotel room is the easiest but one of the most expensive way to communicate abroad from China. The operator can tell you what numbers to dial to access your country. You pay a three-minute minimum and a service charge.

Some hotels have **card phones** in their lobbies. These telephones are also on the streets, in shopping centers, railway stations, and in telecommunications offices. This might not be the cheapest way to call North America but there is no service charge and no minimum. You can buy phone cards from the hotels or the telecommunications offices in set denominations. You use the card until you no longer have a balance. The cost of the call is automatically deducted.

You can also telephone abroad by dialing one of the local numbers below and connecting immediately with an American or Canadian operator. You can then charge the call to your own telephone calling card, or "collect." Some hotels charge a service fee if you call these numbers from your room, but if you call from a public telephone, it is cheaper.

It is probably cheaper if you telephoned overseas after 11pm or did a calling card call home between 11pm and 8am Canadian time.

Calling Card Access Numbers & Country Codes
For the US, **AT&T** is 108-11, **MCI** is 108-12, and **Sprint** is 108-13. For **Bell Canada**, dial 108-186. Some hotels also have "USA Direct" or "Canada Direct" telephones in their lobbies where you push one button and you connect with an American operator. This doesn't work for Canada because you're then asked which language you want, and there's no button to press for that.

China's telephone code is 86. Some other country codes are:

Australia - 61	**Malaysia** - 60
Canada - 1	**Philippines** - 63
Hong Kong - 852	**Singapore** - 65
India - 91	**Thailand** - 66
Japan - 81	**United Kingdom** - 44
Macau - 853	**United States** - 1

Don't forget the time difference. China has forbidden "Call-Back" telephone calls, but you can telephone your own family and have them phone you. Make sure you give them your hotel room number.

A few hotels and business centers like the Portman Ritz-Carlton in Shanghai have call forwarding and conference call facilities. You can lease cellular phones through business centers in some hotels.

Faxes sent overseas are expensive from both hotels and telecommunication offices because they charge a three-minute minimum. It is best to find a friend with a fax machine so you only pay for the amount of time you use. One page usually takes less than one minute. It is cheaper to send a fax to China from North America (before 8am and after 11pm) than to send one from a hotel in China to another city in China.

If you are touring during the day and want to leave a message with someone in the same city during office hours, send a fax from your hotel. Local faxes are reasonably priced and shouldn't have a three-minute minimum.

Many Chinese turn off their fax machines at night, unfortunately making it difficult to reach them from North America.

E-mail is becoming very popular. To send and receive e-mail while you're traveling, just register with *http://www.hotmail.com*. The problem is finding a computer with a program in English without paying a fortune to a hotel. I once spent four hours at Y9 an hour trying to figure out how to send an e-mail on a Chinese program. No one spoke English at the Telecom office in Dalian. Other people around were helpful however. I've also accessed e-mail at a computer mall in Shanghai. The store's owner was so thrilled to meet a Canadian he wouldn't take any money.

Some cities have videophones. Try the telecommunications office on Nanjing Dong Road, near the Peace Hotel in Shanghai.

TIME ZONES

All of China is in the same time zone. Beijing is 13 hours ahead of New York and Toronto. Please make adjustments for standard and daylight savings time.

TIPPING

This is officially forbidden. However, guides and drivers do accept tips and make more money than doctors, university professors, and government officials. First and foremost, you don't have to tip anyone unless you want to. That is the nature of tipping.

You should tip in hotels only for services above the call of duty. Do not tip the attendant who fixes your broken toilet. That is his duty. Avoid tipping in hotels that add a percentage for service. While staff may not necessarily get the service charge, you have paid for their services. In some hotels, tips are accepted as a token of friendship and shared among the staff.

A suggested tip for a bell man is Y5 to Y10 a load and for a porter at the train station Y2 to Y10. As for tour guides and drivers, tip only those who have been exceptionally good, and no more than Y16 per day for the national guide, and Y24 per day shared by the local guide and driver. Cruise ships suggest you put a $5.00 per day per guest into a box on top of a 15% service charge. The $5 tip is split among all Chinese service staff including cooks, and other behind-the-scene personnel. Cruise ships encourage its guests to tip guides and cruise staff in addition if you want.

The Holiday Inns Lido and Crowne Plaza said tipping is not expected nor encouraged. Miserable hours have been wasted in tour groups arguing about tips and gifts.

Asking for tips is strictly forbidden. A few attendants in newly opened hotels will refuse tips. Please thank them profusely. Such purity of spirit should be encouraged. You could perhaps give them a modest souvenir instead and send a letter of commendation to the tourism administration praising them. As for guides, they expect tips and recently have had to share them. Some have had to give a set amount to their travel agencies whether they receive money or not. But this is not your problem.

TOILETS

You are out shopping. Nature calls. What do you do? The best is to head for the closest tourist hotel, barge in as if you were staying there, and use its facilities. Don't expect western toilets except in tourist hotels or on the well-beaten foreign tourist path. The Chinese toilet is the squatting kind over a hole in the ground. These are difficult for people with poor knees. There is usually no place to hang up purses. Toilets are best in your own hotel room.

Some public toilets, especially those in less developed areas, stink unbearably. Foreigners could dab perfume or Tiger Balm under their noses. Sometimes it is better for people traveling by road to stop behind a bush to fertilize the fields. This is certainly better than sharing toilets with writhing maggots. In smaller communities you may find a container of earth or a bucket of water for covering or flushing, but such is well off the tourist track.

TOURISM REALITIES

Going on a group tour doesn't eliminate all problems. But it does mean someone else has to deal with them, and that someone else should find you a clean toilet. Shortages of trained, experienced staff with a good command of English plague all sectors of the industry because it has expanded too quickly. Recent group tourists have complained of inexperienced guides, although most are excellent.

WEIGHTS & MEASURES

China uses both the metric system and the Chinese system.

1 gong-jin (kilogram)	= 2.2 pounds
1 jin or gun (catty)	= 1.33 pounds = .604 kg
1 dan (picul)	= 100 catties = 133 pounds or 60.47kg
1 mi (meter)	= 39.37 inches
1 gong li (kilometer)	= .6 mile = 1 km.

DO NOT BE AT THE MERCY OF YOUR LOCAL GUIDE

It is very important to take a list of what you want to do and see. Usually your itinerary is set but if there's something important you must do, you might be able to work it in on your own. Sometimes, the national guide or escort, is available to help.

If you joined a tour to see the Terracotta Warriors and the local guide is hurrying you through, say no, you want to spend more time there. See Guides above.

1 li (Chinese mile)	= .3106 mile = 1/2 km.
1 mu	= .1647 acres
1 hectare	= 2.471 acres
	= 10,000 square meters
100 hectares	= 247.1 acre = 1 sq. km.
259 hectares	= 1 sq. mile

Kilometer-Mile Conversion Tables

To convert kilometers to miles, multiply by 6 and divide by 10.

Miles	Kilometers	Miles	Kilometers
1	1.6093	1	.621
2	3.2186	2	1.242
3	4.8279	3	1.863
4	6.4372	4	2.484
5	8.0465	5	3.105
6	9.6558	6	3.726
7	11.2651	7	4.347
8	12.8744	8	4.968
9	14.4837	9	5.589
10	16.093	10	6.21
20	32.186	20	12.42
30	48.279	30	18.63
40	64.372	40	24.84
50	80.465	50	31.05
60	96.558	60	37.26
70	112.651	70	43.47
80	128.744	80	49.68
90	144.837	90	55.89
100	160.93	100	62.1
200	321.86	200	124.2
300	482.79	300	186.3
400	643.72	400	248.4
500	804.65	500	310.5
600	965.58	600	372.6
700	1126.51	700	434.7
800	1287.44	800	496.8
900	1448.37	900	558.9
1000	1609.3	1000	621

Metric Conversions

Celsius-Fahrenheit Conversion Table, in Degrees

Centigrade (Celsius)	Fahrenheit
-40	-40

-20		-4
0	Freezing Point	32
10		50
20		68
30		86
40		104
50		122
60		140
70		158
80		176
90		194
100	Boiling Point	212

To convert Fahrenheit to Celsius subtract 32, multiply by five, and divide by nine. To convert Celsius to Fahrenheit multiply by nine, divide by five, and add 32.

–*Charts prepared by Linda Malloy*

8. GETTING AROUND CHINA

AIR TRAVEL

China's air safety record and service have improved considerably since the early 1990s. Northwest Airlines has been helping to train Chinese pilots and the US Federal Aviation Administration has been helping China overhaul the industry, from installing radars to training personnel. On routes between main cities, your flights will probably be on new planes and on time (except in bad weather). Just avoid smaller airlines like Changan Airlines and China United. Their planes are antiques.

If you have a choice of flights, choose the shortest flying time. You are more likely to get a newer plane with bigger seats. Aim for the earliest flights of the day. Delays become compounded as the day progresses.

Tickets have to be paid for by noon, the day before departure. All domestic reservations have to be reconfirmed before noon two days before the flight. Some hotels might do this for you free. Some airlines say that confirmation is not necessary if you are in the city of departure for less than 72 hours. But I have heard of passengers being dropped off overbooked flights for not reconfirming.

Give yourself extra time to get to the airport in rain or snow. It is best to arrive at the airport 1.5 hours before departure for domestic flights and two hours for international flights. Check-in ends 30 minutes before flight time. Prepare to pay either a domestic (Y60) or an international airport tax (Y90). You might want to pay additional personal accident or baggage insurance at the check-in counter.

It is very difficult to get accurate flight departure information over the telephone and sometimes even after you arrive at the airport. If a flight is late, insist on a progress report; if very late, free food. Be sure to confirm delays with more than one official before you go back into town.

Most planes are booked from the front. There may not be room for all the carry-on bags, so try to get there early. Planes have been known to leave early and of course sometimes late. Major airports have luggage carts.

Carry some snacks and a good book. Airport waiting rooms have an information desk with a clerk who might know some English. Some have electronic monitors showing flight numbers. Because boarding announcements are not always audible, check frequently. You could look out the window for your plane. The plane number is painted on the fuselage and should be mentioned on your boarding pass. You could also look for other people with the same color boarding pass and try out your Mandarin. Many Chinese people take a friendly interest in foreign travelers and will tell you when to board the flight.

CHINA TRAVEL GUIDELINES

When you're traveling around China, follow these rules and your travels will be a lot easier:

Whenever you go anywhere alone, carry the name of your hotel in Chinese.

If you are traveling without a guide between cities, take the telephone numbers of your travel agents in both places. If your flight is canceled, at least you can telephone for help.

Always carry lots of small change for shopping and expenses.

Among your highest priorities upon arriving in a new place is to arrange your out-bound travel.

If you are traveling overnight by train or by ferry (not a luxury tourist ship), take your own mug, soap, chopsticks, and towel.

Always carry toilet tissue with you.

And be aware that a cancellation fee is always charged when you make changes in travel arrangements.

Some airports have a room for smokers. Meal announcements are usually not in English, so keep your eyes on fellow passengers if you're delayed. Be prepared to walk to your plane no matter what the weather.

Until recently, **CAAC** was the only airline operating domestically in China. Civil aviation is now broken up into regional subsidiaries of CAAC, and are run by former CAAC personnel with CAAC planes and facilities. China Southern, China Eastern and Air China are the largest. China Southern has a code sharing agreement with Delta Airlines and marketing and scheduling agreements with United Airlines.

Their IATA codes are:
- **Air China** (Beijing) - CA
- **Northeast Airlines** (Shenyang) - CJ

- **Northwest China Airways** (X'ian) - WH
- **China Southern Airlines** (Guangzhou) - CZ
- **Southwest Airlines** (Chengdu) - SZ
- **China Eastern** (Shanghai) - MU
- **Xiamen Airlines** (Xiamen) - MF
- **Xinjiang Airlines** (Urumqi) - XO

There are other domestic airlines including the small GP **China General** Aviation Corp., 3U **Sichuan Airlines**, WU **Wuhan Airlines**, 3Q **Yunnan Airlines** and ZY **Zhongyuan Airlines**.

CAAC continues to manage civil aviation, including safety standards, airports, licensing and international relations.

One schedule book for all CAAC affiliates is available. It comes out twice a year, in November and April, and has been found on sale in some airports. It is easier to get it at Chinese airline offices abroad than in China.

CAAC affiliates have booking offices in major tourist hotels. If you are flying with a Chinese airline from North America, you should be able to make domestic reservations through your carrier, or through China Travel Service. It is much cheaper to book flights in China, but during high season, it's better to pay the extra just to be sure of a seat.

Most domestic flights have only economy class. Hot food has been served on some flights, but food is usually cold, edible and unconventional; for example, Southwest Airlines' box lunch had shrimp chips, sponge cake, plain roll, spicy beef jerky, and sausage in pastry which would have been better hot, but it was okay; Xinjiang Airlines has served cold, smoked fish, chicken and corned beef, a hot rice dish, three kinds of pastry, and an apple. If any domestic airline is responsible for unscheduled overnight stopovers, hotel accommodation should be arranged by the carrier free of charge. (But you might have to insist.)

Buying airplane tickets is not always easy and you may have to fly stand-by. Because many travelers book more than one flight in order to insure a seat, keep trying. Rumor has it that front seats are saved until the last minute for VIPs.

Flying China's Friendly Skies

China is buying many new planes, opening convenient booking offices, and building or expanding airports.

Some planes are small and uncomfortable (especially for big foreigners). A few have broken seat belts and luggage bins that fall open. Cabin crews are not always careful about safety checks, but civil aviation keeps improving. The domestic airlines also need to learn a lot about public relations and computers, but you can book return flights and a whole

APPROXIMATE FLIGHT TIMES FROM BEIJING

Flying time depends on the type of aircraft used and routing.

Beijing to:

Baotou	80 minutes
Beihai	three hours, 10 minutes
Changsha	two hours
Changzhou	one hour, 50 minutes
Chongqing	two hours, 10 minutes
Dalian	one hour
Fuzhou	two hours, 30 minutes
Guangzhou	three hours
Guilin	two hours, 25 minutes
Haikou	three hours, 25 minutes
Hangzhou	one hour, 40 minutes
Harbin	one hour, 40 minutes
Hohhot	one hour, 10 minutes
Hong Kong	three hours
Huangshan	two hours, five minutes
Kunming	three hours, 10 minutes
Luoyang	one hour, 35 minutes
Nanchang	two hour
Nanjing	one hour, 35 minutes
Nanning	three hours, five minutes
Ningbo	two hours, five minutes
Shanghai	one hour, 40 minutes
Shantou	two hours, 30 minutes
Shenzhen	two hours, 45 minutes
Tianjin	25 minutes
Urumqi	three hours, 25 minutes
Wuhan	one hour, 45 minutes
Xiamen	two hours, 25 minutes
Xi'an	one hour, 45 minutes

itinerary now to major cities. Aviation has had 30% increases in passenger volume yearly. China Southern alone flew over 15.2 million passengers in 1997.

If any domestic airline cancels your flight, you'll get a full refund. If a passenger asks for a refund between two and 24 hours before flight departure, the cancellation fee is 10%. If you fail to cancel before flight time, there is no refund. Refunds can only be made at the place of purchase or a place approved by CAAC. Full refunds on international tickets are made if you cancel before check-in time.

Foreign airlines also fly to China but have no domestic services.

Airline Miscellany

Check for uptodate information but in the past, no babies under 10 days of age and no pregnant women almost due were allowed to fly. An infant under two not occupying a separate seat and accompanied by an adult is charged 10% of the adult fare. Children two to 12 are charged 50%-65% of the adult fare.

If a checked bag is lost, the compensation will not exceed Y40 per kilogram. If you want more, you can buy luggage insurance.

Some Chinese airlines operate international flights similar to other international airlines, but with minimal services. Flights have cheap headsets, alcoholic drinks in first class, beer in economy, and movies.

No smoking is allowed on flights under six hours. Helicopter service is available in some cities depending on demand.

BUS TRAVEL

Air-conditioned buses and mini-buses speed along many routes, some of them two-tier for almost horizontal sleeping. Ask about the kind of bus you will be taking because some other buses are small, hard-seated, and very crowded, with little luggage space except on the roof or your knee. They can be uncomfortable for big foreigners, especially if you have to stand. I have heard horror stories of windows impossible to close in freezing weather, and carbon monoxide poisoning because of bad maintenance. So check your bus before you commit yourself.

The main problem with buses are traffic jams getting in and out of cities and onto highways. We have also been delayed by accidents on the road. It is usually better to take a train although China has built many good expressways. Still, buses are more frequent and some even have toilets and video monitors with movies. You should book your trip ahead of time so you will know exactly where the station is. We once showed up at a bus station to find one of three buses a day canceled. We went to another bus station and got the last seats on another bus. You can also try for a last minute bus.

Take your own food. These buses stop at dumpy restaurants with a busload of travelers and you can't expect service immediately. As soon as the driver is finished, the bus leaves. Toilets are usually primitive with line-ups.

Some youth travel agencies and CTS (HK) have tours by tourist bus in Fujian and Guangdong, a great way to see the country.

FERRIES & TOUR BOATS

China has some real antiques crossing harbors and rivers. They are cheap, but avoid them if they look too crowded and tippy. Fatal accidents with boats have recently been blamed on overloading and drunken crews. See Yangtze Gorges for ferries along the Yangtze, Wuxi for ferries along the Grand Canal, and Hong Kong for ferries to China. See also Xiamen, Weihai, Qingdao, Tianjin, and Yantai. On overnight ferries, it is best to take your own mug, soap and towel.

HITCHHIKING

Backpackers have hitched rides with truck drivers. On-your-own tourists in isolated spots have been able to get rides on tour buses. It's a matter of luck. If you have connections with foreign experts, etc., you might be able to use staff cars.

One way to hitchhike is to wait at the door of your hotel. Stop anyone getting into a vehicle and ask for a ride. Or you can go out to the main road and try to wave vehicles down. You could have a note in Chinese asking for a free ride or you could offer to pay for the ride. Always ask beforehand for the price. Hitchhikers have been treated to meals by hospitable drivers. I was once picked up by the police and treated to a banquet. They even refused my cigarettes.

As a precaution, hitchhikers should make a record of the vehicle's license number. And avoid drunk or suspicious-looking drivers as you would in North America.

TRAINS

China has a vast network of railways, linking every provincial and regional capital (except Lhasa and Haikou) to Beijing. Railway lines have been burgeoning and many are being electrified. Diesel is replacing steam. Service has improved, with air-conditioned express tourist trains between Nanjing and Shanghai, Hangzhou and Wuxi, Shenyang and Dalian, Jinan and Qingdao, Shenzhen and Shaoguan, Beijing and Chengde, Guizhou and Anshun, etc.

ALL ABOARD THE IRON ROOSTER!

China is buying better passenger trains, and improvements have started to show. Some travel agents have chartered air-conditioned coaches for their clients. A luxury train trip along the Silk Road is organized by Conference Travel and Tours, and China Express Railway Service. See Chapter 6, "Travel Agents & Tour Operators," for more addresses and phone numbers.

Train tickets can be bought through hotels or travel agencies (usually for a service fee), or at the railway station. In some big cities, special ticket windows are provided for foreigners, but be prepared for frustration, arguing and no English. Lineups can be long, especially for hard class.

Try to buy your tickets at least six days in advance. Travel agencies can usually reserve soft class train tickets a week in advance. It is cheaper but riskier to buy tickets for the same or next day at train stations. There might not be seats left, especially for overnight rides and on holidays. Seasoned travelers say the best time to queue for day train tickets is just before lunch. When the clerks return half an hour later, you'll be first in line.

Scalpers around train stations and in some coffee shops can buy tickets for you with a big markup. While this is illegal, everybody does it; but some scalpers might not be seen again. You pay upon receipt. Travelers have boarded trains using platform tickets and then bought tickets from the conductor on the train. This, however, is risky, as space may not be available.

Hard & Soft Class

Trains are classified as special express, regular, and suburban. Passengers usually have a choice of hard and soft-class seats or berths. The most comfortable are in the middle of a coach, away from noise and wheel vibrations. State your preference when you buy.

Prepaid tourists usually travel **soft-class berth**, which can be almost the same price as going by plane. The berths are the height of bourgeois comfort if you have air-conditioning. Compartments usually have lace curtains, a table with lamp, an overhead fan, and sleeping spaces with bedding and towels for four people on two upper and two lower bunks. An overhead loft stores large suitcases.

It is best to take a small overnight bag too if you are sleeping on the train. Most group luggage is stored at one end of the car and may not be accessible.

Ask the conductor to lock your door when you go to the dining car. The plug for the fan (if you have one), and the switch for the loudspeaker are frequently under the table. Dining-car food is edible, simple, and, on some trains, surprisingly good. Passengers usually give their orders to a steward beforehand and are notified when their food is ready.

Six people share one compartment of **hard-class** berths in the same amount of space as soft class. Berths are padded and tiered in threes, the middle berth being the best.

Hard class is noisy and dirty, with other passengers smoking, frequently clearing throats and spitting on the floor. You cannot turn off the loudspeaker, which starts at six am. Sheets and warm blankets are provided, but if you get on between terminals, these may have been used.

Passengers can eat in the dining car, but can also buy food from vendors on the train itself before the train departs. Don't expect gourmet fare! Food from vendors can be downright unappetizing, like a box of rice with pork (including the skin and hair). Bring your own cups of instant noodles. Steaming hot water is available in each car. Hard-class seats are very crowded. Accommodations can be upgraded after the train is underway if space is available. The conductor is usually in the middle coach.

The **Hong Kong-Beijing train** is great, beautiful and comfortable. If you are travelling alone first class, ask for a compartment for two. Chances are you'll have it all to yourself.

Train Basics

Train schedules should be available in hotels three-stars and up, or at foreigners' counters in railway stations (in Chinese). Give yourself plenty of time to find your train. Platforms are not marked in English, but the train number is posted. The destination of each coach should be marked on its side in *pinyin*. Expect train stations to be very crowded with people sleeping on the floors overnight. Expect people to push and shove. Do protect small children.

Like travel on overnight ferries, men and women are assigned compartments without regard to sex, even in soft class. If this arrangement bothers you, ask for another compartment. The Chinese are used to such travel. Tourist groups usually sort themselves out. I have never heard of sexual harassment on a train in China, so don't feel nervous.

To protect valuables, do not use your purse as a pillow. Things have been stolen that way. Put your valuables in a money belt around your waist or around your neck under your clothes. Tie your camera to your arm.

Toilets look like they've been hosed down and not scrubbed. You might want to use a disinfectant. On coaches reserved for foreign tour groups, you can be sure of toilet paper and soap (in a common soap dish). Soft-class passengers on some tourist trains now have a choice of western toilet seats or a squat. Usually it's a squat.

A washroom in each car offers several sinks with running water. Many prepaid tourists wait until they arrive at their hotels before washing. However, sometimes on arrival early in the morning, hotel rooms have not been vacated, and tourists are taken sightseeing instead.

Some coaches on express trains are air-conditioned. No smoking is allowed but this is not enforced unless you complain. Baggage might be checked for inflammable and dangerous articles. Luggage is frequently pushed in and out of train windows to a waiting guide because it's easier than hauling it. On some trains, the dining car becomes a disco or karaoke bar at night.

Do not discard your ticket. You might be asked for it again at the exit gate of your arrival station, but then again you might not. That's the way China is. Regulations keep changing. Round trip train tickets cannot be booked. So consider booking the next leg of your journey immediately upon arrival.

GETTING AROUND TOWN & COUNTRY

Bicycles

These can be rented from hotels and bicycle-rental shops. Some rented bicycles have fallen apart. Check everything at the shop. You will probably have to leave a deposit or some identification, but do not leave a passport. Clerks have accepted old student cards, expired drivers licenses, anything with a photo. Guard your receipt.

Always park in a supervised parking lot, otherwise your bicycle may disappear. Make a note of the license number and where you left it. Put on some colored tape or a tag so you can find it quickly again among hundreds of identical bicycles. Most cities have bicycle lanes, and some have streets forbidden to bicycles.

If you are staying for any length of time, you might want to buy a bicycle and sell it when you leave.

Officially all bicycles should have bicycle licenses, but most foreigners have had no trouble without one. Some people have taken their own bicycles into China. (To ship a bicycle by train means having to go to the train station a day ahead of time and, at the other end, spending time finding it.) Spare parts for foreign makes are a problem.

You can take a group tour by motorcycle or bicycle, but these tours are not cheap. A truck carrying spare parts follows behind and picks up tired bikers.

Some adventurous bikers have traveled from town to town on their own. Please be aware of the problems. Roads might not be paved. If you get into an accident, you might not be able to communicate. You might secure only substandard accommodations. You might need alien travel permits for some areas. Check about licenses if you want to travel by motorcycle. Police do hassle motorcyclists.

For safety's sake, do not travel alone. If you do, let me know of your experiences.

Motorscooter Rickshaws

For two people or more, these are cheaper than taxis and can take lots of luggage, but they're not comfortable. They swerve and bounce. Prices are often fixed and paid in advance.

Bicycle Rickshaws *(san-lien che)*

Built for two, these cost very little, or a lot in tourist areas, but you can only go short distances. Please consider the driver and get off and walk up steep slopes. Bicycle rickshaws are ideal for leisurely sightseeing in places like Hangzhou. They are on the increase even in Beijing, but taxis might be cheaper. Please don't ride them in heavy motorized traffic since they can be dangerous. Agree on a price in advance, especially in tourist towns. Make sure the price is for the ride, not for each person.

Be careful about your belongings as thieves on bicycles have been known to grab purses and cameras from these.

Taxis

You can get moderate-priced taxis outside tourist hotels, railway stations, airports, passenger-ship quays and places frequented by visitors. You can ask someone to telephone for a taxi, and you can also flag down a taxi on the street in most cities.

If taxis are not easy to find and you have several stops to make, it's better to hire one by the half-day or full day. You can also pay by the meter (or odometer) with a charge for waiting. Always agree on the price before you go. Usually you need not pay for a meal for a driver if you are near his home base, but you might invite him to a meal if you are a long way from his home. Restaurants and hotels have sections for staff if you don't want to eat together.

If you need a taxi early in the morning or for a full or half day, it is best to make a reservation at the taxi stand the night before. Taxi companies also have buses for larger groups.

Not all taxis have meters, but hotels should know prices. While most drivers are honest, a few have added imaginary waiting time in Chinese to the receipts, or charged higher rates. If you feel cheated, don't pay, and ask cheerfully for someone to call a policeman. If you have already paid, get a receipt, take the driver's name and license number, and complain to the manager, dispatcher, or to the local tourism administration. Ask your consulate for advice. Some cities have a taxi complaint office. Letters to *China Daily* have resulted in penalties for drivers and apologies from taxi companies.

Another ploy is to pay what you consider the proper fare, get out, and leave. If the driver follows you, negotiate a settlement. Some drivers charge extra because they have to pay the touts who bring them customers. Try to avoid the middle man.

Some travelers have been greeted at railway stations and airports by a pack of touts grabbing at their bags, a frightening experience indeed, especially if you don't know what these strangers are doing. There is usually a line of legitimate taxis with meters waiting outside.

You can hire a taxi to take you from city to city, but you have to pay the fare back to the driver's base. Ask ahead of time for the price and distance. In isolated regions, ask if you need an alien travel permit. The problem is military zones.

Public Tourist Buses

These are available in a few cities around railway stations. They go to tourist attractions in nearby places and might have a commentary in Chinese. They are a good bargain if you take along a guide book. It's best to take your own lunch to save time and make sure you know how long your bus is staying at each stop. Write down the bus number so you can find it again. Make sure you agree on a price before you hop in, and be aware that some drivers have threatened to leave their passengers behind at tourist attractions unless they pay more.

Self-drive Cars

Generally, you have to be a Chinese resident to get a driver's license in China. You need a medical certificate and your own driver's license translated into Chinese. There is a written test and you are allowed to bring your own translator. You can't use an international license to drive in China.

But – some travel agents can make arrangements to drive your own car into China from Hong Kong or Central Asia. It might cost you up to US$1,000 and a lot of time to get permission. You could drive a jeep with a tour group on the Silk Road, or any other place where tours have been planned. China International Sports Travel in Beijing organizes car rallies from Paris to Beijing. See Concepts East (Canada) or China Merchants Travel in Xi'an.

Most roads are open to foreigners. Four-to-six-lane highways are being built: #107 goes from Beijing south to Shenzhen, #312 from Shanghai west to Yining (Xinjiang.)

GETTING AROUND CITIES

Public City Buses

These are usually oppressively overcrowded, especially during rush hour and Sundays. But they are cheap. Hotel personnel can tell you which bus to take and armed with your destination in Chinese, you should have an adventure asking people for help along the way. Some cities have bus maps in English. Fellow passengers are usually friendly and helpful.

Some public mini-buses have set routes. They are more expensive than city buses but cheaper than taxis, and you do get a seat. In Beijing and Shanghai are now large public tourist buses going to major tourist sites. As in all crowded places, beware of pickpockets.

Shuttle Buses

Shuttles are available at a few hotels. You can take them to airports, Friendship Stores, and a few tourist attractions.

Subways

You can use subways in Beijing, Guangzhou, Shanghai and Tianjin and maps are available. Other cities are building them. Walk down the stairs, pay about Y2, and choose your platform. Signs are in *pinyin*; in Shanghai, they're also in English. If you avoid rush hour, they are a great way to get around.

Walking

Something has to be said about walking because of all the bicycles and cars: crossing streets can be dangerous! Try to let a native upstream run interference. Cross at lights. Some cities have overpasses and underpasses, so please use them.

CHECKLIST FOR TRAVELERS ON YOUR OWN

• *Fax or e-mail your hotel before you arrive to arrange transportation if necessary, giving them your flight number or train and coach numbers. Someone at your destination should hold up a sign with your name or the hotel's name on it. Most hotels charge for picking you up but some have free shuttle buses. If you have less than a day, you could also ask the hotel or a travel agency to reconfirm or book the next stages of your travel.*

• *Consult your hotel travel service or a travel agency about the next leg of your trip, reconfirming plane tickets or booking train tickets.*

• *For your day of departure, book transportation and if there are no porters, ask if the driver can carry your luggage to the train platform or check-in counter. If the driver cannot and you have loads of luggage, ask the hotel to help you. The hotel might send a bellman with you and you only need to pay a tip.*

9. SHOPPING

It's great and prices now are soft, but it's not as cheap as it used to be. The Asian recession means tourism numbers are down and fewer foreigners are buying.

China, which already sells more to the US than it buys, wants to keep selling to the world. Its market includes its own increasingly sophisticated and wealthy shoppers. It has to produce international class goods at competitive prices but also a lot of goods for the proletariat.

You can find great bargains for good quality for a wide variety of merchandise, but you can also find a lot of lower quality wares. Shopping in China is still a rewarding adventure, a challenge.

China has always had fine **arts and crafts**: hand-knotted carpets, watercolor paintings, fine embroidery, porcelain, cloisonne, stone carvings, and feather pictures. China is developing variations of these old crafts. Chinese stores and markets offer marvelous silks and cashmere, and now China is great for modern goods like leather handbags, briefcases, and name-brand cameras. You can find mechanical toys, computers, and cellular phones. China still has antiques and reproductions of antiques, historical souvenirs at good prices.

The most important things to remember are:

- If you want bargains, you have to do your homework and you have to take time. You have to know prices in North America and you have to compare those with prices here in more than one shop. Keep good notes.
- If you only have time for tourist shops, you have to expect high prices but you can haggle there.
- As a general rule, the more Chinese shoppers there are in a shop, the better the prices. If foreign tourists are the only customers, beware.
- Merchants think foreigners are rich, and expect you to pay high prices. When you play by Chinese rules, they suddenly realise you're human too. And it's amazing. They warm up to you. They respect you.
- Haggling is the custom. Merchants know they make you feel good if you get a discount so they put up the prices. You've got to haggle.

HAGGLING

The chance of getting discounts is better in China proper than in Hong Kong. Haggling is imperative particularly in privately-run stores and markets, unless you want to pay three or four times the going rate. You can also haggle in department stores, airport stores, and museum stores. Just ask for a manager who can make such decisions. Aim for the owners, not the salaried clerks.

The secret is to know prices, not to show any enthusiasm for the thing you want to buy, and not to buy the first thing you see. In markets, many stalls sell the same items. If you are asked what you want to pay, suggest a ridiculously low amount: a quarter of the seller's first price. Then walk away pretending you are not interested. You might share a laugh with the dealer. The seller might counter with hand motions for you to give a higher bid, and you could come up a bit if interested. Start to move away again and look at the same thing in the next stall. It is a guessing game. The seller is trying to decide how badly you want it, and you are trying to decide the bottom line for the seller.

The best time for you to haggle is when you're the first customer of the day, no other customers are around, and when the merchant wants to go home. Pretend you're a foreign resident, not a tourist. Make them think you will come back again and again. When you think you have bargained as low as possible, then pull out your US cash and say, "How much is it if I pay US dollars?" At that point, you might get another five percent off.

On the other hand, if the merchant doesn't budge even after you've walked away, make a note of the store's location. If you still want that item after looking around and finding nothing else like it, go back and ask for a lower price. The merchant may or may not come down and you have to make a difficult decision.

- Shops are everywhere. They are at almost every popular tourist attraction but don't assume from the location that they're all tourist traps. Prices in some shops here could actually be reasonable.
- Quality and prices are higher in Hong Kong where clothes are more fashionable.
- If you don't have the time or energy to haggle, shop in the Friendship Store or hotel stores. They speak the best English.

Antiques: Hong Kong offers the best quality because prices are higher there. But China the source has a lot. Dealers in China have to trust you before they close their doors and show you the real old stuff, some of it perhaps stolen. Officially, antiques made between 1795 and 1949 are not allowed out of the country unless they have a red wax seal on them. Only a few stores are allowed to sell anything for export made before 1795. The exception is Hong Kong where they can export anything.

Customs officials rarely search the bags of departing visitors to enforce this rule. But an alert officer might spot the shape of a large vase in a suitcase being x-rayed. I know they did catch one foreigner trying to take out old porcelain and confiscated the pieces until she returned to take them to the Arts Objects Clearance Office. Arts Objects offices are very difficult to find however but any good antique store should be able to help you.

The best antique shopping for knowledgeable shoppers are the **weekend street markets** in Tianjin, Shanghai and Beijing: old clocks, watches, cricket boxes, porcelains, bird cages, curtain holders, silver jewelery, embroidery, and even Qing army boots. Antique markets also can be found sometimes in temples, museums, near other kinds of markets, bird and fish markets, or by themselves. Many cities now have daily markets with fixed stalls in multi-storied buildings (gu dong).

Antique stores run by the government are more reliable but expensive and frequently over-priced. Some won't budge on prices but a lot will. Many are found in museums and tourist attractions like the Forbidden City and Summer Palace. They buy their wares from the markets. Some antique stores are actually contracted to private dealers so haggling can be productive. Only antiques in government stores are guaranteed.

Baby toys: avoid stuffed animals unless you're sure of what's inside. They could be stuffed with dirty materials. Avoid baby toys unless you know there's no lead in the paint. Check for bells and removeable buttons and eyes that babies could swallow. Chinese safety standards are not as strict as those in North America.

Beanie Babies: China makes a lot of counterfeits. Check the Beanie Baby website. They range from Y12 in Sanlitun Market to Y40 in the Friendship Store in Beijing. US Customs allows only small quantities for personal use in spite of copyright violations.

Ceramics: Some of these have been found to contain lead glazes. If you plan to consume food and drink out of them regularly, do test them for lead.

Clothing: The bargains are in the street markets. The best styles and quality are in Hong Kong but Beijing and Shanghai are getting right up there too. Some locally-made brands are very good: Giordano and Bossini for sportwear for example. But you'll see the likes of Victoria's Secret, L.L. Bean, and North Face too.

An American "size nine" doesn't mean a thing in China. If you are buying for yourself, you should try on clothes for size. If you are buying clothes for someone else, you should have their measurements. Wool and cotton will probably shrink if washed in hot water. Do not believe labels. Sometimes they're genuine overruns; sometimes they really don't belong. Check the quality carefully and decide for yourself.

Clothing and other items imported from elsewhere for sale in China are, of course, cheaper in the country of origin. Some of what you see may have been made in Hong Kong or Taiwan. Big international name brands are not bargains as they're aimed at the local market.

Styles can be behind the west or ahead of it. Because it makes clothes ordered by foreign manufacturers, China's goods get onto the local market before it gets abroad. Young people are wearing styles that will show up in America six months later.

Cruise ship stores: these have very limited variety, are highly over-priced but frequently have a sale towards the end of the cruise.

Department stores (*shang chang*) and malls: prices are reasonable to expensive with good variety. Look for sales. Department Stores frequently have arts and crafts, too. Look for good buys in embroidered jackets, clothing, gloves, silks, down coats, furs, novelties, etc. Prices, styles and qualities are frequently better than in the Friendship stores.

Exchanges: Do not expect exchanges except in government stores and department stores. Guard your receipts.

FAKES & REPRODUCTIONS

Learn how to tell fakes from real. Some merchants will tell you the truth. Others can't because they don't know. Going to museums and factories should help you learn.

Rub a pearl on the front of your tooth. If it feels gritty, it's real. If it's smooth, it's fake. As for "antiques" look around. Antiques are usually one of a kind. If other stalls are selling the same thing, it's probably a reproduction. Look closely inside translucent stones. Glass is warmer than stone and has circular bubbles inside. To test for 100% silk, take a few threads and burn it. Silk will not leave a residue but polyester will.

For real hand embroidery, just look for different-sized stitches, and stitches in different directions. The smaller the stitches, the better. For antique embroidery, look for muted vegetable dyes. The brilliant chemical dyes started 150 years ago.

Reproductions can make good gifts too – if the quality is good and the prices are fair.

If in doubt in a market, assume all "antiques" are fake and offer prices accordingly. Offer Y20 to Y50 and see what happens.

Factory stores: Every arts and crafts factory has a showroom where visitors can buy what is made, but prices are usually higher than elsewhere. If you can't get a 40%-50% discount, look for stores around the immediate neighborhood which just might sell the same things, but at cheaper prices. Some showrooms are open all the time; others are open by appointment only. Aim for factories that have overruns from export orders. They should be made to western tastes.

Friendship Stores: these are government stores originally set up for foreigners but now most are like any other modern department store. At least one Friendship Store serves every city. Prices are about the same or slightly higher than other Chinese stores, but the goods are of better quality and some items are unavailable elsewhere. Government stores have a reputation for honesty. If you ask, clerks usually tell you if it's real or fake. The standard of English is usually higher than other stores. At least some signs are in English.

In addition to arts and crafts, the larger Friendship Stores have textiles, television sets, watches, bicycles, sewing machines, lace, silk jewelry bags, cosmetics, herbal medicines, food, jewelry, thermos bottles, camera film, cameras, jackknives, flashlights, cashmere sweaters, and silk blouses, cigarettes and wine – just about everything. Friendship Stores have locally-made goods for sale too.

The best Friendship Stores are in Beijing and Shanghai and they both take credit cards. The Beijing Friendship Store delivers goods to your hotel, takes telephone orders, and ships. It guarantees its goods. If customers have solid evidence of misrepresentation, you should be able to get your money back. You can also try to appeal to the tourism bureau for mediation and a copy of its list of approved stores. Even in some of these shops, you can get a 10% discount if you ask. If you want to buy a lot, you might get a higher discount.

At government stores, clerks tend to ignore you. At private stores, they are aggressive. But private stores usually discount more.

Hotel stores: Stores in fancy joint-venture hotels are not cheap, but you can find some of the best clothing styles, fabrics, and antiques there. In three-star hotels, you might also be able to find a few clothes with name brands like Oleg Cassini, Victoria's Secret, and Land's End. But sizes and color ranges are limited.

Hotels popular with Japanese visitors like the Garden in Shanghai have excellent quality and high priced goods, one-stop shopping for the top of the market.

Jade: The Chinese word for jade is "yu" and means any hard store, usually green. It can be carnelian (red jade), soap stone, serpentine, or whatever. The western definition of "jade" is jadeite or nephrite. Chinese people will sometimes label these harder stones "high quality" jade, and the rest "low quality" jade. But this is not common.

Do be aware that some so-called jades can be doctored. If you look carefully, you might suspect a thin imperial green jade piece on top of a low quality piece with a band of green glue inbetween. The join is covered by a gold setting. In a couple of years, the glue will dry out and your ring will look terrible. Hong Kong has been doing this for decades. China is doing this now. Check everything carefully.

Live plants, birds, and animals: these are usually not allowed into your country without certificates. These are not easily obtainable outside your country. You have to research this before you leave home.

Markets: Markets with lots of similiar shops or stalls, either indoors or out, have the cheapest prices and sometimes have great quality. You have to be extremely careful but these might have genuine name brands and real jade carvings. Markets sell everything: fruits and vegetables, clothes, antiques, curios, pets, flowers and handicrafts. With no changing rooms, people buying jeans have to try them on over their own trousers. They could be seconds, or factory overruns. The colors might run; some clothing will shrink. Check everything carefully.

Minority handicrafts: It is usually more meaningful to buy handicrafts (usually embroidery or batik) directly from the maker in her village. Walk into any minority village, and someone will probably show up with something to sell. Prices are best there. A good embroidered jacket from the Miao nationality costing $60 in a Kaili village would probably sell in New York City for a couple of hundred dollars. If you can't get to a village, look for a peddler. They usually hover around the entrances to hotels in Kunming, Kaili and Guilin.

Consider laundering problems before you buy. Some ethnic skirts could lose their pleats, and the paper lining of applique jackets and baby blankets from Xi'an might disintegrate if washed.

Packing and Shipping: Few stores can crate and ship goods for you. Some hotels can help. Ask before you buy. See Postal Service above. In some cases, the local US consulate might be able to help you if the goods shipped to you are not what you ordered. If you expect to buy fragile porcelains, take your own bubble wrap to the market.

Painted-inside balls: these are a variation of an old art form. Getting the right perspective on a curved surface takes a lot of skill. Prices for these depend on whether it's glass or crystal (more expensive), and the fineness of the work.

Pirated compact discs and recordings: these could be of good or poor quality. They can be purchased in street markets, and at railway stations. If your Customs Service catches these, however, they will be confiscated. The same goes for pirated computer diskettes.

Receipts: save these so you can argue with Customs officials in your own country, or get a refund or exchange. Receipts are usually in Chinese with English numerals, so make a note on it of what each refers to. Put on tags of your own at the time of purchase to remind you where you bought it, how much you paid, and what it is. To help prove to your own Customs people that it's a duty-free antique, you have to get a receipt stating its age.

Snuff bottles: Bottles for snuff, usually with an ivory spoon, is a 250-year old art. Old and unusual ones are collector's items, the most valuable made of carved pink coral and amber decorated with lacquer and pearl. Many are made of Peking glass. Since early in the 19th century, they were painted on the inside surface, an art that continues to this day. Obviously, those pieces are meant for show, not use.

Tailors: they are not as organized as in other places in Asia, like Hong Kong. But they are cheap! Don't bother having clothes tailored here unless a tailor is recommended by Western friends and you have a picture or sample of what you want made. See Crowne Plaza Hotel in Shanghai for a tailor who makes suits for the hotel's western staff and should be good.

Taxes: China does not have taxes on sales.

Tour guides: Many guides take you shopping to stores where they get commissions. But your guides should also be able to get you discounts, good discounts, like 50% if you're in a group. Dont expect guides to be on your side in markets; some have been scolded for telling tourists the price is too high.

Videos and slides: of Chinese tourist attractions are available. Be sure you buy videos tapes labelled NTSC, not PAL. Otherwise they cannot work with North American machines.

Warnings: Peddlers at stalls, especially at the Great Wall, have been known to wrap up a cheaper T-shirt than the one you chose. Always check before you leave. This could also happen in stores. Keep a close watch.

Wholesale Markets: these are also good places to purchase gifts. Groups of silk factories have banded together to form one such market outside Hangzhou. Groups of sweater manufacturers have done the same outside of Ningbo. In Guilin all the merchandise displayed in the tourist markets can be bought at the tourist wholesale market, open to everyone. There's the Hongqiao Market in Beijing where you can get pearls. Prices and selection are generally good.

HOW TO CHOOSE

Before you go to China, learn about quality in museums and prices in Chinatown stores. If you are a serious shopper, plan your trip so you can see how a favorite craft is made. Locally-made crafts are listed under each destination in this book.

In the factory, you can study how the pieces are made and what makes a good piece. Will the wood or lacquer crack in dry, centrally heated houses? You should handle some of the best pieces. Feel the weight and the surface texture. Compare these with ordinary quality goods. For reproductions, study the originals in nearby museums. Remember also that handmade articles are each different - of course! So before you buy, check carefully, not just for flaws, but for the rendering that you like best.

Generally speaking, consider (1) the amount of work involved in the production – the finer and more intricate something is, the better; (2) good proportions, lines, balance, and color; (3) how closely it represents what it is supposed to represent: (4) the quality of the material – will it chip? and (5) whether it will be a joy forever, or will you easily tire of it? (Primitive art doesnt have to be well proportioned or intricate.)

Crafts can also be made-to-order, but most Chinese factories are not set up for easy ordering. These of course take a lot of time. The most difficult part is getting the craftsperson to understand exactly what you want.

Most general tours include at least one handicraft factory and always one Friendship or Arts and Crafts store in every city. Many cities also have handicraft institutes where new crafts are developed and craftspeople are trained.

If you are more interested in handicrafts than temples, it is best to take an individual or special-interest tour. On a regular tour, the average tourist will be back on the bus waiting while you're still talking about the iron content in glazes.

BUYING SOMETHING CHEAP & UNIQUELY CHINESE

China has a good variety of novelties, things distinctively Chinese to take back to your nieces, nephews, and bridge buddies. These are relatively cheap and easy to carry. Unique are **porcelain sherds** made into small pendants, **embroideries**, **pearls**, **silk bags** shaped like little children, **silk scarves** and **ties**, **hand-painted wooden ducks**, **small peasant paintings**, and fancy **Uyger daggers** for paper openers. You can buy hand-painted **T-shirts** and **chops** with rubber stamps both made by artists in hotel lobbies with the names of your friends. Cheap souvenir **pins** with pandas or the names of tourist sites are available. Thimbles, chopsticks, nail clippers, pill boxes and bracelets are made in **cloisonne**. **Dough figurines** in plastic cases of lovely ladies or opera figures cost Y15 each. In markets, you can pay Y20 for **stone rollers** (that help get rid of wrinkles). These have been marked at Y400 on some cruise ships! Expandable **stone bracelets** have cost Y6 in markets.

Posters, **postcards**, and **comic books** are fun and cheap, and so is a **map** of the world showing China in the center, or of Canada and the US in Chinese characters. Look for colored **paper-cuts** for glueing on windows or walls. **Scroll pictures** are easy to carry. How about **Mao caps and buttons?** Now that **green tea** is considered health giving, people should appreciate gifts of it. Not all Chinese tea is green however so read labels.

Other suggestions: porcelain **sherd boxes** that can be stood up for display; **cute tea pots** in unusual shapes, and **hand-stitched quilts** (in American styles). Also typical are **lace tablecloths** (others shrink in hot water). **Cork carvings** are traditional and pretty and can be tiny enough to pack. Look for framed pictures of **two-sided embroidery**, horn or root **carvings**, and carved **balls within balls**.

There's all kinds of **lacquerware, bamboo**, and **feather craft**. Zhejiang province has multi-colored **Qingtian stone carvings. Acupuncture dolls** are about ten inches high and come with genuine acupuncture needles and an instruction booklet (in Chinese) for friends interested in it. Acupuncture posters are found in bookstores. Think about exercise balls for older arthritic people. They can be very heavy.

There are children's story **books** in English or books of Chinese characters. If you're in a foreign language bookstore, you'll find a great many books in English (cheap), all printed in China. Book lovers must visit Liulichang in Beijing to look at samples of fine Chinese printing and **art books**. The Shanghai Museum has a good selection of books in English.

Some **museum reproductions** are quite good and not too expensive. Check out the retail store in any museum you visit.

Consider Chinese **kites**. You can hang them on the wall if you don't fly them. Cloth wall hangings of Chinese **zodiac animals** are best from Beijing and Lanzhou. Xi'an's are not as good. Cheap **tiger slippers** for babies from Xi'an are cute. **Vests** with appliques have been a hit with tourists in Xi'an, where they are cheaper than elsewhere in China.

Furs, **cashmere sweaters**, **down coats**, **and leather jackets** are bargains, but please don't buy any endangered species. A Hong Kong furrier said the quality of the tanning of a lot of Chinese skins is not very good and might later stink when wet, so check items carefully. We've had no trouble with fur hats.

MYTHOLOGICAL & HISTORICAL SUBJECTS IN ARTS & CRAFTS

- Poet Shi Yung of the late Spring and Autumn Period has a knot on top of his head and a sword at his back.
- Wei Tou is the guardian of Buddhism and of the Goddess of Mercy.
- Guan Yin was originally a god, but in recent sculpture, always the Goddess of Mercy. She is depicted with children, or carrying a cloud

duster (like a horsetail whip), or with many heads and arms, or with a vase.

- Princess Wen Chen was the Chinese princess who married a Tibetan king and took Buddhism to Tibet.
- Li Shi-zen was the Ming dynasty author of the classic book on medicinal herbs. He is shown carrying herbs in a basket and a hoe.
- God of Longevity is an old man with a peach.
- God of Wealth is a well-dressed man with a scepter.
- Laughing Buddha or Maitreya is fat and jolly and sometimes is surrounded by children or standing alone with raised arms.
- Eight Taoist Genii - see Taoism, above.
- Fa Mu-lan is the famous woman general who inspired Maxine Hong Kingston's *The Woman Warrior*, and is now a Disney heroine.
- Characters from classical Chinese novels: Water Margin, The Dream of the Red Chamber, Pilgrimage to the West.

10. SPORTS, RECREATION, & ECOTOURISM

China, which tried very hard to host the 2000 Olympics, is sports-crazy. The favorite spectator sport is **soccer** and probably the most popular participatory sport is **billiards**, which you see everywhere. Soccer is a passion and like elsewhere it has deteriorated into fights. The season in Beijing is May to October; in the south the season is all year round. In Shanghai it's played at Hong Kou Stadium; in Beijing it's at Workers' Stadium near City Hotel. Just follow the cheering.

The favorite traditional sport at which the Chinese excel is **ping-pong**. It is less popular than billiards, and the national tournament is usually in May. Another traditional sport is **kung fu**, which has been practised since the Tang dynasty at Shaolin Temple and other temples. Schools are also in Beijing and other cities. For Chinese **martial arts**, look for announcements of demonstrations in tourism materials. See Beijing. The most important place is of course Shaolin Temple itself, which gives demonstration and courses. See Zhengzhou.

The sport taking the most space in recent years has been **golf**, but few Chinese actually play; the courses are mainly for foreigners especially Japanese. You can make arrangements to play through the top hotels, or telephone courses directly yourself. Good courses are also in Zhongshan, Tianjin, Shenzhen, Shanghai, Beijing and a growing number of cities. China Tourist offices should have brochures and maps of courses. See also *http://user.hk.linkage.net/~klaus/golf/sinogolf.html*.

Many sports now emerging are new to China. There's **hot-air ballooning** and **gliding** in Anyang, and gliding in Jiayuguan. China International Sports has **hot-air ballooning tours** over the Great Wall, and along the Silk Road. See *http://sportschina.com*.

Chinese **climbers** can attack over 60 peaks, including Qomolangma (Everest). **Skiing** has been slow in developing but there are now four public resorts and one training resort (Jilin province). The best is at Yabuli in Heilongjiang province, which hosted the 1996 Asian Winter Games. See Harbin. A year-round **ski facility** is the Yulong Alpine Skiing Slope in Yunnan province. Heilongjiang and Jilin provinces have ice hockey teams.

American **football** has not developed much of a following. The Agricultural University has had a team. **Baseball** stadiums are in Chengdu, Lanzhou, Shanghai and Guangzhou. **Rugby** has been developing so well that Chinese teams have participated in Hong Kong's prestigeous Rugby Sevens and done well. Beijing has an annual **Cricket** Sixes in the autumn with Chinese and expatriate teams. The Heineken Open **tennis** competitions brought Michael Chang and Goran Ivanisevic to Shanghai in 1998. The **Beijing marathon** is run during the Spring Festival and there's nothing to stop you from running with it. Shanghai has a world class **squash** court.

Basketball is growing in importance and American coaches have been working with Chinese teams, and American teams playing against them. Get a look at the Sports Bar at the Gloria International Hotel in Beijing. It's big on that sport.

Sailboarding is in Qingdao, Xiamen, Qinhuangdao, Sanya, Dalian, and Qingdao. Sanya has the most sports, among them water polo, scuba diving, para-sailing and sailing. **Whitewater rafting** is in the upper reaches of the Yangtze River in Sichuan and Qinghai. Many groups bring their own rafts, but China Sports can supply tents and bags.

The **Shanghai Acrobats** have a school for professionals with students from all over the country. If you have the right *guanxi* or connections, you might be able to wrangle a visit. Start with the manager at the Shanghai Centre, Shanghai, *Tel. 62798600.*

Horseracing is increasing. Events at the Beijing Country Horse Racing Club are not comfortable, however, because you sit on concrete steps. The minimum bet is five yuan. A board does display the odds and the same eight or ten horses race each time.

For those who want to play against Chinese teams, contact **China International Sports Travel Service** in Beijing, *http://www.sportstravel.com.cn.* On a less formal basis, contact your embassy or consulates, or the sports departments of international schools in China.

RIDE WITH GENGHIS KHAN!

*Travel agents like China International Sports Travel can organize one-week **camel treks** in the Taklamakan Desert or take you riding with those most famous of horsemen, the Mongols.*

Some foreigners who live in China organize their own sports teams and are always looking for volunteers to play hockey, throw frisbees or go skiing. The bulletin boards of supermarkets frequented by foreigners such as those in the China World Hotel or the Holiday Inn Lido in Beijing could have notices too. See above under Nightlife and Recreation about the Hash House Harriers ("a drinking club with a running problem"). For **body building machines**, your best bet is a good hotel. The China World in Beijing has enough to harden a battalion. It also has indoor tennis courts. In Shanghai, the Portman Ritz-Carlton has a good health club, the Regal International has the most tennis courts, and the Regal East Asia Hotel has rooms opening onto the Shanghai Stadium.

See also *http://sportschina.com* and for connections with the expatriate community see *Xianzai Beijing* and *Xianzai Shanghai* in each city. See also Nightlife and Recreation in Chapter 7 for sports opportunities encouraged by the expatriate community.

ECOTOURISM

China is making a good attempt at developing nature reserves, and national forests, with places to hike, bicycle, raft, and breathe fresh air. It is building an international class national park in Yunnan province near Lijiang and Zhongdian with American help. China has over 66 biosphere protection zones and nature reserves, at least fourteen of these are members of UNESCO's Man and the Biosphere Program.

Of the destinations mentioned in this book, these UNESCO programs are accessible from Changchun (**Mt. Changbai**), Chengdu (**Wolong Panda Reserve**, **Jiuzhaigou**), Fuzhou (**Mount Wuyi**), Kunming (**Xishuangbanna**), Yangtze Gorges (**Shennongjia**), and Zhaoqing (**Mt. Dinghu**).

For nature reserves, see Xining for Qinghai Lake's **Bird Island**, and Harbin for the **Zhalong Nature Preserve** near Qiqihar with its red crested cranes. Chengdu is central for **pandas**. Look up Wuhan for attempts to save **river dolphins**, Yichang for **sturgeon**, and Hefei for **alligators**.

Considered World Heritage Sites by UNESCO are **Mt. Taishan** (see Jin'an), **Mt. Huangshan Scenic Area** (see Hefei), **Wulingyuan Scenic Area** (see Changsha), **Jiuzhaigou Scenic Area** (see Chengdu), and **Mt. Lushan Scenic Area** (see Yangtze Gorges).

You might want to add a couple days to your visits to Guilin for the **Longsheng Hot Springs National Forest Park** and to Shanghai for **Sheshan National Forest Park**. There's Dalian for **Benxi National Forest Park** (and cave), Datong for **Mount Wutai National Forest Park**, and Fuzhou for **Wuyi Mountain**.

Major botanical gardens are in Beijing, Chengdu (near Dujiangyan), Guangzhou, Guilin, Nanjing, Jinghong (see Kunming), Lushan, Shenyang, Turpan, Wuhan, and Zhaoqing. There are many others besides. **Flower festivals** are all over the country, peonies in Luoyang, and camellias in Kunming. Kunming is hosting the **1999 Horticultural Expo**. Its province also has the world's biggest rhododendrons on the Burma Road.

All these areas have hiking opportunities. There's also the **Huangguoshu Waterfall** and the **Kaili** area near Guiyang, and many others.

For tame rafting, there's Wuyi, Zhangjiakou/Wulingyuan and Shennongjia above. For serious white water rafting, mountain climbing and skiing, see Sports above. There is talk about rafting on the Yarlung Zangbo River in Tibet and I'm keeping in touch with CYTS in Chengdu about it.

For trekking by camel, contact travel agents in the Silk Road cities, and Hohhot in Inner Mongolia. For bicycling, see Backroads Bicycle Touring, and China International Sports Travel for tours. Very popular for cycling on your own is **Yangshuo** near Guilin.

Accommodations are modest, and serious ecologists will question some of its practices, but China's efforts should be encouraged and enjoyed. It is very aware that these areas should be kept clean. You yourself can help plant trees in Zhengzhou and pick up trash on the Great Wall.

The government has designated 1999 as **Ecotour-China year**. The China National Tourism has published two booklets, *Ecotour Highlights* and *China's National Forest Park,* which are available from China Tourist Offices.

11. FOOD & DRINK

BACKGROUND TO CHINESE CUISINE

The infinite number of Chinese dishes, flavors, textures, and methods of cooking makes eating here exciting. The most famous cooking styles are Beijing, Cantonese, Shanghai, and Sichuan. There are also vegetarian and minority foods. Try the local food. Cantonese is best in Guangdong; Sichuan in Sichuan.

Chinese food is usually chopped up in thin, bite-size pieces, making knives unnecessary at the dinner table. The thinness is for quick cooking, using a minimum of fuel. Chinese food can also appear whole, like fish or pork hocks, but these can be easily separated by chopsticks. When poultry is cooked whole, it is chopped up before appearing at the table. Sometimes the bones are splintered so the food inside the bones can be reached. Do be careful.

HOW TO USE CHOPSTICKS

The bottom stick is held firmly by the base of the thumb and the knuckle of the ring finger. The top stick is the ONLY one that is moved and is held by the thumb and the index and middle fingers. The tip of the top stick should be brought toward the tip of the bottom one. Keep the tips even.

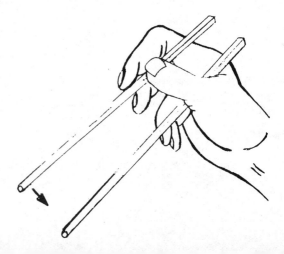

Chinese ingredients reflect the many periods of famine in Chinese history. Everything possible is eaten; nothing is wasted, not even chicken feet, duck tongues, jellyfish, and sea slugs – all famous delicacies.

The Chinese food served to most prepaid groups is usually adequate. If you want to eat better, you can pay more for better restaurants. If food is important, take a gourmet tour.

THINGS TO REMEMBER ABOUT RESTAURANTS IN CHINA

Until recently, restaurants were generally dumpy and tacky, a reflection of revolutionary attitudes. The new economic policies mean many new or renovated eating places, some very striking joint ventures in the gaudy Hong Kong style, and you can even find Starbuck's coffee. International-class hotels import ingredients and executive chefs. Some families and factories have also started restaurants with better food and service than state-run establishments.

The current make-a-profit-or-quit policy has forced improvements everywhere. Provincial and city-state tourism administrations are regulating restaurants. They should have a list of those fit for foreign tourists and if you have a complaint, contact the local tourism administration. Each restaurant should have a plaque that says it's been approved.

You might be put into private dining rooms in restaurants. These are less colorful but cleaner than eating with the masses, and usually cost more. However, you won't be stared at and can make a reservation.

Many state-run restaurants receive guests at 6pm and then rush you out at 8:30 or 9pm so the staff can go home. If you want to linger, choose a privately-owned restaurant or hotel coffee shop.

The days are long gone when you could trust waitresses to give you a correct bill. Hold on to the menu. Check the items, prices, and total.

ORDERING

Menus in restaurants for foreign visitors are usually in English and Chinese and a la carte. Some restaurants have a fixed menu too which you don't usually see. You have to ask. The fixed menu is served to tour groups, who need not worry about ordering. Individuals can order this too for an easy way out. Food on the fixed menu is relatively inexpensive and you get more variety for one or two people; just say *feng fan* or *bao chan*. Menus change every day.

Gourmets avoid fixed menus and buffets because the food is not freshly cooked. But buffets, with their large number of different dishes, are good introductions. If you like a particular dish, ask the name so you can order it again.

Every restaurant has its specialties. These are probably more expensive and are sometimes not worth it. In Ningbo, they included red blood-raw clams which I couldn't eat! Aim also for local or regional dishes like fresh seafood if you're near an ocean. (Top-quality restaurants and hotels everywhere get seafood flown in and charge a lot more.) Meals in the countryside are usually excellent because the vegetables go from the garden to the wok.

It is best to eat with a large group of people to get a greater number of courses. Ten is ideal for a table, and you may get a private room thrown in. When ordering, two people should order three courses plus a starch; five people should order six courses plus a starch or two. Choose only one of poultry, fish, beef, pork, or vegetable. This will give you variety and abundance. If you find you are getting too much, order less next time.

If you need more courses, start the rounds again. If you've already chosen chicken, choose duck or goose. Vary tastes and textures: sweet, pepper-hot, salty, steamed, deep-fried, poached, boiled, roasted, baked in mud – the choice is endless.

Don't feel that every meal should be a banquet. The danger in China is overeating.

For popular restaurants, it is always best to reserve a table and even order meals ahead by telephone, especially for banquets. Restaurants for the masses won't take reservations. Ask your hotel's service desk to make reservations for you, telling the restaurant how much you want to pay but also approving the dishes suggested. One restaurant suggested bears' paws, a local delicacy and an endangered species, which no one ate. Most of the cost went into that one dish!

ELABORATE BANQUET DISHES

These should be ordered at least 24 hours ahead of time and a hefty charge is levied if you cancel.

Don't look for chop suey, chow mein with crispy noodles, or fortune cookies - those are Chinese-American dishes. China has fried noodles, but they are not the same. But with the new economic policies, anything could show up! And be aware that some wild animals used by the Chinese as food are, or may soon be, on the endangered species list. Please avoid them. Tell your host in advance that you don't want them.

SPECIAL DIETS

If you have special food preferences, let your guide know. For an upset stomach, order rice congee, which is rice cooked to a gruel consistency and flavored with salted egg, fermented bean curd, or whatever. Congee is easy on the stomach. Avoid fried dishes, spices, and dairy products. Eat dry crackers, arrowroot biscuits, and apple sauce.

If you have cankers in the mouth, try *hung pean* (chrysanthemum tea). It comes already sweetened in one-cup packages and is an old Chinese remedy.

People on general-interest tours should not expect special diets. Salt-free and diabetic diets are impossible. Chinese cooking uses more salt than western cooking. You could, however, go on a special tour for people with the same restrictions. Vegetarians usually manage on a general tour if you don't mind meat sauces. Vegetarian restaurants exist, but are not on the daily tourist route. Muslim restaurants also exist but so far there is no kosher cooking except in Hong Kong.

DESSERTS

Foreigners on tours will be offered fresh or canned fruits. If you're in Guangdong in May or June, ask for fresh **lichees** - or buy them in markets. Look for **pomelo**, especially in Guilin or Sichuan. It's a sweet grapefruit with a thick rind. Try **Hami melon** on the Silk Road. China also has ice cream, sweet red beans, sweet almond paste, and deep-fried crystallized apples and bananas. Aside from fruit, the Chinese do not have much of a tradition for desserts.

To be absolutely safe, eat only imported ice creams like Bud's, Wall's, and Movenpick's.

BEVERAGES

Most prepaid meals for foreigners include soft drinks, beer, and tea. Canned fruit juice, foreign-brand soft drinks, and liquor cost extra. Coca-Cola and Pepsi have bottling plants in China. The dreaded orange soda has been replaced in some cities by good, fresh, or reconstituted juices. **Laoshan** is the most famous mineral water but others are good.

Tsingdao beer is the favorite. It is made with barley, spring water, and hops from a German recipe. **Five Star Beer** has been designated by the government for state banquets. Local beers are usually good. Locally-brewed foreign beers are increasingly available. Moslem restaurants don't serve alcohol.

The Chinese consider the following three liquors to be the best: **Mao tai**, made from sorghum and wheat yeast, aged five or six years in Guizhou province, very potent and usually served in tiny goblets; **Fenjiu**, mellow and delicate flavor from Shanxi province; **Wuliangye**, five-grain spirit from southern Sichuan, with a fragrant and invigorating flavor.

The best Chinese wines are: **Yantai red wine** from Shandong, **Chinese red wine** from Beijing, **Shaoxing red wine** from Zhejiang, and **Longyan rice wine** from Fujian.

TRY CHINESE WINE

Foreign wines are very expensive; the Chinese version is cheaper. **Dynasty's White Riesling** *and* **Rose** *are good.* **Huadong Qingdao Chardonay** *(the product of an Australian joint venture) and* **Dragon Seal's Cabernet Sauvignon** *(a French joint venture) are popular. Dry red* **Cabernet Sauvignon** *by* **Vinitalia** *is worth trying, a Sino-Italian joint venture from Hangzhou. Xinjiang is starting to produce* **Lanlou**, *an outstanding red table wine.* **Great Wall** *has both a red and white, light, lively and sparkling.* **Chateau St. Pierre** *is an American wine bottled here, red and sweet with a little sparkle. You can get foreign wines with meals mainly in the top hotels, and you can buy wines in supermarkets.*

Dairies have opened, but outside big cities, you only get **UHT**, **powdered** or **canned milk**. If you're uncertain of the pasteurization, order milk hot. It'll probably arrive sweetened. In Tibet you can get **yak butter tea** and in Yunnan, there's crispy fried goat's cheese.

Drinking tea is an art in China. Some springs are famous for their tea-making qualities. If you go to Hangzhou, try **long jing tea** there. A favorite tea in hot weather is **po li**. **Keemun** is good in the wintertime and when you've had greasy food. **Lu an** should help you sleep. **Oolong** is the most common tea in south China, while most foreigners like **jasmine**. Jasmine is said to heat the blood and should be balanced at the same meal with **po li** or **pu er**.

Every Chinese has a personal list of the four most famous green teas. **Long jing** (dragon well), **yun wu** (mist of the clouds), **mao hong** (red straw), and **bi lu chuen** (green spring) are probably among the most popular.

BREAKFASTS

Foreign tour groups in one- and two-star hotels usually receive western breakfast with greasy eggs. You also get lightly toasted bread, coffee, and fruit or canned juice. Four-star-and-up hotels now have western buffets or mixed western and Chinese buffets.

You can opt for Chinese breakfasts if enough people in the group want them. Chinese breakfasts differ regionally: **dim sum** or **rice congee** with peanuts, pickles, salt, or 1000-year-old eggs in south China; in the north, you could get lots of different buns, or **'oil sticks,'** which are like foot-long doughnuts, deep-fried and delicious, but hard to digest. You dip these in hot soy milk. In Shanghai, you might get gelatinous **rice balls** with sugar inside, or baked buns with **sweet bean paste** inside. They are great!

WESTERN FOOD

Most tourist hotels serve western food, but it is rarely as good as Chinese. Bread is cut thick and is usually white. Sometimes it is one Chinese meat-and-vegetable course with bread instead of rice. Excellent western food is available in four-star and up joint-venture hotels and restaurants, especially in Beijing, Shanghai and Guangzhou. Some of these hotels also have delicatessens where you can buy cold cuts. Some restaurants in Northeast China have Russian food.

Local Chinese prefer Chinese food and have rejected invitations to western meals 'because of too much meat' or the lack of familiarity with knives, forks, and western table manners.

COURTESIES

Group tours should be punctual at meals as the food is usually ready on time. Meals are served family style and the dishes may be sitting on the table getting (ugh!) cold.

Guests of honor are traditionally given seats where they face the door. Left-handed people should sit where they can avoid clashes with right-handed chopsticks.

Many restaurants distribute damp towels at the beginning of meals to refresh guests as well as to clean. You can wipe faces, hands and backs of necks with them. Sometimes towels are distributed during the meal and always at the end.

If you pass tea or bowls or calling cards, to be polite, use both hands and bow.

Chinese food is usually served on large platters, which ideally arrive one at a time. The food comes hot off the wok at the peak of perfection to be eaten immediately.

In families, diners pick what they want with chopsticks which are great for reaching across tables, keeping fingers clean, and hitting naughty children. Outside of families, use serving spoons. After guests express admiration for the beauty of the food, Chinese hosts put the best morsels on the plates of the people around them. You could do this, too, after the first round. Since you put your own chopsticks into your mouth, you should use the other end for serving. The host usually invites guests to start eating. Groups of friends can declare a moratorium on such formalities and have everybody dig in. *Hei fai* means 'Raise chopsticks!'

Slurping or even burping indicates that you are rude. If you don't have enough room on your dish for bones and other discards, just leave them neatly on the table itself. Less-polished Chinese will spit them onto the floor!

If you want a tiny plate of hot chili condiment to spice up a bland dish, ask for *la jiang*.

In very fancy restaurants, an attendant distributes every course and guests do not help themselves. Individual plates are removed and replaced with clean ones after most courses. The host usually invites guests to start eating.

GIVING A BANQUET

Hosting a feast is the accepted and most important way to return hospitality or to show gratitude for a favor. If your guide persists in refusing your invitation to eat with you, he may relent and join you the day before you leave as a farewell gesture.

You may want to throw a banquet for some of your Chinese colleagues and people who have been helpful. Discuss your guest list with one of the Chinese involved so you won't offend anybody important by leaving them out. Discuss spouses and times and seating arrangements, but don't be offended if spouses don't show up. The venue is important because some restaurants are more prestigious than others.

Even-numbered days are more auspicious than odd-numbered days. Restaurants may be busier with wedding parties then.

TOASTING & BANQUETS

Chinese people do not like to drink alone. Toasting at banquets is a complicated art, and you are not expected to know the finer points. Just do what you do at home. Stand up, give one or two sentences, make sure everybody is joining you, and drink. *Gan bei!* means 'Empty your glass!'

The first toaster is usually the host, who gets the ball rolling. A frequent toast is to the friendship of the people of your country and China, and the health of friends and comrades present. You can tell a funny story and then talk about your sadness about leaving China and the new friends you have made, and meeting again in your country.

Toasts might continue all evening, and so might the meal, or at least until the restaurant turns out the lights. If the banquet is extremely large, the host might circulate to all the tables, drinking toasts at each one. On smaller, less formal occasions, the Chinese may want to drink you under the table. Be alert; they may be putting tea in their own glasses. You may want to try that yourself after awhile.

I have been to banquets where I didn't touch a drop of liquor. I can't get *mao tai* past my nose - it's so strong. Chinese hosts are not usually offended if you toast with tea or soft drinks. If you don't want to drink liquor, mumble something about a medical problem, like an allergy. Try to divert your fellow diners. Try exchanging songs - but no drinking ones. It may be the only occasion when you'll hear the national anthem of

China. You can turn your cup or glass upside down to signal to the waiter that you've had enough.

If you want to stop eating and your host keeps piling food onto your plate, just lay down your chopsticks. Thank him politely but don't eat anymore. Your host shouldn't feel insulted.

Recently, as an austerity measure, the lavishness of top-level state banquets was curtailed officially to four courses and a soup, and the length limited to one and a half hours. This might be the beginning of a trend, but then again, it might not. Banquets are part of the culture.

EATING WITH THE LOCALS

You can eat quite well for comparatively little money if you're willing to try food stalls and restaurants for the masses. The standard of cleanliness and speed of service are not generally as high as in restaurants for tourists. The cigarette smoke may be suffocating. It is customary to share tables with other diners in busy restaurants.

Payment is made when you order (so you can't stomp out impatiently). Some finicky eaters take their own chopsticks and spoons to places like this, but as far as I can see the dishes are scalded, and if the food is freshly cooked, there should be no problems. The soup sterilizes the utensils (you hope), but you can also scald them yourself with tea.

Hot pot is ideal in places like this for the same reason. I highly recommend James D. McCauley's *The Eater's Guide to Chinese Characters* if you are eating off the tourist track.

FAST FOOD STALLS, MOBILE CANTEENS, & CAFETERIAS

These are recent innovations and are multiplying quickly. Some serve instant noodles. A knowledge of Chinese isn't necessary; you can point.

Outdoor night markets are an adventurous attraction for gourmet as well as budget travelers. Make sure the food is steaming hot and the utensils are scalded or eat directly from the cooking container. Avoid uncooked sauces and condiments.

Sometimes I take my own paper bowls and disposable chopsticks and get food straight off the grill or steamer. It's great, and oh, so cheap. Sometimes in Beijing, you can get steaming hot sweet potatoes, filling enough for breakfast for a *yuan*.

FOOD STREETS

Food streets are usually managed by hotels so are cleaner and more foreigner-oriented. The food is usually light and prices are reasonable: noodles, fried rice, side orders of barbecued duck, cuttle-fish, etc.

EATING PRECAUTIONS

To avoid an upset stomach and intestinal parasites, do not drink water out of faucets. Most bottled drinks are fine, but make sure the seal isn't broken. Steer clear of ice, popsicles, ice cream (except for foreign brands), watermelon, and other fruit. Don't eat anything raw unless it's imported, or carefully washed and peeled. Animal and human manure is used in China as fertilizer. Local people have developed immunities.

Be careful on ferries and small boats. Dishes are frequently washed in river water and are not always scalded carefully afterward. Some people take disinfectants like tincture of iodine. Two drops in a liter of water kills all germs in 20 minutes. When cooking your own food, as in Mongolian Hot Pot, be careful that the utensils you use on raw meat or fish are not the same utensils you put into your own mouth. Sterilize utensils in the hot pot.

OTHER TIPS

The secret of eating a Chinese meal is finding out first how many courses you will be getting. Banquet meals usually have a copy of the menu on the table. If there are 12 courses, take no more than one-twelfth of what

HERE'S THE BEST WAY TO EAT ...

Mantou: the plain steamed roll. Either take bites while holding with chopsticks or fingers, or break apart and stuff pieces with bits of meat. You can also dip it in sauces. Jiao zi are small stuffed ravioli-like pastries, steamed or fried; bao zi are steamed dumplings and may have beans or meat and vegetables inside. The names get confusing.

White rice: served in bowls. Put the bowl up to your mouth and shove the rice in with chopsticks. More genteel people might want to pick up chunks with chopsticks.

1000-year-old eggs: you usually have to either acquire a taste or close your eyes and think of something else; they are best eaten with pickles and are delicious.

Shrimp with shells left on: take a bite of half, then, with your teeth and chopsticks, squeeze out the meat. You could use your fingers to shell them. Cooking shrimp in their shells retains most of the yummy flavor.

Two-and three-foot long noodles: lean over your bowl and pick up a few noodles with chopsticks. Put the noodles in your mouth, biting off pieces and leaving the rest temporarily in your bowl. Don't worry about slurping. The Chinese enjoy long noodles because they symbolize longevity.

Ice cream: ask for a spoon.

you would usually eat in a meal from each plate; otherwise, you will be too full to eat the later dishes. Also take your time. You can't rush through a big meal. Some famous banquets have taken days.

Fish is the last formal course in some places. If you happen to be eating with superstitious fishermen, don't turn a fish over to get at the flesh on the other side. It means their boat will turn over!

Do not worry about 'Chinese restaurant syndrome.' Its symptoms are an increased pulse and a tight feeling around the sinuses. This 'syndrome' is a result of the large amount of Monosodium Glutamate (MSG) in Chinese food in America. Cooks in China use a little, but not as much. You can ask them to leave out MSG (*wei jing* or *Ajinomoto*), salt, chilis or anything else.

Among the beauties of a Chinese meal is the variety. If you don't like one thing, you might like something else. On prepaid tours, you might want to talk with your escort about the overabundance of food when meat for the common man is so limited - if this bothers you.

Menus in English are by translators, not public relations people. Some dishes may sound absolutely terrible, but are really very good. Don't let a name like 'frog oil soup' throw you.

Preserved fruit is delicious, but do not eat too many at a sitting. They are full of preservatives.

Another new development are the health restaurants, with dishes made from Chinese herbal medicines with lots of ginseng, sea horses, deer antlers, and things best left unmentioned. Some foods are known to combat high blood pressure; other foods are good for pregnant women. These are indeed for the adventurous eater because of their unusual flavors, and they can be very delicious.

If you invite average Chinese people to dinner, be sensitive that a meal in a tourist restaurant is a real treat. Normally, they cannot afford it. Since they get little meat, do order more for them. Do encourage them to take the leftovers home. They may be too polite to ask.

REGIONAL CUISINES

For specific dishes, see Chapter 24, *Glossary of Chinese Characters*.

Beijing (or **Peking** or **Northern**) cooking is light and salty with few sauces but lots of garlic, leeks, and scallions. It has flour-made buns, rolls and meat dumplings. Food is baked, steamed, roasted, fried, or boiled in soup. In winter, be sure to try hot pot. And don't forget Mongolian barbecue. It's a Northern dish too.

Cantonese (or **Guangdong** or **Southern**) style has crisp vegetables quickly fried in peanut oil and is somewhat sweet with starch in the sauces. It uses a lot of oyster sauce or fish sauce in cooking, or poured over boiled vegetables. A few dishes are dog, monkey, and snake. (Please, no pangolin and other endangered species!) *Dim Sum* are those small fried or steamed Cantonese pastries served at breakfast or lunch and are ordered from a menu (classier), or chosen from a trolley brought to your table. The trolley attendant can take off any cover for you to see inside. The most famous *dim sum* restaurant is the Panxi Restaurant in Guangzhou. But it's great in most other restaurants in that province. Chicken feet, known as Phoenix feet, are delicious! Honest!

Fujian cooking has lots of seafood and light soups, suckling pig, and non-fat spring rolls. You may recognize Filipino dishes like *lumpia* and *lechon*, originally from this province.

Shanghai cooking from Eastern China is similiar to that of Suzhou, Yangzhou, and Wuxi. It is cooked longer in sesame oil, neither sweet nor salty. It can be very ornamental. *Borscht* is on the menu of most of Shanghai's restaurants because of all the White Russians who once lived in Shanghai. Look for crab in November.

Some **Sichuan** (Szechuan) dishes are highly spiced, peppery hot, and oily. Formal banquet cooking is more bland. Smoked duck with camphor and tea flavor is not spicy hot.

Vegetarian cooking has had a long tradition in China and was first documented 2000 years ago. It developed with Buddhism, which forbids its adherents from killing animals, and restaurants are frequently found near Buddhist temples. Distinctively Chinese are dishes that imitate meat in taste, texture, and looks. While this does not encourage reverence for life as taught by Buddha, it does make it easier for some Buddhists to become vegetarian. Many of the dishes are made of soy bean and use a lot of monosodium glutamate.

12. ACCOMMODATIONS IN CHINA

ABBREVIATIONS & HOTEL JARGON

These are the abbreviations relevant to hotels and accommodations:

BBC – British Broadcasting Corporation with regular world news.

B.C. - Business center or hotel office capable of sending faxes, and offering a secretary for hire, photocopying, and typewriter rentals

CITS - China International Travel Service

CNN – Cable Network News. The major English–language news station from the US

Credit Cards - These are the credit cards accepted by hotels: American Express, Visa, MasterCard, and sometimes Diners

CTS - China Travel Service

CYTS - China Youth Travel Service tours

Executive Floor - a section set aside for higher paying guests usually with complimentary breakfast, a lounge, concierge service, cocktails, and other services.

HBO – Home Box Office, an English language movie channel

Http – the address of a Website

IDD – International Direct Dial

Renovated – means major improvements.

Star TV – a Hong Kong channel offering *The Bold and the Beautiful*, sports, entertainment, and/or music channels in English.

Tourist Hotlines are telephone numbers set up to help with any problems, emergency translating, or complaints of tourists.

Wide twin - twin beds at least 53" wide each

Y - Yuan (Chinese currency).

All dollar prices given in this book, unless otherwise noted, are in US dollars. **One US$=Y8.3**. These are for reference only. Payment should be in Chinese currency.

CHINESE HOTEL CHAINS
& THEIR TOLL-FREE NUMBERS

If you read about an interesting hotel in your destination city, phone its representative in North America here for prices and reservations.

Courtyard by Marriott: *Tel. 800/321-2211, 800/468-3571*
Forum Hotels International: *Tel. 800/327-0200*
Gloria Hotels: *Tel. 800/821-0900*
Hilton International: *Tel. 800/445-8667*
Holiday Inns Worldwide: *Tel. 800/HOLIDAY; http://www.holiday-inn.com*
Hyatt International Corporation: *Tel. 800/233-1234*
Intercontinental: *Tel. 800/327-0200*
ITT Sheraton and Westin: *Tel. 800/325-3535, 325-3589*
Leading Hotels of the World: *Tel. 800/223-6800*
Marriott Corporation: *Tel. 800/228-9290, 468-3571.*
New Otani: *US Tel. 800/421-8795; Canada Tel. 800/273-2294.*
New World Hotels International: *Tel. 800/468-3571.*
Nikko: *Tel. 800/645-5687*
Novotel: *Tel. 800/221-4542, Tel. 800/NOVOTEL (668-6835)*
Preferred Hotels: *The Peninsula and Palace, Tel. 800/323-7500*
Radisson Hotels: *SAS and Shanghai, Tel. 800/333-3333*
Regal Hotels International: *Tel. 800/222-8888*
Ramada International: *Tel. 800/468-3571*
Renaissance Hotels & Resorts: *Tel. 800/468-3571*
Ritz-Carlton: *Tel. 800/468-3571.*
Omni: *Tel. 800/THE OMNI*
Shangri-La International: *Tel. 800/942-5050*
Sofitel: *Tel. 800/221-4542*
Steigenberger: *Tel. 800/223-5652; http://www.srshotels.com.*
Swissôtel: *Tel. 800/637-9477*
Westin and Sheraton: *Tel. 800/228-3000*
Zenith: *E-mail: resvn@zenithhotels.com*

SOME GENERALITIES

The hotels mentioned here are the top hotels in each city and the best hotels in each price category for North Americans. They have been also chosen for location, convenience to downtown and to tourist attractions. Hotel ratings such as 'three-star,' 'four-star,' etc., indicate the government's rating system, with five the highest quality. Most hotels have singles, doubles, and suites. Those of the lowest one and two stars might have dormitories of three or more beds to a room as well.

Most hotels of three-stars and higher will respond with a fax to a request for a reservation if so asked. Those listed here are up to international standards except where noted and you can be sure all have western toilets, private baths, coffee shops with western-type food, a bar, a Chinese restaurant, air-conditioning (except in the cooler regions), money changing facilities, televisions, and telephones in rooms. Most have hair dryers, karaoke, business centers, beauty salons, and gyms. Many have facilities for conventions. Some have in-room safes and satellite television in English.

In a few cases, the "best" hotels in a city may not be very good.

The quality of most facilities four stars and up is usually satisfactory for most North Americans. Those of three stars might be a little worn with dirty carpets, but they are usually acceptable for all but the most fussy foreign tourists. English-language capability has improved but still leaves much to be desired even at the four star level. Usually there's an assistant manager on duty who speaks English.

SERVICE WITH A SMILE?

Service in most of China is not usually up to Bangkok's cheerful or Hong Kong's efficient standards. But it is improving year by year. Some cities have Tourist Hotlines which you can call for help. But a few tours still cannot guarantee their hotels. In far-off Tibet, except for the Lhasa Hotel (no longer the Holiday Inn), it's first come, first served.

The furious pace of hotel construction has continued in the last few years. The range spans huge palaces fit for visiting heads of state to tiny temple hostels for pilgrims. Still new Chinese-managed hotels might be very beautiful, but they can deteriorate quickly. I once tried to grade hotels, but six months later the quality was completely different.

In conservative Chinese-managed hotels, total renovations are made every three to four years, but in the meantime, soft drinks and spit get hopelessly ground into beautiful wool carpets. Foreign-managed hotels try to practice perpetual maintenance.

The joint-venture hotels have raised the level of expectations for all hotels. Tourists used to be happy with a tacky room and private bath, and then, later, an air-conditioner and television set. Today's visitors expect a refrigerator, spotless rugs, non-smoking rooms, and an in-room safe.

BACKGROUND

In 1978, the hotels of China were run by bureaucrats to provide only a place to bathe, sleep and eat. Many were subsidized. One manager said then that he preferred Chinese guests because foreigners were too fussy: 'Americans should learn from the Japanese not to complain!'

In some cities, especially during high tourist seasons, the demand for rooms exceeded supply. In the early 1980s, tour groups for Beijing slept 50 km away in Hubei province. Some business people attending the Canton Trade Fair in 1979 slept in hotel lobbies. Yet other cities had a surplus of rooms.

HOTELS TODAY

Chinese tourism officials now want to attract tourists. While most hotels are still owned by different government agencies, the dramatic increase in hotels has resulted in good old-fashioned capitalistic competition. Big international hotel management chains have arrived. Pleasing visitors has become important! Standards have risen! Hotels that can't meet international standards can no longer serve foreigners.

The joint ventures have given China many hotels of international standards. A few hotels have been built solely by foreign interests. A few like the Kunlun in Beijing and the Jinling in Nanjing have managed to succeed without major foreign help.

Some staff members have been sent on training programs outside China, and regular training programs take place on the job. Many hotels have also imported foreign executives and managers.

In 1999-2000, foreign tourists are usually put into a clean hotel room, or, if they choose to pay more, into a clean, luxurious hotel room. They can also choose, as backpackers will tell you, to live cheaply in a shared dormitory. But most travel agents won't book those!

Hotel rooms are frequently classified from standard/moderate, to superior, and up to deluxe. 'First class' is usually below superior and might even be the same as standard. Hotels with standards deemed unacceptable to foreigners are being phased out.

Brand-new hotels may not have their act together in regard to services, but at least the rooms will be in pristine condition. There is a tendency for Chinese partners to insist on a 'soft' opening before all facilities are ready. A lot of hammering and the hint of better things to come after the 'hard' or 'grand' opening may be annoying to you.

ROOM PROBLEMS?

Many hotels now have Public Relations Departments. Should you have problems in a hotel three stars and above, try the *Gong Guan Xi* during office hours. Almost all tourist hotels have someone on duty somewhere who speaks English. Ask to see a hotel room before you commit yourself to it.

HOTEL STAR RATINGS

Government assessments are a good indication of design, equipment, hygiene, maintenance, management, service quality, and facilities (but not location). To qualify for a rating, hotels must also receive letters from satisfied guests. Write and offer your opinions, good or bad. Star ratings are sometimes given for political reasons.

Each of the following items begets a certain number of points. Each star rating has a minimum number of points. Three stars does not mean that every hotel so graded has special guestrooms for wheelchaired people, for example. (They might only have one wheelchair.)

Local or provincial governments hand out one to three star ratings but the national government must approve the three stars. Four and five stars are determined by the national government.

Only hotels fully opened for one year are formally rated, and a plaque should be prominently displayed. Each successively higher rating incorporates the best criteria of the ratings below it.

Foreigners are not supposed to stay in a hotel with less than one star because the standards are terrible – but many do.

The criteria is roughly:

One-Star hotels must have air-conditioning, coffee shop, dining room, and at least 20 guest rooms, cleaned daily. Of these, 75% must have private baths. They must have central heating, a lobby with information and reception desk, postal service, and 12-hour a day cold and hot running water.

Two-Star hotels must have at least 20 guest rooms, 95% with private baths, 50% with telephones, and 16 hours of cold and hot running water. Western and Chinese breakfast must be offered.

Three-Star hotels must have at least 50 beautifully-decorated guest rooms with dressing table, desk, drawers, and closet; carpet or wood floor; bedside control panel; 24-hour cold and hot water; 110/220V outlet; telephones in every room with international direct dial (IDD); mini-bar and refrigerator; color television sets, in-house movies, music; writing materials; sunproof curtains; and bed turn-down service.

They must have single rooms and suites, western and Chinese dining rooms (with English-speaking attendants, and the last order no earlier than 8:30pm), 16-hour coffee shop, banquet hall or function room, buffet breakfast and bar service (until midnight), and 18-hour room service.

They must also have elevator service, public telephone and washroom, equipment and service for disabled people, disco or karaoke, massage, beauty parlor, barber, bookstore, reading room, 12-hours a day foreign exchange, safe deposit boxes, store, camera film developing, fax and telex services, luggage storage, 24-hour laundry and drycleaning, wake-up calls, shoe polishing, and taxis. They should be able to mend articles of everyday use for guests. They should accept major credit cards. They must have an emergency electricity supply for public areas, medical services, 16-hour a day doorman, and message service. On duty 24-hours a day should be a luggage porter, checkroom service, guest reception, and managers on call. An assistant manager should be in the lobby 18 hours a day. There should be a price list, tourist map (English-Chinese), flight and railroad timetables available. *China Daily* and *China Tourism News* should be on sale (or free).

Four Star hotels should have luxurious and spacious sound-proof rooms, low-noise toilets, and hair dryers. They should have guest and service elevators, background music, health club, swimming pool, sauna, business center, greenhouse, 24-hour doorman, reservations accepted through fax/telex, 24-hour room service, and onward reservations in China for guests. A guest reception and assistant manager should be available in the lobby 24 hours a day. Laundry should be returned by next day.

The restaurants in four-star hotels should provide two kinds of Chinese food with the last order no earlier than 9pm. Bar service should be available to one am. There should be a 24-hour coffee shop and a breakfast and dinner buffet. A clinic should be on-site. A business center with photocopying, typing and translation services should be available, as should a ticketing agency with city tours and babysitting services.

Five star hotels are usually palatial with huge lobbies, their standards not quite matching the best of Paris or New York, but very close. Service should be better than the four-star hotels described above. See Top Hotels section below.

No-Star Hotels

These can be very dirty, with public hole-in-the-floor toilets, no English, heat or air conditioning. A few might have rats, bedbugs and cockroaches. They might have mosquito nets.

Don't be surprised if attendants snarl at guests, are reluctant to carry luggage, answer bells, or give any type of service. A few might be fire traps with stairways locked or blocked. Few have good bedside reading lamps. One Canadian woman was interrupted at 2am by the attendant with a male friend who wanted to sell her souvenirs. But there are no-star hotels where the staff is sweet and helpful.

One & Two Star Hotels

These can be acceptable sometimes. The English and service are not very good, but you might be surprised. An attendant can go to the bank for money changing, or take cables to the post office. Most can get plane or theater tickets, or hail a taxi. You can frequently borrow adapters (for electric razors), portable electric heaters, fans, hair-dryers, and irons. Some also have in-house television (in Chinese), and you can request special programs.

Most have shower curtains, hand or low shower heads, and one day laundry service. The air-conditioning and heat might not be adequate. Many have low-wattage bedside reading lamps. But the carpets will be stained and badly laid. A few of these hotels might have roaches, but I have never experienced bed bugs. A few might also have smelly and clogged public toilets, and poor plumbing in the rooms.

Sometimes gates are locked after 11pm. While most hotels over three stories have elevators, sometimes these are turned off at night. In either case, bang and wake someone up.

Western breakfast selections might be limited to greasy fried eggs, orange juice, toast, and coffee. The Chinese breakfast would probably be better.

Attempts to make reservations by telex or letter might just end up in a pile of unclaimed mail. Few staff, if any, can read English. Just take a chance and show up, or telephone on arrival. Some hotels charge the guest if the hotel has to telex back. This is understandable, considering the cost of telexes and the low room rate.

In some of these hotels, standards might differ according to floors. Foreigners are usually given the best and most expensive rooms. In areas recently opened to foreigners, the local people are not used to western standards of hygiene. If a room is mostly used by local people, the hotel won't bother to do more than mop up.

Top Hotels

There are many hotels of five-star international standard, just as good as hotels in Washington or Ottawa except for the standard of English. Some hotels have their own fleets of Mercedes limousines or Toyota vans that make regular runs to the airport or city center. At least two hotels have Rolls Royces. Many have executive floors with concierges, free continental breakfasts, and fast check-in. Many have magnificent ball rooms and lobbies and cater to foreign business people on expense accounts. They have the best western food and probably the best Chinese food in town, and the most luxurious breakfast buffets. Some leave chocolates on your pillow, or a rubber ducky on your bathtub, nice little touches that bring a smile.

The danger of a luxury hotel, in China as elsewhere, is its great economic disparity with the life of the ordinary citizen. The cost of one night in such a hotel could be the equivalent of several months income. If you go to learn about China, you'll have to make a great effort to do so if you stay in a luxury hotel.

HOTEL BASICS

Air-conditioning and heat: All starred tourist hotels have these, but the quality varies according to cost. Once the heat is turned on for the winter, it takes three days in some hotels to switch back to air-conditioning. If there is a sudden heatwave, you might find your hotel too hot. You could ask the attendant to open the windows, but in some hotels, they can't be opened. It would be best to change to another room, out of the sun.

Beds: These are usually firm and good. Rooms for standard groups usually have twin-size beds, too small for couples. Some beds are too short and narrow for tall foreigners. Be sure you have an extra blanket before the attendant goes off for the night. Top hotels have feather pillows.

Check-out time: usually noon with 50% of the room rate charged if you stay until six pm.

Chinese customs: While some hotels may look like North American hotels, don't be surprised to find staff sleeping in the lobby, and occasionally on the dining room tables.

Discounts: you should always try for one, especially now that occupancy rates are low. Sample dialogue: 'Look, I'll tell all my friends to come here.' 'I'm booked at another hotel but I heard you were cheaper.' 'I'm an Overseas Chinese,' and 'Okay, but how about including breakfast?' 'Can I speak with the sales manager, please?'

Keys: There are different systems. In the lower ranks, you might not get a key at all. An attendant will open and lock your door for you Soviet-style. At the other end of the scale, you might get a customized electronic key system that makes a record of the comings and goings in your room. If something goes missing, security should know the possible time it happened.

In many hotels, the key card also activates the electricity, an energy saving device. However, if there are two people in a room and one wants to read and then sleep while the other goes bar-hopping, there might be a problem with the lights. Many hotels only give one key card. So stick a comb or folded paper in the light slot.

Locks: Even some three-star hotels do not have double locks on their guestroom doors. An attendant could barge in on you at any time after a token knock. A rubber doorstopper helps.

Prostitution: yes, it does exist, even in the best of hotels. You might get strange telephone calls from women at night or hear loud laughing in the hallways. It is of course illegal and hard to control. You can complain to the management if you find these people troublesome. Be aware that some five-star hotels intercept all telephone calls to their guests so they won't be so bothered.

Security: most top hotels have excellent security. You don't usually see anyone but hotel guests and staff on guest room floors. And you might notice security cameras. No unregistered guests can stay in rooms after 10 or 11pm. (This is not always enforced in poorly-managed hotels.) Hotel thefts are rare, especially in the three stars and up range, but don't leave tempting valuables unlocked and in sight. Use the safe deposit boxes. Pilfering by hotel staff is rare but it happens. Items taken recently have included perfume, sweaters, shoes, flashlights, cigarettes, and film. If you are on a lower floor, make sure your windows are locked.

Smoke alarms: these are usually in every room. Fire extinguishers should be on every floor, and fire hoses on higher floors. Most rooms have fire exit maps in English on their doors.

Sports: hotels at all levels could have bicycles for rent, ping pong, badminton, and billiards. Attendants at swimming pools are not necessarily trained lifeguards, and you should supervise your own children. Also personally check the cleanliness of a pool. Many hotels have imported fitness equipment. And you can ask about *taiji* groups you can join at 6am in the parks. Some hotels have aerobics, morning bicycle tours, and jogging maps.

State Guest Houses: these can be palatial, some suites fit for queens with large gardens and lots of privacy. Rooms are frequently big, with high ceilings. The service, service facilities, and maintenance, however, are usually poor.

Suites: some of the top hotels have fancy two-story duplexes, or studios (which can be offices by day). Even medium-range hotels might have incredible luxury suites with gold-plated fixtures, antiques, and jacuzzis. Three people traveling together should ask about a suite. They could be less expensive than you think.

Surcharges: at the higher levels, even Chinese-managed hotels add a service charge of five to 20% on rooms, telephone calls and meals. Part of this is a municipal tax.

Telephones: in most hotels three stars and up, the telephone operator will speak English. There's a telephone in every room. If you're in a cheaper hotel where no one speaks English, you can make local calls by first pushing '0' or '9'. If it is not a dial phone, tell the operator *wai xian* (why she-an). To ask for the service desk, where there just might be someone who speaks English, say *fu wu tai (foo woo tie)*. To get other rooms in most hotels, just dial the room number unless otherwise specified.

Not all hotels will have IDD capability in every guest room. You might have to call the operator or go to a desk in the lobby. If there is no IDD, you can still call from your room. You might have to book the call at the service desk, and pay a service charge beforehand. Or an attendant might come knocking on your door afterwards. It could take hours.

There is usually a service charge, even for collect calls not completed. You might want to ask the rate first. For more information, see Chapter 7, Basic Information.

Tipping: see Chapter 7, *Basic Information*.

University Hostels: these are included because they are inexpensive, and because these give you opportunities to meet and interact with students. Some universities have new, good hostels. Others are dirty and run-down.

Water for Drinking: top hotels now give free bottled water. In addition, hot, boiled water is available in thermoses in all hotels, either in the room, or free on request. Sometimes, there is a flask for cooling. Don't drink water out of the tap, not even in the top hotels.

Some hotels have electric kettles that turn themselves off upon boiling. This does not give enough time to kill all the bacteria. Do not use the non-potable water in these devices. Many hotels also provide ice cubes, probably made of boiled water.

Workmanship: this could be bad. You can't expect people who have never seen a western bathroom to know that paint shouldn't be slopped on top of marble nor bare holes left in bathroom floors.

Hotel Chains: the top chains are the Hilton, Crowne Plaza, Kempinski, Okura, Ritz-Carlton, Shangri-La, Sheraton, Singapore Mandarin, and Westin. I would also recommend the Courtyard by Marriott, Forum, Holiday Inn, Hyatt, New World, Nikko, New Otani, Novotel, SAS, Sofitel and Swiss-Belhotel. The Gloria and KYZ have a range of hotels from three to five stars. Best Western and Harbour Plaza are new to China with very good properties. Days' Inn should be opening a lot of cheaper hotels soon. Of the cheaper chains, Chains City hotels are good, but we have found dirty carpets and grubby walls.

Of the Chinese-managed groups, the Jin Jiang runs the gamut from the pretentious Jin Jiang Tower (Shanghai) and the very good Kunlun (Beijing) down to modest hotels with peeling wallpaper and poor service. The China Friendship Tourist Hotel Group ranges from one or two good properties down to poor ones. Huating is so-so.

HOTEL PRICES

Most hotels give discounts if their occupancy rate is low at the time you want to go. 'Walk-in' discounts can range from 10% to 40% of the published price. Corporate discounts have been up to 60% if your company has signed a contract guaranteeing a minimum number of rooms per year Sheraton hotels give 'Suresavers' with 30% saving if booked 30 days in advance. It also has weekend specials. Also see Saving Money in Chapter 7, Basic Information.

It is almost meaningless to print published prices because actual prices keep changing and are negotiable. For the latest prices for hotels belonging to international chains, use the North American toll-free numbers on page 188, or fax/e-mail the hotel itself. But prices for rooms booked by travel agents might be cheaper. There's also the web or you could telephone the sales manager at the hotel directly. You have to do some homework for your bargains.

China's system of awarding stars to hotels gives some indication of price, but a four star in Beijing is much more expensive than a four star in Guilin. Just don't pay the prices published here. They are maximums.

13. CHINA'S BEST PLACES TO STAY

The hotels listed here are those I particularly like, my favorites. It's been tough deciding because China has so many more I like. For more details and prices, look up the full review in the hotel's respective destination chapter.

GLORIA INTERNATIONAL HOTELS

Gloria International Hotels are not consistently the top of the market, but they have some pretty good ones. Among my favorites are their hotels in Harbin and Sanya.

I especially like its hotel in **Harbin,** the **Gloria Inn**. It is such a jewel because of its location. The inn is right on the Songhua River, on a "walking street," a street without cars, a real plus with me. If you follow the river to the right, there is one of the largest, most exotic street markets in China. To the left is an interesting fresh produce market. Away from the river is the city's main shopping area surrounded by old Russian buildings. The hotel itself is modest, but clean. It has the basics, it's only a three star, and the price is right.

The **Gloria Resort** in **Sanya,** Hainan Island, is in a beautiful tropical setting; I can overlook the growing pains I saw. It is set amid franjipani trees and bourgainvillea bushes, and right on a white-sand beach. Its free-form pool goes under bridges and I'm looking forward to trying its barbecue. Its Chinese food was so great, we didn't want to try anything else. General Manager Pereira says his wine list is the biggest on Hainan island. You can rent all kinds of equipment like sailboards and scuba now, not yet ready when we were there, so I'm anxious to get back. Its presidential villa is one of the most tastefully decorated in China.

If only...

ZENITH MANAGEMENT

Zenith also has a range of properties from five star down to three. The one I like best is the **Garden Hotel** in my father's home county town in **Taishan**, Guangdong. It's got all the basics, and it's set off by itself in a quiet garden. The Cantonese food is great. Maybe it's because I've visited Taishan so many times and stayed in such crummy hotels, that it's a joy in comparison to stay in something clean and good looking for a change. I liked it so much, I expect to return for a month and teach English, just so I can stay there longer. The atmosphere is so informal and friendly.

HOLIDAY INNS

I usually count on Holiday Inns to be clean and well managed, with good western food and good English. Four-star prices are lower than five. I love the one in **Urumqi** because it's been pretty well the only hotel on the Silk Road with real western standards. Going there after the dust of the Gobi Desert, and cruddy hotels elsewhere, is like going home for a while. I love the setting of the **Holiday Inn Riverside** in **Wuhan**. You can walk down to the cruise ships and next door to temples.

I love the **Lido** in **Beijing** because it has every possible service I need, a post office, Bank of China, a Hong Kong drug store (but no pharmacy), and a real supermarket – all under the same roof. It has cheaper Chinese restaurants in the neighborhood. The rooms are big, unpretentious, and comfortable; the twin beds are doubles and I can spread my work out on one. If I happen to be there for Thanksgiving, I know I can get a turkey dinner. I can also get great Thai food in a luxurious Thai setting. It has 25 television channels and every guest gets a *Herald Tribune* as well as *China Daily*. It also has a book shop with other current newspapers and books in English. It's got a deli and a laundry shop. If I use the laundry outlet at the back of the hotel, there's no service charge. Nor is there any if I book at its air ticket office. It is also easy to remember the Chinese name, "Lido Fandian," for taxi drivers.

There always seems to be a Lido representative at the airport. The bellman there hauls my luggage to the shuttle, so there's no wait in the taxi line. Its free shuttle bus can take me downtown and back. Other hotels in China also have many of its services, but the last time I was there, a nice lady at the street market across from the gate gave me a good half-body massage for only Y20. I don't think any can duplicate that.

The market is not as good as those downtown, but it's something to do in the evening. It's only 20 minutes to the Friendship Store, but the Lido saves time and hassle. After a couple of nights there, I feel recharged and ready to go back to places with no international news, and no weather reports.

SHERATON HOTELS

I don't like big, brassy hotels with giant chrome pillars. So, no matter how good the service and the rooms, I have avoided the Great Wall Sheraton in Beijing. This past year however, Sheraton has been opening some marvelous new hotels. I think the **International Club** in **Beijing** is one of the most beautiful in the country. The service and location off Jianguomenwai are great too.

But the **Sheraton** in **Suzhou** takes the cake. It is built in Chinese style, not gawdy stereotypical Chinese palace style, but quiet Suzhou Song and Ming dynasty garden style. It even has an adaptation of maze-like courtyards in which you can get very lost. It too is one of the most beautiful in the country. And its location inside the city moat, surrounded by history, is excellent.

SHANGRI-LA HOTELS

The Shangri-La Hotels are an Asian-based chain. My favorite is the **Island Shangri-La** in **Hong Kong** because it's so beautiful, with its multi-storied Chinese landscape painting and its profusion of Venetian chandeliers and art work. Its location is ideal too, so handy to everything, including one of Hong Kong's best parks and shopping malls. It is close to the metro, trams, a walk to the ferries and the British relics of the city.

I also like the **China World Hotel** in **Beijing** for its beautiful lobby and good location on Jianguomenwai. The China World is also a self-contained world, a convenience desperately needed when time is short. It too has a good supermarket, a good bakery, a deli, a gym, and several places to reconfirm plane tickets. It has a wide range of restaurants in the complex including one where you can get a quick, cheap lunch. And there's a cyber cafe nearby. No one needs to go outside at all. It has more stores than the Lido but it doesn't have its park. It is a quick drive to Tiananmen Square and the ghost market. But it's a lot more expensive. You're paying for a very luxurious and palatial hotel, a marvelous lobby lounge, good rooms and service. You're paying for a downtown location, and a very spacious and private hotel setting, within walking distance of offices, the very special Silk Market, and department stores.

If I rave about Shangri-La Hotels, it's because they are excellent. The service and the food are usually superb and lavish. Their locations are usually the best. The **Pudong Shangri-La** has one of the best situations in **Shanghai**, in relatively uncrowded Pudong, right on the waterfront. From there is one of the best views of the lights on Shanghai's historic Bund. It's also a walk to an incredible ferry and, for only for Y1, a close-up view. The ferry docks close to Nanjing Road, the Opera, the Shanghai Museum, and the Yu Garden. It is also close to the offices on the Bund.

I also like the **Shangri-La** in **Hangzhou** because of its old European atmosphere and its quiet garden setting. I've liked its site even before it was taken over by the Shangri-La people. I can just walk out the door, past the trees, across the road, and there's lovely West Lake, *Sai Woo* in Cantonese, the name of a favorite Toronto Chinatown restaurant. I like to walk early in the morning and the lake, especially at dawn, has a magic quality about it. Out onto the nearby causeway with water on either side, I can see the morning sun, a rosy one on my last trip, peeking out from behind strings of weeping willow branches, bare in winter. And if I stand in the right spot, I can frame the sun under a deeply-curved Song-dynasty roof while the mist hides the line of modern skycrapers on the tranquil horizon. I can breath deeply as everything seems to blend together in a living, classical Chinese painting.

The last time I was there, a group of white-haired seniors on bicycles, came charging along, yelling for people to get out of the way. They wanted to speed up so they could ride over the humpback bridge without having to stop and walk up. It was so unexpected and fun, I think I want to live in Hangzhou when I retire.

The hotel itself is romantic, old in a nice way, quiet, warm, not marred by glitz. The rooms are bigger than its rival, the Dragon; the atmosphere is more classy but simple and not pretentious. The lake is an extension of the hotel's garden.

I could continue raving about other Shangri-Las too. They are all beautiful, a fusion of east and west, with good locations, good rooms, and fine service. I like them all.

NEW WORLD HOTELS

One of my favorite New World Hotels is in **Hong Kong**. Now known as the **Renaissance Harbour View**, it is right on the waterfront and a short walk to a ferry and to the metro. New World Hotels do tend to look institutional, almost like banks. But this one has a great roof-top garden, one of the best places to watch the New Years' fireworks. It has a daily hungry hour, an all you can eat cocktail buffet for the price of a drink. The services are good. There's a great view of the busy harbor and is attached to the Convention Centre. I can use the e-mail at a cheap cyber cafe nearby.

I also like the **Grand New World Xi'an**, its lobby warmed by an amazing carpet, and punctuated by giant statues, ministers of the Qin emperor. I can get excited about its Tang Dynasty show, especially a segment about the Terracotta Warriors. It's too bad other people haven't discovered it yet. I love its Food Street; I revel in hotels where I don't have to go far to save money.

HARBOUR PLAZA HOTELS

The Harbour Plaza chain is new and growing. I've only seen two and especially like the **Harbour Plaza Chongqing** because of its location right downtown on a "walking" street, close to shops, offices, and the ferry pier. In the past, I've hated shopping in Chongqing because of traffic-congested streets. But now it's great, and I can shop without fear and bumping into people and leave purchases at the hotel to go back for more.

I'm anxious to get back to the **Harbour Plaza** in **Beijing** with its all-you-can eat *dim sum*. It's making such an effort to compete with the nearby Lido. It's not one of my favorite hotels yet, but it could be soon.

GUANGZHOU & HONG KONG FAVORITES

One great hotel in **Guangzhou** is the **White Swan**, because of its magnificent atrium garden, and its location on historic Shamian Island beside the Pearl River and next to the US Consulate. I like sitting in its coffee shop and watching the river traffic go by, and I like its good quality shops. I like wandering around almost car-free and historic Shamian Island, a quiet oasis away from the crowded city. But the hotel is close enough to walk to the very special, very exotic Qingping Market.

The other preferred hotel is the **Garden**, because of its magnificent lobby and its proximity to stores, other hotels, and restaurants with which it is joined by a convenient overpass. No risking my life crossing busy streets here. I like its cheaper food street, its buses with Hong Kong, and downtown checking on China Southern Airlines.

To choose the best hotel in **Hong Kong** is another struggle. It's a toss-up between the Peninsula, the Grand Hyatt and the Island Shangri-la:

At the **Peninsula**, my junior suite was marvelous, huge, decorated in rich Indian prints, with more telephones than I could count. It had a fax machine, a giant desk, and a thermometer reading outside temperature. It also had a magnificent bathtub flush to a window, where I could soak and enjoy the view. But the sight of the harbor from the living room – it was the 16th floor – especially with its 19th century Bombay telescope was worth the long flight across the Pacific. The telescope was permanently set up and strategically located to catch just about anything in the harbor, from tiny pilot boats to giant cruise ships, from little junks to navy cruisers. It was so stunning with all the lights I didn't want to close the curtains.

The **Grand Hyatt** has the same great roof-top garden as the Renaissance Harbour View and the same marvelous view of the harbor. But it is a more beautiful hotel, more luxurious, and of course, more expensive. I had high tea here, Devonshire cream and the whole bit. I don't think England could have done better.

The **Island Shangri-la** is mentioned above under the Shangri-la Hotels section. As for **The Salisbury YMCA**, it's been a favorite since my first trip to Hong Kong in 1961, the place to stay when a company expense account is not picking up the bill. But it's not only the price. The Y has a million dollar location next door to the Peninsula, and this time I found the food and service vastly improved. It used to have these old surly waiters. It's now also the place to meet for city tours and it's got the only Laundromat found so far in town. You can now also make a reservation by e-mail or fax. In the old days, I had to personally pay one night in advance, rooms were in such short supply. Now with its extensions, it's so much easier to get a room.

MOST IMPROVED HOTEL NOMINATIONS

Both of these hotels are in Shanghai:
*I'd like to nominate the **Cypress** in Shanghai for the "most improved," transformed as it has been from a dumpy, plain hotel with a marvelous garden setting, to one decorated with flair in a marvelous garden setting. I'll tell you about the service after I've had a chance to try it.*

*Second prize goes to Shanghai's **Peace Hotel**, which used to be a badly managed socialist hotel. It's now a better managed modern hotel, still with its faults yet, like its famous jazz band, full of bad notes but overall a tribute to history. Service has improved a lot in the last few years.*

14. BEIJING & THE GREAT WALL

BEIJING

(Peking; Northern Capital)

The capital of China – **Beijing** – is surrounded by Hebei province on the northern fringe of the North China plain. It is 180 km west of the sea and about 44 meters above sea level, with mountains to the north, west, and east. The population is about 12 million (seven or eight million urban) and a couple of million "floaters."

The best time to visit is autumn. It is at almost the same latitude as Philadelphia with similiar temperatures. The hottest days are in July and August, up to 38 C; the coldest are in January and February, down to -20 C, sometimes with snow. Dust storms occasionally blow from December to late March, and sometimes into May. The winter air is heavily polluted and very dry; hopefully your hotel will supply humidifiers. Beijing is switching to natural gas rather than relying on coal for fuel, one of the measures it's taking to clean up the air. The annual precipitation is 683 millimeters, usually from June to August. There's a chronic water shortage which should be alleviated in the future by diverting water from the Yellow and Yangtze Rivers.

ARRIVALS & DEPARTURES

By Air

Beijing is about four hours flight west of Tokyo, three hours north of Guangzhou or Hong Kong, and two hours northwest of Shanghai. It has air links with 76 Chinese cities and at least 35 foreign cities. Its new airport was due to open October 1, 1999. Approximate flight tickets to Beijing cost one way Y1360 from Guangzhou, Y2710 from Hong Kong, Y1930 from Urumqi, and Y900 from Shanghai. If you're flying into Beijing, be aware that fog might delay flights in winter. The "left luggage" storage room at the airport is not open 24 hours. Charges range from Y4-Y25 per day depending on size.

Taxis from the airport downtown should cost Y60-Y90. From the airport, public "A" airbuses leave about 8am-9:30pm for the main Beijing East Railway Station and to the airport every 20-30 minutes between 6:30am-6:30pm for Y16. A1 stops at the Hilton, A2 at the Lufthansa Center, Kempinski, Landmark, Great Wall Sheraton and Huadu Hotels. A4 goes to the Swissôtel and Beijing Asia Hotel, and A6 goes to the Beijing International Hotel and Wangfujing. For information, *Tel. 65265019.*

For **general airport inquiries**, call *Tel. 64563604* for international flights and *Tel. 64562233* for domestic flights.

Airlines servicing Beijing are:

- **Aeroflot**, *Tel. 65002980, 65002412*
- **Air China**: the booking office for all Chinese airlines is at 15 Chang'an Xi Avenue, west of the Telegraph Building (clock tower) and Zhongnanhai gate, *Tel. 66017755.* For domestic flights, *Tel. 66013336;* for international flights, *Tel. 66016667;* for the information counter at the airport, *Tel. 26892689 x 2580, 64663698*
- **Air France**, *Tel. 65881388, 65051818, 65051431*
- **All Nippon Airways**, *Tel. 65053311*
- **Alitalia**, *Tel. 65610378*
- **Austrian Airlines**, *Tel. 64622161/4, Fax 64622166*
- **British Airways**, *Tel. 65124070, 65124075, Fax 65123637*
- **Canadian Airlines International**, *Tel. 64682001, Fax 64637906. Web: Http://www.cdnair.ca*
- **Dragonair**, *Tel. 65182533, Fax 65183455*
- **Ethiopian Airlines**, *Tel. 65050314*
- **Finnair**, *Tel. 65127180, Fax 65127182*
- **Japan Airlines**, *Tel. 65130888*
- **Kazak Airlines**, *Tel. 65126688*
- **KLM Royal Dutch**, *Tel. 65053505*
- **Korean Airlines**, *Tel. 65050088, 65051047*
- **Kyrgyszstan Airlines**, *Tel. 65229799*
- **Lufthansa**, *Lufthansa Center, Tel. 64654488, Fax 64653223*
- **Malaysian Airlines**, *Tel. 65052681-3*
- **Mongolian Airlines**, *Tel. 65079297*
- **Northwest**, *Tel. 65053505, Fax 65051855*
- **PIA**, *Tel. 65051681-4, Fax 65052257*
- **Qantas**, *Tel. 64674794, 64673337, Fax 64669494*
- **SAS**, *Tel. 65183738, Fax 65183736*
- **SIA**, *Tel. 65052233, Fax 65051178. Web: Http://www.singaporeair.com*
- **Swissair**, *Tel. 65123555, 65123556, Fax 65127481. E-mail: swissair@public3.bta.net.com*

• **Thai International**, *Tel. 64606995, 65123881-3*
• **United Airlines**, *Tel. 64631111, 65128888*

By Train

Beijing is a minimum 30 hours north of Hong Kong and 19 hours northwest of Shanghai. It can also be reached by train from Ulan Bator (Mongolia), and, beyond that, from Moscow. Trains leave Hong Kong every other day and are due in Beijing at the West Railway Station the following night. This high-speed train costs Y1028 for soft sleeper, and Y777 for hard sleeper. Tickets can be booked 30 days in advance.

The new Xi or **West Beijing Railway Station** building is in southwest Beijing on Lianhuachi Dong, 6.7 km from Tiananmen Square, *Tel. 63216263, 63216253*. It has been the terminal for all trains going through the city of Zhengzhou, including those from Hong Kong. The old east (dong) main station known as Beijing Station, near the Beijing International Hotel, has been the terminal for three international lines (Trans-Siberian, Mongolia, and North Korea) and trains from Shanghai and Inner Mongolia. It is currently being renovated and this division might change. So ask when you book your tickets, *Tel. 65128931*.

For **train inquiries**, *Tel. 6554866, 65776851, 65129525*. To purchase tickets for foreigners, *Tel. 65581032*.

TRAIN PRICES

At the West Railway Station, these prices in Chinese yuan were posted in late 1998 for the following Chinese cities. "X" means the frequency per day for express trains.

	Soft Berth	Hard Berth	Hard Seat	
Hefei	Y237	147	66	
Zhengzhou	263	173	92	4X
Wuchang	428	279	152	2X
Changsha	528	343	189	1X
Guangzhou	704	456	251	3X
Shenzhen	719	465	255	1X
Guilin	657	428	236	
Kunming	889	576	318	1X
Chengdu	641	416	229	2X
Chongqing	658	429	237	2X
Urumqi	1005	650	361	1X
Yichang	485	317	173	1X
Xi'an	417	273	149	1X

If you're planning on traveling to **Russia** by train, check first with the US Embassy and Monkey Business Info for tips regarding travel there. The Chinese train (#3) leaves Beijing on Wednesdays at 7:40am via Datong. The Russian train (#19) leaves on Saturdays at 11:10pm via Shenyang and Harbin. They take seven days to reach Moscow. You can buy tickets at China International Travel Service (Beijing International Hotel), and at the Monkey Business Infocenter. Monkey Business seems to have the best English and orientation for travelers. See Practical Information at the end of this chapter.

ORIENTATION

Beijing is the most important place to visit in China. It is the nation's capital and it has a 3,000-year history, beginning in the Western Zhou, when it was known as **Ji** (Chi). Its most impressive historical monuments date from the 13th century A.D. The museums here have the best collections in China, the temples among the most impressive. The palaces are the biggest and most elaborate. For most Chinese people, visiting Beijing has been and still is a lifetime ambition and many are now able to do it.

The **Liao** (916-1125 A.D.) were the first to build a capital here. They called it Nanjing, Southern Capital, as distinct from their old capital farther north in Manchuria. The name was changed again to **Yanjing** (Yenching) in 1013. In 1125, the Jin, a Tartar dynasty, overthrew the Liao and enlarged the city, calling it **Zhongdu**, Central Capital. The Mongols (Yuan) under Kublai Khan overthrew the Jin and built a new capital called **Dadu** (Ta Tu). In 1368 the Ming drove out the Yuan and established its capital at Nanjing in 1409, with Beijing, then called **Peiping Fu**, as an auxiliary capital.

Beijing became the main capital again in 1421 (Ming) and continued as the Qing capital into the early 1900s. In 1860, it was invaded by foreign troops, mainly English and French. The foreigners completely destroyed the Yuanmingyuan Palace. The Boxers took over in 1900 and laid siege to the Foreign Legation section, but were repelled by an international military force while the Qing Empress Dowager fled temporarily to Xi'an. In 1928, the Nationalist government moved its capital to today's Nanjing, and Beijing became **Peiping** (Northern Peace). The Japanese held it from 1937 to 1945. When the Communists took over in 1949, it regained its old name and former position as capital of the nation.

During imperial times, no structures taller than the Forbidden City were allowed. Fortunately, Beijing escaped the Pacific War relatively intact. In 1959, ten massive buildings were completed for the tenth anniversary of the founding of the People's Republic. Built in the heavy, plain Soviet style, these included the Great Hall of the People, the Museums of History and the Revolution, and the Palace of the Minorities. They are period pieces now.

Beijing is centered around the **Forbidden City** and **Tiananmen Square**. The old legation area is east of the square, between the Beijing, Xinqiao, and Capital hotels. The few remaining European buildings there reflect that period of its history. The Chinese city was south of the Qianmen Gate on the southern edge of Tiananmen Square.

Beijing now consists of ten districts and nine counties. Rural villages raise the famous force-fed Beijing ducks. Over 2000 factories, mainly in the suburbs, produce iron and steel, mine coal, make machines, basic chemicals and petroleum, electronics, and textiles.

The people of Beijing speak **Mandarin** (*putong hua*), the official national language, but they twirl their tongues more and go heavy on the "r's". They are predominantly **Han**, but you will see flat, wide Mongolian and Manchu faces too. Beijing people tend to be reserved compared to other Chinese. Don't be put off by this, for they are warm and friendly once they get to know you.

GETTING AROUND TOWN

You need at least six days to cover the important attractions in Beijing.

Bicycle rickshaws should be cheap for short distances but decide on a price before you hop aboard. About Y10 is fair for one kilometer and these can frequently get around traffic jams. You can rent bicycles at some hotels, among them the Palace and Crowne Plaza.

Large **public tour buses**, numbers one to five, follow regular routes to major tourist attractions. For example, Tour Bus One goes from Qianmen (No. 17 bus station) to Badaling Great Wall and the Ming Tombs. Tour Bus Two goes from the 103 trolley bus stop at Beijing East Railway Station to the Badaling Great Wall and Ming Tombs. For detailed information in English, phone the **Beijing Tourism Hotline**, *Tel. 65130828.*

Many individual travelers use **public transport** successfully if they have the time. Just avoid rush hours especially 4pm-7pm. Public buses and subways operate from 5am-11 or 11:30pm and cost Y.50-Y2. Bus and subway maps are available in many hotels. Subway trains operate every three-eight minutes.

The **east-west subway line** goes from Pinggouyuan in the east along Jianguomenwai Avenue past the World Trade Centre (the stop southeast of the Trade Center south gate opens Oct. 1, 1999), along Chang'an Avenue and past Tiananmen with a stop at Xidan, and on to Tong Xian County. The **circular subway**, a 16-km line, makes a rectangle around

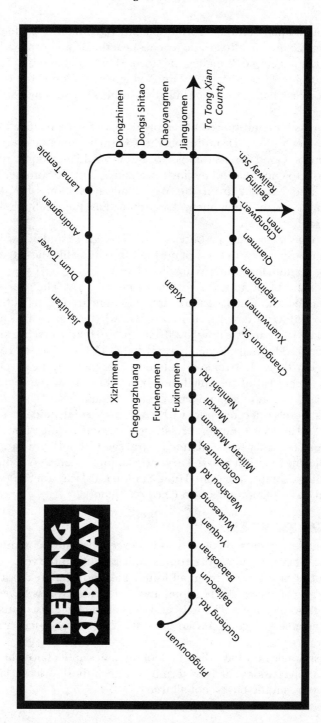

Tiananmen Square and the Forbidden City (Qianmen stop the closest) following Second Ring Road, and reaches near the Beijing Zoo (Xizhimen) and the Lama Temple (Yonghegong stop). Maps with the subway stops in *pin yin* are inside each station. The Fuxingmen station is the only one where you can change from one line to the other. The subway is still being expanded.

Express air-conditioned buses ply the city for Y2 for five km, and then another Y1 for each additional three km. They operate every five to ten minutes. Good for visitors is No. 801 from Liangmaqiao near the Kempinski to Qinghua and Beijing universities, and the Summer Palace. There's also No. 802 from the West Railway Station with stops in Fuxingmen, Xidan, Tiananmen, Wangfujing, East Railway Station, Ritan Road, and Panjiayuan.

Among the best regular buses are the 1, 4, 37, 52 and 57, which link Tiananmen Square with the Friendship Store, the Silk Market, and the Jianguo, Jinglun and China World hotels.

Taxis are plentiful and available 24 hours a day. The cheapest are those marked with Y1.00, very uncomfortable and frequently with drivers who don't know the city. Taxi prices went down (heavens! what's happening?) in late 1998, and are now Y1.20 per km, Y10 for the first five km, then Y1.20 every additional kilometer. Taxis marked Y1.60, charge Y10 for the first five km, then Y1.60 for every additional. Apparently the government is trying to get rid of the small mini-buses that follow the regular bus routes, as they can't pass emission control standards.

Most hotels can offer **tours with English-speaking guides** and lunch in the Y270 and Y320 range. A relatively inexpensive tourist bus service for about Y60, entry fees and lunch extra, can be booked at backpacker hotels like the Jing Hua below. These regular **join-in tours** go to the Great Wall, Ming Tombs, Fragrant Hills, Summer Palace, Tanzhe Temple, Yunshui Cave, Qing tombs, and Chengde (Jehol).

WHERE TO STAY

There are plenty of hotel rooms, except in late September and October. There are now more rooms available than three years ago and some hotels have lowered their published rates and offer breakfast as well. Some travel agencies like Hualong and American Express have special deals with some but not all hotels, and can get you huge discounts. So try several agents, and your chosen hotel itself; compare prices and even haggle.

Most hotels now have direct telephone lines and a booth at Beijing airport's international arrivals terminal. Check those prices too. Many have airport shuttle buses, not all free.

Beijing has a lot of good hotels now. Below are those I recommend because of quality and location with a wide price range. They include cheaper and not-so-good ones for budget travelers. There are other noteable hotels not mentioned for lack of space.

The most luxurious and classy hotel with top services is the **Beijing International Club Hotel**. You pay a premium for exclusivity. The **China World** and **Shangri-La** are not quite as lavish, but they are also tops for service and quality. These are followed by the **Kempinski, the Great Wall** and **Palace**. This order will probably change as these hotels are redecorated and services upgraded. The late 1990's is a good time to visit as many hotels are being refurbished and buildings spiffed up because of China's fiftieth anniversary.

The best of the four-star hotels are the **Holiday Inn Lido, the Jianguo, Traders**, and the **Capital**. Up and coming is the **Harbour Plaza**. The **Song He** is the best three-star hotel because of its central location and tolerable standards. There are better three-stars in the suburbs. The most popular for backpackers is the **Jing Hua**.

Prices listed here are in US dollars or Chinese yuan (roughly US$1 = 8.3 yuan). These prices are subject to change, negotiations, a 10% to 15% surcharge and Y6 tax per bed per day. Some hotels have recently discounted 10%-60% off these published prices even during high tourist season but you might have to ask for it. Local telephone calls range from free to two yuan. Some hotels have in-room safes only in suites or executive floors; listed are those that have them in every room.

Hotels here are all international class except for the cheapest ones, with money exchange, credit card service, business centers, beauty salons, western coffee shop, and international direct dial. The top hotels can organize theme parties for groups: an imperial banquet hosted by the "emperor," or traditional Chinese folk celebrations: lion dances, acrobats, and magicians. The best sports facilities are at the **Holiday Inn Lido**, **Movenpick**, **China World**, and **Kempinski**. Because traffic jams downtown are endemic, we suggest you consider a hotel closest to the places you need to visit.

The following are roughly in order of price based on single rooms.

Around the Forbidden City & Tiananmen Square

The best location for tourists and some business people is east of Tiananmen Square. The **Grand Hotel** here is the only hotel with beautiful Chinese decor in all its rooms and most of its restaurants. The English, however, is not five-star standard and it looks worn. It's the closest hotel to the Forbidden City and has the best location in town for tourists. For a view of the Forbidden City, try the 10th floor bar at sunset on a clear day. The Beijing Hotel next to it is of lesser quality but improving soon.

Around the corner is Wangfujing Avenue, with its mix of modern chrome-plated shopping malls and tiny old stores with latticed wooden fronts. Nearby and also within walking distance of the Forbidden City are the **Palace** and **Crowne Plaza**, which are the best in this area and preferred over the Grand and Beijing except for the location. Next and a long way behind are the **Wangfujing Grand**, **Prime**, **Tianlun Dynasty**, **Peace**, and **Song He** roughly in order of quality with the Wangfujing the best. This area is also near Beijing municipal government offices, good restaurants, and is very congested. The **Grand Hotel** here is in a special category. It makes you feel you're really in old Beijing. It has few services and limited English.

An 84-room five-star hotel should open here in the Oriental Plaza across Wangfujing from the Beijing Hotel operated by Hutchison Whampoa in 2000.

Further from the Forbidden City, south of the old Legation section and east of Tiananmen are the **Capital**, **the New World Courtyard**, and the **Xinqiao** in that order of quality, with the Capital best and closest to Tiananmen, and the New World a close second for quality. The Xinqiao and New World are in a very crowded, traffic-congested neighborhood to the southeast of the square. The New World is new and looks good.

Unless otherwise mentioned, hotels here are about 30-35 km from the airport, two-three km from the east railway station and 8-10 km from the west train station.

THE PALACE HOTEL (*Wangfu Fandian*), *8 Goldfish Lane (Jinyu Hutung), Wangfujing Street, 100006. Five stars, Tel. 65128899, Fax 65129050, 65127118. E-mail:info@peninsula.com. In North America, Tel. 800/223-6800. $280-$430 for rooms, and $400-$3500 for suites.*

Built in 1989, the Palace has 17 stories and 530 classy rooms with safes, molded ceilings, CNN and bathroom panic buttons. It has duplex suites, non-smoking floors and three executive floors. It has room service, business center and pressing service – all 24 hours. In the building is a Bank of China. Especially good are its Italian, Bavarian and international restaurants. It has a year-round indoor pool, spa, two Rolls Royces and a Bentley. It has an acupuncture clinic, bicycles for hire, and a florist. It did have signs of wear like cracked paint in bathtubs and paint worn off gold frames. These hopefully should be repaired by now. Managed by the Peninsula Group. The Palace is a member of the Leading Hotels of the World, and Preferred Hotels.

GRAND HOTEL BEIJING (*Gui Bin Lou Fan Dian*), *35 Chang'an Dong Avenue, 100006. E-mail: ghbj@mail.chinapro.net.cn; or sales@mail.grandhotelbeijing.com.cn. Http: www.grandhotelbeijing.com. Five star standard, Tel. 65137788, Fax 65130048. In North America, book through Leading Hotels of the World 800/223-6800. $275-$300 for rooms, $400-$2700 for suites.*

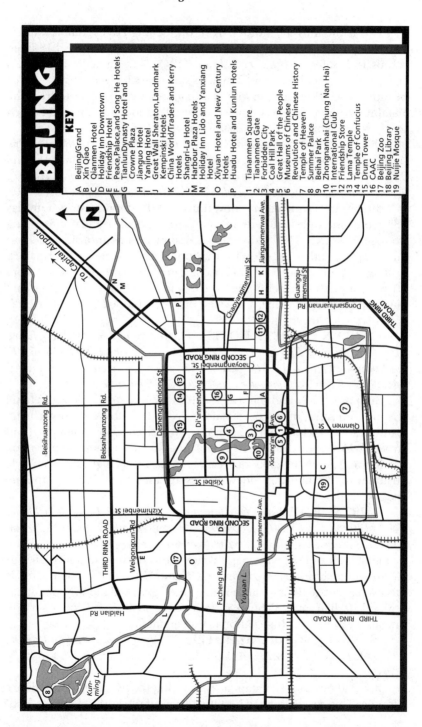

BEIJING

KEY

A Beijing/Grand
B Xin Qiao
C Qianmen Hotel
D Holiday Inn Downtown
E Friendship Hotel
F Peace, Palace, and Song He Hotels
   TianlunDynasty Hotel and
   Crowne Plaza
G Jianguo Hotel
H Yanjing Hotel
J Great Wall Sheraton,Landmark
   Kempinski Hotels
K China World/Traders and Kerry
   Hotels
L Shangri-La Hotel
M Harbour Plaza Hotels
N Holiday Inn Lido and Yanxiang
   Hotel
O Xiyuan Hotel and New Century
   Hotels
P Huadu Hotel and Kunlun Hotels

1 Tiananmen Square
2 Tiananmen Gate
3 Forbidden City
4 Coal Hill Park
5 Great Hall of the People
6 Museums of Chinese
   Revolution and Chinese History
7 Temple of Heaven
8 Summer Palace
9 Beihai Park
10 Zhongnanhai (Chung Nan Hai)
11 International Club
12 Friendship Store
13 Lama Temple
14 Temple of Confucius
15 Drum Tower
16 CAAC
17 Beijing Zoo
18 Beijing Library
19 Nuijie Mosque

This is the most beautiful part of the Beijing Hotel complex and is separately managed. Built in 1989-90, this 10-story hotel has 218 large rooms with safes, CNN, Star TV and HBO. It has a 24-hour business center, indoor pool, gym and sauna. Its small dark lobby contrasts with its beautiful seven-story atrium with amazing zodiac reproductions from the Yuanmingyuan Palace. Cantonese, especially good Sichuan, and French food are available. The breakfast buffet costs $16.

CROWNE PLAZA BEIJING (*Wang Guan Jia Re Jiudian*), *48 Wangfujing Avenue, 100006. Five stars, Tel. 65133388, Fax 65132513. In North America, Tel. 800/HOLIDAY. E-mail:hicpb@public3.bta.net.cn. Http:// www.crowneplaza.com/hotels/pegwf. $200-$220 for rooms. Suites from $400.*

Built in 1991 with major renovations in 1999, this nine-story hotel has 385 rooms and wide twin beds, in-room safes, executive and non-smoking floors. It has CNN, HBO, Australia television, a 24-hour business center, an art gallery and an art salon for traditional Chinese music. It also has a grill room, Cantonese food with live crabs in a tank, and a spacy eight-story atrium coffee shop. It rents out bicycles and has a health club with steam bath and tanning machine, and a view of the Forbidden City. Its driveway is too crowded for big tour buses.

TIANLUN DYNASTY HOTEL (*Tianlun Fandian*), *50 Wangfujing Street, 100006. Four stars, Tel. 65138888, Fax 65137866. E-mail:tianlun@public.bta.net.cn. In North America, reserve through 800/ 44UTELL. $186-$210 for rooms, and $260-$578 for suites.*

Built in 1991-92 and renovated 1998, this nine-story, 408-room hotel has in-room safes, dirty carpets and CNN. It has a bake shop, Sichuan, Cantonese and Huaiyang restaurants, and a cheaper basement food street (Y3-Y49 per dish, Y16 for hot pot). It has a gym, indoor pool, bowling and tennis. Its 2500-square meter, seven-story high European-style atrium with fountain and "sidewalk" restaurant is huge. It has an antique shop.

CAPITAL HOTEL (*So Du Dajiudian*), *3 Qianmen Dong Jie, 100006. Tel. 65129988, Fax 65120321, 65120309. E-mail: cptlhtls@public3.bta.net.cn. $180-$288 for rooms and $320-$2,000 for suites. Four stars.*

First built in 1989 with major renovations finished in mid-1996, this 22-story hotel has 326 large rooms, CNN and HBO, and in-room safes. It has two executive floors, four bowling lanes, gym and indoor pool. It has seafood, Italian, and Sichuan restaurants, and 24-hour room service. Singapore Mandarin International Management.

WANGFUJING GRAND HOTEL, *57 Wangfujing Avenue, 100006, Tel. 65221188, Fax 65223816. $180-$200 for rooms, and $300-$1800 for suites.*

It has about four-star standards, is trying for five, but standards are slipping. This has the second best hotel view of the Forbidden City. Built in 1996, it has 14 stories, 227 rooms, and in-room safes. It has an executive floor, Sichuan and Cantonese restaurants, a gym, indoor pool, sauna, and gym.

PRIME HOTEL BEIJING *(Hua Qiao Da Sha), 2 Wangfujing Avenue, 100006. Five stars but looks like a four, Tel. 65136666, Fax 65134248. E-mail: sales@phb.com.cn. Http://www.srshotels.com. $160-200 for rooms, $300-$1200 for suites and includes breakfast.*

The building here was a hotel in the 1960s. It is on the same street as the back gate of the Forbidden City, about a 15 minute walk. It has 10 storys, and 400 rooms, said to be largest in town, but the beds are narrow. It has CNN, an executive floor and non-smoking rooms. There's a Scandinavian grill room and imperial Chinese, Italian, Mexican, and Cantonese restaurants. There's a gym and indoor pool. It looks worn, but is otherwise okay.

BEIJING HOTEL *(Fandian), 33 Chang'an Dong Street, 100004, Tel. 65137766, Fax 65137703 (sales), 65137307. E-mail: business@chinabeijinghotel.com.cn. Http://www.chinabeijinghotel.com.cn. Five stars, awarded especially because of its long history and special status. East Building $150-$170 for rooms, $300-$680 for suites.*

The Middle and West Buildings are being renovated and should be re-opened in late 1999 with a pool, bowling, karaoke and tennis. It has three connecting buildings with at least 900 rooms, CNN, in-room safes, and Cantonese, Sichuan, Japanese and Huaiyang restaurants. It has a famous acupuncturist, gym and a marvelous nine-dragon, gold medallion in its lobby lounge. The East Wing has 583 large rooms with 3.6 meter-high ceilings, stained carpets, and some rooms with balconies. It has 40-watt reading lights and its bathrooms have heat lamps and moldy grouting. There's lots of good shopping, and a real post office. Breakfast buffet Y45.

NEW WORLD COURTYARD MARRIOTT *(Xinshijie Fandian), 3C Chongwenmenwai, Chongwen District, Tel. 67181188, 67088013 (reservations), Fax 67081808, 67088031 (reservations). E-mail: nwcybj@ht.rol.cn.net Four star standards not yet official. $148-$168 for rooms, $238-$488 for suites. One km from the East Railway Station and close to the Chongwenmen Subway Station. It is 40 km from the airport, 1.5 km from Tiananmen Square, and two km from the Temple of Heaven. Tunnels get you safely under busy streets here.*

This 1998 hotel has 280 small rooms, in-room safes, and ticketing service, indoor pool and gym. It has a garden, voice-mail, CNN, HBO and Star Movies. There are an English pub, Cantonese restaurant, attached department store, office towers and apartments, and free city/airport shuttle bus.

XINQIAO HOTEL *(Fandian), 2 Dong Jiao Min Xiang Street, 100004. Three and four star towers, Tel. 65133366, Fax 65125126, 65128902. 35 km from the airport, 0.75 km from the east railway station, and 10 km from the west railway station. Four-star section charges $120-$180 for rooms, and $240-$660 for suites. Its three-star section charges $42-$80 for rooms, and $145 for suites.*

Built in 1954 and expanded in 1998, this six- and 14-story hotel has 400 rooms with CNN, and some rooms with small bathrooms. It has bicycles for hire, in-room safes, Cantonese, Shandong and Japanese food, and natural hot spring water. In the old section, the carpets are dirty, moldy grouting is around the bathtubs, and the wallpaper is peeling. The new section is much better with an English-speaking elevator. It has bicycles for hire, and is generally good except for the maintenance and English.

PEACE HOTEL *(Heping Binguan), 3 Jinyu Hutong, Wangfujing Avenue, 100004 (across from the Palace Hotel), Tel. 65128833, Fax 65126863, 65266989. Its four-star east building costs $110-$180 for good-sized rooms and $250-$1500 for suites.*

Built in 1952, it says it'll finish redecorating all rooms in 1999. It has some non-smoking rooms and executive floor. It has a small indoor pool and gym, carpet stains, and CNN. It has no free bottled water nor in-room safe and English might be a problem. We found the breakfast buffet good, but the western dinner buffet poor. It has a cheaper three-star west building attached.

BEIJING SONG HE HOTEL *(Song He Dajiudian), 88 Dengshikou, Dongcheng District 100006. Three stars, Tel. 65138822, Fax 65139088. E-mail: songhe@cen.pok.net. $90-$110 for rooms, $200 for suites.*

The best rooms are above the fifth floor. Built in 1992, this hotel has 310 rooms with safes, no minibars, and bad grouting. It has CNN, Thai and Cantonese restaurants, low hall ceilings and dirty carpets. The breakfast buffet is Y110.

HAOYUAN BINGUAN, *53 Shijia Hutong (Lane), Dengshikou Street, 100010, Tel. 65125557, 65253179. Y450.*

On a lane east of the Tianlun Dynasty Hotel, 164 steps east of the Holison Clothing Store (on Dong Dan Nan Da Jie), look for two white lions outside a rust-colored gate. Built in 1984, this inn has 17 rooms, some with private baths and none with television in English. It is clean but in need of maintenance. It has few services (not even money exchange) and little English, not even on the gate. But it's charming, cheap and in traditional Chinese style. It is operated by the All-China Womens' Federation.

Jianguomenwai

The second-best location, especially for business people but also for shoppers and tourists. It is about four km east of Tiananmen Square on Jianguomenwai Avenue, which is the same as Chang'an Avenue, the street between Tiananmen Square and the Forbidden City. On the southwest side of Jianguomenwai from west to east bunched together are the **Gloria Plaza**, **Jing Du Yuan** and **New Otani Hotels**, the **Beijing Tourism Tower**, **Scitech Building**, and the **Scitech Hotel**. On the north side spread out west to east for about two km are the **Beijing International Club Hotel**, C.I.T.I.C. Building, Friendship Store, Gui You Department Store, Silk Alley, **Jianguo** and **Jinglun Hotels**. Next are **China World** and **Traders Hotels** in the China World Trade Center (CWTC). The new Kerry Center, due 1999-2000 north of Traders' Hotel at Third Ring and Guang Hua Roads, should have offices, apartments and a 487-room hotel.

The **China World Trade Center** (CWTC) is a city in itself with hotels, an arcade, apartments, offices and shops. It has exhibition and conference centers, and the offices of Ethiopian, Northwest, Korean, Malaysian and Singapore airlines, CITS, and Bank of China. It has a cyber cafe, deli, coffee shops, restaurants, DHL and American Express. It also has a supermarket (open 9am-9pm). Its late-1999 addition should have an indoor ice skating rink, fitness center and more stores and restaurants. It is about 27 km from the airport, three km from the main East Railway Station, and 20 km from the West Railway Station. All other hotels in this area are closer to these stations.

The western part of this less crowded area is within walking distance of the United States embassy, Ritan Park, and the international post office.

The **Beijing International Hotel** is between these two areas, and walking distance to the East Railway Station. It is a nice compromise but Tiananmen is still at least a half-hour walk away. A newer hotel is across the street from this station but there's been no time to review it. A good deal here for budget travelers is the **Jing Du Yuan Hotel**, back of the Gloria Hotel.

BEIJING INTERNATIONAL CLUB HOTEL (*Beijing Guoji Ju Le Bu Fandian*), *21 Jianguomenwai Avenue, 100020, Tel. 64606688, Fax 64603299. Http://www.sheraton.com. Five star standard. $375-$465 for rooms, $595-$3800 for suites.*

This 1997-98 hotel has 273 spacious rooms and suites with large twin or king-size beds, fluffy pillows, big bathrooms with tub and shower stall, walk-in wardrobes, safes, and CNN and in-house movies. Rooms have computer outlets and black-tailed butler service with packing and unpacking, light pressing on arrival, and wake-up tea or coffee. This boutique hotel has western, Asian, Italian, Japanese and Cantonese restaurants, and 24-hour room service. It has a 24-hour business center. The decor is Asian and western, classical and current, a mix of styles put together with considerable flair. Look carefully at the details, even at the hand-made paper under the Chinese calligraphy. Its health club with pool and entertainment should open in 2001. Member of the Luxury Collection ITT Sheraton.

See also Chapter 13, *China's Best Places to Stay*.

CHINA WORLD HOTEL *(Zhong Guo Da Fandian), 1 Jianguomenwai Avenue, Da Bei Yao, 100004. Five stars, Tel. 65052266, Fax 65050828, 65053165. E-mail: cwhbc@public3.bta.net.cn. Http://www.Shangri-La.com. $230 and $330 for rooms, $2000 and $2400 for suites.*

Built in 1990, this 21-story hotel has 737 large rooms with good-size desks, CNN, second data ports, and safes. It has non-smoking and executive floors. There are a deli and bake shop, eight bars and restaurants including Cantonese, American and Nadaman Japanese restaurants, and Expresso Bar (with Y35 lunch) in the complex. Its conference hall can seat 800 people banquet style. Facilities include gym, squash, indoor tennis, golf simulator, pool, and bowling. It has a 24-hour business center. Its new Aria Bar and Grill should have a choice of 100 wines, open kitchen with steaks, seafood and entertainment. Managed by Shangri-La International Hotels and Resorts.

The executive floor breakfast at the China World included two kinds of smoked fish, stir-fried vegetables with corn, three kinds of cheeses, nine different fresh fruits, and *dim sum*. There was also bacon, sausages, three kinds of yogurt, boxed cereals, toast, nine different sweet buns, eight kinds of rolls, congee, noodles, rice, hamburgers, four juices, and two kinds of milk.

See also Chapter 13, *China's Best Places to Stay*.

JIANGUO HOTEL *(Fandian), 5 Jianguomenwai Dajie, 100020. Four stars, Tel. 65002233, Fax 65002871. E-mail:sales@hoteljianguo.com or res@hoteljianguo.com. Http://www.hoteljianguo.com. $190-$240 for rooms, and $310 for duplex suites.*

Built in 1982 with Mediterranean-style architecture and courtyard garden, this 462-room hotel has exemplary standards, and room renovations in 1999. It has duplexes, some with balconies or second bedroom. It has four storys with a nine-story tower, and a 24-hour business center and room service. Its twin beds are wide, and its televisions receive CNN, HBO and Star TV. It has an executive floor with complimentary use of a computer and printer. There's a fine French restaurant (see below), American bistro, Cantonese food, and gourmet food/bake shop. Try the cheese parfait and the tarts. They're heavenly. It has a gym, indoor all-year pool and bicycles to rent. Asiana, Alitalia and Tarom Romanian airlines have offices in the building. Affiliated with Steigenberger World Hotels.

HOTEL NEW OTANI CHANG FU GONG HOTEL *(Chang Fu Gong Fandian), 26 Jianguomenwai Avenue, 100022. Five stars, Tel. 65125555, 65125711 (Sales), Fax 65125346, 65139810. Y1530-Y1870 for rooms, and Y2550-Y5525 for suites.*

Opened in 1990, this 24-story hotel has 500 rooms with hand showers, low bathroom ceilings and molded plastic sinks. It has CNN, Japanese and continental restaurants, and a pretty classical garden. It has a narrow indoor pool, lighted tennis court, and a good gym. Its ANA airlines office here has a free airport shuttle for its own passengers. Managed by New Otani International.

GLORIA PLAZA HOTEL *(Kai Lai Dajiudian), 2 Jianguomennan Avenue, 100022. Four stars, Tel. 65158855, Fax 65158533. $160 and $190. Presidential Suite $1,200. Four star standard.*

Built in 1992, this hotel has 423 large rooms and suites, and executive floors. The west-side rooms have a great view of the old Qing observatory. It has in-room safes, CNN, 24-hour business center and room service, and Korean barbecue, international, European and Cantonese seafood restaurants (see below). Its gym also has a good view, and it has an indoor pool, sauna, and there's an amazing sports bar, Sports City Cafe. The carpets are a little stained.

SCITECH HOTEL *(Saite Fandian), 22 Jianguomenwai Dajie, 100004. Four stars, Tel. 65123388, Fax 65123542, 65123543. E-mail: sthotel1@sw.com.cn $160 for rooms, and $260-$620 for suites.* Standards and discounts here are especially good. You might be able to get them down to $55 through the right travel agent. Built in 1991, this 15-story, 294-room hotel has small bathrooms and beds, in-room safes, CNN and Star TV. It has a Cantonese restaurant, 24-hour room service and business center, gym, indoor pool and tennis. Guests can use the billiard tables, bowling and steam room in the Scitech Club next door.

TRADERS HOTEL *(Guo Mao Fandian), 1 Jianguomenwai Dajie, 100004. Http://www.Shangri-La.com. Four stars, Tel. 65052277, Fax 65050818. $140 and $210.*

Built 1989 with a west wing in 1998, this 567-room hotel has non-smoking rooms, in-room safes, and CNN. Guests can use facilities like the pool and tennis courts at sister China World Hotel next door. This comfortable, well-managed hotel has good service and high standards, its own small fitness center, and offices. Two executive floors should be added soon. Managed by Shangri-La Hotels and Resorts.

JINGLUN HOTEL *(Jinglun Fandian), 3 Jianguomenwai Dajie, 100020. Four stars, Tel. 65002266, Fax 65002022. E-mail: jinglun@public3.bta.net.cn. $130-$150 for rooms, $230-$300 for suites.*

Built in 1984, this 12-story glitzy hotel has 659 rooms with small bathrooms, wide twin beds and safes. It has the Aeroflot office, an indoor pool, gym and bicycles. It also has a clinic, Japanese, Cantonese and snake restaurants. The pedestrian and taxi access here is unpleasantly crowded with cars, and it needs some refurbishing which should be done soon. It is otherwise well maintained and managed by Nikko Hotels International.

JING DU YUAN HOTEL, *8 South Avenue, Jianguomen, 100022, Tel. 65291166, Fax 65291882-3. Three stars. This is in the big building behind the Gloria Hotel on Second Ring Road with the official five-star government seal in front. Go to the south side door however. $100 for a single or double. For a big discount, book at the Hualong International Travel Service also on the ground floor. The Hualong is open 8am-5pm, Tel. 65191166 X 2172.*

This is a new 106-room hotel with business center, health center, sauna, and billiards. It offers CNN and Star World, refrigerator, a few dirty carpets, and key cards. The only hitch found so far is the Y60 an hour for swimming even for guests, and the poor English.

BEIJING INTERNATIONAL HOTEL *(Beijing Guoji Fandian), 9 Jianguomenwai Dajie, 100005. E-mail: bih@ht.rol.cn.net. Four stars, Tel. 65126688, Fax 65129972. $85-$148 for rooms, $218 for suites. Cheaper No. 2 building charges Y298 for rooms. 28 km from the airport, and 0.5 km from the East Railway Station.*

Built in 1987, this 29-story, curved hotel has 1008 large rooms with huge windows, Italian, Korean, Shanghai and Cantonese food, a revolving restaurant and 24-hour room service. It has CNN, HBO and Star TV, an executive floor, Kazak Airlines, and CITS and Hualong travel services. There's tennis, bowling, gym and a worn-looking heated indoor pool and sauna. It has lots of shops, a supermarket and florist.

Further Away But Still Downtown

The **Jing Guang Hotel** is about two km due north of the China World Trade Center. A little further out near Beijing Workers' Stadium, the Sanlitun markets, and lots of bars and restaurants, are the **City** and the **Zhaolong hotels.** These are still central and close to embassies and restaurants. Of these the Jing Guang is the best, then the Zhaolong and the City.

JING GUANG NEW WORLD HOTEL *(Jing Guang Zhong Xin), Jing Guang Centre, Hu Jia Lou, Chao Yang Qu, 100020. Five stars, Tel. 65018888, Fax 65013333. In North America, Tel. 800/44UTELL. E-mail: jghef@ht.rol.cn.net. Http://www.newworld-intl.com. $200-$300 for rooms, and $460-$1300 for suites. Five km from the East Railway Station, 25 km from the airport, seven km from the Forbidden City and 22 km from the West Railway Station.*

Built in 1990, this hotel has good standards, 52 stories (not all hotel) and 492 guest rooms. The standard rooms are small. It has a non-smoking floor, two executive floors, CNN, and HBO. It has a Food Street,

Cantonese and Korean food, deli, and 24-hour room service. It has an indoor pool, steam bath, jacuzzi, and gym, and shuttle bus. A Marriott Hotel.

ZHAOLONG HOTEL *(Fandian), 2 Congti Bei (Workers Stadium) Road, Chaoyang District, 100027. Four stars, Tel. 65972299, Fax 65972299. Y1290-Y1480 for rooms, Y2260-Y8800 for suites.*
This 1985 hotel has 19 storys, 259 rooms and small bathrooms. It has a year round indoor pool and gym.

CITY HOTEL BEIJING *(Cheng Shi Binguan), 4 Gongti Dong Road, Chaoyang District, 100027. Three stars, Tel. 65007799, Fax 65008228, 65007668. Y680-Y1020 for rooms, Y1180-Y3600 for suites.*
This 1989 hotel has 85 big rooms with safes, CNN and Star World. There are electric hand dryers in rooms, 135 studios and apartments. It has a shuttle bus, small gym, Cantonese and hot pot restaurants. Managed by Chains International (Hong Kong), it's a bit scruffy and modest but comfortable and used to North Americans.

The Great Wall-Kempinski-Kunlun Cluster
This area is further out in the northeast but still close to some embassies, about nine km from the main East Railway Station, and about 24 km from the airport. It is about 15 km from the West Beijing railway station. Hotels here are the **Great Wall Sheraton** and **Kempinski**, then close on, the **Kunlun**, followed by the **Landmark Towers**, and **Huadu** hotels in descending order of quality. The **Yuyuan** is over a kilometer from the western edge of this group and is better than the Huadu. This group is relatively close to two diplomatic areas, including the Australian and Canadian embassies, and the Agricultural Exhibition Centre. The **Beijing Hilton** is on the north edge of this area, and all but the Yuyuan are within walking distance of each other. This is now one of the centers of the city.

You should consider staying at the Kempinski, Landmark or Great Wall Hotels if you are going on foot frequently to the Lufthansa Centre. This centre has the Youyi Shopping Centre and the offices of Thai Airways, Lufthansa, Canadian Airlines, United, Asiana, Qantas, an international-quality medical office, and the South African Embassy. Heavy traffic endangers guests in other hotels here and an overpass to the south makes for a long walk.

GREAT WALL SHERATON HOTEL *(Changcheng Fandian), Donghuan Bei Road, Chaoyang District, 100026. Five stars, Tel. 65905566, 65004555, Fax 65003398, 65001919. E-mail:business@greatwall.linkexcel.com.cn. Http://www.sheraton.com\greatwall. $260-$305 for rooms, $350-$2400 for suites.*
Opened in 1984, the Great Wall is currently upgrading its guest

rooms, a three-year winter project. This 21-story hotel has its own private garden and 1007 rooms with CNN, BBC, and HBO. Its standard twins have wide beds. You can borrow a modem if necessary from housekeeping if you want to use the e-mail. It has executive and non-smoking floors. Its business center, coffee shop, room service and money exchange never sleep. Its buffet breakfast is lavish and includes 21 kinds of toppings for congee, probably a record. It has a daily barbeque May-October. It can seat 800 people at tables for a banquet.

The Great Wall also has Air China and CITS offices, You can work out in its indoor pool, Clark Hatch health club, and outdoor tennis court. This hotel can arrange champagne and hors d'oeuvres at sunset on the Great Wall as you listen to an adventurer speak about running the whole length of it. It is active in programs to clean up the litter at the Great Wall's Jinshanling pass; contact Lydia Lu. Its architecture is patterned after a glitzy Dallas hotel.

KUNLUN HOTEL *(Fandian), 2 Xin Yuan Nan Road, Chaoyang District, 100004. Five stars, Tel. 65903388, Fax 65903228. In North America, Tel. 800/44UTELL. E-mail:kunlun@public.bta.net.cn. $260-$310 for rooms and $440-$2800 for suites.*

Built in 1986-88, this 29-story hotel has 900 rooms and office suites with difficult-to-open safes, CNN, and internet plug. It has a revolving restaurant, Japanese, Korean, Vietnamese, Shanghai, and Cantonese restaurants, and 24-hour coffee shop. It has an indoor pool, gym, outdoor tennis and a shuttle bus. Its staff is friendly, lively and helpful. This is a good, dependable hotel with a play room for children, cigar store, and golf shop. The other problem was finding someone before 7:30am who speaks English. At 8am, it was okay. Managed by the Jin Jiang Group.

KEMPINSKI HOTEL *(Yan Sha Zhong Xin, Kai Bin Si Ji), Beijing Lufthansa Centre, 50 Liangmaqiao Road, Chaoyang District, 100016. Five stars, Tel. 64653388, Fax 64653366. E-mail: khbsales@public.east.cn.net. In North America, Tel. 800/426-3135. $250-$320 for rooms, $400-2500 for suites.*

Built in 1992, this well-run 18-story hotel has 530-rooms with safes, Star Plus and HBO, and executive and non-smoking floors. It has eight handicapped rooms. All suites have executive floor benefits. It has Bavarian, Vietnamese, and Italian restaurants and its own brewery. Service is good and its ballroom seats 1600 banquet style. It has an indoor pool, solarium, gym, and lighted tennis courts. A Lufthansa hotel. Leading Hotels of the World.

BEIJING HILTON INTERNATIONAL *(Xi Er Dun Fandian), 4 Dong Sanhuan Bei Road, 1 Dongfang Road, 100027. E-mail: hiltonbj@public3.bta.net.cn. Http://www.hilton.com. Five stars, Tel. 64662288, Fax 64653052, 64672970. $230 to $310 for rooms. Presidential suite $1500.*

Built in 1993, this 25-story, 363-room hotel has executive floors, satellite television, in-room safes and in-house movies. It has 24-hour room service and business center, Cantonese, Japanese and American fusion cuisine. It has an indoor pool, squash, tennis, and gym, and bicycles for hire.

BEIJING LANDMARK TOWERS *(Liangmahe Fandian), 8 Dong Sanhuanbei Road, Chao Yang District, 100004. In the same compound as the Great Wall Sheraton Hotel. Four stars, Tel. 65906688, Fax 65900503, 65906513. E-mail:lmt@public.gb.com.cn. Standard Rooms are $150 and business suites $200.*

This 1990 hotel has 15 stories, 479 rooms and 240 apartments. Its decor is charming but the air inside smells of food and mold, but other than this it's okay. It has Cantonese, Sichuan, and Korean restaurants, and the Hard Rock Cafe. It has CNN, HBO and CNBC, a small indoor pool, gym and sauna.

YU YANG HOTEL *(Fandian), 18, Xin Yuan Xili Zhong Jie, Chao Yang, 100027, Tel. 64669988, Fax 64666638, 64667316. Two blocks from the Canadian and Australian embassies. Four stars. $130 for rooms, and $230 for suites.*

The Yu Yang has 440 rooms, narrow halls, CNN, HBO and Star Plus. It also has 66 offices for rent, 24-hour room service, a mini-golf course, health club, and indoor pool. Its Green Garden cafe has had Y65 no tax international dinner buffets including unlimited local beer, soft drinks and ice cream.

HUADU HOTEL *(Fandian) 8 Xinyuan Nan Road, Chaoyang District, 100027. Three stars aiming for four, Tel. 65001166, 65001754, Fax 65001615. Y758-Y888 for rooms and Y1168 for suites.*

Built in 1982, this six-story, 500-room hotel has in-room safes, and a real post office. It is grubby even after its recent renovations, and badly managed, the air stuffy and the grouting falling apart. It lacks signs in English, has 40 watt bulbs, but has kettles, in-room safes, CNN and Star TV. The English isn't bad for a three star. It is adequate for budget travelers if you get a good discount, not just the 20% they offer everybody. Just don't expect it to honor reservations nor pass on messages. The breakfast buffet costs Y50.

The Holiday Inn Lido/Harbour Plaza Cluster

This cluster is in a residential area, about 14 km from the east and 25 km from the west railway stations. It is 15 km from Tiananmen, and 15 km from the airport. The hotels here are within walking distance of each other, restaurants, and bars in Beijing's northeast quarter, and four km from the Kempinski-Great Wall cluster. Almost in between is pretty Lido Park with lots of greenery and water.

HOLIDAY INN LIDO (*Lido Fandian*), *Jichang Road, Jiang Tai Road,* *100004. Four stars, Tel. 64376688, Fax 64376237, 64376540. E-mail:lido@ht.rol.cn.net. $190-$265 for rooms, $300-$600 for suites. Senior's discount on request.*

Across from Lido Park with its fish pond and childrens' playground, this 1984-85, five-story hotel has 720 spacious rooms. Its standard twin beds are wide and you need a flashlight to read directions for its in-room safe. It has an executive floor, CNN and HBO. Its business center, clinic and coffee shop never sleep. It has a post office, Bank of China and China Travel Service counter. CTS is open 8:30am-5:30pm Monday-Friday, 8:30am-12 noon Saturdays.

There's a yummy pizzeria, deli and pub, Cantonese and Indonesian restaurants, and especially good Thai and good German farmhouse food. Its Texan Bar & Grill has satisfying steaks. It has non-smoking areas, bicycles for hire, and 20 lanes of bowling, a gym and heated indoor pool. There's a sports bar, hi-tech disco/karaoke and fun pub. Japanese, German and international schools are on the premises as are a good supermarket that takes credit cards and is open 8:30am-9pm. Watson's "drug store" (no pharmacist) has the same hours. This hotel is Asia's largest Holiday Inn and growing. The buffet breakfast costs Y110. The downtown shuttle bus is free and its airport shuttle Y20.

The Lido Club next door, open 6am-11pm, has squash, golf, four indoor tennis courts and heated indoor pool. A small curio and clothes market is across the street. For Y20 and hard haggling, you should be able to get a good outdoor 30-minute above-the-waist massage from masseuses across the street.

See also Chapter 13, *China's Best Places to Stay.*

HARBOUR PLAZA HOTEL (*Haiyi Jiuduan*), *8 Jiang Tai Xi Road, Chao Yang District, 100016. Four stars, Tel. 64362288, Fax 64361818 or 64376310 (Sales). In North America, Tel. 800/44UTELL. $140-$240 for rooms, and $380-$600 for suites.*

Built in 1990 as the Grace Hotel, and managed by Hutchison Whampoa since 1997 (a great improvement), this attractive 17-story hotel has 429 rooms, some of them small, and service suites with microwaves. It has executive and non-smoking floors, and in-room safes that operate with credit cards. It has Japanese, Continental, California, Shanghai (Meilongzhen), and Cantonese food, and 24-hour room service. It has CNN, BBC and HBO, free downtown and airport shuttle, and reflexology and massage clinic. Its Formula One Grand Prix pub has monkey wrenches for door handles. Head for its all-you-can *dim sum* lunch for Y58. But there's no pool and no sauna.

YANXIANG HOTEL *(Fandian), A2 Jiang Tai Road, Dong Zhi Men Wai, 100016. Three stars, Tel. 64376666, Fax 64376231. Y680 for rooms and Y988-Y1688 for suites. It is behind the Lido.*

This socialist-style hotel has an attractive garden and Shandong restaurant, an indoor pool but no CNN. Its lobby is very dark, depressing, but its newly renovated rooms should be all right. It is poorly run with poor English, dirty carpets and mold.

Airport Hotel

The most convenient major hotel to the airport (three km away) is the fancy **Beijing Movenpick Hotel**, now also promoted as a resort. This hotel is good even for a two-hour stop between planes, or an unexpected overnight because of its good food, English, and services. It is especially good for children.

BEIJING MOVENPICK HOTEL *(Guo Du Fandian), Xiao Tianzhu Village, Shunyi County. P.O. Box 6913, 100621. E-mail: bjmphtic@iuol.cn.net; Http://www.movenpick-hotels.com/beijing_fs.htm. Four stars, Tel. 64565588, Fax 64565678, 64561234. North American Tel. 800/34HOTEL. $135. China Express Tours & Travel in San Gabriel, California, Tel.(626)312-3858 gives especially good rates. While a taxi could charge Y60 to downtown Wangfujing, the Movenpick provides free airport and downtown shuttle buses.*

The Movenpick is in a small village and has bars and restaurants across the street. It is a few meters off the main airport road. Built in 1990, it has 12 stories with 427 rooms, half of them with bare wooden floors and some with small televisions. It offers CNN, in-house movies, and non-smoking floors. You have a choice of Cantonese, Mongolian, Japanese, and Swiss restaurants (with cheese fondue and 30 *grappa* wines). The Sunday brunch is good but the elevators are small and hallways are narrow. Its health club claims Beijing's only outdoor swimming pool and its largest indoor pool. It has squash, aerobics, tennis, and acupressure and therapeutic massages. It has a golf-putting range, activities for children on weekends, and a camel named Amanda. Breakfast buffet $12. Chinese breakfast $7.

The Northwest Hotels

The **Shangri-La, Xiyuan**, and **New Century Hotels** are 35-38 km from the airport, about 15 km from the east railway station and about seven-11 km from the west railway station. The Third Ring Road (Xisanhuanbei Road) express highway has made these hotels and the Friendship quickly accessible from the city center (15-20 minute drive), and the airport. The **Exhibition Center Hotel** is next to the Beijing Exhibition Center, but the Xiyuan and Shangri-La are in the same neighborhood and are of better quality. The Xiyuan, New Century, and Shangri-La are within walking distance of each other and the zoo, and Temple of the Great Bell, Beijing Art Museum, high-tech district of Zhong Guan Zhun, new Beijing Experimental Zone, the Negotiations Building, and a Pizza Hut. The Xinjiang Cun (Village) moslem food market is close by.

The Friendship Hotel is north of here, about four km from the Shangri-La. These are the closest hotels in this book to Beijing, Qinghua and other major universities, Yuanmingyuan, the Summer Palace, and Western Hills. The city has been talking about opening the nearby canal between the Summer Palace and Purple Bamboo Park to tour boats, the Qing emperors' old route.

SHANGRI-LA HOTEL *(Shang Gorilla Fandian), 29 Zizhuyuan Road, 100081. Five stars, Tel. 68412211, Fax 68418006. E-mail: slbbc2@ht.rol.cn.net. Http://www.Shangri-La.com. $190-$240 for rooms. $285-$1300 for suites. This hotel is in a residential area across the road from the beautiful Beijing art museum and close to countryside, wooded hills, Holstein cows, pagodas, and peach trees. It is a 20-minute drive to the botanical garden, and 30 minutes to the Fragrant Hills hotel.*

This hotel opened in 1987 with 657 spacious rooms, each with lounge chair, foot stool, and lighted clock. It has offices, executive floor, a 720-square meter grand ballroom, and conference facilities. It has a non-smoking floor and 24-hour business center, CNN, HBO, ABN, CNBC, voice mail, and in-room safes. You can choose from its delicatessen, Cantonese, Continental, Nishimura Japanese and Italian restaurants. The hotel sells great pastry as well as food. There are indoor tennis, indoor heated pool, basketball, gym and squash, and its own garden. You can take its shuttle bus downtown. The breakfast buffet costs about Y150. This classy hotel displays Chinese paintings in its elevators protected by carved wooden frames; its pool area is decorated with stained glass. A 22-piece orchestra plays classical western music for high tea, 3pm on Sundays. Managed by Shangri-La International Hotels and Resorts.

BEIJING NEW CENTURY HOTEL *(Xinshiji Fandian), 6 Southern Road, Capital Gym, 100044, Tel. 68491841, 68491835, Fax 68319564. Five stars. $170-$210 for rooms, and $260-$1400 for suites.*

This 1992 hotel has shuttle bus service three times a day downtown. It has 738-rooms with CNN and HBO, kettles, safes and 24-hour room service. It has small rooms with stained carpets. It has an indoor pool, steambath, gym, bowling, golf practice range, and lighted outdoor tennis. It has Japanese, Sichuan and Cantonese food and snacks, and 24-hour room service. Aside from the lattrine smells on the 32nd floor, it's fine. ANA Hotels International.

XIYUAN HOTEL *(Fandian), 1 Sanlihe Road, 100046. Four stars, Tel. 68313388, Fax 68314577. E-mail:xyhotel@public3.bta.net.cn, Tel. in North America 800/821-0900. $150 for rooms and $200-$1000 for suites.*

The Xiyuan boasts a main 26-story building with 707 spacious rooms and two Moslem floors, and 10 four-story villas. This recently resurrected old hotel with garden now has in-room safes, in-house videos, CNN and Star TV, and a 24-hour business center and room service. It has a German brewery with American food, a good Moslem restaurant, and Shandong and Sichuan restaurants. It also has a revolving restaurant and a fast food restaurant. It has a small heated pool and steam bath, and a health club. The breakfast buffet costs $10. A Cathay International Hotel.

FRIENDSHIP HOTEL *(Youyi Binguan), 3 Baishiqiao Road, 100873, Tel. 68498888, Fax 68498866. E-mail:fhtjcn@public.3.bta.net.cn. $130-$220 for rooms, $380-$1600 for suites. Four stars. 35 km to the airport, 16 km to the East Railway Station, and 10 km to the West Railway Station. It is in a residential suburb close to the Third Ring Road Bei San Huan exit. You can walk to Bai Shi Qiao (high tech area) and two shopping malls.*

Built in 1954 for Soviet experts, this is currently home also for many foreign teachers. Services are geared to long-staying guests. It has five- and six-story buildings set in a huge garden. Building One is the best with an executive floor. Building Three has baby sitting service and rooms for the disabled. Its 26 restaurants have Russian-style, Cantonese, western and Sichuan food. It has indoor and outdoor pools, gym, tennis, bowling, golf driving range, and a track. It arranges hiking tours. It has a total of 1900 rooms, most small to medium sized with small baths, and each with kettles, mini-bars, safes, and CNN. Its brass could be better polished and its bulbs are only 40 watts, but if you can get a good discount, it's okay.

EXHIBITION CENTRE HOTEL *(Zhan Lan Guan Binguan), 135 Xi Zhi Men Wai Street, 100044. Three stars, Tel. 68316633, Fax 68347450. E-mail: gljtbech@public.bta.net.cn. $70 to $100 (in high season). 33 km from the airport, 12 km from the East Railway station and eight km from the West Railway Station.*

This 1988 hotel has a quiet setting in a large garden by its own small lake. It has seven stories, 250 rooms, CNN, American pub, Chaozhou and Shandong food. It has a small gym and bicycles. But it is getting very run down and hopefully promised renovations will have been completed by the time you get there.

The In-Between Hotel

HOLIDAY INN DOWNTOWN, *98 Beilishi Road, Xichengqu, 100037, Tel. 68338822, Fax 68340696. Four stars. $130-$140 for rooms, and $230-$250 for suites. It is in the northwest but not too north and west. It's only six km to the Forbidden City. It is also five km to the west railway station, and a few meters from Second Ring Road and its growing financial street with bank headquarters and computer companies.*

This small, friendly hotel is comfortable and unpretenious. It has 346 rooms, a small indoor pool, small gym, but a great Indian restaurant. It is next to Isetan department store and Kenny Roger's Roasters Restaurant.

Within One Kilometer of the West Railway Station

The best here is the Beijing Telecom, but the Media Centre is good value.

BEIJING TELECOM HOTEL *(Beijing Dian Xin Fandian) 6, Shifangyuan, Haidian District, 100036, Tel. 63901166, Fax 63901273. Across the road from the train station. About four star standards.*

This hotel's 325 rooms have Star TV, CNN and 33 international channels, safes, and high-speed data lines. Some of its restaurants have Internet corners. They also serve French, Korean and Chinese food. It has simultaneous translation systems and high definition conference videophones. It has an indoor pool and gym, and can pick you up at the airport in a Red Flag (Hong Qi) stretch limo.

BEIJING RAILWAY MANSION *(Tie Dao Da Sha) 102 Beifengwo Avenue, Haidian District, 100038, Tel. 63229199, Fax 63229155. Three stars. Y550 for rooms, and Y800 and Y900 for suites.*

This 1998 hotel is on a quiet side street. It looks good for a three-star but you might have problems with English. No CNN but you can get Voice of America.

MEDIA CENTRE *(Meidiya Zhongxin), 11B Fuxing Road, 100038, Tel. 68514422. 68516288, Fax 68515240. Beside the CCTV building and the military museum, one km from the west train station. Y430-Y830 for rooms, Y760-Y1780 for suites.*

This eleven-story, 272-room hotel with apartments, has in-room safes, medium-sized beds, and mini-bar. A Japanese joint venture, it has Cantonese, Sichuan, and Japanese food and a 700 square meter multi-function hall. It has a health club and billiards. Its Media Centre has satellite transmission, equipment leasing, and television production services. English might be a problem but this is one of the best deals in town if you bring your own light bulb. It only has 25 watt ones. Its buffet breakfast is Y48.

Other Locations

RADISSON SAS HOTEL *(Huang Jia Fandian), 6A Beisanhuan Dong Road, Chaoyang District, 100028. Four-star standard, Tel. 64663388, Fax 64653186, 64653183. E-mail:sas@public.gb.com.cn. In North America, Tel. 800/333-3333. Four stars. $170 to $210. Presidential suite $800. Seniors' rates. Twenty km from the airport and 10 km from Tiananmen. The Radisson SAS Hotel is adjacent to the China International Exhibition Center (CIEC) in the* *north of the city. It is not near anything else except Carrefour with its cheaper goods, a McDonald's, and a couple of small restaurants.*

Built 1992-93, this 15-story hotel has 374 smallish rooms with kettles. You have a choice of different decors, some with striking colors like black leather and light yellow walls. The least radical is the art-deco. Some desks have no drawers but have in-room safes and trouser press machines. It has executive floors and non-smoking rooms, and narrow twin beds. It has CNN and HBO with speakers in its relatively large bathrooms, a Scandinavian Grill room, Sichuan and Cantonese food served European style, a deli and bake shop. For sports, there's an indoor pool, tennis, squash, gym and express three-hour laundry service. This hotel is very clean, bright and cheerful. The breakfast buffet costs Y125.

QIANMEN HOTEL, *175 Yongan Road, Xuanwu District, 100050, Tel. 63016688, Fax 63013883. Three stars. $75-$100 for rooms, $120-$200 for suites. Three km from Tiananmen, seven km from the Beijing East train station, and 36 km from the airport.*

This 410-room hotel is all right with HBO and Star TV, and in-room safes, if you don't mind stained carpets and moldy grouting. It is the home of the Li Yuan Beijing Opera show and is close to Liulichang antique market in the southwest part of the city. It has also been giving 60% discounts to individual travelers booking through travel agents in the US. As long as standards keep up, this is a good deal.

FRAGRANT HILL HOTEL, *Fragrant Hill Park, Haidian District, 100093, Tel.62591166, Fax 62591762. E-mail:xshotel@midwest.co.cn. Four stars.*

The pretty 1982 Fragrant Hill Hotel has amazing architecture (by American I.M.Pei) and good convention setting isolated in the Western Hills, but it is badly managed and borderline, still with moldy grouting. So it's here without enthusiasm, even though it was redecorated in 1997 and Europeans living there liked it. The only complaint was no daily change of towels. It now has in-room safes, bowling, tennis, an indoor pool, and a spa but no CNN. English could be a problem. A shuttle bus goes to the Friendship Hotel and Shangri-La five times a day and a line of taxis is outside. One tried to charge Y100 to two nearby temples and the Yuanmingyuan but settled on Y60.

SUMMER PALACE GUEST HOUSE *(Yiheyuan Binguan), Summer Palace, 100091, Tel. 62581144 X 462. Rate varies.*

It is very difficult to get a room here because of its long-staying guests, but it's worth a try for the incredible setting and antique furniture. The guest house is a long walk from the main gate and there is no English spoken. Even people in neighboring stores do not know of it and travel agents will not book it. But the Summer Palace is real historical imperial China.

Start looking for it a few meters before the west end of the Long Corridor, before the stores, under the three-story pagoda on the hill. Look on the right, the north side, for a red wall with gray around the entrance with white trim, and green-and-red framed windows in front painted with flowers. There's gold trim on its red door and vines cover its entranceway. Look for the sign on a tree that reads BO9446 (or on a cypress marked BO8552). The guest house only has six suites with beds for 20 people. Some mahogany beds are carved with imperial dragons. It also has thick carpets, antique plumbing and poor English. Pay whatever they ask. How many foreigners can say they slept at the Summer Palace?

The Cheaper Hotels

OVERSEAS CHINESE HOTEL *(Huaqiao Fandian), 5 Santiao, Beixinqiao, 210336, Tel. 64016688, Fax 64012386. 15 minutes walk to Lama Temple at Yonghegong metro stop through hutongs. No need to take the rickshaw tour. About a two-star standard. Y330-Y460 for rooms, Y750-Y800 for suites.*

This hotel is a 30-45 minute drive from downtown but is near the subway. Its rooms have ill-fitting stained wallpaper, safes and scales, and receive CNN and Star Plus. The grouting is dirty and the light bulbs are 40 watts. This 1954 hotel has one Chinese restaurant.

LU SONG YUAN HOTEL *(Binguan), 22 Banchang Hutong, Kuan Jie, East District, 100009. Two stars, Tel. 64040436, 64011116, Fax 64030418. No credit cards. Y168-Y260 for singles, Y298-Y358 for doubles. Two dorms with six beds each at Y80.*

North of the Art Gallery, you can reach this hotel by buses #104, 108, 113, and 2, plus a short walk. It has 31 rooms and is the only hostel in Beijing affiliated with the World Youth Hostel Federation. It gives 10% discounts on rooms to federation members and is a good deal considering its location close to downtown.

JING HUA HOTEL, *Xi Luo Yuan Nan Lu, Yongdingmenwai, 100077, Tel. 67222211 (and ask for Ms. Waley who speaks good English and can give you directions). Fax 67211455. Take the 17 bus from the Temple of Heaven. It is almost due south at Third Ring Road South, 40 km from the airport, 11 km from the East Railway Station and 14 km from the West Railway Station. Y140-Y200 for rooms with private baths but no shower curtains, Y300 for suites. Beds in a four-bed basement dorm costs Y30; beds in a new dormitory in its better back building costs Y35.*

Internet service is Y15 for 30 minutes, one of the cheapest in hotels, but the line-up is long. It hopes to be offering coin-operated washing machines too. It has CNN and cheaper tours, Y50 to the Great Wall at Simatai, and Y50 to see the acrobats including the bus. Taxies cost about Y30 from the railway station. The Jinghua is a favorite of foreign backpackers who don't mind the dirt, cobwebs and roaches.

WHERE TO EAT

Beijing is a gourmet's delight, with excellent food from all over the country and the world. The top restaurants now fly seafood in from the Gulf of Thailand and import China-grown produce from Hong Kong because the best is sent there. So far, I've found five hotels with restaurants offering over 100 different wines. These are in the **Kempinski**, **Great Wall Sheraton**, **Hilton**, **Jianguo** and **Palace**, and there's probably more.

Dress codes are not mandatory anywhere, but you might feel more comfortable dressing up a little at restaurants in top hotels, or in case you're invited to the **Great Hall of the People** or the **China Club** (which has sharp-dressing Hong Kong members.) Even then, Justine's at the Jianguo says "no shorts."

Quality is consistently good in these hotels, but you can find cheaper gems too. Many tour groups say the best meal is the home-cooked one prepared for the **Hutong Tour** by the occupant of one of the houses. And you might find something incredibly tasty in a street market.

Prices listed are subject to change and except for the markets, there's usually a 10-15% service charge.

Beijing Food

You do have to try good local dishes in Beijing. It is much like Shandong's, but influenced by Manchu and Mongol imperial tastes. It is usually salty (as opposed to sweet) and is not highly spiced. Sauces are used less frequently than in Cantonese cooking. Everyone must try **Peking duck** at least once! The best part is the crispy skin, which is dipped in sweet, dark brown hoisin sauce, seasoned with a green onion, and then wrapped in a thin pancake and eaten by hand.

Peking Duck

QUANJUDE KAOYA DIAN RESTAURANT, *13 Shuaifuyuan, east of Wangfujing, Tel. 65253310, 65228384. It's open 10:30am-1:30pm and 5pm-8:30pm.*

For eight people, they suggested two Peking ducks at Y88 each; salted beef for Y20; mushrooms and pine nuts for Y20; stir-fried mustard greens Y18; chicken with cashews Y30; shelled prawns with chili oil Y130; duck soup Y4 and fruit Y80. This restaurant has clean white table cloths, charming Chinese decor and bright chandeliers. This is the more elegant Wangfujing branch (known as "Sick Duck" because of the nearby hospital). They have another restaurant, the Quanjude branch, at *32 Qianmen Avenue, Tel. 65112418* (known as the "Big Duck"). This is said to have fatter more delicious birds, but it is very crowded with no place to park.

Qing Imperial Food

LI JIA CHAI (*Li Family Restaurant*), *11 Yangfang Hutong, De Nei Avenue. Have your driver or hotel telephone 66011915 or 66180107 for directions. The Li Jia Chai is very difficult to find, unless a sign has now been posted outside the gate. It costs Y200 and up per person, but Y480 is better, and Y600 is the best.*

Located across the lake from Soong Ching-ling's residence, this restaurant has only two tiny rooms in a private home in a lane full of tiny traditional houses. It has three tables and seats a maximum of 22. But it has great imperial cooking and classy table settings, a special and exotic experience especially when Mr. Li talks about the different dishes and his grandfather who cooked in the Qing court. A reservation might have to be made weeks in advance but give it a last-minute try anyway. You must consult about the set menu. Please do not cancel without several days' notice; the restaurant will have bought food only for you.

FANG SHAN RESTAURANT *in Beihai Park, along the lake by the White Dagoba at 1 Wenjin Jie, Xichengqu, Tel. 64011879.*

The cooks in this unique restaurant were taught by the Empress Dowager's cooks. Unfortunately the food here isn't as good as it used to be, but it's still worth a try for its historic building and lakeside setting.

The **TINGLIGUAN** (Pavilion for Listening to Orioles) in the Summer Palace formerly a favorite, is no longer recommended. The best cooks have been probably lured away by better-paying restaurants.

While we're on poor food, that at the **Great Hall of the People**, China's parliament, isn't any good either.

Mongolian

For all these popular restaurants, you should make reservations in advance on weekends.

Mongolian food is local too, especially hot pot which you cook yourself at your table. For the barbecue, you select the raw ingredients and sauces, and then someone else cooks it for you. For Mongolian food in a relatively authentic setting, you can eat in a *gher* or *yurt* at the **Movenpick Hotel** (see *Where to Stay* above) and at the **Swissôtel**, *Hong Kong Macau Center, Dong Si Shi Tiao Li Jiao Qiao, Tel. 65012288, open 5:30pm-10pm and reservations are required.* There's also the **Fang Jhuang** in south Beijing, near the Temple of Heaven.

DONGLAISHUN restaurant, *198 Wangfujing Avenue, Tel. 65253562.* The Mongolian food is famous here.

KAOROJI RESTAURANT, *14 Di'anmenwai Avenue, Tel. 64045921, 64042554.*

Located near the Drum Tower, Kaoroji is among the best for barbecue.

Doing It Cheaply

At the opposite end of the scale are onion and sesame buns hot out of the oven, or steaming hot sweet potatoes in their jackets cooked in huge bins on the street for next to nothing, Y1-Y2 each. A typical breakfast is deep fried oil sticks (like long donuts) dipped in soy milk and you can find these in street stalls and tiny canteens too. Look also for *jiao zi* meat dumplings, either steamed or boiled in soup. Take your own chopsticks and bowl.

For the Romantic

Some foreigners have celebrated their weddings with dinner on a boat in Kunming Lake at the Summer Palace, or enjoyed picnic suppers under a full moon at the Ming Tombs or Great Wall. Catering can be done by any top hotel.

For other than Beijing food

Superb food is available in the top hotels but there are also a lot of good restaurants.

Around the Forbidden City & Tiananmen Square

CROWNE PLAZA HOTEL, *48 Wangfujing Avenue, Tel. 65133388.* Try either the lunch buffet (Y88) or dinner buffet (Y128).

HANWOORI KOREAN RESTAURANT, *in the Peace Hotel, 3 Jinyu Hutong, Wangfujing Avenue (across from the Palace Hotel), Tel. 65128833 X 6605, 6607. Open 11am-2:30pm and 5pm-10pm and takes credit cards.*

This is a good Korean restaurant with the same menu as its sister restaurant, the Sorobal in the Kempinski area (listed below).

COURTYARD RESTAURANT, *95 Donghuamen Avenue, Tel. 65268883. Open 6pm-10am. Accepts credit cards.*

The food here is a fusion of east and west. It's near the East Gate of the Forbidden City. The bar is open to 1am. Champagne costs Y78 a glass and wine Y45. Entrees in this pleasant, modern restaurant range from Y120-Y195, appetizers Y55-Y90 and soups Y35-Y55.

HONG KONG FOOD CITY *18 Donganmen Avenue, just west of Wangfujing, Tel. 65136668 and open 11am-3am. It takes credit cards.*

This place looks dumpy but the food (especially Cantonese) is good. There's sweet and sour pork for about Y42, and your pick of live fish from a tank for Y250. Good *dim sum* 7am-11am. The first floor has seafood and Cantonese food. The third floor has lighter food and hot pot: roast goose with soy sauce Y36; Golden Label suckling pig Y48; sharks fin with chicken for one person Y98, and enough sweet corn soup with chicken for four people for Y38.

The Qianmen area on the south side of Tiananmen Square has the best branch of the **Quanjude Kaoya Dian Restaurant**. Qianmen also has the best vegetarian restaurant in town, the **Gongdelin**, at *158 Qianmen Nan Avenue, Tel. 65112542. 10:30am-9:30pm.*

For Kosher food, consult the Israeli embassy.

Jianguomenwai

DANIELLI'S, *the International Club, Open 11:30am-2:30pm and 6pm-10:30pm. The hotel's entrance is on the side street behind the club, Tel. 64606688.*

This is an excellent Italian restaurant. Try the *spaghetti al arogosta* Y165, crab soup with seafood and scallops scented with sambuca Y65, and an *antipasto* of deep fried *calamari* with chili garlic mayonnaise Y140.

JUSTINE'S, *the Jianguo Hotel, 5 Jianguomenwai Avenue, Tel. 65002233, open 6:30am-9:30am, 12 noon-2:30pm, and 6pm-10pm.*

With draperied ceiling, and maroon-and-gold striped chairs, this restaurant offers some of the best European food in the city. Try the goose liver terrine appetizer for Y159 and escargot Y98. Grilled steak is Y345 to Y570 (for two), prawns, and mushrooms flambéd with Calvados is Y258.

TRADERS HOTEL COFFEE SHOP, *1 Jianguomenwai Dajie, Tel. 65052277 is behind the China World Hotel.*

This coffee shop has a great lunch buffet and Starbuck's coffee, Y138 plus 15% weekdays, half price for ladies on weekends.

SAMPAN RESTAURANT, *Cantonese, etc. Gloria Hotel, 2 Jianguomennan Avenue, 100022. Four stars, Tel. 65158855. Credit cards. It is open 11:30am-2pm; 5:30pm-10pm.*

The Sampan has braised sharks' fin with shredded chicken Y148; combo platter appetizers Y88; hot and sour soup Beijing style Y28 per person; sauteed mixed seafood with macadamia nuts Y98; pan-fried boneless duck with lemon sauce Y68; beef steak Cantonese style on sizzling platter Y68.

BLEU MARINE, *French. 5 Guang Hua Xi Road, a block north of the Gui You Department Store, Tel. 65006704. It is open Monday-Saturday from noon-2:30 or 3pm, and then 6:30pm-10:30pm or whenever. It accepts no credit cards.*

This hotel is charming and casual with comfortable captains' chairs. For Y80 you can get a substantial entree and dessert, with a glass of wine or soft drink at dinner.

WINDOWS ON THE WORLD, *Cantonese. CITIC building next to the Friendship Store. It is open 12:30 noon-2pm, and 5pm-10pm.*

Dim sum here ranges from Y10 to Y16 per basket. Appetizers include suckling pig and roast meat combo Y88, or roast crisp duck Y42. Entrees: vegetable broth in *taiji* shape Y20 per person; whole baked fortune chicken ordered in advance Y260; steamed vegetables with Yunnan ham in fan shape Y52; deep-fried stuffed crab claws Y30 per piece; banana or apple fritters Y15 per person.

Look in the **Yong An Li vegetable market** one block east and opposite the Friendship Store on Jianguomenwai. Around the tomato, green pepper, and cilantro stalls here are several, not necessarily clean restaurants. Of these, especially good if the right cook is on duty is the "hot and prickly" **Sichuan Home Town Restaurant** (no credit cards). Ask for *dan dan* noodles, *mapo* beancurd and chicken with peanuts. Forget about Uncle Sam's. Avoid Maxim's. But don't ignore the **Baskin-Robbins** at the Friendship Store because you can get donuts for Y4 each, a soft drink for Y4.50, and ice cream (Y19 for a double cone). It's open 24 hours.

The **Pizza Hut** next to it is open 11am-10pm on week days, and 10:30am-10pm on weekends. Telephone 65017768 for take-outs. A **Haagen-Dazs Cafe** is close by in Room 196 of the Beijing International Club at 21 Jianguomenwai Avenue, the entrance on Ritan Road.

East of the International Post Office & North of the Friendship Store

OMAR KHAYYAM INDIAN RESTAURANT, *Indian. Asia-Pacific Building, 8 Ya Bao Road, Tel. 65139988 X 20188/20203. Open daily 11:30am-2:30pm and 6pm-10:30pm. It accepts credit cards.*

This is a Singapore company with cooks from North India. Reservations are recommended on weekends or for big groups. Chicken *tikka* costs Y55; *tandoori* chicken Y25, Y50 and Y95; *palak paneer* Y55; *roganjosh* Y69; and mutton *vindaloo* Y76. I personally prefer the Holiday Inn Downtown because of the Mumbai flavors, but others think this is more authentic. In any case, the food is great. Beer costs Y22-Y35.

AMERICAN CHILI'S GRILL & BAR RESTAURANT, *Tex-Mex. Gateway Building (next door to the Asia-Pacific Building), Unit 03-01, at 10 Ya Bao Road, Tel. 65925317, Fax 65925340. It is open 11am-11pm daily and takes credit cards.*

Take your tacos with live music. Recently it's had a solo singer from the Philippines Tuesday and Thursday nights, the popular Touchstone Jazz band on Wednesday nights, and the Red Zebra pop band on Friday nights. The yummy chicken chili is Y30-Y35, fajitas Y118-Y210, margaritas Y50-Y75, and beer Y30-Y35.

SPAGEDDIES ITALIAN KITCHEN, *Italian. Same building as Chili's but at Unit 01-01/03-02. Hours are the same and it also takes credit cards, Tel. 65925215.*

Its fried calamari is Y65, spaghetti carbonara Y62, margherita pizza Y65, spaghetti with garlic and olive oil Y62. These are both casual restaurants.

Ritan Park

XIHE YA JU RESTAURANT, a*t the northeast corner of Ritan Park (west side). Sichuan. Moderate, Tel. 65941915, 65010385. It's open 11am-2pm and 5pm-10pm.*

This is a cute little cafe with green and white checked table cloths, very popular with foreigners. One section is air-conditioned and decorated with plastic grapes and gourds.

RITAN PARK RESTAURANT, *southwest corner inside Ritan Park, is within sight of the sign on top of the CITIC Building, Tel. 65005883. Open daily 11:30am-2:00pm; 5pm-8pm.*

It has good *jiao tze* dumplings, Sichuan, Huiyang, and imperial food with moderate prices. You can eat in its Chinese palace-like building or in summer, on its patio.

BAIKAL CAFE RESTAURANT, *See Cat Calls and Whistles below. Russian. 2 Beizhong Street, Dongzhimennei, Tel. 64052380, 64054902.*

Near the Russian embassy, this restaurant has shows daily between 7:30pm-11:30pm. The restaurant is open 11am-midnight. A Russian band plays nightly.

Full Link Shopping Center (Feng Lian Guang Chang), *18 Chaoyangmenwei Avenue northwest of Ritan Park*, is a popular mall. **Tully's Espresso Bar** is in the basement.

NYC MUSIC KITCHEN, *Shanghai. Moderate. 4/F. Tel. 65881791/ 1792. It's open 11am-10:30pm Sunday-Thursday, closing at midnight on Friday and Saturday. Happy Hour is 5pm-7pm, two for one.*

This is a modern-looking cafe with a disc jockey playing mainly US pop music. Live jazz, rock, and pop music are offered regularly on some evenings. Recently it's had a Singapore duo Saturday, Sunday and Monday nights. You can get Starbucks coffee during 2pm-5pm "tea time." Popular dishes include steamed mini-shrimp dumplings for Y25, pan-fried bun with pork filling for Y16, minced meat ball and cabbage in clay pot Y42, and roasted baby back ribs with scallions for Y38. It also offers sweet and sour chicken for Y38, and sauteed shrimp in green tea for Y98. Delicious.

Further Away But Still Downtown

The **City Hotel-Zhaolong Hotel-Sanlitun area** has very casual and moderate-priced dining. See also bars with food in this area in the *Nightlife & Entertainment* section below.

METRO CAFE, *Italian. 6 Gong Ti Xi Lu (by Workers Gymnasium), Tel. 65527828. Open 11:30am-10:30pm daily and accepts credit cards.*

This restaurant has good pasta and reasonable prices, served in an attractive patio garden with fountain in summer. It's known for its *lasagne bolognese* for Y52, *fetuccini* with chicken and pepper cheese sauce for Y67, and Y25-45 *Caesar* salad. Manager Marvin Lau is from Hawaii.

FRIDAY'S, *American. 19 Dong Sanhuanbei Road, one block south of the Zhaolong Hotel on the west side of Second Ring Road, Tel. 65975314, Fax 65975240. E-mail: tgif@public.cmit.cn.net. It is open 11am-midnight, and takes credit cards.*

The first restaurant of this Dallas chain in China has great ribs for Y66 a half rack or Y98 for full. It also has *fajitas*, fried *mozzarella*, and buffalo wings, *nachos*, hamburgers, soup and salad, and loaded potato skins. The waiters dress in cute costumes and it has tiffany lamp shades, striped red and white plastic table cloths and Rock Hudson movie posters. You'll see more FRIDAY'S in other cities. It's expanding to 40 restaurants in the whole of China.

SCHLOTZSKY'S DELI, *16 Gong Ti Dong Road, near Workers Gymnasium, Tel.65041246.*

It's open 7am-1am and has great sandwiches, just like home.

AL FRESCO DINING IN BEIJING

*Summer is patio time especially along Jianguomenwai where hotels have tables on the street in front. Also prolific and informal is **Sanlitun Market** (which might be in the process of moving because residents have complained of the noise.) Notable here is the **Kebab Kafe** on the west side, Tel. 64155812, and open 11am-11pm. It accepts credit card. **Bella's Bake Shop** here is also good especially for cinnamon buns and cookies, Tel. 64168785 and open 8am-midnight. At number 54 is the **Side By Side Cafe**, Tel. 64164191, open 9am-2am. You can get an American breakfast for Y35.*

Great Wall-Kempinski-Kunlun

LOUISIANA RESTAURANT, *Fusion. Expensive. Beijing Hilton, 4 Dong Sanhuan Bei Road, 1 Dongfang Road, Tel. 64662288, 64674754. It's open 11am-2pm; 6pm-10:30pm.*

This restaurant has a marvelous blend of Pacific Northwest, Creole, and Asia-Pacific cooking. The menu changes frequently so there's always some variety introduced by guest chefs like Claus Mayr and Charles Saunders. It also matches local and foreign wines to each dish. This makes it a very exciting place. Popular are the winter squash bisque, and gumbo soups. Highly recommended is the rack of lamb smoked with coffee beans, after marinating in sugar cane juice. Also great is the butterfly Norwegian salmon. Or try the tender supremo of free-range chicken with mango sauce. The most popular dessert is the Mud Bug.

LA FRANCE RESTAURANT, *French. Expensive. Great Wall Hotel, Donghuan Bei Road, Tel. 65905566. Credit cards.*

Every Monday evening at 7 pm, you can share General Manager Bruno Huber's passion for jazz in this intimate restaurant while you eat. Reservations are recommended. Recommended also any time are the smoked salmon and Sri Lanka crab parcel with avocado and truffle dressing, lobster cappuccino, fillet of Baramundi on sauteed baby spinach, roasted cherry tomato and balsamic sauce, roast veal tenderloin with caramelized apple, and goose liver topped with Morel mushroom sauce. Then there's the mascarpone cheese with white coffee bean sauce. This is too much for one person, but any or all should make you happy.

YUEN TAI RESTAURANT, *Sichuan. Expensive. 31st floor of the Sheraton Great Wall Hotel, Donghuan Bei Road, Tel. 65005566 X 2295. Open 11:30am-2pm and 6pm-10pm.*

Try the Sichuan beef, Chengdu smoked duck, hot and sour soup, and stir-fried seasonal vegetables. It has a great view too.

SEASONS RESTAURANT, *Kempinski Hotel, Beijing Lufthansa Centre, 50 Liangmaqiao Road, Tel. 64653388. It accepts credit cards.*

It has a great Sunday champagne brunch for Y245 including champagne and beer, Y195 including coffee, tea and soft drinks. Its daily buffet lunch is Y170 and dinner Y180. All these plus 15%. Try other restaurants here too.

The **SHANGHAI RESTAURANT**, *at the Kunlun Hotel. It is open 11:30am-2pm, and 5:30pm-9:30pm. It accepts credit cards.*

This restaurant is especially good. Popular are braised hairy beans Y38, bean curd skin rolled with fungus Y38, crystal shrimps Y138, stir-fried shredded eels Y68, braised Mandarin fish with pine nuts Y320 for 1.5 kilograms, and sauteed egg plant in spicy sauce Y58. Believe me, these taste better than they sound.

The Cantonese restaurant in the Kunlun is also good for lemon chicken, bean soup, and sweet and sour pork.

THE RED BASIL THAI RESTAURANT, *Thai. moderate. Sanyuan Dong Qiao, Third Ring Bei Road, northwest of the Hilton. Tel. 64602339-2344. It is open daily 11:30am-2pm, and 5:30pm-10pm.*

This restaurant has amazing Thai cooking. The numbers are from its menu: We really liked #4, *Kai Hor Bei Teoy*, balls of marinated chicken with *pan dan* leaf; #12, *Yum Woon San Talay*, is a spicy glass noodle salad for Y60; #16, *Tom Yum Koong*, spicy and sour soup with fresh prawns for Y40; #41, broccoli *Phod Pla Muek Koong*, sauteed broccoli with fresh squid for Y40; #60, crystal water chestnuts and coconut cream for Y25; and #63, sweet golden egg yolk silk thread.

SORABOL KOREAN RESTAURANT, *Korean. Basement of the You Yi Shopping Center, Lufthansa Center, 50 Liangmaqiao Road, Tel. 64651845. Open 11am-2:30pm, and 5pm-9:30pm daily It accepts credit cards.*

You can get good *Boolgahlbi* or marinated short ribs for Y75, or *Boolgogi* (marinated beef) for Y60. *Haemool Pahjuhn* (spring onion and seafood pancake) goes for Y60. This restaurant is part of a chain of good Korean restaurants. While you're in the basement, there's a bake shop and edible snacks in the supermarket next door for the budget minded.

HONG KONG FOOD CITY, *Cantonese. Moderate. 9 Dongsanhuan Bei Road,* across from the Hilton. See main listing above.

ADRIA RISTORANTE PIZZERIA CAFE, *Italian. Moderate. It is open 11:30am-2:30pm; 5:30pm-11pm. This is near the Lufthansa Center, Tel. 64600896. A branch is also near the Beijing Hotel on Wangfujing Street, Tel. 65229556.*

This has the best pizza in town, some would say in Asia. It has green and white table cloths with red napkins, and the scrumptious *quattro stagioni* was Y79 for a 12-14" pizza and the *capricciose* was Y82.

MATSUKO, *Japanese. Moderate. Across the street from the Kempinski. Telephone 64654331.*

This modest Japanese restaurant has plastic models of dishes in its window and a good reputation.

NEW ARK RESTAURANT, *Sichuan. Moderate. 300 meters east of the Great Wall Sheraton at 4, Mai Zidian Street, Tel. 85016649.*

This restaurant is used by tour groups and isn't too bad.

YU YANG HOTEL, *Chinese-American cooking. Xin Yuan Xi Li 18 Middle Street, Tel. 64669988.*

This is close to the Canadian and Australian Embassies.

GOLD (OR GOLDEN CAT) RESTAURANT, *at the East Gate of the Tuanjiehu Park, Zhaoyang about two km south of the Great Wall Hotel. Tel. 65985011, 65985113. It is open 7:30 am-6am – yes, all night!*

This is your place for cheap dumplings. It is noted for its 19 varieties of dumplings, each order with five pieces costing about Y3.50. Two orders are enough for a light lunch. In this Chinese courtyard building - with a smelly front room and a backroom decorated with tacky fake flowers – I wondered if President Clinton really ate here as some people claim. While the dumplings are good, and what dumplings aren't, the ambience is far from presidential quality. Note: there is no sign in English on the outside, but it's worth asking around.

Holiday Inn Lido/Harbour Plaza area
BOROM PIMAM THAI RESTAURANT, *Thai. Moderate to expensive. Holiday Inn Lido, Jichang Road, Jiang Tai Road, Tel. 64376688. It is open 11:30am-2pm and 6pm-10pm, and accepts credit cards.*

This outstanding restaurant decorated in traditional Thai style is worth the trip out from downtown. It is another romantic setting, a place for lovers. You can sit on the floor or on chairs. Soups cost Y40-Y45; salads Y45-Y61; vegetarian entrees Y35-Y52; noodles and rice Y45-Y60; fish and seafood Y52-Y175; curries Y40-Y45 for two, Y65-Y75 for four people; and meat sautés Y40-Y60.

TEXAN BAR & GRILL, *Tex Mex. Moderate. Holiday Inn Lido, Jichang Road, Jiang Tai Road, Tel. 64376688. Credit cards accepted.*

This is almost like home. Nachos are Y53, chili con carne Y45, Texas burgers with mushrooms and sour cream Y60, and US Angus beef tenderloin steaks are good and worth Y65 per 100 grams.

YUMMY DIM SUM!

A great buy has been the unlimited **dim sum** *for Y58 at the Harbour Plaza Hotel daily from 11:30am-2:30pm. This Hong Kong hotel claims the largest variety of dim sum in China, and they should know how to make the best. It also has a Japanese lunch buffet for Y118 from 11:30am-2:30pm, and a Friday and Saturday barbecue from 6pm-10pm, all you can eat for Y78. Tel. 64362288. It's at 8 Jiang Tai Xi Road.*

BEIJING LIDO HANCHENG RESTAURANT, *Korean. Moderate. Jiang Tai Road, Tel. 64371517, between the Harbour Plaza and Holiday Inn Lido. It is behind, but has no other relation to the Holiday Inn Lido. It is open 11:30am-9:30pm. and accepts credit cards.*

Good value for your money, an all-you-can-eat barbecue for reasonable prices from a choice of 60 dishes, including dog. You can also order grilled sliced prime rib, *kimchi*, and beef short rib soup. No tablecloths.

HOME AWAY FROM HOME, *Beijing. Moderate. Across the street from the Lido's main entrance. Tel. 64360023.*

In this modest restaurant, good were the barbecued sliced chicken at Y22, sauteed shredded chicken with red pepper for Y12 (a little oily), and stir-fried broccoli for Y18.

CHUAN JIA XIANG JIU JIA, *Sichuan. Moderate. Jianwai Avenue, Fang Guan Suo, Tel. 65957688. No credit cards.*

This is next door to the Home Away from Home and open 11am-11pm weekdays, and closed midnights on weekends. It has good noodles for Y10, and hot sour soup.

Near the Northwest Hotels

NISHIMURA RESTAURANT, *Rabatayaki Japanese. Shangri-La Hotel, 29 Zizhuyuan Road, Tel. 68412211. Accepts credit cards.*

Rabatayaki is Japanese peasant food, where the shaved dried fish wiggles like worms. This restaurant offers *sushi*, grilled vegetables on skewers, steak and onions. Try the delicious sampler for Y120 that arrives in a lacquer box. The atmosphere is casual.

SHANG PALACE, *Chinese. Shangri-La Hotel, 29 Zizhuyuan Road, Tel. 68412211. This restaurant is open 11:30am-2pm, 5:30pm-10pm and accepts credit cards.*

Try the sweet corn soup with crab at Y45 per person, sweet and sour pork with fresh fruits Y52, wok-fried beef with spring onion Y68 and traditional Beijing duck for Y50.

MOSLEM RESTAURANT, *very moderate. Ground floor, Xiyuan Hotel, 1 Sanlihe Road, Tel. 68313388. Credit cards accepted.*

Try the Xinjiang fried rice for Y20, snow peas for Y30, and lamb kebabs for Y8 per skewer. It has a great choose-your-own-ingredients hot pot which included jumbo prawns. You have to get there at the right time because customers grab them all immediately. On the grounds of this hotel is a cheaper snack food street open 11:30am-2:30pm, and 6pm-10pm.

BEIJING'S MOSLEM FARE

*For Moslem food, try **Uygurville**, a street market with cheap food and great shishkebobs, meat on skewers, and nan bread. Also known as **Xinjiang Village** or **Xinjiang Cun**, it's on Baiwanzhuang Xi Road, Ganjiakou. It is north and west of the Holiday Inn Downtown, and south of the Xiyuan Hotel. It is not clean so if you eat there, be careful. Kebobs straight from burning coals should be okay. The best looking are the restaurant at no. 3, the **Huang Tian Fan Jiang**, and another called **Hantan Ri**. No one speaks English. The soups and stews can be very spicy hot, and the food can be great.*

Elsewhere

SHAMIANA RESTAURANT, *Mumbai Indian. Moderate. Holiday Inn Downtown, 98 Beilishi Road, Tel. 68338822. Open 11:30am-2:30pm, 6pm-10:30pm. It accepts credit cards.*

This restaurant is special. It has great seafood and North Indian cooking. Chef Aniruddha Kalele has worked at the five-star Oberoi Hotel in Mumbai where the food is fantastic, and it shows. A set Indian lunch is Y80 plus 15% tax, and *samosas* are Y18, *nawabi tangdi* (chicken drumstick), *kebabs* are Y48, *jhinga masala* (marinated prawns with ginger, garlic, onions, tomatoes and spices) costs Y78, and the chicken *tikka* is Y48.

CAT CALLS & WHISTLES

*Beijing is no longer the quiet, puritanical city of the pre-1980s where you arrived at restaurants at 6pm and had to leave by 9pm. It has recently developed a lot of fun restaurant-bars, like **Henry J. Bean's** in the West Wing Building, China World Trade Center (open Sunday-Thursday 11:30am-1:30am, and Friday-Saturday 11:30am-2:30am). This place has juggling bartenders, waitresses dancing on table tops, and similiarly-inspired customers–if the mood is right. A Canadian band has been playing Monday to Saturday at 8:30pm. Chicken quesadillas with salsa, sour cream and guacamole are Y60, and brownies with real whipping cream Y45. Telephone 65052266 X 6540.*

*Very popular is the **Afanti** or A-fun-ti where guests are crowded together into long tables (a fire trap). The food is Uygur from China's western Xinjiang province, and great. A couple 20-minute shows highlight a dancer, her floor-length hair waving wildly as she twirls in high heels amid whistles and cat calls. She also throws caps into the audience to a heavy tambourine beat and lively middle eastern music. Some diners might get up to join her. It is open 11:30am-10 or 11pm. A full meal costs Y80, Y180, or Y260 each for 10 people, beverages extra. Take your friends. The menu could include a whole sheep, salad, and mutton shashlik or Arabian sweets. Afanti is at Jia 2 Hou Guai Bang Alley, Chaonei Street, Dong Cheng District, Tel. 65272288, 65251071.*

*The **Daijiacun** (Dai Village) **Restaurant** is more subdued but cooks could kill live snakes at your table–if you want. Dai minority women cheerfully dance between tables with the grace usually associated with Thailand. The Dai and Thai are related. They also invite customers to join them. The food is good: bacon cooked in bamboo costs Y30, spicy hot stewed fish in coconut Y30, roast beef on hot stone Y40, and bamboo rice Y10. Open 10am-2:30pm, and 5:30pm-10:30pm with performances starting at 6:30pm. It's at Guandongdian Nanjie, Chaoyang, north of the China World. Ask a Chinese speaker to phone for reservations. Tel.65942455, 65089186.*

***Baikal Cafe** is Russian of course. It's at 2 Beizhong Street, Dongzhimennei, near the Russian embassy. Tel. 64054902, 64052380. It has shows daily between 7:30pm-11:30pm. The restaurant is open 11am-midnight. A Russian band plays nightly.*

*See also **Durty Nellies Irish Pub** and other bars with food below.*

Cheaper Food

For budget travelers, there are the **food stalls** at night near the East Gate of the Forbidden City with food from all over China. They serve everything from scorpions to frogs to corn on the cob and are open from about 6pm. If you want a snack to fill you up, **fast-food Cantonese restaurants** are in the basements of the Jing Guang New World Hotel (shrimp dumplings or noodle soup for Y22), and the Tianlun Dynasty Hotel (Gourmet Bazaar, open 11:30am-2pm; 5:30pm-9:30pm). Shopping malls also have fast food restaurants. You don't have to deprive yourself.

Bake shops are all over. On the southeast side of the Xinqiao Hotel is the good **Xinqiao-Sapporo Mian Bao Dian**, open 7am-9pm. Grocery shops everywhere sell dried noodles in cups, cookies and biscuits. The hot pots can be cheap. One of the branches of **Deli France**, the Hong Kong company, is on the second floor of the Sun Dong An Plaza. It serves relatively cheap sandwiches Y8-Y12.50, soup for Y9.80, fresh milk for Y2.80, soft drinks for Y3.80, milk shakes for Y5.80, and coffee for Y7.80. It is open 9am-9:30pm.

McDonald's are all over Beijing. One is across the street from the zoo. McDonald's will deliver Big Mac's and cheeseburgers for Y100 minimum orders, and you have to pay taxi fare. *Tel. 65513192.* **KFC** will also deliver fried chicken, *Tel. 63034430.*

SEEING THE SIGHTS

I have arranged this section as a six or seven day plan. This is a very heavy schedule and you may have to squeeze your shopping and strolling into the evenings. One really needs a week, and then some. Stay two weeks if you can. Don't miss the **Beijing Opera**, the acrobats, the **Lao She Tea House**, and the pandas. Do see something of modern Beijing too: one of the new malls, perhaps, or the **China World Trade Center** or **Henderson Centre**, and take a ride on the subway. Visit the **Blue Zoo** and relax in a pub. Take advantage of the cheaper prices or unique opportunities for international cultural events like Turandot performed in the Forbidden City (under the baton of Zubin Mehta) or the Johann Strauss Orchestra of Vienna or the Kirov Opera; Beijing isn't just ancient relics. It's becoming a world class, cosmopolitan city.

Tours from major hotels cost about Y310 for the Great Wall and Ming Tombs, Y300 for Forbidden City and Temple of Heaven, and Y280 for Summer Palace and Lama Temple. **Panda Tours**, which operate many of these, can be reached at *Tel. 68036963, or Fax 68037044; E-mail:bjpanda@public.bta.net.cn.* Tours from backpacker hotels cost Y50 to the Great Wall; see Jing Hua Hotel, *Xi Luo Yuan Nan Road, Yongdingmenwai, Tel. 67222211,* listed under hotels above. See also public tour buses.

As a reminder, an asterisk next to a site indicates that the site is genuine and under the protection of the national government.

DAY ONE

Tiananmen Square is 98 acres and great for kite-flying in the spring. Try to imagine 1966 at the beginning of the Cultural Revolution, when a million school children filled this square, chanting slogans and waving Chairman Mao's little red book of quotations. The father of Communist China stood in front and acknowledged the screams and cheers of the youngsters. Besides giving them a vacation from school, he also gave them a mandate to travel around the country on the trains with room and board in each city, all free.

Unfortunately, the Cultural Revolution had a serious downside as well, with many people killed and persecuted throughout the country. It was in effect a civil war.

It will be hard for many foreigners to forget the much televised, idealistic young students demonstrating nonviolently for democracy in early 1989. An estimated 300 to 3,000 people were killed in or around the square in what the Chinese government calls "the quelling of the counter-revolutionary rebellion." Chinese government accounts of the turmoil and western sources do not agree, as you might expect.

The square is bounded on the north by **Tiananmen Gate** and on the west by the **Great Hall of the People**. On the east is the **Museum of the Chinese Revolution** and the **Museum of Chinese History**, and on the south you can't miss the imposing **Qianmen Gate**. In the center, from the north to south, are the **Monument to the People's Heroes** and the **Chairman Mao Memorial Hall**. The portrait of Chairman Mao on Tiananmen Gate is changed every year on October 1.

Let's start with **The Great Hall of the People**, also known as People's Congress Hall, China's parliament, *Tel. 66801188*. It is open to tourists 8:30am-3pm if not used for meetings. Built in 1959, the Great Hall measures 171,800 square meters. Three main sections include a 5000-seat banquet hall, a three-story, 10,000-seat auditorium, and lounges in the style of each of the provinces. To some observers, the People's Congress is merely a rubber-stamp group of representatives. To others, it is a forum for the opinions of citizens.

Magnificent, beautiful **Qianmen Gate** to the south has a folk museum. To the south of that is Dazhalan, the old Chinese shopping area.

THE GATES OF BEIJING

Beijing's gates are marvelous. Each had a very specific purpose; for example, night soil could only go through Andingmen in the north and prisoners to be executed plodded through the west gate, Xuanwumen. Departing soldiers marched through another of the north gates even if they had to fight in the south. The impressive Deshengmen (Victory Gate) can be climbed.

In the **Monument to the People's Heroes**, the sculptures represent the burning of opium and the Opium War, 1840-42; the Taiping Heavenly Kingdom, 1851-64; the Revolution of 1911; the May 4, 1919 demonstration against the Versailles Treaty and for the New Cultural Movement (calling for literature in the colloqial rather than the generally incomprehensible classical language); the May 30, 1925 Incident in Shanghai, a protest against foreign powers in China after a Chinese worker was killed by a Japanese foreman. Look also for the August 1, 1927 uprising in Nanchang and the Anti-Japanese War, 1937-45.

In April 1976, during the Qingming (Ching Ming) festival, when the dead are honored, attempts by the Gang of Four to remove wreaths brought by private citizens in memory of Premier Zhou Enlai were resisted by pro-Zhou supporters at this monument. Hundreds were wounded and thousands arrested. This protest is now referred to as the April Fifth Movement against the Gang of Four, and encouraged pro-Zhou politicians like Deng Xiaoping to attempt to overthrow them. In 1989, this monument was central to the student demonstrators.

The **Chairman Mao Memorial Hall** *(Tel. 65131130, 65249831, open 9:30am-3 or 4pm daily)* was built in 1977. Whether it remains open depends on the political climate. In this mausoleum rest the remains of China's great leader. The simple white building, with 44 granite columns and glazed yellow trim, is 33.6 meters high and 105 meters square.

Foreign tourists used to get priority to enter but now there's no distinction, and the visit takes less than 30 minutes. As a token of respect, visitors are advised not to wear bright colors, especially red, but I've never seen anyone stopped. No cameras or purses are allowed. You first enter the North Hall where there is a seated, three-meter-high marble statue of the leader. Then, quietly, two by two, you enter the Central Hall where Chairman Mao (1893-1976) lies in state.

The **Museum of Chinese History** *(Tel. 65128321, open 8:30am-3:30pm, closed Mondays)* has the best of China's artifacts but it has only a few titles in English. Books with photos of the collection are Y30 and Y98, a little expensive just to identify what you see. The museum is divided into four sections: primitive society, slave society, feudal society, and semi-colonial-semi-feudal society. You can walk through without absorbing much in an hour, it is so large. You need at least a half day to do it justice. Please take it in short doses, especially if your feet tire easily. The entrance to the museum is opposite the Great Hall of the People. The history museum is to the right.

Relics here date from 1.7-million-year-old pre-human teeth to 1911. They include a model of the cave where the Peking Man was found. Also on display are a 14th-century B.C. ivory cup inlaid with jade, a Shang bronze wine vessel with four protruding ram's heads, and a Western Zhou sewer pipe with the head of a tiger. Intriguing, too, are a model of a Warring States irrigation system, tomb figures galore, and a model of a first-century B.C. wheel used to operate a bellows to melt iron. Here, too, is the Flying Horse of Gansu, which people around the world waited many hours to see when it was exhibited abroad. No queues here!

There is also a model of a 1700-year-old drum chariot with a figure of a child on top, always pointing south, and another miniature drum chariot with a figure that beats a drum every 500 meters, a Yuan water clock, and some Yuan rockets attached to spears. I can only whet your appetite. It is best to take a friend who reads Chinese.

Tiananmen (Gate of Heavenly Peace) is the second most famous structure in China. From its high balcony the imperial edicts were read, and this is where, on October 1, 1949, Chairman Mao Zedong (Mao Tse-tung) proclaimed the People's Republic of China. It is a symbol of old and new China. The country's leaders frequently appear here on national days to review the parades and festivities. It was built in 1651 and stands 33.7 meters high. The rostrum where Chairman Mao stood is open to tourists for a fee.

Through the gate under Chairman Mao's portrait and to the left is **Zhongshan Park**, the memorial park to Dr. Sun Yat-sen. To the right is **Working People's Cultural Park**. These two parks are great for an early morning walk because of the magnificent walls, towers, gates, moats, and pavilions, and also because of the people limbering up for the day. You might hear some very beautiful voices resound off the walls from very shy singers hiding behind bushes and screens. Where else can they practise without neighbors complaining?

In the square between the two parks is a tiny white marble pavilion looking much like a Japanese lantern. In imperial times, if an official made a serious error, his black gauze cap was placed inside and he was taken out to be executed at the *Wumen* in front of the palace. Commoners were executed at the marketplace seven km southwest of here near the Qianmen Hotel.

The **Gu Gong** or **Imperial Palace** (also known as **Palace Museum** or **Forbidden City**), *Tel. 65132255, is open 8:30am-4:30pm (summer) or 9am-4pm (winter) and costs Y30-Y50.* No one is admitted after 3:30pm. Visitors usually enter by the Wumen (Meridian Gate) inside the Tiananmen Gate between the two above-mentioned parks, and head north. An acoustiguide, recorded by British actor **Roger Moore**, giving details about a limited area, is recommended for travelers without guides for additional payment. You can photograph exteriors with still or video cameras, but not interiors. You can also enter from the north gate but most use the south. Except for pavilions on the right and the left of the north-south axis, you cannot enter buildings. A toilet is at the entrance to the left.

The Gu Gong was the home and audience hall of the Ming and Qing emperors. Many buildings here are as the Qing left them, minus relics now in the National Palace Museum in Taiwan. Many of the buildings are exhibition halls for historic treasures from all over China. Thousands of imperial robes are stored here. You can see the queue of the Last Emperor Pu Yi, which he cut off himself, his bicycle, and his cricket box. To walk at a leisurely pace from one end to the other takes about 30 minutes, but to explore it thoroughly takes at least a full day, some would say a week. Tour groups usually whiz through the center, following the north-south axis, the center of the world. If you want to see it all, and the side chambers are all worth seeing, see the center first, and then go back for the east chambers, following the signs to the important exhibits. Then see the west-side exhibits.

In some places, visitors have to pay for bootees to put over street shoes to protect the floors. You might want to carry a pair of heavy socks and wear those instead. The bootees fall apart.

The Forbidden City was originally built from 1406 to 1420 as the palace of the Ming emperors. It lies on more than 720,000 square meters (178 acres) of land. Over 8600 rooms cover a total floor space of about 150,000 square meters. The surrounding imperial red wall is over 10 meters high. Only imperial palaces were allowed to have yellow ceramic roofs. (Commoners could only use gray.) This massive city was built by 100,000 artisans and a million laborers.

Toward the end of the Qing, 280,000 taels of silver were needed annually to maintain the palace, the money collected in taxes and rents from 658,000 acres of royal estates. 2000 ladies-in-waiting and 3,000 eunuchs served here. Some eunuchs became more powerful than the self-indulgent emperors. Sacked by foreign powers in 1900, the Forbidden City was restored and now maintains a permanent staff of painters and carpenters so that every 20 years all the buildings are renewed.

The Forbidden City is divided into two major sections: the outer palace (for business) and the inner residential courts. Directly inside the

Meridian Gate at the south entrance are the five marble bridges "like arrows reporting on the emperor to Heaven." The River of Gold below is shaped like a bow. Note the gates; red was used only for important structures. Each has 81 studs - nine times nine, an imperial number. Seven layers of brick line the courtyards so no one could tunnel in from below. Note the white squares, on each of which a royal guard stood whenever the emperor ventured past.

Throughout the palace, huge cauldrons of water stand ready for possible fires. On the north side, beneath the cauldrons, are air vents that fan fires set in winter to keep the water inside from freezing. Note the lack of hiding places for possible assassins.

The first building is the Taihedian (Tai Ho Tien; **Hall of Supreme Harmony**), the most stately of all the buildings. It is surrounded by incense burners, 18 bronze ones representing the then 18 provinces, and others in the form of a stork (longevity) and a dragon-headed tortoise (strength and endurance). Note the copy of an ancient sundial and the small openings on the side of the pavilion to allow air to circulate inside. This building was used for major ceremonies like the emperor's birthday, for imperial edicts, and for state affairs.

Imagine the area in front of the Hall covered with silk-gowned ministers and officials kneeling in rows, their heads to the ground while smoke poured from incense burners and musicians played on the balcony. Can you see the child emperor being carried by a palanquin above them to the highly carved throne? If you can't, try to see the Chinese historical movie *Power Behind the Throne* and the American movie *The Last Emperor*. Good books to read are *Inside Stories of the Forbidden City*, published in China, and E. Behr's *The Last Emperor*.

Each of the 18-meter-high cedar pillars was made from one piece of wood. Each of the floor tiles took 136 days to bake, after which it was immersed in oil for a permanent polish. The bricks are solid, about five inches thick and 18 inches square. The base and throne are carved sandalwood.

The second building on the north-south axis is the Zhonghedian (**Hall of Complete Harmony**), used by the emperor to receive his ministers, to rest, and to dress before he entered the Taihedian. The two Qing sedan chairs here were for traveling within the palace. The braziers were for heat, the four cylindrical burners for sandalwood incense. Note the imperial dragon symbols on the ceiling.

The Baohedian (**Hall of Preserving Harmony**) the most decorative of these halls, was for imperial banquets and, during the Qing, the retesting of the top scorers in the national examinations. Note the ceilings and beams. Behind this hall, between the stairways, is a giant carving of dragons from one piece of marble, 16.5 meters by three meters and

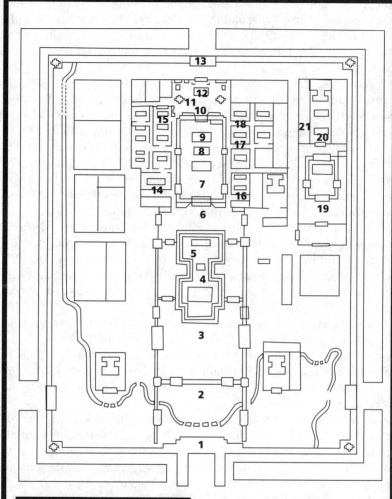

FORBIDDEN CITY PALACE MUSEUM

1 Wumen Gate
2 Tianhemen Gate
3 Taihedian Hall
4 Zhonghedian Hall
5 Baohedian Hall
6 Qianqingmen Gate
7 Qianqinggong Palace
8 Jiaotaidian Hall
9 Kunninggong Palace
10 Imperial Garden

11 Thousand Autumn Pavilion
12 Qinandian Hall
13 Shenwumen Gate
14 Yanxindian Hall
15 Chuxiugong Palace
16 Hall of Bronzes
17 Hall of Ceramics
18 Hall of Arts & Crafts of the Ming
   & Qing Dynasties
19 Hall of Paintings
20 Hall of Jewelry
21 Qianlong Garden

weighing about 250 tons. Anyone caught touching this imperial symbol was executed. The carving and the timbers were brought here in winter by sliding them over ice made from water out of wells especially sunk for the occasion. Nothing was too extravagant for the representative of Heaven!

A photographer is stationed between two of the large pavilions and can take photos of you or your group in the morning, and deliver them as ordered to your restaurant at lunch time or to your hotel for Y60 each with booklet. These are quite good and you don't pay until delivery.

Several buildings on both sides of these main halls were used for study, lectures, a library, and even a printing shop. Beyond this third hall are the Inner Courts, the three main buildings, similar to the three in the outer palace; the Qianqingong (**Hall of Heavenly Purity**) where the emperors used to live and where deceased emperors lay in state.

Cixi (Tzu Hsi), the infamous Empress Dowager, received foreign envoys in the Jiaotaidian (**Hall of Union**) where ceremonies involving empresses took place. (Women were not allowed in the outer palace!) The Kunninggong (**Palace of Earthly Tranquility**) was a residence in the Ming and a shrine in the Qing. One of the Qing emperors used its eastern room as a bridal chamber.

East of the Kunninggong is a hall where **clocks** from all over the world are exhibited, gifts from foreign missions. In the back of the inner court is the Imperial Garden, where you can find a snack bar. The Imperial family sipped tea, played chess, and meditated in this beautifully designed but tiny garden. Can you imagine living in this crowded space with little or no grass?

Then, continuing northward, you arrive at the back gate where tour groups usually meet their buses, poor things, because they miss out on a lot. But you're not finished yet! Retracing your steps to the entrance of the inner court, turn left (east) at the Qianqinggong, past the washrooms and the Nine Dragon Screen, and then turn left again.

Here are several pavilions with exhibitions well worth seeing, including a stunning collection of gold artifacts, bells, incense burners, table service (with jade handles), and scepters. There are also precious Buddhist relics and the biggest jade sculpture in China, a five-ton Ming statue depicting one of the earliest attempts in the Xia Dynasty to control the Yellow River. Look for paintings and antique jewelry, pottery and bronzes. Also notable, north of this area, is the 12-inch diameter well in which the obviously-thin Pearl Concubine was drowned by a eunuch after she incurred the wrath of the Empress Dowager in 1900. A clean toilet is in this area near the jewelry exhibit.

In each building, look at the ceilings and the palace lanterns, the distinctive blue Manchu cloisonne, and the western clocks. Where were the Imperial toilets? the kitchens? Think of the children who grew up within these walls and never set foot outside! Think of the eunuchs who gave up their manhood for a job that would benefit their families!

There are also two halls of ancient bronzes, and a Qing opera exhibit. Some have titles in English. American Express has placed wooden signboards in the palace with historical information in English but there aren't enough.

There are also exhibit halls in the west side too.

Jingshan (Coal) **Hill**, outside the north gate of the palace, was originally the site of a Ming coal pile. It was built with earth excavated from the moats and is 43 meters high. It is now a park with a good view of the Forbidden City and the lakes to the west and north. As the Manchus were breaking into the city, the last of the Ming emperors hung himself on a locust tree at the foot of the hill on the east side.

The ***Tiantan** or **Temple of Heaven**, *Tel. 67022242)*, is about five km south of the Forbidden City. People usually enter by the south gate and exit by the east gate. Think of the processions of incense-swinging priests, spear-bearing palace guards, and the palaquin bearers carrying the emperor, all marching from the palace unseen by anyone else. Setting eyes on the emperor was a crime punishable by death.

The temple is set in the middle of a 667-acre park with many pine and cypress trees, some over 500 years old. Give yourself at least 20 minutes for a quick look, an hour for a more thorough tour. The Temple of Heaven was built in the same period as the Forbidden City (1420), and ranks among the most famous structures in China. It was used a couple of times a year when the emperor, bearing all the sins of the Chinese people, humbled himself before Heaven and performed the rituals calculated to bring good harvests. The temple has two concentric walls, both round at the north and straight at the south, heaven being round and earth square, or didn't you know!

To the south is the **Imperial Vault of Heaven**, originally built in 1530 and rebuilt in 1752. In this building without horizontal beams were stored the tablets of the God of Heaven, the Wind God, the Rain God, etc. Sacrifices were made on the circular Sacrificial Altar on the winter solstice. The surrounding wall has a strange echo effect. You can hear people talking softly beside it from an unusual distance but not if a lot of noisy people are around. Also count the number of stone slabs on the floor, staircases, and balustrades. They are in multiples of nine.

The raised, 360-meter passage between the main buildings is the Red Stairway Bridge. To the north is the famous Qiniandian (**Hall of Prayer for Good Harvests**) with triple eaves, 38 meters high and 30 meters in diameter. The four central columns represent the four seasons. Around these four are two rings of 12 columns each, the inner symbolizing the 12 months and the outer the 12 divisions of day and night. Here, the emperor performed the rites on the 15th day of the first moon of the lunar calendar.

DAY TWO
The Hutong Tour

This tour was started by a photographer obsessed with recording the old architecture and trying to save it. It can now be booked direct or with travel agencies.

Before the 1970s, the whole of Beijing consisted mainly of these tiny courtyard homes now quickly disappearing. The privately operated Hutong Tourist Agency has at least 50 bicycle rickshaws and drivers. While blankets are provided in cold weather, we do recommend it only when it's warm and dry.

The three-hour tour starts twice a day from 100 meters west of the north entrance to Beihai Park. Look for tricycles with maroon canopies. It goes past Xi Sha Lake to the **Drum Tower** on the north-south axis with 69 high stairs. Here is an exhibit of hutong photographs, one 13th century Yuan dynasty drum and a good view. From there you go to the old Silver Ingot Bridge and one of the houses. We had tea with a 78-year old Communist cadre, then went to the other extreme to Prince Gong's digs where over tea in cracked crockery you can chuckle about the piece of the Great Wall he had built to remind him of his Manchu past. The mansion was originally built by a Ming eunuch in the southern style in 1776-1785.

Prince Gong's Mansion *is at 23 Lu Yin Street and can be visited even if you're not on a tour. It is open 8:30am-4pm daily.* It was owned at one time by the great-uncle of the last emperor. Go for the pretty garden, the theatre, and the traditional style buildings.

Some tours then go for lunch in a home, and try to make *jiao zi* dumplings. The delicious home-cooked meal and opportunity to talk with ordinary Beijing inhabitants is frequently one of the highlights of a tour. Did you know garbage is collected there three times a day? and the postman comes twice a day?

Contact: **Beijing Hutong Tourist Agency**, *26 Di An Men Xi Avenue, Xi Cheng, 100009, Tel. 66159097, Fax 64002787*. Ask for Tony He. Tours leave at 8:50am and 1:50pm.

Next head over to **Beihai Park** (North Sea Park), open 7:30am-4pm, only a few blocks west of Coal Hill. If you are short of time, just look for the Baita Shan (**White Dagoba Hill**) and then the **Nine Dragon Screen** (1756) on the opposite side of the lake. While the whole area is a historic site protected by the State Council, these are the highlights of this big, 168-acre park full of intriguing old buildings, the recently renovated **Jingxinzhai** (Serenity Study), winding paths, and interesting rocks that could take a half day to explore. Rowboats are for hire and, in the winter, ice skating on the lake is an exotic experience (but bring your own skates).

The **Fang Shan Restaurant** near the White Dagoba serves the same fancy, delicate dishes (well, almost!) once presented to the Empress Dowager.

In the 10th century (Liao), an imperial residence was built on the site and called Precious Islet Imperial Lodging. In the 12th century (Jin), auxiliary palaces were constructed here and a lake excavated, the earth used to build the artificial hills and the *Round City** at the southern edge. Rocks from Kaifeng were also used. During the Yuan, the Qionghua Islet was expanded and the palace of Kublai Khan was made the center of the city. This palace is no longer standing.

Also on the islet, the 35.9 meter-high, bell-shaped **White Dagoba** was first constructed in 1271. The current stupa was built in 1731.

Also noteworthy is Kublai Khan's 3000-liter jade liquor container (1265) and the Jade Buddha in **Chengguang Hall** in the Round City on the mainland, by the White Dagoba causeway.

The **Nine Dragon Screen** on the north side of the lake is of glazed brick and is five by 27 by 1.2 meters. Successive dynasties added buildings to Beihai, but this park was also looted by the foreign powers in 1900.

Zhongnanhai, south of Beihai, has not been generally open to the public because it contains the residences and offices of China's leaders. Very special tour groups have successfully requested a visit. The Qing Guangxu (Kuang Hsu) emperor, who attempted to make modern reforms, much to the displeasure of the Empress Dowager Cixi, was imprisoned here during the winters when he was not at the Summer Palace. The historically important Pavilion of Purple Light and Fairy Tower were recently repaired. The South Gate, brilliant red and fancy, is on Chang'an Avenue west of the Tiananmen, too prominent to miss.

DAY THREE

The Summer Palace, Temple of the Azure Clouds, Temple of the Sleeping Buddha, and Fragrant Hill are all within 10 km of each other, 20-30 km northwest of Tiananmen. Because of traffic jams, avoid this area on the weekends.

The **Summer Palace** or Yiheyuan (Garden of Cultivating Peace) is about 15 km from downtown and was opened to the public in 1925, *Tel. 62881144*. It can be reached on public buses 801 from Liangmaqiao. It is open 8:30am-5:30pm or 6pm, but parts are open earlier. A visit to this 717-acre garden usually takes half a day. It is three-quarters water. Originally built in the 12th century, it was expanded in 1750 for the 60th birthday of Emperor Qianlong's mother and burned in 1860 by the British-French army. It was rebuilt by the Empress Dowager Cixi (Tzu Hsi) on the occasion of her 60th birthday (1895) and financed with funds meant for the Chinese navy. It was badly damaged by the foreign powers in 1900; the existing buildings were restored in 1903.

The imperial court lived here every year, when possible, from April 15 to October 15, receiving diplomats and conducting business in the **Renshoudian (Hall of Longevity and Benevolence)**. Empress Dowager Cixi, who was the power behind the throne from 1861 to 1908, lived in this hall near the Deheyuan (Grand Stage) where she could indulge in her passion for theatricals. The stage floor is hollow so that ghosts could emerge from it. The Grand Stage is now a separate museum requiring an additional fee. It contains Cixi's jewelry and dinnerware, and wax figures of Cixi and two imperial concubines. Attendants are in Qing palace costumes and you can have your photo taken in costume here. In the exhibition hall behind the stage is the 1898 automobile given to the emperor by General Yuan Shikai.

Twenty-eight ladies in waiting, twenty eunuchs, and eight female officials waited on the Empress Dowager. For lunch, she was offered at least 128 courses daily.

In the **Hall of Jade Ripples**, to the south of the main entrance, she kept the Guangxu (Kuang Hsu) emperor imprisoned every summer from 1898 to 1908 after he tried unsuccessfully to institute reforms to modernize China and to take his rightful power back. Note the walls around the compound. The rooms here and elsewhere are furnished as they were then.

The **Long Corridor** extends 728 meters along the lake to the famous **Qingyan** (Marble) **Boat** whose second floor is actually wood. There are 1,400 paintings here; some guides say 10,000, a spectacular display. To the north up the hill are the Hall of Dispelling Clouds, the Tower of Buddhist Incense, and the Temple of the Sea of Wisdom where the empress used to hold her birthday celebrations and religious services. The Xiequyuan (Garden of Harmonious Interests) was designed like the Jichangyuan (Garden) in Wuxi. Also on the hill is a Tibetan-style **Lama Temple**. Across Kunming Lake is a 17-arch bridge and, on an island, the Dragon King Temple.

The **Summer Palace Hotel** is in the garden, near the Hall of Scalloped Clouds, an exotic experience if you don't mind being isolated. Accessible from the palace is **Suzhou Street**, reconstructed on its original site. Built in the 18th century, and destroyed in 1860 by foreign soldiers, it was the shopping area used by palace residents. Attendants in Manchu dress give demonstrations of crafts and music. Photos are best late morning and early afternoon.

Visitors usually enter by the east gate and walk to the marble boat and onwards to the west gate. Or you can take a boat back the way you came and end up at the east side again near the 24-arch bridge. The boat trip costs Y4 per person and gives another view of the palace.

Northwest of the Summer Palace are the **Beijing Botanical Garden** (Y4) and the **Temple of the Sleeping Buddha** (also known as Wofusi, or Temple of Universal Spiritual Awakening). Do not expect to do any of these western temples in a hurry as a lot of walking is involved from the parking lot. The **Temple of the Sleeping Buddha** was first built in the Tang and reconstructed and renamed in the Yuan, Ming, and Qing. The lacquered bronze Sakyamuni, which was cast in 1331 (Yuan), is 5.33 meters long and weighs 54 tons. The Buddha here is giving his last words to his disciples before his transition from earth. Because he is barefoot, successions of emperors have presented the statue with 11 pairs of huge hand-made cloth shoes, which are on display in the same room. You can also stay in the temple overnight.

The **Biyunsi (Temple of Azure Clouds)** is less than a kilometer from the Fragrant Hill Hotel but it is a kilometer from the parking lot, and open 8am-4:30pm. It is more important than the Sleeping Buddha because of its stunning collection of religious statues and the Diamond Throne Pagoda. The Biyun was first built in the Yuan as a nunnery. During the Ming, it was the burial place for powerful eunuchs. In 1748, Emperor Qianlong ordered built the Hall of Five Hundred Arhats and the Diamond Throne (or Vajra Throne) Pagoda. The 508 gilded, wooden Buddhist saints are life-size and strikingly beautiful, each different, and protected behind dirty glass. How many are not sitting? Which have two heads?

In 1925, the body of Dr. Sun Yat-sen lay in state at this temple until the completion of his mausoleum in Nanjing. A tiny museum is at the spot. The unique 34.7-meter Diamond Throne Pagoda consists of five small pagodas in the Indian style and has some excellent carvings.

Xiang Shan (Fragrant Hill) Park *is open roughly 7:30am-5:00pm, Tel. 62591155.* It was a 150-hectare (384 acre) hunting ground for many emperors. A 20-minute chairlift to the top of the mountain now gives a spectacular view of the area, especially in autumn, when the air is less dusty and some leaves are red. The highest peak here is 557 meters above sea level. The lift goes by a small Glazed Pagoda, a western-style mansion that was presumably the hunting lodge, and a Tibetan-style temple, which you can inspect later.

If time permits on the way back to town, glimpse the **Yuanmingyuan ruins** *(Y3), open 7am-7pm, Tel. 2551488.* This Garden of Clear Ripples was built in an area full of bubbling springs and was used as an imperial resort from the 11th century. A major palace was built here in 1690 and later rebuilt as a favorite 160-hectare palace garden by Emperor Qianlong, with buildings copied from Suzhou, Hangzhou, and Yangzhou. Sacked by

Anglo-French forces in 1860 (after Qing forces tortured their envoys), it was partially repaired only to be destroyed again in 1900. Foreigners wanted to punish the emperor for the siege of the legations.

The few remains of this Garden of Gardens and Palace of Palaces can be glimpsed in 20 minutes if you enter by the correct gate. But it's a good place to walk and you might want to stay longer. Enough remains of the marble archways of the Evergreen Palace to show the influence of the European missionaries who helped design it early in the 1750s. Since the imperial families favored the Yuanmingyuan over the Imperial Palace, they kept their most precious treasures and books here. The 1860 burning took two days and is documented in a good Chinese-made movie, *The Burning of the Summer Palace*. One of the best accounts in English is Garnet J. Wolseley's *Narrative of the War with China in 1860*. A small exhibition near the entrance tells the story. The maze and some other buildings have been reconstructed.

DAY FOUR

Some people prefer to take their own box lunch to the *Great Wall even though restaurants are available. For an excursion to the Great Wall *(Tel. 63011864)*, see *The Great Wall* section later in this chapter. Remember, Badaling is not the only place to see it, nor is it the best.

The **Ming Tombs**, *Shisan Ling, are among the most famous sights in China. Open daily 8 or 8:30am-4 or 4:30pm, the tombs are usually combined with a trip to the Great Wall at Badaling another 30 km beyond that. The Tombs are about a 60-km, one-hour drive northwest of Tiananmen.

These 13 imperial tombs were built from 1409 to 1644 and spread over 40 square kilometers. Each tomb consists of a Soul Tower, a Sacrificial Hall, and an underground palace where the bodies were placed, surrounded by a wall. Approaching from the south, you can see a big, carved white marble archway, erected in 1590, beyond which are the Great Red Gate, ornamental pillars, and the Tablet Pavilion. The Sacred Way has 24 stone animals (lions, unicorns, camels and elephants), 12 larger-than-life-size humans (military officers and government officials), and an army of enterprising hawkers (also an old China tradition) selling everything from furs, porcelain, and fruit to junk.

Two of the tombs are set up for visitors: **Chang Ling** is the biggest and earliest which you cannot enter. But there is a good museum there with the gold crown, headdresses, jade belt – items found in the tombs. **Ding Ling**, has been excavated and can be entered. It is the tomb of the 13th Ming Emperor Wanli, who ruled for 48 years, starting at age 10. The tomb was begun when he was 22 years old. It took six years and cost eight million taels of silver to build. *Tel. 60761196*, open 9am-4:30pm.

The underground palace consists of three halls, the central one with passages to annex chambers, totaling 1195 square meters. The marble doors each weigh four tons and were closed from the inside by propping two large stone poles against them. Note the two triangular depressions in the ground inside the door where the poles rested. Note also the blue and white porcelain jars with the dragons, which were half filled with oil when the tomb was opened. The oil was burned to create an oxygen-free vacuum inside.

In the central hall are three marble thrones, two for the empresses, one for the emperor, all real. Note the Five Altar Pieces and the porcelain lamp. The rear hall has the three coffins and plaster replicas of 26 chests.

The best place for lunch is the restaurant at the nearby **Beijing International Golf Course** but it's expensive. Some tour groups go to the not-too-bad **Nine Dragon Palace Restaurant** (pay 30 jiao extra for toilet). Its setting on a reservoir is lovely, and the deep-fried tomatoes and fries are good, but otherwise don't expect much. It is two km south of the gate to the Spirit Way.

If you have time, you should also wander around the other tombs, which are not repaired and are usually free of tourists. Enjoy the rural beauty. These others have not been opened because of the high cost of careful archaeological work. Besides, no one knows where the entrances are because their builders were executed and no records have survived. The exterior of the tombs and the Great Wall are best seen at dusk, when one feels the presence of ghosts. Seeing weeds growing on imperial terraces and birds making nests on once glorious beams is a good time to reflect on life and death.

The Beijing Municipal Government and a Japanese firm have opened a recreation complex nearby with roller coasters, ferris wheels, hotels and camel-racing tracks – to break the spell.

DAY FIVE

Head for the furthest first. The **Arthur M. Sackler Museum of Art and Archaeology** is at **Beijing University**, *Tel. 62501667, 62751667*, open 9am-4:30pm. You can go to the west gate and bear left once inside. It's the other side of the pond. Buses 801 and 332 go by. The Sackler contains fourteen galleries from Paleolithic to Ming from the university's own collection: 1100 year old silver chopsticks, and an ancient bronze rabbit. It is worth the trip to see these, and this beautiful 100 year old university that was involved in the Tiananmen demonstrations.

Next is the Da Zhong Si, the **Temple of the Great Bell** with its 6.75 meter tall and up to 2400 year old bells. It is at *31A Beisanhuan Xi Road, Haidian District, Tel. 62550843*, Y10 entrance fee and open 8:30am-4:30pm. This temple houses over 40 different ancient bells. The most spectacular was cast during the reign of Emperor Yongle (1403-1425 A.D.) in a clay mold and weighs 46.5 tons. How did they bring it here without a crane and truck? In 1733, the Chinese slid it on ice in winter or on wheat shells in summer and put it on a mound. After attaching the bell onto the beams, they dug out the mound and built the hall around it. The 220,000 handsome Chinese characters decorating it are Buddhist scriptures and prayers.

The other bells in the exhibit were for various purposes. In religious ceremonies they drove away worldly worries and attracted the attention of the gods. Some bells here announced the time of day and the closing of the city gates. Some were used in music rituals. (See also Wuhan.) Look for the exhibit on how the bells were made.

Do visit the **Beijing Art Museum** in the exotic 16th century Wanshou temple complex across the road from the Shangri-La Hotel. It has 18 larger-than-life arhats or saints, Tibetan statues, and multi-colored *shoushan* stone carvings. It has imperial seals and robes, paintings, pottery, jades, and buddhas–a small but beautiful collection worth making a trip out here to see. It is open 9am-4 or 4:30pm and closed on Mondays, has titles in English and costs Y10. *Tel. 68413382.*

The **Beijing Zoo** is across the main street from the Xiyuan Hotel, *Tel. 68314411,* and is open 7:30am-5pm daily. The pandas are near the main entrance to the left. The zoo is currently constructing a huge aquarium here with 800 species of saltwater fish, 500 species of fresh water fish and sea mammals. It will have 50,000 specimens.

The **Blue Zoo ocean aquarium** is at *Worker's Stadium (South Gate), Tel. 65913397, 65913398 X 1178, Fax 65935262. E-mail:market@ public.bta.net.cn.* This is a New Zealand joint venture. A 120-meter clear, acryllic tunnel allows 6000 sharks, rays, sturgeons, and other creatures to swim over and beside you as you pass by on a moving sidewalk. The sharks are fed by a human in scuba gear at 10:30am and 2:30pm and also on request. Staff give lectures for no extra charge (English on request). It is open 9am-8pm daily, and probably to 8pm in the summer. Adults pay Y75, children under 18 years Y50, family of three Y150, and kids under one meter free.

DAY SIX

The *Yonghegong (**Lama Temple**), is spectacular. *It is open roughly 9am-4:00pm, and maybe closed Mondays, Tel. 64041408. The entrance fee is Y15.* Count on spending at least 40 minutes here. First built in 1694, this Mongolian-Tibetan temple is at the Yonghegong subway exit. Beautifully renovated, it reveals pavilion after pavilion of increasingly startling figures, the largest in the back hall 18 meters high. This Buddha was carved from one piece of sandalwood from Tibet and the temple was built around it.

The steles are incised with Han, Manchurian, Mongolian, and Tibetan script. The statues in the main halls resemble those in most Buddhist temples, but some statues wear the pointed Himalayan caps and white Tibetan scarves, a gift of respect. The building on either side have the more typical Tibetan demons, human skulls, and *tankas*. Another admission ticket is required for the exhibition hall with fine silver utensils worth seeing.

The Yonghegong was built in 1694 as an imperial residence for Emperor Yongzheng, then still a prince. It was transformed into a temple in 1744 during Emperor Qianlong's reign. Prayer wheels are on sale.

This temple was part of his attempt to unite the Han, Manchu, Mongol, and Tibetan peoples into one country. He also took a Uygur princess into his court, one of his favorite empresses. For more on Tibetan Buddhism, see also Lhasa and Chengde.

The Shudian (**Capital Museum**), in the old Yuan dynasty **Confucius Temple**, is almost across Yonghegong Avenue from the Lama Temple. It is at *3-13 Guozijian Street, Dongcheng District, Tel. 64012118*, and is open daily except perhaps Mondays, 9am-4pm. It is the second largest Confucian temple in China. The exhibits on Beijing history, Qing armor, and the stone drums are worth seeing. Look for maps and relics of the old Yuan city too.

If you have more time and interest, Beijing has at least 101 museums and many other things to see. Listed here are only the most prominent. Stay another week or even a month if you want to see it all!

Walks

Carry a scarf or mask to cover your nose if the polluted air bothers you. You might begin with the area north of the Xinqiao Hotel and south of the Beijing Hotel for the old European architecture. This **foreign**

FOLLOW PRESIDENT CLINTON'S BEIJING ITINERARY!

In 1998, President Clinton took the Hutong Rickshaw tour, visited the Great Wall at Mutianyu, and went to the Forbidden City and Beijing University. Daughter Chelsea visited the Summer Palace. They or their staff ate at the Golden Cat Restaurant. A state dinner was held in the Great Hall of the People and the president stayed at the Daiyutai State Guest House. The press corps and secret service stayed at the Shangri-La Hotel and press conferences were held there.

legation area was under siege during the Boxer uprising from June 13, 1900. On June 20, most foreign diplomats and missionaries and 2,000 Chinese Christian refugees took shelter in the British Legation until the International Relief Force arrived on August 13. That British Legation building has been torn down to make way for a housing project. But many of the old buildings are still there, some now used by the Beijing Municipality and the Communist Party.

Head north and west for the **Forbidden City** and the two parks in front of it. This area is full of old houses with antique doors, carvings, grinding stones used as steps, and fancy, carved stone door hinges. Such crowded courtyards are fascinating and are an endangered species. The names of the alleys evoke another age: Nai Zi Hutong (Wet Nurse Lane) was where the new mothers who nursed the imperial babies lived. Flower Lane was for those who hand made all the silk flowers for the imperial ladies. There were also Goldsmith Lane, Laundry Lane, and Bowstrings Lane.

NIGHTLIFE & ENTERTAINMENT

There's a lot of good stuff here: opera, ballet, symphony orchestras, movies, art exhibitions, martial arts and bars. Beijing's large expatriate community is a market for many activities so consult your consulate, tourist handouts or the *Xianzai Beijing* e-mail newsletter below for events and times. The web sites under Practical Information can give you the latest information on exhibitions, concerts, ballet, jazz, and acrobatic shows.

Many hotels have a box of cards with maps and addresses in Chinese for the following. In some cases, the card merits discounts.

For traditional Chinese arts, a good introduction to Beijing Opera is the pleasant **Li Yuan Theater** *in the Qianmen Hotel, 175 Yongan Road, just south of Liulichang antique street, Tel. 63016688.* Performances are held every evening at 7:30, usually with English titles to help you understand the plot. Real opera can be long and boring. This is a good introduction with just excerpts. Prices are Y30, Y90, Y120 and Y150. You don't have to take a tour. You can do it by yourself. The ticket office at the hotel is open 9am-8pm.

For a traditional Chinese variety show, there's the delightful **Lao She Tea House** *in the Da Wan Cha Building, third floor, 3 Qianmen Xi Avenue, 50 meters west of Kentucky Fried Chicken at the south end of Tiananmen Square, Tel. 63036830. No credit cards* At 7:40pm, it offers 100 minutes of Beijing's top talent, including opera singers, magicians, cross-talk, and comedy acts that require no language to enjoy. Go at 5pm for dinner if you want. Y40-Y120 includes snacks, Y60-Y200 includes dinner. Reserve two days in advance. There's also the **Tianqiaole Tea House**, *113 Tianqiao Market,*

Tel. 63040617. Credit cards accepted. Performances are at 7pm, with folk art shows and dinner, Y330. The show only costs Y180. Reservations are recommended

Every second Friday at 7:30pm, **Cherry Lane** shows good Chinese movies with English subtitles at the *Sino-Japanese Youth Exchange Centre, 40 Liangmaqiao Road, Tel. 65004466 X 103.* The film maker is frequently present to answer questions. This costs Y50 per person. For information, *Tel. 65224046, Fax 65224047 or E-mail: Primont@cherrylane.com.* Try also the **Art Salon** *at the Crowne Plaza, Tel. 65133388,* to learn about Chinese movies with English subtitles every other Friday evening. It also has concerts on Thursdays and Saturdays.

The 95-minute **Chinese Soul Show** put on by **China's National Acrobatic Troupe** is as good as Shanghai's, with more artistry, creative lighting, good costumes, and less muscle. It's not the same old stuff; it's developed the art of plate spinning to new heights, and barrel spinning is now child spinning. Book through your hotel at Y50-Y500 or at the International Theatre in the Poly Plaza (near the Hong Kong and Macau Centre), *Tel. 65001188 X 5126,* box office open 9am-6pm. The show starts at 7:15pm. The cheaper seats get bottled water and peanuts. This troupe toured the US twice in 1997. Performances are not always daily so ask.

The Swissôtel and China World hotels have western and Chinese **classical music** with symphony orchestras in their lobbies on Sundays, not the quietest place to listen, but it goes with high tea from 3pm-6pm. And there's an interesting open-air **night food market** near the East Gate of the Forbidden City open 6pm-9pm.

For complete relaxation, there're **massages** at the hotels or outside the hotels. You can also watch the fish swimming at the Blue Zoo. The larger hotels have cocktail lounges with live music.

Beijing's Jazz & Classical Hot Spot

If you're tired of things Chinese, Beijing also has other fare. The second floor of the **Sanwei Book Store** has live, smoke-free jazz, the same good group every Friday evening (with not-so-good food) at 9pm. It has live classical music on Saturday evenings. Admission Y30. This tiny book store is on a side street across the street south from the Cultural Palace of the Nationalities which is on *Fuxingmennei Avenue, Tel. 66013204.*

In the Jianguomenwai area

One of the more popular hotel bars among foreigners is **Charlie's Bar** at the Jianguo Hotel. Many pleasant, small, privately-run Chinese bars have also opened, but have also been periodically closed for prostitution or drugs.

Other Watering Holes Frequented By Foreigners
   MEXICAN WAVE RESTAURANT *(poor food), Guang Hua Xi Road, Dongdaqiao Xie Street, Tel. 65063961.*
   This is one block behind the Gui You Department Store, open 11am-2am and is usually packed after 11pm because it has a good bar. It has sidewalk tables in the summer and moderate prices.
   THE JOHN BULL PUB *at 44 Guang Hua Road, next to the Brazilian and British Embassies and behind the International Post Office, Tel. 65325905, open daily 10:30am-1am, weekends to 1:30am. Major credit cards are accepted.*
   Fish and chips, and steak and kidney pie are Y90 each. It has Guinness, Kilkenny and Tetley beers, Yorkshire pudding, and bangers and mash. You'll find it hard to believe you're in China.

In the Sanlitun Area
   There are three groups of restaurants and bars here:
   FRANK'S PLACE, *East Sports Stadium Road, Tel. 65072617, 65891985 is near the City Hotel.*
   American-owned. Hamburgers are Y35 and considered by some the best in town. Try also the fried cheese for Y35. Beer costs Y20-Y35 a bottle which you can enjoy *al fresco* in warmer weather. A good bake shop, **Bella's**, is next door.
   BERENA'S BISTRO, *6 East Sports Stadium Road and is open 11am-2pm, and 5pm-midnight, Tel. 65922628.*
   Close by to Frank's Place and Bella's, Berena's is a moderately-priced Cantonese restaurant also favored by foreigners.
   South of Gongrentiyuchang Bei Avenue, and a couple of blocks behind Frank's Place and the City Hotel on Dongdaqao Xie Street, are several other restaurants and bars. Near the corner is **Minder's Cafe**, *No. 1 Houpingfang, Xinyi Building, Nan Sanlitun, Tel. 65006066, and E-mail: shaiming@public.east.cn.net.* This has a casual pub atmosphere, and good steaks, sandwiches, burgers, and spaghetti. It has a band every evening and serious darts on Thursday evenings. Open 11am to whenever, its happy hour is 2pm-8pm and it has a disco on weekends after midnight. *Filet mignon* is Y98, *osso bocco* Y72, and *chili con carne* Y35.
   DURTY NELLIES IRISH PUB, *is on the same lane, at 12 Nan Sanlitun, Tel. 65022808. It is open 12 noon-1am daily and accepts no credit cards.*
   It has Guinness and Kilkenny beer for Y50 a pint, and Chinese beers for Y25. It has stews, steak and roasts on Sunday, a Belgian chef, and at least one Irish person on hand at all times. It has Irish music, darts, stone floor and paintings of Michael Collins and Oscar Wilde on the walls, and a live band on weekends.
   NASHVILLE, *on the same alley as Durty Nellies, above.*
   Come here for country music, blues, rock and roll. The house band

plays nightly from 9:30pm with no cover charge. The food is western, barbecues, kebobs and sausages. It takes Visa and American Express cards and is at *14 East Building, Dongdaqiao Xie Street, Tel. 65024201.*
Then on Sanlitun near the market, there's another group of bars.

In the Kempinski-Great Wall Sheraton Area
HARD ROCK CAFE, *in the Landmark Arcade next to the Great Wall Sheraton Hotel, 8 Dongsanhuan Bei Road, Tel.65906688 X 2571.*
The Hard Rock has great fries and brownies (Y48) but the rest is mediocre. It is open Sunday through Thursday 11:30am-2am; Friday and Saturday 11:30am-3am. Yankee burgers cost Y68-Y98; pig sandwiches Y90; thick fountain shakes Y38. Tee-shirts are on sale for Y100-Y130. This is one of the best discos, very noisy after 10:30pm.
PAULANER BRAUHAUS *is in the Kempinski Hotel, Lufthansa Centre, 50 Liangmaqiao Road, Tel. 64653388 X 5731, open 11am-1am. It accepts credit cards.*
This is a boutique brewery with huge shining beer vats, long tables, and benches. It has good food, too, like half-grilled pork knuckles with sauerkraut and roast potatoes for Y125 and Nuernberger sausage with sauerkraut and mashed potatoes for Y85. Half a liter of beer will set you back Y45.

SPORTS & RECREATION

The weekly cyber newsletter *Xianzai Beijing* is mainly for foreigners living in Beijing and it should be helpful. A recent edition calls for ice hockey players *(Tel. Markus Benz at 1391087653 or E-mail:benzmarkus@hotmail.com)*, where to paraglide *(Tel. 62344230)*, and bungee jump *(Tel. 69860701 or 69379170)*. For rock climbing, *Tel. 64063777 or E-mail shirley@ihw.com.cn*; for horse racing and organized betting, *Tel. 69401499.* For frisbee addicts, contact *Sungene@public.bts.net.cn* or Carolyn, *e-mail: frisbee@public.gb.com.cn.* For a free subscription see Practical Information below.
The **Hash House Harriers** are not really sports people. They are "a drinking club with a running problem." But meeting up with this group of friendly fun lovers is a good way to meet Beijing residents. For information, e-mail Ratchucker at *rdrhead@uop.com*; or call Bumper at *64376688 X 2735.*
The **Beijing International Golf Club** is at *Shisanling, Changping County, Tel. 60762288, 69746388, Fax 60761111.* It's the best and has a remarkable setting near the Ming Tombs. It also has squash courts, pool, huge fitness center and aerobics room. Major hotels can arrange.
Many hotels have bowling and one alley near Workers' Stadium has about 60 lanes and is open 24-hours. Outdoor ice skating at the Summer

Palace or Beihai Park is an old tradition. The Movenpick has curling. The Beijing New Century Hotel has tennis and a serious pool. The Australia, British and Indian embassies should know about cricket. The Gloria Hotel has a huge Sports City Cafe with batting cage, basketball hoops, and darts.

If you want to learn more about acrobatics, go to a show with an interpretor, and ask where you can learn too. Contact the **Yuanmingyuan Ruyi Martial Arts School**, *152 Yuanmingyuan Road, Tel. 62571596, 62587485*. There's go-carting (*Tel. 65064991*), and horseback riding (*Tel. 64364250*).

Festivals

The **Beijing Marathon** and is now open to everyone. It is held annually in mid-October and China Travel Service can make arrangements. The week before and after the lunar new year, a temple fair takes place at the Temple of the Earth, the Ditan. The **Golden Autumn Festival** is at the Yuanmingyuan. Look for dragon boat races in June and kite-flying contests in the spring.

SHOPPING

Beijing is a great place to shop because its large international community demands high-quality goods at competitive prices. Locally-made are cloisonne, silk, dough figurines, lacquerware, chops, jade carvings, pearls, filigree jewelry, and carpets. The **factories** are essentially tourist traps because prices are higher than in the stores even if you haggle. You should first go to the **Friendship Store** and make notes of what things cost and then aim for less. See below.

For one-stop souvenir shopping at the cheapest prices, go to the **Hongqiao Market** in the building with the traditional Chinese roof across the street and east of the Temple of Heaven on Tiantan Dong Road. The third floor has tiny **antique** stores, reasonably priced fresh-water pearls, cloisonne, and crafts wholesale, and you should still haggle. There are also antique and curios stalls here: **Zhang's Textiles** at no. 78, *Tel. 67132301*, 10am-6:30pm, has good embroideries and will take credit cards; **Zhang Shu Hua** at No. 39 has good prices and everything imaginable. *Tel. 67038039*. Best go during the week; Saturdays and Sundays are crowded. Open 9:30am-6:30 or 7pm. Some merchants have credit card service, and other merchants can use these for a Y10 fee.

For **silk**, go to the crowded **Xiushui Free Market/Silk Alley** (open 9am-6:30pm daily) between the Jianguo Hotel and Friendship Store on Jianguomenwai, the best such market in China. Here are mainly clothes, ties, scarves, and linens, name-brand jackets, and also crafts from all over the country–not just silk. These are fashionable export-quality overruns and seconds, Calvin Klein's and North Face, so look goods over carefully before buying. There are also 100% polyester pieces labelled "100% silk," to be avoided.

Less hectic, more reliable and more expensive for silk is the **Yuan Long Embroidery and Silk Store**, *55 Tiantan Road, Tel. 67020682*, at the southwest end of the Temple of Heaven. It's open 9am-6:30pm and has silk textiles, carpets, embroidery, and clothes. It also has jewelry and furs. There's the **Rui Fu Xiang Silk shop** at *Rui Fu Xiang*, south of the Qianmen gate. All have ready-made clothes and yard goods. Cheap **batiks** are for sale in **Chinese Ethnic Culture Park** (open 8:30am-6pm) in the north but it's a long way there and you pay an entry fee. It's at *Yayuncun, Asian Games Village* just west of Beichen Road, *Tel. 62063626 or 62063640*.

Of the **department stores**, the Lufthansa Friendship Shopping City (**Youyi Yensha Shang Cheng**) at *52 Liang Ma Qiao Road, Tel. 64651188*. It is beside the Kempinski Hotel and north of the Great Wall Sheraton and has lots of variety. I found cheaper fancy silk jackets, robes, and pyjamas there than at the Friendship store. There's also **Parkson Shopping Center** *(Bai Sheng Gouwu Zhongxin, 101 Fuxingmennei Street, north of the Fuxingmen Flyover, Tel. 66072841)*. The Jianguomenwai area has the good **Gui You Department Store** (Gui You Dasha, open 9:30am to 9:00pm). Almost across the street from the Friendship Store is the **CVIK-Yaohan** department store at *22 Jianguomenwai Avenue*, a little more expensive. Both are near the Friendship Store so you can compare prices.

Cheaper department stores like those in Xidan don't have anyone speaking English, nor signs you can read.

The **Friendship Store**, on *Jianguomenwai Avenue* between the International Club and Jianguo Hotel, shouldn't be avoided entirely. You can find things there unseen elsewhere without the crowds. There are furs, down coats, cashmere sweaters, silk underwear and textiles, groceries, books in English, cloisonne, stone carvings, wines, carpets, antiques, and even fresh flowers. The Friendship Store can reset jewelry and develop photos, and a tailor here does a reasonable job in three weeks. A directory in English is on the ground floor and the store is open 9am-9pm. Like most other department stores, this one takes credit cards.

Wangfujing, Beijing's main traditional shopping street on the east side of the Beijing Hotel, is very crowded and might still have some old stores for traditional musical instruments and fur hats and traditional pharmacies. This area is in the process of being transformed from an interesting old shopping area with latticed wooden store fronts to an expensive, modern shopping area with giant malls and goods like anywhere else in the world. The **Sun Dong An Centre** here near the Beijing Hotel has opened with the likes of Montagut Paris, Burberry's, Ports International and Esprit. The **Arts and Crafts Centre** at *200 Wangfujing*

(Tel. 66124165) might still be there with its good prices. The **Foreign Languages Book Store** might be still at 235. There's also the **Beijing Department Store** (on the west side, *Tel. 65126677).*

For China-made name-brand clothes or fakes, avoid the **Yabaolu Market** near Ritan Park unless you want bargains in large sizes. Here rude vendors sell in large quantities to rude Russians. The **Sanlitun market** north of the City Hotel across Gongrentiyuchang Bei Avenue, has name brand seconds, and good styles. Generally markets don't accept credit card payments but a few individual shops might.

The **Palace Hotel** has top-of-the line international name brand clothes like Louis Vuitton, Hermes, Gianni Versace, Hugo Boss, and Givenchy.

For **factories**, some tours on the way to the Great Wall stop at the cloisonne factory, the **China Beijing North Suburbs Industrial Art Factory**, *Ding Fu Huang Zhuang, Shahe, Tel. 69732942, 69737417.* It is 20 minutes south of the Ming Tombs. It is open 8am-6pm, and takes major credit cards, but "only for US$25 and up." Don't let that fool you. Threaten to report them to the credit card company. They are not supposed to impose a minimum purchase price. But do get a look at the manufacturing process. It's interesting.

A pearl factory is also on the way to the Great Wall, its wares cultured in the Miyun Reservoir. You get only the opening of one mussel, a come-on for this over-priced store.

The telephone number of the **Jade Carving factory** is **67128899**, and the **Beijing Arts and Crafts Wood Carving Factory** is **67110006**.

For **antiques**, the best bargains are at the weekend **Ghost Market or Panjiayuan**, two blocks west of Second Ring Road, behind the Le You Hotel, west and north of the imposing Henan Building. Private dealers lay goods out on tables under a huge roof. Go early (about 5:30am) for the best selection and smaller crowds. The place is jammed with tourists and locals at 10am and dealers start to pack up about 3:00pm. This street market is full of reproductions and fakes, ethnic textiles, stone carvings, wood carvings, porcelains, etc. but people with a good eye can find real treasures especially if they haggle well and don't mind being hassled and pushed and subjected to cigarette smoke. No credit cards nor receipts are used. (The similar Sunday antique market in neighboring **Tianjin** is also good for prices and variety, and both are fun.)

Permanent stalls are here too and open daily 9am-6pm, *Tel. 67334023* (dealer Chen Si Qiang here speaks English).

Collections of other small private dealers are at **Beijing Curio City** (Guwanchung, behind the Duty-Free Store), *the west side of Hua Wei Qiao Bridge, Dongsanhuan,* open 9:30am-6:30pm. It has three stories (with escalators) of shops: curios, pearls, furniture, jewelry, silver, paintings, and embroideries. A restaurant there has good food.

The **Liangma Antique Market** is full of antiques and curios too and is open daily across the road from the Kempinski Hotel. It has fine antique embroidery already framed (and unable to be checked but they look good. Are they machine or hand stitched?) It's open 9am-8:30pm. Prices at the **Jin Song Antique market** – are uneven, some very reasonable and others outrageously high. A few take credit cards. It has fewer fakes than Liulichang and Hongqiao markets but you still have to be careful. Open daily 9 or 10am-6pm.

A great place to buy jade and other stones is the small store in the **Round City** at Beihai Park and they take credit cards. The park also has shops with tapes of classical music for Y8 each near the pagoda.

There's also the **Chai Wai market** mostly for antique furniture beyond the northwest corner of Ritan Park (open 10am-5pm). And the **Ping'anli flower and bird market**, north of Beihai Park, and south of Houhai Lake, also sells a few curios.

For **upmarket antiques and curios**, take a look at the magnificent stone carvings (Qingtian and Shoushan) in the shop off the lobby lounge in the China World Hotel. The Shangri-La and Grand Hotels, Summer Palace and Forbidden City have good stores too. The Friendship Store also has some good pieces. For large buddhas, look in the shop at the back of Ghost Market. They look good but who knows if they're real antiques. Owners of stalls everywhere will sometimes close their doors and produce some illegal Tang or Song dynasty pieces. The **Huaxia Antique Store** is at *293 Wangfujing Avenue*, and open 9am-7pm. This government store has lots of porcelains, carvings, rugs, etc. and you can get an official red wax seal and receipt for purchases. It is more reliable than the markets.

The largest collection of stores selling real antiques, reproductions and fakes, and arts and crafts, is **Liulichang** (on both sides of Xuanwumen Wai Avenue), the main street where the buses stop. It is open roughly 10am-5:30 or 6pm, later in summer. This is more expensive and has better goods generally than the markets and stalls and is less crowded. It also has art books (mainly in Chinese). You could spend hours poking around.

In 1277, artisans made glazed tiles here. In the Qing, it was a market with 140 shops selling the same sort of arts it does today, including reproductions of paintings, the Dunhuang murals, bronzes, and porcelains. Some of the merchandise then was stolen from the Forbidden City and other wealthy homes. Small shops are also next to and behind the **Rong Bao Zhai** art store on the west side at No.64. Good is **Xie Yan Fang** at No.3 with great embroideries and old books at reasonable prices. *Tel. 63017979*. Try **Kui Jin Ge** at No. 115 for porcelain, wood toggles, and gold jewelry. *Tel. 63017979*. Prices here could be better than the Friendship

Store if you haggle. It is less crowded too. The **Beijing Cultural Relics Store** at *64 Liulichang Dong Street, Tel. 63033848,* is allowed to sell pre-Qing relics.

If your antiques are expensive, they need a red wax seal for export. Ask your store to get one before you buy.

EXCURSIONS & DAY TRIPS

See separate entries in this guide for Beidaihe, Chengde, Datong Shanhaiguan, and Shijiazhuang for overnight trips nearby. Zunhua with its Qing imperial tombs and Tianjin can be one-day trips.

THE GREAT WALL
(Wanlichangcheng; 10,000 li-long wall)

The length of *The Great Wall has been officially given as 12,700 Chinese li, or 6,350 km (3,946.55 miles) long from Jiayuguan to Shanhaiguan. Some scholars, however, add another 1,040 km all the way to the Yalu River on the Korean border. The length depends on what you measure, as there are many offshoots and parallel walls. The Wall is in various states of repair.

The best time to see the wall is in the afternoon. Stay to see the sunset if you can. The autumn is especially good when the air is clearer and red leaves add interest to photos.

Orientation

The Great Wall was first built in shorter pieces, starting in the fifth century B.C., as a defensive and boundary wall around the smaller states of Yen, Chao, and Wei. The first Qin emperor (221-206 B.C.), who unified China for the first time, linked up and extended the walls from Liaoning in the east to Gansu in the northwest as protection from the Huns and other nomadic tribes. The wall was subsequently repaired and extended by succeeding dynasties, especially the Ming.

Originally built by slave labor, it has been called the world's longest graveyard because many of its builders were buried where they fell. It was designed in places to allow five horsemen or ten soldiers to march abreast along the top. It was almost a superhighway, considering the rough mountain terrain. A system of bonfires communicated military information to the emperor at a speed considered rapid for that period.

Visiting the Wall

The Great Wall is most frequently visited at *Badaling** (Padaling), about 75 km (one hour) by expressway northwest of Beijing. It and the Ming Tombs are open 8am-4:30pm, *Tel. 69121383.* The entrance fee is

Y25. It is extremely crowded. Avoid weekends. Most tourists leave Beijing by tourist buses between 8am-9am and stop at both the Great Wall and Ming Tombs. To avoid crowds, arrive later or avoid Badaling.

Tours range in price. See *Getting Around Town* above.

Badaling is about 1000 meters above sea level. Here the wall averages 7.8 meters in height, is 6.5 meters wide at the base, and 5.8 meters wide at the top. Watchtowers are located every few hundred meters. Note the giant rocks and bricks of uniform size, the gutters, and the waterspouts. You can walk, and in some places climb, for several hundred meters in either direction or you can take a cable car. Most visitors don't need to take the cable car, and it is a long way from the main entrance, back by the bus parking lot. Skateboarding on the wall has been allowed, but is not recommended when it is thick with people, which is most of the time.

A shaggy Bactrian camel or pony for photographing are available. Taking a box lunch is recommended, especially in pleasant weather, so you can spend more time at the wall rather than waiting for service in a crowded restaurant.

Also of note is the gate in the center of Juyongguan (Chuyungkuan Pass), about 10 km south of Badaling which you pass on the way. It is built of finely-carved marble and called *Guofie (Cloud Terrace)*. Originally the base of a tower built in 1345 (Yuan), the walls are decorated with carved buddhas, four celestial guardians, and the text of a Buddhist sutra in Sanskrit, Tibetan, and four other languages. Tours do not usually stop here except by request and as you can see as you go by, it is considerably steeper than Badaling.

A three-km-long section of the Great Wall is at **Mutianyu**, 70 km northeast of Beijing in Miyun County, *Tel. 69626505*, open 8:30am-4:30pm. It is less crowded and more beautiful, less commercial, with more rugged hills than Badaling. But you do have to ask for it. A 720-meter-long Swiss-built cable car can take you from the parking lot uphill to the base of the Wall. You still have to climb or take the cable car down. All buildings including a restaurant are tastefully built in matching Ming style. Open 8:30am-4:30pm. You can also go by road from Mutianyu to the Ming tombs.

You'll find a very steep section about 90 km from Beijing at **Huang Ya Pass**. Also open for tourists is the Wall in **Huairou County** (two-km-long reconstruction), 60 km northeast of Beijing. You can go by road from Beijing to Chengde following the Wall with stops at Simatai and Jinshan Ling.

Simatai, 140 km from Beijing, is spectacular but you may have to walk about one km from the parking lot to the base. At **Jinshan Ling** (150 km from Beijing and 110 km from Chengde), there is camping (bring your own tent). Officials here say you can see the lights of Beijing from the top.

About two kilometers of the wall have been repaired here. This is the area where volunteer crews have been organized by the Beijing's Great Wall Sheraton Hotel to pick up litter left by tourists.

An 850-meter section is open in **Jixian County**, 60 km northeast of Tianjin but closer to Beijing, and two sections are available near **Datong**. The Great Wall has also been restored and opened to visitors at 3,000-year-old **Shanhaiguan** (with cable car), over 40 km north from Beidaihe, and about 30 km from Qinhuangdao in the east. The tower was built in 1381. Nearby, at **Old Dragon Head**, the Great Wall meets the sea.

In west China, you can see it in Ningxia close to **Yinchuan**, and in Gansu at *****Jiayuguan**, its western terminus where it is much narrower but still fascinating.

Museums are at Jiayuguan and Shanhaiguan. See separate listings under these destinations for more details.

PRACTICAL INFORMATION

Beijing Tourism Administration, *Beijing Tourism Tower, 28 Jianguomenwai Avenue, 100022, Tel. 65158255, Fax 65158215. E-mail: bta.soc@bjta.gov.cn, and http://bjta.gov.cn (in Chinese).*

Business Hours: for offices 8:30am to 4:30 or 5:30pm with lunch 12 to 1:30 or 2pm. Store hours on Wangfujing about 9am-8:30 or 9pm. The stores in the Beijing Hotel are open at 8:15am.

China National Tourism Administration, Division of Europe & Americas, Dept. of Marketing & Promotion, *9A Jianguomennei Avenue, 100740, Tel. 65201413, 65201412, Fax 65122851.* For brochures. It is best to go to China Tourist Offices abroad. See Chapter 6, *Planning Your Trip.*

Embassies (Da She Guan):
• **Australia**, *21 Dongzhimenwai Street, Sanlitun, 100600, Tel. 65322331.*
• **Canada**, *19 Dongzhimenwai Dajie, Chao Yang District, 100600, Tel. 65323536; Fax 65324311, 65325544, 65323034.* Monday-Friday, 8am-5pm
• **CIS** (most of the former USSR), *Dongzhimen Bei Zhong Street, Number 4, 100600 (Not open daily), Tel. 65321267, 65322051.*
• **France**, *3 Sanlitun Dong Road, Chao Yang District, Tel. 65321331, 65321332.*
• **Germany**, *5 Dongzhimenwai Avenue, Chaoyang District, Tel. 65322161.*
• **Israel**, *China World Trade Center, Tel. 65052970.*
• **Japan**, *7 Ritan Road, Jianguomenwai, Tel. 65322361.*
• **Kazakhstan**, *9, Dong 6 Road, Sanlitun, Tel. 65326183.*
• **Mongolia**, *2 Xiushui Bei Jie, Tel. 65321203, 65321810, Fax 5325045.* Not open daily. Phone for hours. Accepts only US$ for visas.
• **Myanmar** (Burma), *6 Dongzhimenwai Avenue, Tel. 65321425, 65321488.*
• **Nepal**, *1, Xiliujie, Tel. 65321795, Fax 6532325.*
• **Netherlands**, *4 Liang Ma He Nan Road, 100600, Tel. 65321131, Fax 5324689.*

• **New Zealand**, *1 Ritan Dong Er Street, Chaoyang District, 100600, Tel. 65322731, Fax 65324317.*
• **Pakistan**, *Dongzhimenwai, Tel. 65322504, 65322660.*
• **Philippines**, *23 Xiu Shui Bei Street, Jianguomenwai, 100600; Tel. 65321872, 65322451, 65324678* (Consular).
• **Poland**, *1 Ritan Road, Jianguomenwai, 100600, Tel. 65321235.* Not open daily, mornings only.
• **Thailand**, *40 Guanghua Road, Tel. 65321903, 65323955.*
• **UK**, *11 Guanghua Road, Jianguomenwai 100600, Tel. 65321961; Fax 65011977.*
• **US**, *Xiushui Beijie 3 (Chancery), 100600, Tel. 65323831, Fax 65054574.* American Citizen Service, *2 Xiushui Dong Jie, 100600, Tel. 65323431 X5648, 5344, Fax 65324153 or 65323178.* For after hour emergencies, *Tel. 65321910.* Monday-Friday, 8:30am-12 noon, and 2pm-4pm. Closed weekends and holidays. USIS, *17 Guang Hua Road, 100600, Tel. 65321161, Fax 65322039.* US Customs Service, *31 Technical Club Companies Ltd., 15 Guanghua Road, 100020, Tel. 65002392, Fax 65003032.*
• **Vietnam**, *32 Guanghua Road, Jianguomenwai, Tel. 65321155, 65321125.* **Fire**, *Tel. 119.*

Internet Cafes: one is in the China World Trade Center in the building to the right as you enter from Jianguomenwai. Another is outside the east gate of Beijing University on Chengfu Street. *Tel. 62527602* SIS Bar.

Medical Concerns: for minor ailments, consult your hotel. For more serious problems:
• **Ambulance**, telephone 120. Ambulances are equipped with defibrillators.
• For the **International First Aid Center** *(Gi Jou Chong Xin), near KFC on Qianmen, Tel. 65255678, 66014336.* For a local hospital: Xiehe Hospital (also known as Capital Hospital or **Peking Union Medical College Hospital**), the Foreigners' Clinic is at *53 Dongdanbei Avenue, 6/F, Tel. 65295296 or 65135002.* The Emergency Room entrance is at *No. 1 Shuaifuyuan Hutong, behind the hospital. Tel. 24 hours 65295284.* This hospital is behind the Palace Hotel downtown.
• For **international medical service**, foreign doctors and higher prices: The **International Medical Center**, Lufthansa Center, Suite 106, has a pharmacy, dental and medical office. Its 24-hour service telephone is *64651561-63, fax 64651984.* For non-members, a flu shot cost $35, an office consultation $80-$110, a hepatitis A shot can be $105-$147 each. A full physical can be $250.
• Information about the **International Hospital** can be obtained from its office in the *Fuhua Mansion, Building "B", 6/F, 8 Chaoyangmen Beidajie, Dongcheng District, 100027, Tel. 65541728, Fax 65541734.* E-

mail: hospops@btih.com.cn. Http://www.btih.com.cn. This is a new hospital joint venture with a Canadian company and has Canadian standards.

• For women and children, there's also the **Beijing United Family Health Center**, *2 Jiangtai Road, Chaoyang District, 100016, Tel. 64333960, Fax 64333963.* It's near the Holiday Inn Lido.

• For emergency medical services including death and evacuation, try **Asia Emergency Assistance** *(AEA), Building C, BITIC Leasing Center, 1 North Road, Xing Fu San Cun, Chaoyang District, 100027, Tel. 64629100 (24 hours), Fax 64629111.* It has a pharmacy. There's also **International SOS Assistance**, *Kunlun Hotel, Room 447, 2 Xin Yuan Nan Road, 24-hour Alarm Center, Tel. 65903419, Fax 65016048;* and **MEDEX Assistance Corporation**, *Regus Office 19, Beijing Lufthansa Center, No. 50 Liangmaqiao Road, 100016. For its 24-hour Alarm Center, Tel. 64651264, Fax 64651269.*

Police, *Tel. 110;* Foreigners' Section of the **Beijing Public Security Bureau**, *Tel. 65255486, 65253102.* Open 8:30am-11:30am, and 1:00pm-5:00pm. Closed Saturday and Sunday. Extensions of visas take one week, but you can pay double for express service. It is half a block north of the East Gate to the Forbidden City at *85, Bei Chi Zi Avenue, Tel. 65253102.*

Religious Services in English: A non-denominational Christian group has church services in English at the Sino-Japanese Youth Exchange Center, *40 Liangmaqiao Road,* near the Kempinski Hotel. It's at 10:30am Sunday mornings, *Tel. 1391104943* for information. Proof of foreign citizenship needed. There's also the Congregation of the Good Shepherd, 10am, Capital Club Athletic Center, next to the Capital Mansion across from the Huadu Hotel, *Tel. 65954558, 64155276.* The Canadian embassy hosts a Catholic mass in English on Sunday evenings, *Tel. 65323536.*

Telephone Operators: information *Tel. 114;* long-distance information, *116;* overseas operator, *115*; time *117*; weather *121.*

Tourist Complaints: Supervisory Bureau of Tourism Quality of *Beijing Municipality, Room 1001, Beijing Tourism Building, 28 Jianguomenwai Street, 100022, Tel. 65130828 (24 hours), Fax 65158251, 65158255.*

Tourism Hotline, 24 hours, *Tel. 65130828.* Questions, complaints, and compliments.

Travel Agents: check all of these for good hotel discounts, and cheaper city tours:

• **American Express**, *21/F, China World Trade Center Tower, 1 Jianguomenwai Avenue, Tel. 65052888, Fax 65054972.*

• **Beijing Tourism Tower**, (between the Gloria and New Otani Changfugong Hotels), *28 Jianguomenwai, 100022.*

- **China International Sports Travel**, *Weitu Mansion, C3 Longtan Road, Chongwen District, 100061, Tel. 67117364, Fax 67117370. E-mail:office@sportstravel.com.cn. Http://www.sportstravel.com.cn.*
- **China International Travel Service**, **Beijing branch**, *Beijing Tourism Tower, ground floor, 28 Jianguomenwai, 100022, 8:30am-11am; 1:30pm-4:30pm. Saturday 8:30am-12 noon, Tel. 65158844, 65158587, Fax 65158251, 65158602.* The **Beijing CITS Sales and Management Center** is here too, *Tel. 65157796, 65158844 X 2402, Fax 65158602.* Its office in the Beijing International Hotel, *Tel. 65126688 X 1751/2, Fax 65121369* books only airlines. That at *Tel. 65120507/8, Fax 65120503* books only international trains and ships. Both these offices are on the ground floor, open Monday-Friday, 8:30am-11:30pm and 1:30am-4:30pm, Saturdays 8:30am-12 noon.
- **China International Travel Service Head Office**, *Room 711, CITS Building, 103 Fuxingmennei Avenue, 100800, Tel. 66053632, Fax 66012021. E-mail:xiemz@cits.co.cn.* Contact Xie Mengzhu for tours.
- **China Travel Service Head Office**, *China Travel Service Tower, North American Department, 2 Dong Beisanhuan, 100028, Tel. 64622288, Fax 64612502. Otherwise Tel. 64612571, 64612572, Fax 64612567. E-mail: cts-europe@immedia.ca.*
- **China Travel Service Beijing**, *Beijing Tourism Tower, 28 Jianguomenwai, 100022, Tel. 65158264, 65158844, 65158565, Fax 65158557.*
- **CITIC Travel Inc.**, *Room 1201, Capital Mansion, Xinyuan Nan Road, 6, Chaoyang District, 100004, Tel. 64660088, Fax 64661660, 64654712. E-mail:citictvl@public3.bta.net.cn. Http://www.spyspy.com.* For business travelers.
- **CYTS Tours Co. Ltd.**, *23C Dong Jiao Min Xiang, 100006, Tel. 65274896, Fax 65272290. E-mail:market@cyts.com.cn and xfyuan@cyts.com.cn. Http://www.chinatour.com/cyts/* Attention: Sales Manager, North American Department.
- **Grand Holidays**, *Room 8222, Xin Yuan Cun, Beijing Hotel, 100006, Tel. 65271970, 65223451, Fax 65275368. Http://www.grandholidays.com.*
- **Helen Wong's Tours**, *Room 3040/3041, Beijing International Hotel, 9, Jianguomennei Avenue, 1000005, Tel. 65254385, Fax 65257667. E-mail:hwtpek@public3.bta.net.cn.* Contact person: Sam Chen. This is the first wholly Australian-owned tour company in China.
- **Hualong International Travel Service**, *Room 916, 9/F, No. 2 Building, Beijing International Hotel, 9 Jianguomennei, 100005, Tel. 65126688 X 7915, 7916, Fax 65229299.*
- **Monkey Business Infocenter**, *Forbidden City Hotel, 48 Guang An Men Nan Street, South Building, 3/F, Xuanwu District, 100054, Tel. 63562126, Fax 63562127. E-mail: MonkeyChina@compuserve.com. Http://www.monkeyshrine.com.* Open 10am-8pm; Tuesday, Friday and Satur-

day until 6pm, and Sunday from 2pm-8pm. Specialists in train travel to Russia and the Silk Road.

• **Panda Tours**, which operate city and Great Wall tours can be reached at *98 Beilishi Road, Western District, Holiday Inn Downtown, Tel. 68036963, 68338822 X 7180, or Fax 68037044, 68340696. E-mail:bjpanda@public.bta.net.cn.*

Websites and Information on Beijing: *Http://www.chinatour.com. Http://www.cbw.com* for weather, map, hotels. For a subscription to the helpful weekly e-mail newsletter *Xianzai Beijing,* write to *Xianzai@ListServe.com* with "Subscribe" as the subject. It has about 12 pages of bargain airfares, restaurant specials, jobs, and used furniture and appliances for sale. It also lists sports opportunities, current festivals, and orientation for newcomers.

Look for tourist handouts like *Welcome to Beijing, Beijing This Month, Beijing Beat,* and *Metro.* These are distributed in hotels and expat hangouts like the San Wei Bookstore and Mexican Wave Cafe. You should be able to get *Beijing Beat on e-mail: beijingbeat@bigfoot.com. Otherwise it's at 18 Guanghua Road, First Floor, No. 1 North (Ritan Middle School), 100020, Tel. 65927381, 67630642, Fax 67699296.*

15. SHANGHAI

Shanghai is China's second largest city, its busiest port and an industrial city making Volkswagen and Buick cars, electronics, telecommunications equipment, iron and steel, home appliances, and petrochemicals. It is an important trading city and has China's major stock market. Think of it as China's New York.

Shanghai straddles the **Huangpu River** and reaches the Yangtze River on China's east coast, about 28 km from its Bund or downtown waterfront. It borders on Jiangsu and Zhejiang provinces and is due west of the southern tip of Japan. The urban population is approximately 7.5 million plus three million "floaters." The greater Shanghai area has at least 13.4 million people. Its population density is about 50,000 people per sq km, a world high. It covers roughly 120 km north-south, and nearly 100 km east-west. The hottest temperature is 35 C in July and August; the coldest is minus 5 C in January and February. Most of its 1200 mm. of rain falls May-September. Shanghai is at about the same latitude as Jacksonville, Florida. Its natives speak a dialect unlike that of Beijing and more akin to that of Hangzhou and Suzhou, only faster.

History

This municipality, directly under the control of the central government, started out 6,000 years ago as a tiny fishing village. It celebrated its 700th birthday in 1991. It became a port in the 16th century. By 1840 its population was 500,000. In 1842, the British seized it, and although the Chinese paid a $300,000 ransom to keep it from being sacked, British soldiers and Chinese thieves severely looted it.

The **Treaty of Nanking** of that year opened Shanghai to foreign trade and settlement. This led to its partition into British, French, and, later Japanese concessions, which are still reflected in its downtown architecture. The British concession became the International Settlement. These concessions continued until the 1940s. Each of the concessions had its own tax system, police, courts, buses, and electrical voltage. A criminal could escape justice simply by going from one concession to another.

Shanghai thrived as a port, trading principally in silk, tea, and opium. Most of the foreign trade was British, and one fifth of the opium reached China in fast American ships. From 1853 to 1855, the **Small Sword Society** seized the walled section of Shanghai. This was a Cantonese-Fukinese secret society that wanted to restore the Ming dynasty and prohibit opium. It was helped in its struggle by some foreign seamen, but many other foreigners supported the Manchus and regained the city. In 1860, the **Taiping Heavenly Kingdom** tried unsuccessfully to take Shanghai. In 1915 students and workers demonstrated here against the Twenty-One Demands of Japan. And in July 1921, the first **Congress of the Communist Party of China** met secretly here.

In 1925, a worker striking for higher wages was killed at a Japanese factory. This led to a demonstration by workers and students in the International Settlement, during which the British police killed several demonstrators. A rash of nationwide anti-imperialist protests followed. In April 1927, **Chiang Kai-shek** ordered a massacre of the Communists here, and **Chou En-lai** barely escaped with his life. The 1920s was the golden age of Shanghai.

In 1932, Shanghai resisted a Japanese attack for two months and made a truce. China appealed to the League of Nations and the United States, neither of whom did anything to help. Japan attacked again in August 1937. The Nationalists fought back for three months before retreating to Nanjing and later to Chongqing. The movie and book *Empire of the Sun* is set in this period and parts were shot in Shanghai. The Japanese stayed until 1945. In May 1949, the **Communists** took the city. During the Cultural Revolution, it was the scene of many intense political struggles, especially in January 1966.

Today Shanghai is a boom town, but look carefully. Many of its huge new high-rise nickelodeon buildings and fancy single-family houses are empty. It's old 19th century neighborhoods are being torn down. It is still experiencing double digit economic growth and its average per capita income of about Y11,000 is one of China's highest. It is the "dragon's head" of the burgeoning Yangtze River basin, a modern 20th century city.

ARRIVALS & DEPARTURES

Shanghai is joined to other parts of China by air, land, and water services. Driving from Suzhou to the north of Shanghai takes less than an hour on the expressway. If you are in a car, be aware that between 4-7pm, Shanghai restricts the number of motor vehicles entering and leaving from outside.

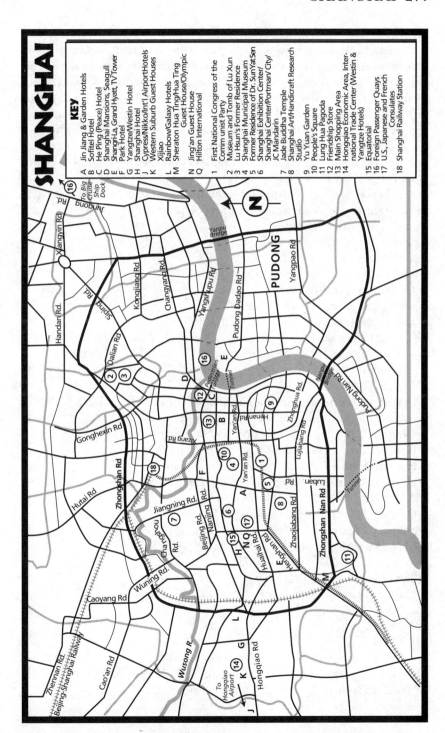

SHANGHAI

KEY

A Jin Jiang & Garden Hotels
B Sofitel Hotel
C He Ping (Peace) Hotel
D Shanghai Mansions, Seagull
E Shang-La, Grand Hyatt, TV/Tower
F Park Hotel
G Yangtze/Westin Hotel
H Shanghai Hotel
J Cypress/Nikko/Int'l Airport Hotels
K Western Suburb Guest Houses
   Xijiao
L Rainbow/Galaxy Hotels
M Sheraton Hua Ting/Hua Ting
   Guest House/Olympic

N Jing'an Guest House
Q Hilton International

1 First National Congress of the
   Comm unist Party
2 Museum and Tomb of Lu Xun
3 Lu Hsun's Former Residence
4 Shanghai Municipal Museum
5 Former Residence of Dr. SunYat-Sen
6 Shanghai Exhibition Center/
   Shanghai Center/Portman/City/
   JC Mandarin
7 Jade Buddha Temple
8 Shanghai Art/Handicraft Research
   Studio
9 Yu Yuan Garden
10 People's Square
11 Lung Hua Pagoda
12 Friendship Store
13 Main Shopping Area
14 Hongqiao Economic Area, International Trade Center (Westin &
   Yangtze Hotels)
15 Equatorial
16 Foreign Passenger Quays
17 U.S., Japanese and French
   Consulates
18 Shanghai Railway Station

By Air

Shanghai is about a two-hour flight northeast of Hong Kong and less than two hours southeast of Beijing. It is also linked by air with at least 74 other cities including Los Angeles, Macau, New York, Osaka, Paris, San Francisco, Seattle, Seoul, Tokyo (two hours 20 minutes), and Vancouver. After the opening of the **Pudong International Airport**, international flights will gradually shift to the new airport, and only domestic flights will go from the current **Hongqiao Airport**. It should take about 90 minutes to drive between the airports. In 1999, the left luggage room was open 8am-7pm, Y10-Y15 per bag.

A Travel Service Centre where you can book tickets without a service fee is at the domestic arrivals level after you leave the baggage-claim area.

Major airlines include:

· **Aeroflot**, *Tel. 64146700*
· **Air China**, *Tel. 63277888*
· **Air France**, *Tel. 63606688. Airport 62688899 X 5325*
· **Air Macau**, *Tel. 62684019*
· **All-Nippon Airways**, *Tel. 62797000*
· **Ansett Australia Airlines**, *Tel. 64155209*
· **CAAC/China Eastern Airlines**, *200 Yan'an Xi Road, Tel. 62475953 for domestic, 62472255 for international, Fax 6276761.* Ticketing offices in many hotels. Airport information, *Tel. 62683659, 62688918, 62537664*
· **Canadian Airlines International Limited**, *Central Plaza, Tel. 63758899, Fax 63758386. E-mail: shatocp@uninet.com.cn*
· **Dragonair**, *Tel. 62798099, Fax 62797189. Airport 62558899 X 5307*
· **Japan Airlines**, *Ruijin Building, Tel. 64723000*
· **Korean Airlines**, *Equatorial Hotel, Tel. 62786000*
· **Northwest Airlines**, *Shanghai Center, Tel. 62798088; airport Tel. 62558899 X 5319*
· **Qantas**, *Tel. 62798660, Fax 62798650*
· **Shanghai Airlines**, *Tel. 62688558*
· **Singapore Airlines** *(SIA), Tel. 62798000, 62798090*
· **Swissair**, *Tel. 63758211, 62797381*
· **Thai Airways**, *Tel. 62487766*
· **United Airlines**, *Hilton Hotel, Tel. 62798009. At airport, Tel. 62558899 X 5304*

By Train

If you are arriving at the main train station, you can walk directly to the subway without coming up for air and vice versa. The train with Hangzhou is three hours, with Suzhou one.

SOME GOOD BOOKS TO GET YOU IN THE MOOD FOR SHANGHAI

*Try Noel Barber's **The Fall of Shanghai;** Pan Lin's **In Search of Old Shanghai;** and especially Sterling Seagrave's **The Soong Dynasty** – a very readable and revealing book about the Soongs, sons-in-law Gen. Chiang Kai-shek and Dr. Sun Yat-sen, son T.V. Soong (reluctant premier and finance minister), and their Soviet, gangster, and wealthy Christian, American and Chinese friends. For the Cultural Revolution, there's **Life and Death in Shanghai** by Nien Cheng.*

If you're departing Shanghai by train, you can book tickets yourself at the Foreigners' Ticket Office in the **Shanghai Railway Station,** *Tel. 63179090.* Tickets are also at the **Longmen Hotel** near the railway station, *777 Hengfeng Road, Tel. 63170000.* Any travel agent can book a ticket and charge for service. You should be able to book six days in advance.

By Bus

A bus to Nanjing's Jinling Hotel leaves from the front of the New World Yangtze Hotel twice a day, and buses leave for Suzhou and Wuxi from the airports and frequently from the Long Distance Bus Stations.

By Ship

The ticket office for **international passenger ships** is at the *2/F Dongfang Hotel, 12 Zhongshan Road E2.* For **domestic ships**, it's *1 Jinling Dong Road.* The **Shiliupu Passenger Terminal** is at *111 Zhongshan Road, Tel. 63261261,* south of the Bund. The Gongping Road Passenger Terminal is at *60 Gongping Road, Tel. 6326126.*

ORIENTATION

Shanghai is pleasant because the people are outgoing and lively, and eager to learn. They are less reserved than Beijing people; making friends is easier here. **Shanghainese** have been known for centuries for their quick wit, business talents, and efficiency.

Today, parts are reminiscent of Manhattan or Paris. It is striving hard to clean up the air and has had campaigns to forbid spitting, littering, foul language, jaywalking, and the burning of coal – not always successfully. The air is still dirty but not as bad as before.

Shanghai's cosmopolitan heritage is reflected in its architecture and in the relative sophistication of many of its citizens. Its fashions and standards for products and services are the result of its longer, more concentrated period of dealing with fussy foreigners. Its shopping is the best in the country.

It is a big, very crowded city that is more redolent of trade, commerce, and industry than it is of ancient Chinese culture. Its attractions are mainly outside the city. Many visitors think Shanghai can be missed, especially if you're not interested in shopping. But I think you should at least look at this city with six million bicycles and 300,000 motor vehicles, that is expecting to surpass Hong Kong in the next century. Get a feel for its vibrancy. It is the most liveable city now for foreigners in China.

GETTING AROUND TOWN

Streets running east-west downtown are named after cities and those running north-south after provinces. Shanghai floods when it rains, so you need extra time to get around then, an extra hour to get to the airport from downtown unless you take the superhighway. The second Metro line between the two airports and the second elevated superhighway should open by October 1999. Major hotels give out free maps.

The most efficient way to get around is by car or tour bus with guide and driver. These are booked in most hotels or with a travel agent and are the most expensive. Guides are available through travel agencies, hotels, or schools. Taxis cost Y10 at flagfall.

By Public Bus

Good buses to know are the Number 20 from the Jingan Temple, past the Shanghai Centre and down Nanjing Road almost to the Bund. The Number 505 goes from People's Square, past the Hilton, Westin, Zoo, Nikko Longbai Hotel to the airport. The double-decker Number 911 goes past the Isetan Department Store, the Crowne Plaza and then to the airport. Buses are incredibly crowded. Mini-buses ply fixed routes and seats are guaranteed.

By Public Tour Bus

These are a recent god-send because they go directly to places frequented by tourists and are relatively cheap. Go the day before and check out locations and times. Buses leave every 45 minutes to an hour from the **Jin Jiang Hotel** (Jin Jiang Fandian), *59 Mao Ming Nan Road, Tel. 62582582, 62701667*. These go to People's Square, the Oriental Pearl TV Tower in Pudong, Yaohan Department Store, Nanpu Bridge, Yuyuan Garden, the Bund, People's Square and back to the Jin Jiang Hotel. Monday-Friday 9am-5:15pm; Saturday-Sunday 8:45am-5:45pm. Take this bus first without stopping as a good overall introduction to the city and then go back to spend more time in places that interest you.

Outside the **Shanghai Stadium** (Section 27) towards the Hua Ting Hotel, within half a block east of the Shanghai Stadium Metro Station is another bus terminal. Fares are generally in the Y2-Y12 price range. Comfortable buses leave once every 30 minutes to an hour, usually between 6:30am and 5pm. (Coffee shops are in the Regal Hotel and Olympic Hotel close by if you need to wait.)

Route No. 1 goes to **Sheshan** and **Song Jiang**, with departures between 6:30am and 5pm. *Tel. 64648536* for details. Route No. 2 goes to the **Wild Animal Park**. Route No. 3 goes to **Pudong**. Route No. 6 goes to **American Dreams Park** and **Jiading**, *Tel. 59598686*. Route No. 7 is a historical and cultural tour. Route No. 8 is city sightseeing. Route No. 9 goes to **Wuxi**. These are especially convenient for places outside of town, a cheap way to see the countryside.

Make sure you know the time of the return bus. The bus company has a good bus map in Chinese, hopefully soon in English, and though no one speaks English, they do try to be helpful. Your hotel should write your destination in Chinese and "what time does the bus leave here to go back to Shanghai Stadium?" Consult the Tourism Hot Line below.

By Metro (Di Tie)

The first 14-km stage of Shanghai's subway system is now operating. The line now starts from the Shanghai Railway Station with stops at **Han Zhong Road**, **Xin Zha Road**, **People's Park** (Nanjing Road, Shanghai Museum, Grand Theatre, Flower and Bird Market; this is the closest to the Bund), **Huang Pi Nan Road** (Huai Hai Road and Isetan shopping center), **Shan Xi Nan Road** (Garden Hotel, Jin Jiang Tower, Huai Hai Road), **Chang Shu Road** (Hilton and Shanghai Hotels, US, French and Japanese consulates), **Heng Shan Road** (Heng Shan Hotel), **Xu Jia Hui** (Jianguo Hotel, Orient Shopping Centre, Pacific Department Store), **Shanghai Stadium** (Hua Ting Hotels and Regal East Asia Hotel), **Cao Bao Road** (near carpet and jadeware factories, and Mongolian barbecue), **Xin Long Hua**, and **Jin Jiang Amusement Park**.

The new subway (set to open October 1, 1999) is 22 km long and goes from Hongqiao Airport to Baoshan Road, Qiujiang Road to Dalian Road, and the tunnel under the Huangpu River to Lujiazui Road Station, Dongchang Road, Dongfang Road, Yanggao Road, Central Park and Longdong Road, the last six in Pudong. You should be able to change lines at the new Henan Road Station and People's Square.

Look for the logo, a circle with two mountain peaks or "M" inside. Signs in the Metro are in English and Chinese. Fares are Y2. You pay with a plastic card, obtained from a vending machine.

By Taxi & Rental Car

Taxis cost Y10.80-Y14.40 for the first three kilometers. Reliable taxi companies are the **Da Zhong** *(Tel. 62581688)* and **Friendship Taxi**, *Tel. 62584584*. The quickest way to get around by car is by elevated expressway, one of which, the six-lane Inner Ring Road, is 48 km long and takes 36 minutes to circle the city. This is connected by the east-west expressway and the new north-south expressway, like a pizza roughly cut into four pieces. The expressway between the airports is part of this system. These elevated expressways are frequently the longer more expensive and fastest routes but on ground level you risk time-consuming traffic jams.

WHERE TO STAY

The best five-star hotels are the **Garden**, **Portman**, **Westin**, **Hilton** and **Pudong Shangri-La**, all top rate. The best four stars are the **Crowne Plaza** and **Yangtze New World**. Also good are the **Sofitel** and then the **Equatorial**. The best three-star downtown is the **City Hotel** especially for business people, and with hesitation the **YMCA** for tourists. Further out, the **Jianguo** Hotel and **Huating Guest House** are good choices for individual tourists on a budget. Closer to the Hongqiao Airport is the **International Airport Hotel** and the **Cypress**. Isolated by itself with good discounts is the adequate **Novotel**. The best for sports fans is the **Regal Shanghai East Asia Hotel** with its rooms opening into the Shanghai Stadium. All the hotels listed here are recommended unless specified otherwise.

There's no reason to fear walking alone in streets surrounding these hotels after dark as long as they are full of people. Some of these hotels still have problems with English, more so with the lower stars. Because of the recession in Asia, hotels have been full only in late-September and October or during a convention. The **low season** when prices are soft goes from late November or December to mid-March. July-August is the not-quite-so-busy 'shoulder season.' Because of the five-day work week, you should also haggle on weekends in top hotels when business people return home.

The cheaper hotels here are the **Seagull** and then the **Pujiang**, included because of their fantastic locations near the Bund. Service is poor however, English bad, and the Pujiang is a fire trap. The food and service in the Seagull are downright awful but other restaurants are close.

If you want a feeling of old Shanghai, do consider the **Peace**, **Peace Palace**, **Jin Jiang** or **Garden** – all of which have some 1920s ambiance. Service at the Peace has improved in the last few years. If you want something different, ask about the hotel rooms 140 to 230 meters up on the television tower in Pudong where so-so rooms cost from about Y500 to Y1600, and you can rent a telescope for Y30 a day. But you might feel trapped after the novelty wears off. It has no restaurant. See *Seeing the Sights* below.

The top hotels here have international class services like credit cards, beauty salons, coffee shops with western food, foreign exchange, and business centers. English is good in the five-star hotels but only in some four and three stars. Shanghai has a lot of other acceptable hotels too.

Prices listed here are subject to change, negotiation, and a 10 or 15% surcharge. Discounts have ranged from 20% to 60%. Hotels charge about Y1 for local telephone calls and an excessive amount for e-mail (over Y100 an hour). See below for Internet Cafes. Again, prices are given either in US dollars or Chinese yuan; remember, the rate at press time was about US$1=Y8.3.

The Bund/Waterfront Area

The best location for visitors and some business people is near and along the Bund. It is only 30 minutes from Hongqiao Airport by expressway, it has a subway stop in 1999, and it's close to the new pedestrian tunnel to Pudong. The flavor of old Shanghai is still here, the crowds, the European buildings, and the ships in the harbor. The view of Pudong at night is spectacular. The Nanjing shopping area here is visited by at least 200,000 people daily, the roads very congested, and on weekends, Nanjing Dong Road might be closed to vehicular traffic.

Still, if you're willing, the **Peace Hotel** is the best here for atmosphere and location, across the street from the Bund. The service is quite good but could be better, and tour buses cannot easily park and wait for groups. But the historic atmosphere is here and in the **Peace Palace** across Nanjing Road. Both are worth a look even if you don't stay there. The Peace is almost next door to the Telecommunications Building and is the closest major hotel to the Friendship Store and some good department stores.

The **Sofitel** a few blocks west has better service and more modern facilities, and almost as good a location. It is more convenient to Nanjing Road shopping and the subway, but the area around it is more congested with pedestrians. Rooms are smaller, but it is also within walking distance of the Bank of China, the Friendship Store, and Bund offices.

The **YMCA Hotel** is about 1 km from Nanjing Road towards the Yuyuan Garden, a very modest hotel with poor English and service, but it's a good location for tourists. All but the **Ocean Hotel** are about five km from the railway station and about 20 km from the airport. The Ocean is about nine km from the railway station and is nearest to the Yangpu Bridge. Plans are in the works to move the cargo port and build a waterfront walkway from near the Ocean to the Bund, three km west. The best quality hotel here is a trade-off between the Sofitel and the Peace, between efficiency and history.

HOTEL SOFITEL HYLAND SHANGHAI *(Hailun Binguan), 505 Nanjing Dong Road, 200001. Four stars. Tel. 63515888, Fax 63514088. E-mail: Sohyland@uninet.com.cn or sohyland@prodigychina.com. $190-$350. Ten-minute walk to People's Square subway station, Shanghai Museum and Grand Theatre.*

Built in 1993 and all rooms renovated in 1998, this compact, modern hotel has 30 stories, 389 rooms, with poor bedside reading lamps but good service. It has CNN and HBO, in-room safes, executive and non-smoking floors. It has international, western and Cantonese food. You can watch the activity on Nanjing Road from the comfort of its restaurants. It has its own brewery and 24-hour room service. There's a health club with an Alpha 33 relaxation pad but no pool.

PEACE PALACE, *23 Nanjing Dong Road, 200002. Star rating unknown. Tel. 63291888, Fax 63297979. Across Nanjing Road from the Peace Hotel. $160 for rooms and $220-$350 for suites. Recently it gave 55% discounts.*

The rooms in this 1906 hotel have been beautifully renovated in Victorian style but with 20th century safety features and amenities, like televisions and in-room safes. It re-opened in 1998. It has six storys, 100 rooms, and a good view of the harbor, especially from its roof garden. It is worth a look but judging by the service before the renovations, any recommendation is clouded with hesitation. Ask for an inspection before a commitment. It was not considered for my evaluation of top Shanghai hotels because it is so new.

PEACE HOTEL *(Heping Fandian), 20 Nanjing Dong Road, 200002. Four stars aiming for five. Tel. 63216888, Fax 63290300. E-mail: peacehtl@public.sta.net.cn. Http://www.shanghaipeacehotel.com. $120-$250 for rooms, $250-$350 for suites.*

Built in 1929 and renovated in 1997, this 11-story hotel has 279 large rooms, many with walk-in closets, televisions in bathrooms, and non-smoking rooms. It has CNN, and a good Sichuan-Cantonese-Shanghai restaurant on its eighth floor. This hotel is for romantic travelers, not for tightly-scheduled business people. Do ask Public Relations for a tour and don't miss the charming Indian suite, Victor Sassoon's own tower apartment, the Lalique glass, and the old ballroom. Sassoon made his money from real estate and opium. There's also the room where Noel Coward wrote "Private Lives" in 1930. Its famous 1920's jazz band plays off-key daily from 8pm-11pm, more corn than music.

OCEAN HOTEL *(Yuan Yang Binguan), 1171 Dong Da Ming Road, 200082. Four stars. Tel. 65458888, Fax 65458993. $110 to $180 for rooms, $280 for suites. Next to a department store, old Jewish ghetto and close to a post office. Three km from the Bund, and two km from the International Port.*

Built in 1988, this 28-story building has 370 rooms, and executive floors. Its standard rooms are medium-sized. It has a 24-hour business center, health club, CNN and Star Plus. There's a Japanese restaurant and a revolving restaurant with good western food.

PARK HOTEL *(Guoji Fandian), 170 Nanjing Xi Road, 200003. Four stars. Tel. 63275225, Fax 63276958. E-mail: parkgj@public1.sta.net.cn. Http://www.jjusa.com. $105 for rooms, $170 for suites including tax and service charge. Near People's Square subway station, this is the best location for Nanjing Road shopping, Shanghai Museum, Grand Theatre, and bird market.*

Built in 1934 and renovated 1997, this 24-story, 208-room hotel has small baths, safes, CNN, and Cantonese, Beijing, and continental food. English might be a problem. A Jin Jiang Hotel.

SHANGHAI MANSIONS *(Da Sha), 20 Suzhou Bei Road, 200080. Three stars aiming for four. Tel. 63246260, Fax 63065147. E-mail: shds@public1.sta.net.cn. Y850-Y930 for rooms, Y1100-Y8000 for suites and includes breakfast.*

Built in 1934 and renovated 1997, this 19-story, 254-room property has sound-proof windows and a great view of the Bund. It has Yangzhou food and coffee shop, HBO and CNN. It's okay for budget travelers who aren't fussy and want to learn Chinese.

YMCA HOTEL *(Qian Nian Hui Binguan), 123 Xizang Nan Road, 200021. Three stars. Tel. 63261040, Fax 63201957. E-mail: ymcahtl@isdnnet.sta.net.cn. Http://www.ymcahotel.com. 15 km from the airport, five km from the railway station. Walking distance to the Shanghai Museum, Nanjing Road and Yuyuan Garden. $55-$82 for rooms, $145-$300 for suites, and $15 per bed in dormitory.*

Built in 1929 with 11 stories, this hotel has 165 small worn rooms with dirty carpets and 24-hour coffee shop. Budget travelers only. English could be a problem. Jin Jiang group.

SEAGULL HOTEL *(Hai Ou Fandian), 60 Huangpu Road, 200080, north of Beidu Bridge from the Bund and close to Shanghai Mansions. Two stars, Tel. 63251500, Fax 63241263. Y440-Y530 for rooms; Y880-Y1320 for suites.*

Built in 1985, this 12-story, 104-room, basic hotel has a business center. Its south side has a great view of the Bund, but it has grubby carpets, poor food and sluggish staff. For desperate budget travelers and seamen who aren't fussy.

PUJIANG HOTEL, *15-17 Huang Pu Road, 200080. Tel. 63246388, Fax 63243179. One star. Across the street from the Seagull Hotel. Y300-Y330 for rooms, Y55 per bed in dormitory.*

This 116-room hotel was founded in 1846, Shanghai's first hotel. It was moved here in 1857 and renamed the Astor House Hotel. It should be a museum, rather than a favorite backpacker hotel. Its beautiful dark wood panelling, wooden floors, and its marvelous hallway look like a period movie set. It has a restaurant. Check the fire exits.

The Old French Concession Area

The most popular hotel area is the old French Concession. It is about 13 km from the airport and six km from the Bund in a pleasant residential area increasingly becoming commercial with tourist stores, restaurants and bars.

The **Jin Jiang Hotel**, **Jin Jiang Tower** and **Garden Hotels** are close together and within walking distance of shopping, the Shanxi Road subway stop, and Huaihai Road. **The Hilton, Shanghai** and **Equatorial Hotels** are clustered together near the Children's Palace, and are closest to the US Consulate. **The Portman** (in the Shanghai Centre), **City** and **JC Mandarin** surround the Shanghai Exhibition Center with its tourist stores and restaurants. They are near the Ruijin Center.

The **Shanghai Center** is the main international business center with offices and apartments. It has one of the theatres of the Shanghai acrobats, Hard Rock Cafe, and United, Thai, Qantas, Dragonair, and Northwest airlines, DHL, travel agents, supermarket and a "drug store." You can walk to Jinan Temple. These three groups are within about three km of each other. The Hongqiao-Pudong expressway goes right by the Equatorial and the Hilton. The Hilton and Portman both have slow elevators.

The best hotels here are the **Hilton**, **Portman**, and **Garden** (inspite of its plastic soap dishes), all aiming for excellence.

SHANGHAI HILTON INTERNATIONAL *(Jinan Dajiudian), 250 Hua Shan Road, 200040. Five stars. Tel. 62480000, Fax 62483848. E-mail: shhilton@public.sta.net.cn. $230-$290 for rooms, $540-$1960 for suites. Http://www.hilton.com to reserve. At Jingan subway stop.*

Built in 1988, this 43-story hotel has 800 spacious rooms each with at least three telephones, CNN and HBO. It has western, Cantonese and Sichuan cuisine and *teppanyaki*. Its basement, fast Asian food restaurant is budget-priced and good. (The set lunch is Y45. *Won ton* soup Y20.) It has a Clark Hatch gym, indoor pool, lighted outdoor tennis, and squash. It has executive and non-smoking floors, and two Japanese-speaking floors, Lufthansa Airlines and United Airlines. This hotel can book a whole train car for groups to Suzhou, clean out a coach and cater it with food and open bar. It has classical Chinese gardens indoors and outdoors with waterfall.

THE PORTMAN RITZ-CARLTON *(Po Ter Man Jiu Dian), Shanghai Center, 1376 Nanjing Xi Road, 200040. Five stars. Tel. 62798888, Fax 62798999, 62798887. E-mail:portman@public.sta.net.cn. Http://*

www.ritzcarlton.com. $220-$360 for rooms, $500-$2000 for suites. 1.5 km from the Shanxi Nan subway stop.

Opened in 1990 and managed by Shangri-La until the end of 1997, this hotel was taken over by Ritz-Carlton in 1998 with its European tradition. Since then, it has been undergoing major renovations. It has 50 stories and 600 huge rooms with at least three telephones each and non-smoking floors. Its executive club floors offer drinks and food all day and after-dinner. Snacks have included shrimp cocktails, stuffed eggs, nuts and cheeses. Its executive club breakfast has made-to-order eggs, *dim sum,* bacon, sausage, cheeses, smoked salmon, buns and yogurt. All rooms have voice mail, CNN, HBO, NBC and in-room safes.

The hotel has Cantonese, American, and Japanese restaurants, and a grill room, all with dress code: smart casual, no shorts. There's a 24-hour coffee shop and room service. It has one of the largest health clubs in the city: indoor tennis, squash, aerobics, gym, and *taiji* classes, and an indoor-outdoor lap pool. It has access to Deng Xiao Ping's boat for parties, and free airport shuttle. Its concierge has some of the best seats reserved at the Grand Theatre.

GARDEN HOTEL SHANGHAI *(Huayuan Fandian), 58 Maoming Nan Road, 200020. Five stars, Tel. 64151111, Fax 64158866. E-mail: garden@online.sh.cn. Http://www.gardenhotelshanghai.com. $220-$300 for rooms and $550-$3000 for suites. Set in a large 27,000 square meter garden.*

Opened in 1989-90 with major renovations 1997 and 1998, this hotel incorporates the 1926 *Cercle Sportif* with its marvelous old ball room into its building. It has 34 stories, 500 spacious rooms each with safes, at least three telephone jacks, HBO and CNN, and gleaming white bathtubs. It has non-smoking and executive floors, a classy-looking business center, voice mail, and 24-hour room service. There's a pool with retractable roof, gym, and lighted outdoor tennis court, Japanese and continental food. It has parking for 240 cars and free airport shuttle bus. Hotel Okura management. Member of Leading Hotels of the World.

SHANGHAI JC MANDARIN *(Jing Chang Wen Hua), 1225 Nanjing Xi Road, 200040. Thirty minutes from the Hongqiao airport. Five stars. Tel. 62791888, Fax 62792314, 62791822. E-mail:shjcm@public1.sta.net.cn. Http://www.jcmandarin.com. In North America, Tel. 800/44UTELL. $210-$270 for rooms, $410-$1460 for suites.*

Opened in 1991 and renovated in 1998-99, this 30-story hotel has 600 large rooms each with three telephone jacks, HBO, safes, and contact-free key card system. It has non-smoking and executive floors, continental cuisine, a *patisserie,* and especially good Cantonese cuisine. It has a clinic, tennis, squash, and a gym, an all-weather pool, sauna, jacuzzi and steamroom. There's also a playroom for children. A marvelous lacquer painting of Ming Admiral Cheng Ho dominates the lobby. Managed by Meritus Hotels and Resorts. Member Leading Hotels of the World.

HOTEL EQUATORIAL SHANGHAI (*Gui Du Da Fandian*), *65 Yan'an Xi Road, 200040, Tel. 62481688, Fax 62481773. E-mail: equatsha@public.sta.net.cn. Http://www.equatorial.com. Four stars. Y1650-Y2100 for rooms, Y2600-9500 for suites.*

Built in 1991-92 with renovations in 1998-99, this hotel has 26 stories, 526 rooms and small bathrooms. It has executive and non-smoking floors and guests have the use of the International Club with its heated indoor pool, bowling, gym, tennis and squash. It has Thai, Japanese, Chaozhou, and Cantonese food. There's a 1000-seat theater, CNN and HBO, in-room safes and UPS office. Managed by Equatorial International Singapore.

JIN JIANG TOWER (*Xin Jin Jiang*), *161 Changle Road, 200020. Five stars. Tel. 64151188, Fax 64150045. Http://www.jjusa.com. $190 for rooms, $350 for suites.*

Built in 1988-1990 with some floors renovated in 1998-99, this 43-story hotel has 728 rooms, tiny twin beds, in-room safes, CNN and HBO. It has executive floors, gym, year-round outdoor pool and jacuzzi. It has a revolving restaurant, Korean barbecue, and French restaurant.

JIN JIANG HOTEL (*Jin Jiang Fandian*), *59 Mao Ming Nan Road, 200020, Tel. 62582582, Fax 64725588. Http://www.jjusa.com. $155 for rooms, $150-$240 for suites, including surcharges. Avoid the South Building $100, which looks like a cheap American motel.*

First built in 1929, this is a complex of hotel buildings. It has 505 rooms, HBO, CNN, and ABN, and a famous Sichuan restaurant. Its North Building is good with big rooms and four stars. Its middle building is now five stars, with classy art deco lobby, and all suites. It has a book store, crafts stores, and supermarket. It expects to upgrade its North Building to five-star standard soon with convention centre, health center, and bowling. English might be a problem.

CITY HOTEL (*Chen Shi Jiu Dian*), *5-7 Shanxi Nan Road, 200020. Three stars. E-mail:cityh@uninet.com.cn. Tel. 62551133, Fax 62550611, 62550211. $115-$155 for rooms, $240 for suites.*

Built in 1988-89, it redecorated its 14th-17th floors in 1997. It has 270 small rooms with soft beds, CNN and 40-watt bulbs, executive floors and popular Sichuan and Shanghai restaurants. Its worn and stained carpets should be replaced soon.

SHANGHAI HOTEL (*Binguan*), *505 Wulumuqi Road, 200040. Three stars, Tel. 62480088, Fax 62481310, 62481056. Y858-Y1588 for rooms, Y2028-Y3888 for suites.*

Built in 1983, and renovated in 1997, this hotel has 23 stories and 562 rooms. It has Chaozhou and Japanese food, a gym, jacuzzi, CNN and Star Movies. Huating group.

Shanghai Stadium Metro Area

This is the third best location, a great location for individual travelers near tourist buses, and subway stop. The **Hua Ting Hotel**, **Regal East Asia**, **Jianguo Hotel**, and **Hua Ting Guest House** are in this area (in order of quality, with the Hua Ting Hotel the best). They are also close to the elevated highway. There are two relatively good shopping areas nearby, new restaurants, the Shanghai Gymnasium, the 80,000-seat soccer stadium, and a little further away, the Cao He Jing High Tech park. This area is about 12 km from the airport and about 15 km from the train station. The Hongqiao Development Zone is six km away.

HUA TING HOTEL AND TOWERS *(Hua Ting Binguan #1), 1200 Caoxi Bei Road, 200030. Five stars. Tel. 64391000, Fax 62550830, 64390130. Http:\\www.huating-hotel.com. $215-$285 for rooms, and $305-$1500 for suites. The Hua Ting used to be managed by Sheraton. It has been offering about 60% discounts.*

Built in 1986, this 26-story hotel renovated several floors in 1998 and 1999. It has 885 spacious rooms with large beds, voice mail and CNN. It has Japanese, executive and non-smoking floors. It has an indoor pool, gym, bowling and tennis, Cantonese, Sichuan, Japanese, Continental, and Asian food. There's a popular 24-hour American sit-down deli and a good shopping center. Its shuttle bus connects with the airport.

REGAL SHANGHAI EAST ASIA HOTEL, *666-800 Tian Yao Qiao Road, Xu Hui District, 200030. Four stars. Tel. 64266888, Fax 64265888. $160-$240 and $260-$650 (but it's been giving a very good discount). E-mail:rseah-c@online.sh.cn. This is part of the Shanghai stadium.*

This 1997 hotel has 350 rooms with data ports, CNN, CNBC, and HBO. Guests in some rooms above the 10th floor can see into the stadium and have to pay an extra charge if there's a game. It has non-smoking and executive club rooms, Japanese, Chinese and western restaurants. Its 12th floor Sports Bar also has a view of events inside the stadium. The concierge should have a schedule of games and also of the tour buses outside. It has aerobics, steam room, and whirlpool. Guests can use some of the facilities in the stadium like the track if free. Let me know if you can hear the roar of the crowd from your room.

JIANGUO HOTEL *(Binguan), 439 Caoxi Bei Road, 200030. Four stars. Xujiahui metro station. Tel. 64399299, Fax 64811578. Y1100-Y1500 for rooms, Y2600-Y5600 for suites. Eleven km from the airport and eight km from the railway station.*

This hotel is within one km of the Hua Ting Hotel towards the Orient Shopping Centre. Opened in 1991 and renovating executive floors in 1999, it has 23 stories and 473 rooms with small bathrooms. It has a gym, CNN and CNBC, Cantonese, Shanghai, Chaozhou and French food, and a 24-hour coffee shop. Carpets are a little dirty, there's no pool, and English might be a problem. Shanghai New Asia Group.

HUA TING GUEST HOUSE *(Hua Ting Binguan #2), 2525 Zhong Shan Xi Road, 200030. Three stars. Tel. 64813500, 64391380, Fax 6390322. Y680 for rooms. This is not to be confused with its neighbor, the Hua Ting Hotel and Towers.*

Built in 1987 with floors 13-16 renovated in 1998, this hotel has 17 stories and 187 rooms. It has a non-smoking floor, CNN, and slow elevators. The food is pretty good but the service is sluggish. Its standards and prices are not as high as its sister hotel next door. Guests here can use facilities next door but must pay cash.

In-Between Hotels

CROWNE PLAZA YINXING *(Yin Xing Jia Re Jiudian), 400 Panyu Road, 200052. Four stars. Tel. 62808888, Fax 62808888, 62822014. E-mail: hicpsha@uninet.com.cn. Http://www.crowneplaza-shanghai.com. $210-$310 for rooms, and $400-$800 for suites. 15 km from the airport, nine km from the railway station, five km from the Hongqiao area, and five km from the US Consulate. It is 1.8 km from the Xu Jia Hu metro stop. This is the best hotel for the Shanghai film and television festivals next door. It's in a residential neighborhood with small restaurants and bars and Iranian consulate. Across the street is a bowling alley.*

Built in 1991-92, this hotel has 26 storys and 534 spacious rooms, with wide twin beds, in-room safes, CNN, and in-house movies. It has executive and non-smoking floors and handicapped rooms, a gym, good size indoor pool, steam bath, sauna, squash, and tennis. It has Cantonese, Sichuan, and international food, 24-hour room service and coffee shop. Its bar claims the longest happy hour in town 11am-7pm. Children have a playground with free nanny service at lunch and for some kids free food. Ask about special rates for teens and seniors. And enjoy its friendly, professional staff. It has a complimentary shuttle bus service.

REGAL INTERNATIONAL EAST ASIA HOTEL, *516 Hengshan Road, 200030. Five star quality. Tel. 64155588, Fax 64458899. E-mail: rieah@prodigychina.com. Http://www.regal-hotels.com. In a residential district southwest of the Hengshan Road Metro stop. $200-$270 for rooms, and $500-$1400 for suites.*

This 1997 hotel has 300 rooms, CNN, HBO and safes. It has non-smoking rooms and executive floor. It looks good and is included primarily because of its eight outdoor and two indoor tennis courts with 1200-spectator places. It also has a 25-meter heated pool, 12-lane bowling alley, golf simulator, squash, *kungfu* classes and gym. It is ideal for athletic business people and tennis players.

Near the Hongqiao Exhibition Centre

This could be the best location for you if you're involved with exhibitions here. The closest subway stop is about three km away at Changning Road on Number 2 line (2000). The Hongqiao Development Zone (HQDZ) is less than 10 km from the airport, about 12 km from the train station and from the Bund, and 18 km from Pudong. This area has a couple of exhibition centers, including the Shanghai Mart for big trade shows. It also has some major government offices, apartments, a recreation center, two department stores, consulates, restaurants, and several hotels: **Westin Tai Ping Yang** (top), the **Yangtze New World**, then the **Galaxy**, and the **Rainbow** in that order of quality.

New hotels, luxury housing and supermarkets have been built nearby. An entertainment center, two department stores, shopping center, bars and restaurants are also here. Towards the airport is a government guest house, the zoo, and a growing number of expensive single family houses for foreigners.

THE WESTIN TAI PING YANG SHANGHAI *(Tai Ping Yang Da Fandian), 5 Zunyi Nan Road, 200335. Five stars. Tel. 62758888, Fax 62755420. E-mail: westin@uninet.com.cn. $210 and $345 for rooms and $398-$468 for suites.*

Opened in 1990-92, this hotel has 27 stories and 578 spacious rooms with safes, voice mail, and BBC, NBC, and HBO. All rooms have a swivel chair and an executive desk with three electrical outlets, and two lamps. It has non-smoking and executive floors. Expect especially good Italian and Japanese food and 24-hour room service. There's a gym and small outdoor pool. Fortunately, the tediousness of its constantly bowing staff in its elegantly-decorated lobby has been replaced by a rubber ducky on each bathtub, a refreshing change. It has a shuttle bus. Independently owned and managed.

YANGTZE NEW WORLD HOTEL *(Yangtze Jiang Da Jiudian), 2099 Yan'an Xi Road, 200335. Four stars. Tel. 62750000, Fax 62750750. Y1550-Y1950 for rooms, Y2950-Y10650 for suites.*

Opened in 1990-91, this 34-story hotel has 570 rooms with data ports and safes, CNN and HBO. It has non-smoking and executive floors, a gym and small outdoor pool. It has Asian, Sichuan, Chaozhou and the best Cantonese food in town. Its bar has a "hungry hour" with substantial snacks free with drink. There are frequent shuttle buses with the airport. It also has Cadillac limousines.

GALAXY *(Ying He Binguan), 888 Zhongshan Xi Road, 200051. Four stars. Tel. 62755888, Fax 62750201, 62750039. $160-$200 for rooms, $260-$1000 for suites.*

Built in 1990, this hotel has 35 stories and 685 rooms with soft beds, CNN and Star World, and 40-watt bulbs. They should have in-room safes soon. It has two lobbies, Cantonese, Sichuan and Korean food, a gym and bowling. English might be a problem. Huating Group.

RAINBOW HOTEL *(Hongqiao Binguan), 2000 Yan'an Xi Road, 200051. Four stars, Tel. 62753388, Fax 62757244 (reservations), 62753736 (guests). Http://www.cbw.com/hotel/rainbow. In North America, Tel. 800/ 44UTELL. $150-$170 for rooms, $300-$600 for suites.*

Built in 1988, this 31-story hotel has 630 rooms, narrow halls and beds, and small bathrooms. It is clean and adequate with 40-watt bulbs, CNBC and NBC, CITS airline ticket desk and Asiana airlines. It has 24-hour room service, a pool and gym. English might be a problem. Huating Group.

Slightly Outside the Hongqiao Development Zone (HQDZ)

MAN PO BOUTIQUE HOTEL, *660 Xinhua Road, 200052. About three star standard. Tel. 62801000, 62806660. About one km east of the Hongqiao area. $150-$180 for rooms, $230-$350 for suites, both including breakfast.*

This tiny 76-room hotel is included because it looks very beautiful, intimate, and clean. The quality of its service has yet to be proved and so it's outside this survey. It has limited facilities, good-looking western and Chinese restaurants, satellite television, a gym and billiard room. It has spacious rooms with surge protectors and the English is basic. Managed by the City Hotel.

The Nikko-Airport-Cypress Hotels Area

Here are the **Nikko**, **Cypress**, and **Airport** Hotels, in order of quality with the Nikko best, the Cypress next, and the Airport International a close third. These are within two km of the airport and 19 km of the railway station. The closest to the airport is the International Airport Hotel. These three hotels have co-operated with frequent shuttle buses from the airport.

HOTEL NIKKO SHANGHAI *(Re Hong Longbai), 2451 Hongqiao Road, 200335. Four stars. Tel. 62689111, Fax 62689333. $160-$220 for rooms, and $280-$500 for suites.*

Built in 1987 with renovations in 1998, this 11-story hotel has 419 smallish rooms and attractive garden. It has tennis, a gym and outdoor pool. It has Cantonese and western food, and 24-hour room service. There's CNN and Star TV, plastic bathrooms, disco and *karaoke*.

CYPRESS HOTEL *(Long Bai Fandian), 2419 Hongqiao Road, 200335. Three stars but moving up it seems. Tel. 62688868, Fax 62681878. E-mail: cypress@stn.sh.cn. Http://www.jjusa.com. In North America, Tel. 800/223-5652. $140-$240 for rooms, $260-$400 for suites.*

Built in 1982 and renovated in 1996, this hotel has six stories and 150 small rooms with CNN, ABN and HBO. It should be given the prize for the most improved hotel in the last three years. It is set in a vast garden. It has always had a China Eastern booking office, book store and recreation center with indoor pool, bowling, tennis, and squash. There's a lovely patio cafe, German food, and smartly uniformed bell men, miniskirted clerks and flight monitors. It has non-smoking rooms and it looks like it's kicked out the guys who used to smoke up the lobby.

SHANGHAI INTERNATIONAL AIRPORT HOTEL *(Guoji Ji Chang Binguan), 2550 Hongqiao Road, 200335. Three stars, Tel. 62688888, Fax 62688393. $75-$110.*

Built in 1988, it has eight stories and 308 small rooms. This Japanese joint venture transit hotel also has CNN, massage, and *teppanyaki*. There's a China Eastern ticketing office, flight departure monitors and free check-in for some China Eastern flights. It is five minutes walk from Hongqiao airport.

Less Touristy Neighborhoods

If you want totally Chinese neighborhoods, look for isolated hotels like the **Novotel** which is, however, very far out for tourists. It is also frequently full of long-staying guests. And inspite of the nearby Botanical Garden and its suburban location, the air isn't much better than downtown.

NOVOTEL SHANGHAI YUAN LIN *(Yuan Lin Binguan), 201 Bai Se Road, 200231. Three stars. Tel. 64701688, Fax 64700008. E-mail: caticyih@public.sta.net.cn. About $100-$120. Fifteen km from the airport, 17 km from the railway station, and 16 km from the Bund. Free access to Botanical Garden next door.*

Built in 1990, this six-story, 183-room hotel has a once-a-day shuttle bus downtown (otherwise a Y38 trip by taxi to Nanjing Road), two non-smoking floors, CNN, and Star TV. It has an indoor pool, gym and tennis, and 40 Canadian-style villas.

By the Railroad Station

EAST CHINA HOTEL, *111 Tian Mu Dong Road, 200070. Four-star standard. Tel. 63178000, Fax 63176678. In front of the railway station. Y780-Y880 for rooms, Y1560-Y2340 for suites.*

This should be okay for an overnight between trains. It has no CNN, and no room safe. It has small bathrooms, but it's clean and assistant managers speak English. Managed by Huating Group.

Pudong

The **Shangri-La** is the top hotel here until the **Grand Hyatt** opens, and then it's anyone's guess. The 555-room five-star Grand Hyatt is within

PUDONG

*Tourists should not ignore **Pudong**. Business people, of course, have already found it. Pudong means "east of the Huangpu River." The older part of Shanghai is Puxi, "west of the Huangpu River." Pudong is between the Huangpu River and the mouth of the Yangtze River. In 1990, this community south and east of Shanghai proper was nothing but rice fields and villages. The national government gave it first priority for economic development and you can see the results today. It is booming. Its major investors are from Hong Kong, Japan and the United States. Its annual growth rate in some areas has reached 30% to 50%. Its population is at least 1.5 million, and officials expect the population to reach two million people by the year 2000. Pudong hopes to exceed Hong Kong.*

*You can get there by two vehicular tunnels (one more is planned), one pedestrian tunnel in late 1999 (two more are planned), two bridges, or by any of seven ferries. People who take taxis have to pay an additional Y15 extra for crossing a bridge or tunnel. The best ferry for tourists is from the **Yan'an Road Ferry Terminal** (Yan'an Lu Ma Tou). This disembarks close to the **Shangri-La** and **Grand Hyatt Hotels** and the television tower. This ferry costs Y1 for a return trip, payable on the Puxi side, a nice reminder that all is not glitz and high prices in this burgeoning city. This ferry and nearby park are highly recommended evenings as the ideal place to see the lights on the Bund. It's also a touch of Old Shanghai. The trip is short and passengers stand. It will be relocating one km south after the opening of the pedestrian tunnel.*

The pedestrian tunnel should move a maximum of over 5000 people an hour from Nanjing Dong Road (across from the Peace Hotel) to the Oriental Pearl TV Tower in five minutes. It'll have lots of pictures to look at but it won't be as nice as a ferry ride.

*The metro should soon link the Hongqiao airport with the Pudong International Airport (1999), the largest airport in China. Pudong already has **Asia's biggest department store** (Yaohan/Next Age/Babaiban), its highest television tower, the world's tallest building, and the Shanghai Stock Exchange.*

Pudong is a planned city with lots of open park space, and hotels here are 30 minutes drive from either airport. The Yan'an Dong Road tunnel in Puxi becomes Central Road, Shi Ji Dadao, the main road to the airport in Pudong. The closest Metro stops to the hotels below should be Dong Fang Road Station at the Tower.

walking distance of the Shangri-La. It has 40-square meter rooms, the largest in town. It is on the 55th-87th floors of the delicate-looking 88-story Jin Mao building. Two of its 61 elevators should be able to zip you up to the 88th floor observation deck in 45 seconds. From 1999 to 2003, this will be the **highest hotel in the world** at 420.5 meters.

The Hyatt has windows beside its bathtubs so you can soak and enjoy the view. It has a 31-story atrium lobby, voice mail, at least two telephone lines, seven executive floors, Cantonese, Japanese and Italian restaurants. All rooms have inter-active television.

In early 1999, the **New Asia Tomson Hotel** was the second best. The lobby of the **Holiday Inn** is cavernous and bare but the rooms are fine. The **Purple Mountain Hotel** is good value. These three are closer to downtown Pudong, near the Yaohan Department Store.

PUDONG SHANGRI-LA HOTEL *(Pudong Shang Gorilla), 33 Fu Cheng Road, Pudong, 200120. Five star standard. Tel. 68828888, Fax 68826688. Http://www.Shangri-La.com. On the edge of Lujiazui commercial area, beside the Huangpu Riverside Garden and television tower. $220-$330 for rooms and $450-$2950 for suites.*

This 1998 hotel has 612 large rooms. Rooms have data ports, kettles, safes, executive work desks, CNN, and electronic keycards. It has an executive club, 24-hour room service, Japanese and Chinese restaurants, and an amazing entertainment center with metal menus and a different view of the world. Its grand ballroom can seat 1470 people banquet style. It has a gym, indoor pool, tennis, jacuzzi and steam bath. There is a complimentary airport shuttle and a world-class view of the Bund from its two-story high coffee shop, its lounge, ball room, business center, pool, and running machines. It is decorated with hundreds of paintings.

See also Chapter 13, *China's Best Places to Stay.*

NEW ASIA TOMSON HOTEL, *777 Zhangyang Road, Pudong, 200120. Five-star standard. Tel. 58318888, Fax 68756761. E-mail: nathsha@uninet.co.cn. In Lujiazui trade and financial zone. $210-$280 for rooms, $280-$2388 for suites.*

Opened in 1996, this 24-story hotel with 21-story atrium, has 400 large rooms, in-room safes, voice mail, and CNN, NBC and CNBC. It has executive floors, Cantonese, Chaozhou and Italian restaurants, and 24-hour fast food and business centres. There's also a delicatessen, and a grill room. It has a gym, golf and indoor-outdoor pool.

HOLIDAY INN PUDONG *(Pudong Jia Ri Fandian), 899 Dong Fang Road, Pudong, 200122. Four stars. Tel. 58306666, Fax 58304719, 58305555. E-mail:hipudongsha@poboxes.com. Http://www.hi-pudongsha.com. It is 20 km from Hongqiao airport, and eight km from the railway station. $160-$235 for rooms and $220-$1,200 for suites.*

This 1998, 25-story, 294-room hotel has room safes, three executive floors, and room data ports. It has airport shuttle service, 24-hour room service, and seven floors of office space for rent. Enjoy its Irish pub, brasserie with fusion dishes, Cantonese, curries, and Shanghai food. Its Shanghai suite can seat 500 at a banquet. It has a 1000 sq meter health club with gym, aerobics room, jacuzzi, steam room and pool. Its Deli Corner has apple pie, Black Forest cake, and lemon meringue pie for Y20 a slice. Rooms receive CNN, NBC, MTV, and Star World.

PURPLE MOUNTAIN HOTEL *(Zi Jin Shan Dajiudian), 528 Lao Shan Dong Road, 200122, Tel. 68868888, Fax 68868800. E-mail: pmhotel@prodigychina.com. $100-$200 for rooms, $120-$1880 for suites. Price includes breakfast.*

This four-star standard, 260-room hotel is between the Holiday Inn and the New Thomson in Pudong. It has been giving 40% discounts and as such is a good deal. It has an airport shuttle bus, CNN, NBC, Star Plus, and 24-hour coffee shop.

WHERE TO EAT

The Asian recession has hit restaurants too. Hotel restaurants have been advertising discounts in tourist or hotel handouts, like 50% dim sum weekends or Norwegian salmon for Y65 at the JC Mandarin, and all-you-can-eat *dimsum* for Y59 on Sundays from 10am-2:30pm at the Pudong Shangri-La. Both have great Cantonese food. The Crowne Plaza has had live lobster on Wednesdays, 30% off Y65 per 100 gms, and two-for-one birds' nest soup.

Every top hotel should be able to lay on a great Chinese banquet. But if you want to impress anybody, take them to the JC Mandarin, Westin, Garden, Hilton, Shangri-La or Portman Hotels. Then there's the Meilongzhen. The Hilton's lunch buffet is Y160-Y168.

So far we haven't found the equivalent of Hong Kong's Lan Kwai Fung or Beijing's Sanlitun sidewalk restaurants. There are groupings of restaurants in and around the Shanghai Centre, around the Hua Ting Hotel, and across from the New World Yangtze Hotel. There are a few good-looking restaurants around the Gap at 4 Hengshan Road, places to look into, smell, compare menus and choose.

Shanghai food is sweeter, lighter and prettier than other Chinese foods. It has a delicate consistency. See Chapter 11, *Food & Drink.*

MEILONGZHEN, *Nanjing Xi Road, 22 Lane 1081, Tel. 62535353, about 100 meters east of the JC Mandarin Hotel.*

This is the old-tried-and-true It is especially good for crabs in November. It also has pleasant traditional Chinese decor, moderate prices, and is open 11am-2pm and 5pm-9:30pm.

LU BO LANG RESTAURANT, *10 Wen Chang Road, (18 meters south of Seven-Bend Bridge in Old Town Temple), Yuyuan Garden, Tel. 63550500, 63554408.*

Since President Clinton ate here, you must try it. It's great for typical Shanghai snacks. Y50 gives you a sample of 12 different dumplings and cakes, enough for a light lunch. The service however is slow for us mortals.

XIAONANGUO SHANGHAI RESTAURANT, *1848 Hongqiao Road, Tel. 62425209.*

This is a chain with moderate prices, good for spare ribs and drunken crab soaked in wine.

CAFE 1931, *112 Mao Ming Nan Road, Tel. 64725264.*

Worth a try. They successfully duplicate the ambience of the 1930's.

PARADISE RESTAURANT, *on the ground floor in the Hua Ting #2 Guest House.*

Standard and satisfying. The service is slow, the table cloths crisp and white. Try the sauteed pork with peppers Y28, fried shrimp Y98, sweet and sour pork Y34, bean curd with spicy sauce Y24. It is open 6am-10pm and takes credit cards.

If these are still too pricy for you, there are loads of cheaper places to try all the way down to the **Deng Guang Ye Shi** (Lighted Lantern Night Market). This is at Nanjing Dong Road and Yunnan Road from 7pm to midnight. It is closed in winter. Take your own bowl and chopsticks if you're worried about hygiene. You can fill up for less than Y10 on satay and noodles.

Western Food

Try any of the top hotels. The Westin and Hilton have great Italian restaurants and a choice of over 100 wines, mostly French in the Westin's **Giovanni's** restaurant, *Tel. 62758888.* The Giovanni has good US sirloin steak with Arugula and fine herbs for Y136, and grilled US beef tenderloin for Y149. The grill room in the Garden Hotel is great. Try also:

PAULANER BRAUHAUS, *50 Feng Yang Road, Tel. 64745700.*

They brew their own German beer and serve up authentic sausages and sauerkraut.

ATRIUM CAFE, *at the Hilton.*

Good food, and there's a live band.

PARK 97, *2 Gao Lan Road in Fuxing Park, Tel. 63180785.*

Park 97 has a quiet, sylvan atmosphere. Its cafe is open at 11am daily to whenever. Its dining room is open 6pm Monday to Saturday with a weekend brunch from 11am-2pm.

A.D.,*3896 Hong Mei Road, Tel. 62625620.*

Expensive Italian.

BLUE HEAVEN REVOLVING RESTAURANT, *in the Jin Jiang Tower, 161 Changle Road, Tel. 64151188.*

For more American food, this restaurant has a nice atmosphere and changing scenery. It's open 11:30am-2pm, 6pm-10pm.

THE HARD ROCK CAFE, *in the Shanghai Centre, Suite A05 & 110, 1376 Nanjing Xi Road, 11am-2am, Sunday-Thursday, and 11am-3am Friday-Saturday. Tel. 62798133.*

The Hard Rock here seems to be better here than in Beijing.

MALONE'S AMERICAN CAFE, *near the Portman, 257 Tong Ren Road, Tel. 62472400.*

You can't get any more American than this place.

TONY ROMA'S, *in the Shanghai Centre, Tel. 62797129.*

Expensive-but-worth-it ribs, open 11am-10:30pm.

SWENSEN'S, *139 Ruijin Yi Road, Tel. 53065005.*

For dessert as well as dinner.

McDonald's has a branch at *88 Nanjing Xi Road, Tel. 63589690.* Open 8am-11pm. **Pizza Hut**, *700 Xizang Zhong Road, Tel. 63523026,* is open 11am-10:30pm. You should be able to telephone for take-out.

EAST & WEST

Sasha's, in the old French concession, has a setting as interesting as its menu. Built in the 1920's for a Jewish taipan, the house was also lived in by Chiang Kai-shek and owned by his in-laws the Soong's. Jiang Qing, Chairman Mao's widow, also used it for her theatricals. The bar is on the ground floor, the main dining room on the second. The food has unusual flavors, a fusion of Asian and western and tastes good: a great poached salmon with Black Thai Risotto with parsley sauce for Y140; a Caesar salad (Y60) with too many anchovies, a good tea-smoked duck with creamy polenta; teppanyaki vegetables with apricot brandy sauce for Y130 and Haagen Dazs ice cream in a sugar basket. There's a 73-item wine list – including French, Spanish, Australian, Italian, and Californian. The wooden latticed interior with white marble table tops was unusual and charming. Sasha's is at House 11, 9 Dong Ping Road (at Heng Shan Road), Tel. 64746166, Fax 64746170. Credit cards accepted.

THE GAP RESTAURANT AND BAR, *ground floor, Jing Ming Building, 8 Zun Yi Road, Tel. 62782900, 62704693. It takes credit cards.*

The Gap is across from the Yangtze New World Hotel in an alley to the left of the Friendship Department Store. It has a mixed menu of Chinese and western food, including very good Gapburgers with excellent fries. Its Hainan chicken rice was tasty but not authentic. Ask for the German braised pork knuckles and the Dai Yu, the deep fried fish Chinese style. The Gap even offers a choice of Italian, French, Australian and South African wines. Decorated with Charlie Chaplin and James Dean posters, it has a cute atmosphere and sometimes a live American band.

The Gap has many other branches, one of which, **Mini One**, is behind Giordano's to the left as you go out the Hua Ting Hotel. Other branches are the **Xiao Ting Hot Pot** and its **Sea Food Restaurant**, *7/F, International Shopping Center, 527 Huaihai Zhong Road, Tel. 53065449.* It has a branch on the fourth floor of the West Gate Mall. The quality of the food has not been consistent, but the decor of all its restaurants has been fun and imaginative.

Other Chinese Food

If you want great *dim sum*, try either **The Yangtze New World Hotel** or the **JC Mandarin Hotel**. In fact, the Yangtze New World's **Dynasty Restaurant** has the best Cantonese food in town.

JIE ER JING SICHUAN RESTAURANT, *82 Yandang Road, Tel. 63728574.*

Old and famous.

WAN BAO HE RESTAURANT, *603 Fuzhou Road, Tel. 6307609.*

Known for its Shanghai crab. Open 11am-1:30pm, 5:00pm-9:30pm.

FU RONG ZHEN SICHUAN RESTAURANT, *Crowne Plaza Hotel, 388 Panyu Road, 200052, Tel. 62808888. It accepts credit cards.*

This Sichuan restaurant has perfect *dan-dan* noodles for Y10 a small bowl. It has better Sichuan food than some restaurants in Chongqing. Try the sliced pork with garlic sauce for Y27, deep-fried shrimp with chili sauce for Y96, tea-smoked duck with dumpling for Y77, shredded chicken with Sichuan sauce for Y31, and boiled beef with chili and onions for Y42. Yummy. You can request different degrees of fire.

SHANG PALACE, *33 Fu Cheng Road, Pudong, 200120, Tel. 68828888,*

In the Shangri-La Pudong, it is very good and somewhat pricey: try the barbecued meat combo, hot-sour soup, pan-fried chicken, braised Shanghai cabbage, and stir-fried sliced beef with peaches and vegetables. The buffet in its Garden Cafe includes Mongolian barbecue all the time.

MONGOLIAN BARBECUE RESTAURANT *(Qing Xiang Co), 33 Chao-Bao Road, Tel. 64360126, 8:15am-8:30pm, south of the Hua Ting. You should make reservations for lunch. Credit cards accepted.*

This is a favorite. How can you go wrong with Mongolian barbecue when you pick your own ingredients and sauces? But you might not enjoy its factory-like atmosphere, noise, and line-ups. Over-priced up-market shopping is next door. (see Shopping below).

LU LU RESTAURANT, *No. 1, Lane 88, Shui Cheng Road, Tel. 62706679.*

This place has the best seafood. It is expensive and open 24 hours a day. You pick your own live fish from a tank.

International Cuisine

TANDOOR, *in the Jin Jiang Hotel, Food Street, 59 Mao Ming Nan Road, Tel. 64725494, 62582582 X 9301. It is open 11:30am-2:00pm and 5:30pm-10:30pm.*

This is the only Indian restaurant in town, and is very good, authentic, and expensive.

VIVA EL POPO MEXICAN RESTAURANT, *in the Gubei New Area No. 12 Lane 19 Golden Lion Garden, Tel. 62199279.*

This is out near the Westin Hotel. The food is reasonably priced.

JIA JIA LE RESTAURANT, *next to the domestic airport terminal at Hongqiao, Tel. 65371688 X 81881, or 62684018. Open daily 9am-9pm.*

This is a modest cafe with good, authentic Singapore and Malaysian food, and affable manager Peter Yap. The pork spare rib soup (*bak kut teh* for Y20) tasted just like my Cantonese father's. Popular are the chicken rice for Y25, the *laksa* (fiery, spiced noodles with coconut milk soup) Y24, *choi tau kueh* (carrot cake) Y20, *nasi lemak* (coconut milk rice) Y28, *satay* Y18 a dozen, and *mee siam* (spiced vermicelli soup) for Y20. the food here is especially good if the boss is around.

THE GRAPE (Pu Tao Yuan), *142 Xin Le Road and 55 Xin Le Road, Open 11am-1am. No credit cards.*

These have been the current 'in' restaurants among knowledgeable expatriates, but I found nothing special. It serves Cantonese and Sichuan specialties on only a few tables, and accepts no reservations. It's usually hot, crowded, and noisy. The service is surly. Get there early for lunch. Friends say I should have asked for pork ribs fried in salt and pepper, or aubergine, or spicy beef.

XU'S DUMPLING HOUSE, *1, Lane 142 Xin Le Road.*

Also in the same neighborhood as The Grape above, dumpling fans should try this tiny unpretentious place serving great *jiao tze*.

SEEING THE SIGHTS

Huangpu Park is the oldest and smallest park in the city, *Zhongshan Dong-1 Road, across the bridge from Shanghai Mansions. Open daily from 5am-10pm,* even for foreign tourists. Started in 1868 by the British, next to the Suzhou and Huangpu Rivers, this once displayed the infamous sign 'No Dogs and Chinese Allowed.'

The **Bund** (riverside embankment) starts at Huangpu Park on the east and follows the **Huangpu River**, about 400 meters wide at this point. It was even more active between the mid-19th and mid-20th centuries when 240 foreign banks flourished here: look at the grandeur of the Bank of China lobby and the Greek columns of the Customs House. Look into the lobbies especially of the **Pudong Development Bank**, which used to be the Hongkong and Shanghai Bank building. It has some marvelous 1923 mosaic murals of London, New York, and Paris, cities where the bank had branches. Historical plaques are posted outside important buildings.

The Bund is now an elevated walkway beside the river. There are plans to extend it south beyond Yan'an Road. If you make it from the Peace Hotel to Yan'an Road, you can walk about the same distance onward to Yuyuan Garden.

If you like temples, see the **Jade Buddha Temple**, *170 Anyuan Road, Puto District, Tel. 62663688. It is open daily, 9am-5pm,* but closed for lunch at noon. This is a good introduction to Buddhist temples, but nearby Suzhou has better, older and less crowded ones. The Jade Buddha Temple

SHANGHAI'S JEWISH HISTORY

Jews in Shanghai? Yes, there have been three main migrations. A handful of **Sephardic Jews** *arrived from west Asia in the mid-1800s. These were the Kadoories, Hardoons, and Sassoons, who invested in much of Shanghai's real estate.*

Then came **White Russian Jews**, *refugees from the Communist revolution who arrived in the early 1920s. The third and latest group came to escape Hitler's Europe in the late 1930s. The 19,000 or so who reached Shanghai were mainly from Poland, Germany, and Austria. They were encouraged to stay by the then Japanese rulers even though Japan was an ally of Germany. The Japanese incorrectly thought they could borrow large sums of money from them. This group arrived with only their clothing, choosing Shanghai because they needed no visas and passports here. They just walked off their ships or trains, and were helped by earlier migrants and Jews from other parts of the world.*

There were also Jews from Russia who arrived via Harbin. In 1943, the Japanese forced all Jews into Hongkou district. They endured US bombs and a few married Chinese people.

After the war, most discovered they had no family in Europe. With the communization of China, they left for other parts of the world. The last of the resident Shanghai Jews died in the 1980s.

Part of the **Ohel Moshe Synagogue**, *built in 1927, is now a museum organized by the district government. A good sign in English points to two rooms with a few relics and photos. Located on the second floor of 62 Chang Yang Road in Hongkou District, Tel. 65120229, and 65416312; open 9am-4:30pm Monday to Friday. It is behind the Ocean Hotel, where a memorial plaque (in English and Hebrew) also sits in a nearby park. Ask for guide Wang Fah Liang, a neighborhood resident who can tell you in English about the area.*

was built in 1882 in the southern outskirts of Shanghai. It was bodily moved to Shanghai in 1918 and now occupies about two acres in the western part of the city. Many monks live in this temple, and you might hear them singing or reading the scriptures. At your request and donation, monks will chant prayers for the well-being of your soul.

In the first hall, a 2.6-meter-high, gold-faced **Wei Tuo**, the military protector of the Buddhist scriptures, menacingly greets visitors. On each side are two temple guardians. The three largest figures inside the next parallel building are **Sakyamuni** (center), to his right the **Amitaba Buddha** (with lotus), and the **Yuese Buddha**, carrying the Buddhist wheel of law. Along the sides are the 20 guardians of heaven. **Guanyin** is centered behind the three main Buddhas. Note the very thin Sakyamuni, above, paying homage, and the 18 arhats.

On the second floor the seated 1.9-meter-high Jade Buddha, carved from one piece of white jade in Burma, was brought to China in 1882. The shelves on both sides of the room contain 7240 volumes of Buddhist scriptures, printed in the Qing 200 years ago. In another building is a Reclining Buddha, also of white jade.

Many group tours include a visit to a **Children's Palace**. These are after-school programs for seven to 16 year-olds, much like community centers. Specially-chosen children get extra opportunities to learn and practice art, sciences, music, and sports. Some of the 23 palaces in the city are in old mansions built by wealthy capitalists. A visit to one will not only give you a chance to learn something of the education of children but also to explore the buildings themselves.

Best set up for tourists is the **Children's Municipal Palace**, *64 Yan'an Road, Tel. 62481850*. It has been open Wednesday and Saturday for visitors but not during school vacations.

The *****Yuyuan Garden**, *Yuyuan Road, Tel. 63283251, 63260830*, is a major tourist attraction. Open daily, 8:30am-4:30pm, Y20. Should you see it if you are also going to the gardens of Suzhou? It depends on how much time you have and how much you like gardens. This one is pretty good, but it is crowded in the mornings. It was originally laid out between 1559 and 1577 by a financial official from Sichuan and now covers 20,000 square meters.

From 1853 to 1854, this garden was used as the headquarters of the Small Sword Society, which staged an armed uprising and held part of Shanghai for 18 months. The pavilion opposite the exquisite stage is now a mini-museum. The top of Rockery Hill is an artificial mountain made with rocks carried from Jiangxi province. Until it was dwarfed by Shanghai's skyscrapers, this was the highest point in the city from which you could see the Huangpu River nearby.

The five dragon walls wind concentrically around the garden. Look for their heads. Note the unusually-shaped doors, some like vases, and, of course, the lovely moon gates. Look for the Pavilion to See the Reflection of the Water on the Opposite Side (these names are really something!) and don't trip over the step-over doorways. The south side of the garden was for the aristocratic women, kept out of sight of all but family members. There's a snack bar and souvenir store. An antique market is on a nearby street.

About 100 years ago, a part of the Garden was sold to merchants, and that is now the 98-shop **Yuyuan Market**, once the busiest in the city and still bustling. Its old architecture helps make it a fun place to visit. In the market you can buy dressmaking patterns (six sizes on one pattern) and novelties, and watch *jiao zi* and other Chinese dumplings being made. It is a good place for souvenirs and antiques. President Clinton ate here. Take a peek at the old **Huxin Ting Tea House**, *Tel. 63736950*, the most famous tea house in the city and learn about this Chinese institution. Count the number of local women here.

The excellent **Shanghai Museum**, China's best, is in People's Square, *201 Renmin Da Dao, 200003, Tel. 63723500, 63270271. It is open Monday through Friday, 9am-5pm, no admissions after 4pm; and Saturdays 9am-4pm, with no admissions after 3pm. Admission is Y60* including a recommended "acoustiguide," Y20 otherwise. From the outside, this four-story building looks like a giant Chinese bronze with four huge handles, its shape symbolizing that heaven is round and earth is square. The exhibits are well lit and signs are in English and Chinese, galleries full of marvelous bronzes, Buddhist statues, fine porcelains, paintings, minority costumes, and furniture. Look for the Tibetan skulls and demon masks, the polished mirrors, and Qianlong's jade wine goblet. Nearby is the **Grand Theatre**, especially beautiful at night. Underneath People's Square is the **Hong Kong Mall** (Di Tie Shang Cheng), with decent clothes shopping, supermarket, bakery, and tourist information.

The **Shanghai Zoo**, *2381 Hongqiao Road, Tel. 62687775, is usually open daily, 6:30 or 7am-5 or 5:30pm (depending on the season)*. Check before you go. One of the better zoos in China, it's on 70 hectares and has 280 species, including giant pandas, rare Chinese birds, and Yangtze crocodiles.

The new **Shanghai Library**, *1555 Huaihai Dong Road, open 8am-8pm with free admission*, deserves a visit as the most efficient and largest in Asia, the third largest in the world. It has 13 million books of which 1.7 million are old, up to 1400 years old. It has a music room, computers and high-tech retrieval system. Foreign academics can get a tour. Apply at the reception counter.

The 80-hectare **Botanical Garden**,(Je Oo Yuan), *1100 Longhua Road, Tel. 64513369 X 1157*, is also worth a visit for plant lovers. It's open

**FOLLOW PRESIDENT CLINTON'S
SHANGHAI ITINERARY!**

*The president ate at the Luboluo Restaurant in the Yuyuan Garden,
and had official receptions at the Peace Hotel, on a cruise, and at the
Shanghai Museum. The latter was catered by the Yangtze New World
Hotel. He visited Pudong, the General Motors Plant, and the Shanghai
Library. His party took 585 rooms at the Portman.*

6:30am-7pm daily in summer and is in the southwestern suburbs. There
are lots of birds, rock gardens (with rocks, no flowers), medicinal plants,
ferns, peonies, bamboo, and potted miniature trees, some several hundred years old. Y6 admission, free for guests at the Novotel next door if
you enter across from the Novotel's front door.

Shanghai also has **private museums** of folk arts, theatrical costumes,
calculation instruments, paper fans, boat models, coins and rock sculptures. There is a traditional Chinese medicine museum and a navy
museum. The Shanghai Tourism Administration has the addresses.

Modern History

The former residence of **Dr. Sun Yat-sen**, *7 Xiangshan Road, is in the
old French Concession, and open 9am-4pm Monday to Friday, and 1:30pm-4pm
on Sunday. Y4.* Once inside, you are back in the 1920s. The house was
bought by Chinese-Canadians for the father of republican China for
16,000 pieces of silver. Dr. Sun lived here with his wife intermittently from
1920 to 1924, just before his death of cancer in 1925. His widow, Soong
Ching-ling, lived in the house until 1937, when the war forced her to move
to Chongqing.

Here, in 1924, Dr. Sun met Communist leader Li Dazhao (Li Tachao)
publicly for the first time to work out Nationalist-Communist cooperation. Dr. Sun was much influenced by Marx and Lenin. Besides the
antiques, there are some old photographs, a 1920 China train map, Sun's
medical instruments, clothes, and glasses. The map is significant because
Dr. Sun was in charge of railways for a short time after he resigned as
president. The house contains his library: a 1911 Encyclopedia Britannica,
biographies of Bismarck, Cicero, Lincoln, and Napoleon in English,
books in Japanese, and ancient works in Chinese. No photos are allowed.

Soong Ching-ling was the sister of Mme. Chiang Kai-shek. She eloped
with the already-married Dr. Sun and was virtually disowned by her
wealthy Christian father, up to that point one of Dr. Sun's strongest
supporters. She was tolerated by her family and her powerful in-laws,

although she was outspoken in her opposition to their exploitation of China. She was, after all, the widow of the widely respected father of the country. She chose to remain in China after Liberation, and worked to promote the welfare of children. See also Nanjing and Zhongshan for more about Dr. Sun.

There's also the site of the **First National Congress of the Communist Party**, *76 Xingye Road. It is open Tuesday-Sunday 8:00am-11pm, closed Thursday mornings.* This was the living room of a small rented house in the former French Concession. There, 12 representatives of the Party from all over China including Mao Zedong, met secretly for four days in 1921.

Pudong

The **Oriental Pearl Television Tower** *(Dongfang Ming Zu), 2 Lane 504 Jujiazui Road, Pudong, 200120, Tel. 58791888, 58827333, Fax 58796660, open 9am-9:15pm. Y50.* At 468 meters, it has been the tallest such structure in Asia and the third highest in the world. You can see it as you look east on Nanjing Road. It has an elevator, observatory, and soon the Shanghai History Museum. The food is no good. It would certainly be cheaper to take the elevator to the top of the Grand Hyatt or Shangri-La. The food would probably be better there too. The tiny old building near the base is a history museum. The Ocean Aquarium with its 120 meter-long sightseeing tunnel is due here the end of 1999.

The **Shanghai Stock Exchange** was founded in 1990. A visit will give you some indication of the vast scope of China's capitalism. Unfortunately the guides speak poor English and give a murky description but you can see its immense trading floor. Ask for its booklet. *It's at 528 Pudong Nan Road, 200120, Tel. Ms. Li Qian, 68808888, 68806146, Fax 68803459. E-mail: qli@sse.com.cn. Open 9am-11:30am and 1pm-5pm, weekdays.*

NIGHTLIFE & ENTERTAINMENT

Tourist and expat giveaways are full of sports and entertainment events. See Practical Information below.

Shanghai has high standards of international music, art, and drama, a contribution of its many immigrants. No one can miss Shanghai's magnificent and imposing **Grand Theatre** in People's Square next to the Shanghai Museum. It is meant to look like an eagle about to take off, and is lit up at night. It claims the largest stage in the world. Your hotel concierge might be able to get tickets. *You can get one-hour tours of the theatre from 9am-11:30am, and 1pm-4:30pm for Y50, Tel. 63276562, 63868686 X 3303.* Recent performances were by Jose Carreras for Y400-Y1500, and of Faust by the Opera Comique de Paris Y120-Y600. The American Ballet Theatre, Washington National Symphony Orchestra, Vladimir Ashekenazy, and the UK Royal Ballet have or will perform here. Chinese companies also perform here. It has three theatres, the largest seating 1800 people, the smallest 250. It has three restaurants and is at the People's Square Metro stop.

Look for what's playing at the **Shanghai Art Theater** and **Shanghai Concert Hall** as well.

For everybody, the **Shanghai Acrobatic and Magic Troupe** is a fun show with magicians, sword-swallowing, juggling and sometimes performing pandas. Troupes display their skills at the **Lyceum Theatre** (for classier seats, *Tel. 62178530*), and the **Shanghai Center**, *Tel. 62798888*. Accept nothing else as sometimes tours are taken to cheaper shows of lesser quality.

The **Portman** has a 14-member orchestra playing Beethoven and Mozart on Sunday afternoons in Zhou's Bar.

The best evening **walk** is the promenade between the Shangri-La Pudong Hotel and the Huangpu River when the Bund lights are on sometime between 7pm and 10:30pm. This does not always happen at the same time every night. The park costs Y5 and is less crowded than the Bund.

For sheer relaxation, try a massage in your hotel.

The Bar Scene

Much of the bar scene is still in the hotels: the **Golden Age** in the Garden Hotel is good; **Charlie's** at the Crowne Plaza has a Filipino band. The **Long Bar** is a hangout of usually boisterous Americans. Happy hour is about 5pm-8pm. It's at the Shanghai Center, *1376 Nanjing Xi Road, Tel. 62798268, 62798888,*. There's **Hyland 505**, *second floor, Hyland Sofitel Hotel, 505 Nanjing Dong Road, Tel. 63515888*, which has a happy hour 6pm-8pm daily, a mini-brewery and pub with darts, pool and live entertainment.

Be careful about scams: in some bars you'll pay unreasonably high prices for hostesses to drink with you.

MALONE'S AMERICAN CAFE, *near the Portman, 257 Tong Ren Road, Tel. 62472400.*

Usually lively with sports on television.

O'MALLEY'S IRISH PUB, *42 Tao Jiang Road near the US Consulate, Tel. 64370667.*

Foreigners, not just Brits, hang out here, even though it's somewhat expensive.

L.A. CAFE at *188 Huai Hai Road, Tel. 63587097*, has draft beer, sandwiches, and a good salad bar.

COTTON CLUB & PARK 97, *1428 Huaihai Zhong Road, Tel. 64377110.*
Booze as well as dinner.
SHANGHAI SALLY'S, *4 Xiang Shan Road, Tel. 63580738, 63271859, close to the Sun Yat-sen house. It's open 5pm-2am daily.*
An English pub with pool and darts.
ZOO BAA, *593 Fu Xing Zhong Road, Tel. 64151583.*
PEACE HOTEL, *20 Nanjing Dong Road. Tel. 63216888.*
The famous Peace Hotel jazz band is a Shanghai institution, where seniors and near-seniors drink and sometimes dance. Don't expect Oscar Peterson.
GALAXY DISCO, *888 Zhongshan Xi Road, Tel. 62755888.*
The younger crowd heats this place up, especially on weekends.
CASABLANCA *,2000 Yan'an Xi Road, Tel. 62753388.*
This is a disco on the top floor of Rainbow Hotel.
NEW YORK NEW YORK, *146 Huqiu Road, Tel. 63216097, 63215611.*
A good disco with reasonable prices. It appeals to the younger crowd.
B.A.T.S., *at the Pudong Shangri-La Hotel.*
The entertainment center for those who like funky things.
YANG YANG'S (Y.Y.'s), *1127 Yan'an Zhong Road, Tel. 62481691.*
Foreigners might prefer this place over B.A.T.S. This was formerly J.J.'s until the police closed it down.

Festivals

The annual **Shanghai Tourism Festival** is between October 17 and November 8 with special events. In 1998, the festival organized jogging from the Stadium to the Botanical Garden, a group wedding with 999 couples at the Garden Hotel, 1500 people on a bicycle tour of Pudong, and a race to the top of the world's tallest building.

SPORTS & RECREATION

The tourist and expat giveaways below under Practical Information can tell you about **Bunjee Jumping** at the *Jinjiang Amusement Park, 201 Hong Mei Road, Tel. 74840844,* the **Wushu** Centre at *595 Nanjing Xi Road, Tel. 62153599* and **kick-boxing and karate** at the Shanghai International Martial Arts Association, *Tel. 1381787445, e-mail: simaa@parsmail.com.*

The US Consulate has a list of interesting things to do, like the regular matches of the **Shanghai Darts League** or the **Hash House Harriers** (they run on Sundays: call Adrian at *63512312* or Angie at *62816275* or e-mail: *Adrian@public1.sta.net.cn.*) This is "the drinking club with a running problem" which welcomes all nationalities and ages. American Citizen

Services also has a list of clubs for long-stay expatriates to join. *Xianzai Shanghai* can tell you about the **Hairy Crabs rugby players**, *call Mark Thomas at 64155588.*

At least six **golf courses** are in Shanghai, 12 within an hour of the city. Among the best is the 18-hole Shanghai International Golf Club in Hongqiao, *Tel. 59241969, Fax 59728520.* Hotels, especially the Westin Hotel can make arrangements. There's also the 18-hole Tomson Golf Club primarily for members and for guests of the New Asia Tomson Hotel. It's at *1 Long Dong Da Dao, Pudong, Tel. 58555858, Fax 58554500.* The Holiday Inn can arrange for you to play at the Suzhou Golf Club.

Popular are motor-driven **go-carts**. Some operate to 2am and separate ones are for kids and for adults. There's one at the Shanghai Stadium. The **Xian Xia Tennis Centre** near the Xijiao Guest House hosted the Heineken **tennis** championships with Michael Chang battling Goran Ivanisevic. You can play there too. It's at *1885 Hongqiao Road, open 6am-10pm weekdays, and 6am-10pm on weekends, and charges range from Y30-Y120 an hour. Tel. 62626720.* See also the Regal International East Asia Hotel above.

SHOPPING

Shanghai is the best place in China (outside of Hong Kong) for selection and quality, and time should be set aside here to shop if interested. Produced in the city are jade, ivory and whitewood carvings, lacquerware, needlepoint tapestries, silks, carpets, embroideries, gold and silver jewelry (especially filigree), artificial flowers, painted eggs, reproductions of antique bronzes, and such proletarian articles as jogging suits, bedroom slippers, winter jackets, heavy tee-shirts, gloves and fake Beanie Babies.

You'll find most places cheaper than Hong Kong for clothes, crafts and antiques but the best selection is in Hong Kong.

Last minute shopping in the **international departure lounge** at the airport is actually quite good: it has a few books and magazines in English, clothes, arts and crafts, the usual duty-free items, and 21 bottles painted on the inside with portraits of US presidents for Y45,000, negotiable.

Antiques and curios: If you don't trust your judgment, head for the expensive tourist shops or just assume everything's a reproduction or fake, and haggle accordingly. I usually offer Y20 and frequently pay just that for pearls, and Y50 for brass figurines and nephrite carvings.

The best bargains in antiques is at the Saturday and Sunday morning **Fuyou Market** which is no longer on Fuyou Road but one block away on Fang Bang Zhong Road and Henan Nan Road. This is beside the Tianyu Department Store near the bus stop at the front of the Yuyuan Garden complex. It is in a building which opens at 9am-6pm weekdays, and 5am-6pm on weekends, with weekend merchants on the top floors.

The next best market is the basement of the **Old Town Gods' Temple Market** in the *Hua Bao Building, 265 Fong Bang Zhong Road, Yuyuan Garden, Tel. 63557011, 63559999. This is open 9:30am-6:30pm.* Then there's the semi-outdoor **Dongtai Antique Market**, around *54 Dong Tai Road.* It has about 200 shops. If you have problems finding it, telephone Tom Tang one of the vendors at *63080117.* He speaks English. The market is open 11am-5pm daily. It's near the site of the First National Congress of the Communist Party.

Guides are reluctant to take you to these markets partly because they don't get any commissions. But the markets are fun; you can find tiny shoes for bound feet, old silver jewelry with real kingfisher feathers, and cricket boxes - things you see in museums.

For the top-of-the-line antiques and for people who would rather pay extra and avoid crowds, look at the **Shanghai Antique & Curio Store** for antiques guaranteed by the government. It's at *192-246 Guangdong Road, Tel. 63215868, Fax 63216529.* Other antique shops are in the area. There's the #**Antiques and Curio Branch, Friendship Store**, *694 Nanjing Xi Road, Tel. 62539549.* Several antique stores are between the Hilton and the Shanghai Hotels on Hua Shan Road. Especially good is the **Kuo Yue Cha Artware shop** in the Hilton itself on the second floor with good quality stone carvings, porcelain and jade – and negotiable prices.

For antique furniture and new furniture in Chinese style, try **Antique Alley** around *1438 Hongqiao Road* towards the airport from the Westin and Yangtze New World. There are several shops and workshops here and you should be able to ship purchases at horrendous prices. *Tel. 62199229.* Try **Chine Antiques**, *1660 Hongqiao Road west of Xi Jiao Guest House, Tel. Julie Yu, 62701023.* It's open 9am-4pm weekdays for refinished antique furniture. It also has a warehouse and can ship.

Art: Shanghai has lots of galleries. ShanghART is on *Level two of the Portman Ritz-Carlton, Tel. 62797135. Http://www.shanghart.com.*

Arts and Crafts: Serious souvenir shoppers should check out the prices first at the **Arts and Crafts Shopping Centre**, *190-208 Nanjing Xi Road (next to the Park Hotel, and near the Shanghai Museum), Tel. 63276530, e-mail:sharts@public.sta.net.cn. Open 10am-10pm.* Jewelry is on the ground floor and crafts on upper floors. Here you can buy silver chop sticks, silk, tee shirts, quilts, clothes, shoes, gloves, ties, children's dresses, carpets, cloisonne, yard goods and furniture. Across the road is a KFC.

Check also the **Friendship Store** for moderate prices and stores in and around the **Old Town Gods' Temple Arts and Crafts** in Yuyuan Garden for cheaper quality and prices. The **Shanghai Museum** has some good reproductions.

Books: The best for books in English is the **Foreign Language Book Store** at *390 Fuzhou Road, 200001, Tel. 63223200. Open 9am-5:30pm.* It will mail books and has a branch in Pudong named the **Shanghai Book Trader**. They take credit cards. Other stores with books in English are in the **Jin Jiang** and **Cypress Hotels**, and in the **Friendship Store**. For art books look in the **Shanghai Museum**. There's also the top floor of the **Shanghai Book City** at *717 Huai Hai Zhong Road, Tel. 63271914* and **Shanghai Art Bookstore**, *3/F, 42 Hua Shan Road, Tel. 62487476.* Most art books are in Chinese and relatively cheap.

Carpets: The **Shanghai Carpet Factory** is at *15 Cao Bao Road, Tel. 64365091* (across from the Huaxia Hotel beyond the Hua Ting Hotel). Good selections are in the **Arts and Crafts Shopping Center** and **Friendship Store**.

For over-priced crowd-free shopping with poor service, there's the **Shanghai Arts and Crafts Trading Corp.**, *1000 Yan'an Zhong Road, Shanghai Exhibition Center, open 9:00am-6pm, Tel. 62474781.* In another building is the **Zhonghua Tourist Souvenir Corp.**, *Tel. 62472180, 62790279* with the same quality. For good service, there's the **Qing Xiang Tourist Store** next to the Mongolian barbecue restaurant at *33 Chao-Bao Road* where our test item was about nine times the price at the Arts and Crafts Store near the Park Hotel.

Clothes: For sportswear, the **Huating Market** off Huaihai Road near the Hilton is good for better quality factory overruns and seconds than other street markets. Look for great buys on silk shirts, boots, jeans, and jackets in its 300 or so booths. It's got lots of junk too.

At the other end of the price range is **Maison Mode**, *1312 Huaihai Zhong Road, Tel. 64310100, near the Garden Hotel.* Expensive and crowdless.

Friendship Store and other Department Stores and Malls: The **Shanghai Friendship Store**, *40 Beijing Dong Road, Tel. 63294600, Fax 63218200. Open 9:30am-10pm,* two blocks north of the Peace Hotel, is one of the largest in China. It can crate and ship purchases. Prices are higher than other department stores but it has a good variety of lacquerware, cinnabar, eggs, peasant paintings, cloisonne, teapots, old porcelain shard boxes, pearls, musical instruments, ordinary stone carvings, painted silk screens, calligraphy, cross-stitch, antique embroidery, and dough figures.

The best general shopping no longer is along crowded Nanjing Dong Road, though that is still good. Shopping malls and department stores in other areas have developed, a favorite of which is the moderate-to-expensive **Meilongzhen Plaza/West Gate Mall** at *1038 Nanjing Xi Road, Tel. 62187878. It is open 9:30am-10pm* and has curios, sporting goods like backpacks and tents, clothes, toys, cosmetics, art gallery, music cd's, optical store, jewelry, Watson's drug store, Isetan department store, a wine shop, travel agent, and a Haazen Dazs ice cream parlor. It also has a bakery, Japanese restaurant and a branch of The Gap restaurant.

Another favorite department store is the moderately-priced **New World**, *2 Nanjing Xi Road, at the circular overpass opposite the Number One Department Store, Tel. 63588888. It is open 9am-10pm.* Crafts are on the ground and fourth floors. Prices are better than the Meilongzhen but this means oppressive crowds. The Shanghainese themselves shop along Huaihai Road, a very long street with fewer people than Nanjing Road. Good there with moderate prices is **Parkson Department Store** at *918 Huaihai Zhong Road, near the Shan Xi Nan Road metro stop, Tel. 64158818.* The **Orient Shopping Center** is at *8 Caoxi Road, Tel. 64870000, open 10am-9pm* near the Jianguo and Hua Ting Hotels. A modern shopping mall is under **People's Square**.

Musical Instruments. A small store is at 114 Nanjing Dong Road. Try the department stores or the **Shanghai Piano Co.**, *369 Yunnan Road at Nanjing Road.*

Pharmacies. Check with the international medical providers in Practical Information below. Watson's is a Hong Kong "drug store" chain with patent medicines. It has a branch in the **Shanghai Center**, but no pharmacist. For Chinese medicines, try the **Lao De Ji Dispensary** at 51 Nanjing Dong Road, the **Friendship Store**, or **Shanghai No. 1 Pharmacy** at *616 Nanjing Dong Road, Tel. 63224567.*

Photography. The **Guan Long Photo Store** can fix cameras, has a wider variety of films, and has unusual-sized camera batteries. It's near the Peace Hotel at *180 Nanjing Dong Road at Jiangxi Zhong Road, Tel. 63218699.* Most hotels, department stores, and the Friendship Store have cameras and film.

Porcelain. **Jingdezhen Ceramics Art Center**, *1253 Daduhe Road (between Jinshajiang and Meichuan Roads, Tel. 63856238, Fax 62855979, open 9am-4:30pm.* It has demonstrations, store and museum.

Silk: A good selection is in the **Friendship Store** and **Arts and Crafts Shopping Center** but markets in Suzhou and Hangzhou have better prices for ready-made garments.

Supermarkets: are everywhere especially in malls and department stores. Geared to foreigners are those in the **Friendship Stores**, **Shanghai Center** and the **Jin Jiang Hotel**.

Tailors might take two weeks to three months to make anything. Make sure they know the latest western styles. Contact Mr. Wei Guo Rong through the Public Relations office of the Crowne Plaza Hotel, *Tel. 62808888.* He makes suits for Y800-Y900 including materials, takes three days and speaks no English.

EXCURSIONS & DAY TRIPS
OUTSIDE OF TOWN TO THE SOUTHWEST

Longhua Pagoda and Temple, *2853 Longhua Road, Tel. 64397797, 64385963, open 7am-4pm*, can be combined with the Botanical Gardens, She Shan, and Songjiang county for a one-day trip if you have your own car. It is a noted scenic spot, the park formerly was an execution ground. It was originally built by Sun Quan of the Three Kingdoms (222-280 A.D.) for his mother and rebuilt several times since, the latest in the early 1980s. It is considered the oldest temple in Shanghai district. Note the fine brick carvings on its walls. The seven-story brick-and-wood Song dynasty pagoda stands about 40 meters high. It tolls good luck bells on New Year's eve.

Songjiang County, about 40 km southwest of the city, has a history of 2,500 years. The rare **Square Pagoda** in the **Xingsheng Monastery** is 48.5 meters high. It's on *Sangong Street, Songjiang, Tel. 57833310, open daily 5:30am-5pm*. It was first erected in 949 and rebuilt in 1086-94 in the basic Song dynasty style with the tetragonal shape of the Tang. It still has some original brick and wooden brackets. Its nine stories lean slightly seaward to compensate for prevailing winds.

The screen in front is the oldest brick carving in the area, erected in 1370 to keep evil spirits out of the Temple of the City Gods, which no longer exists. Very well preserved, the mythical animal is a *tuan*, greedily eating everything in sight. Note the money in its mouth. Other ancient relics have been assembled here from different parts of the county.

The **Roman Catholic Basilica** (Xu Jia Hui, **She Shan**), *Zao Xi Bai Road, Tel. 57651651, 57813349*, is high on a hill beside the Academy of Science's Observatory. It is northwest of Songjiang. It looks most impressive but intriguingly and incongruously European. The Jesuits built both, the observatory in the 1860s and the basilica in the 1920s. A Jesuit seminary is still at the base of the hill and it has a tiny guest house, *Tel. 57651521*. Stations of the cross line the driveway up and pilgrimages take place in May. See Public Tour Buses above.

TO THE WEST

The **Daguanyuan** (Grand View) **Garden**, *65 km north of Shanghai on Dianshan Lake west of Qingpu town, Tel. 69266629, 69266831, open 8am-4:30pm*, is not international class but people who know the 1886 book *Dream of the Red Chamber-Mansions* might want to see this theme park. It can be combined in a one-day tour if you have your own car with 900-year old **Zhouzhuang village**, about 60 km from Shanghai towards Suzhou. This is a beautiful little place with narrow streets, canals like Suzhou's lined with Song, Ming and Qing-style cottages. There are boats to ride and hump-back bridges. The **Shenting Restaurant** on the main street is dumpy but has very good food.

See Jin Jiang Tours below for a Zhouzhuang tour and equally charming **Tongli** on Saturdays. Suzhou can also be a one-day trip though it is better done in three.

Other excursions can be easily arranged from Shanghai to Hangzhou, Ningbo and Putuo Shan, and Wuxi. See separate listings.

SHANGHAI FOR CHILDREN

*American Dream Park is an amusement park with roller coaster. It's at 4498 Caoan Road, Huang Du Zhen, Jiading County, Tel. 59598686. You can also take kids to the **zoo**, **go-karts**, **acrobats**, and **Sun Island** (Y40). The latter is a resort with pool in Shenxing, Qingpu County, Tel. 59830888. Take the bus to "Shang Tai." See Public Tour Buses above. See also Xianzai Shanghai in Practical Information below.*

Walks

Downtown Shanghai is too crowded and the air too polluted for much walking, but there are parks near the Jin Jiang Hotel. People's Park and Square don't have much greenery but they're interesting. You can also head for the suburbs or air-conditioned urban malls. Or follow the circular route of the old city wall and moat that winds in a big loop around the Yuyuan Garden. Start at Ren Min and Zhong Hua Roads, and then head north on Ren Min Road.

In the suburbs are the Botanical Gardens and the zoo. There's interesting hiking on the hill around the She Shan Basilica.

PRACTICAL INFORMATION

Business Hours: Most offices are open five days a week; some offices 8:30am-5pm, or 9am-5:30pm. Lunch time goes from 11:30 or 12 noon to 1 or 1:30pm. The Friendship Store is open 9am-10pm. Many stores open 9:30 or 10am-9:30 or 10pm. Store hours vary.

ATMs: Money machines are in the Citibank, outside the Peace Hotel, and on the sixth floor of the Union Building near the Bund and Yan'an Dong Road. You can get cash from your Visa card at most branches of the Bank of Reconstruction. Many are around the city.

Consulates: Hours are usually Monday to Friday, about 8:30am-5:00pm. If you are traveling independantly, it is a good precaution to register with your country's mission. In the event of a lost passport, replacement should be faster. Should there be an emergency, you will be notified.

- **Australia**, *Tel. 64334604, Fax 64376669*
- **Canada**, *Tel. 62798400, Fax 62798401*
- **France**, *Tel. 64377414, Fax 64377073, 64339437*
- **Germany**, *Tel. 64336953, Fax 64714488, 64714448*
- **Israel**, *Tel. 62098008, Fax 62098010*
- **Italy**, *Tel. 64716980*
- **Japan**, *Tel. 64336639, Fax 64331008*
- **Korea**, *Tel. 62196417, Fax 62196918*
- **New Zealand**, *Tel.64711108, Fax 64333533*
- **Poland**, *Tel. 64334735, 64339288*
- **Russian Federation**, *Tel. 63242682, Fax 63069982*
- **Singapore**, *Tel. 64370776, Fax 64334150*
- **Switzerland**, *Tel. 62700519*
- **UK**, *Tel. 62797650*
- **US**, *1469 Huaihai Zhong Road, 200031,* passport required for identification before entry. *Tel. 64379880, 63242682.* American Citizen Services, *Tel. 64336880 X 247, X 293, Fax 64375173, 64711148.* Open 8:30am-11:30am or 12pm, and 1 or 2pm-4 or 4:30pm, Monday through Friday.

  Emergencies:
- **Ambulance**, *Tel. 120*
- **Fire**, *Tel. 119*
- **Police**, *Tel. 110*

  Medical Concerns:
- **Hua Shan Hospital**, *12 Wulumuqi Zhong Road, Foreigners' Clinic, 18/F and 19/F, Tel. 62483986.*
- **Sino-Canadian Dental Clinic**, *Ninth People's Hospital, 7/F, main building, 639 Zhi-Zhao Ju Road, Tel. 63774831 X 5279.*
- **World Link Medical Center** (US and expat doctors; imported vaccines), *Shanghai Center, 1376 Nanjing Xi Road, Suite 203, Tel. 62797688* (24 hours).

  Internet Cafes: Y5-Y15 an hour. *3/F Haodu Plaza, 400 Jinling Dong Road (entrance on Guangxi Road), open 1pm-11pm, Tel. 63557070 X 306; 3C and T at 238 Shanxi Nan Road, 1/F, Tel. 64730814;* O'Richard's Bar and Restaurant, *2/F Pujiang Hotel, Tel. 63246388 X 174; InfoHighway, 181 Ruijin 2 Road, Tel. 64155009.* Shops in malls selling computer services might let you use their e-mail. *Http://Shanghai-ed.com* has a list.

  Shanghai Municipal Tourism Administration, *2525 Zhong Shan Xi Road (in Hua Ting Guest House), 200030, Tel. 64391818 extensions 2414, 2309, 2311 or Miss Cheng Mei Hong, Tel. 64810905, Fax 64391519.* (*Administration, complaints, brochures.*)

  Telecommunications Telegram and Telephone office (open 24 hours), *30 Nanjing Dong Road.* Has videophone and card phones.

Taxi Complaints, *Tel. 63216611*

Tourist Complaints, contact Supervisory Bureau of Tourism Quality of Shanghai Municipality, *Room 501, 2525 Zhong Shan Xi Road (in Hua Ting Guest House), 200030. Tel. 64393615, Fax 62553615.*

Tourism Hotlines and Information in English, for help with translations, logistical questions, telephone numbers, etc.: *Tel. 62688899 X 56750* 10am-9:30pm (lobby of international arrivals at airport); *Tel. 64381693* 8:30am-5pm (People's Square Metro Station); *Spring Travel Service Tel. 62520000, 24 hours.*

Tourist and expatriate handouts: *Shanghai Star* and *Shanghai Buzz* are free at many of the hotels and expatriate hangouts. Subscribe to the free weekly cyber newsletter in English *Xianzai Shanghai* (e-mail: *shanghai@xianzai.com*) with "subscribe" as the subject. *Shanghai Talk* is a monthly magazine aimed at expatriates which charges Y50 for a one-year subscription, *939 Yanan Xi Road, #201, 200050. Tel/Fax 62121832 and e-mail: 75223.1646@compuserve.com.* There's also http://www.shanghabc.com especially for people moving to Shanghai, and it lists cultural events.

Shanghai Pictorial covers shopping, travel, restaurants, bars, medical, and is free in bars. *E-mail:cshpph@online.sh.cn or Tel. 62475697.* There's also www.shanghai-ed.com which is the best organized with sports, clubs, discounted air tickets, sports, cyber cafes, and Chinese consulates. *Http://shanghai.muzi.net* has a lot of good stuff too and even a map. *Http://www.chinavista.com* has recipes, telephone numbers, current weather, news, business and travel. Http:www.sh.com can arrange for you to send a gift to Shanghai and gives the day's weather forecast, among other things.

Travel Agencies:

• **American Express Travel**, *Room 206, Retail Plaza, Shanghai Center, 1376 Nanjing Xi Road, Tel. 62798082, Fax 62797183.*

• **Shanghai China International Travel Service**, *CITS Building, 1277 Beijing Xi Road, 200042, Tel. 62154440, 62892512, 62897829, Fax 62897838. North America Division, Tel. 62892077, Fax 62893018. Individual Travel division, Tel. 62892512, Fax 62897838. Booking office, 66 Nanjing Dong Road, Tel. 63234067, 63233384, Fax 63291788. Head office, 2 Jinling Dong Road, 200002 (near Yan'an Road and the Bund), Tel. 63238748 for tickets.*

• **China Shanghai Spring International Travel Service**, *1558 Ding Xi Road, 200050, Tel. 62520000, Fax 62523734.* Ask for Sally Shao, Sales Manager, open daily 9am-9pm. Contact Shanghai Spring in the United States for cheaper Shanghai hotels, etc.: *300 N. Continental Blvd., #450, El Segundo, CA 90245, Tel. 310/7260183, Fax 310/7260185.*

- **China Travel Service**, *881 Yan'an Zhong Road, 200040 (domestic tours),* *Tel. 62478888, Fax 62475521. 62792281. E-mail: webmaster@scts.com.* For domestic flights, *61 Nanjing Dong Road, Tel. 63616730, 63614058 or Fax 63616730. For international flights 88 Tongren Road, Tel. 62189283, Fax 62189282.*
- **CYTS Tours**, *2 Heng Shan Road, 200031, Tel. 64331826, Fax 64733349. E-mail: cyts@public.sta.net.cn.*
- **Jin Jiang Tours**, *2/F Peace Hotel, 23 Nanjing Dong Road, Tel. 63610071.*
- **Jin Jiang Optional Travel Service**, *191 Changle Road, Tel. 64459525, 63276675, Fax 64720184. E-mail:sjtsjt@online.sh.cn. Http:// www.JJtravel.com.* City tour Y250; Suzhou Y300, Zhouzhuang-Tongli Saturdays only. Y350. This website also gives performance dates at the Grand Theatre and Jin Jiang Travel can arrange tickets.
- **Shanghai Railway Bureau**, *Tel. 63171880* between 8am-11:30am. and 1pm-5:30pm. It and other agencies here can book train tickets and deliver them to you for a fee.

16. EAST CHINA

FUZHOU

(Foochow)

The capital of Fujian province, on the east coast across from Taiwan, **Fuzhou** is an important coastal city especially for business people and those with relatives in Taiwan. It is on the way to the mountain resort of Wuyi.

The Fujian dialect is distinct, neither Cantonese nor Mandarin. This language is spoken also by the majority on Taiwan, just across the straits. The weather is subtropical, and most of the province is mountainous.

ARRIVALS & DEPARTURES

Flights arrive from Hong Kong, Macau, Singapore and 37 other Chinese cities. Flights with Macau connect directly with Taiwan. The international airport is modern and gleaming, almost a quarter-kilometer long. A left-luggage room and hotel booths are outside the arrival hall. The airport should be forty minutes (50 km), southeast of the city by four-lane highway in 1999.

Buses take six hours from Fuzhou to Xiamen, four hours from Quanzhou. With the 1999 opening of the new highway, it should take a little over three hours from Xiamen. The Jiang Hotel has air-conditioned bus service to Xiamen, about six times a day. The Dong Hu Hotel also has buses to Xiamen.

Fuzhou is a 30-33 hour train ride from Guangzhou, 35 hours from Beijing and 21 hours from Shanghai.

Passenger ships from here go only to Xiamen. Currently only cargo ships arrive directly from Taiwan, but hopefully this might change soon.

ORIENTATION

Fuzhou is a 5000-year old city. In the Tang dynasty, it was expanded to include the three hills and the waterfront Bund was constructed. Opened to foreign trade in 1842 because of the Opium War, Fuzhou had

British and American dockyards, and factories for making tea bricks. It was once home to about 10 foreign consulates. The old British Community Church is still a church. Across the street is the Hua Nan Women's College which is looking for native English-speakers to teach English in return for room and board.

The city is noted for its **hot springs**, with over a dozen in Fuzhou itself. It became provincial capital in 1949. Prominent is a statue of Lin Zexu (Lin Tse-Hsu), 1785-1850, the minister born here who destroyed the opium in 1840. The population is 1.5 million urban, four million total. The Min River runs through town from Wuyi. The hottest temperature is 39 C in July and August; the coldest, -0.8 C in February. Most rain falls May and June.

WHERE TO STAY

The most important hotels here for business people are centered around the Foreign Trade Center (FTC) where the Hot Spring and Foreign Trade Center Hotels are the best. The best for tourists is the four-star **Lakeside** with the best pool. The best three-star is the **Min Jiang Hotel**. A new five-star should open in 2000. All the downtown hotels have hot spring water and are convenient to shopping. They all take credit cards and have business centers and international direct dial services. Hotels add a 10-15% surcharge.

HOT SPRING HOTEL *(Wen Quan Daxia), Wusi Zhong Road, 350003. Five stars, Tel. 7851818, Fax 7835150. Reservations in North America 800/ 44UTELL. Y988-Y1380 for rooms, and Y1780-Y2800 for suites. Four km from the railway station.*

Built 1986, and renovated in 1998, this 15-story, 311-room hotel has a large outdoor pool open May 1 to October 1. It has a garden, gym, tennis, and bowling. Standard rooms are large with balconies, small closets, and no drawers but it has an executive floor. It has a Japanese restaurant, night club and 20-seat cinema, and is a Hong Kong joint venture.

FUJIAN FOREIGN TRADE CENTER HOTEL *(Wai Mao Zhong Xing Jiudian), 73 Wusi Road, 350001. Tel. 7523388, Fax 7536552. Email:ftchotel@public.fz.fj.cn. Five stars. Y838-Y1420 for rooms, Y1467-Y2446 for suites. Three kms from the railway station.*

Built in 1985 and renovated in 1997 and 1999, next door to the Foreign Trade Center, this seven-story, 385-room hotel has attractive rooms, pool, tennis, book store, and conference hall. Its south section was built in 1996. It has two non-smoking floors, in-room safes, CNN and BBC. It serves French, Japanese, Cantonese, Huaiyang and Fujian food.

LAKESIDE HOTEL (Xihu Dajiudian), *158 Hubin Road, 350003. Four stars, Tel. 7839888, Fax 7836585. Email:L78398@public.fz.fj.cn or public.fz.fj.cn. Http://www.lakeside-hotel.com. Four stars. Y838-Y1390 for rooms; Y1980-Y6980 for suites. Three km from the railway station.*

Built in 1988 and renovated in 1998, the Lakeside has 22 stories and 436 rooms with safes. It also has a gym, disco, outdoor pool, Japanese and Cantonese restaurants. Even-numbered rooms have a lakeview. It has non-smoking rooms and executive floors, CNN, Star Plus and BBC. Buffet breakfast is Y55.

MIN JIANG HOTEL (Fandian), *Wusi Road, 350001. Three stars. Tel. 7557895, Fax 7551489. Y380-Y560 for rooms; Y840-Y1980 for suites.*

From the railway station, it's 3.5 km. Across the street from the Bank of China, this China Travel Service hotel has 412 rooms, Cantonese and Huaiyang cuisines. Its lobby has a marvelous stone carving of horses, like waves in the sea, but it is old and worn.

WHERE TO EAT

In addition to the hotel restaurants, try the famous **Ju Chun Yuan Restaurant**, *130 Bayiqi Bei Road, Tel. 7533230* near the Dong Bai Department Store. The **Dong Hu Hotel** (*73 Dongda Lu, Tel. 7557755*) near the Trade Center has good steamed prawns, spectacularly cooked on hot rocks, and excellent razor clams in chicken soup. Ask also for the Buddha-climbed-over-the-wall-noodles with scallops, mushrooms and bamboo shoots. The best locally-made beer is Huiquan.

SEEING THE SIGHTS

In one day, you can visit Drum Mountain, Yu Mountain, Xichan Buddhist Temple, and West Lake. **Gushan** (Drum Hill) is topped by a huge drum-shaped boulder in the eastern suburbs, at least 969 meters high. It is 10 km outside the city, open 7 or 7:30am-6pm. Here is the **Yongquan Si** (Surging Spring Temple) which was founded in 908 A.D. and has a white jade buddha. Monks chant twice a day for one hour. **The Qianfo Taota** (Thousand-Buddha Pottery Pagoda) and the **Shuiyun Ting**

(Water and Cloud Pavilion), east of the Yongquan Si are both from the Song dynasty. Views from the 18 caves west of the temple are famous.

The most famous temples are the plain-looking **Baita** (White Pagoda) on the west side of Yushan Hill (open 8am-6pm), and the **Wuta** (Black Pagoda), at the base of Wushi Hill, both in the center of town. The main hall of the *Hualin Temple, from the Song, is worth seeing. The **Jinshan** (Gold Mountain) **Temple** is snugly perched on an island west of the city. The **Xichan Si Buddhist Temple** is at *Yang Ziao Road*, open 8am-5:30pm.

Especially worth a visit is the **Memorial Hall of Lin Zexu**, the official who destroyed the 20,000 chests of opium near Canton in 1839. It is a small shrine to the national hero who is known also as a calligrapher and a poet. Lin was one of the first Qing officials to take an interest in things foreign. Because the British attacked as a result of Lin's actions, the emperor exiled Lin to Xinjiang.

NIGHTLIFE & ENTERTAINMENT

There's a disco and bowling at the Hot Springs Hotel and a night food market and dancing near May 1 Square. Travel agents can arrange for you to use the Wusi Road Sports Centre. Fuzhou has four golf courses. The **Festival of Goddess Mazu** is held in April and May on Meizhou Island in Putian City, 108 km south.

SHOPPING

In the main shopping area, Jin Tai Street, a 10-minute walk from the Hot Spring Hotel at Dong Lu, is the biggest department store, the **Dongbai**, *Tel. 7531949*. Look for the **Fuzhou Shoushan Stone Carving Factory**, *229 Liu Yi Zhong Road, Tel. 0591-7550758*. Bodiless lacquerware and cork carving are also made and sold here.

EXCURSIONS & DAY TRIPS
WUYI

Wuyi is a place for hiking, for getting away from city noises and air pollution, and bamboo rafting down the jade-green Min River. Its highest mountain is 717 meters. You can even stay in farm houses overnight. It is in the northwest side of the province, divided into two parts, a normal town, and a tourist section with a 60 sq km scenic area, and a 570 sq km nature reserve with a United Nations Biosphere Reserve. The airport is in between, 14 km away from the town, and about 11 km from the tourist area with the hotels. The total population is 218,000.

It is very cold in winter, sometimes with snow, and hot in summer, humid all year round. The best time to go is autumn. Over 200 mm. of rain falls each month in April, August and September.

The easiest way to go is to fly, but the scenic way is by air-conditioned train leaving once a day from Fuzhou at 8:43am and arriving at 2:11pm. Trains also go every other day from Xiamen at 4:52pm overnight. You can also go by road along the beautiful Min River, past terraced hills growing jasmine flowers, sugar cane and rice. The drive usually takes six hours but don't go by road unless you're sure you won't be delayed by road construction.

From April 1 to October, one 40-minute flight leaves daily from Fuzhou at 10:10am. Flights also go from five other Chinese cities and Hong Kong.

Hotels are basic, a step above camping, and are interesting architecturally. Staff English is generally poor even in the best hotels. The Wuyi Villa and the Jade Maid Hotel are the best, but don't expect much.

You can hike for a couple of days directly from the hotels. From the hotels, you can hire a Chinese-speaking guide for about Y40 a day, or an English-speaker for about Y100. You can stay at farm houses, negociating on the spot, after checking out the facilities. Hotels here add 10% service charge. Food at the Jade Maid Hotel is not so good, but you won't starve. The Wuyi Guesthouse (Binguan) in the main town has considerably better. Try the sticky rice with red mushrooms and pork.

WUYI MOUNTAIN VILLA, *Wuyi Palace, 354302. Tel. 5251888, Fax 5252567. Y380-Y480 for rooms, Y600-Y1280 for suites.*

This hotel, owned by CTS Fujian, is set in a large garden. Its 112 rooms are in connected two- and three-story buildings. Opened in 1984, it claims the largest presidential suite in China (700 sq meters). Standard rooms have soft beds and poor reading lights, but heat and air-conditioning. It gives demonstrations of the local tea-making ritual, an 800 year old art.

THE JADE MAID HOTEL, *Country Tourism Holiday District, Tel. 5252988 X 8608, Fax 5252258 is the best. Y390-Y600 for rooms, Y1200-Y1800 for suites.*

It has 300 rooms and was inspired architecturally by the uniquely Fujian cylindrical, Hakka farmhouse style from Sanming. This Taiwan joint venture has four stories, no elevators, and a beautiful courtyard garden. Water in taps is murky and no western food is available, but it has *dim sum*, and somewhat greasy offerings.

You should climb the 800 steps up to 409-meter-high **Tianyou (Heavenly Tour) Peak** which is open all year round, entrance Y21 to Y26. Sedan chairs are available (about Y80 one way) but they don't go up the side with the best view which is narrow and precarious. On top is a temple inspired by a famous high-ranking official Peng Zu who retired here with his two sons, thousands of years ago.

ABOUT WUYI TEA

The first cup clears your thirst.
The second cup calms you down.
The third cup helps you use all your wisdom.
The fourth cup starts you sweating,
And all your troubles leave your body.
The fifth cup makes your skin smoother.
The sixth cup makes you feel clean, and immortal.
The seventh cup makes your soul float.
—ancient Ming poem

The 9.5 km relaxing **rafting trip** takes 90 minutes to negociate 18 curves, from the Xingcun Village "Ma Tou" or port. It's a Song dynasty-designed raft for six people, Y300 a raft or Y50 per person. Some raftsmen tell jokes in Mandarin as well as stories about the rocks ("two copulating turtles"). You pass caves with 3800 year old coffins in the fourth curve, and if you're lucky, you see birds. The raft stops at Ancient Street with its Song architecture near Great King Peak in town.

Wuyi produces black mushrooms, bamboo shoots, cloud's ears, local wine, and Wuyi tea. **Shops** are down the hill and across from the Jade Maid Hotel. **China Travel Service** is at the *Wuyi Villa, 354302, Tel. 5252981, Fax 5252567, 5252839.* **CITS'** *telephone is 5303808, Fax 5302161.* The telephone code is *0599.*

PRACTICAL INFORMATION

China International Travel Service Fujian, *7/F Lippo Tianma Plaza, 1 Wuyi Bei Road, 350001, Tel. 3370065, 3370070. North America department Tel. 3370110, Fax 3370077, 3370076. E-mail: fujicits@public.fz.fj.cn.*

CTS, Fujian Branch, *116 Wusi Road, 350001. Tel. 7539219, 7554215, Fax 7553983, 7535110. E-mail:ctsfj@public.fz.fj.cn. Http://www.fjcts.com.*

CYTS, *20th Floor, International Plaza, Wusi Road, 350003. Tel. 7810001, 7810015, Fax 7810021.*

Fujian Overseas Tourist Enterprise Company, *1/F and 9/F, Lippo Tian Ma Plaza, 1# Wuyi Bei Road, 350001, Tel. 3370065, 7526496, Fax 7535159; e-mail: otcfji@public.fz.fj.cn.*

Fujian Provincial Tourism Bureau, *1, Daying Street, Dong Da Road, 350001, Tel. 7559379, Fax 7538758.*

Hours: Offices, 8am-5pm. (some until 6pm); stores, 8am-9pm.
Telephone code: *0591*

Tourist complaints: contact Supervisory Bureau of Tourism Quality of Fujian Province, *1 Daying Street, Dongda Road, 350001, Tel. 7553794*. **Tourist Hotline**: *Tel. 7568474, 7555048*. For complaints and questions.

XIAMEN

(Hsiamen, Amoy)

Xiamen is on the southeast coast of Fujian (Fukien) province, over 200 km across the straits from Taiwan, but just 2.5 km from one of Taiwan's offshore islands. It is important because it is one of the cleanest cities in China, well-run and very pleasant. It is the ancestral home of millions of Overseas Chinese now living in other parts of Asia, a port city, and an important trading city. Over 2000 joint-venture companies operate here but no heavy industries are allowed on downtown Xiamen Island.

Xiamen was the home base of **General Zheng Chenggong** (known as **Koxinga**), who repelled the Manchu invaders and then rid Taiwan of the Dutch in 1662. Xiamen was a minor trading port when the British seized it in 1839. In 1842, the Treaty of Nanking allowed foreigners to build residences and warehouses here. For many years, especially in the late 1950s, both explosives and propaganda shells were lobbed onto Xiamen from Kinmen in Taiwan. Today Xiamen has a 131 sq-km Special Economic Zone.

ARRIVALS & DEPARTURES

You can reach Xiamen by sea. Heping Port, the passenger quay for ships from Hong Kong, is near the Gulanyu ferry. One passenger ship a week goes between Hong Kong and Xiamen, a journey of 17 hours. Ships are clean with good restaurants and bars.

Xiamen is a 1.5-hour flight southwest of Shanghai and one hour flight northeast of Guangzhou. It is linked by air with 46 other Chinese cities and by direct flights with Hong Kong, Jakarta, Kuala Lumpur, Macau, Manila, Osaka, Penang, and Singapore. Its airport is one of the largest in China with a capacity of 10 million passengers a year because Xiamen is the closest city to Taiwan. It will be the major gateway from there, when direct travel is resumed. Its departure lounge has a smoking room, lots of purple and jade-colored seats, and had an overabundance of good quality merchandise for sale. It had no books in English but is otherwise one of the best organized airports in China. It is on the north tip of Xiamen Island.

You can also reach Xiamen by air-conditioned express bus in nine hours from Shenzhen, and in one hour from Quanzhou. It should soon take only 3.5 hours from Fuzhou.

ORIENTATION

The population is 550,000 urban, the total 1.2 million. Local people speak the Xiamen dialect in addition to Mandarin. Fukienese is also spoken by the majority on Taiwan. Xiamen is one of China's best governed cities: traffic jams are rare, city buses are modern and efficient, and bicycles are few. Motorcylists wear helmets! Fines are imposed for littering. Officially no spitting is allowed and only natural gas is used.

Downtown is 131 sq. km Xiamen Island, where most of these hotels are located. To any other place on this island, it's no more than a 30-minute drive. Taxis cost Y10 for four km. An expressway around the island should be finished in 1999.

The hottest weather descends in July and August when the temperature soars to 38 C for a couple of weeks; the coldest is in February, when it could dip to -4 C. The annual precipitation is about 1206 millimeters, mainly from May to July.

WHERE TO STAY

The best hotels are the **Mandarin**, the **Marco Polo** and the **Crowne Plaza**. The Mandarin has a quiet, isolated garden setting on a hill closer to the airport above factories. It is the best for people with business in the Huli area. The other hotels are better located for tourists and people with business downtown. Many new hotels have recently been built and there is a glut of hotel rooms, making prices softer for travelers. Among the new hotels is Zenith's four-star **Hong Du Hotel**.

The three-star **Lujiang** has a special location on the waterfront, close to shopping and the Gulangyu ferry pier. It's got beautiful old architecture, but it was rundown the last time seen. With a new partner from Hong Kong, renovations and hopefully a Hong Kong manager, it should be a pretty good three star now.

Other acceptable three-stars are the **Xiamen Plaza** and the **Min Nan**. **Xiamen University** has an adequate two-star **hostel** booked through the university travel service, *Tel. 2088481, 2181252, Fax 2088481*. This is an opportunity to get to know English-speaking students.

The hotels here three stars and up have international standards, foreign exchange services and accept credit cards. Hotels add 7%-15% service charge to the following prices which should be discounted.

XIAMEN MANDARIN HOTEL *(Yue Hua Jiudian), Huli District, 361006. Five stars. A 400-room five-star New Mandarin Hotel should be completed soon. Six km from the airport, 10 km from the railway station. Tel. 6023333, Fax 6021035. Email:mandarin@public.xmn.fj.cn. $160-$230 for rooms, $360-$530 for suites; $450-$12,000 for villas.*

Built in 1984, this complex of several buildings set partly on a hill is very modern, sparkling clean, and well maintained. It has several buildings of three and seven stories. It also has 22 two-story villas. It has non-smoking rooms and an executive club. It has a 600-seat conference center, health club, pool, bowling, mini-golf, tennis, and free shuttle bus downtown. There's men's underwear for sale and safes in its rooms. It serves French, Japanese, Sichuan, and Cantonese food. The reception area is in the Tian Feng hall. Its three-story presidential villa is spectacular, furnished in imitation European Louis XIV style with rococo chairs and Chinese touches, a combination that some guests might not like. Other guests can use its indoor pool in winter if no presidents are in residence. Two bellmen here refused tips, and should be commended. A Famous Hotel Club.

HOLIDAY INN CROWNE PLAZA HARBOURVIEW *(Haijin Jiari Dajiudian), 12-8 Zhen Hai Road, 361001. Four stars aiming for five stars. Tel. 2023333, Fax 2036666. Email:hixmnch@public.xm.fj.cn. 15 km from the airport, six from the railway station, and 0.6 km from the ferry pier. $160-260 for rooms, $350-820 for suites.*

Built in 1992, this 22-story, 367-room hotel has CNN, in-room safes, large twins, non-smoking rooms and executive floors. It serves Sichuan and Cantonese food and has 24-hour room service. For your health, it has a pool, gym and clinic and is planning a tennis court and golf packages.

THE MARCO POLO HOTEL, *8 Jianye Road, Hubin Bei, Yuandang New Urban District, 361012, Tel. 5091888, Fax 5092888. Email: mpxhotel@public.xm.fj.cn; http://www.marcopolo.xm.fj.cn. In North America, call 800/THE-OMNI. High four-star standards. $160-$205 for rooms, $230-$980 for suites.*

The Marco Polo is in a residential district near government offices, Bank of China, the Trade Centre, Yuandang Lake, and the port. It is 15 minutes' drive from the airport. With seven stories (one is executive), this luxury hotel has 350 rooms (including disabled and non-smoking), and large twins. It has in-room safes, voice mail, fax modems, and eight television channels in English. Available is a gym, aerobics room, sauna, and 24-hour room service. It has a Japanese restaurant. Its eight-story atrium has a waterfall, mural of Wuyi, lounge, and Filipino band. A Hong Kong joint venture.

XIAMEN PLAZA, *908 Xiahe Road, 362004, Tel. 5058888, Fax 5058866. E-mail:xmplazah@public.xm.fj.cn. Three stars. Y918-Y998 for rooms, Y1398-Y2388 for suites.*

The hotel has a non-smoking floor, 287 rooms, pool and gym.

LUJIANG HOTEL (Binguan), *54 Lujiang Road, 361001. Three stars, Tel. 2022922, Fax 2024644. About $69.*

Built in 1989, it had a major renovation in 1998. This six-story hotel in colonial architecture has large rooms, Sichuan, Cantonese, Chaozhou, health-giving, and continental food. It has an open roof-top patio with a good view of Gulangyu's neon lights.

MIN NAN HOTEL (Dajiudian), *Hubin Nan Road, 361004, Tel. 5181188, Fax 5180460. Three stars. $50-$90 for rooms, $180-$380 for suites.* It has a revolving restaurant, tennis court, pool, and gym but no in-room safe.

WHERE TO EAT

Fujian food is much like Cantonese, and heavy on fresh seafoods, of course, with some distinctive dishes. See Chapter 11 for recommended local dishes. Try the **Hao Qing Xiang Restaurant**, *1 Hubin Zhong Road,* and the vegetarian food at the **Nan Putuo Temple** *(Tel. 2085908, 2087281).* The **Jia Li Restaurant** is a huge floating seafood palace at *Lundu Port, Tel. 2041475.* There's also the **Shuyou Seafood Restaurant** on *Hubin Bei Road, Tel. 5098888.*

Hotels have very good food too. The Chinese restaurant in the **Marco Polo Hotel** has good herbal soup, and Peking duck. It also has a *teriyaki* bar. Its buffet breakfast costs Y110, lunch buffet Y68, and dinner buffet Y138.

The ambience at the Chinese restaurant at the **Lujiang Hotel** should improve with its renovations. It usually has a translator to explain its interesting medicinal banquet and each dish's effect on your body. The banquet is delicious and different: cashews, beancurd, celery, bamboo shoots, *dangui* (osmanthus flower) and fish. Tiny red *goujizi* seeds are to brighten the eyes. *Manyu* fish should heal wounds and "dispel the water in the body." Bamboo, meat and pancreas of squid are good for the breath. A menu in English is available.

SEEING THE SIGHTS

If you only have one day for sightseeing, take in **Gulangyu Island**, **South Putuo Temple**, and hurry through **Jimei**. Try to squeeze in the museum at **Huli San Fort**. Better stay a second or third day.

The adventurous might want to hire a boat from a fisherman or travel agent for a tour of the harbor, and see the Taiwan-held island of **Kinmen** a little closer. The **botanical garden** is for plant lovers. A new **ocean park** is now open and people searching for their roots here might want a look at the **Overseas Chinese Museum**, between downtown and Xiamen University.

The southern part of the city contains the downtown shopping area, and the **botanical gardens** where President Richard Nixon planted a redwood tree among the tropical and subtropical plants. Also in this area are the South Putuo Temple, Xiamen University (built by Tan Kah Kee in 1921), and the ferry pier to Gulangyu.

The 1,000-year-old **Nan Putuo** (South Putuo) **Temple** is named after the home of the Goddess of Mercy. Most of the current buildings are recent, but the tablets, scrolls, sculptures, bells, etc., are from the Song and Ming. On the lotus base of the statue of Buddha is carved the biography of Sakyamuni, and the story of the monk Xuanzang who went to India. Most famous is the stunning, three-faced, multi-armed statue of Guanyin. A festival is held here New Year's Eve. Behind the temple is **Five Old Men Peaks**, which you can climb for a good view of the Taiwan Straits. At its foot is the **Overseas Chinese Museum**, *Fongchaon Hill, Tel. 2085345,* outlining the contributions of natives who emigrated overseas.

Extra special is the **Ronguang Treasures Museum** in the old **Hulisan Fort**, Bo Wu Yuan. It is one km south of Xiamen University. Take no. 17 bus from the railway station which goes every 15 minutes for Y2. It's open 7am-6pm daily, *Tel. 2099603.* This museum has 4,600 fascinating rocks with natural pictures on them. Look for Emperor Qianlong's pet rock. These were collected by seven generations of a Singapore family. There's also an exhibit of fire-arms ranging upwards from 11 cm long, and including a 12th century cannon, believed to be the oldest in the world.

A bonus is a view of Taiwan's **Kinmen** through powerful binoculars from this fort. The Taiwan government's sign there has said "The Three Democracies Unite China."

The new **Underwater World**, with 400 kinds of aquatic animals, is at *2 Long Tou Road on Gulang Island, Tel. 2069363.*

See the Islands

Gulangyu (Drum Wave) **Island** is 1.7 hilly sq. km, seven minutes across the 'Egret River' by ferry. Ferries leave every five to 15 minutes. The Gulangyu population is about 25,000. Formerly the foreign ghetto with 14 consulates, it has the best beach – **Gangzi Hou** – the Moon Garden, and is decorated profusely with frangipani, flame trees, and heavily scented plants. A charming collection of old mansions have now been converted into guest houses. You could spend a whole day here.

Gulangyu is a car- and bicycle-free resort area, great for children and relaxing. It is cleaner and more prosperous-looking than Hong Kong's outlying islands to which it bears some resemblance. Staying here, however, makes it difficult for hectic sightseeing. The dominating statue is of Koxinga. Gulangyu has two small museums, two churches (one from 1882), a temple, and a concert hall. Many music lovers live here and you might hear Bach and Verdi floating on the evening breeze.

Everyone must climb 90-meter-high Riguang Yan (**Sunlight Rock**) for the view and the story of two devoted egrets, the male killed by a greedy, unromantic goshawk. Also here is the Lotus Flower Nunnery (**Sunshine Temple**), the camp where Koxinga stationed his men, and **Zheng**

Chenggong Memorial Hall, with souvenirs of his life, and a history written by a Dutchman about the fall of Taiwan/Formosa. The city museum is nearby.

The **Shuzhuang Garden** was built in the late 1890s. Unlike most gardens in China, it incorporates the sea into its design. 'The garden is in the sea and the sea is in the garden.'

Jimei, 2.83 sq km, is worth an hour and is 15 km north of downtown. A 2.8-km causeway connects it with Xiamen Island on the road to Quanzhou. Eighty percent of its 23,000 people have relatives abroad.

On Jimei is a monument built by Overseas Chinese philanthropist, **Tan Kah Kee**, who made his money from rubber, rice, and pineapples in Singapore. Turtle Garden, built in 1950, is an encyclopedia in stone, full of pictures of what Mr. Tan wanted to teach people about the world outside China: factories, machinery, exotic animals, Chinese literature, history, and culture. His elaborate, horseshoe tomb has pictures of his life.

Nearby is the huge Jimei Middle School, one of many he financed. Here, Overseas Chinese students from all over the world come to study. For those curious about the man, a tiny museum is nearby.

NIGHTLIFE & ENTERTAINMENT

During the **moon festival** here in the autumn, people buy cakes in different shapes. The bigger the pancake, the bigger the wished-for fortune. Four hundred years ago, Koxinga started the popular local dice game of Bobian during the festival because his troops from Xiamen were homesick. A **night market** thrives from about 6pm-10:30pm on Ding An Road. You can also try the **Arcadia Disco Pub**, *Building N, Bailuzhou, Tel. 5088888 X 3788, 1766.*

Gulangyu has parasailing, water skooters, and sail boarding. It has three golf courses. The **Kai Kou Golf Club** is at the *Hillside of Fair Lady, Fu-Xia Highway, 361100, Tel. 7011682, 7011679, Fax 7011882.* It has a 36-hole course designed by Greg Norman, and is one of Asia's largest. The Mandarin and Crowne Plaza have tennis. The Marco Polo has aerobic lessons. **Dongshan Island Resort**, four hours' drive south of Xiamen, is the best resort in the province.

SHOPPING

Locally made are Caiza silk figures, lacquer thread-decorated vases, colored clay figures, and bead embroidery. You may want to try the *yupi* peanuts, the *gongtang* crisp peanut cakes, dried *longan* fruit, and preserved olives. Locally grown are *longan, litchis, oolong* tea, and sugarcane. **Ports International** has a factory outlet in Jimei 30 minutes drive from the Marco Polo with good bargains, but somewhat outdated fashions. *Tel.*

6069998. The main shopping street is near ancient **Zhongshan Road**, rebuilt in its original style. It is hard to park, but look for the white sign with green characters indicating a taxi or bus stop.

Good shopping is at the **Hua Hui Department Store** on *Zhongshan Road, Tel. 2040018*, and the **Lai Ya Department Store**, *Wuhan Building, Xiahe Road, Tel. 5201588*. There's the **Bailuzhou Tourist Shopping Street** in Bailuzhou off the Sifu Dadao Antique Store, and for antiques, the **Xiamen Cultural Relics Store** is at *52 Si Bei Road, Tel. 2023363*. For arts and crafts, the **Xiamen Arts and Crafts Factory** is at *Baihe Road, Tel. 2017610*, and the **Gulangyu Arts and Crafts Interchange Center** is on *Gulangyu Island, Tel. 2062140*.

EXCURSIONS & DAY TRIPS

This province is mainly for those interested in maritime history, in the warrior Koxinga (see museums in Xiamen above and Quanzhou below), in the relics of Arab traders, and in Manichaeanism and Nestorian Christianity. Some of its native sons have returned prosperous from Southeast Asia to build monuments, schools, hospitals, and temples. The religious buildings are uniquely flamboyant with cosmopolitan touches.

Xiamen is the most developed for tourists in the province, with good hotels (see above). Quanzhou is next with some unique things to see. Fuzhou has less to offer tourists. A 300 km expressway linking Xiamen, Quanzhou and Fuzhou should be finished in late 1999.

QUANZHOU

Quanzhou is 103 km by road north of Xiamen and takes about an hour. It's 98 km from Xiamen airport. Quanzhou was considered one of the two largest ports in the world by Marco Polo, who knew it as Zaiton or Citong. Today it is one of the 24 cities protected by the State Council as a historical monument. It has China's largest collection of Nestorian Christian and Manichaean relics.

If you want to stay in the area to take in these excursions, the best hotels are the Quanzhou and the Zai Tong:

QUANZHOU HOTEL (Fandian), *22 Zhuang Fu Lane, 362000. Three stars. Tel. 2289958, Fax 2182129. E-mail:quzhhtl@publ.qz.fj.cn or public.*

This hotel has 132 four-star rooms and suites ($126.50-$172.50), and 172 three-star rooms and suites ($53.59-$196.50). It also has non-smoking floors and receives CNN. Four-star rooms have safes. It has bowling, swimming, gym, and tennis.

ZAI TONG HOTEL (Fandian), *Yingbin Road, 362000. Three stars, Tel. 2102222, Fax 2102108. 177 rooms. $45-$108.*

It was last renovated in 1998 and receives Star TV.

Among the unusual sights here is the **Kaiyuan Temple**, one km northwest of the Overseas Chinese Hotel. It dates from the Tang. The main hall has 100 heavy stone Greek-type columns, with gaudy bird-women musicians. Look also for the 1000-armed, 1000-eyed Guanyin. Note the corners of the roof, the curled swallow tails, and the lively dragons that are distinctively southern Fujian.

There is also the nine-story **Museum of Maritime Navigational History**, which houses relics from many religions, including Nestorian Christian, Manichean, Hindu, and Islamic. Look for the Franciscan tombstone with a cross. It also has the remains of a 13th-century ship, 24-meters long, found in Quanzhou Bay.

Old God Rock is four km from the city. This five-meter high stone statue of Laotze, the founder of Taoism, is 600 years old.

The *****Qingjing** (Grand Mosque) on Tushan Street, half a kilometer from the Overseas Chinese Building, is one of the few mosques in eastern China with west Asian architecture.

Wanshan Peak has some rare Manichaean relics. This religion, brought to China in the seventh century from Persia, was a combination of Zoroastrianism, Christianity, and paganism. At one time, St. Augustine was an adherent. On a stone tablet near the site of the monastery are inscribed the activities of the cult during the Song, when it was associated with Taoism. Behind the ruins is a circular Manichaean statue of a man.

About 13 km outside the south gate of Quanzhou is the **Caoan Temple**, the only Manicaean temple left in China and the best preserved such temple in the world. It was first built in the Song and renovated in the Yuan. It has a 1.5-meter-high carving of Mani Buddha inside dating from 1339.

The **Tomb of Zheng Chenggong** (Koxinga) is at Nan'an, about 25 km northwest of Quanzhou.

The hometown of the **sea goddest Mazu or Tianhou**, who is worshipped by fisherfolk in 1,500 temples around the world, especially in Hong Kong, Macau, and Taiwan, is on **Meizhou Island**, near the city of Putian. It is about 88 km from Quanzhou. Mazu was originally a woman named Lin Mo or Lin Mazu who lived from 960 to 987 A.D. and is credited with saving members of her own family and later other fishermen from shipwreck.

The nearby **Tianfei Hot Spring Hotel** is at the foot of Phoenix Hill near the Fuzhou-Xiamen Highway (*at the entrance to Xue Yuan Road, 351100. Tel. 265588, Fax 265068*).

Travel agents in Quanzhou are **China Travel Service**, *Overseas Chinese Building, Baiyuan Road, 362000, Tel. 2195935, Fax 2282366*. There's also **China International Travel Service**, *Tumen Road, Tel. 2281805, Fax*

2182056. **Quanzhou Tourism Administration** is at *3/F, Jinwei Building, M. East Street, Tel. 2160976, Fax 2160975.* The telephone code is *0595.*

PRACTICAL INFORMATION

American Express Travel Service, *Room 212, 2/F, Holiday Inn Crowne Plaza Harbourview, 12-8 Zhen Hai Road, Tel. 2120268, Fax 2120270.*
CITS, *25/F, Zhenxing Building, Hubin Bei Road, 361012, Tel. 5051825, Fax 5051819.*
Consulate of the Philippines, *2 Lianxiang Li Lianhua Xinchun, 361009.*
Consulate of Singapore, *9/F United Overseas Bank Building, No. 19 Hubin Bei Road, 361012.*
CYTS, *7 - 13 Bai Road, 361003. Tel. 5076881, 2053188, Fax 2020024, 2282366.*
Hours: 9am-5pm or 5:30pm weekdays and 9am-12 noon Saturdays for offices. 9 or 9:30am-9:30 or 10pm for stores.
Telephone Code, 0592
Travelers' Consulting Service Center, *6/F Xing Ye Building, 78 Hubin Bei Road, 361012, Tel. 5318985.* Information and complaints.
Xiamen Overseas Tourist Co., *361012, 64 Hubin Sili Road, Tel. 5076881, Fax 5083553.*
Xiamen Tourism Bureau, *Xing Ye Building, 78 Hubin Bei Road, 361012, Tel. 5318898, Fax 5318880.* Information.
Xiamen Tourism Co. Ltd., *15/F Huajian Building, 78 Xinhua Road, 361003, Tel. 2117021, Fax 2079297.*

GRAND CANAL

The oldest and longest in the world, the **Grand Canal** was built in the Sui dynasty (581-618 A.D.) and originally extended 1,794 km from Hangzhou to Beijing, an inland shipping route safe from sea-faring pirates.

Today, visitors can still take tour boats on parts of the canal for an intimate look at life on the water. You can sleep on ferries between cities to save paying for a hotel room. But the water is dirty and the trip can be noisy as traffic moves on the canal all night. However, that was the way it was 1000 years ago!

At individual cities along the route, you can visit parts of the canal. **Wuxi** has a 36.5-meter-long, two-storied 'dragon boat' with flashing eyes. Tours cruise mainly between **Yangzhou** and **Suzhou**.

HANGZHOU

(Hangchow)

Hangzhou, the capital of Zhejiang province, is famous for beautiful **West Lake**, its temples and gardens, its tea, and its history as the capital of the Southern Song dynasty. It is on the **Qiantang River** at the southern end of the **Grand Canal** on the east coast of China. The coldest weather is in January, a little below -10 C; the hottest is in July, with highs of 37 C. The annual precipitation is about 1452 millimeters, mainly May-June. The population is 1.8 million urban.

ARRIVALS & DEPARTURES

Located 140 km southwest of Shanghai, Hangzhou is best reached from there by a two-hour express **train** leaving at 7:29am. A new railway station is due in 1999 which will be about six km from the lake. It is also linked by a 1999 expressway. Non-stop trains leave Hangzhou for Shanghai at 7:23am, 9:10am, 2:40pm, 3:26pm, 4:42pm, 6:28pm, and 6:38pm. It costs Y40 or Y50 one way.

Hangzhou has **air** connections with Hong Kong and 31 Chinese cities. A new international airport is due in 2000 which should be 18-20 km from the lake. Its current airport is about 14 km from the lake. **Taxis** are old and dirty but changes are in the works as Hangzhou competes with 60 other cities for the best tourist city in China.

ORIENTATION

Hangzhou is one of the most famous beauty spots of China because of **Xihu** (West Lake). It is also of historical importance. Founded over 2,200 years ago in the Qin, it began to prosper as a trading center after the completion of the Grand Canal in 610. It was the capital of the tiny state of Wuyueh (893-978), at which time the first dikes forming the lake were built. It was also capital of the Southern Song after 1127.

The best book giving a detailed picture of the city from 1250 to 1276 is Jacques Gernet's *Daily Life in China on the Eve of the Mongol Invasion,* essential for visitors who want to know a lot of history, to compare life then with now, and to look for old ruins. The city was seized by the Mongols under **Kublai Khan** in 1279 and visited by **Marco Polo** the next year when it was known as Kinsai. The Venetian explorer raved about it, then the largest and richest in the world, its silks and handicrafts much in demand in China and abroad.

Hangzhou has been a famous **resort** for centuries, attracting painters, poets, and retired officials as well as tourists. It is also an industrial city now, with machine-making, chemicals, an oil refinery, and electronics. Of tourist interest are its crafts factories, temples, and museums. Villages

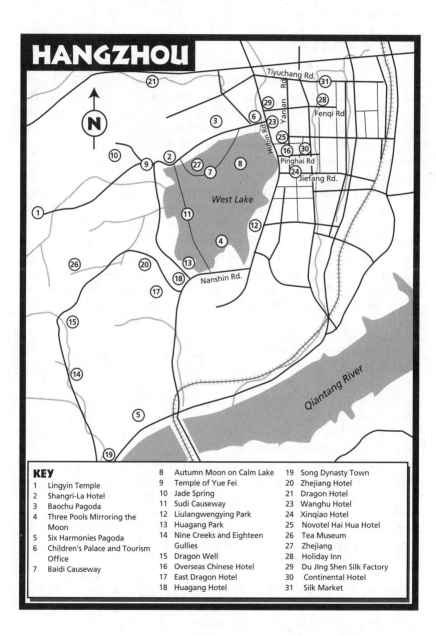

HANGZHOU

West Lake

Qiantang River

Tiyuchang Rd.

Yanan Rd

Fenqi Rd

Pinghai Rd

Jiefang Rd.

Nanshin Rd.

KEY

1 Lingyin Temple
2 Shangri-La Hotel
3 Baochu Pagoda
4 Three Pools Mirroring the Moon
5 Six Harmonies Pagoda
6 Children's Palace and Tourism Office
7 Baidi Causeway
8 Autumn Moon on Calm Lake
9 Temple of Yue Fei
10 Jade Spring
11 Sudi Causeway
12 Liulangwengying Park
13 Huagang Park
14 Nine Creeks and Eighteen Gullies
15 Dragon Well
16 Overseas Chinese Hotel
17 East Dragon Hotel
18 Huagang Hotel
19 Song Dynasty Town
20 Zhejiang Hotel
21 Dragon Hotel
23 Wanghu Hotel
24 Xinqiao Hotel
25 Novotel Hai Hua Hotel
26 Tea Museum
27 Zhejiang
28 Holiday Inn
29 Du Jing Shen Silk Factory
30 Continental Hotel
31 Silk Market

here grow the famous *Longjing* (Dragon Well) tea, and silk worms. Today Zhejiang province produces one-third of China's silk. These make a rural excursion especially worthy.

WHERE TO STAY

My favorite hotel here is the **Shangri-La**, because it's romantic, close to the lake and away from urban congestion. See Best Hotels. The **Dragon** is more for business people with the World Trade Center close-by. The **Novotel** and **Wanghu** are together by the lake, but in the busy town. The **Continental** and **Holiday Inn** are each about 2.5 km from the lake and next to the north-south freeway and accessible to the economic zone. The **Continental** is beautiful and romantic too with the most elegant lobby in town, but it doesn't have the lake.

The best quality hotel is the Shangri-La then the Continental which has a good location for shoppers. Of the four stars, the Novotel is best. The Novotel and Wanghu are neighbours almost beside the lake but the Wanghu is badly managed with hardly any English, so isn't worth considering except for its lower prices.

The high tourist season here is April, May, September, and October. The shoulder season is March, June through August, and November. All prices listed below are subject to change, 20%-50% discounts and 20% surcharge. Hotels here have international standards with credit card and foreign exchange services, business centers, etc.

SHANGRI-LA HOTEL HANGZHOU *(Shang Gorilla Fandian), 78 Beishan Road, 310007. Five stars, Tel. 7977951, Fax 7073545, 7996637. $170-$250 for rooms, $295-$1065 for suites. E-mail:slh@public.hz.zj.cn. Http://www.shangri-la.com. In North America, Tel. 800/942-5050. On the north shore of West Lake.*

The East Building has seven stories, 156 rooms and Chinese decor. Its West Main Building dates from 1956 and has six stories, 199 rooms with smallish bathrooms. It is more convenient to its store and restaurants. These two buildings are joined by a covered walkway. It also has three villas, a total of 387 rooms. It has two 24-hour business centers, conference facilities, satellite television, Italian and Cantonese restaurants. A fast-food restaurant is on the grounds. It has a gym, boating, bicycles and games, and a pool is planned. The hotel has been under Shangri-La International management since 1985.

See also Chapter 13, *China's Best Places to Stay.*

HANGZHOU CONTINENTAL HOTEL, *2 Pinghai Road, 310006, Tel. 7088088, Fax 7077618. Close to night antique market. Y1000-Y1350 for rooms, Y2500-Y7560 for suites. Five star standards.*

This 1997 hotel has 21 storys, 380 rooms with executive and non-smoking floors. It has bowling, small outdoor pool, small gym, sauna and lighted outdoor tennis court. It has CNN and CNBC, safes, kettles, and small baths in its standard rooms. It has western and Cantonese food, a Bavarian beer garden, and conference facilities.

DRAGON HOTEL (Huang Long Fandian), *7 Shuguang Road, 310007, next to the World Trade Center. Four stars, Tel. 7998833, Fax 7998090. 15 km from the airport, seven km from the railway station. Five minutes walk to Dragon Cave. $130-$180 for rooms, $280-$700 for suites.*

Built in 1987-88 with most rooms renovated in 1998, this six, seven and nine-story hotel has 525 spacious rooms, most with small baths, CNN and CNBC. It has Singapore International Airlines and Dragonair offices, a gym, lighted outdoor tennis courts, bicycles, and outdoor pool. It has a beautiful inner courtyard garden, and airport shuttle service. Its ballroom seats 350 people banquet style. The buffet breakfast is $15.

HOLIDAY INN HANGZHOU, *Fengqi and Jianguo Bei Road, 310004, Tel. 5271188, Fax 5271199. Email:hihz@public1.hz.zj.cn. 10 km from Jian Qiao airport, and five km from the East Railway Station. In the new financial and trading district of Hangzhou, close to the Itokin Department Store, 1.5 km from the wholesale silk market, and 30 minutes drive from the economic zone. Four star standards. $110-$160 for rooms, $260-$800 for suites.*

I haven't seen this 1999 hotel yet. It has 294 rooms, three executive floors, and some floors for non-smokers and the physically challenged. It has in-room safes, CNN, and kettles. It claims the largest recreation centre in town with eight bowling alleys, indoor pool, and gym. It has a delicatessen, Cantonese, western, and international restaurants, and conference facilities. Its function room seats 350 banquet style. It will bake bread fresh for you.

NOVOTEL HANGZHOU HAI HUA (Hai Hua Dajiudian), *298 Qing Chun Road, 310005. Tel. 7215888, Fax 7215108. Email:novohz@public.hz.zj.cn. It should be four stars by now. $140.*

Opened in 1997 with pretty pink marble pillers in its bright lobby, the Novotel has 247 rooms, its standard rooms small with 40-watt bulbs, no CNN or HBO but BBC and CNBC. It has a steam room, small heated indoor pool, fitness center, massage, and dance hall. Its internet is free for sending or receiving e-mail, but Y4 a minute for web browsing. It has beautiful wood walls and every evening in the lobby you can hear a classical western string quartet.

WANGHU HOTEL (Binguan), *2 West Huancheng Road, 310006. Four stars. Tel. 7071024, Fax 7071350. Email:whhotel@public.hz.zj.cn. Http:// www.chinapages.com/zhejiang/hangzhou. Y980-1280 for rooms, Y1600-Y3600 for suites. Economy rooms Y350-Y500.*

It has 410 rooms with safes, hair dryers, and robes. It has an executive floor, CNN, health club and pool, and Cantonese and Sichuan restaurants. It has a second building with two and three star rooms that look clean and adequate. Renovations to some rooms were made in 1998. Economy rooms have CNN, kettles, no tubs, just showers, no refrigerators, and no elevator service. This hotel lost my reservation, the bulbs are 40 watts, and the English is very poor.

WHERE TO EAT

Hangzhou claims "beggar's chicken," the first made with lotus leaves and mud from West Lake, as its very own. The lake fish is very bony.

The food and ambiance in the hotels are generally but not always the best. For good local food, the **Lou Wai Lou Restaurant** is at *30 Gushan Road, Tel. 7969023, 7029023* near the Shangri-La. The **Lan Bao Restaurant**, at *431 Baochu Road, Tel. 5118866* is between the Wanghu and Shangri-La Hotels. Vegetarian food is featured at the **Lingyin Temple**. The **Hu Qing Yu Tang Restaurant** serving "healthy food" is across from the **Traditional Medicine Museum** (*Da Jin Lane, Wu Shan, Tel. 7025896*). For cheap local pizza, Y18 for an 8", try the popular **Pizza** restaurant at *120 Wushan Road, the night antique market, Tel. 7081450.*

SEEING THE SIGHTS

Xihu (West Lake), is a 5.6-sq km lake, originally part of the Qiantang River until its outlet silted up. It was first dredged under the leadership of the famous Song poet, Su Dong Po, then mayor. It is now 15 km in circumference, with an average depth of 1.8 meters. The lake is now linked again with the Qiantang River and is usually renewed with fresh water once a month. Just strolling around the edge of the lake is worthwhile. Many of the tourist attractions are close to its shore.

Visitors with only one day to spend in the city should take a boat ride with stops at various famous sites. Then take in the **Pagoda of Six Harmonies**, **Lingyin Temple**, **Jade Spring**, and a **silk factory**. You can hire boats at different places around the lake like in front of the Shangri-La.

The best times to see the lake itself is in the mist, in the moonlight, or just at sunrise before the sun makes strong shadows, and when the birds are singing in the willows. One of the favorite spots for viewing the lake, especially during the harvest moon, is at **Pinghuqiuyue** (Autumn Moon on Calm Lake Pavilion) at the southeastern end of Gu Shan (Solitary Hill). But don't expect to be alone.

On an islet is the **Wenlan Ge** (Pavilion for Storing Imperial Books), built in 1699 (Qing), and one of the seven imperial libraries. This one was especially built to store the *Sikuzhunsu*, a 33,304 volume Chinese encyclopedia ordered by Emperor Qianlong. It took 10 years to copy it by hand. The stone **Chamber to the Three Venerables** (Han San Lao Hui Zi) here

SEEING HANGZHOU ON WHEELS

*You can rent a bicycle from a hotel or hire a pedicab. That way in one day you can ride along the 1.8 km, 1,000 year old **Baidi Causeway** with stops at the **Autumn Moon on Calm Lake Pavilion**, **Wenlan Ge** (next to the Zhejiang Provincial Museum), **Xiling Seal Engraver's Society**, **Tomb and Temple of Yue Fei**, and **Jade Spring**.*

*Explore **Lingyin Temple** and then visit the **Feilaifeng Grottoes** across the stream from the temple. Turn back to the Yue Fei Tomb and then south onto **Sudi Causeway**. Follow Nan Shan and then Hubin roads. Stop to enjoy **Liulanwenying Park** if only for its name, which means Park to See the Waving Willow and Hear the Singing of the Birds.*

was carved in 52 A.D. The island has the provincial **museum** and a good restaurant, the **Lou Wai Lou**.

You can look for lively giant golden carp at **Huagang Park** at the southwest end of the lake, beyond the Sudi Causeway.

The 2.8-km **Sudi Causeway** is the more beautiful of the two causeways here, lined with grass, willows, and peach trees. No motor vehicles are allowed because of its hump-backed bridges. It's a pleasant bicycle or pedicab ride, but please give the driver a break. Get off and walk up those bridges.

The famous **Zig-Zag Bridge** is on the islet **Xiaoyingzhou (Three Pools Mirroring the Moon)** and can be reached only by boat. It is east of Sudi Causeway. Did you know that bad spirits can only move in straight lines? Stand on the bridge here and nothing can harm you. This islet was first constructed in 1607 (Ming) with mud cleared from the lake. Look for the 'island in a lake and the lake in an island.'

During the Moon Festival, candles light up the small pagodas, thus creating 'Three Pools Mirroring the Moon.' In June, this is a good place to enjoy water lilies and lotus flowers. Everywhere around West Lake are exquisite gardens, some with artistically cobbled foot paths.

You can also go by boat to **Ruangongdun Island** on the northwest side of West Lake just south of Gu Shan Hill. Here you'll find **Huanbi Zhuang**, an attempt to reproduce a Song Dynasty village with period costumes, sedan chair rides, wine shop, and music. Some tourists have found it fun, but others think it too commercial and poorly done. June to mid-September has a show. Book through travel agents. The acrobatic show below is better.

The **Liuhe Ta** *(Pagoda of Six Harmonies), *91 Zhijiang Road, Tel. 7038911, 6082980,* is on the north bank of the Qiantang River. Built in 970

A.D., it is 59.89 meters or 13 stories tall, octagonal, and made of brick and wood. It can be climbed for a good view. West of this temple is the shallow and clear Nine Creeks and Eighteen Gullies, which cut through the rugged but tranquil Yangmei Hill. Great for hikers, the paths wind for about seven km.

The **Lingyin** (Soul's Retreat) **Temple**, *One Fa Yun Si Nong, Tel. 7996657, 7968665,* is nine km from the city, west of West Lake. Founded in 326 A.D., its Celestial King's Hall and 33.6-meter-high Buddha Hall are all that is left of the original 18 pavilions and 72 halls. Lingyin at one time housed 3000 monks. The statues have been replaced now. The seated Sakyamuni inside is 19.6 meters high. The temple guardian behind the Four Celestial Kings was carved from camphor wood during the Song. Lingyin is still one of the largest and most magnificent temples in China.

Across from Lingyin temple is **Feilaifeng (Peak that Flew from Afar), named by an Indian monk after a similar-looking Indian peak that must have flown here! The 380 carvings along the narrow, hilly trails are from the Five Dynasties to the Yuan.

It could take three or four days to cover all the important spots in Hangzhou. The 45-meter-high **Baochu** (Precious Stone Hill) **Pagoda** is on a 200-meter-high hill north of the lake, two km from the city. It was first built in 968 to pray for the safe return of the unjustly arrested Qian Hongchu, a successful effort. The pagoda, last reconstructed in 1933, is now filled with dirt and no one can enter.

The ***Tomb and Temple of Yue Fei**, *Tel. 7969670,* is at the northwest corner of the lake, next to the Shangri-La Hotel. He was a famous Song general who was unjustly executed in 1142. Public reaction forced a retrial 20 years later that reversed the verdict. A temple was built with statues of his four accusers kneeling for forgiveness before his grave. These four are spat on even today.

Yue Fei was also a calligrapher and poet who came from a family that valued patriotism. His mother tattooed his back with four characters to remind him of his duty to his country. His son was murdered on the day of Yue Fei's death. Their tombs are together but only contain their clothing. An exhibition hall illustrates Yue Fei's battles and shows his handwritten proposals to the Song emperor.

At the **Hupao** (Tiger) **Spring Park**, *Tel. 7967213,* you will find water that will not overflow from a full cup even though you add coins to it. The high surface tension will also support a carefully placed Chinese coin, a trick that also works in Toronto, so don't be gullible. The spring is near the **Hangzhou Zoo**, about six km from the city southwest of the lake on Hupao Road. A handy tea house is here. The well is named after a tiger who revealed the location of the water in a dream to a monk.

The **Longjing** (Dragon Well), *Tel. 7986060*, to the northwest of Hupao, is another spring. The water here has a curious ripple effect when you stir it, especially on rainy days. This phenomenon is explained by the differences in the specific gravity of the rain water and the spring water, and is a good ploy to encourage business in wet weather.

Two km southwest is **Longjing Cun** (Dragon Well Village) where you can see the famous tea growing on hillsides. It is usually picked in late March or early April. Connoisseurs of good tea pay fabulously high prices for the best of the harvest, the most tender leaves hand-picked before the spring rain. The quantity is also limited because only a few villages have the proper soil and water.

The third of Hangzhou's famous springs is **Jade Spring** on *Yugu Road*, off the northwest corner of the lake within walking distance of the Shangri-La Hotel. It is for gold fish and flower lovers, as multi-colored ornamental fish are bred here. It is inside the 200-hectare **Hangzhou Botanical Garden**, *Tel. 7961908*, which has 3700 species of plants, including 120 varieties of bamboo.

A **cable car** runs 8am-5pm between Beigao Feng (North Peak) and near the Lingyin Temple, giving a good view of the lake. You can also drive up Wushan Hill, east of the lake, the highest spot in the city. This has an 800-year-old camphor tree and the ruins of the former Song palaces, trashed by the Mongols. At 6am it is full of *taiji* and disco people.

The **Tea Museum** has good exhibits and is open daily 8:30am-4:30pm all year, *Tel. 7964778*. It's four km from the Shangri-La past the Xihu Guest House west of the lake.

The **Silk Museum**, just south of the lake, has the oldest weaving machines in China, ancient silks and Ming and Qing court robes. It also has a silk fragment from 2715 B.C. It is open 8:30am-4:30pm.

The **Hu Qing Yu Tang Museum of Traditional Chinese Medicine** on *He Fan Street, Tel. 7027507*, should be seen for its beautiful old wood panelled building as well as its exhibits, one of the two most famous herbal medicine stores in the Qing. Open 8am or 8:30am-5pm Monday to Friday, it closes for lunch from 11am-12noon and has titles in English. It is in an old area full of interesting old buildings east of the lake. All these museums have signs in English.

You should be able to visit a silk factory to see the process. Try the **Dujinsheng Silk Weaving Factory** downtown close to the Wangpu Hotel, *215 Fengqi Road, Tel. 7061103, Fax 7913360* (closed Sunday), or the **Hangzhou Silk Printing and Dyeing Complex**, far from city center, *Tel. 8017824*.

New and good is the **Song Dynasty Town** with demonstrations of Song weaving, pottery-making, puppetry. It's at *148 Zhijiang Road,*

310008, Tel. 7090470, 7321785, Fax 7090471. Y50. Open 8:30am-9pm, with many show times.

Ask about the special events: the marathon race (October) and international boat festival (September), traditional medicine festival (May), and New Year's Eve.

NIGHTLIFE & ENTERTAINMENT

Try **Casablanca Bar**, *23 Hubin Road, Tel. 7025934,* five minutes by taxi from the Shangri-La with loud music. Nearby is the **L.A.Disco**, frequently packed with young people and costing about Y90 per person. And there are the quieter hotel bars.

An **acrobatic show** performs daily at 7:30 during high season, and every other day during low season. It's at *51 Wulin Road, 5174339.* The **Continental Hotel** has a good nightclub show at 8pm nightly.

Hotels have packages for the **West Lake Golf Club** at *200 Zhejiang Road. Tel. 7970060, Fax 7961005.* Its 36 holes were designed by Jack Nicklaus. *Email:golf@public.hz.cn. Http://www.eastgolf.com.*

Tennis is at the hotels and at **Huanglong Tuixun Zhongxin** near the Yellow Dragon Hotel.

SHOPPING

This province is known for silk textiles, woven silk pictures, satin, brocades, silk parasols, lace, mahogany and boxwood crafts. It also produces fresh water pearls, *Longquan* celadon, sandalwood fans, woven bambooware, distinctive *Tianzhu* chopsticks, and stone and wood carvings. Look for the incredible multi-colored stone carvings from Qingtian. Hangzhou also makes some fancy scissors that are useful souvenirs. Now that green tea is fashionable for health, a package should be a welcome gift at home. Loose leaves are better quality than tea bags.

The main shopping areas are **Jiefang Road** and **Yan'an Road**. For a local department store, try the **Hangzhou Department Store** on *Jiefang Road, Tel. 5158800.* For a good selection of arts and crafts at reasonable prices, the **Gong Lian Da Xia** is on Yan'an Road.

For **silk** fabric and garments, check out prices and quality in the department stores and then go to the **Hangzhou Sichou Shichang** (wholesale silk market), *Tel. 5159166.* It is open daily about 9am-4 or 5pm and about a 20-minute taxi ride from the lake. This market has three blocks of shops with overruns and seconds from all the different silk factories here and prices are great, better if you haggle. Avoid the store at the **Silk Museum**. While the tourist quality silk is cheaper than some, the fine art quality is twice the price of other stores.

Lots of tea pots are for sale in the **Tea Museum**. The cheapest prices for curios are at the **Bird and Flower Market** (Hua Niao Shichang). It is open 9am-5pm. Three tiny charming real jade (nephrite) carvings have cost Y50 each here after haggling first thing in the morning.

Wushan Road (Wushan Yeshi) in the same neighborhood and near the Friendship Hotel is a good place for serious antiques. It has about five stores. Especially good is the **Siu Shu Keung** at *Number 118, Tel. 7060926,* for ancestral portraits (at one-third Hong Kong prices), jade, and porcelain. In the evening from 7pm-10pm, this road turns into a curio market with stalls of **Qingtian stone carvings** and reproductions of brass dragons. The stone carvings are direct from Qingtian county itself and you can contact Mr. Wu Song Lin, in Hangzhou, *Tel. 8952364, (*Mobile phone: *9102562*; in Qingtian, *Tel. 578/6824835.* The **Dragon Hotel** has some magnificent Qingtian carvings on display.

The government **Cultural Relics Company** at *90 Dongpo Road just east of the lake, Tel. 7013447,* has good quality but prices are a little high. It gives export seals.

EXCURSIONS & DAY TRIPS

For Ningbo (about 150 km southwest) and Shaoxing (about 50 km southeast), see below. For Huangshan (200 km west), see separate listings under Hefei.

Mogan Mountain, 700 meters high (about 75 km northwest), is a well-known summer resort with over 300 hectares of waterfalls, bamboo forests, stone trails, ponds, and caves. It's good for hiking and relaxing in beautiful surroundings. You can stay at the modest **Mt. Mogan Hotel** in Deqing, Tel. 8033184.

Between Hangzhou and Huangshan is the 30 year-old 1,000 Island Lake, a two-day trip with an overnight at the **Thousand Island Lake Hotel** (Qian Dao Hu), *Danzhu Township, Chun'an County, Tel. 571/ 4872181, 4782181, Fax 4872788.* This 105-room, three-star hotel is on the southeast side of the lake near a small village, about a five-hour drive from Hangzhou. Though it has five storys, it doesn't have an elevator. In 2000, the Sofitel should be opening a resort nearby.

This largely undeveloped lake is 580 sq km, very pretty and pristine. Mountains rise up to 200 meters. On its 1078 islands are a couple of temples. One island has 200 wild, free-roaming monkeys (15-minute stop but no disembarking). Another has a thousand snakes in pits (a worthwhile 30-minute stop). From the hotel, you can take a ferry to Anhui province on the other side of the lake and then go by road to Huangshan.

In **Tiantai**, about 100 km from Hangzhou, the Guoqing Temple is the home of the Tiantai Buddhist sect.

The **Tidal Bore** of the Qiantang River is most spectacular on the 18th day of the eighth month (lunar calendar). In 1974 it reached a height of nine meters, but it is not usually that dramatic. You can best see it in Yanguantown at Zhan'ao Pagoda, 45 km from Hangzhou, or at Haining. Check with a travel agent for dates and bus tours if you are in Hangzhou in late September or early October. This is a one-day trip.

Huzhou, about two hours' drive or train north of Hangzhou plus boat trip, is a silkworm breeding centre. Here you can also watch the silk-making process on a large scale, an opportunity to see the countryside.

PRACTICAL INFORMATION

Hours: offices, 8:30am-5:00 or 5:30pm with lunch about 11:30am-1:30pm, Monday to Friday; stores daily 9am-8 or 9pm; banks 8:30am-5pm five days a week; most temples open daily from 8:30am-5:30pm, museums 9am-4 or 4:30pm daily. Some parks close at 6pm.

CITS, Zhejiang, *1 Shihan Road, Hangzhou 310007. Tel. 5152888, Fax 5156667, 5156576.*

China Hangzhou Overseas Tourist Company, *45 Shuguang Road, 310013. Tel. 7993888, Fax 7994365. E-mail:OTCHZ@public.hz.zj.cn.*

Hangzhou Tourism Administration, *484 Yanan Road, Tel. 5165224, Fax 5152645.*

Zhejiang Overseas Tourism Corp., *58-A or 380 Fengqi Road, 310006. Tel. 5064273, 5064276, Fax 5064242. E-mail:zjotc@public.hn.zj.cn.* Contact Mr. Yu Xiao Qiang, Americas Department. Office in the New World Dragon. ZOTC has one-day tours to Tonglu, Shaoxing, and Suzhou; two-day tours to 1000 Island Lake, and three-day tours to Huangshan Mountain.

Zhejiang Provincial Travel and Tourism Bureau, *1 Shihan Road, Hangzhou, 310007. Tel. 5156631, Fax 5156429.* Brochures available.

Tourist complaints, contact Supervisory Bureau of Tourism Quality of Zhejiang Province, *Tel. 5156631, 5158831, Fax 5156429.*

NINGBO

(Ningpo)

Ningbo is on the Zhejiang coast south of Shanghai. A community of 1.13 million people, Ningbo is known for its great ship builders and prominent business people and booming commerce. It is also noteworthy for the oldest extant library in China, two major temples, and the nearby home of the Goddess of Mercy in Putuo Shan.

ARRIVALS & DEPARTURES

Ningbo can be reached by train (in about 1.5 hours) or by road (over two hours) from Hangzhou. It can also be reached by expressway from

Shanghai. Express highway buses go frequently from the Eastern bus station in Hangzhou. It is linked by plane with about 23 Chinese cities and Hong Kong, and from Shanghai it's a 30-minute flight or a four-hour ferry and bus ride – a convenient weekend trip.

ORIENTATION

The Ningbo area has been settled with an advanced culture at least since 4800 B.C. and some scholars now claim the cradle of Chinese civilization was here, and not confined to the Yellow River.

Ningbo has been recorded since the Spring and Autumn Period (700-476 B.C.). It has been a major port since the Tang, trading with Korea, Japan, and Southeast Asia. Ice-free, it was made a treaty port, open to foreign trade and residence in 1842. After 1860, a French military detachment was stationed here. Ningbo was reopened as a port for foreign trade in 1979 for the first time in 30 years. Today its population is 5.2 million.

If you have only one day, see **Hemudu**, the **library** and the two **temples** to the east. If you have one more day, there's **Chiang Kai-shek's home town** and the **temple home of the Laughing Buddha** in Xikou Town, Fenhua city. From Ningbo, **Putuoshan** could be a three-day trip. Forget about crafts shopping. There isn't much.

WHERE TO STAY & EAT

Hotels here have international services like credit cards, business centers, and international direct dial room telephones. The East Port Hotel is best, then the Asia Garden. Add 15% tax to prices. We haven't had a chance to see the **Citic Ningbo Hotel** but hear it's good. It's at *One Jiangdong Bei Road, Tel. 7757888, Fax 7334739.*

EAST PORT HOTEL, *52 Caihong Bei Road, 315040. Four stars. Tel. 7373188, Fax 7333646. Email:eshotel@public.nbptt.zj.cn. Three km from the railway station, 15 km from the airport. Y880-Y1250 for rooms, Y1800-Y7500 for suites, both including one western breakfast. It also has a sub building with cheaper rooms Y560 and suites Y930-Y1100.*

In the commercial district near big department stores, this 1994 hotel has 14 stories, 228 rooms, CNN and ABC, 24-hour room service, Japanese and Cantonese food. There's an indoor pool, gym, and clinic. It has a shuttle bus meeting flights from Hong Kong and Shanghai, and a Dragonair office. China Famous Hotel VIP Club.

ASIA GARDEN HOTEL (Yazhou Huayuan Binguan), *72 Mayuan Road, 315012. Three stars, Tel. 7116888, Fax 7112138. E-mail:agh@nbnet.com.cn. Http://www.nbnet.com.cn. Y580-Y930 for rooms, and Y1450-Y3500 for suites. 15 km from the airport and 0.5 km from the railway station. Close to the Friendship and antique stores.*

Built in 1987, this 10-story, 170-room hotel was renovated last in 1998. It has been clean and adequate and has four non-smoking floors, CNN and Star Plus, and in-room safes. It has French and Japanese food and charges Y45 for buffet breakfast.

SEEING THE SIGHTS

The *Tianyige Library, completed in 1561 (Ming to Qing) is half a kilometer from the Asia Garden Hotel. It still has more than 300,000 books. It started as a private library and now has in its more modern extension next door over 80,000 rare books, mostly from the Ming, plus numerous stone tablets. Scholars can see these books upon request. The library is worth visiting for its simple elegance and its peaceful, tastefully-designed gardens. It was the blueprint for the other seven imperial Qing libraries.

At the entrance to the library is a sign that says something like 'This is not an amusement park. No fun inside. Keep out.' Don't be intimidated by the blunt Ningbo manner. Note also the conversations of the man-in-the-street, which might sound like intense, bitter arguing.

Both the Tiantong Temple, (35 km) and the Ayuwang (King Asoka) Temple (30 km) are east of the city in rural hill country, and are bigger and more impressive than city temples, with bigger-than-life-size statues. The Ayuwang, *Tel. 4880624* (open daily 8am-5pm) was founded in the third century. The Ayuwang Temple has about 70 monks, and relics of Sakyamuni (Buddha) in its highest hall. The famous Buddhist monk Jianzhen (see Yangzhou) once lived here after he failed in his third attempt to reach Japan in the Tang dynasty.

The Tiantong Temple is one of the largest temples south of the Yangtze, with over 700 halls and over 100 monks. The Tiantong has sent many teachers to Japan and consequently attracts many Japanese visitors. It is the second holiest shrine of the Zen or Chan sect. Zen Buddhist statues are supposed to have deepset eyes looking at their noses as the nose safekeeps one's heart to avoid temptation. See if you can find any. Better still, try crossing your eyes when you feel tempted to sin.

On the way back to Ningbo from these temples, you might be interested in a huge wholesale market for sweaters made in the area.

The Hemudu site is west of the city in Yuyao County about 90 minutes by road in the flourishing countryside. It has a small but good museum, *Tel. 2670158*, with English signs. The display includes a still-playable 6,000 to 7,000 year-old bone flute, rice, plough shares, weaving, inlaid-bone and wood carvings, and jade ornaments. Open daily 8:30am-4:30pm year round.

The *Bao Guo Temple, built in 1013 (Northern Song), is the oldest extant wooden structure south of the Yangtze, and is in Yuyao, 20 km north of the Asia Garden Hotel. Unlike other temples, which have large beams for support, this one uses many small ones. The **Tainfeng Pagoda**, built in 695, was traditionally a place for scholars to gather to compose poems and enjoy the scenery. It is hexagonal, seven stories high, but not as beautiful as younger pagodas. This needs another half day to see.

EXCURSIONS & DAY TRIPS

Putuo Shan is the home of Guanyin (Kuan Yin), the Goddess of Mercy, and is one of the Four Sacred Buddhist Mountains. I've been told that this 12.5-sq-km island is reached by **ship** from Ningbo, a two-hour trip offered four times a day, and that a ferry is also available from Shanghai (a three-hour speed boat from Pudong's Luchaogang Port, or overnight from Shiliupu Port). An **airport** is at Zhu Jia Jian with flights from Shanghai. This is a 30-minute ferry trip away from Putuo Shan.

Do check these directions because of changes and transfers from neighboring islands which might mean tiresome delays. In summer and on weekends, do reserve a hotel room.

On the way you pass the famous **Zhaoshan-Qundao fishing ground** with triangular fish nets, a picturesque view, especially at sunset. Expect to pay a Y40 entry fee upon arrival, and take anti-mosquito precautions. Do not leave valuables in your room.

Putuo Shan has been a religious site since 847 A.D. It once had over 200 temples and nunneries, but the years and the Red Guards have done their worst, and about 80 are now open. Those who remember hiking from innumerable nunneries to innumerable temples may be disappointed. No more tiny Buddhist statues inscribed with religious poems to help keep one single-mindedly devout, line the narrow mountain paths. But you can still climb thousands of steps and hike through bamboo groves, and along the rocky shore and beaches. Along with the hospitable and warm hearted villagers, enough of the religious atmosphere remains for first-time visitors to enjoy.

Visitors can also see the *kowtow*ing pilgrims, forehead to ground every three steps, as they pay homage or ask special favors of this favorite deity. Especially touching are the sick and handicapped, carried on the backs of friends or family, who come to pray for healing. Devout Buddhists try to make a trip to Putuo at least once in a lifetime.

It is customary to purchase a yellow sack from one of the temples and, for a fee, have each temple rubber-stamp its seal on the sack to prove you've been there.

Putuo Shan is especially famous because repeated storms kept some Japanese worshippers from carrying away a statue of Guanyin from China. Near a cliff is the **Won't Go Temple**, to commemorate the goddess's desire to remain in China.

The prices below are subject to 10% tax and discount. Among the hotels here is the four-star, 150-room **Hoi Tak Putuoshan Resort**, *Sijifan Road, Putuoshan, 316107, Tel. (580)6092828, and Fax 6091818. Y621-Y1668 for rooms, Y1238-Y3168 for suites. Credit cards.* The best three-star is the **Putuo Shan Zhuang**, Tel.580/ 6091666 or Fax 6091667, but the 160-room **Xilei Xiao Zhuang Hotel**, *316107, Tel. 6091522, 6091505 or Fax 6091023*, is more convenient. It's beside a temple and the chanting might awaken you early in the morning. It's also a three-star hotel.

CITS **Putuo Shan** is at *25 Wenhua Road, Ding Hai District, Zhongshan City, 316000, Tel. 580/6091183, 2024931, Fax 2027342.*

PRACTICAL INFORMATION

Ambulance, *Tel. 120*
CITS Ningbo, *75 Yan Yue Street, Tel. 7312805 or Fax 7298690.*
Ningbo China Travel Service, *5/F Golden Dragon Hotel, Ningbo 315010, Tel. 7307998, Fax 7329429.*
Ningbo Overseas Travel Co., *3 Lane 5, Xinchangchun Road, 315010, Tel. 7364451, Fax 7364481. Try also 16 Xian Xue Street, Tel. 7280483, Fax 7280014.*
Ningbo Travel and Tourism Bureau,*35 Changchun Road, Yinhe Building 3, 315012, Tel. 7303716, Fax 7291266.*
Police, *Tel. 110*
Telephone Code, *0574*

SHAOXING

(Shaohsing)
Shaoxing is in Zhejiang province. The urban population is 240,000.
You go to Shaoxing to get a feel of old traditional China. It is a 2000 to 3000 year-old town, best known for its wine. Its charm will not last forever so go soon. It was the birthplace of China's most famous pre-Liberation writer, Luxun (Lu Hsun). Some of his stories, notably *The Story of Ah Q*, were set in this town, and a highly recommended but very sad 1982 movie was made of the Ah Q novella here. Literary types should pay a visit to his former residence and the Luxun Memorial Hall.

Shaoxing was the capital of the State of Ye during the Spring and Autumn period. The 'tomb' of **Emperor Yu**, the Xia dynasty founder, is in the south suburbs at the base of Mt. Kuaiji. No one knows if the remains of this third century B.C. pioneer in irrigation are actually here in Yuwang Miao Temple. In any case, he died in Shaoxing during a visit. The name Shaoxing means 'gathering place,' for example, of the people celebrating the miraculous engineering feats of Emperor Yu.

Shaoxing is famous throughout China for its distinctive opera. It is less formal, full of emotion, action, and audience-pleasing lyrics, gorgeous costumes, and flashy sets. All parts are played by women.

ARRIVALS & DEPARTURES

Shaoxing is 60 km from Hangzhou by train or road, three hours from Ningbo. It is 65 km from the closest airport in Hangzhou.

ORIENTATION

Shaoxing is attractive because it still has many houses, streets, canals, and boats from centuries ago. Much time can be spent walking around in this time warp. Changes have been made however: the addition of a local television station and the lovely sycamore and plane trees lining the streets. The Second Hospital was the former mission hospital.

Shaoxing today is the capital of one of the ten most prosperous small counties in China, its wealth based on textiles. Don't miss the Wine Festival if you're here in September.

WHERE TO STAY & EAT

These hotels take credit cards, have international direct dial phones, air-conditioning, and are subject to 10% surcharge and discounts. The two four-star hotels are the best.

XIANHENG HOTEL, *680 Jiefang Road, 312000, Tel. 8068698, 8068698, Fax 8051028. E-mail:xianheng@public.sxptt.zj.cn. Four star standard. Y298-Y560 for rooms, and Y600-Y6800 for suites.*

This 22-story hotel has 236 rooms.

SHAOXING INTERNATIONAL HOTEL, *100 Fushan Xi Road, 312000, Tel. 5166788, Fax 5166778. Four stars. Y380-Y680 for rooms, Y800-Y6600 for suites.*

This is near Fushan Hills in a western suburb, eight-minutes drive from the train station and 50-minutes drive from the airport.

SHAOXING HOTEL (Binguan), *9 Huanshan Road, 312000. Three stars. Tel. 5155888, Fax 5155565. 67 km from the airport, three km from the railway station. Y300-Y550 for rooms, Y3800 for suites. The price includes breakfast.*

The traditional late Ming garden-style architecture is beautiful, but the hotel smells mildly of mold. The dining hall is an old family temple.

SEEING THE SIGHTS

If you want to visit **East Lake**, **Yuwang Miao**, **Lang Ding** (Orchid Pavilion), **Luxun's home** and **museum**, **Qiu Jin's home**, and stroll about the town, you need at least two full days. You could also ask about the story of the scholar writing with a brush made of mouse whiskers. Tours can visit a home for the aged.

Shaoxing is known for its lovely canals and lake, alive with **boats** of all descriptions. Especially striking are its distinctive foot boats, the oars worked by feet. Do take a lake boat trip through its canals, and into caves cut out of the lake's quarried cliffs to see the hanging gardens. You can also glide under some of its 3,000 stone-arched bridges to old temples and the market, a good way to see the city.

Also of interest are the **Orchid Pavilion**, dating back to the fourth century, and the **Shen family garden**, which commemorates the meeting between Song dynasty lovers. The home of the early 20th century female revolutionary Qiu Jin is open as a museum. Premier Chou En-lai, though born in Jiangsu province, was brought up in this city and you can visit his home.

You can take another boat trip near ancient **Keqiao**, 12 km from Shaoxing, pulled in the old way by two men along part of a five-km long stone towpath to a 800-year old stone bridge. Travel agents can also arrange a demonstration of Shaoxing opera on board.

SHOPPING

Shaoxing wine, brewed with two thousand years of experience, is a "must purchase" item. You can savor a sample at the **Xian Heng Wine Shop**, *44 Luxun Road,* named after a Luxun short story. Other locally-made items include lace, felt hats, paper fans, silk, porcelain, bambooware, and ink stones. The **Shaoxing Antique Store** is on Jiefang Nan Road.

PRACTICAL INFORMATION

CITS Shaoxing Branch, *366 Fushan Xi Road, 312000, Tel. 5167672, Fax 5167672.*

Telephone Code *0575.*

Zhejiang Shaoxing Tourism Bureau, *412 Fushan Xi Road, 312000. Tel. 5155353, Fax 5155592.*

HEFEI

(Hofei)

Hefei is the capital of Anhui (Anhwei), a province on the north bank of the Yangtze River. Its only international class destination is marvelous **Huangshan Mountain**, the inspiration for Chinese landscape painters, poets, and mystics. It does have a lot of traditional culture and architecture, Three Kingdom's and early Ming dynasty history.

ARRIVALS & DEPARTURES

Flights from 22 cities and Hong Kong are available now. There's also train service from Beijing (12 hours), Nanjing (six hours), and Shanghai (11 hours). Hefei is connected by expressway to Nanjing, a 185 km trip taking two to three hours, and to Shanghai six hours.

ORIENTATION

Anhui is famous for its dramatic mountains. In the province live Han, Hui, She, and other nationalities. Because of its strategic location, numerous battles were fought here in the ancient past. Hefei's tourist attractions can be squeezed into one day. It would take a week to see the province. Hefei's urban population is 1.2 million. The coldest weather in January is -5 C; the hottest in July and August is 39 C.

WHERE TO STAY

The best hotels here are the **Anhui Hotel**, the **Holiday Inn** and the **Novotel**. The latter two have the best location, two minutes walk to the Bao Zheng Temple. The Holiday Inn is near the shopping street. Hotels add 15% surcharge, accept credit cards, and have foreign exchange.

HOLIDAY INN HEFEI, *1104 Changjiang Dong Road, 230011, Tel. 4291188, Fax 4291166. E-mail:hihfe@public.hf.ah.cn. This 1998 hotel is close to Xiaoyaojin Park, Hefei's largest, three km from the railway station, six km from the hi-tech industrial zone, and 12 km from the international airport. Four star standard not yet official. Y920-Y1410 for rooms, Y1500-Y7800 for suites.*

This 341-room hotel has an indoor pool, gym, steambath, and jacuzzi. It also has CNN, CNBC and HBO, Korean, Cantonese and western food, in-room safes, and a free airport shuttle.

NOVOTEL HEFEI, *199 Wuhu Road, 230001, Tel. 2887777, Fax 2884341. Email:novotel@public.hf.ah.cn. Ten km from the airport. Close to the Bao Zheng Memorial Temple. Tel. in North America 800/221-4542. Three to four-star standard. $95-$150 for rooms, $180 for suites.*

This new 246-room hotel has non-smoking floors, CNN and Star Plus, in-room safes, Sichuan, Cantonese, continental and French food. $7 for buffet breakfast. An Accor Hotel.

ANHUI HOTEL (Fandian), *18 Meishan Road, 230022. Tel. 2811818, Fax 2817583. E-mail:anhuihtl@public.hf.ah.cn. 12 km from the airport, and 10 km from the railway station. Four stars. Y600-Y980 for rooms, and Y930-Y5880 for suites.*

This 305-room hotel, renovated in 1998, has non-smoking floors, CNN and Star Plus, in-room safes, and Cantonese and western cuisine.

WHERE TO EAT

Anhui specialties are fresh-water crabs and locally-produced *Gujing Gongjiu* wine, once sent as tribute to the Ming emperors. Try cured Mandarin fish, stewed turtle, *Fulizi* braised chicken, *Wenzhenshan* bamboo shoots, and sesame cakes. Dishes are somewhat salty and slightly spicy hot with thick soups.

Try the restaurant in the **Anhui Hotel** for Anhui food, *Tel. 2811818.* The **Novotel** has a western bakery. The Holiday Inn has good Cantonese food. There's also the **Huishang Restaurant** on *Yangtze Road, Tel. 2653088.*

SEEING THE SIGHTS

If you have a half day, do a city tour. If you have a full day, go to Fengyang. The charm of this province is its old architecture and its countryside.

In **Xiaoyaojin Park**, near the center of the city, during the Three Kingdoms period 1700 years ago, General Zhang Liao of the State of Wei fought against General Sun Quan (Sun Chuan) of the State of Wu. The site is now a park with three islets, on one of which is the tomb and statue of General Zhang. Near the park is a zoo.

Two km south of Ximaoyaojin, the **Lecturing Rostrum/Archery Training Terrace** is where Emperor Cao Cao trained Wei troops in using crossbows. These sites are marked with pavilions in traditional architecture. The **Mingjiao Temple** (from the Tang dynasty) is on the terrace. Destroyed in the 19th century during the Taiping War, it was rebuilt by General Yuan Hongmo of the Taiping Heavenly Kingdom.

The **Temple to Lord Bao Gong**, in the center of the city, was built in honor of this honest and outstanding magistrate and vice minister of the Northern Song. The **Provincial Museum** has a pleasant dinosaur garden.

MULAN'S BIRTHPLACE!

Anhui province also claims to be the birthplace of the Disney heroine **Mulan**, *specifically the city of Bo Zhou 330 km from Hefei. It also has a wine museum and a huge medicinal herb market. For more information, contact the* **Bo Zhou Tourism Bureau**, *Tel. 551/3630018, or* **Bo Zhou International Travel Service**, *25 Xinhua Road, Bo Zhou, 236800, Tel. 558/5522247, Fax 5525348. See also Wuhan.*

SHOPPING

Pears, pomegranates, grapes, kiwi fruit, and herbal medicines are grown in the province. Made are candied dates, tea, bamboo mats, and iron pictures. Hefei is also noted for its four scholarly treasures: *Xuan* writing brush, *Hu* ink stick, *She* ink slab and *Xuan* paper. Try the **Hefei Department Store**, *124 Yangtze Road, Tel. 2647133* or the **Shang Zhi Du Department Store** on *Suzhou Road*. The **Chenghuangmiao shopping center** was built in the Ming style and surrounds the 900-year-old Town God's Temple. It has lots of antiques and curios for sale.

EXCURSIONS & DAY TRIPS

Near Bengbu in **Fengyang County**, on the railway line between Beijing and Shanghai, 169 km from Hefei, is the ancestral home of the first Ming emperor, who proclaimed it a royal city. A new expressway in 1999 should cut down travel time. Among the **Ming tombs** here are Tang He's, one of the Ming dynasty founders. The ***ruins of the Imperial City of the Middle Capital**, and stone inscriptions at the Imperial Mausoleum, are now under State Council protection.

Bengbu also has the **Temple of King Yu**. One of the first attempts at the 'Responsibility System' was started here in 1978. This is a one day trip from Hefei. If you need it, there's the three-star **Zhanggongshan Hotel**, *128 Zhanggongshan Road, Bengbu, 233010. Tel. 4091888, Fax 4091588.* It takes credit cards and has international direct dial service. **Bengbu International Travel Service** is at *161 Zhongshan Street, 233000, Tel. 2068666, Fax 2042025.* The telephone code is *0552.*

Jiuhuashan (Mt. Jiuhua), one of the Four Buddhist Mountains (altitude 1,341 meters), is at least an overnight trip by road taking three hours each way. It is 301 km south of Hefei. It has 78 Ming and Qing temples, 6,800 buddhas which were untouched by the Red Guards, and 99 peaks. Motor vehicles can drive up to 600 meters. There is a 1350-meter-long cable car service to **Tiantai Temple**. Roushen Hall and Qiyuan Temple are both important sites. In Baisui Gong (Buddhist Mummy Hall), there is a 400-year-old gold-plated monk. There's a temple fair on the 30th of the seventh lunar month for 10 days.

The coldest mean temperature in January is -3 C. The hottest mean temperature is 18 C in July. The best hotel is the two-star **Julong Hotel**, *Jiuhua Street, Qingyang County, 242811. Tel. 5011368, 5011227, Fax 5011022.* This hotel is on the mountain, and accepts no credit cards. Another two-star is the new 70-room **Foguyuan Hotel**, *Tel. 5011011, 5011479, Fax 5011484.* Y320-Y400 for rooms, and Y480-Y980 for suites. **CITS** is on *Jiuhua Street, Jiuhua Mountain, Qinyang County, 242811. Tel. 5011318, Fax 5011202.* For **China Travel Service**, *Tel. 5011588, Fax 5011587.* For **cable car information**, Tel. 5011719. The telephone code is *0566.*

Tunxi is the administrative part of **Huangshan City** and is 60 km from the Huangshan Mountain Scenic Area. Flights arrive from Hong Kong and from nine other cities. Here you can see **Tunxi Old Street** (with antique and curio market), and the **Tangyue Memorial Arches** (with China's only hall for women) in **Shexian** (five km from Tunxi). The best hotel here is the three-star 201-room **Huangshan International Hotel**, *Xiaohuashan, Tunxi, 245000. Tel. 2526999, Fax 2512087. Y680 for rooms, Y1280-Y6000 for suites.* It is four km from the airport, and two from the railway station. It has international direct dialing, credit card service, and tennis. It is a CTS Hotel.

The following agencies and offices can help you with information and travel arrangements: **Anhui Overseas Tourist Corporation**, *60 Qianyuan Nan Road, Tunxi District, Huangshan, 245000. Tel. 2514266, 2518464, 2516635, Fax 2514689, 2514000;* **Huangshan CITS**, *6 Xizhen Street, 245011. Tel. 2515231, 2515618, Fax 2514014;* **Huangshan Municipal Tourism Administration**, *63 Yan'an Road, Fax 2514019, 2511850* for brochures. **CTS**, *Tel. 2511467, Fax 2516605.* Tunxi's telephone code is *0559.*

Wuhu, in the southeastern part of the province, is where the Qing-yi River joins the Yangtze. On the railway line between Nanjing and Hefei, it is the main foreign trading river port for the province and the fourth largest port on the Yangtze. It also produces silk and those lovely pictures made of forged iron, usually painted black. Its **Alligator Breeding Center** (4,000 alligators) is in Diadulin District in the southern suburb of Xuancheng County. **Xuancheng International Travel Service** is at *Ningguo County, 242300, Tel. 563/4021888.*

PRACTICAL INFORMATION

Anhui Overseas Travel Corp., **Anhui Tourism Administration**, and **CITS** Hefei Branch, are together at *8 Meishan Road, 230022. Tel. 2821418, 2812930, Fax 2812855.* **CITS'** telephone is *2812930, Fax 2812855.* It can arrange home stays with local families. The **OTC** telephone is *2812978, Fax 2812855, and e-mail:caote@public.hf.ah.cn.* Ask for Mr. Zhang Ming. For **tourist complaints and hotline**, *Tel. 2821821.* For information, *Tel. 2812930, 2812931.*

Anhui Provincial Tourist Bureau, *8 Meishan Road, 230022. Tel. 2821038, Fax 2824001* for tourist information.

China Travel Service Group, *Jiuzhou Building, 381 Jinzhou Road, Tel. 2651522, Fax 2654308.*

Hours: offices 8 or 8:30am-5 or 6pm, lunch 12-2pm. Bank of China, 8am-5pm.

Huangshan CITS, Planning and Reception Centre, *6 Xizhen Road, Tunxi, 245011, Tel. 2515263. Fax 2514014.* For help or information.

Huangshan Comfort Travel Service, *12 Qian Yuan Bei Road, Tunxi, 245000. Tel. 2515835, Fax 2514040.*
Telephone Code, *0551*
Tourist Complaints, contact Supervisory Bureau of Tourism Quality of Anhui Province, *4 Meishan Road, 230061, Tel. 2821825, Fax 2824001*

HUANGSHAN SCENIC AREA

Located in southern Anhui province, **Huangshan Mountain** is one of China's top ten tourist attractions, and has been designated a UNESCO World Heritage site. Climbing the mountain has been described by one writer as 'walking into an unending Chinese landscape painting.' It is part of Huangshan City.

The coldest month is January, with a low of -6 C; the warmest is July, with a high of 20 C. The annual precipitation is 1600 millimeters, mainly from June to September.

ARRIVALS & DEPARTURES

Huangshan can be reached by road from Hangzhou via 1,000 Island Lake. From Tunxi, the closest airport and railway station, you can go by public bus (68 km). By train from Nanjing it takes seven hours or by bus eight hours. The Beijing train takes 23 hours, and from Shanghai it's 11 hours by tourist train. It can be reached from Hefei by bus in 6.5 hours.

ORIENTATION

Huangshan Scenic Area is 154 sq. km with three cable cars and 45 km of paved paths. It is not really a plateau on top. Even after you get to the top, there's still a lot of climbing. At two of its best views, the **Peak for Dispelling Clouds** and **Lotus Flower Peak**, lovers can put a padlock on a fence and throw away the key into the clouds below.

As with most mountains in China, paths are crowded with hikers during the summer. The end of April is the most beautiful time, and hiking is good to the end of October. Winter is also beautiful with wizened trees laden with snow. The cable car works all year round.

WHERE TO STAY & EAT

Hotels here are only two and three star quality. We haven't found any yet with satellite television. The best hotel is the **Peach Blossom**. The **West Sea** and the **North Sea** are on the mountain, and the Peach Blossom and the **Cloud Valley** are at the base. The summit hotels lend coats to unprepared shivering guests. Travelers should leave heavy bags at the base and take only what they are able to carry in case they can't find help. High season is March 1 to November 15.

WEST SEA HOTEL (Xihai Fandian), *Xihai Scenic Area, 242700. Three stars. Tel. 5562132, Fax 5562988. $150. Only hotel on summit accepting credit cards.*

The 1988-built West Sea has 208 rooms. At 1600 meters, it is a half hour (one km) walk and climb from the top of the first cable car. It is 300 meters from the third cable car.

PEACH BLOSSOM HOTEL (Tao Yuan Binguan), *3 Yanan Road, Hot Spring area, 242709. Three stars. Tel. 5562295, 5562502, Fax 5562888. Y580 for rooms, Y1880 for suites. No surcharge.*

This hotel is near stores and a swimming pool, two km or 7.5 km to a cable car terminal. It has 200 rooms, traditional Chinese architecture, a non-smoking floor, no CNN and great view. Buffet breakfast costs Y30.

NORTH SEA HOTEL (Beihai Binguan), *242709. Three stars, Tel. 5562555, Fax 5562707. $60. Altitude 1630 meters. Half kilometer walk including a 340-meter uphill climb from upper cable car terminal.*

Built in 1958 and expanded in 1996, this hotel has 506 rooms of different qualities.

CLOUD VALLEY VILLA HOTEL (Yungu Binguan), *Yungu Si, 242709. Three stars, Tel. 5562188, Fax 5562121. $45. Credit cards. Altitude 800 meters.*

This 102-room hotel is set in a beautiful valley surrounded by bamboo and pines. As a result, it rarely gets sun and smells musty. It has charming Ming architecture, built like a maze on the side of a mountain, with connecting three-story buildings.

SEEING THE SIGHTS

Huangshan is worth making an effort to visit. But you have to take a chance with the weather. For serious photographers, the weather should be cloudy, which it is 208 days a year (mainly in the spring). For perfect photos, you must patiently wait for clouds to float to the right place between the mountains, silhouetting twisted, horizontal 400-year old pines that add depth. One full day on top is enough for covering all the designated photo spots but not for taking the perfect photo.

The highest of the 72 peaks, **Lian Hua** (Lotus Flower) rises 1,864 meters above sea level. To reach the valley before the final ascent to the top means climbing 800 stone steps cut into a 60-70 degree angle cliff, nose almost to rock.

One section of the second highest peak, **Tian Du** (Heavenly Capital Peak, 1,830 meters), has a ridge less than a meter wide called **Carp's Backbone**. Although iron chain railings are there to assure the unsure, some people resort to crawling to get across. This is just to say that

Huangshan is for the strong and adventurous, who will be rewarded by giant vertical peaks, pines (some over 1,000 years old), hot springs (42 C), lots of streams, mist, magnificent views, and a great feeling of achievement if you make it.

Foreigners usually go up and down on the same day by cable car. But you can spend the night on the summit to see the sunrise. The summit is not for people prone to heart attacks nor for the fussy. And one must consider cable car maintenance days.

Built in 1986, the 2800-meter-long **cable car** on the east slope leaves from near the Cloud Valley Hotel and makes the ascent in eight minutes to near the North Sea Hotel. Otherwise it takes 2.5-three hours by foot up 15,000 stone steps. The cable car operates daily 7am-6pm in busy season and 8am-4pm otherwise. One car leaves every 15 minutes with a maximum of 40 people. Expect up to an hour's wait during high season. The cable car runs all year except for a half day between the 22nd and 26th of each month. It is closed once a year from December 20 to 31. It does not operate during windstorms, nor during maintenance.

You can also ride human-powered **sedan chairs** up and on the mountain. One way up the mountain costs at least Y600. You can also negotiate for a porter to carry bags.

SHOPPING

Paintings of Huangshan, Huangshan tea, bamboo, and straw curtains are made here. It is traditional to buy a special stone and find someone to carve your name on it. And don't forget the padlock.

PRACTICAL INFORMATION

Business Hours: Offices 8am-6pm. Bank of China 8am-5:30pm.

Huangshan Tourism Development Co., *Huangshan Scenic District, Hot Spring Area, Tel. 5561311, Fax 5561110.* For information.

Telephone code, 0559

Travel Agents: see Tunxi above.

JINAN

This capital of Shandong province is an industrial center producing trucks, textiles, and paper, and has been famous primarily for its springs, its Buddhist temples, and its proximity to Taishan mountain and Qufu, the hometown of Confucius. It is due south of Beijing, 15 km from the south shore of the Huanghe (Yellow River).

Jinan was settled more than 5000 years ago by the neolithic Dawenkou and Longshan peoples. It dates from the sixth century B.C., when it was the gate city to the state of Qi and the starting point of the ancient Qi Great Wall. It was named Jinan, meaning south of the Ji River, a name it has kept even though that river dried up centuries ago.

Jinan was a busy commercial center during the Tang, and Marco Polo spoke favorably of its garden atmosphere and its thriving silk industry. It has been the capital since the Ming.

The climate is temperate. The hottest in late July to early August is 33 C; the coldest in January, -10 C. The annual precipitation is about 700 millimeters, mainly in July and August. The urban population is 2.4 million, total 5 million.

ARRIVALS & DEPARTURES

Jinan is at the junction of the Beijing-Shanghai and the Qingdao-Jinan railways. It takes five hours from Beijing. Jinan can also be reached by plane from Hong Kong and 24 cities. The airport is 40 km from town. Express buses to Qingdao and Yantai leave about seven times a day from the South Bus Terminal, *Tel. 2984344, 2984345.*

ORIENTATION

A geographer first recorded the excellent quality of the water in this **City of Springs** 2,500 years ago. The Chinese kept records of pretty much everything! During the Jin (1115-1234), someone else listed 72 springs on a tablet. He missed a few; a 1964 survey mentions 108 natural springs.

The springs were not just holes in the ground spouting water. They were embellished with gardens, rockery, pavilions, and tea houses. A subterranean wall of volcanic rock forced the water to the earth's surface. But alas, a lowering water table due to the overuse of water dried up the springs. However modern technology has come to the rescue and the waters should start gushing again in 1999 from late August to March, worth a visit.

WHERE TO STAY

The best hotel for tourists and business people is the **Qilu**. The glitzy **Pearl** is better located for business people but standards are lower. The **Zhonghao Grand Hotel** and **Hua Neng Hotel** are worth considering. The **Guidu** is new and looks good. The following prices are subject to change, discounts and 10% service charge.

QILU HOTEL (Binguan), *8 Qianfoshan Road, 250014. Four and five stars. Tel. 2966888, Fax 2967676. E-mail:qilu@shell.sdcmt.co.cn. 40 km from the airport, six km from the railway station, and walking distance to the provincial museum. $80-$120.*

This hotel has a good comfortable suburban feeling about it, and is convenient to downtown. It has a garden and faces 1000 Buddha Hill. It has 255 rooms from 1986, and 450 rooms added in 1998, a "fashion show," tennis, indoor pool, gym, and satellite television. It has a revolving restaurant, Korean, Shandong, Sichuan, and Chaozhou food. The breakfast buffet costs Y66.

PEARL HOTEL (Zhen Zhu Dajiudian), *164 Jingsan Road, 250001. Tel. 7932888, Fax 7932688. E-mail:lhw@pub.online.jn.sd.cn. Three stars. $47-$59 for rooms and $104 for suites. 38 km from the airport and 1.5 km from the railway station. It is within walking distance of the city hall.*

Built in 1991-92, this hotel has 24 stories, and 153 rooms with in-room safes on floors above the 14th. It also has CNN, and a revolving restaurant and hot pot. It has a very small driveway, carpets are dirty, and maintenance poor.

ZHONGHAO GRAND HOTEL *(Zhonghao Dajiudian), 165 Jiefang Road, Tel. 6968888, Fax 6993200. E-mail:Zhgh@jn-public.sd.cninfo.net. Four stars. $100.* This hotel has 260 rooms, a pool and a gym.

HUA NENG HOTEL (Hua Neng Binguan), *17 Quancheng Road, Tel. 6036888, Fax 6039888. Four stars. $70.* This 147-room hotel has a pool and gym.

GUI DU HOTEL, *1 Shengping Road, Jingyi Weisan, 250001, Tel. 6900888, Fax 6900999. E-mail: 1guidu@public.jn.sd.cn Three stars. $60.*

Located 30 km from the airport, 0.2 km from the railway station and in a crowded area full of markets and shops.

WHERE TO EAT

Exotic local fare are cattails, lotus roots and lotus seeds from Daming Lake, roast duck, winding-thread cakes, and monkey-head mushroom. In addition to the hotels, there are the **Jinsanbei Restaurants**. The most convenient of this chain is across the road from the Jilu Hotel at *5, Qianfoshan Road, Tel. 2961616, 2961446.*

SEEING THE SIGHTS

The **Shandong Provincial Museum** is at *14 Jingshi Yi Road at the foot of Qianfo Hill, Tel. 2967179, 2962722. It is open 8:30am-11:30am and 1:30pm-5pm, closed Mondays.* It contains both historical and natural history relics. These date from neolithic times and includes Sun Bin's famous treatise on the art of war, written on bamboo about 2000 years ago. Also note the frescoes from Sui dynasty tombs, musical instruments, paintings from the tomb of the Prince of Lu (Ming), and musical instruments from the Confucian Family Mansion in Qufu.

The **Qianfo** (Thousand-Buddha) **Hill**, *Tel. 2951792, open 24 hours,* is 2.5 km south of the city. The entrance is beside the Qilu Hotel and there's a Y6 fee. The cableway only operates on request. Here are Buddhist images carved into the side of a cliff. Much climbing is involved for the

Xingguo Si (Revive the Nation Temple), with 60-70 buddhas from 20 centimeters to over three meters tall, ranging from the Sui to the Tang.

Look for three caves at the foot of the cliff, and in the rooms of the west courtyard of the temple. There you find, yes, more buddhas. In the **Yilan Ting** (Pavilion of Panoramic View), the tallest building around, you can get a good view of Jinan. On Jueshan you can see the 10-meter-high cave with the head of a buddha, seven meters tall.

West of Xingguo Temple about three km is the **Yellowstone Cliff**, a 40-meter-high rock around which were carved more buddhas, and heavens! – flying devas – some of them nude! These were made during the Northern Wei, about 1,600 years ago. A stimulating time to visit this temple is on the ninth day of the ninth lunar month, when the hill is full of chrysanthemums and market stalls are set up for a festival.

If you want to get out into the countryside, the ***Lingyan Si Temple**, *Tel. 7463198,* 55 km south of Jinan on the way to Taishan is one of the "four finest temples" in China. It was founded in 354 A.D. The current temple is from the Tang.

SHOPPING

Made in the province are human hair and silk embroidery, lace, wool carpets, straw articles, kites, feather pictures (lovely), and dough figurines. The **carpet factory** is at *108 Beixiao Xin Zhang Dong Street, Tel. 7963608* and open 8am-5pm. The province also produces the popular Tsingtao Beer. The main shopping area is **Quanchen** and also along **Jin 2-Road**. The **Silver Star Plaza** at 66 Leyuan Avenue is good for general shopping and is open 9am to 9pm. The **Shandong Silk Store** is at *No. 2 Yongqin Street, Jingsi Road, Tel. 6915469.*

NIGHTLIFE & ENTERTAINMENT

Across the road from the Qilu Hotel is the **Xi Jiao Fang** where you can get a relaxing foot massage for Y60-Y70. Several bars also await you. A favorite is the **Boiling Point Bar** at *9 Qianfoshan Road, Tel. 2960014,* open 7pm-midnight with a band at 10 every night. It has no minimum and happy hour is 7pm-9pm with 20% discount. It takes only Chinese credit cards. Beer ranges from Y10 to Y25 and owner Wei Xue Jun speaks English.

At 5 Qianfoshan Road is the **Down Town Cafe**, its staff in overalls. Open 2pm-about 2am daily, it accepts no credit cards. It has different jazz or hard rock bands and it has been giving discounts to foreigners on weekends. It has darts and beer is Y10-Y30 a bottle.

EXCURSIONS & DAY TRIPS

You really need a couple of days to take in Tai'an, 80 km away, and Qufu, 160 km south. Both are very worthwhile. Nearby is **Linzi**, a day trip. In the province also are Qingdao, with excursions to Yantai, Weihai, and Weifang. See separate listings.

***Linzi** is one hour's drive east of Jinan and about five km east of Zibo. It was the capital of Qi state that existed from the 11th century B.C to 221 B.C. It has several on-site museums, the most impressive of which is **The Ancient Chariots' Museum**, built over the actual site of buried chariots and horses. These were uncovered during the building of the expressway and is worth an hour's stop. Telephone 533/7080468 for exact directions. It is at Linzi exit 8, and is open 8am-5:30pm daily. The building is ultra-modern, the most obvious part a pyramid with its top flattened. Part of the museum is under the expressway and can be entered from either side. The toilets are bad but the exhibit is amazing: about 32 pairs of horse skeletons in two neat lines, buried in the mid-Spring and Autumn period (770 B.C.-476 B.C.). The museum also contains reproductions of ancient camel and elephant carts, and war chariots.

Nearby in **Qidu town**, *Linzu District, 255400,* is the **Qi Ancient Capital Museum** with armour belonging to the first king of Qi state (11th century B.C.) and wax figures and diaoramas. *Tel. 7030229.* A guide is necessary if you want to see more than the Ancient Chariots Museum because the other museums are hard to find.

Food in Zibo at the **Century Hotel** (Qidu Dajiudian) is good and reasonably priced. Try the chicken with egg white and pea shoots, snow shell fish with carrots and cucumbers, steamed fish with soy sauce and onions, deep-fried steamed bun, and egg white custard with pork. *Tel. 2288688 X 4483, Fax 2186731.* The 185-room **Zibo Hotel** is old fashioned, dirty, and badly maintained but cheap. This hotel and **CITS** are at *189 Zhongxin Road, Zhangbian, Zibo, 255037.* Here too the food is superb: diced fish in chicken soup, phoenix fish, deep fried spare ribs, green beans with sesame, crystal potatoes and chicken and egg white balls in tomato sauce. It takes Visa and MasterCard. The hotel's telephone is *2288688.* That of CITS *2186731.*

The **Zibo Tourism Bureau** is also at *189 Zhongxin Avenue, Tel. 2183407, Fax 2184990.* The **telephone code** is 0533.

PRACTICAL INFORMATION

China Shandong Tourism Corporation, *180 Quancheng Road, Suite 606A, 250011. Tel. 6025270, Fax 5025290. E-mail:sdotc@public.jn.sd.cn.*

Fire, *Tel. 119*; **Ambulance**, *120;* **Police** *110.*

Shandong CYTS, *2-1 Yingxiong Shan Road, 250002, Tel. and Fax 2016806.*

Shandong China International Travel Service, *88 Jing Shi Road,* *250014. Tel. 2965858, Fax 2965651. E-mail:sdcitsaa@public.jn.sd.cn.*
Telephone Code, *0531.*
Tourist Complaints, contact Supervisory Bureau of Tourism Quality of Shandong Province, *Tel. 2963423, 2965858, Fax 2964284.*
Tourist Hotline, *Tel. 2963423.*

QUFU

(Chufu)

The hometown and grave of **Kong Fuzi** (Master Kong), known to the west as **Confucius**, is a good place to be immersed in old China. Take your time. Meditate in these beautiful, exotic surroundings. Read the *Analects of Confucius*. The discipline he advocates might be just what your hectic life lacks. Go back in time.

Confucius was born in Nishan, 35 km southeast from his temple. He moved with his mother to Qufu after the death of his father, when he was three. His father was a general of the State of Lu. He preached his social and political theories while traveling around China, and after he died, his disciples, the most famous of whom was Mencius, spread his teachings. The Qin emperor later burned his books, but the succeeding Han dynasty adopted his philosophy officially. Succeeding emperors continued this practise in varying degrees until the early 20th century.

Qufu was the capital of a minor kingdom during the Shang (14th-11th century B.C.). The city is named **Winding City Wall** after the old wall built 3,000 years ago. The current wall is Ming.

Today, one-fifth of the people in Qufu are surnamed Kong, and those in a direct line of descendance once received state pensions (with no need to earn their living otherwise). Currently living are the 69th to 80th generations. The sage's birthday, September 28, is now celebrated with a festival from September 25 to October 10 and a re-enactment for tourists of the sacrificial ritual and homage by an emperor. This performance is in the hypnotic, slow movements and music of the times. A telephoto lens is necessary for photographers.

The hottest temperature in summer is 39 C; the coldest temperature in winter is a chilly -7 C. About 800 millimeters of rain fall annually mainly in July and August.

ARRIVALS & DEPARTURES

Qufu is about 150 km south of Jinan, the closest major **airport**. You can get there by expressway from Jinan and from Tai'an (70 km). Public **buses** take about two hours, and leave every ten minutes from the Long

Distance Bus Station near Jinou Park in Jinan. These arrive in the eastern part of Qufu. You can go by **train** from Beijing and from Jinan. From the station, taxis and buses can take you the remaining 18 km to Qufu, far away because officials didn't want a railway to disturb Confucius' grave and its *feng shui*.

ORIENTATION

Spend at least two days in this small, charming city, one day for the three Kongs (mansion, temple and forest), and one day for the tomb of Mencius, the birthplace cave of Confucius, and the Temple of Shao Hao.

This is a good place for bicycling or hiking. It is relatively flat and has many interesting things to explore. At least a week is necessary for adventurous bicyclists. You can rent bicycles near the Qufu bus station or in the Forest of Confucius.

The old city is centered around the Confucian monuments. The business area is south of it. Qufu is in southwestern Shandong province. The urban population is 60,000, the total 600,000.

WHERE TO STAY

The only hotel for tourists is the charming **Queli**, which has western food, but needs work. Its English is poor, it's grubby and badly maintained. It has the best location within walking distance of the Mansion, Temple, and shops, and just a ten-minute taxi ride from the forest. The four-star **Long Xing Hotel** in the old city near the Drum Tower should be finished in 1999.

QUELI HOTEL (Binguan), *1 Queli Street, 273100. Three stars and aiming for four, Tel. 4411300, Fax 4412022. Almost adjacent to the Temple of Confucius. Y398 for rooms, Y988-Y3288 for suites. No clear television channels in English.*

First built in 1986, this hotel has exquisite Chinese architecture with courtyards and ponds. The statue in its lobby is based on a mythical bird, a symbol of peace, from the Spring and Autumn period. It has two stories and 160 rooms, striking murals and sculptures. It provides concerts of classical Chinese music if enough guests are interested. It has conference facilities and a video of Confucian ceremonies on request. It also has a gym. A Singapore management company should have taken over and made improvements by now.

WHERE TO EAT

Confucian food is not as salty as Shandong and each dish has a meaning, for example, turtle for longevity. A genuine banquet used to have 400 courses! The food at the **Queli Hotel** is Confucian, interesting and adequate but not exciting. The **Qufu Grand Hotel** on *Jing Xuan Dong Road, Tel. 4418888* has good smoked bean curd and *jinko* nuts, both unique to Qufu. You might want to try the 39 proof Confucian Family liquor.

SEEING THE SIGHTS

The Confucian monuments are in and near the old city, and can be seen in a day. The *Confucian Temple** (Y20), occupying more than 20 hectares (about 50 acres), is the most important one in China and the largest in the world. First built in 478 A.D., it was rebuilt and enlarged to its present size during the Ming and Qing. Its gold-tiled roofs, its arches, red doors, and carved tile dragons are Ming. Live egrets and cranes nest in the gardens here. The two stone generals, over two meters tall and near the gate, are from the Han Dynasty (917-971). They once guarded a noble's tomb in another part of the city.

The **Dacheng Hall** is the main hall for paying homage. Only an emperor could be carried over the carved dragons up to its door. The hall is over 31 meters tall and 54 meters wide, with a resemblance to some of the buildings in Beijing's Forbidden City (copied from this temple, some say). Important are the ten carved stone columns, two dragons with a pearl on each, slithering between clouds and a pearl. Note the set of ritual bronze bells which are played on ceremonial occasions. (See also Provincial Museum, Wuhan.)

The *Kong Family Mansion** (Y20) has nine courtyards, over 400 rooms and a garden, on 14 hectares. The gate in front is Ming. The Main Hall, Second Hall, and Third Hall were offices of the Duke of Yansheng, who was made a noble by Emperor Renzong of the Song. These offices, with his desk under a yellow canopy and painted beamed ceiling, give authenticity to opera stage sets of the period. Ancient weapons, banners, and drums line the walls. The mansion was started in 1038 and is currently falling apart while a dispute between the local, provincial and national governments rage over who should pay to fix it.

Gifts to the family from emperors and high-ranking visitors include Zhou and Shang dynasty bronzes. Visitors would do well to read *In the Mansion of Confucius' Descendants* by Kong Demao and Ke Lan before arriving. From it you can feel the human drama that took place here. Kong Demao, who is still living in Beijing, was the daughter of the second wife of the Duke of Yansheng. Her mother was believed to be poisoned by the first wife. Her tale of being confined behind these walls is very sad, but she was also party to great events as well as family misfortunes. Some photographs of the family are on display. The current Duke of Yansheng is living in Taiwan. The Kong Family Mansion Hotel has an exhibition of antiques.

THE PHILOSPHY OF CONFUCIUS

Confucius lived from 551 to 479 B.C. during the Spring and Autumn Period, a time of small warring kingdoms and political chaos. He was an itinerant teacher who preached that stability could be achieved by a return to the classics and the old Zhou dynasty rituals. He defined and promoted an already existing system of interpersonal relationships with its emphasis on responsibility and obedience.

The virtuous or benevolent man does not lose his temper; the virtuous man thinks ill of people who criticize others in their absence, who talk badly of other people to make themselves look better, or who persist in promoting deceptions they know are false. He did not concern himself with insignificant things, material gain, fame or ambition. He was moderate in all things.

He was no democrat. People who do not hold office in a state should not discuss its policies, he said. He advocated that subjects be unquestionably subordinated to rulers, sons to fathers, younger brothers to older brothers, wives to husbands, younger friends to older friends.

His philosophy was the official ideology in China for over 2,000 years, promoted because it supported the oligarchic power structure. Filial piety was essential to the system, and the state enforced this policy. If a child failed to care for his aged parents or was rude to them, the authorities would punish the child. Children owed their lives to their ancestors. They were obligated to respect and worship these people.

The philosophy deteriorated into a religion where descendants performed rituals to keep ancestral spirits happy, so the dead would influence the fortunes of the living.

One finds elements of his theories still stifling Chinese people everywhere. Confucius was behind the famous civil service system, based on the memorization of the classics and his analects. The imperial examinations and the arrogant, insular thinking did, however, outlive their usefulness. The civil service examination system was abolished in the early 1900s.

In some family temples, food is still shared with ancestors, heads bowed and incense burned in worship especially during the Qing Ming Festival in spring, and the autumn equinox. Vestiges of the traditions surrounding the cult remain to this day, in spite of governmental discouragement of things like arranged marriages, marriages between two deceased people, or between one living and one deceased person, etc. This is not, however, as common as it was before 1949. Rote memory is still the basis of much education, but hopefully this is changing soon.

The **Confucian Forest** (Y10) contains 200,000 family tombs and is reputedly the oldest and largest cemetery in the world. The trees were collected by disciples from all over the country. It is about three by four km and has over 30,000 trees. Elaborately crafted gates, stone lions, and a stone-arched bridge punctuate the lovely greenness. Tall stone nobles and animals guard the gate to the *Tomb of Confucius, a tumulus marked with stone tablets and fancy incense burners.

A small brick house, **Zi Gong's Hut**, stands nearby. One of the master's disciples built it and lived there for six years after Confucius' death, to show respect. **Lady Yu's Arch** was named after a daughter of Qing Emperor Qianlong, who was married to the then Duke of Yansheng. The title was hereditary until the Nationalists officially stopped the practice.

Also in Qufu is a **Sacred Way** with stone animals and steles, the Temple of Yan Hui, the Temple of the Duke of Zhou, and the remains of the former capital of the State of Lu.

The **Tomb of Shao Hao**, one of the five legendary rulers, is about eight km away. The Temple of Mencius is 27 km south of the city. Here is also a small museum, a temple to the mother of Mencius, and a hall for the wife of Mencius.

The **Birthplace of Confucius** in Nisan is also open as a museum. A theme park based on the **Six Confucian Arts** is between the Forest and his temple. Ignore the theme park. It is tacky and unprofessional. It is made up of different buildings with different Confucian themes; its music hall has a 30-minute show, its archery hall has arrows to shoot and darts to throw. A tiny train goes through exhibits with life-size figures of the life of the sage. But it needs work.

SHOPPING

Locally produced are wood carvings, stone rubbings, carpets, and Nishan inkstones. The **Antique Store** attached to the gate of the Family Mansion, *Tel. 4412757,* sells beautiful carved and gilded wooden beds and can ship them. A souvenir market is on the road from the Queli Hotel to the cemetary. A market in Ming architecture is one block to the left as you leave the Queli Hotel. A souvenir store, the **Spring and Autumn shop**, is on the same street as the Mansion, *Tel. 4411014.*

PRACTICAL INFORMATION

CITS, *1, Kuiquan Road, 273100. Tel. 4412491, 4422001, Fax 4412492.*
Qufu Tourism Bureau, *Xingtan Hotel, 273100, Tel. 4412576, 4419863, Fax 4412709.*
Telephone Code, *0537*
Tourist Complaints, *Apricot Terrace Hotel, 250014, Tel. 4414002.*

TAI'AN

Tai'an is where you ascend **Mt. Tai** (Taishan), one of China's Five Sacred Mountains and a UNESCO World Heritage site. It is 2.5 billion years old, one of earth's oldest mountains. In ancient times, emperors came here to offer sacrifices to Earth and to Heaven; if they went up the mountain, they were probably carried up, and visitors today have the same choice, but by bus, taxi or cable car. The summit is 1545 meters above sea level. The city itself is at 150 meters.

The hottest time (37 C) is in July and August; the coldest is December and January, -10 C. The annual precipitation is 700 millimeters, mainly from July to September. It is about 10 degrees cooler at the top of Mt. Tai. The best time to climb is from April to October, but you can climb all year round except in inclement weather. The urban population at the base is over 300,000, the total population six million.

ARRIVALS & DEPARTURES

Tai'an is accessible by road and rail, and is usually combined with a visit to Qufu, 80 km away. It is about 75 km south of Jinan, which has the closest airport. It can be reached by the daily overnight no. 51 **train** from Beijing in about seven hours (10:10pm-5:02am). A second train leaves shortly afterwards. An expressway is being built that will hopefully shorten the trip from Jinan to 35 minutes before 2001.

WHERE TO STAY

At the foot of the mountain, the best hotel is the **Overseas Chinese Hotel**. The **Taishan Hotel** is second best for tourists because it has better English, but don't expect much. The three-star **Laodong Hotel** (Labor Hotel) is actually better than the Taishan but its English is non-existent. The Labor charges Y350-Y380 for rooms, Y680 for suites and is at *Dongyue Zhong Street, 271000, Tel. 8331888, Fax 8226577.* On the summit, the best is the **Shenqi**. If your schedule is tight and a strong wind threatens to cancel cable cars, you had better stay down below.

Being built is the four-star, **Taishan International Hotel**, with seven stories, and 100 rooms. It is in the suburbs, a 40-minute drive from the city and due in 1999. CITS can arrange home stays in **Buyang Zhuang Village**, *Tel. 8601579,* 17 km southeast, for about Y100 per day including meals.

Prices listed below are subject to change and 10% surcharge. Hotels here generally have relaxed standards, but have foreign exchange, international direct dial, airconditioning, etc.

TAISHAN HOTEL, *26 Hongmen Road, Tel. 8225888, 8224678, Fax 8221432. 2.5 km from the railway station. Three stars. Y380 for rooms.*

Built in 1980, this 110-room, six-story hotel has Shandong, Sichuan and Cantonese restaurants. It has a gym, clinic, and ticket office, but no CNN and takes American Express credit cards only.

TAISHAN OVERSEAS CHINESE HOTEL (Huaqiao Dasha), *Dongyue Zhong Avenue, 271000. Four stars, Tel. 8228112, Fax 8228171. Two km from the railway station, close to Daimiao Temple, and across the road from a department store. Y480-Y680 for rooms, Y780-Y880 for suites. Credit Cards but no Diners.*

Built in 1995, and renovated 1997, this 19-story, 205-room hotel has Cantonese, Italian and western food, heated indoor pool, bowling, gym, and night club. It has two television channels in English. Famous Hotel VIP Club.

SHENQI HOTEL (Binguan), *10 Tian Street, Taishan, 271000. Three stars, Tel. 8223866, 8337025, Fax 8333150. Y680.*

About two km upward from the top of the cable car, 20 km from the railway station, this hotel is at 1500 meters. Built in 1991 with two stories, and 102 rooms, it has a sauna, clinic, great view, seven restaurants, and a traditional medicine and wild vegetable banquet. It also has Cantonese and Sichuan food. But note: because of a water shortage, this hotel might be closed or no baths allowed December through March.

WHERE TO EAT

The hotel restaurants are good here and so is Taishan Beer. Tai'an's liquor is 29, 39 and 44 proof. The **International Restaurant**, *Longtan Road, Tel. 8214593* is also recommended, especially its toffee bean curd, roasted sesame-coated pork, and Sichuan spicy chicken. It is open 11:30am-2pm; 6pm-9pm. The Chinese restaurant in the **Taishan Hotel**, *Tel. 8225888, Fax 8221432* is especially good. Its bean curd banquet is famous, Y1000 for ten people. Delicious were the deep fried crispy bean curd balls, fried pancakes, and beef with oyster sauce.

At the **Overseas Chinese Hotel**, good dishes are the shredded turnip, garlic fried crisp chicken, fried fresh milk, spicy beef with bamboo shoots and oyster sauce, and stir-fried snow peas. The best western food is also in the Overseas Chinese Hotel, but don't expect much. Only the hotels accept credit cards.

SEEING THE SIGHTS

An **Information Center for Tourists** is at the *Hongmen Hotel, Hongmen Road, 271000. Tel. 8259899, Fax 8253024.*

If you have only one day, you can be driven halfway up the mountain to the **Zhongtian** (Middle Celestial) **Gate**. Then you can take the 2078-meter-long suspended cable car almost to the top at Nantian (South Gate of Heaven) between 7am and 7 or 8pm. During the summer and autumn, the cable car starts at 4:30am so you can see the sunrise. From the top of the cable car to the peak at an altitude of 1,545 meters are 500 more steps.

A second 2100-meter cable car from Peach Blossom Ravine on the northwest side also reaches the South Gate of Heaven. This side has no temples but lots of natural scenery. You can lunch at the **Shenqi Binguan** near the summit and then return to see the Daimiao Temple and a free market.

Ascending on Foot

The longer, more satisfying way is to climb (at least one way) because the mountain has 30 old temples and 66 well-documented scenic spots, including beautifully carved memorial arches, Han dynasty cypress trees, white water, breathtaking views of forests and crags, and a stone pillar that looks suspiciously like a lingam. If you do it the hard way, you are following in the footsteps of Confucius!

The top can be reached in five or six hours through the Path of Eighteen Bends. Note the 7,000-plus stone stairs, each carefully placed by human labor! Like an almost vertical Great Wall! And they are not narrow! It is difficult to get lost. The stairs are very steep and in some places difficult to climb.

The **Temple of Azure Clouds** on the mountain is over 970 years old (Song). Note the bronze or iron roof ornaments, rafters, bells, and tiles of the main hall, made of metal to endure the severe mountain storms. Inside are nine huge gilt statues. Can you imagine having to carry these and the bronze Ming tablets up here! The top is at Tianzhu Feng (Heavenly Pillar Peak), which is also known as Yuhuang Ding (Jade Emperor Peak).

The **Tomb and Museum of Feng Yuxiang** (Feng Yu-hsiang) may be of interest to students of modern Chinese history. This was the famous Christian General who fought with the Nationalists against the Japanese and baptized his men with water hoses. He is known more for his eccentricity than his military successes. His tomb is at the east end of Dazhong Bridge, downhill from the Dragon Pool Reservoir. These are on the north part of Puzhou Street.

Seventy-two visiting emperors used to offer sacrifices at the **Daimiao** (Temple to the God of Taishan), Hong Men Road. This is close to the Taishan Guest House at the base and is open 7:30am-5pm. On special occasions like the Climbing Festival or on request in advance, actors perform a re-enactment of the rituals by Song Emperor Zhengzong at this impressive building. Though slow-moving, this should not be missed. The main hall has a mural 3.3 by 62 meters, painted in the Song, showing the pilgrimage of this emperor here. It includes 570 to 657 figures. (Count them!) This hall was built in 1009 A.D. and is considered one of the three eminent halls of China.

Travel agencies can arrange sightseeing by helicopter. A nunnery with seven nuns is open 8:30am-6pm daily near Tiger Hill.

Festivals: From September 6-8, there is the mountain climbing festival. The third day of the third lunar month is the birthday of the grandmother of the mountain whose shrine is at the Azure Cloud Temple.

SHOPPING

Carpets and baskets are made locally. Peaches, walnuts, chestnuts, and dates are grown. The **Tai'an Antique Store** is at *No. 1 Hongmen Road*, near the back of Daimiao Temple. *Tel. 8222416.*

PRACTICAL INFORMATION

Ambulance, *Tel. 120.*

CITS Taishan Branch, *22 Hongmen Road, 271000, above the Dai Temple and the Taishan Arch, Tel. 8223259, 8221183, Fax 8332240, E-mail: tscits@public.taptt.sd.cn.*

City Center Hospital, *Tel. 8224161* (but no English).

Tai'an Tourist Bureau, *45 Hongmen Road, 261999, Tel. 8233423, Fax 8333150, 8221613. E-mail:mttic@public.taptt.sd.cn.*

Taishan Tourism (Group) Co., *West Dong Yue Street, 271000, Tel. 8418777, E-mail 8332240.*

Telephone Code, 0538

QINGDAO

(Tsingtao)

Qingdao lies on a peninsula on the southern coast of Shandong province, 393 km east of the provincial capital Jinan. It is an important manufacturing center, ice-free port and pretty summer resort, famous for its beer, mineral water, wine, and European heritage.

Starting as a fishing village, Qingdao (pronounced Ching Dow) has been an important trading port since the seventh century. During the Ming, it was fortified against pirates. The Germans seized the area in 1897 in retaliation for the assassination of two German missionaries. Here they built a naval base and trading port, and protected them with at least 2000 men. The large number of Germans accounted for its German architecture and its beer recipe.

In 1919, the Versailles Peace Conference confirmed Japan's 1915 capture of the German territories in Shandong. The Japanese stayed long

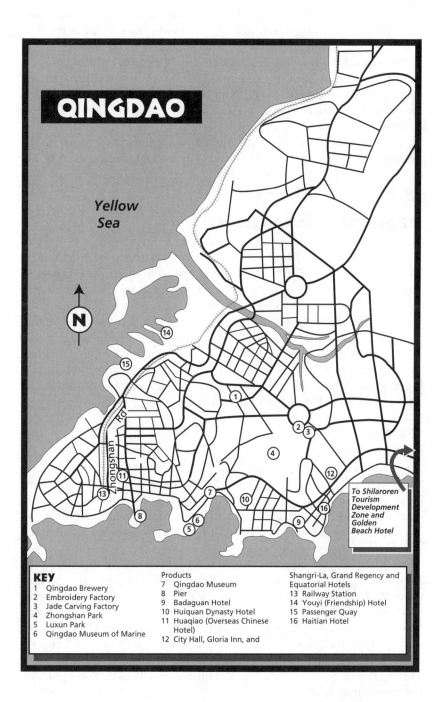

QINGDAO

Yellow
Sea

N

Zhongshan Rd

To Shilaroren
Tourism
Development
Zone and
Golden
Beach Hotel

KEY

1	Qingdao Brewery
2	Embroidery Factory
3	Jade Carving Factory
4	Zhongshan Park
5	Luxun Park
6	Qingdao Museum of Marine

Products
7 Qingdao Museum
8 Pier
9 Badaguan Hotel
10 Huiquan Dynasty Hotel
11 Huaqiao (Overseas Chinese
    Hotel)
12 City Hall, Gloria Inn, and

Shangri-La, Grand Regency and
Equatorial Hotels
13 Railway Station
14 Youyi (Friendship) Hotel
15 Passenger Quay
16 Haitian Hotel

enough to build huge cotton mills before they were forced to withdraw in 1937. During this period, the British built cigarette factories. The Japanese navy regained the city early in 1938, but not before a Chinese mob smashed the breweries, sending rivers of beer into the streets!

Qingdao's breweries were rebuilt, of course, and still produce the most popular **Tsingtao Beer**. Qingdao also bottles Laoshan mineral water, and now makes Huadong Riesling wine, the product of a recent German joint venture.

The climate is temperate: the highest in August an average, 25 C; the coldest in January an average -1.2 C. The annual precipitation is 715 millimeters. Fog in June and July might delay flights. The urban population is two million, the total seven million.

ARRIVALS & DEPARTURES

Qingdao can be reached by train from Beijing in 10-13 hours and from Shanghai in 17-18 hours once a day. Trains also arrive from Jinan (in four hours), from Tai'an (in 5.5-6 hours), and Yantai (in four-4.5 hours). It's a one-hour flight south from Beijing or north from Shanghai. There are or will be direct air connections with at least 35 other Chinese cities and Fukuoka, Hong Kong, Macau, Munich, Osaka, Seoul and Singapore.

Qingdao is on the Huanghai (Yellow Sea) and you can reach it by ship twice a week from Shanghai (26 hours, but sometimes with last minute changes in schedule), once a week from Simoseki in Japan, and twice a week from Inchon in Korea. There's also an expressway from Jinan (3.5 hours) and from Yantai (three-3.5 hours).

ORIENTATION

Qingdao should be put at the end of a hectic, tight schedule in summer because of its beaches. Full of hills, trees and red-tiled roofs, it is very pretty for walking. Laws insure that the red roofs will continue in the west part of town. It also has 200 buildings in 25 different Asian and European architectural styles, most from its imperialist past. Many of these are no longer seen in Germany. Qingdao is now concerned about preserving the best of them.

Qingdao is the largest city and industrial center in Shandong. Its factories make diesel locomotives, automobiles, television sets, and cameras. Its oceanic research institute is internationally famous. Huangdao District, on the west coast of Jiazhou Bay, is its economic and technical development zone. Qingdao is one of the 14 original Open Coastal Cities.

Qingdao has good public buses (Y4 and Y5). Taxis start at Y7 and Y9. The city is building a subway, starting from Xizhen in the south and running to the Number Nine Textile Mill in the north, a 16.68 km line with 13 station due in 2000.

WHERE TO STAY

The best hotels are the **Shangri-La**, the **Haitian** and **Grand Regency**. The best four-star is the **Huiquan Dynasty** but it is dark and standards somewhat sloppy. The four-star **Seaview Garden** is all right. The **Huanhai Gloria Inn** is the best three-star. The **Equatorial**, **Shangri-La**, **Haitian**, and **Gloria** are all close to the city government and World Trade Centre. A new five-star national holiday resort should be finished soon east of the Shangri-La. A Holiday Inn should open in 1999.

On the other end of the market is a student hostel. Travel agents can arrange home stays on farms and fishing villages for about the same price.

Hotels listed here have offered discounts of at least 20-30% even in high season, and have international standards such as credit cards, currency exchange and air-conditioning.

SHANGRI-LA HOTEL, *9 Xiang Gang Zhong Lu, 266071, Tel. 3883838, 3886868. E-mail:slqbc@qingdao.cngb.com. Five star standards. 45 minutes drive from the airport. $155-$230 for rooms, $290-$1500 for suites.*

This 1997 hotel is not as lavish as other Shangri-La's in China but is very attractive. It has 502 rooms and three executive floors, German, Asian and western food. It has a gym, indoor pool and outdoor tennis court. Rooms have safes, bidets, and smoke hoods. They also have voice mail, CNN, Star World and HBO, and fax and computer outlets. It was relatively new when reviewed and the workmanship needed fixing, but it should be okay now.

GRAND REGENCY HOTEL (Lijing Jiudian), *1 Taiwan Road, 266071. Tel. 5881818, Fax 5881888. E-mail:regency@ns.qd.sd.cn. Five stars. $138-$180 for rooms and $228-$2888 for suites.*

This 448-room hotel has a Kaiser Clock with Snow White and other interesting "European Renaissance" relics in its lobby. It has four executive floors, non-smoking rooms, and 24-hour room service. Rooms have CNN and in-room safes. It has a gym, squash, bowling, tennis, and indoor pool, and Cantonese, French, and Japanese restaurants, and coffee shop. Its ballroom can seat 600 banquet style.

HAITIAN HOTEL (Dajiudian), *48 Xianggang Xi Road, 266071. Five and four stars. Tel. 3871888, Fax 3871777. E-mail:htsales@ns.qd.sd.cn. $100-$178 for rooms, $168-$1800 for suites. 25 km from the airport; five km from the railway station; 200 meters from Number Three Swimming Beach.*

Opened in 1989 with an extension completed in 1993, this hotel has 15 floors (two of them executive), and 641 rooms with safes, and satellite television. Its standard bathrooms are small and carpets worn but it's otherwise very good. It has a lighted tennis court, indoor heated pool, gym and bowling. Its ballroom can seat 600 guests banquet-style. Daiichi management group. VIP China Club.

HUIQUAN DYNASTY HOTEL (Huiquan Wang Chao Dajiudian), *9 Nanhai Road, 266003. Four stars. Tel. 2873366, Fax 2896204, 2871122. Reserve through UTELL. About Y670-Y1350 for rooms, Y1680-Y25200 for suites. 35 km from the airport; five km from the railway station. Across a busy street with no stoplights from Number One Swimming Beach.*

This 1979, 12- and 25-story hotel has over 500 rooms and a non-smoking floor. It has two-story penthouse suites, CNN, Air China office, a Korean, a western, and a revolving restaurant. There's a gym, bowling, pool and tennis and it's managed by Dynasty.

GOLDEN BEACH HOTEL, *Stone Old Man National Tourism Resort, 266101, Tel. 8897888, 8897052. 17 km from downtown (about Y30 taxi), but a walk to Beer City. Three stars and aiming for four. $65-$95 for rooms, and $150-$660 for suites.*

This simple but adequate 164-room hotel owns a part of Qingdao's best beach but its carpets don't fit. It also has tennis and nearby horse rentals, and is building an addition with indoor pool. It has Chinese, western, Japanese and Korean restaurants, and three television channels in English. Buffet breakfast Y26. You need a reservation one week in advance in summer.

HUANHAI GLORIA INN (Huanhai Kailai Shangwu Jiudian), *21 Donghai Road, 266071. Tel. 3878855, Fax 3868511, 3864640. In North America, Tel. 800/821-0900. E-mail:gloriahl@hkstar.com; http://www.hotel-web.com/gloria/index.htm. Almost on the waterfront, 30 minutes from the airport. Y436-Y620 for rooms; Y864-Y1080 for suites.*

This charming hotel has 410 rooms. Its standard rooms are spacious with small bathrooms and continental beds, kettles and fridges, but no in-room safes. It has four television channels in English, and a Sichuan and Cantonese restaurant with hot pot. On weekends it has shuttle buses to the JUSCO department store. Its business center can issue air tickets only. Guests can use pool and sports facilities ten minutes walk away. Gloria Hotels and Resorts.

FOREIGN STUDENT HOSTEL, *Ocean University, 5 Yushan Road. Telephone the Foreign Affairs office (Wai ban) at 2032436 at 7:30am-5pm weekdays, or E-mail:waishi@lib.ouqd.edu.cn.*

This good six- or seven- story hostel has no elevator but is air-conditioned and available all year round. It has three storys, 25 rooms with private baths for tourists for Y180 during peak season. Guests eat with teachers.

WHERE TO EAT

You have to try seafood here, of course, especially abalone and prawns. It is especially good in the top hotels. The **Shangri-la** and **Gloria Inn** have good western food. The hot pot at the Gloria Inn costs Y78, its lunch and dinner buffet Y72, and its breakfast buffet Y68. At the Shangri-La, buffets are Y90 for breakfast, Y52-68 for lunch and about Y98 for dinner.

QINGDAO HOTEL, *on the waterfront 200 meters from Little Qingdao, on the second floor.*

This is a cheaper hotel restaurant option, serving dishes of raw ingredients ready to cook. Its fresh clams were Y12, boiled prawns Y50 a piece, abalone with green vegetables Y50-Y80, and fried cashew nuts with scallops Y22 and Y38. Beer was Y4.50.

888 RESTAURANT, *18 Nanhai Road, Tel. 2861970.*

Moderately priced.

BRIGHT RESTAURANT (Mingguang Jiu Lou), *127 Yanan No.3 Road (near the Haitian and Shangri-La), Tel. 3870709.*

This unpretentious restaurant has steamed crab for Y80 (500 grams), and steamed pork with minced garlic for Y30. Open 10:30am-11pm.

HUIQUAN DYNASTY HOTEL, *9 Nanhai Road. Tel. 2873366,*

If you just want a sample, the hotel restaurant here has cooked-to-order snacks: *jiaotze* (three for Y10), spicy barbeque squid Y6, and steamed shrimp Y26.

SILVER CITY SEAFOOD SQUARE, *60 Xionggang Zhong Road, Tel. 5712272,*

Two stories of restaurant, with Y30-Y50 meals.

GOLDEN SIAM RESTAURANT, *No.1 Lane 3, Zheng Yang Road, Tel. 3861409 or 3864953.*

Come here for good Thai food. Try the pineapple fried rice.

The city also has at least four **KFC's** and two **Pizza Huts**. Jusco has a **McDonald's**. A **KFC** is on *Zhongshan Road.*

SEEING THE SIGHTS

You can cover all of Qingdao's urban attractions in a day, unless you want to walk leisurely through this museum of European architecture. You need a second day or two for Laoshan Mountain if you enjoy hiking in exotic settings and want to savor it all. Qingdao's four km of city beaches slope gently into the sea and are protected by four large bays east from **The Pier** (1891). This 440-meter pier is a good place to absorb the sunrise. Southeast of the Pier and linked with the shore by a 700-meter-long dyke is Xiaqingdao (**Little Qingdao Island**) with a lighthouse.

Among its ten hills, **Zhongshan Park** is best seen when its 700 cherry trees bloom in April. **Luxun Park** has an excellent view of Number One Beach, Xiaoqingdao, and the European buildings. Look for the Christian church on Jiangsu Road and the Catholic Church on Hubei Road.

Travel agents can arrange tours of the **Tsingtao Brewery** (*May 4th Square, Xianggang Zhong Road, Tel. 5711119*), and the **Shell Carving**

Handicraft Factory at *106 Yanan San Road, Tel. 3873162*. You can go on your own to the **Beer City** theme park with its folk performances and competitions.

If you can borrow a bicycle you can explore the Badaguan area, where each street is lined with a different kind of blossoming tree: cherry, peach, or crape myrtle. Behind the trees are individually-designed houses with spacious gardens, a bit of old Europe. The most famous is at *18 Huanghai Road*. Built in 1903 in the shape of a castle, it was originally a hunting lodge for the German governor and protected by Qingdao as a historical monument. The **Stone House** can be visited for Y10 or so. CTS says it can be rented.

The 18-hole **Qingdao International Golf Club**, *Gaozhi Road, Tel. 7891133* in the high-tech park near Shaolaoren is the best. The largest, best, and probably cleanest of the seven city beaches is at the **Shilaoren National Tourist and Resort Area** (*Tel. 3861667, Fax 3875344*). The **Number One Beach** downtown with lifeguards, medical station, shark nets, and changing facilities is too crowded. Beaches are open from early July to the end of September. Shilaoren is 17 km east of downtown and should be less crowded. If you are worried about pollution, **Yangkou Beach** is being developed as the pollution-free bathing beach. It is on the east coast of Laoshan, 1.5 hours from the city. Both are accessible by public bus.

Qingdao Ocean Park, China's largest, is in *Shilaoren National Holiday Resort, Tel. 5882373*. It has a dolphin show (April- October), water sports, Aquatic Museum, and hotel.

The **Qingdao Sailing and Water Skiing School**, *Tel. 3880816*, has sailboards and skiis for rent.

NIGHTLIFE & ENTERTAINMENT

The expatriate community is very active here and has a newsletter in English with social events, Bible study, travel tips, and book exchange. If you're staying a while, John Lombard at the Grand Regency or any of the managers of the major hotels can put you in touch.

Festivals: The annual **International Beer Festival** begins July 8 and runs for 15 days. The **Candied Haw** (Crab Apple) **Festival** has attracted 500,000 people at the Haiyun Temple on the 16th day of the lunar new year.

SHOPPING

Shops are along **Zhongshan and Jiaozhou Roads**. **Jusco's** department store there is huge and expensive. Local products include beautiful shell pictures, feather pictures, carpets, weaving, embroidery, and knitting. A large market is on **Jimo Street** with clothes, handicrafts and bicycles for sale. The **Cultural Market** with curios, handicrafts, stamps and coins is at Changle Road and Yixian Road. Look also in the **Qingdao Museum**.

In addition to the crafts factory above, you might be able to visit the **Double Star shoe factory** at *5 Guizhou Road, Tel. 2891907* and look for bargains. The **Foreign Languages Book Store** is on *Zhongshan Road*. The **Pearl Market** on *Zhongzhan Road* has antiques and curios.

EXCURSIONS & DAY TRIPS

The **Laoshan Mountains** are roughly 40 km east of the city, reached by bus, and said to be the home of the Eight Taoist Immortals.

You may have to choose one of three routes to tour Laoshan. The most popular one is the south **Taiqinggong route** with the Taoist temples, but the most beautiful is the **Yangkou route**. The waterfalls can be seen only in summer and autumn. A leisurely three-day trip to include them all would be ideal for hikers. There's a 400-meter-long chairlift.

Do not expect fancy, large temples. The meditative Taoists didn't and don't want to be distracted in their search for eternal peace, their communion with nature. Laoshan is famous for the masculine shape of its mountains and its rushing waterfalls. The highest peak, Mt. Laoding, is 1,333 meters above sea level. The mountains extend over 386 sq km and are full of granite canyons, grotesque crags, old temples, rivers, streams, and the Laoshan reservoir. The **Taiping** (Great Peace) **Taoist Temple** was founded in the Song. The home of Qing writer **Pu Songling** (1640-1715) is open to the public. He lived in a very modest corner of the Taiping Temple. Pu wrote his famous *Strange Tales from a Lonely Studio* here. The trees he described are still standing. The biggest temple, Taiqing Taoist Temple, has over 150 buildings.

An inscription about the visit of the first Qin emperor in 219 B.C. is also on the mountain. The builder of the Xi'an ceramic army searched here too for pills of immortality.

Other day trips can be to Yantai, Weihai, or Weifang. See separate listings below.

PRACTICAL INFORMATION

CITS, *9 Nanhai Road, 266003. Tel. 2861513, Fax 2870983.*

Consulate of South Korea, *Huiquan Dynasty Hotel, Tel. 2873366.*

CTS Qingdao, *No. 41 Xianggang Zhong Road, 266071, Tel. 5722021, Fax 5736574.*

Internet cafe has been behind the World Trade Centre, and is hopefully still there.

Qingdao Overseas Tourist Company, *Room 1603, Fu Tai Plaza, No. 18 Xianggang Zhong Road, 266071, Tel. 5719819, Fax 5722979, 5716506. E-mail:qdotc@ns.qd.sd.cn.* Ask for Howard Song.

Qingdao Tourism Administration, *11 Xianggang Zhong Road, 266071, Tel. 5912027, Fax 2912028.* Information.

Telephone Code, 0532

Tourist Hotline Center, *Tel. 5912000.*

Website: *Http://www.chinaqingdao.net.*

Weidong Ferry Co., *10 Xinjiang Road, Tel. 2803574, Fax 2821152.* Ferries from Inchon.

WEIFANG

Weifang is almost in the center of Shandong province, 180 km from Qingdao and 250 km from Jinan. Weifang is noted for its **international kite festival** (the first five days in April) every year, its unique kite museum, and home stays. The urban population is 500,000, the total 8,200,000.

ARRIVALS & DEPARTURES

You can reach it by twice weekly flights from Beijing, Changchun, Dalian and Guangzhou with more flights during the kite festival. The airport is 10 km southeast of the city. The Qingdao airport is one hour's drive from Weifang, the Jinan airport is two hours away. Express trains between Jinan and Qingdao, and Jinan and Yantai stop here. It is two hours by train from Qingdao and is on the Jinan-Qingdao expressway.

WHERE TO STAY

Hotels here have higher prices during the kite festival, but discounts of about 30% at other times. All rates are subject to 10% surcharge.

FUWAH HOTEL, *No. 168, Fushou Dong Road, 261031. Five stars. Tel. 8881988, Fax 8880766. E-mail:f-hotel@public.wfptt.sd.cn. Y780-Y1080 for rooms, and Y1380-Y7800 for suites. Located in the hi-tech development zone 15 km northeast of the airport, and seven km from the railway station, it is next door to the Fuhua Amusement Park with its waterworld.*

This 1996, nine-story, 246-room hotel also has 322 three- and four-star rooms in its adjacent international convention centre. Together they have CNN and BBC, in-room safes, Shanghai, Cantonese, Japanese and Korean restaurants. There're also 12 bowling lanes, gym, heated indoor pool, sauna, steam bath and tennis. In its lobby, a long-tailed phoenix looking suspiciously like dripping strings of money, hangs from the ceiling, five tons of copper. It has an executive floor, and carpets in general could be cleaner.

YUAN FEI HOTEL (Dajiudian), *31 Siping Road, 261041. Tel. 8236901, Fax 8233840. Five km from the airport and 2.5 km from the railway station. Also near the kite museum. Three stars: 204 rooms, built in 1987, $35-$45 for rooms and $60-$650 for suites; four stars: 150 rooms, built in 1995, $65 for rooms, $120-$600 for suites. Only Visa and MasterCard accepted.*

This 21-story, 225-room hotel has CNN and Star TV, Shandong, Cantonese, French and Japanese restaurants. It has seafood and hot pot and usually a fashion show with lunch and dinner. It has a gym, sauna, bowling, indoor pool, tennis and dirty carpets.

WHERE TO EAT

One of the food treats here is fried scorpions or cicadas, actually quite tasty. Your best bet for good food is in the top hotels. Try celery and madadamia nuts, Beijing duck, crabs, *luo bo dun pai gu* spare ribs, and corn bread.

SEEING THE SIGHTS

There are Buddhist relics from the Sui and Tang dynasties here, and a 7.5 meter high stone longevity character, the biggest such character in

KITE HEAVEN!

Kites are the main draw and they are fun. You can visit the kite and woodblock print-making village of **Yangjiabou** *to watch the process. Here you can see professional adult kite fliers testing their goods. It's about 10 minutes drive east of the Fuwah hotel, Tel. 7252050, and is open 7:30am daily expect Sundays for eight hours. You can buy a kite here or from peddlars on the road and learn flying techniques from the champions. They are cheaper here than in Beijing. Did you know that silk kites fly better and last longer, but paper kites fly higher? That China invented kites during the era of Confucius? Do explore the kite museum with room after room of the world's best kites from 350 meter-long centipedes to tiny matchboxes that fly. It's at 66 Xingzheng Street, 261041, Tel. 8237313, Fax 8880099. It's open daily 8am-6pm.*

*The **festival** itself draws 300,000 spectators. You should book early or go on a tour to ensure transportation and hotel. Contestants have come from all over the world and every foreign kite flier gets a prize. The world headquarters of the international Kite Federation is in Weifang at the Kite Museum.*

China, carved over 500 years ago. It is in the **Shi Hu Garden**, *49 Hujia Daifang Street, open 8am-11:30am and 2pm-5:30pm.*

In Shanwang, southwest of the city, 18-million-year-old prehistoric fossils and unique stones have been found. The **Shanwang Paleontological Museum** there has 10,000 specimens. Tourists can live with farming families in **Shijiazhuang** village.

Students of modern history might be interested in the **Second Middle School**. This was once the Weihsien Concentration Camp. British, Canadian, and American prisoners were held here by the Japanese in the 1940s, including Eric Liddell, the hero of the movie *Chariots of Fire.* A gold medalist in the 1924 Olympics for winning the 400 meters, this Scottish athlete refused to race on Sundays. He later became a Congregational missionary in China and died of a brain tumor in 1945. He was buried near the prison camp six months before the end of the war. Look for the seven-foot-high memorial stone in Chinese and English. Some of the original prison-missionary buildings are still standing.

SHOPPING

Made locally are woodblock prints, kites, mahogany furniture inlaid with silver, cotton toys and bronze imitations.

PRACTICAL INFORMATION

CITS, *31 Siping Road, Weifang, 261041, European and Asian Department, Tel. 8277725, Fax 8213854. E-mail:citswf@public.wfptt.sd.cn.*Ask for Song Jinlin.

Hours, 8:30am to 6pm (summer) or 5:30pm (winter) five days a week in offices; 9am to 6:30pm for stores.

Telephone Code, *0536*

Weifang Tourism Bureau, *127 Shengli Street, 261041. Tel. 8236901, Fax 8233840*for information and complaints. Tel. for complaints 8236473.

WEIHAI

(Wei-hai-wei)

Weihai is a beautiful little open-port city on the Bohai Sea, with small but good beaches and hot springs. Natives are proud of its appearance and cleanliness. There are no fancy resorts. It is 90 km east of Yantai and 307 km northeast of Qingdao with an urban population of about 230,000, total 2,430,000.

Weihai was developed in the Ming because of its excellent harbor. Some of the funds to strengthen the navy base here were squandered by Empress Dowager Cixi on her Summer Palace in Beijing. In 1894, the

Japanese won a naval base on a 25-year lease, which was used to monitor the Russians at Port Arthur (now Dalian), 100 km north. The British tutor of the Last Emperor, Reginald Johnson - remember Peter O'Toole in the *Last Emperor* movie? - was the British administrator here. It has a navy museum and factories that produce carpets, leather goods, embroidery, artificial fur, etc. Nearby is the easternmost tip of China at Chengshan Gap, where the Yellow Sea meets the Bohai Sea. A fishing village, **Yuanya**, five km from Weihai, has been available for overnight home stays.

The hottest temperature is 28 C in August; the coldest is -12 C in January. 700 mm of rain falls mainly in August.

This off-the-beaten track family vacation city can be reached by road or soon by rail, flights from five other cities, and a ferry from Dalian and Inchon, Korea.

The best hotel is the four-star **WEIHAIWEI MANSION** (Dasha) at *82 Haigang Road, 264200, Tel. 5232542, 5247888, Fax 5232281. About Y780 a room. It is 100 meters from the port and 30 km from the airport.*

It has 17 stories, 153 rooms, hot spring water, and satellite television. It offers French, German, Korean, Sichuan, and Cantonese food.

CITS is at *96 Guzhai Dong Road, 264200, Tel. 5817211, Fax 5817456.* It charges $30 for an eight-hour day for guide service for two people, $45 for a car for one day, and $5 booking a domestic flight. The **telephone code** is *0631.* For **Weihai Tourism Bureau,** *Tel. 5222335.*

YANTAI

(Chefoo, Cheefoo or Zhifu)

Yantai is an ice-free port city, of interest primarily to business people. It also hosts international cruise ships. Yantai is one of the original Coastal Cities opened to accelerated industrial development. It is about three hours by expressway northeast of Qingdao. Inhabited almost 2,200 years ago, this fishing village was visited by the first Qin emperor early in its existence. In 1398, during the Ming, a military post was set up, and beacon towers built for transmitting messages. Yantai means smoke tower. Yantai was first opened to foreign trade in 1862. It was a summer resort for the US Navy's Yangtze Patrol (with White Russian bar girls). The China Inland Mission operated a school here for missionary children; the buildings now are used by the Chinese Navy. Its seaside Yantai Hill once housed 10 foreign consulates.

The weather is hottest (28.3 C) in July and August; the coldest is -10 C in January. The annual precipitation is about 700 millimeters mostly in June. The urban population is now 1,544,000, the total about six million.

ARRIVALS & DEPARTURES

You can reach Yantai by train from Qingdao in four hours twice a day or by a five-hour superhighway (350 km). You can go there by plane from Seoul, Macau and Hong Kong and 17 Chinese cities. It can also be reached by ship from Dalian taking three to eight hours. A direct 15-hour train from Beijing takes 15 hours, and from Shanghai 23 hours. The airport is about 20 km from town.

ORIENTATION

Yantai is one of China's prettiest little cities, nestled between the sea and, on three sides, gentle hills. Many of its buildings are topped with orange tiles, and some are of rose-colored stone. It has a cheerful atmosphere of vitality and prosperity. Off the main tourist track, it is more for relaxed family sightseeing and swimming than hectic tourism. Its old colonial city is near the Bund waterfront and Yantai Hill.

It farms prawns, abalone, scallops, and jelly fish. It grows peanuts (one fifth of China's crop), cherries, grapes, apples, and white asparagus. It mines one quarter of China's gold. The closest mine is about 80 km from the city.

WHERE TO STAY

PACIFIC HOTEL, *74 Shifu Street, 264001, Tel. 6206888, Fax 6224421. E-mail:tpybc@public.ytptt.sd.cn. Four stars. Y660. 17 km from the airport.*

The Pacific has 148 rooms, Cantonese and Chaozhou food, a bowling alley, pool, and health club.

YANTAI ASIA HOTEL *116 Nan Avenue, 264000. Tel. 6247888, Fax 6242625. Tel. in North America 800/860-2345. E-mail: asia@public.ytptt.sd., cn. 18 km from the airport. Three stars. Y428-Y488 for rooms, Y688 for suites.*

This hotel has 147 rooms including 12 non-smoking. It was renovated in 1998. It has a gym, CNN and Star Plus. It serves western, Cantonese, Shanghai, and Sichuan food. Its breakfast costs Y20 and Y28.

Home Stays

Yantai is a pioneer in home stay programs for tourists bored by temples. By Chinese standards, some of the rural villages here are incredibly wealthy, and a visit will explain why. Xiguan Village, 23 km away is one of the places where you can spend the night with a family, usually part of a package and not cheap. Contact a travel agency.

WHERE TO EAT

Fresh seafood, of course, is the food of choice here! The best restaurants are in the hotels. Shandong food is not peppery hot or overly sweet, but it has lots of garlic, onions, and salt. Yantai people say that Beijing duck originated when two indigent Yantai peasants went to Beijing and found a dead duck on the road. Improvising an earthen oven, they cooked the duck. An official happened by, liked the smell, and asked for a taste. Pleased, he presented the dish to the emperor, who rewarded the official and the poor peasants.

SEEING THE SIGHTS

Penglai Pavilion is the most important tourist attraction here and is 83 km northwest of the city, past the Yantai Economic and Technology Development Zone. A visit to Penglai can take a day.

It was from Penglai Pavilion that legend says, the Eight Taoists Immortals flew across the seas. After getting drunk, each tried to compete with the other using his or her own treasure. Ask to see the room where the Immortals partied! (See Attributes of the Eight Taoist Genii in Chapter 5, Land & People). Some people say they flew to Japan. A Japanese legend speaks of seven "fairies." But some people say they achieved immortality or arrived in paradise. Myths vary. The pavilion was first built in the Northern Song (960-1127) and extended in 1589.

From the Penglai Pavilion, **mirages** have been seen by many people. A recent sighting was in 1998. CITS says a video was made and can only be shown in Penglai. Natives have conflicting opinions about the ideal conditions for mirages, but they seem to be in summer and autumn, with the east wind blowing shortly after a gentle rain, between 2 and 3pm. The mirage is of a high mountain, an island or old city, which some people believe to be Dalian or Korea across the straits.

Movies about the Immortals are shown regularly on television. Ask about them at your hotel. A good Hong Kong movie is the *Eight Immortals Cross the Sea*. These mythical people were each from different periods of history but legend says they did get together during the Song! Fairies can do anything!

Among the other buildings nearby are the **Temple of the Sea Goddess** Tian Hou, a Taoist temple, and the Wind Protection Hall, where lit matches will not blow out even if the wind is from the north. Important is the room full of calligraphy by a famous Ming calligraphist who lived here for three years waiting unsuccessfully to see a mirage. Let that be a lesson to you!

The **Penglai Water Town* or Beiwocheng, immediately to the south of the pavilion, was built as a fortress, particularly against Japanese pirates. The Song and Ming navies trained here, and the Ming expanded the defenses. Intriguing is the water gate. In the old days, the Chinese lured in pirates and closed the gate behind them. Then, after the water level rose, the gate was opened and the dead pirates flushed out. Originally built in 1376, the gate was rebuilt in 1596.

A replica of the Ming town Dengzhou, including an old style bazaar, is on the way from the bus stop to the pavilion. Two recently built Ming "warships" take visitors for rides. Nearby is the **Dengzhou Ancient Ship Museum**. On special occasions, spear-carrying guards in Ming dress, waving dynastic flags, stilt and boat dancers, and firecrackers enliven the gateway and market.

The **Eight Immortals Palace** is a nearby exhibition with moving figures of these famous mythological people. It can give you some background, but it's not Disneyland.

Also important downtown is the **Yantai Museum**, *2 Yulan Street, Tel. 6222520. Open daily, except perhaps Mondays, 8:30am-5pm.* It is in a flamboyant Fujian-style guild hall with a temple dedicated to the sea goddess. This beautifully restored building was constructed from 1884 to 1906 in Fujian, and brought in three sections here. Note the jawbone of a whale and the remains of a giant sea turtle. A statue of the goddess, destroyed during the Cultural Revolution, has been replaced in wax. The museum has a few relics from 8000 B.C. with labels in English and can be seen in 40 minutes.

Pleasant to visit is the 600-year old white **Yuhuang** (Jade Emperor) **Temple**, *23 Yuhuang Bei Street, Tel. 6242283.* It's open 8am-5pm at 70 meters above sea level, with a good view of the city. The temple building is original, the tower built in 1984, and the memorial arch in 1876. A 600-year old white **pomegranate tree** here still bears fruit. Nearby is another garden, Little Penglai, inspired by the real one to the north.

You can visit the **Zhang Yu Wine Company** and its museum at *56 First Road, Tel. 6244616.* If you have more time, a lighthouse was built on top of a Ming dynasty beacon tower on Yantai Hill. It has a good view of the harbor.

Yangma Dao (Horse Racing Island or Elephant Island, because of its shape) is one hour by road away. Here the first Qin emperor raised horses and visited three times. A one-km horse-racing track with bleachers opened in 1985.

Yantai has two **bathing beaches** in the city proper: Number One Bathing Beach, in central Yantai, and Number Two Bathing Beach farther east. Both have all facilities. The swimming season goes from June to early September.

SHOPPING

Manufactured here are Riesling wines, vermouth, Gold Medal Brandy, lace, tablecloths, straw weaving, wooden-framed clocks, and partially completed woolen needlepoint pieces. Try the factories and department store.

PRACTICAL INFORMATION

CITS, *181 Jietang Road, 264000, Tel. 6234145, 6234144, Fax 6234147.*
Yantai China Comfort Travel Service, *115 Dama Road, Yantai, 264000, Tel. 6610543, Fax 6205559.*
Telephone Code, *0535*
Yantai Municipal Tourism Bureau, *Tel. 6246929.*
Yantai Shanshui Travel Service, *28, Xingfu Zhong Road, Tel. 6805742, Fax 6823124.*

NANJING

(Nanking: Southern Capital)
Located in the southwest part of Jiangsu province of which it is the capital, **Nanjing** lies on the Yangtze River. It is important because of its magnificent Ming wall and gates. Many of its ancient relics are Ming, built by Zhu Yuanzhang (Chu Yuan-chang), first emperor of the dynasty who reigned from 1368 to 1399. After his death, his successors moved the capital to Beijing, where they built the Forbidden City and were buried in elaborate tombs north of it.

Nanjing was settled 6,000 years ago and became a walled city 2,400 years ago. From 229 to 1421 A.D., it was intermittently the capital of the Eastern Wu (229-280 A.D.), Eastern Jin (317-420), Song (420-479), Qi (479-502), Liang (502-557), Chen (557-589), Southern Tang (937-975), Ming (1368-1421), and Taiping Heavenly Kingdom (1853-64).

In 1842, England and China signed the Treaty of Nanking, ending the First Opium War, and the city became an open port. From January 1 to April 5, 1912, it was the capital of the Sun Yat-sen government after which the capital moved to Beijing. After a period of much confusion, Chiang Kai-shek unilaterally declared Nanjing the capital again in 1927.

The Japanese captured Nanjing in 1937, and massacred 300,000 civilians in what is referred to as the Rape of Nanking. A museum was recently opened to commemorate this tragic event. Nationalists' headquarters moved to Chongqing but returned to Nanjing after the Japanese surrender in 1945. Most buildings survived the war. The Communists took the city in 1949, and moved the capital to Beijing. Nanjing is still the provincial capital.

Two thousand factories make metallurgical and chemical equipment, ships, telecommunication instruments, and synthetic fibers. The Zhong Xin Yuan Silk Factory manufactures brocade, and the Arts and Crafts Carving Factory works in ivory and wood.

For background on Nanjing, read Barry Till's *In Search of Old Nanking*. Nanjing's hottest temperature is a rare 40 C in August; its coldest is -7 C in January. The annual precipitation is more than 1,000 millimeters with rain mostly in summer. The humidity can be incredibly high in late spring and summer. The population is 5.3 million (three million urban). A good time to visit is late October to mid-November when the streets are lined with chrysanthemums.

ARRIVALS & DEPARTURES

Planes arrive from Hong Kong and 40 Chinese cities. It is a 1.75 hour flight by air southeast of Beijing and a one-hour flight (300 km) northwest of Shanghai. The airport is about 40 km from the city. The 274 km Nanjing-Shanghai expressway should be finished now with signs in English and service centers along the way. A bus leaves twice a day from the New World Yangtze Hotel in Shanghai for Nanjing as well as from other bus stations there.

Buses leave for Shanghai every 30 minutes or so from the Hanzhong bus station near the railway station in Nanjing.

Nanjing is a 2.5-three hour trip by train (Y86) from Shanghai.

ORIENTATION

Nanjing is a beautiful city of broad avenues thickly lined with 240,000 sycamore trees. Centrally located is the Drum Tower, with Zhongshan Road, the main shopping street, running south, northwest, and east, intersecting in the center of town. Xuanwu Lake dominates the north-eastern sector. Above it to the east looms 450-meter Zijin (Purple Gold) Mountain. The magnificent Ming city wall snakes around most of the urban area. The Yangtze River borders the western part of the city with the most important bridge at the northwest corner.

The city is building a 16.4 km south-north subway line from the Zhonghua Gate to the train station due in 2004.

WHERE TO STAY

The best hotels are the five-star **Jinling**, the **Hilton** and probably soon the **Sheraton**. The Jinling has been one of the best Chinese-managed hotels in the country with lots of experience hosting North Americans. It is still very good. The Hilton was recently opened and shows lots of promise. The Sheraton, Jinling and **Holiday Inn** are central. The Holiday Inn is good, unpretentious and reliable. If you want to sleep more cheaply, there's the four-star **Dingshan** and then the three-star **Nanjing Hotel**. For getting closer to things Chinese, the **Mandarin Chamber Hotel** is smack in the middle of the Confucian Temple area.

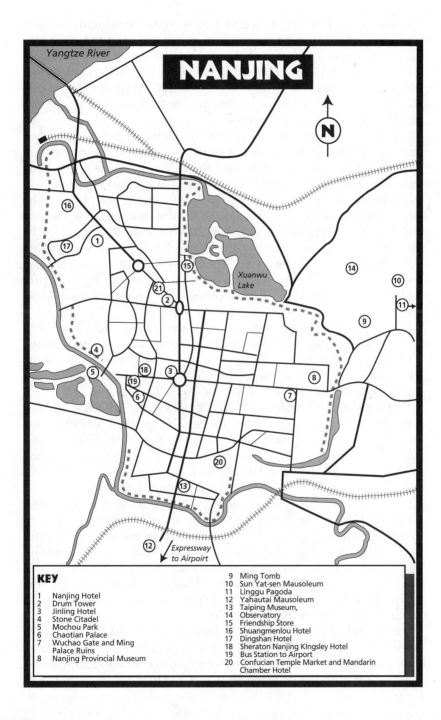

Yangtze River

NANJING

N

Xuanwu Lake

Expressway to Airpoirt

KEY

1 Nanjing Hotel
2 Drum Tower
3 Jinling Hotel
4 Stone Citadel
5 Mochou Park
6 Chaotian Palace
7 Wuchao Gate and Ming Palace Ruins
8 Nanjing Provincial Museum
9 Ming Tomb
10 Sun Yat-sen Mausoleum
11 Linggu Pagoda
12 Yahautai Mausoleum
13 Taiping Museum,
14 Observatory
15 Friendship Store
16 Shuangmenlou Hotel
17 Dingshan Hotel
18 Sheraton Nanjing KIngsley Hotel
19 Bus Station to Airport
20 Confucian Temple Market and Mandarin Chamber Hotel

The hotels listed here accept major credit cards, have business centers, minibars, air-conditioning, money exchange, and add a 10%-15% surcharge. Prices are subject to change, negociation, and discounts.

HILTON INTERNATIONAL HOTEL, *319 Zhongshan Dong Road, 210016. Tel. 4808888, Fax 4809999. E-mail:PR_NANJING@Hilton.com. Http://www.hilton.com. 559 rooms, and non-smoking floor. Five stars. $170-$260 for rooms; $250-$1500 for suites.*

The "S" shaped, 620-room, 42-story Hilton is set on 45 acres, conveniently located next to the city wall, and the provincial museum in a residential part of town. You can also walk to the ruins of the Ming Palace. It is the closest hotel to the Nanjing-Hangzhou Highway. You might encounter traffic jams if you go downtown however. It has a big, airy lobby with two grand staircases, a coffee shop and murals of Einstein and Galileo. Its restaurants have Italian, Cantonese and Japanese food. Its ballroom which can seat 1200 for dinner is in Italian marble with padded walls and slithering gold dragons. The business center has padded arm chairs. Rooms are very spacious with stuffed arm chairs and leg rests, safes and in-house movies. It has a health club with aerobics, pool and a 700 sq meter sauna.

While it is very classy indeed, the workmanship could have been better, and the decor needs work. The pictures in the room matched nothing. A few switches and buttons didn't work. It should have fixed these glitches by the time you get there. It should soon have bowling and simulated golf. The Hilton is owned by China Travel Service.

SHERATON NANJING KINGSLEY HOTEL & TOWERS (Kingsley Binguan), *169 Hanzhong Road, 210029, Tel. 6668888, 6519990, Fax 6656132. E-mail:nanjing.kingsley@ittsheraton.com. Five-star standard not yet official. On the edge of the commercial, business and government area, 500 meters west of the Jinling Hotel, and next to the Stock Exchange, hospitals, and CAAC office. 42 km from the airport and five km from the railway station.*

This 42-story, 371-room hotel opened in 1998 with a big incense burner and fountain in front. Standard rooms are 37 sq meters with floor to ceiling windows, separate shower stalls and safes, second modem lines, irons and boards. It has executive and non-smoking floors, an Irish fun pub, cigar bar, 24-hour coffee shop, and piano bar with high tea. To help you keep fit, there's a bowling alley, 100-meter running track, putting green, 25-meter lap pool, lighted tennis court, gym and traditional medicine center. It has offices for hire.

JINLING HOTEL (Fandian), *2 Han Zhong Road, 210005, at Xinjiekou Square. Five stars, Tel. 4711888, 4711998, Fax 4724849. 4704141. Http://www.jinlinghotel-nanjing.com. E-mail:hotel@jinlinghotel-nanjing.com. 35 km from the airport, 10 km from the railway station. Y1410-Y2325 for rooms; Y2490-Y16600 for suites.*

Opened in 1983 and renovated in 1998, this 37-story, 600-room hotel is next to the 17-story World Trade Center. Services include a gym, sauna and tanning machine. It also has a very pretty indoor pool, bowling, golf simulator, and snooker. There're a grill room, Japanese, German, and Sichuan food, scheduled shuttles with the airport and train station. Rooms have CNN and CBS, safes, coffee makers, and 24-hour room service.

HOLIDAY INN HOTEL, *45 Zhongshan Bei Road, Tel. 3308888, 3301688, Fax 3309898, 3309688. Http://www.holiday-inn.com. E-mail: nkgch@public1.ptt.js.cn. It's in a downtown location near the Drum Tower and close to Xuanwu Lake about two km from Xinjiekou Square, 35 km from Lukou International Airport and seven km from the railway station. $120-$165 for rooms, $170-$1988 for suites.*

This 34-floor, 277-room hotel has executive floors. Standard rooms are relatively small. It has a 24-hour business center and coffee shop, Italian, Cantonese and Asian restaurants. It has an indoor pool, sauna and steambath. The housekeeping needs some improvement. We found a hair on our towels, for example, and the carpet needed cleaning. But generally the hotel is good and improvements should have taken place by now. Two internet centers are in the immediate neighborhood.

DINGSHAN GARDEN HOTEL (Binguan), *90 Chahaer Road, 210003. Four stars, Tel. 8802888, 6601868, Fax 8821729. Isolated on a hill in the northwest corner of the city. Rooms $98-$118; suites $238; serviced apartments $238-$438.*

This hotel is 51 km from the airport and seven from the railway station.

MANDARIN CHAMBER HOTEL (Zhuang Yuan Lou Jiudian), *9 Zhuang Yuanjing, Fuzi Temple, 210001. Three stars, Tel. 2202555, 2202988, Fax 2201876.*

On a narrow street north of the Confucius Temple, you can sit in its fancy lobby and watch 'old China' outside.

NANJING HOTEL (Fandian), *259 Zhongshan Bei Road, Tel. 3411888, Fax 3422261. E-mail:njhotel@pub.nj-online.nj.js.cn. 47 km from the airport, and five km from the railway station, it's in a good location northwest of the Holiday Inn. In its Zi Jin block, rooms cost $96-$108 and suites $158-$806. In its Zi Xia Block, rooms cost $32-$52, the quality of course much lower. Breakfast is included.*

This 1936-built hotel has several buildings set in a garden. No safes and CNN in rooms, but it is generally clean and okay but don't expect excellence. It has Chaozhou and western food, gym and sauna.

WHERE TO EAT

Nanjing people say the recipe for Beijing roast duck originally was from Nanjing, so you might want to try the Nanjing version. Among the other local specialties are: salted duck, especially August Sweet Osmanthus duck, salted duck gizzard, roast chicken with coriander, salted shrimps, casserole cabbage heart, big flat pork croquette (outside crisp, inside soft), chrysanthemum-shaped herring, long-tailed shrimp, and squirrel-like mandarin fish.

The best food is in the hotels. The **Hilton** has had a great dinner buffet for about Y98 that included roast beef, *sushi*, fish, *won ton*, salads, and brie cheese. For good western food, try also the **Holiday Inn** and **Sheraton**. The Jinling has a **Brauhaus Brewery** where you can hide behind the beer tanks and gorge on German-type sausages and slurp soup from a chunk of crispy bread.

The Dingshan has good Jiangsu food. There's the related **Dingshan Restaurant** chain, one near the Confucian Temple at *5 Zhanyuan Road, Tel. 6627555, one at 458 Zhongshan Dong Road, Tel. 4456614, and one at 79 Hunan Bei Road, Tel. 3220077.* The **Nanjing Palace Restaurant** is at *31 Beijing Dong Road, Tel. 3364600.*

For cheaper fare:

WU HUA GUO, *near Nanjing University on Yu Dao Jie Street.*

A small restaurant where the fish and shrimp are great.

ZHONG LU YUAN RESTAURANT, *on the second floor, 313 Zhongshan Bei Road, Tel. 3425726.*

China Travel Service runs this restaurant, and serves a good but scrawny roast pigeon, bean curd fish with chili peppers, dumplings, and spinach with chicken egg in the moderate-priced range.

SEEING THE SIGHTS

Nanjing takes two days to see, but if you only have one day in the city itself, most important are the Sun Yat-sen Mausoleum, Linggu Temple, and Ming Tomb in the eastern part of the city, usually combined in a half-day tour.

In the afternoon, you can choose from the Observatory (for the view), the museum, and the Drum Tower. The Zhonghua Gate and city wall, the Confucian Temple, Qinhuai River, and the Taiping Museum are close together.

The **Dr. Sun Yixian** (Sun Yat-sen) **Mausoleum**, *Tel. 4446458, open daily,* is on an 80,000-square-meter site. The building was designed to be more impressive than those of the emperors whom the father of the Chinese republic overthrew. Eight km from the Jinling Hotel, it is on the south side of Purple Gold Mountain, its *feng-shui* ideal. Dr. Sun (1866-1925) was buried here in 1929 in the rear of the hall. The mausoleum, 158 meters above sea level, has 392 steps and a five-meter-high statue, and is well worth visiting. But you must leave bags and purses behind.

Sun Yat-sen was born of peasant stock in Guangdong province, near Macau, in what is now called Zhongshan County, renamed after its most distinguished son. Zhongshan was Dr. Sun's honorific name. Dr. Sun actually spent most of his life outside China, leaving home at the age of 12 to study at an Anglican school in Hawaii, where his older brother had settled. He studied medicine in Hong Kong and for a short time set up practice in Macau. He spent much of his life traveling in Europe and America, living in Japan, writing and plotting against the Manchus, and planning a government for China.

An intriguing, complex man, Dr. Sun became a Christian early in life and, although he attacked missionaries as being imperialists, he admitted on his death bed that he remained a Christian. He fought the Manchus because they could not rid the country of the foreign imperialists. After becoming president, he formally informed the first Ming emperor of what had happened! Dr. Sun did not remain president for long. Because he wanted to unite the country, he abdicated in 1912. The north was not willing to accept a southerner as head of state, he reasoned. He later accepted a post as director of railways for the country. At the same time, he flirted with socialism, coming under the influence of Russian advisers.

He was married first to a peasant woman and later to Soong Chingling, much against her father's wishes. The second marriage shocked the Christians but not most Chinese, who were used to the idea of several wives. Mme. Sun was the sister of Mme. Chiang Kai-shek. See also Shanghai and Zhongshan.

Linggu (Valley of the Soul) **Temple**, open daily, is the only survivor of a whole complex of Buddhist structures, its statues destroyed during the Taiping war when the Qing army slept here. Eight km from the Jinling Hotel, a Liang princess built it originally in 513 A.D. in memory of the famous monk Xuan Zhang. The first Ming emperor moved it to its current location at the eastern foot of Zijin Mountain because he wanted the original site for his own tomb. Built without beams, it is reminiscent of medieval Europe because of its arches. Nearby is a nine-story pagoda built in the 1920s to complement the area around the mausoleum, two km to the northeast. You can climb the pagoda for a good view of this beautiful, wooded area. The Sun Yat-sen Museum is nearby.

The **Xiaoling Mausoleum** (Ming Tomb) *is open daily, Tel. 6642990.* This mausoleum, for the first Ming emperor, Zhu Yuanzhang, and his empress is not as impressive as those north of Beijing, but is worth a visit only for its Sacred Way with over a dozen well-proportioned, larger-than-life mythical animals, generals, and ministers.

Zhu Yuanzhang was an unemployed peasant and former Buddhist monk and beggar who fought his way to the throne and was a brilliant emperor. Most of the buildings were destroyed in the early days of the

Qing, who overthrew the Ming dynasty. The mausoleum is six km from the Jinling Hotel. The **Botanical Garden**, with tropical and subtropical plants, is on one side of the Sacred Way.

Zijinshan (Purple or Bell Mountain) dominates the northeastern skyline. **The Observatory**, *Tel. 6642270*, is on the west side and you can combine it with a visit to Xuanwu Lake. This major research center of the Chinese Academy of Science, built in 1934, is involved with space research and man-made satellites. You can go there for the view and to see copies of ancient instruments outside.

Chinese astronomers invented the armillary sphere (four dragons and spheres) 2000 years ago to locate constellations. They invented the abridged armillary sphere (three dragons) in the Yuan for the same purpose. The Germans and French stole both of these 500-year-old replicas in 1900 but returned them later. Astronomers used the gnomon column next to the abridged sphere (a 3,000-year old invention), to survey the seasons and calculate the days of the year. It faces due south and north. In the large column is a small hole through which the sun shines at noon, casting light on the gauge below. Because of this instrument, the Chinese decided very early that there were 365 1/4 days a year.

Xuanwu Lake is outside Xuanwu Gate, northeast of the city, five km from the Jinling Hotel. *Tel. 6633154*. Twenty-five km in circumference, this lake is now used for recreation and fish farming. One to two meters deep, it was originally built in the fifth century, and several emperors used it to train or review their navies and for private recreation. A black dragon was spotted here in the fifth century, so if you visit it on a dark and stormy night, you might want to look for it. You can walk from the railway station and take a ferry.

The **Jiangsu Provincial Museum** (Nanjing Museum), *Zhongshan Dong Road, Tel. 6641554*, is a traditional Chinese-style building and contains exhibits ranging from the era of Peking Man to revolutionary times. Three thousand items are on display, among them a 3,000-year-old genuine duck egg; the jade burial suit that was exhibited in America in 1973 (Eastern Han, from Xuzhou City, Jiangsu); a sixth-century Soul Pot covered with many birds, placed in a tomb so the birds could fly the soul of the deceased to paradise; maps of the early capitals in Nanjing from 229 to 589, a 20-meter scroll showing the inspection tour by Qing Emperor Kangzi (Kang-shi) from Nanjing to Zhenjiang; the anchor from a British merchant ship lost in Zhenjiang; a photo of a British-built electric company in 1882; and a list of institutions set up by the United States in China, with numbers of Chinese students and foreign teachers.

The **Gulou** (Drum Tower) is at the intersection of Zhongshan Bei Road, and Zhongyang and Beijing Roads, in the center of the city. Built in 1382, it holds a six-foot diameter drum and an ancient giant stone tortoise carrying a stele added in the Qing, a report on the inspection tour of Qing Emperor Kangxi. Nearby is the Big Bell Pavilion.

The **Nanjing City Wall** is 12 meters high, 33.4 km in circumference, and from 7.62 to 12 meters thick. Built from 1368 to 1387, it once had 13,616 cannons on top. Roughly 10 km north-south by 5.62 km east-west, it is believed to be the longest city wall in the world. The bricks were made in five provinces, and each is inscribed with the name of the superintendent and the brickmaster, plus the date made. The mortar was lime, tung oil, and glutinous rice paste. Originally built with 13 gates, 11 more were added later. You cannot miss this magnificent wall.

The **Zhonghua Gate**, *Tel. 6625752*, on the south side, is the best gate to see. It has four two-story gates in succession (in case the enemy breaks through one), 12 tunnels, and room to garrison 3,000 soldiers. You can walk along the top of the wall here.

If You Have More Time or Special Interests

The **Confucius Temple** (Fuzimiao), adjacent shopping center, hotel, and free market, are major tourist attractions, featuring Ming and Qing architecture, and worth a visit. The Temple was originally built in 1034 A.D. as a place of sacrifice. Wars destroyed it many times and the current building is a post-Liberation reproduction. Moving wax statues of scholars in period dress demonstrate how examinations were written. Birds, fish, and clothes are on sale. Nearby on the **Qinhuai River** is the former residence of famous Ming sing-song (courtesan) girl Li Xiang; you can rent boats (but the ride is short and the water dirty).

A relic of the Taipings well worth seeing is the **Tianwang Mansion** (The Heavenly King's Mansion), *292 Changjiang Road* in the eastern part of the city, *Tel. 6641131*. The mansion was made for Hong Xiuquan (Hung Hsiu-chuan) the head of the Taipings, with materials from the Ming palace. It is now the Taiping Museum, *Tel. 6623024*. Read *God's Chinese Son* by Jonathan Spence.

Prominently displayed inside the museum is a plaque 'in memory of the organizer and leader of the Ever Victorious Army, erected by the Frederick Ward Post, American Legion, May 27, 1923.' Frederick Ward was an American mercenary who fought against the Taipings and died in 1862.

You can study the **Ming Palace ruins** near the Hilton in about five minutes. It was built between 1368 to 1386 for the first Ming emperor. The Forbidden City is about the same size. Qing troops partially destroyed it in 1645 and the Taipings pulled down the remainder. In 1911 only a gate was left standing, but in 1958 the government restored a few pieces.

Also in the city is a memorial hall to **Zheng He**, the Muslim eunuch who became one of China's most famous maritime commanders, making seven voyages to 30 countries of Asia and Africa from 1405 to 1433. His tomb is 10 km south of Nanjing. Read *When China Ruled the Seas*.

From more recent times is the **Memorial of the Nanjing Massacre**, *7 Jiang Dong Gate, Tel. 6501033*.

The **Meiling Palace** is about three km outside the Zhongshan Gate. This 1930s building was the weekend home of Generalissimo **Chiang Kai-shek** and his wife from 1945 to 1949. They held church services here, sometimes with the American ambassador.

Walks

Great walks include Purple Mountain and along the top of the city wall.

NIGHTLIFE & ENTERTAINMENT

The best disco is in the **Jinling Hotel**, *Tel. 4711888*. The **Manhattan Disco** on Baixia Road is very popular as is the **Casablanca** in the Xuan Wu Hotel. The disco in the **Zhongshan Hotel** attracts foreign students, *Tel. 3361888*. The **Jinling Folk Music Performances** are in the Golden Hall, *Tel. 4547903*.

The **Nanjing Acrobatic Troupe** has won international prizes. Favorite watering holes of local foreign residents are the **Tequila Bar** (Xu Ri Dong Sheng) on *Shenzhou Road*, and the **Swede & Kraut**, *137 Ninghai Road, Tel. 6638020*.

SHOPPING

Made in Nanjing are 'Yunjin (Figured) Satin' brocade, velvet flowers, tapestry and carpets, imitations of ancient wood and ivory carvings, silver jewelry, and paper cuts. Made in the province are inlaid and red lacquer (Yangzhou), purple sand pottery (Yixing), Huishan clay figures, fresh water pearls, silk underwear, batik (Nantong), and Suzhou embroidery. Prices for double-sided embroidery seems to be the best here. Don't pay more than Y500 for a large one.

A worth-while antique and curio market is in the **Confucius Temple** with many private and a few government shops. The latter says they will accept credit cards but will try to charge you a service charge, a no-no. You could tell them the credit card company will no longer work with them if they do. This market had grossly over-priced agate, fluorite, serpentine, and other stones. Pearls should be relatively cheap here. Aim as low as Y15 for a woven necklace, the pretty ones with one line of real pearls, the rest tiny fakes.

For curios and antiques, try also the **Co-op Antique Building** upstairs at *99 Gong Yuan Road across from McDonald's and KFC, Tel. 3226811.* It is open 9am-7pm weekdays or 8pm on weekends. Prices have come down to 25% of the first price asked.

The **Nanjing Arts and Crafts Industry Corp.** at *31 Beijing Dong Road, Tel. 7711193* and is open 9am-6pm daily. It claims "set prices" and takes credit cards. But prices are steep. Serious shoppers might want to visit its factory instead. Unique here are human hair embroidery, and elegant brocade at Y1800-Y2300 per meter and used for Japanese *obis*. Prize-winning crafts people demonstrate on the upper floor and offer to sell their products at a 20% discount. The **Chaotian Gong Palace** near the Jinling Hotel has a courtyard of shops and vendors. More show up on weekends. Stores at the **Provincial Museum** have given 20% discounts.

Prices at the gift shop at the Sun Yat-sen mausoleum bus parking lot are ten times that asked elsewhere.

You can visit the **Brocade Research Institute**, *240 Chating Dong Road, Tel. 6611377;* **The Arts & Crafts Company**, *31 Beijing Dong Road, Tel. 7711193;* and **The Nanjing Jade Workshop**, *233 Zhongshan Dong Road, Tel. 4412910.*

There's lots of shopping in the **Golden Shopping Centre** next to the Jinling Hotel, *2 Hanzhong Road, Tel. 4455888.* An antique store is at the Zhongshan Gate and the **Cultural Relics Shop** is at the *Nanjing Museum, 321 Zhongshan Dong Road, Tel. 4450324.* The **Shizhuzhai, Nanjing Cultural Relics Shop**, is at *72 Taiping Nan Road, Tel. 6643313.* The **Nanjing Central Department Store** is at *79 Zhongshan Nan Road, Tel. 4408288.*

EXCURSIONS & DAY TRIPS

You can make day trips from Nanjing to Changzhou, Yangzhou and Zhenjiang but it's better to spend more time in Suzhou, Wuxi, and Yixing.

Changzhou is the home of a still productive, 1,500 year old imperial comb factory and the *Tianningsi (Heavenly Tranquility) Temple with its 500 Tang arhats. It is a stop on some Grand Canal cruises and 20 km southeast are the ruins of Yancheng, the capital of Yan State (11th century B.C.), with a small museum, ongoing excavations, and pearl farming in its moats. It is halfway between Shanghai and Nanjing on the Grand Canal, three hours by boat from Wuxi. Flights arrive from 13 other cities. The urban population is 600,000.

You can stay at the **Changzhou Grand Hotel** (Dajiudian), *65 Yanling Xi Road, 213003. Four stars. Tel. 8109998, Fax 6607701. Credit Cards. It has a downtown location, 30 km. from the airport, and five km from the railway station.* Look for its diet therapy restaurant with food to 'prolong life and beautify women.'

You can contact **CITS** at *Tel. 8100481 or Fax 8109455*. **CTS** is at *70 Cheng Zhong Nan Road, Tel. 8118299, Fax 8118677*. The telephone code is *0519*.

Yixing, due west of Shanghai and Suzhou and on the west side of Lake Taihu, is the home of purple clay pottery in Dingsu which you see everywhere in this area. You can visit factories and the huge exhibition hall. It's also known for its limestone caves.

Shanjuan Cave, 25 km southwest of the city, was discovered about 2,000 years ago. The 700-meter walk takes about an hour. It has a 120-meter-long underground river. The **Zhonggong Cave**, 22 km southwest of Yixing was the home of Zhang Daoling (one of the founders of Taoism), and Zhang Guolao (one of the Eight Taoist Immortals). With 72 small, interconnected caves, its one km walk includes 1,500 stone steps. **CITS** and **CTS** are in the *Yixing Guest House, 214200. Tel. 0510/7992172, Fax 7905491 or 7995491*.

PRACTICAL INFORMATION

China Comfort and **Zhongbei Travel Service** have daily day tours booked at some hotels.

CITS and **Overseas Tourist Co.**, *202-1 Zhongshan Bei Road, 210003. Tel. 3428999, Fax 3438954*.

CTS Jiangsu, *313 Zhong Shan Bei Road, 210003. Tel. 3431502, Fax 3426533. E-mail:JSCTS@pub.jlonine.com*. This agency and Nanjing Normal University give foreign students diploma courses in Chinese language and culture. It also has join-in-whenever tours around China with regular Friday departures.

CYTS, *160 Hanzhong Road, Tel. 3344124, Fax 6523355. E-mail:CYTSYQ@public1.ptt.js.cn*. Contact Miranda Wang Lan, Asian & Oceanian Department.

Hours: offices 8am-11:30am, 1:30pm-5 or 5:30pm; department stores 9am or 10am-10pm.

Jiangsu Tourism Administration, *255 Zhongshan Bei Road, 210003, Tel. 3427144, Fax 3433960*. For complaints, *Tel. 3418185, Fax 3427495*.

Jinling Business International Travel, *2 Hanzhong Road, Tel. 2269370, Fax 2264842*.

Nanjing Municipal Tourism Bureau, *4 Donggushi Nan Road, Tel. 3362686, Fax 7711959*. Complaints, *Tel. 3606085*.

Telephone Code, *025*.

Tourist Hotline, *202-1 Zhongshan Bei Road, Tel. 3428999; 313 Zhongshan Bei Road, Tel. 3431502*.

SUZHOU

(Soochow)

Located on the ancient Grand Canal in Jiangsu province, **Suzhou** is famous for its gardens, silk, moats and canals. One of China's oldest and most beautiful cities, it is known for its half-moon bridges and architecture. UNESCO has listed four of its classical gardens as World Heritage sites. The old city proper is under national government protection as a historic and cultural treasure. Its renovated old buildings and even new ones are exquisite and in traditional white Huaihai Chinese style. No new construction is allowed to be higher than the North Temple Pagoda. No one can build any new factories, and existing factories that pollute must move to the suburbs.

Suzhou's streets are thickly lined with plane trees and some of its tiny white-washed cottages are original Ming. Unlike other Chinese cities, the Japanese war inflicted little damage here. Suzhou is known primarily as a cultural and scenic city, similar in this respect to Japan's Kyoto.

Choosing between a visit to Suzhou and its rival, the silk resort city of Hangzhou, is not easy. Both are among the best of old China. Suzhou is closer to Shanghai, but you can fly direct to Hangzhou from Hong Kong and Singapore. Hangzhou has West Lake. Both are romantic, and for lovers.

The hottest temperature is 36 C (usually one to two days in late July, early August); the coldest is -9 C around the end of January, averaging 0 C to 7 C. It snows once or twice a year. 1063 mm of rain fall mainly from May into early September. The population is 5.7 million, of whom one million live in the city.

He Lu, King of Wu, founded the city as his capital in 514 B.C. Iron was smelted here more than 2,500 years ago and silk weaving was well developed in the Tang and Song. **Marco Polo** visited in the latter half of the 13th century and proclaimed it another Venice. Textile manufacturing flourished during the Ming. From 1860 to 1863, 40,000 troops of the Taiping Heavenly Kingdom controlled the area. During the Japanese occupation, the Jiangsu provincial puppet government had its headquarters in the Humble Administrator's Garden.

People here speak the Wu dialect which is similar to that of Shanghai, only with softer tones and more adjectives. Industries include the manufacturing of television sets, wristwatches, chemicals, and electronics. Among its sister cities are Portland, Oregon and Victoria, Canada.

Here you can see the factories where artisans spin and weave silk, make sandalwood and silk fans, and create one of the four most famous embroideries in China. They also make musical instruments. The villages raise silkworms, jasmine flowers for tea, shrimp, and tangerines.

ARRIVALS & DEPARTURES

The fastest way to Suzhou is by express train leaving Shanghai's downtown railway station at 6am, and arriving in about one hour (86 km). Other trains leave every 30 minutes but take a few minutes longer. The railway station is in the north outside the city moat. If you are going to Suzhou directly from Shanghai's Hong Qiao airport, look for a bus from there. It's 1.5 hours. Suzhou has a small military airport 30 km away but it only has a few flights with Beijing and Foshan.

There's also a 3.5-hour direct bus from Hangzhou March to November only. The Hangzhou train takes about the same time. Air-conditioned, express buses leave Shanghai's bus station on Gong He New Road. By tourist boat on the Grand Canal from Wuxi it's a very pleasant three hours; by bus or car it's an hour, and by express train 40 minutes.

Buses leave Suzhou's North Bus Station every hour or so for Wuxi and elsewhere.

ORIENTATION

The old formerly walled city is still surrounded by a rectangular moat. The Shanghai-Nanjing Expressway runs parallel outside and close to its north side. The old city is about 2.5-4.6 km north-south, and about 2.6-three km east-west. It is criss-crossed by many canals (many in need of cleaning). The western and southern moats are actually branches of the famous Grand Canal (610 A.D). Immediately to the east is the 70 sq km Sino-Singapore-Suzhou Industrial Park, a Singapore joint venture. To the west is the 60-square-km High and New Technology Zone. Beyond that is Lake Taihu 20 km east of the old city.

The main street, **Renmin** (People's) **Road**, runs north-south; **Guanqian Street** runs east-west, meeting with Renmin almost in the center of the city. The city wall was built in 514 B.C. and remnants, including three gates, remain. Also remaining is one of the eight water gates. Taxis are double Shanghai's rates but the city is small. You can also get around cheaply by bicycle rickshaw (Y10 for a couple kilometers) or public bus.

WHERE TO STAY

The five-star hotels here are the **Sheraton** and the **New Suzhou International**. The latter is beautiful but too far away from downtown for anyone but business people associated with the Industrial Park. The Sheraton is at the southwest corner of the old city at Pan Men Water Gate, a marvelous location for its history. The next best hotel is the beautiful **Bamboo Grove** with its own restful classical garden and architecture, good service, and convenient location in the old city. Next in quality is the **Gloria Plaza Hotel** and for those who want to save money, don't care about a little wear and lower service, the Suzhou hotel is fine, its location fantastic. The **Aster** is adequate for business people as is the **New City Garden Hotel**. These two are west of the city moat in the business district close to Suzhou Customs and the trade center. The New Garden is newer and brighter than the Suzhou Hotel and the Aster and its staff seem friendlier.

Prices mentioned below are subject to seasonal discounts, and a 15% surcharge. Hotels here all have money exchange, business centers, mini-bars, international direct dial, and take credit cards. They all add 10% to 15% surcharge.

SHERATON SUZHOU HOTEL AND TOWERS, *388 Xin Shi Road, 215007. Tel 5103388, Fax 5100888. Http://www.ittsheraton.com. E-mail: sheraton_suzhou@ittsheraton.com. Aiming for five stars. Rooms start at $160 and opening discounts have been over 50%.*

The Sheraton has five stories and 328 rooms, including a presidential suite the size of 14 regular hotel rooms. Four cabana rooms overlook the pool. I can't emphasize too much its amazing architecture, decor and location. The hotel captures the flavor of gracious old Suzhou with its white walls and gardens. It has lovely touches like a curtain of dripping water at the entrance to its coffee shop. And you can walk to the ancient Pan Men Water Gate on a branch of the Grand Canal. If Suzhou still had its king, his palace would probably look like this if built today.

See Chapter 13, *China's Best Places to Stay.*

NEW SUZHOU INTERNATIONAL HOTEL (Xin Su Guoji Dajiudian), *Jinji Lake, northeast corner of the Sino-Singapore Suzhou Industrial Park, 215021, Tel. 7616688, Fax 7612288. Http: www.suz.int.hotel.com.* Twenty minutes' drive from the railway station, and near an international school. Five-star quality. $120-$145 for its 70 medium-sized rooms, $200-$300 for suites, and $800-$6000 for apartments in its ten villas. All have safes, coffeemakers, and satellite television. Executive rooms have data ports. This beautiful lake-side hotel has western decor with oriental touches. It has a heated indoor pool, gym, minigolf, and squash. It is good for small conferences, has a 100-seat theatre, and its ballroom can seat over 500 banquet style. The business center operates 24 hours. It has a shuttle bus and you can surf the Net in its Olympic Bar.

BAMBOO GROVE HOTEL (Zhu Hui Fandian), *168 Zhu Hui Road, 215006. Four stars, Tel. 5205601, Fax 5208778. E-mail: bghsz@public1.sz.js.cn. Http://www.bamboo.sz.js.cn. $120-$170 for rooms; $230-$2200 for suites. Six km from the railway station.*

Built in 1990, this hotel has five stories, three connecting buildings and 356 rooms. It has an executive floor, Cantonese and Japanese food. Sports include a gym, tennis, indoor pool, bicycles, and sauna. Rooms have CNN and HBO. Lee Garden International management.

NEW CITY GARDEN HOTEL, *Shishan Road, 215011. Tel. 8250228, Fax 8250573, 8257179. E-mail:xcnetl@publicl.sz.js.cn. Four stars. Rooms are $100-$150, suites are $200-$500.*

This 1997 hotel is about five km west of the west moat, and has 182 rooms with safes, CNN but little drawer space. It has an executive floor. There's bowling, gym and squash and should have a pool and tennis by now. It has Japanese, Chinese and western food. E-mail is relatively cheap.

GLORIA PLAZA HOTEL, *535 Ganjiang East Road, Tel. 5218855, Fax 5218533. E-mail:gloriasz@public1.sz.js.cn. Http://www.hotel-web.com/gloria/index.htm.*

This 300-room hotel won't give discounts because its "prices are good." Y680-Y900 for rooms; Y1530-Y2970 for suites. Prices are reasonable here and include the surcharge. You should be able to get a choice of soft or hard mattress and enjoy live music and very cold beer in the lobby every evening. We found a "message" light that wouldn't turn off and a phone that rang for no reason. Otherwise it was fine. Managed by Gloria International Hotels and Resorts.

ASTER HOTEL (Yadu Dajiudian), *156 Sanxiang Road, 215004. Four stars, Tel. 8291888, Fax 8291838. E-mail:aster@public1.sz.js.cn. Four km from the railway station.*

This 1991, 29-story hotel with a cheerful two-story lobby decorated in bright colors does not have a reputation for snap-to-it service. But it's okay if you're not fussy. It has 396 medium-sized rooms. You might want to aim for its 27th floor with larger rooms renovated in 1998. It has satellite television, a Food Street with Cantonese, Chaozhou and Suzhou snacks, and a revolving restaurant. It has Japanese and western food, and 24-hour room service. Assets are its large shopping area, indoor pool, and bowling alley. It was charging only Y25 for thirty minutes e-mail. English might be a problem.

SUZHOU HOTEL (Fandian), *115 Shi Quan Street, 215006. Four stars, Tel. 5205298, 5204646, Fax 5204015. $70-$100 for rooms, $150-$1000 for suites. Six km from the railway station. Quiet setting in large garden next to CITS.*

Built in 1958 and renovated in 1996, this hotel has three buildings with a total of 350 rooms, the better ones with kettles, small televisions, scales, CNN and CNBC. It also has a sauna and gym. The air could be better and it's poorly maintained.

WHERE TO EAT

The **Bamboo Grove Hotel**, the **New Suzhou International** and the **Sheraton** have the best western food. All the hotels here have good Chinese food. Try the braised fish balls with ginger sauce for Y28 and pan fried dumplings at the Gloria Plaza's **Suzhou Express restaurant**.

The next two are on the same street downtown near the Taoist Temple off Guanqian Street and are tourist restaurants:

SONGHELOU (Pine And Crane Restaurant), *141 Guanqian Street, Tel. 7277003.*

This place has been famous since Qing emperor Qianlong's time for its squirrel-shaped mandarin fish, snowflake crab meat, and duck in spicy sauce.

WANGSI RESTAURANT, *23 Taijian Lane, Tel. 5227277.*

Wangsi specializes in local food like beggar's chicken.

Jia Yu Fang Street, *near Joyous Garden*, is where the locals ea. Along this much more popular two-block long "L"-shaped street, menus are only in Chinese and restaurants are all privately owned. A favorite along this street is:

SPRING STORY (Chun Tian Gu Shi), *No. 2, Tel. 5239023.*

Take a Chinese-speaking friend and try this place. Good choices here are the green beans in cao wine, the potted duck soup, the silk squash and fried *jiaotze*. Ask about the famous Chinese artists who hang out there.

A night food street market is on **Guanqian Street**.

SEEING THE SIGHTS

If you only have one day, you might consider visiting two of the gardens. Explore the **Master of Nets** at dusk and then stay on for the show. See **Tiger Hill** and one handicraft factory. On a second day, there's **Tongli** (25 km from the city) and **Zhouzhuang**, both charming ancient villages. There is enough to enjoy for three or four days, if you just want to poke around in museums, meditate in temples, and indulge in shopping for silk. If you have more time, Suzhou has 70 gardens in traditional Chinese style. Most gardens are open 8:30-5pm with seasonal variations. The Master of Nets stays open later in summer.

Shizilin Yuan (Lion Forest) **Garden**, *23 Yulin Road, Tel. 7272428*, four km from the Suzhou Hotel, was built in 1350 during the Yuan and is so named because the teacher of the monk who built it lived on Lion Rock Mountain. It is a UNESCO heritage site. Some of the rockeries are shaped like lions. It was once owned by the granduncle of American architect I.M. Pei and takes about thirty minutes to see but more to relax in and enjoy.

At the entrance, the maze inside the rockeries is notable, and some of the rocks have clearly been carved and then weathered in Lake Tai for scores or hundreds of years. The rock structure above the stone boat was a waterfall, which in the early days was hand-poured. The Standing-in-Snow Study is exquisite, so named because a student once went to visit his teacher there and, too polite to awaken him, waited patiently in the snow.

Changlang Ting Yuan (Gentle Wave or Surging Wave) **Pavilion**, *3 Canglang Street, Tel. 5306148*, is one km from the Suzhou Hotel. About two acres, it is the only garden that is not surrounded completely by a view-blocking wall. A pond lies outside to be enjoyed from a View-Borrowing Pavilion. A hall houses 125 steles with the images of 500 sages, dating from the Kingdom of Wu to the Qing. Carved in relief in 1840, the deeds of each one are confined to 16 poetic characters. The poet Su Tzu-mei founded the garden, one of the oldest in the city, in 1044 (Song). In the Yuan and early Ming, it was a Buddhist nunnery.

Look for the set of dark brown furniture made from mahogany tree roots that look like giant chocolate-covered peanuts. This garden is not as spectacular as the others, so if you're short on time, skip it. Normally it takes about 30 minutes to see.

Yi Yuan (Joyous) **Garden**, *340 Renmin Road, Tel. 5249317,* was built by a Qing official and, at 100 years old, it is the newest. It has taken the best of all the gardens, concentrating them into about an acre. The rockeries are from other older gardens. The dry boat is an imitation of the one in the Humble Administrator's.

*Liu Yuan (Lingering) **Garden**, *79-80 Liuyuan Road, Tel. 5337940,* six km from the Suzhou Hotel, was originally built in 1525 (Ming). The eight-acre garden consists of halls and studios in the east sector, ponds and hills in the central, and woods and hills in the western section. In late autumn, these woods are red. Look through some of the 200 different flower windows at the scenes beyond. You are in a living picture gallery. A huge five-ton, six-meter-high rock from Lake Tai stands in the eastern section. This garden takes at least 30 minutes to see.

Wangshi Yuan (Master of Nets) **Garden**, *11 Kuotao Xiang, Tel. 5223550,* 0.5 km from the Suzhou Hotel. Originally built in 1140 (Southern Song), it is one of the best and a UNESCO Heritage site. Usually it take 40 minutes to see. The Metropolitan Museum of Art in New York City has reproduced its Peony courtyard as the Astor Chinese Garden Court.

This garden is very pretty, especially when decorated with colorful palace lanterns for the Classical Night Garden in summer when tourists rotate among the pavilions to hear musicians and storytellers. Don't miss this charming experience.

*Zhuozheng Yuan (Humble Administrator's) **Garden**, *178 Dong Bei Street, Tel. 77536224,* five km from the Suzhou Hotel, is the largest in Suzhou and a UNESCO heritage site. A humble administrator, a dismissed official, laid it out in 1522 (Ming). Later it was divided into three gardens after the owner lost it gambling. The largest and most open of the gardens, three-fifths water, is typical of the water country south of the Yangtze. Almost all buildings are close to water. If you only have a short time, visit the central part. At Fragrant Island, there is a two-story stone 'dry boat' complete with gangplank, 'deck,' and 'cabin.' The Mandarin

Duck Hall has blue windows and classical furniture, with live ducks in a cage at the side of the hall. A covered walkway in the western section follows the natural contours of the land. Note the Lingering and Listening Hall for listening (of course) to the raindrops on the lotus leaves. Ramps instead of stairs make one wonder about wheelchairs back then. Look for the wood carving and the cloud designs on the glass. A 200-year-old miniature pomegranate tree is included in the excellent collection of *penjing* miniature trees. A museum of gardens with titles in English is near the exit.

Important but not spectacular is the ***Huqiu** (Tiger) **Hill**, *8 Huqiu Shan, Tel. 5314921*, nine km from the Suzhou Hotel. Take no. 5 bus. The 45-acre site is northwest of the city outside the moat and takes about an hour to see. The grounds were an island many years ago, but are now about 100 km from the East China Sea. Named Tiger Hill because a white tiger appeared here at one time, the entrance is the head, the pagoda is the tail, and in-between is the back of the tiger.

On the right after entering is the Sword Testing Rock which He Lu, King of Wu, was supposed to have broken in the sixth century B.C. On the left is a large magic rock. If the stone you throw stays on top, you will give birth to sons, so beware! On the right is a pavilion with red characters, the **Tomb of the Good Wife**, a widow sold by the wicked brothers of her deceased husband to another man. Forced to be a courtesan, she committed suicide.

Here is also where Fu Chai, King of Wu, is said to have built a tomb for his father, He Lu, in the early fifth century B.C., after which the tomb builders were slaughtered to keep the location a secret. Hence, no one is sure if this is indeed the right place. If you look carefully, you can still see the red of the blood on the large flat rock!

The tomb of He Lu is believed to be beyond the moon gate. In 1956, unsuccessful attempts were made to enter it. The foundation of the pagoda started to protest. Inside are supposed to be 3000 iron and steel swords. You can see the cave, blocked by large, cut stones, from the bridge to the pagoda. Is it or isn't it the 2500-year-old tomb? The two holes on the bridge were for hauling up buckets of water.

Northwest of the park is the **Tiger Hill Pagoda**, known also as the "Leaning Tower of Suzhou." This was built originally in the 10th century A.D. (Northern Song) but was burned down thrice. The latest repairs were made in 1981, when its foundation was strengthened. At 47.5 meters high, it tends to tilt to the northwest. Pilgrims used to climb the 53 steps here on their knees. Note the Indian arches.

If You Have More Time

North inside the moat: The **Beisi Ta** (North Temple) **Pagoda**, *Tel.*

7531197, at the north end of Renmin Road inside the old city at 652, is nine stories and 76 meters high, the tallest pagoda south of the Yangtze River. It was first built in the 10th century. You can climb it. On the grounds are exhibition halls and across the street to the northwest is the excellent Silk Museum (see below).

The **Embroidery and Folk Arts museums**, and the **Humble Administrator's** and **Lion Gardens** are relatively near this pagoda and are also worth visits. The **Mahogany factory** is nearby to the west and the **Theatre Museum** is near the east moat at *14 Zhangjiaxiang, Tel. 727-5338*. It is in a fancy old Shaanxi Provincial Guild Hall.

The **Silk Museum**, *661 Renmin Road, Tel. 7276538*, open 8:30am-5pm. It should fascinate lovers of textiles. You can see reproductions of ancient brocades, giant looms (with weavers balanced on top), and 'stone washing' which is actually stone grinding. The **Folk Arts Museum**, *Tel. 7271478*, is charming.

The **Suzhou Museum**, *204 Dongbei Street, Tel. 7274203*, near the Humble Administrator's Garden was the official residence of a royal Taiping prince, first built in 1860.

West of the old city: **Han Shan** (Cold Mountain) **Temple**, *8 Hanshansi Long, Tel. 5336317*, open 8:30am-4:30pm. 10 km west of the Suzhou Hotel, this was the home of two Tang monks, Han Shan and Shide. To the right of the central, gold Sakyamuni Buddha is Wu Nan, the young disciple who wrote the sutras; the older man is disciple Ja Yeh. Japanese pirates stole the original bell but Japan replaced it with a bell cast about 100 years ago. Originally built in the Liang dynasty (sixth century), the current buildings are Qing and the pagoda was built in 1993.

Travel agents organize special excursions to hear the bronze bells here on midnight December 31, New Year's Eve. If you hear the bells chime 108 times on this night, you should have few troubles in life! Monks chant and pray for guests. Lions and dragons dance. The temple is open 7pm-1am on this occasion.

Xiyuan (West Garden) **Temple**, *18 Liuyuan Road, Tel. 7232911*, open 8:30am-4:30pm. It is also very beautiful. Between the Han Shan Temple and the old city, it is the largest group of Buddhist buildings in Suzhou. It was originally built in the 16th century but was destroyed by fire, and rebuilt in 1892.

The ceiling in the main building is ornamented with magnificent bats (happiness) and cranes (long life), as in Beijing's Forbidden City. The central Buddhas are seven meters tall, including base and mandala. Behind the Buddhas to the right is the Bodhisattva of Wisdom, with a crown on his head. To the left is the Bodhisattva of Universal Benevolence.

The 500 arhats here are worth studying, each face so real, expressive, profound, individual. Outstanding is the crazy monk, who can look sad, happy, or wry, depending on the angle from which you look at him. Gilded on modeled clay, each statue is larger than life. But can you find any women? Enjoy those incense burners. During the Great Leap Forward (1958-60) they were supposed to be smelted. But the CITS director said no! Look also for the five-colored carp and giant soft-shelled turtles in the pond in the back garden.

Inside the moat south and central: this area has the major tourist hotels, the Master of Nets and Joyous Gardens. The Confucian Temple (Wen Miao) can take about 40 minutes. It is on Renmin Nan Road with a miniature tree collection, and a small museum with Song dynasty astronomical and city maps. It also has lots of antiques and reproductions for sale.

The newly renovated **Xuan Miao Guan** (Mysterious Wonder Taoist Temple), *Guanqian Street, Tel. 7274348*, is in the middle of the city, near the Renmin (People's) Department Store, and car-free shopping. Three giant, gilded sculptures of the founders of Taoism dominate. Originating in the Jin (265-420 A.D.), the temple's current central Sanqing Hall was built in the Southern Song. The Twin Pagodas, almost in the middle of Suzhou, are known as the big and small 'brushes' (used by Confucius for writing). They were built in the Song in honor of the sage.

A visit to the **pearl farm** in the eastern suburbs is fun for groups. After a 15-minute boat ride, you can choose a living, breathing oyster from the lake, and keep the pearls found within. (Pick a big one.) Contact *Suzhou Fishery Industry, Marine Tourism Service, Huangshiqiao, Fengmen, Suzhou 215006. Tel. 7261987, open 8:30am-3pm.* A pearl wholesale market is open daily 5am-7pm 20 km from Suzhou.

In **Guang Fu**, 25 km east of the city, is a tiny village amid fields of stunted mulberry trees. Here all the women embroider in their homes. I watched a 73-year old work on a Japanese *obi*. A visit can also give you an opportunity to experience rural life.

Nearby

Zhouzhuang is 70 km from Suzhou and 45 km from Shanghai. It is a tiny charming village, where you can take a short 20-minute boat trip along the canals, and eat great food in a dumpy restaurant. It still has Ming architecture, some of it original. **Tongli** is 25 km from Suzhou and has gardens, bridges, and old mansions from the Ming and Qing. Travel agents can arrange for you to travel by boat one hour from one to the other.

The Singapore Labour Federation and Suzhou Municipality has built a huge industrial, commercial, and tourism project in the eastern suburbs. Its 'integrated resort facilities' will include a 36-hole golf course and amusement park. All should be completed before the year 2003. In the meantime, there are several golf courses here.

One of the best is the 18-hole Jack Nicholas-designed **Sun Rise Golf Course** 20 minutes by car west of the Sheraton.

Walks

The gardens are good but can be crowded at times, a little difficult if you want fast-moving exercise. They are lovely, however. Try the large Humble Administrator's and Tiger Hill.

Explore the alleys and follow the canals near the Nan Lin, Suzhou, and Bamboo Grove Hotels.

NIGHTLIFE & ENTERTAINMENT

From mid-March to late November, 7:30pm-10pm daily, Chinese artists perform in the **Master of Nets Garden**, a not-to-be missed experience. See above. Popular bars are in the Aster and Bamboo Grove Hotels. A night market is in front of the Taoist temple on Guanqian Street.

For the **Hash House Harriers** contact Dean and Wendy at *Tel. 6510582* or foreign staff at the Sheraton. The Hash are the drinking people with a running problem. Expat hang-outs are the **Indiana Bar** and the **Jiu Ba** on the same street as the Aster, and the bars between the Nanlin and Suzhou Hotels on Shi Quan Street. Look here for the Tao Yi Ba where you can take your frustrations out in clay and make yourself some pots, while you enjoy a beer. A Silk Festival takes place in early September.

SHOPPING

The main shopping streets are Guanqian Street, Shi Lu Road and Nanmen. The **People's Department Store** (Renmin Shang Chang) at *22 Bei Road* near the Taoist temple is popular. Look for sales and for silk. *Tel. 5221252*. It takes Visa and MasterCard and is open 9am-9pm on weekends, and 9am-8:30pm on weekdays.

Some stores here welcomed US travelers checks and especially cash, if you can show a passport and visa card. Suzhou is a major tourist city; a great variety of crafts are on sale. Available are inkstones, brushes, jewelry, embroideries, silks, traditional musical instruments, antiques, iron reproductions of ancient relics, excellent woodblock prints, and reproductions of some of the *arhats*. Onyx vases here have nice colors and patterns. Also on sale are turquoise carvings, fossils (that could or could not be real), and crystals. It is the best place to buy sandalwood fans but they might just be perfumed so buy from the **Suzhou Sandalwood Fan Factory** and make sure you get a receipt saying they are real. It's at *58 Xibei Street, Tel.*

7537334 and open 8:30am-5pm. **The Jade Carving Factory** is at *33 Baita Road West, Tel. 7271869, 7274169.*

Good to buy here is double-sided embroidery because of the variety available and the prices. Some of the embroideries have embroidered signature chopmarks which implies they might be of high quality from well-known artists. They are not necessarily one-of-a-kind. Good also to buy here are fresh-water pearls.

There are also lots of small polychrome porcelain shard pendants with a curious thumb-size mark on the back which makes us suspect reproductions. But if you get them for Y10 or so, they should make a cheap gift. There are also many small **snuff bottles** painted on the inside, the crystal ones more expensive than glass. Valuable are the ones with recognizable famous people and fine quality painting.

There's good shopping in the tiny curio shops on **Shiquan Road** near the Nan Lin Hotel and Nanyuan Guest House. This quaint tree-lined street has old facades and is being rebuilt to look even older. Many shops are open during the day but most come to life at night until 10pm. Stalls are around the entrance to the Master of Nets Garden (where we found good silk dress shirts for Y40 to Y80.) Look for paintings by local farmer artists. A good antique dealer who seems honest is Mr. Xu Zhi Cheng, **Shyuee Lahng Antiques**, *200 Shi Quan Street, Tel. 5295084.*

There are also antique shops around the **Confucian Temple** open at different times of the day, starting from mid-morning. Vendors in the courtyard don't have much to offer but you might find one or two treasures. Haggling is easier here for textiles, reproductions, old silver, porcelains, Cultural Revolution items, wood carvings, stones, scrolls, paintings, stamps, coins, and old books. The more expensive government **Suzhou Antique Store**, *238 Renmin Road, Tel. 5224972,* has lots of variety.

Guides can take you to a **mahogany furniture factory** making Ming dynasty style furniture. It's on a back street not easy to find on *Liao Jia Lane, Tel. 7532883.* The **night market** is on car-free *Guanqian Street.*

Silk in most stores to which tourists are taken and offering credit card service is good but expensive. Insist on a 50% group discount. Local Chinese buy silk in department stores, or at the **Dong Hu Silk Factory Store**, *540 Renmin Road, Tel. 7274691* or at the **Yuan Long Silk Market**, almost across the road at *532 Renmin Road, Tel. 7272405, 7202942.* Take a look at the **Gusu Silk Bazaar**, *Tel. 531936.* The **No 1 Silk Spinning Mill** can show you the silk-making process.

You can watch double-sided embroidery done at the **Embroidery Research Institute** between 8:30am-5pm. It has a small embroidery museum, *Tel. 5225756,* and is at *262 Jingde Road, Tel. 5222403.* There is a silk market – probably wholesale – which I'm looking for on my next trip. Keep in touch.

We found Y20 woven pearls in a store on the grounds of the North Temple pagoda, while other stores were selling them for Y400 or so.

PRACTICAL INFORMATION

Boat Tours are usually booked through any of the following travel agencies. To book directly, the office is at *271 Sichuan Street, 215006, Tel. 5192930.*

CITS, *115 Shiquan Street* (on the grounds of the Suzhou Hotel), *215006. Tel. 5223783, Fax 5233593, 5223573;* **CITS Group**, *Tel. 5209362, Fax 5233593.*

CTS, *251 Ganjiangxi Road, 215002, Tel. 5231918, Fax 5225931.*

CYTS Tours, *102 Zhu Hui Road, 215007. Tel. 5292774, Fax 5291929.*

Hours, 8am-11am and 1pm-5pm for offices, five days a week.

Jobs: The Suzhou International Foreign Language School has been looking for teachers. *Tel. 5490201, 54909211.*

Suzhou Tourist Bureau, *115 Shiquan Street, 215006. Tel. 5213140, Fax 5192980.* For tourist complaints, *Tel. 5223327, Fax 5192980.*

Telephone code, *0512*

Tourism hotline, *Tel. 5223377, 5223327.*

WUXI

(Wushi)

Wuxi is one of the oldest cities in China, founded over 3000 years ago. After deposits of tin became depleted here, inhabitants changed its name to Wuxi, meaning 'no tin.' It is worth visiting now because of **Taihu Lake**, famous for the rocks used in many of China's classical gardens, and its sail-filled image (October only). It is also known for its gardens, silk and pearls, and the ancient Grand Canal.

The population is 4.2 million of whom one million are urban. The hottest weather is in July at 38 C; the coldest in January, minus four C. The annual precipitation is 1056 millimeters mainly in June.

ARRIVALS & DEPARTURES

Wuxi is 25 minutes by No. 4 express train (8:44am) from Suzhou on the Beijing-Shanghai railway. It is 130 km west of Shanghai's Hongqiao airport (1.5 hours by expressway and about Y600 by taxi). You can get a bus from the Shanghai Stadium leaving once an hour. It is 180 km or two hours plus traffic jams from Nanjing, or one hour (58 km) from Suzhou (Y200-Y500 by taxi, and cheaper by frequent buses) via the Nanjing-Shanghai expressway. It is over five hours by train from Hangzhou.

You can also take a boat between Hangzhou and Wuxi but expect a long uncomfortable overnight trip with nothing to see.

ORIENTATION

Wuxi sits on the northeast shore of Lake Taihu, south of the Yangtze River in southern Jiangsu province. The main tourist area is along the lake with its peninsula and islands. To the east about 12 km is downtown with shops, crafts factories, temples, and the Grand Canal.

WHERE TO STAY

The best hotel is the **Sheraton**, which along with the **New World** is in the bustling downtown area convenient for business people and shoppers. The **Wuxi Grand** is also near the top, while the New World is the next best downtown. The **Milido** is worn-looking except for its new fancy recreation center. The Sheraton and the New World are the closest to the railway station. Only about seven minutes drive southwest near the Grand Canal in a residential district are the Wuxi Grand and the Milido. They are near the main bus station and a morning street market, separated from each other by a steady stream of motor vehicles all day.

About eight km away beside Lake Taihu and accessible by expressway without having to confront traffic jams downtown, the older **Hubin Hotel** is next to Liyuan Garden and is one of the best hotels in town. Newer, more beautiful, and more luxurious is the **Lakeview Garden**, a few kilometers closer to the big buddha and the Three Kingdoms theme park. I haven't had a chance to try it, so if you do, tell me about the service.

Hotels here add 10% to 15% service charge. All accept credit cards, have money exchange, business center, air-conditioning, etc. The following prices are subject to change, and discounts.

SHERATON WUXI HOTEL & TOWERS (Shi Lai Tun Dafandian), *Garden City Mall, 443 Zhongshan Road, 214001. Tel. 2721888, Fax 2752781. Http://www.ittsheraton.com. Five stars. 396 rooms and 66 apartments. $155 for rooms, and $250-$880 for suites.*

Every room here has a swivel chair by the desk, voice mail, one-touch service buttons, safes, HBO and CNN. Each also has an ironing board and iron. This hotel has a gym, a heated, indoor pool with retractable roof, and attached shopping center. It has day care and a marvelous bar, each booth with its own Fosters' tap, a gauge measuring the amount drunk, and a sign giving the table's record. Someplace Else has great fries and good pizza. It also has an outdoor lighted tennis court and function rooms with access to its garden. The decor is contemporary with Chinese touches.

MILIDO HOTEL WUXI (Milido Dajiudian), *2 Liangxi Road 214062. Three stars, Tel. 5865665, Fax 5801668, 5807348. Email: milido@public1.wx.js.cn. Twenty km from the airport, five km from the railway station, and four km from Lake Taihu. $105-$148 for rooms and $190-$888 for suites.*

Opened in 1987-1988, this ten story, 251-room hotel also has apartments with kitchenettes. It boasts the largest pool in Wuxi, a gym and squash. Rooms are small, clean with stained carpets, and have kettles, safes, and six television channels in English. Formerly a Holiday Inn, this is now managed by Shanghai Huating Hotels.

NEW WORLD COURTYARD BY MARRIOTT WUXI (formerly Ramada and now Xin Shi Jie Wan Yi Jiudian), *335 Zhongshan Road, 214001. Tel. 2762888, Fax 2763388. Three stars. The 280 rooms here include 22 apartments with kitchenettes. $105-$125 for rooms; $160-$200 for suites.*

Standard rooms are medium sized with small baths and all rooms should have safes and HBO now. The carpets however were stained and you need to ask for a room with no one on either side, but it's otherwise fine.

WUXI LAKEVIEW PARK RESORT, *Tai Lake Shanshuicheng Tourism Zone, 214081. Tel. 5555888, Fax 5556909. Five km from the Three Kingdoms theme park, and seven km from downtown. Four stars. Y588 to Y688 for rooms, Y1188 to Y1888 for suites. Its 151 rooms have safes, HBO and should have CNN soon.*

This Hong Kong joint venture has a small indoor pool, gym, snooker, four tennis courts, bowling, and archery. It also has conference facilities, free shuttle bus and a beer garden. From its 250 meters of lake front, you can see Istanbul (in the theme park across the bay).

LAKESIDE HOTEL (Hubin Fandian), *Hubin Road, Li Yuan, 214075. Tel. 5101888, Fax 5102637. Four stars. Twenty-three km from the airport, 12 km from the railway station, and five km from city center. Y580-Y830 for rooms, and Y996-Y1245 for suites in the 10-story main building; Y996-Y2075 for rooms, and Y4150-Y16600 for suites in the Jing-Xuan building; Y200-Y450 for rooms and Y760 for a suite in the lesser-quality Shuixiu Garden.*

Opened in 1978, this hotel is set in a 30,000 sq. meter lake-side garden. Some of its 365 rooms are small and modest. It has a pool, CNN and clinic. It is noted for its good food and floating restaurant.

PAN PACIFIC HOTEL WUXI/WUXI GRAND HOTEL (Wuxi Dafandian), *1 Liangqing Road, 214061, Four stars, Tel. 5806789, Fax 2700991. In North America Tel. 800/327-8785. E-mail:bc.pwgh@public1.wx.js.cn (Public Relations). 22 km from the airport and four km from the railway station. Y520-Y1460 for rooms, and Y960-Y3240 for suites.*

Built in 1989, with renovations 1996-1999, this 22-story, 342-room hotel has suites with kitchens. This Japanese joint venture has non-smoking and executive floors, Japanese, Cantonese, Shanghai and Sichuan food, and live music. Its ballroom can accommodate 500 people banquet-style. It has a gym and clinic. A shuttle service connects with the railway station. It can make arrangements for you to golf. Pan Pacific management.

WHERE TO EAT

Local specialties include ice fish, spareribs, deep-fried eel, crabs, and shrimp. The hotels listed above will be your best bet here. We like the **New World's** goodlooking Chinese restaurant, especially the chicken and shrimp balls, baked barbecue pork puff pastry, and *dim sum*. The **Sheraton** can arrange for boats to take you along the Grand Canal, even from Wuxi to Shanghai. It can of course cater the food here and on train coaches.

SOUTH CHINA RESTAURANT, *near the railway station, Tel. 2707483.* This is a good place.

JIAN NAN RESTAURANT, *61 Tong Yuan Road near the train station, Tel. 2707483.* Moderate prices, no credit card service.

WUXI ROAST DUCK RESTAURANT, *222 Zhong Shan Road, Tel. 2729435.* Wuxi food, no credit cards, located near the New World Courtyard.

SEEING THE SIGHTS

We highly recommend the three-hour daytime tour boat from Wuxi to Suzhou along the **Grand Canal** for about Y100. Tour groups have also taken a speedboat from Wuxi 1.5 hours to Huzhou (ancient writing brush factory), and then a two-hour bus to Hangzhou. Ask a travel agent.

Near the Hubin Hotel, the **Liyuan Garden** has a 'thousand-steps veranda,' with 89 windows on the inside wall. At the **Meiyuan** (Plum) **Garden**, the plum blossoms are best appreciated in the early spring. These are both beside Lake Taihu. On the peninsula is **Yuantouzhu** (Turtle Head) **Park**, 17 km west of the city. South of here, movie and television companies have opened their sets to tourists.

The best sight to see is **The Three Kingdoms** (220-265 A.D.) with its twenty reproduced miniature 1800-year old warships from which flames explode. This theme park also has a show with real galloping horses and fighting costumed riders. But prepare for no shade, and lots of walking between interesting buildings, the waterfront, and reproductions of famous sites from the book. Better still, make notes from the book and try to identify the sites. The entrance fee is Y60 and it's open 8am-4pm. English-speaking guides alas are not available. *Tel. 5805117.* Don't waste time at any of the other nearby theme parks in this neighborhood.

Twenty km southwest of the city on the other side of Taihu Lake is a 101.5 meter-high (including base) cheerful **standing Buddha**, 760 tons of bronze. (The Statue of Liberty is 93 meters high including the base.) It's worth the trip if you consider the amazing workmanship going into something that big. But you might get turned off too by the commercialization of a religious symbol.

Wuxi is also a silk-producing center, the hills around the city filled with mulberry trees. Tourists can learn about silk, from silkworm rearing through the printing and dyeing process at a **silk factory**. You can take cruises on the lake and along the Canal. You can also visit Huaxi Village, 1.5 hours away for demonstrations of ancient farming and village life. These can be arranged by travel agents. A good time to visit is the Mid-Autumn Festival, with lots of colored lanterns, moon cakes, and an evening cruise on the lake and, one hopes, a full moon.

Festivals: The week-long Lake Tai Arts Festival features folk dancing and singing; and the Cherry and Pottery festivals are held in April.

SHOPPING

Good locally-made products include hand-painted clay figurines, embroidery, fresh-water pearls, pearl face cream, and silk. Also made in the province are porcelain, and Yixing purple sand pottery (especially tea pots in collectible shapes and sizes).

The **Bird**, **Fish and Pet Market** opposite CITS at the **Nanchan Temple** has the best prices for old coins, pearls, stamps, art work, pearls, antiques and reproductions. Some prices are marked but vendors come down from them easily. This is a fascinating market around a wonderful old temple with huge deities and monks burning incense and open about 9am-5pm. Just out of curiosity, look for the unusual puppies for sale displaying orange squares, circles and stripes on black coats. How were they dyed that way? Were they dyed that way? No credit cards are accepted here.

The **Purple Sand Pottery Special Sales Corporation** has two government stores back to back, open 8:30am-5:30pm daily. *Tel. 5868742 or 5883943* for directions. This is a typical government tourist trap but if you want collectors' items with certificates of famous potters, you can get them here for up to Y10,000. Avoid the other over-priced goods. Try the shops across the smaller tree-lined side street for better prices, like the **Wuxi Bao Feng Shi Ye Gong Si**, *Tel. 5807496*. It is open 8am-5pm.

You should do a lot of hard bargaining at the expensive **Wuxi Antique store**, *Tel. 5883943*. It is open 8:30am-6:30pm daily. Pearls were reasonable at the **Orient Pearls and Jewels Co.** which takes credit cards. It's at *Bao Jie Bridge, Tel. 5802619*. It is open 8am-6pm daily.

The **Wuxi Clay Figurine Research Institute** is open 8am-4pm daily. It is at *8-1 Xiahetang, Huishan,* in a charming neighborhood of old houses, *Tel. 3709594.* You should be able to see artists make these cute hand-painted clay figures in the mornings, a folk art from the Ming dynasty. It also produces embroidery and accepts credit cards. Prices, however, are cheaper at the stores just outside and down the block.

Number One Silk Spinning Mill has a display of silkworms and reasonable prices for garments. *Tel. 5012461, 5014649.* **Parkson's Department Store** is across from the New World Courtyard. Avoid the **Pearl Research Center** on the peninsula north of The Three Kingdoms where an English-speaking guide misinformed us about pearls. The woven pearls here cost 30 times the price of the same thing in the market.

EXCURSIONS & DAY TRIPS

You can take excursions to **Yixing** and the nearby (69 km) Yixing purple sandware ceramic factory (the best teapots in China), ceramic museum, and tea plantations. There's also the Yixing limestone caves, bamboo forest, and **Jiangyin** (home of Ming dynasty scientist and traveler Xu Xiake). Jiangyin and Huaxi village can be combined in one day's sightseeing. These are on the west side of Lake Taihu.

The best hotel is the **International Hotel** at *52 Tongzhengguan Road, 214200. Tel. 7916888.* **CITS** is at *2 Renmin Zhong Road, 214200, Tel. 7982372.* See also Nanjing and Shanghai above.

PRACTICAL INFORMATION

CITS, *7 Xin Sheng Road, 214002. Tel. 2700268, 2700416* for the English Dept. *Fax 2701489.*

CYTS, *6/F, the Youth Culture Center, Jin Yan Dong Bridge, 214023. Tel. 5748904, Fax 5757653.*

Hours 8am-5pm five days a week (offices). Department stores are open 9am-7 or 8pm, daily, and street markets all day or from 7pm-9pm.

Telephone Code *0510*

Wuxi China Travel Service, *88 Chezhan Road, 214005, Tel. 2304030, Faz 2302743.*

Wuxi Municipal Travel and Tourism Bureau, *7 Xinsheng Road, 214002. Tel. 2704314, Fax 2729644 or 2703851.* **Complaints** *Tel. 2728218 or 16801111* voice mail.

Wuxi Overseas Tourist Corporation, *7 Xinsheng Road, 214002, Tel. 2754026, 2762480, Fax 2716780. Email:wxotc@public1.wx.js.cn. Complaints to Xu Jirong or Wang Bosheng.*

Wuxi website: *http://wxtour.opchlna.com.*

YANGZHOU
(Yangchow)

Yangzhou is a charming little city 20 km north of the Yangtze on the Grand Canal in Jiangsu province. It is almost 2,500 years old and famous for its gardens and classical architecture. It is worth a special trip, a nice change from the hectic pace of other Chinese cities. Because of its location, it was a very prosperous port after the building of the canal in the seventh century. In the Tang dynasty, it was the residence of over 5,000 foreigners. One of the Prophet Mohammed's descendants is buried here, and from 1282 **Marco Polo** is said to have spent three years as inspector here. Yangzhou's wealth declined with that of the canal, and by the Qing it was famous only as an imperial resort city.

The hottest temperature is 34 C in July-August; the coldest is -2 C in January-February. The annual rainfall is about 1000 millimeters, mainly from June to September. Its population is 4.4 million of whom 500,000 live in the city proper.

ARRIVALS & DEPARTURES

Yangzhou can now be reached in less than two hours by the expressway from Nanjing. You must cross the Yangtze River either by ferry or bridge. You can go by boat along the Grand Canal from Hangzhou but it is a very long trip. Overnight steam boats ply between Wuhan, Shanghai and Yangzhou, or just from Shanghai to Yangzhou, cheaper, slower and less comfortable than the train. The closest airport is at Nanjing 80 km away. The closest railway is in Zhenjiang on the other side of the Yangtze 28 km away. A new four-km bridge should be built here in 2002 over the Yangtze.

ORIENTATION

Yangzhou is one of the 24 historical and cultural cities protected by the State Council. All new buildings must be in traditional Chinese style and industries must be confined to the suburbs.

WHERE TO STAY

The best located hotels for tourists are the **Xi Yuan** and **Yangzhou**, with good gardens close to the museum and tourist stores in the northwestern suburbs. The **State Guest House** is a possible alternative although English is a problem, and service is more oriented to domestic travelers. The **Yangzhou** has the best service and is a good place to eat. Hotels here add 10% surcharge.

YANGZHOU HOTEL (Binguan), *5 Fengle Shang Street, 225002. Four stars, Tel. 7342611, Fax 7343599. Credit Cards. Y480 in its old wing; Y704 in its new wing.*
Built in 1985 and renovated in 1998, this nine-story, 150-room hotel has a business center, gym, indoor pool and CNN. You can request a safe in your room.
STATE GUEST HOUSE. *1 Changchun Road, 225002. Tel. 7325288, Fax 7331674. Close to Slender West Lake. Y480-Y800 for rooms, Y1380-Y8800 for suites.*
The section for tourists has small rooms and baths, a safe in your room on request, and CNN. This is a beautiful-looking hotel in traditional Chinese architecture with spacious lawns and indoor pool.
XI YUAN HOTEL (Fandian), *1 Fengle Shang Street, 225002. Four stars, Tel. 7344888, Fax 7233870. Main building Y620-630 for rooms, Y1456-Y8728 for suites. Cheaper, less luxurious rooms for Y256 and up. Credit cards.*
Built in 1976 and looking beautiful in 1998, this five-story hotel has 210 beds for foreigners, small baths, and dirty carpets. It has an outdoor and indoor pool and lighted tennis court on the roof but unfortunately no elevator.

WHERE TO EAT

"Thousand-layer oily cake" may sound awful, but it is delicious. People also go to Yangzhou from Nanjing for the dumplings. Both the **Yangzhou** and **Xi Yuan hotels** can reproduce a banquet from the novel *Dream of the Red Mansion*; the author's father lived here.
At the Yangzhou Hotel, delicious dishes include salty goose, double-colored Mandarin fish slices, sliced dried bean curd in chicken soup, and duck's blood with green soy beans.

SEEING THE SIGHTS

The highlight is the boat trip on **Slender West Lake**, but Yangzhou has other things to offer. Both Qing Emperors Qianlong and Kangxi took this five-km long cruise about six times each. It will take you about two hours with stops. You board near the Yangzhou Hotel and you'll see 24 of Shouxi (Slender West) Lake's relaxing, exquisite scenic spots: curled-roof pavilions, potted landscape garden, and imposing White Dagoba (Qing). You can also follow the river by road and visit many of the same places more cheaply but a boat is more fun and historical.
The **Five Pavilion Bridge** was built for Qianlong's visit. It is best seen on the night of a full moon, when 15 moons are supposed to reflect in the water under the arches, a Chinese puzzle that must be seen to be understood. You'll see the **Daming Temple**, founded in the fifth century,

with its 18 three-meter-high carved Buddhist statues. The beautiful **Jian Zhen Memorial Hall** here was built in 1973 to commemorate the 1,200th anniversary of the death of Monk Jian Zhen. It is a copy of the Toshodai Temple in Nara, Japan. This abbot of Daming Temple persisted in going to Japan to teach Buddhism in spite of five unsuccessful attempts and his blindness. He succeeded at age 66. Because he and his disciples also introduced Tang literature, medicine, architecture, sculpture, and other arts to Japan, he is highly honored in that country, where he died and is buried. The statue of Jian Zhen is a recent copy of a 1,000 year-old-plus statue, a national Japanese treasure. The original was brought back for a visit in 1980 'because it looked homesick' but was destroyed in a fire in Japan in 1998. *Tel. 7340720.*

Along the way, you can also look for the bird and fish market, the former city moat, and the 24-Maid Bridge. The four larger-than-life jade buddhas can only be seen between 7:30am-5pm and are lovely. There are also a 70 meter-high pagoda and two three-ton iron cauldrons used to feed the dragon king and control floods. You can visit all these places on foot or by bus,

Prepaid tours might also visit a lacquerware, jade-carving and paper-cutting factory.

The **Yangzhou Museum** next to the Yangzhou Hotel was originally a temple, later turned into a temporary palace. It has a Marco Polo Hall to which modern day Italians sent a bronze lion, the symbol of Venice. There are two Italian tombstones on display, dated 1342 and 1344. An antique and curio market is here, liveliest on weekends.

The charming **Geyuan Garden** in the east of the city, started as a private garden, and later became the home of the Ye Chun Poet's Society in the Qing. It is full of gnarled rockeries, moon gates, bamboo, latticed doorways, wavy walls, and real picture windows. The rockeries are built around a spring-summer-autumn-winter theme. Do these inspire you, too, to poetry? It's on *Dongguan Zhong Street.*

The **Heyuan Garden**, in the southeastern part of the city on *Xu Nin Men Street* is typical of Yangzhou's gardens. The Islamic-styled **Tomb of Puhaddin** is on the east bank of the Grand Canal, near the Heyuan. Built in the 13th century, it contains the remains of this 16th generation descendant of Mohammed, the founder of Islam. Puhaddin (Burhdn Al-Dan) came to China as a missionary in the Southern Song. The 700-year-old **Xianhe** (Crane) **Mosque** is one of the four most famous in China, and was built between 1265 and 1275. It is worth a visit and is open daily except Fridays.

Further afield, you can visit **Zhenjiang** and **Nanjing** from here on day trips. 50 km east is **Gaoyu County** where farmers have trained wild ducks to respond to human commands. This trip is available every month except April and May through travel agents.

SHOPPING

Good local products are lacquerware, red lacquer carving, jade carving, velvet flowers, paper cuts, and silk lanterns. Yangzhou also exports potted landscapes, miniature trees and tiny mountains. Better quality goods than the museum market but less fun to buy are at the **Yangzhou Cultural Relic and Antique Shop**, *1 Yanfu Xi Road, Tel. 342987, 349610.* It is open 8:30am-6pm. The **Yangzhou Jadeware Factory** is at *6 Guangchumen Outer Street, 225002, Tel. 7348040, Fax 7348324.* The **Lacquerware Factory** is at *50 Yanhe Street, Tel. 7347127, Fax 7340265.* The **Friendship Store** is at *454 Guoqing Bei Road,* with adjacent antique store.

PRACTICAL INFORMATION

CITS, *6 Fengle Shangjie Street, 225002, Tel. 7348925, Fax 7344278*
Telephone Code, 0514
Yangzhou Tourism Bureau, *1 Fengle Shangjie Street, 225002, Tel. 7343669, Fax 7343646. Email:yz.lyj@public.yz.js.cn.*

ZHENJIANG

(Chinkiang, Chenchiang, Chenkiang)

Zhenjiang should be visited because of **Pearl S. Buck**. It is in central Jiangsu province, where the Grand Canal meets the south bank of the Yangtze. It is bounded on three sides by hills and on the north by the Yangtze River.

Zhenjiang is an historic old city, the streets lined with plane trees, some of its houses small and whitewashed like Suzhou's, others black brick with courtyards. The city was founded in the Zhou. It boasts 2,500 years of history, including seven years as the capital of the Eastern Wu (third century), when it was called Jingko (entrance to Nanjing). In the Qin dynasty (221-206 B.C.), 3,000 prisoners were sent here to build canals and roads. Many battles were fought in the area and the city is mentioned in the novel *The Romance of the Three Kingdoms*.

During the Yuan, Zhenjiang was visited by Marco Polo. The first British missionaries arrived in the 17th century. Toward the end of the First Opium War, it was the only city that strongly resisted the imperialists. After that failed, however, about 1,000 foreigners, mainly merchants and missionaries from Britain, Germany, and the United States lived here. The foreigners left their mark on some of the architecture and on education.

In 1938, Marshall Chen Yi's New Fourth Army was stationed about 50 km away, and some skirmishes with the Japanese took place in the area. In April 1949, the British warship *H.M.S. Amethyst,* while rescuing British citizens upriver, was caught in the crossing of the Yangtze by the People's Liberation Army and held for over three months here. The captain refused to cooperate or admit his ship fired first. Under cover of a passing passenger boat, the Amethyst finally escaped.

Its hottest temperature, in July and August, is 35 C, with breezes from the Yangtze; its coldest is -3 C from the middle to the end of January. The annual precipitation is 1000 millimeters mainly in July. The urban population is 500,000.

ARRIVALS & DEPARTURES

Zhenjiang is about one hour by train (63 km) east of Nanjing, and about four hours (220 km) northwest of Shanghai. The closest airport is about 60 km away at Nanjing.

WHERE TO STAY

The **Zhenjiang Hotel** is better for business people and Pearl Buck fans. It is downtown near her home. Hotels add 10% surcharge and accept credit cards.

INTERNATIONAL HOTEL ZHENJIANG, *218 Jiefang Road, 212001, Tel. 5021888, Fax 5021777. Four stars. $68-$88 for rooms, and $108-$988 for suites.*

This 31-story hotel has a pool and revolving restaurant.

ZHENJIANG HOTEL, *92 Zhong Shan Xi Road, 212004. Tel. 5233888, Fax 5231055. 300 meters from the railway station. Four stars.*

Built in 1963 and expanded since, this hotel has BBC and CNN, 188 rooms and 10 suites, an indoor pool, tennis court, bowling and a gym.

WHERE TO EAT

The best restaurants are in the hotels.

A local specialty is crab cream bun, a steamed meat pastry. Make a hole first and slurp out the soup inside. Food here is concerned with fragrance, shape, and color, and is neither too sweet nor too salty. You might find your *hors d'oeuvres* looking like butterflies, peacocks, or fans. Everything can be dipped in vinegar.

SEEING THE SIGHTS

If you only have one day, consider seeing Jinshan Hill, Jiao Shan Island, the museum, Pearl S. Buck's house, and the Thousand-Year-Old Street.

PEARL S. BUCK, FRIEND OF CHINA

The American Nobel and Pulitzer Prize-winning author Pearl S. Buck (1892-1973) grew up here, studied in what is now the Zhenjiang Second Middle School (founded 1884) and taught here (1914-17), a total of 18 years. In the past, China criticized her for being 'imperialist' and ignored her writings. In the 1950s, US Senator Joseph McCarthy accused her of being a Communist. Zhenjiang and sister city Tempe, Arizona, have renovated one of her homes as the Zhenjiang Friendship House or Sino-US Cultural Exchange Center, for the 100th anniversary of her birth.

The home is also for the study of foreign missions and her books. They would appreciate copies of her books: Good Earth, Imperial Women, Dragon Seed, My Several Worlds, etc. You can talk with some of her old students. Pearl S. Buck has a foundation based outside Philadelphia supporting American-Asian children.

Friendship House, her home is at 6 Runzhoushan Road, 212004. Tel. 5234174, Fax 5236425.

Thousand year old tiny **Xiao Matai Street** has an unusual Song or Yuan stupa built above the sidewalk. **Jiao Hill** (150 meters high) on **Jiao Shan Island** is less than half a kilometer from the city. For the ferry to Jiao Shan Island, *Tel. 8815502*. It operates 8am-5pm. Up 250 steps is a magnificent view of the Yangtze. All three of Zhenjiang's hills have magnificent views of the Yangtze, and you can see the place where the Chinese held the Amethyst. What would you have done if you were captain?

Back at the base of Jiao Hill, you can look at the **Battery**, which was used against the British in 1842. Also below is a garden with steles of many calligraphers, including that of the father of modern calligraphy, Wang Hsi-chih, who lived 1,500 years ago. At the loquat orchard and the Din Hui Buddhist Temple, the Red Guards destroyed most of the Ming statues. The existing statues were made in 1979.

Jinshan (Golden Hill), at *62 Jinshan Road, 212002, Tel. 5281631*, one km from the Jinshan Hotel, looks better from afar than close up. The temple here was first built 1500 years ago (Jin) and rebuilt several times since, a victim of lightning, fire, and weather. The current pagoda was finished in 1900 with animal carvings, in time for the Empress Dowager Cixi's birthday. It reflects her crude tastes. Seven stories tall, 30 meters high, it is easier climbing up the 119 steps than down because the steps are shallow.

There are some fun caves, all the more interesting because of the presence in one cave of the white, ghastly-looking, life-size figure of the monk Fa Hai, and in another the two beautiful women said to be the White Snake and the Blue (sometimes Green) Snake, both fairies. The cave is said to reach Hangzhou!

Other Sights & Tours

The **museum** is housed in the former British consulate building, *85 Boxian Road and Daxi Road, 212002, Tel. 5277317, 5277143,* open 8am-5pm daily. It includes the former Southern Baptist mission residences. Its permanent collection includes an anchor from the British ship Amethyst, a land lease refers to the 'former British Concession lot and the tomb stone of the famous missionary Hudson Taylor.' A tiny silver coffin found under the nearby Iron Pagoda contains two gold coffins and the ashes of a Buddhist saint. Charming is the Song porcelain pillow in the shape of a sleeping child. No titles are in English.

SHOPPING

Dashikou is Zhenjiang's main shopping area. Factories here make elaborate palace lanterns and are famous for their 'crystal' meat and vinegar. Also made in the city are silk, jade carvings, paper cuttings, and silk birds.

THE SNAKE STORY & CHINESE OPERA

The story of the Snakes is also the plot of a famous Beijing opera. Briefly, the several thousand-year-old White Snake from Mount Emei (the Blue Snake is the maid) becomes a beautiful woman and goes to Hangzhou. There, at the Tuanqiao (the Bridge of Breaking Up), she falls in love with a scholar, and eventually the two marry.

The White Snake, using her magic powers, takes money from a government official to build a house, but because the official's seal is still on the money, the young man is arrested and ordered beaten for theft. The White Snake again uses her magic so that whenever her husband is beaten, the official's wife feels the pain. Consequently, the young man is expelled to Zhenjiang.

After his arrival, the monk master Fa Hai, jealous of their happiness, tries to separate the couple, but the White Snake floods the area, including Jin Shan temple. They are reunited at the Tuanqiao. The unrelenting monk master retaliates by imprisoning the White Snake under the Leifeng pagoda in Hangzhou. There she is rescued by the Blue Snake. The White Snake, her husband, and her son are reunited and live happily ever after.

This is a popular Chinese tale and a study of its symbolism and the psychology of its popularity could keep a folklorist busy for years.

PRACTICAL INFORMATION

CITS, *25 Jianking Road, 212001, Tel. 5237538, Fax 5244818.*
CTS, *6 Jiankang Road, 212001. Tel. 5016926, 5207663, Fax 5017911.*
Telephone code *0511*
Zhenjiang Culture Travel Service, *25 Jiankang Road, 212001. Tel. 5231806, Fax 5012245.*

Zhenjiang Travel and Tourism Bureau, *92 Zhongshan Xi Road, 212004. Tel. 5232959, Fax 5236425.*

17. NORTH & NORTHEAST CHINA

TIANJIN

(Tientsin)

Tianjin is China's fourth largest city. The urban population is six million, the total nine. It's a good shopping city (cheaper than Beijing) as well as a museum of 19th European century architecture and history. Go there for the antique market.

Tianjin has been inhabited for 2500 years. It was not until after the Grand Canal opened in the seventh century that inland commerce and Tianjin's fortunes started to improve. During the Ming (1404), city walls were built and the city was called Tianjinwei by the Duke of Yen, who crossed the Haihe River here on a military expedition.

The British and French invaded Tianjin in 1858. In June of that year they and the Chinese signed the **Treaty of Tientsin** giving Christian missionaries freedom of movement and protection "because the Christian religion as professed by Protestants and Roman Catholics inculcates the practices of virtue, and teaches man to do as he would be done by." In 1860, British and French troops from Tianjin marched on Beijing and forced the Qing rulers to ratify the Treaty of Tientsin; they then burned down the Summer Palace. The resulting Treaty of Peking opened Tianjin and nine other ports to foreign trade.

Nine countries eventually controlled over 3,500 acres of this city: Britain, France, Germany, Japan, Russia, Italy, Belgium, Austria, and the United States. The concessions lasted from 20 to 80 years and, as in Shanghai, left the Chinese some very interesting old European architecture as well as bitter memories. The **Treaty of Peking** also forced the Chinese to permit French missionaries to own or rent property in China, and further helped to inflame smoldering anti-Christian and anti-foreign resentment.

Many of these feelings resulted from what the Chinese saw as Christian arrogance, which insisted that the Christian god was the only true god. Added to this were cultural misunderstandings. Quite a few

Chinese actually believed that the children in Catholic orphanages were either eaten by nuns or ground up for medicine. The French Catholics did pay money for female babies - to keep them from being killed. By 1870, the atmosphere had grown so tense that after the French consul fired at a minor Chinese official, the consul was immediately hacked to death. Ten nuns, two priests, and another French official were also brutally killed in what is now known as the Tientsin Massacre, or what the Chinese prefer to call the **Tientsin Revolt**. In 1976, an earthquake centered in nearby Tangshan severely damaged the city.

The weather is hottest in July briefly at 40 C, and coldest in January, -10 C. The annual precipitation averages 600 millimeters, mostly in July and August.

ARRIVALS & DEPARTURES

Tianjin, 80 km from the Bohai Sea, is two hours (120 km) southeast of Beijing by train on the Beijing-Shanghai and Beijing-Harbin railway lines. There are three express trains a day with Beijing.

It is also joined by expressway to Beijing by a fleet of air-conditioned Korean buses, Y30 one way, leaving every 30 minutes from the Hongqi bus station in Tianjin. Buses from Beijing to Tianjin go from the Beijing East Railway station and Zhaogongkou in Fengtai District. Count on 2.5 hours plus traffic jams in both cities between the Hyatt Hotel and Beijing airport. Taxis range from Y500 and up. From the Hyatt Hotel, it also takes 50 minutes (70 km) by car to the port of Tanggu via the expressway. There are four trains a day there, about an hour's trip.

Tianjin has air connections with Hong Kong, Nagoya, and 29 Chinese cities. International flights to Tianjin have been cut back recently and some foreign airlines provide buses from Tianjin to connect with their flights at Beijing airport. CAAC also has a bus from its ticket office in Tianjin every hour to the Beijing airport for about Y70.

Tianjin also has sea passenger routes with Inchon (a 28-hour trip leaving Korea every five days), Kobe (a 48-hour trip leaving Japan every Thursday), Dalian (leaving Tianjin on even days) and Yantai (leaving Tianjin six times a month).

ORIENTATION

Tianjin is more of a gateway to elsewhere than a tourist destination in itself. It is a port city, the largest commercial seaport in north China. It is now one of China's biggest industrial centers. Tianjin is mainly for business travelers but in between appointments, there are things to do in addition to golf and sports. Resident foreigners say it is a good place to live because the people are friendlier and more polite than in Shanghai and Beijing, and the sightseeing is less crowded. Many of Beijing's residents drive the two hours to Tianjin on weekends for a change of pace and its **antique and curio market**.

Tianjin is one of four municipalities directly under the central government. It has eight urban and four rural districts, and five suburban counties. The Dagang Oil Field, for example, is 60 km away, but it's part of Tianjin. Its factories make Flying Pigeon bicycles, Seagull watches, petrochemicals, textiles, and diesel engines. Its counties grow walnuts, chestnuts, dates, rice, and prawns. The city is rather smoggy. You might be interested in seeing its arts and crafts factories.

The city proper sprawls on both sides of the Hai River. The area immediately southwest of the Jiefang (Liberation) Bridge was formerly French. The section south of that, around the Astor Hotel, was formerly British. Liberation Road was Victoria Road.

WHERE TO STAY

The **Sheraton** and the **Hyatt** are the best hotels here. Both are good and luxurious with executive floors. The Sheraton is best for families. The Hyatt borders the Haihe River and is more central, closer to government offices and the antique market. The Sheraton is in a quieter district within walking distance of the 400 meter-high telecommunications tower, CITS, and the Friendship store. It is also near the World Economy Trade and Exhibition Centre which has its own hotel, the Geneva, a cheaper alternative.

The **Astor Hotel** is almost next door to the Hyatt, both about 20 km from the airport and three km from the railway station. Hotels here all take credit cards, book tickets, change money and have business centers. All hotels add a 15% surcharge and about Y5 tax.

SHERATON TIANJIN HOTEL (Sher Er Don), *Zi Jin Shan Road, Hexi District, 300074. Five stars. Tel. 23343388, Fax 23358740. It is 15 km from the airport, and nine km from the railway station. It has a complimentary scheduled airport shuttle. $185-$195 for rooms; $205-$780 for suites.*

Built in 1987, this six-story, 282-room hotel also has 64 apartments. It has non-smoking rooms, CNN, HBO and BBC, and Japanese, western and Chinese restaurants. It has bicycles for rent, gym, two lighted tennis courts, putting green and steam bath. For families, it has a lounge with baby sitter and toys, and a supermarket. An ATM (Visa Plus and Cirrus) is in its lobby. Its internet is one of the cheapest for hotels. Its rooms for women have pink bathrooms, nail files, and makeup mirrors.

HYATT TIANJIN (Kai Yue Fandian), *219 Jiefang Bei Road, 300042. Four stars. Tel. 23318888, Fax 23310021. E-mail:hyatttj@public1.tpt.tj.cn. $185 for rooms, and $230 to $1200 for suites.*

Built in 1986, this 19-story, 450-room hotel is in great shape. It has CNN and HBO, kettles, and mini-bars in its rooms. The river view is best.

It has 24-hour room service and business center, and Cantonese, Chaozhou, Tianjin, western and Japanese restaurants. Its two executive club floors have only suites. It has bicycles, a well-equipped gym with steam bath and sauna, golf-driving range, basketball court and children's playground. Its ball room seats 300 for dinner.

HOLIDAY INN TIANJIN, *290 Zhong Shan Road, Hebei District, 200141. About four-star standard. Tel. 26288888, Fax 26286666. Http:// www.holiday-inn.com. E-mail:hotel@mail.hitianjin.com. $130-$150 for rooms, $280-$300 for suites.*

A long block from the Hai River, four km from the railway station, and 18 km from Tianjin international airport, this 1997 hotel is a little bit out of the way. It would make a good conference site. Its ballroom can serve a sit-down dinner for 300. With 263 rooms and suites, executive and non-smoking floors, this 29-story hotel has a handy ATM (Cirrus, Visa Plus) in its spacious soft-beige lobby, and 24-hour room service and business center. It has a delicatessen, western, Cantonese and Asian food. Its unusual-shaped rooms have CNN, HBO, CNBC, safes, and kettles. It has a gym and indoor pool.

ASTOR HOTEL, (Lixun De Fandian), *33 Taier Zhuang Road, 300040. Four stars. Tel. 23311688, 23311112, Fax 23316282. E-mail: astorbc@mail.zlnet.com.cn. $130-$150 for rooms; $220-$880 for suites. You should be able to get a good discount. Two executive floors.*

Originally built by the British in 1863, and expanded in 1924 and 1987, it's provided a bed for US President Herbert Hoover. The charming old wing has 94 big rooms. The new wing has 129 rooms. This is the hotel for people who like history, and much of it is in English on plaques and in its stunning lobby mural. Look for "the reproduction of Emperor Guang-Xu's dick," a line from its booklet "The Sightseeing of the Hundred Year's History of Astor Tianjin, China." But it also has modern facilities like CNN and safes in its rooms, and an ATM (Cirrus, MasterCard, Visa Plus) in the lobby. But "The ATM doesn't always have money," said a clerk.

WHERE TO EAT

The top hotels have the best food, but you might want to try one of these too:

NANSHI FOOD STREET, *Tel. 27351784 or 2350900*, has three stories of shops, restaurants, wine shops, and tea houses – but very little English. The food here is from all over China and abroad, and includes typical Tianjin snacks such as *goubuli* (steamed meat dumpling), *erduoyan* (fried cake), and *shibajie* (deep-fried dough twist). For Japanese food and hotpot try the **Fusoen Restaurant** here, *Tel. 27283333*.

COSY CAFE AND BAR, *To the left as you leave the Hyatt Hotel, towards the river, under the overpass. Tel. 23127870. It's open 10:30am-2am and accepts no credit cards.*

This cute, little place with checkered table cloths, live music and reasonable prices has good sandwiches, good light western food, but stale popcorn.

BROADWAY CAFE,*74 Munan Street, Tel. 23300541.*

This is moderately priced with a good reputation, but we had poor Mexican food (Y50 Friday evening special). Its summer time patio is so pleasant, however, do give it another chance. The English is good.

SGT. PEPPER'S MUSIC HALL GRILL AND BAR, *62 Jiefang Bei Road, Tel. 23128138.*

This popular restaurant has good food, Beattle decorations, and loud music after 7pm.

The **TOP TEN: EAST SEA FISHING VILLAGE RESTAURANT**, *23, Chongqing Dao, Heping District, Tel. 23118888, and is open from 11am-9:30pm.*

This place is frequently recommended for Cantonese food, which is good, the table cloths snow white. During our visit however, the staff looked so glum, the experience was actually unpleasant. The *dim sum* is good and inexpensive.

SEEING THE SIGHTS

The standard city tour includes the Water Park, Ancient Culture Street, a carpet factory, television tower, Food Street, and New Years Picture factory. Do consider the Art Museum, the Catholic Cathedral, and the Theatre Museum.

The **Dabei Zen** (Grand Mercy) **Temple**, *40 Tianwei Road*, near the Holiday Inn, Tel. 26352320, is the city's biggest Buddhist temple, founded in 1656. The **Grand Mosque** on Dafeng Road, in the same direction, was built in 1644 (Qing). The **Tianjin History Museum**, *4 Guanghua Road, Tel. 24314630*, contains exhibits on the ancient and revolutionary histories of Tianjin, and has some bronzes, jade, paintings, and calligraphy.

The newly renovated **Tianjin Arts Museum**, *12 Chengde Road, Tel. 23991127*, has sculptures and other traditional works of art from ancient times and is highly recommended. The **Catholic Cathedral** is at *9 Xining Road, in Heping District, Tel. 27811929*, 27301929. It is next to the International Market.

The **Friendship or Cadre's Club**, *268 Machang Dao*, was built in 1925. Formerly the Tientsin Club, it reeks of Britain in the early 1900s, with beautiful, high mahogany paneling, and a drab, dismal interior. It's good mainly for tennis.

The new **Zhou Enlai/Chou En-lai Museum**, *Tel. 27371961*, is in the western part of the city, south of the Grand Mosque at *20 Sima Street, Nankai*. The former premier studied at Nankai Middle School here from 1913 to 1917, and briefly at Nankai University (1919), where he led student uprisings. No titles in English.

The 100-room, 1875 **Grand Mansion of the Shi Family** is in a back alley off a park in *Yangliuqing Township, Xiqing District, Tel. 22355062*. A 50-minute drive from downtown, it is worth seeing for the architecture and its folk arts, life-size models of a wedding sedan, a real wedding bed, and demonstration of woodblock printing. It is however not beautiful. Open 9am to noon; 1:30pm-5pm. It has no signs in English, alas. And alas again, no one seems to care about visitors. Y8 entry fee.

Near Food Street is **Ancient Culture Street** in Qing dynasty style, and the 1326 A.D. **Temple of the Sea Goddess**. But the street is nothing like Beijing's Liulichang or Nanjing's Confucian Temple area. I found nothing much to buy except traditional musical instruments. It does have a well-stocked **antique shop** and a tiny **folk museum**, *Tel. 27275062*. Do let me know if it's worth a trip.

The **Theater Museum**, *31 Nanmennei Street, Nankai District, Tel. 27275062*, is a must for theater lovers. The building itself is a gem in the gaudy south China style, a guild hall for Guangdong merchants built in 1907.

NIGHTLIFE & ENTERTAINMENT

Chat's Bar at the Hyatt is lively. The beach at **Tanggu** is "tacky." The **Blue Whale night cruise** on the river leaves from the pier at the Railway Station when there are enough customers after 7:30. It's cheap (Y10) and pleasant enough, if you like loud popular Chinese music and don't mind the occasional mosquito, but can be skipped as there isn't all that much to see. (Longer boat trips go from here during the day.)

You can bowl or rent skates at the **ice rink** on the eleventh floor of Isetan Department Store (Jili Dasha) open 10am to midnight. Y30 an hour. *Tel. 27221086 X 166*.

Festivals are held on Ancient Culture Street (Men Hui Jie) with stilts and dragon dances and special exhibits. On the first Sunday of April is the International Marathon; the Rose Festival is in May; the Great Wall Mountain Produce Festival is in the autumn; and the New Year Picture Festival is during the Spring Festival. Cultural presentations here sometimes include traditional opera, Tianjin ballet, acrobats, and puppets.

SHOPPING

The main shopping streets are **Binjiang Dao** and **Heping Road**, and **Nanjing Road**. Made in Tianjin are wool carpets, painted clay figurines by

Master Zhang, New Year's pictures, porcelain vases, tablecloths, accordions, cloisonne pens, soccer balls, basketballs, kites, jade, Dynasty wine, pictures painted on feathers, and inlaid lacquered furniture. Cloisonne is better in Shanghai and Beijing.

Tianjin Friendship Corporation is at *21 Youyi Road, Hexi District, 300201, Tel. 28135588 and open 9:30am-8:30pm.* This department store sells most of the above and more. It also ships purchases, tailors clothes, and arranges certificates of origin and orders.

Isetan is a Japanese Department Store on Nanjing Road and eight minute taxi ride from the Hyatt. It is open 10am-8:30pm daily and sells major international brands and Japanese merchandise. **Tse Sui Luen**, the Hong Kong jewelry store is on the top floor. Major credit cards are accepted. Packing and shipping service available. Next door is the **International Market Place**, a local store with lower prices, services and quality.

The **Sheraton Hotel** has the largest amount of hotel shop space. The gift shop was willing to drop prices easily by half for some items. It was selling "Beanie Babies" for Y40 to Y80.

You may also want to shop at: **Quan Ye Chang Emporium**, *290 Heping Road, Tel. 27303771;* **Wenyuange Antique Store**, *191-263 Heping Road, Tel. 27303450;* **Yangliuching New Year's Picture Studio**, *Gu Wenhua Street, Nankai District, Tel. 22355191.* Good prices for scrolls, reproductions, and prints; **#Tianjin Cultural Relics Company**, *161 Liaoning Road, Tel. 27300308.* Branches in the Friendship Hotel, and Astor Hotel. A traditional **Chinese furniture factory** is at Wuqin on the road to Beijing.

The **Antique Market** (Shen Yang Dao) is open daily from about 8:30am-about 2pm with goods spread out for about seven blocks alongside three regular blocks of full-time more expensive antique shops. Individual peddlers let you peek inside their bags at what they hope you think is a genuine Ming vase. There must be over 100 merchants here with Victrolas, old handsewn clothes, jewelry, old silver and clocks. You can see plenty of the cricket boxes. Be prepared for some hard haggling and crowds. A good store here in the middle of the market is **Tianjin Han Bao Tang**, *No. 27 Rehe Road, Shenyang Street Heping District, Tel. 27227320.* The **Tingbaozhai Antique Shop**, opposite the party school on *Shandong Road,* had lots of embroidered shoes for bound feet. *Tel. BB, 127-5383056, 9097, 6900, or evenings Ms. Zhang at 27303660.* The **Bird and Flower Market** is behind the Cathedral.

Visit a Factory
Tianjin is a good place to visit factories. The **Number Two Carpet**

Factory, *Heiniucheng Road, Hexi District, Tel. 28331920*, is one of the biggest carpet factories here, and has been making Junco-brand carpets for more than 100 years in Tianjin. These include thick carpets of pure wool, with no synthetics. Knots are made by hand, either 70 rows per square foot (ordinary) or 120 rows (refined). Embossing is also done by hand. Washing in a chemical solution adds gloss.

Other factories you might want to visit: **Tianjin Special Handicrafts Factory**, *16 Liuwei Road, Hedong District, Tel. 22344105*. The **Yangliuqing New Year Picture Society** is at *111 Sanheli, Tonglou, Hexi District, Tel. 27351531*. It has New Year's pictures of deities, like the Kitchen God, who informs Heaven of family events during the year past. These folk pictures are much brighter and more cheerful than traditional Chinese art.

You can also visit and buy from factories making Pierre Cardin clothes, and Italian bicycles. The Sales Manager at the Hyatt should know about these factory outlets and about factory overruns at the **Arts and Crafts Centre** on Heping Road.

Notes: visitors allergic to dust or wool should avoid carpet factories. Some factories are open on Sundays but closed one day during the week because of electricity rationing.

EXCURSIONS & DAY TRIPS

Beidaihe and Qinhuangdao are 3.5 hours northeast by train. Other nearby excursions include Beijing, Chengde, and the Qing Tombs (about three hours drive northeast). Other excursions include:

Jixian City: *****Dule** (Temple of Solitary Joy), 170 km north, about two hours drive from the Hyatt, is in the western part of Jixian city and can be combined with a trip to Panshan Mountain, the Great Wall and Qing Tombs in two days. It was founded in the Tang. Its Guanyin (Goddess of Mercy) Hall and the Gate to the Temple were rebuilt in 984 A.D. (Liao). The magnificent **Guanyin Hall**, 23 meters high, is the oldest existing multi-storied wooden structure in China. The 16-meter-high, 11-headed goddess is one of the largest clay sculptures in China. The **Great Wall** at Huangyaguan is 28 km north of Jixian County town. It has a museum, and usually is free of peddlars and tourists and can be reached in less time from Beijing. See also Great Wall.

The **Panshan** (Screen of Green) **Mountain** (about 12 km north of Jixian City) has been a mountain resort since the Tang. The highest peak is 1000 meters above sea level, on top of which is a pagoda said to contain a tooth of Buddha. Its 70 Buddhist temples were burned by the Japanese during World War II. Some of the buildings have been replaced or renovated.

This is an overnight trip, especially good in the autumn. The Hyatt can arrange for you to stay in an old Chinese house. There are two trains a day between Tianjin and Jixian town, taking almost three hours each way.

ZUNHUA
(Tsunhua)

Located in Hebei province, **Zunhua** is about 125 km northeast of Tianjin and 135 km east of Beijing. It's a day trip from these two cities. There are no decent hotels to recommend here, so make this a day trip. The two-star **Zunhua International Hotel** is the best hotel here, but is dirty.

Among the **imperial Qing tombs** (built 1743-1799) at **Dongling** (Eastern Tombs) are those of Emperor Qianlong (Chien Lung) at Yuling. Qianlong was the man who snubbed Britain's envoy. He is buried with his five wives. A devout Buddhist and patron of the arts, his tomb is covered with religious statues and sutras in Indian, Tibetan, Chinese, Manchurian, and Mongolian.

The tombs of **Empress Dowager Cixi** (Tzu Hsi) and Empress Cian are together at Dingdongling about one km from Qianlong's. Cixi was the fascinating, outrageous, scheming, brilliant, scandalous but short-sighted woman who built the Summer Palace in Beijing. Her tomb, covered with phoenixes deliberately and arrogantly placed above the dragons (symbolizing the emperor), was completed in 1873 and renovated in 1895, with an additional 4590 taels of gold as decoration. She died in 1908.

Both mausoleums can be entered. The carving is more elaborate than that in the Ming tombs, with Buddhist sutras (in Tibetan and Sanskrit) and figures inside. You can study an exhibition of her clothes, utensils, a coat for her dog, and photos. Her tomb was robbed in 1928 by a Nationalist warlord who used explosives to open it. He stripped over 500 pearls off her clothes.

Like the Ming tombs, there is also an animal-lined **Sacred Way**, the figures here smaller but more elaborately carved. It seems each dynasty tried to outdo its predecessors, the Ming being more elaborate than the Song (see Zhengzhou). The tombs of the emperors and empresses have glazed yellow roofs. Tombs of lesser importance have green roofs.

These tombs are a fast one-day trip from Beijing, a slight detour on the way to Beidaihe or Chengde. The Qing Tombs here are less spread out than the Ming Tombs. At least six of the 15 are open to the public. The atmosphere is quieter, less commercial. In the vicinity live 10,000 Manchu farmers.

The **Xiling** (Western Tombs), 120 km southwest of Beijing at Yixian are not as illustrious. The 14 mausoleums hold the remains of Emperors Yongzhen (Tailing), Jiaqing (Changling), Daoguang (Muling), and Guangxu (Chongling), plus the usual retinue of wives and children. Visitors can enter Chongling, the last royal tomb in China, but it has no funeral objects as it was robbed.

CITS is at *3/F, Municipal Government Building, Tel. 315/6613419*, or in Beijing *Tel. and Fax 10/65137796.*

PRACTICAL INFORMATION

Church Services for foreigners: *InterTech Building on 25 Youyi Road,* 10am Sunday.

CITS and **Tianjin Overseas Tourist Corporation**, *22 Youyi Road, 300074, Tel. 28350104, 28350821, Fax 28358479. E-mail: citstj@mail.zlnet.co.cn.* Also **O.T.C**, *Tel. 28350821, 28350104, Fax 28358479.* **CITS** *Tel. 28358501, Fax 28352619*

CITS, *46 Qianjindao, Meishiyan, Tel. 28358563*

CTS, *10 Youyi Road, 300074, Tel. 28353925, Fax 28353924*

CYTS Tours, *11 Mu Nan Road, He Ping District, 300050, Tel. 28309818, 23115017, Fax 23318017. Also No. 1 Leyuan Road, Hexi District, 300201*

Human Resources Consulting Services, Ms. Cindy Read, *Hyatt Tianjin, Room 824. E-mail: 102353.1766@compuserve.com.*

Internet: see Sheraton Hotel and Holiday Inn above. An internet cafe is also on Nanjing Road across the street from the International Trade Plaza (look for a big soccer ball with Carlsberg in front.

Telephone code, *022*

Tianjin Tourism Bureau, *18 Youyi Road, 300074, Tel. 28354860, Fax 28352324.* (Information)

SHIJIAZHUANG

(Shihchiachuang, Shihkiachwang)

Shijiazhuang is the capital of Hebei province. With a total population of six million, Shijiazhuang is primarily an industrial city.

It is of importance to Chinese revolutionary history as the burial place of the Canadian who became a Chinese hero. **Dr. Norman Bethune** arrived in China in 1938 to help the Communist Eighth Route Army in its fight against the Japanese. Working almost in the front lines, he died of blood poisoning on November 12, 1939, in Huangshikou village, Tangxian county, in Hebei.

That year, Chairman Mao wrote a much publicized article, pointing him out as an example of utter devotion to others without any thought of self. He became known to every school child, and statues were made of him all over the country. Highly recommended is the Canadian feature film, *Bethune, the Making of a Hero.*

ARRIVALS & DEPARTURES

Shijiazhuang is 2.5 hours by train south of Beijing, on the main line to Guangzhou, east of the Taihang Mountains on the Hebei Plain. It is also three hours by the 224-km long Jingshi Expressway with Beijing and now linked by air with 12 Chinese cities and Hong Kong. The airport is 33 km from city centre and is one of Beijing's alternatives, should Beijing's airport be unexpectedly closed.

WHERE TO STAY & EAT

These hotels are the same quality. Both take credit cards.

HEBEI GRAND HOTEL (Binguan), *23 Yucai Road, 050011. Three stars, Tel. 5815961, Fax 5814092.*

INTERNATIONAL BUILDING, *23 Changan Xi Road, 050011. Three stars. Tel. 6047888, Fax 6034787.*

SEEING THE SIGHTS

The **Bethune International Peace Hospital**, first set up in 1937 in the Shanxi-Chahar-Hebei Military Area, was moved here in 1948. Dr. Bethune is buried in the western part of the **North China Revolutionary Martyrs' Cemetery**, where there is also the **Bethune Exhibition Hall** and the **Memorial Hall for Revolutionary Martyrs**. The city also has the **Hebei Provincial Exhibition Hall and Museum**.

SHOPPING

Locally made are painted-on-the-inside snuff bottles, paper cuts, and ceramics. There are also white marble carvings from Quyang County, and Liuling wine. Elsewhere in the province are made golden-thread tapestry (Zhuoxian), shell crafts (Qinhuangdao), horse saddles (Zhangjiakou), ink slabs (Yishui), woven straw (Chengde), Handan ceramics, and Tangshan porcelain.

For good shopping, go to the **Dong Fang Shopping Center** in the west, and the **Beiguo Shopping Center** in the east.

PRACTICAL INFORMATION

Hebei Overseas Tourist Corporation, *175 Yucai Street, Tel. 5815102, 5873974, Fax 5815368. E-mail:otchb@sjz.col.com.cn.*

Hebei Oriental Travel Service, *437 Zhong Shan Dong Road, Tel. 5657058, 5657268, Fax 5657218.*

Tourist Complaints, contact *Supervisory Bureau of Tourism Quality of Hebei Province, 22 Yuzhong Street, 050021, Tel 6014239, Fax 6015368.*

Hebei Tourism Bureau, *175 Yucai Street, 050021, Tel. 5814319, Fax 5872864. E-mail:mddHB@990.net.*

Telephone code, *0311*
Tourist Hotline, *Tel. 5814319.*

CHENGDE

(Chengteh, Chengte, Jehol, Jehe)
    The historic mountain resort of **Chengde** is in Hebei province, 250 km northeast of Beijing. It is at an altitude of 340 meters, and has an urban population of over 130,000.
    Chengde oozes with history. The Qing court lived here from May to October each year. It was in a *yurt* here in 1793 that **Lord Macartney** of Britain refused to *kowtow* to Qing Emperor Qianlong. The emperor dismissed the Englishman as a bearer of tribute from King George III, and refused his requests for trade.
    In 1860, the Manchu court fled to Chengde as Anglo-French forces approached Beijing. The death of Emperor Xianfeng in 1862 led to the rise of **Cixi**, the Empress Dowager, as regent. Think of the plotting that went on as he lay on his deathbed. Cixi visited here again, by train, in 1900.
    In the 1930s, warlord Tang Yu Liu looted and destroyed many of the buildings. The most important have been repaired. Chengde's coldest temperature is -19 C; the hottest is 35 C for a very short time. Most rain falls in June and July.

ARRIVALS & DEPARTURES

    Express train 225 leaves Beijing daily at 7:29am, arriving at 12:10 noon. Train 226 leaves Chengde daily about 2:31pm arriving in Beijing at 7:14pm. (Times subject to change.) To join Panda Tours' two-day train package, telephone CITS in Beijing. The trip should take 2.5 hours by highway and the drive could follow the Great Wall past Simatai and Jinshan Ling. (In the last century a one-way trip took the Manchus three to 20 days by horseback, palanquin, or bumpy chariot).

ORIENTATION

    The **Qing Imperial Summer Resort** was built for Emperors Kangxi and Qianlong, not just to relax in, but to curry favor with the Mongolian nobles in the area. To help win them over, Emperor Kangxi (1703-1790) built 12 Buddhist temples also. Chengde is well worth seeing, especially if you don't go to Tibet. It is one of the 24 historical cities protected by the State Council and is an **UNESCO Heritage site.** The Imperial Summer Resort covers an area of 5.6 million square meters, which is larger than the Summer Palace in Beijing. Most of it is surrounded by a 10 km-long wall.

WHERE TO STAY & EAT

The best hotel is the four-star, 70-room **Qianyang Hotel**, built in 1998. The **Guest House For Diplomatic Missions** is an okay three star, located on *Wutie Road, Tel. 2021970, Fax 2021967.*

SEEING THE SIGHTS

You can explore the main palace and garden in one day and five of the outer temples on a second day. If you rush and avoid the climb to the Club Stone, you can cover all the open temples and the summer resort in one full, hurried day.

The **Imperial Summer Resort** has nine courtyards. It is not as palatial as Beijing's Summer Palace, but it is worth seeing. The building to the right inside the second gate has a painting of the Macartney visit and a hunting scene with officials wearing animal head masks and imitating mating calls to attract the animals.

To the left is the **Hall of No Worldly Lust but True Faith**, also called the Nanmu Hall because of the scented wood from which it is made. The emperor received subjects and envoys in this ceremonial hall. On either side are waiting rooms, one for foreign visitors and one for relatives and tribal leaders. Among the exhibits in these and other halls are Manchu coats with sleeves shaped like horses hooves, sedan chairs, an elephant dotted with pearls, and brilliant blue kingfisher feather ornaments. In a hall displaying fine porcelain are Qing imitations of Ming vases.

The **Refreshing-at-Mist-Veiled-Waters Pavilion** was the imperial bedroom. On either side are the pavilions of the two empresses. The imperial bedroom has a hollow wall (seen from the back) where Cixi listened carefully as the emperor lay dying inside. As a result of her eavesdropping, she was able to seize power. Cixi lived in the Pine Crane Pavilion, which was originally built for the mother of Emperor Qianlong. The emperor used the two-story pavilion beyond to enjoy the moon with his concubines. It has no interior stairs.

The **garden** is beautiful and great for walks. Visitors should be able to rent ice skates and bicycles. The trees planted by the Qing are tagged with identifications numbers. These two most influential emperors chose 72 scenic spots and wrote poems about each. Kangxi's poems have four characters; Qianlong's have three. Thirty of these places are still marked by pavilions from which you can enjoy the view, including one on the top of the hill to view the snow. There is even one to view the Club Stone.

Among the buildings counterclockwise around the lake is the Jinshan Pavilion, copied from one of the same name in Zhenjiang, and the Yanyulou (Misty-Rain Tower), the latter built by Qianlong, a copy of one now destroyed in Zhejiang. It was used to watch the misty rain, of course, and to read.

On the flatland area here, Emperor Qianlong stooped to receive the equally arrogant Lord Macartney, the envoy from Britain. The walled garden on the Changlang Islet is a copy of the Changlang Garden in Suzhou. Some people collect postcards when they travel; the Qianlong emperor collected buildings! Nearby, on a side road, is a herd of spotted deer, started here during the Qing because some of the emperors drank deer's blood as a tonic.

The two-story **Imperial Library** has a pond in front and a few trees as a precaution against fire. The library is a copy of one in Shaoxing. It is approached through the rockeries. If you notice tourists in front of the library staring into the water, its because they are looking for the reflection of a crescent moon.

As a Chinese garden, this imperial summer resort is one of the best, a microcosm of the whole country with lake, grasslands, and mountains.

The **Eight Outer Temples** outside the walls are a mixture of Manchu, Mongolian, Tibetan, and Han Chinese architecture with a similar mix of artifacts inside. Once housing 1,000 lamas or monks, they are now primarily museums. The steles usually have Manchu writing in front, Chinese behind, and Mongolian and Tibetan on the sides. If you are short of time, the Putuozongsheng and Puning are the most important to include. Otherwise, start with the ***Pule**, which is also known as the Round Pavilion, as it was built in 1766 to resemble the Temple of Heaven. Inside is a statue of two hard-to-see copulating gods from the tantric sect of Tibetan Buddhism. From this temple you can climb or take a cable car to the **Club Stone**, the giant, mallet-shaped stone, for a marvelous view.

The small **Anyuan Temple** is patterned after a temple in Xinjiang that no longer exists. Inside is a statue of Lu Du Mo, a female goddess. The **Puren** should be open for your visit.

Inside the gate of the ***Puning Temple** is a stele about Qianlong's suppression of a rebellion of the minorities. The Puning Temple contains a copy of the spectacular 1,000-headed and 1,000-armed Guan Yin, Goddess of Mercy, which should not be missed. Actually he/she has only 42 hands and arms, each representing 25. On each palm is an eye. The statue in Mahayana Hall is 22.28 meters high. A warlord stole the original.

The Puning Temple is patterned after the Sumeru temple in Tibet and is known also as the Temple of Universal Peace or Big Buddha Temple. Inside are a drum and a bell tower, a laughing Buddha, and four guardian kings. About 100 larger-than-life-size *arhats* remain of the original 508; the others were destroyed by fire. Only eight of the saints are Chinese. The mural of the 18 *arhats* is 230 years old and original, remarkable for its preservation. Look for the big bronze cooking pot that fed 1000 lamas. The number of buildings and stupas are symbolic. The center of the world was Sumeru Mountain, with four great continents around it.

In the Puning are live, chanting red-robed monks, probably from Inner Mongolia and Qinghai on a three-year contract. They chant every morning. If you can't go to Tibet, this is the place to come.

The **Xumifushou** (Longevity and Happiness) **Temple** was inspired by the Tashilhunpo/Zhaxilhunbu Temple in Shigatse, Tibet, and used as a residence for the sixth Panchen Lama. Dragons seem to scamper along the edges of the roof, most unusual for a Han temple. Built in 1780, it is the newest of the temples and commemorates Qianlong's 70th birthday, at which point he started to learn Tibetan. In the main building is a statue of the founder of Lamaism and behind him Sakyamuni. The tent-like pagoda in the back is similar to the one in Fragrant Hill Park in Beijing.

The ***Putuozongcheng Temple** is patterned after the Potala Palace, home of the Dalai Lama, in Lhasa. It was built from 1767 to 1771 for the 60th birthday of Qianlong and for the 80th birthday of his mother. The elephant symbolizes the Mahayana sect. (One elephant equals 500 horses.) The five pagodas on several of the buildings symbolize the five schools of Buddhism. Dancers might perform here.

Not to be missed is the **Donggang Zi Dian** (East Hall). Statues here are from the Red Hat sect of Tibetan Buddhism, where sex with a person other than one's spouse was part of the religious ritual. In the opposite hall on the same level are other metal Buddhist statues. Another 164 steps lead up to the main building, which is decorated by Buddhas in the niches - the 80 at the top representing Qianlong's life. Some birthday cake! The temple was built to commemorate the birthdays, as well as a visit by tribal leaders. This temple is the largest. Finally, the **Yongning Temple**, built in 1751, is worth a quick look.

PRACTICAL INFORMATION

CITS and **CTS**, *6 Nanyuan Dong Road, 067000, Tel. 2030746* for CTS, and *2026418* for CITS. *Fax 2027484* for CITS and *2028930* for CTS.

Chengde Tourism Bureau, *11 Zhong Hua Road. 067000, Tel. 2020876, Fax, 2021706.*

Telephone code, *0314*

QINHUANGDAO

(Chinwangtao)

Qinhuangdao, at the northeastern tip of Hebei province on the Bohai Sea, is more of a commercial than a tourist city though it is a center for sea sports. It is the capital of the prefecture that includes Beidaihe, 15 km away, the better seaside resort. Qinhuangdao is also 20 km from Old

Dragon Head, where the Great Wall meets the sea. The city is one of China's busiest harbors. Ice-free, it is the port for a nearby oil field to which it is joined by a pipeline. With an urban population of about 448,000, it is one of the 14 Open Coastal Cities.

ARRIVALS & DEPARTURES

Qinhuangdao is a 280 km, three-hour expressway trip from Beijing, or a 2.5 hour express train trip. Buses leave from Qianmen in Beijing. The closest airport is 15 km away near Shanhaiguan. Flights arrive from 10 other cities. Migrating birds also make Qinhuangdao beach a stop in autumn and winter.

ORIENTATION

Originally a small village, Qinhuangdao was opened as a seaport in 1898 and became a base for foreign (especially British) shipping. In 1902 the British army also built a small pier. The railway was finished in 1916.

The city is named after a legend. The Qin emperor passed through here about 2,200 years ago looking for pills of longevity. Suddenly, he recognized a special tree described by his teacher. Surprised and afraid, he bowed to the tree and a branch bowed back.

WHERE TO STAY & EAT

QINHUANGDAO CINDIC HOTEL, *Yinbin Road, 066000. Three stars. Tel. 3062243, Fax 3032253. 0.5 km from the railway station and 12 km from the airport. Five km from the beach.*

Built in 1984, this hotel has over 100 rooms, satellite television, Cantonese, Sichuan, and French-style food.

SEEING THE SIGHTS

Dong Shan (East Mountain) is where the Qin emperor searched for the pills of longevity and boarded his ships. There's a good view of the sea and the sunrise. A cruise boat goes to a **fishing village** at the mouth of the Xin Kai River and sometimes visitors can come across teams of fishing boats going out together, dragging their big nets between them. In the old days, the fishermen used to sing to each other.

You can visit a **shell-carving factory** and the **Sea God Temple**, where the Qin Emperor searched for those longevity pills. You can also go swimming at **Dong Shan beach**. A natural wildlife park is now open.

SHOPPING

Grown locally are peaches, pears, sea cucumbers, and crabs (biggest in September-October). Made locally are pictures, lamps and ashtrays of shell. Also manufactured are mirrors, magnifying glasses, painted eggs, painted stones, butterfly and insect specimens, bird-feather crafts, and necklaces of red beans (symbol of longing between lovers).

EXCURSIONS & DAY TRIPS

A good nearby excursion is to **Beidaihe**, primarily a seaside resort 10-15 km south of Qinhuangdao. See below.

Shanhaiguan in northeastern Hebei province 20 km north of Beidaihe is an important pass in the Great Wall. Its Qinhuangdao airport can be reached by air from seven Chinese cities. It's a five-hour train ride from Beijing.

Six km north is the **Meng Jiang-nu Temple**, built in memory of another of China's chaste, almost supernatural heroines. Lady Meng traveled on foot during several winter months in search of her husband, one of the hundreds of thousands of workers building the Great Wall. Her deep sorrow and tears moved heaven so much that the Great Wall collapsed to reveal her husband's bones. The temple was originally built in the Song dynasty, but the Red Guards destroyed the statues. The government restored them in the late 1970s in gaudy, crudely painted clay. But the view of the hills to the north is interesting.

Laolongtou (Old Dragon Head), the place where the **Great Wall** meets the sea, is four km south of Shanhaiguan. Chenghai Tower, on the seashore, was originally built in 1579. It has been rebuilt and decorated with soldiers in Ming costume. The Great Wall Festival in June has races, 18 to 40 km up and down the Wall. It also has costumed Ming and Qing performances, lantern shows and large scale fireworks at Old Dragon Head. A small temple to the Sea Goddess is nearby.

At **Jiao Shan**, where the Great Wall is very steep, there is an 1,833 meter-long chair lift almost to the top. The town itself is surrounded by a well-maintained wall of its own. Hotels are better in nearby Qinhuangdao and Beidaihe.

PRACTICAL INFORMATION

CITS, *8 Wenhua Bei Road, Tel. 3035974, Fax 3034765.*

Qinhuangdao Haiyan International Travel Service, *Hebei Street, 066000, Tel. 3044666, 3045555, Fax 3045558. E-mail:qhyits@public.he.cn.*

Telephone code *335*

BEIDAIHE

Beidaihe is primarily a **seaside resort**, built after the completion of the Beijing-Shanhaiguan railway in 1893. By 1949, 706 villas and hotel buildings had been completed, many of them for foreign diplomats and missionaries as well as wealthy Chinese. After Liberation, the Chinese government rebuilt some of the old buildings and added new ones as rest and recreation centers for its employees. The urban population is around 20,000.

ARRIVALS & DEPARTURES

Beidaihe is about 40 km from Shanhaiguan, 10 to 15 km south of Qinhuangdao, and about a 3.5 hour train trip or a six hour drive due east (290 km) of Beijing. The railway station is about 18 km away. Cars are generally not permitted into the downtown area, but you can get permission to access the hotels there. The closest airport is Qinhuangdao.

ORIENTATION

The resort stretches along 12 km of hard, golden sand sloping gently out into the Bohai Sea, a good place to walk. Swimming is good too though there may be a few jellyfish. Rock promontories divide the beaches. At the **Pigeons Nest** in the east, you can look at Qinhuangdao across the bay and the best sunrise. At the **Tiger Stone** in the center, crab fishermen sell their catch in the summer.

Several swimming areas are attached to each of the hotels, manned by life guards and protected by nets. Each hotel has changing rooms on the beach with hot and cold fresh-water showers, open 8am-10pm. The swimming season is from May to September, depending on how cold you like your water. The hottest days are in August (maximum 36 C for a few days), but the high is usually 31 C, sometimes dropping to 24 or 25 C at night.

WHERE TO STAY

The top hotel is the Jinshan close to the beach. The airport is 30 km east and the railway station 12 km north.

JINSHAN HOTEL (Binguan), *Dongshan Road, East Beach, 066100, Tel. 4041678, Fax 4042478. Three stars. It accepts credit cards.*

Built 1986, it has several buildings joined together by covered walkways and beautiful private gardens. It is half a block from the beach. It has satellite television, an outdoor pool and bowling. The high season is July 1 to September 15 and it's open all year.

SEEING THE SIGHTS

A **Guanyin Temple**, built in 1911, is on the grounds of the West Hill Hotel. The building was beautifully restored in 1979, the two statues and frescoes inside replaced after being destroyed by the Red Guards. The temple is about 1.5 km behind the hotel's service bureau, a nice walk. The **Xiaobaohezhai Village** is also a good place to visit. It was one of the first in China to have pensions for its older citizens and one of the first with a birth-control program. It grows apples, peaches and pears for export, so an ideal time to visit is late August-September.

An incredible **seaside playground** built by Changli County is located less than 60 km south of Beidaihe. It has fake castles, sand slides, water slides, cabanas, hotels, amusement parks - none of which appears to be up to North American standards. Only foreigners wanting a do-nothing seaside vacation with something to amuse the children would probably be interested.

PRACTICAL INFORMATION

See Qinhuangdao.
Beidaihe International Travel Service, *4 Dongsan Road, Beidaihe, Tel. 4041748, Fax 4042474.*
Telephone code, *0335.*

TAIYUAN

Taiyuan is in the center of Shanxi province, of which it is the capital. It has a couple of interesting tourist attractions, one certified world class.

Taiyuan was founded in the Western Zhou (1066-771 B.C.). Because of its strategic location, it was the site of many wars, changing hands five times between 396 and 618 A.D. It was a silk center under the Sui and has been growing grapes for a thousand years.

The hottest temperature is 35 C for a few days in August, the coldest is -14 C in January. The annual precipitation is 400 millimeters from July to September. The altitude is 800 meters. The population is 2.05 million.

ARRIVALS & DEPARTURES

Taiyuan is over an hour's flight southwest of Beijing, and 2.5 hours north of Guangzhou. Taiyuan can be reached by air from 25 other cities, and by train from Beijing (10 hours), Xi'an (12 hours), Hohhot (14 hours), and Datong (nine hours). It can also be reached in six hours from Beijing 540 km away by express air-conditioned bus every 20 minutes.

ORIENTATION

Although it used to be a highly cultured city with many architectural wonders, the wars and modern industry have changed its complexion.

WHERE TO STAY

The five star **Shanxi Grand Hotel** should open in 2000. The four-star Shanxi Grand is currently the best in town.

SHANXI GRAND HOTEL (Shanxi Dajiudian), *5 Xin Jian Nan Road, 030001, Tel. 4043901, Fax 4043525. E-mail:sxdjd@public.ty.sx.cn. $82. Credit Cards.*

Built in 1989, this hotel has 14 stories, and 168 rooms, satellite television, Cantonese and Russian restaurants. There's an indoor pool, bowling, and a gym.

YINGZE HOTEL, *189 Yingze Street, Tel. 4043211, Fax 4043784. $65. 294 rooms. Four stars.*

SAN JIN INTERNATIONAL HOTEL, *30 Yingze Street, Tel. 4049988, Fax 4129360. $52. 531 rooms.*

WHERE TO EAT

Shanxi people love noodles and vinegar-flavored dishes. Five hundred-meter-long **Food Street**, in the southern part of the city, has 46 food shops and restaurants. There's the **Xiangjiang Restaurant** at *155, Fuxi Street, Tel. 3534518*, and the **Sanqiao Hotel Restaurant**, *4 Hanxi Guan, Xin Jian Bei Road, Tel. 3045885, Fax 3043286.*

SEEING THE SIGHTS

Taiyuan is most famous for the **Jinci Temple**, 25 km southwest of the city at the foot of Xuanweng Mountain, reached by bus No. 8 from the railway station. One source says it was initially built in the Northern Wei (386-534) in memory of the second son of King Wu of the Western Zhou. The Jin Temple was renovated, with additions, in 1102 (Northern Song). The temple has female statues, which, aside from goddesses, is very rare in China. Was this second son a lush? A son much pampered by women? Are the women here to continue indulging him in the after-life?

Alas, no! Centuries ago, Shanxi was very short of water. Sea and water deities have usually been female. In Shanxi a spring was found near Jinci, so people started worshipping Shuimu (Mother of Water). The maids-in-waiting and the mermaids were her retinue.

The temple is the oldest wooden structure in the area and is charming. In the Shengmu (Sacred Lay Hall) are 43 dusty, lifesize clay figures, 30 of these court maids-in-waiting, all lithesome, each different in expression, and still retaining much color. They were made in the Song.

Uphill from the Jinci about 40 minutes by road (Bus No. 8 still), the **Tianlong Shan** (Mountain of Celestial Dragon) has a little temple with four lohan and 24 small caves with many old, damaged statues.

The **Chongshan Monastery** in the city itself is believed to have been a Sui palace once. Only part of the original (Tang) monastery is standing, and part of that is the Shanxi Provincial Museum. The monastery is famous for its ancient 1000-handed, 1000-eyed Goddess of Mercy. It, along with the two other *bodhisattvas* are eight meters tall. The beams and ceiling are quite remarkable. During the Sino-Japanese War, a bomb went through the ceiling without exploding, and the repair work is still visible. It is three km from the Yingze Hotel.

Next door is the **Shanxi Provincial Museum**. Museum Number One has a vast collection of neolithic artifacts. So far, 200 paleolithic and 500 neolithic sites have been unearthed in the province, plus over 500 tombs and other ancient ruins. Provincial Museum Number Two is considered more important than Museum Number One. Located at the site of the Chunyang Palace on the west side of May 1 Square, the palace itself was built between 1573 and 1619, and renovated in the Qing. It contains 20 exhibition halls with ceramics, bronzes, carvings, lacquer, calligraphy, embroidery, books, and other documents unearthed around the province. There is also a huge **coal museum**.

The **Shuangta Temple**, also known as the Yongzuo Monastery, has twin pagodas, symbols of Taiyuan, eight km from the Yingze Hotel. The pagodas were built in the Ming and are over 50 meters high. They are octagonal and of carved bricks. Inside the monastery are exhibitions of old coins, pottery, etc., and a corridor with 207 stone tablets of Ming calligraphy.

There are also a great number of important historical monuments in Shanxi province: 100 km southwest is the **Qiao Family Compound** and folk museum, originally the home of a wealthy Qing merchant. This is highly decorated with carvings and should be of interest to those who saw the internationally-acclaimed Chinese movie *Raise the Red Lantern*. Built in 1755 in Qixian County, it was used as the main set for this Oscar-nominated movie. The mansion has 313 rooms.

Long-distance buses pass it 10 km before Qixian.

SHOPPING

Locally made are fur coats, including rabbit and wild rat(!) skin, gold and lacquer inlaid crafts, reproductions of ancient ironware, black-glazed porcelain, Junco brand carpets, Fen Chiew wines, vinegars, fine glassware, lacquerware, jade carving, and brass and copperware (especially fancy charcoal-burning hot pots). Grown locally are dates, pears, persimmons, walnuts, and wild jujubes.

EXCURSIONS & DAY TRIPS

The following can be covered in a two-day tour. In the southern tip of Shanxi province is *Yong Le Palace in Ruicheng County, with beautiful

400-meter-long Yuan dynasty murals. From it, you can also study social and architectural history.

Nearby in Yuncheng County is the **Guan Di Temple**, founded in the Sui and completely renovated in the Qing. **Pingyao**, about 100 km southwest of Taiyuan, is a well-preserved ancient city with 6.7 km of city walls, and shops and homes untouched since the Ming and Qing. It is a UNESCO heritage site.

At Hongdong, about 200 km southwest of Taiyuan, is the ***Guangsheng Temple**, listed as Yuan and Ming. It has excellent colored ceramic figures and frescoes. An intricate, stunning collection of about 1,000 lively Buddhist and animal figures over 300 years old is at the Xiaoxitian (**Miniature Western Paradise**), northwest of Guangsheng Temple and north of Xixian county town. These are also worth a visit. Be prepared to climb and crane your neck. Take a flashlight and binoculars. And recently opened for tourists is a **Ming dynasty jail** in Hong Dong County. There, a woman, wrongly accused of poisoning her husband, was incarcerated.

***Dingcun paleolithic ruins** are in Xianfen county, roughly 25 km southwest of Hongdong. Also in this area is a Han (nationality) **folk museum**, with 19 Ming and Qing courtyards, the oldest built in 1593. **Houma**, another 50 km southwest of Linfen, is a Jin site from the Eastern Zhou. A low but spectacular (depending on the season) **waterfall** is at Hukou on the Yellow River, northeast of Dingcun. Guesthouses are at Yuncheng City. You could spend a fruitful month exploring this province alone! Much of the Chinese collection in Toronto's Royal Ontario Museum is from southern Shanxi.

See Datong for the Yungang Grottoes, the Great Wall, Wutai Mountain, Sakyamuni Pagoda, the Huayan and Shanhua Monasteries and the Mid-Air Temple.

PRACTICAL INFORMATION

Shanxi CTS, *8 Xinjian Nan Road, 030001, Tel. 4043377, Fax 4035024.* **Shanxi CITS**, *A38 Ping Yang Road, 030012, Tel. 7042188, Fax 7040312. E-mail:sxcits@public.ty.sx.cn.*

Shanxi Provincial Tourism Administration, *282 Ying Ze Avenue, 030001, Tel. 4080073, 2027161, Fax 4048289.* (Information); for **Tourist Complaints**, *Tel. 4047544, Fax 4048289.* Contact: Liang Hai Hong.

Telephone code, *0351.*

DATONG

(Tatung)

Datong is most famous for the **Yungang** (Yunkang) **Grottoes**, said to be the best-preserved, the largest, and the oldest sandstone carvings in

China. Founded during the Warring States, about 2,200 years ago, this was a garrison town built between two sections of the Great Wall. The Northern Wei (386-534) declared it their capital and instructed Monk Tanyao to supervise the carving of the caves.

The population is 520,000 urban, 2.7 million total. The highest temperature in summer (July-August) is 37.7 C, the lowest (December-February) -29.9 C. Rainfall is a scant 400 millimeters a year, mainly May-October. The best time to visit is May-October. The altitude is 1000 meters.

ARRIVALS & DEPARTURES

Located in northern Shanxi province, Datong is 7.5 hours by train No. 205, the fastest from Beijing. It leaves at 11:20pm and arrives at 5:50am. You can continue from here by once-a-week train to Ulan Bator and thence onward to Moscow.

ORIENTATION

Datong is basically a coal-mining town, one of the largest open pit coal-producing areas in the world, with a 600-year supply at the current rate of production. The city is industrial and heavily polluted. Outside Datong, you can see the coal deposits with all kinds of coal transport equipment on the roads. Some of the equipment is the most advanced in the world.

The mining may be ugly but it is worth your time. Because the mines have unearthed many old burial grounds, Shanxi has an extremely large number of excavated tombs and neolithic sites.

WHERE TO STAY

DATONG GRAND HOTEL, *1 Yingbin Dong Road, 037008, Tel. 2032476, Fax 2035174. Three stars.*

This is the best hotel.

YUNGANG HOTEL (Fandian), *21 Yingbin Dong Road, 037008. Three stars. Tel. 5021601, Fax 5024927.*

WHERE TO EAT

Look for people preparing Knife-cut Noodles on the street. Ask about the chefs who put noodle dough on their heads and slice the dough with a knife into a cooking pot. Try The **Hong Qi Restaurant** on *Yingbin Dong Road*, or the **Yong Ho Restaurant** on *Nan Guan Street*.

SEEING THE SIGHTS

If you only have one day to spend in the city, good choices are the

Yungang caves, Huayan Monastery, Shanhua Monastery, and the Nine-Dragon Screen. Take a flash light for the grottoes and a flash camera. Nine of the caves have wooden protectors in front and many are dark.

You can reach the *Yungang (Yunkang) Grottoes by taxi about 20 km west from Datong. Fifty-three caves here contain over 51,000 stone carvings of buddha, *bodhisattvas, apsaras* (angels), birds, and animals. These statues range from 17 meters to a few centimeters high and some of them still retain their original color. They were restored in 1976. The grottoes are at the southern foot of Wuzhou Hills. They were built between 460 and 494 A.D. after a period of persecution against the Buddhists supposedly led to the illness of Emperor Taiwu. The grottoes extend east-west for a kilometer. The Wei dynasty later moved its capital to Luoyang and built another set of grottoes there.

Although the exposed caves have suffered natural erosion as well as damage by man, they are nicely preserved and well worth visiting. The walking is easy. The best are at the **Five Caves of Tanyao** (Nos. 5, 6, 16-20), which include the largest statues. The large ears mean deliberate poverty (no earrings). Although Datong was not on the Silk Road, the carvings carry strong Indian, Persian, and even Greek influences. You can expect to spend at least half a day here, strolling from cave to cave. During tourist season, English-speaking guides are available for hire. There are several restaurants.

The *Huayan Si (Huayan Monastery) is one of the largest temples in China. You can easily spend from two hours to a half day there, there is so much to absorb. It is in the southwest of the city, three km north of the main tourist hotel. An antique store is at the temple. The monastery is well preserved and is separated into the Upper Huayan and the Lower Huayan. You pay two entrance fees. In Upper Huayan is the magnificent main hall, Daxiong Bao Dian, built in 1062 and rebuilt in 1140. It is 53.75 meters wide and 29 meters long. The beam structure, murals, five large Ming buddhas, and 26 guardians are most impressive. In Lower Huayan is the main hall, the Bhagavan Stack Hall, built in 1038. Along its walls are 38 two-story wooden cabinets housing the Buddhist sutras. The temple's exquisite 31 clay statues were made in the Liao.

The **Datong Municipal Museum** has prehistoric fossils and cultural relics and is in the Municipal Exhibition Hall.

The *Shanhua Monastery, in the south part of the city, was founded in 713 A.D. Surviving are relics of the Liao and Jin. **The Nine Dragon Screen**, in the southeast of the old city, is almost 600 years old, and at 45.5 meters, larger than the two in Beijing. The morning is better for photographs. A nearby Christian church is worth at least a 10-minute visit. The **Steam Locomotive Museum** is on the way to the Grottoes.

SHOPPING

Locally made products include porcelain, knitting wool, furs, leather, silk dolls, and carpets.

EXCURSIONS & DAY TRIPS

If you have more time, the 67.3-meter-high ***Sakyamuni Wooden Pagoda at Foguang Temple** should be worth the 1.5 hour drive if you are interested in unusual pagodas. It is the tallest ancient wood-frame structure in China. It was constructed in 1056 (Liao), with eight corners and nine stories. From the outside it looks like five stories. Local folklore says that the pagoda only sits on five of its six vertical beams. One of the beams is always resting, and you can pass a piece of paper underneath it. Each beam takes its turn at being weightless. Bring a piece of paper and test it for yourself. It is 75 km south of Datong in Yingxian county. The Great Wall is 40 km and 150 km away.

You can also visit **Hengshan Mountain**, 80 km south, for the Xuankongsi or **Temple in Mid-Air** (or **Hanging Monastery**). This is a two-hour drive southeast of Datong, a marvel of cliff-side architecture. The temple literally clings to an almost vertical mountainside. It was first built over 1400 years ago (Northern Wei) and rebuilt in the Tang, Jin, Ming and Qing dynasties. Its clay statues are poor. The bronze and iron castings and stone and wood carvings are better and probably older. Take lunch in Hongyun County town nearby. From here it's another four hours to Wutai Mountain, 240 km south of Datong. You pass some 11th century Liao dynasty tombs.

On **Wutai Shan**, one of the Four Great Buddhist Mountains of China, there are about 50 temples from the fifth century. Important are the ***Main Hall of the Nanchan Temple** (Tang to Qing), ***Foguang Temple** (Tang to Qing) and the ***Xiantong Temple** (Eastern Han). The main halls of the Nanchan and Foguang temples are the oldest extant wood-frame buildings in the world. Both have histories of over 1200 years and are worth the white-knuckle trip through the mountains.

Visitors can hike on a paved path to the summit. The liveliest time to visit is during its festival here in July and August. Dr. Norman Bethune's model hospital is also in the area. You can stay at the three-star **Yindu Hotel** in Taiwai Village at the foot.

PRACTICAL INFORMATION

China Comfort Travel Service, *5-28 Yingbin Dong Road, opposite the Yungang Hotel, Tel. 5101107, 5103222, Fax 5103222.*

CITS, **CTS**, and **Datong Tourist Bureau**, *21 Yingbin Dong Road, 037008, Tel. 5102265, Fax 5102246.*

CYTS Tours, *Floor 3 Building, One Drum Tower Dong Street, 037008, Tel. 2069205, Fax 2063303*
Telephone code, *0352*.

HOHHOT

(Huhehot, Huhehaote)

Hohhot, the capital of Inner Mongolia (Nei Monggol Autonomous Region), is northwest of Beijing in the south central part of this 1800-km-long region. The urban population is over 800,000.

Genghis Khan united the tribes living here in 1206, and his descendants went on to conquer the rest of China and then parts of Europe. The traditional religion, as reflected now in its monasteries and temples, is a distinctive branch of Buddhism and is related to that practiced in Tibet.

Hohhot dates from the Ming, at least 400 years ago. It was called Guisui under the Nationalists. After Liberation it was renamed Hohhot (Blue City), the name preferred by the natives. In the past, Inner Mongolia has been a temporary home for nomads.

The best time to visit is June through September. The highest temperature in Hohhot is 30 C, but the nights are cool. The winters are very cold and windy, with an occasional -32 C low in January, and you need long johns even in early May. The spring has a few sandstorms. The annual precipitation is between a scant 50 and 450 millimeters, mostly late summer and early autumn. The altitude is 1500 meters above sea level and it has from 90 to 160 frost-free days.

ARRIVALS & DEPARTURES

Hohhot can be reached by train or plane from Beijing and twelve other Chinese cities, and from Ulan Bator, Mongolia.

ORIENTATION

Today Hohhot's population includes Han, Daur, Ewenki, Oroqen, Hui, Manchu, Korean, and, of course, Mongolian nationalities. The Mongolians are now actually a minority. Hohhot looks like any other Chinese city, except for the horse statues.

WHERE TO STAY

PEARL INNER MONGOLIA HOTEL, *2 Xin Cheng Bei Avenue, 010010. Three stars, Tel. 6280088, Fax 6910499. E-mail:pearl-hotel@pearl-hotel.com.cn. 12 km from the airport and two km from the railway station. Y380-Y700 including breakfast.*

This, the best hotel in Hohhot, has 112 rooms, satellite television, *dim sum,* western and local food, and a business center. There's a gym and sauna.

ZHAO JUN HOTEL *(Zhaojun Dajiudian), 53 Xinhua Road, 010050. Three stars, Tel. 6962211, Fax 6968825, 6967645. 15 km from the airport, 0.5 km from the railway station, 200 meters from city hall. Credit cards. Y320-Y540.*

Built in 1987, this hotel has 262 rooms, satellite television and international direct dial.

XIN CHENG (Binguan), *Hu Lun Nan, 010010, Tel. 6963322, Fax 6968561. Rooms start at Y200 and it takes major credit cards.*

WHERE TO EAT

Meat, mainly mutton but also beef, is the big thing here. Notable dishes are barbecued lamb, mutton hot pot, sesame pancakes, braised oxtail, beef kebab, *yu mian* noodles, ox tendon in egg white, camel hoof, and *facai* (the edible black hair-like moss that is a favorite in China.)

Mongolian food is better in Hohhot at the **hotels** than in the grasslands. Outside and to the right of the Zhaojun Hotel you'll find a place for good Mongolian hotpot.

SEEING THE SIGHTS

In summer, visitors can travel out from here, if they wish, and sleep in a *yurt* in the beautiful sparsely settled grasslands. You can drink tea laced with milk, butter, and grain, said to be very filling and great for cold winter days - it's too greasy for hot weather. Visitors can go to one of several rural communities located 90 to 180 km away, on roads cut through the rolling prairie lands.

Mongolian **yurts** or tents are made of compressed sheep's wool with no windows unless you count the roof. They are shaped somewhat like igloos, and can be folded up and carried by camel. Eight people can put up a large one in 40 minutes. Visitors staying in *yurts* sleep on padded earthen mattresses. Everything smells of sheep. (Put a bag between you and the wall if the smell keeps you awake.)

Up to three people to a *yurt* is very comfortable, and over six very crowded. Sometimes you can hear bugs eating the felt. A mosquito net might be useful. Most Mongolians now live in houses but keep *yurts* around because they are cooler in summer.

In some *yurt* hotels, there is a separate bathhouse with running water and flush toilets (when the pump is working). The people are charming and wear their traditional costumes. The food might be barely edible, with tough fresh-killed mutton, fried millet, boiled millet, rice, boiled eggs, and cake. Do not expect traditional Mongolian hot pot or barbecue except in winter or in the cities. Take some snacks to fill up. Also soap. Each travel agency has a different hostel on the grasslands, some better than others.

You can visit Mongolian homes and an *aobo*, the rock mounds at high points where people worship, gather, and leave messages for each other. Mongolians now ride motorcycles much more than horses. Hohhot used to have many temples but the Red Guards destroyed them during the Cultural Revolution. Among the survivors is the oldest, **Dazhao Temple** (Ming), with a rare silver Buddha and many musical instruments, and the **Xiaozhao Temple**. At the **Wutasi Temple**, the tallest of its five pagodas is 6.26 meters and all are made of glazed bricks carved with Buddhist symbols and inscribed in three languages: Mongolian, Sanskrit, and Tibetan. Behind the pagodas is a Mongolian astrological chart.

The **White Pagoda** on the eastern outskirts of the city at the Xilitu Lamasery (monastery) is from the 10th century and is 40 meters or seven stories high. Inside are native tapestries. For more on Tibetan Buddhism, see Tibet.

The **Tomb of Wang Zhaojun** is about 10 km southwest of the city. In 33 B.C., she was an imperial Han concubine, married off to a Xiongnu tribal chief to form an important political alliance. The story goes that the Han emperor picked his bed partner from paintings of his many concubines. Consequently, the women bribed the painter to make them look beautiful. Wang Zhaojun refused and he made her look awful. She was continually ignored. In choosing a gift for the tribal leader, the emperor decided on the ugliest of his wives. He never saw Wang Zhaojun until the day of the presentation. She was beautiful, but it was too late. The Xiongnu liked her too. And the peace was kept for 40 years! A Han Chinese, she helped to bridge the two groups.

The **Great Mosque**, built in Chinese style, is worth seeing, as is the **Provincial Museum**, *2 Xin Hua Avenue, Tel. 6964924,* with a highly recommended exhibition about the Mongolians. For those serious about Mongolians, there is a Mongolia Society in the US. You might also be interested in the **Mongolia Art Performing College** and the **Horse Rodeo School** with displays of singing, dancing, and horsemanship. Ask about them at the local tourist office.

Walks

Out in the rolling grasslands, you can see for miles, and hiking is a pure joy.

Festivals

The dates of the **Nadamu Festival** are now set by the province and depend on the harvest. Some areas celebrate in July, others in August. This annual fair in Hohhot is held around August 15-20th. Tourists then go on to celebrations outside Hohhot.

For example, at **Sitenghuile**, 100 km north of Hohhot on a poor road, there is a demonstration of Mongolian culture with a parade, wrestling, archery, horsemanship, and traditional songs and dances. You eat Mongolian food, sleep in a concrete *yurt* with cement floor, use flush toilets, and visit Mongolian homes. You can ride horses and camels. Tourists sometimes outnumber Mongolians.

At **Xilinhot**, 700 km from Hohhot, foreigners might sleep in *yurts* or in town and commute about 40 minutes to the fair grounds carrying their own food. The 10,000 Mongolians attending Nadamu sleep in *yurts*, put up booths to sell kitchenware, boots, carpets, and motorcycles, but no native clothes or jewelry. They wear traditional dress, and used muddy open pit toilets with canvas covers. There could be circus acts, wrestling, archery, and horse- riding competitions with lots of chaos and no explanations, no dancers, and no horseback rides. Only a few foreigners attend.

You have to choose. Because of the crowds, I urge you to book a place through a travel agency and expect no star accommodations. These will probably improve as organizers get more experience.

SHOPPING

Today, in addition to less exotic goods, Inner Mongolia produces woolen textiles, cashmere sweaters, carpets, and tapestries. It also manufactures Mongolian-style boots, daggers with chopsticks, silver bowls, brass hot pots, cheap but fancy tweezers, wrestlers jackets, saddles, stirrups, and felt stockings. Also available are antique bottles of jade or agate.

Try the **Inner Mongolian Minorities Handicraft Factory** and Minzu Shang Chang (**Nationalities Market**, *Tel. 6968822*), the **Hohhot Antique Shop**, *10 Xilin Nan Lu, Tel. 6968430, 6966748* and the **Hohhot Carpet Factory**. There's also the **Tian Yuan Department Store** opposite the Minzu Shang Chang. Shopping is better in Hohhot than in the grasslands.

EXCURSIONS & DAY TRIPS

Baotou in western Inner Mongolia, 20 km north of the Yellow River, is 144 km from Hohhot. It is 800 km from Beijing, about a 12 hour train trip, or a 1.5 hour flight. It is connected to nine other cities by air. The average altitude is 1000 meters, its annual rainfall a sparse 312 mm. The city was founded in the 17th century (Qing) on a neolithic site. The urban population is about 1,700,000, of whom the Han are 90%, the Mongolians 2.5%, and the rest 21 other national minorities.

Locally produced in this region are carpets, cashmere knitwear, leather and furs, porcelain, and arts and crafts.

If you only have one day, you might want to visit the Wudangzhao Lamasery and take a quick city tour. The **Wudangzhao Lamasery** is 70 km east of town in Huluntu Mountain, Guyang county. It is a massive 2,500 room complex established in 1794 (Qing), once home to 1,200 monks and covering about 50 acres. The largest monastery in western Inner Mongolia, it contains statues, murals, and *tangkas* typical of the yellow sect of Tibetan Buddhism. (More about Tibetan Buddhism under Lhasa and Chengde.)

If you have more time, also visit the **Meidaizhao Lamasery**, originally built in the Ming, which is at Tumd You Banner, 80 km east of Baotou. It is also known as the Sanniangzi Temple after Wang Zhaojun. Her husband, the temple's founder, is buried here.

The *Tomb of Genghis Khan** was moved 170 km south of Baotou to Ejinhoroq (Elinhoro) in 1954. It contains ashes, said to be his. Pilgrims gather here to pay homage for one day in the third, fifth, ninth, and tenth lunar months.

You can also visit the **Great Wall**, 40 km and 70 km north of Baotou. And all places of interest are open 8am-6pm daily.

The best hotel here is the **Qingshan Hotel**, three stars.

CITS and **CTS** are at the *Baotou Hotel, Kundulun District, 014010, Tel. 5156655, Fax 5154615*. Address tourist complaints to the *Baotou Tourism Bureau, City Hall, Kundulun District, 014010, Tel. 5152255*.

PRACTICAL INFORMATION

Business Hours, offices 8:30am-5:30pm. Stores 9am-7pm.

China Comfort Travel Service, *32 Xin Hua Avenue, Tel. 6951385, 6967066, Fax 6967336*.

CITS Group, *32 Xinhua Avenue, 010020, Tel. 6951385, Fax 6967336*.

CYTS Tours, *9 Zhong Shan Dong Road, 010020, Tel. 6964968*.

Inner Mongolia Tourism Bureau, *95 Yishuting Nan Street, 010010, Tel. 6914197, 6965978, Fax 6968561*.

Inner Mongolia Railway International Travel Service, *112 Xilin Bei Road, 010057, Tel. 6244822, Fax 6932586. E-mail:tglint@public.hh.nm.cn*.

Police, *Tel. 110*.

Telephone code, *0471*.

Tourism Administration of Inner Mongolia, *Inner Mongolia Hotel, 010020, Tel. 6964233. For complaints, Tel. 6914196*.

CHANGCHUN

Capital of Jilin province, **Changchun** is noted mostly as an industrial city manufacturing automobiles, trucks, railway carriages, tractors, and textiles. It was also the capital of Japanese Manchuria and it has Puyi's palace. The total population is 6.5 million; the urban population is 3.8 million. Changchun is very cold in winter (lowest -30 C). The average annual rainfall is 600-700 millimeters, mainly in July and August. There are about 150 frost-free days!

ARRIVALS & DEPARTURES

Changchun is a 90-minute flight northeast of Beijing. It can also be reached by plane from about 22 other Chinese cities, Seoul, Vladivostok, and Hong Kong. From Shenyang, you can take a train now but after 2000, you will be able to drive there in four hours. From Harbin it is a five-hour train ride.

ORIENTATION

Changchun was founded in 1800. Invaded by Tsarist Russia in the 1890s, it became a Japanese concession in 1905 and the capital of Japanese-controlled Manchukuo from 1931 until 1945. Parts can be very attractive with lovely broad avenues flanked by beautiful hospital and university buildings.

The province of Jilin borders on Korea and Russia. Its 24 million people include Koreans, Manchus, Hui, Mongols and Xibos. Settlements have been recorded since the Qin dynasty.

WHERE TO STAY

The luxurious **Shangri-La Hotel** is the best place to stay. The **Swiss-belhotel** is good but too far from downtown to consider. The **Noble** is better located but needs work. The **Paradise** is too old and run down. The **International Trade Centre Hotel**, while well located, was not up to international standards. Most hotels add 15% service charge, and some also add a Y5 tax and Y2 social security fund. All accept major credit cards, have discounts, money exchange, direct dial telephones, and business centers.

SHANGRI-LA HOTEL, *9 Xian Road, 130061 at Chongqing Road. Five stars. Tel. 8981818, Fax 8981919. In North America, Tel. 800/942-5050. $140-$210 for rooms; $340-$1200 for suites.*

Located in the diplomatic, financial, business and entertainment district, the Shangri-La is 2.5 km from the railway station, 10 km from the airport, and one km from the city hall. Opened in 1996, it has 458 rooms plus 63 serviced apartments and 84 offices. It also has three executive floors, a Cantonese restaurant, and karaoke lounge. There's also a gym, jacuzzi, sauna, steambath, indoor pool, children's playground, and lighted tennis court. Rooms have safes, and five television channels in English. The decor is western style, and it has been lacking the antiques, art work, and fancy chandeliers that make its sister hotels in Hong Kong and Beijing so special. But it is attractive with frosted glass accents and comfortable stuffed arm chairs. The service is very good.

NOBLE HOTEL, *135 Renmin Street, 130021. Tel. 5622888, Fax 5665522. Five stars. $100-$140 for rooms; $260-$1500 for suites.*

With 25 floors and 301 rooms, sloppy standards spoil this otherwise good-looking hotel: a broken window and unpolished brass. It has narrow halls and low ceilings. But it has safes in rooms, bowling, sauna, indoor pool, and CNN, Thai and Singaporean food. An extra bed costs $20.

WHERE TO EAT

Changchun has some exotic specialties: *houtou* (golden orchid monkey head) mushrooms, *ginseng* chicken, thick deer antler soup (with sea cucumber, prawns, egg white, ham, and chicken), and frog oil soup. Frog oil is said to be very nutritious and tastes better than it sounds. Please, no endangered species! And yes, you can get other dishes too! Ask for the carmelized potatoes.

The best restaurants are in the hotels but for a change, you can try the **Nong Jia Restaurant,** *23 Bei Jing Da Jie, Tel. 2734137*; or **Papa's Korean Restaurant,** *20 Da Jing Road, Tel. 8738504.* The **Shangri-La's** prices are moderate: silver garlic cod Y80, broccoli Y28 and sizzling beef Y65.

SEEING THE SIGHTS

If you have only one day in Changchun, you must see the **Museum of the Former Palaces of the Last Emperor Pu Yi**, 10 km from the Changbaishan Hotel. From 1932 to 1945, Pu Yi lived and worked in this complex. He was made Emperor of Manchukuo by the Japanese. The **Ton De Palace** was actually used as one of the sets in the movie *The Last Emperor*. (The movie company put in the chandelier). Only one of Pu Yi's wives lived in this palace which was built for Pu Yi by the Japanese and now holds provincial relics. A good guide can tell you which rooms she lived in. Pu Yi himself lived in a neighboring building; he believed the Ton De Palace was bugged and used it only for receptions.

You can see the emperor's throne and his living quarters in the white trim Qian Ming building. Wax figures, photographs of the emperor, his wedding, wives, and English teacher are on display. The palace was looted after the Japanese surrender and Pu Yi was exiled to the Soviet Union. During the Cultural Revolution, Mao badges were produced here. (Many are still on sale.) A tunnel goes from here to the railway station.

In Changchun, you might want also to include: the **Changchun Film Studio**, one of China's largest. The **Changchun Movie City**, a theme park, is more for domestic tourists. At the **Changchun Number One Motor**

Vehicle Plant, you can watch a more labor-intensive manufacturing process than in America or Europe. You won't believe the wages! **Ice sculptures** are at South Lake in winter.

On summer evenings you can find dancers in costume in **People's Square**. And you should be able to relax across from the Shangri-La at **Second Home** (songs in English), and **Friday Bar**.

The **Changbaishan Nature Reserve**, with tigers, deer, and sable is in Antu County about 300 km southeast, with its own mythical monster and at least two hotels.

For fans of **steam locomotives**, especially in wintertime, photos are good at the East Junction (Tong Har Tao Kao), 15 minutes by taxi from the Changbaishan Hotel. Another good site for photos is the South Bridge (Quan Ping Tao Quo, tram 53 or 54).

Festivals: A fascinating time can be had at the **Mongolian Festival** in Baicheng, 400 km from Changchun, five or six days of horse racing, archery, wrestling, and dances. A **Ginseng Festival** is held for three days, usually in August, in Fusong county at the foot of Changbai Mountain. In August-September is the **Port Wine Festival**. A **film festival** takes place every two years in August. Check exact dates with travel agents.

SHOPPING

Changchun manufactures wine, ginseng, sable, deer antlers (aphrodisiacs), and frog oil (tonic). It also produces carpets, embroidery, mushrooms, azalea wood carvings, and bark pictures. Please avoid furs from endangered species. **People's Department Store** near the Shangri-La is open 9am-5:30pm; **Changchun Department Store** at *77 Dajing Road, Tel. 8985720* has five floors of goods. Good buys are leather coats, fur hats and jackets but check the tanning carefully.

The four-story **antique center** at *75 Qing Ming Street* is open 9:30am-4:30pm. It has old cameras, stamps, coins, onyx vases, "Tang" figurines, silver Qing hair ornaments, etc. The **Ginseng and Pilose Antler Market** at *27 Tongzhi Street, Tel. 5677275*, specializes in ginseng, *Tel. 8922318 X 2214*. Valuable are the ones with strings, the longer and most human-like the better. Red and Korean are more popular.

EXCURSIONS & DAY TRIPS

The **Deer Town** is at Shuang Yang, 46 km south of the city, a holiday resort with the largest herd in China. Nearby is the biggest wooden buddha in the northeast at *No. 29 Shuang Yang Street, Tel. 4223002, or 4223764*.

Jilin is in the center of Jilin province, 90 km east of Changchun, and about 100 minutes away by highway. You can get a bus every 30 to 60 minutes from the Jilin Bus Station on Renmin Bei Road in Changchun. You can reach it by rail from Beijing, Changchun, Shenyang, Harbin, and Tianjin. You can fly there twice a week from Beihai, Beijing, Changchun and Changsha. The airport is 25 km away. The population of Jilin is nearly one million.

Tourist attractions include the **Jilin Exhibition Hall** with a 1770-kilogram meteorite, believed to be the largest in the world, and **Songhua Lake**, a 480-sq-km man-made lake, 20 km from the city center. The Songhua River runs through the city and beautiful hoarfrost forms on the trees lining its banks in -20 C weather. the **Rime Festival** celebrates this phenomenum. Ice lanterns are sculpted in the winter.

Jilin has **skiing**. Jingye, Beida Lake and Tonghua all have lifts and hotels. The **Changbai Mountains** have alpine skiing with lifts operating from December to February.

The Changbai mountains are 380 km southeast of the city, their highest peak 2,691 meters. The famous crater is beautiful Heaven Lake with its own mythical monster. The mountains can be reached by road from Jilin and Yanji, by rail from Tonghua and tourist helicopter from Yangji. The other side is Korea.

You can also see **Arladi Village**, 70 km from Jilin, where Korean customs are still practiced.

Local specialties include venison, frog oil soup, steamed whitefish, raw salmon and carp, and chicken and **ginseng** in earthenware pots.

Visitors can stay at the four-star **Crystal Hotel. CITS** and **CTS** are at *4 Jiangwan Road, 132001. For CITS, Tel. 443451, Fax 453773.* The telephone code is *0432.*

PRACTICAL INFORMATION

Changchun Overseas Tourist Corporation, *37, Jie Fang Road, 130041. Tel. 8692002, 8692178, mobile 1384323751, Fax 8692001.*

China Jilin Changbaishan International Travel Service, *2 Nanhu Road, (Nanhu Hotel), 130021. Tel. 5688919, 5684242, Fax 5684300.* (Mainly tours to Changbaishan).

CITS Jilin, *7th floor, Yinmao Da Sha Building, 14 Xinmin Street, 130021, Tel. 5609039, mobile 1394338866, Fax 5645069.*

Hours: *8:30am to 4:30pm Monday through Friday (offices). Stores are open 8 or 9am to 5:30 or 6:30pm.*

Telephone Code, *0431*

HARBIN

(Haerhpin)

Harbin is the capital of China's northernmost province of Heilongjiang, formerly part of Japan's Manchuria. It produces the likes of helicopters, boilers and coal. Important for visitors are its **Siberian tigers**, its amazing **morning market**, and its **ice sculpture festival**. Outside the city is a red-crested crane reserve, the best skiing in China, and day trips to Siberia.

Its highest summer temperature is 36 C; its lowest in winter is -38 C with an average daytime temperature in January of -15 C. The July average is 27 C. The winter is six months long, so take your longjohns. Wintertime, however, is brightened by the Ice Sculpture Festival, its major tourist attraction. You can also bring skates and skis. The annual precipitation is 250-700 millimeters, mostly June through August.

ARRIVALS & DEPARTURES

Harbin is a 90-minute flight or 12-hour train ride northeast of Beijing, or a five-hour train ride from Changchun. Flights are with Hong Kong, Khabarovsk, Seoul, and Vladivostok and 33 Chinese cities. After the expressway is completed in 1999, the airport will be 30 km south of the city. It should make driving easier from Changchun as well.

ORIENTATION

The area was first settled by people of the Nuzhen nationality in 1097. In the Yuan, the city was renamed Harbin. In 1898 it became a Russian concession with Tsarist police in charge. After the Communist revolution it became home for thousands of White Russians who built synagogues as well as Russian churches. From 1932, the Japanese occupied it until the war's end in 1945. You will see a lot of imperialist Russian and Japanese architecture, and cobblestone streets (in Dao Li District). The sprawling city has a few convenient expressways but is still subject to traffic jams and air pollution. Harbin is planning a mass transit railway.

Harbin has a total population of nine million, of whom at least three million are urban. Heilongjiang province numbers among its 35 million people Han, Manchu, Korean, Hui, Mongolian, Daur, Orogen, Ewenki, Kirgiz, Hezhen, and other nationalities.

WHERE TO STAY

The most beautiful hotel currently is the five-star standard **Singapore** with its magnificent water park next door. The **New World Hotel** is second best for quality and is close to government buildings, the Trade Exhibition Center, the Russian Market and Museum. The best for group tourists are the **Gloria Inn** because of its fantastic location, and the

Holiday Inn (the second best location). Between them is the very pleasant car-free Central Avenue (Zhongyang Dajie), the main shopping area. Nearby are St. Sophia Cathedral, a European-style neighborhood, and city hall. The morning markets here are really amazing; they cling to the riverside for at least three km west of the Gloria Inn, full of flowers, food, clothing, pets, snakes, antiques, and women hobbling on bound feet. People gather and dance on summer evenings in the square in front of the Gloria.

The **Flamingo Hotel** is a cheaper alternative for business people with relatively good English, good service, and a good breakfast buffet. But its carpets are stained and its uninspiring. In an industrial area, it is near provincial government offices, a developing high-tech zone, and far from shopping. Cheaper and near the Flamingo is the older **Swan Hotel** with poor English. If this is still too expensive, check out the **Central Hotel** behind.

All hotels listed except for the Central have money changing, business centers, international direct dialing, minibars, and credit card service. You can also get discounts.

A 346-room **Shangri-La Hotel** should open in 1999 with apartments and offices as well, tennis, pool, health club, and a grand ballroom that can fit 1300 people. It should rival the Singapore in quality. It will be at *555 Youyi Road* on the river to the east of the Gloria. *Tel. 4607296.* Also being built is an **Intercontinental Hotel**, due in 2000. Prices below are subject to 15% surcharge, a small tax and discounts.

SINGAPORE HOTEL (Xinjiapo Dajiudian), *68 Ganshui Road, Xiangfang District, 150036. Tel. 2336888, Fax 2331818. Managed by Ananda Hotel Management Limited. In Xiangfang Economic Development Zone, with 21 storys and 338 rooms, rooms here range from $275-$240. Suites cost $320-$3380. The presidential suite has nine rooms.*

With its curved staircases, and wood-trimmed, pink and beige marble interior, the lobby here is a joy to see. Rooms are western style with safes and CNN, and the grand ballroom can seat 600 for dinner. The Singapore also has executive floors and 24-hour room service, shuttle bus, tennis and indoor pool. See below.

HARBIN FLAMINGO HOTEL (Shang He Dajiudian), *119 Minsheng Road, Dongli, Tel. 2603677, Fax 2657028. E-mail:flamingo@public.hr.hl.cn. Three stars. $105-$125 for rooms; $140-$170 for suites.*

Built in 1994-96 and near an economic zone, provincial and city government offices, this 180 room property gives a generous supply of feather pillows. It has offices, 24-hour room service, Cantonese and western food, a gym and sauna. A Zenith Hotel.

HOLIDAY INN CITY CENTRE HARBIN (Wanda Jia Ri Jiu Dian), *90 Jingwei Street, Daoli District, 150010. Four-star standard. Tel. 4226666. Fax*

4221661. $98-$140 for rooms. It's a 30 minute drive from the airport and four km from the railway station. 144 rooms. Buffet breakfast Y75.

The lobby here is simple with a gorgeous jade pagoda. Rooms receive only CNN, and no safes. Though it opened in 1995, this is not the usual Holiday Inn Asia standard although it does have a non- smoking floor, in-house movies, e-mail service, a gym with sauna and steam room, Cantonese, and Northeastern food. It does not however have a pool nor tennis.

NEW WORLD BEI FANG HOTEL HARBIN (Beifang Jiudian), *403 Huayuan Jie, Nangang Qu, 150001. Four-star. Tel. 3628888, Fax 3622828. E-mail:BFHOTEL@public.hr.hl.cn. Reservations in North America 800/637-7200. Y650-Y1920. 45 km from the airport, and five km from the railway station.*

Set in the business and commercial district next to the Trade Exhibition Centre, this 1995 hotel looks very institutional. It was originally built as a Russian guest house. It has 329 rooms, three executive floors, CNN and inhouse movies. It also has a clinic, gym, and billiards.

SONGHUAJIANG GLORIA INN (Kaili Fandian), *257 Zhongyang Avenue, Daoli District, 150010. Tel. 4638855, Fax 4638533. Tel. 800/821-0900. $59-$71 for rooms; $118-$166 for suites. No discounts, it says, but try. 304 rooms and duplex apartments.*

This simple, unpretentious hotel functions well. The location is great (see above). It's exotic and romantic. In the winter, you can enjoy the sunset and river from its front rooms (though the windows are small). In the summer, you can walk along the river or look for onion-domed Orthodox churches nearby and try to visualise the bushy-hatted czarist police patrolling the streets here. We found the hotel's ambience light and airy, the business center very helpful. Don't expect a pool but it does have CNN, in-house movies and room service. It has a seafood restaurant and coffee shop.

SHIRBLE SWAN HOTEL (Tian E Fandian), *95 Zhongshan Road, 150036. Three stars, Tel. 2300201, Fax 2304895. 45 km from the airport; five km from the railway station. Y450-Y790 for rooms; Y580-Y1680 for suites.*

Built 1983 and renovated 1998, this modest, 15-story, 258-room hotel has small rooms and baths, only CNN in English, and no room safes. We found a few cracked dishes, but a cheap all-you-can-eat hot pot with crab, shrimp and goat, etc. cost only Y38. There's also a 12-lane bowling alley, a pool, and its own brewery.

CENTRAL HOTEL (Gong Xin Binguan), *95-2 Zhongshan Road, 150036. Tel. 2327758, Fax 2310676. Behind the Swan Hotel. Two stars. Y188-Y228, and cheapest for the top fifth floor.*

This 39-room hotel is a tourism training school, and has no elevator, nor television in English. It does have 24-hour hot water, restaurant, and private rooms.

WHERE TO EAT

The most exotic dishes are moose nose and hazel grouse. Please, avoid endangered species! For those who want something less questionable, try monkey-head-shaped mushrooms.

The hotels have excellent food and the **Singapore Hotel** has been giving 50%-off specials for women. Many department stores have adequate cheap food. The **Holiday Inn** has had a Y58 lunch buffet.

HUA MEI RESTAURANT, *142 Zhongyang Street, Tel. 4617368.*
This place has the best Russian food in town.

HARBIN RESTAURANT, *Shang Zhi Street.*
The Harbin has good northeastern food.

SEEING THE SIGHTS

Come for the natural scenery, China's best skiing, and the ice sculpture festival. Come for the red-crested crane sanctuary and the Siberian tigers. Come for the cooler summers and Siberia. How many people can say they've been to Siberia?

The magical **Ice Sculpture Festival**, from early January to February 25, depends on the weather. You can easily spend three hours here. Its twinkling colored lights are best seen at dusk around 5pm, before it gets too cold. Teams compete from all over the world with giant ice pagodas, bridges, lanterns, human figures, and palaces.

If you have a couple of days to spare, you could add Siberia to your list of exotic destinations. **Heihe** on the border is 600 km north and travel agents can arrange. They can also get you bird-watching, gold panning, horse riding (Mongolian), and skiing. You can take steam locomotive tours on narrow-gauge mining and logging trains.

If you only have one day in Harbin, it only takes a couple hours to visit the eight or so very healthy **Siberian tigers** and watch them gobble down live chickens, rabbits, deer or calves in their huge home. On the other hand, the gore might turn you off. The animals however are beautiful. Just imagine trying to move these big cats during the recent floods. Take a taxi three km south of the toll booth beyond the Song Wan Jeung Gong Lu Da Qiao Bridge. The bridge is near Sun Island on the Song Hua River. Turn right, a few meters past the huge red mansion and drive about one km to the only "Tiger Park" sign on the way. The Y33 entrance fee gives you a 30-minute ride on a bus with barred windows. Attendants request additional money for the live sacrifices. You can join a tour, a Chinese one if an English-speaking guide is not available. It doesn't take much language to enjoy them.

If You're a Bird Watcher

China's biggest bird sanctuary, the 210,000-hectare **Zhalong Nature Preserve** is near Qiqihar, 180 km from Harbin. Its cranes, storks, swans, geese, and herons are best seen from April to September. The famous red-crested cranes are considered a symbol of luck. For more information, contact **CITS**, *4 Wenhua Street, Qiqihar, 161005, Tel. (0452)2712016, Fax 2715836.*

NIGHTLIFE & ENTERTAINMENT

Ask about the annual **Harbin Summer Music Festival** in July. Singapore Hotel's **Dreamworld** is a great place to swim all year round. Safety standards are high. Waves in its 1000 sq. meter pool churn for 15 minutes per hour and slides drop you from a height of 15 meters. Open 10am-10pm weekdays, 9am-11pm on weekends, it puts on a short laser show projected on mist every evening. The fee for three hours is Y20 for children, and Y60 to Y70 for adults. Credit cards are accepted. Dreamworld also has bowling, disco and a night club. *Tel. 2336888.*

SHOPPING

Sable, mink and muskrat hats, jackets, and collars are made here. Handicrafts include straw patchwork, horn carving, knitting, and ivory, jade, stone, and wood carving. Good to eat are its pine nuts and good for you, is *ginseng*. A tiny store at the cruddy **International Hotel** has been selling antique porcelain, archer's thumb rings, jade pieces, old cameras and pocket watches. The **Swan Hotel** had the most hotel stores: over-priced pearls, fur coats, antique wall clocks (Y200-Y350), phonographs, and local paintings. The stalls at the **Chinese-Russian Street Market** on *Zhongyang Street* are worth a look. For information, *Tel. 2511078.* Open 8am-5pm, daily, it had Y20 fresh water pearls, mink pelts, fur hats (Y150-Y650), Russian dolls and imports, Chinese antiques of ivory, jade and coral, fossils, and petrified wood.

The upmarket **New World Department Store** near the New World Hotel takes major credit cards, and is open 9am-8pm. It has up-to-date styles and imported brands. **Central Street** (between the Gloria Inn and the Holiday Inn has the popular **Zhong Yang Shang Chang Department Store**, **Bossini's** and **KFC**. Stalls here operate after the stores close. The **Antique building** is at *62 Hoang Jun Street, Nan Gang District,* near many gold stores. It is across the square from the International Hotel and provincial museum, and is open 8:30am-4pm five days a week. Stores here sell porcelain and old jewelery.

EXCURSIONS & DAY TRIPS

Heilongjiang has China's biggest ski resort: **Yabuli Ski and Vacation Resort**, *Tel. 451/3455066, Fax 3455058.* It is 195 km by expressway from Harbin, about 1.5 hours from Mudanjiang. Buses leave twice a day at 8am and 1:20pm daily from the Longyun Road bus station in Harbin. By train it takes four hours.

On 2,255 hectares, with an elevation of 1000 meters, Yabuli is used also for training China's national ski team.

WINDMILL VILLAGE, *150631, in the Yabuli Ski and Vacation Resort. Tel. 3455088, 3455168, Fax 3455138.*

This three-star ski lodge has 500 beds, Chinese and western restaurants, and a conference room seating 500 people. It has international direct dial, business center, and fax service, and was open for the 1996 Asian Games.

The skiing season goes from early November to April. The resort has three lifts, three beginners' tows, and night skiing. It offers lessons and has two first-aid stations, 11 runs totalling 30 km for all levels. It also has five km of cross-country trails. Yabuli is open in the summer with bob-sled runs, mini-golf, hot air ballooning and gliding. See also Chapter 10, *Sports Recreation, & Ecotourism.*

Closer to Harbin and less challenging is **Yuquan**. In both places you can rent skis and clothes. Lift tickets cost about Y40 per day. For the **Heilongjiang Yabuli International Travel Service**, *call Tel. 2334783, Fax 2309722.* The **telephone code** is *0451.*

PRACTICAL INFORMATION

Ambulance, *Tel. 120.*

Internet Service: *China Telecom, 127 Zhongyang Street, 3/F, Tel. 4689312.* Open daily 8:30am-5:00pm. Y9 an hour for e-mail.

Harbin Air Tickets Centre, *171 Zhong Shan Road, Tel. 2651188.*

Office Hours, 8am-5pm; stores 9am-7 or 8pm.

Railway enquiry, *Tel. 6420115.*

Harbin Tourism Bureau, *Tel. 6225009, 6208756.*

Heilongjiang China International Travel Service, *95-1 Zhongshan Road, 150036. Tel. 2302579, Fax 2302476.*

Heilongjiang CTS, *72 Hong Jun Nangang District, 150001. Tel. and Fax 3644679.*

Heilongjiang Overseas Tourist Corporation, *8/F, Dongfang Building, 235 Huayuan Street, Nangang District, 150001. Tel. 3633611, 3642671, Fax 3621088.*

Heilongjiang Tourism Administration, *4 Xi Dazhi Street, Nangang, 150001, Tel. 3630860, 3635223, 3641441 X 826, Fax 3630860, 3635223.*

Police, *Tel. 110.*
Telephone Code, *0451.*

SHENYANG

(Formerly Mukden)

Shenyang is the capital of Liaoning province which borders on North Korea. In the news recently because of its recently discovered fossils of bird dinosaurs, it was inhabited by apemen 280,000 years ago. It has a history of over 2,700 years. Shenyang was the Manchu capital from 1625 until 1644. After that, the Manchus moved to Beijing as the Qing dynasty. Shenyang is the biggest industrial city in this region, which was formerly Japanese-held Manchuria. The **Mukden Incident** on September 18, 1931, a surprise attack on the Chinese army stationed here, marked the beginning of Japanese aggression in China.

The weather is hottest in August, averaging 23.8 C; the coldest in January is -30 C. Rain is mainly from June to August with an annual 760 mm. The urban population is about 6.12 million, total 6.8 million. Shenyang is a sister city of Chicago.

ARRIVALS & DEPARTURES

Shenyang is 75 minutes by air northeast of Beijing. Flights with Hong Kong, Irkutsk, Macau, Osaka, Seoul and 41 Chinese cities are available. You can also reach it by train and expressway (in four to five hours), from Dalian, about 375 km away. Trains connecting with Beijing and Harbin use the Shenyang North Station at *102, Bei Zan Road, Shen He District;* with Dalian, the South Station, *2, Sheng Li Nan Street, in He Ping District.*

ORIENTATION

Shenyang today is an industrial and cultural center, with many institutions of higher learning and research. It has two ring roads around the city, one 30 km long, and the other 80. You should always add extra time for traffic jams.

WHERE TO STAY

The top hotel is **Traders**, then the austere **New World**, both within a block of each other in the downtown commercial area, about 27 km from the airport and 15 from the railway station. When the five-star **Sheraton** is opened in 1999, it should rival Traders in quality, but it will be in the southern part of the city, catering to the expatriate community and high technological zone, another market. It should be followed shortly by its rival the **Marriott**, both only about 15 minutes from the airport and 15 minutes from downtown. Both are across the road from the Summer Palace indoor pool, and a big supermarket and suburbia. The **Gloria Plaza** has a good location near the railway station to be developed by 2003 into the financial and trading district. Within a kilometer is the city government building, and China Telecom. A five-star 350-room **Crowne Plaza** and 200-room **Holiday Inn** should open in 1999. Shenyang has a hotel boom, lots of choices, and lots of soft prices. Take advantage of them.

Hotels listed here all have money changing, credit cards, and business center services. Prices are subject to 15% surcharge and discounts.

TRADERS HOTEL (Shang Mao Fan Dian), *68 Zhong Hua Road, Heping District, 110001. Four stars. Tel. 23412288, Fax 23411988. In North America, Tel. 800/942-5050. $150-$210 for rooms; suites $310-$1300.*

This 595-room hotel has an Irish fun pub, northeastern, western, and Cantonese food. Its health club has a gym, jacuzzi, sauna, and steambath. Rooms have safes, in-house movies and 24-hour room service. Executive floor rooms are very spacious with wide twin beds. Shangri-La Hotels and Resorts.

SHERATON SHENYANG, *370 Qingnian Street, Heping District, Shenyang, 110003. Tel. 23842874, 23921096, Fax 23921070, 23921121.*

This 1999 hotel has two towers of 570 rooms plus apartments.

NEW WORLD COURTYARD SHENYANG, *2 Nanjing Nan Street, Heping District, 110001. Four stars. Tel. 23869888, Fax 23860018. In North America, Tel. 800/321-2211. Four stars. 30 km from the airport and 15 km from the railway station. $120-$155 for rooms; $200-$1600 for suites.*

Built in 1994, this 22-story, 263-room hotel has non-smoking and executive floors, CNN, indoor pool, gym and sauna. Its ballroom is able to serve 350 sit-down dinner guests. It also has bowling, disco, karaoke and undercover parking. A Courtyard by Marriott Hotel.

GLORIA PLAZA HOTEL (Kailai Fandian), *32 Yingbin Street, Shenhe District, 110013. Tel. 22528855, Fax 22521112. Http://www.hotel-web.com/ gloria/index.htm. Four stars. Y998 for foreigners, Y498 to Y568 for domestic, Hong Kong and Macau guests. The price includes breakfast.*

Opened in 1995, this hotel has a higher standard of English than other comparable hotels. It has 289 rooms, with mini-bars, satellite television, Cantonese, Shanghai, and western cuisine, gym, sauna, and business center.

WHERE TO EAT

Local delicacies like frog oil soup are available in the autumn only. The best food is in the top hotels. At **Traders** the lunch buffet offered very tasty fare that included curries, sushi, and salads. No stinting on the spices here! The executive floor breakfast buffet included *dim sum*, scrambled eggs, bacon, and Danish pasteries.

PHOENIX HOTEL, *Fenghuang Fandian, near the Palace, 109 Huanghe Nan Street, Tel. 86805858.*

Although only a three-star hotel, the food and service has been good. Try the crispy bamboo shrimp, stir-fried Phoenix special, pork cutlets, and pork hocks. The dumplings were delicious too.

OVERSEAS TOURISM CORPORATION, *113 Huanghe Nan Street, Tel. 86248150.*

This has a small restaurant where the food is less spicy and the price reasonable. Edible were the beef and green peppers, the Mandarin fish, crystal sweet potatoes, and sweet and sour pork cutlets.

SEEING THE SIGHTS

If you only have one day, do consider the not-to-be-missed Imperial Palace and Beiling Tombs. The 19-year reigns of Nurhachi (Nulhachi) and Huangtaiji (Huang Tai Chi) were enough to build the very impressive *Imperial Palace, 171 Shenyang Road, Tel. 24844192, 4843227.* The palace dates from 1625 to 1636, and is now restored to its original gaudy splendor. In an area of almost 60,000 square meters, be prepared for lots of walking. Although this palace has a lot of Han influence, look for Mongolian and Manchu-style touches. The most impressive section is the eastern one, with its octagonal Dazheng Dian (**Hall of Great Affairs**) and Shiwang Ting (**Pavilions of Ten Princes**). Does the Beijing Palace have such dragons on its pillars and the yurt-like design? The hall was used for important ceremonies and meetings with top officials.

Huangtaiji commanded his military forces and conducted business from the Chongzhen Dian (**Hall of Supreme Administration**). At the back of this hall is a road to the Fenghuang Lou (**Phoenix Tower**) and the Qingning Gong (**Palace of Pure Tranquility**). The families lived in the Qingning Gong, which is the most distinctively Manchu.

In the western section is the Wenshuo Ge (**Hall of Literary Source**), especially constructed for the Complete Library of the Four Treasures of Qing Emperor Qianlong. Unfortunately, no signs are in English.

The *Beiling (or North) Tombs, also called the Zhaoling Tombs, are on *Beiling Street, Tel. 86896203, 86896337,* in the north of the city. They are of Huangtaiji and his wife Borjigid (Poerchichiteh). Huangtaiji was the son of Nurhachi. Begun in 1643, the tombs were completed in 1651. If you still want to study more Manchu tombs, the **Dongling** (East) **Tombs** (or Fuling Tombs), of Nurhachi and his wife Yihnaran, are 20 km from the city, *Tel. 88416474, 88842494.* During the Ming, Nurhachi unified the tribes, became Khan in 1616, and made Shenyang his capital in 1625.

Other Sights

Also of interest is the **Shenyang Steam Locomotives Museum**, *Sujiatun Jiwuduan, Sujiatun District,* open daily 9am-4pm with exhibits from nine countries. The best place to see the real thing is at Chaoyang City, six hours southwest of Shenyang. This has more locomotives than Shenyang and the slope is better for taking photos. See also Anshan below.

The **Liaoning Provincial Museum** is located at *26, Shiwei Road, Heping District, Tel. 22822936, 22821316* in the mansion of a former warlord's son. It had an excellent exhibition of photos of the city taken 1901 to 1912 by a French photographer. It also has exhibits with a few English titles starting from 280,000 years ago. Open 9am-4:30pm daily May 1 to October 30; otherwise 9am-3pm. Closed Mondays. Its store had outrageously high prices, ten times the prices at this Imperial Palace. It takes credit cards.

NIGHTLIFE & ENTERTAINMENT

Evenings from 8pm-1am around **Chairman Mao Square** can be fun. This is where many Chinese people relax and dance. You could also try it at 6am too. Look for the nearby **Liaoning Hotel**, a relic from the Japanese past. The art deco stained glass windows, dark mahagony woodwork and rattan furniture are worth savoring. They are from the time this hotel was the most fashionable in the city.

You might consider swimming in the **Summer Palace**, claimed to be China's biggest water activity center. It's at *No. 215, Shen He District, Qing Nian Street, Tel. 23848779,* beside the Singapore Hotel. It has other sports as well. Shenyang also has Go-Karts, golf and bowling.

SHOPPING

Produced in the province are diamonds, ginseng, sable and carvings of jade, agate, jet, and amber. Also produced are ceramics, root carvings, the musical instrument *zheng,* shell carvings, feather pictures, and paintings. Ask about the jade factory and the feather picture factory.

The main shopping area is around the **Dong Ya Commercial Square** on *212 Zhongjie Street,* around the **Liaoning Department Store**, *63 Zhonghua Road, Tel. 23863312,* and around the **Zhongxing-Shenyang Department Store**, *86 Taiyuan Bei Street, Tel. 23838888.* On Taiyuan Street walking street at the side of Traders Hotel is the **Korean Department Store** with a good selection of arts and crafts on the 4th and 5th floors at reasonable prices: buffalo horn carvings, linens, paintings, enamelware, shell pictures and screens. Paintings can be mounted on scrolls here. *Open 9am-6pm daily, Tel. 23834184.*

Look for antiques and curios at the **Shenyang Eastern Folk Art Exchange City** (Friendship Street City), *5, You Hao Street, Shenhe District, Tel. 22525687, 22525689 or Fax 22520485.* Open daily 8:30am-5pm. This building houses four stories of tiny private shops with collectors' teapots, root carvings, black porcelain, serpentine carvings, and jewelry (Y400-Y1000). It also had Shaoshan stones with tiny calligraphy by master artist Zhao Wen Guang at reasonable prices, and items with a crystalline glaze, cheap and attractive. Lots of fossils and meteorites, good antique embroidery, Korean celadon, Egyptian papyrus!!!, and neolithic objects, probably illegal to export. Unfortunately there was no air-conditioning nor elevators.

The **Imperial Palace** is full of arts and curios stores; the **Liaoning Antique Shop** is at *48 Chaoyang Road, Heping District, Tel. 24842454.*

EXCURSIONS & DAY TRIPS

Also in Liaoning province and worth side trips if you have the time are Anshan, Dandong, Fushun and Dalian. Dalian is treated separately below as a destination in its own right.

ANSHAN

Anshan is 75 minutes by train or expressway, about 90 km southwest of Shenyang. Its mines date from the second century B.C. It is today the home of China's biggest iron and steel works where fans of **steam locomotives** should be able to ride over 1000 km of tracks.

New and very spectacular for art lovers is the 7.95 meter high **Jade Buddha**, carved out of one piece of Liaoning nephrite in 1996. Photographs do not do it justice. On the spot, the light keeps changing to highlight its different features. Decide for yourself if the carvers used the natural colors of the jade, darker for the face, lighter for the palm and hair. If so, this is an amazing achievement because until it was cut, no one knew if the different colors would fit the design. At 230 tons, the statue will never travel abroad, so do make an effort to see it here.

Even though the area outside is an amusement park, the buddha's own temple-like setting is reverent and spectacular, the same type of ceiling as in Beijing's Forbidden Palace, only newer, and better lit. The whole project has 9999 dragons (count them!), and 392 lions and should be viewed from all sides, including the top. Open daily 6:30am-7pm. The Y30 admission pays for guide service. It's at *58 Luhua Street, Tiedong District* on the east side of Anshan within one km of downtown. *Tel. 412/5566716.* Take No. 8 bus from the railway station. Its store has been selling carvings made from jade not needed in the original carving. It also sells locally-made root carvings.

Anshan has a **jade market** in Xiuyan Town, said to be the largest such market in China.

A good, convenient place to eat here is The **Familiar Place**, in the Laodifang Hotel, outside the Jade Buddha Park. Good was the *taiji yin-yang* soup, spinach noodles and black beans, beef and green peppers, and fried milk. The park is planning a vegetarian restaurant.

The best place to stay is the five-star **320 International Hotel** (Guoji Jiu Dian), *219 Yuan Lin Road, Tiedong District, 114001. Tel. 5555888, Fax 5555988. Y680*. This 23-story hotel has a decent-sized indoor pool, gym, CNN and HBO. It is 30 km from the airport, five km from the railway station, next to the soccer stadium, and near the Buddha.

CITS is at *29 Shengli Road, Tiedong District, 114002. Tel. 5553685, Fax 5530465*. The telephone code is *0412*.

Benxi Water Cave is in a pretty area with Guilin-type hills southeast of Shenyang and 35 km east of Benxi city. Here you can take a 50-minute motorboat trip on a 12 C, 2,800 meter long, five million year old underground river for about Y50. (Coats are provided but take a sweater, socks and headgear.) It is 25 minutes from Shenyang airport, about 80 km from city center, and open 8:30am-5:00pm. While the lighting is not as skillful as other caves in China, this one is still pretty impressive and relaxing, especially if you are the last boat of the day. Each boat seats nine to 12 people.

Only 26 km outside Shenyang near the airport, is **Aerolite Hill Park**, the home of a giant 160 meter-long, two million ton aerolite/meteorite. It is believed to have landed here 1.9 billion years ago.

DANDONG

Dandong is at the border with North Korea and can be reached by air from five Chinese cities or by a five-hour train ride from Shenyang. A train goes from Beijing every other day. Shenyang has the closest North Korean consulate and travel agents need two days to a week to process visas. You can't land in Korea without one, but you can boat on the **Yalu River**. This river is known to those who remember the Korean War. You might want to visit the **King of Medicine Temple** on Feng Huang (Phoenix) Hill, a visit to which should cure you of all ills.

The best hotel here is **DandongInternational Hotel**, *88 Xinan Street, 118000, Three stars. Tel. 2137788 X 3004, Fax 2146644*. It is 30 km from the airport, and five km from the railway station.

CITS is on *No. 1 Square, 118000, Tel. 2137493, Fax 2131853*; and **Korea International Travel Company**, *Room No. 3, 2/F, 25, Xianqian Street, Yuanbao District, Tel.2812542, Fax 2818438*. Both offer tours and can help you obtain visas for North Korea.

FUSHUN

Fushun is 50 km northeast of Shenyang and known now for the **War Criminal Prison Museum** where the last Qing emperor spent the years 1950 to 1959. You can see the greenhouse where Pu Yi learned gardening, and the room where his concubine stayed with him for 48 hours (and afterwards filed for divorce). You can see the bed platform where he slept. His captors moved him in 1952 from this room along with 11 other Manchu companions because he didn't know how to tie his shoelaces.

Fushun is also important as the first Manchu capital (1616) with the **oldest imperial Manchu tombs**. At **Soldier Lei Feng's Museum**, you can muse about how today's heroes are made and visit the **Fushun Open Coal Mine**.

The best hotel is the **Fushun Friendship Hotel**, *4 Yongning Street, Xi Fu District, Tel. 413/2622181, Fax 2626773*. It's three stars but don't expect much; it's dirty.

The **tourist office** is at *4 Yongning Street, 113008, Tel. 2429756, Fax 2438647*.

PRACTICAL INFORMATION

Hours: most tourist attractions are open 9am-5:00pm in summer and shorter hours are possible in winter; the large department stores above are open 8:30 or 9am-6 or 7pm in winter, or 9pm in summer.

CITS, *113 Huanghe Nan Street, Shenyang, 110031, Tel. 86807005, Fax 86808772*. It can book trains to Russia and Korea.

CYTS Tours, *21 Wu Jing Bei Road, Heping District, 110003. Tel. 22714356, Fax 22712917*.

Liaoning Overseas Tourist Corporation, *26 Kun Shan Zhong Road, 110031, Tel. 86248150, 86271592, 86225075, Fax 86228632*. They can arrange tours to North Korea but not for US citizens.

Japanese Consulate, *50, 14 Wei Road, Heping District, 110003, Tel. 22322749*.

Liaoning Tourism Administration, *113 Huanghe Nan Road, 110031. Tel. 86807316. E-mail:gaoyupi@pub.sy.lnpta.net.cn*. For information and brochures.

Telephone Code, *024*

Russian Consulate, *Phoenix Hotel, 109 Huanghe Nan Street, Tel. 86805858 - 1004*.

US Consulate, *52, 14th Wei Road, Heping District, 110003, Tel. 23220848, 3221198, Fax 2322374*.

DALIAN

(Talien, or Luda)

Dalian is worth visiting because it is a beautiful little well-run city. It is an ice-free port near the southern tip of Liaoning province on the Yellow and Bohai Seas and an important industrial center. It appears to be more progressive, better organized and more prosperous than Shenyang. For example, you don't have to wait longer than three minutes for a bus, and traffic lights are co-ordinated. Occasionally you hear talk that the provincial capital should be moved here instead. Its government has decreed that all new construction be in western-style architecture, and this uniformity makes it look very attractive, as does its seaside location. It has lots of fresh seafood, peaches, pears, strawberries, and 100 varieties of apples. Dalian is a sister city of Oakland, California, and Vancouver, Canada.

Dalian has a total population of 5.38 million. While its weather is generally moderate, its hottest temperature (August) has been 34 C, and its lowest -21 C (for one or two days). The annual precipitation is 600-800 millimeters. The best time to visit is May 1 to October 1.

ARRIVALS & DEPARTURES

Dalian is south of Shenyang, a forty-minute flight, or a four to five hour train trip, or drive (375 km) on the expressway. Taxi prices from Shenyang airport range from Y900 to Y1200. You can reach Dalian by express train from Beijing in 12 hours and by frequent plane in less than an hour from Beijing, and two hours from Shanghai. You can also fly here from Fukuoka, Hiroshima, Hong Kong, Osaka, Pusan, Pyongyang, Seoul, Tokyo, and 41 Chinese cities. You could however be delayed by fog.

You can get there by ship every four days from Shanghai in 32 hours, or from Tianjin daily in 15 hours. From Inchon a ship leaves twice a week and takes 18 hours, from Yantai four times a day in three hours, and from Weihai once a day in 3.5 hours. Ocean cruise ships sometimes also stop here. It has one of the two biggest cargo ports in North China.

ORIENTATION

Known during imperialist times as **Port Arthur**, Dalian was seized briefly by the Japanese in 1894, but was leased as a naval base for 25 years to Russia in 1898. Russia was also given the right to build a railroad connecting the base with the Trans-Siberian railroad. As the result of the Russian defeat by Japan in 1905, Japan took over the base until 1945. It left behind a high standard of education.

Dalian has Japanese and old tsarist architecture and a high percentage of first-rate hotels. It also has 1,800 km of coastline, its commercial area on a 15 by eight kilometer peninsula, easily accessible from the expressway. You can walk to most places downtown and air pollution is minimal.

WHERE TO STAY

The top hotel is now the **Shangri-La** followed very closely by the new tower of its neighbor the **Furama**. This is a highly competitive situation you might want to exploit. The service at the Shangri-La is slightly better. The next best in town is the **Holiday Inn**. All these hotels are within two km of each other, close to shopping and the harbor, and about 12 to 14 km from the airport. The Shangri-La is a tad closer to a walking street with shops and a good Friendship Store. The airport is about 20 minutes drive away to the north.

All hotels listed add an additional 15% service charge and have such services as credit cards, money exchange, business center, etc. All these hotels give discounts and packages during low business season, some as high as 50%. Hotels can arrange golfing. Though the city has many, I couldn't find any three-star hotels to recommend but discounts should bring four-star hotel prices to three-star levels.

SHANGRI-LA HOTEL DALIAN, *66 Renmin Road (at Zhi Gong Street), 116001, Tel 2525000, Fax 2525050, 2823232. E-mail: slda@shangri-la.com. One km from the harbor and two km from the railway station. $190-$260 for rooms; $290-$1200 for suites.*

This hotel has 520 rooms, each with coffee makers, big fluffy pillows, and safes. It also has a health club with gym, pool, two tennis courts, steam bath and sauna. Three executive club floors have fax lines in rooms, late checkout, and good friendly service. The club's complimentary breakfast has offered smoked salmon, carrot and other juices, and made-to-order eggs. Its regular Y115 breakfast buffet has one of the best selection in China, and includes omlettes, eggs benedict, hash browns, cheeses, and *dim sum.* Each elevator has two sets of buttons, a lower one for wheelchair travelers.

FURAMA HOTEL (Fulihua), *60 Renmin Road, 116001. Five stars, Tel. 2630888, Fax 2639128. E-mail:framahtl@pub.dl.lnpta.net.cn. Old building: Y979-Y4814; new tower, Y1560-Y20750. No relation to the Furama Hotel in Hong Kong. But it has ties with the New Otani Reservation system. In North America, Tel. 800/44UTELL.*

The Furama's old 22-story, 456-room wing was built in 1988 and renovated in 1992. The older section has small bathrooms and dark hallways. Its new wing, opened in 1995, has an additional 376 larger rooms with separate shower stalls, beautiful hall carpets, and chandeliers in its elevators. It is renovating in 1999. It offers CNN and HBO, safes in rooms, and Japanese grill room, Chaozhou, Cantonese and Shanghai restaurants. Its huge classy lobby has upscale stores like Hugo Boss, Bally and D'Urban. It has office suites and free shuttle bus. Its health club has an indoor pool (with a sign that says "no swimming when drunk,"), a gym, putting green, squash, aerobics, and lit tennis courts.

GLORIA PLAZA HOTEL, *5 Yide Avenue, Zhongshan District, 116001. Tel. 2808855, Fax 2808533. Four stars. $110-$130 for rooms; $180-$280 for suites.*

The Gloria Plaza is a 240-room hotel with tasteful but unpretentious decor and a small lobby. It has small rooms, comfortable beds, some with the smell of smoke – so ask for its non-smoking floor. There's satellite television and in-house movies. It has Cantonese food and a ballroom that sits 180 people theatre style, but no pool.

HOLIDAY INN DALIAN (Jiu Zhou Jia Ri Fandian), *18 Sheng Li Square, Zhong Shan District, 116001. Four stars, Tel. 2808888, Fax 2809704. E-mail: hidlgm@pub.dl.lnpta.net.cn (reservations). Opposite the railway station, Shengli/Victory Plaza, and next to a "walking" street, it is about one km from the harbor. Rooms range from $110 to $160, and suites $220 to $380.*

Built in 1988, this 23-story, 405-room property has an executive club with computer jacks in rooms, and late check-out. It also has a non-smoking floor, pub, Cantonese and Sichuan food, and Hong Kong food street. For fitness, it has a gym, small indoor pool, and tennis. There's a free scheduled airport shuttle. Rooms receive CNN and twins have double beds and small bathrooms.

GRAND HOTEL (Bolan), *1 Jiefang Street Zhongshan Dist, 116001. Tel. 2806161, Fax 2809680, 2806334. $78 to $280. Three stars.* This dark, old fashioned hotel has poor English but should be okay if you need something cheap. It is clean, has room safes and CNN, and is downtown near Zhongshan Square.

In the **Dalian Economic and Technical Development Zone** 30 km to the northeast, the best hotel is the 27-story, 270-room **Jinyuan** (Golden Imperial) **Hotel**, a four-star with good standards, but little English. *Tel. 7618888, Fax 7618770. Y600 to Y790 for rooms; Y1400 to 2100 for suites.*

WHERE TO EAT

Seafood is the main specialty here. The best food is at the top hotels, especially the **Shang Palace** in the Shangri-La for spicy jelly fish and lemon duck.

NEW ORIENT SEAFOOD CITY, *on Harbor Square, near the port.*

This is the most popular seafood restaurant in town, where you can choose from many tanks of swimming fish, from 10 kinds of crab, or abalone, squid, turtles, snakes, and lobster. Prices are moderate up to the top stewed sharks fin and abalone with black chicken at Y1380. There's also dumplings and *sushi,* and stir fried vegetables.

SEEING THE SIGHTS

There are no world-class attractions to bring you here but enough to keep you busy for a couple of days. Tourists might be interested in its **ornamental glass factory**, the centrally-located **zoo**, the **harbor** (tour boats from Tiger Beach), and its beautiful **beaches**. The best **swimming beach** is at the **Bangchuidao Hotel** (Y10 entrance fee) on *Binhai Road* only a few kilometers from downtown. Dalian has at least three **golf** courses of which **Golden Pebble** is the best. It costs Y1500 for 18 holes and a meal. It has night golf and is planning a total of 54 holes. The season is nine months.

Travel agents can also arrange for **scuba diving** (water temperature is 16 C to 22 C in summer), **fishing**, and **mountain climbing**.

You can visit part of old **Port Arthur**, the 1900 tsarist-built fort on Jiguanshan Hill and prison. With permission, you can cruise to **Snake Island**, 25 nautical miles away, northwest of Lushun. With an estimated 13,000 pit vipers, this is a snake sanctuary. It supplies a research center studying the medical benefits of the venom.

You can also hike and raft in the small but exquisite **Bingyu Valley** with its Guilin-like scenery, 90 minutes by expressway northeast from Dalian and 40 km from Zhuanghe city. (You will also be close to North Korea.) It is best to go by taxi because there's only one train a day. Minibuses do leave from the railway station in Dalian but schedules are not regular. Bingyu has 40 peaks and 20 caves to be explored in a 47-sq km park. Here the best hotel is the three-star 104-room branch of the Dalian Furama. The **Bingyu Furama** has a pool, disco, sauna and two restaurants, *Tel. 411/8220237, Y480.*

This national park is a pleasant day trip, a chance to see the countryside. You do have to bring your own interpretor. Another guest house here has served good fresh-water shrimp, celery and conch, and deep fried silk worm cocoons. The **Tourism Bureau** is at *296, Xiang Yang Road, Zhuanghe, Dalian, 116400, Tel. 8612315.*

NIGHTLIFE & ENTERTAINMENT

Head for the two main squares in the evening for badminton, dancing, games, concerts and just hanging out. The **Kylin stage** is a theatre for Peking opera that performs upon request or every Saturday 6pm-8:30pm. It's at *One, west lane of Kylin, Kunming Street, Zhongshan District, Tel. 2305411. Tickets Y120.* There's a **Brunswick Bowling Alley** behind the Shangri-La with over 20 lanes.

PRACTICAL INFORMATION

CITS, *4/F, One Changtong Street, Xigang District, 116011, Tel. 3687660, 3687806, 3696273, Fax 3687733.* European and American Department, *Tel. 3691165.*

CYTS Tours, *94 Shenyang Road, Xi Gang District, 116011, Tel. 3600608, 3601774, Fax 3686070.*

Dalian Overseas Travel Agency, *5/F, One Changtong Street, Xigang District, 116011. Tel. 3589859, 3680857 (European Department), Fax 3687831.*

Dalian Tourism Bureau at *One Renmin Square, 116012. Tel. 3631258, Fax 3637872* for brochures and complaints. *E-mail:dttb@dalian-gov.net.*

Employment: Mr. Peng Jiansheng, Office Director, *Dalian Association International Exchange of Personnel, 259 North, No. 1 People's Square, 116012. Tel. 3631831, Fax 3623469*

Hours: the main stores open from 9:30am-9:30pm here, especially in summer. Office hours are 8:30am-5:30pm with a one-hour lunch break at 11:30am. Rush hour is 7am-9am, and 5pm-7pm.

Telephone code is *0411.*

Tourism Complaints, Quality Supervision Office of Dalian Travel and Tourism Bureau, *31-2, Wansui Street, Sha Hekou District, Dalian. Tel. 4623959, 4623962, Fax 4623959.*

18. NORTHWEST & CENTRAL CHINA

SILK ROAD

The term **Silk Road** was first used by a German author in the 19th century and is still used because it is so apt. Silk was the main commodity carried along the caravan routes between Cathay and Europe. It dazzled the eyes of Marco Polo who traveled here in 1275. Bales of silk were buried in ancient tombs along the way, it was that highly valued.

Informal trade between China and West Asia goes back over 2,000 years. In 138 B.C. (Han), **Emperor Wudi** sent his emissary **Zhang Qian** (Chang Ch'ien) on missions westward to get help fight the Huns. Zhang returned 13 years later, having been imprisoned most of that time by hostile tribes, but he fired the emperor's interest in trade. The Han emperors encouraged trading caravans with imperial protection and the building of beacon signal towers.

From then on, the routes flourished periodically until the 14th century, especially in the Tang. It declined because sea-going ships were able to trade more efficiently and because of hostilities along the land routes.

Trade was mainly in high-value or easily transported goods. The Chinese exchanged silk, tea, and seeds for peach and pear trees. They also exchanged skills, such as iron-, steel-, and paper-making; they received grapes, pomegranate and walnut trees, sesame, coriander, spinach, the Fergana horse, alfalfa, Buddhism, Nestorianism, and Islam.

Goods were exchanged along the route especially with India and West Asia. A few items even reached Rome. The road went west from Xi'an along the Weihe River valley, Hexi Corridor, Tarim Basin, and

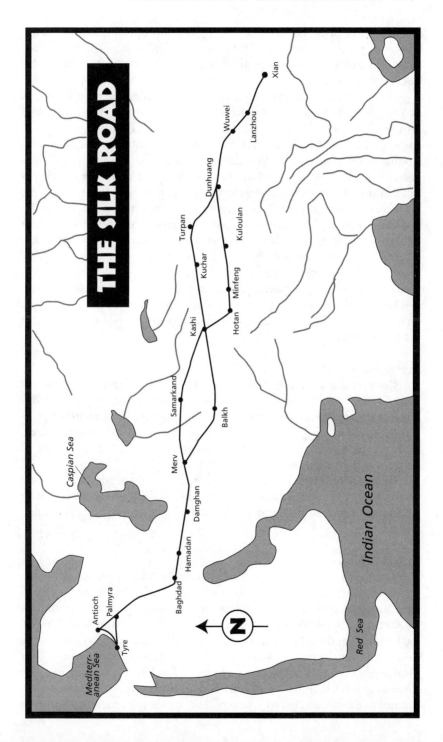

Parmirs (in Central Asia). Then it continued through Afghanistan, Iran, Iraq, and Syria. It was about 7000 km long (2,700 kms within China). Northern and southern routes divided at Dunhuang on either side of the Taklamakan Desert.

Many Arab and Persian merchants settled in Xi'an and even as far east as Yangzhou. Many of the Silk Road cities are open to foreigners, and tourists find themselves in a world of onion-domed mosques, bazaars, oasis, grapes, central Asian and Turkish faces, embroidered caps, and languages their national guides cannot understand. Spontaneous dancing and singing, uncontrolled by Han reserve, make people here delightful. Visitors are frequently asked to join in and contribute to the festivities.

You can find giant rock carvings and murals, some of the best in the world, and can explore earthen-walled ghost cities, the western end of the Great Wall, old tombs, and Buddhist temples. You can look for mummies. Try to figure out how and what the beacon towers communicated and learn how water is channeled to make this desert flourish. Carpets, jade goblets, jeweled daggers, and musical instruments are good buys here.

But the Silk Road is not Turkey, Pakistan, or Afghanistan. It is China, an ingredient that makes this region of mixed cultures special and worth the hardships.

Arranging Travel

Conference Travel & Tours (see Chapter 6 under *Travel Agents & Tour Operators)* and **China Rail Express Travel Service** (*9 Yongan Xi Li, Jianguomenwai Avenue, Chaoyang District, Tel. 65633239, Fax 65013528; E-mail:crts@public.fhnet.cn.net*) have deluxe train tours through this area. Several agencies have less elegant land tours. China Nature Tours of Urumqi can arrange week-long camel treks.

Regular charter flights during the April to July tourist season have served Dunhuang, Jiayuguan, Lanzhou, and Xi'an. Kashi and Dunhuang should not be missed. Major tourist attractions are usually open 8am-5pm.

Travel Realities

Tourists in this area should be fit and adventurous. It is not for the finicky and inflexible. While good hotels exist, there are few luxury hotels here. Do not expect good plumbing, air-conditioning, or a constant flow of electricity. Some visitors get sore throats and upset stomachs. Careful backpackers and the adventurous traveler who want to jeep through the desert and eat in canteens and street markets where no foreign tour groups go, should take their own chopsticks and bowl. You are okay on the tourist track in hotels three stars and up, and even in tourist two-stars, but not in all one and two-star hotels. The area is extremely dry and cold

EATING & DRINKING ON THE SILK ROAD

If you don't want to risk spoiling your trip with diarrhea, read about how to avoid upset stomachs in Chapter 11, Food & Drink. Do not eat anything from the local markets unless it's right off the fire. The meat beyond Xi'an is mainly mutton. Wise is the traveler who says something like 'I would love to try it, but it doesn't agree with me. Thank you anyway,' when handed a glass of mare's milk buzzing with flies. The well-meaning tribesman in his yurt is not going to appreciate the pain you will go through later. If you drink it because you don't want to hurt his feelings, you are the one who will suffer!

even on summer nights. Long train and bus rides through the desert are not comfortable. Tourist buses, but not all trains are air-conditioned. Buses have broken down in the desert and the coolest retreat has been the shade of a rock or a sand dune, if you're lucky.

Be prepared for delays and be pleasantly surprised if they don't happen. While waiting, think about the peasants and herdsmen who struggled to raise crops and animals here while sandstorms howled mercilessly. Think of the sand smothering the crops. Think of the caravans passing through. What did the camels and traders do when they couldn't see a foot ahead of them?

Carry your own liquid refreshments and something to protect your nose and eyes from stinging grains of sand. Also imperative for travel here is an inflatable pillow to cushion bumpy roads, a strong flashlight for caves, a flask for water, and if you want to buy a carpet, a folding bag with lock. Try to plan your trip for the Sunday bazaar in Kashi.

The government is in the process of upgrading services in this area. By the time you go, planes may be flying into most of the cities on the route. Paved roads already reach the most important cave temples.

Ethnic Groups

As you travel around, try to pick out the characteristics of the different nationalities. Attempt to identify people from their facial features and their distinctive dress. Among the groups here are the Han, Huns, Huis (Moslems), Kazaks, Kirghiz, Manchus, Mongols, Russians, Tarjiks (Tajiks), Tartars, Turfans, Uzbeks, Uygurs (Uighurs), and Xibos.

Guides leave visitors in minority villages to fend for themselves, with no introudctions or suggestions as to what to do. Do some reading beforehand. Prepare some questions about lifestyles, schooling for no-mads, number of children allowed, handicrafts and courtship customs.

Many guides know nothing about these people. On the other hand, one of our highlights was stopping spontaneously on spotting a nomad yurt by the road, and being invited in for a look.

Read William Dalyrimple's *In Xanadu, A Quest*, about his 1986 trip here and Peter Hopkirk's *Foreign Devils on the Silk Road* about archaeological raids here in the early 1900s. There are many books on China's national minorities.

See Xian, Dunhuang, Kashi, Lanzhou, Turpan, and Urumqi.

LANZHOU

(Lanchow)

In the western province of Gansu, of which it is the capital, **Lanzhou** is almost in the center of China. Founded about 2200 years ago, Lanzhou was called the 'Gold City' after gold was found here. Gansu province today has a population of 25 million, including Han, Hui, Tibetan, Uygur, Dongxiang, Bonan, Mongolian, Kazak, Tu, Salar and Manchu nationalities.

The area was settled 200,000 years ago. Three thousand years ago, the inhabitants started farming the eastern part of Gansu. The province is the setting for Yuan-Tsung Chen's excellent autobiographical novel *The Dragon's Village*, a book based on her own experiences with land reform shortly after Liberation in 1949.

Situated on the Yellow River and at an altitude of 1,524 meters, the coldest winter temperature is -10 C in January; the hottest is 35 C in summer. The annual precipitation in the province is 30-800 mm, the rain mainly in the southeast. Sandstorms occur in April and May sometimes in the Hexi Corridor once every four or five years. The best time to visit is April-November.

With an urban population of 1.4 million, Lanzhou is industrial, with petrochemicals, machine building and smelting.

ARRIVALS & DEPARTURES

Lanzhou can be reached by air from Hong Kong and 25 Chinese cities including Beijing, Dunhuang (1165 km away), and Xi'an (800 km). The airport is about 70 km from the city by expressway. The CAAC bus is the cheapest means to get downtown. Lanzhou is also serviced by irregular express train from Urumqi (30-36 hours) and tourist trains with X'ian (12-16 hours). From Xining it's 4.5 hours by train; from Jiayuguan, it takes 14.5 hours.

ORIENTATION

Lanzhou is important as a stop on the **Silk Road** and as a gateway to two cave temples, the ***Bingling Si Grottoes** and the ***Maijishan Grottoes**. The infamous pollution here has been reduced by the growing use of electricity instead of coal. A whole mountain, Daqingshan, is being removed and wind will hopefully blow the polluted air away.

WHERE TO STAY

The best hotel is the Lanzhou Legend, then the Jincheng.

LANZHOU LEGEND HOTEL, *599 Tianshui Road, 730000. Four stars, Tel. 8882876, Fax 8887876. 76 km from the airport, and two km from the railway station.*

This hotel has 389 rooms, a gym, and Korean restaurant. It has Singapore management and charges $95 a room, but CITS will book it for $80. You might do even better.

JINCHENG HOTEL (Binguan), *363 Tianshui Road, 730000. Three stars, Tel. 8416638, 8827759, Fax 8418438. 76 km from the airport and three km from the railway station. $70 a room; CITS charges $55.*

In the center of town, this hotel offers 300 rooms, and a gym. It was built in 1982, the earliest tourist hotel in Gansu.

WHERE TO EAT

Local specialties include roast piglet (delicious), sweet and sour Yellow River carp, *facai* (black moss), steamed chicken, fried camel hoof (ugh), and fried sheep's tail. The hotel food is best, but try the **Lidu Restaurant**, *opposite the Legend Hotel, Tel. 8416321*, the **Chao Shan Restaurant**, *361 Tianshui Road, Tel. 8889494, 8416638*, or the **Feicui Moslem Restaurant**, *410 Pingliang Bei Road, Tel. 8824830*, for beef noodles.

SEEING THE SIGHTS

In Lanzhou itself, of mild interest is the **Baita** (White Pagoda Park) on the north bank of the Yellow River. First built in the Yuan, then rebuilt and expanded in the Ming and Qing, the Baita has seven stories and eight sides and is about 17 meters high. It's open 8:30am-4 or 5pm.

Five km from the Jincheng Hotel is the **Wuquan** (Five-Spring) **Hill** with genuine temples, the oldest, the spooky Ming dynasty Chung Wen. Legend credits General Huo Qubing (Huo Chu-ping), in 120 B.C., with stabbing the ground with his sword after finding no water for his horses. Five streams of water appeared and have been flowing ever since. Other important relics to see are the **Taihe Iron Bell**, three meters high, weighing five tons, and cast in 1202; and the **Tongjieyinfo Buddha**, cast in bronze in 1370 and weighing nearly five tons. It's open 8:30am-5pm and walks are good here.

The **Yellow River cruise** is not special, but the **Provincial Museum** at *3 Xijin Xi Road* opposite the Friendship Hotel and five km from the Jincheng Hotel is worth a visit. It is closed Saturday-Monday, but *telephone 2334106* for hours. Here is the famous 1,800-year-old **Galloping Horse of Gansu** that toured the US and Canada. It was found in Wuwei in the middle of the province. A replica in the lobby of the Jincheng Hotel shows how it was originally presented. Also important are the 2000-year-old-wooden 'slips' (documents of history and medicine) from north and west Gansu, and 8,120-year-old painted pottery.

In the evening until midnight, people relax in **Dong Fang Hong Square** or go to **night food markets** on Hezhen Road, Xiguan Cross, or Nongminxiang Lane (near the Lanzhou and Jincheng hotels.)

SHOPPING

Lanzhou produces many kinds of melons, red dates, the best tobacco for water pipes, carved ink slabs, luminous 'jade' cups, and bottle gourds. It also manufactures carpets, lanterns, and reproductions of ancient paintings based on the Silk Road murals. Beautiful are the buddha heads from the Maiji Grottos. Some of its replicas of the famous Flying Horse are made from molds directly from the original. There are also whimsical cloth animals. See the **Gansu Cultural Relics Shop**, *3 Xijinxi Road, Tel. 2336587.* Try the **Provincial Arts and Crafts Shop**, *67 Donggang Xi Road, Tel. 8827233.*

For buddha heads reproductions, **Le Seine Culture and Art World** is at *45 Qinan Road, 730000, Tel. 8828987, 8828989.* The **Huangmiao Market**, five minutes by taxi from the Jingcheng Hotel, is especially good on weekends. It has curios, stamps, coins, and some reproductions. The **Hong Tudi Restaurant** opposite has Lanzhou beef noodles. The best department store is the **Xiguan Pass**.

EXCURSIONS & DAY TRIPS

For the two caves, you need at least three days and the energy to climb. The elaborate fifth-century *Bingling Si Grottoes** are 129 km southwest of the city, near Linxia, open April to November, depending on the water level. From Lanzhou, you go 75 km by road to Yongjing county town, and then 54 km (2.5 hours) by ship on the Liujiaxia reservoir (a 10-hour excursion in all). It's not easy. Here you'll find 183 caves and shrines with 694 stone Buddhist statues and 82 clay ones, the biggest Buddha is 27 meters high. The smallest only 25 cm. Be aware that there are many stairs. The statues range from Northern Wei to Ming, the youngest, at least 350 years old. The most spectacular are the **Xiasi** (Lower Temples). CITS has a one day tour for $85 with private car, etc. For over 10 people, it's $30 each. The *Maiji Grottoes, also Northern Wei to Ming, are 45 km southeast of Tianshui, itself about 380 km southeast of Lanzhou.

You can take an eight-hour train to Tianshui from Lanzhou or an overnight eight-hour train from Xi'an and then a one-hour minibus for the last 45 km from Tianshui or Beidao railway station to the base of the mountain. Tianshui was a trade distributing center on the Silk Road and has two smaller temples, the important Fuxi (with the ancestor of all Chinese people), and the Nanguo. Better do these temples by car.

CITS is at *Huancheng Zhong Avenue, Qingcheng District in Tianshui, Tel. 938/8213621, 8217683.* For **Nature Travel Service,** *Tel. 2734220, 2734226.* CITS has a three-day tour with two nights hotel for $140 per person. With your own taxi and guide, it's $490.

At **Maiji,** there are 194 caves with over 7,200 stone and clay Buddhist statues, and 1300 square meters of murals dating from the end of the fourth century to the 19th, a period of 1500 years. These caves are on a mountain, which rises almost vertically, and are reached by wooden staircases. Some of the statues are completely unsheltered; others have doors and windows. One 15.28 meter high statue is from the Sui. The work on the mountain was done by craftsmen who piled blocks of wood up to the top and started carving while standing on them. As the artisans worked their way down, they gradually removed the blocks. The Maiji is better than Bingling, more beautiful and more important. Most are well preserved.

Buses leave early in the morning from the West Bus Station in Lanzhou for **Xiahe,** altitude about 3000 meters, so bring warm clothes. It's 280 km southwest of Lanzhou, a six-to-seven hour trip. Here is the **Labrang/Labuleng Lamasery,** the largest outside of Tibet, built in 1709. It's best seen in July, but it has twice yearly festivals (lunar January 11-17 and lunar July 8) during which a giant 60-meter long Buddha *tangka* is put out to sun. These are interesting times to visit. In 2000, this takes place Feb. 17 to Feb. 19, and July 28-August 14. Belonging to the 'Yellow sect,' with about 1,000 monks in residence, the monastery has a 10 meter-high statue of Maitreya.

Xiahe has a population of 120,000 people, mainly Tibetan. The **Labuleng Hotel** here is two stars and is at *Laizhou Cun, Xiahe, 747100, Tel. 941/7121849.* It is two km from the monastery, has 300 beds, and is built in Tibetan court tent architecture. It advertises $60 a room but CITS charges $50. You might be able to do it for even less. You can also stay in tents for a little more.

CITS can arrange performances of Tibetan songs and dance. If you have 10 people, CITS has a three-day bus tour from Lanzhou to Labrang for $130 each.

Because it is difficult or very expensive for individual travelers to get to Labuleng, and the grottos, do check with travel agents in Lanzhou about your joining existing tours at a reasonable price. For Labuleng, **Gansu Overseas Tourist Corporation** charges Y1645 for one person, Y1100 each for 2-3, Y750 for 3-6, and Y550 for 6-9 people.

Also in the province are Dunhuang and Jiayuguan. See separate listings and ask about the 6,000 Roman troops (Han dynasty) who 'lost' their way and ended up in Wuwei.

PRACTICAL INFORMATION

Ambulance, *Tel. 120.*

Business hours: Bank of China, 8:30am-11:30am; 2:30pm-5:30pm, Monday to Friday. Travel agents 8 or 8:30-12 noon; 2 or 2:30-6pm.

China Comfort International Travel Agency, *22/F, Changyun Plaza, 22, Xiao Shao Men Wai, 730000, Tel. 8813133, 8842417, Fax 8842424.*

China Everbright International Travel Service, *10 Nong Min Xiang Road, 730000, Tel. 8410953, 8811715, Fax 8883167, 8863860.* Contact Ms. Lydia Wang. It has Silk Road and Inner Mongolian automobile tours.

China Lanzhou Railway International Travel Service, sponsors a luxury express train tour. *Tel. 8886124.* Mr. Wang Bo.

CITS Gansu, and Gansu Tourism Administration (brochures and complaints) are both at *10 Ningmin Xiang Lane, 730000. CITS Tel. 8821705, 8819394, Fax 8418556, 8819393. E-mail: sgg1@public.lz.gs.cn. Http://www.lz.gs.cninfo.net.* It can arrange coach tours to Lhasa and along the Silk Road, and Yellow River rafting tours. For the **Gansu Provincial Tourism Administration**, *Tel. 8418443 or Fax 8418443*, and ask for Mr. He Xiaozu.

Gansu Overseas Tourist Corporation, *10, Nongmin Xiang Road, 730000, Tel. 8821251, 8825047, Fax 8824670, 8418442.* Contact Ms. Wang Zhiger, Tel. 8821966.

Gansu International Sports Travel Service, *17 Xiaogoutou, 730030, Tel. 8823583, 84319530, Fax 8413192/8419530. E-mail: GISTS@Public.lz.gs.cn.* This has motorcycle, bicycling, ballooning and gliding tours. It also has trekking and camel tours.

Gansu Silk Road International Tours, *Euro-American Department, 361 Tianshui Road, 730000, Tel. 8830138, 8416638X6587, Fax 8830138. E-mail:hualin@public.lz.gs.cn.* Contact Ms. Lin Hua.

Police, *Tel. 110*

Telephone code, *0931*

Tourism Hotline, *Tel. 8418443*

Tourist Complaints, *Tel. 8826860, Fax 8826860.*

DUNHUANG

(Tunhuang, Tunhwang)

In isolated western Gansu province lies one of the world's greatest art treasures, now a UNESCO Heritage Site: the **Thousand Buddha Mogao Grottos**.

ARRIVALS & DEPARTURES

Eight trains go daily to Dunhuang from Lanzhou in at least 24 hours (1,148 km), and from Turpan to Dunhuang in 11 hours. Public mini-buses and taxis are at the Dunhuang train station in Liuyuan which is 128 km northeast of Dunhuang. From Lanzhou, Jiayuguan, Xi'an, Beijing, Urumqi and Nanjing one or two flights a day go March-October, and at least three flights a week fly to Dunhuang November-March. Dunhuang is 12 km from the airport. Frequent mini-buses from Jiayuguan take five to six hours to cover the 382 km to Dunhuang.

ORIENTATION

Dunhuang was an important cultural exchange center and oasis on the Silk Road. It was founded in 111 B.C. during the Western Han. From here, the Silk Road west splits into northern and southern routes and ends 7,000 km away at the Mediterranean Sea. Dunhuang was a military outpost under the Tang. In 400 A.D., it became the capital of the Xiliang kingdom. It changed hands several times. In 1227, **Genghis Khan** seized it, and in the Han, it was a military headquarters. You can see the ruins of the Han walls and a 16-meter-high tower in the old part of town, 250 meters west of the current one. The population now is 60,000 in the city, 150,800 urban and rural.

Between the fourth and 14th centuries, more than **1,000 caves** were cut out of the cliffs. They are 25 km southeast of the city. These were filled with Buddhist carvings, sculptures, gilt and colored frescoes, and murals– the now famous caves.

Summers are hot, the warmest about 41 C in July, the coldest has been briefly -21 C in December, but it can be -15 C in April. The annual rainfall is only 39 mm. The best time to visit is May, June, September or October. The altitude is 1,000 to 1,200 meters.

WHERE TO STAY & EAT

The **Grand Sun Hotel** is currently the best place to stay. For restaurants, the hotels below are your best bet. Apricots, jujubes, pears, melons, peaches, and wine grapes are grown locally.

GRAND SUN HOTEL DUNHUANG, *5 Bei Road Shazhau, 736220, Tel. 8829998, 8822306, Fax 8822019, 8822121. Y450-Y6800. Three stars aiming for four.*

This 12-story, 220-room hotel is downtown, has satellite television, a conference hall, sauna, steamroom, gym and snooker. It has a 24-hour business center, and travel service office. Attached is the two-star **Solar Energy Hotel** (Y200-Y560). These take credit cards and can change money.

DUNHUANG HOTEL (Binguan), *13 Yangguan Dong Road, 736200, Tel. 8822008, Fax 8822915. Three stars. 13 km from the airport, and 128 km from the railway station. $60 for a double but $49 if bought through a travel agent.*

This 1980 hotel has 130 air-conditioned rooms. The hotel gives 50-minute performances of folk dances when there are enough guests from 6pm-11pm at Y30 each guest. (Contact the Recreation Department, *extension 1290*). It accepts credit cards and can change money.

SEEING THE SIGHTS

At the *Mogao Grottoes**, 491 caves remain today in three or four rows on a 1.6 km-long wall. They are open 8:00am-5:00pm with the last admissions about 3:30pm, *Tel. 8869060. Y75.* Knowledgeable guides are available for hire on the site to show you around, and some speak English. The State Council has renovated murals like the **Feitian** (Flying Apsaras) **Fresco** (Tang) and repainted over 2,400 statues. Some of the statues, in about 20 caves, were repainted in the Qing. Note the intricately painted ceilings.

The most important cave is the **Cangjing** (Preserving Buddhist Scriptures) Cave, now Number 17. Dating from the Jin to Song (or late Tang to Western Xia, depending on sources), a span of over 800 years, this is where 50,000 important old documents were found, including the **Diamond Sutra** (868 A.D.), said to be the oldest existing printed book. It is now in the British Museum in London.

Other important caves include number 45 (clay figures); number 158 (the 15.6 meter-long **Sleeping Buddha**), and number 96. Both also have 26- and 33-meter-high Maitreya Buddhas respectively.

The caves have stories. One of the most famous is outlined in a series of pictures about a woman who was badly treated by her husband. While returning to her mother, she encountered a wolf that killed her two children. After becoming a nun, she learned that her miseries were punishment for mistreating her stepsister in a previous incarnation.

Some of the statues are damaged, many by Moslems adhering to the Ten Commandments and a few by the Red Guards. Signs indicate which museums abroad have stolen the pieces originally here. Some of the colors are still original and vivid. The red might be from pig's blood or cinnabar. One can get a real mystical feeling of history here. Caves were used as temples because they were conducive to meditation and felt secure, like in a mother's womb. Perhaps they symbolized reincarnation.

The caves are a half-day trip at least and there is a decent restaurant and lots of souvenir shops. You could take your own lunch. Taxis that will wait for you cost about Y100. Mini-buses from Dunhuang city leave every half hour from the Dunhuang bus station arriving 30 minutes later. Make sure you find out what time the last bus leaves or hitch a ride with a friendly tour group. As with all cave temples, it is best to take a flashlight to zero in on what you want to see. (You can also rent them.) And do not expect to observe an entire mural as you would in a spacious museum. You have to piece each section together in your own mind. A heavy metal door protects each cave.

Cameras and bags are not generally allowed. Entry to specific caves (Y50 to Y200 additonal per person) and photography need special permission in advance. Tourists cannot wander around the site without a guide. Only 30 caves are open at a time and these are rotated every year. The best caves are opened on request.

Other Sites

Visitors also can see the **White Horse Pagoda** (only a 12-meter-high pagoda in the suburbs and a five-minute stop). It commemorates the horse of the Indian monk Jumoluoshi, which died here. It is two km from town.

The **Yangguan Pass** (75 km southwest of Dunhuang) is just a beacon tower now. It was a military command post from the Han to the Yang, but desert sands have buried it. The **Yumen Guan** (Jade Gate) **Pass** is a 100-km drive on a new road northwest of the city. Jade from Hotan used to be carried through here and it now has a restaurant. It also has 600 meter-long earthen remains of the Han Great Wall six km west, and the **Hecang** (Military Supply) **Depot** (276 A.D.) 13 km east. These three sites are now joined by an improved road. Here you can easily visualize the hardships of the camel caravans supplying the wealthy homes of Europe, and the envoys bringing tribute to the emperor. Twenty km south of the city is a movie set of old Dunhuang which gives you a feel for the era. Do see the movie **Dunhuang**.

At the **Mingsha** (Singing Sand) **Hill**, six km southwest of town, a sandstorm buried a whole army. Their ghosts are still heard from time to time playing military drums and horns! You can get a short **camel ride** to Crescent Moon Spring, climb sand dunes, and visit a folk custom **museum** nearby.

SHOPPING

Dunhuang has a carpet factory and tourist souvenir street. Shops are in the **Dunhuang Museum** (*Tel. 8821981*), **CITS** (*Tel. 8825942*), and the **Dunhuang Research Institute**, *Tel. 8825217.*

PRACTICAL INFORMATION

China International Travel Service Gansu, *Dunhuang Branch, 29 Minshan Road, Dunhuang, 736200, Tel. 8823012, 8825071. Http:// www.lz.gs.cnifo.net*

Dunhuang International Travel Service Gansu, *32 Mingshan Road. 736200, Tel. 8823312, 8822598, Fax 8822173*

Dunhuang Solar Energy International Travel Service, *5 Shazhou Bei Avenue, 736200, Tel. 8822464, Fax 8822121*

Dunhuang Tourist Bureau, *14 Yangguan Dong Road, 736200, Tel. 8822234, 8822529, Fax 8822234.* Tourist complaints, *Tel. 8822403*

Gansu Overseas Tourist Corporation, *Dunhuang Branch, 14 Yongguan Dong Road, Tel. 8824937, 8822008, Fax 8822666. E-mail:ghy@otcgs.com.cn. Http://www.otcgs.com.cn*

Gansu Silk Road International Tours, *1 Dong Dajie, 736200, Tel. 8824726, Fax 8824727*

Fire, *Tel. 119*
Police, *Tel. 110*
Telephone code, *0937*

JIAYUGUAN

Jiayuguan is at the western end of the Great Wall in the Hexi Corridor in the western part of Gansu province. It is in the eastern Gobi desert. The altitude is 1500-1800 meters, the population 130,000 of whom 90,000 live in the city proper. The hottest weather in August is 34 C. The coldest, in January, is - 21 C. The best time to visit is May-October. Sandstorms sometimes occur March to May, especially around Anxi, and strong winds in November and December could make for an unpleasant trip.

ARRIVALS & DEPARTURES

Jiayuguan can be reached by infrequent summer flights from Lanzhou. During the high tourist season, there are more frequent chartered flights. The airport is 13 km away. Trains between Urumqi and Beijing, Shanghai, Xi'an, Chengdu, and Lanzhou stop here.

From Dunhuang, Jiuquan, and Lanzhou there are public buses. A tour bus on the 383-km paved road takes five or six hours from Dunhuang, more if you lunch at the Yumen Guest House or Anxi Hotel. Some stop in Qiao Wuan town to see the 300-year-old earthen ruins of an imperial scam, 85 km east of Anxi.

WHERE TO STAY

CHANGCHENG BINGUAN or **GREAT WALL HOTEL,** *6 Jianshe Xi Road, 735100, Tel. 6225288, 6225213, Fax 6226016. Y350-Y880. 14 km from the airport and two km from the railway station. It accepts credit cards. Three stars.*

Built in 1990-91 like a fort, on the edge of town with a great view of the snowcapped Qilian Mountains, this five-story, 156 room hotel is close to the Great Wall Museum. It has 24-hour hot water, international direct dial (IDD) telephones, a gym, sauna, steam bath, and pool.

JIAYUGUAN HOTEL (Binguan), *1 Xinhua Bei Road, 735100. Two different buildings with two and three stars, Tel. 6225804, 6226185, Fax 6227174. Y380-Y1280 (cheaper through a travel agency). 14 km from the airport and five km from the railway station. It accepts credit cards.*

This five-story, 172-bed hotel has IDD, air-conditioned cars, foreign currency exchange, store, sauna and gym.

SEEING THE SIGHTS

The **western end of the Great Wall** is marked by a **fort**, seven km from town. It was originally built in 1372 when the first Ming emperor had the wall repaired to keep out the defeated Mongols. He sent government and military officers to develop the region and to protect commerce on the Silk Road. The fort covers over 33,500 square meters and has three imposing gates with fancy 17-meter-high towers. In addition to military structures, it has a theater built in 1502, a reading room for officials, and a temple to the God of War. The god must have worked. No army ever captured it. *Tel. 6225518 and open 8:30am-8pm.*

The end of the Great Wall here is a mere trickle of its eastern magnificence but it still fascinates. It continues from here south for 7.5 km to the first beacon tower.

The **Wei and Jin Tombs** (220 to 420 A.D.) are 20 km northeast of the city and open 24 hours. You can enter them to study the famous bricks with their delightful paintings of old lifestyles and mythology. The modest museum is well worth seeing.

Jiayuguan also has a **Great Wall Museum**, *Tel. 6225881, open 8:30am-12:30am and 2:30pm-6:30pm.* It has a glacier (136 km away and a one-day trip). You can also go gliding at the gliding base of the civil airport 10 km northeast of the city which claims one of the three best airflows in the world. Contact a travel agency in advance. A gliding festival takes place mid-July.

For shopping, there's the **Friendship Shop** at *1, Xinhua Bei Road, Tel. 6225042*, and the **Grand Desert Gale Tourist Arts Handicraft Workshop**, *8, Jianshe Xi Road, Tel. 6225598*.

Jiuquan is 22 km away, with a Bell and Drum Tower originally built in 346 and renovated in the Qing, an Eastern Jin tower, and a carpet factory. The **Wine Spring Park**, the Western Han relic after which the city is named, should be seen. The other city attraction is the **Luminous Jade Cup Factory** (open 9am-6pm) which makes almost eggshell-thin goblets of 'jade'. There is also the Jiuquan **City Museum**, open 9am-5:30pm.

PRACTICAL INFORMATION

Jiayuguan International Travel Service, *2 Sheng Li Bei Road, 735100, Tel. 6228668, 6226598, Fax 6226931*.

Police, *110*.

Telephone code, *0937*.

URUMQI

(Urumchi; pronounced Oo-roo-MOO-chi)

Urumqi, the capital of the Xinjiang (Sinkiang) Uygur Autonomous Region, has an area one-sixth of China's total, and 5,700 km of borders with Mongolia, Russia, Kazakhstan, Kyrghzstan, Tajikistan, Afghanistan, Pakistan and India. The region has 16 million people and is four times the size of France.

Urumqi is at an altitude of 650-910 meters and is surrounded on three sides by mountains. Its hottest weather is in August, 40.9 C. Its coldest weather is in December, -41.5 C. Pack also for cold summer nights. In May and June, the coldest has been -8.9 C! Consider yourself warned. Maybe you can use the weather as an excuse to buy a fur jacket! The annual precipitation is 200 to 800 mm. There is snow between November and March. The best time to visit is May to September.

The urban population is 1.6 million, the total 17 million. The people are mainly Uygurs, but also Hans, Kazaks, Mongolians, and Huis. The city has 13 nationalities, the region 47. The region produces oil, ketchup, sheep, pears, grapes, and grain.

ARRIVALS & DEPARTURES

You can reach Urumqi by plane from Beijing (2,631 km in 3.5 hours), Lanzhou (three hours), and Shanghai (4.5 hours). Flights connect with Almaty, Bishkek, Islamabad, Moscow, Novosibirsk, Tashkent and 38 Chinese cities. Flights with Hong Kong are irregular. The Beijing-Urumqi express train covers almost 4,000 km in 61 hours, and the Shanghai-Urumqi train takes 74 hours, the longest train ride in China. Passenger and freight train service arrive from Almaty in Kazakhstan and beyond that from Moscow and Rotterdam. See Chapter 6, Planning Your Trip.

ORIENTATION

Urumqi dates from the Tang, 618 to 907 A.D., but its attractions are its people and nearby scenery. It is a bustling city, at least 25 years behind eastern China but starting to catch up commercially. Tourists usually go here on the way to somewhere else.

WHERE TO STAY

The **Hoi Tak** is new and should be near the top. It is far from downtown and closer to the airport. The better-located hotel is the attractive **Holiday Inn Urumqi**. The **Hotel World Plaza** is next but back towards the airport. The **City Hotel** is the best three star. The **Islam Grand** is better located for business people. Hotels here can change money and accept credit cards.

Except for the joint-venture hotels, don't expect much. The high tourist season is June through October. Prices listed below are subject to 15% surcharge and 3% tax, change, discounts, and negotiation.

HOI TAK HOTEL, *1 Dong Feng Road, 830002. E-mail:hthxjbc@mail.wl.xj.cn or hosec@htintl.com.hk. Five star standards not yet official. Y950-Y1050. 22 km from the airport and 7 km from the railway station.*

This 318-room hotel has executive floors, Moslem rooms and restaurant, Chinese and western food. There's also a gym, indoor heated pool, bowling center and sauna.

HOLIDAY INN URUMQI (Xinjiang Jia Ri Da Jiudian), *168 Xinhua Bei Road, 830002. Four stars, Tel. 2818788, Fax 2817422. E-mail:holiday@public.wl.xj.cn. Y1000-Y1200 for rooms, Y1700-Y4350 for suites. 20 km from the airport. Six km from the railway station.*

With a good central location, this 1992 hotel has 24 stories and 383 rooms. It has CNN, non-smoking and executive floors, Moslem, Sichuan and Cantonese food. It has a deli, pub, and beer garden. There's a gym, sauna, jacuzzi, tennis court, solarium and steam bath. It has a video projection room and free shuttle service for Beijing flights. Work should start on a bowling alley and pool in late 1999.

See also Chapter 13, *China's Best Places to Stay.*

HOTEL WORLD PLAZA (Huan Qiu Dajiudian), *2 Beijing Nan Road, 830011. Four stars, Tel. 3836360, 3836409, Fax 3836399 or 3839007. $90 to $100 but $62 through a travel agent. 17 km from the airport and 12 km from the railway station. In the South Road Technological Development area.*

Built in 1992, this hotel has 24 stories and 400 rooms. It has a non-smoking floor, satellite television, gym, sauna and indoor pool. There's 24-hour room service. Lee Garden (H.K.) management.

ISLAM GRAND HOTEL, *22 Zhong Shan Road, Tel. 2811017, Fax 2811513, Three stars.*
This hotel is cheaper than the other hotels here. It's in Moslem style with good food, but I haven't had a chance to review it.
XIN JIANG CITY HOTEL, *119 Hongqi Road, 830001, Tel. 2309911, Fax 2301818. 15 km from the airport and four km from the railway station. Y280-Y600.*
220 rooms with in-house movies and satellite television. It has conference rooms, a Ladies Club, tea house, 24 hour international restaurant, and 24 hour room service. There also a gym and sauna.

WHERE TO EAT

Local specialties include roast whole goat or sheep, *kebabs*, thin-skinned steamed buns with stuffing, fried rice (eaten with bare hands), deep-fried *nan* bread, mare's milk, and dried sour cheese. The food can be chili hot. Local fruits include seedless white grapes, pears, Hami melons, apples, and raisins. The meat in Xinjiang is mainly mutton, because Moslems do not eat pork.

The **Holiday Inn** has had the best food, both western and Asian. Food at the **World Plaza** and the **Overseas Chinese Hotel** , *51 Xia Hua Street, Tel. 286079,* is okay. Try the crispy chicken and fake crab soup in the Cantonese style. A **night food market** has Moslem food with questionable hygiene at **Tuan Jie Ye Shi**, but it's fascinating.

SEEING THE SIGHTS

A one-day trip is possible to **Tianshan** (Heaven Mountain) and **Lake Tianzi** (Heavenly Lake), 115 km south of the city. These are about 1,980 meters above sea level and colder than Urumqi. They've had snow in early May. Take something extra for warmth, especially if you want to climb. Tianzi has beautiful scenery but the boat trip on the lake can be missed as you can experience the same scenery while walking. The lake is five sq km and 100 meters deep. An ancient glacier, about 100 meters thick and two by five km wide, sprawls near ice caves and valleys. But visitors are frequently too cold to stay to explore. Your visit to a *yurt* is usually not well planned as guides explain very little.

This area might look like the Rockies or Switzerland. But did you ever find *yurts* and herds of cashmere goats near Lake Louise?

On a second day you can drive about 75 km south of Urumqi to the **Nanshan Pasture** for more mountains, valleys, fountains, waterfalls, and cypress and pine trees. Horseback riding, mountaineering, and digging for valuable *ginseng* roots are among the attractions.

Here, if you are lucky, or unlucky, you might find a game of polo played with an initially live goat instead of a ball! Shades of Afghanistan!

THE UYGURS

The different minority groups make this an interesting region. The **Uygurs** *(or Uighurs) controlled northwest China during the Tang. In 788 A.D., a Tang princess married a Uygur khan, by no means a love match. In subsequent years, Chinese silk and sugar were exchanged for Uygur horses and furs. Uygur cavalry often helped the Tang emperors. Strangely enough, the Uygurs were the main supporters of the Manichaean religion (see Quanzhou).*

The power of the Uygurs declined after their capital was sacked by the Kirghiz of western Siberia. In 842, a food shortage turned the Uygurs into very aggressive raiders and China retaliated with force and the execution of Uygurs in Xi'an. The Uygurs also fought with Genghis Khan but because they had a written language, they were the bookkeepers and administrators, not the warriors.

Or you might cheer on women chasing and beating men on horseback, a courtship ritual. You might also be able to dine and sleep in a *yurt*. Barbecued mutton drowned by tea with mare's milk has been offered to some groups. The **Kazaks** are traditionally nomadic herdsmen, whose ancestors rode and plundered with Genghis Khan.

In the winter, you can hire boots and skiis and get a horse to pull you uphill at **Ju Hua Tai** on Tianshan 60 km from Urumqi to **downhill ski**.

In Urumqi itself, you can visit the nine-story Hong Ding Shan Ta (**Red Pagoda Hill**), *Tel. 2828416,* founded in the Tang, the current building finished in 1788. There is a good view of the city from the pagoda. The excellent **Xinjiang Museum**, (*132 Northwest Road, Tel. 4816436, closed on Sundays*) has gold Roman coins, silver Persian coins, and other artifacts from the Silk Road. One hall contains murals; another displays 4,000-year-old mummies. A special exhibition hall shows traditional relics and the customs of 12 major minorities in Xinjiang. The museum is good for at least two hours.

The **Moslem Market** near the Grand Mosque, *11 Jiefang Road*, is dirty and not well organized, but you can see local Moslem snacks, *halal* meats, and local vegetables there. The **Russian market** is interesting because it has goods from Central Asia and Russia like cameras, shoes, and appliances. But the trade is more from China to Kazakstan. The **Qiao Livestock Market** has camels and horses.

SHOPPING

Urumqi is just about the best place on the Silk Road to shop for minority handicrafts. These include carpets, decorated Yengisar daggers, jewelry, embroidered caps, red copper ware, jade carving, embroidery, musical instruments, and fur and leather articles. Hand-knotted wool carpets in Persian designs are especially good buys but are probably cheaper in Pakistan. The **Overseas Chinese Hotel** has a shop with reasonable prices for cashmere sweaters. The **Holiday Inn** has books in English and some unusual crafts, at high prices.

Other outlets of interest are the **Urumqi General Carpet Rug Factory**, *40-64 Jinger Road, Tel. 5813297;* **Musical Instrument Factory**, *245 Jiefang Nan Road, Tel. 5813293, 2823284;* **Xinjiang Antique Store**, *325 Jiefang Nan Road, Tel. 2825161;* **Jade Sculpture Factory** (jasper, topaz, crystal, Hotan jade), *7 Pearl River Road, Tel. 5812395;* **Urumqi Foreign Trade Carpets Factory**, *14 Li Yu Shan Road, 830000, Tel. 5812395.* There is also a **Cashmere Sweater Factory** at *7 Juan Jue Road, Tel. 2863678.* **Tian Shan Department Store** is the biggest in Northwest China. It's near People's Square and has fashionable items. Near the Market is the **Department Store**.

A daytime street **bazaar** is at *ErDao Qiao* near the Overseas Chinese Hotel, with food, clothing, antiques and carpets.

EXCURSIONS & DAY TRIPS

Xinjiang is a huge region, the largest in China. It is much less populated than other parts of China as most of it is desert and mountain. Two cave temples are at **Baicheng** and **Kuqa**, almost halfway in between Kashi and Urumqi, and 285 km from Urumqi. (Turpan's caves are better; see below). Kuqa has an airport, so you can fly there if you want to see the ***Kezil/ Kerzil Thousand Buddha Grottoes**; these caves are from the Han and have 236 grottoes. Xinjiang has at least eight important groups of grottoes.

Another interesting place is **Yili** via Yining, near the Kazakstan border where you should be able to see hundreds of *yurts*. This can also be done from Almaty on a long weekend if the border is not closed due to holidays. See Chapter 6, section on Getting To China Via Central Asia. A new highway should be finished in 1999 between Urumqi and Yili.

Travel agents can arrange jeep, camel, motorcycle, bicycle or bus tours on the Silk Road, a tour of the southern, less traveled route to Tibet and Pakistan, treks in the mountains or the Taklamakan Desert, and a land tour from Urumqi to Almaty in Kazakhstan and back through Kashgar.

For other caves and tourist attractions in the region, see Silk Road, Turpan, and Kashi. Ask about the Corban Festival, the Moslem New Year, with its songs, dances, horse races, courtship rituals on horseback, wrestling, and lamb snatching.

PRACTICAL INFORMATION

Business Hours, 10am-12am, 3:30pm-7:30pm (winter) and 9:30am-1:30pm and 4pm-8pm (summer) for offices five days a week. 10am-7pm (summer) and 11am-8pm (winter) for stores.

China Xinjiang Nature Travel Service, *9 Dong Hou Street, 830002, Tel. 2643454, Fax 2617891. 2617174.* Attention Song Yong, Manager, European and American Department. Specialists in bird watching, trekking, jeep, horse and camel tours, and in off-the-beaten-track areas around the Silk Road.

CITS and **Overseas Tourist Corporation**, *51 Xinhua Bei Road, 830002, Tel. 2825913, Fax 2810689, 2818691.* **OTC**, *Tel. 2814490.*

CTS, *51 Xinhua Nan Road, 830001, Tel. 2860238, 2861806, Fax 2862131.* Attention Kingway Joe.

CYTS, *9 Jianshe Road, 830002, Tel. 2827172, 2818447, Fax 2817078, 2832331* (Muhtar).

Telephone code, *0891*

Tourism Hotline, *Tel. 2831902* for information and complaints.

Xinjiang Tourism Bureau, *16 Hetan Nan Road, 830002, Tel. 2846342, 2831907, Fax 2818439.*

Tourist Complaints, contact Supervisory Bureau of Tourism Quality of Xinjiang, *Tel. 2831902, Fax 2824449*

KASHI

(Kashgar)

At the far western tip of Xinjiang province, 164 km from the former Soviet republic of Kyrghyzstan, **Kashi** is one of the highlights of a Silk Road trip because of its Central Asian ambience, architecture, and extraordinary Sunday market.

Kashi has about 300,000 people, urban and rural, of whom 74% are Uygur. The altitude is 1,289 meters. The annual rainfall is below 100 millimeters so take precautions against dust. The highest temperature in summer is 40 C. The lowest in winter is -24 C. Early May to early September is fine to visit. The end of September can be cold.

The **Sunday market** is a medieval crush of 100,000 Uygurs, Afghanis, Pakistanis, Kyrghyz, Tajiks, and Mongols, blacksmiths, barbers, 'dentists,' and donkey carts. Peppercorns, mutton *shish kebabs*, pomegranates, grapes, cloth, bright felt carpets, jeweled knives, and boots, camels, and goats are traded here. Tinkerers repair kettles and bicycles. This market is more interesting for photographing than for buying, and needs at least three hours. Most residents don't mind cameras. Go early to avoid the heat.

Government officials, hotels and tour guides operate on Beijing time, but some shops keep 'Kashgar time,' and others keep 'Pakistan time', which could be a three-hour difference.

ARRIVALS & DEPARTURES

From Urumqi, you can get there by air (1,085 km in 1.5 hours at least once and sometimes twice a day–on weekends). You can go non-stop by long-distance bus in 36 hours, or more leisurely by jeep in three days. You can also get there by land from Lhasa but it's even harder. You go via Korla, Kuqa, Aksu – four days and three nights. Ask about the state of the roads.

A railway should be finished between Urumqi and Kashi in 1999.

Kashi is also accessible by road, but not without a long, tiring, and sometimes spectacular journey from Pakistan (520 km), or from Kyrghyzstan (quite risky). You need two weeks for a travel agent to get you a special permit to go through Kyrghyzstan.

ORIENTATION

Kashi is over 2,000 years old and has been fought over by many contenders. In the mid-10th century, a Uygur-Turkish coalition, the Karahanid (Qurakhanid) Dynasty took over the area. Its leaders later converted to Islam and made Kashi their capital. Today it grows rice, wheat, fruit, and cotton. It exports tomato sauce.

WHERE TO STAY & EAT

Prices listed here are subject to change and negotiations. Kashgar's accommodations are generally poor with limited services. The **Friendship Building** of the **Qiniwak Hotel** is the best. It is aiming for three stars and has 60 rooms. The **Seman's** new section is second. Dine only in the top hotels.

KASHGAR HOTEL (Binguan), *Tazris/Tawuguzi Road, 844000. Building Number Four is two stars, Tel. 2822367, Fax 2824679. $60. American Express credit card only.*

This hotel is nine km from the airport and four km to town center. Set in a large garden, it is the closest hotel to the Sunday market, and has a Moslem dining room. There's been good hot water but terrible plumbing, and IDD. It's okay for backpackers.

QINIWAK HOTEL (Qinibah), *93 Seman Road, 844000. Two and three stars, Tel. 2822103, 2825006, Fax 2823842, 2823087. 12 km from the airport. $38. Credit Cards.*

The old British Consulate building is still there. The hotel's 1990 addition has five stories and 140 rooms. It has IDD, bigger bathrooms than at the Kashgar Hotel, and CITS nearby. Read *The Antique Land* by Diana Shipton, who lived here in 1946.

SEMAN HOTEL, *170 Seman Road, 844000. Two stars, Tel. 2822129, 2822150. 13 km from the airport.*

The Seman is more central with a notice board for travelers. It has bicycles, a western coffee shop, exchange desk and IDD.

SEEING THE SIGHTS

You can get around locally by taxi, but if you want to try something different, go for the bumpy donkey cart experience! Just wave one down.

Like other cities of Xinjiang, Kashi gives you a feeling more of Central Asia than of China. It is the only place in China where women veil their faces, by choice. The city centre is near the **Idkah Mosque**, *Tel. 2823235,* (1442 A.D.) which holds 7,000 people. Nearby is a giant pomegranate, symbol of the city (and fertility). Just sitting in this square is like watching a movie of life and death in the Middle Ages. I saw a funeral pass by, the deceased on a stretcher, not a coffin. Behind the mosque are streets with old buildings, wrought-iron balconies, and alleyways with mud townhouses more typical of north Africa than China. The local people are friendly. Carpet and musical instrument factories are close by, the best instruments made of snake skin. The area has 9,500 mosques.

You should go to the huge **Abakhojia Tomb**, *Tel. 2822638* (Ming and Qing), the final resting place of 70 descendents of Muhatum Ajam, an Islamic missionary. It is five km from the Kashgar Hotel and has a jewelery shop. A museum is being built close to this hotel. The **San Xian** (Three Immortals) **Buddhist Caves** are 16 km north of the city with a decent road. Three rectangular holes high in the side of a cliff beckon the fit and curious. Unless they have been recently repaired, the frescoes inside are not in good condition.

Recent visitors have seen the snow-covered Pamir Mountains from **Scholar Mohamed Kashgari's Tomb** 45 km southwest of Kashgar on the road to Pakistan. You can visit **Karakuli Lake**, 196 km west of the city, on a one-day excursion.

Thirty km east of Kashi is the town of **Hanoi**, abandoned after the 11th century and now just a ruin. In the area, you can also cruise **South Lake**, but it is only a respite from all the dryness. South of the city and east of the Sino-Pakistan Highway towards Afghanistan are the 7,719-meter-high Mt. Kongur and 7,546-meter-high Mt. Muztagta, part of the Pamirs. If you keep in mind that Hunza in Pakistan and Kashmir in India are also to the south, you will get an idea of the magnificence and isolation of the area here. Think Himalayas!

There's a good walk behind Idkah Mosque. Actually, this whole city is good for walking and bicycling. You can rent bicycles from the hotels.

SHOPPING

Kashi produces gold and silver ornaments, leather boots, bronzeware, jewelry, rugs, jade carving, embroidered caps, daggers, and musical instruments made of apricot wood. The jewelry bazaar is on Zhiren Street. The **Odali Bazaar** on *Jiefang Bei Road* sells daggers and caps. The **Handicraft Centre** is on the same road.

If you buy the fancy 'jewelled' daggers, put them in your checked luggage during your flight, or leave them with the cabin crew (for a fee).

PRACTICAL INFORMATION

CITS, *Qiriwak Hotel, 93 Seman Road, Tel. 2823156, 2828473, Fax 2823087.*

Kashgar China Travel Service, *144 Seman Road, Tel. 2822262, Fax 2822552.*

Telephone code, *0998*

TURPAN

(Turfan)

Turpan is located in the desert of northeast Xinjiang province. With so many Chinese cities clogged with traffic and frentic with activity, it is refreshing to find this sleepy, charming, exotic little town. It still seems to have more donkey carts than cars and traveling by bicycle here is not the ordeal it is in Chengdu, for example. In fact, it is downright pleasant, especially under the grape arbors that line the downtown streets. They in turn are bordered by canals of rushing water.

The weather here is the hottest in China! Turpan is in the Turpan Basin, which is known as 'the oven.' Air temperatures reach over 48 C in summer. Rainfall averages 16.6 mm. a year, and in very dry years, it has been as little as four mm. Strong winds blow more than 30 days a year. The hot air from the basin and cold air from the north create violent storms.

An old Chinese saying goes: In winter, Turpan people wear fur coats in the morning, light silk clothes at noon, and dine on watermelon in the evenings around hot stoves. The temperature has fallen to minus 17 C in January. For summer nights, you need a sweater. It is an area of extremes. Weather people and geographers would love it. The best time to visit is late May to October. A few sandstorms blow in April and early May.

The lowest point of the basin is **Aydingkol Lake**, its water surface 154 meters below sea level. It is second only to the Dead Sea as the world's lowest body of water. It is not usually included on tours because of the poor road. Nearby is **Bogda Mountain** with a peak at 5,445 meters. The population is 200,000, 80% Uygurs.

But wait! Don't stop reading! Those of us who have been there say the dust and plumbing are worth it!

ARRIVALS & DEPARTURES

Roughly 200 km, or a 2.5 hour drive southeast of Urumqi, Turpan can be a 3.5 day tour by road or train from there. Turpan is also 680 km or 12 hours by train from Dunhuang. The train station is 50 km from town at Daheyan.

Your tour should include visits to Gaochang, Jiaohe, the Baziklic Caves, Astana Tombs, Imin Minaret, Grape Valley, and the Karez wells.

ORIENTATION

Turpan was once an oasis on the Silk Road. It existed then and now because of subterranean water from **karez wells** some dug 2,400 years ago. During the Western Han (206 B.C.-24 A.D.), soldiers were sent to develop agriculture here. Some sources say the technology for the wells came from Shaanxi province. Other historians say it arrived from farther west, since *karez* is a Persian word. In any case, the wells are most common in Turpan and nearby Hami, to the east.

In spring, snow from the Tianshan Mountains melts, and this water flows into the Turpan Basin, soaking into the ground and stored in vast natural underground reservoirs reached by sloping channels tapped in turn by the wells. You can see the desert dotted with lines of wells.

Visit the **Karez Well Museum**, which explains with diagrams just how those 40 km-long irrigation tunnels were dug. There are 5,000 km of these tunnels.

Modern irrigation methods based on these wells have transformed Turpan into an agricultural area. Californians, and anyone else who has made deserts produce food, should be fascinated. Grain, cotton, and the famous Hami melons are grown here. Grapes have grown here for 2,000 years. The wooden huts with the holes are for drying the September-harvested fruit in the hot, dry air. Ask to see the drying process. Hami melons are much in demand. They have a sweet perfume, somewhat like face powder, with the texture of cantaloupe and the taste of honeydew.

Grape Valley (Pu Tao Gao) is 10 km northeast of the city. Turpan's grapes are very sweet with a 15-20% sugar content. Grapes grow almost everywhere, along streets and beside private homes. Turpan is also a good place to experience the different **cultural minorities**. Uygur and Hui nationalities live here with the Han.

WHERE TO STAY & EAT

The **Oasis** is the best hotel now but this keeps changing. Both it and the **Turfan Hotel** have air-conditioning (turned off for the winter in September and October). They are within walking distance of each other and the markets. The Turfan has a good Uygur dance show in the evenings. Both hotels are capable of very good Moslem banquets.

The cheaper **John's Cafe** across from the Turfan Hotel is a hangout for foreign backpackers and should be safe for western food. It is only open during tourist season. Some hotels might be closed in winter.

OASIS HOTEL (Liuzhou Binguan), *41 Qinian, 838000. Two stars aiming for three, Tel. 8522478, 8522491, Fax 523348.*

This hotel has a post office, karaoke hall and rooms for backpackers. It was renovated in 1998.

TURFAN HOTEL (Tulufan Binguan), *838000. Two stars, Tel. 8522301, 8522642, Fax 8523262. $50 for rooms but $38 through a travel agent.*

This five-story hotel has money exchange and good service considering its isolated location. It has an attractive dining room and wide twin beds. It has dorms for backpackers and a small pool.

SEEING THE SIGHTS

The 37-meter-high **Imam Minaret** (1778) stands two km east of Turpan, its geometric patterns in the Uygur style. However, its smooth inverted-cone shape with rounded top is reminiscent of those towers south of New Delhi on the road to Agra.

There's a small **museum** near the Turpan Hotel with five well-preserved 1,300-year old human mummies on display. It is open 9:00am-8pm daily in high tourist season (May 1 until the winter).

Walking around town is good if it's not too hot, as some streets are topped with shady grape arbors. The Grape Festival is on August 20.

EXCURSIONS & DAY TRIPS

The dry climate has preserved historical monuments. The area has many ancient tombs, Buddhist grottoes, and the ruins of ancient cities all worth seeing.

The ghost city of *Gaochang, 40 km southeast of Turpan, was capital of the State of Gaochang (500-640 A.D.) and reached its peak in the ninth century, with a population of 50,000. Try to imagine it as it was then. It was on the Silk Road and flourished from the first century B.C. until the Mongols ravaged it in the 14th A.D. Here were once 30 to 40 monasteries! The buildings were made of mud bricks and are now without roofs. Take a donkey cart if it's too hot to walk.

The equally ancient city of **Jiaohe** on the other hand shows the effect of its UNESCO and Japanese help: a scale model, signs in English saying the likes of "five minutes to the temple," or "Do not enter." UNESCO has opened new areas like the small northeastern temple. The paths are now paved and it is hard to get lost.

*Jiaohe (also known as Yarkhoto, and possibly Yaerhu), 10 km west of Turpan, existed from the second century B.C. to the 14th A.D. Its mud brick buildings are better preserved than Gaochang's and are in an area 1.65 km x 0.3 km. It also had a population of 50,000. In the northwestern part are temple ruins with the remains of Buddhist images. There is also a rare brick Buddhist temple. Take a donkey cart if you tire easily. Jiaohe is different in structure from Gaochang; the city was carved out rather than built. One source says it was abandoned in the Ming for lack of water; another source says it was destroyed by fire during fighting in the Yuan dynasty.

Eight km from Gaochang and 40 km southeast of Turfan are the **Astana Tombs** dating from the third century to about the eighth A.D. This is where 500 mummies, plus their belongings, were found, along with 2100 documents and books. Take a flashlight. Visitors routinely see only a couple of Tang mummies in a dark room. The dry weather has preserved the bodies with still discernible eye lashes and eyeballs. Was Astana the Uygur capital? Astana means capital in Uygur.

The *Pazikelik (or Baziklic, Bazeklik) **Thousand-Buddha Caves** are 16 km northeast of Turpan by dusty road, by a cliff on the Flaming Mountains. About 80 of the grottoes are still intact but in poor condition, destroyed by looters, earthquakes, and archaeologists. Many of the murals were taken to the Berlin Museum in Germany and destroyed by bombs during World War Two. (Read *Foreign Devils on the Silk Road* by Peter Hopkirk.) Faces were mutilated by Moslems. They were built over a period of 1,400 years, starting in the Southern and Northern Dynasties (420-550 A.D.). Dunhuang's are more interesting and younger, but it is good to compare the two.

The **Flaming Mountains** themselves are historical, so named because the incessant sun is supposed to make the red rocks seem on fire from a distance. Perhaps this happens at sunset only in the classic fairy tale *Pilgrimage to the West*. In that story, the monkey king helps put out the fire so that Monk Xuan Zhang can go to India. The mountains are 100 km long and 10 km wide, their highest peak 800 meters above sea level. Unless you know the story, this is just another set of hills and may not be worth a special stop. They are between the Caves and Turpan in the hottest part of the depression.

Travel agents can arrange for you to go to **Aydingkol Lake** by bus leaving Urumqi between 7am and 8am a one or two day tour. The lake has now shrunk to a basin of crystals from its original 22.5 sq kilometers and is at 154.43 meters below sea level.

PRACTICAL INFORMATION
CITS and **CTS**, *Oasis Hotel, Tel. 8522907, Fax 8522768*
Telephone code, *0995*

XI'AN
(Sian, Chang An)
    Xi'an, the capital of Shaanxi province on the Guanzhong Plain, borders on the Loess Plateau to the north and the Qinling Mountains to the south. It was the center of China's world from the 11th century B.C. to the early 10th A.D.

    Xi'an was the capital intermittently for 1,183 years of 11 imperial dynasties, including the Western Zhou (of the ritual bronzes), the Qin (of the Great Wall and terracotta army), the Western Han (of the jade burial suits), the Sui (of the Grand Canal), and the Tang - ah, the Tang! Commerce on the Silk Road thrived west of here to the Mediterranean and beyond. (See Silk Road.) Thousands of foreigners lived in the Western Market then.

    In spite of the occasional invasions and sackings by rebels and tribesmen, Xi'an, then named Chang'an (Everlasting Peace), reached its peak in the Tang, when the population was nearly two million. It was one of the world's largest cities, with walls measuring 36 km in circumference. It declined because of late Tang debauchery and corruption, the eunuchs ruling the court, and increasingly powerful governors-general controlling the provinces. In 906, one of the last Tang emperors allowed one of his generals to take complete charge while he enjoyed his lady love. Xi'an rolled downhill from there on, following the fortunes, also, of the Silk Road. Read Cooney and Alteri's marvelous novel about this period, *The Court of the Lion.*

    A short-lived peasant regime made Xi'an a capital again in the 17th century, but it never regained its past glory. Xi'an did, however, continue to be a tourist resort and destination for religious pilgrimages because of its Buddhist roots. In 1900, when the Empress Dowager fled Beijing, she went to Xi'an.

    In 1936, one of his top officers, known as the Young Marshall, kidnapped Generalissimo **Chiang Kai-shek** here in what is known as the Xi'an Incident. They forced him to cooperate with the Communists against the Japanese, and the Communists set up a liaison office here which is now the *Museum of the Eighth Route Army. On May 20, 1949, the Communists took over the city.

    The altitude is 400 meters. The hottest weather is 40 C in July; the coldest is -14 C in January. Rain falls all year round, but especially July through early September with an annual precipitation of 550-770 mm.

The best weather is May-June when the pomegranates are in bloom, and September-October. The air can be badly polluted at times but the government is taking measures to improve it. The total population is over six million, 3.6 million urban.

ARRIVALS & DEPARTURES

Xi'an is a 1.75 hour, 1,165 km flight southwest of Beijing. It is a seven hour train ride west of Luoyang and a 570 km trip from Chongqing. Air routes with 42 cities now include Fukuoka, Hiroshima, Hong Kong, Macau and Nagoya. Check with travel agents about summer flights with Tianshui and Dunhuang.

Upon arrival at the airport, be prepared to walk from your plane to the terminal. The airport at Xianyang is 38-53 km from the city's hotels. The one-hour CAAC airport bus is 10% of the price of most hotel airport transfers and operates frequently between 5am-6pm. Taxis cost about Y180. On the way, look for the 2,200-year old Qin imperial burial tumuli (pointed tops) and almost as old Han imperial burial mounds (rounded top).

Early morning taxis to the airport from hotels might charge less (about Y100) since they have to go there anyway, but do insist that your taxi won't stop for other passengers; otherwise the trip will be much longer. CAAC buses go from its office outside the West City Gate.

The airport transit lounge has lots of shops including a supermarket with better drink prices than the cafe. Announcements are made in beautiful English. Be warned that the Xi'an airport is notorious for charging for overweight luggage, or is it a scam by the porters who transported our group luggage? This was the only place that billed our group for the same amount of luggage on four flights in China.

ORIENTATION

Next to Beijing, Xi'an is the best city to visit in China, especially if you are interested in ancient Chinese history, traditional culture, and archaeology. It is one of the 24 historical cities protected by the State Council and, unfortunately, it has been sinking due to lack of water.

Just to glimpse what it has to offer takes a full week. To savor Xi'an slowly, to study it deeply, to read about Empress Wu and her lover-protector-henchman while sitting in the shadow of a Tang pagoda - or to read about that crafty fictional Tang detective Judge Dee, two giant silk-flower petals sticking sideways out of the back of his magisterial cap - that kind of depth could take months.

Ancient Xi'an is the setting for many Chinese operas, their sweet young heroines waving flowing ribbon sleeves, and their flag-pierced generals galloping away to battle amid the clash of cymbals. Here the foreign caravans, the traders on camels exchanged silver, furs, horses, and sesame for Chinese silk and porcelain with Europe. It is here that the egomaniac Qin emperor ordered the burning of all books except those he liked, and demanded that his subjects create an army of life-size soldiers to maintain his empire forever.

Xi'an today is a textile and manufacturing center. It also produces Chinese and western medicines, and airplanes. It is an educational center, with about 40 colleges, universities, and research institutes. Xi'an Jiaotung (Communications) University is the best known, and one of the 11 'super-key' universities in the country. The municipal government has embarked on a program to bring Xi'an up to international standards between now and 2010. It plans to make the city more green and develop its high-tech industries.

Xi'an's **farms** grow cotton, maize, wheat, vegetables, pomegranates, and persimmons. Many houses and walls have been made of loess soil mixed with straw. If cared for properly and protected with bricks on top, mud walls can last 100 years. Cheap too! But today many farmers are rebuilding entirely in brick.

GETTING AROUND

Taxis are relatively cheap within this small city and there are public buses. You can book tours through the hotels or travel agents for about Y270 which pays for lunch, entrance fees, movie?, and transportation. The Jiefang Hotel across from the railway station has a Y50 tour to the Terracotta Warriors (but in what language?). The May First Hotel on Dongda Street has even cheaper tours (Y35 and Y45 in English). Tours booked at the YMCA are Y44 for the Terracotta Warriors, Y60 for Hua Shan, and Y54 for Famen Temple, *Tel. 7436790, 7427508.* This is only for transportation.

You can rent cars at hotels like the New World which charge Y200 to the airport, Y480 for the Terracotta Warriors, Banpo and Hot Springs, Y700 for the western route, Y850 for Famen and Y70 an hour for city sightseeing. China Travel Service charges about Y300 a day for a car in the city. Be aware that not all taxi drivers use their meters. Settle on a price before you get in. Judge distances by the city wall.

The walled city is a grid, a rectangle. The downtown commercial area is on Dongda Jie or East Street. Nearby is the city hall. North (Bei), South (Nan) and West (Xi) Streets meet it at the Bell Tower. The Railway Station is at the north end of Jiefang Road. West Street ends at the very impressive West City Gate. Xi'an is building a 34 km expressway around the city due in 2000.

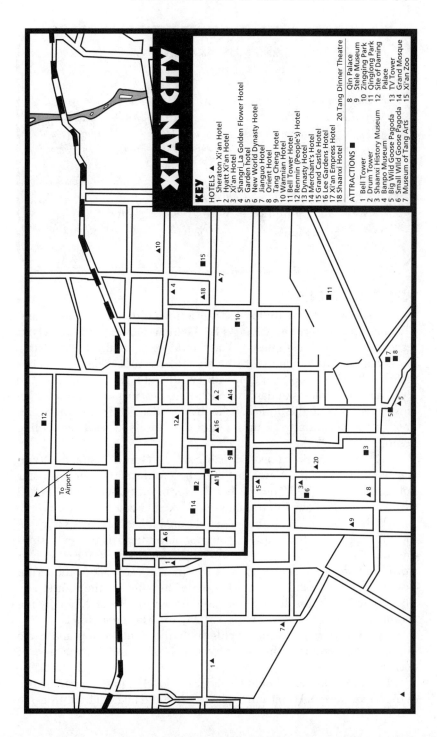

XI'AN CITY

KEY

HOTELS ▲

1 Sheraton Xi'an Hotel
2 Hyatt Xi'an Hotel
3 Xi'an Hotel
4 Shangri_La Golden Flower Hotel
5 Garden hotel
6 New World Dynasty Hotel
7 Jianguo Hotel
8 Orient Hotel
9 Tang Cheng Hotel
10 Wannian Hotel
11 Bell Tower Hotel
12 Renmin (People's) Hotel
13 Dynasty Hotel
14 Merchant's Hotel
15 Grand Castle Hotel
16 Lee Gardens Hotel
17 Xi'an Empress Hotel
18 Shaanxi Hotel
20 Tang Dinner Theatre

ATTRACTIONS ■

1 Bell Tower
2 Drum Tower
3 Shaanxi History Museum
4 Banpo Museum
5 Big Wild Goose Pagoda
6 Small Wild Goose Pagoda
7 Museum of Tang Arts
8 Qin Palace
9 Stele Museum
10 Zingqing Park
11 Qinglong Park
12 Site of Daming Palace
13 TV Tower
14 Grand Mosque
15 Xi'an Zoo

To Airport

TOURIST SIGHTS IN XI'AN BY LOCATION

In Xi'an and immediate vicinity: Wild Goose Pagodas, Bell Tower, Drum Tower, City Wall, Great Mosque, Xi'an Stele Museum, Shaanxi Provincial History Museum, Xingqing Palace Park, Banpo Museum, Memorial Museum of the Eighth Route Army, Xi'an Film Studio.

West and South of Xi'an: Chariot and Horse Pits, Xingjiao Temple, Xiangji Temple, Qinglong Temple, Temple of Du Fu, Cao Tang Temple, Peasant Painting of Hu County.

East of Xi'an: Huaqing Hot Springs, Qinshihuang's Tomb and Terracotta Army, and Bronze Chariots.

North and Northwest of Xi'an: Xianyang Museum, Maoling, Zhaoling, and Qianling tombs, Famen Temple and the international airport.

WHERE TO STAY

Some hotels charge for local as well as long distance telephone calls. The best hotels are the **Shangri-La Golden Flower** and the **Hyatt** (especially for business guests). The **Sheraton Xi'an** also has top standards but is a little isolated for tourists. All are modern-day world class palaces, the Hyatt and Sheraton with grand and beautiful lobbies. The Hyatt has the smallest standard rooms, but the best furniture. The Golden Flower seems to be the busiest, its lobby crowded. The Sheraton makes note of the taxis that pick up its guests, in case you leave something behind.

Also of international luxury quality are the **Grand Castle**, the **Xi'an Garden** and the **Grand New World** (the best four star). Of the three-star hotels, the modest **Bell Tower** is best for location and service. It has had the benefit of Holiday Inn training but broke ties in 1998.

The best location for business people and individual tourists is inside the city wall but traffic jams are common and the air is not as fresh as outside. The Bell Tower Hotel is the most convenient. You can walk to stores, an internet center, and Bell Tower. You can walk to the Drum Tower, the Mosque and curio market, Stele Museum, and the South Gate. The other hotels inside the wall are the Hyatt, Royal Xi'an (going downhill), Grand New World, the YMCA, and May First Hotels.

The Xian Grand Castle is closest to the South Gate, and Stele Museum. Forget about the City Hotel. It is dirty and I saw a nest of cockroaches there.

Romantic travelers should consider the lovely Chinese architecture of the **Xi'an Garden Hotel** and forget its price and high humidity for one night. Budget travelers should stay at the **May First Hotel** or the **YMCA**, right on Dongda Street. The top hotels here are all international quality unless noted, with money exchange, credit card service, business centers, international direct dial, etc. The prices here are subject to change, discounts from 10%-60% or more, and 10%-15% surcharge.

HYATT REGENCY XIAN (Kaiyue Fandian), *158 Dongda Street, 710001. Five stars, Tel. 7231234, Fax 7216799, 7277650. E-mail:hyattrsv@public.xa.sn.cn. Http://www.travelweb.com/hyatt.html. 45 km from the airport and two km from the railway station. It is across the street from Parkson's Department Store and close to the East Gate. $140-$180 for rooms, $260-$1800 for suites.*

Built in 1990, the Hyatt has 8, 10 and 12 stories. It has 404 classy rooms, some of which have attractive Japanese paper windows, and apartments. It should have three executive floors and internet room now. There's 24-hour room service, Cantonese and Italian cuisine. Its pizzeria has live music. It has a gym, aerobic, steam room, HBO and CNN. Bicycles are for hire. It has the largest indoor heated pool in Xi'an, and a high-tech gym. It charges Y50 an hour for its computer and internet service.

SHANGRI-LA GOLDEN FLOWER HOTEL (Shang Gorilla or Jinhua Fandian), *8 Changle Xi Road, 710032. Five stars, Tel. 3232981, Fax 3232888. E-mail: SLXXIAN@public.xa.sn.cn. 45 km from the airport, three km from the railway station. A night market is outside with cheap food and clothes. $130-$230 for rooms, $230-$1500 for suites.*

Shangri-La took over this 1985 hotel in 1993. It has seven and 11 story wings with 446 rooms (including apartments with kitchenettes). It has executive and non-smoking floors, in-room kettles, safes and voice mail. There's CNN and HBO, 24-hour room service, a superb bake shop, great breakfast, and good coffee, a gym, jacuzzi, sauna, and Xi'an's largest indoor heated pool.

SHERATON XIAN (Xilaidun Jiudian), *12 Feng Hao Road, 710077. Five stars, Tel. 4261888, Fax 4262188, 4262983. 45 km from the airport, 4.5 km from the railway station. In a quiet location, two km west of West Gate, this 1991 hotel finished major renovations in 1998. $120-$170 for rooms, $230-$498 for suites.*

This hotel has 16 stories and 450 rooms with safes, satellite television, and electronic door locks. It has an executive floor and 24-hour business center, non-smoking floors, and Cantonese and international food. Its relatively formal continental restaurant has a stringed western quartet, something to dress up for. It has a small heated indoor pool, gym, sauna, steambath and jacuzzi.

XI'AN GARDEN HOTEL (Tang Hua Binguan), *4 Dong Yan Yin Road, Da Yan Ta, 710061. Four stars, Tel. 5261111, 5255840, Fax 5261778,*

5261998. 53 km from the airport, eight km from the railway station. $110-$160 for rooms, $250 for suites.

This garden-style hotel on the southern edge of the city is within walking distance of the Xi'an Film Studio (theme park) and Big Wild Goose Pagoda. It is small but good with its own little museum of Tang dynasty artifacts, titled in English. It has its own theatre restaurant. Built in 1988 in Tang courtyard style, it has four stories, 301 rooms, and non-smoking floors, some with Ming-style furniture. Its twin rooms, televisions and bathrooms are small, and you might have to walk a long way between the lobby and your room. It has Star TV but no CNN or in-room safe. It has Japanese, Chinese and fast food restaurants and a gym. Member Prima Hotels. Managed by Mitsui.

GRAND CASTLE HOTEL XIAN (Chang'an Cheng Bao Dajiudian), *12 Xi Duan Huan Cheng Nan Lu, 710068. Five stars, Tel. 7231800, Fax 7231500, 7231244. Just outside the South Gate but difficult to walk there because of relentless traffic. $120-$180.*

Built in 1993, this 10-story, 340-room hotel looks like a castle and has a huge atrium lobby with a life-size camel and driver. It has Japanese, Cantonese, and Mediterranean cuisines, and health foods. It has 24-hour room service, Star TV and CNN, kettles and a gym but no inroom safes, and no pool. Managed by ANA Hotels.

GRAND NEW WORLD HOTEL (Gu Du Dajiudian), *48 Lian Hu Road, 710002, Tel. 7216868, Fax 7214222, 7317043. Four stars. 45 km from the airport, four km from the railway station. Near West Gate and park in the north west part inside the wall. E-mail:gnwhxian@sein.sxgb.com.cn. $100 for rooms and $180 for suites.*

Built in 1989, this 14-story hotel has 491 attractive medium-sized rooms with unusual color schemes, two business floors and one executive floor. It has a Cantonese restaurant and cheaper food street, a large heated indoor pool, gym, sauna, steam bath and lighted tennis court. Its 1130-seat theatre on odd-numbered days during high season has an excellent historical dance drama. Its rooms should have CNN, two telephone jacks, electronic keys, and room safe soon. Managed by Marriott International.

See also Chapter 13, *China's Best Places to Stay.*

JIANGUO HOTEL (Fandian), *20 Jinhua Nan Road, 710048. Four stars, Tel. 3238888, Fax 3235145. E-mail: jianguo@pub.xaonline.com. 50 km from the airport, five km from the railway station, and in a residential area outside the west wall about one km south of the Golden Flower Hotel. $98-$150 for rooms, $200-$800 for suites. It has economy rooms for $68.*

Built in 1989-90, this six and 14-story hotel has 888 large rooms with big beds and televisions in beautiful cabinets, wicker furniture, Star World but no CNN and no safes. It has 24-hour room service and a coffee shop, Sichuan and Cantonese food. There's an executive floor, gym, indoor pool and sloppy standards. But it's okay if you're not fussy.

HOTEL ROYAL XI'AN (Huang Cheng Binguan), *334 Dongda Street, 710001. Four stars, Tel. 7235311, Fax 7235887. Across the street from a marvelous produce market and near good shopping. $90-$500.*

Built in 1992, this 12-story, 439-room hotel has kitchenettes in all suites. It has satellite television, Cantonese food and 24-hour room service. There's also un-inspired architecture and almost non-existent English. Nikko Hotels International (JAL).

BELL TOWER HOTEL (Zhong Lou Fandian), *southwest corner of Bell Tower, 710001. Three stars, Tel. 7279200, Fax 7271217, 7218767. E-mail: belltower@ihw.com.cn. 45 km from the airport, three km from the railway station. Overlooking both Drum Tower and Hua Jue Xiang (with its modern underground Ginwa shopping center). $80-$100 for rooms, $120-$160 for suites.*

Built in 1982, this hotel has seven stories and 321 rooms. The best view is from odd-numbered rooms. It has CNN and HBO, a Cantonese restaurant, gym and bicycles for rent. Needless to say, I like staying there.

WANNIAN HOTEL XI'AN (Fandian), *11 Changle Zhong Road, 710032. Three stars, Tel. 3231932, Fax 3235460. Y480-Y580 for rooms, and Y880 for suites. It is outside the west wall about one km north of the Golden Flower.*

This is a good basic hotel with very good food and non-smoking rooms but no CNN nor in-room safes. It is renovating some rooms in 1998 and building a four-star addition for 2000.

YMCA, *33 Dongda Street, Tel. 7235479, Fax 7275830. About 2.5 star standard, aiming for three. This hostel has a great downtown location east of the Bell Tower and west of the Hyatt. Opened in 1988, it has 60 rooms at Y268, and four suites at Y488. No discounts.*

It has a health club, Chinese and western food, foreign exchange, and tour desk. This is a basic seven-story hotel, no television channels in English, nor safes in rooms. Carpets are stained but the manager promised to have them cleaned during the winter. Light bulbs are 25 watts. The bathroom floors look dirty. The YMCA also has accommodations for travelers now in Beijing, Shanghai and Guangzhou.

MAY FIRST HOTEL (Wuyi Binguan), *351 Dongda Street, Tel. 7213824, 7215932, Fax 7213824. About $25.* The entrance to this well-located 110-room hotel is through a Chinese cafeteria with open kitchen serving Qin dynasty snacks. The hotel has dirty carpets, dim lights and a musty smell. Otherwise it's fine for low-budget travelers.

WHERE TO EAT

Xi'an food is similar to that of Beijing: somewhat bland. Its famous local dishes are crisp fried chicken or duck, and dried fish shaped like grapes. Much of its food has been inspired by imperial tastes.

Two celebrated **wines** are made here: one is thick and sweet with the appearance of milk. Served hot, Chou Jiu wine inspired Tang poet Li Po, who drank 1000 cups and wrote more than 100 poems. The other wine is Xifeng Jiu (55% alcohol), one of the eight Most Famous Wines in China.

Most hotels have good Chinese food, but joint ventures have the best western food. At The **Sheraton**, the western dinner buffet costs Y118 but it also has hot dogs for Y22, and hamburgers and fries for Y40. During warm weather it has an outdoor barbecue. It has great US beef steaks, T-bone cost Y158 for 350 grams, sirloin Y138 for Y250 grams, filet Y122 for 250 grams, and rib eye Y148 for 250 grams. A **Kenny Rogers Roasters** and **Deli France** are in the mall below the Bell and Drum Tower (Hua Jue Xiang) Square. A whole chicken at Kenny's costs Y62.

For Chinese food, the best and most expensive are in the top hotels. The Cantonese Restaurants at the **Garden Hotel** has great frogs and hot peppers, celery and macademia nuts, steamed *Gui* fish, mushrooms and cabbage.

TANG DYNASTY THEATER RESTAURANT, *39 Changan Road, Tel. 7211633, 7211655, across from the Xi'an Hotel.*

It has an international menu, now very good. The dinner and show costs $49. The show only costs $19, and the buffet lunch $14. There's a discount if you book through Xian CITS.

DE FACHANG *on the other side of Drum and Bell Tower Square from the Bell Tower Hotel. Tel. 7214065.*

This famous *jiaotze* dumpling restaurant serves over a hundred different kinds of dumplings.

SCORPIAN RESTAURANT, *118, Dongda Street, Tel. 7219623.*

This restaurant is for those who want to try something new. I've had a whole meal of them, dishes with different variations, and survived. You can too. And they were delicious.

WANNIAN HOTEL, *1 Changle Zhong Road, Tel. 3231932.*

Good dumplings, and a well-served hot pot banquet (Y50). Its food generally is good and moderately priced.

Moslem food is important here and a typical Moslem dish is Yang Rou Pao Mutton Soup. A good place is the **Tong Sheng Xiang Restaurant** with its pancake-in-mutton soup. It's on *Xi Dong Street* near the Bell Tower, *Tel. 7214636, and 2482828*. The food at the **Moslem Markets** is cheap and quite good, but also of questionable hygiene. One market is at *Xi Da Street* and *Da Mai Shi Street*; the other is at *Xi Da Street and Ma Jia Shi Zi*.

There are **street food markets** in the evenings near the Jianguo Hotel, the Xi'an Hotel, and New World Xi'an. Take your own bowl and chopsticks. You can get good Cantonese snacks and *dim sum* (best in the morning) at the **Grand New World Hotel's Food Street**. Their fried rice and noodles range from Y26-Y32 and congee is Y5-Y14. **KFC** is south of the Bell Tower.

SEEING THE SIGHTS

The city was spruced up for President Clinton's visit in 1998. Trees were planted; repairs made to the wall. He was greeted at the South Gate with an elaborate welcoming ceremony, the lowering of the draw bridge, and the gift of an ancient passport with an official seal. Officials, dancers and singers in Tang-dynasty costumes greeted him and his party. Travel agents can arrange the same for you at the larger north gate, not the traditional one, but closer to the airport. The south gate is too congested. The price depends on the numbers and the arrangements and you can have camels and horses too.

President Clinton visited the Terracotta Warriors, the Tang frescoes and the basement of the Shaanxi History Museum. He stayed at the Xi'an Hyatt Hotel. Near the Warriors, he visited Xiahe village with an annual per capita income of Y2601. Its life had been changed by tourism.

If you only have one day, you must see the Terracotta Warriors, then Banpo Village, the Big Wild Goose Pagoda, the Provincial Museum, the Bell Tower, and the City Wall. If you've never experienced a Chinese-style mosque, try to fit in the Great Mosque, too. This is a very rushed itinerary, better done in two days. Most tourist attractions are open 8:30am-5pm.

*The **Museum of Emperor Qin's Terracotta Army** (Qin Yung Bo Wu Guan) is a 40-minute drive northeast of the city. The entrance fee is Y45. *Tel. 3911961. Http://www.bmy.com.cn (Chinese).*

This is one of the most spectacular and important places to visit in the world. It has a 2,200-year-old painted-ceramic army of more than 8000 soldiers buried to 'protect' the tomb of the first Qin emperor. Upon entry you are given a "smart card" which you can use later to get into other buildings. You can purchase slides, photos and books of reasonable quality in souvenir shops. In Pit Number One, the staff can take a photo of you or your group in front of the soldiers for Y150.

The terracotta army is a puzzle because the emperor left no record of its existence. Excavation started in 1976. A permanent building protects the army and tourists from most of the elements, and you are able to walk around the periphery of these once-buried relics. If you look carefully, you should see bits of the original colors, most lost because they were exposed to air.

There are three pits. Vault Number One, opened to the public in 1979, is 62 X 230 X 5 meters deep. Most of the army was found facing east, toward the tomb, 1.5 km away. The soldiers were in lines of roughly 70 across and 150 deep, separated by 10 partition walls and 11 corridors.

TERRACOTTA ARMY MUSEUM TIPS

Do not allow guides to hurry you through this exhibit. Take your time. They have to wait for you. Do not even raise your camera. If you are caught taking photos indoors without permission, the fine is Y300-Y800, payable to the museum. Get a receipt. Guides have been known to pocket this themselves.

Local peasants digging a well discovered the relics in 1974. Some of these men now spend their time signing autographs on books you buy inside for Y180, and outside for Y95. Look for them in the Cinema.

The men are hollow from the thigh up and made in two parts; they are 1.78-1.87 meters tall. The soldiers in front hold crossbows; also in front were bells and drums. Charioteers hold their hands out before them as if clutching reins. The horses originally wore harnesses with brass ornaments and are a breed native to Hechu in Gansu. You can distinguish the officers from the soldiers by their clothing and armor. Is every one of the 600 faces here different? Judge for yourself. This pit actually had 6000 warriors but only 600 are visible. The rest will be replaced when repaired.

Researchers believe that kilns were built around the molded figures (probably two horses at a time) and destroyed after firing. An exhibit explains this on the second floor of Vault Number Two. There are remains of 30 wooden chariots.

In a separate building, there's Vault Number Two, 124 X 98 meters, holding 1,400 cavalrymen, archers, charioteers and infantrymen, some kneeling and shooting. There's also Vault Number Three which has 68 officers and was probably the 'command post.' You pay extra to visit these two others unless you have your card. In Vault Number Two, look carefully for the charred remains of the ceiling, believed burnt by farmers angry at the emperor. Near the main museum is the Bronze Chariots and Horses Exhibition Room with two of the 20 tiny bronze chariots found. These are also outstanding and you should see them at close range.

Seven human skeletons believed to be of noble family are on display in one of the museums. Were they competitors for the throne killed by the second emperor as some people believe?

The 19-minute circle-vision movie is worth Y40 to see. It makes the history come alive and all around you and shows you the costumes, the war, the making of the ceramic army, and its burning. Groups have to request a showing in English, but you don't need any language to understand it.

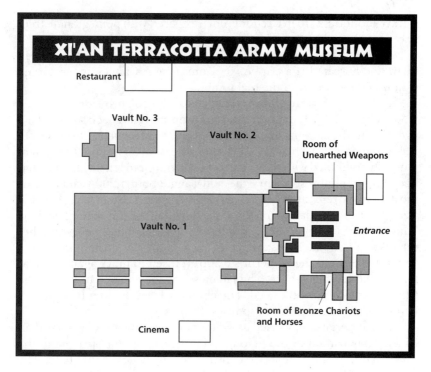

A new building with restaurants and more stores is currently being built. In the meantime, many tourists eat at the **Li Shan Hotel** restaurant which is quite good and about one km away. We liked the chicken there, the sweet potatoes, cauliflower and bean sprouts, carmelized potatoes, and the noodle soup.

Shopping here at the Warriors is almost fun. Peddlars are controlled now; they used to pull you to their stalls. But you must still haggle to get the bargains.

You pass the **Tomb of Emperor Qinshihuang** (Chin Shih Huang-ti) on the way to and from the Terracotta Warriors. The first emperor of the Qin Dynasty, the builder of the Great Wall, and first unifier of China, lived from 259 to 210 B.C., and became King of Qin State at age 13. What he achieved in so short a reign is incredible, and it is no wonder that he searched his empire for pills of longevity. Over 700,000 people worked on his magnificent underground palace tomb, begun in 246 B.C. when he was 14 years old.

Archaeologists have made preliminary excavations at this site and so far believe that the tomb has not been robbed, and that the ancient records are correct. 'Rivers of mercury' probably flow through it. Lack of money and technology have postponed its excavation. All you can see is a grave mound six km in circumference, covered with pomegranate trees and a small pavilion.

A theme park, a reconstruction of the first Qin emperor's tomb based on the 2,000-year old description by Szuma Chien, China's first historian, is now 200 metres from the real tomb.

The *Huaqing Hot Spring, the site of the Xi'an Incident, is open 7:30am-7pm daily in summer, shorter in winter. It has been so overshadowed by modern events that its ancient history is frequently overlooked. It is at the base of Lishan Hill, 30 km northeast of Xi'an, and a visit here is usually combined with the Terracotta Warriors and lunch. Huaqing has been an imperial resort since the mid-Tang, about 1,200 years ago. Its most famous tenants were Emperor Xuanzong (Hsuan-tsung) of the Tang, and the woman blamed for his downfall, his favorite concubine Yang Guifei (Kuei-fei). The influence of Concubine Yang and her relatives caused much dissatisfaction at court. In 755, an adopted son of hers rebelled, and the emperor's troops refused to move against him as long as she remained alive. The Japanese say she escaped to Japan. The Chinese say she was strangled. The emperor lived on even though they had vowed to die together. Promises! Promises!

The imperial couple used to winter here because it was warmer than Xi'an. They bathed in the Jiulong (Nine Dragons) Hot Spring and the Lotus Bath. You can find a reconstruction of her personal bath. The current buildings are post-Liberation in the old Tang style.

You can also trace the flight of Chiang Kai-shek, the Chinese Nationalist leader, from his bedroom as he panicked at the sound of gunfire at 5am on a cold December morning in 1936. He left behind his false teeth and wore only one shoe. A pavilion today marks the spot up the hill where the "Young Marshall" captured him and forced him to cooperate with the Communists against the Japanese.

The *Dayan Ta Pagoda (Big Wild Goose Pagoda) of the Da Ci'en Temple (south of the city wall), along with the Little Wild Goose Pagoda, are the most famous pagodas in China because of their age and history. They are not, however, the most beautiful or spectacular. The bigger pagoda was built to house the *sutras* brought back from India in 652 A.D. (Tang) by the famous monk Xuan Zhang. It was probably named in memory of the temple in India where the monk lived, on a goose-shaped hill. Or it could have acquired its name because some monks were starving and Buddha, in the form of a wild goose, dropped down close to them. The monks, being vegetarians, refused to eat it.

The pagoda has seven stories, 248 steps, and a great view from the top. In the adjoining Da Ci'en Temple (647 A.D.) are painted-clay statues of 18 *lohan* (Ming), most with strong Indian rather than Chinese features. These buildings are usually full of tourists.

The *Little Wild Goose Pagoda (Xiao Yan Ta), south of the wall, is 45 meters high and was constructed of brick in 684 A.D. Thirteen stories high, it is missing two of its original stories, which were destroyed during earthquakes in 1444. This is all that remains of the great Da Jianfu Temple, so important in the Tang.

While both pagodas are state-protected historical monuments, only a stop at one is really necessary. The little one is in a park, no longer a temple. It is a pleasant place to rest and enjoy because there are few people.

The **Shaanxi Provincial History Museum** (Shaanxi Li Shi Bo Wu Guan), *91 Yanta Zhong Road, 710061,* is south of the walled city and is open 9am-5:30pm daily, with the last entry at 3:30pm, *Tel.5234421, 5255966.* The Y38 fee includes a locker for your purse. This separate entrance for foreigners has a shopping area, toilets, and a snack bar. This is one of China's best museums and is worth seeing. It is well laid out with some explanations in English. It requires a minimum of one hour, more if you want to savor it. It covers prehistory 1.5 millions years ago to the end of the Qing and has original Tang frescoes. Look for the tiny gold Tang dragons and the great but tiny Han tomb figures.

The 36-meter-high *Bell Tower (Zhong Lou) in city center was first built in 1384 (Ming) in another location, and moved to its current site here 200 years later. Three sets of eaves weaken 'the force of the rainfall,' and actually only two stories are here. The furniture is gorgeous (Qing) and the very fancy traditional ceiling is Ming. From the second story you can look at all four gates of Xi'an. Parking is impossible. Park inside the Bell Tower Hotel compound, pretend you're eating there, and take the tunnel.

The nearby **Drum Tower** (Gu Lou) within walking distance to the west is also impressive. The tower was built in 1384 and is original. Drums used to be beaten about 800 times in 10 minutes before the city gates closed for the night.

The *Great Mosque, *Qing Zhen Si, Tel. 7271504, 7272541,* the largest in Xi'an, is on a back street north past the Drum Tower. It was founded as a mosque in 742 (Tang) by Moslems from Xinjiang and Guangzhou with the permission and help of the Tang emperors. The present buildings are mainly Ming.

The buildings are a good example of the sinofication of foreign religious buildings right down to the bats, dragons, unicorns, and mother-of-pearl-inlaid furniture–contrary to Moslem practice. The **Great Hall** (Ming) is, however, west Asian, the writing Arabic, the arches and flowers more like Istanbul or Baghdad. You remove your shoes if allowed to enter. Prayers are said five times a day. Its gilded wooden Koran, the largest in the world, was carved here. Today in Xi'an, 14 other mosques and this one serve at least 60,000 Moslems.

Banpo Neolithic Museum, *Banpo Wu Guan, Tel. 3279240, 3279248,* is open 8am-6pm daily is in the eastern suburbs of the city. It is the actual archaeological site of a 6,000-year-old neolithic village. The site covers 50,000 square meters, of which the museum encloses 3,000. There you see living quarters, one of the oldest pottery kilns in the country, and a graveyard.

The museum encompasses a communal storage area, moat, grave-yard (skeletons under glass), and fireplaces. In the museum are a bow drill, barbed fish hook, clay pots, and pottery whistle believed to be the earliest musical instrument in China. Among its other artifacts are hairpins, stone axes, and a pot with holes in the bottom, probably used as a steamer. Its narrow-necked, narrow-based water jugs, with two handles, look surprisingly like *amphoras* also used by the ancient Greeks and Romans! Is there a connection? The exhibits are labeled in English.

This culture is believed to be matrilineal:

• because of the burial customs; most of the 174 graves had one skeleton each, and the few graves that contained more than one skeleton had no male-female couples.

• the women gathered wild food at first while the men hunted. After the women discovered how to plant seeds, land became valuable and it was passed on from mother to daughter.

• because of the burial system (with no couples), scientists concluded that there were no fixed marriages. Besides, did neolithic people know where babies came from?

• the village consisted of one big house in the center for old and young, and smaller houses for visiting males. The men kept their belongings in their native villages, where the men were later buried.

As agriculture developed, men started pursuing it too. As surpluses grew (and probably the basic principles of physiology were discovered), fixed families started. In later neolithic gravesites in Gansu, male skel-etons were found lying straight, females leaning toward them. Since the women were bound, they were probably buried alive. So much for early women's lib! Now, what is your theory?

The new theme park **Banpo Village** on the same grounds as the Banpo Neolithic Museum is a waste of time and money. The dances are poorly choreographed and executed. The costumes are not authentic. Did they really wear sneakers 6,000 years ago? The buildings are badly made, so forget it.

The ***City Wall** was built from 1374 to 1378 (Ming), probably with material from the old Tang wall: 3.4 km (north-south) by 2.6 km (east-west), and 12 meters high. The walls follow the boundaries of the

Tang imperial city. The gates open to the public are on each of the four sides. From these you can climb the wall. Six new gates have been added to the original four to facilitate the flow of traffic. You can see a small section of the south wall in its original Tang dynasty state. You can walk on top of most of the wall and an electric car can take you to the East or West Gate for Y10 one way. But it's a good place to walk and watch people go about their lives down below. Entry fee Y8.

If You Have More Time or Interest

The **Xi'an Stele Museum**, *Bai Shu Lin Street, Tel. 7213868*, is at the first gate east of the South Gate. It is in an old (Qing and Ming) Confucian temple, and is primarily of interest to calligraphers. The museum has the most important collection of steles in China, with over 3,000 from the Han through the Qing, used by centuries of scholars.

Important for Christians is the 7th century **Nestorian stele**, written in Syriac with a cross at the top, a rare piece of church history marking the establishment of the church in Xi'an. This stele is in the second pavilion at the back of the museum, the first stele on the left. You can buy rubbings of this and other steles in the souvenir shop. The Nestorian sect started in the fifth century but was declared heretical by Rome in 431 A.D. The sect flourished in west Asia, but relics have also been found in Quanzhou, China.

This museum also has giant stone carvings, the largest from the eastern Han, including a life-size rhinoceros and ostrich (inspired by live animals given as tribute). Four of the bas-reliefs of horses from the Zhaoling tombs are here. (One is in Philadelphia.)

You might also want to go to *Qianling, Tomb of Tang Emperor Gaozong (Kao-tsung), and the Empress Wu, 79 km northwest of Xi'an. She was as ruthless and outrageous as Qing Empress Dowager Cixi, but a more successful ruler. He died in 683 A.D. and she in 705 A.D. This unexcavated tomb is a worthwhile full day's excursion that can include other tombs as well. While earlier tombs were built to create their own artificial hills on the plains, the Tang tombs were built into existing hills. This one is 400 meters high, 1049 meters above sea level.

Approaching the hill, you pass statues of horses and ostriches, and three to four-meter high guardian figures holding swords. Then on the left are the life-size statues of guards, tribal heads, and foreign diplomats who paid their respects at the funeral. The 61 statues are now without heads, alas; look for names on their backs. One is labeled "Afghanistan." The wall around the tomb is 4470 meters long. There are plans to open the actual tomb to the public. Although many of the structures at Qianling were destroyed in the war at the end of the Tang, the museum here contains about 4000 pieces.

Some of the minor tombs in the neighborhood are excavated, and you can also go underground to find the coffin and fine murals of court scenes in the tombs of **Princess Yong-tai** and **Prince Yide**.

Famen Temple, 120 km from Xi'an, can be included in a one-day trip along with the Qianling Tomb. The temple was founded in the Han Dynasty, 2000 years ago. It is extremely important because it houses a **finger bone of Prince Gautama**, the founder of Buddhism whose statue is in every Buddhist temple in China and who lived in the fifth century B.C. Unfortunately a tourist town has been built around this shrine. This and loud rock music have destroyed the mystical atmosphere but the museum is worth the trip. While tourists will not normally be shown the rare relic, you can see some of the 900 treasures that were buried with it: well-preserved gold-inlaid ceremonial vessels, ancient glass and jade, gilt buddhas, jewelry, gold walking stick, gold chain basket, fake 'bones' of jade - the largest group of Tang artifacts found since 1950. They were gifts from Tang Emperors Yi Zong and Xi Zong. Empress Wu donated gilded embroidery with threads finer than those made today. Titles are in English and the museum air-conditioned.

More Tombs?

*****Maoling** on a plateau north of the Wei River, 40 km northwest of Xi'an, has more than ten tombs, small grassy pyramids, about 46.5 meters high. The main tomb is that of the fifth Han emperor, built 139-87 B.C. According to records, it contains a jade suit with gold threads (seems to be a Han fad), and, in a gold box, more than 190 different birds and animals, jade, gold, silver, pearls, and rubies.

The other identified tombs are of the emperor's favorite concubine, Madame Li; General Huo Qubing, who fought the Xiongnus/Huns, and strengthened the dynasty from the age of 18 until he died of disease at 24!; General Wei Qing; his horse breeder Jing Min Ji, who remained faithful even after the emperor defeated Jing's tribe; and General Huo Guang.

You can also study some of the earliest and, therefore, most primitive massive stone carvings, originally placed in front of the tombs. Look for the horse stomping a Hun aristocrat. Each stone has a few lines added to the natural shape of the rock.

Near Maoling is the **Xianyang Museum**, containing 3,000 painted terracotta warriors and horse figures from the Western Han (206 B.C. to 24 A.D.). They are each between 55 and 68 cm high, and artistically better than the Qin Army.

Also near Maoling is the **Tomb of Yang Guifei**, the beautiful, tragic imperial concubine. Women have taken earth from here to put on their faces, hoping it will make them equally alluring.

*Zhaoling, 70 km northwest of Xi'an near Liquan, is the tomb of the second Tang Emperor Taizong. You can visit its small museum with Tang pottery, stone tablets, and murals. This tomb is not worth visiting unless you can read classical Chinese. The six famous bas-reliefs of the emperor's favorite horses in the Stele Museum are from here.

The **Horse and Chariot Pit**, Zhangjiapo, Chang'an county, can be combined with Huxian county for a half-day tour. It is the burial site of two chariots, six real horses, and one slave (11th century B.C. to Western Zhou) and is the best of seven such pits found. It is of special interest to archaeologists.

Tired of Tombs?

In town, the **Xian Film Studio** is worth a visit if only for the magnificent reproduced Qin palace used for the strongly recommended Sino-Canadian movie (and book), *The First Emperor*. There are other exhibits as well. It is near the Garden Hotel.

The **Kaiyuan Men Gate**, in the western part of the city, was the starting point of the Silk Road and is now marked with a huge recent photogenic statue of a caravan. The ruins of *Daming Palace, built in 634 A.D. (Tang) are about two km north of the railway station. Now reconstructed, it should be furnished in the Tang style.

Head southwest of Xi'an about 30 km to Huxian County Town. Here you can visit the **Huxian Peasant Painting Exhibition Hall** with arrangements through the Huxian Tourism Bureau, *Tel. 4818901 or 4818902, Fax 4812260*. Some of the 2,000 painters in the county have also exhibited abroad these recordings in gay colors of their everyday lives and achievements. While you can buy these paintings everywhere in Xi'an and many of them are now mass-produced, you might want an opportunity to meet the artists.

About 25 km away from the city is the thatched-cottage **Caotang Temple** (Tang), where Indian monk Kumarajiva Jiumoluosi translated the Buddhist *sutras* into Chinese. He died in 413 A.D.

*Xingjiao Temple, about 25 km east of the city wall, is on a sylvan hillside, which, with a little mist, could look like the lonely setting of the famous Japanese movie *Rashomon*. The place oozes with atmosphere although the buildings are recent. It was founded by Tang Emperor Gaozong in 669 A.D., but destroyed and rebuilt several times. The remains (at least some of them) of monk Xuan Zhang, who brought back the *sutras* from India, are buried in the small, five-story pagoda here. About 20 monks are in residence. It is peaceful with few tourists.

The **Louguan Taoist Temple** has now been restored. It is beyond Huxian, about 70 km west of Xi'an. It is said to be the place where Lao Tzu, founder of Taoism, taught. The temple has resident monks and makes traditional medicines. The setting and especially the entrance gate are very fine. A big yearly fair is held here.

NIGHTLIFE & ENTERTAINMENT

There's not much aside from the theater restaurants or their shows. The **Tang Dynasty Theater Restaurant** has an international-quality show of Tang-inspired dances and music. It's at *39 Chang'an Road, Tel. 5261633, Fax 5261619*, nightly at 6:30pm-8pm for dinner; 8:30pm for the show. The food is very good. See Where to Eat above for prices. A second newer dinner theatre is the **Shaanxi Grand Opera House, Song and Dance Theatre**, at *5 Wenyi Road, Tel. 7853295, Fax 7853299*, Attention Ms. Su San Cui. It is also very pleasing. The dinner is at 7pm, the show at 8:15pm. For lunch, it's 11am-2pm.

The Grand New World, Royal Xi'an, and Garden Hotels also have shows but not on a regular basis. The **Grand New World**'s "The Charms of Ancient China" show is at 8pm and just as good as the Tang Dynasty dinner theatre's show. Especially moving was a segment on the Terracotta Warriors with very stirring music. 8pm-9:10pm from April 1-Oct. 31; Y80; *Tel. 7211868.*

Some visitors feel that these shows are tourist traps. Of course they are. But they are entertaining, they make a good attempt to give you the flavor of ancient times, and the food is delicious. If you want to eat with real Chinese, you should get your request in early. Try the night food markets too.

Parkson Department Store across from the Hyatt has a many-splendored entertainment center on its 12/F with a bar, lounge, karaoke, and night club. Its international show has good costumes, fancy lighting, billowing smoke, loudly played popular Hong Kong songs, Korean folk songs, a *passo doble,* and even a scene from a revolutionary opera. It was worth Y100 plus drinks to watch it from a comfortable arm chair.

Hotels have the usual discos and karaoke, the best at the **Hyatt** and **Sheraton**. Unfortunately there are lots of prostitutes frequenting locally-run bars, but not bars in these good hotels.

The **City Wall** has some drink stands on summer evenings. You can probably see some local outdoor dance halls from the top of the **South Gate**. The Wall is lighted and decorated with huge lanterns during festivals and is very pleasant up on top especially at dusk. Groups can arrange a fireworks display. Ask about the powerful **Shaanxi waist drum dancers**. A **night food market** is near the Drum Tower, and other places around town.

The nine-hole **Ya Jian Golf Club** is at *Cao Tang Village, Tel. 4955235;* the **New Century Golf Driving Range** is at *New Century Square, Gao Xin*

Road, Tel. 8226699. The annual **Cultural Arts Festival** in September is highly recommended.

SHOPPING

The main shopping area is east of the Bell Tower on Dongda Dong Street. Made locally or in the province are: rubbings, reproductions of three-color Tang camels and horses, and murals. Also made are inlaid lacquer, cloisonne, stone and jade carvings, gold and silver jewelry, peasant paintings, silk embroidery, and celadon. Cloisonne seems cheaper in Shanghai and Beijing than here. You should haggle with everyone, especially in the over-priced factories, and during low tourist season. Some have settled for 50%-60% on carpets and silk scarves.

You will also find cheap reproductions of the Terracotta Warriors. Some of these are not kiln-fired and are easily broken. The better quality is usually found in government-approved stores like the **Xi'an Art Ceramics Factory**. It's at *5, Dian Chang Dong Road, Bu Zi or Puzi Village, 710038, Tel. 3519063.*

A 200-meter-long Tang Dynasty-style street, with food, souvenirs and actually good-quality modern paintings is near the **Big Wild Goose Pagoda**. Silk stores are on **Xiao Zhai Xi Road** near the east side of the Orient Hotel. At stalls outside many tourist attractions, you will find cheap tiger slippers for children and red cotton vests with appliquéd snakes, scorpions, lizards, and pandas. These are very popular and are the cheapest in China here. The yucky bugs are to frighten away the evil spirits. The **Xi'an Friendship Store**, *Nanxin Street, near Dongda Street, Tel. 7273749,* has batik, linens, silk jackets, cloisonne, cashmere sweaters, carpets, clothes, jewelry, stone carvings, decorated tiles, opera shoes, ceramics, a few antiques, lacquer, and folk crafts.

Among the factories you could visit are the **Jade Carving factory** near the museum where you can see a demonstration and its big showroom full of beautiful stones. It is open 9 am-6pm and is at *9 Yan Ta Road, Tel. 5523421.* The **Phoenix Embroidery Factory** and the **Cloisonne Factory** are at *33 Dong Road, 710005, Tel. 7277689, 7271437.*

The best shopping for antique embroidery and curios has been in the alley **between the Drum Tower and Mosque**, open 9am-6pm. At the South Gate behind the head of the gold dragon is **Shu Yuan Men Street** in ancient architecture where some traditional arts like writing brushes are made and curios and antiques sold. The **Xi'an Antique Store** is here near the Stele Museum, *Tel. 7213672.* **#Shaanxi Cultural Relics Store** is in the Shaanxi Provincial Museum, *Tel. 7213691* and the **#Xi'an Cultural Relics Shop** is at *375 Dongda Street, Tel. 7215874,7441572.* An antique store is in the **Drum Tower**.

The **Tang Cheng Department Store** is on Dongda Street at An Ban Street, west of the Friendship Store. From it, you can cross Dongda Street, turn right and then left at **Lo Ma Shi** for an alley of stalls selling cheap clothing. **Parkson Department Store** is across the road from the Hyatt Hotel at *119 Dongda Street*, open 9am-9pm in winter, to 10pm in summer, *Tel. 7450287 X 101*. It should take credit cards by now but don't count on it until you check. It has no arts and crafts or silks. The supermarket is on the third floor. Lucy, the public relations person speaks English. Below Drum and Bell Tower Square is the modern underground **Ginwa shopping center** with supermarket, open 9am-10pm, *Tel. 7212166*. It takes only MasterCard. The **Minsheng Department Store** has arts and crafts of medium quality and reasonable prices. It's at *103 Jiefang Road*, near the railway station, and is open 9:30am-9pm, Saturday and Sunday 9am-9pm.

EXCURSIONS & DAY TRIPS

*Huangling County is almost halfway between Xi'an and Yan'an, about four hours by road. Important there is the ***Tomb of the Yellow Emperor Xuan Yuan**. This is 3.6 meters high and 50 meters in circumference, originally built in the Han but moved here to its present site in the Song. The Yellow Emperor is the legendary ancestor of the Chinese people believed to have lived about 2,000 B.C. The tomb is at the top of **Qiaoshan Hill**, one km north of Huangling town. At the base is **Xuan Yuan Temple** built in the Han. The throne stands in the middle with information about Xuan's life on both sides. In ancient times, travelers had to dismount from their horses and pay their respect to their First Ancestor as they passed by. His memorial day is the 5th day of the fourth lunar month.

Of its 63,000 cypress trees, the Yellow Emperor himself is supposed to have planted one. It is the largest known ancient cypress in China.

Huashan Mountain is 120 km east of Xi'an, three hours drive each way. It has a cable car and 80-degree cliffs (there are iron chains to hang on to) and a '1000-foot-long Flight of Stone Steps.' You can also squeeze through the '100-foot-long Gorge.' Famous as one of the Five Sacred Mountains, it is dotted with old temples and has peaks up to 2,100 meters.

The best hotel here is the three-star **Financial Hotel**. There's also the two-star 90-room **Huashan Binguan**, *Tel. 913/4362836, 4362603, Fax 4363124 or 4364705* at the foot of the mountain but it's not great. Hostels are on the slopes. The 1550 meter-long cable car is a Sino-Singapore joint venture using Austrian hardware. It is otherwise a nine-hour climb.

Yan'an, in northern Shaanxi, was the headquarters of the Communist army and revolution at the end of the famous **Long March**. In 1936, it had a population of 3000 and grew to 100,000 in 1945. Today it has about

50,000 people. It is of interest to revolutionaries and students of modern history. For others it has only a 44-meter Tang pagoda famous primarily because of the revolution, and a tiny cave of 10,000 Buddhas (used as the Communist print shop). The city is now largely industrial.

Yan'an has **flight** connections once a week with Xi'an and Beijing. You can also get there by road or rail north from Xi'an in about eight hours. Its altitude is 800 to 1000 meters. During the rainy season, planes may be postponed or canceled.

Important to see are the **Yan'an Revolutionary Memorial Hall** and the four **Residences of Chairman Mao** (now museums and 'caves'). Ask about performances of the Waist Drummers, and the Ankle and Wrist Drummers, and China's second largest waterfall, 210 km from Huangling County on the Yellow River. Ask about the **Mausoleum of Hua Mulan**, the warrior woman who inspired Maxine Hong Kingston's famous book and the movie.

The main hotel is the 168-room **Yan'an Guest House** (Binguan), *Zhong Xing Street, 716000, Tel. 2113122, Fax 2114297*, 10 km from the airport. It has 168 rooms. **CITS** is at *106 Main Street, Tel. 2116285*.

A Note on Mulan

Many provinces claim the warrior woman as their own. Contrary to the Disney movie, officials here say she was in the army for about 20 years and was praised because of her faithfulness to her father, not for her military exploits. See also Wuhan.

PRACTICAL INFORMATION

Business Hours, 8:30am-5:30pm, five days a week for offices; 9am-8 or 8:30pm for stores. About 5pm-about 11pm depending on weather for night food and clothing markets.

China Merchants International Travel, *333 Chang'an Nan Road, 710061, Tel. 5263841, Fax 5261387. E-mail:cmxian@public.xa.sn.cn*. It has self-drive jeep rides on the Silk Road. For e-mail bookings and enquiries, contact Wang Jun, *jwang@pub.xaonline.com*.

CITS, *Xi'an Branch, 32 Chang'an Bei Road, 710061, Tel. 5262066, Fax 5261453. E-mail:xacitswl@public.xa.sn.cn*. Branches in many hotels.

Internet Cafe, *2/F China Telecommunications Office* across the square north from the Bell Tower Hotel. Open daily 9am-8:30pm. Y10 for 30 minutes, Y18 an hour.

Shaanxi China Travel Service, *45 Xingqing Road, 710048, Tel. 3232999, 3244352, Fax 3241060, 3241070. E-mail:CTSSALES@ihw.com.cn*.

Shaanxi CYTS Tours, *24 Xiao Zhai Xi Road, 710068, Tel. 5256422, Fax 5256409*.

Shaanxi Overseas Travel Corporation, *Room 201, Tian An Building, 2 YuCai Road, 710061, Tel. 5233941, Fax 5261399. E-mail:cwd_3939@Yahoo.com.*

Shaanxi Provincial Tourism Administration, *15 Chang'an Bei Road, 710061, Tel. 5261337, 5261179, Fax 5250151, 5261483.*

Telephone code *029.*

Tourist Complaints, contact *Supervisory Bureau of Tourism Quality of Shaanxi Province, Tel. 7295646, 5261437, Fax 5250151, 5261437.*

Xi'an Tourism Administration, *159 Beiyuanmen, Xi'an 710003, Tel. 7295670, 3233131, Fax 7295607.*

YINCHUAN

Yinchuan is the capital of the Ningxia Hui Autonomous Region, which lies between Inner Mongolia and Gansu on the north central border of China. It has no international class tourist attractions and, if you go there, you should be adventurous and intrigued by its mysteries.

In the northern part of the province, Yinchuan is a few kilometers west of the Huanghe (Yellow) River, and in the middle of a mesh of irrigation canals in the plains, but close to mountains and sandy deserts. Its regional weather is coldest in January at -22 C; its hottest is 33 C in May to September. It has very little rain, but a few sandstorms blow hard in spring and autumn.

ARRIVALS & DEPARTURES

Yinchuan is linked by air mainly with Beijing (1.5 hours) and Xi'an (1.3 hours) but also nine other Chinese cities. It is also reached by train from Beijing (22 hours), Shanghai (36 hours) and Xi'an (16 hours) by direct express once a day. It is on the Lanzhou-Baotou-Hohhot railway line.

ORIENTATION

Yinchuan has only recently been opened to tourists, It is not as far from Beijing as the Silk Road, but the weather is more severe, and it is still being developed. Today, 850,000 people live in the urban part of Yinchuan.

It was founded in the Tang and was the capital of the Western Xia dynasty during the early part of the Song (1038), when it was known as **Xingqing**. The Xia kings reigned for about 190 years until Genghis Khan destroyed them. Very little is known about them.

Ningxia was inhabited 30,000 years ago, and archaeologists have collected 8000-year-old neolithic relics here. It was home to the Yong and

Di tribes in the Western Zhou dynasty. The first Qin emperor conquered the tribes and connected parts of the Great Wall. He sent thousands of men to settle and defend this area but the Xiongnu tribal federation took it over in the fifth century.

Ningxia was close enough to the trade routes for Persian coins to be buried in its Northern Wei tombs. It exists because parts have been irrigated by the Yellow River for the last 2000 years. Its fight against the relentless sands is admirable. Visitors from places like California will be interested in how the Chinese manage. A great deal of the region is covered by the Liupan Mountains, through which the Long March passed in 1935.

Ningxia Hui Autonomous Region was founded in 1958, and the Cultural Revolution sent many people here from urban China in the 1960s. Today, it has many national minorities, including the Huis (31.7%), Mongolians, Manchus, and Turfans. The provincial population is 4.65 million. It produces an edible black hair-like moss called *facai*. The region exports coal and also produces petroleum, mica, asbestos, and lime.

WHERE TO STAY & EAT

INTERNATIONAL HOTEL, *25 Bei Huan Dong Road, 750004, Tel. 6028688, Fax 6711808. Three stars. Y325-Y439 for rooms, Y788-Y1020 for suites, plus 16% surcharge. It is 27 km from the airport and 13 km from the railway station and accepts credit cards.*

This 159 room hotel is the top hotel in town. It has CNN, Star Plus and non-smoking rooms. It charges Y28 for continental breakfast.

A four-star hotel is also being built. The food here is mainly Moslem (mutton, no pork). Corn on the cob and oil sticks (like long donuts) are delicious. The hotels are the best place to eat.

SEEING THE SIGHTS

Of importance to visitors is the **Chengtian Monastery Pagoda**, built in 1050 A.D.(Western Xia) and renovated in the Qing. Like many of the area's pagodas, it is unusually plain. The old **Tanglai Canal** and **Hanyan Canal** (Han) should be seen as examples of ancient irrigation efforts. Note the old waterwheels. The **South Gate Mosque**, *Tel. 4012704*, is recent, with an onion dome. The **Zhongda Mosque** is more in the Chinese style. Both these mosques are downtown.

The **Tongxin Mosque** is from the early Ming and was repaired in the Qing. It is one of the largest mosques in the region. The imposing **Jade Emperor Pavilion** (Ming) is good for photographs, with its delicate towers, as is the unusual **Drum and Bell Tower**. The *Haibo (Sea Treasure) or **North Pagoda** is also unusual, a naked structure without fancy eaves, and appearing more like a strange sort of Masonic temple, perhaps of Indian origin. Dating from the early fifth century, it was destroyed by an earthquake but rebuilt in the 18th century in its original style. It is one km north of the city.

The **Twin Pagodas** at the Baizi Pass on **Mt. Helan**, and the **Western Xia Mausoleum** at the base of Mt. Helan, are 80 km southwest of Yinchuan. The mausoleum is rather crude and of interest primarily to people keen on history. In treeless surroundings, it has a stark kind of primitive beauty.

The founder of the Western Xia kingdom built over 70 tombs, most as decoys. The nine imperial tombs are being rebuilt. Archaeologists believe that octagonal glazed-tile pagodas once stood by each tomb. For atmosphere, tourists should visit at night when the tombs are illuminated and accompanied by ancient music. You can enter the **tomb of Li Yuanhao**, the dynasty's founder. The 23rd grandson of the last emperor of the Western Xia Dynasty is still living and doing research into his family history.

Adventurers can also take **river rides on rafts** buoyed by inflated sheep skins. Normal watercraft are also available. At **Qingtongxia** south of the city is a gorge and an impressive dam. Nearby on a barren hill, the mysterious **108 white dagobas** have been arranged in the shape of a triangle in 12 rows from one to 19 across in odd numbers. The smallest one is about six feet and three arm-spans around. They are Buddhist structures from the 13th and 14th centuries, apparently built to ward off the '108 human frustrations' and are unique in China.

The city also has a museum and a Russian Orthodox Church (another mystery to be solved). The Guyuan grottoes, the mosque in Tongxin county, the Kangji Buddhist Pagoda in Tongxin County, and the Wanshou Pagoda (the latter two dating from 1038 to 1227 A.D. respectively) were all renovated in 1988.

Also in the region are **2,000-year-old rock paintings** on Helan Mountain, and the ruins of the **Great Wall** (Warring States: 475-221 B.C.), mainly earthen mounds, no stone. Especially important are the *Buddhist grottoes on Mt. Xumi** (also known as Sumeru) in Guyuan County. They are Northern Wei to the Ming and have a 19-meter-tall bust of Buddha rising from the floor of a cave. In the south of the province, these caves are impressive, although many of their 300 statues are damaged. Unless they have been recently built, few, if any sidewalks and stairs connect the 132 caves. This cave temple covers an area one by two km and the trip is rugged.

The **Gao Temple**, in Zhongwei County in the western part of the province, is striking because of its sandy monotone. A temple for Confucianism, Buddhism, and Taoism, it also has statues of the Jade

Emperor, the Holy Mother, and Guan Yu, the God of War. These point to the eclecticism of Chinese religion. Multi-purpose temples of this broad range, however, are rare.

The **Yellow River Festival** is celebrated in Yinchuan every September.

SHOPPING

The region produces sheepskin garments, licorice root, Helan inkstone carvings, rugs, and blankets. Its Eight Treasure Tea (Babao Cha) is well-known. Try the **Shopping Center** on *Gulou Nan Street, Tel. 6023046.*

PRACTICAL INFORMATION

Business Hours, for offices, 8am-12noon, 2:30pm-6 or 6:30pm; 9am-9pm for stores.

China Comfort Travel Service, *6 Gongyuan Street, 750001, Tel. 5045678, 5019234, Fax 5045600. E-mail:cct@public.yc.nx.cn.*

China Travel Service of Ningxia, *150 Jiefang Xi Street, 750001, Tel. 5044485, 5043734, Fax 5044485.*

Ningxia CITS, *77-8 Hubin Xi Street, Tel. 5019512, Fax 5033254. Try also 4/F, 116 Jiefang Xi Street, 750001, Tel. 5043720, Fax 5043466.*

Ningxia Tourism Bureau, *49 Jie Fang Xi Street, 750001, Tel. 6022744, Fax 5064674.*

Ningxia Overseas Tourist Corporation, *International Hotel, 25 Bei Huan Dong Road, 750004, Tel. 6714998, 6728688 X 2608, Fax 6720783. E-mail:nxotc@public.yc.nx.cn. Http://www.nxotc.com.*

Telephone code, *0951.*

Tourist Complaints, contact *Supervisory Bureau of Tourism Quality of Ningxia, Tel. 6022265, Fax 6041783.*

XINING

Xining is the capital of Qinghai (Tsinghai) province. It is important because of Taer Lamasary and the bird sanctuary in Qinghai Lake. It is the main land gateway to Tibet, and the birthplace of both the **Dalai Lama** and the **Panchen Lama**, an important province for those interested in Tibetan buddhism.

The Qinghai region covers one-thirteenth of China. It has less than four million people, Han (60%), the rest Tibetan, Hui, Mongolian, Kazak, Salan, and Tu. Many of these are nomadic herders. Ninety-six percent of its land is pasture for 22 million horses, yak, and sheep. Livestock breeding has been practiced here for 4000 years. Half of China's yak and one third of all the world's yak are in Qinghai.

Times are changing however: recently, a 3,500-gram gold nugget was found, and a gold rush is on. The national government has been focusing its economic development on the northwest region. Pasture land is now contracted to herdspeople for 30 years, thus encouraging wise management. Counties give bonuses to families who send their children to school, not an easy task for nomads. The government is building railways and highways.

Qinghai's eastern section is a grass-covered plateau ranging from 2,500 to 3,000 meters, up to 5,000 meters. You could be affected by altitude sickness. If you go in summer, you might be kept awake by open-air karaoke bars too.

Qinghai is the source of both the Yellow and Yangtze rivers and has a lot of hydro-electric power. It is rich in aluminum, coal, and oil. Its hottest weather is about 30 C in July and August, but thermometers could hit 50 C or more out in the desert sun in its northwest. Its coldest temperature is -20 C in January and December. The annual precipitation is 450 mm in July and August. The urban population of Xining is about 500,000.

The region is also known as the **Gulag of China**. Here criminals who have served their sentences continue to live because they cannot get residence permits elsewhere. Stores in Xining are stocked with products made from prison labor.

ARRIVALS & DEPARTURES

Xining is a two-hour flight from Beijing. It also has direct flights with three other Chinese cities. A daily tourist train arrives from Lanzhou in 3.5 hours, and a bus in 5 hours.

WHERE TO STAY & EAT

QINGHAI HOTEL (Binguan), *20 Huang He Road, 810001. Three stars, going on four in 1999, Tel. 6144888, Fax 6144545. 27 km from the airport and three km from the railway station. It accepts credit cards and is near government trade offices.*

Built in 1989, this 23-story hotel has 395 rooms, a gym and BBC. It is the best hotel.

XINING GUEST HOTEL (Binguan), *215 Qiyi Road, 810000. Three stars, Tel. 8238701, Fax 8238798. 12 km from the airport and four km from the railway station.*

Built in 1957, it has 600 rooms.

SEEING THE SIGHTS

A one-day visit to Xining can include the Taer Monastery, Dongguan Mosque, and North Mountain Temple. The **Dongguan Mosque**, one of the biggest in northwest China, was built in 1380 and is two km from the Qinghai Hotel. The **North Mountain Temple** is also two km from the hotel.

The *****Taer Monastery** (Ming), the center of the Yellow Hat sect of Tibetan Buddhism, is at Huangzhong, about 40 km south of the city. Built in 1379, it is worth a visit if you are interested in Tibetan culture. Its kitchen has three bronze cauldrons that are said to cook 13 cattle at one time to serve 3,600 people. Ask why meat is served in this Buddhist monastery! In the winter, frozen butter, two meters high by 26 meters long, is sculptured into Buddhist scenes and displayed on the 15th day of the lunar new year. It also has 20,000 religious paintings and embroideries. In 2000, the draping outdoors of a giant *thanka* takes place May 17-18, and July 8-9. Check these dates however with a travel agent. **CTS** has a branch in the *Taersi Hotel, Tel. 233126, 233810, Fax 233810.*

The two-star **Taersi Hotel** is at *57 Yingbin Road, Lushaer Town, Huangzhong, 811600, Tel. 233189, Fax 233810.* The telephone code is *0972.*

You can visit the birthplaces of both the current **Dalai Lama** and the 10th **Panchen Lama**, 100 km by good road west of Xining. About 60 km east of Xining in Lu Du county is the *****Qutan Monastery** (Ming). Also in the vicinity is the 6282-meter high **Ma Qing Gang Re** (Anyemaqen) **Mountain** (two to 10 day trip). Ask about the **Regong Tibetan artists** with their 300-year old tradition.

Qinghai is for mountaineers with several peaks up to 6860 meters and **trekking** between April and November. There is also **white water rafting**.

SHOPPING

Good buys are handicrafts made by the minorities like wooden bowls inlaid with silver. There's also *facai* (edible moss), a favorite ingredient of new year's banquets.

EXCURSIONS & DAY TRIPS

Golmud is a new industrial city in the Gobi Desert in the western part of the province. It has a population of 200,000, is 800 km from Xining, and is a trans-shipment point for Tibet. The highway to Lhasa from here is now asphalt, the highest highway in the world. A railway joins Xining with Golmud (and also with Lanzhou and Xi'an, eastward). Currently being built is a 1200-km rail line from Golmud to Lhasa. When it is finished in the next century, it should be one of the most spectacular train rides in the world.

The **Golmud Hotel** is modest but adequate. For **CITS** and **CTS**, *Tel. 979/412764, Fax 412817.* It's at *157 Kunlun Road, 816000.*

Qinghai Lake (China's largest saltwater lake) is 3,196 meters above sea level and 151 km from the capital. A bird sanctuary, **Bird Island**, is about 300 km away from Xining in the northwest section of the lake and is best seen April to July. The small island attracts 100,000 migrating geese, black-neck cranes, gulls, Griffon vultures, Mongolian larks, minivets and skylarks. The island has bird-watching pavilions and Tibetan-style hotels. This trip can be a two-day tour from Xining. Birders should ask also about the Longbao Black-necked Crane Sanctuary. The province has wild antelope, yak, donkeys, camels, lynx, deer, snow leopards, and pheasant, all protected.

PRACTICAL INFORMATION

China Travel Service Group, *348 Qiyi Road, 810000, Tel. 8238701 X 4228, 8235744.*

CYTS Tours, *Qinghai, 7/F, 136 Huzhuxi Road, 810007, Tel. 8133466, Fax 8144248.* Try also *3/F Overseas Chinese Hotel, 30 Bei Da Street, Tel. 8239687, Fax 8244073.*

Qinghai CITS, *156 Huanghe Road, 810001, Tel. 6143950, 6131081, Fax 6131080. E-mail:qhcits@public.xn.qh.cn.*

Qinghai Provincial Tourism Administration, *156 Huanghe Road, 810001, Tel. 6157011, Fax 6131080.* Brochures and information.

Telephone code, *0971.*

Tourist Complaints, contact Supervisory Bureau of Tourism Quality of Qinghai Province, *57 Xida Street, 810000, Tel. 8239630, Fax 8239515.*

CENTRAL CHINA

ZHENGZHOU

(Chengchow)

Zhengzhou is the capital of Henan province, one of the cradles of China's civilization, with much to offer visitors. It was one of the first cities to be built in China. This was during the Shang dynasty 3,500 years ago. It is also important because of its proximity to Shaolin Monastery, known to every *kung fu* fan. Zhengzhou is a good place to start a week's driving tour.

For historians and archaeologists, Zhengzhou is important. It was in nearby Anyang that the oracle bones with the first Chinese writings were found. The capitals of the Eastern Zhou, Han, Wei, Jin, Northern Song, Tang, and Liang were in this province. At least one of the capitals and possibly four of the five other capitals of the Xia dynasty were also here.

The Xia was China's first dynasty, and until recently was clouded in legend, traditionally dating from the 16th century B.C. China's first Buddhist temple, the Longmen Grottoes, and the earliest astronomical observatory are also located in the province.

More recently, Zhengzhou was the site of the February 7th Beijing-Hankou Railway Workers' General Strike of 1923, part of a larger workers' movement for better wages and conditions. Over 100 railroad workers were killed. The strike is commemorated with a modern 14-story double pagoda-like clock tower in February 7th Square, built in 1971.

The coldest average temperature is -10 C in January; the hottest can be 40 C briefly in July. The annual rainfall is 500-900 mm. especially July through September. The urban population is two million, the total six million.

ARRIVALS & DEPARTURES

On both the Beijing-Guangzhou and the Shanghai-Xi'an railway lines, Zhengzhou is about 20 km south of the Yellow River on the main railway line between Luoyang (two hours away) and Kaifeng (one hour). It is a two-hour flight south of Beijing and an eight hour train trip, and can be reached by air from 26 other Chinese cities and Hong Kong. It is on the North-South China freeway finished in 1999 and is 700 km south of Beijing. The airport is 35 km from the main hotels. The railway is seven km away.

ORIENTATION

Zhengzhou itself doesn't have much to offer tourists unless you can get excited by a seven km stretch of 3500 year old wall. One day is enough for its marvelous provincial museum and sightseeing along the Yellow River at Mangshan Mountain. If you are interested in ancient relics, there are the Shang ruins and the old city wall, and better still, a day trip to Anyang for its Shang capital.

WHERE TO STAY

The top hotel is the **Crowne Plaza** and then the **Holiday Inn**. The four-star **Novotel** is next. The five-star **Hotel Sofitel** should be near the top when it opens in 1999. All four are together in a restaurant and bar district near the provincial government offices. They are three km from the airport and four km from the railway station. The Crowne Plaza and Holiday Inn are joined together by a corridor and have airport shuttle service, two telephone lines per room, in-room safes, and non-smoking rooms. They share a recreation center which has a 21 meter-long indoor year-round pool and gym. Look for the Chinese restaurant with naked

Roman ladies built for Russian experts.

The Novotel and Sofitel are also close together. Information can be obtained from *E-mail:asiapac_res@accor.com,* and *http://www.hotelweb.fr.* They are both Accor Asia Pacific hotels.

If you want to avoid chain hotels, the next best is about two km away. The **Weilai Hotel** is a badly managed four-star at *East Wei Si Road, 450003, Tel. 5612288, Fax 5613366.* Prices range from $95-$450.

All hotels here take credit cards, have money exchange, ticketing services, and business centers. Prices below are subject to change, 20% surcharge, and discounts.

HOTEL SOFITEL ZHENGZHOU, *289 Cheng Dong Road, 450003. Five-star standard. E-mail:Sofitel@public2.zz.ha.cn. Rooms range from $120-$150, suites from $200-$700.*

This 1999 hotel should soon have an indoor pool, gym, and bowling.

CROWNE PLAZA ZHENGZHOU, *115 Jinshui Road, 450003. Five star standard. Tel. 5950055, Fax 5953851, 5990770. E-mail: hicpzz@public.zz.ha.cn. Http://www.crowneplaza.com/hotels/cgoch. $118-$170 for rooms, and $200-$670 for suites.*

This five-story hotel has 222 rooms (including 32 two-story suites and executive floor), BBC, CNN, HBO and some non-smoking rooms. It has a bank, and bicycles for rent. It has a patisserie, pizzeria, Cantonese and western restaurants. There's an English pub, night club and karaoke.

HOLIDAY INN ZHENGZHOU *E-mail, address, telephone and fax are the same as the Crowne Plaza above. Http://www.holiday-inn/com/hotels/cgcch. Four star standard. $98-$113 for rooms, and $160-$260 for suites and apartments.*

This 1997 hotel has seven floors, 143 rooms, six two-bedroom apartments, 11 offices, and non-smoking rooms. Rooms have kettles, CNBC, and NBC.

NOVOTEL INTERNATIONAL HOTEL ZHENGZHOU, *114 Jinshui Dong Road, 450003. Tel. 5956600, Fax 5951526. E-mail:edp123@public.zz.ha.cn. Three stars. Three km from the airport, five km from the railway station. $57 for rooms, $111-$184 for suites.*

Built in 1981-82 with renovations and extension in 1996, this 496-room hotel has Star Plus and Star TV, and small standard rooms. It also has dirty carpets, no room safes, a gym, sauna and clinic. A pool, bowling and tennis are due soon. It is the best three star hotel.

WHERE TO EAT

The best food is in the top hotels but there are also some good restaurants nearby. The modest **Yue Xiu** (Cantonese) is 100 meters west of the Holiday Inn. The **Hai Xian Chen Restaurant** is nearby. The

International Hotel has fried milk, chicken with peanuts, steamed fish, fried or steamed buns with sweetened condensed milk, all good.

SEEING THE SIGHTS

You can't miss the recently-built **Henan Museum**, considered China's second best after Shanghai. It's on *8 Nongye Road, Tel. 3511063, 3511066, open 8:30am-12 noon; 2pm-6pm*. It has a dinosaur exhibit, a jade burial suit held together with gold thread, tortoise divination shells with the earliest Chinese writing, gold and silver inlaid in bronze, some unusual ancient bronzes, and tomb figures. It has a display of the lost-wax process of putting designs in bronze, and it has signs in English.

You can miss the **Dahecun Village**, a 5,000-year-old site of the Yangshao and Longshan neolithic cultures, especially if you're going to see the better organized Banpo Museum in Xi'an. This one is poorly presented and boring.

The **Mangshan/Yellow River Scenic Area** is a park on the south shore, about 40 km north of the city, an opportunity to get out into the countryside. On the way a market at **Laoyacun village** sometimes blocks the road, a good chance to mingle with people. At Mangshan, you can climb the mountain or take a lift to 300 meters and slide down (Y20) on tiny bob sleds. The Y20 entrance fee includes the lift. You can take a second lift parallel to the river for a good view of China's second longest river. The Yellow is 5646 km long. Note the dikes and the water level (if there's water), sometimes three to ten meters higher than ground level. We've had a near accident on this lift because of the lack of English here so be careful.

The 45-minute cruise (Y60) of the Yellow River 8am-6pm daily (from the pier a couple of kilometers away from the mountain) not only gives a view of the impressive 5.5 km-long bridge (a train goes over every five minutes) but you can actually bounce on a mud flat on the most heavily silted river in the world - as if it were a bowl of jelly. Riding a hovercraft on mud is a unique experience. Sometimes horses are available on the island for riding.

The water has gotten so low through sedimentation, diminished rainfall, and overuse recently that plans have been made to divert water from the Yangtze River to this one, and onward to Beijing. It has not even been able to reach the sea at times. The **Xiaolongdi Dam** is being built nearby toward Luoyang. It is almost as big as the controversial Three Gorges Dam, but no one has made a fuss about it.

SHOPPING

Made here are reproductions of three-color Tang porcelain figures, jade and lacquerware, calligraphy and paintings. It's a good place to buy

Chinese writing brushes, paper, inkstones, and inkbars. Made in the province are also Jun porcelain, and embroidery from Kaifeng. The **Zhengzhou Jade Carving Factory** cuts saffires, jades, rose quartz, and cat's eyes. The **Friendship Store** is at *96 Erqi Bei Road, north of People's Park.* The **#Henan Cultural Relics Shop** is at *4 Jinshui Dadao, Tel. 5955347.* The largest department store is the **Hualien**.

EXCURSIONS & DAY TRIPS

In the province, there's **Kaifeng** which is 70 km away from Zhengzhou. **Anyang** is also a one-day trip from Zhengzhou. You can take in the other highlights of this varied and interesting province in another four-day road trip, visiting **Gongxian**, **Dengfeng** (overnight), **Luoyang** (overnight), and **Sanmenxia** (overnight) in that order. There are flights between Hong Kong and Zhengzhou, and a train goes from Sanmenxia to Xi'an.

For destinations close to Zhengzhou in Shanxi province see Taiyuan. For Hebei province, see Shijiazhuang.

Anyang and the four-day road trip mentioned above are included in this section. Kaifeng and Luoyang are treated as separate destinations with their own entries below.

ANYANG

In the northern part of Henan province, **Anyang** lies about 200 km (2.5 hours) north of Zhengzhou by express highway or via the Beijing-Guangzhou railway line. A quick visit can be made by car in one day from Zhengzhou. The population is 700,000.

Anyang is one of the oldest cities in China, inhabited at least 4,000 years ago. It was a capital of the State of Yin during the Shang dynasty for 273 years. It was here that the oracle bones, an ancient means of divination were found. The earliest writings were inscribed on tortoise shells and the shoulder blades of oxen and then cracked with heat. The direction of the crack foretold the future.

Visitors can see a reproduced Shang palace and tomb, a Shang museum, the mausoleum of the man who proclaimed himself emperor after the republican revolution, some temples, jade carving and carpet-weaving. This is also the birthplace of the *I Ching*. Anyang is primarily of interest to people who like history, archaeology and air sports.

Important sights include the 24-sq-km. *****Yin Ruins** on the edge of town, *Tel. 331689.* These include the palace foundations, 11 royal tombs, bronze and jade artifacts, and a small but good museum. There are reproductions of the palace, Shang chariots, guardian tomb figures, and the largest bronze vessel found anywhere in the world, the 875-kilogram

Simuwu Tripod. (The real relics are in museums in Beijing and Zhengzhou.) You can also see the **Tomb of Fu Hao**, concubine of King Wuding. She was the first woman general in Chinese history. Many of the pits hold remains of human sacrifices. One pit has 16,000 oracle bones. The annual **Shang dynasty festival** takes place September 16 to 25.

The five-story 40-meter high **Wen Feng Pagoda** is unusual. It is wider above than below and is crowned with a tiny white stupa. Built in 952 A.D., it can be climbed if you don't mind high stairs. The **City Museum**, 2.5 km from the Anyang Hotel, is in the **Mausoleum of Yuan Shi Kai**, *Tel. 425959.* Yuan was the warlord, an overly ambitious, brilliant official of the Qing court who took over the presidency of republican China from Dr. Sun Yat-sen in 1913. He declared himself emperor in 1915 and died of a heart attack in 1916. He reigned for 83 days.

If you have the Chinese surname Lin or Lim (as in 'forest'), you might be interested in the **temple of the first Lin**, a Shang dynasty prime minister. At **Bigan Miao Temple**, a short way off the expressway halfway between Zhengzhou and Anyang, you can learn about the maligned Bigan who had to take out his own heart to prove his honesty. His son changed the family name to Lin.

If sky sports are essential to your visit here, you can make arrangements with the **Anyang Aerial Sports School**, *Tel. 424686, 422675;* the Aviation Sports Association; or a travel agency before you go. It is the main place in China for hang gliding, parapente, sky diving, hot air ballooning and parachuting.

In Anyang, your main choice is the three-star **Great Wall Hotel** at *5 Xinxing Road, Tel. 5910669,* but it's not very good. At least the food isn't too bad. It is between the long distance bus and the railway stations. The two-star **Feiying Hotel** is at *118 Renmin Zhong Road, Tel. 5935888.* For more travel information: **CITS** is at *Zhongyuan Guest House, 62, Beimen Dong, 455000, Tel. 425650, Fax 427740.* The telephone code is *0372.*

CAVE TEMPLES & TOMBS
Zhengzhou-Deng Feng-Luoyang-Sanmenxia

If you can take the four-day trip from Zhengzhou and are looking to get well off the beaten path, go to Gongxian County on the way to Songshan Mountain, where you can see the *****Gongxian County Cave Temple**. Its 7,743 small Buddhist figures date from 517 A.D. (Northern Wei) to the Song dynasty. Some are very well preserved. They are not as big or as impressive as Luoyang's, but they are certainly worth a look.

There are also several groups of imperial *****Song Tombs** here, at least one with 60 impressive giant stone statues, among them foreign envoys wearing turbans. The tombs themselves are less spectacular than those of the later Ming and Qing emperors and are spread over an area 15 km long. They were built in a much shorter time than those of their successors, and without the personal supervision of the emperors who were going to reside there. These are worth visiting if you are in the area, 65 km west of Zhengzhou. They are from the Northern Song.

The **Tomb of Song Emperor Hengzong** is the most popular because of its location in Gongxian County town. That of Emperor Yong Ding is in the suburbs.

The cave home of **Tang poet Du Fu**/Tu Fu also in the neighborhood is not worth a visit unless you're into Tang poetry. There are also the **Han Tombs** at **Dahuting** (Tiger-hunting) **Pavilion** in **Mixian County**. They are worth a short stop for their lively paintings and stone carvings. They are about a 15-minute drive from Dengfeng.

DENGFENG COUNTY AREA

You should go here to see the Shaolin Temple. Bare, rugged, Songshan Mountain is about 80 km southwest of Zhengzhou (its closest airport and railway station), and 180 km from Luoyang. The mountain stretches more than 60 km east to west. The highest peak is 1,512 meters above sea level. It is one of China's Five Sacred Mountains, and emperors used to come here to worship. During the Southern and Northern Dynasties (420-589 A.D.), 72 temples and monasteries flourished here. It is well worth visiting also for the lovely Chinese countryside, and air so clean you might want to stay an extra day.

From your hotel in **Dengfeng County town** (population 50,000), you can bicycle or drive to China's largest Taoist temple, China's most famous temple, and a pagoda from 520 A.D. Thirteen km northwest of Dengfeng County town is **Shaolin Temple**, *Tel. 2749116*, the home of *kung fu*. Shaolin Temple was first built in 495-496 A.D. and became famous in 728 A.D. because 13 fighting monks from here supported the prince who became the first Tang emperor. Here you can see 48 depressions in the floor worn by generations of monks practicing martial arts.

Among the murals and frescoes are some of the 500 arhats (Ming), and some depicting fighting monks. At its peak in the 15th century, 2,000 to 3,000 monks lived here. In the seventh century there were 500, and now there are about 80-100. All monks take the surname Su.

The *Ta Lin (Forest of Pagodas) is the largest group of memorial pagodas in China. A cemetery for abbots, it has over 240 miniature pagodas, two to seven levels high, dating from 791 A.D. to 1995. The platforms are used for Ching Ming festival rituals. Clean toilets are here and outside the main temple. Prepare yourself for this visit by seeing the movie *The Fugitive Boys of Shaolin* starring Li Lianjin, China's Bruce Lee. It was shot here.

Northwest of the temple is a cave where the sixth century Indian missionary Bodhidharma, was reputed to have spent nine years in meditation before achieving Nirvana. He was the founder of Chan Buddhism, more popularly known as *Zen*, and is frequently depicted in art in his robes, crossing the Yangtze River standing on a reed. The **Shaolin Martial Arts Training Center** (Wu Shu Guan), *Tel. 2749120,* is also close to the temple, and it gives exhibitions and classes. Athletes jump on a bed of nails, breaking bricks with a head, and inviting visitors to smash a midruff. The *kung fu* here is somewhat different in style from North American *kung fu*. Foreigners can also study and live at the school, but foreigners cannot become monks. The 20-room hostel at the school is spartan and you can stay there too. It is the only state-run school and some consider it the best. Dengfeng has at least 43 private *kung fu* schools, the largest of which has 7000 students. Private schools are cheaper (but six to a room). The state school has two to a room. These schools have grown in popularity lately because the skills learned are valuable for teachers, policemen and body guards.

If You're Staying Overnight

From the temple you can see a cable car to a small nunnery at the peak of Song Mountain. The scenery is magnificent. It takes about an hour. There is only one nun living there.

The 43-meter-high ***Songyue Pagoda at Fawang Temple** is the oldest proven extant pagoda in China, and is four km from Dengfeng. Built of brick about 520 A.D. (Northern Wei), it is also unusual because it has 12 sides and is curved like an Indian *sikhara* tower. It is important to those studying pagoda architecture. The **Songyang Shuyuan** (Songyang Academy of Classical Learning) at the foot of the mountain has two cypress trees said to be over 3,000 years old, each measuring 12 meters in circumference. The school was one of the four imperial academies preparing students for the imperial examinations.

Zhongyue Miao (Central Mountain Temple) at the base of Taishi Peak and four km east of Dengfeng town, was founded in the Qin and moved here in the Tang. It has four feisty 3.5-meter-high iron figures (Northern Song) guarding it. Children pat these 'to gain strength.' This is one of the earliest Taoist temples (it's huge) and the largest extant monastery in the province. It was enlarged during the Qing, along the lines of the Forbidden City in Beijing. The ***Taishi Tower** is from the Eastern Han. You can climb to the top of **Huanggai Peak** for an overall view of the 400 or so buildings and the 300 2,000-year-old cypresses. 10-day temple fairs take place during the third and tenth lunar months.

SEARCHING FOR CHINA'S OLDEST DYNASTY

A search for the first Xia capital, China's oldest dynasty, has been centered in Dengfeng County, half a kilometer west of the town of Gaocheng at Wangcheng Gang (Royal City Mound). This site is not usually included in a tour, but people interested in archaeology might ask about it. City walls, skeletons (probably of slaves buried alive in foundation pits), wine vessels, bronze fragments, and ceramic pots have been uncovered. However, Wangcheng Gang was found to be of a later date.

Across the river and half a kilometer northwest of Gaocheng is another site where the earliest bronze vessels in the province were found and carbon-dated to 2000 B.C.

The *Shaoshi Tower** and the *Qimu Tower** also on the mountain, are from the Eastern Han too. The *Astronomical Observatory**, 14 km from Dengfeng town, was built early in the Yuan, based on a Zhou dynasty concept. It is the oldest in China. Ancient astronomers here proved that the earth revolved around the sun once every 365.2425 days, 300 years before the Gregorian calendar. China's first astrological museum is nearby.

The hotels here are not good, alas. The best seems to be the three-star **Shaolin International Hotel** at *16 Shaolin Road, Tel. 2870890.* Another three-star is **Tianzhong Hotel**, *Zhongyue Dong Road, Tel. 2871560.* The **Shaolin Inn** has bad management and is not warm in winter. *Kung fu* students stay at the two-star **Shaolin Wushu Training Center**. Food here is good but facilities are below standard. There's talk of a five-star hotel. Let's hope it's here soon.

You can also stay and eat at the **Shaolin International Kung Fu Training Center**, *Shaolin, China 452479. Tel. 2749018. Fax 2749017. No credit cards.* Book through CITS. The food is basic but good: cauliflower Y20; beansprouts Y18, egg plant Y18. It has meat dishes too.

CITS is at *48 Zhongyue Street, 452470, Tel. 2872137, 2877038, Fax 2873137;* **Dengfeng Tourism Bureau** is at *177 Zhongyue Street, 452470, Tel. 2873043, Fax 2873137.*

Hours are 8am-6pm for tourist attractions and *kung fu* demonstrations in summer, 8am-5pm in winter. The telephone code for Dengfeng is *0371.* Shaolin has a **Wushu** (martial arts) **Festival** around September 10.

PRACTICAL INFORMATION

Henan China International Travel Service, *15 Jinshui Road, 450003, Tel. 5951134, 5944305, Fax 5957705. North American Department, Tel.*

5954501, 5945850. E-mail: lhm@public.zz.ha.cn. It can arrange for visitors to work on farms.

Henan China Travel Service, *Tel. 3935117, Fax 3935361.*

Henan China Youth Travel Service, *17 Jinshui Da Road, 450003, Tel. 5935235, 5965187, Fax 5952191. Http://www.henantravel.com.*

Henan CITIC Travel Inc., *4/F, 4 Jinshui Road, 450003, Tel. 5930430, 5939039, Fax 5930420. E-mail:hcitic@public2.zz.ha.cn.* It can arrange for visitors to plant trees if they want.

Henan Tourism Administration, *16 Jinshui Road, 450003, Tel. 5957880, Fax 5955656,* for information. For tourist complaints: contact the *Supervisory Bureau of Tourism Quality of Henan Province, Tel. 5955913, Fax 5955656.*

Henan Tourism Group, *288 North Section, Chengdong Road, 450003, Tel. 5961133 X 5721, 5961431, 5962187, Fax 5952273. E-mail: hntc@public.zz.ha.cn.*

Hours: People in this small city go home for lunch so offices open 8am-12 noon; 2pm-6pm in winter, and 3pm-6:30pm in summer.

Telephone code, *0371*

KAIFENG

The former imperial capital of **Kaifeng** is in northern Henan province. It is 10 km from the southern bank of the Yellow River, and is highly recommended for its history and quiet, exotic charm. It also has a new economic zone in its west suburbs.

With a history of 2,600 years, Kaifeng was the capital of several imperial dynasties, including the Wei, Liang, Later Jin, Han, Later Zhou, Northern Song, and Jin. During the Song it was an important commercial and communications center, producing textiles, porcelain, and printing. It was sacked by Jurched tribesmen in 1126 and never recovered.

With 120 recorded Yellow River floods due to dikes breaking near Kaifeng between 1194 and 1948, you might wonder why Kaifeng exists at all. In 1642, during a peasant uprising, Ming forces destroyed an embankment and completely inundated the city killing 372,000 people. In 1938, the Nationalists destroyed the dam upriver near Zhengzhou to stop the Japanese, and 840,000 people died. Today, the river bed, raised by centuries of silt deposits, is about 10 meters higher than ground level near Kaifeng. Since Liberation, the Chinese have given top priority to controlling the Yellow River.

The population is about 620,000. The hottest weather in July to early August is 38 C; the coldest in January is -9 C. Its annual rainfall is about 600 mm. mainly in July and August. Spring is dry, dusty, and windy.

ARRIVALS & DEPARTURES

On the Shanghai-Urumqi railway line, Kaifeng is accessible to Zhengzhou to the east, its closest airport, about a 90 km expressway trip away. You could take a taxi from the airport–or more cheaply, go into Zhengzhou to the long distance bus station and hop a bus there–if you arrive early enough. Kaifeng is on National Highway 106 (Beijing-Guangzhou) and Highway 310 (Tianshui- Lianyungang).

ORIENTATION

Kaifeng is one of the 24 historical cities protected by the State Council. It is laid out in the classic Chinese style, and has a well-preserved but decaying earthen Song city wall. It has a downtown shopping area built in Song architecture. It is easy to get around because it is small. Except for the Yellow River, all important sites are inside or near the four by eight km-long wall.

WHERE TO STAY & EAT

The two main hotels are terrible, run down with poor service and poor English. Hopefully the situation will be better by the time you get there or you'll have to make it a hurried day trip from Zhengzhou. Two days is better for more leisurely sightseeing. The **Dongjing** has bigger rooms, and is within walking distance of the museum, the old wall, and the lake. It is on the No. One bus route downtown to Song Dynasty street. The **Dongyuan** however is better.

DONGJING HOTEL (Dongjing Dafandian), *99 Ying Bin Road, 475000. Three stars. Tel. 5958936, 5958938, Fax 5956661. It accepts no credit cards.*

In the southwest part of the walled city, this 1988-89 hotel has three stories, 200 rooms, no elevators, and not bad Sichuan and Shanghai food.

DONGYUAN HOTEL (Dajiudian), *1 Xin Song Road at Gongyuan, 475002. Three stars. Tel. 2918888, Fax 2925588. 3.5 km from the railway station, it is just outside the east city wall. It accepts no credit cards.*

Built in 1992, this 14-story hotel has 198 small rooms and a gym.

SEEING THE SIGHTS

Kaifeng has 22 historic and cultural sites, a large number for such a small city. You need two days to see everything important: temples, museum, reproduced Song dynasty city, Jewish relics and iron pagoda. The annual Song Dynasty Culture Festival in Kaifeng is celebrated every April.

The 13-story, 55.6 meter-high *Tie Ta ('Iron Pagoda') in the northeast corner inside the wall was built over 900 years ago. It is actually made of glazed brick. The **Xiangguo Temple** in its south-center, built in 555

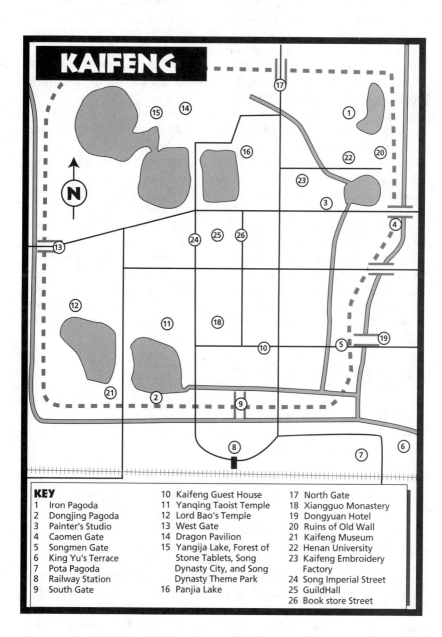

KAIFENG

KEY

1 Iron Pagoda
2 Dongjing Pagoda
3 Painter's Studio
4 Caomen Gate
5 Songmen Gate
6 King Yu's Terrace
7 Pota Pagoda
8 Railway Station
9 South Gate

10 Kaifeng Guest House
11 Yanqing Taoist Temple
12 Lord Bao's Temple
13 West Gate
14 Dragon Pavilion
15 Yangjia Lake, Forest of
   Stone Tablets, Song
   Dynasty City, and Song
   Dynasty Theme Park
16 Panjia Lake

17 North Gate
18 Xiangguo Monastery
19 Dongyuan Hotel
20 Ruins of Old Wall
21 Kaifeng Museum
22 Henan University
23 Kaifeng Embroidery
   Factory
24 Song Imperial Street
25 GuildHall
26 Book store Street

A.D., was rebuilt in 1766 after a flood. It has a famous thousand-armed, thousand-eyed Buddha of gingko wood. The **Longting (Dragon Pavilion)** in the north center is at the site of the Northern Song palace. The existing buildings here are from the Qing, the stone lions in front from the Song.

Also worth seeing are the **Yanqing Taoist Temple, Lord Bao's Memorial Hall** (wax figures) on Baogong Lake, and the very fancy **Guild Hall of Three Provinces**, all within walking distance of the Dongjing Hotel. The Yuwang Miao (**King Yu's Temple**) was built in the Ming in honor of Emperor Yu, who tried to control the floods; it is outside and to the south of the east wall. Near the Yuwang Miao is the **Pota Pagoda**, its bottom built in 977, and its top section replaced in the Qing.

A theme park, the **Riverside Scene during the Qing Ming Festival** is based on the famous painting of the ancient Song city. It's at *5, Longtinxi Road, Tel. and Fax 5955770, 5951982*. It's open 8:30am-6pm with wedding ceremony and stilt walking 9am-11am, and 2pm-4pm.

Kaifeng is great for bicycling. Walks are interesting along the path on top of the old Song wall and in any of the monuments.

Canadians in particular might be interested in the grave of Canadian **Dr. Tillson Lever Harrison**, who died in Changqiu in 1947 after delivering three box cars of medical supplies under horrendous conditions through Nationalist areas to the Communists. It is in the **Revolutionary Martyrs Cemetery** with a stone almost two meters high. There is also a **Tillson Lever Harrison Memorial School** in the city.

The Jewish Community of Kaifeng

Jews first arrived here at least 2,000 years ago. Most came as silk merchants and migrants from Persia. In the Song dynasty, thousands of Jewish merchants arrived from India. Most left in the Ming because of the floods. Marco Polo came across groups of Jews in Beijing, Hangzhou, Suzhou, Guangzhou, and Kunming.

In the late 13th century, there were about 2,000 Jews in Kaifeng. The original 1163 synagogue was founded by Jews who passed the imperial examination. Jews from other communities, such as Hangzhou, contributed to the rebuilding of the Kaifeng synagogue each time it was destroyed by flood or fire. The last synagogue was destroyed between 1850 and 1866.

About 200 Jews still live in Kaifeng today although they don't practice Jewish traditions. The **Kaifeng Museum** *(open 8:30am-5:00pm daily except Mondays)* has a top floor room with a reproduction of a seventh century drawing of the synagogue, and steles dated 1469, 1512, and 1679 describing the history of the community, etc. A photographic exhibit donated by the Sino-Judaic Institute of Palo Alto, California (contact

Professor Al Dien, president of the institute at *aldien@leland.stanford.edu*) is located in the nearby Qingming Shanghe Yuan park.

Tourists can still visit the house of **Zhao Pingyu**, *at #21 South Teaching Scripture Lane* (Nan Jiao Jing Hutong), which is in back of the original site of the synagogue. Zhao was the major spokesperson for the descendants until his death. Several artifacts from the original synagogue can also be seen in the local **Great East Mosque** (Dong Da Si). These include the stone lotus bowl and the original blue roof tiles from the synagogue.

If you are asked to donate money for rebuilding the synagogue, ask if it's to be a place for local Jews to gather or worship, or just a tourist attraction. Ask if the descendants of the Jews are now registered as"Jewish/ Youtai" or "Han."

For more information and tours, contact Dr. Wendy Abraham, **JewishHistorical Tours of China**, *P.O. Box 9480, Stanford, CA 94309, Tel. 800/446-9494 or e-mail: wabraham@leland.stanford.edu). Http:www.jewishchinatours.com.*

SHOPPING

Kaifeng is famous for its embroidery and fighting kites. Shopping is extensive at the **Xiangguo Temple Market's** 3,000 stalls. For antiques, try the ***Kaifeng Cultural Relics Shop**, *23 Madao Street.*

PRACTICAL INFORMATION

Kaifeng CITS, *98 Yingbin Road, Tel. 5955130, Fax 5955131. Contact Liu Wenqing.*

Kaifeng CTS, *15 Shengfuqian Street, Tel. 5966129, Fax 5955743. Contact: Yan Xinzhu.*

Kaifeng Tourism Administration, *98 Yingbin Road, 475000, Tel. 5954370, 5950485.* Contact Xia Feng. (For complaints and information).

Telephone code, *0378*

LUOYANG

(Luoyang: North bank of the Luo River)

Luoyang, about 25 km south of the Yellow River, is important because of the **Longmen Grottoes**, the **White Horse Temple**, and **Mrs. Yang**. Because it was an imperial capital for many centuries and the site of many battles, many relics were buried here – almost as many as in Xi'an. It is one of the 24 cities of historical importance protected by the State Council.

Luoyang was built in the 11th-century B.C. From 770 B.C. it was the capital at one time or another of the Eastern Zhou, Eastern Han, Wei, Western Jin, Northern Wei, Sui, Tang, Later Liang, and Later Tang dynasties. The imperials moved here frequently because of drought in Xi'an, a city they preferred.

Because there are hills on three sides, it was relatively easy to defend, and whoever wanted to control western Henan had to take Luoyang. Consequently, many battles were fought in this area and many treasures were buried to save them from the soldiers.

Luoyang was one of the earliest centers of Buddhism, dating from the first century A.D. During the Tang, it was the biggest city in China. It declined later because the capital moved away. Luoyang people will proudly tell you that the Silk Road actually started from here and not from Xi'an, as is commonly supposed. 'Knowledgeable merchants always came here for silks,' they say. 'It was cheaper.'

The hottest temperature is 39 C in July and August; the coldest in January and February -12 C. The weather is usually mild. The altitude is 145 meters above sea level. The population is at least 1,290,000 in the city, between five and six million including the suburbs. The city has had a quiet, provincial atmosphere, but is starting to get lively.

ARRIVALS & DEPARTURES

Luoyang is two hours by train or expressway west of Zhengzhou, a 160 km trip. It's a 6.5 to 8.5 hour train ride east from Xi'an. There are infrequent air connections with seven Chinese cities. The long-distance bus station is near the Guan Yu Temple.

ORIENTATION

The older, eastern part of Luoyang is more interesting than the newer sectors. It has old architecture and old shops with traditional arts, but it's not worth making a trip to see. Today, there are over 400 factories manufacturing everything from truck cranes to ball bearings. It has one of the biggest free markets in North China, serving 50,000 people a day. This is near the Guan Yu temple and Longmen Grottoes. Visitors might be interested in its arts and crafts factory which makes palace lanterns and reproductions of three-color Tang porcelains and Shang bronzes.

Area farms grow cotton, corn, winter wheat, a little rice, sesame, sorghum, sweet potatoes, apples, pears, and grapes. They also raise yellow oxen, goats, and donkeys. The city is also noted for its **peonies**, first grown 1400 years ago in the Sui! Flower lovers should aim for the Royal City (Wangcheng Park) between April 15 and 25.

WHERE TO STAY

The best hotels are the **Peony** and the **Peony Plaza**. The Peony Plaza has a great location for tourists at one end of Peony Square where people dance in the morning and evening and peddlars put up stalls. Tourists can join the dancing for Y1 each. While it is a relatively new hotel, the service and English are not as good as that at the three-star Peony, a km away. The Friendship Hotels are also near Peony Square and are both grubby and badly managed. An "antique and curio" market is nearby. Closer to the White Horse Temple in the east of town is the three-star **Goddess** which isn't bad, but again English could be a problem. The **Baoyuan Hotel** is a three star, close to the dam, too far from town for tourists, *Tel. 6910918, Fax 6911328.*

The five-star **Central Asia Hotel** (Zhong Ya Fandian) and the four-star **Small Swan** (Xiao Tian E Binguan), a US joint venture should open soon. Hotels add a surcharge of 15% and prices are subject to change and discount.

PEONY PLAZA HOTEL,(Mudan Cheng Binguan), *2 Nanchang Road, Jianxi District, 471003, Tel. 4931111, Fax 4932514. Three stars. Y788 for rooms.*

This glitzy hotel, shaped like a 26-story silo has 163 small rooms, its carpets cleaner near the top, but still stained. A toilet room on the ground floor near the elevators stank. Air-conditioning goes on in rooms only after 7pm and the sound for CNN is poor. Guest room doors do not lock automatically when closed and need a key. The buffet breakfast is sparce but edible and could be better. It does have good showers.

LUOYANG PEONY HOTEL (Mudan Dajiudian), *15 Zhong Zhou Xi Road, 471003. Three stars, Tel. 4013699, Fax 4013668. Y580 for rooms and Y1260 for suites. 15 km from the airport, four km from the railway station and in the center of the city.*

Built in 1990, this 15-story hotel has 196 rooms, a gym, in-room safes, CNN, and business center.

GODDESS HOTEL (Luo Shen Da Jiudian), *Luoyang Glass Factory Nan Road, 471009, Tel. 3944878, Fax 3935050. Y450-Y980. Three stars.*

This hotel has a pleasant atmosphere, is clean, and the food is good (see below). We found goods in its store cheaper than the factories.

WHERE TO EAT

This is a small provincial city so don't expect much. The best was behind the Friendship Hotels, like the Ya Xiang Lou restaurant below.

YA XIANG LOU, *Anhui Road, no. 4, Tel. 4911993. Second floor.*

Good dishes here include curried beef, chicken with fruit (#2515), stir fried bean curd (#2536) Y18; and flat noodles Y16, and fried rice. Noodles are made by hand in the dining room.

GODDESS HOTEL RESTAURANT (Luo Shen Da Jiudian), *Luoyang Glass Factory Nan Road. Tel. 3944878.*

The Goddess restaurant has excellent food with interesting spices. Parrots are painted on the ceiling and a grand piano is in the lobby bar. We liked the eggplant with fish flavor Y38; chicken with mushrooms Y32; sweet and sour pork Y36; dried soy bean string and stringed potatoes at Y15 each as appetizers. It is a 25-minute drive east of the Peony Plaza, and 15 km from the White Horse Temple.

LUOYANG PEONY HOTEL, *15 Zhong Zhou Xi Road. Tel. 4013699.*

Food is good here; they have banana fritters.

NEW FRIENDSHIP HOTEL, *6 Xiyuan Road, Tel. 4913770.*

Food isn't too bad here but the crockery was chipped. They accept credit cards.

SEEING THE SIGHTS

The following can be covered in one day if you don't dawdle. The *Baima Si (White Horse) **Temple,** *Tel. 3789053,* 25 km from the Friendship Hotel, was founded in 68 A.D. after the second Han Emperor Mingdi dreamed that a spirit with a halo entered his palace. His ministers convinced him that the spirit was the Buddha, so he sent scholars to India to bring back the *sutras*. After three years, the famous Indian monks Shemeteng and Zhufalan arrived here with the scriptures, having made the last part of the trip on a white horse. Here they translated the scriptures into Chinese. Both monks died in China and were buried in the east and west corners of the grounds beyond the moon gates. This was the first Buddhist temple in China.

None of the buildings here are original: the red brick foundation of the Cold Terrace is Han, and none of the others are earlier than Ming. The State Council lists them as Jin to Qing. The abbot here was one of Tang Empress Wu's boy friends.

In the main hall to the right of Sakyamuni is Manjusri, the Bodhisattva of Wisdom carrying the *sutras*, and at Sakyamuni's left, Samantabhara, Bodhisattva of Universal Benevolence. In the next hall are 18 clay arhats, each with a magic weapon. These are the oldest statues here (Yuan). One is Ceylonese, one Chinese (the Tang monk Xuan Zhang went to India), and the rest Indian. Inside the back halls are statues of the two Indian monks, the Pilu Buddha (Sakyamuni), and the drawers where the scriptures are kept.

The 13 story **Qiyun** (Cloud Touching) **Pagoda** nearby is in the Tang style, first built in 1175. You get a strange echo effect if you stand either north or south of it and clap your hands. This temple is a good place for meditation, for enjoying the peonies and fresh air. There are, however, some very deformed beggars waiting outside, giving you an opportunity to gain some merit.

The **Luoyang Municipal Museum**, *Tel. 3937107*, has a special exhibit on the second floor with English titles and it's worth a stop. The museum has 2,000 pieces on display and roughly 50,000 pieces in its collection. Relics include historical maps of the city that show the imperial cities. Other items include a meter-wide bronze tripod incense burner, a sandalwood pagoda, and two mammoth tusks found right in town. There's a double boiler used 3,700 years ago; a crossbow with a trigger (476-221 B.C.); iron farming tools (Han); figures from the tomb of a Northern Wei prince, including a band with one musician falling asleep; and original three-color Tang horses and camels from which copies are made. Study these carefully for comparison if you want to buy reproductions. It is open 8:30am-5:30pm daily in summer, winter to 5pm, and has a shop.

Longmen Grottoes

China has 19 important 'cave temples' and the *Longmen (Lungmen) **Grottoes**, *Tel. 5981650*, is among the top three. Although predating these caves and built also by the Wei, those at Datong are better preserved, more elaborately colored, and bigger. The stone at Longmen, however, is better. The grottoes are about 18 km south of the Peony Plaza Hotel and extends north along the Yi River for about 1000 meters. They were not touched by the Red Guards, but the heads and hands of some were damaged by farmers wanting the stone for fertilizer. The buses stop by a 303-meter copy of a famous Sui bridge. Pedlars here are among the most persistent. Just say "Boo yow!" (I don't want) and they should go away. There's lots of climbing of stairs to look into caves. And you can dress up in costume for photos.

Work on the caves began about 494 A.D., when Emperor Hsaio Wen of the Northern Wei moved his capital here from Datong. Work continued at a great pace from then until the Tang. A few statues were added during the Five Dynasties and Northern Song. There are 1352 grottoes, over 750 niches, and about 40 pagodas of various sizes. They contain more than 100,000 Buddhist images, ranging in size from two centimeters to 17.14 meters. The most important have signs in English.

The **Wan Fo** (10,000 Buddhas) **Cave** actually has 15,000 buddhas on the north and south walls. It was completed in 680 A.D. (Tang). Note the musicians and dancers at the base. The back wall has 54 *bodhisattvas,* each sitting on a lotus flower. Outside the cave is a Guanyin with a water vessel in her left hand and a whisk in her right. There used to be two lions here, but they are now said to be in the Boston Museum of Fine Arts. The Guyang Cave was the earliest, built around 494 A.D.(Northern Wei). The corn-like design represents a string of pearls. The ceiling is covered with buddhas, lions, and tablets.

Fengxian Temple, the largest and most spectacular, was completed in 675 A.D. The main statue (17.14 meters) is the Vairocana Buddha (i.e. Sakyamuni), the face said to be modelled after Empress Wu. The square holes around the statues were used to hold the roof structure that was taken down when it was found that sunlight was good for limestone. Behind the smaller disciple to Sakyamuni's right is an imperceptible cave large enough to hold 400 people and from which climbers used to negotiate the top of the head. This is now blocked. On Sakyamuni's far left is Dvarapala, whose ankles are worn black and smooth by individuals trying to embrace them in return for happiness. A western toilet is at ground level in the store at the base of these statues.

Compare the dress of the statues. Some are clothed in the plain robes of Indian holy men; others wear female Chinese court dress, sometimes with jewelry, a later development. You can understand that wealthy, devout worshippers wanted to clothe their gods in the best fashions of the day. This practice is much like that of medieval European religious art. The narrow, regular pleats are characteristic of the Northern Wei. The Tang statues tend to have rounder faces. While it is said that gods could change their sex at will, the feminine faces are because, as one adherent said, 'We want people to look at the face of Buddha. Since women's faces are more attractive than men's, the statues are made to look more feminine. It seems that Guanyin changed from male to female in the third century Wei dynasty.

A highlight of many tours is a visit to charming **Mrs. Yang Xiu Hua** in her late 80s. Her feet were bound at age six and her once wealthy family lost its money to opium. She will let you photograph them and ask questions. She lives by preference in a 200-year old cave hollowed out of the ground and sells a few cheap souvenirs. Arrangements have to be made through travel agencies as she is not always there. A nearby masseur might entice you into some treatment, but don't pay more than Y20 negociated beforehand. The place is not clean.

Other Sites

The **Tomb of Guan Yu**, *Tel. 5975746, 5962018* or at least that of his head is nearby. Guan Yu was one of the heroes of The Three Kingdoms period, and he is also known as the Chinese god of war. His tomb, between the grottoes and the city, was built in the Ming. He was beheaded about 219 A.D.

Outside of the city is the **Tomb of Liu Xiu**. He was first emperor of the Eastern Han 1,900 years ago. A visit could be combined with a trip to see the Yellow River. The **Luoyang Ancient Tombs Museum** is seven km from the city near the airport and is worth a visit if tombs interest you. These 22 are from the Han, Tang, Ming and Qing dynasties, some genuine, some reproductions. Mainly in one building and underground, this museum is cool in summer, dark and spooky. Take a flashlight. Children would love it. An imperial Wei tomb is next door.

The **Folk Customs Museum**, *Tel. 3957064*, is charming if you have a good guide explaining the symbols on tiny women's shoes, embroidered headbands and children's clothes. It has a special display of birthday and wedding customs and religious influences. The tombs and folk customs museums are not on the regular tour and you must ask for them.

The **Yellow River Theme Park** has recently opened here, a Singapore joint venture. Let me know if you like it. You can visit the 154 meter-high **Xiaolongdi Dam** project on the Yellow River, 40 km north of Luoyang and due to finish in 2000.

SHOPPING

A department store, the **Guangzhou Market**, is behind the Friendship Hotel. The **Arts and Crafts Store** and **Luoyang Antique Store** on *Zhongzhou Zhong Road*, are near the Zhongzhou Bridge and the Peony Hotel. The Arts and Crafts store sells palace lanterns and reproductions of Shang bronzes, and artistic tiles. Tang horses and camels are made upstairs. It's at *503 Zhongzhouzhong Road, Tel. 3935387, open 8am to after 6pm daily*. The workshop is closed on weekends. The Antique Store is in the *Old Town Gods' Temple, Tel. 3955018*. It takes credit cards and is open 9am-6:30pm.

We found prices at the **Luoyang Artistic and Ceramic Corporation** excessively expensive, especially compared to the store in the **Goddess Hotel**. But it had a good selection and you can see the process. It's on *503 Zhongzhou Road, No. 503, Tel. 3935387*.

EXCURSIONS & DAY TRIPS

Sanmenxia is 122 km west of Luoyang, about a four-hour drive. It is almost halfway between Zhengzhou and Xi'an. You can cruise the Yellow River, and visit two very impressive 3,000-year old horse-and-chariot pits. You can spend a second day visiting Hangu Pass. A performance of the Sanmenxia "monks" with lamps on their head is very worthwhile but takes some organizing in advance. The monks are actually farmers, and they are very good.

The best hotel is the four-star **Royal Hotel International**, *Tel. 2898088*, close to the Yellow River, 20 minutes from the city.

The three-star **Minzu Hotel**, *Xiao Shan Zhong Road, Tel. 2821506, Fax 2821509* is in town. **CITS** is at *Heping Zhong Road, 472000, Tel. 2824623, Fax 2823404*. The telephone code is *0398*.

PRACTICAL INFORMATION

CITS, *Tourism Mansion, Jiudu Xi Road, 471003, Tel. 4323200, Fax 4325200. E-mail: citsly@public2.lyptt.ha.cn*

CTS, *6/F, Zhangfang Mansion, 26, Zhong Zhou Xi Road, 471003, Tel. and Fax 4856504.*

CYTS, 1 Nanchang Road, CYTS Building, 471039, Tel. 4945360, Fax 4325200. E-mail: lyq1@public2.lyptt.ha.cn. Ask for Tony Wang or Zhang Sheng Li.

Luoyang Tourism Bureau, *4/F, Tourism Mansion, Jiudu Xi Road, 471003, Tel. 4313824 and Fax 4313825.*

Telephone code, *0379.*

19. TIBET

LHASA

Lhasa, the capital of **Tibet,** is your main point of entry to the 'roof of the world.' Lhasa is situated north of Bhutan and Bangladesh and almost due south of Urumqi.

Tibet is generally safe for visitors, except those who get involved in local politics or can't take the altitude. Avoid getting close to the many stray dogs here.

Tibet is one of the more exotic places in the world to visit, almost a country in itself, with an area about the size of France, Spain, and Greece combined. It is isolated by the highest mountains on earth. It is important to see because of its unique culture, its celebrated monasteries, and its stark, spectacular scenery. You should go so you can make up your own mind about its controversial situation.

Good books to read before your trip here include Heirich Harrer's *Seven Years in Tibet,* about his adventures there in the 1940s, a good picture to compare with today's Tibet. Harrer, a German, taught the Dalai Lama English and was his cameraman. See the movie too but believe the original source, the book. A sequel relates Harrer's return trip. Take also the movie *Kundun* with a grain of salt.

See the movies the *Saltmen of Tibet* and *Red River Valley.* Also recommended are the classic books *Tibet and Its History* by Hugh E. Richardson, and Peter Fleming's *Bayonets to Lhasa.* For current travel information, ask the China Tourist Office for the bimonthly *Tourism in Tibet,* or call *(891) 683-6042, Fax 683-4632* in Lhasa. And look up the websites below about the different factions within the Tibetan community.

Lhasa's population is about 175,000, Tibet's population 2.3 million.

ARRIVALS & DEPARTURES

Lhasa is reached by two daily two-hour flights from Chengdu, and two flights a week each from Beijing, Kathmandu and Chongqing. It also has one flight a week from Xi'an. The Kathmandu flights might or might not continue all winter. (See also Chapter 6, Planning Your Trip, about Getting to China Via Nepal.)

Lhasa's **Gonggar Airport**, the third highest in the world at 3,542 meters, can now accommodate 747s. There is talk of direct flights from Hong Kong. The airport is about 100 km from Lhasa and the road follows the Yarlung Tsangpo River, the highest river in the world, which becomes the Brahmaputra in India.

You can also go to Lhasa by daily bus from Golmud (1,100 km) with an overnight stop in Amdo or wherever the driver wants to sleep. It's about 30 hours driving time with the possibility of snow in the high passes, even in June. Take warm clothing, motion sickness pills, and your own food. Buses have no toilets and heat.

Travelers have also been going overland from Kathmandu; you can travel from the Nepal border to Lhasa in one long day if you don't stop to sightsee or sleep, but some people have gotten very sick this way. And they have had to get out and walk around the landslides. Three days is better for this route. A good basic hotel is at Tingri (Y300). It's clean with 25 rooms and electricity. From Tingri to Shigatse, the road is bumpy and dusty.

Some guides feel it is better to get used to the altitude by flying to Lhasa first before attempting this rough route from the border.

You can also go by land from Chengdu via Chamdo to Lhasa, from Kashi, and via Yunnan province. Most of these roads are very poor, however, and you should expect delays due to landslides in summer, and weeks to get permits.

From Lhasa are buses to Tsedang, Shigatse, Nyingchi, Nagqu, Gyantse, and Gormu which leaves the Long Distance Bus Terminal at 8am daily.

Arranging Travel to Tibet

Tibet has been officially open (except during times of civil unrest) only for prepaid tours with a guide, even for one person. Any Chinese travel agent can arrange these. You will need authorization sent from the **Tibet Tourism Bureau** to the Chinese mission where you are applying for

BRING CASH TO TIBET

Recent travelers have found a stronger demand for US cash than for travelers' checks. Only the Lhasa Hotel will change money for its own guests. The main Potala branch of the Bank of China will cash travelers' checks. It is open weekdays and also on Saturday morning. Don't count on changing money easily after arrival, and don't count on credit cards.

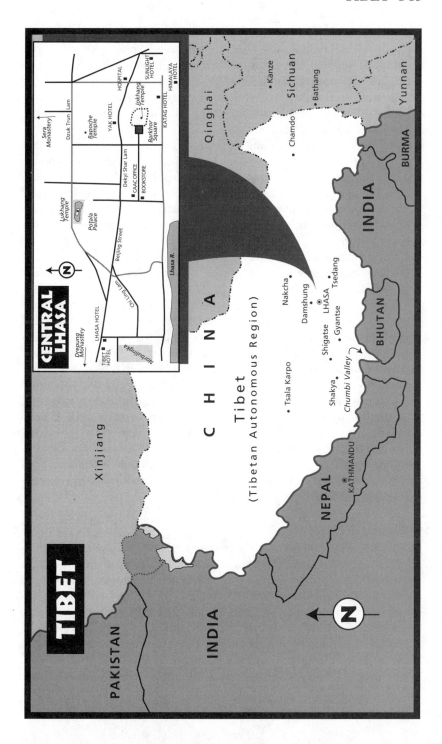

a visa. You can also arrange tours after you arrive in China. *If you wait until you get to China, do not mark 'Tibet' on your visa application form.* If you mention Tibet, the Chinese consulate will need to see your permit from the Tibet Tourism Bureau first.

Waiting until after your arrival could mean a cheaper trip depending on the number of people in your group. It can take three days to get permission, but better give yourself a week. For diplomats assigned to countries other than China and traveling as tourists, legal entry to Tibet is decided on a case-by-case basis which could take three weeks to a month once authorities receive your name and passport number.

As for journalists, what is a journalist? As long as you call yourself something else, and behave like any other tourist, journalists should have no problems. Just don't put "journalist" on any form, not even a hotel registration form.

From time to time, these official restrictions have not been enforced and a few people have entered without a permit. You do risk a fine and deportation if caught.

If you want an ethnic Tibetan rather than Chinese guide, make your request when you book your tour. A Tibetan guide might not speak English as well as a Chinese one, but a Tibetan guide will be able to communicate better with Tibetans. Tibetans can be hostile to Chinese guides. You can also request a guide with good English but you might not get one. Some travel agencies specializing in Tibet are listed in Chengdu.

Because tourists have complained of guides with little knowledge and poor English, please take this guide book with you or get something more detailed. If you are worried about political unrest, contact the **US consulate in Chengdu** for current information. There could be demonstrations on important Tibetan anniversaries, but guides will steer you away from them. If something happens before your trip, your travel agent can always cancel it.

ORIENTATION

This is colorful *National Geographic* land: you can see prostrating pilgrims, fierce-looking tribesmen, and people spinning prayer wheels on the street. You can photograph a great variety of tribal dress, maroon-robed monks, and unusual handicrafts and architecture. You will thrill at great snow-covered mountains. You will also find smiling, friendly people, most of whom don't mind having their picture taken when asked, and some of whom take baths once a year. It's best to take a long lens for the ones who have never seen foreigners or cameras before.

Feel lucky if you encounter groups of monks challenging each other with questions catechism-style amid much laughter and the clapping of hands. And there are yaks – oxen who live at these high altitudes.

While visiting Tibet is no longer an experience just for the adventurous few, it is still not for the weak. The average altitude in Tibet is over 5000 meters (very hard on the lungs, and on the skin, so take some good sunscreen). Usually it takes about two days to decide whether you'll be sick, and two weeks to feel at home. Just don't push yourself too hard. Taking it easy is difficult, as a lot of climbing is involved just to sightsee. Do not go if you have asthma or other pulmonary problems. In addition to the altitude and dust, the temples are full of incense smoke and butter lamps, both of which might make breathing difficult. Qualified doctors may not be available.

Since most food, energy and building materials have to be imported by truck or plane, the cost of accommodations and sightseeing is higher than in other parts of China for the same quality. You should take your own flashlight, drinking flask, medicine for altitude sickness, and an alarm clock.

The Climate

The altitude in Lhasa is about 3,607 meters. Most of the year can be very dry with lots of dust blowing. A nose mask and goggles are helpful. Only light clothing is needed in summer for Lhasa, but warmer clothes are needed for higher altitudes. Winter days can be warm with highs of 20 C and you can get a sunburn. But the nights can be cold. The best weather is September to November. The hottest temperature in Lhasa is 27 C in July and August; the coldest, -15 C in December to February. The annual precipitation is about 500 mm, mainly in June and July.

When to Visit

The busiest tourist months are April, May, and July through October. From November one to March 31, the valley is full of colorful nomads going on pilgrimages from monastery to monastery, and living in tents. A good time to go is when fewer tourists are about, especially March, with lots of sunny 15 C days. At night the temperature dips to near freezing but there's nothing to do outside anyways. Be warned however that there may not be any decent heat and hot water in hotels except in the Lhasa and Shigatse Hotels, nor is there adequate heat in mini-buses.

At New Year's in the spring, houses and mountains look glorious with fresh prayer flags. Monasteries have special ceremonies, but markets are only partially open, and stores and factories are closed for two weeks. This is the best time for photography and tourist market haggling. Just take a hot-water bottle. You can visit Gyantse, Shigatse, and Zetang year round.

ALTITUDE SICKNESS

*If you only have two days, it is worth going because it takes so much time to acclimatize. In Lhasa you get about two-thirds the amount of oxygen at sea-level. In Shigatse, you get 50%!! In summer you get more than in winter. Jogging or any physical exertion makes matters worse. About 60% of new arrivals get a headache. If you are one of the small minority afflicted with severe **altitude sickness**, you could spend much of your time in bed.*

You won't know you are susceptible until you get to about 3,000 meters. You can travel successfully in high altitudes 20 times and get it on the 21st. It seems to hit the young and strong more than the old and weak. Young people have passed out checking into hotels. You should not jump onto a bicycle or jog upon arrival, even though you feel fine.

The symptoms are severe headache, dizziness, insomnia, nausea, vomiting, and difficulty in breathing. People who make a gradual ascent by road rarely get it, if at all. People who fly in are prone. So are people with colds, breathing difficulties, poor health, and heart disease. Pregnant women should stay below 3,600 meters, says the Himalayan Rescue Association in Hints on High Altitude, circulated by the Holiday Inn.

It is better to let your body adjust naturally. Avoid smoking, alcohol, and sleeping pills. Move about in slow motion. Drink over three liters of liquid a day. Get plenty of bed rest especially if you feel any of the symptoms. Open your windows. Breathe deeply. Relax. Do not panic.

Some hotels have oxygen in the rooms. This will give relief but will retard the time it takes the body to adjust. Some people have found aspirins helpful. Some have successfully taken the diuretic Diamox available in North America by prescription only. Many doctors will not prescribe it because they don't know its effect at high altitudes. With a few people Diamox has caused vomiting, confusion, and, of course, urination. Discuss it with a mountaineering club or travel agency doctor before you go. You have to start taking it a day before you arrive.

In very severe cases of altitude sickness, the only recourse is evacuation to a lower altitude – but you may not get a plane out for days.

Tibetan History

Tibetans were nomadic herdspeople or farmers who raised barley, yak, and sheep. In 233, King Tho-tho-ri-Nyantsen received a book of Buddhist doctrine from India as a gift, but it was written in Sanskrit and no one in Tibet could read it. The king did nothing about it, nor did his successors for hundreds of years; it was finally translated in the mid-600's, by officials working for King Songtsen Gampo. It was this king who took the Nepalese princess Bhrikuti Devi in marriage; she brought with her an image of the Aksobhya Buddha. Apparently not satisfied with one wife, and looking to settle border skirmishes with China, he asked for a Chinese wife as well, and was given Princess Wen Cheng, daughter of the Emperor. Wen Cheng brought with her an image of the Shakyamuni Buddha (the "original" Buddha, as it were – Gautama, the fellow who started it all). Each princess had temples facing toward their homeland; one east to China, one south to Nepal, and both promoted their own brand of Buddhism. In 779, **Buddhism** became the state religion.

In the seventh century, the king of Tubo conquered the other tribes and made Lhasa his capital. He also invaded neighboring Sichuan, and although he was repulsed, his request for a Chinese wife was granted. His marriage with Tang princess Wen Cheng and his interest in Tang culture introduced much Chinese culture into Tibet. Among the innovations were silk, paper, and the architecture of the palace he built for her. His marriage to a Nepalese princess also meant Nepalese-Indian influences. Tibetan script is derived from Sanskrit, which was developed in India.

The Tibetan kingdom subsequently expanded to include parts of Yunnan and northern India. The Mongols invaded Tibet in 1252 and adopted Tibetan Buddhism for themselves and propagated it to help control their subject tribes in other parts of China. Some Tibetan lamas, or high priests, became very powerful during the Yuan. **Kublai Khan** appointed a lama as king, to maintain overall power himself. This system has continued with varying degrees of Chinese enforcement ever since. Qing Emperor Qianlong (Chien Lung) especially asserted his authority in Tibet.

In 1624, the Jesuits were the first western missionaries to arrive here. During the lifetime of the **fifth Dalai Lama**, the office of Dalai Lama became political as well as religious. The first British mission arrived in 1774 and a British military expedition (Younghusband's) forced the Dalai Lama to flee to Mongolia from 1904 until 1909. In 1910, the Chinese again asserted their control and the Dalai Lama retreated for a time to India.

In 1911, the Tibetans repelled the Chinese. The British tried to maintain some control, but the Tibetans pretty much ruled themselves until the Chinese People's Liberation Army invaded in 1950-1951. The 1950's saw periods of turmoil as well as calm as the Chinese strengthened their hold.

An uprising by many Tibetans and a fierce Chinese crackdown in 1959 caused the current Dalai Lama (the 14th) to fear for his life; he and a large number of Tibetans fled to India. He has been living in Dharamsala, India, ever since, along with tens of thousands of Tibetans who live in exile throughout India, Nepal, and to a lesser extent Bhutan. Many live in North America.

In 1964, China made Tibet an "autonomous region" within China. During the Cultural Revolution, the Red Guards destroyed most of the monasteries. Today, Tibet has at least 50 monasteries open, including seven for nuns, with at least 3,000 monks in residence and 138 nuns. In 1980, the government agreed to rebuild a number of monasteries, which it has been doing. The Tibetan and Chinese governments maintain and regulate the monasteries. Before the Chinese army took over, Tibet had 2,770 monasteries.

The Chinese have started to train Tibetans to replace Han administrators. Tibetans here are over 95% of the population, not counting the Chinese military. Due to government incentives, many Han Chinese are moving into Tibet, especially Lhasa. Some estimates put the number of Chinese soldiers and security forces in Tibet at 300,000.

In 1987, again in 1989, and sporadically in the past few years, a number of Tibetans (led by monks) have demonstrated for independence. Several dozen people have been killed and hundreds imprisoned.

The **current Dalai Lama** was awarded the **Nobel Peace Prize** in 1989, for his nonviolent resistance in exile to Chinese occupation of his country, and for a peace plan offering the Chinese sovereignty of sorts in exchange for genuine autonomy in everyday life, with guarantees of political and religious freedom. China accused the United States and other countries then (and still does) of interfering in its internal affairs.

Not all Tibetans agree with or follow the Dalai Lama. For information on the current conflict between the Dalai Lama and Tibetan followers of deity Dorje Shugden, read *Asiaweek*, September 11, 1998, and *http://www.tibet.com*; the Dalai Lama's talk published in *http://www.tibet-society.org.uk/aptrans.html; http://www.he.net/~shugden; http://38.216.63.6/public/dg1.htm*.

See also the newsgroup, "talk.politics.tibet" at *http://www.phoaks.com/talk/politics/tibet*. Our thanks to Colman Jones for these addresses.

Tibetan Buddhism

Tibet's Buddhism is different from that of the rest of Asia, aside from Mongolia and northern China. It believes in reincarnation and there are both wrathful and peaceful aspects: the wrathful side includes a torturous hell for sinners, which is reflected in its art, full of demons and human skulls, witchcraft and magic, much influenced by the pre-Buddhist polytheism of the Tibetans.

The peaceful side of the religion is also reflected in Tibetan art. It has also many pre-Hindu influences and much recitation of spells. You might hear the chant *Om Mani Padme Hum*, which means 'Hail to the Jewel in the Lotus,' a mantra that helps the individual communicate with the eternal. Buddhism also has many mystical elements, and a highly developed theology. The goal of Buddhism is the end of continuous reincarnations.

WANTED - DALAI LAMA PHOTOS

As you move around the region, be sensitive to the feelings of people. I have been appalled by the loud talking of my Chinese guide during Tibetan prayers. Walk clockwise around temples. If you hand a picture of the Dalai Lama to a Tibetan, make sure no Han Chinese is around because you and your Tibetan friend could get in trouble. Hold the photo (postcards are great) in both hands, put it to your forehead and then bow your head as you hand it over.

The Dalai Lama is considered by Tibetans to be an incarnation of God, and they might ask you for a 'Dalai Lama picture' in every monastery. You probably could give out 40 in the Potala alone. However, if you have pictures of the Dalai Lama in your possession, the police could conclude that you support Tibetan independence. They have arrested some foreigners for getting involved in this dispute. In the early 1990s, you could see photos of the Dalai Lama in monasteries, but in 1996, the authorities confiscated them.

At one time, a quarter of the male population of Tibet were monks, and the theocracy was such that no matter how cold it was, on whatever day spring was proclaimed by the Dalai Lama, everybody had to change into summer clothes!

Like other religions, Buddhism is divided into sects: the two main ones in Tibet are often referred to as the Red Hats, where sex with a person other than one's spouse is part of the ritual, and the Yellow Hats (the **Gelukpa sect**), which practises celibacy and other Buddhist monastic traditions. The Dalai Lama is head of the Gelukpa sect.

The title Dalai Lama comes from combining *Dalai*, which is a Mongolian word meaning '*ocean*,' and *Lama*, which means 'revered one,' 'teacher,' or, in this case, 'wisdom.' So Dalai Lama means Ocean of Wisdom.

Determining Reincarnated Lamas

How successive Dalai Lamas are chosen is a fascinating story. Toddlers recognizing objects used by themselves in their previous incarnations, answering questions correctly, and so on, is the usual way it's done. The current incumbent is from a peasant family from **Amdo** (northeastern Tibet, now in Qinghai province). The Dalai Lamas are believed to be earthly incarnations of the four-armed god **Chenrezi**, the God of Compassion or Mercy. When each incarnation dies, his spirit takes on the body of another Tibetan child at birth. (See the movie *Kundun*.)

Disputes have arisen over who is the real reincarnated Dalai Lama or any other lama, and the issue is politically sensitive. To the chagrin of his followers, the current Dalai Lama has said there should be 'no more Dalai Lamas,' and 'there is no need to preserve this institution.'

Lamas are very learned monks or recognized reincarnations of previous lamas or monks, and their identities are determined in a similiar way. One American woman has recently borne the reincarnation of a high lama. In 1995, the Dalai Lama proclaimed one child as the reincarnation of the Panchen Lama while the Chinese government proclaimed another. The Chinese pointed to a Qing dynasty agreement that said it had to approve the appointment.

Tibetan Customs

Tashi delek is the Tibetan greeting. It means "good luck." Hello is *Wei.* Among traditional Tibetan customs is the giving of a *kata*, a long silk scarf, as a token of esteem and good luck. The sticking out of the tongue is a sign of respect. At one time, Tibetans practiced polyandry, brothers sharing one wife because of poverty. Every summer a festival celebrates the annual washing and cleaning.

Funeral workers cut up the remains of the deceased at dawn to feed vultures, a 1,000-year-old tradition. Tibetans believe these birds take the spirits to heaven. Those who cannot afford this expensive rite, like beggars or victims of serious illnesses, are fed to fish, which is why Tibetans don't eat fish. Burial in the ground is for the very poor and unfortunate, such as criminals or victims of murder. Some high lamas are covered in butter and cremated. The highest lamas are buried in monasteries; the previous Dalai Lamas are in the **Potala Palace** (see below).

Tourists are forbidden from seeing the birds at work, because the families fear strangers will scare the birds away. Look for the *tangkas* hung on monastery walls. These are the scrolls used by preachers to illustrate the teachings of the Buddha and the best are valued by art collectors. You'll also see **prayer wheels**, with a written prayer inside, which adherents spin in the belief that each rotation sends a prayer to Buddha. Monasteries have giant prayer wheels. Prayer flags are blue symbolizing the sky, white for clouds, red for fire, green for water and yellow for earth. They are for protection.

Religious institutions usually decide the time and date of ceremonies and special events at the last moment. You have to telephone each morning for the time if you want to see these. No one really knows what is going on when, and you could find many changes to your itinerary.

TIBETAN-CHINESE PLACE NAMES

In this section, I've attempted to use the Tibetan name, but please forgive the errors. Guides might know only the Chinese name, here in parenthesis. With many thanks to Steve Powers: Chonggye (Qonggyai), Drepung (Daipung) Monastery, Ganden (Gandan), Gyantse (Gyangze, Chiang-tze, Jiangxi), Jokhang (Juglakang, Tsuglag Khang, Dazhaosi) Temple, Lhasa (Lasa), Lhoka (Shannan), Norbulingka (Norpulinkha, Luobulinka) Summer Palace, Potala (Budalagong) Palace, Sera (Sela) Monastery, Shammo (Zhangmu), Shigatse (Xigaze, Xigatse, Rikaze), Tashilhunpo (Zhaxilhunbu), Tibet (Xizang), Tingri Shegar (Xegar), Tsedang (Zedang), and Yarlung Tsangpo (Yarlung Zangbo) River.

WHERE TO STAY

The best hotel is the **Lhasa Hotel** (with the best English), then the **Lhasa Tibet Hotel**. Third is the **Himalaya Hotel**. The Lhasa and Tibet are within walking distance of each other and the Norbulinka. The Kirey, Banok Shol and Yak are normally clean Tibetan inns. Aside from the Lhasa, few hotels honor reservations. You might have to send a scout a day ahead to secure rooms in high tourist season. Hotels outside of Lhasa's top three can be downright crude.

The cheaper Tibetan inns are within walking distance of each other and the central Jokhang Monastery in the old Tibetan city and have been off limits to foreigners from time to time. The best is the Yak, and second best the Kyichu. Other hotels are being built here or expanded. Expect to have your luggage searched while you're away from your room. The following prices are subject to change, discounts and negociations. You can e-mail agents in Chengdu.

LHASA HOTEL *(Lhasa Fandian), One Minzu Road, 850001. Three stars aiming for four. Tel. 6832221, (Sales office) Fax 6835796. $156 for rooms, $231 for suites, April 1 to October 31. 95 km from the airport. Credit cards. In the western suburbs.*

Built in 1986 with renovations 1998-99, this 468-room former Holiday Inn is in five and six story buildings with exotic Tibetan-style suites, non-smoking floors, CNN and BBC. Heated in winter, it has satellite television, Sichuan, western, Indian and Tibetan food. Its outdoor pool is open April to the end of October. It has western and Tibetan herbal clinics, and its own airport bus. CITS, CYTS and the Tibet Tourist Bureau have offices on the premises. The buffet breakfast costs $16. The Holiday Inn did not renew its contract here because it could not get this hotel up to its usual standards.

LHASA TIBET HOTEL *(Xizang Binguan), 100 Beijing Xi Road, 850001. Three stars. Tel. 6833677, Fax 8636787. Renovations in 1998.*

Located behind the Lhasa Hotel, this 1986 hotel has a clinic with rooms from about Y580.

LHASA HIMALAYA HOTEL, *6 Linguo Dong Road, Tel. 6831111, 6332675. One star. Renovations in 1998.*

SUNLIGHT HOTEL LHASA, *27 Linju Road, Lhasa, 850000, Tel. 6322853. Surly staff.*

YAK HOTEL, *100 Beijing Dong Road, 850000, Tel. 6833496, 6323496. About Y250 for rooms with bath, Y110 for no private bath, and Y25-Y50 for beds in a dormitory.*

This bright and friendly hotel was built in 1985, renovated and expanded since. It has a new wing with about 40 rooms, some private ones with western toilets, and remote controlled heaters. It has a great view from the roof and problems with water pressure. Bicycles are for rent.

HOTEL KYICHU *(Kechu), 149 Beijing Dong Road, 850000, Tel. 6338824, and Fax 6320234.*

There are 22 rooms, Y230 and Y420. 24-hour room service. Near the Yak.

WHERE TO EAT

Tibetan tea is drunk with yak butter and salt, and tastes more like an overly rich beef broth. It does tend to give much needed energy for survival and is said to be good for colds. The proper way to drink it is to lightly blow the top cream away from you and allow it to settle on the sides of your cup. The thicker the cream, the more generous the host. Fresh, hot yak milk is sweet and 'heavenly' and has a higher fat content than cow's milk. Barley-like flour is often added to the milk or tea to form a dough. **Chang**, a barley wine, is another favorite drink offered to guests. Most foreigners do not like yak butter and yak-butter flavored Tibetan food – it's too rich.

The best restaurants are in the Lhasa Hotel. Except for the hotels, restaurants here are generally dirty and the food is not good. There are few vegetables. You can get Tibetan food (yak meat and cheese), Moslem (mutton or lamb), and Chinese food in Lhasa. The park at the front base of the Potala has food stalls, but take precautions when you eat there. If you are going outside of Lhasa, stock up on snacks before you leave for Tibet.

SNOW LAND RESTAURANT, *4 Yiyuan Road, Tel. 6337323.*

Come here for great pizza.

HARD YAK CAFE *at the Lhasa Hotel, One Minzu Road.*

This is the place for yak burgers and spaghetti.

BARKHOR CAFE, *Tel. 6326892, in the main square in front of the Jokhang Temple.*

Good and clean, run by former Holiday Inn staff in the summers. It has a problem getting orders straight, however.

TASHI ONE or **TASHI TWO**, *around the corner from the Barkhor.*

Backpackers often eaten at either one of these places, which are good.

CRAZY YAK SALOON, *at the Yak Hotel, 100 Beijing Dong Road. Tel. 6833496.*

Great atmosphere, slow service.

THE THIRD EYE, *down the street from the Yak Hotel.*

Decent but very greasy food.

SEEING THE SIGHTS

The most important buildings to see in Lhasa are the **Jokhang Temple**, **Potala Palace**, **Sera Monastery**, and **Drepung Monastery**. You should also see the **Barkhor** or bazaar, and **Norbulingka Palace**. You might want to visit a carpet factory or traditional medicine hospital.

In your spare time you may want to go out on your own. The Yak Hotel has bicycles. You can flag down one of the frequent public mini-buses or take a bicycle rickshaw; jeep-type vehicles are expensive (almost three times the taxi rate in any other Chinese city). Monastery hours keep changing, so ask your hotel to telephone. The Potala has been open Mondays and Thursdays to the public, and daily except Sundays to tour groups, 9am-12:30 noon. Do check before you go. To travel to other parts of Tibet, ask your hotel, travel agents or other travelers. The Yak, Kirey, and Sunlight Hotels have notice boards with messages.

You can see the temples and palaces of Lhasa in two days if you are in good shape. You must not miss the *Potala Palace, Tel. 6324587.* It costs Y40 to enter, Y50 to photograph *each* chapel, and Y100-Y150 extra to video. Then there's Y10 to go to the roof. The Potala is 3.5 km from the Lhasa Hotel and one km from the Jokhang. It dominates the city from its lofty cliff. Your group gets driven up to the entrance, but individual travelers have to climb the 300 meters to the door. In spite of its 13 stories, there are no elevators. If you follow the crowds and go into every open doorway, you should be able to take in everything worthwhile in three hours. Unless things have changed since my last visit, there are no signs in English or arrows. There are a lot of stairs, and the only toilet is near the east entrance.

Originally built in the seventh century by Songsten Gampo, the Potala was the official residence of the Dalai Lama, the religious and secular head of Tibet. The first Dalai Lama lived from 1391 to 1474. The Potala has 1,000 rooms, 10,000 chapels, and the tombs of eight Dalai Lamas, some gold-plated and studded with diamonds, turquoises, corals, and pearls. The largest tomb is 14.85 meters high. More than 200,000 pearls cover the Pearl Pagoda. The tombs are not always open so ask about them. Additional payment is worth it. Every room has a helpful monk-guide.

The building was destroyed and rebuilt several times, the latest structure dating from 1642. Among its 200,000 statues are those of King Songsten Gampo and his Chinese wife. Every wall is covered with murals. Noteworthy are those in the Sishiphuntsok Hall. In the West Grand Hall, the murals record the life of the Fifth Dalai Lama, including his meeting with Qing Emperor Shunzhi in Beijing in 1652.

The palace is 400 meters by 350 meters, and is made of stone and wood, its brightly colored walls between three and five meters thick, yellow for living quarters, and red for chapels. Black around doors is good luck. The White Palace was built during the time of the Fifth Dalai Lama (1617-1682) and the Red Palace afterward. From the 18th century, with the construction of the Norbulinka Summer Palace, the Potala was used only in winter. Can you imagine a child growing up here? The current Dalai Lama was brought here at the age of four. Think of him flying his kite from the Potala's roof and exploring the city and its people with a telescope!

The *Jokhang Temple (Juglakang), *Tel. 6323129,* is the most important Buddhist temple in Tibet. It is here that most pilgrims prostrate themselves and you can take a great photo of them from its second floor. It is here that China's largest concentration of policemen seem to be, ready to show up whenever a crowd gathers. The Jokhang is 4.5 km from the Lhasa Hotel and is the heart of the city. It was built in the mid-seventh century, also during King Songsten Gampo's time. It has been expanded several times since. Note the Nepalese and Chinese features. Princess Wen Cheng brought with her from China the seated statue of the child Sakyamuni. The Tibetans believe that the statue was made by the Buddha himself. The **Great Prayer Festival** is held annually here from the third to 25th of the first month of the Tibetan calendar.

The *Sera Monastery, *Tel. 6323139,* in the northern suburbs 10 km from the Lhasa Hotel and four km from downtown, was built in 1419. It was extended in the early 18th century, and is one of the four major monasteries in Tibet, at its height housing 10,000 lamas and monks. Today it has about 500. The 18 sandalwood *arhats* and four heavenly kings here were gifts from a Ming emperor. Look also for a gold statue of an 11-faced Guan Yin, the Goddess of Mercy.

The *Drepung Monastery, *Tel. 6323149,* is in the western suburbs six km from the Lhasa Hotel and 10 km from the Jokhang. You can climb to the roof for a view of the valley. Financed by the same nobleman who built the Sera, the Drepung was founded in 1416 and extended several times.

It is one of the four major monasteries. Among its treasures is a white conch and a gilded Buddha. Inside the abdomen of the statue in the main hall are the remains of a master translator named Dorjidak. At one time, this monastery also had a population of over 10,000 monks and lamas; today it has about 600.

If you have more time, the **Norbulingka**, *Tel. 6322157*, was the summer residence of the Dalai Lamas. With 370 rooms, it is four km from the Potala and set in a 100-acre garden. Kalsang Podang, the first building, was originally erected in 1755. The New Palace for the 14th Dalai Lama was built in 1954 and 1956. It is also full of statues and murals. The murals are of Princess Wen Cheng and her marriage to the king, the three worlds, and Buddha preaching under a banyan tree. The bedroom is as the current Dalai Lama left it when he fled to India. In the 1940s, the German mountain climber Heinrich Harrer set up a movie theater for the Dalai Lama here.

An exhibition of *tangkas* is usually in one of the temples in the back. Study it so you'll know what good quality it. Some *tangkas* look like paint-by-number products. If you don't like the toilets, go over to the Lhasa Hotel nearby.

One of the temples in Lhasa has a bronze bell with Latin inscriptions. It should be from 17th-century Catholic missionaries. Ask about it if you're interested. Also of interest is the **Sunday market**, down the hill and across the street in front of the Potala, a delightful innovation with rides for children, market stalls, and food to eat. At the **Tibetan traditional medicine hospital**, you can also learn about Tibetan medicine. If you want to ride a **yak-skin raft**, that should be possible too; inquire at your hotel. Ask about the **Nechung oracle monastery**. It's small, less crowded, with very interesting chapels.

Festivals
Dates are hard to pin down and some festivals have been canceled at the last minute.
• October-November: the **Gods Descending Festival**
• November-December: the **Fairy Maiden Festival** (Jokhang Temple)
• December: **Tsong Khapa's Festival**
• January-February-March: **Tibetan New Year**
• February-March: **Great Prayer Festival** (Jokhang)
• February-March: **Butter Lamp Festival**
• July: **Giant Tangka Festival** (Shigatse)
• August: **Shoton (Tibetan Opera) Festival**

SHOPPING

Tibetan boots, rugs, saddle blankets, jewelry, temple bells, prayer wheels, and woolen blankets are for sale. Look in the market around the Jokhang Temple, the **Barkhor**. There you can also buy Nepalese-made Tibetan *tangkas* which are finer than Tibetan ones, at several times the price of those in Nepal but cheaper than in North American. Several upmarket store are here.

Many Tibetan crafts are actually made in Nepal and a stop in Boda there to check prices beforehand would help serious shoppers. I've also seen the cheap jewelry sold by peddlars in the square in Jordan for about the same price. The Silk Road still thrives. *Tangkas* and original art have also been seen at **Potala Arts & Crafts**, at the foot of the Potala (bus stop). Unmounted prints of Tibetan *tangkas* are a great buy and have been found in the Lhasa Hotel and at the Potala. There's a Chinese-run **Friendship Store**, Renmin Road.

You can watch carpets being woven in Lhasa of Tibetan highland sheep wool with traditional Tibetan-inspired designs. The **Khawachen Carpet Factory**, a US joint venture, will also sell carpets at prices considerably lower than in the US. It is 20 minutes drive from the Jokhang and 10 minutes form the Lhasa Hotel at *103 Jinzhu Xi Road, Tel. 6835226, 6833255, Fax 6833250.* For a preview before you go, contact **InnerAsia Trading Company** *236 Fifth Avenue, New York, NY 10001, Tel. 212/532-2600. E-mail:104437.2251@compuserve.com.*

EXCURSIONS & DAY TRIPS

SHIGATSE & GYANTSE

The most important town outside of Lhasa is **Shigatse** for the *Tashilhunpo Monastery. On the new highway, this is about a five-hour, 260 km journey west of Lhasa. It can be combined in a two-night, three-day trip with Gyantse. You can return on the older, longer and more spectacular road that includes the monastery in Gyantse, a climb up to a 5,000-meter pass full of stone cairns, and thousands of prayer flags, vibrating in gale-force winds. You can leave a cairn there yourself if you're not too cold. You also get spectacular views of snow-covered **Najun Gsancy glacier** and mountain (7,220 meters high). This is a journey of about 10 hours, including a picnic lunch and a drive around sacred **Lake Zambok**.

Shigatse is at an altitude of over 3,900 meters. The Tashilhunpo is usually open 9:30am-12:30 noon and sometimes 3:30pm-6:30pm. It was founded in 1447 and was the home of the Panchen Lamas, the reincarnations of the Buddha of Eternal Light. The Chinese consider the Panchen Lama a political equal to the Dalai Lama, but this is also a very sensitive and controversial point.

At one time, the Tashilhunpo had a population of 3,800 monks. Today there are about 650. This monastery also has many halls and chapels, and statues of the 18 arhats. The Hall of the Buddha Maitreya Champa/Qiangba was built from 1914-18 with a 26.7-meter statue of the Buddha in gold and copper. The gold-plated reliquary of the fourth Panchen Lama is 11 meters high and is decorated with precious stones. The tenth Panchen Lama died here in 1989. Look for the photos of British Prime Minister Major and US President George Bush on a stupa. There are also 15th century paintings. You can probably hear the lamas chanting in the Grand Chanting Hall three times a day. A good market for Tibetan handicrafts and unique boots is nearby.

Shigatse is a good place for walking around, except for the vendors who grab you, hoping for a sale. It is flat and interesting especially around the market. Shigatse also has a traditional **Tibetan medicine hospital** to visit and the **Gang-Gyen Carpet Factory**, *9 Mount Everest Road, 857000*, with traditional Tibetan designs, which is owned by the Tashilhunbo monastery. It makes carpets, bags and jackets with sheep's wool and natural Tibetan-grown dyes. It's open 9:30am-12:30 noon then 3:30pm-6:30pm.

The **Xigatze Hotel** *(Binguan) at 13 Beijing Zhong Road, 857000, Tel. (892) 8822550, Fax 8821900 has at least 123 rooms and growing.* It has heat and hot water. It's less than one km to the Tashilhunpo and almost next door to the Bank of China, and not recommended bars.

Gyantse is almost a two-hour drive from Shigatse, and 205 km from the airport outside Lhasa. It is worth a stop, unless you're tired of monasteries by now. Gyantse's is the spookiest of the lot and has about 85 monks, but few visitors because of its isolation. The town itself looks positively medieval with the remains of an impressive old fort above it. Gyantse has a carpet factory and the two-star Gyantse Hotel, *Tel. 892/ 8172222, Fax 8172366.*

ROYAL TIBETAN TOMBS

The *Royal Tibetan Tombs, from the seventh century, are at Chonggye in Lhoka prefecture, about 180 km southeast of Lhasa. A hotel is in **Tsedang**. The **Yumbulakang Palace**, built in 228 B.C. by the first Tibetan King, is on a hilltop. **Lake Yamdrok Yamsto** is a one-day excursion from Lhasa, a large undeveloped lake, but an opportunity to enjoy the stark countryside.

GANDEN MONASTERY

The *Ganden Monastery, 60 km east of Lhasa, is listed as early Ming to Qing. At least 10 buildings have been restored. Less than 100 monks live there now. At one time, it had over 8,000 monks.

ELSEWHERE IN TIBET

Nyingchi County, 400 km from Lhasa, has the new Parsong Co. Lake Vacation Village (Namuchuo in Chinese) on a 12-km long lake but we haven't had a chance to review it yet. The Nyingchi Hotel *is on Shuangyong Road, August 1 New Village, Tel. 894/5821300, Fax 5821655.*

Tsedang is the first Tibetan capital, boasting the best hotel and food outside of Lhasa. On the way is **Samye**, reached by a beautiful 1.5 hour ferry ride and a white-knuckle ride standing in the back of a truck as it bounces on the dunes. This is the oldest remaining monastery of the Red Hat sect (8th century) and it has its own very basic guest house (smelly hole-in-the-floor toilets, and barking dogs all night). The three-star **Tsedang Hotel** *is at 21 Nedong Road, 856000, Tel. 893/7821668, Fax 7821688.*

Tsurpu is the new 'hot spot.' Two hours' drive from Lhasa, it has the newly rebuilt **Tsurpu Monastery**, the seat of the Karmapa, the head of the 'Black Hat' sect. He is the 17th reincarnation, discovered in 1992 at the age of eight years, but an old soul. The lineage is older than the Dalai Lama's. This remarkable child has given blessings (from a distance) to visiting tourists. Security is heavy and no cameras and purses are allowed. Audiences are not always possible and involve a one-day trip from Lhasa. Travel agents can make arrangement if the monastery is willing.

Zhangmu, on the Tibet side of the Nepal border, is now open to tourists, with a 100-bed guesthouse. It is not worth staying there as the town is the pits. The hotel however isn't bad with a good breakfast buffet, and electricity only after dark. Y420 for rooms.

There are also tours to the **Quangtang grasslands**, a 200,000 square km nature reserve with 60 kinds of rare wild animals like yak, argali, bear, and wild donkeys. Zhangmu is between 840 km and 900 km from Lhasa. Sources and routes differ.

ELSEWHERE IN CHINA

See also *Zhongdian* in Kunming, *Taer Monastery* in Xining, and Chengdu for other Tibetan regions of China.

TREKS

Several tour agencies now offer **treks** in Tibet, and prices for these are higher than similar treks in other countries. Mountaineering can be organized through the **Chinese Mountaineering Association**.

The best trekking months are June-July and September-October. August has the most rain and landslides. There are treks to **Kailash** and **Rongbuk** (Everest Base camp) and various lakes, and soft treks from Ganden to Samye (four-six days). (See also Chapter 6, *Planning Your Trip,* Getting to China Via Nepal.)

PRACTICAL INFORMATION

CITS, *Beijing Xi Road, 850001, Tel. 6822980, 6832980.*

CTS, *Tel. 6822980, 6836626, Fax 6835277.*

CYTS, *331 Zin Zhu Dong Road, 850000, Tel. 6823329, Fax 6835588.*

Medical Emergencies The Lhasa Hotel should be able to put you in touch with a Chinese or European doctor.

Nepalese Consulate, *13 Norbulingka Road, Tel. 6822880.*

Telephone code, *0891*

Tibet Foreign Trade Travel Agency, *Tel. 6331453, Fax 6338606.* Contact: Tenpa Gyaltsen.

Tibet Holiday International Travel Service, *Tel. 6824305, Fax 6834957.*

Tibet International Sports Travel, *6 Linkhor Dong Road, 850000, Tel. 6334082, 6834082, Fax 6334855, 6834855.* Very reliable.

Tibet Tourism Bureau, *208-218 Beijing Xi Road, 850001, Tel. 6826793, 6832980, Fax 6835277, 6833241.* For permits and complaints, *Tel. 6824584.* Offices in Tibet Hotel, Chengdu and *149 West Gulou Street, Beijing 100009, Tel. Beijing 64018822 X 1601, Fax 64015883 or 64019831.* Office also in the US, *Tel. 909/629-8888, Fax 909/629-8889.*

Tibet Wind-Horse Adventure, *Tel. 6833009, Fax 6836793.*

Tourist Complaints, contact Supervisory Bureau of Tourism Quality of Tibet, *208 Yuanlin Road, 850001, Tel. 6834913.*

See also Chengdu, Kathmandu and US for travel agents there specializing in Tibet.

20. SOUTH CHINA

CHANGSHA

Located south of the Yangtze River, **Changsha** is the capital of Hunan province. It is partly famous because Chairman Mao was born in nearby **Shaoshan**. He studied for about five years at the First Hunan Normal School (1912-18) in Changsha. Yale University started a mission here about 1904 and eventually established a medical school, hospital, and middle school. The Americans left shortly after 1949. Changsha is also known for its important 2100-year old Han excavation. Its embroidery is one of the four most famous in China. It is also the gateway to **Zhangjiajie**, a UNESCO World Heritage site.

Changsha, in one of China's main rice-growing areas, was a small town 3,000 years ago. It was almost completely destroyed during the Japanese War. The coldest temperature is about -8 C in January; the hottest about 30 C in July. The rainfall is from 1250 to 1750 mm mostly April to June. The population is about five million, with 1.5 million in the city proper.

ARRIVALS & DEPARTURES

The city is a 95-minute flight southwest of Shanghai, one hour northeast of Guilin, and 100 minutes south of Beijing. It has direct flights with Hong Kong, and 38 other cities. Changsha is on the main Beijing-Guangzhou railway line, 726 km and nine hours north of Guangzhou. It is 18 hours by train from Beijing.

ORIENTATION

The novel and movie *The Sand Pebbles* was set partly in Changsha during the Northern Expedition in the late 1920s. The hero was an engineer on an American gun boat, which sailed up the Yangtze through Lake Dongting and along the Xiang River. Changsha is also the setting of a more recent book, Liang Heng and Judith Shapiro's autobiographical *Son of the Revolution*, a refreshing look at growing up in Communist China and beating the system. The excellent but sad novel *A Small Town Called Hibiscus* is set in the southern part of this province during the Cultural Revolution.

In addition to Han, Hunan has many national minorities, including Tujia, Miao, Dong, Yao, Hui, Uygur and Zhuang.

WHERE TO STAY & EAT

The best hotels are the Huatian and the Grand Sun City Hotel. The Furama is the best four star. The Lotus is the best three star. Hotels here having been giving up to 55% discounts and adding a 10% service charge and 5% tax. The top hotels take credit cards and can change money.

DOLTON HOTEL, *149 Shaoshan Bei Road, 410011, Tel. 4168888, 4160901, Fax 4169999, 4160900. Y918-Y1118 for rooms, and Y1380-Y26888 for suites including 15% surcharge.*

GRAND SUN CITY HOTEL *(Shenglong Dajiudian), 298 Furong Nan Road, 410007, Tel. 5218888, Fax 5218288. E-mail: gschotel@public.cs.hn.cn. Five stars. Y880-1280 for rooms and Y1680-Y2380 for suites.*

There is an entertainment center, pool, and 375 rooms. A Zenith Hotel.

HUATIAN HOTEL *(Dajiudian), 380 Jiefang Dong Road, 410001, Tel. 4442888, Fax 4442270. Five stars. E-mail: resv@huatian.com. $98-$158 for rooms, and $188-$2380 for suites. 23 km from the airport; 1.5 km from the railway station.*

Built in 1990, this 17-story, 288-room hotel has an eight-story recreation building, executive floor, Chaozhou and Thai food. It also has a pool, bowling, gym and disco.

HUNAN FURAMA, *Four stars, Tel. 2298888, Fax 2291979.*

ZI DONG GE HUA TIAN HOTEL, *68 Ba Yi Dong Road, 410001, Tel. 2288888, Fax 2281688. Three stars. Y598-Y2360 for rooms and Y1560-Y3160 for suites.*

This is a branch of the Huatian Hotel above, two blocks away. This 400-room hotel has executive floors. Its big rooms have been discounted to $40 including Chinese food. With its downtown location, it's a good deal.

LOTUS HOTEL *(Furong Binguan), 8 Wuyi Dong Road, 410001. Three stars, Tel. 4401888, Fax 4465175. 15 km from the airport, and one km from the railway station. Y338.*

This 1984 hotel has 15 storys and 265 rooms.

SEEING THE SIGHTS

If you only have one day, the Hunan Provincial Museum, the embroidery factory, the Yue Lu Academy, and a walk on Orange Island are good choices.

The **Hunan Provincial Museum**, *28 Dongfeng Road, Tel. 4513123, open 8am-12 noon and 2:30pm-5pm,* is the main tourist attraction. Skip everything else if you are short on time. You must see the relics from these three 2,100-year-old Han tombs because of their excellent state of preservation and vast numbers. It takes about one hour.

The three tombs were of Li Tsang, chancellor to the Prince of Changsha and Marquis of Dai, his wife, and his son. The son died in 168 B.C. The body of the woman, 1.52 meters long and weighing 34.3 kilograms, is incredibly well preserved, with flesh, 16 teeth, and internal organs. The lungs, intestines, and stomach were removed after disinterment and preserved in formaldehyde. They are all on display in the basement. An autopsy revealed arteriosclerosis, gallstones, tuberculosis, and parasites. Death came to her suddenly at age 50; there were undigested melon seeds in her stomach. The body was wrapped in hemp and nine silk ribbons, and sealed from oxygen and water in three coffins surrounded by 5,000 kilograms of charcoal and sticky white clay. She died after her husband; maybe that is why her tomb is the largest, and she is the best preserved of all. She probably planned it herself.

The 5,000 relics include 1,800 pieces of lacquerware, many of which needed only cleaning to appear new. Look for the ear cups for wine and soup, and a make-up box with comb, mirror, powder, and lipstick. For her after-death use, she also had incense burners, clothes, silk fabrics, medicinal herbs, and nine musical instruments. Maybe she did play them! An inventory of the relics was written on bamboo strips, paper still being rare then.

The **Han tomb site**, only four km away in Mawangdui, is now just a large hole in the ground under a roof. You can see the pyramid-shaped hill, the neat, earthen walls, and staircase inside. Geomancy students can figure out the *feng shui*. Was it practiced then? Did the tomb face south?

The **Hunan Provincial Embroidery Factory**, *70 Bayi Xi Road, Tel. 2291061, 2291952 is open 8:30am-12 and 2:30pm-5pm.* It is a worthwhile visit. You can see this ancient craft being practiced and be amazed at the number of workers not wearing eyeglasses. Look for embroidery so fine it can be displayed from either side. Admission has been free.

A tour of the city includes **Tianxin Park** *with its small section of 600-plus-year-old city wall. It is open daily, 6am-8pm.* Five km-long **Juzi (Orange) Island** is in the middle of the Xiang River, probably the 'long sand' after which Changsha is named. It is just a pretty walk.

The **First Hunan Normal School**, *Shuyuan Road,* outside the south gate of the city, has a small museum. Mao studied and taught here in 1913-18 and 1920-21. The current structure, built in 1968, is a copy of the 1912 school and reflects its European connections. The entrance fee is Y15.

The **Changsha Museum** *is at 81 Bayi Road, Tel. 2257307.* It is new and centered on a recent find of 1700-year old bamboo slips or books.

NIGHTLIFE & ENTERTAINMENT

Local Huagu opera originated from provincial folk songs and ditties. The **Hunan Provincial Puppet Show Troupe** is well known. Performances can be arranged through travel agents if booked in advance. **Windows of the World Theme Park** has international song and dances performances at 7pm. *It's at Liuyang River Dong Bridge, Tel. 4256737, 4256763.*

SHOPPING

Made in the province are embroideries, brocade, batik, porcelain and pottery, chrysanthemum stone, peach stone and bamboo carvings, fans, firecrackers, lacquer reproductions, smoky quartz and bloodstone carvings, minority handicrafts and duck-down clothing. Look for these items at the **Friendship Store** and **Apollo Store**, *on Shaoshan Road near the Hua Tian Hotel.*

EXCURSIONS & DAY TRIPS
ZHANGJIAJIE

Zhangjiajie is 400 km northwest of Changsha, nine hours by bus; the express train leaves Changsha at 7:30am and arrives at 7:45pm. There's also a 30-minute flight, three times a day in summer, once in winter. It has flight connections also with seven other cities.

This is a 369-sq. km national forest, 35 km from Zhangjiajie in the western part of Hunan province. This well-maintained park has lots of guides and sedan chair porters eager to help you and it's full of beautiful hills, stone pillars, flowers and wild boar, monkeys and leopards. Thirteen different ethnic groups live here including the Miao, Zhuang, and Tujia in Jishou City. There are karst caves in Longshan county and white-water rafting on the Mongdong River in Yongshun County. A Forest Protecting Festival takes place the end of October. Visitors can walk to their hearts content.

The best hotel is the four-star Dragon International in town. The Pipaxi Guest House is in the forest. Hotels add a 14% surcharge.

DRAGON INTERNATIONAL HOTEL *(Xianglong Guoji Dajiudian), 46 Jiefang Road, Zhangjiajie, 416680. Four stars, Tel. 8226888 or Fax 8222935. Credit cards. Hong Kong joint-venture. $50. Hong Kong Tel. (852)2520-2266 or Fax 2529-1868.*

Built in 1994, this 260-room hotel is a 30-minute drive from the park, and six km from the airport.

PIPAXI GUEST HOUSE, *Zhang Jia Jie National Forest Park, 427401. 35 km from the airport. Tel. 5718888, Fax 5712257. Http:// www.hunan˜window.com/pipaxi. Three stars. Y200-Y480 for rooms, Y1280 for suites, plus 14% surcharge.*

Built in Tujia style, the Pipaxi was renovated in 1999. It has CNN and BBC, Y12 buffet breakfast, and takes credit cards. If you stay inside the park here, you only need to pay one entry fee.

Hunan CITS is at *55 Lingyuan Road, 427000, Tel. 8300136, Fax 8300139. E-mail: citszj@public.zj.hn.cn.* Try also the CITS Building, *Tianmen Road, Zhangjiajie, 427000, Tel. 8223968, Fax 8223668.* For **Hualong Travel Service**, *Tel. 8232858, Fax 8233333.* The telephone code is *0744.*

SHAOSHAN

Shaoshan is 104 km southwest of Changsha, a worthwhile 2.5 hour trip by road, 90 km by train. There is an airport but no flights scheduled. The countryside is lovely with tea plantations, orange groves and rice fields. This is the ***Birthplace of Chairman Mao**, a simple mud-brick farmhouse where the founder of the People's Republic was born on December 26, 1893.

He lived in this charming, and apparently peaceful village until 1910, when he left to study in Changsha. He returned briefly several times, holding meetings and conducting revolutionary activities. The Nationalists confiscated and destroyed the original house in 1929, but after 1949, the Communists rebuilt it along the original lines. Two families shared the house, the section on the left as you enter being Mao's. It is very sparsely furnished. The dining room still has the original small table, typical even for large families. The master bedroom has portraits of the parents and the bed in which he was born. Another room holds original farm tools.

The **museum**, with ten large galleries, is a ten-minute walk from the farmhouse. It is full of exhibits depicting his life. Also open is the **Water-Dropping Cave** where Mao Zedong stayed hidden for 11 days in 1966 and planned the Cultural Revolution. It is three km from Shaoshan. You can also visit the **family temple** and stay at the modest two-star **Shaoshan Hotel** *(Binguan), 108 Yingbin Road, Tel. 5685111, a five-minute walk from the museum.* **CTS** and **CITS**, *Tel. 682197, Fax 682197.* The telephone code *is 0732.*

YUEYANG

Yueyang, 2,000 years old, is on the north shore of Lake Dongting, just south of the Yangtze River, and is sometimes a stop on a Yangtze River cruise. It is 160 km north of Changsha and is close to the mother of all dragon boat races every June. The 19 meter-high **Yueyang Tower** was first built in 716 A.D. to train the navy. It was rebuilt in 1867 in the original Tang style. One of the eight Taoist genii, Lu Tung-pin with the supernatural sword, is credited with saving the tower from collapsing.

You can also visit **Junshan Island** which grows Junshan Silver Needles tea and a tree with red leaves on one side and green on the other. It is a bird-watcher's paradise. Try to imagine the Song dynasty when 10,000 troops were stationed here.

As for the **dragon boats**, in 278 B.C. in the nearby Miluo River, **Qu Yuan**, the great patriotic poet, drowned himself in protest against the destruction of the State of Chu by the first emperor of China. Ever since, this tragic event has been commemorated with races, usually held in June to feed the fish before the fish can eat Qu Yuan! The races are on Nan Lake north east of Yueyang. Travel agents can arrange the best place to watch, which is the east watchtower.

The best hotel in town is the three-star **China Bank Hotel** (*Zhong Yin Dajiudian*), *1 Front Road at the train station, Yueyang, Tel. 827-0666, Fax 8270111, 8262119. Y348.* For **CITS** *Tel. 8222482 or 82222386* and for **Yueyang CYTS Tours**, *Tel. 9013339. E-mail: qnix@public.yy.hn.cn.* The telephone code *is 0730.*

HENGSHAN MOUNTAIN

Hengshan Mountain is about 160 km south of Changsha, one of the Five Great Mountains of China. It has 72 peaks and about 20 Taoist and Buddhist temples. The most noteworthy is at **Nanyue**, occupying 98,000 square meters. First erected in 725 (Tang), it has Song and Ming architecture.

If you're planning on staying overnight, the two-star **Yinyuan Hotel** is best. It is at the foot of the mountain near the cable car at *70 Zhurong Road, Nanyue Town, Hengyang, Tel. 5661329.* A botanical garden is also there. You can eat vegetarian food at the **Zhusheng Temple**. A 1,800 meter-long cableway is now operating.

PRACTICAL INFORMATION

Business Hours, 8:30am-6pm for offices; 9am-9pm for stores.

Hunan China International Travel Service and **Overseas Tourist Corporation**, *11/F Xiaoyuan Mansion, Wuyi Dong Road, 410001. E-mail: citsgaow@public.cs.hn.cn. For the Euro-American Department, Tel. 2280439. E-mail: citsamer@public.cs.hn.cn. Http://www.hncits.com.*

Hunan Hua Tian China International Travel Service, *380 Jiefang Dong Road, 410001, Tel. 4442888 X 82737, Fax 4118148. E-mail: welcome@htcits.com.cn. Http://www.htcits.com.cn.*

Hunan Provincial Travel Bureau, *Chunhua Road at Bayi Dong Road, Wulaipai, 410001, Tel. 4724017, Fax 4720348.* Complaints and brochures.

Telephone Code, *0731*
Tourist Complaints, *contact Supervisory Bureau of Tourism Quality of Hunan Province, First Floor, Provincial Tourism Administration Building, Wulipai, Changsha, 410001, Tel. 4717614, Fax 4720348.*

NANNING

The capital of Guangxi Zhuang Autonomous Region, **Nanning** is in the southwestern part of Guangxi near the northeastern border of Vietnam. The urban population is one million.

Nanning has a subtropical climate, resulting in great fruit, flowering trees, and mild, humid weather. Its hottest is 38 C; its coldest is 5 C. The annual precipitation of about 1300 mm. falls mainly May to September. Nanning is worth visiting because of its minorities, its karst caves, medicinal herb garden, and its location as a gateway to Vietnam.

Founded in 214 B.C., Nanning was the provincial capital from 1912 to 1936, and after 1949. Guilin, its sister city in Guangxi, is more famous. It has light industries like pearl farming, arts and crafts, sugar refining, soft drinks, beer and food processing.

ARRIVALS & DEPARTURES

You can reach Nanning in about seven hours by train leaving Guilin at 7:50am and arriving at 2:40pm. The Nanning-Kunming railway should be open for passengers in 1999 and takes 12 hours from Kunming. An expressway should be completed in 2000. Currently the once-a-day long distance bus takes 12 hours. You can also get to Nanning by air from 16 cities, Hanoi (30 minutes) and Hong Kong (over an hour). It is about a 33-km, 40-minute drive now from the airport, but it'll be 20 minutes soon with the opening of the new expressway.

WHERE TO STAY

The top hotels are the Majestic and Nanning International Hotel. Rates are approximately Y800 but have been discounted recently by 40%. Hotels add an 11% surcharge. The Majestic has a three-star section known as Mingyuan Fandian.

MAJESTIC HOTEL (*Mingyuan Xindu Fandian*), *38 Xin Min Road, 530012, Tel. 2830808, Fax 2830811. E-mail: myxdhtl@public.nn.gx.cn. 3.5 km from the railway station. $100 including western breakfast. Five stars.*

The Majestic sits in a 100,000 square-meter park in Nanning's commercial district. Built in 1995, it has 300 rooms with in-room safes, in-house movies, and CNN and Star Sports. It has executive floors, a call-waiting feature on its telephones, and a 24-hour business center. It

serves Cantonese, Asian and American food, and has a deli. For your health, it has a gym and outdoor pool, jacuzzi, jogging, tennis, and golf. **NANNING INTERNATIONAL HOTEL** *(Guoji Dajiudian), 88 Minzu Dong Avenue, 530022, Tel. 5851818, Fax 5886789. E-mail: pimtbc@public.nn.gx.cn. Four stars. Rooms cost Y768-Y888; suites cost Y1128-Y11888.*
It has an executive floor.
YONGJIANG BINGUAN, *Tel. 2803072. E-mail: yjhng@public.nn.gx.cn.* This is the best three star hotel in Nanning.

WHERE TO EAT

The food here is much like Cantonese. Please avoid eating endangered species. The **Sun City Restaurant** in the three-star Yongjiang Hotel is good. It's at *41 Jiangbin Dong Road, Tel. 2808123 X 5085.* Otherwise, the restaurants in the top hotels are where you should eat.

SEEING THE SIGHTS

The **Guangxi Museum,** *Minzu Road, Tel. 2810907, 6020420* has botanical and zoological specimens, historical relics, and Taiping history. It also boasts the largest collection of bronze drums (over 500) in China. The 126.5 hectare **Nanhu** (South Lake) **Park** in the southeast has 1200 varieties of medicinal herbs, orchids and miniature landscapes. The **Guangxi Botanical Garden of Medicinal Plants**, eight km from the city in the eastern suburbs, has 2100 kinds on 200 hectares. It also raises animals for medicinal purposes.

The **Yiling Cave**, 32 km north in Wuming County, is much like a Guilin cave, with colored lights to highlight weird rock formations. Visitors usually walk 1100 meters. Outside is a pavilion built in the elaborate style of the Zhuang people, *Tel. 6225114, 3219052.*

For those interested in the customs of national minorities, visit a **Zhuang village** in Wuming County, and in Nanning, the **Guangxi Minority Nationality College** *(Tel. 3214141, 5313138).* The **Guangxi Art College** *(Tel.5322571)* teaches the art, music, and authentic dances of the minorities. The **Ethnic Garden** displays the real houses of the Zhuang, Yao, Miao, and Dong nationalities, and a Dong bridge and drum tower. Arts and crafts are demonstrated.

Twelve different nationalities live in the region, of whom the Zhuang form over one-third. They are somewhat similar to the hill people of northern Thailand. The colorful Miao and Yao live here also. This makes Nanning a good place to look for handicrafts to study and buy.

The Taiping Heavenly Kingdom originated from *****Jintian village**, 272 km northeast of the city. This was the most extensive peasant uprising in Chinese history. It started in 1851 and took over a large portion of the country with a capital in Nanjing. Its disruptions were largely responsible for the immigration of Chinese people from south China to America, Australia, and other parts of Asia. At the home of Wei Changhui, one of the leaders, revolutionists made weapons. Read *God's Chinese Son, The Taiping Heavenly Kingdom of Hong Xiuquan* by Jonathan Spence.

SHOPPING

Locally made are Zhuang brocade, ethnic embroidery, bamboo, and pottery ware. The province also sells artistic shell, horn, and feather products, and stone carvings. Also produced are Xishan tea and Milky Spring Wine. You can visit the silk factory. Locally grown are jack fruit, mango, almond, and longan fruit.

You might want to check out the following stores: **Arts and Crafts Service**, *Xinhua Road, Tel. 2822779;* **Foreign Languages Bookstore**, *Minsheng Road, Tel. 2827033;* **Nanning Antique Store**, *19-2 Gucheng Road, Tel. 2807810;* and **Guangxi Tourist Produce Market**, *Tel. 2803019.*

EXCURSIONS & DAY TRIPS

The most important tourist destination is of course **Guilin** (see separate entry below), but there's also **Beihai** for its beach, and **Liuzhou** for its terraced hills and more minorities. **Vietnam** is also nearby (see sidebar below).

BEIHAI

Beihai is Guangxi's sea port, and one of the 14 Open Coastal Cities. A tourist train from Guilin connects it with Nanning and Liuzhou. It has a splendid ten km beach, and the largest holiday resort in Asia is being built there. It grows pearls and seafood, and should have cruises to Vietnam now.

SHANGRI-LA HOTEL, *33, Chating Road, 536000, Tel. 2062288, Fax 2050085. Http://www.Shangri-La.com. Four stars aiming for five stars. $95-$155 for rooms, $476-$1524 for suites. It is 20 km from the airport, nine km from the railway station and 12 km from Silver Beach, the main tourist attraction. It is on the CAAC bus route from the airport.*

This 1996 hotel is the best in town. It has 425 rooms, an outdoor pool, two tennis courts, gym and sauna, CNBC and Star Plus. Its ballroom can accommodate up to 2000 guests.

FURAMA (Fuli Hua), *31 Beibu Gulf Chating Road, 536000, Tel. 2050080, Fax 2050085. Three stars. About $60.*

CITS has a desk at the Shangri-La Hotel. It's office is at *10 Beibuwan Dong Road, 536000, Tel. 2062999, 2062777 and Fax 2062525.* **CTS** is at *2F,*

Huangdu Hotel, Guizhou Road, Beihai, Tel. 3033935, Fax 3035256. Beihai's telephone code *is 0779.* Business hours are 8am-12 noon; 2:30pm-5:30pm; store hours are 9am-9pm.

LIUZHOU

Liuzhou is two hours by express bus or train from Guilin with many Dong, Hui, Miao, Yao, and Zhuang nationalities and festivals. It has the **Liuzhou Temple** and tomb of the famous Tang writer who worked to free women from being bond slaves. There are also the **Dule Caves** (much like Guilin's) and the Bai Lain Cave where **Liujiang** (Liuchiang) **Man** lived 20,000 to 30,000 years ago. Open now is the **Longshen Minority Area** (Long Ji Ti Tian) with Yao, Zhuang and Dong minorities and somewhat primitive Y20 hotels. You really need an extra one or two days to see the spectacular rice terraces.

JINGDU HOTEL, *40 Yuejin Road, Tel. 2860188, Fax 2816409.*

This German joint venture is the best hotel here. It has an excellent western restaurant with real ground coffee, tennis and good English. A room costs Y300.

LIUZHOU GRAND HOTEL *(Fandian), 2 Longcheng Road, 545001, with IDD and pool. Tel. 2828336, Fax 2821443. Three stars. $45.*

A new four-star hotel should open in 1999.

A good time to visit is during the **Dragon Boat Festival** (5th day of the 5th month), the **Zhuang Song Festival** (3rd day of the 3rd month), **Lantern Festival** (15th day of the 1st month), and **Mid-Autumn Festival** (15th day of the 8th month). All are according to the lunar calendar. At the Song Festival, small groups of male and female singers compete with each other in wit, knowledge, and vocal quality. Then the boys chase the girls they like to continue the contest with more privacy. The festival also includes throwing embroidered balls, and dragon and buffalo dances.

The **Zuojiang Huashan Tourist Area** has the **Mount Hua Rock Paintings** which are found along the Ming River, 180 km away from Nanning near the Vietnam border. Here you can take a boat trip to wonder at primitive riverside paintings, and the dances inspired by the paintings. You can also watch local people pan for gold and visit the **Longrui Nature Reserve**, the only place in the world where you can find rare white-headed langur monkeys and golden camellias.

You can also travel to **Guilin** from here.

CITS is at *3 Youyi Road, Tel. and Fax 280180.* **China Travel Service** is at *334 East Lane, Yayu Road, Tel. 2855409, Fax 2828417.* The telephone code is *0772.*

GOING TO VIETNAM

*You need a valid Vietnam visa, not available in Pingxiang nor Nanning, but in Guangzhou. You can fly from Nanning to Hanoi any Monday or Thursday, or take the No. 617 train four hours from Nanning to Pingxiang. After crossing the border, you change to the Vietnamese train. To Hanoi from there takes another four hours or so. **Pingxiang CITS** is at 68 Beida Road, Tel. 8523475, Fax 8521745. An overnight boat goes from Beihai in China and arrives next day in Haiphong in Vietnam.*

PRACTICAL INFORMATION

Business hours: offices 8am-12 noon and 2:30pm-5:30pm; stores, 9am-10pm.

Guangxi Nanning China Travel Service, *14 Jiaoyu Road, Nanning, Tel. 5320165, Fax 5320753, 5321294. E-mail: nncts@public.nn.gx.cn.*

Guangxi Professional Worker's International Travel Service, *27 Xinghu Road, 530022, Tel. 01397864073, Tel. and Fax 2816147. E-mail: chang@public.nn.gx.cn. Contact: Ms. Chen Ying.*

Nanning China International Travel Service, *68 Chaoyang Road, Nanning, 530012, 68 Chaoyang Road, Tel. and Fax 2824742.*

Nanning Municipal Tourism Bureau, *68 Chaoyang Road, Tel. and Fax 2824742.* Write for a list of interesting tour possibilities including forest preserves, Zhuang traditional medicine, hot sand treatment, and dates of festivals.

Nanning Prefectural Tourism Administration, *38 East Mingxiu Road, Tel. and Fax 3124900.*

Tourist Complaints, contact Supervisory Bureau of Tourism Quality, *Tel. 2802312, Fax 2801248.*

Telephone Code, *0771*

GUILIN

(Kweilin: City of Cassia Trees)

In northeast Guangxi, the first 'province' west of Guangdong, **Guilin** was founded as a prefecture in 214 B.C. It is famous for its vertical limestone mountains rising above flat tree-lined streets, rice and water chestnut fields, and the meandering Li and Taohua (Peach Blossom) Rivers. It is also known for its caves. The **Li River cruise** is the main reason tourists flock here.

Guilin developed with the opening of the Ling Canal over 2200 years ago. It was the provincial capital until 1014 A.D. and a command post for

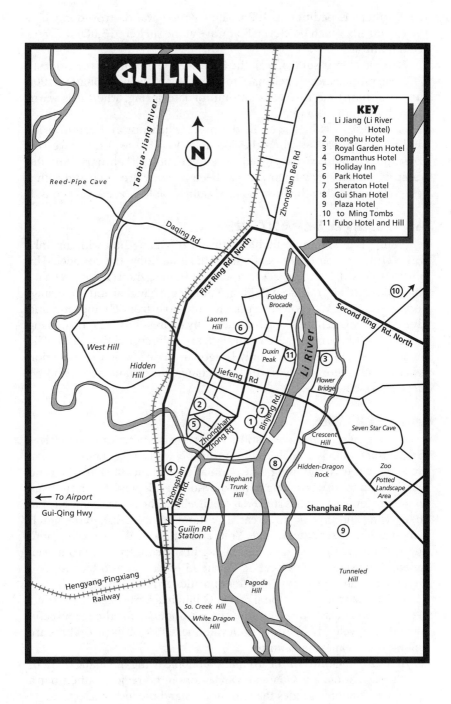

the Northern Expedition in 1928. The Japanese war destroyed much of the city during which the Seven Star Cave alone sheltered 5,000 refugees from bombs.

The weather is subtropical, the hottest 36 C in August; the coldest - 3 C. The rainy season is February to May, the annual precipitation 1900 mm. The best time to visit is autumn or late spring, when it is warm enough to ignore the rain.

The scenery is best seen in the mist, which inspired centuries of landscape painters, or when the sun and clouds conspire to give you constantly changing scenes. From November until the February rains, the water in the river may be low. It has been recently dredged, and with a reservoir controlling the flow, boats should be able to use it year-round.

ARRIVALS & DEPARTURES

Guilin is a 55-minute flight northwest of Guangzhou with air links with 22 other cities, and direct flights with Hong Kong. It is connected by tourist train with Nanning (seven hours) and Guangzhou (14 hours!). You can also reach it by rail from Beijing, Kunming, Shanghai and Zhanjiang, and by bus with Wuzhou (the port for the boat from Guangzhou and Hong Kong). Liuzhou is one hour away by express bus. The Liangjiang airport is 40 km from the city and a taxi could cost about Y120. The Sheraton's shuttle bus meets only Dragonair flights. A new train station is being built in north Guilin which will change the distances to the hotels after it is open.

ORIENTATION

Guilin has only one international-class tourist attraction, the **Li River cruise**. But Guilin is a small and beautiful city with a relaxing pace, clean air, and fun tourist shopping. The population is about 400,000 urban and 1,280,000 in total, nearly one in ten of whom are dependent on tourism. In the last few years, it has started to get livelier. The land is generally flat so bicycling and walking are great. The standard of English in the hotels is higher than other cities its size. You can spend a week here poking into alleys, climbing rice terraces, and hiking in the countryside. From even quieter Yangshuo you can canoe on the Li River and also bicycle. You could take side trips to investigate minorities around Nanning.

While many tours see the sights in Guilin in a fairly hectic pace (tour groups need at least two days), the city is wonderful for the resourceful individual traveler, a favorite of honeymooners. Best of all, prices here are among the cheapest in China.

Because one-third of the 10 million people living in Guangxi are of the Zhuang nationality, Guangxi is an 'autonomous region' rather than a 'province.' National guides may not understand the local dialect.

Guilin is one of the 24 historical cities protected by the State Council. Some of its houses are antiques and you should stroll through the past at your leisure. Taxis are plentiful.

WHERE TO STAY

Foreign tourism is down, so haggle on prices here all year round.

The top hotels are the **Sheraton** and the **Royal Garden**, then the **Gui Shan** and the **Holiday Inn**. The **Garden** is the most beautiful. The less luxurious **Universal** and **Fubo** are also good, especially for their location and Cantonese food. The Fubo is better than the Universal. The **Plaza** looked acceptable but is too far out to be considered except as a last resort. The Royal Garden and Holiday Inn have the widest twin beds.

The **Ronghu** is a "socialist" hotel with a noisy atmosphere. The Osmanthus seems to be going downhill, and is in a crowded neighborhood. The English is poor.

The best location for business people are the Holiday Inn and the Ronghu on a lake near the city hall but the city is small and location not all that important. The best location for tourists is the west bank of the Li River close to tourist shopping and the night cormorant tour.

On the east bank are the Royal Garden and the Gui Shan, less convenient to shops but still good. The Park is pretty, but even further out in the suburbs. The Lijiang Hotel is good for budget travelers.

The following prices are subject to change, discounts, and an 18% tax and service charge. Top hotels have money change, business centers, western coffee shops, and gyms. They take credit cards.

GUILIN ROYAL GARDEN HOTEL *(Di Yuan Jiudian), Yanjiang Road, 541004. Five stars. Tel. 5812411, 5813611, Fax 5815051. E-mail: glrghtl@gl.col.com.cn; http://www.cbw.com/hotel/royalgarden. Six km from the railway station. Five stars. $110-$120 for rooms; $230-$1500 for suites. You can walk to the ethnic village from here.*

Built in 1987, this beautiful hotel has eight stories, 335 spacious rooms, wide beds, but smallish bathrooms. It has good furniture and decor but rooms could be a long walk from its elevators. There's CNN, Australian TV and Star TV. It has a huge atrium garden coffee shop, Japanese and continental restaurants, and 24-hour room service. There's also a clinic, outdoor pool and tennis, and it has mountain bikes for rent.

SHERATON GUILIN *(Wen Hua Fandian), Bing Jiang Nan Road, 541001. Five stars. Tel. 2825588, Fax 2825598. $110-$160 for rooms, $225-$385 for suites. Five km from the railway station.*

This 1988 hotel has six stories and 430 large rooms, some non-smoking. It has satellite television, 24-hour room service, Cantonese and Sichuan food. To keep you in good shape, it has a 20-metre outdoor pool, sauna, gym, and bicycles for hire. Its beautiful atrium lobby and garden with waterfall has a pianist playing evenings. Reservations are usually held until 4pm the same day. It has a Dragonair office.

HOLIDAY INN GUILIN *(Jia Ru Binguan), 14 Ronghu Nan Road, 541002. Four stars, Tel. 2823950, Fax 2822101. E-mail: glhi@public.glptt.gx.cn. $110-120 for rooms, $230 for suites. 3.5 km to the railway station.*

Built in 1987, this nine-story, 259-room hotel has a nice intimate atmosphere. It has Cantonese, Sichuan and Asian food, satellite television, health club and bicycles. It can provide lunch boxes for boat trips, or if groups book a whole boat, it can provide food and beverage service. It can also set up a barbecue on Yao mountain. There's a gym, steambath and outdoor pool.

WINDSOR GUI SHAN HOTEL *(Guishan Dajiudian), Chuan Shan Road, 541004. Four stars. Tel. 5813388, Fax 5813856, 5814851. E-mail: guishan@public.gl.ptt.gx.cn. Http:/www.windsorhotel.com.hk. $90-$250. Five km from the airport. Suburban setting between two rivers near Seven Star Park.*

This good institutional-looking hotel was built in 1988 and should be renovating again in 1999. It has five stories, four connecting buildings and could be a long walk to your room. Its 607 rooms include some for non-smokers and some designed for Moslems. It has western, Cantonese and Moslem restaurants, and a good room service menu. There's an outdoor pool, gym, steam room, jacuzzi and bowling. It also has bicycles to rent, CNN and Star Plus, and lots of shops. Managed by Windsor Hotels International (H.K.)

FUBO HOTEL *(Fubo San Zhuang), 121 Binjiang Road, 541001. Four stars. Tel. 2829988, Fax 2822328. E-mail: fubo@public.glptt.gx.cn. $80-$150. About eight km from the airport and next to Fubo Hill with a great view of the mountains.*

This 1992 hotel should be renovated in 1998-99. It has four stories, 150 rooms, some non-smoking, CNN and Star Plus, Cantonese and Sichuan food. It has generally friendly and thoughtful service, but the hotel is a bit scruffy. English might be a problem.

HOTEL UNIVERSAL GUILIN *(Huan Qiu Dajiudian), 1 Jiefang Dong Road, 541001. Three stars, Tel. 2828228, Fax 2823868. Seven km from the railway station. $80-$150. Closest hotel to Liberation Bridge.*

Built in 1988, this hotel has seven stories, 230 rooms, and no CNN. It has Cantonese and Italian restaurants and a disco, and lower standards than other hotels.

GUILIN PARK HOTEL *(Gui Hu Fandian), 1, Luosi Hill, Laoren Shan Qian, 541001. Three stars aiming for four. Tel. 2828899, Fax 2822296. $70-$90. 5.5 km from the railway station. Very pretty suburban setting in northwest part of town next to the Laoren Hill and thought to have good feng-shui.*

This 1990 hotel has five stories, 268 rooms, satellite television, Cantonese and Zhejiang food. It has a gym, steam bath and sauna, and outdoor pool. It is a bit run down and English is a problem. Managed by Merit International Hotels.

GUILIN PLAZA *(Guan Guang Jiudian), 20 Li Jiang Road, 541004. Three stars. Tel. 5812488, Fax 5813328. E-mail: glgg@glcol.co.cn. $70-$400. Five km from the railway station and one km from Zhishan Bridge. In the eastern suburbs near the International Exhibition Center, nowhere near good shopping.*

Built in 1991, this hotel has 13 stories, 288 rooms, European, Cantonese and Sichuan restaurants. It has bicycles, Star TV, an outdoor pool, gym, and sauna. It is primarily for tour groups, is difficult to get a taxi, and English is a problem. Macau CTS Management.

OSMANTHUS HOTEL *(Dangui Fandian), 451 Zhong Shan Nan Road, 541002. Three stars. Tel. 3834300, 3832261, Fax 3835316. E-mail: glosmh@public.glptt.gx.cn. One km from the railway station. Three-star west wing $70-80.*

Built in 1986, this hotel has 14 stories and 214 rooms, its even-numbered rooms with river view. It is somewhat rundown and has soft beds, health center with outdoor pool, and Cantonese *dim sum*. Its rooms are stuffy but they should be okay after the airconditioning is turned on. It has a disco, bicycles for rent, and problems with carpets and English. Vista International Hotels management.

RONGHU HOTEL *(Fandian), 17 Ronghu Bei Road, 541001, Tel. 2823811, Fax 2825390. $65-$180. Four km from the railway station. Buildings Five and Six are three stars. Five has smaller rooms and fewer services. Eight buildings on large hilly grounds, total 455 rooms.*

The atmosphere here in this government guest house is noisy. It has a Japanese restaurant, good Chinese food, and brews its own German beer. It has a gym, tennis court, bicycles for rent, and conference services. Both buildings have satellite television but no CNN. Other buildings are older, with high ceilings, old-fashioned decor and are not as conveniently located.

LIJIANG HOTEL, *1 Shanhu Bei Road, 541001, Tel. 2822881, Fax 2822891. Three stars.*

This, one of the oldest hotels in town, has 388 large guest rooms, Star TV, sauna, a relaxing western restaurant and bar, and is spotlessly clean.

WHERE TO EAT

Chinese food here is usually Guangxi or Cantonese. Food is served with chili sauce and fermented bean curd as condiments. You should like bean curd if you like blue cheese. Mix a bit with your rice. The local rice wine, Sanhua, is made from a 200-year-old recipe. The top hotels are the best for Chinese and western food. **Night food markets** are outside the Osmanthus.

SHERATON GUILIN, *Bing Jiang Nan Road, Tel. 2825588.*

The Sheraton has especially good pizza. Its **Studio Cafe** (above its Food Street), is famous for hamburgers. Its **Food Street** has noodles and *won ton*. Both are on the southwest side of the hotel.

GUILIN ROYAL GARDEN HOTEL *(Di Yuan Jiudian), Yanjiang Road. Tel. 5812411.*

The Royal Garden Hotel has good Japanese food, as well as good Chinese cuisine.

YI YUAN FAN DIAN RESTAURANT, *106 Nan Huan Road, Tel. 282-0470.*

With its wooden exterior, this is a good restaurant.

JIULONG RESTAURANT, *almost across from the Osmanthus Hotel.* Good Cantonese food.

LONG ZHE TEA TAVERN, *outside the gate of Seven Star Park, just around the corner from the Royal Garden. Tel. 5812852.*

This is a decent vegetarian restaurant.

SEEING THE SIGHTS

For those in a hurry, one morning could be spent at Fubo Hill and Seven Star Park, and the afternoon at Reed Flute Cave, Diecai Hill and Elephant Hill. Tourist attractions usually open 8am-5pm. The Li River boat trip could be enjoyed on a second day. The Ming Tomb Museum, the **Guilin Museum** at *Xishan Park, Tel. 2822892,* Gao Shan for the view, a handicraft factory, shopping, just walking or cycling or the Ling Canal can complete your third or fourth day.

Diecai (Folded Brocade) **Hill**, *Tel. 2822326,* 3.6 km from the Sheraton Hotel, is the tallest hill in town at 73 meters. The peaks are named Bright Moon, Crane, and Seeing Around the Hill. Partway up, past the ornamental arch, is the Wind Cave with Ming and Song poems and memorials on its walls. You can get a good view of the area from the top.

Fubo (Whirlpool) **Hill**, *Tel. 2823620,* a short walk north of the Sheraton Hotel, named after famous Han Marshal Ma Fubo, is 60 meters high. At the base is a 7.5 ton iron Qing bell belonging to the temple originally here. To the right is the **Cave of the Returned Pearl**, where guides used to tell you a dragon left a gift of a pearl for a poor family, who returned it. 'This illustrates the honesty of working people.' Nearby is a rock where Ma Fubo tested his sword, and a cliff with Tang buddhas. Partway up on the east side is a pavilion with a view of the river.

Qixing (Seven Star) **Park**, *Tel. 5813652,* 2.7 km from the Sheraton Hotel, is about 10 sq km. It contains a zoo, Camel Hill (with nearby miniature garden), and Seven Star Hill whose seven peaks are positioned like the stars in the Big Dipper. **Seven Star Cave** on the west side of **Potaraka Hill** has three levels; visitors enter the middle one. It is bigger than Reed Flute Cave, one km long, 43 meters at its widest, and 27 meters at its highest. Colored lights highlight the grotesque limestone formations. Just think, you will be following in the footsteps of tourists from the Sui (581-618) dynasty!

A forest of cassia trees blossom in spring and a 700-year old stone replica of the **Flower Bridge** (Song) spans a stream. Originally built of wood but destroyed in a flood, the bridge was designed so that the water below reflects its arches to form a complete circle.

The **'Cave for Hiding a Dragon'** looks like it could snugly fit a dinosaur. The most famous of the stone Song steles nearby lists people doomed for execution. The emperor sent copies around China (although paper was invented by then), and when the verdict was reversed, all but the stele in Guilin were destroyed. Also on the west side of **Putuo** (Potaraka) **Hill** is the Yuanfeng (Deep and Windy) Cave, and on top, the **Putuo Temple** (good views) and Guanyin Cave.

Ludi (Reed Flute) **Cave**, *Tel. 2602241*, is eight or nine km from the Sheraton Hotel. One km long, this cave takes about 40 minutes to explore. The temperature inside is a cool 20 C. The lighting is cleverly placed so that with a bit of imagination, the limestone resembles a giant goldfish, a Buddha, a wall of assorted vegetables, etc. The reeds that grow at the entrance gave this cave its name.

Xiangbi (Elephant Trunk) **Hill**, *Tel. 3850544*, 1.4 km from the Sheraton Hotel, at the junction of the Li and Taohua Rivers, really does look like an elephant drinking. **Shuiyue** (Moon-in-Water) **Cave** is between its trunk and front legs. **Elephant Eye Cave** is where you would expect. The Samantabhadra Pagoda tops the hill.

Duxiu (Unique Beauty) **Peak** was the site of the mansion of Zhu Shouqian, grandson of Emperor Hongwu of the Ming, which dates from 1393. Destroyed during the Qing, and again during the Japanese war, it is now the teachers' university. Today, only the original wall, its gates and steps remain.

The **Jingjiang Ming Tombs** are a good place to bicycle to. You pass old villages, water buffalo herds, mountains and several intriguing Ming cemeteries, a total of 320 tombs in 100 sq km. All persons buried here in relatively simple graves are descendants of the Ming emperor's family. A museum, *Tel. 5827276*, and several guardian statues of animals, servants and officials are at the unexcavated tumulus of the grandson Zhu Shou Qian Chi of the dynasty founder's older brother. He died in 1370 A.D. Much smaller and less elaborate than the Ming tombs near Beijing, they are worth a visit if you have the time. The museum is open daily 9am-5pm.

There's also **Yao Shan** (Broadcast Mountain), which is 300 meters high with a road to the top, but there's nothing more there than good views. To see if the chair lift is working, *Tel. 5814592*. It should be operating 9am-4pm. You can hire one of the Royal Garden Hotel's mountain bikes, and take off between the rice paddies and water chestnuts fields.

There is the **Li River Folk Customs Center** (Feng Qing Yuan) beyond the Royal Garden Hotel on Yanjiang Road. It now has Miao, Dong and Zhuang buildings, a lovely wind-and-rain bridge, Dong drum tower - all great for photographs. But its show isn't very good and not daily. The center is open 8am-10pm daily.

You can still visit the **Lingqu** (Ling Canal, *Tel. 6221913*) dug in 214 B.C. to connect the Chang (Yangtze) and the Zhu (Pearl) rivers. It was an inland route to Guangzhou, used as such until the 1930s. It is still important for irrigation, of interest to engineers and history fans. It has 18 locks and sections, and starts about 57 km north of Guilin in Xing'an County. You can ride a small bamboo raft and enjoy its tranquillity and ancient bridge.

Visits to the rice terraces at Longsheng and minority villages can be done in a hurried day.

Li River Trips

You can book the **Li River boat trip** directly (*Tel. 2825502)* or with a travel agent or your hotel. The price is about the same. If you want to try for a cheaper trip, you could shop around for boats for Chinese tourists. These leave near the Universal Hotel. Be aware that guides here speak only Chinese, the boats are not as clean, and there is no air-conditioning.

Boats for foreigners leave from **Zhu Jiang wharf** about 20 km from the city. Only some are air-conditioned and not all have protection from the rain or sun on the roof deck. The ride from Zhu Jiang to **Yangshuo** is 59 km and takes about four hours. Prices usually include lunch and the bus back to Guilin from Yangshuo about mid-afternoon.

For more information directly from the cruise folks, contact the **Guilin Tourism Motor Boat Co.**, *3 Fuxing Road, Tel. 5815595, 5813306.*

The Li River, normally 50 to 100 meters wide, winds its way between some incredible stone peaks, the highest about 80 meters. Pollution control has been upgraded, but you still notice dishes being washed in the river.

Look for **Crown Cave** (shaped like the British imperial crown), a cock with tail up bending down to pick up rice, followed shortly by the U-shaped **Ram's Hoof Mountain** on the right. On the right is **Conch Shell Hill**, then a temple on a cliff. If you're trying to save on camera film, the most beautiful area is between Yangdi Village and Snail Hill, that is, between Number Nine and Number 16 on the map they give you.

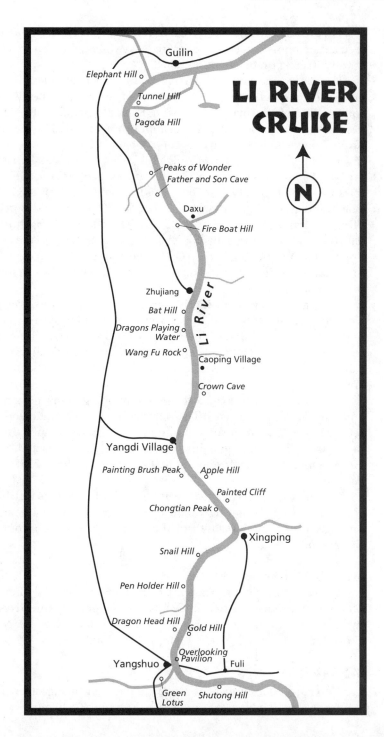

Guilin

Elephant Hill

LI RIVER CRUISE

Tunnel Hill

Pagoda Hill

N

Peaks of Wonder
Father and Son Cave

Daxu

Fire Boat Hill

Li River

Zhujiang

Bat Hill

Dragons Playing
Water

Wang Fu Rock

Caoping Village

Crown Cave

Yangdi Village

Painting Brush Peak

Apple Hill

Painted Cliff

Chongtian Peak

Xingping

Snail Hill

Pen Holder Hill

Dragon Head Hill

Gold Hill

Overlooking
Pavilion

Yangshuo

Fuli

Green
Lotus

Shutong Hill

On the way, look for large **cormorants** (real birds, not stone), usually seen sitting on fishing boats. If you're lucky you might even watch them at work, fishing on behalf of humans.

Yangshuo, the tiny town at the end of the boat ride, has a park, museum, good curio shopping, and an old temple. If time allows, you could walk along the main street to the right of the landing. The **museum** has copies of famous paintings of galloping horses and Li River scenes by **Xu Beihong** who lived here between 1935 and 1938.

You might want to stay overnight, bike, hike, or rent a banana boat for Y15. Good for bicycling at Y5 a day is the road to Camel Hill Resort towards Moon Hill. A favorite hang-out for foreigners is the **Cafe Under The Moon** at *83, Xi Jie (West Street), Tel. 8825000*. The best hotel is the three-star **Paradise Hotel** *(Tel.8822109)*. The cheaper **Yangshuo Hotel** has rooms with private baths for Y20 but hot water only in the evening. You can take a public bus back to Guilin the next day giving you more time to stroll along Xi Jie Street and relax over a cappuccino. You can still enjoy the same lovely scenery.

A variation is a **two-day Li River cruise** with stops at Daxu village and a minority cultural center. There is overnight camping at Crown Cave in tents, or the simple **Misty Cloud Hotel**, *Tel. 3609523*. Twenty-nine km south of Guilin at Cao Ping village, **Crown Cave** has several levels and a cable car. It also has a subterranean river on which you can boat for three km.

After caving, people can also swim, rent boats, sauna, get a massage and visit the nearby villages. The only access seems to be by boat. The setting is beautiful and gives photographers a chance to capture the river in a variety of different lights. For information, contact the **Guilin Huazhiguan Tourist Development Co.**, *Tel. 2835968, 2835989, Fax 2835988*.

President Clinton changed the unknown **Yu Cun village** with his 1998 visit. Other tourists now also want to go there. You take a boat for 45 minutes from Xingping south of the Crown Cave, or 1.5 hours from Yangshuo.

Festivals & Theme Parks

Festivals include the **Cassia Festival** in March, and the annual **Mountain and River Festival** in October or November (three days). One night is spent in the mountains with the minorities. See also Nanning above for Liuzhou, 140 km by highway from Guilin.

SHOPPING

You can buy locally-grown oranges, pomelo, and mangosteens (*luohan guo*) in season. Guilin also produces artistic pottery, bamboo, new and old-style wood carvings, redwood chopsticks, woven and plated bamboo, dough figures, stone exercise balls, tablecloths, embroidery, and proletarian items like bicycle bells and down jackets.

The main shopping area is along **Zhongshan Zhong Road** where you can find the best department store, **Nikko Nikko Do**, between Jiefang and Zhongshan Roads, open 9am-9:30pm, Tel. 2819856.

Haggling is imperative in the markets and antique stores. You can visit the **Myer Guilin Jewelry Manufacturing Company**, at 211 Li Zhong Road, Tel. 2834442. It exports to the United States and Europe but does not usually sell in China.

The **night tourist market** between the Universal and Sheraton hotels has 100 stalls and is full of jewelry, tea pots, old gilded wood carvings, silk shirts, table cloths, porcelain, wooden ducks, 'opium pipes.' etc. Occasionally you can find something really valuable like 12" long, old, gilded wood carvings for Y100 a pair, circular crocheted table cloths six feet in diameter for Y80, and a fine child's silver necklace with bells (I bought one; they asked Y600 but gave in at Y140). Avoid ethnic earrings because they have big stems requiring big ear holes.

Yangshuo's riverside market is huge and has the same sort of curios for sale but day trippers only have about 20 minutes between the boat and the bus.

Prices are cheaper in Guilin at the **Wa Yiao Tourist Wholesale Market** which supplies both these markets. It is also open to the public, and is 15 minutes by car southeast of the Sheraton on the way to the river cruise.

NIGHTLIFE & ENTERTAINMENT

The **night boats** to watch the **cormorants** can take a minimum of 45 minutes from the Er Hao Mao Tou, Number Two Pier near the Universal Hotel. Cormorant fishing is traditionally done at night by men so their wives can take their catch to market the next morning. The process is fascinating, the light on the fisherman's bamboo raft attracting the tiny fish. The birds swim underwater and jump back on board the raft with fish tails sticking out of their beaks. Alas, they give up their catch to the fisherman.

There are **'ethnic' dance and song performances** at the Gui Shan (Y80) and Royal Garden Hotels (about Y60). Both are entertaining, the same quality, and start at 8pm every evening. The **acrobatic and minority show** at the **Spring Theatre** near Ronghu Lake has a good reputation and Sheraton can arrange for tickets (about Y100 including transportation). If you want a **real minority show**, it's best to go on the trip to Longsheng, where performances are sometimes held. Better still, go to a minority festival.

Local bars are around the Sheraton: look for the **Yiren Bar** behind it, and **Lovers' Bar** opposite it on *Renmin Road*. The best disco is the **Go Go** on *Yiren Road, Tel. 2856821,* behind the Sheraton. It has games and a variety show as well for Y15. **Men Bin** has a good karaoke bar with songs in English. It is also behind the Sheraton. Be forewarned of bars outside hotels that overcharge for the drinks of hostesses who invite themselves to sit with you.

The 18-hole Twin Peaks and 18-hole Golden Fortune **golf courses** are both good. The latter is near the pier where you board the Li River cruise.

PRACTICAL INFORMATION

Ambulance, *Tel. 120*

CYTS Tours, *Guangxi Branch, Tel. 5812336, Fax 5813974.*

Guilin CITS, North American Department, *41 Binjiang Road, 541002, Tel. 2828304, 2828314, Fax: 2805303, 2827205. E-mail: pack@public.glptt.gx.cn or christin@chinahighlights.com.* As you leave the Sheraton, it's to the right.

Guilin CTS, *4/F, 202 Zhongshan Nan Road, Tel. 3830295,2860988, Fax 3852315, 2860688.*

Guilin Municipal Tourism Bureau Inspection Station, *Ground Floor, 14 North Ronghu Road, 541001, Tel. 2824344, Fax 2826230.* For tourist complaints.

Guilin Overseas Tourist Corportation, *8, Zhisan Road, Tel. 3834116, Fax 3835395.*

Guilin Tourism Bureau, (information), *No.2, Luosi Hill, 541001, Tel. 2836044, Fax 2820869.*

Police, *Tel. 110*

Telephone code, *0773*

GUANGZHOU

(Kwangchow, Canton)

Guangzhou is the bustling capital of Guangdong province, which has been one of the fastest developing areas in the world. It is important for business people, and those who have ancestral roots in the area. While it is not a major tourist city, there is enough to do here for about four days. It is 165 km to the northwest of Hong Kong on the Zhujiang (Pearl River).

Guangzhou is known as the **Goat City** because five fairies came here supposedly in 1256 B.C, riding goats from whose mouths the fairies drew the first rice seeds. In 214 B.C., the first Qin emperor set up the Prefecture of Nanhai here. It has been south China's largest trading city since at least the Tang dynasty when Arab traders started arriving. The Portuguese settled in Macau, 150 km away in 1557, and foreign traders moved here seasonally after that. More recently, it was the site of the Canton Trade Fair (China Export Commodities Fair) for 23 years China's main foreign trade institution.

Being far from the political center of China, the people here developed an independent spirit. Guangzhou was the starting point or site of many important historical events, including the fight against the importation of opium. Chinese officials destroyed 20,000 chests of it near here in 1839. The Taiping Heavenly Kingdom's Leader Hong Xiuquan (Hung Hsiu-ch'uan) was born about 66 km north and was given the Christian tract that changed his life and China's history in Guangzhou. Dr. Sun Yat-sen was born south of the city in Zhongshan county. He led the Republican campaign in the early 1900s. The officers of the Northern Expedition were trained at the nearby Huangpu (Whampoa) Military Academy. Chiang Kai-shek was director and Chou En-lai was in charge of political indoctrination.

Many foreign missionaries established schools and churches here after the Treaty of Nanking in 1842 opened the city to foreigners. From 1938 to 1945, the Japanese occupied Guangzhou. The Communists took over in 1949. Guangdong has 11 institutions of higher learning, including Zhong Shan University, which is on the site of the missionary-founded Ling Nam University.

In recent years, Guangdong has been one of the main suppliers of food, water, and electricity for neighboring Hong Kong. It is rich in livestock, fruits, and vegetables and is a major manufacturing center.

Guangzhou is at the same latitude as Cuba. The weather here is subtropical, the coldest about 0 C in January and February; the hottest and most humid about 38 C in July and August. The average rainfall is 1680 mm. The best time to visit is October to February before the rains. The urban population is 3.85 million, the total about six million. While Mandarin is understood by almost everyone, the language in most homes is Cantonese.

ARRIVALS & DEPARTURES

From downtown Hong Kong, you can take buses in about three hours (depending on traffic) direct to Guangzhou's Garden Hotel at least 20 trips a day for about HK$160-$190. Hong Kong buses arrive at other hotels as well. From Hong Kong, Guangzhou is a non-stop two-hour train ride, a three-hour hydrofoil ride, or a 20-minute flight. It is a Y80 train ride from Shenzhen on the Hong Kong border. See Hong Kong.

BY BUS FROM HONG KONG

*China Travel Service **buses** leave from **Hong Kong International Airport** daily for hotels in Guangzhou at 10:10am, 1:25pm, 3:20pm and 5:30pm. The Customer Service Counter No.2A in the Meeters and Greeters Hall, Level 5, can book tickets for HK$175-$185. Buses from other Guangdong cities arrive across from the China Hotel.*

There are overnight boats, fast catamarans and hovercraft leaving several times a day from Hong Kong China City at 35 Canton Road in Hong Kong. Ferries arrive at Zhoutouzui *(Tel. 84448218)*, or Dashatou *(Tel. 83829933)* south of the Pearl River in Guangzhou.

Buses to Hong Kong from Guangzhou are cheaper but not faster than taking the train. After booking (preferably three days in advance, but even last minute sometimes) you only need to arrive at your hotel terminal fifteen minutes before departure. Buses leave also from bus stations. The double decker Citibus is less comfortable than those of the GD-HK Bus Company, but it has connections to Admiralty MTR station on the Hong Kong side. The three-to-four hour trip means shorter train lines but struggles with luggage at the two border points. Avoid arriving in Hong Kong during rush hours. Some buses stop at Shatin and Kowloon Tong MTR stations and then continue on.

Guangzhou is a 24-hour train ride south of Beijing. To get train information, call the Railway Station, *Tel. 87140612, 87777112, 86661789, 87752409*. Trains from Shenzhen and Hong Kong use the East Guangzhou train station at Tianhe. Trains from elsewhere use the main railway station near the Liuhua Hotel and Trade Fair building.

Airlines
- **Flight Information**: *Tel. 86666123, 86596123.*
- **Air China**, *Tel. 86681399.*
- **China Northern**, *Tel. 86682488.*
- **China Southern**, next to the main railway station, *Tel. 86661818. 86662749, 86661830, 86681803* (international); *Tel. 86662969. 86671583* (domestic); Airport Service Desk, Departure Lounge, Tel. *86666123, 86678901.*
- **China Southwest**, *Tel. 86673747.*
- **JAS**, *Tel. 86696688, Fax 8666-5603.*
- **Malaysian Airlines**, *Tel. 83358828, 83338989.*
- **Shanghai Airlines**, *Tel. 86681149.*
- **Singapore Airlines**, *Tel. 83358999, 83338898 X 1056.*
- **Vietnam Airlines**, *Tel. 83827187.*

HOLIDAYS & HONG KONG CROWDS

Every time there is a long Hong Kong holiday, over 100,000 visitors try to get from Hong Kong to China and back, so avoid traveling then. The lunar new year holiday in late January or early February is the worst. Don't even think about it. Christmas and New Year week is a very stressful time too, with long line-ups, pushing and shoving.

ORIENTATION

The city is divided by the **Pearl River**, which is crossed by seven bridges, a tunnel and innumerable ferries to be avoided at rush hours (roughly 7:30am-9am and 4:30pm-7pm). **Tianhe** is seven km east of the Garden Hotel and its modern highrises make it look more like a suburb of Hong Kong. The rest of the city is drab in comparison. Most of the tourist places are on the north side of the river. Taxis are plentiful. An 18 km-long metro line goes from the Guangzhou Steel Plant to the East Railway station with 16 stations. A second line should be finished in 2001.

The city is plagued with traffic jams. More elevated highways and bridges are being built to relieve them. Cars from outside of town are now banned from the center of the city, and bicycles from some streets. But ring roads, wider roads, and express roads and multi-storied car parks have opened. Guangzhou is also trying hard to clean up the air so motorcycles are also restricted, leaded gas is forbidden downtown, and trees are being planted.

WHERE TO STAY

Do not pay the rates listed here. All hotels here have given 20-50% discounts depending on availability to walk-in guests who ask. Rooms are

GUANGDONG'S GIFT TO THE WORLD: HER PEOPLE

Guangdong province is the provincial 'home' of many Chinese immigrants to Australia, the United States, Canada, Hong Kong and Southeast Asia. These people have contributed to the economic development of their adopted lands and have also brought or sent back expertise as well as money to their ancestral home. Many are playing a leading role in China's modernization program, and are largely responsible for Guangdong's economic boom.

cheaper too when booked through travel agents or 800/ numbers. Ask about packages.

Guangzhou's hotels, however, certainly do not give discounts during the Canton Trade Fair when prices double or triple and reservations must be secured by a deposit for at least the first week.

The top five-star hotels are the **White Swan**, the **Garden** and the **China**. The best four star is the **Holiday Inn**, and the most convenient three star is the **Bai Yun** which has had much experience with foreigners. All hotels listed here of three stars and more have television reception from Hong Kong, sometimes in English. The higher rated hotels also have CNN and Star television. Downtown check-in on domestic China Southern (CZ) flights can be done at five-star hotels like the Garden and Guangdong International Hotel. Most hotels add 10% service, 5% tax and 5% subway tax, and rates are in US dollars or Chinese yuan (remember, the exchange rate is about US$1=Y8.3).

Canton Trade Fair area

The China and Dong Fang are the best located for the Canton Trade Fair, City Hall, and tourists. It is within walking distance of parks, the Orchid Garden, the Han Museum, the Six Banyan Tree Temple, Zhenhai Tower (museum), China Southern Airlines/CAAC, CITS, and the main railway station.

CHINA HOTEL *(Zhong Guo Dajiudian), Liu Hua Road, 510015. Tel. 86666888, Fax 86677014, 86677288. In North America, Tel. 1-800-1HO-TELS. E-mail: gzchinar@public1.guangzhou.gd.cn. Http://www.chinahotel.com. Five km from the airport. $148-$225 for rooms, $225-$1500 for suites.*

Built in 1983, this international class property has 19 stories and 1013 rooms including 85 suites. It has executive floors, a separate check-in for commercial guests in the lobby, and a Bank of China. It has a deli, Asian and Chaozhou food, and a hot pot restaurant. It even has an expresso bar with latte and Starbucks' coffee. Sports include a gym, tennis, bowling, golf simulator, and 25-meter outdoor pool. An 18-piece orchestra plays evenings. A Marriott hotel.

DONG FANG HOTEL *(Dong Fang Binguan), 120 Liu Hua Road, 510016. Five stars, Tel. 86669900, 86662946 (reservations), Fax 86662775. E-mail: dfhtlbc@public.guangzhou.gd.cn. In North America, Tel. 1-800-44UTELL. Five km from the airport and attached to the Trade Center by escalators over the street. $90-$120 for rooms; $145-1930 for suites.*

Built in 1961, this hotel has eight and 11-story buildings with 1300 rooms, some very spacious. CNN is available on smallish televisions and not all rooms have safes. It has been a generally charming hotel with a large beautiful Chinese courtyard garden, until it added a busy shopping mall. It has an executive floor and the old wing has larger rooms and

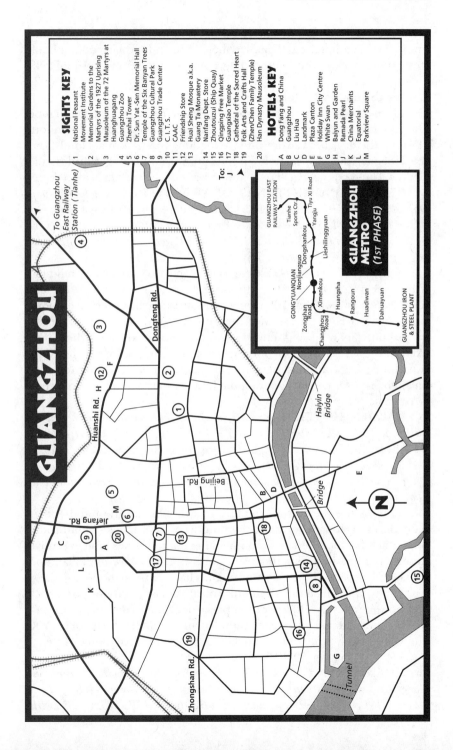

GUANGZHOU

SIGHTS KEY

1 National Peasant Movement Institute
2 Memorial Gardens to the Martyrs of the 1927 Uprising
3 Mausoleum of the 72 Martyrs at Huanghuagang
4 Guangzhou Zoo
5 Zhenhai Tower
6 Dr. Sun Yat-Sen Memorial Hall
7 Temple of the Six Banyan Trees
8 Guangzhou Cultural Park
9 Guangzhou Trade Center
10 C. I. T. S.
11 CAAC
12 Friendship Store
13 Huai Sheng Mosque a.k.a. Guang Ta Monastery
14 Nanfang Dept. Store
15 Zhoutouzui (Ship Quay)
16 Qingping Free Market
17 Guangxiao Temple
18 Cathedral of the Sacred Heart
19 Folk Arts and Crafts Hall (Zhen/Chen Family Temple)
20 Han Dynasty Mausoleum

HOTELS KEY

A Dong Fang and China
B Guangzhou
C Liu Hua
D Landmark
E Plaza Canton
F Holiday Inn City Centre
G White Swan
H Baiyun and Garden
J Ramada Pearl
K China Merchants
L Equatorial
M Parkview Square

GUANGZHOU METRO (1ST PHASE)

GUANGZHOU EAST RAILWAY STATION
Tianhe
Sports Ctr.
Tiyu Xi Road
Yangju
Dongshankou
Lieshilingyuan
Nonjianguo
GONGYUANQIAN
Zonghan Road
Changshou Road
Ximenkou
Huangha
Rangoun
Huadiwan
Dahuayuan
GUANGZHOU IRON & STEEL PLANT

To Guangzhou East Railway Station (Tianhe)

Dongfeng Rd.

Huanshi Rd.

Beijing Rd.

Jiefang Rd.

Zhongshan Rd.

Haiyin Bridge

Bridge

Tunnel

To: J

higher ceilings than the newer west wing. Rooms have smoke hoods and umbrellas. The hotel has Thai, Japanese, and Indonesian food, a book store, supermarket, four-lane bowling, outdoor pool, tennis and mini-golf.

Garden & Holiday Inn area

The next best area is about three km east of the Trade Fair, about nine km from the airport, and three to five km from the main railway station. Here are the Bai Yun, Garden and Guangdong International Hotels, and the Holiday Inn City Center, Friendship Store and the World Trade Center. The zoo is nearby. The Tianhe area is six or seven km east of here.

GUANGDONG INTERNATIONAL HOTEL *(Guangdong Guoji Dajiudian), 339 Huanshi Dong Road, 510098. Five stars. Tel. 83311888, Fax 83313490, 83311565. E-mail: sales@gitic.com.cn; http://www.gitic.com.cn. $140 for rooms, $170-$250 for suites. If you book through American Express, you might get 35%-50% discount.*

Built in 1992, this four-building complex has a 63-story main building. It has a Bank of China, DHL, Bud's ice cream, American Express and several consulates. It has 702 rooms, non-smoking and executive floors. Rooms have CNN, "Please wait" buttons, and wide twin beds. There's Chaozhou, Japanese and European food (Swiss executive chef). For exercise there're an outdoor pool, lighted tennis, gym, mini-golf, bowling, squash, jogging track and hi-tech karaoke. The lobby is decorated with naked marble ladies representing the four seasons and a helicopter pad is available.

GARDEN HOTEL *(Huayuan Jiu Dian), 368 Huanshi Dong Road, 510064, Tel. 83338989, Fax 83324534. In North America, Tel. 1-800-44UTELL. E-mail: gzgarden@public.guangzhou.gd.cn. Http:// www.gardenhotel-guangzhou.com. $140-$210 for rooms; $290-$2000 for suites. Built in 1984-85, it has good standards, 30 stories, 1,002 rooms, suites and apartments.*

Its immense, beautiful, wood-trimmed lobby, location and convenient buses to Hong Kong make this hotel a favorite. It has 24-hour room service and business center, a non-smoking floor, business and executive floors. Its retro Red Flag limousines are special, as are its Italian and French restaurants. It houses Malaysian, Thai, Garuda, and SIA airlines. Among its sports facilities are tennis courts, squash, outdoor pool, a 20-lane bowling alley (AMF), children's playground, and a decent health club with a sauna, jacuzzi and steam bath. Its convention hall banquets 1200 guests and has a three-ton chandelier. A Summit International Hotel.

See also Chapter 13, *China's Best Places to Stay.*

HOLIDAY INN CITY CENTRE *(Wen Hua Jia Re Jiudian), Huan Shi Dong Road, Overseas Chinese Village, 28 Guangming Road, 510095. Four stars. Tel. 87766999, Fax 87602063, 87753126. E-mail:*

resvn@holidayinn_guangzhou.com. *$130-$180 for rooms; $230-$1000 for suites. It provides free shuttle buses from the railway station and airport.*

This 1989-90, 24-story, 431-room hotel has an exhibition center, gym, outdoor pool, and 500-seat cinema. Data ports are on floors above the tenth and pagers are for rent. It has wide twin beds, two executive floors, a clinic and children's games room. Children 19 and under are free in parents' room.

BAI YUN HOTEL *(Binguan), 367 Huanshi Dong Road, 510060. Three stars. Tel. 83333998, Fax 83336498. Six km from the airport and next to the Friendship Store. Y398-Y548 for rooms, and Y658-Y9888 for suites. In its East building, Y300-Y430 for rooms.*

Built in 1975, the Bai Yun has 34 stories with wide hallways and over 700 large rooms and suites. The 28th floor is best but don't be surprised by worn carpets or poor English.

OCEAN, *412 Huanshi Dong Road, Tel. 87765988, Fax 87765475. Four stars. Rooms there are $76-$110, and $128-1000 for suites.*

You can try this nearby hotel if you don't like the Bai Yun.

Other areas

The **White Swan Hotel** is relatively isolated on historic Shamian Island, but an elevated highway means only a 15-minute drive to the Trade Fair Building. It hosts the US Consulate, and you can walk to the Qingping Market. Also on the island are the cheaper **Victory Hotel** *(Tel. 81862622, 81861062, HK$530-HK$620 for rooms, no CNN)* and a **youth hostel** *(Tel. 81884298, Fax 81884979)*. Within steps of the Pearl River Bridge downtown is the Landmark Hotel, close to CTS and shopping.

The **Ramada** is in a less crowded area to the east, far from anything but the river. The White Swan has the most beautiful lobby, its bar and coffee shop the best view of the busy Pearl River, but the Ramada's river view includes a genuine pagoda.

RAMADA PEARL HOTEL *(Hua Mai Da), 9 Ming Yue Yi Lu, Dong Shan District, 510600. Four stars. Tel. 87372988, Fax 87377481. E-mail: gzramada@public.guangzhou.gd.cn. Http://www.ramada.com. From Tianhe station it's five km From the airport, it's 15 km $125-$180 for rooms; $210 for suites.*

On 150 meters of waterfront, the Ramada is generally too far to walk to anywhere else of importance. It is a 10-minute drive to the International School and the closest international hotel to Tianhe.

Opened in 1991, this 25-story, 331-room hotel has non-smoking rooms, executive floor, an office tower and apartments. It has an Asian buffet, California cafe and 24-hour room service. For getting into shape, there's a gym, squash, tennis, indoor and outdoor pools, and mini-golf. It has lots of space for children. It receives CNN, HBO and Australian television. A shuttle bus is available.

WHITE SWAN HOTEL, *(Baitian E Binguan), 1 Southern Street, Shamian Island, 510133. Tel. 81886968, Fax 81861188, 81882288. Eleven km from the airport; seven km from the railway station.*

Opened in 1983, this charming, 28-story hotel has 834 spacious rooms. It has smoke hoods, a 24-hour business center, and executive floor. It has a good grill room, Japanese food, and a marvelous Chinese restaurant. There's a gym, tennis, squash, beautiful outdoor pool and 20-meter lap pool. You can practise on its golf-driving range and enjoy its Rolls Royces. It has a convention center, US, Philippines, and Thai consulates. Member Leading Hotels of the World.

See also Chapter 13, *China's Best Places to Stay.*

HOTEL LANDMARK CANTON *(Huaxia Dajiudian), 8 Qiao Guang Road, Haizhu Square, 510115. Four stars. Tel. 83355988, Fax 83336197, 83331564. E-mail: gzhuaxia@public1.guangzhou.gd.cn $78.30-$180.70 for rooms, $180.70-$241.00 for suites. 10 km from the airport; six km from the railway station; 13 km from Tianhe.*

Built in 1992-94, this 39-story, 730-room hotel has business studios and two executive floors. It has CNN, a gym, indoor heated pool, tennis and Chaozhou food. Its tea house has its own waterfall and garden. Managed by Macau CTS.

Tianhe

The commercial center is shifting to Tianhe. These two hotels are adequate if you don't want to go downtown.

CHINA MAYORS' TOWER, *189 Tianhe Bei Road, Tel. 87553838, Fax 87550099. Y628-Y688 for spacious rooms, Y898-Y1088 for suites. It is about 300 meters from the East Guangzhou Railway Station and close to the Tianhe Sports Centre.*

This beautiful, 1997 hotel is small and lacks luxury services.

STAR HOTEL, *89 Linhe Xi Road, 510610, Tel. 87552888, Fax 878553288. Four stars, Y500-Y680 for rooms, and Y730-Y1200 for suites.*

The Star has a gym and large outdoor pool.

WHERE TO EAT

Look for *Clueless*, the helpful magazine in English about bars and restaurants in Guangzhou. You can find it at Kathleen's (below), major hotels, or E-mail: *editor@clueless.nu*, on the web at *Http://www.clueless.nu*, or *Tel. 83571215, or Fax 83509254.*

The restaurants in the top hotels – the **Garden**, **China**, and **White Swan** are excellent for both Chinese and western food. They are however very expensive. The **Garden's Cantonese restaurant** has good, fresh abalone, suckling pig, and *Qing Yuen* steamed chicken. It's lunch buffet costs Y188. The **China Hotel's lunch buffet** costs Y178 plus 15% and offers the likes of sushi, barbecue, roast beef, and smoked salmon. A special treat at the China are its marvelous chocolates and fruit tarts, as well as *dim sum*. The **Baiyun** and **Dong Fang Hotels** are good for moderately priced Chinese food. Try the 'drunken' or steamed prawns and the crisp-skinned pigeon.

PAN XI (Ban Xi) **RESTAURANT**, *151, Long Jin Xi Road, Tel. 81815955 or 81817038.*

This historic place is the only garden restaurants left with good food and location. It is famous for its hundreds of varieties of *dim sum* (6:30am-12:30 noon only, egg tarts are Y2 each, double dragon rolls Y5 each, suckling pig Y280, and winter melon pond Y130). It is generally open 6:30am-12:30 midnight every day and takes no US credit cards. A reservation here is mandatory for its fancy, private banquet rooms, especially the Reception Dining Hall with its traditional, redwood Chinese furniture and beautiful blue glass windows.

GUANGZHOU RESTAURANT has five branches of which the most convenient is at *112 Tiyudong Road*; the telephone number of the one near the Tianhe Railway Station is *87579138*; a branch is at *2 Wang Nam Road,* closer to the White Swan Hotel, *Tel. 81380388.*

One of the best Cantonese restaurant chains in town, it has great *dim sum* and been inventing new dishes. Try the sauteed clams with XO sauce and peppers, and sauteed shrimp with vegetables stuffed with Yunnan ham and mushrooms. There's also vegetables with soup and sauteed preserved egg. A whole *Wenchang* chicken costs Y140.

For lighter, cheaper food like noodles, congee, and *dim sum*, try China Hotel's **Food Street** or the Holiday Inn's **Dai Pai Dong Food Alley**. At the Garden Hotel's **Lai Wan Market**, Yangzhou fried rice costs Y35, roast goose and *wudong* noodles in soup cost Y23.

Near the Garden Hotel & Holiday Inn

The area around the Garden Hotel and Holiday Inn has many good restaurants and bars.

LEI YUAN GARDEN RESTAURANT, *33 Yi An Street, out the west side door of the Garden. Cantonese. Tel. 83861338. It takes Visa, MasterCard and American Express and is open 11am-3pm; 5:30pm-11pm daily.*

A fancy upscale restaurant with little or no English, the most popular dishes here are braised boneless spareribs in sweet and sour sauce Y68, deep-fried taro with almond flakes Y48, *dim sum* at Y24 a plate, Singapore-style spicy crab for Y78, and fresh prawns baked French style Y88.

BANANA LEAF CURRY HOUSE, *8 Luhu Road, Tel. 83591288 X 3119, 3123, 3118. North of the Friendship Store in the Broadcasting and Television Hotel. It is open daily 11am-11pm and accepts Visa and Master Card. Foreigners get 15% discount*

Its cooks moderately priced Singaporean and South Asian food from an illustrated menu. Curried crab is Y52, chicken and cashews Y28, Vietnamese spring roll Y18, *satay* Y20 for 6 pieces, and beer Y20-Y48.

KATHLEEN'S CAFE & BAR, *60 Tao Jin Road, 510095, Tel. 83598045, Fax 83581787. E-mail: Kathleen's@888.nu.*

This little cafe is modest but if Kathleen Lau is there, the place oozes with warmth. It has pizza (Y45-Y70), soup (Y20-Y35), sandwiches (Y35-Y45), *fajitas* (Y45), and salads (Y20-Y35). Follow the neon signs to the 360 Bar next door. It has been open Monday-Thursday 10:30am-11pm, Fridays to 12pm. A blues band plays 7pm-llpm Fridays.

Other Restaurants

KIU MEI RESTAURANT, *56 Shamien Main Street, Tel. 81861412, 81884168.*

In the street off the side door of the White Swan Hotel, this modest restaurant advertises a luncheon special for Y68. But steamed rice noodles in lotus leaf only cost Y15 and deep-fried pigeon only Y29. Delicious!

HARD ROCK CAFE, *China Hotel. Tel. 86666888, Fax 86683146.*

Ribs have been Y100, a chicken Caesar sandwich Y65, and beer Y35 until 10:30pm. A simple set lunch is Y55. Tee-shirts are about Y100.

Fast Food

Mei Xin (Maxim's) is in *Liu Hua Park*; **Cafe de Coral**, **KFC**, and **Pizza Hut** are everywhere. **McDonald's** is at the *GITIC* and *Dong Fang Hotels.* McDonald's (*Tel. 86669900 X 2162*) and Pizza Hut will deliver.

The **Xihu Market** also has food stalls (mostly dirty and not well developed) but some foreigners love it. It is open evenings to about midnight, and is near the White Swan and the Cultural Park. **Xigong Fishing Harbor Food Street** can be fun, *Tel. 83834418.* The annual food festival is 10 days in late September to early October.

SEEING THE SIGHTS

If you only have one day, do visit the Chen Family Hall, the Han Dynasty Mausoleum Museum, the Temple of the Six Banyan Trees (for exotic Chinese architecture), and the Qing Ping Free Market (for genuine local color). You could also decide on a garden (if you like plants), or an arts and crafts factory.

Be sure to try *dim sum* and a drink in the riverside coffee shop or bar at the White Swan Hotel. If you have more time (at least a day), go to Foshan for the ancestral temple, 61.9 meter high sitting Buddha, and ceramic factory.

The **Chen** (Zhen) **Family Hall**, *Liwan Bei Road, Tel. 81814559,* is open 8:30am-5:00pm daily. It was built in the 1890s with nine halls and six courtyards. Its windows, door frames, and pavilions are all lavishly decorated with carvings and sculptures, almost too much to absorb at once. Take it in small doses. Because the army occupied these buildings during the Cultural Revolution, the artwork suffered very little damage.

The **Guangdong Folk Arts and Crafts Museum** is located here now, and it is a good place to shop for linens. Just don't let the bargains distract you from the ceramic opera scenes on the roofs and the charming carved mice eating the *lichees* on the pillars.

The **Liu Rong** (Six Banyan Trees) **Temple**, *Liu Rong Road, Tel. 83357754,* open 8am-5pm daily, was founded 1,400 years ago. It was so named because the famous Song poet Su Dong Po found six luxuriant banyan trees here in 1100. The present buildings are recent. Its nine-story Flower Pagoda is 57.6 meters high and originally built in 537. It can be climbed for a good view and the exercise. Monks chant Tuesday and Friday mornings.

The **Qing Ping Free Market** *(Qing Ping Ziyou Shi Chang),* is the largest herb and vegetable market in the city (about five blocks). Here you can find dehydrated lizards, snakes, plants, and weird-looking roots. It has some live fish and animals, too, for pets or food, including pangolins (an endangered species) and civet cat. This market is not for children nor the squeamish as it has skinned barbecued dogs dangling in the stalls. It also has one block of antiques for sale.

This market is filthy especially in the rainy season, always crowded, but fascinating even if you don't want to buy anything. It is within a 20-minute walk of the White Swan Hotel, across the north bridge to the mainland, and about three blocks in each direction. It is open 6am-6pm. As in all crowded places anywhere beware of pickpockets!

Museum of the Nanyue King

Guangzhou has a 2100-year-old "imperial" tomb now officially known as the **Museum of the Western Han Dynasty Mausoleum of the Nanyue King**, *about half a block behind the China Hotel on 867 Jiefang Bei Road towards the river, Tel. 86664920, 86678030, open daily 9:30am-4:45pm.* You need at least 1.5 hours here. The Nanyue Kingdom was founded by one of the ruling generals of the first emperor Qin. After Qinshihuang's death in 210 B.C., his son and successor who lacked his father's fanatical drive, let loose the reins of empire. Zhao Tuo, the surviving general in charge of south

China declared himself Emperor of Nanyue in 204 B.C.

The Han dynasty took over China in 206 B.C. Five years later, the Nanyue Emperor was given the choice of renewing his allegiance to the Chinese empire, or bringing suffering on his people. Zhao Tuo chose the former, and died at age 93 in 137 B.C. The tomb here is of his successor, the second Nanyue King. Included in the find of over 1000 burial objects are the oldest jade burial suit so far found in China, a chariot, ritual bronzes, gold and silver vessels, ivory and lacquerware, musical instruments, weapons, and tools. Also found were human sacrifices, concubines, and servants buried with him. The relics are beautifully displayed, with English titles, at the actual site. Don't miss the video, in English, of the excavation.

If You Have More Time or Interest

Shamian (Shamien, Shameen) **Island**, in the Pearl River in central Guangzhou, became a British and French concession in 1859-60. It was then an 80-acre sandbank, later built into a European ghetto. The architecture is European, but, unfortunately, so many of the old buildings have been destroyed that its overall charm has almost disappeared. The island is joined to the mainland by bridges. At the western tip is the White Swan Hotel, built on reclaimed land, one of the top hotels in China.

The **Guangdong Provincial Museum**, *Wenming Road, Tel. 83832195,* displays relics of local primitive society and is not as good as the Guangzhou Museum. The **Guangzhou Museum**, *Tel. 83832195,* open 9am-5pm daily, is in the **Zhenhai** (Sea-dominating) **Tower** in Yuexiu Park and is better organized. The original tower itself was built in 1380 to assert the power of the Ming dynasty. It has been rebuilt several times since then. Located at one of the highest points in the city, it starts with prehistory on the second floor, to revolutionary history on the fifth. The exhibits include some interesting old clocks, ceramics, and a painting of the burning of the 20,000 chests of opium.

The **Mausoleum of the Seventy-two Martyrs at Huanghuagang** *(Yellow Flower) Hill on Xianlie Road* is east of the Garden Hotel on the road to the zoo. This commemorates Dr. Sun Yat-sen's unsuccessful attempt to overthrow the Qing in 1911. Of special interest to visitors of Chinese ancestry, this 260,000 sq-meter park was built by Chinese Nationalists' Leagues around the world. The stones are inscribed in English with the names of the donors, among these Chicago, Illinois; Moose Jaw, Saskatchewan; and Lima, Peru.

The **Dr. Sun Yat-sen Memorial Hall**, *Tel. 83332430,* is a theater seating over 4,500, built in 1931 and expanded in 1975. This building is architecturally important because its huge hall is supported by four vertical concrete beams that branch out on top to form the octagonal roof.

The modern technique and pure Chinese style, with its bright blue circus-tent-shaped ceramic roof, is unique. (For more on the life of Dr. Sun, see Nanjing.)

The *Guangxiao Temple, *109 Sheshi Road at Guangxiao Road, Tel. 81087421* has the longest history in the city. It was founded on the site of the Nanyue King's residence. The temple was built in 397 A.D. to commemorate the visit of the Indian monk Dharmayasas, and is the largest temple in south China. The present buildings are from the Five Dynasties to the Ming. The attractive Sixth Patriarch's Hair-burying Pagoda is a miniature of the Flower Pagoda.

The **Huaisheng Mosque** and **Guangta Minaret**, *56 Guangta Road, Jiubuqian, Yide, Tel. 83336737,* are of historical value and not the least bit attractive. Considered the oldest mosque in China, it was built in 627 A.D. by Arab traders and is open daily.

The **Shishi** (Cathedral of the Sacred Heart), *Yide Road, Tel. 83336737,* was constructed in 1863-88. Its 57.95 meter Gothic spire was probably designed deliberately taller than the pagoda nearby. Shishi means Stone House. During the Cultural Revolution, it was used as a storehouse. Mass has been celebrated weekdays at 6am and Sundays and festivals at 6, 7:30, and 8:30am.

You can book the **Pearl River** boat ride with dinner through your hotels from April to October (about 7:30pm, *30 Pier, Xiti*) but don't expect luxury.

If you are interested in crafts, visit the **Guangzhou Jade Factory**, *28, Xinsheng Street, Changzhou Xi Road, Tel. 81861605,* and the **Daxin Ivory Carving Factory** at *415 Daxin Road, Tel. 81882870.* You should also visit Foshan.

Gardens, Parks, & Zoos

Depending on the season, don't forget to bring your own insect repellent. The **Orchid Garden**, *Dabei Road,* at the foot of Yuexiu Hill, *Tel. 86677255,* is a delight for orchid lovers. It has over 300 species on five hectares. The **Xi Yuan** (West Garden), next to *Dongfeng 1-Road; Tel. 81885867,* specializes in *penjing,* miniature trees and landscapes. The **Guangzhou Zoo and Ocean Park**, *Xianli Zhong Road, Tel. 87752702,* are in the northeastern suburbs. They have 200 species, including pandas.

Festivals

The **Happy Festival** with performing arts groups is in the autumn. A fine food festival takes place during the autumn Trade Fair. The **Export Commodities Fair** is held annually from April 15-April 30, and October 15-October 30. North Americans can make arrangements through the **US China Travel Service**, *San Francisco, Tel. 415/398-6627 or 800/332-2831,*

Fax 398-6669. E-mail:ctsusa@aol.com. You can also apply for an invitation through a Chinese trading corporation or the **China Foreign Trade Center Group**, *117 Liu Hua Road, 510014, Fax 86665851.* Pickpockets as well as traders visit Guangzhou for the event, so be careful.

Further Afield

Worth a stop on the way to Shenzhen is the **Humen Fort** on the north shore of the Pearl River, *under the Humen Bridge, south of Dongguan County city. Tel. 750/6288551.* This is about a 90-minute drive towards western Shenzhen on the coastal road. The fort was built against the foreign invaders during the Qing and is quite impressive. At Humen, Minister Lin Zexu destroyed the opium in 1839.

The **Huangpu Military Academy** (1924) should be of interest to modern history buffs. It's on *Changzhou Island, Huangpu, Tel. 82201082* and can be reached by boat from the Xidy Wharf, Yanjiang Xi Road, or *Tianzi Wharf, Yanjiang Zhong Road, Tel. 81888932, 81908191, Fax 8188932.* The **Taiping Museum** at leader Hong Xiuquan's Former Residence is in *Guanglubu Village, Huaxian County.* Read *God's Chinese Son* by Jonathan Spence.

Another escape from crowds is a nearby village, many of which grow and preserve fruit for export. Guests are frequently given samples. Lucky are those who go during the *lichee* season! It is in June.

The **Flying Dragon World Fun City** *(Feilong Shi Jie),* in Panyu about 10 km from Guangzhou, is a theme park centered on snakes. Here you can eat snakes, and see a show featuring women playing with snakes. Getting there is difficult except by taxi. It is unusual, but not great.

See also Foshan, Taishan, Zhaoqing, Zhongshan, and Zhuhai below.

NIGHTLIFE & ENTERTAINMENT

The bars in the top hotels are popular with foreigners. The Garden's **Lotus Bar** has a multi-colored lighted floor. Across the street to the west of the Garden Hotel at the base of the underpass is the **Cave** (beer Y15-Y28). It has Tex-Mex food, live music, billiard table, and manual soccer game. It takes all credit cards and is in the *basement of the Zhujiang Building, 360 Huanshi Dong Road, Tel. 83863660.* The best golf is at the **Nansha Golf Club** an hour away in Panyu. Closer to town is the small but beautiful **Nan Hu** golf course.

You can rent **bicycles** near the back door of the White Swan Hotel, and from some other hotels. They are not allowed on main streets. Ask your consulate about the Hash House Harriers ("a drinking club with a running problem.") You'll probably be able to join them for a run on weekends.

> ## BEWARE THE KARAOKE CRAZE IN GUANGZHOU!
> *Some Guangzhou people are karaoke mad, though it's not as bad as three years ago. They sing into a microphone at lunch and dinner. Many private restaurant dining rooms have karaoke machines. If you can't stand amateur singing, let it be known, before you insult your host, that you'd like a nice quiet place in which to eat – without music.*

In the Garden Hotel building is film star Jacky Chan's expensive **Star East night restaurant** with Asian and western food, the oriental version of Planet Hollywood. It's open 8pm-3am daily.

SHOPPING

Locally made goods are carvings of ivory, jade, bamboo, and wood, and gold and silver jewelry. Shantou (Swatow) drawnworks and embroidery and Foshan's ceramics are famous, and should be cheaper here than outside the province.

The main shopping area is around **Zhongshan 5-Road and Beijing Road**. The **Guangzhou Department Store** is popular at *12 Xihu Road (and Beijing Road), Tel. 83331817*. Also proletarian is the **Nan Fang Da Sha department store** at *49 Yan Jiang Xi Road, Tel. 81886022*.

The shops in the **World Trade Centre** in front of the Friendship Store on Huanshi Dong Road are the most expensive in town. The **Friendship Store** is at *369 Huanshi Dong Road, Tel. 83336628*, and open 8:30am-9pm. It is expensive with imported name brands and locally manufactured goods and next to the Baiyun Hotel.

The **Qing Ping Free Market** has been selling antiques like old coins, water pipes, and old porcelain, with many fakes and reproductions. Lots of fun also is the antique street market at about *10 Da He Road* near Qing Ping Road. This lane is across the street from the hospital with a red gate and curved gold Chinese roof. **Da He Lu Market** has about 300 stalls and is open daily from about 9am-5pm. The goods are the usual "silver" jewelery, old ceramics, tea pots, reproductions and reproductions, more fun than serious, but you might find some treasures there.

The stores at the **White Swan Hotel** have good quality and variety for silks, crafts and antiques. The **#Guangdong Cultural Relics Store**, is at *696 Renmin Bei Road, Tel. 86678608*. The **Guangzhou Antique Store** is at *170 Wende Bei Road, Tel. 83330175*. **Books in English** are at the White Swan and Dong Feng Hotels.

The **Xihu Road Night Market** (open from 7-10pm) has over 900 stalls with casual clothes, factory overruns and seconds. Prices for Hong

Kong-made items can be about three to five times Hong Kong prices, so beware.

PRACTICAL INFORMATION

Ambulance, *Tel. 120*
Consulates:
• **Australia**, *Tel. 83350909, 83311888.*
• **Britain**, *Tel. 83336520, 83311888.*
• **Canada**, *China Hotel, Tel. 86660569, Fax 86672401, 86679380.*
• **Netherlands**, *Tel. 83311888.*
• **France**, *Tel. 83321955, 83311888.*
• **Germany**, *Tel. 81922566.*
• **Japan**, *Garden Hotel, Tel. 83338999.*
• **Italy**, *Tel. 83311888.*
• **Korea**, *Tel. 83340170.*
• **Malaysia**, *Tel. 87395660.*
• **Phillipines**, *Tel. 81886568.*
• **Poland**, *63 Shamian Street, Tel. 81861854.*
• **Thailand**, *White Swan Hotel, Tel. 81886968 X 3310.*
• **US**, *White Swan Hotel, Tel. 81888911 X 256, 81862441, Fax 81862341. American Citizen Services Unit, Tel. 81862418. United States Information Agency, Garden Hotel, Tel. 83354269, 83338999 X 7351. Trade Office, China Hotel, Tel. 86660569.*
• **Vietnam**, *Tel. 83580555 X 1001 or X 604.*
Travel Agents and Officials:
• **American Express Travel**, *C1, G/F, Central Lobby, Guangdong International Hotel, 339 Huanshi Dong Road, Tel. 83311771, Fax 83313535.*
• **China International Travel Service Guangzhou**, Open Monday-Saturday 8:30-12 noon and 2pm-5pm. Sunday 9am-5pm. *179 Huanshi Xi Road, 510010 (next to main railway station), Tel. 86677881, 86677151, 86666271, Fax 86678048.* For tickets, tours and other services, *86677449, 86666089.* Air tickets *Tel. 86666273, Fax 86678048, 86677462. E-mail:citsgzy@public.guangzhou.gd.cn.*
• **China Travel Service**, *Guangdong branch, 23/F, Yanjiang Building, 197 Yanjiang Zhong Road, 510115, Tel. 83336888 X 3212, X 3201, Fax 83394375.*
• **CYTS Tours Corporation**, *3/F, 69 Dadao Road, Dongshan District, 510600, Tel. 87761040, 87752402, Fax 87762509, or 3/F Bao Shan Plaza, 509 Huan Shi Dong Road, 510075, Tel. 57784047, 8667741, Fax 87765112, 86665039.*
• **Guangdong Provincial Tourism Bureau**, *185 Huanshi Xi Road, 510010, Tel. 86666889, Fax 86665039. E-mail: gdlyjscc@public.guangzhou.gd.cn. Http://www.gznet.com/travel. For brochures, promotion department exten-*

sion 8630. *For complaints and suggestions, contact: Business Management Department, Tel. 86677422.*
• **Guangdong Railway China Youth Travel Service**, *69 Dadao Road, Tel. 87662865, Fax 87752409.*
• **Guangzhou Tourist Bureau**, *180 Huanshi Xi Road, 510010, Tel. 86678043, 86661275, 86673220, Fax 86673220, 86678083. Ask for Wu Yi Ming.*
• **Guangzhou Tourist Corporation**, *4 - 155 Huanshi Xi Road, 510010, Tel. 866632314, 86663725, Fax 86677563, 81877563.* Organizes tours from abroad for foreigners and outbound for Chinese people. Ask for Michael Sun.
Medical emergencies: *Consult your consulate above.*
Telephone code, *020*
Tourist Compaints, *Supervisory Bureau of Tourism Quality, Guangdong Province, Tel. 86681163, 86687042, Fax 86661267.*
Tourist Information Center, *Tel. 86696882, 86687051.*

EXCURSIONS & DAY TRIPS

Most of these places in Guangdong are mainly for business people and for visitors trying to connect with their Chinese roots. They are, however, worth seeing. The countryside is lush and beautiful except for the hills carved bare to fill in Hong Kong's harbor. It is full of villages with black brick buildings and watchtowers built against tigers and bandits. Some of the places like Foshan, Shenzhen, Zhaoqing, Zhongshan and Zhuhai could be of interest to other people as well, and Hong Kong has short tours. This is a quickly developing area which is losing much of its distinctive architecture and way of life. But it still has many charming aspects.

Shenzhen and Zhuhai are treated as separate entries below.

FOSHAN

Foshan (Fatshan) is about 25 km southwest of Guangzhou by expressway. It is important because of its Ancestral Temple, and its handicrafts. It is usually reached by road from Guangzhou, a one-day excursion from Guangzhou. Named 'Hill of Buddhas' because a mound of Buddhist statues was excavated here, Foshan is one of the Four Ancient Towns of China. The city is over 1,300 years old.

The **Ancestral Temple**, now the **Foshan Municipal Museum**, was founded in the 11th century, expanded and rebuilt after Liberation. It contains sculptures, ancient relics, and a 2,500 kilogram bronze figure named Northern Emperor. Note the decorations on the bases of the arches, and the stone, wood, and brick carvings. Four of the statues are made of paper, the others of wood or clay. The roof, decorated with

Shiwan pottery figures, is one of the most elaborate in the country, quite gaudy, but artistically and culturally important.

Locally made are also cuttlebone sculptures, brick carvings, silk, lanterns, paper-cuts, and of course the famous Shiwan ceramics. The **Foshan Folk Art Institute** also produces palace lanterns, T-shirts, and paper cuts. **Shiwan Artistic Ceramic Factory** across the street is one of the most famous ceramic factories in China and is worth a visit, not only for its temple-top figures, but also for its maroon-robed lohan saints, with expressive, bulging eyes and unglazed faces. Its exhibition hall has works by master artisans. Tours usually visit a **silk factory** too. A 61.9 meter high **Sitting Buddha** should be finished soon.

Both hotels below have Hong Kong television reception, and are about eight km from the Foshan Airport and three km from the railway station. They both take credit cards and add a 10% surcharge plus Y5 per person tax. Consider them for food.

FOSHAN HOTEL *(Binguan), 75 Fenjiang Nan Road, 528000. Four stars. Tel. 3353338, Fax 3352347. E-mail: gzfshl@pub.foshan.gd.cn. $56-$69 for rooms, and $110-$1783 for suites. You should be able to get at least a 20% discount.*

This attractive downtown garden hotel was opened in 1973 and renovated in 1998. It has eight stories, and 395 rooms with safes and CNN. Some rooms are non-smoking. It has an outdoor pool, gym, and Japanese and Chaozhou food.

GOLDEN CITY HOTEL *(Jin Cheng Dajiudian), 48 Fenjiang Nan Road, 528000. Three stars. Tel. 3357228, Fax 3353924. Downtown location across from Exhibition Center.*

Built in 1989, this 19-story, 180-room hotel has an outdoor pool and gym. A standard double should cost about $40 through a travel agent.

The **Foshan Tourist Bureau** is at *3/F, 107 Renmin Road, Foshan, 528000.* The **Foshan Travel Co.** is at *2-3/F, 107 Renmin Road, Foshan, Tel. 2284595, Fax 2223098.* For **Foshan CITS,** *Tel. 3322387, Fax 2101019* and **Foshan Tour Service,** *Tel. 2101051, Fax 2101054.* The telephone code is *0757.*

JIANGMEN

Jiangmen (Kiangmen or Kongmoon in Cantonese) is about 100 km south of Guangzhou, the closest airport. You can reach this old port city by road or ship from Guangzhou, or by daily non-stop four-hour ferry from Hong Kong and Macau. Jiangman City is made up of five counties: Xinhui, Heshan, Kaiping, Enping, and Taishan. The best hotel is the **Crystal/Celeste Palace**. The **East Lake** is a good garden-style hotel. Both are close together in the suburbs, take credit cards, and are five km from the port and two km from the bus station. Prices from travel agents are in the $45-$60 range.

CELESTE PALACE *(Yin Jing Jiudian), 22 Kong Kou Road, 529051. Four star standard. Tel. 3183288, Fax 3183001. E-mail: jmcph@pub.jiangmen.gd.cn.*

Opened in 1990 with renovations in 1999, this 216-room hotel has 216 spacious rooms some of them non-smoking. It has a large outdoor pool, CNN, a gym, bowling and tennis.

EAST LAKE HOTEL *(Dong Hu Binguan), 15 Guang Hou Road, 529051. Three stars. Tel. 3363611, Fax 3361010, 3351010.*

Built in 1973, this three-story hotel has 208 small rooms and a pool. Its Azalea Villa has only suites.

Travel agents for Jiangman: **General Tour Corporation**, *5 Xiqu Road, Tel. 3516888.* **Jiangmen China Travel Service**, *15 Kongkou Road, 529051, Tel. 3336361, 3333611, Fax 3351010.* **CITS**, *13 Nonglin Road, 529000, Tel. 3356562, 3353384;* **Jiangmen Travel Co.**, *5 Xiqu Avenue, Jiangmen, Tel. 359221, Fax 355872.* The telephone code is *0750.*

SHANTOU

Shantou (Swatow), a port city and Special Economic Zone in northeastern Guangdong province, is also charming, famous for its handicrafts and Chaozhou food. It is 350 km by air north of Guangzhou, and should soon be reached by expressway from Shenzhen in three hours. Flights currently connect with Hong Kong, Bangkok, Kuala Lumpur and 29 Chinese cities.

Shantou is the ancestral home of innumerable Chinese emigrants to Southeast Asia, Japan, and Africa, some of whom were kidnapped from here and sent to Cuba in the late 1800s. Today about 15% of the population receives remittances from overseas.

Shantou is a 2,000-year-old town to which disgraced officers of the Tang were exiled. Europeans used its port to import opium. In addition to its famous lace and embroidery, it produces carpets, painted porcelain, jewelry, bamboo carvings, lacquer, and stone, shell, and gilded wood carvings.

In Shantou city, 30 km south of Chaozhou, are the **Arts and Crafts Exhibition** and **Zhong Shan Park**, with its 'gardens within gardens.' To the east of Shantou is tiny **Maya Islet**, seven km by ferry with a **Mazu goddest temple** and the old British Customs House. A globe at Shantou University marks the **Tropic of Cancer**.

Chaozhou is one of the traditional Four Famous Ancient Towns, and still has Tang and Song architecture. Among the attractions in Chaozhou City are: the **Kaiyuan Temple** from the Tang dynasty, **West Lake Park**, the arts and crafts, and embroidery **factories**. None of these are world class.

The weather is mild, with an annual rainfall of 1,400 to 2,000 mm. mainly in the summer. Both of these top hotels are in the Special Economic Zone within the main urban area, add a 15% surcharge, and have foreign exchange and credit card services. Prices are subject to change and discounts.

GOLDEN GULF HOTEL *(Jin Hai Wan Da Jiudian), Jinsha Dong Road, Shantou, 515041. Five stars. Tel. 8263263, Fax 8265163. E-mail: stgghotl@pub.shantou.gd.cn. Y1100-Y2500. 12 km from the airport.*

Built in 1991 with renovations 1999, this hotel has 28 stories, and 307 rooms, CNN and some non-smoking rooms. It has a pool, sauna, tennis, and gym and is managed by the Dong Fang Group of Guangzhou.

SHANTOU INTERNATIONAL HOTEL *(Guoji Da Jiudian), Jin Sha Dong Road, 515041. Four stars, Tel. 8263263, Fax 8451796, 8293678. E-mail: stih@pub.shantou.gd.cn. Http://www.shantou.gd.cn/travel/hotel/stih/ 15 km from the airport. Y930-Y1380 for rooms; Y2100-Y8300 for suites.*

Built in 1988, this 26-story property has 353 rooms, a gym, revolving restaurant, in-house movies, and 24-hour room service.

Travel agents: **Shantou Tourist Corporation** is at *136 Yuejin Road, Tel. 8297615, Fax 8293456,* and **China Comfort Shantou** is at *53 Changping Road, Tel. 8240232, Fax 8539776.* **China Travel Service**'s *Fax is 8254118.* **Golden Gulf Tourism**'s *Fax is 8534111.* The telephone code is *0754.*

TAISHAN

Taishan (Cantonese, Toishan; Toishanese, Hoishan) is important as the ancestral home of many who left China for the Chinatowns of North America, Southeast Asia and Australia in the early 1900s. For tourists, the attractions here are rural, a restful exposure to south China, towns that still retain old over-the-sidewalk architecture and charm, and villages with watchtowers. But things are changing so get there soon. The population of the main city Taicheng is about 980,000.

This Taishan should not be confused with the mountain in Shandong farther north, also called Taishan. This Taishan is a county on the southern coast of Guangdong province, 146 km southwest of Guangzhou and about 80 km as the crow flies, west of Aomen (Macau). You can reach Taicheng, the county seat, by at least 20 public mini-buses from Xiao Bei on Deng Feng Road from Guangzhou, about 1.5 hours by freeway away. Add more time for traffic jams. A new expressway between Taishan and Guangzhou, due in 2000, should take one hour from the Guangzhou border. The bus terminal is beside the Overseas Chinese Hotel in Taishan. From Macau, Taishan is about three hours by road, from Jiangmen and Xinhui, about an hour.

From Hong Kong you take a 3.5 hour ferry to the port of Gong Yi, then a public bus 20 km to the city. It leaves Hong Kong once a day in the morning and leaves Taishan about 1:45pm to go back.

You can explore villages in this area. If you don't have an ancestral village to visit, travel agents can arrange one for you to see. Near the Overseas Chinese Hotel is a statue of **Chen Yu Hi**, a Chinese-American who returned to China to start in 1906 the first railway line by a private company in China. The 100 km-long track was used from 1912 to 1942 when it was destroyed by the Japanese. The old railway station still standing nearby is patterned after one in Seattle at the time.

The town's "cultural area" has a tiny **museum** at *Huan Bei Da Dao Shi Shan, 529200, Tel. 5529446, 5524045.* It has exhibits of the history and development of the city, its emigrants, and some antiques. Unfortunately, it has no titles in English. You can visit Taishan **Ma Lan Fang Kindergarten**, at *168 Huan Bei Road, 529200, Tel. 5502959,* an obviously well-endowed child care centre with 15 tiny computers and 24 electric pianos. You can visit the **No. 1 Middle School** on *Stone Flower Road* which has volunteer teachers from abroad (*Tel.5523252*). The city makes good billiard tables.

Shang Chuan Island's **Fei Sa Beach** is about 40 km south of Taicheng, plus a 30-minute jetfoil ride. It has four km of beach and clear water. Nearby is the **St. Francis Xavier Church** where the Jesuit died in 1552. To the east is Zhongshan county, **birthplace of Dr. Sun Yixian** (Sun Yat-sen).

The Garden Hotel is the only place where **taxis** wait outside. But you can hire a car from **China Travel Service**, or the **Taishan Tourist Co.**, *Tel. 5534714, Fax 5529999* for about Y500 a day. The only international standard hotel here is the Garden.

OVERSEAS CHINESE HOTEL *(Huaqiao Dasha) has rooms for Y218-Y278 and suites for Y308, Tel. 5524768.*

This hotel is dumpy and old.

GARDEN HOTEL *(Yuanlin Jiu Dian), Nanmenxi Road, 529200. Less than one km south of the bus station. Tel. 5525890 or Fax 5518015. E-mail reservations: resvn@stamfordkyz.com. Four stars. Y380-Y700 for rooms; Y880-Y3000 for suites. Villas with 5-13 rooms cost Y6,200-Y10,800 plus 10% tax.*

This is an attractive garden-style hotel on the edge of a man-made lake with lots of song birds and frogs. It has hot spring water in all 148 rooms but no CNN. Its central location is ideal for walkers who want to see both the old town and the newer suburbs. The food is worth a trip here. And its standards of cleanliness and service are exceptional for a four-star in such a small town. It is the only hotel here good enough for western visitors, and it cares enough about us to make an effort to improve the English of the staff. A Zenith Hotel.

See Chapter 13, *China's Best Places to Stay.*

Taishan food is basically the same as Cantonese, but there are some dishes that are unique, like mud fish, steamed minced pork with salted egg (*yuk beng*), peanuts fried with water chestnuts, and double boiled soup. The **Garden Hotel** has the best restaurant here and does a good suckling pig for Y30, lobster for Y260 per 500 gms., and stir-fried vegetables for Y18. Great also are the steamed shrimp, barbecued pork, and stir-fried spinach. You can get hamburgers for Y10 and spaghetti for Y20. Other restaurants are available but check out the hygiene before you try them.

The **Taishan Bureau of Travel and Tourism** and **Taishan Tour Company** are at *19 Stone Flower Overseas Chinese Village, Huan Bei Street, 529200, Tel. 5534602, 5525847, Fax 5529999.* The **Overseas Chinese Affairs Office**, is at *38 Huan Nan Street, Back Building, Tel. or Fax 5522567.* It should be able to give you information about summer camps for young foreigners with roots in Taishan. Ask for Steve Liu at the **Foreign Affairs Office**, *19 Huan Bei Avenue, Shihua Huaqiao Xincun, Tel. 5503379, 5501286.* **China Travel Service** is at the *Overseas Chinese Hotel, 1 Tong Ji Road, 529200, Tel. 5524768, Fax 5529405.* The telephone code is *0750.*

XINHUI

Two hours by car south of Guangzhou, and 20 minutes from Jiangmen, **Xinhui** is of interest to people whose roots are in the area. For information contact Harvey Chan, Director, **Xinhui Tourism Bureau**, *36 Zhuzi Road, Tel. (750)6612698, 6619035, Fax 6612122 and Pager 996862033.*

ZHAOQING

Zhaoqing (Chaoching) is about 100 km west of Guangzhou on the west bank of the Xijiang River. You should visit it for its Seven Star Crags, and its relatively tranquil atmosphere, a good town for walkers and bicycles. It is also famous for its *Duan* inkstones. It can be reached by ship, bus, or train from Hong Kong, Shenzhen, and Guangzhou. It is building an airport. The population is about 200,000. The weather is subtropical, with an annual precipitation of 1599 mm. mainly from April to August.

Known since ancient times, Zhaoqing was the home for six years of the Italian **Jesuit missionary Matteo Ricci**. He lived in 'Shuihing' in the 1580s. While no one knows exactly where Ricci's house was, an educated guess places it between the boat landing and the Ming pagoda in the old city by the river. The district here has a Song dynasty gate with houses that look like they haven't changed since Ricci's time. An earthen wall circles the old city. For good background, read *The Wise Man from the West - Matteo Ricci and His Mission to China* by Vincent Cronin.

Zhaoqing was not really developed as a resort until 1955. Then, 460-hectare Star Lake was created for irrigation, fish breeding, and tourism.

Seven Star Crags, so named because they appear placed like the seven stars of the Big Dipper, is like a potted miniature garden. Its mountains are very much like those of Guilin. You can climb 130-meter Heavenly Pillar for the view.

The seven crags are named Langfeng (Lofty Wind), Yuping (Jade Screen), Shishi (Stone Chamber), Tianzhu (Heavenly Pillar), Chanchu (Toad), Shinzhang (Stone Palm), and Apo (Hill Slope). The biggest cave is at the foot of Apo Crag and you can enter it by boat. If you hit the rocks at **Musical Instrument Rock**, you get different musical notes. A giant musical fountain, believed to be the biggest in Asia, is in front of the Seven Star Crag Square near the Star Lake Hotel.

Zhaoqing also boasts the **Baiyun** (White Cloud) **Temple**, built in the Tang (618-907) and the Chongxi, Wenming, and Xufeng pagodas. **Qingyun Temple** is at the middle of 1000-meter-high **Dinghu** (Tripod) **mountain**, 18 km northeast of Zhaoqing. The mountain, which is a nature preserve, has a 30 meter-high waterfall on its northwest side.

Made in the area in addition to famous **inkstones**, are ivory and bone carvings, sandalwood fans, paintings, straw products, umbrellas, and jewelry. **Ginseng Beer** is made here too. An interesting store is the **Guangdong Zhaoqing Duanxi Factory of Famous Ink Stones** on Gongnong Road. The **night market** with some clothes, curios, and crafts is between the Overseas Chinese Hotel and the Star Lake Hotel.

The best hotel by the lake in town is the **Star Lake Hotel**. Second is the **Overseas Hotel**. If you want to be away from town beside the lake, there's the Songtao but it isn't as good. These are all 80 km from the closest airport in Foshan. Hotels here are in the $60 or less range.

STAR LAKE HOTEL (*Xing Hu Sing Dajiudian*), *37, 4th Duan Zhou Road, Four stars. Tel. 2221188, Fax 2236688.*

This downtown hotel is quite good, but its windows were constantly fogged up. It's close to the lake, and well located for the night market outside. It has 31 stories, 400 rooms, a swimming pool, mini-golf, and gym.

OVERSEAS CHINESE HOTEL *Four km from the railway station and near the bus station, stores, night market and lake.*

Built in 1987, this hotel has 239 rooms, and satellite television.

SONGTAO HOTEL (*Binguan*), *Seven Star Lake Resort, 526040. Three stars. Tel. and Fax 2824412.*

This hotel is four km by road from the bus station, two km by boat across the lake, and six km from the river port. Set in the park between two of the crags (one 90 meters high), this 1978 hotel has three and four stories, 211 rooms, and satellite television.

MT. DINGHU INTERNATIONAL YOUTH HOSTEL, *Tel. 2621668, Fax 2621665.*

The hostel is in the UNESCO nature reserve and the entry fee is refunded for hostel guests. It has 100 beds at $5-$10.

For Zhaoqing travel information: The **Zhaoqing Tourism Administration** is at *9 Kangle Bei Road, 526020, Tel. and Fax 2825721.* **CTS**, *Tel. 2833699 or Fax 2229983, 2231197;* **CITS**, *Tel. 2826984, Fax 2234492.* The telephone code is *0758.*

ZHONGSHAN CITY

Zhongshan is important because of the former residence of Dr. Sun Yat-sen (Sun Yixian) in **Cuiheng** village, 26 km from **Shiqi** (the main city), Tel. 5501691. The father of the Chinese republic himself designed the house, a blend of Spanish and local styles. The flossy **Sun Yixian Memorial Middle School** and an interesting **folk culture museum** are nearby. For more about Dr. Sun Yat-sen see Nanjing.

Close to Macau, and across the Pearl River delta south of Hong Kong, Zhongshan can be directly reached by 1.5 hour hovercraft from Hong Kong at least five times a day, or via road from Macau and Zhuhai in about 30 minutes. It is about two hours by six-lane expressway, southwest of Guangzhou. An expressway with Shenzhen should open soon. You can obtain visas for the whole of China at the port about 10 km from Shiqi in 15-20 minutes. An instant camera is available for visa photos if working.

Shiqi (Shekki, Shekket) is the cultural, economic, and political center of Zhongshan City. Its urban population is 220,000. It is in water country, full of intriguing waterways begging to be explored. It has a lot of activity and new buildings, yet the canals and the age-old river boats, might remind you of a much smaller, older Bangkok. A visit to the **Zhongshan Hot Spring Golf Club** can be arranged in Hong Kong, *Tel. 852/28335666, 28335723.* The Arnold Palmer Course Design Company planned the 18-hole, par-72 course. It now has 36 holes. The club, which is one of the best in China, can make arrangements.

The top hotels in Shiqi are the **Zhongshan International** and the **Fu Hua**, both about 15 km from Zhongshan port and 56 km from the closest airport in Zhuhai. They are almost together near the bridge in the center of Shiqi, night market and shops. They are about even in quality. All hotels here receive Hong Kong television programs. Most add a 15% service charge to the following prices (which should be discounted) and some add an additional 10% surcharge on weekends and Hong Kong holidays.

FU HUA HOTEL *(fiudian), 1 Fuhua Road, Shiqi, 528401. Four stars. Tel. 8866888, Fax 8861862. Built in 1986, this 19-story, 242- room hotel is set in a garden.*

This hotel has smoke hoods and emergency flashlights, a revolving restaurant, Bank of China, and satellite television. A separate building for sports has a large swimming pool, night club, 30-piece gym, six-lane bowling, and sauna. It has western (of sorts), Cantonese and Chaozhou food.

ZHONGSHAN INTERNATIONAL HOTEL (*Guoji Jiudian*), *142 Zhongshan Road Section Number One, Shiqi 528401. Four stars aiming for five. Tel. 8633388, Fax 8833368.*

This 1986, 22-story, 369-room hotel has a revolving restaurant and good quality stores. It also has four bowling lanes, a sauna and outdoor pool open all year round but not heated.

For Zhongshan travel information: **CTS**, *Fuhua Hotel, Tel. 8866888, Fax 8861888 or 8822369;* **CITS**, *142 Zhongshan Road, First Section, Shiqi, 528401, Tel. 8811888, Fax 8611376.* **Tourist Hotline**, *Tel. 8611888, 8806928;* **Zhongshan Tourism Bureau**, *38 Zhong Shan 2nd Road, 528400, Tel. 8805211, 8806928, Fax 8806615.* The telephone code is *0760.*

SHENZHEN

(*Shumchun*)

On the Hong Kong border, this Special Economic Zone has been the wealthiest and the fastest growing in China. In 1979, **Shenzhen** had 20,000 people. Today, urban and rural, it has at least 3,580,000 and growing. Aspiring to become the next Hong Kong by the year 2010, it has its own stock exchange and a tightly-packed garden of skyscrapers. Fifty percent of all "foreign" arrivals into China pass through its Customs Houses. Most are Hong Kong commuters. Shenzhen has the highest cost of living in China, but it is still cheaper than Hong Kong.

Shenzhen is Hong Kong's weekend playground. It has China's best theme parks, amusement parks and resorts. Its golfing is among China's best. Prostitution seems to be out of control.

ARRIVALS & DEPARTURES

Fast and frequent electric trains arrive from Hong Kong's Kowloon Railway Station in less than one hour. You might have to endure lineups up to 30 minutes during holidays in both Customs Houses. Trains are the fastest and most convenient way to get to downtown Shenzhen from downtown Kowloon because of sluggish road traffic.

There are also city and hotel buses between the two cities, and direct buses to Splendid China and some of the hotels and resorts. No Hong Kong taxis are allowed into Shenzhen. Ferries with Macau should be starting soon.

Double-decker Citibuses go 20 times a day from 7am-2:30pm from Admiralty MTR station and China Hong Kong City (Canton Road) with stops at City One Shatin, Sha Tau Koh border point, Shenzhen City, Honey Lake, Shenzhen Bay (for Splendid China theme park), Xili Lake, and Hot Spring Lake. The last bus leaves Shenzhen Bay at 5:30pm, too early alas, for the parade at the Folk Cultures Village. The fare is about HK$75, *Tel. Hong Kong (852) 27458888 or Fax 27865876.*

Ferries also go from China Hong Kong City to Shenzhen's Shekou and to the Shenzhen airport. (You go to Fuyong and take a connecting bus). Buses leave four times a day from Hong Kong International Airport for hotels in Shenzhen. Check with the 5th Level service desk, Arrivals Hall.

Shenzhen is reached by air from at least 46 Chinese cities, and Manila. **Huangtian Airport** is 40 km west of the city and has luggage storage open from 6am-8:30pm, and four restaurants, *Tel. 7776156.* The Sunshine and Shangri-La Hotels have downtown check-in counters for China Southern flights.

Formalities

You can enter China at Shenzhen with the usual China visa, but you can also enter Shenzhen and Shekou without a visa for 72 hours. You can obtain a five-day visa for Shenzhen at the Shenzhen Customs House if you enter from the Hong Kong border by train between 7:30am and 10pm. The border is currently open from 6:30am-11pm daily. Hours however might be extended soon to 24 a day.

ORIENTATION

Shenzhen is about 7 by 10 km, spreading mainly east and west from the railway station. A 39.5 km east-west subway should be finished in 2002 from the main railway station to Shenzhen airport.

The main resorts are in the suburbs, or toward Shekou, which is 29 km west. At least two resorts have amusement park rides, the biggest at the **Honey Lake Country Club** (eight km from the train station), boasting the longest roller coaster ride (two km) in the world. Its monorail is 4.5 km long.

WHERE TO STAY

Shenzhen has over 100 hotels for foreigners. Hotels and food here are cheaper than in Hong Kong for the same quality. The English is generally not as good as Hong Kong's.

The top hotel is the **Shangri-La**, then the **Sunshine** and **Landmark**, all downtown. The best for business people depends on where you are doing business. Around the railway station closer to the International Trade Centre are the **Shangri-La Hotel** and the **Forum**. Not far away are the **Sunshine** and the **Landmark**. These are 30 km from the airport. In Shekou, the best is the **Nan Hai Hotel**.

The **Shenzhen Bay**, the **Nan Hai** and **Evergreen** have the most garden space and would be best for children, but are far from good shopping. Until the new five-star hotel opens close to Splendid China in 1999 or 2000, the best and most convenient to four of the theme parks is the **Shenzhen Bay Hotel**.

From the higher floors of the hotels downtown, you can make out Hong Kong's Sheung Shui, a neat switch after decades of tourists peeking at China from Hong Kong. Really good three-star hotels are scarce here.

Hotel prices listed here are subject to change, negotiation and a 10%-15% service charge. Walk-in guests might get 20%-50% discount just for asking. Hotels might quote their prices in Hong Kong dollars (one US dollar = about HK$7.80.) The hotels listed here receive television in English from Hong Kong and take credit cards. They have foreign exchange and business centers. All except the rustic Evergreen have IDD and services expected of international standard hotels.

SUNSHINE HOTEL *(Yanguang Jiu Dian), 1 Jiabin Road, 518005. Five stars, Tel. 2233888, Fax 2226719. In North America, Tel. 800/44UTELL. E-mail: resvr@sunshinehotel.com. Http://www.sunshinehotel.com. In North America Tel. 800/44UTELL. Y1633-Y2185 for rooms, Y2783-Y4807 for suites. 30%-50% discounts. Across plaza from Seibu Department Store.*

This hotel has a free shuttle for guests from the railway station, or downtown Hong Kong once a day. It was opened in 1991, with a two-story lobby, 10 floors and 307 rooms and 20 suites. It has wide halls with low ceilings, CNN, and a 24-hour business center. It also has an indoor pool, gym, putting green, and executive and non-smoking floors. There's a 24-hour buffet and 24-hour room service, Japanese, western and Chaozhou restaurants, and a McDonald's. You can get a milk bath in its spa for Y437.

LANDMARK HOTEL SHENZHEN, *3018 Nanhu Road, 518001. Five stars. Tel. 2172288, Fax 2290473, 2290479. E-mail: landmark@szwd.net.cn. Http://www.szwd.net.cn/~Landmark/ Y1450-Y2100 for rooms, Y2200-Y9800 for suites. Three km from the railway station.*

Built in 1994, this hotel has 27 stories, 351 rooms, CNN, an executive floor (with butler service), and non-smoking floor. It has a gym, outdoor pool and driving range, Chaozhou and seafood restaurants. A Cathay International Hotel.

SHANGRI-LA SHENZHEN HOTEL *(Shang Gorilla), East Side, Railway Station, Jianshe Road, 518001. Five stars, Tel. 2330888, Fax 2339878, 2330470. E-mail: bcslzch1@nenpub.szptt.nett.cn. HK$1200-HK$15000. Direct buses from Admiralty MTR station and China Hong Kong City in Hong Kong arrive several times a day.*

Opened in 1992 and renovated in 1999, this hotel has 31 storys, 523 large rooms and CNN. In-room safes and voice-messaging system due soon. There are executive and non-smoking floors, revolving restaurant and 24-hour room service. There's a clinic, gym, jacuzzi, sauna, steambath, outdoor pool and excellent security.

FORUM HOTEL SHENZHEN *(Fulin Jiudian), 67 Heping Road, 518010. Five stars, Tel. 5586333, Fax 5561700. In North America, tel. InterContinental at 800/327-0200. Y1148-Y2132. West side of railway station.*

Built in 1990, this one has 25 stories and 541 rooms with twin beds, in-room safes and satellite television. It has a deli, Sichuan, Japanese and international food. There're executive and non-smoking floors, an outdoor pool, gym, 24-hr room service and coffee shop. It claims the largest ballroom in the city.

BAMBOO GARDEN HOTEL *(Zhuyuan Binguan) Three-star. Dong Men Bei Road, Tel. 5533138, Fax 5534835. Y348-Y480 for rooms, Y568-3219 for suites.*

This hotel isn't too bad but has no CNN and room safes.

Near the Theme Parks

The **Shenzhen Bay Hotel** is the best here, comfortable and basic with good restaurants but it needs to improve its service and English. There are other cheaper hotels in this neighbourhood but the Shenzhen Bay is most convenient to the parks. Many of its rooms overlook the Folk Culture Village. You can sometimes see flocks of egrets in nearby mangroves, and the skyscrapers of Hong Kong's New Territories across the bay. Another five-star hotel, the Yu Yue, should be finished the end of 1999 near Happy Valley.

SHENZHEN BAY HOTEL *(Shenzhen Wan Dajiudian), Overseas Chinese Town, 518053. Five stars, Tel. 6600111, Fax 6600139. About Y770 for a standard room and Y130 taxi from the airport. There are 308 rooms with narrow twin beds and some with balconies.*

A sign in English in this hotel says "Please dress properly." It has a beautiful outdoor pool, tennis, gym and night club. There's a grill room, and *dim sum* (7am-11am). A CTS Hotel.

SEAVIEW HOTEL *(Haijing), Overseas Chinese Town, 518053. Three stars, Tel. 6602222, Fax 6606831.*

This is also within walking distance of the theme parks, across the road away from the ocean. It's okay but has no western breakfast. Y495-Y1078 for rooms, Y1936-Y2178 for suites.

Shekou

Shekou is 30 km from downtown Shenzhen, about 25 km from the airport. It has 50-minute hovercraft service with Hong Kong four times a day. Shekou is near the science park with its many factories and is about

10 km from Splendid China. Here are the lovely five-star waterfront **Nanhai** and the cheaper but adequate **Ming Wah International** on a mountain.

NAN HAI HOTEL *(Da Jiudian), Gong Ye First Road, Shekou Industrial Zone, Shenzhen, 518069. Five stars, Tel. 6692888, Fax 6692440, 6679476. E-mail: sznanhai@public.szptt.net.cn. Http://www.nanhai-hotel.com. In a residential area near town and close to the ferry to Hong Kong. It charges Y926-Y1329 for rooms, Y1610-11914 for suites.*

This Hong Kong joint venture was built in 1985 and has non-smoking rooms. It has 11 stories and 396 rooms with safes, smoke hoods, 24-hour room service and CNN. It has lighted tennis courts, mini-golf, disco, and bicycles for rent, a small gym, outdoor year-round pool, and foot reflexology. A direct bus once a day arrives from Hong Kong. A shuttle bus goes to Splendid China and the Shenzhen railway station. Managed by Miramar International Hotels Management Group (H.K.).

MING WAH INTERNATIONAL, *Gui Shan Road, Shekou Industrial Zone, 518067. Three-star standard applying for four. Tel. 6689968, Fax 6687356, 6679615. Y555. It has a shuttle bus going to the Hong Kong ferry.*

This six story, 113-room hotel has small bathrooms, CNN and BBC and a pleasant college dormitory atmosphere with relaxed standards and dirty hall carpets. It also has a gym, heated indoor pool, squash, bowling, steam room, gym, and golf-simulator. In the complex are a conference center, service apartments and offices. Hua Ting management group.

Resorts

Mission Hills (see *Sports & Recreation below*) has a beautiful little five star hotel in another suburb. At the other end of the spectrum is the Evergreen:

EVERGREEN RESORT, *Yueliangwan, Nanshan District, 518054, Tel. 6646988, Fax 6406322. Rooms cost Y960-Y1080 and camping Y120-Y200; discounts available if booked through travel agencies.*

This resort is isolated in the northwest part of the city and surrounded by *lichee* groves. It's a Y25 taxi ride from Shekou. It has 100 cabins and 88 rooms. It has large models of dinosaurs, huge pool, pottery making, handicraft center, butterflies, fishing, tennis courts, hiking trails, and real mosquitos. It has in-room safes, but no television in English. Ask for Paul Tai who speaks English.

WHERE TO EAT

Vegetables here are fresher than Hong Kong's. The hotel restaurants are best, but these restaurants are good too:

SEAFOOD MARKET RESTAURANT (*Hao-shi-jie*) *at Bagua 4th Road, Bagualing, Tel. 2264817, 2423099. It's open 11am-10pm.*

There's no menu in English but you can point. You can get a fish hot pot for Y48, stir-fried vegetables for Y40 and five-spice pork leg for Y65. You can also get ostrich for Y78, but the seafood is more expensive.

PANXI RESTAURANT, *Jianshe Road near the Shangri-la Hotel.*

HENRY J. BEAN'S, *at the Shangri-la Hotel.*

You can get steak, potatoes and vegetables for Y108, ribs for Y85 and up, wings for Y68 and hot dogs for Y58. It is open 5:30pm-2am daily with a happy hour 5pm-7pm. At Shangri-La's Japanese restaurant, a set lunch is Y90. In its revolving restaurant, the Asian buffet is Y98 for lunch, and Y148 for dinner.

SUNSHINE HOTEL, *1 Jiabin Road. Tel. 2233888.*

The lunch buffet costs Y138 and the dinner Y168.

BAMBOO GARDEN HOTEL, *Dong Men Bei Road, Tel. 5533138.*

The scallops, prawns and squid in birds' nest is Y80, stir-fried scallops and brocolli Y98, and seafood salad Y55. It is open 6:30am-3pm, and 5:30pm-9:30pm. For *dim sum* it's 6:30am-11am. All credit cards accepted.

NAN HAI HOTEL, *Gong Ye First Road. Tel. 6692888.*

The breakfast buffet is Y88, the executive lunch is Y98 and the dinner buffet Y148.

And you can find **McDonald's** everywhere.

SEEING THE SIGHTS

The day trippers can view China's greatest concentration of skyscrapers. They might note the reservoir that supplies half of Hong Kong's water supply. Shenzhen has no historical monuments save the modest grave in Shekou of the last Song emperor, who fled here to escape the Mongols.

Four theme parks are together around the Shenzhen Bay Hotel, about a 25 minutes' drive from the railway station towards Shekou. They should be linked together now by monorail and are worth one or two days if you like theme parks. If you visit Splendid China and Folk Culture Village, adults pay Y130 for both. For Splendid China only it's Y70. Folk Cultures has a place to leave luggage.

Splendid China (Jinxiu Zhong Hua) is on 29 hectares with over 80 of China's top tourist attractions in 15:1 miniature. It is highly recommended (but not in the rain). Take a guide as no explanations are in English. Thousands of tiny ceramic people, each different, in period or ethnic dress, and in scale, add liveliness. They include Mongolian wrestlers in their leather vests and baggy pants, and emperors paying homage at the Temple of Confucius. *Open 8:30am-5:30pm daily. Tel. 6600626 X 2005.* Mr. Wu Yan is an official with Splendid China who speaks English and can answer questions on the telephone.

The **Folk Culture Village**, run by the same company as Splendid China but a separate park, is next to the miniatures. This is a 180,000 square meter exhibition of 24 different life-size minority buildings, with demonstrations of handicrafts, cooking, and three shows a day of dances and songs. It is a lot more interesting than Splendid China because it has real people. With samples of full-scale Tujia, Uygur and Wa architecture, and of course real Miao, Jinuo and Tibetan people in ethnic dress, you can really get a good introduction to China's 55 minorities.

If you want to do more than just shoot photos, take an interpretor so you can ask questions. There is only one small sign with a limited amount of information in English beside each exhibit.

You can spend two to six hours at Folk Culture Village, plus the parade. It is open 11:30am-9pm weekdays, and 10am-9pm weekends and holidays. The 50-minute 7:30pm dance show is in the Central Theatre. The daily 8:30pm Carnival Parade is outside, lively and professional with permanent floats and show-biz adaptions of minority dances and costumes. In case you missed it the first time, the parade goes around twice. Its happy-happy atmosphere with 500 performers should not be missed. Seats cost Y15 and Y20 extra.

Photo opportunities abound and attendants willingly pose. No one runs shyly away nor asks for money. While the dirt and poverty of the real villages are missing, and the variety within cultures are absent in each exhibit, there are enough farm implements, hanging husks of corn, and looms to show how these people differ from the Han majority. In some cases, you can sample ethnic food. And the toilets are clean! For lazy tourists, this is the next best thing to reality.

You can go there even as late as 4pm, snack on the grounds, and explore until the 7:30pm parade, *Tel. 6602198, 6600626.*

On the other side of the Shenzhen Bay Hotel is **Windows of the World**, a 480,000 square meter theme park with miniatures of world monuments like the Golden Gate Bridge and Eiffel Tower (which you can climb for the view). Shows are all day but the big one is 7:30-8:45pm with galloping "British" horsemen, lavish costumes, and international performers. Avoid the front seats; you'll have to turn around. *Tel. 6608000, Fax 6602590.*

Nearby is the new **Happy Valley** with water sports, rides and interactive exhibits aimed at children. *Tel. 6608088, 6908866.* Two golf courses are also in the neighborhood.

For all parks, *E-mail:szocthv@public.szptt.net.cn.*

Food is available at the theme parks. At the **Tujia Pavilion** in the Folk Culture Village, you can buy sticky rice wrapped in lotus leaves. The best restaurant here is the **Tian Eye Ge** with large servings of good Yunnan-style minced pork on cabbage (Y68), steamed fish (Y88), lightly fried mushrooms (Y118), and steamed pot chicken soup (Y128). **McDonald's**, open 7am-11pm, is outside Windows on the World (Y18 for a big Mac). The Chinese restaurants in the nearby **Shenzhen Bay Hotel** are fine. The breakfast buffet for Y66 was basic. Near the Seaview Hotel are several smaller local restaurants.

Safari Park, a wild animal park with 15,000 animals is in another part of the city, at *Xili Lake, 518055, Tel. 6622888*. It takes at least two hours to tour and at 4pm has a parade of animals and clowns. You take buses through the various habitats but there's lots of walking. Among the 150 species are pandas, golden monkeys, Asian elephants, red-crested cranes, and Asian tigers. It is all right if you have time and haven't been to such a park elsewhere, but if you have to choose, go to Splendid China and Folk Culture Village because they are uniquely Chinese and better done.

Festivals

During the summertime *lichee* season, tourists come here to pick this sweet fruit. The tour price usually includes all-you-can eat and 2.5 kilograms to take home. A **Lichee and Fine Food Festival** takes place the end of June and early July.

SHOPPING

At the theme parks, there's the usual tourist stuff, mostly poor quality. Some good minority embroidery is at the **Folk Culture Village** and across the road is a **fine arts exhibition hall** with theatre and concerts. In town, a shopping mall with a branch of **Dickson's**, the Hong Kong department store, is in the *Tian An International Building, Renmin Nan Road, Tel. 2296161*. The **Friendship Department Store** is at *Friendship City, Youyi Road, Tel. 2178210, 2178245*. It is open 10 am-10pm daily.

Although Shenzhen makes many international name brand clothing, I couldn't find any stores with factory overruns. Things are cheaper in Guangzhou. China's first **Wal-Mart** is in the *Hujin Garden Building, Honghu Road, Tel. 5607060*.

NIGHTLIFE & ENTERTAINMENT

In Shekou, the expat hangouts are the **China Beach** and **Red Rooster** bars, near Sea World. A **night market** is at Nanguo Square near the Sunshine Hotel from 8:30pm-midnight.

SPORTS & RECREATION

One of China's best courses is the world-class **Mission Hills Golf Club**, about 30 minutes drive north of Shenzhen, used for the 1995 World

Cup. This 72-hole course was designed by Jack Nicklaus, Nick Faldo, and Masashi Ozaki and is open 6am-11:30pm. It also has 50 lighted tennis courts and a 3000-seat stadium, an outdoor pool and a 64-bay driving range, squash court, gym, and children's play area. Its 228-room resort is a real oasis from the crowds and noise of cities. Its restaurants offer about 65 mainly French wines. Rates are Y1210-Y2420 for rooms, Y1925-13068 for suites. It's very beautiful.

To book a room, contact the Mission Hills Golf Club at: *Mission Hills Road, Guanlan Town, 518110 Tel. 82020888, Fax 8010713. Its office in Hong Kong can make arrangements, Tel. 852/29730303, Fax 28699632, and it takes credit cards.*

The 27-hole **Xili Golf course** is exclusive and good, about 45 minutes from downtown. Book through any Shangri-La or in Hong Kong, *Tel. 29672592, Fax 29671972.*

The best swimming beach is at **Xiao Meisha**, 30 km east of the Shangri-La.

PRACTICAL INFORMATION

Business Hours, 8:30 or 9am-5:30pm, mostly five days a week for offices; 9am or 10am-10pm for stores daily.

China Comfort Shenzhen Travel Service, *Flat C, 5/F, Shenzhen Textile Building, 3 Huaqiang Bei Road, 518031, Tel. 3218064, Fax 3219049.*

Shenzhen China International Travel Service, *2 Chuan Bu Street, Heping Road, 518001, Tel. 5588411, 5588401, Fax 5577969, 5572151; also 15/F, CITS Hotel, 6 Yan He Nan Road, 518005, Tel. 2338822, 2329829, Fax 2329832.*

Shenzhen CTS, *5/F, China Travel Service Building, 40 Renmin Nan Road, 518001, Tel. 2258447, 2255888, Fax 2235576, 2227907.*

Telephone code, *0755*

Tourist Information and brochures: **Shenzhen Trade Development Bureau Tourism Department**, *Block 4B, 8/F, Saige Science Industrial Garden, 518028, Tel. Mr. Ou Yang, 3369461, Fax 3369459.*

Tourist Complaints. *Tourist Quality Monitoring Institution, Room 821, 8/F, Building 4, SEG Industrial Park, Zhenxing Road, 518006.*

ZHUHAI

Zhuhai is adjacent to the Portuguese colony of Macau across the Pearl River delta southwest of Hong Kong. Most visitors come for conferences, on business, or on their way from Macau to somewhere else, like Zhongshan next door. It produces electronics, and trains airplane pilots. It is one of the most pleasant cities in China. It does have one international class tourist attraction. It also has an **annual air show** every two years from November 1998. Its **Formula One Grand Prix car races** are in October-November, and will probably be held every other year after 1999.

There are also two golf courses and an international trade and exhibition center. See Zhongshan (in Guangzhou's excursions section above) for a better golf course. The urban population is about 160,000. The Pearl Land Amusement Park is over 30 minutes by road north of the city. It is huge with a 1.8 km roller coaster, and a 36-seat, four-abreast ferris wheel.

ARRIVALS & DEPARTURES

You can reach Zhuhai Special Economic Zone direct by ferry every 15 minutes from Hong Kong, or from Shenzhen. You can go by road or foot via Macau at Gongbei and in late 1999 at Hengqing, an island off Zhuhai and Macau. Zhuhai is also a two-hour 140-km drive from Guangzhou but traffic jams in Guangzhou could add an additional hour. Its small but very modern airport has links with 25 other Chinese cities. The world's longest bridge extending 50 km from here to Hong Kong should be finished about 2003 or 2004.

The border with Macau is open from 7am to midnight at Gongbei. You can get a three-day visa upon arrival in China without photos. You can extend this visa in Zhuhai (photos needed). But you might not find a porter for the long walk through the Customs' House.

Frequent mini-buses and air-conditioned highway buses go from two bus stations near the Gongbei Customs House to Guangzhou (Y50), Shenzhen, Zhongshan (30 minutes) and Taishan. The Kee Kwan Motor Co. has new air-conditioned buses. The airport is about 35-40 km away.

WHERE TO STAY

Zhuhai has at least 83 hotels and resorts. The top hotel has been the restful **Grand Bay Hotel** but the newer **Harbour View Hotel and Resort**, as yet unseen, should have better international standards. These are followed by the **Yindu** (Silver Capital) **Hotel** in the downtown area. A new hotel, the **Paradise Hill Tourist Centre**, aiming for five stars, is very beautiful, but needs a lot of work. The carpets in its villas were dirty. A **Youth Hostel** is at the **Zhuhai Holiday Resort**, on the ocean. Reservations are needed weekends, July-August and Hong Kong holidays. 10%-15% surcharge is added but prices below should be discounted.

HARBOUR VIEW HOTEL & RESORT ZHUHAI, *Haijing Road, 519015, Tel. 3322888, Fax 3371385. E-mail: harbour@pub.zhuhai.gd.cn. Five star standards. Y840-Y1180 for rooms, Y1380-Y1680 for suites.*

This 1998 hotel has four restaurants, two bars, gym, pool, mini golf and bowling.

GRAND BAY VIEW HOTEL *(Haiwan Dajiudian), Shui Wan Road, Gongbei, 519020, Tel. 8878998, Fax 8878998. E-mail: zhgbvhzh@pub.zhuhai.gd.cn. Http://www.gbvh.com. Five stars. Y830-Y1180 for rooms, Y1380 for suites.*

This 1996 hotel has 244 rooms in its old wing, 180 in its new. In low season it was offering 40% discounts on weekends, and 50% on weekdays. It is 43 km from the airport, about one km from the Customs House, and a 45-minute taxi ride from the airport. Carpets and wallpaper are being renovated in 1999. This very restful, attractive property has 19 and 14 story wings and non-smoking rooms, CNN, Star TV, and HBO. It is located on spacious grounds overlooking Macau. It has good standards aside from its health club. It has a decent but not lavish breakfast buffet with made-to-order omlettes, and there are a pool, gym, and in-room safes. It should now have a night club with Russian dancers. Its convention hall seats 800 guests, which it claims is the largest in town.

Note: The manager of the health club told me rudely that they didn't serve women, only men. The giggles of the other patrons suggested that something illegal was going on. The management of this central government-owned hotel said the health club was under separate management and had no control over the policy there.

YINDO HOTEL, *Yuehai Road, Gongbei, 519020, Tel. 8883388, Fax 8883311, 8892896. Y820-Y1180 for rooms, Y1300-Y22000 for suites. Five stars.*

Built in 1989, this 299-room hotel with European-type decor is surrounded by stores, and is two km from the Gongbei Customs House. It has an outdoor pool, gym, tennis, bowling and mini-golf. It has a Food Street with snacks, western grill room, north Chinese and Cantonese food. It was playing Christmas music in March, whatever that means.

ZHUHAI HOLIDAY RESORT *(Dujiachun Jiu Dian), Shi Hua Shan, 519015. Four stars, Tel. 3332038, Fax 3332036. E-mail: zhr@pub.zhuhai.gd.cn. Y598-Y830 for rooms, Y830-Y1280 for suites, and Y2380-Y4980 for villas.*

This attractive 468-room resort is set in a vast garden, a 15-minute walk from the Hong Kong ferry pier and direct bus service from the Gongbei Customs House. It was built in 1986 and has about 10 villas. Rooms are medium-sized with kettles, continental beds, safes, and CNN and CNBC. It has tennis, bowling, outdoor pool, roller skating, horses, archery, shooting gallery, go-karts, and water sports.

The 120-bed **Zhuhai Youth Hostel** here has dorm beds for US$5-$10. The hostel guests are entitled to use the resort's recreational facilities, which include bowling, tennis, a swimming pool, etc.

WHERE TO EAT

Food in the hotels is good. A moderate-priced restaurant with lower standards is on the third floor of the **Tourism Building**, *Haibin Nan Road.* Its stir-fried pinenuts and corn for Y15 is a good novelty. Watercress soup at Y30 is delicious. Its egg plant, hot pepper and minced meat for Y22 is also good.

SEEING THE SIGHTS

The only tourist attraction worth stopping for is the **New Yuanmingyuan** (see Beijing chapter, *Seeing the Sights (Day Three)*, for information about the real summer palace). The park is open 9:30am-10:30pm and costs Y80-Y90 for adults, less for seniors and kids. It's at *Lanpu Jiu Zhou Road, Tel. 8610388.* This is a theme park based on the favorite palace of several emperors. It was built in 1709 with the help of Italian missionaries and destroyed by foreign troops in 1860. You could spend two hours walking around here, and another two hours at the evening show. This reproduction is quite good, and enlivened by "soldiers" and "court ladies," dancers, musicians and storytellers in Manchu costume. Unfortunately there are no signs in English but you can hire an English-speaking guide.

A food court with stalls from various provinces and countries will keep you from going hungry. Wine is available in the second floor restaurant which serves imperial Qing food. Manager Jack Tam promises English labels and menus on each stall but you can point if he hasn't followed through. And you pay with tokens. The food court is open 11am-9pm daily.

The evening show is at a 5000-seat outdoor theatre behind the Lama Temple and only the front seats require an additional Y10 payment. The lighting of the park is very good and you should visit just before dusk. The show however has only a few good moments like 16 real galloping horses, and an impressive burning scene; it has too many slow arty dances too. Hopefully it will improve.

PRACTICAL INFORMATION

CTS, *G/F, A Block, 23 Building, Yinhai Xin Village, Gongbei, 519020; Tel. 8881981, Fax 8888456. E-mail: zhctswxy@pub.zhuhai.gd.cn.*

Zhuhai Tourism Administration, *12/F Tourism Building, Haibin Nan Road, Jida, Tel. 3366905, Fax 3366902.*

Tourism Complaints should be directed to: **Zhuhai Tourist Service Complaint Center**, *13/F, Tourism Mansion, Tourism Building, Haibin Nan Road, Tel. 3336061; Fax 3366902.*

Zhuhai Mondial International Travel Service, *3, Changsheng Road, Gongbei, Tel. 8873873, Fax 8885272. E-mail:zhmits@pub.zhuhai.gd.cn.*
Telephone code: *0756*

HAIKOU, HAINAN ISLAND

Haikou is the capital of Hainan, China's second largest island and its 31st and smallest province. Hainan is 30 km off China's southern coast, and includes the Xisha, Nansha, and Zhongsha Islands. It is important because it is China's tropical playground and agricultural area, wonderful in winter. Though it has no heavy industries, it is a major stop for business people. Its air is among China's cleanest.

The weather is tropical, with 2000 mm. of rain a year. Summer has high temperatures but is usually cool at night. Typhoons could hit from March to October. The high tourist season is Christmas to the end of March, but could start earlier. The island is at the same latitude as the southern tip of Hawaii.

ARRIVALS & DEPARTURES

A new airport is due in 1999 or 2000. It is expected to be huge, 26 km from downtown and capable of landing 747s. Until then, the airport is three to six km from the hotels downtown. Haikou has flight links with Bangkok, Hong Kong, Kuala Lumpur and Macau and 37 Chinese cities. In Haikou and Sanya, you can get a Chinese visa at the international airport. The government is working on a visa-free entry but don't count on it yet.

Infrequent ships arrive from Zhanjiang, Guangzhou, Beihai and Shenzhen. You can also go by almost direct train and ferry in 52 hours from Beijing twice a week.

ORIENTATION

Han dynasty troops first colonized Hainan. From the Tang dynasty, disfavored scholars and officials were exiled here, a tropical Siberia. During the 1930s and 1940s, a Communist army detachment fought here, and after Mao's victory in 1949 part of the island became an autonomous region because a large percentage of the population are national minorities: mainly Li and Miao, but also Hui.

Hainan Island with 34,000 square km is just about as big as Taiwan. The Chinese government is developing it as a very special economic zone with more flexibility and openness than other such zones. The island has a 1528 km coastline, 60% of this sand beaches. The government has targeted Sanya and Yalong Bay in the south as major resorts areas.

The island produces tea, coffee, rubber, fish, sugar, coconut and rice. The population is over seven million. Haikou itself has an urban population of 300,000 and who knows how many transients. Its road traffic does jam up and it has a frontier attitude. People are out to make a fast yuan.

HEALTH SITUATION ON HAINAN ISLAND

Doctors at the People's Hospital in Haikou where ambulances are international standard, provided by AEA, insist they haven't had any **malaria** *cases in "many years." The World Health Organization suggests that visitors to this island get protection for malaria (larium). "Malaria is found only in the deep forests," said Dr. Liu Shu Yong. I found no one who lives here taking any precautions, not even foreigners.*

The decision is up to you. I found only two mosquitos during my stay in November, and only a few in April. Bring long sleeves and trousers for the evening.

Compared to five or 10 years ago, there are more sexually transmitted diseases here now, but the rate has recently gone down. "The government is paying attention to the problem," he said. "Most patients have high blood pressure or stroke. Many old people have hepatitis."

GETTING AROUND

Haikou has three sections – the north (old Haikou), north tip with the university and Golden Coast Hotel, and the financial section. The architecture in old Haikou is much like Hong Kong's in the early 1960s– a charming mix of old buildings hanging over the sidewalks, and huge palacial hotels. English could be a problem except in the top hotels.

WHERE TO STAY

The best hotels in Haikou are the **Golden Coast Hotel** and the Mandarin. The Golden Coast has the better location. The second best is **Huandao Tide Hotel**, then the **Bao Hua Harbourview**. The **Haikou Tower Hotel** is popular with moderate-priced tourists. The **university hostel** is good for backpackers. The four-star **International Financial Center Hotel** has gone downhill and can't be recommended in spite of its great business location unless it's had a complete recent renovation. Hotels below are good and add a 15% service charge. Prices listed are subject to change, discounts and a surcharge.

HAINAN MANDARIN HOTEL, *18 Wen Hua Road, 570105. Tel. 8548888, Fax 8511228. E-mail: resvn.sjm@meritus-hotels.com. Http://www.smi-hotels.com. Five stars. Four km from the airport. Y1360-Y6560. 318 rooms located on the 9th to 23rd floors, each with a safe.*

The hotel has a gym, steam bath, indoor and outdoor pools, and nightclub.

GOLDEN COAST LAWTON HOTEL (*Jin Hai Dajiudian*), *68 Renmin Avenue, 570208, Tel. 6259888, Fax 6258889. Six km from the airport. Five stars. Y1100-Y13800.*

Opened in 1993, the Golden Coast has 12 stories and 351 rooms, non-smoking rooms and executive floors. It offers Shanghai, hot pot, seafood, Chaozhou and Japanese restaurants, and has three western food outlets. The breakfast buffet included congee, made-to-order omelettes, Japanese *odon* noodles, *dim sum*, salted eggs, good croissants and cookies. It has a 72-item wine list.

The exterior was patterned after Hong Kong's Peninsula Hotel, but spoiled by red neon advertising its karaoke night club. The interior was inspired by Hong Kong's Grand Hyatt with graceful twin staircases (but in beige Italian marble). The staff is always smiling "good morning." It has an Internet bar at a reasonable Y38 an hour, minimum Y19, and a golf shop with imported clubs. It has a golf package and a gym. Emergency telephones are in every hallway (in case of a forgotten key.) While it's not yet perfect, it is trying hard. The bathroom gleams. Even the standard rooms have hallways, privacy when the door is open. The television offers ABN, inhouse movies, CNN, Star movies, CBS and NHK. But the windows are small, like the old Peninsula.

BAO HUA HARBOUR VIEW (*Jiudian*), *69 Binhai Avenue, 570105, Tel. 8536699, Fax 8538958. Four stars. Y920-Y1280 for rooms, Y1580-18800 for suites.*

This 1996, Hong Kong-managed hotel has a four-story atrium lobby and 31-story hotel tower. Its Qing style Chinese suite and Japanese suite with *shoji* windows but no *tatami* cost Y3100 each. Ask for a harborview room. The 12-room presidential suite has Forbidden City red-studded doors, and Ming-style furniture and includes two saunas. Standard rooms have small bathrooms. It offers Thai, Sichuan, Shanghai and Suzhou food.

YANTAI INTERNATIONAL HOTEL, *No. 18, The 5th East Haidian Road, 570208, Tel. 6250888, Fax 6270533. Four stars. Y880-Y1080 for rooms, Y1580-Y4600 for suites.*

This 1997 hotel is isolated in a residential area with a good view of the coast, 15 minutes by car from downtown. It has 302 rooms, 19 floors and garden, and a conference hall seating 400 for dinner, and 800 for meetings. It is equipped for simultaneous translation.

HUANDAO TIDE HOTEL (*Dajiudian*), *18 Peace Avenue, 570208, Tel. 6265222, 6368888, Fax 62655588. Tel. in North America 800/821-0900. Five stars. Y588-Y1336 for rooms, Y2596-18000 for suites.*

Opened in 1994, this hotel has 23 stories and 408 rooms with relatively small televisions and potable tap water. The lobby is covered by a giant pyramid (with dirty glass windows; other windows are clean and give a nice feeling of openness to its 6.5 acre garden outside). The Presidential Suite has two bedrooms and one secretary's room, the decor except for the mahjong table, more suited to western taste than the Lawton's. The furniture was made in Canada. It also has garden suites. It has one non-smoking floor, some narrow halls, and an executive lounge, Chaozhou restaurant, Korean barbecue, and 24-hour western coffee shop. It is related to the Asiana hotel group.

HAIKOU TOWER HOTEL *(Tai Hua Jiudian), Binhai Road, 570105. Three stars, Tel. 6772990, 6773962, Fax 6773966. Near bus station and three km from the airport. Y472-Y660 for rooms, Y1438-Y3500 for suites. Built in 1986, this two-story, 240-room hotel has tennis, pools, bowling and a gym.*

This hotel has satellite television, free in-house movies, and air-ticketing. It is well-maintained, set in a small garden and has snap-to-it service.

HAINAN UNIVERSITY GUEST HOUSE *(Hainan Da Xue Shao Yi Fu Xue Shu Zhong Xin), 570228, Tel. Foreign Affairs (Wai Ban) office, 6259949 or Fax 6258369. Y120 per room. Y50 a day for food. 56 clean, air-conditioned rooms with television, private bath, and basic services.*

This is a beautiful spacious campus with friendly staff, palm and flame trees, but little English.

WHERE TO EAT

The province produces all kinds of fruit: pineapples, mangosteens, mangoes, *lichees*, watermelons, jackfruits, and rambutans. It also has fresh, fresh seafood. Famous dishes are *Wenchang* Chicken (known elsewhere as Hainan chicken, poached with ginger), *Jiaji* duck, *Hele* crab, and *Dongshan* mutton. Some restaurants serve dog meat too, so beware. At the top are the hotels. You can't go wrong in the **Chaozhou restaurant** at the **Golden Coast Hotel** where you choose your own ingredients and spices for Beijing, Huaiyang or Sichuan hotpots for Y88. Your choices range from sandworm and eel, to the usual beef, mutton, shrimp, fish, crab and vegetables. And popcorn! The hotel also serves black chicken which melts in your mouth.

In its **Shanghai restaurant**, good were pork balls (hong shao shi zitou) for Y55; steamed shrimp Y128; Peking duck Y188; steamed black fish (*hong you yu*) Y150. The **Mandarin Hotel** has a good Italian restaurant.

At the lower price end are food streets on **Haixiu Road** and **Jin Long Road**, open 7pm-midnight.

SEEING THE SIGHTS

In Haikou, you can visit the restored **Five Officials Memorial Temple**, originally built in 1889 in honor of its banished officials. A

butterfly museum is adjacent. Near this is the **Su Temple**, a memorial to the famous Song poet, Su Dong Po, who was exiled to Hainan in 1097. Travel agents will also send you to the **Hai Rui Tomb**. While mildly interesting, you can ignore all these if you want. The only important tourist attraction in Hainan are the southern beaches and resorts.

Not worth a special trip, but good for people just wanting to see some countryside, is a drive to the **mangrove forest** at Haikor, 30 km northeast of Haikou. You can take a small boat for an hour's tour for Y25. A good, seafood restaurant, the **Hong Shu Lin**, is at the entrance. Best go by taxi.

The **Dong Jiao Peninsula** is a little further south. There you have to take a short Y45 ferry ride by small noisy motor boat past fish farms to a string of dumpy open-air beach-side restaurants. The better ones have signs "Designated Tourist Unit," and you can gorge cheaply on coconut rice, and fresh crab, squid, abalone, and mackerel.

Swimming however is better elsewhere. Sad however are the stalls selling stuffed endangered sea turtles. Nearby within 10 minutes walk is a **statue of the three Soong sisters**, a remarkable family. Wenchang was the home of Charlie Soong, the father of these three influential women. (See Shanghai).

NIGHTLIFE & ENTERTAINMENT

The **Golden Coast** has a night club with performances and disco from 8:30 or 9-11pm. Russian women do an underwater and stage ballet for Y80 at the **Holiday Beach Water World** to American pop music for Y80. Bars are safe in four and five star hotels.

Note: Standards of morality in Hainan are more "flexible" than in other parts of China. While prostitution is illegal, it is pretty obvious. You might get a call at night about 'special services.' Five-star hotels at least monitor all telephone calls so guests won't be disturbed.

SPORTS & RECREATION

The island has **17 golf courses** completed or in construction in a variety of beach and mountain settings. Sanya and Yalong Bay are one of the country's best places for **water sports**. Hainan also has six **hot spring resorts**.

SHOPPING

Local are saltwater pearls, rubies, rose quartz, coconut and ox horn carvings, hand weaves and embroidered ethnic textiles. Pictures are made of butterfly wings. Department stores are on **Haixiu Road**. The Golden Coast has a small **antique shop**.

EXCURSIONS & DAY TRIPS

See **Sanya** below for a full description.

Three roads go from Haikou south toward Sanya. If you take the 296 km central road through the mountains, you can stop at the **Feng Mu Deer Farm** (arrangements in advance), and then visit a Miao village. There's a modest hotel and the **Museum of Nationalities** in Tongzha but this road is not great. If you go via the eastern expressway route, you can also visit Kangle Garden Resort at Xinlong, and stop at the Chao Yin Si Temple on Mount Dongshan. The western road is longest at 405 km and non-stop this would be a 3.5 hour drive to Sanya.

Hot Springs Resort

KANGLE GARDEN RESORT *(Kangle Dajiudian), Xinglong, Wanning, 571533. It should have a five-star rating when extensions are finished. Y858-Y1500 for rooms; 1288-3000 for suites, plus 10% tax. This beautiful resort is on the east coast, about 170 km from Haikou, and 80 km from the Sanya airport. Tel. (0898) 2552008, Fax 2552038, 2554140. E-mail:Kangle@public.hk.hq.cn.*

This is the best of the **hot spring resorts**, built in 1989. Rooms and suites, some with terraces attached, are in two-story buildings. All rooms have CNN, ceiling fans, air-conditioners and American decor. A conference room holds 500 people classroom style, 700 for cocktails. The food and service here is good, the surroundings beautiful. The outdoor swimming pool is 120 meters long (24 C). It also has outdoor jacuzzis but there's tennis in the works, bowling, pingpong, and billards.

Dinner in the Chinese restaurant has been good: egg and local wild greens soup Y6 a cup, lightly cooked green beans Y15; squid and bitter melon Y35 (not bitter at all). It could have a cook from France by the time you get there so the western food should improve.

This is a beautiful, well-maintained international class resort, primarily for people who want to soak in natural hot spring water. It is not for those who want to be on the ocean. The closest beach is an eight km, nine-minute drive away. Only umbrellas and a small hotel are on **Riyue** (Sun and Moon) **Beach** but it does have showers and the Kangle's driver (if available) can take you there for free. Beach people had better head for the more developed Yalong Bay.

From here you can also make day trips to Sanya, trips to Li and Miao villages, and hike in the mountains. Hiring taxis by the day costs between Y300 and Y500. The town and tropical botanical garden are within walking distance. You can rent bicycles from Kangle for about Y40 a day. Nearby is the **Haiwang Nanyanwan Golf Club** designed by American Bob MacFarlane on Nanyan Bay, three km from the Shimei Exit of the Eastern Expressway.

XISHA (PARACEL) ISLANDS

While the government has given permission for tourists to visit this controversial group of islands about 400 km southeast of Haikou, arrangements to do so on a regular basis might not be ready yet. Do contact travel agents for the latest information. Recent visitors have arrived there by a very unstable ship in 20 hours, too long a trip just to be able to say you've been there. There's not much to see, but the water and air are clean.

These islands are very sensitive, the source of conflict between China and its neighbors. Known also as the Spratly Islands, this archipelago is situated on a strategic shipping route thought to be rich in oil. The islands are claimed wholly or partly by China, Malaysia, the Philippines, Brunei, Taiwan and Vietnam.

PRACTICAL INFORMATION

Ambulance, *Tel. 120.*

CTS, *17 Datong Road, 570001, Tel. 6772652, Fax 6772095.*

China International Travel Service Hainan, *3/F Changlong Mansion, West Airport Road, 570203, Tel.5358269, Fax 5358187.*

Hainan China International Travel Service, *No. 33, Jichan Road, Tel. 5358432, Fax 5353174. Contact Ye Xian Yeng.*

Hainan Overseas Tourist Corporation, *14/F Nanyang Mansion, Seaside Avenue, 570105, Tel. 8511426, Fax 8512639.*

Hainan Provincial Tourism Administration, *3/F Changlong Building, Tel. 5363619, Fax 5363172.* Brochures.

Hainan Tourist Corporation, *HNTC Building, 2# Long-She Road, Tel. 5350264, Fax 5351647.* Contact Yang Wen Bo.

Hainan Tourist Corporation, *8 - 1 Hailu Building, Airport Road East, 570203, Tel. 5352431, Fax 5351647.*

Hours: government: 8am-12 noon; 3pm-6pm; travel agents 8:30 or 9am-11:30; 3-5:30pm. Department stores: Monday-Fridays 8 or 8:30am-9:30 or 10pm. On Saturday and Sundays open to 10:30pm. Smaller shops close at 12 noon, reopen about 3pm.

People's Hospital, *Renmin Avenue*, is near the Golden Coast Lawton, *Tel. 6269383, 6256555.*

Telephone Code, *0898*

Website: *www.hainanisland.com*

SANYA, HAINAN ISLAND

Sanya is at the southern tip of Hainan Island. Here no one will get you up at 7am and onto a tour bus at 8:30 for 12 hours of sightseeing and eating – unless you want to, of course. Sanya is for relaxing, for sun and sand, for water sports, hiking, and golf. Of course you can visit a Moslem fishing village, a pearl farm, and the rocky "Ends of the Earth." Forget Monkey Island; its animals are vicious.

About 3000 to 4000 Moslems live in Yanlan village near the End of the World, and many wear a distinctive dress. During the Ming and Yuan dynasties, the emperors sent Moslem soldiers to secure the borders. Some are also descendants of traders from Central Asia – and many are poor and aggressive.

ARRIVALS & DEPARTURES

You can fly direct to Sanya from Haikou but you can fly from nine other Chinese cities and Hong Kong. Chinese visas are available on arrival. The international airport is 15 km north west of Sanya City.

Air-conditioned buses go from hotels in Haikou to Sanya. You can get an air-conditioned bus with television and toilet for Y100 at the East Haikou Bus station, on Hai Fu Road, one an hour between 6am and 8pm. A car costs about Y800 a day.

ORIENTATION

Tourism is the only industry here. Ten airlines now bring visitors here, not all on a regular schedule. The port at Sanya is being deepened to accommodate more cruise ships. Cruise ships currently arrive from Malaysia and Hong Kong.

It has many water sports, golf and hiking. It is great for lieing on the beach or soaking up tropical beauty.

Sanya has 16 sea ports, 10 islands, and 180 km of coastline. It should now have 20,000 hotel beds and more scenic spots. The urban population is about 120,000, the total 380,000. The high tourist season is October to February.

The best resort hotel in Sanya City is the **South China Hotel**. It maintains its own stretch of Dadonghai Beach which is beautiful but of questionable hygiene. The English in most hotels is not good.

OLD CHINESE SAYING

"May your luck be as deep as the eastern sea (Da Dong Hai) and your life be as long as South Mountain (Nan Shan)."

WHERE TO STAY

SOUTH CHINA HOTEL *(Nan Zhong Hai), Dadonghai, 572021. Four star standard. Tel. 8213888, Fax 8214005. Three km from the bus station; four km from the pearl farm. Y680-Y5800. On three km-long Da Dong Hai Beach.*

Built in 1992 and renovated in 1998, this pretty 438-room hotel includes 20 three-bedroom villas, each differently decorated, all somewhat crowded together. Most of its rooms have views of the sea and bright tropical plants: pink bourgainvillea and red hibiscus flowers. Rooms have rattan furniture, safes, no carpets, no CNN now but maybe later.

The hotel has a sauna, gym, tennis courts, outdoor swimming pools, and water park. It rents sailboards, catamarans, kayaks, and cabanas. Its medium-sized lobby is decorated in pink marble with a magnificent porcelain vase with 108 characters from the classic novel Water Margin. South China Hotel is building the five star Nan Zhong Guo Dajiudian.

PEARL SEAVIEW HOTEL SANYA, *Da Dong Hai, 572021, Tel.8213838, Fax 8215822. Its 184 available rooms range from Y788-Y1528, with the honeymoon suite about Y1328. Major credit cards.*

Built in 1995, its lobby has stained glass windows, brown marble tones and a baby grand piano. It has three, circular three-story villas set in a garden about 200 meters from Da Dong Hai beach. Rooms are small and pretty, have dim reading lights and no CNN. Otherwise they are fine. It has a pool, a night club, Chinese and western restaurants, and the manager speaks English. It should have a gym now.

JINLING HOLIDAY RESORT *(Do Jia Chang), Lu Ling Road, Dadonghai, 572021. Four stars. Tel. 214081, 214088, Fax 214088. Y618-Y978 , Suites Y1658. Set above the beach in a garden.*

This 1989, three-story hotel has 147 suites with seaviews and big televisions. It has a fresh water pool, tennis and should now also have night club, water-cycling, parachuting, windsurfing, water sking, and scuba diving.

SANYA INTERNATIONAL HOTEL *(Guoji Dajiudian), Jiefang Road, 572000. Four stars. Tel. 8273066, 8274041, Fax 8273069, 8275049. 15 km from the airport, and on the waterfront in downtown Sanya near the city center and city hall. It is convenient to public transportation. On an inlet of the Sanya River, it has a view of fishing boats, and its own nearby pier. Y580-Y860 for rooms, Y1688 for suites.*

This huge 1991 hotel is generally drab, dark, and uninteresting. Don't bother with it unless you check first for a recent renovation, and a cheap price. It has three-connecting four-story buildings, with an elevator only in number five building. Its 14-lane bowling alley is the biggest in the city but it has no CNN. The service generally is sluggish. Restaurant serves individual hot pots for Y26 and a relatively cheap Chinese buffet, A CTS Hotel.

PEARL RIVER GARDEN HOTEL (*Zhujiang Huayuan*), *Dadonghai,
572021, Tel. 8211888, 6302280, Fax 8211999. Y630-Y980 for rooms, Y1380-
Y3380 for suites.*
Built in 1995, this hotel is aiming at four star standards, and comes
close. It is very pretty. Its lobby has carved wooden gold-painted scenes of
life in Hainan and its bar has an ocean view. Some rooms have large
balconies, and jacuzzis. Standard rooms have safes, and blond furniture.
The hallways are curved and have badly fitting carpets. Covered walkways
are between buildings, and the beach. The pool has a mountain view.

WHERE TO EAT
Only the major hotels accept credit cards. The **South China Hotel** has
the best western food. The **Dong Bei Restaurant** is best for Chinese food
if you like northeastern style. **Sanya Seafood City** (Jia Yuan Fang) is the
cleanest and has a good view. It is near Da Dong Hai and the South China
Ocean Diving Club and is relatively expensive. This restaurant is basic and
large, with plastic on top of its white table cloths. Try the fried squid Y56,
oysters (Y268-358 per kilogram), steamed abalone for Y118, medium
shrimp for Y98 and fried chicken for Y68. Nearby is the **Shuntian Seafood
City**(Hai Xian Chen) in about the same price range.
You can get a nice view of the city on the way to the **Liu Hui Tou
Restaurant** (Coconut Forest Restaurant), in the northwestern part of the
city, near Xiao Dong Hai Beach, two to three km from downtown Sanya.
Nearby is the **Ye Lin Jiu Jia Restaurant**, behind the Liu Hui Tou Binguan
Guest House, *Tel. 8214228*. This caters to groups and has a set menu
which individual guests can order four hours ahead. Y150 for individuals;
Y80-Y100 each for groups of at least eight. It includes coconut pork, crab,
steamed medium shrimp, prawns, and abalone, all Hainan dishes. The
table cloths are plastic.
An adventurous place to eat fresh seafood are the restaurant stalls on
Lu Hui To Beach, at the west side of downtown Sanya, two km west of Da
Dong Hai beach.
The **Ka Yuan Restaurant** has white tablecloths, a great view of fishing
boats, and takes credit cards. It is expensive, but less than the hotels for
Hainan, Chaozhou, Korean, Japanese, Taiwan and Sichuan dishes. Try
the chicken fried with bananas for Y38, fried pork Y38, and steamed
medium shrimp Y68. Open 9:30am until the last guest leaves. It has a tank
of live fish outside. And is close to the Coconut Forest in the north part
of the city.

SEEING THE SIGHTS
End of the Earth is so named because it was the end of the political
career of high ranking officials from the Song and Tang dynasties. It is

about 30 km west of downtown Sanya City and is a pleasant rocky place to explore. There's also a **Pearl Farm**. At **Monkey Island**, the monkeys can be vicious, and it's not recommended.

NIGHTLIFE & ENTERTAINMENT

Nov. 18 every year is the **Wedding Festival**. Chinese and foreign couples getting married or celebrating 5th, 25th, and 50th anniversaries get special treatment. Contact travel agents.

Hotels have sports and shows. You can hike to the top of **Lu Huitou Garden** for a view of the city, or do a night dive. Bars in the better hotels have no annoying girls pestering customers. See Yalong Bay.

EXCURSIONS & DAY TRIPS
YALONG BAY

Yalong Bay is about 20-25 km (about a Y40 taxi ride) southeast of Sanya City, and 17-30 km from the Sanya airport. It is located between the beach and mountains. The main Yalong Road, follows the beach and passes all the hotels which are all within two km of the town square. Yalong Bay is more spread out than Sanya City and its beach is cleaner and safer for swimming. Ten years ago, it was just beach. The water is clear and usually peaceful (like a 18-year old girl, said one tourism official). Today it is a nationally-protected marine reserve. No commercial fishermen are allowed to fish there nor harvest or destroy coral. Yalong Bay Development Company is building a water treatment plant and planting trees.

Until others open, the best resort is the Gloria, then the Tide, and finally the Cactus.

Hotels listed here accept credit cards and have money exchange. They add a 10% surcharge.

LOVELY YALONG BAY

Yalong Bay is my favorite tropical resort in China and should remain so because the number of resorts are restricted to six, ranging from two-to-five star ratings. Resorts have to be approved by Beijing. Its goal is "fewer people spending more to maintain a good environment." No resort can be closer than 100 meters from the 7.5 km-long beach. It is the only place in Sanya where I would swim in the ocean.

GLORIA RESORT, (*Kai Lai Du Jiajiudian*), *Yalong Bay National Resort District, Sanya City, 572000, Tel.8568855, Fax 8568533.E-mail: gloria@public.syftt.ha.cn. Five star standard. Y200 for a Sanya airport pickup. Travel agents can book this hotel for rooms Y1088-Y1490; suites Y2488.*

This sprawling eight-story 1996 hotel with house-size villas, is set in a huge, beautifully-tended garden bordering on the beach, full of bourgainvillea, and palm trees. It is aiming at five-stars, and when I visited, was pretty close to that.

The lobby is open to sea breezes which blow most of the year. (July to September is hot.) With its louvered shutters, which protect guests from wind and rain, its immense size and ceiling fans, the lobby looks like a 19th century railway station. The coffee shop staff, dressed in Hawaiian shirts, set an informal tone and most staff have relatively good English.

Rooms are comfortable with rattan furniture, and televisions providing HBO, CNN, CBS, and Star Movies in English. Guests can sailboard, sea kayak, hobie cat, waterskoot (but not within 200 feet of the beach), or boat. Part of its huge pool is set up for water polo. It also has four all-weather tennis courts, Japanese restaurant, and disco.

The South China Dive Club should have a shop here now to organize dives and rentals. Across the road, a golf course should have 18 going on 36 holes. There are also archery, four lighted tennis courts, beach volleyball, croquet, foccia, darts, pingpong, billiards and mah jong. It should soon have mountain bikes to rent with a map of the area. The future should also bring a convention and exhibition center.

The three-bedroom presidential villa is full of tastefully selected art and antiques with rattan furniture, large potted plants, curved staircase, and gold fish pond. It is one of the best decorated such suites seen in China, with stained glass, a glass bottle collection, and carved wooden African heads. It is the closest building to the beach, has its own swimming pool and costs about Y20,000 a night.

See also Chapter 13, *China's Best Places to Stay*.

RESORT HORIZON, *Yalong Bay International Resort, 572016, Tel. 8566411, Fax 8567890. Five stars. 151 rooms now, 217 more later. Fresh water pool, tennis courts and night club. Y980-1390 for rooms, and Y1580-2580 for suites.*

HUANDAO BEACH HOTEL (*Haidi Shi Jie*), *Yalong Bay International Resort, 572016, Tel. 8565588, Fax 8567788. About four star standard. Prices range from Y798-Y6668. It is 25 km from Sanya, and 35 km from the Sanya airport.*

This hotel has 57 rooms now, and will eventually total 70. As a result, it is more intimate than the much larger Gloria. It has a small business center and shop, but no non-smoking areas, no CNN, no western food and no tour desk. It demands a Y100 deposit for a hairdryer. The English is very poor.It has four separate three-story buildings (with no elevators) joined by covered walkways and is across the road from the beach. A kiosk here can arrange sea sports and boats. See below.

CACTUS RESORT SANYA, *Yalong Bay National Resort District, 572016, Tel. 8568866, Fax 8566816. Three stars. About Y480-Y560 for rooms, Y780 for suites.*

Opened in 1998, the Cactus has 600 rooms with safes, satellite television and in-house movies. It claims China's largest swimming pool, and has beach volley-ball, tennis, water sports, and a children's playground. It has a lobby lounge and pool bar, and a tour desk. There's a "mud" tennis court, lake-side restaurant.

As for **restaurants** in Yalong Bay, **Gloria Resort** is best for Chinese food, and unless it's improved in the last year, no good for western. In its Chinese restaurant, try the the poached *Wenchang* chicken, the *Dongshan* mutton, steamed crab, and fried rice. The Chinese restaurant is decorated in fishermen's style with wooden buckets, fishnets and straw hats. Performances of ethnic dances are at its outdoor barbecue, which also has good food.

The **Huandao Beach Hotel** restaurant in Yalong Bay is quite good and moderately priced. Delicious were the snow peas at Y18; steamed shrimp Y80; and Gong Bao chicken with peanuts, chilis and peppercorns Y34. Wintermelon soup with clams was Y28 for a big bowl.

The public beach at **Yalong Square** has showers, beach umbrellas to rent and life guards daily from 8am-7pm, all year round. Golf is near the Gloria Resort.

Sights & Sports

In **Yalong Bay**, you can walk to most places of interest from its hotels. The square has a public beach, shops, rentals, and has a restaurant and delightful **sea shell museum** underneath *(Tel. 8568899 X 8339)*. The museums's exhibits are displayed like fine jewelry. For sports see above.

The outdoor netted **Butterfly Garden** *(hu die yuan, jia yuan hai xuan fang)* has a mountain hiking trail and stream and is worth an hour if you can find it behind the Huandao Tide Hotel. Hopefully, directional signs will be up by the time you visit. It's on *Nan Bian Hai Road, Tel. 8215526, 8568720.* Ask for directions at the Cactus Resort. This is the 1500 sq. meter home of 500 varieties of live, fluttering butterflies. Trees and some butterflies are labelled in English, Chinese and Latin. Butterfly specimens and products are for sale.

Yalong Bay is a work in progress. It expects to develop its hot spring resources and also open a magnolia garden and factory making Magnolia products in 1999. It is building about five more golf courses. It expects to have a submarine cruising eight to ten meters underwater, at Y150 an

SCUBA WARNING

Scuba diving can be a dangerous sport and should not be attempted without at least hours of training. If a store wants to rent you gear without asking for proof of training, do be suspicious about its other standards. The gear may not be carefully maintained or cleaned between customers.

*The Hainan tourist office has approved only one scuba diving company in Sanya, the **South Sea International Ocean Club** (SSIOC) which has shops in the South China Hotel and soon in the Gloria Hotel. It has a map of the 10 good diving spots on the island. Its general manager Edward Chan speaks English and is concerned about protecting the environment. It has 100 sets of imported equipment, five dive boats and a staff of 15 full-time certified dive masters and instructors. It has Padi, Navi, and CMAS certification. The SSIOC charges Y500 for one or two dives and can tell you about the **underwater garden** with bubbling underwater fountain. Telephone or Fax 8212079.*

*Another club, the **Ten Thousand Happiness Diving Club** might also be approved by now. The navy hospital in Sanya has a decompression chamber. At the dive shop at Yalong Square, we found no one who spoke English and questionable standards, so avoid it.*

hour, out of Da Dong Hai. *Tel. 8263741, 8211821.* It should now have a Buddhism theme park and a 108-meter high Guan Yin with four faces, higher than the Statue of Liberty. Look for it 300 meters away from the beach and connected to the mainland by a glass passageway. It should now also have farm visits and agriculture tours.

The **Underwater World** kiosk across from the Huandao Beach Hotel has things to do but there are no signs in English, *Tel. 8565588, or Fax 8567776.* A visit to the **Submersible** costs about Y150; snorkeling (including transportation to the reef and rentals) about Y120 an hour, better take your own mask and snorkel; parachuting (5 minutes) for Y160; speed boating for four people, 10 minutes Y60. It can also arrange scuba diving: 1-3 people Y480 each.

You take a short motor boat ride to its 45-seat Australian glass-bottom submersible which circles a relatively good plot of staghorn, tube, black and fan coral with mostly tiny but some decent-sized fish. No one can tell you the names in English. The trip takes about an hour and is good for people who don't want to snorkel or scuba. You can also rent fishing gear and a boat. And there should be waterskiing soon. The Huandao has been looking for someone to start a sailboarding business.

You can also hire a boat to visit **Pig Island** nearby. The above **snorkeling** package includes a motorboat ride to a ship anchored near an island reef. There you can get masks, snorkels, fins, lessons, and mandatory life jackets. Leering male swimmers might get close enough to females to kick. Be careful also of sea urchins which can sting painfully. See also facilities at the Gloria above.

Note: Topless bathing is contrary to local custom, but no separate beaches are planned, nor is it forbidden. You can expect a lot of stares and even harrassment from the locals on public beaches.

PRACTICAL INFORMATION

    Ambulance: *Tel. 120.*

    Complaints: *Tel. 6250780.*

    Telephone Code: *0899.*

    Yalong Bay Holiday Travel Service, *No. 2, Shang Pin Jie Da Dao, Sanya, 572000, Tel. 8279870, 8278411, Fax 8279435.*

    Edward T.W. Chan, South China International Ocean Club, *China National Diving Training Centre, Sanya City, 572021, Tel. and Fax 8212079.*

    Sanya Tourism Bureau, *7/F, No. Second Building West River Government, 572000, Tel.8268452, Fax 8268450. Contact Cai Shi Dong.* **Website:** *www.hainanisland.com*

21. SOUTHWEST CHINA

CHENGDU
(Chengtu)

Chengdu is important because of its pandas, its marvelous new Sanxingdui Shu Museum, the Dujiangyan Dam, and the Divine Light Monastery. It is the main gateway to Tibet, Zigong, Emei Shan and the giant Buddha in Leshan. Eco-tourists should aim for Jiuzhaigou, and people interested in China's satellite projects should go to Xichang. Sichuan of course is the home of Sichuan cuisine.

Located in central Sichuan province of which it is the capital, Chengdu has a history of over 2,000 years. In the fourth century B.C., the King of Shu moved his capital here and named it Chengdu ('Becoming a Capital'). In the Han, after brocade weaving became successfully established, it was called the Brocade City. During the Three Kingdoms, it was the capital of Shu. Many American, Canadian, and British missionaries and teachers lived here in the late 19th and early 20th centuries.

With an altitude of 500 meters, its hottest temperature is 38 C in July and its coldest – 3 C in January. The tourist season is April to November, with July and August uncomfortably hot. Annual precipitation is about 1000 mm., mainly in July and August. The population is over two million urban. Minorities in the province include Naxi, Qiang, Yi, Jingpo, Miao, Lili, Tujia, and Tibetan.

ARRIVALS & DEPARTURES

Chengdu is slightly over two hours by air southwest of Beijing. There are direct flights from 53 other cities in China, Bangkok, Singapore and Hong Kong, It can also be reached by a 22-hour train from Kunming through 250 km of tunnels, and in 17 hours from Xi'an. Buses from Chongqing are faster than the train. From there, it is a 3.5-4 hour, 340 km expressway trip costing Y98 on an express bus with movie and toilet.

For buses to Leshan and Dazu, use the Xinnanmen Bus Station; to Chongqing use the Wuguiqiao Bus Station; to Jiuzhaigou and Wolong, use the Ximeng bus station.

ORIENTATION

Chengdu is an educational and an industrial center with metallurgy, electronics, and textiles. The area grows rice, wheat, canola, chilis, and sweet potatoes. It also grows medicinal plants and herbs that are sold all over the country. It has so much to offer, you need at least two days to cover it, and more for nearby excursions.

Its notorious traffic jams have been relieved somewhat by three ring roads around the city, but its downtown areas are crowded especially around the Jin Jiang and Minshan Hotels and north towards one of the few remaining statues of Chairman Mao, the big department stores, the Crowne Plaza, and Inter-Continental Hotels. A 46-km subway is being built.

WHERE TO STAY

The top hotels are the **Crowne Plaza** and the **Jin Jiang**, and then the **Yinhe Dynasty Inter-Continental**. The best three stars are the **Tibet** and **Chengdu**. The **Jin Jiang**, near the Jinjiang River, CAAC and CITS offices and the night market, is good but showing its age, and seems to be losing its English. From the **Yinhe Dynasty** and **Crowne Plaza Hotels**, you can walk to department stores. The **Chengdu Hotel** is further away but still central. The **Yinhe Dynasty** is generally good, but it needs work on its plumbing, linens, and other necessities. The **Chengdu** is adequate but not classy, with moldy grouting in its bathrooms.

The **Traffic Hotel** is popular with foreign low budget travelers who are not fussy. The **Arong**, far from the city center, was opened as a Holiday Inn but was not up to Holiday Inn standards. If you can get a price lower than the three stars here, it could be a great deal for budget travelers. At least the building is new.

Prices here are subject to 10%-15% service charge. Some hotels have been giving 20%-50% discounts, free breakfasts, and free airport pickups. The railway station is about seven km to downtown. Hotels here have business centers, western coffee shops, and money change. Top hotels accept credit cards.

HOLIDAY INN CROWNE PLAZA (*Zong Fu Huang Guan Jia Ri Jiudian*), *31 Zhon Fu Street, 610016, Tel. 2786666, Fax 6789791. E-mail:ahicp01@shell.scsti.ac.cn. 18 km from the airport and 0.5 km from the Provincial Exhibition Centre. Five star standard not yet official. Free airport shuttle five times a day, and no service charge on long distance calls. Y1411-Y1909 for rooms, Y2158-Y6640 for suites.*

This 33-story, 424-room hotel has in-rooms safes, non-smoking floors, a grill room, Japanese, Sichuan and Cantonese restaurants. Its great breakfast buffet included smoked fish and egg plant, Japanese *miso* soup, hash brown potatoes, four different *dim sum* dumplings, congee with 10 toppings, three cheeses, and superb pasteries. Its lobby is decorated with huge marble pillars, and European-style art including a Sistine Chapel-like ceiling, sort of. It has floor-to-ceiling windows, a gym, indoor pool, bowling alleys, and tennis court. There are CNN, CNBC, HBO and Star movies.

YINHE DYNASTY INTER-CONTINENTAL HOTEL *(Yin He Wang Dajiudian), 99 Xia Xi Shun Cheng Street, 610016. Four stars. Tel. 6618888, Fax 6624313, 6748837. In North America, Tel. 800/327-0200. E-mail:chengdu@interconti.com. 22 km from the airport and close to the Sichuan Exhibition Centre and Chairman Mao's statue. Y1100-Y1490 for rooms, and Y2150-3150 for suites, both including breakfast.*

Opened in 1995 with six and 26 stories, this 380-room hotel has a Three Kingdoms theme in its lobby, CNN, HBO and National Geographic Channel, in-house movies, and a clinic with free consultation. It has executive floors and one non-smoking floor. It has Asian, Cantonese, Chaozhou, Italian, and Japanese food, Sichuan hot pot, and a ballroom big enough to care for 650 people at a sit-down dinner. There's a gym, steam bath, sauna and probably the largest outdoor pool in the city.

JINJIANG HOTEL *(Binguan), 80, Section 2, Renmin Nan Avenue, 610012. Five stars. Tel. 5582222, Fax 5582348, 5581849. E-mail:ajjhsw@shell.scsti.sc.cn. Http://www.chengdujinjianghotel.com. 17 km from the airport; eight km from the train station. Y780-Y1980 for rooms and Y1580-Y46000 for suites. Airport shuttle three times a day.*

This 1962 hotel has nine stories and 523 rooms, some with three telephone jacks and in-room safes. It has international, Sichuan, Cantonese and Korean cuisines and executive suites. It rents out bicycles and has a gym, bowling, tennis, and pool. There's satellite television, a clinic, and post office. China Famous Hotel, VIP Club.

ANRONG HOTEL, *132 Zheng Street, Chadianzi, 610036, Tel. 7526688, Fax 7540689. Three or four-star standard. It is 27 km from the airport, and 2.5 km from the railway station. In the northwest part of Chengdu close to the Exhibition Centre, it is three minutes from the Tuqiao Industrial Zone, and on three bus lines to downtown. It is on the way to Dujiangyan, and is better value for money than downtown hotels like the Tibet. Y650-Y830 for rooms, Y990-Y1100 for suites.*

This 280-room hotel has two executive floors, international, Sichuan, and Cantonese restaurants, and hot pot. Rooms have large twin beds, CNN, Star Sports, and safes. It has an indoor pool, gym, sauna, steam room, and night club.

CHENGDU HOTEL *(Fandian), Dongyiduan, Shudu Road, 610066. Three stars. Tel. 4444888, Fax 4441603, 4432083. 18 km from the airport.* This hotel was built in an industrial area in 1984. It has 12 stories, 310 small rooms, indoor pool, gym, and clinic. It also has CNN, Korean, Chinese and Japanese restaurants, and executive floors. Try haggling for a discount. Member of China Friendship Tourist Hotel Group.

TIBET HOTEL *(Xizang Fandian), 10 Renmin Road, 610081. Three stars. Tel. 3333988, Fax 3333526. Y368-Y780 for rooms, and Y938-Y1188 for suites.*

In the north part of the city four km from the center, this modest, 359-room hotel has Sichuan, Cantonese and western food. Its advantage is its Tibet Travel Bureau office, convenient for arranging trips to Tibet. The hotel's service however is not good, rooms are small, and don't expect CNN or in-room safes. But it does take credit cards.

TRAFFIC HOTEL *(Jiaotong Fandian), 77 Linjiang Road, 610041, Tel. 5551017, Fax 5434699, 5531877. E-mail:traffic@public.cd.sc.cn. Near the Xinnanmen Bus Station. Rooms are Y120-Y210 or for one bed Y40. Ask if western breakfast is included. It's been giving 60% discounts.*

This hotel has Star TV and dirty carpets, but no CNN. It is a favorite of foreign backpackers.

WHERE TO EAT

This is one of the best cities for **Sichuan food**. Flower petals and herbs are used in such specialties as fried lotus flower, governor's chicken, diced chicken with hot peppers and peanuts, and smoked duck with tea fragrance. Try also the *dan dan* noodles.

If you don't like hot spices, ask the restaurant to tone them down. The food is still good without chilis. If you want more hot spices, ask for *la jiao*. Local snacks are *lai tang yuan* dumplings or *long chao* dumplings.

Restaurants in hotels are very good; the ninth floor Chinese restaurant at the **Jin Jiang Hotel** is especially good, as is the western food at the **Crowne Plaza**. But try any of the following:

BOYAYUAN RESTAURANT, *3, 4th section, Renmin Nan Avenue, Tel. 5221007, on the grounds of the Sichuan Provincial Museum.*

The Boyayuan is used to tourist groups, so if you're with a group they can handle it.

NU LICAN RESTAURANT, *1 Jinhe Street, Tel. 6633382, 6635181.*

Come here for traditional peasant food. Ask for the beef simmered in soy sauce and five-star annis, the shoe-string potatoes, and egg custard.

MAPO DOUFU RESTAURANT, *197 Xi Yu Long Street, Tel. 6754512, 6627005.*

This famous 18th century is still here, but with mixed reviews. It originated the well-known spicy hot bean-curd dish and still offers 30 other variations of bean-curd.

BRICK CAFE PUB, *77 Ke Hua Bei Road, Tel. 5214065.*

A modest but good restaurant. Menu in English.

HIGHFLY CAFE, *18, No.1, Renmin Nan Road, Tel. 5501572.*
They also have a menu in English. Highfly has e-mail service and a book exchange, and is cheaper than the Brick.

NIGHTLIFE & ENTERTAINMENT

Bars in the top hotels are best, but there's the **Huigui** (Reunion) **Bar** at *4 Renmin Nan Road* (inside the Huachuan Hotel), and the **Hei Ma Yi Pi Jiu Guan** (Black Ant), beside Southwest Nationality College.

SEEING THE SIGHTS

A one-day city tour usually goes to Dujiangyan, Green City Mountain, Funanhe river park, Dufu's cottage and the Temple of Marquis Wu. You should be able to haggle over tour prices in travel agencies in back-pack hotels through the **Traffic** (Lida) **Travel Service**, *Tel. 5531877, 5551017 X 2803.*

West

***Du Fu's** (Tu Fu) **Thatched Roof Cottage** is a 20-hectare park with a replica of the modest residence of the famous Tang poet who lived here and wrote 240 poems in four years from 759 A.D. A temple and garden memorial were first built in the Song. The pavilions here are from the Qing era. Among the exhibitions are some translations of his poems in 15 foreign languages which might help you understand his importance. It is open daily.

South & Southwest

The **Sichuan Provincial Museum** is about two km south of the Jin Jiang Hotel. It has an amazing display of bronzes from the Ba Culture that developed in the Yangtze valley to the east. These are the people whose coffins you look for in the hills along the Yangtze river. Unique to the Ba/ Shu culture are these incredible humanoid figures. It's at *3, Section 4, Renmin Nan Road*, and open daily. A good tourist restaurant is on the grounds. For more on these mysterious people, see the Sanxingdui Museum.

The **Temple of Marquis Wu**, at *231 Wuhouci Avenue* was originally built in the sixth century in memory of Zhuge Liang, a famous strategist and prime minister of Shu during the Three Kingdoms (220-265 A.D.). Here are tablets written during the Tang, larger than life-size statues, and the still unexcavated Tomb of Liu Bei, the King of Shu. The current buildings are Qing. The ***Zhuge Liang Memorial Hall** is a national historical site.

The **Guanyin Temple**, *Bao Qiao village, Xingjin county*, 32 km from Chengdu on Dajian Road (the old road to Leshan), is 500 years old and has original murals and painted clay sculptures. This small temple off the main tourist route is a gem for art-lovers. As yet, undeveloped for tourists, it is home for 10 nuns. Open daily 8am-9pm, *Tel. 2450282.*

North

The 25-hectare **Chengdu Zoo** is six km north of the city and boasts five giant pandas. The zoo also has rare golden-hair monkeys among 2,000 animals of over 200 varieties. Open daily. The **Chengdu Giant Panda Breeding and Research Base** costs Y12, and also has pandas. The animals there should be living in habitats, not cages and attempts to breed them by the zoo and this base have resulted in at least 27 pandas. Sichuan is the home of 80% of the world's pandas, and reserves are under the control of Chengdu.

The ultra-modern **Sanxingdui Museum** was built on the 3000 year old, 12 sq km site of the Shu (also known as Ba) culture. It is one of the most exciting new museums in China, beautifully displayed with magnified pictures above tiny artifacts, creative lighting, and titles in English. It has sacrificial pits, gold-leaf masks, huge bronzes, and one of the earliest dragons, not bad for people with no written language. The relics are unique to this area, never before seen anywhere in the world. The museum is open daily from 9am-4:30pm or 5:30pm, with entrance fee Y20 and is worth a special trip to see. It's 38 km from downtown Chengdu in *Guanghan, 618300, Tel. 5222917, 5240907, Fax 5227645.*

The **Baoguangsi** (Divine Light Monastery) should not be missed. It is 18 km north of the city at Xindu, and famous. Originally founded about 2000 years ago, it became the site of a palace ordered built by Tang Emperor Li Huan. During the Ming, war destroyed the monastery but it was reconstructed on its original foundation during the Qing in 1671. Pagodas, five halls, and 16 courtyards make it most impressive. The Tang **Pagoda** is 30 meters high, 13 stories with a glazed gold top. The 500 arhats are from the Qing in 1851, each about two meters high, unique and vivid. Look for the 175-centimeters-high stone Thousand Buddha Tablet, carved on four sides in 450 A.D., and for the Buddhist scriptures written on palm leaves from India. Open daily.

Northwest

The *Dujiangyan Irrigation System*, a one-hour drive (57 km) out in Guanxian county, usually takes a full day when combined with Green City Mountain. It was originally built in 256 B.C., the oldest such project in the country. Impressive because of its age and scope, it controlled floods and diverted half of the Minjiang River to irrigate the fertile Sichuan plain. Here are also old temples with murals. It has a 240-meter-long swinging bridge first built before the Song, but most recently rebuilt in 1974, so don't be afraid to walk on it. The Fu Long Kuan (**Dragon Subduing Temple**) houses a statue of Li Bing, the project's mastermind. The **Erwang** (Two Kings) **Temple** is a memorial to Li Bing and his son.

Also near Dujiangyan and 90 km from Chengdu is **Qingcheng** (Green City) **Mountain**, one of the birthplaces of Taoism and still a Taoist center, with 38 left of its original 70 temples, shrines, and grottoes. There's a 15-minute cable car almost to the top, but you have to hike a way first.

With some of its cliffs shaped like city walls, this strikingly beautiful mountain rises up to 1,600 meters. It was a base for a peasant insurgency led by Zhang Xianzhong, who captured Chongqing in 1644 and occupied Chengdu. Visitors can reach the Jian Fu Temple (Tang dynasty) by road. There are guesthouses midway up and on top.

The **Cavern of Taoist Master Temple** was founded in 617 to 605 B.C. The building is from the Tang and contains a portrait of Master Zhang Daolin, stone carvings of the Three Emperors, and murals of the Eight Taoist Fairies. The mountain is full of legends.

SHOPPING

The main shopping is on **Renmin Road**, **Yanshikou**, and **Chunxi Road** with many big department stores, including the huge Pacific, open 10am-10:30 daily. Prices at the Pacific are higher generally than other stores for local products, but not as high as in North America. The **Chengdu Bamboo Weaving Factory** is at *12 Jiefang Road, Section 1,* and **Number Two Shu Embroidery Factory** is at *11 Heping Street.*

In the evening, the **street market** beside the Jin Jiang and Minshan Hotels is a half-km-long sidewalk art gallery of ethnic crafts and paintings, stuffed animals, and "antiques." Tibetan relics and ethnic textiles are beside the Minshan Hotel. On the Jin Jiang Hotel side is a line of antique and craft shops that sell tourist junk but also some genuine antiques from Tibet that look like human skulls, ceremonial daggers, scriptures and *tankas.* The **Minshan Hotel** has a book store and over-priced shops on the second floor. Try the **Sichuan Antique Store**, *6, Shaocheng Road, Tel. 6636329.*

There's a daytime **antique market** at *Chao Tang Bei Road,* in the western part of the city, 30 minutes from the Jin Jiang Hotel. *Tel. 7319023 X 6257 or 6257* for information. Unique are the designs of local snuff bottles painted on the inside.

EXCURSIONS & DAY TRIPS

See also separate entries for Chongqing and Dazu, below.

Baoxing County, 350 km west of Chengdu, has a wildlife preserve that is bigger than Wolong with 100 pandas, but park officials cannot guarantee you'll see any pandas. Baoxing also has Tibetan minorities, with traditions stronger than at Jiuzhaigou. It is best to go here in a tour.

EMEI SHAN

Emei Shan is 140 km southwest of Chengdu and 31 km from Leshan by train or frequent bus. Together they make an interesting trip of at least three days, but either Emei or Leshan can be a quick one-day or overnight trip if you don't climb. Travel agents offer a two day tour of both.

Emei Shan is one of China's four great Buddhist mountains. You can reach the base by tourist train from the North Railway Station in Chengdu in less than two hours. The climb to the summit and back can be done on foot in one day if you're energetic, or two days for the less agile. Along the 60-km stone paths are 23 monasteries, intriguing caves, gushing waterfalls, magnificent views, and birds. Be careful of monkeys; they can be vicious.

A **cable car** can take you from Jingshui to **Wannian Temple**; Land Rovers drive within six km of the peak at **Jieyin Hall**, at 2,670 meters. From there another **cable car** can take you from Jieyin Hall to the **Golden Summit**. At that height, it can be very chilly, about - 20 C at the top in January. Hostels are at the base of and on the 3,100-meter-high summit, and there are restaurants along the way. Guides are available.

The best time to climb is from April to June, and September to November. It may be too hazardous December to March, but the mountain is beautiful. The rainy season is July and August.

Baoguo Temple, at the base, has a scale-model map of the mountain with lights. The temple originates from the Ming. **Wannian** (Samantabhadra) **Monastery** on the slope dates from the fourth century. Its bronze and iron buddhas are Song to Ming. The bronze Samantabhdra on a white elephant is 7.4 meters high and weighs 62 tons. How did they carry it up here? The beamless brick hall, its roof, and square walls, are said to be typically Ming.

RED SPIDER MOUNTAIN HOTEL *(Hong Zhu Shan Binguan), 614201, Tel. 5525727, Fax 5525666. 130 km from the airport, 10 km from the railway station. It costs about Y300 and takes credit cards. It is near the Baoguo Temple.*

This is the best place to stay. Built in 1935, this hotel has three stories, 180 rooms and 10 buildings. It has two three-star buildings, the best "Number Five" opened in 1998. It is the largest hotel in the city.

EMEI SHAN GRAND HOTEL, *Baogao Temple, 614201. Two stars. Tel. 5522579, Fax 5522061.*

This hotel is near the main street up the mountain, with 340 rooms. The telephone code for Emei Shan is *0833*.

JIUZHAIGOU & LESHAN

For **Jiuzhaigou**, you'll need at least three and preferably five days to visit this beautiful wilderness area which was the setting for the Hollywood movie *The Little Panda*, about two children saving a panda from poachers. The Long March passed through here. You can go by long-distance bus from the West Bus station, taxi or join a tour group.

Jiuzhaigou is a nature preserve about 450 km north of Chengdu, an eight-10 hour drive. You can stay in the **Jiuzhaigou Hotel** (Binguan) with its 100 three-star rooms and 24-hour hot water, but it has no credit card service nor IDD. The Jiuzhaigou should be upgrading to four stars in 1999. There's also the two-star 1998 **Jingding Hotel** on a 3000 meters high mountain with 100 rooms at Y300. The three-star **Jiulong Hotel** (Binguan) costs about Y400, has international direct dial and credit card service. An airport is being built.

The preserve comprises 60,000 hectares of primitive forest with species earlier thought to be extinct. Naturalists should go wild with excitement here. Expect exotic animals, forested hills, carpets of flowers, lakes and waterfalls. Jiuzhaigou means Nine Stockades Canyon, three of which are about 2500 meters above sea level. **Tibetan** and **Qiang** minorities live in the area. The best time to visit is September and early October. In the vicinity is the renovated **Nyingma Longchen Nyingtik** (Maiwa) **Tibetan Temple** in Hong Yuan County, originally built in 1646.

Leshan is about 168 km southwest of Chengdu (the closest airport) and 3.5 hours by road. At the end of 1999, a new expressway should shorten the trip to 150 km or 1.5 hours, making it the best way to go. Its train station is 31 km from Leshan. Buses are more frequent. It is 40 km from Emei Mountain.

Warm rains from April to June add to the mystical atmosphere. It is a small 1,300-year-old town of 200,000 people, a good place for pedicab rides. On the *Dafu (Great Buddha) **Temple** grounds sits a Buddha (either 58.7 or 70 meters in height, depending on sources) started in 713 A.D. and completed 90 years later. It is believed to be the second largest ancient Buddha in the world. From Leshan city across the river, visitors can take a public bus to the front gate, or arrive by ferry. The view from the water is better; otherwise you can't see the temple guardians. From the water, you should see an even bigger, more **virile**, **reclining Buddha**, head to the right, formed accidentally by the shape of the hills and a pagoda. At the confluence of three rivers (Min, Dadu, and Qingyi), the monastery buildings stand at Buddha's eye level.

This huge statue was built to offset the large number of serious accidents on the river. Since statistics were probably kept before and after, it would be enlightening to know if the statue was worth it. You can reach the **Wuyou (Black) Temple** in 15 minutes by footpath from the Dafu

Temple. It has a good museum for its tiny size. There is also an **Eastern Han Dynasty Museum** at Mahao Cliff Tomb, south foot of Lingyun Mountain.

JIA ZHOU HOTEL *(Binguan), 19 Bai Ta Road, 614000. Three stars, Tel. 2134415, 2139888, Fax 2133233. About Y450. Credit cards. It has a good location on a main street across the river from the Great Buddha.*

This is the best hotel here. Built in 1953 with a second building in 1987, this 13-story, 296-room hotel has bicycles for rent. It is on the site of a former Canadian mission, near shopping, a park, and boat to Great Buddha Temple.

Leshan CITS is at *129 Renmin Nan Road, Changchen Building, 614000. Tel. 2124570, 2133198, Fax 2132154.* The **tourist hotline** is *Tel. 2124570.* Contact the **Leshan Tourist Bureau**, *23 Boshui Street, Leshan, 614000, Tel. 2131968,* if you have any complaints. The city's telephone code is *0833.*

ELSEWHERE NEAR CHENGDU

Tibet is most easily reached from Chengdu with at least twice-a-day flights leaving at 6:40am and 6:50am. You can book flights and tours from most large travel agencies in China, but Chengdu has branches of Tibetan travel agencies. Try the travel agencies above. You need a pre-paid tour, and a permit from the Tibet Travel Bureau, Tibet Hotel, before you can buy a plane ticket. It should only take two days to get permission. For more details, see Chapter 19, *Tibet.*

Wolong Nature Preserve is about a 150 km, three-to-four hour trip on a bumpy, narrow road from Chengdu. Public buses go from the Ximen West Bus Station to Dujiangyan (1.5 hours). Then you get another bus from there to Wolong (2.5 hours), a total cost of Y12 but difficult and uncomfortable. Better take a tour or taxi. The scenery is great and there should be hiking trails with maps. It gets cold at night because of the altitude. There are many pandas in the wild, but you might not see any except in cages; there are usually about six around. Some can be seen only on video monitors. Recent visitors found they had to pay to take photos. Some refused the offer to pat these wild creatures not wishing to disturb them.

There's a panda museum here. Read *The Last Panda* by George B. Schaller. Naturalists estimate that there are now about 1,000 pandas in the wild. Ask about the September Panda Festival.

There's lots of room for hiking. The best hotel is the 150-room **Wolong Shanzhuang**, *Tel. (08489) 664877, 664874.* For about Y200-Y300 you get a room with a private shower, no tub.

Xichang has China's satellite launching center and tourists are welcome. From Chengdu, it is an overnight train ride on the

Chengdu-Kunming railway line. Xichang has an airport with flights twice a day from Chengdu.

Be sure you get permission through a travel agent before you go if you want to see a launch. Xichang also has the **Museum of Liangshan Yi Slave Society** on Qionghai Lake in a southeast suburb. It was a stop on the southern Silk Road and claims a visit by Marco Polo. It is the home of the largest Yi community in China.

The **Xichang CITS** is at *2 Xiyanjing Bei Lane, Shengli Nan Road, 615000, Tel. 3223061, Fax 3222678. E-mail:xits@moon.ls.scsti.ac.cn.* The telephone code for the area is *0834.*

Zigong 190 km from Chengdu and 200 km from Chongqing by road, is noted for its locally-found dinosaurs and giant lanterns. There's a daily train from Chengdu. It has a **dinosaur museum** (built at the site with over 100 specimens) and a dinosaur festival, a **salt museum** (showing 2,000 years of the industry), and a **Chinese lantern museum**. The city makes huge spectacular lanterns and a good time to visit is the Lantern Festival which lasts about 20 days before and after the spring festival, every three years from 2000. The very fancy **Shaanxi Guild Hall* houses the salt museum. The hall was first built in 1736 A.D. and has lots of gilded wood and stone carvings. It is at *107 Jiefang Road, Ziliujing, 643000, Tel. 222746, 222083.*

The best hotel is the three-star **Shawan Hotel**, *3 Binjiang Road, 643000, Tel. 2208888, Fax 2201168.* It's 107 km from the airport and one km from the railway station. Y308-Y418 for rooms, Y748-Y925 for suites.

CITS Zigong is at *2 Tangkan Shang Road, Zigong 643000, Tel. 2203569.* The Control Department, **Zigong Tourism Bureau**, *Number Three Building, Tan Mulin Hotel, 643000, Tel. 222141,* should be contacted if you have any complaints. The city's telephone code is *0813.*

PRACTICAL INFORMATION

Business Hours: stores open 9am-9 or 10pm; offices 8am-12 noon, 2pm-5:30pm.

Hash House Harriers: check with Alan Brooks at the Yin He Dynasty Hotel.

Internet bar: *Dian Xin Shang Cheng, Tai Sheng Nan Road, (near Children's Hospital).* Try the **Highfly Cafe**, *18, No. 1, Renmin Nan Road, Tel. 5501572.*

Sichuan China Youth Travel Service, *99 Dong San Duan Yi Huan Road, 610061, Tel. 4318971,4332333, Fax 4339911. Ask for Maria. E-mail:scyt@mail.sc.cninfo.net.* It is working on boat trips down the Yalu Zhangbu River in Tibet, self-driving trips on the Silk Road in foreign-made jeeps in May-September and other adventure tours.

Sichuan Overseas Tourist Corporation and **Sichuan China International Travel Service**, *65 Section 2, Renmin Nan Road, 620021, Tel. 6659474, Fax 6655042.*

Sichuan Tourism Administration, *65 Section 2, Renmin Nan Road, 610021, Tel. 6659653, 6622065, Fax 6671042, 6674460.* For brochures.

Tourism Quality Control Bureau, *Tel. 6654780, 6657308.* For complaints.

Tibet Tourism Office, *Room 229, Tibet Hotel, 10 Renmin Bei Road, 610081, Tel. 3333988X38, Fax 3333526.*

Telephone code, *028*

Traffic (Lida) **Travel Service**, *Traffic Hotel, 77 Linjiang Road, Xinnanmen, 610041, Tel. 5531877, 5551017X2803; Fax 5582777, 5574699. E-mail:traffic@public.cd.sc.cn.* Contact Liao Xiao-Kang. Open 8am-9pm. Specialises in Tibet, Kathmandu, and Russia and should soon be able to book by e-mail.

US Consulate, *4, Lingshiguan Road, Section 4, Renmin Nan Road, Tel. 5583992, 5589642, Fax 5583520.*

Websites on Chengdu: *www.sc.cninfo.net; www.travel.com.hk/china/chengdu.html; Http://www.chinats.com/cchengdu.html.*

CHONGQING

(Chungking)

For tourists, **Chongqing** has been a gateway to the Yangtze River cruises, but with the opening of an expressway, it now has a day trip to a major tourist attraction. As the capital of Nationalist China during the Japanese war, it is of interest to students of modern history. It is an industrial center, the sister city of Toronto and Seattle, and important for business people.

Urban Chongqing is located between the Yangtze and Jialing Rivers and its immediate surroundings and is at an altitude of 168-400 meters. The urban population is about six million, the total about 30.2 million.

WORLD'S LARGEST CITY?

In 1997, with the stroke of a pen, Chongqing became China's and probably the world's largest city. Because of the Three Gorges Dam, it has joined Beijing, Shanghai and Tianjin as municipalities directly under the central government. It is no longer in Sichuan province and at 82,304 sq. km, it is bigger than Belgium. Its borders extend to the provinces of Hubei, Shaanxi, Hunan, and Guizhou as well as Sichuan, and includes Wanxian/Wanzhou and two of the three Yangtze Gorges.

Chongqing is over 3,000 years old. It was the capital of the Kingdom of Ba in the 12th century B.C. During the Song, it was named Chongqing, which means double celebration. During the Qing, a 10 meter-high, seven-km wall was built around the city. In the 19th century, Chongqing was one of the treaty ports open to foreigners, and foreign missionaries and teachers worked here before 1949. Innumerable books have been written in English about this area.

In the late 1930s, during the Sino-Japanese War, the Nationalist government moved its capital here, and Han Suyin's book *Destination Chungking* reflects that period. Unfortunately, Japanese bombs destroyed much of the city, and few ancient relics survived the war. Zhou Enlai (Chou En-lai) lived here as he tried to work with the Nationalists against the Japanese. American missions (Stilwell, Hurley, Marshall and Wedmeyer) attempted to get the Nationalists to work with the Communists. Read Theodore H. White's *In Search of History* for more information on that period in the 1940s.

The highest temperature in summer is 40 C; the lowest in winter, 6 C. The annual precipitation is 1000 mm. Chongqing is one of the "three furnaces of China." There are clear skies only in summer, and fog between November and March might affect flight and ship schedules. The cheaper Suzuki taxis are weird when it's hot; sometimes you find your seat wet because of water from air-conditioning.

ARRIVALS & DEPARTURES

Chongqing is a little more than a two-hour flight southwest of Beijing, or a 7-9 hour train ride from Chengdu. It's better to take a bus. There are flights from Hong Kong, Macau, Bangkok and Nagoya, and 43 Chinese cities including Lhasa (twice a week). Jiangbei Airport is 30 km from downtown. When departing by air, give yourself at least one hour from downtown to the airport, more if it's raining, however. Congestion around the Jialing River Bridge should be relieved soon when the new Huang Hua Yuen Bridge over the Jialing River is opened, hopefully in 1999. The CAAC shuttle bus terminal is at Meizhuanxiao Street and Zhongshan San Road. It departs and leaves for the airport every 10 minutes and charges Y15. It also stops at the Southwest Airline ticket office next to Cygnet Plaza.

There are air-conditioned express buses (Y110) on the four-lane highway between Chongqing and Chengdu (3.5-4 hours plus traffic jams). They leave every ten minutes or so. The countryside is beautiful, hilly and full of sorghum and Tudor-like farm houses. The bus and railway stations in Chongqing are both together about one km west of the bridge to the Holiday Inn at Caiyuanba Square and can be confusing. From it, you might find yourself going west through the tunnel and then east to get

CHONGQING'S CLEAN ROUTINE!

As part of the mayor's attempt to make this the cleanest city in China, trucks and buses cannot go into the city during the day without a permit (they can only enter after 11pm and before 7am). Be sure to ask about this if you hire a vehicle.

downtown because of the one-way roads. The soft-class waiting room is to the right as you approach the station. To the left is the bus station for Chengdu, Zigong, and Yibin. Do ignore the scalpers who try to sell you tickets. The real ticket offices are inside the buildings, more reliable and cheaper. The highway between Chongqing and Yichang should be finished in 2002.

Chongqing is a water city.

Most cruise ships leave from quay No. 3 at Chaotianmen Wharf which has very dirty elevators (Y2). But at least you don't have to climb stairs there. Wharfs 4 to 9 should be improved in 1999. Obnoxious porters might fight for your bags everywhere. It should be Y10 per reasonable load. Wait at the top of the stairs and hope a member of your ship's crew sees you. Learn to say, "Wo bu yao," meaning, "I don't want."

Many ferries and hovercraft leave from Wharves 2,3,4 and 5. You can get tickets from travel agents like CITS or at the counter inside the Navigation Office Building at Chaotianmen, under the Chaotianmen Hotel. Ignore the other so-called government-run tour agencies which charge you higher prices than inside, or promise you all meals and shore excursions, unrecognized later by your ship. See Yangtze Gorges.

The Yangtze is navigable to Yibin, 400 km upstream to the west. You can take a ferry from the pier at Caiyuanba outside the railway station at 6pm bound for Hejiang in Guizhou, but get off at Luzhou. There you change to another ferry to Yibin. You can go another 100 km by sampan.

ORIENTATION

Today, Chongqing is crowded. Downtown is a hilly peninsula, the wharves and main commercial area at its eastern tip and the airport to the north. The Three Gorges Dam will raise its water level only four or five meters and ships over 10,000 tons will be able to reach here after 2009. It has no bicycles because of the narrow, winding, and hilly roads. The houses clinging to the hillsides are fascinating. But the hills, bridges and prosperity have brought traffic congestion and air pollution downtown. Relief is in sight with the building of two more bridges across the Jialing River and a riverside road. Three bridges across the Yangtze River should be in use by the end of 1999.

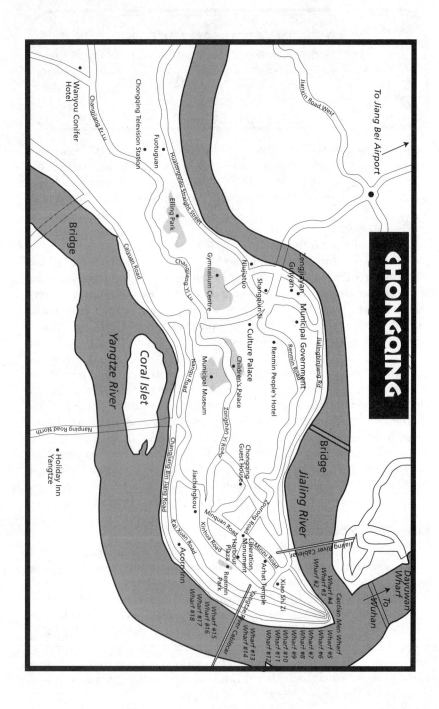

The city seems to be moving ahead internationally faster than Chengdu. New consulates should be opening and a diplomatic area north of the Jialing is developing. Diplomats might prefer to stay downtown.

WHERE TO STAY

The best hotels are the Harbour Plaza, the Holiday Inn Yangtze, and the Best Western Wanyou Conifer. The **Harbour Plaza** has a great location beside the downtown "walking street," near department stores and offices, and five minutes drive to the Chaotianmen wharfs. The **Holiday Inn** is on the south bank of the Yangtze River, a little isolated especially at rush hour, but with good, much experienced staff. It is in the Nanping economic development zone, close to the Nationalists' sites, and you pay an additional Y5 taxi when you cross the bridge from downtown. The **Best Western Wanyou** is furthest from the Chaotianmen Wharves but near other economic zones, and has great looking buffets. At $60 or less a night, you get excellent value, the best deal in town if you don't mind the location and early morning traffic jams to your ship.

Closer downtown is the **Chongqing Guest House** with poor service except for its VIP Section which is better quality than rooms at the **Renmin Hotel**. The latter is isolated on the top of a hill, its former Nationalist congress hall an impressive Temple-of-Heaven clone.

The Renmin has better service than the **Cygnet Plaza** which is on the way to the airport and one of the better three stars. The tiny, basic **Best Western Acorn** has a good location between the Chaotianmen wharves and the Yangtze River Bridge. It is clean and adequate (except for its carpets, bathroom mold and few chipped crockery), convenient and ideal for budget travelers because it's under the eye of the international Best Western chain. All the top hotels have international standards, foreign exchange, credit cards, and business centers.

Around the ferry pier are three very poor hotels not worth mentioning except for their convenient location. Foreign backpackers go to the **Huixianlou** which has dorms for Y50 a bed. It is near Liberation Monument. A five-star **Grand Zenith Hotel** should open soon.

The airport is about 30 km from downtown, the train station about three to five km. Hotels here add a 10%-15% surcharge, accept major credit cards, and have business centers. Some have been giving discounts of 20%-40%.

HARBOUR PLAZA CHONGQING (*Hai Yi Jiudian*), *Wuyi Road, 400010, Tel. 63700888, Fax 63700778, 63726304. E-mail: hpcq@public.chongqing.cngb.com. Reservations in North America Tel. I-800-44UTELL. Five stars. Y1250-Y1600 for rooms, and Y1750-Y9960 for suites.*

This 1997 downtown hotel with 391 spacious rooms, 34 suites, and 3.5 meter high ceilings, is near offices and banks, the Metropolitan Plaza

Mall and Sunshine Building. It has wood-panelled halls, CNN and Star TV, medium-sized bathrooms, kettles, and big closets. There's a coffee shop and restaurant serving Cantonese and Sichuan food, and 24-hour room service. It also has a good gym, heated indoor lap pool, lighted tennis court, sauna, and steam bath. It has an airport shuttle. A Cheung Kong and Hutchison Whampoa Hotel.

See also Chapter 13, *China's Best Places to Stay.*

HOLIDAY INN YANGTZE *(Yangzi Jiang Jia Ri Fandian), 15 Nan Ping Bei Road, 400060. Four stars. Tel. 62803380, Fax 62800884. E-mail:hickg@public.cta.cq.cn. Http://www.holiday-inn.com/hotels/chgch. $135-$140 for rooms, $185-$998 for suites.*

Built in 1989, the Yangtze offers CNN, HBO, and CNBC television. It has 21 stories, 379 rooms with irons and ironing boards, and coffee makers. It has a non-smoking and an executive floor, a local snack restaurant, Italian restaurant (with choice of 32 different wines, German beer house, coffee house and grill room, and 24-hour room service. Its extensive breakfast buffet included congee with 26 toppings, and waffles with cream and real maple syrup. It has an outdoor pool, steam bath, lighted tennis court, and putting green, but no downtown shuttle bus.

CHONGQING GUEST HOUSE *(Binguan), 235 Minsheng Road, 400010, Tel. 63845888, Fax 63830643. The four-star VIP Building is the only section recommended (with hesitation). $110-$131 for rooms; $210-$772 for suites.*

This very Chinese hotel has small televisions with CNN, Cantonese restaurant, Korean barbecue and hot pot restaurants. It has a large recreation center with indoor pool, karaoke, disco, night club, billiards, games and mini-golf. Dirty carpets are in its public areas.

RENMIN (PEOPLE'S) HOTEL (Renmin Binguan), *173 Renmin Road, 400015. Three stars, Tel. 63851421, Fax 63852076. Y600-Y750 for rooms, Y1200-Y1700 for suites.*

Across the street from the city hall and the former home of the Soong sisters, this 248-room hotel was built in 1953. North Americans are usually put in the East Wing, but the North Section is better with big twins, bidets, and inroom safes. It has no real western restaurants, just a coffee shop. It has a 24-hour business center, BBC but no CNN, and no English-language newspapers. It has dirty carpets in its public areas.

BEST WESTERN WANYOU CONIFER HOTEL, *77 Changjiang 2nd Road, Daping, 400042. Tel. 68718888, Fax 68713333. E-mail:hotel@wanyou.com. Four star standard. 37 km from the airport, eight km from Liberation Monument, ten km from the railway station and two km from Eling Park. It is also three km from the high tech zone, and two km from the Southeast Economic Development Park. A supermarket is almost adjacent.*

Telephone in North America 1-800-528-1234. Four stars (but not yet official). $60-$132 for rooms and $156-$988 for suites and duplex apartments.

This 1998 hotel has 30 floors, 332 spacious rooms, and is in a complex with offices. All rooms have safes, goose-down pillows unless otherwise requested, and at least 19" televisions receiving CNN, CNBC, HBO and the National Geographic channel. Executive floor rooms also have fax machines. It has a shuttle bus, Chinese restaurant and 24-hour coffee shop. Lunch and dinner buffets have cost Y88 each.

CYGNET PLAZA HOTEL *(Xiao Tian E), 78 Jian Xin Bei, 400020. Three stars. Across from the Foreign Trade Building on the road from the airport 20 minutes away. Three stars. Y400-Y638 for rooms, Y888 for suites.*

The 119 or so rooms here have small bathrooms, CNN, plants, and free mineral water. Thirteen rooms are non-smoking. Its buffet breakfast costs Y48. It has an airport shuttle and dirty carpets.

ACORN INN, *22 Kaixuan Road, 400012, Tel. 63809597, 63806699, Fax 63821807. Http://www.coniferhotels.com. Two km from the railway station, about three km from the Chaotianmen Wharf and next door to a school. No money exchange. Two stars. $35-$40 for rooms, $50 for suites.*

This 1996, ten-story building has 60 small rooms and small baths. It accepts American Express and Visa, and has Star Sports and Star World but no CNN. It has ticketing service, shuttle buses, Cantonese, *dim sum,* Sichuan food, and a simple western menu.

WHERE TO EAT

The international hotel chains have the best western and Sichuan food. Not all Sichuan food is chili hot. See Sichuan Dishes in Chapter 11, Food & Drink, and Chapter 24. The restaurants in the hotels are best for Sichuan food.

The **Sichuan Hot Pot Restaurant** on *Jiao Chang Ko Street* is famous and privately run. The **Tianzi Hotpot Restaurant** is at *8 Shixiao Road, Shapingba, Tel. 65316648.* The **Friendship Restaurant** (and Hotel) is at the south end of the bridge to the Holiday Inn with great hot pot for Y40 a person. The price includes *dim sum* and all the beer you can drink, *Tel. 62812321.* Fun is the **American Cowboy Restaurant**, *178 Renmin Road* (south of and down the hill from the Renmin Hotel), *Tel. 63620045.* Its buffet has uncooked dishes which you or staff can stir-fry at your own table. It also has cooked dishes. The **Xiao Tian E Hotel** in Jiangbei District, has good hot pot for Y30-Y48. It is clean and air-conditioned. *Tel. 67870700.*

There's the **Beiyuan Restaurant** at *96 Jiang Bei District, Tel. 67851316.* Tour groups go to the **Yangtze Island Club Restaurant** *(Yantzi Dao Can Ting), opposite the Holiday Inn, at No. 13-2 Nanpin Bei Road, Nanpin District, Tel. 62805977 or 62805975* for Sichuan food, but it doesn't have western toilets. The **Chongqing Modern Art Gallery Restaurant** is a couple kilometers beyond the airport. It has good deep fried lotus seed balls, sweet and sour fish, and lots of paintings for sale.

SEEING THE SIGHTS

CITS charges $27 to $60 each for a one-day tour depending on the number of people. This could include Eling Park, the cable car, the Stilwell Museum, Zoo and Painters' Village.

For art lovers, **Painters' Village** in Huang Kuo Ping District is worth a visit. The institute is one of the best in China for traditional styles, wood block prints, oils and water colors, good technique but not much creativity. The government has supported most of these 17 artists for 40 years and you can watch some of them work. Some have exhibited abroad. It has a three-story gallery with art for sale. Open daily, it is at *24 Huacun, Hualongqiao, Tel. 63862177.*

For modern history and especially Americans, there's the tiny **Stilwell Center**, open daily 9am-6pm but closed December-May. Telephone for directions *63850085.* It is good for people who remember the Japanese War and it has videos to see. Nanshan (South Mountain) Park on the south bank of the river was the **home of General George C. Marshall**, the American mediator, and **Chiang Kai-shek**. The Nationalist leader lived in Yun Xiu, now renovated and open to tourists.

You can learn a bit about China's version of modern history at the Hong-yan Cun Revolutionary Memorial Hall (**Red Crag Village**) at 13 Hongyang Village. This was the office of the Communist Party and the Eighth Route Army between 1939 and 1946. It was also the residence for Chou En-lai and other revolutionary leaders including, briefly, Mao Tse-tung. This office was opened as a result of the kidnapping of Nationalist leader Chiang Kai-shek in Xi'an in 1936.

For older history, the **Chongqing Museum**, *Pipashan Zheng Street*, near Loquat Park, is open daily, with a display of Ba relics and ship coffins. You strain your neck looking for Ba coffins in Yangtze River caves. Here they are! This museum is dirty, dark, with no English nor air-conditioning. If you want to go back farther than that, try the **Chongqing Museum of Natural History**, Beibei District, 43 km northwest of the city. Dinosaur bones were found in this region and some are on view here. Open daily. See also Zigong under Chengdu.

There is a rundown **zoo** here, with half a dozen pandas. Better wait until you get to Chengdu where conditions are better. You can pet a panda for a fee, but please don't do it. These are wild, endangered creatures.

A 800-meter-long **cableway** goes across the Jialing River from Cangbailu Station in Jiangbei District to Jinshajie Station near Liberation Monument for a bird's-eye view of the area. Another cableway goes across the Yangtze at Xinhua Road to the south side close to Yikeshu. It costs Y1.50 one way and closes at 10pm.

NIGHTLIFE & ENTERTAINMENT

China Travel Service organizes **dinner cruises** with performances on two ships, the Jia and the Yang for Y68. In **Eling Park** at 350 meters up you can see both the Yangtze and Jialing Rivers and all the lights. **Pipashan** is a good place for an evening stroll. If you want bright lights, head for Liberation Monument. The Metropolitan Plaza there has **ice skating** and **bowling**.

On warm evenings, people **dance** and *taiji* at People's Congress Hall (below the Renmin Hotel). Its square has a musical fountain. Every Saturday and Sunday at 7:30pm, there's Sichuan Opera in the **Sichuan Opera Theatre** at Jintang Street. It costs Y5-Y10 and you can watch the actors put on make-up. A nine-hole **golf** course should be open soon.

SHOPPING

Chongqing makes umbrellas, silk, satin, bambooware, glassware, jewelry, knitting wool, carpets and motorcycles. See Painters Village above. Going to stores around Liberation Monument (Jiefeng Bei) and the Harbour Plaza Hotel is now actually very pleasant. Cars are banned. A big mall is in the Metropolitan Plaza (open 10am-10pm) where the **Pacific Department Store** is uncluttered and reasonable priced. A Watson's drug store is next door.

Also downtown is the dirty **Chongqing Antique Market** with a few private booths at *Yu Zhong District, 982 Tiao Changkou,* open daily, 8:30am-5:30pm. It has stamps, coins, antiques and fakes.

The **Chongqing Museum** has an overpriced third floor gift and antique shop where one clerk easily came down 50%, and would probably come down more if pressed. "Purple jade" stone carvings were considerably cheaper at the markets around the Dazu grottoes. Serpentine rollers (for cooling the face) cost Y600 at the museum but Y10 to Y20 in the markets, and Y160 to Y180 in local department stores. Down the hill to the right as you leave the museum are about eight other antique shops, where you can haggle too. Beyond them at *No. 72* is a **teapot shop** with nice selection and fair prices. It is open 9am-6pm.

The **Oriental and Fine Arts Academy store** just inside the zoo (*Tel. 68420069*) had damp and very moldy paintings, of ancient and contemporary artists. It really does give more than a 20% discount if you persist in spite of a sign to the contrary.

EXCURSIONS & DAY TRIPS

Dazu County is the home of the **Dazu Stone Buddhist Sculptures** and is about 105 km northwest of Chongqing, about 95 minutes away mainly by expressway. It can also be about a 2.5 hour drive from Chengdu or reached by train; the station is 15 km from Dazu town. This is an outstanding historical and artistic site. Do not miss it.

You can go by public bus from Chongqing, or travel agents can arrange tours. CITS' one-day trip to the highlights at Baodingshan and Beishan ranges from Y440-Y1450 each, depending on the number of passengers. Taxis are about Y800 a day. Public tour buses go from the Chongqing bus station.

These original outdoor sculptures are better preserved and of finer quality than those in Luoyang, Datong, or Dunhuang. Started in the Tang, and mostly added to in the Song, a few were carved in the Ming and Qing. Because there was no road then, they were untouched by the Red Guards but many are weather damaged. China has applied to UNESCO to make this a world heritage site too. About 50,000 sculptures are located in 76 places in Dazu County, most still not readily accessible by car. Roads are currently being improved.

Under State Council protection are *Guangdashan, *Longtan, and *Linsongpo. Easiest to reach are those at **Baodingshan** (Y30), 15 km northeast of the Dazu Guest House in a horseshoe-shaped mountainside with one or two levels of carvings. It takes about half an hour to take in the most famous: a mother sleeping next to a bed-wetting child, a village girl tending ducks, the 31-meter long Reclining Buddha, and the beautiful *bodhissatvas*, one with 1000 arms. Some of the standing figures are seven meters high. Only still cameras are allowed and photos only of selected relics. There's hardly anyone around to enforce this rule in the other groupings however.

The sculptures here were mostly made by one monk, Zhou Zhifeng, from 1179 to 1249, and centered on the theme Life is Vanity. It is essential that you obtain a tour guide to explain.

*Beishan has about 400 stairs to climb in total. It gets fewer visitors than the more famous Baodingshan but has the largest concentration and pagodas. It takes about 30 minutes and is two km north of the Dazu Guest House. Look for the elegant Goddesses of Mercy.

Another group of sculptures, carved in the Song dynasty, is at **Shimenshan**, 20 km southeast of the Dazu Guest House. These are Buddhist, Taoist and Confucian (smooth and simple). The **Nanshan Carvings** are 1.5 km south of Dazu town and are Taoist from the Southern Song dynasty. Look for the flying stone dragon.

Peddlers at the sites can be a real pain, but they can also save you money. A one foot high carved purple-jade stone statue here (Y200) costs twenty times as much at hotels in Chongqing. They are heavy to carry however.

Dazu county is a relaxing pleasant place to spend a couple of days. You can hike, explore Longshui Lake, and wonder how many of its locally-made switchblades will be used by gangs abroad.

DAZU HOTEL *(Binguan), 47 Gongnong Street, Longganzhen, 402360, Tel. 43721888, Fax 43722827. Three stars.*

This is the best place to stay or eat. This hotel was renovated in 1995 and has 133 attractive rooms with small bathrooms, Star World, but no CNN. It has worn and poorly fitting hall carpets, and grouting just starting to mold, but otherwise it is adequate. You might get a 10%-40% discount off depending on the season. The high season is August to October. Its restaurant is the best place to eat in Dazu; the fried rice is good, as are the pressed smoothed bean curd, three-fresh sliced fish, and sizzling dumplings. It has a gym and sauna.

CITS and **CTS** are at *47 Gonglong Street, 402360. Tel. 43722245, Fax 43722827. Dazu's telephone code is 023.*

DIAOYU CASTLE

*At Hochou/Hechuan, about 100 km north of Chongqing is a fortress which changed the history of Europe. At **Diaoyu Castle** in 1259, five km southeast of Hochou, the Mongolian King Mangu/Mongke, elder brother of Kublai Khan, was killed while personally trying to take this castle with an army of 70,000. His death stopped the invasion of Europe as Mongol leaders in the field withdrew to war among themselves for the leadership of the Mongol empire. Only the walls and a few structures remain. There is no museum and the road will not improve until 2002.*

Flights go to **Tibet** from here twice a week but you need a special permit obtainable from CITS or other travel agents. It takes four days.

For other places of interest within Chongqing, like two of the Three Gorges, Wushan, Shibaozhai, Fengdu and Wanzhou/Wanxian, read the Yangtze Gorges section below.

PRACTICAL INFORMATION

China International Travel Service, *Chongqing Branch (CITSCQ), 63 Zaozi Lanya Street, Yu Zhong District, 400015, Tel. 63850806, 63851362, 63850693. Tel. 24-hour 65315294, Fax 24 hours 63852490.* It has a liaison office for information about cruise ship movements. *E-mail: citscq@cq.col.com.cn.*

China Merchants International, *173 Renmin Road, 400015, Tel. 63855762, Fax 63856128.* Try also *17/F, Hua An Building, 99 Zhongshan Second Road, Tel. 63516386, Fax 63516500.*

Chongqing CYTS, *125 Renmin Road, 400015, Tel.63857071, Fax 63850951. E-mail:Info@mailwebone.com.cn. Website:www.CQCYTS.COM.CN.*

Chongqing Overseas Tourist (Group), *63 Zao Zi Lan Ya Street, Yu Zhong District, 400015, Tel. 63850598, Fax 63850095. E-mail:long@chinatourwest.com.*

Chongqing Tourism Administration, *63 Zaozilanga Zhong Street, Tel. 63850612, Fax 63851448.*

Complaints: Tourism Quality Monitoring Agency, Chongqing Tourism Administration, *Tel. 63890134, 63621101, Fax 63851448.*

Consulates:

Consulate of Canada, *Room 1705, Metropolitan Tower, Wuyi Road, Yu Zhong District, 400010, Tel. 63738007, Fax 63738026. E-mail:cdncon@public.cta.cq.cn.*

Consulate of Japan, *Tel. 63733585, Fax 63733589.*

Hours: most tourist attractions are open 8 or 9am-6pm. Business hours: 8:30am-12:00 noon, 2pm-5:30pm, Monday-Friday.

Orient Royal Cruises (East King and East Queen), *Rm 5315, Chongqing Hotel, 41-43 Xinhua Road, Tel. 63822702, Fax 63822701.*

Regal Cruises, *Tel.63830507 X 6377, 5282.*

Telephone code, *023*

Victoria Cruises, *3 Xin Hua Road, 3/F,Zuzhong District, 400011, Tel. 63820264, 63815260 (for reservations), Fax 63814474.*

Website: *www.chinatourwest.com* for information about the ten western provinces as well as Chongqing, hopefully in English.

GUIYANG

(Kweiyang)

Guiyang, the capital of Guizhou (Kweichow) province, is due south of Chongqing. Guizhou is a landlocked region known for its minorities, many of whom still wear their unique costumes even for work in the fields. It has some of the best ethnic embroidery and batik in China, and cultures that are still intact. It also has beautiful mountains, and China's largest waterfall. This is National Geographic-land, the frontier, truly exotic and amazing. Don't expect it to be like Kansas.

The province is rich in minerals like aluminum, coal, iron, lead, gold, silver, and zinc. It has China's largest mercury deposit. It grows rice, corn, tobacco, cork, raw lacquer, and timber. But many of its people are poor.

ARRIVALS & DEPARTURES

Guiyang has direct flights with Hong Kong Monday and Friday, and air links with at least 29 other Chinese cities. Its Long Dong Bao Airport, big enough for 747s, is ten km from downtown. Guiyang is at the hub of railway lines with Chengdu (967 km), Nanning (865 km), Kunming (639 km), and Changsha. It is 786 km northwest of Guilin and 463 km south of Chongqing by train.

ORIENTATION

Guiyang is a big, lively, modern city with dirty air and not much unusual to see. The urban population is about 800,000.

Guizhou province on the other hand is one of my favorites. Its high percentage of ethnic groups is due to its hard-to-cultivate land and karst mountains. China's dominant Han people did not want it and the minorities had no choice. Today, out of a total population of 30 million, 36.5% are minorities: Miao, Bouyei, Dong, Yi, Shi, Hui, Gelo, Zhuang, and Yao. They have fascinating architecture and more than 100 lively unique festivals a year with bullfights, horse races, and *lusheng* (bamboo pipes) dancing.

Because this province has only recently been opened to tourists, people will find the exotic here but don't expect private baths and hot water outside of Huangguoshu, Guiyang and Kaili. You'll be lucky to get a clean, functioning hotel room. Think of your accommodations as camping, and you'll be okay. New hotels are being built however, but with more tourists, do not expect the minorities to remain unchanged.

MIAO SONG

Welcome,
Today is not a festival but
Since you have come,
Today should be a festival.
The vegetables were planted by me,
The rice was planted by me,
The chickens were fed by me,
And the wine was made by me.
The more you drink the happier I will be.
I don't know which wind brought you here.
If I knew which wind brought you today,
I hope every day that kind of wind will come.
–Miao song translated by Pan Xin Xiong

You can still find villages effusive with genuine hospitality, a brilliant bouquet of ethnic clothing. You will experience elaborate welcoming ceremonies, totem worship, a coffin on a back porch to make its future inhabitants happy, and unusual music. It is, in places, a time warp. Some women's hairstyles are from the time the group arrived in the area, each village different. You can actually see real Tang and Song hair-dressing!

Contact the tourism offices and travel agencies for festival dates.

They are mainly in the spring and subject to many last-minute changes. The dragon boat races are around July and the weather is best in September and October (but no festivals).

WHERE TO STAY

The best hotel in Guizhou should be the new Holiday Inn, then the Park. Both are in downtown Guiyang. The Baicheng shows much promise and could be better when it gets finished but its standard rooms are smaller. These hotels take major credit cards, have money change, business center, IDD, etc. and are subject to 15% surcharge and discounts.

HOLIDAY INN GUIYANG *(Sun Qi Jia Re), No. 1 Guikai Road, 550001, Tel. 6771888, Fax 6771688. In North America, Tel. 800/HOLIDAY. 12 km from the airport, seven km from the railway station and near the Park Hotel in a commercial shopping area.*

This 230-room 1998 hotel should have this US chain's usual four-star standards. Y750-Y900 for rooms, and Y1100-Y4800 for suites.

GUIYANG BAICHENG HOTEL *(Baicheng Jiudian), 246 Zhonghua Nan Road, Tel. 5866888, Fax 5824985. Four star standards. In a 25-floor building next door to a movie theatre and lots of shopping.*

This 1997, 180-room hotel has Mongolian hotpot and Cantonese food, revolving restaurant, bank, swimming pool and gym. A fountain in front responds to music. It has CNN and BBC.

PARK HOTEL *(Guizhou Fandian), 66 Beijing Road, 560004. Three stars, aiming for four. Tel. 6822888, Fax 6824397. Ten km from the airport, six km from the railway station. Y320-Y680 for rooms, Y1380-Y4800 for suites.*

The Park has 410 rooms, bowling, billiards, and piano bar. It has money changing 24 hours a day, safes, and cleaner rooms on upper floors but dirty carpets. We found the food in the Chinese restaurant good but the service and food in the coffee shop terrible. It might have since improved. Its location, off a main street, is convenient to restaurants and a food market. The English is poor and standards are sloppy.

GUIZHOU UNIVERSITY HOSTEL, *Huanxi, 550025, Tel. Foreign Affairs Department, 3851187 or Fax 3851381. Home Tel. Zhang Chengxia, Section Leader of Overseas Students Affairs, 3852921. 50 rooms. $10 for a single; $6.50 per bed in double. Restaurant.*

This university hostel is 17 km from the railway station. Catch No. 1 bus to the Big Cross intersection in city center, then change to No. 90 (Guiyang-Huaxi bus) which stops in front of Guizhou University. The university can send transportation to the railway station or airport if notified in advance, and arrange tours with guides. Backpack quality only.

WHERE TO EAT

The best and safest food is in the hotels, especially the Holiday Inn. Local food is frequently chili hot, but you can get cook-it-yourself hot pot spiced to your own liking. Restaurants in Guiyang do not yet take credit cards. Guizhou wine is 35% alcohol – check contents before drinking. This is *maotai* country. Like other **Holiday Inns** in China, this should have the best western food in this city. The **Yayun** is famous and good for seafood. It's at *138 Beijing Road, Tel. 6820330*. The **Jinlong Jiu Jia Restaurant**, at *68 Yan'an Zhong Road, Tel. 5824661*, serves good roast duck for Y68. The stir-fried *Ji Yu* fish with red chili peppers cost Y48, and the steamed pork meatballs (*Mi zhi tan zi rou*) cost Y58. The staff here is friendly and helpful, and the decor attractive with frosted glass. Just ignore the filthy stairway, the chipped dishes, and the plastic table cloths.

The service at the moderately-priced Chinese restaurant in the **Jin Qiao Hotel** (*26 Ruijin Bei Road, Tel. 5829958,*) was excellent. Good were the white eel, chicken pie, crispy fried potatoes and quick fried black chicken, fried beans with condensed milk, and fried chicken steak.

SEEING THE SIGHTS

Guiyang itself has little to see beyond karst caves, wild monkeys, some temples, and visits to Sinocized Bouyei and Miao villages. It does have a **provincial museum**, a good introduction to the region. This is open 9am-5pm daily except Mondays at *47 Beijing Road, Tel. 6825674*. It is worth a stop for its collection of minority costumes, especially if you are looking to buy good embroidery and genuine textiles. Look also at the fossilized fish and plants, and relics of the 2000 year old Yelang culture found in the province. This is half a block from the Park Hotel, to the right as you leave.

Outside of town, however, it's wonderful. Among the day trips available is **Xiangzhigou**, 32 km from Guiyang where you can see paper-making for funerals, and have a meal with a family. You can see the highlights of **Anshun** in a day tour, though it's best to stay longer. **Kaili** needs at least two nights, preferably more.

SHOPPING

The main shopping streets are **Yan'an Zhong Road**, **Yan'an Dong Road**, and **Zhong Hua Road** – around two traffic circles. The **Guiyang Department Store** is at *No.2 Zhonghua Zhong Road, Tel. 5822262*. The

Guiyang Antique shop is at *No.9 Gongyuan Road, Tel. 5824109*. Guiyang has stores with embroidery but the place to buy is in the countryside where women will sell their grandmother's baby carrier to you.

EXCURSIONS & DAY TRIPS

FYI: toilets in this province are especially gross. The best seem to be in gasoline stations, government guest houses, specific restaurants, or behind a bush. Food however is available everywhere, and hot pot is hygienic and good. (You can sterile chopsticks in its boiling soup.) The area has the infamous five-step snake (before you die after being bitten), the cobra, golden pheasant and wild pig. Summer and rain are in May to September when the rivers are high enough for boats. August is hottest and it can go up to 34 C for several days.

WHEN IN ROME...

• *A local custom is hitting the table instead of clicking glasses while toasting.*

• *A Dong custom is to single out the poorest person in a village, one day a year, dress him up, and invite him to eat.*

• *When a baby is one month old, the parents place the child outside on the ground at the first intersection. The first man to pass by is asked to be the godfather.*

• *When a couple gets married, the woman gives more gifts to the man's family and pays for most of the wedding.*

• *Kissing is unknown in Miao culture. "He bit me!" exclaimed an old woman after an Italian tourist thanked her with a kiss for a delicious dinner.*

• *Villagers experiencing their first flash from a camera thought it was lightening, and covered their ears expecting thunder.*

HUANGGUOSHU FALLS

These are 150 km west of Guiyang and 40 km south of Anshun. It is most convenient to take a taxi from Guiyang, especially if you want to see more than the falls and Dragon Cave. Taxis and rickety, dangerous motorcycle rickshaws are available in Huangguoshu. The rickshaws are big enough for one big foreigner or two small ones.

You should be able to join a day tour from Guiyang. Some were advertised in Guiyang hotels for Y60 to Huangguoshu Waterfall and the Dragon Cave in a shared air-conditioned van. Most of these tours leave about 6:40am and return at 6:40pm. Check to see if you get an English-speaking guide, and whether you stop at a village. Cheaper public tour buses also leave early morning from the railway station, definitely without English.

A day trip by taxi to the falls from Guiyang could cost you about Y700. For two days, it's Y800. If you want to travel more cheaply and spend a few days, you could have a tour bus drop you off at the Huangguoshu Hotel and from there, you can take mini-buses or risk the motorcyle rickshaws. You can pick up the tour bus on subsequent days back to Guiyang, if you want, or get public transport to the train station in Anshun or wherever. Public buses park on the east side of the Huangguoshu Hotel. Public minibuses stop briefly at major sightseeing spots and drivers try to tell you what time they are leaving in Chinese. Buses leave irregularly for Anshun between 8:30am and 11am from the hotel. I feel there is enough to do in this area for at least three days and it's beautiful.

Huangguoshu Falls, China's biggest, is best seen after the rains from June to early October, when they are 74 meters wide and 81 meters high, In November, they could be one-third this maximum; in April, they can be just a trickle. You can walk behind them any time and later enjoy world-class views of the countryside nearby. Don't expect Niagara Falls. This area is still undeveloped for tourism, thank goodness.

The daytime entry fee of Y20 includes a cable car ride which operates daily, year round 7:30am-6pm, when full. *Tel. 853/3592110.* You could spend two hours exploring. Colored lights shine at night on the falls on weekends all year round, and ethnic dances are performed here during high season from about 9:15pm to 10pm on weekends for about Y40.

The **Huangguoshu Hotel** and waterfall are at an altitude of 1000 meters, across the road from each other. Mosquitos are pests from July through September. From December to mid-March, the temperature averages 7 or 8 C, going down below zero for a couple of days in January.

If you want to stay overnight:

HUANGGUOSHU HOTEL, *Huangguoshu National Park, 561208, Tel. (853)3592110. It accepts no credit cards and cannot change money. It has 3000 sq meters of grounds and good and bad rooms: the best is in its 1998 three-star 60-room Courtyard Number Three (Y380) with a Chinese and western restaurant. Its cheapest rooms are Y140 in its Fan-Shaped House with big bathrooms, small beds, and no heat, a total of 300 rooms. All rooms however have poor bedside reading lights.*

The Huangguoshu Hotel has CNN and 24-hour hot water. It should have a sign in English at the gate soon. The dining room has polished stone floors and stained old table cloths. Deputy Director Li Yingxian has asked for help teaching western dishes to his cooks. Maybe you can share some recipes. The food is good but not great, some dishes greasy and chili hot: deep fried beef, lily with Yunnan beef, steamed Lu fish, fried dumpling and hot sesame cake. Women in minority dress tour tables and offer drinks and toasts in the traditional style. The old V.I.P. House is closest to the falls and its best view is from No. 15 and 16. This section has had noisy air-conditioning, heat, and private bathrooms with broken tiles. Fortunately it is due for renovations and should soon have better rooms, a barber shop, sauna, business center, and bar.

The hotel's travel desk should have maps in English, and hopefully an English-speaking guide for about Y100 a day. On your second day, you could hike five km or hitch a ride from the hotel, downhill to the **Garden of Stone Bamboo Shoots** which is an attempt to improve on nature. You follow the green **Bai Shui River** below the waterfall on a parallel road. At the bottom is the **Tenxing Qiao**, a wooded area with lots of little waterfalls and paved pathways where you can look for wild monkeys, parrots, and other birds. This whole area is full of old banyan trees with their roots clinging to 200 million year old limestone.

In the Tenxing parking lot Number Three, you should be able to see an incredible pair of human **tight-rope walkers** performing daily on a 200 meter-long cable, 300 meters above you. They do their stuff hourly from 9am to 5pm for twenty minutes at a time with a bicycle, but no safety net. When you hear music, look up.

Here also is a decent fast-food snack bar and a regular restaurant with good table cloths and moderate prices. At the snack bar you might get a tray with bony fried fish, pork dumpling soup, and some raw **medicinal root**. Nearby is the tiny 16-room **Yin Lian Dui Tan Inn** with no screens, but CNN and karaoke. It is in a pretty sylvan setting by a waterfall. Rooms there cost Y180.

From here, you can walk or take a 200-meter **cable car ride** to board rubber rafts to float downstream. Each of the 50 rafts can seat 12 at Y80 per person including a bus ride back to the Yin Lian Inn. Make sure you have transportation back to your hotel. It's a long, hard uphill hike back.

In this 115 sq km scenic area, you can also spend two or three more days climbing mountain roads, finding a 300 meter-high waterfall, and dropping in to visit **Bouyei villages** at leisure. People are friendly, but none speak English. In some villages you may be attacked by swarms of women trying to sell you batik and embroidery. Don't expect the pleated skirts to stay pleated after washing. They're originally pressed by finger nail. You can get small embroidery pieces for as low as Y20.

The **Long Gong Dragon Palace Cave** is open 8:30am-6pm daily, *Tel. 853/3223969*. Transportation could be as cheap as Y4 by mini-bus (47 km) from the waterfall, but none of the drivers speak English. The entrance fee is Y33 which includes the 40-minute row boat ride in a 1.6 km-long, cave. It's peaceful if other tourists are quiet and your guide is not singing folk songs. A cable car should be finished the end of 1999.

On the other side of Anshun is **Chaiguan village**, a 20-minute drive (nine km) northeast, and about 60 km north of the waterfall. The **masked peasant opera** here glorifies the soldiers sent by the Tang emperor to quell a rebellion. One story is of Mu Gui Ying, a woman, who successfully led an attack against the minorities and became a famous general.

For about Y500, the farmers, some of whom have performed in France, will put on an opera for tourists if you contact the village chief. Otherwise all you might see is a small **mask museum** (about 100 masks, some with 13th century designs). You might also see families carving masks which they sell for about Y100 to Y200 each. Travel agencies can make arrangements if given 24 hours notice. *Telephone 412/5534403 or Fax 5534403.* **CTS** is at *Tel. 3223173, Fax 8224537.* The **Tourist Office** telephone in Huangguoshu is *853/3224747.*

Chaiguan people are **Old Han**. To this day, some of them and the other 100,000 Old Han in Anshun area wear clothing styles unchanged since their ancestors first arrived here from Nanjing. Look for women wearing a white headband in mourning for the soldiers who died then. Also in Anshun is a **batik factory**.

PRACTICAL INFORMATION

Guizhou China International Travel Service, *20 Yan'an Zhong Road, 550011, Tel. 5825873, 5925292, 5814829, 8222506, Fax 5824222.*

Guizhou China Youth Travel Service, *334 Ruijing Zhong Road, 550003, Tel. 5824266, Fax 6825024.*

Guizhou Overseas Travel Corporation, *20 Yan'an Zhong Road, Tel. 5815342, Fax 5823095,* and *3/F, Zilin Hotel, 10 Yan'an Zhong Road, 550001, Tel. 5813432, Fax 5823095.*

Guizhou Provincial Tourism Administration, *746 - 5 Zhonghua Bei Road, 550004, Tel. 6892357, 6892434, 6892360, Fax 6892309, 6832574.* (Brochures)

Hours: most tourist attractions are open daily 9am-6pm. Office hours are 8:30am-6pm, five days a week. Store hours are 8:30am-7pm. **Bank of China**: 8:30 or 9am-12; 2 or 2:30pm-5pm. Monday to Friday.

Tourist Complaints, contact Supervisory Bureau of Tourism Quality of Guizhou Province, *346-5 Zhonghua Bei Road, 550001, Tel. 6892360, Fax 6892309.*

Telephone code for Guiyang, *0851*

KAILI

Kaili is a small city of 150,000. The air in town is cleaner than Guiyang's, but black smoke belches from its factories. Its hotels are basic, badly managed and maintained. From here you can make day trips to villages by taxi or public bus. Or if you're adventurous enough, you can try even dumpier hotels further out, or spend the night in a village.

This area has a large percentage of people below the poverty line. Roads are generally paved but bumpy except to the individual villages where they can be muddy after rain.

ARRIVALS & DEPARTURES

Kaili is 196 km east of Guiyang. It is on several main train lines: Beijing-Kunming, Shanghai-Chongqing, and Guangzhou-Chengdu. You can also fly to Guiyang, the closest airport, or take the once-a-day express train which leaves Guiyang at 8:30am and arrives 3.5 hours later. But it's only hard class. There are two other trains, but they are not express. Buses leave from the Guiyang train station. You might want to hire a taxi in Guiyang.

The trip to Kaili by road can be done in 3.5 hours. It should take three hours after the expressway is completed in 2000. The scenery is not as dramatic as Huangguoshu's but the rice fields and architecture are marvelous. In the spring, the fields are gold with canola blossoms, and in November, the leaves of popular trees turn yellow.

Kaili has three bus stations: one is near the museum and the Kaili Hotel, and one is at the teachers' college. The buses are dumpy too but can usually get you to villages.

WHERE TO STAY

No hotels take credit cards yet, and IDD calls are made only from the front desks. You can change money only at the Bank of China. The hotels here are really crude and worn with badly stained carpets.

KAILI HOTEL *3, Guang Chang Road, 556000, Tel. 8234666, Fax 8221658. Y218 per room. Two stars.*

This hotel looks good after you've seen the others. It has a good location near a bus station, main street and museum. It is five km from the railway station and has heat and air-conditioning. The tourist bureau is on the second floor.

YING PAN PO NATIONALITIES HOTEL, *53 Ying Penpo Dong Road, 556000, Tel. 8234600. Rooms start at Y218. It is two km from the Kaili Hotel.*

The back building of this place has two-star quality rooms. It is older than the Kaili Hotel and is next door to CITS.

XIAO JIANG NAN INN, *Chonganjiang town (between Kaili and Huangping). Tel. 855/2451208.*

If you're eager to really rough it outside of town, look at this family-run no-star. For Y50 a room, it has a good location for hikers, is clean, has air conditioning, heaters, and a tiny museum of local embroidery and batik. Beside a river, it has its own boat. Hot water is in thermoses only and its menu is limited. It only has 10 double rooms but from here you can hike in all directions. Owned by Gong Ming Yu.

A very special opportunity is provided at **Lande Village**, where travel agents can arrange a stay in a real Miao house in a very pretty real Miao village for Y50 a night. But be prepared for real Miao standards of hygiene and food. You can eat with local neighborhood families, and hike during the day to neighboring villages or even pick your own vegetables and slaughter your own chicken. The public toilet next door is filthy, but you can pay someone Y5 to clean it up. We suggest you have someone who speaks English and Miao or Chinese with you.

WHERE TO EAT

FLYING DRAGON TENG LONG RESTAURANT, *Shao Shan Nan Road, near the Wuyi Binguan and close to the Big Cross (Da Shi Zi), Tel. 8233120, 8226424.*

This is the best restaurant in town, and is air-conditioned. The service is good, and they have the highest prices (relative to the rest of Kaili). It serves Cantonese, Sichuan and sea food. Fish Miao style is Y58. Its most popular dish, pig's leg costs Y45. Try also the throat of ox, a delicacy here, monkey's head mushrooms with chicken feet, and sizzling beef on an iron board. Also good are steamed egg and bean curd. The decor is simple and it has dirty table cloths.

The **Kaili Hotel** has edible but not memorable food. Try the pork and garlic shoots, the soup with pork balls, and vegetables and gold needle mushrooms. Avoid the beef in tomato juice (too tough). The spicy noodle soup is good.

INTERESTING CUISINE CHOICES

*Dog is a favorite food around here, especially in **Pan Jiang town**, 60 km from Guiyang towards Kaili. In front of over a hundred dog restaurants you'll see naked, cooked rumps and tails.*

SEEING THE SIGHTS

The **Museum of National Minorities** in Kaili is worth visiting, though it lacks titles in English. It is not always open. Do try to telephone the day before at *8223557*. The entry fee is Y10. Get a guide to explain. It is full of good exhibits of minority life and crafts. Downstairs is an unrelated furniture store and a sewing factory.

The huge **Sunday Market** is for local people to shop and is good to see but not many people are in costume. It's open 11am-4pm, and near the Ying Pang Po Nationalities Hotel. It's better to get out to the villages.

Outside of Kaili

A relatively clean rest room with a great view of rice fields is in **Quiding**, 85 km from Guiyang, and 110 km from Kaili, at the **Dong Fang Fandian** hot pot family restaurant. It's at 10 East Huan Chen Dong Road, the main highway, and is across from a long stone wall. The Y80 hot pot is good. Try to ignore the chipped crockery and enjoy the owner's collection of *penjing* miniature trees. The dogs here are pets, and not to be eaten.

Close to Kaili are many **Gejia** and **Miao** villages. You can arrange a village visit through CITS or drop in on your own. If the visit is arranged, be prepared for a traditional welcome drink from a buffalo horn, during which your hands should be behind your back. Some women should be in costume for you to photograph and music played. Miao music is sung high and loud, as if from mountain to mountain. Do take a tape recorder as well as lots of film.

If you drop in unexpectedly, you can still request somebody to put on a costume and the 15 kg. silver head dress. You might want to give a tip for their trouble.

The **Gejia village** of Matang, 23 km from Kaili, has been extremely well organized for tourists and the dances are good. The official costume of Gejia women is of male military origins because of the bravery of the women who fought Han soldiers during the Qing dynasty. The skirt is short for riding horses. Though the Gejia say they are a separate group, the government classifies them as Miao. Their founder General Da Sa was probably Manchu. He was a general married to a Miao woman and forced to flee to the mountains.

The town of **Taijiang**, 50 km from Kaili, is the center of Miao culture with a 97% Miao population. You can visit many nearby Miao villages here too. These include Qinman, Wengxiang, Xijiang, and Upper Langde. In **Baiying village** (Majiang County), the pattern of the cloth looks Scottish and you can get a bull-fighting demonstration on request and payment.

Huangping County, east of Kaili has a **Museum of Minority Festivals** in the Feiyun Temple. Zhenyuan, about 140 km east of Kaili, is near the **Black Dragon Cave**. The Miao and Dong are descendants of dragons or water buffaloes who believe these animals were born of butterflies. If you are prepared to rough it, the **Wuyang Guest House** in Zhenyuan has a very pretty river setting.

There is also a **Museum on Marriage Customs** in Xinyi, a bird sanctuary at Grassy Lake in Weining County, its black neck swans seen in winter and early spring. From Kaili, you can actually drive to Guilin.

Visiting areas where **Dong** people live with their elaborate multi-gabled bridges and drum towers, is still difficult. The road from Kaili to Rongjiang is currently being improved however, and a five-hour road trip should be possible in the future.

Trekking trips are great here if you don't mind the lack of decent hotels. There is also a problem of getting an English-speaking guide willing to sleep in villages with you. You are lucky if you can get **Mr. Pan Xin Xiong** of the Guizhou Tourism Administration in Guiyang who speaks Miao, and is known to most of the people in the area. This remarkable Shanghai native who owes his life to Miao people, can also keep you entertained for hours with games, demonstrations of Chinese opera, and local folklore, some of which he makes up himself. Travel agencies here do have tents and rubber boats to rent for white water.

Festivals are worth attending because of the costumes, and the rural flavor – an opportunity for courting, competing on a ladder of swords, and water buffalo fights. Animal lovers should avoid the fights because the buffaloes are motivated by a kick in the genitals. They are separated if the going gets too rough. Buffaloes can lock horns and throw each other like human wrestlers. The loser usually runs away.

SHOPPING

In Kaili peddlers wait at the gate of the hotels. The museum has a shop. Stores on the street and inside the hotels have antique pieces. You are expected to haggle. A reasonable price for an embroidered fanny pack is Y15-Y20; for a good, embroidered fancy baby hat Y25 and Y20, and fine small embroidery pieces Y20-Y50. You can frame the pieces or sew them on your own clothing. You can hang baby carriers and aprons on walls. Be careful of the jackets. They are not tailored and tend to slip back when worn. The indigo dye might come off. The brown color is made from pig's blood. The shine could be from egg white.

VILLAGE WARES

Each village sells only its own unique styles. Expect to be surrounded by a lot of competing women peddlers. Also look for silk funeral boots, caps, purses and sleeve pieces. Be aware that handicrafts are getting mass produced and commercial now. If you want the real thing, look for old pieces, quality, fine workmanship, and muted natural dyes. Please note that some of the costumes on sale are worn only for weddings, funerals, and religious ceremonies. If you grow tired of them later, offer them to a museum in your own country, especially if you've kept a record of its purpose, the name of the village, and the woman from whom you bought it.

There's a tiny one-man silver jewelry factory in the village of **Tang Bai** near Zhenyuan (Shidong), but not much silver on sale unless you order it. An **embroidery factory** (seeded by UNICEF) is in Taijiang at *444 Heping Street*. Both are within a few hours drive of Kaili.

PRACTICAL INFORMATION

China International Travel Service, *No. 53 Yinpun Dong Road, 556000, Tel. 8229441, Fax 8222506*. Ask for Mr. Xie Min.

Hours: offices 8am-noon and 2pm-6pm in winter; department stores 9am-5:30pm daily.

Kaili Tourism Bureau, *Kaili Hotel, Tel. 8222547*. For brochures and complaints. Write Ms. Pan Qi Zhi here for dates of festivals and bull-fights. This office covers the whole Southeast Guizhou region. Taxis will take you most places in town from the railway station for Y10. Taxis cost about Y2.50 per kilometer.

Telephone code: *0855.*

KUNMING

(Kunnanfu)

Kunming is the capital of Yunnan province, which borders Vietnam, Laos, and Burma. It is beautifully situated on 330 sq km Dianchi Lake, China's sixth largest. Because of its altitude (1600-1894 meters) and its subtropical location, it is blessed with the best weather in China, spring all year round. (It occasionally gets snow.) The hottest temperature is 29 C in May and the coldest is -one C in January. Precipitation is 1,500 mm. mainly from May to August.

One of the loveliest times to visit is February when the camellias are in bloom. The best times to visit are February to May, and August to November. The urban population is 3.8 million, the total provincial population is over 40 million.

ARRIVALS & DEPARTURES

You can reach Kunming by train from Beijing in 54 hours, Chengdu in 24 hours, Guangzhou in 52 hours, and Hanoi in 30 hours. It has flight links with 52 Chinese cities, Yangon/Rangoon, Bangkok, Kuala Lumpur, Macau, Singapore and Hong Kong. More routes are expected in the future probably with Chiang Mai and Vientiane. The airport is five km from the city.

ORIENTATION

Yunnan province is the third most desirable tourist destination in China, another of my favorites. You could easily spend two weeks here. It is important because of its mountain scenery, its national minorities, the artistry and history of its temples, architecture, the Burma Road, Shangri-La, and the Stone Forest. From here you can travel to Laos, Myanmar and Thailand.

In the province are several unusual sights. These range from almost year-round snow-capped mountains to tropical jungles where elephants and monkeys roam freely. One third of its people belong to 25 national minorities. Many of the groups, especially the women, still wear their distinctive clothes, even while working in the fields, and practice old customs like the Dai Water-Splashing Festival.

Kunming is completely surrounded by mountains. Sightseeing here can be a little rugged. The Dragon Gate necessitates a climb of 200 stairs, but the effort is well worth it.

WHERE TO STAY

This is a good time to visit. Hotels have been spiffed up for the Horticultural Expo '99. The best hotels are four stars: the Green Lake, Holiday Inn and King World. The new Harbour Plaza should be among the top later in 1999. A new five star at the Camellia Hotel should be ready in 1999. The best three star is the Kingtown Hotel.

Regarding location, the **Holiday Inn** and **Kunming** are nearest to the fancy Sakura department store, the City Hall, and main square. The **Golden Dragon** and **King World** are almost neighbors, around the corner and a couple blocks down the street from the Holiday Inn, and closer to the railway station. These four are slightly more convenient for travelers. But the **Green Lake** and **Harbour Plaza** are next to Green Lake, and are walking distance to the Bird and Flower Market and many shops. The **Harbour Plaza** is at the south end of the lake, closer to town, and near the museum.

The following published prices are subject to change, 10%-15% surcharge, discounts, and negotiation. All hotels here have foreign exchange, private baths, and take credit cards unless stated.

HOLIDAY INN KUNMING *(Yinghua Binguan), 25 Dong Feng Dong Road, 650011. Four stars. Tel. 3165888, Fax 3135189. Http://www.holiday-inn.com. $138-$224 for rooms and $324-$488 for suites. Five km from the airport; two km from the railway station.*

Built in 1993, this hotel has 18 stories and 180 rooms with small bathrooms. It has the widest twin beds in town. It also has executive floors, and a 24-hour business center. To keep you healthy, it has a gym, year-round indoor pool, 16-lane bowling alley and clinic. You can eat Italian, Cantonese and Sichuan food.

GREEN LAKE HOTEL *(Cuihu Binguan), No 6 Cui Hu Nan Road, 650031, Tel. 5158888, 5155788, Fax 5153286. $90-$150 (new wing). 15 km from the airport, and eight km from the railway station.*

This hotel has four-star standards and 306 deluxe rooms in its 1993, 17-story section. Its old front section is currently being rebuilt.

GOLDEN DRAGON *(Jinglong Fandian), 575 Beijing Road, 650011. Four stars, Tel. 3133015, Fax 3131082. E-mail:gdhotel@public.km.yn.cn. Http://www.dragonhotels.com. Seven km from the airport, and 450 meters from the railway station. About $88-$120.*

Built in 1988-89, the Golden Dragon has 17 stories and 290 rooms, most with small bathrooms. It should now have in-room safes. It has an executive floor, in-house movies and English language television. It also has a gym, bicycles for rent, tennis and an outdoor hot spring pool.

KING WORLD HOTEL *(Jinhua Dajiudian), 28 Beijing Nan Road, 650011. Four stars, Tel. 3138888, 3138656, Fax 3131910. About $80-$108 for rooms and $200 for suites. The price includes buffet breakfast and free airport shuttle. $60 through Edward's below. It's 400 meters from the railway station, and five km from the airport.*

The King World is near the Yunnan Foreign Trade Building in a busy commercial area. Built in 1992-93 with 22 stories and 320 rooms, it has television in English, a gym, massage, chess and mahjong. It also has a clinic, bake shop, French, Italian, Sichuan, Yangzhou and Cantonese cuisines. Managed by Jin Jiang Hotels.

HARBOUR PLAZA KUNMING, *20 Hong Hua Qiao, 650031, Tel. 5386688, Fax 5381188. E-mail:ivyh@harbour-plaza.com.*

This 1999 hotel should have a Formula One Grand Prix pub, Japanese and Chinese restaurants, 321 rooms, and executive floors.

KUNMING HOTEL (Fandian), *145 Dong Feng Dong Road, 650051, Tel. 3162172, 3162063, Fax 3163784, 3138220. Five km from the airport; three km from the railway station. $70-$100 for rooms, and $118-$650 for suites. Its three-star South Building was built in 1982 with 122 rooms. Its better four-star back section North Building was built in 1989 with 248 rooms.*

This hotel has a business center, gym, indoor pool and garden. It has television in English, 24-hour coffee shop, and room service.

CAMELLIA HOTEL *(Cha Huan Binguan), 154 Dongfeng Dong Road, 650041. One and two-star buildings. Tel. 3163000, 3162918. Y120-Y230; dorms Y30 a bed. No credit cards.*

A favorite of budget travelers, the Camellia was built in 1985. From here go buses to Dali, and tours to the Stone Forest. The staff speaks some English and a message board is up for travelers. It has some television in English.

WHERE TO EAT

Specialties include Rice Noodles Crossing the Bridge, Yunnan ham and crispy, deep-fried goat's cheese. The adventurous could try snake, deep-fried bees, dog, or congealed blood. Dai food includes grasshoppers. Try the cook-it-yourself hot pot. The best local food and minority dance restaurant is the **Jixing Yunnan Flavor Food City**; see Nightlife section below.

For Yunnan cuisine, there's the **Kunming Hotel** and the **Yunnan Crossing-The-Bridge Rice Noodles Restaurant**, *39 Nan Hua Street, Tel. 3131453.* The **Holiday Inn** is good for western food. Outside is the tiny **Jiuqi Cafe**, good for pizza.

SEEING THE SIGHTS

If you only have one day, you have to choose between a tour of the city or going to the Stone Forest. It is better that you stay at least two days, preferably more. Important in the city are the Western Hills, Golden Temple, Black Dragon Pool, Bamboo Temple, Yuantong Temple, Daguan Park, and Green Lake.

Xishan (Western Hills), *Tel. 8182211,* is about 26 km from the Holiday Inn. The 14th-century Huating Temple is the largest in the city. South of here is the **Taihua Temple** (Yuan) with the best view of the sunrise over the lake. The **Sanqing Tower**, two km farther south, was the summer resort of Emperor Liang of the Yuan. It has nine tiers each about 30 meters above the other. On the top is the **Long Men** (Dragon Gate) with another great view of the lake. The stone corridors, chambers, paths, and intricate carving of the Dragon Gate were cut from 1609 to 1681.

The coppercast *****Golden Temple**, *Tel. 5154306,* 11 km northeast of the city, is 300 years old, 6.5 meters high and weighs 200 tons. The **Qiong Zhu** (Bamboo) **Temple**, 18 km northwest of the Holiday Inn has 500 life-size arhats carved in the Qing. These are very expressive and well worth a visit. The temple was founded in 1280.

The **Daguan Lou Pavilion**, *Tel. 4142335,* across the lake from Xishan Hill (seven km from the Holiday Inn), has a 180-character couplet at its entrance, the longest ever found in China. Composed by a Qing scholar, the first half praises the landscape while the second deals with Yunnan history. Also important is the **Black Dragon Pool**, *Tel. 5150395,* with its Ming temple and tomb. The Heishui Shrine here may be from the Han. Nearby are the **Botanical Gardens**. **Yuan Tong Si**, the only Tang temple in town, is a little over one km from the Green Lake Hotel.

The **Yunnan Ethnic Group Village** on Dian Chi Road is worth a visit for the architecture (Bai, Dai), and an introduction to Yunnan's minorities. It is 12 km from the Holiday Inn. There are dance demonstrations and a sampling of the water-splashing. But unless you are there during these demonstrations, you can find very few people in minority costume to photograph. If you are going to real minority villages, skip this. But if you are shopping for minority crafts, go for a look.

The **Stone Forest** is one of the highlights of a Kunming visit. It is 80 km southeast of the city. It can be a day trip or an overnight in the adjacent two-star **Stone Forest Hotel** *(Shilin Binguan), Lunan County, 652211, Tel. 7795401, Fax 7795414.* Many tour groups eat at this hotel. Hardly any stay here. On the way to the Stone Forest is a new golf course and a lake, which is usually a pit stop for tourists. Singapore money is developing a 34-sq-km tourist resort with casino and villas. Many tourist buses now stop at a huge store owned by a collective under the Yunnan Provincial Tourism Administration so it should be okay. It sells jade and other stones, and all manner of tourist goods. You can watch them carve jadeite from nearby Myanmar.

About 270 million years ago this area was covered with water. The sea receded and rain continued to corrode the limestone into these artistic pinacles. One-fifth of its 64,000 acres is open to visitors. Here too are many steps. The shortest of the two routes is 2.5 hours long, but you can get the picture in much less time.

Near the hotel is a Sani ethnic village with minority-type handicrafts for sale. If you want to visit a real Sani village, this is not the place; this one is too touristy. While much is machine-made, you should be able to find some fine-quality pieces here.

Peddlers can be a real nuisance. Groups of local dancers in ethnic costume have entertained hotel guests in the evening. The blandness of the Stone Forest makes it difficult to photograph. You can hire a local guide in Sani costume to take you around.

The trip between Kunming and the Stone Forest is remarkable because of the hilly scenery and the eucalyptus trees. A fascinating cave 100 meters straight down is located 93 km from Kunming and 24 km from the Stone Forest at **Jiuxiang** in Yiliang county. A word of warning: one of our group was overcome by the humidity, particularly towards the bottom. He spent an hour negotiating the stairs back up, a few at a time. The waterfall there was pretty however, but not worth that experience.

Other Attractions

If you have more time, take a two-hour boat cruise on 340-sq-km **Lake Dianchi** but go only for the rest, as not much can be seen (except for Daguan Lou, fish farms and people fishing with large triangular nets). The **Provincial Museum**, *Tel. 3163694*, is towards the Green Lake Hotel. Open daily except Sundays from 9am-4:30pm, it has a worthwhile exhibit of minority costumes. The **Institute for Nationalities** also has a good exhibit of minority costumes but you have to make arrangements through a travel agent well in advance as it is not generally open.

Along the west shore of the lake is **Sleeping Beauty Hill** and a series of swordlike peaks. On the southern tip of the lake is **Jinning** county town, the birthplace of the famous **Ming navigator Zheng He**, who sailed to East Africa half a century before Vasco da Gama. The **Memorial Hall to Zheng He** is on a hill above the town. Read *When China Ruled the Seas*.

Festivals & Markets

Festivals and markets are worth experiencing: in addition to the Water-splashing Festival in Jing Hong in April, there's the Yi Torch Festival (in late July or early August) in the Stone Forest and Chuxiong, the Third Moon Market (usually April, sometimes May) in Dali, and the Horse and Mule Market (about early April in Lijiang).

Ask about regular minority markets. Lijiang's is especially mind-boggling. An arts festival with performances by most of China's national minorities has been held mid-February to early March.

The **Horticultural Expo 99** (May 1-October 31, 1999) is in the **Jindian (Golden Hall) Scenic Resort**, four km from downtown. Plant lovers who are lucky enough to go, will see exhibits of Chinese and international landscape art, rare plants, tea gardens, bamboo gardens, miniature gardens, and vegetable-and-fruit gardens. This is an international class exposition.

NIGHTLIFE & ENTERTAINMENT

The best dinner and minority dance restaurant is the **Jixing Yunnan Flavor Food City**, inside the gate of the Camellia Hotel. The show is daily at 7pm, *Tel. 3178508*. The **best disco** is at the Holiday Inn. Also good are the **dance halls** at the Kunming and the Golden Dragon Hotels. Be wary of bars outside of hotels because you might have to buy drinks at high prices for the girls who sit with you. At least one of these bars has been known to give a guest an incredibly high bill at the end of an evening and threatened him with violence unless paid.

SHOPPING

Look for batik, feather products, minority handicrafts, embroidery (especially shoulder bags and clothes), tin and spotted copperware. You can get minority crafts at the **Yunnan Ethnic Group Village**, though the cheapest handicrafts are from peddlers at the gate of every hotel. The cross-stitching is an excellent buy.

The **Yunnan Antique Store**, *Qingnian and Dongfeng Road, Tel. 3161198, 3161296*, open 9am-7pm, is worth a look. Try the **Bird and Flower Market** about five blocks behind the Green Lake Hotel where antique jewelry and porcelain, real and fake, share space with live gold fish and budgies. In this area too are a growing number of real antique stores. An **arts and crafts store** is at *200 Qingnian Road, Tel. 3162200,* on the same street as the Holiday Inn but beyond the square. The **Golden Dragon Department Store** is on *Bai Ta Road,* near the Holiday Inn. The **Southwest Plaza** (Xi Nan Da Xia), on *Chaochang Street at Qing Nian Street* is one of the largest department store.

EXCURSIONS & DAY TRIPS
JING HONG

This is a town where you visit minorities and their villages. It is southwest of Kunming in Xishuang Banna region (pronounced She-Schwan-Ban-NA), about a 740-km, 24-hour drive on paved roads. Planes fly there in 50-minutes daily. Air connections between Jing Hong, Bangkok (two hours), and Chiangmai (Thailand) should start any day now. The city is 10 km from the airport.

At an altitude of 550 meters, Jing Hong is humid but not overly hot in May, but can get pretty steamy in July and August. The area rises up to 2,300 meters, and grows rubber and tea. There are 1,200 to 2,000 mm. of rain annually. Take precautions against malaria. Jing Hong's urban population is about 30,000 people.

Thirteen minorities inhabit this region. The ethnic cultures here are similar to those of the northern Thai and Laotian hill tribes, but the standard of living is higher.

The best hotel in Jing Hong is the Tai Garden, then the three-star **Cai Xin**. The four-star **Tai Garden** *(Daiyuan Jiudian) is at 8 Nonglin Road, 666100, Tel. 2123888, 2130558, Fax 2126060.* The telephone of the **Cai Xin** is *2139888, Fax 2133721.*

The hostels in the Dai village (Manjinglan) are just barely recommended for backpackers. But many backpackers stay there and like them. No hostel has IDD.

Just outside the Dai Village is a park with a replica of a beautiful white stupa or pagoda next to a genuine Buddhist monastery with a friendly abbot. A museum of Dai costumes should open in Jing Hong soon.

There has been talk of boat tours on the **Lancang River** which becomes the Mekong 30 km south in Laos. This river is 293 km long in China, but so far there are only ferries. In Yunnan this river falls 1,780 meters, and 14 power stations will eventually harness it for electrical power.

You can visit **Hani** and **Jinuo villages** in the mountains. Guides tend to just drop you off at villages allowing you to wander around on your own. Don't be afraid to knock on doors. You can even ask them to don their costumes for photos. They understand sign language. (Tip them five yuan or buy something.) Interested visitors should go armed with questions about life styles, unique customs, technology, child rearing, courtship rituals and the percentage of women on village councils.

A visit to a **Dai village** could include songs, dances and a demonstration of the Water-Splashing Festival (below) any time of the year if you're expected. Some of these villages can also provide good meals in a Dai home. Some of the temples are similar to those in neighboring Laos. You can take an organized tour or rent a bicycle or car and go off on your own. You could also take public buses, but they are infrequent. You can be splashed at the **Local Customs Garden of National Minorities**, Chunhuan Park too.

The **Menglun Botanical Garden**, 75 km west of Jing Hong has been badly maintained. Hopefully it is better now but the drive there through intensely exotic and lovely countryside is worth the trip. **Simao** with an airport is the mother of all the world's tea; 23 kinds of tea still grow wild there. Simao is 540 km from Kunming (a 40-minute flight) and 160 km from Jing Hong. There is also the wild life reserve with elephants and buffalo at **Sanchahe**, 47 km north of Jing Hong. 250 Asian **elephants** lived here in 1994 but poachers, now executed, have killed many. There are now very few. Visitors can see only a small part of the reserve, ride tame elephants and visit Dai and Jinuo villages. There are tree-top hotels to see the animals but no guarantees you will spot any.

TRAVEL TO LAOS

"Officially westerners can't go to Laos by land. But lots of backpackers do so, and I believe they succeed. A Laotian consulate is in the Camellia Hotel in Kunming," says David Huang of the Yunnan Overseas Travel Corporation in Kunming, who can help you.

Shopping is best at the various tourist attractions or factories: silver jewelry, embroidered purses, natural marble pictures, and tie-dyed cotton. You can buy handicrafts directly from villagers. In Jing Hong, there's the early morning food market to see and craft stores outside the gate of the Xishuangbanna Hotel.

The **Water-Splashing Festival** marks the Dai New Year. If it's well-organized, there will be minority dances and demonstrations, dance dramas, and bamboo rocket competitions. Wa tribesmen, former headhunters, may sacrifice a bull. CITS has a boat for you to watch the dragon boat races. The water-splashing is confined to certain areas between 10am and 4pm on one designated day. Take a water pistol and shower cap. Guides loan you basins. Local youths attack you gleefully. It is a lot of fun, but keep your mouth closed. Keep your valuables at the hotel and your camera in a plastic bag.

For help with travel, **CITS** Xishuangbanna Sub-branch is in *Nakunkang District, Jing Hong, 666100, Tel. 2122032, Fax 2125980.* It can arrange day trips to villages. The telephone code is *0691.*

XIAGUAN & DALI

You can now fly from Kunming to Dali in 35 minutes, two flights every morning. The airport is 15 km from the city. The flight however would cheat you out of a 344 km six to eight-hour road trip through fascinating countryside. Part of the fun and adventure is getting there. Public air-conditioned buses are crowded and can be booked at the Camellia Hotel in Kunming. The best view is the side behind the driver. You should be able to take the new train in 1999 too.

About three-hours' drive west of Kunming along the Burma Road is Chuxiong where you can lunch in the hotels. If you take precautions about hygiene, the stalls along this road can also provide memorable meals of congealed blood, pork kidneys, squirming eels, and hot chilis, cooked before your very eyes.

Xiaguan is at an altitude of 1,980 meters, the capital of Dali Bai Autonomous Prefecture. The highest temperature here is 29 C in June. The coldest is -3 C in December. Annual rainfall is 1,200 mm. mainly May to August. It's windy all year round but the strongest winds are from November to March. Xiaguan is at the southern tip of 41-km-long Lake Erhai. There is a tea brick factory and a temple to the Tang general who failed to conquer Xiaguan.

You'll see an abundance of signs in English advertising tours, trips, food and accommodations. You can take boat trips on the 2,000-year-old man-made lake to see 4092-meter-high **Cangshan Mountain**, snow-capped most of the year. Have you ever heard of an antique lake before?

Be aware that there is a tendency to confuse the names Dali and Xiaguan. Xiaguan was the old term for greater Dali, and the name is still used. **Dali** town is 14 km north of Xiaguan, an old walled town with marble factories, and some of the best marble in China. Some houses are made of marble. Look for a large obelisk erected by conqueror Kublai Khan. Dali is a good place for hiking, generally flat in the valley, with inviting mountains. The fascinating **Shapin Market** is about 45 minutes by bus from Dali, with local produce, and a tacky tourist alley. Buses stop running at 8pm. Taxis start at Y5.

Dali was the capital of the Nanzhao and Dali kingdoms. The Tang emperors never conquered the Nanzhou empire but the Mongols subdued it in the 13th century and Marco Polo visited. It has the **Sanyuejie** (Third-Moon market), the 15th to 20th day of the third lunar month, with caravans of horses and mules, and containers of traditional medicines arriving to be traded. About 30,000 people take part in the market which is enlivened by races and perhaps gambling. The site west of Dali at the foot of the mountain is a former Nationalist execution grounds.

The San Ta Si (**Three Pagoda Temple**) on the west shore of Lake Erhai, one km outside the north gate of Dali, was first built in the Nanzhao/Tang period over a thousand years ago. The view of the lake, the three towers (70 and 43 meters tall), and the mountains behind are famous.

Butterfly Pool on the northern tip of the lake is a natural spring with one huge tree covering it. In May, strings of different kinds of butterflies appear. **Xizhou**, just north of Dali, has especially remarkable Bai architecture, incorporating marble, white-washed walls and black trim. The much-decorated houses are courtyard style. The women's dress is basically white with red or black vests and a colorful bonnet. The **Tian Zhuan Hotel** (Binguan) is built in the Bai style and is charming but not up to standard.

For **hotels** in Dali, the four-star **Asia Star** is the best, then the three-star **Man Wan** at *Canglang Street, 671000, Tel. 2188188, 2181739, Fax 2181742*. The **Asia Star Hotel** is in the *Holiday Distict, South Suburbs of Gucheng, 671003, Tel. 2670009, Fax 2672299*. It is one km from Dali. It costs $88 for a room but $66 including breakfast if booked through Edward's Adventure Tours below. Check with other travel agents too. The two-star **Jinhua** is new. It's on *Renmin Road, Tel. 2673344, Fax 2670574*. Rooms are $24, but Edward's below charges $20. Backpackers should like **No. 4 Guest House**, just outside the South Gate on *Fuxing Road*. It has shared baths. There's also the **Old Dali Inn** for Y20 a bed.

For **food**, very popular are the **Tibetan Cafe** and **Jimmy's Peace Cafe**, both popular with backpackers. Also interesting is **Mr. China's Son Cafe**, *67-5 Bo Ai Road, 671003*. The owner He Li Yi is the author of two books in English, including his autobiography *Mr. China's Son* published in the United States.

From Dali, you can travel on to **Shizhong Shan** near Jianchuan (a long, one-day excursion north), which has a unique Buddhist grotto reached by a steep 45-minute climb. Women there rub a one-meter-high female genitalia for fertility and boys rub it for courage. It also has some of the earliest Buddhist carvings in China, several styles, including some humans with long curly hair, foreigners perhaps. At the base of this mountain lies an exotic old monastery.

Shibao Shan nearby also has temples and an annual singing contest in late August or early September by young people of many minorities.

During the festival, thousands sleep under the trees or in temples. Courtship here also is by song. Fish is the local specialty, but the cooking is not outstanding. **Dali Overseas Travel Corporation** is at *216 Renmin Bei Road, Xiaguan, Dali, 671000, Tel. 2120209, Fax 2121935.* **CITS Dali**, is in *Room 232, Huaxing Building, Zhenxing Road, Xiaguan, Dali 671000, Tel. 2124707, 2124902, Fax 2124902.* You can also contact Edward He at **Edward Adventure Tours**, *19 Gan Wu Road, Dali 671003, Tel. and Fax 2670222, or e-mail:edad@public.km.yn.cn.* He charges $8 for a day trip on Erhai Lake including lunch, $12 for hiking to the top of the mountain, and $28 for two days cycling around Erhai Lake, food and guesthouse included.

The telephone code is *0872.* For **tourist complaints**, *Tel. 2670384.*

LIJIANG

From Dali, Lijiang is about 200 km north, five hours by public bus (Y25). It's also about a 40-minute flight twice a day in the morning, about 544 km from Kunming. It has the UNESCO world heritage, 800-year old **Dayan Ancient Town**, and the 5596-meter high Yu Long (Jade Dragon) Mountain. 15 km north is **Yulong Mountain** where you can take a 2968-meter long **cableway** up to 4500 meters above sea level.

Lijiang is an old town with winding streets and old bridges, completely rebuilt in the same style after an earthquake destroyed it. It is wonderful, a good place for walks. Also important to see are the **Liuli Temple** and **Dading Temple**, both in Ming architecture. **Basha**, 10 km from Lijiang, was the political and economic center of the Naxi during the Ming. The **Dabaoji Temple** has Ming and Qing murals, a combination of Lamaism, Taoism, and Buddhism. Lijiang has good tourist shopping, ethnic goodies, paintings, textiles, and the delicious Naxi Jiu, Naxi wine.

Lijiang is cooler than Kunming and padded jackets are needed in spring and autumn. It has year-round snow on the mountains. Its airport is at Heqing 28 km north of town. In Lijiang the Naxi people still use hieroglyphic writing and wear sheepskin capes on their backs for warmth and to cushion heavy baskets. On the sheepskin are seven small embroidered moons to show how hard they work (until the moon and stars appear).

Some of the **Naxi** and **Mosuo** people are matriarchal with walk-in marriages. At age 14, the boys are put out of their homes and have to find girlfriends to sleep with. Without a girlfriend, a male sleeps with the dogs. There are no marriages. Men eat breakfast with their mothers. Children are supported by all the males in the community. Joseph F. Rock, Peter Goullart, Li Lingcan, and Yang Fuquan are scholars who have written books on the Naxi people. Rock wrote for the National Geographic Society. See Zhongdian below.

The best located hotel is the three-star **Grand Lijiang** overlooking the old town, *Xingyi Street, Tel. 5128888, Fax 5127878*. $56 a room. Edward in Dali charges $45 including breakfast. The four-star **Guanfang Hotel** is the best and is at *Xueshan Zhong Road, 674100, Tel. 5188888, Fax 5181999*. $100 a room. Edward charges $70 including breakfast.

The three-star **Black and White Rivers** (Heibaishui) **Hotel** is on *South Huancheng Road, 674100, Tel. 5126688, Fax 5124887*. The two-star Guluwan Hotel can be reached at *Tel. 5121446, Fax 5121019*.

Good for backpackers is the **First Bend Inn** at *43 Mingshixia, Xingyijie*, Old Town with public shower and toilet. $10 for twin rooms, and $11 for rooms with three beds. There's also the **San He Hotel** at *4 Jishangxia, Xingyijie, Old Town*, $25 for a twin, and $3 a bed in a dorm.

Popular with foreigners is the **Market Cafe** in the old town near the market square. The **Naxi Family Cafe** is at the entrance to the old town.

Lijiang International Travel Service is on *Dongdajie Street, Dayan, 674100, Tel. 5187554*. For **tourist complaints**, *Tel. 5123432*; the telephone code is *0888*.

ZHONGDIAN TO TIBET

Zhongxin town is 315 km north of Lijiang about five hours by road. It is an eight hours drive from Dali. It is toward the Tibet border at an altitude of 3,000 meters, almost the same as Lhasa so do read about altitude sickness in **Tibet**. It is a 45-minute, 659 km flight from Kunming and is the capital of the Diqing/Dechen Tibetan Nationality Autonomous Prefecture and Zhongdian County. This county has 470 mountains over 4000 meters high. A new airport should be completed in 1999; 41 percent of its people are Tibetan, 18 percent are Naxi.

Now promoted as the "real" **Shangri-la**, the city is generally a tourist trap, grey and miserable. From here you can take tours and horse treks, visit Tibetan villages, and see the upper Yangtze and Mekong Rivers. You can stay with Tibetan families.

Five km from town, you can visit the once prosperous Tibetan Buddhist **Ganden Sumtseling Monastery**. This is also known as Gukhua Si or Songzanlin Monastery, first built on this hilltop in 1679. During the Cultural Revolution, the Red Guards almost totally trashed it. The main hall has been reconstructed and a visit to this remote area is rewarding. The temple has a simple inn and 800 monks.

The three-star **Diqing Hotel** is at *11th Changzhen Road, Tel. 8227599, Fax 8226568*. $40. Popular with backpackers is the **Tibet Hotel**, *16 Fengqu Road, Tel. 8222448*. $22 for a twin, or $3 a bed in dorm.

Interesting is the 52-room **Gyalthang Dzong Hotel** (*Jiang Tang Binguan*). It is built in Tibetan style, offers Tibetan food, and is also a cultural center, giving lectures, demonstrations and tours on Tibetan medicine, the local flora, dance, and music. It's at *Zhongdian, Deqing Tibetan Autonomous Prefecture, 644000, Tel. 8227610, Fax 8223620.* It's a 30 minute drive from the Zhongdian airport and a 20-25 minute walk from town. $40 for a small room with twin beds. The telephone code is *0887.* **InnerAsia Trading Company** can arrange tour packages from the US. Contact them at *236 Fifth Avenue, New York, 10001, Tel. 212/532-2600 or Fax 532-5230. E-mail is 104437.2242@compuserve.com; Http:// www.gdh.innerasia.com/romance.html.*

The scenery from Dali to Zhongdian is especially great for bird watchers from March to September. It is full of lakes, forests, and mountain views. Read C.P. Fitzgerald's *Tower of Five Glories* about his experiences in this area in the 1930s. And if you can find them, look up 1924-1935 National Geographic magazines, for Joseph F. Rock's articles and photographs. These are said to have inspired James Hilton to write the novel "Lost Horizon" which in turn inspired the 1937 movie. The US Nature Conservancy Organization and the Yunnan government have signed an agreement to set up a national forest park here in the northwest of Yunnan.

For **tourist complaints** and information, *Tel. 8223786.* The **telephone code** is *0887.*

180 km by bus further north from Lijiang on the Tibetan border is **Deqin** where you can ramble around spectacular mountains and enjoy the Langcang/Mekong River. The highest mountain here, the snow-covered Shanzidou, rises to 6740 meters. It has glaciers and French churches. The best hotel is the **Ka Wagebo**, *Wenhua Street, Shengpin Town, Tel. (887)8413188, Fax 8412688.* Y340 a room. The **Deqin Hotel** charges Y40.

You need a permit to go on to **Tibet**. This could take three working days and cost Y500 from a travel agent. Don't expect to enter from Zhongdian immediately. From Zhongdian to Lhasa, it can be another 11 days by land cruiser, camping overnight in snowy mountain passes or in the gorges of the upper Lancang River. **CITS** is at *Jiantang Dong Road, 674400, Zhongdian, Tel. (887) 8222364.*

THE BURMA ROAD

The **Burma Road** goes from Kunming as far as Xiaguan, and instead of going north to Lijiang, it runs south to the Myanmar (Burmese) border. From Xiaguan onward, don't expect luxury hotels. Do not expect air-conditioning, heat, IDD, money exchange, credit cards, carpets, coffee shops, bars, 24-hour electricity, or hot tap water. Take cash for buying from villagers and lots of small change. **Dali/Xiaguan** is usually an overnight stop on the Burma Road, first used as part of the southern silk route from Sichuan to India in the fourth and fifth century B.C.

The Burma Road was built 1937-1939 by 160,000 Chinese and Burmese laborers. The United States financed it to supply China in her fight against the Japanese. It was used by the Allies until 1942 when the Japanese captured Burma. It was extended and reopened between India and Kunming in 1945 and renamed the **Stilwell Road** after the American general.

Unfortunately, there is nothing in Yunnan to mark this Sino-US achievement except for a small, hard-to-find pillar in Kunming. Local people seem to know nothing about it. There is a monument to the Chinese soldiers who fought in the Japanese war (near historic Tengchong).

Along the road live Yi, Dai, Bai, Lisu, Deang, and Achang minorities. Ask about the famous bronze drums. There are also neolithic sites and takins, pheasants, camphor trees, coffee and pepper, all indigenous to this area.

The drive south from Dali is also paved and takes about nine hours through the mountains, the highest elevation reaching 4,000 meters. Many World War II battles took place here. **Tengchong** also sits near 97 dormant volcanoes and hot springs with geysers. It has a huge **rhododendron forest**, with the biggest tree 16 meters high. You can get a lovely room with balcony at the **Tengchong Guest House** for Y30 a night.

Ruili is 88 km southwest of Luxi/Mangshi which has an airport. On the Myanmar border, it has China's largest diamond market and of course you can buy Burmese jadeite, rubies and sapphires. You can take an eight km rafting tour on the Ruili River or rent a **bicycle** from the Jue Jue Cold Drinks' shop and explore the Burmese-style temples. Here the best hotel is the **Kai Tong Hotel**, on *Bian Cheng Street, Tel. 4149526* at Y360 a room. The **Nan Yang Hotel** charges Y25 a room, Y50 a suite. The city itself is the pits but renting a bicycle and exploring the countryside is marvelous. The people here are mainly **Jingpo** and **Dai**.

GETTING TO BURMA

"Burma anyone? Foreigners cannot go on tours to Myanmar by land. They can only go by air from Kunming. There are two flights a week. The Myanmar Consulate is in Kunming," says David Huang of the Yunnan Overseas Travel Corporation, Kunming, who can help you.

Flights go between Kunming and Baoshan City, 176 km from the Myanmar border, and between Kunming and Dehong at the border. At **Baoshan** (571 km drive from Kunming or 45 minutes flight), you can stay at the **Yindou Hotel** for Y40 a night in a big room. Baoshan was on the southwest Silk Road, 160 km east of Tengchong County. A **museum** is in

Yuhuang Pavilion. The **Temple of the Sleeping Buddha** is 16 km north of Baoshan and was founded in 716 A.D.

At **Dehong**, you should be able to see the barter trade between the two countries and pigs sniffing for heroin. The urban population is 920,000. **Manshi**, also close to the Burmese border, has an airport.

PRACTICAL INFORMATION

Airport Info, *Tel. 3133216*

Consulates: The Thai Consulate is in the King World Hotel. The Laotian and Myanmar Consulates are in the Camellia Hotel. A Vietnamese consulate should open soon.

CYTS Tours, *23 Lao Hai Geng Road, 650034, Tel. 4141037, Fax 4167841.*

First Aid, *Tel. 120.*

Kunming China International Travel Service, *218 Huan Cheng Nan Road, 650011, Tel. 3132895, 3134019, Fax 3132895, 3132332.* Dept. of Europe and America, *Tel. 3535448, Fax 3535448. Manager Wang Ping. E-mail: ynkmcits@public.km.yn.cn.*

Kunming Municipal Tourism Administration, *28 East Dongfeng Road.*

Telephone Code, *0871.*

Tourist Hotline, *Tel. 3135412.*

Yunnan China Travel Service, *16/F Zhong Ming Plaza, 36 Beijing Road, 650041, Tel. 3514788, (24 hours), or Fax 3179878, 3515155.*

Yunnan Overseas Travel Corporation, *154 Dong Feng Dong Road, 650041, Tel. 3543560, 3537361, 3123281. Fax 3546204. Ask for David Huang.*

Yunnan Travel and Tourism Administration, *218 Huan Cheng Road, Kunming, 650011, Tel. 3557861, 3543560, Fax 3546204* for brochures and information. For complaints, *Tel. 3139197, 3537351, 3164961 or Fax 3174343.*

WUHAN

Wuhan, the capital of Hubei province, is really three cities: **Hankou**, **Hanyang**, and **Wuchang**. These are separated from each other by the Yangtze and Han Rivers, and joined by bridges and expressways. You might find yourself there because of business or a Yangtze River cruise. You should go there because of its ancient chime bells. There are no other international class attractions. Students of modern history might be interested in the beginning of the Sun Yat-sen republican revolution and Chairman Mao's house there. And eco- travelers might pass through on the way to Shennongjia Prime Forest or to look for fresh-water dolphins. Taoists would be interested in the Wudang Mountains.

Wuhan has been an important port for at least 2,000 years. The city itself dates from the 11th century B.C. (Shang). The city wall in Hanyang, no longer standing, was first built almost 2000 years ago. The Wuchang wall was constructed during the Three Kingdoms (220-265 A.D.), by Sun Quan, King of Wu, and can still be seen at the Small East Gate. Hankou and Hanyang were originally one city, but in the 15th century, the Han River changed its course.

Several foreign nations forced concessions here after the Opium War, and some of Hankou's architecture still reflects old Europe. Wuchang is especially famous because on October 10, 1911, the first victory of the Sun Yat-sen revolution against the Manchus took place here, an accidental explosion of a bomb on Shouyi Road in Wuchang, now the **1911 Revolution Memorial Hall**. Wuhan later became the headquarters of the left wing of the Nationalist party. In 1923, the Communists led a successful railway workers' strike.

The Communists took the city in May 1949. The three cities merged administratively shortly afterward. During the Cultural Revolution, it experienced some of the heaviest fighting between factions. Today it is the home of the huge Wuhan Iron and Steel Works. Other industries include Citroen automobiles, electronics, textiles, and computer software. It is developing quickly, largely because of the Three Gorges Dam.

The weather is hottest in July and August at 42 C, and coldest in January and February at 5 C. The annual precipitation is 1,200 mm., mainly February to May. The population is seven million, of whom 3.8 million are urban.

ARRIVALS & DEPARTURES

Wuhan is 12 hours by train south of Beijing, north of Guangzhou, and east of Shanghai. The capital of Hubei province can also be reached by air from 44 Chinese cities. It is 70 minutes, 800 km west of Shanghai. The main Tian He International Airport is 20 km north of the city and also has flights from Hong Kong, Macau, and Fukuoka in Japan. Only the Wuhan Air Company uses the downtown airport; other airlines use the Tian He. Both are in Hankou.

Good highway buses arrive from Yichang in 3.5 to four hours, and from Jingzhou in three. In Wuhan, buses leave about once an hour from the Hankou and Wuchang bus stations for Yichang and Jingzhou. Cruise ships and ferries arrive from Chongqing and other points upstream. (Tickets from Chongqing cost from Y166 (fourth class) to Y542 (second class). There is no first class. A hovercraft arrives at least once a day from Jiujiang in 3.5 to four hours.

ORIENTATION

Hankou is the main downtown area with department stores and the main ship piers. This was the old European section. It and Hanyang are on the northwest bank of the Yangtze. The main tourist attractions, the provincial museum, East Lake and the Yellow Crane Tower are in Wuchang on the south bank.

Wuhan has recently opened a circular beltway around the city, alleviating somewhat the traffic jams downtown.

WHERE TO STAY

The best hotels are expected to be the new **Shangri-La** which is aiming for five stars, and then the four-star **Holiday Inn Tian An**. The **Wuhan Asia** is good and the new **Holiday Inn Riverside** should be between three and four stars and special.

The **Holiday Inn Tian An** and the **Shangri-La** are close to the main Wuhan Pier, good locations for business people and close to municipal government offices. The **Holiday Inn Riverside** has a fantastic location for tourists across the Yangtze River Bridge from the main tourist attractions but also next to the TV Tower, the Qingchuan Pagoda, Guishan Hill, and the Han River. It is the closest of these hotels to the provincial government in Wuchang.

The **Holiday Inn Riverside** is convenient if you're cruising on the Splendid China, President, Yangtze, Yangtze Paradise or Star Dipper as these ships dock at its pier. Victoria Cruises ties up at Pier 16, and the Blue Whale, Yangtze Angel, and the Regal princesses berth at Pier 19 across from the Metropolitan Hotel. The East King and East Queen are at Pier 14. These others are close to the **Hankou hotels**.

The high tourist season is April to June, September and October. Prices listed below are subject to change, negotiations, and 15% surcharge. Hotels below all have business centers, foreign exchange facilities, ticketing offices, etc.

SHANGRI-LA HOTEL (*Shang Gorilla*), *700 Jianshe Avenue, Hankou, 430015, Tel. 85806868, Fax 85776868. Located in a business district near a shopping mall, tax bureau and municipal government offices. About 25 km from Tianhe Airport and eight km from Wuhan Port.*

This 1999, 21-story hotel has 506 spacious rooms, executive floors, 13 long-stay apartments and 17 serviced offices. Rooms have Fax and computer outlets, coffee-making, safes, and full executive-size desks. It has valet parking, 24-hour room service, and underground car parking. It has a Cantonese restaurant, delicatessen, sports bar, and coffee shop with open kitchen. Its ballroom can seat 1,200-1,350 for banquets, and is equipped for conferences. It has a gym, jacuzzi, steam room, 12-meter indoor pool and outdoor tennis court, and its own garden and playground.

HOLIDAY INN TIAN AN *(Tianan Jiu Dian), 868 Jie Fang Da Dao Avenue, 430022. Four stars. Tel. 85867888, 85845484, Fax 85845353. E-mail: wuhchsal@public.wh.hb.cn. In good downtown location near stores, and two km from the Port. It's 27 km from Tian He airport and five km from the railway station. $120-$160 for rooms; $290-$1600 for suites.*

Built in 1996, this pleasant 394-room, 27-story hotel has five executive floors, non-smoking rooms, Cantonese and Asian cuisine. It has a revolving restaurant, 24-hour room service, gym, outdoor pool and tennis court. It has a night club, offices, rooms for the physically challenged, and Dragonair office.

WUHAN ASIA HOTEL *(Yazhou Da Jiudian), Wuhan International Convention Centre, 616 Jiefang Dadao Avenue, Hankou, 430030. Four stars. Tel. 83807777, Fax 83808080, E-mail:asiahotel@iname.com. $115-$150 for rooms, $170-$650 for suites. 25 km from Tian He airport, 15 km from the railway station, and six km from the Pier.*

This 265-room hotel has a good reputation, BBC and Star movies. It has 24-hour room service, and a revolving restaurant. There's Cantonese and Sichuan food, disco and karaoke rooms, an outdoor pool and gym.

HOLIDAY INN RIVERSIDE, *88 Xi Ma Chang Street, Hanyang, 430050, Tel. 4716688, Fax 84716181. E-mail:hirwgm@public.wh.hb.cn. About 3.5 stars but not yet official. $80-$160 for rooms; $180 for suites. 29 km from the Tian He airport, eight km from the railway station, and five km from the port. Complimentary airport shuttle for international flight arrivals.*

This 336-room hotel was originally built in 1984 and renovated extensively in 1998-99. It has a gym, tennis, CNN, HBO, and Star World. It has executive floors, non-smoking rooms and three telephone jacks in every room. Its ballroom can seat 300 guests banquet style, and it has simultaneous translation equipment. It has an international buffet, Italian restaurant, Cantonese food and a Filipino band. It gives free unlimited ice cream for one child under 12 accompanied by a parent, and free buffet meals for one child under 12 when accompanied by one adult per child. Children under 19 years are free when sharing a room with parents. It has two executive floors with their own workout room, and mini-bar prices 50% of its restaurant prices.

See also Chapter 13, *China's Best Places to Stay.*

WHERE TO EAT

Among the well-known Hubei dishes are: steamed Wuchang fish, three steamings of fish, pork and vegetables, stir-fried boneless eel, and lotus root soup. Food is good in the hotels. The **Holiday Inn Tian An** has good buffets in its Revolving Restaurant. It costs Y95 for breakfast, and

Y118 for dinner, plus 15%. It also has an outdoor barbecue dinner from 5:30pm-10pm every Saturday, weather permitting.

YINZUO RESTAURANT, *159 Yan Jiang Avenue in Hankou, Tel. 82836657*

LAOTONGCHENG RESTAURANT, *1 Dazi Road, Hankou, Tel. 82814966,*

Both above restaurants are good for Wuhan food.

MR. XIE'S RESTAURANT, *in the same block as the Holiday Inn Tian An, at 910 Jiefang Da Dao, Tel. 85813580.*

Everybody recommends this place.

CHU TOUR PALACE RESTAURANT, *20 Shouyi Park Road, Wuchang near the Yellow Crane Tower, Tel. 88874155.*

This is a great restaurant. We loved the *mayuen* sesame balls, steamed grass carp, cabbage and pork balls, lotus root and rice balls, rice and pork dumplings. It's also a dinner theater. See below.

SEEING THE SIGHTS

Wuhan only has one major tourist attraction. You cannot miss the **ancient chime bells** next to the Hubei Provincial Museum, *188 Dong Hu Road, Wuchang, Tel. 86783683, 86783685.* It is open daily with two hours off for lunch from 11:30am or 12-2pm or so. In 1978, 7,000-20,000 articles were excavated from the Zenghouyi Tomb, just outside of Suizhou city. Dating from the Warring States period 2,400 years ago, the tomb of Marquis Yi of Zeng contained bronzes, weapons, lacquer, musical instruments, gold, and jade. The contents were found in water in which oxidized copper was accidentally dissolved. This saved most of the pieces from decay. Some of the lacquer is still preserved in water and shows the original brilliant red at its best. 30 of his concubines took poison and died with him.

Most important in the find is a complete set of **64 ritual bells** of different sizes, a total of 2,500 kilograms, the heaviest musical instrument in the world. When struck, they emit a perfect 12-tone system covering five octaves. Each bell also has two tones depending on where it is struck, a quality that has not yet been found in any other bell anywhere else in the world. In addition, the name of the tone and the date were inscribed on each bell in both the Zeng and Chu scripts. The two languages side by side here are as valuable to linguists as the Rosetta stone.

The bells were a gift from the King of Chu. Since the reigns of the donor and the recipient overlapped by only a few years, the technology to produce them must have been at an astoundingly high level. Not only are their tones precise, they were probably cast in a short length of time. The heaviest is 203.6 kilograms and 1.5 meters high. Imagine pouring hot metal into a mold that size! And of the exact amount to produce the prescribed tone!

Ritual bells were only played for ceremonies, not for pleasure. Only aristocrats and royalty were allowed to possess them, and only in certain numbers. Musicians can play ancient Chinese music on reproductions of the bells for an additional fee. Foreigners are usually deeply moved by a rendition of *Ode to Joy*. The original bells are played on very special occasions like the return of Hong Kong in 1997.

The five-story, 51 meter-high, **Huang He Lou** (Yellow Crane Tower), Y30, in Wuchang is a symbol of the city and has a good view. Open 7:30am-5:30pm. It was first built in 223 A.D. and inspired many famous poets, including Li Bai. It was destroyed and rebuilt several times, the latest in 1981 when it was reconstructed and expanded. The current design is based largely on the Qing version (1768-1884). Pictures of previous versions are inside. There are 70 steps to climb to the base and more stairs inside, a hard climb in spite of the two elevators which cost an additional Y2 each way.

The legend of the wine shop on the original site has inspired poets. The owner used to give free wine to an old man who drew a picture of a yellow crane on the wall in gratitude. After the old man left, the crane came to life and danced for the customers, and the owner became rich. When the old man returned decades later, he mounted the crane and flew off into the sky.

If you're looking for other things to do while you wait for your ship, the **Minority Museum** is at *Zhongnan Minority University, 13 Lu Xiang, Wuchang, Tel. 87492050,* open daily 8am-11:30am; 2pm-4:30pm, but closed during school vacations. The 45-meter-high, seven-story **Hongshan Pagoda**, *Wuluo Road, Wuchang, Tel. 87884539,* dates from the Yuan (1279) and is open 7am-5pm. The **Guiyuan Temple**, *20 Cuiwei Heng Road, Hanyang, Tel. 84841367,* open 8am-4pm, was founded over 300 years ago. It is the most important Buddhist temple in the city, and is one of the 10 biggest in China. It contains 500 clay arhats, each life-size, distinctive, and 250 years old. The Guiyuan is relatively close to the Holiday Inn Riverside.

Chairman Mao's House where he stayed when he took his famous Yangtze River swims is one block from the provincial museum. It's an opportunity to see how he lived, a big house with a four-meter high ceiling at *56 Dong Hu Road, Tel. 86796106,* open 8am-5pm daily. Y20 entrance fee. Tours also go to pleasant **East Lake** which is bigger than West Lake in Hangzhou.

A **river dolphin research center** is at the *Institute of Hydrobiology, Chinese Academy of Sciences, Luojiashan, Wuchang, 430072, next to Wuhan University. Tel. 87801331.* Only one dolphin is there. Fee Y50.

You can take a half-day trip to the museum at the *Ancient Copper Mine** in *Tonglushan Daye county*, described by a Canadian metallurgist as "incredible." One hour by road from Wuhan, it takes another half-hour to explore. It is now an open pit with mining tools, shaft, ropes, and baskets, started in the Zhou about 3,000 years ago. Nowhere else in the world at the time was mining technology so far advanced.

Note: Be aware that some guides in Wuhan have convinced their groups to substitute some cheaper (Y5) tourist attraction for the more expensive (Y30) Yellow Crane Tower ("because it has a lot of steps," or "it's too hot"). The savings were not passed on to the group who should have gotten extra drinks, a meal upgrade, another stop, or reimbursement. Do make enquiries if this happens, unless you want the agency to pocket the money.

THE WARRIOR WOMAN

Mu Lan, one of Walt Disney's recent heroines, was a real historical person, who lived in the Southern/Northern Dynasties or the Tang dynasty. Sources differ. Her family name was Zhu but she is known as Fa Mu Lan, "Fa" meaning "beautiful lady." She disguised herself as a man and fought in place of her elderly father for 12 years and became a general. Then she returned home to care for her parents. Several places claim her as their own. Hubei province says her birthplace was Mulan Hill in Huangpi County, about 50 km north of Wuhan. A tomb tablet with her name and story was erected there in the 17th century. Six km north of Mulan Hill is 57 km-long Mulan Lake. No mention of her is in the provincial museum.

NIGHTLIFE & ENTERTAINMENT

Noteworthy cultural groups include the Wuhan Acrobatic Troupe, Beijing Opera Troupe of Wuhan, and the Wuhan Song and Dance Drama Troupe. Some of these perform at the **Chu Tour Palace Restaurant** noted above for its food. Its theatre has a different show each month. It could be acrobatics, a performing panda or Beijing opera, and goes from 7pm-8:30pm for Y30 daily. It's at *20 Showyi Park Road, Wuchang, 430060, Tel. 88874155, Fax 88874155*. All of these troupes have performed abroad.

For fun, there's **J.J.'s Disco**. The **night market** is on *Jianghan Bei Road* near the Holiday Inn Tian An. The 18-hole **Wuhan International Golf Club** is out towards Tian He airport and open all year round.

SHOPPING

Local products are gold and silver jewelry, lacquerware, carpets, shell carvings, carved turquoise, boxwood carving, feather fans, colored pottery, jadeware, and paintings. The main shopping area is near the railway station in Hankou and along **Zhongjiacun** in Hanyang. For general shopping there's **Wuhan Plaza**, *Jiefang Avenue, Hankou*, and the **Masses Paradise Shopping Centre** (lower quality), at *608 Zhongshan Da Dao, Tel. 85719060*. The **Galaxy Plaza** is near the Holiday Inn Tian An. The **Wuhan Carpet Factory** is at *32 Ruiqiang Road, Hankou, 430017, Tel. 82832003*. The **Wuhan Jade Factory** is at *226 Hangkong Road, Hankou, 430030, Tel. 83635898*; and the **Wuhan Arts and Crafts Store** is at *646 Zhongshan Avenue, Hankou, 430021, Tel. 85843460*. The **Dingxin Folk Arts Gallery** is inside *East Lake Park, Wuchang, Tel. 86778312*.

Hubei Antique Store is at *68 Donghu Road, Wuchang, 430077, Tel. 86783678*. Other stores and markets are in this area. The **Wuhan Antique Store** is at *999 Zhongshan Avenue, Hankou, 430017, Tel. 82836243* and *167 Zhongshan Avenue, Hankou, 430030, Tel. 83786538*. Antique stores are located in **Sangyang Road** with peddlers' stalls at the back. Near the Holiday Inn Tian An on the 3rd junction of Jianghan Road is a "**silk alley**" for clothes.

EXCURSIONS & DAY TRIPS

Shennonjia Prime Forest Scenic Spot in the west of the province adjacent to Chongqing is 3,250 sq kilometers of virgin forests, mountains, minority villages, and the home of the Chinese "Big Foot." It is a three-hour trip by bus west of Yichang to **Shennong Resort Hotel**, *A1 Muyuzhen, Muyuzhen Town, Shennongjia Region, 442400, Tel. (0719) 3452513, Fax 3452514*. See also Yangtze Gorges below.

Tian Er Zhou, Shishou, 300 km west of Wuhan near the Yangtze, is for animal lovers. Here is a reserve where the government with the help of Hong Kong's Ocean Park is trying to save fresh-water **dolphins** or *baiji* from extinction. There could be six dolphins resident by now. Scientists estimate that only 100 of these mammals are left in the wild. No one is allowed to kill dolphins or speed on a 135-km section of the river west of Wuhan. Cruise ship passengers have seen dolphins swimming between Wuhan and Jingzhou.

Wudang Mountain is about 200 km northwest of Wuhan and needs at least five days. It is the home of the Wudang style of martial arts. This important Taoist center has an impressive collection of religious buildings. Mostly built in the Ming, it includes eight palaces, two temples, 36 nunneries, and 62 grotto temples, all along a 30-km mountain path. The highest of its 72 peaks, Tianzhu, is over 1,600 meters. On top is the *Golden Hall (Yuan and Ming), made of gilded copper. Wudang is not as strenuous as other mountains. New hotels are at the foot.

Zhangjiajie is a national scenic spot in the south of the province, about 300 km southwest of Wuhan and accessible by air. See Changsha.

For the Yangtze Gorges and other important destinations along the river, keep reading. From Wuhan, you can take a regular ferry or one of the luxury cruise ships through the Yangtze Gorges to Chongqing.

PRACTICAL INFORMATION

Business hours: 8:30 or 9am-5 or 5:30pm for offices, five days a week. 9am-12 noon and 1:30pm-4:30pm for the Bank of China. 8:30am or 9am-7 or 8:30pm for stores.

Changjiang Cruise Overseas Tourist Corporation, *55 Yanjiang Avenue, 430014, Tel. 85701025, 85655362, Fax 85701040. E-mail: ccotchw@public.wh.hb.cn.* (Mainly wholesale) Contact: Ai Yong Hong. For M.S. Yangtze Angel and other ships.

East King and **East Queen**, Orient Royal Cruiser Limited, *Dock No. 14, Yanjiang Avenue, Hankou, 430021, Tel. 85703553, 8566-9988, Fax 85666688, 85673795.* For 1999, East King and East Queen will be running between Chongqing and Yichang only.

Hubei CITS, *7/F, Xiaonanhu Building, 26 Taibei Yi Road, 430015, Tel. 85784100.* (Reservations for cruises and tours: *Tel. 85672651, Fax 85784089.*) *E-mail:citswuh@public.wh.hb.cn. Contact James Lin.*

Hubei Overseas Cruise Co.: (M.V.Yangtze Paradise and M.V.Yangzijiang), *88 Ximachang Street, Hanyang, 430050, Tel. 84715302, Fax 84715301.*

Hubei Overseas Travel Group, *88 Xima Changjie Street, Hanyang, 430051, Tel. 84715293, 84715297, Fax 84715301. E-mail:kathyyin@126.com or e-mail:citshub@public.wh.hb.cn*

Hubei Provincial Tourism Administration, *178 Lanjiang Road, Hanyang, 430050, Tel. 84843024.*

Hubei Yangtze International Travel Service, *3 Dandong Road, B-21/F, Hankou, 430022,* (next to Holiday Inn Tian An), *Tel. 85826436, Fax 85824549. E-mail:yangtze@126.com. Http://www.yangtzetour.com.* Contact Ben Chen. The Cruise Department should know about ship movements.

Telephone Code: *027.*

Tourist Complaints, contact Supervisory Bureau of Tourism Quality of Hubei Province, *Building 2, Qingshiqiao Area, Hanyang, 430050, Tel. 84818760, Fax 4822513.*

Wuhan Overseas Tourist Corporation, *48 Baofeng Road, 430030, Tel. 83638312, 83620672, Fax 83626601. E-mail: whotc@public.wh.hb.cn.* Contact Toby Lee Xiang Bin.

Wuhan Tourist Administration, *17 Hezuo Street, Hankou, 430017, Tel. 82833107, 82844081, Fax 82177868, 82817868.* For information.

Yangtze Bright Star Cruise Ltd., *282 Qintai Road, Hanyang, 430050, Tel. 84830478 84762856, Fax 84843324.* (For MV President Cruise Ships, see also CITS Head Office, Beijing.)

YANGTZE GORGES

(also known as Yangzi or Changjiang River Gorges)

The boat trip through the **Yangtze Gorges** and on the great river itself is highly recommended, not just for its spectacular scenery but also for its history and tranquility. Bring binoculars, a telephoto lens if you're a camera bug, and some books about the river.

The scenery includes sheer cliffs and mountains rising up to 1,000 meters on both sides of narrow, rushing water, old towns cut by slender lines of stone steps, and a hill almost lined from top to bottom with a pagoda. You can hear reproductions of ancient chime bells, and see a 2,000-year old gentleman. You might race a dragon boat and look for wild monkeys and hanging coffins. You will see signs on hills showing the new water levels after 2009, towns and temples that will be flooded, and the largest dam in the world being built.

You will see social history: ships still unloaded by strings of men carrying coal in baskets on their backs. If you go up the Daning River or Shennongjia Stream, you might see Tujia men pulling boats upstream with shoulder harnesses and chanting in the old way.

The Yangtze Gorges were created 30-50 million years ago as a result of collisions between the Indian and the Eurasian continental plates. These formed the Himalayas and its foothills, primarily made of limestone, except for the site of the Three Gorges Dam which is granite. The Yangtze River is a busy highway. Aside from a few short sections, there has been no road along the river between Yichang and Chongqing. (There is one being built now.)

Guides should tell you stories of the Three Kingdoms, but bring your own books and maps along because the ships' information is sketchy: a copy of Richard McKenna's *The Sand Pebbles,* John A. Hersey's *A Single Pebble,* or Caroline Walker et al's *On Leaving Bai Di Cheng, the Cultures of China's Yangzi Gorges.* Probe International's *Damming the Three Gorges* is an environmental group's readable critique of the feasibility study of the proposed dam. Van Slyke's *Yangtze, Nature, History and the River* also describes the foreigners who lived here. *The Romance of the Three Kingdoms,* a historical war novel, has been translated into English, and you will

BUYER'S MARKET FOR YANGTZE GORGE CRUISES!

In 1998, with the recession in Asia, the floods and misinformation about the dam closing the river, most cruise ships were far from full. Sailings on many had to be canceled. This year it is still a buyers' market. The Three Gorges Dam will not affect water levels until the year 2003. There is still time to see it and it's worth the trip. The river and gorges are beautiful.

encounter the names, statues and temples of the heroes in many places in the Yangtze valley: Liu Bei, Zhang Fei, Guan Yu, and Zhuge Liang – and their arch enemy, Cao Cao.

When To Go

The best time to go is September and October. The rainy season is May to August. There are landslides due to heavy rains and floods in July and August which could disrupt land excursions. The winter is cold, the hotels and ferries inadequately heated. A padded jacket or sweater and windbreaker is necessary for the wind in the gorges even in mid-October and into April. Expect delays by fog from early November and March. Also expect delays waiting for berths in Chongqing and Wuhan.

History

Among the highlights of the archaeology and history in this area are the **Ba**, a little known group who lived here from about the 16th century B.C. to the third century B.C., their capitals in Chongqing and Chengdu. They were worshippers of white tigers and left behind some very distinctive and impressive bronzes in humanoid forms. See Chengdu. There are also some relics in the Chongqing museum. These are the people whose hanging coffins you look for in the streams above the Yangtze.

The **Kingdom of Chu** dominated what is now Hubei from about 770 B.C. until it was taken over by the King of Qin, the first emperor of China in 221 B.C. This was the period of the poet-statesman Quyuan, whose death inspired the first dragon boat races.

The **Three Kingdom's** period started about 220 A.D. with an oath in a peach orchard, and ended in 265 A.D. during which battles were fought between contending kingdoms, the Wei, Shu and Wu. Ask about the famous Battle of the Red Cliffs west of Wuhan.

The Yangtze was also frequented by **foreign merchants**, **gunboats**, and **missionaries** in the late 1800s and early 1900s, but guides will not give you much information about this embarrassing period. This is the background of the novel and movie, *The Sand Pebbles*. Nobel and Pulitzer prize winner **Pearl S. Buck** lived and worked in Zhenjiang downstream.

Sailing the Gorges

I have never heard of anyone getting seasick on this river and it is safe. Between Wuhan and Chongqing, it is under three km wide and in some places only 100 meters. River traffic controllers are strict. Ships have fire alarms, smoke detectors, life boats and jackets. Traffic is heavy so if there is trouble, help is close by. Ships have radar and captains are in radio contact with control towers along the way.

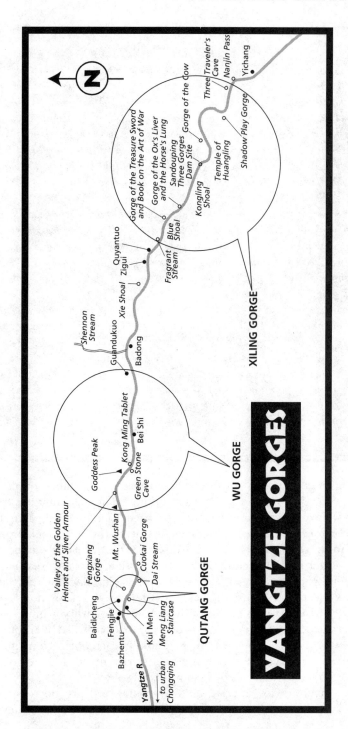

THE DAM CONTROVERSY

*A controversial dam is currently being built that will displace over a million people, raise the water level upstream, and decrease the dramatic effect of the gorges by over 100 meters at the site, and less elsewhere. The dam will help control floods, provide irrigation and 84 million kwhs of hydroelectric power, and enable ocean-going ships to reach Chongqing. You should be able to see the furious construction activities in **Sandouping**, day or night, unless you sleep through it. It is lit at night but not well enough for photos or to satisfy people who want a good look. Let's hope you get there during the day.*

Some but not all cruise ships stop for a visit at the site. Buses take them to the highest point, a look-out tower called Jar Hill and nearby exhibition room with a scale model. Plans for the largest civil engineering project in the world call for submerging 632 sq km of land, and creating a lake at Chongqing. The project includes new bridges, more flights, airports, easier navigation and better hotels.

While construction of the dam has now started, cruise ship movements will not be affected except for one month in 2003. After this, the water will start rising, and larger ships will use the five-stage locks (three hours) and smaller vessals like cruise ships will use the lift (45 minutes).

Critics argue that sedimentation will destroy the dam's turbines in less than 10 years, that it will affect the ecology, and destroy archeological sites. They say that the costs far outweigh the benefits, especially in terms of disrupted lives. If you get the chance, ask local people how they feel about it.

Warning: on passenger ferries and Tianzi cruise ships, you usually pay only for the fare and bed ahead of time. Some unscrupulous travel agents will try to get you to pay for a package, food included. The ships don't recognize these packages and make you pay for food. Book through one of the travel agents listed here or directly at the ticket office at the Pier. After you get aboard, second class and up passengers could ask for a Y60 a day food package; you eat after everyone else has lined up and eaten.

The cheapest ships are the **passenger ferries**. But if you don't speak Chinese, how will you make your wishes known? How will you buy a ticket? And get a berth assignment once on board? How long will it be before you see the Gorges? How long will the ship stop in each port? Don't go this way unless you're very short of money, love adventure, and are good at charades. You also have to be healthy and flexible.

Passenger ferries operate all year round and are decreasing in numbers because of the faster hovercrafts and the new roads. They are crowded with little privacy. The top second-class has a lounge, bunks for four people to a cabin, and soap, toothbrushes, towels and tea. The public bathrooms might have a tub, shower, western toilet and lots of water all over the floor. Try for an outside cabin. The inside ones can get pretty stuffy in summer, and you might find other passengers gambling noisily on the floor outside your room all night.

In second, third, fourth, or fifth class, you share a room with an increasing number of people, get suffocated by cigarette smoke, or worry about thieves. Aim for a cabin with a window. In "No Class" you rent a blanket and sleep on the floor.

Below second class, you have to bring your own towel, mug, soap, etc. Steaming hot water is available. Fourth class has 12 bunks to a cabin. Hope for a spot near the door. If you want to sit indoors, you have to book a berth, essential in cold weather. Up to recently, no one got private toilets, private baths, or air-conditioners but second class cabins on some ships are being converted to first class with these conveniences.

These ferries leave Chongqing between 8-9am. It you want your choice of cabin, you could pay extra (not much) and check in the night before, also saving yourself a hotel room.

Stops on ferries are short and not necessarily at tourist sites: Badong, Zigui, Wanxian, Fengjie and Fengdu. Nor can you be sure your ship will get close enough to take a photo of the lovely 11-story pagoda at Shibaozhai. You only pay for passage to where you get off. And by ferry you can get closer to Chinese people and experience with them the loudspeakers blaring announcements at 6am and queues for showers. After all, didn't you come here to meet the people?

The food is usually edible but with little variety. The basic dining hall with chairs and tables is crude.

Tianzi Cruise ships for Chinese tourists or sightseeing ferries cost a little more than regular ferries. These stop at tourist attractions for a couple of hours and you can pay extra for shore excursions and food (breakfast Y10). In spite of the name, you can book these through travel agents. From Chongqing to Yichang, first class has cost about Y930 each (two people to a room) and second class (Y466) has two to four to a room. These are filthy and many but not all slovenly backpackers would be content.

These ships leave Chongqing at 6pm daily and arrive about 7am in Wuhan after four nights on board with stops in Fengdu, Shibaozhai, Wanxian, the Lesser Three Gorges, and Yueyang. Conditions are in no way modern and international quality. Expect the worst. These are so bad that CITS Chongqing suggests you pay a little more and take one of the low-class cruise ships instead in the $200-$300 range.

Hovercrafts leave Chongqing and arrive in Yichang the second day. They are meant for speed, not sightseeing, and they are bouncy, noisy and in summer, hot. It costs Y380 plus hotel at Y20 a bed. From Chongqing to Wanxian, it's Y185. Jet foils also service Badong, Zigui, Wanxian, Fengjie and Fengdu. It is best to avoid the noisy back end. Travel agents can ticket these for you. To book in Chongqing, *Tel. 63827717.* If you have more than your own weight in luggage, you pay for a second ticket.

Town Hopping

It is possible to go along the Yangtze by ferry spending the nights on land. The road between Chongqing and Yichang won't be finished for a while. Grubby but adequate hotels are in Fengdu, Jingzhou, Wanxian, Yichang, Yueyang and Zigui. Hotels elsewhere might be terrible: no toilet seats, no workable plumbing, no air-conditioning, and no 24-hour hot running water. Few rooms will have private baths.

Many hotels are high on a mountain; you have to climb with your luggage. Few towns have porters and English-speaking travel agents. While every major community has ferry service at least once a day, it can be canceled because of fog and bad weather. Taxis are hard to find. Few people speak English and few restaurants are good. Only banks can change money and few hotels accept credit cards.

However, town hopping means you can do a lot of hiking and climbing, spend time seeing monuments and views that cruise tourists can't. The Yangtze from a mountain top is glorious. The scenery away from the river is also great.

Expensive, Tourist-Class Cruises

Currently most foreign tourists take one of the 80 much more expensive air-conditioned **tourist cruise ships** that ply the Yangtze from mid-March to late November or early December. About 10 of these meet standards suitable for the average middle-class North American tourist but don't expect the services of bigger, more luxurious cruise ships elsewhere in the world–like soft comfortable lounge chairs. Prices range from $200 and up for Chongqing-Wuhan, with better quality the more you pay.

You can book the top ships through travel agents in North America or China to ensure your dates during high season, or at the last minute on the spot at other times. You are isolated from all but rich Chinese people or bureaucrats on junkets, and crews. But you can expect more comfort than ferries and few of the hassles. The government has tried to regulate these ships and their safety, and rates them with stars the same way it rates hotels. Five stars is the top with all the services of the previous ratings.

On **one-star ships** half the cabins should have private baths, and all get heat and air-conditioning, and twelve hours of hot water a day. They should also have money-changing services, stamps for sale, and English-speaking guides. (The quality of the English will not be very good.)

On **two stars ships and up**, cabins should have televisions, toilets, and telephones, and the ship should have a karaoke dance hall, reading room, clinic and massage. Linens should be changed every other day and managers speak English.

On **three stars and up**, you get color televisions, satellite telephone service, a gym, and 24 hours a day hot and cold water in your cabin. Linens get changed daily, and you have a card room, business center and a library. On **four stars** and up you get credit card service, Star television satellite reception with news in English, and background music. On **five stars**, you could have a swimming pool, jacuzzi, and bathrobes.

These ships should have same-day laundry service, refrigerators, currency exchange, postal and safe deposit services, beauty salons, lounge, pool (rarely working), bars, and a small store. Television programs are usually in Chinese. Some of these ships have dancing, *mah-jong* and *taiji* classes, cooking and medical demonstrations, and karaoke. In the evening, they could have fashion shows (of goods available in the

CRUISE WARNINGS

• *Shipboard satellite telephone service costs about $16 or so a minute plus 15% starting from the time you dial! You should wait until you get on shore to phone, or ask for someone's mobile. Zigui and Fengdu CITS have long-distance telephone service near the quay.*

• *Porters in Chongqing have been so obnoxious, I've had to call the police once. They will grab your bag. Two have seized a tiny woman tourist and carried her and her bags protesting down the stairs. You might want to wave at your ship and hope it will send its own bell man. Help is nearby at your ship. Officers there will tell you what a fair tip is (Y10). But before that, learn to say, "Wo bu yao," or "I don't want to."*

• *Stops usually necessitate **climbing a lot of stairs**, part of the Yangtze lifestyle. Chongqing has an elevator at Chaotianmen from the ship to the street above (Y2). Ship personnel should be able to arrange for a sedan chair to take wheelchair-confined travelers up and down stairs and through the streets in some but not all places on shore. Ships themselves also require climbing. Most ships have four or five storys and none have elevators. Wheelchair travelers have difficulties unless they travel with help or make some such arrangements beforehand.*

store), and variety shows. Service staff double as performers and it's good to see them in another role. Service staff are usually friendly and pleasant.

What to Wear

Dress is generally casual but most ships have a captain's banquet or cocktail party and your crew could be dressed in white. You might want to take something dressy (but not too dressy) for that occasion. Definitely take good walking shoes or boots for shore excursions. For the Lesser Three Gorges and Shennongjia excursions, it is best to take life jackets from your own cabins. The ones available outside have been smelly.

Prices

Check with travel agents for prices and discounts which could range upwards from $840 upstream and $910 downstream (MV President) between Chongqing and Wuhan. The Victorias charge a minimum of $920 upstream in shoulder season plus $75 each for shore excursions. It seems to be the only one where excursions are not included in the package price.

If space is available, you can upgrade to more spacious suites on all ships. If stops are canceled, you might want to ask for a refund. You've paid for the guide and transportation. You should get it back.

The Most Popular Cruise Ships

The most popular with North Americans are the East King and East Queen, the four Victorias, and the three Regals. I would recommend the five stars and the Victorias. The Regals are okay but have major problems. Some sailings are better than others.

None of the cruise ships is perfect. They age quickly and are not well maintained. They range in size from 130 to 270 passengers. The longest are the Regals, the smallest the Yangtze Paradise.

The **East King** and **East Queen** are five stars, generally very good, but guides, entertainment, and food have been better on some of the **Victorias**. On the **East King**, we found the Chinese food excellent but the western mediocre. The cabins are bigger (166 sq. feet) than the Victorias and the Regals, and they have room safes and larger television, but not much cupboard space. The English of the staff giving lectures and translations was poor, not much better than the Regals. All cabins are "outside," and you can leave your curtains open to enjoy the view in almost total privacy. The only outside decks are on the top with no shade or protection from rain.

The **Victorias** (I, II, III, and Pearl) have been among the best but it depends on the staff. Each ship is different.

Cabins on the four-star **Regals** (Princesses Sheena, Jeannie, and Elaine) are the smallest, and the food needs improvement. If the ship is full, buffet line-ups can be long and people at the end get short-changed. The Regals were built in Germany and are the best made, but they were designed for tourists on the Volga River and at 129 meters, are the longest ships.

The other ships were made in China. Repairs and maintenance are sloppy. The televisions are small with old (but good) Chinese movies with subtitles. None have CNN. The exercise equipment even on the five stars is outdated. The Regals and Victorias have decks outside their cabins – great for walking, but not for privacy. All these ships could do better cleaning jobs and need a coat of paint. Some ships have smelly toilets, even the top ones. Some have mold. I haven't found any with working swimming pools. Most have thin walls.

Sometimes excellent American cruise staff have been on board the Regals and the Victorias but you can't count on it. Shore excursions are usually well organized, but being on a five-star does not guarantee a guide with good English on shore. The English of the management staff is usually good, but that of service staff, quite poor. Doctors don't usually speak English.

Do not expect the Love Boat but there's usually a captain's dinner or reception, and a final dance (to ancient music, so bring your own cassettes). There might even be a farewell banquet. There's drinking water in each cabin. (You can buy bottled water on the ship or on shore.) Merchandise in stores on board can cost ten times the price on shore. Discounts are better towards the end of the trip. Avoid the front cabins over the engines, and cabins near bars and night clubs. Get on the higher floors for the best views.

Cruise staff give life jacket briefings and passengers should check window exits in cabins and locations of life jackets early on.

No ships announce points of interest along the way in English unless you ask. They do give you a blow-by-blow description as you go through the Gorges and past the Three Gorges Dam.

Other Cruise Ships

Unfortunately, I haven't been able to experience other cruise ships. By reputation, the four-star **Yangtze President** should be among the top, some cabins with private balconies and more Chinese food and bigger rooms than the Regals. But does it have fluent English-speaking guides? The **Yangtze Princess** should be acceptable. The **Shenzhou** was a state guest house with waterfall, and two-story dance hall. The **Blue Whale** and **Yangtze Angel** should be five stars now and good. The **Star Dipper** (Bei Dou) has very good food. Also good is the four-star **Splendid China** with big cabin owned by China Travel Service. Of the cheaper three stars, the **MV Three Gorges** and **MV Three Kingdoms** seem to be okay.

The quality of the ships differ; they are owned by different companies. Avoid the **Ping Hu 2000** with its poor service. The **Qiao Feng** has large cabins but a reputation for poor food, poor service, and no planned activities. Avoid ships that cater primarily to Chinese passengers; their staffs don't know how to serve foreigners adequately and the English is even poorer.

Itineraries

Between Chongqing and Wuhan, you travel 1286 km, and between Chongqing and Yichang it's 660, and Jingzhou and Chongqing it's 808. Itineraries differ depending on which direction you are going, up or down river, and which ship you book. Upstream is cheaper and longer with fewer passengers and it's fine if you have the time, and books to read.

If you have a particular site you must visit, make sure you take a ship that will stop there. If you are going upstream, make sure that your ship will stop for all announced sightseeing spots. They don't always. And there could be last minute changes.

All ships are regulated through the gorges by the navigation authorities and some have no choice but to pass through after dark or during meal times. You might have to get up at four in the morning if you don't want to miss these, or take your food out on deck.

The highlight for many tourists is the day trip on the **Lesser Three Gorges** on the Daning River, or the similar **Shennongjia Stream** at Badong. Ships only stop at one. These are on smaller boats through narrower canyons with hanging coffins, wild monkeys (rarely seen), and Tujia villages. The water is crystal clear when not white and bubbly. The better trip is the Shennongjia Stream, more like rafting, and glory be, with no diesel fumes, no engine vibrations, or noise.

You may want to ride only between Chongqing and Jingzhou or Yichang. Between Jingzhou and Wuhan by ship isn't all that interesting and you can do it by bus in three hours. Many deluxe shuttle buses go back and forth hourly each way. On the other hand you might prefer to relax on a ship than bounce in a bus.

A typical itinerary would be downstream: **Day One** board in Chongqing with a stop in Fengdu; **Day Two** Qutang and Wu Gorges and shore excursion in Shennongjia or Three Lesser Gorges, and the Three Gorges Dam or boatman show in Zigui; **Day Three** Three Gorges Dam, Xiling Gorge and shore excursion in Jingzhou; **Day Four** arrive Wuhan.

It might be possible to board the ship the night before you sail, and stay overnight the day you arrive.

Alternative Itineraries

Victoria Cruises also has a Shanghai-Chongqing service with additional stops in Mt. Lushan, Mt. Huangshan, Nanjing and Yangzhou, 11 days upstream and eight days downstream. The Regals also have a Shanghai-Chongqing run. The East King and East Queen have two-day and three-night Yichang-Chongqing schedules. The Regal takes longer and has a Shanghai-Chongqing run too.

Downstream Schedule

These differ with the speed of the ship, of course, but the following should give you an idea of what to expect:

Leave **Chongqing** early and note white pagoda and Buddha on the north bank. At about three hours out, you pass **Fuling**; at 8.5 hours out, **Zhongxian**. At about 10 hours out, you reach **Shibaozhai**. At 12.5 hours, you're at 2,000-year-old **Wanxian/Wanzhou**.

About 4.5 hours from Wanxian, you pass **Fengjie** and **Baidicheng** and arrive at the **first gorge**, the **Qutang**. Near the entrance of the gorge on the north bank is a two-story pavilion with red lacquer columns, which marks the beginning of the gorges. On the south side of Kui Men Gate are two stone towers and five Chinese characters, which mean "The Kui Men Gate is an unmatched pass."

The Qutang Gorge is eight km long. It is the most imposing and shortest of the gorges, only 100-150 meters wide. Prepare for a very windy passage, as the wind as well as the water, is funneled between the cliffs. Canadian and Chinese tight-rope walkers once crossed here and you can still see their parallel wires.

The **Wuxia** or **Wu Gorge**, starts 30 minutes after you leave the Qutang. It is 44 km long and takes about 1.5 hours (upsteam 3.5 hours) to pass through. Look for the "Twelve Peaks Enshrouded in Rain and Mist," of which you can see six on the north bank and three on the south. Of these Goddess Peak is the highest, at over 1,000 meters. It has a tall stone column on top that looks like an anorexic young woman. Look for a table-shaped rock with six Chinese characters meaning "The Wu Gorge boasts craggy cliffs," said to be written by a prime minister of the Shu Kingdom in the third century. Look for coffins in caves here.

The town of **Wushan** is between the Wu and the Qutang Gorges. From here cruise ships might stop for a shore excursion on the Daning River through the **Lesser Three Gorges**. Continuing on, twenty minutes after leaving the Wu Gorge is the town of **Badong** on the south shore. You have left Chongqing and are now in Hubei province.

About one hour from Badong you see **Zigui** on the north shore. This is the **birthplace of Quyuan** and some ships stop for a dragon boat race or show at the pier.

Five or so minutes after Zigui is Xiang Xi (**Fragrant Stream**) on the north side, where the lovely imperial concubine **Wang Zhaojun** accidentally dropped her pearls 2,000 years ago. A white statue marks the spot. The water here is said to be limpid and fragrant as a result. There's more about this woman, who is considered one of the four famous beauties of China. See Hohhot in the North China section. Ship guides say this is where the waterway between the Yangtze and Yellow Rivers will be built after 2009 to alleviate water shortages there and in Beijing.

Shortly after Xiang Xi is the 75 km-long **Xiling Gorge**, which takes about 1.5 hours (upstream two hours) to pass through. It is the longest and has been the most treacherous of the three. Thirty minutes beyond the entrance, on the south side, is Kuang Ming village, with a large temple, Huang Ling Miao. Then comes Five Sisters Peaks, Three Brothers Rocks, and the Needle. While still in the Xiling Gorge, you'll see **Zhongbao Island** and **Sandouping**, the site of the new dam. You can't miss it; much has been completed.

The end of the Xiling Gorge about 37 km later is marked by a large Buddha, and a **statue of Zhang Fei** of The Three Kingdoms on the north side. Then you reach the east part of **Yichang**, and go through the **locks** of the 1988-built 70-meter-high **Gezhouba Dam**. If you stay on board you pass hundreds of miles of levees and you might stop at **Jingzhou** 148 km later on the north side, or **Yueyang** on the south 247 km beyond that. **Wuhan** is 231 km beyond Yueyang.

Important Stops on the Yangtze Gorges Trip

Badong is where you get off for a tour of **Shennongjia Stream** - about a six-hour trip by bus and boat. This is a very difficult excursion to do on your own. The tourism office has decent buses. The village in the Gaolin Scenic Area where you get an 18-passenger boat is about 47 km from the ferry pier on the north side of the Yangtze, about two km west of Badong. Gaolin has made a good attempt at clean toilets compared to toilets in other rural area. You drift 3.5 hours downstream from there helped by three boatmen on each boat. You might have a lunch stop and look for 1400 year old coffins. Only a couple noisy engines might disturb the serenity. The scenery here is very beautiful, the air clear and it is wonderful.

Most cruise ship however prefer to send their passengers on three-hour tours to better fit into their schedules. This is another aspect of history. Trackers actually pull you upstream for two hours with ropes and harnesses, as they did in the old days. No toilets are available on this trip and you end up surrounded by peddlers.

I prefer the six-hour trip up into the mountains, seeing a village, and many more people – even though the people might be sticking things into your face to buy. The **Shennongxi Travel Service Co.** is at *9 Kueihua Street, Xinliu Town, Badong, Tel. (718)4224347, Fax 4223388.*

Fengjie, at the western end of the Qutang Gorge, was the capital of the state of Wei during the Spring and Autumn Period (722-481 B.C.), the time of Confucius. The tomb of Liu Bei's wife is here. Here on a hill top, reached by a ferry and 300 steps, is **Baidicheng** or **White King City** with its great view of the river. Wax statues show you how Liu Bei entrusted his son to Zhuge Liang.

Fengdu (170 km east of downtown Chongqing on the north bank) has been regarded as hell, a gathering place for ghosts since the seventh century. This is because two men lived here whose combined names Yu and Huang meant King of the Underworld. Here believers built 48 Taoist and Buddhist temples, all destroyed in the 1960s by the Red Guards. Rebuilt recently by Fengdu townspeople, it now has tacky statues of demons and hell, of no artistic merit, probably no different from the originals. These will give you an idea of the folk concept of the after-life, and the role of religion in their lives.

Guides here make you go through various tests of agility and strength, most of which you can probably pass, and make it to heaven (instead of hell). Don't bother with the fortune sticks. Y18 is too much to throw away on a one-line "fortune." But the Qing Ming Festival celebrated here is special.

The **ghost city** is on a 288 meter-high hill reached by stairs or a cable car (Y15 return). It often remains open after hours (7am- 5:30pm) to accommodate cruise ships. While well lit, you should take a flash light after dark. CITS puts on an acrobatic show at its store in town which can be missed. This lowland town will be moved across the river to a new site. The ghost city will remain high and dry here.

Many tourists don't like the Fengdu stop, but it is a historical folk tradition and belief, crudeness and all. You might prefer to wander around the town instead. Terribly disfigured beggars wait on the stairs at the pier. But a marvelous little Catholic church is across from the pier with Sinofied statues of Jesus and Mary, and very friendly clerics.

Jingzhou, at 3000 years old, is one of the famous 24 cultural cities, and is about ten hours east of Yichang by ship. It is a recent union of the cities of Jingzhou (the capital of the State of Chu), and Shashi (a 2000-year old transshipment port), opened to foreign trade in 1895. It was known as Jinsha for a year or so. It is one of the best places to stop because of its good **museum** where if you're lucky, you can hear reproductions of the ancient chime bells played (See Wuhan.) They were found in this county. This museum is also the home of **2150-year-old Mr. Sui**, a county governor who died of a bleeding ulcer, his silks and hemp shoes on the second floor, lacquerware and bronzes on the ground floor. You can photograph his remarkably well-preserved remains. The museum is open from 8:30am-5pm daily or until the last boatload leaves, and is protected by vicious dogs at night.

In another part of the city is a **300-year old gate** and 10.9 km long wall, first built 1700 years ago. The present one is at least 300 years old, so well preserved that costume movies are made here. Jingzhou is a well-governed city with no beggars and annoying peddlers (so far)! **CITS** in Jingzhou is at *52 Jingdong Dong Road, 434100, Tel. 8445446, 8467999, Fax 8466429.* Shashi has an airport and links with Guangzhou. The telephone code is *0716.* The flood of 1998 crested here 46 meters above normal.

To visit the **Lesser Three Gorges**, see Wushan.

Lushan is 40 km south of the port of Jiujiang. This 1,094-1,400 meter-high mountain-top plateau has been a summer resort since the mid-1800s. Its tourist belt is about eight by four km. It has been a stop on some Yangtze River cruises. It has great views of Poyang Lake and the Yangtze River and has sites related to the Taoist Immortals and the first Ming emperor. It has an alpine botanical garden.

About 9,000 people live in **Gulin**. The three-star **Lushan Hotel** is best. It's at *446 Hexi Road, 332900, Tel. 8282060, Fax 8282843.* The best hotel for business people is the two-star **Villa Village Hotel**, *179 Hedong Road, 332900.* The hottest weather is a rare 32 C at noon in July; the coldest, -16 degrees in January with snow from the end of November through February. The best time to visit is June through October. The **Lushan CITS** is at *4 Hexi Road, Jiujiang, 332900, Tel. 7010/8282497, Fax 8282428.*

For **Shennongjia**, see Badong above.

Shibaozhai (Precious Stone Village), or Shibao Block on the north bank about 10 hours downstream from Chongqing, has an 11-story Qing pagoda. It is built on a limestone rock hill that rises to 160 meters above the river. Smaller ships can stop here but the Regals and Victorias are too big.

In the main temple here are statues of Liu Bei, Zhuge Liang, Guan Yu, and Zhang Fei. Three of these swore oaths in a peach orchard to support each other. They are immortalized in *The Romance of the Three Kingdoms* novel. Emperor Liu Bei, who led an unsuccessful army to avenge the death of Guan Yu, retreated here and died in sorrow.

Wanzhou, formerly Wanxian, is a district of Chongqing. It became a treaty port in the 1890s when its biggest crop was opium. It is the largest town between Chongqing and Yichang. In 1926, the British accused the Chinese of interfering with a foreign steamship company here. Two British gunboats started shooting and over 3000 people were killed. Some historians consider this one of the first successful assertions of Chinese power against the imperialists.

You have to climb about 85 steps to get to this town of 300,000 for the **Zhang Fei Temple** (to be relocated because of the dam). Ships have stopped here for the tiny but worthwhile **Three Gorges Museum** and dinner at the **Sote Hotel**, a nice change. It has an airport with connections to Guangzhou and Chengdu.

The top hotel is the three-star **Wanzhou International Hotel**, *Tel. 5810888*. The two-star **Taibai Hotel** has been alright in the past, at *30 Baiyan Road, Wanzhou, Chongqing, 404000, Tel. 58223976*. About 80 rooms. No money change, but it is near the Bank of China (closed Sundays). **CITS** is at *56 Baiyan Zhi Road, Wanzhou City, 400400, Tel. 8222071, Fax 8224163*. The telephone code is *023*.

Wushan is where you change to a small boat for about 3.5 hours on the Daning River through the 50 km Lesser Three Gorges. This is between the Wu and Qutang gorges. If the water level is low, you might have to climb up a steep slope to get to the bus for the short ride to the boat pier. You should however be able to get a sedan chair ride (don't pay more than Y20) if you can't handle the climb. If the water level is high, you will be able to get on the motor boats right from your ship, and avoid the aggressive peddlers. This should be a five-hour excursion, not to be attempted if diesel fumes bother you. The boatmen push with poles to help the straining engine climb up the foamy white rapids. You might have to queue up behind other such boats or get out and walk for a few meters around the most difficult parts.

Look for the square holes made in rock walls for horizontal posts for the **plank roads**. If you're lucky, you can go past the restaurant in **Shuanglong/Double Dragon village** to an attempted reproduction of such a plank road and look for wild monkeys. Downstream of Double Dragon village where groups have lunch, look up near the sky in two narrow horizontal caves for the old coffins of the Ba people. Enjoy the clarity of the water, and the vertical cliffs. Much will disappear with the completion of the Three Gorges Dam. If it is raining hard, trips here will probably be canceled.

Yichang is a 2,400-year old settlement which became a treaty port in 1876 and was almost leveled by Japanese bombs during World War II. It grew dramatically with the building of the 2,605 meter-wide Gezhouba Dam in the late 1980s. Your ship will probably take a 12 minute, 30-meter high water-borne elevator ride in its locks. In Yichang itself, you can visit by land the eastern end of Xiling Gorge at Nanjin Pass with its statue of Zhang Fei of The Three Kingdoms, a giant welcoming Buddha, and the Three Travelers Cave.

It is worth a visit for the scenery high above the river. In the city also, the **Sturgeon Research Institute** is good for ecologists and those who want to look at a couple of live specimens of this huge, ugly fish from the dinosaur era, an endangered species.

From Yichang, there are flights to 13 other Chinese cities. An express train leaves Yichang at 3:35pm and arrives next day in Beijing at 1:22pm. (A direct express train has been leaving Beijing daily at 5:30pm and arriving in Yichang about 4:07pm on the second day.) The train between Wuhan and Yichang takes 11 hours. The bus is only four hours on an express highway.

Yichang has two four-star hotels. The best is the **Yichang International Hotel**, *127 Yanjiang Avenue, 443000, Tel. 6222888, Fax 6228186*. Y428-Y668 for rooms, Y998 for suites. It has a beer hall, night club, gym, revolving restaurant, and accepts credit cards. There's also the **Taohualin Hotel**, *29 Yunji Road, 443000, Tel. 6442244*.

In the three-star category, **Hui Feng Yuan Hotel**, *18 Shenzhen Road, Dongshan Development Zone, Yichang, 443000, Tel. 6330999, Fax 6330888. Http:www.HBCININFO.NET*. It's 15 km from the airport. Y323-Y365 for rooms, Y545-Y981 for suites. It has 22 stories including non-smoking floors, and 160 rooms with safes. It has an indoor pool, bowling, gym and tennis and is managed by Xi'an Jianguo Hotel.

The **airport** is about 18 km away from downtown Yichang. **CITS** is at *42 Yanjiang Road, 443000, Tel. 6739888, Fax 6738165*. The **Three Gorges International Travel Service** is at *40 Yanjiang Road, Tel. 6731848, Fax 6731683*, contact Ms. Gao Xiao. The **Yichang Overseas Travel Co**. telephone is *6458527, Fax 6458527*. Contact Mr. Zhang Bai Qing for jet foils to Chongqing, *Tel. 6746043*. Yichang's telephone code is *0717*.

For **Yueyang**, see separate listing in Chapter 20, *South China*.

Zigui, west of Yichang, can be reached from Yichang in about one hour by ship. The **Quyuan Temple** here was built in 1976-85 and will be moved again. The original ninth century Tang site was flooded by the Gezhouba dam. Quyuan (see sidebar below) was the poet/statesman who drowned himself in the third century B.C. because the King of Chu did not heed his warning about the threats from the Kingdom of Qin. You can pay respects at his tomb which contains some of his clothes. The temple has 1976-made slate tablets of his poetry based on Qing designs, a painting of Quyuan by Yang Chu, and a 400-year old statue of Quyang. He was born in this county.

Cruise ship passengers have raced fellow tourists in **dragon boats** here. This is the traditional way to honor Quyuan (and save him from the fish). Boat men also perform a powerful boat dance at a dockside theatre right beside your ship in the evening and CITS provides a convenient store.

LI SAO

*This is the poem "Li Sao," by the poet/statesman **Quyuan**, in whose memory dragon boats are raced in June all over the world. Quyuan tried unsuccessfully to save the Kingdom of Chu from the first emperor of China:*
The conspirators steal their heedless pleasures;
Their road is dark and leads to danger.
What do I care of the peril to myself?
I fear only the wreck of my lord's carriage.
I hastened to his side in attendance
To lead him in the steps of the ancient kings,
But the Fragrant One would not look into my heart;
Instead, heeding slander, he turned on me in rage.
*–**Reprinted from China Tourism, translator unknown.***

PRACTICAL INFORMATION

Tipping: you don't have to give any tips but if you want, each guest could give Y10 to your guide on shore excursions, and Y20 for the whole crew pushing your little boat upstream. You might want to give more after you see how hard they work. Cruise ships have boxes for tips to be shared by the whole crew with a suggested Y40 per day per passenger.

US addresses for the major cruise ships:

• **China Travel Service** in the US (Splendid China).

• **Orient Royal Cruiser Ltd.** (East King and East Queen), *119 South Atlantic Blvd., Suite 208, Monterey Park, CA 91754. Tel. 626/289-5384, Fax 626/289-4895. E-mail:orc-usa@worldnet.att.com; e-mail in China:dfhjle@public.wh.hb.cn.*

• **Regal China Cruises**, *57 West 38th Street, New York, NY 10018, Tel. 212/768-3388, or 800/808-3388, Fax 212/768-4939.*

22. HONG KONG

Hong Kong is unique in the world – the partnership, at times reluctant, of British law and capitalism, an 1100-sq. km. Chinese territory, Chinese labor, and Chinese entrepreneurship. The official relationship lasted from 1840 to 1997 but the spirit continues. It has been a success.

It is now the **Hong Kong Special Administrative Region** (HKSAR) of China, but with its own flag and currency. It is allowed to keep its own social and economic systems for 50 years after the handover. But China is in charge of its foreign affairs and defense.

Hong Kong is on the southeast coast of mainland China attached to the province of Guangdong near Shenzhen and Guangzhou. It is still one of the most modern, most vibrant cities in the world. You should visit to see what changes have been made by the Communists – if any.

Judges may still wear their powdered wigs and Christmas is an official holiday. Have they changed the name of the naval headquarters from the Prince of Wales Building? Is the Royal Hong Kong Jockey Club still royal? Is there self-censorship of newspapers? Do read the Hong Kong newspaper *South China Morning Post* before you go. On the web it's at *www.scmp.com*. On the surface, nothing much has been changed. Or has it?

Hong Kong is an exciting mix of life styles and architecture, of exotic religions and customs that flourished and developed while those on the China mainland were periodically suppressed. Here amid the money-making are the world's largest seated bronze Buddha, and the world center of *feng-shui*, the art, the belief that the placement of buildings and furniture affect one's fortunes. Here are bustling stock and vegetable markets, huge skyscrapers, and beautiful ocean, beaches, gentle mountains and vast parks. Enjoy its world class hotels and the best Chinese food in Asia. Explore its air-conditioned shopping malls, its cheap street markets and factory outlets. The bargains are actually coming back.

And don't worry. English is still an official language; street signs are in both languages. Rugby and cricket are still played. It is the easiest place in China for foreign tourists to visit on your own. There's a lot to see and do, much of it cheaply.

Hong Kong, which means *Fragrant Harbor*, was a remote, unpopulated part of China to which the last emperor of the Song dynasty escaped temporarily – he was then only ten – in the thirteenth century.

In the nineteenth century, the British needed China's trade to pay for its passion for tea and silk; the Chinese wanted only gold in exchange. Britain forced the Chinese to take opium. The Chinese fought back and lost. In 1841, Britain got a "barren island with hardly a house upon it," today's Hong Kong Island.

This centre of British trade flourished and with subsequent wars, the British acquired the Kowloon peninsula up to Boundary Street in 1860, and then leased the much larger New Territories and islands in 1898 – a lease that resulted in the handing back of all three now-interdependant parts to China.

The Japanese occupied Hong Kong from 1941 to 1945. In 1945 it had about 600,000 inhabitants. It has been growing ever since with refugees from China's communism, and now with legal immigrants eager for bright lights and jobs. It has flourished as a manufacturing centre, and as a trading centre for China as well. Today its population is 6.5 million.

The first thing to do when you're thinking of a visit is to contact the **Hong Kong Tourist Association** (HKTA). Its website is great for uptodate information like special hotel bargains, and the latest visa requirements. You can make reservations for hotels on it without a credit card guarantee and book your airport shuttle. You can telephone and get its generous collection of free literature, this month's cultural and sporting events, and lists of tours. It can help you get tickets for its world class cultural events. See Practical Information below.

US-HONG KONG EXCHANGE RATE

Price quotes in this section are in Hong Kong dollars. **One US dollar is worth about HK$7.80** *but exchange rates vary. You usually get a better rate through banks but most banks charge upward from about $30 each time you change money. The best rate however has been at one of the money changers in the back of the sleazy Chungking Mansions on Nathan Road near Middle Road. You have to shop around even for money.*

The Asian recession means prices in Hong Kong are soft and the services have improved as hotels compete for customers. The shopping, hotel, and food prices are the lowest they've been in decades. It's a great time to visit.

ARRIVALS & DEPARTURES

Visa requirements are different here than in the rest of China. Citizens of the United States and 20 other countries can enter Hong Kong with a valid passport without a visa, and stay for one month. Citizens of Canada, Australia and other Commonwealth countries need a valid passport, no visa, and can stay three months.

Visitors are allowed to import duty free only one-liter of alcohol, 200 cigarettes, 60 ml. of perfume, and 250 ml. of toilet water.

By Air

Hong Kong has international flight connections with about 110 countries, and at least 51 Chinese cities. You can fly from New York on Cathay Pacific in 15.5 hours *(http://www.cathay-usa.com)*. The airport is joined to Western in downtown Hong Kong (34 km, about a 23-minute trip), and to Kowloon by the **Airport Express Railway**. This train leaves every four to eight minutes between 6am and 1am and costs $90 to Kowloon and $100 to Central. Innummerable cheaper buses link it to the **Mass Transit Railway** (MTR subway) at Lai King station and downtown.

Buses are slower (one to two hours) and a **hotel shuttle** could cost $80 and up. An airbus costs a maximum $45 to Causeway Bay. Buses can take you downtown all night, at the most, a 20-minute wait. **Taxis** are about $350 to Hong Kong Island. **Helicopter** service is on request, *Tel. 2802-0200*. **Ferries** go to Tuen Mun in the New Territories. The airport is open 24 hours a day.

By Bus

Dozens of public buses arrive daily from Guangzhou and Shenzhen. But buses are difficult unless you avoid rush hour traffic jams. You have to lug your luggage out at the border, and struggle with it back onto the bus or even some trains for inspections.

By Ferry

Ferries from Macau run every 15 minutes during the day and take less than an hour. The main terminal is west of the Star Ferry on the Hong Kong side, close to the Sheung Wan MTR station. **China Hong Kong City** is the terminal for all China-linked ships and some buses. It is on Canton Road a few hundred meters north of the Star Ferry in Kowloon. Here ferries arrive from such Chinese cities as Guangzhou, Haikou, Shekou, Shanghai, Shantou, Taishan, and Xiamen. You can also arrive by cruise ship on such lines as Cunard, Holland America, P & O Cruises and Princess Cruises. These berth at Ocean Terminal in Tsim Sha Tsui next to the Star Ferry in Kowloon.

By Train

Five trains arrive from Guangzhou a day, a 102-minute trip. One train a day arrives from Zhaoqing. From Beijing a super high-speed train makes the journey in about 27 hours six minutes every other day for about $1170. This train leaves from Beijing West, and stops briefly in Zhengzhou, Wuchang, Changsha, Shaoguan, Guangzhou and Dongguan. The train station is in Hung Hom in Kowloon and both trains have good service.

HONG KONG TRANSIT PASSENGERS

Transit passengers can wait in the transit hall. You can take a shower and change, swim or workout, plug in your computer, or take a room at the adjacent Airport Regal Hotel. You can also check in for your next flight there. See Where to Stay/Islands, below. You can shop at the airport's 140 shops and restaurants which advertise "downtown" prices.

If you have more than four hours, you can pay $120 plus $50 airport tax for return fare to Kowloon Airport Express station, from where you can take a Transit Bus Tour. These leave Kowloon Station five times a day between 9:15am and 1:45pm. Take your transit pass to the Tai Fung Kiosk 4A opposite Exit B of the arrival hall, Tel. 2186-6883, and you'll see something of Hong Kong.

Departures

All passengers taking the Airport Express rail service can check-in downtown at its terminals and then go to the airport. They also get a free hotel transfer to the terminal. The airport departure tax is $50; the marine ferry terminal passenger fee is $18.

ORIENTATION

Hong Kong is on the South China Sea on the north shore of the Pearl River estuary across from Macau. In a sub-tropical zone, it rarely experiences frost. Summers, especially in August, can be extremely humid and hot (33 C), and most people then find themselves drawn by 70% discounts to air-conditioned malls, or to northern climes. The best time to visit is cool, dry, sunny October to early December with an average temperature of 22.6 C. Chinese New Year's in late January or February is usually the coldest time but not intolerable. Rain comes mainly from March to mid-May which is not bad, but it's not sunny enough for good photos. Typhoons do hit from July to September, so look at weather maps for circles near the Philippines. They could affect your travel plans a few days later.

Hong Kong has three distinctly different areas: 14 km-wide Hong Kong Island, tiny Kowloon, and the vast New Territories and outlying islands. You must spend at least one day in each area. Highly developed historic **Hong Kong Island** is a short five-minute ferry ride south of Kowloon.

Kowloon, with its sky scrapers and tourist stores, is on the China mainland, attached to the suburban **New Territories**. Hong Kong island and the mainland are joined together by four tunnels and numerous ferry, bus and subway train routes. The **235 islands** are spread on all sides. They range in size from Lantau which is much bigger than Hong Kong island, down to a few rocks.

FIRST FLOOR?

Hong Kong uses the British system of numbering floors. The first floor is the American second floor. The Chinese system is the same as the American but is written in Chinese.

GETTING AROUND TOWN

Get a good map and booklets from the **HKTA**. Kiosks are in the buffer hall of the airport (8am-10:30pm daily). Hong Kong is easy to get around but avoid rush hours 8am-10am and 4pm-7pm, especially through the Cross-Harbour Tunnel. Other tunnels usually have less traffic.

Do not be shy about asking for directions. Filipinas, western residents, most Chinese business people wearing suits, and policemen with a red shoulder patch speak English well. All train stations have neighborhood maps and signs in English.

If you are using a lot of **public transport**, do buy a **stored-value Octobus Card** for use in most buses, trains, and the MTR. You can buy these at any MTR station. It is the most convenient and cheapest way to get around.

SENIOR DISCOUNTS

Generally, people over 60 or 65 and children under 11 get a discount on public transportation including the Macau ferry. 65 and older seniors are free on the Star Ferry, and HKTA can give you a pass, discounts on tours, and a "Mature Traveller's Guide." But you only need to wave a passport at the Star Ferry. Some coffee shops give discounts. Always ask.

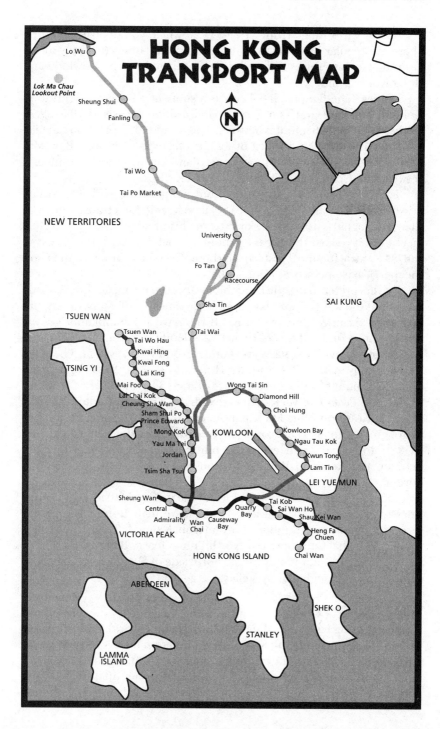

Buses: Fares range from $1.20-$34.20 which you deposit on entry. There are regular buses, express buses, and mini-buses (where you are assured of a seat). Buses with red signs on top go between Kowloon and Hong Kong Island.

Ferries: The famous Star Ferry is a short hop between Central on Hong Kong Island, and Tsim Sha Tsui in Kowloon. It costs $1.70 to $2.20 and leaves every 3-10 minutes between 6:30am and 11:30pm. You can take a cheap tour of the harbor just by taking a ferry to Silvermine Bay (Mui Wo) or Discovery Bay. On Hong Kong Island, the main ferry terminal is between the Central and Sheung Wan MTR stops.

Taxis: You can wave down taxis but not at yellow curbs. Most taxi drivers do not speak English but can call on a radio for a translation. The charge at flagfall is usually $15 for two km plus $1.40 for every 200 meters thereafter. If you use the Cross-Harbour Tunnel, you must pay $20 extra, and $45 extra for the Western Harbour Crossing. Other tunnels are cheaper. Taxis operate 24 hours a day.

Drivers prefer to use the faster highways even if it means going a long way out of the way (at your expense). Sometimes it's one-way streets, but taking a taxi can get very expensive. If you have any complaints, get the taxi's number and call the 24-hour Police Hotline, *Tel. 2527-7177*.

Trains: Hong Kong has a great underground train system. The **Mass Transit Railway** or **MTR** Enquiry Hotline, *Tel. 2993-8880*. Trains run every five minutes 6:00am-1am. Fares range $4-$23.00. Ask for a free *MTR Guide Book*. The MTR connects with the **Kowloon-Canton Railway** (KCR) at Kowloon Tong MTR station, exit B. The KCR operates mainly above ground and is a cheap and jam-free way to see the New Territories. KCR trains usually run every 4-6 minutes between 5:30am-12:25am between the Kowloon Railway Station and Lowu at the Guangdong border.

Trams: These are one of the best and cheapest ($2.00) though slowest rides in town, great for tourists. Trams leave their terminals every 45 seconds. They run from about 6am-1am from Kennedy Town to Western-Central-Wanchai-Causeway Bay-North Point-Quarry Bay and then Shau Kei Wan. They operates only on the north side of Hong Kong Island and some detour through Happy Valley.

WHERE TO STAY

Hong Kong has some of the best hotels in the world. Unfortunately we can't list them all. Hong Kong has a reputation for overly high prices but these actually started dropping in mid-1997. During low occupancy times, these hotels were giving 25%-65% discounts off the following published Hong Kong dollar prices, sometimes with breakfast. Some prices have been half that of the previous year and have included free local telephone calls and a 15% discount on food. HKTA, travel agents, and hotel 800/ numbers and websites can tell you about specials. Some travel packages were including six room nights for the price of a discounted airfare. So don't let these prices frighten you. Ask about honeymoon discounts or whatever.

All hotels here take major credit cards and most charge 10% service and 3% tax. The low seasons are around the January-February Chinese New Year, and June to early September. But low could be any time riots are in Indonesia, and banks are failing in Japan. Do not pay these prices; they are only for reference.

All hotels listed have international standards unless noted. Most have peep-holes and double or triple locks in doors and many have helpful concierges. All have Cantonese restaurants and western coffee shops. The more expensive hotels also have highly recommended restaurants for fine dining.

All hotels here accept major credit cards unless indicated otherwise. They have at least two television channels in English and the top hotels have ten or more. The Kowloon Hotel has computers in each room free. Many have rooms for the disabled. All these hotels are close to an MTR station unless noted. But beware: local telephone calls can range from free to $6 each. For more about my favorite hotels, see Chapter 13, *China's Best Places to Stay*.

HONG KONG ISLAND

The best place for business and old Hong Kong scenery is Central, Wan Chai and Western on Hong Kong island.

Expensive

GRAND HYATT HONG KONG, *1 Harbour Road, Wan Chai, Tel. 2588-1234, Fax 2802-0677. Http://www.hyatt.com. 572 rooms of which over 70% have harbor views. $3200-$4000. Suites $5500-$25000. Extra bed $350.*

This magnificent, 36-story hotel is indeed grand with curving staircases swirling down to the impressive black marble lobby, its public areas works of art worth studying. There is an elegant disco, a Champagne Bar, a coffee shop with a good harbor view, and some of Hong Kong's best restaurants. Try the Milanese, Japanese (with extensive *sake* menu), or Cantonese. The latter captures the romantic flavor of a 1930s taipan's home. Outdoor recreational facilities on a 11,000-sq meter, roof-top terrace include a 335-meter jogging trail, golf-driving range, two flood-lit tennis courts, and a sizeable gym. Its 47-meter outdoor pool is downtown Hong Kong's longest. There's also 24-hour room service, and eight executive floors. It has separate shower stalls in rooms and shuttle service in a London taxi to Central and Pacific Place. Room decor is simple and European. At rush hour taxi service is slow to arrive but from the Wan Chai MTR station 350 meters away or the ferry pier on the other side of the Renaissance Harbour View, the rest of Hong Kong is a snap to get to. See also Chapter 13, *China's Best Places to Stay.*

RENAISSANCE HARBOUR VIEW, *1 Harbour Road, Wan Chai, Tel. 2802-8888, Fax 2802-8833. 862 rooms of which 65% have a harbor view. $2700-$18800.*

This 42-story, modern, glitzy, comfortable 1989 hotel is less elegant than its sister, the Grand Hyatt next door. It is very good nonetheless. They share the same, great roof-top garden and pool, and both have direct access to the Hong Kong Convention and Exhibition Centre. It has Cantonese, European and international restaurants, a deli, and well-lit medium-sized rooms. Its well-equipped business center has computer rentals. The four executive floors have CD players. It also has a health center, steam bath, sauna, jacuzzi, and BMW and Mercedes limousines. It is about 300 meters by covered walkway to Wanchai MTR and is close to the frequent ferry to Tsim Sha Tsui. It's the best for children. All rooms have fax machines and voice mail. Its conference room has LCD Data Projector, wireless microphones and Wyteboard with instant print-out capability. You can rent its 50-passenger cabin cruiser. Renaissance Hotels International.

See also Chapter 13, *China's Best Places to Stay.*

ISLAND SHANGRI-LA HONG KONG, *Pacific Place, Supreme Court Road, Central. Floors 5-8 and 39-56, Tel. 2877-3838, Fax 2521-8742. Http:/ /www.shangri-la.com. E-mail: ISL_guest@yahoo.com (for guests.) 565 spacious rooms. $2300-$3650. Suites $5300-$26000.*

As with all Shangri-La's, if you pay the published rate, you get free transfers, laundry, breakfast, etc. But you don't have to pay the published rate. This 1991 hotel has good Peak and harbor views and is very well located, classy and opulent. It is close to the giant, upmarket Pacific Place shopping mall, Hong Kong Park and Admiralty MTR station. Facilities include a 24-hour business center, a heated outdoor pool, a deli, and 24-hour room service. It also has a good gym, aerobics, tanning machine, massage, steam bath, sauna, jacuzzis, and personal training. There's a lighted tennis court. Rooms have separate shower stalls and tubs, bidets, double sinks, two desks, and three telephones.

See also Chapter 13, *China's Best Places to Stay.*

CENTURY HONG KONG HOTEL, *238 Jaffe Road, Tel. 2598-8888, Fax 2598-8866. E-mail:bcentre@century.com.hk, or booking@century.com.hk. 516 rooms. $1850-$2660; suites $4080-$8280.*

This 23-floor, 1991 hotel is located in a crowded neighborhood a couple short blocks from the Wanchai MTR station. Compact and basic with small rooms, baths and beds, it is a good deal if you can get a good discount. There's a small outdoor pool, business center, very good New York-style Italian Restaurant (try the cod), and a Shanghai restaurant. It has 24-hour room service, executive and non-smoking floors, golf-driving range, and well-equipped gym.

TWO MACDONNELL ROAD, *2 Macdonnell Road above Central, Tel. 2132-2132, Fax 2131-1000. 220 rooms and 32 stories. $900-$1050 for rooms; $1500-$2100 for suites. No 3% tax. No credit cards.*

This St. John's Ambulance Society hotel is across the street from the Garden View. It is newer and looks better than its neighbor but has no bar nor room service. It is across from the lush Botanical and Zoological Gardens but a 20-minute walk up from Central and the MTR. Public mini-buses 12A and 1A from the Star Ferry make access easier.

GARDEN VIEW INTERNATIONAL HOUSE, *1 MacDonnell Road, above Central, Tel. 2877-3737, Fax 2845-6263. E-mail:gar_view@org.hk. 130 large rooms. $880-990 for a double. Monthly rates. No 3% tax.*

The YWCA manages this 1990 hotel. It has a restaurant, 24-hour business center with computer rental, outdoor pool, and badminton court. It has a gym, chapel and babysitting, but no room service.

KOWLOON

Shoppers and tourists should aim for Kowloon, especially Tsim Sha Tsui. It is slightly closer to the airport than Hong Kong Island and the railway station is in Tsim Sha Tsui East.

Expensive

THE PENINSULA, *Salisbury Road, Tsim Sha Tsui, Tel. 2366-6251, Fax 2722-4170. E-mail: pen@peninsula.com. Http://www.peninsula.com. 300 rooms. $2900-$4600; suites $5200-$39000. Extra bed $500. Book through Leading Hotels of the World.*

This, the oldest and most beautiful hotel in Hong Kong, is in a great location a few minutes walk from the MTR, the Star Ferry and the best shopping. It has some of the best and most expensive restaurants in town. It is also a historic tourist attraction and deserves at least a look. The high lobby ceiling in the original wing has carved gold trim and rams' head pillars. The Peninsula's restaurants include **Gaddi's** (European with an average meal price of $1200 to $1500) and **Chesa** (Swiss with an average price of $600, but the three-course set lunch is only about $195). It also has *dim sum*, a Japanese restaurant, 500 different wines and a caviar bar. Its health spa has a waterfall, year-round Roman-style pool with retractable screen, steam bath, sauna, jacuzzi, large gym, and massage. Its shops are upmarket and it has its own helicopter.

See also Chapter 13, *China's Best Places to Stay.*

GREAT EAGLE HOTEL, *8 Peking Road, Tel. 2375-1133, Fax 2375-6611. E-mail:resv@gehotel.com. Http://www.gehotel.com. 500 rooms. $2400-$3600 for rooms and $4000 to $15000 for suites. Add $200 for double occupancy. Extra bed is $440.*

This restful, 19-story, 1989 luxury hotel exudes informality and quiet efficiency. It is the closest of these hotels to Hong Kong China City, and a couple blocks from the MTR and Star Ferry. It is above a Duty Free department store and half a block from the Ocean Terminal/Harbour City mall. Its Bostonian American Bar and Restaurant are fun and papered with customer drawings. Its well-lit rooms have wide beds, separate shower stalls, voice mail, and three telephones, two with hands-free speakers. Its four executive floors have fax machines, safes, its own lounge, and lots of other goodies. You can unwind in its health club and squash court. The roof-top pool is heated. However we found no foam bath and a torn pillow slip, minor glitches. Great Eagle Hotels International management, and a member of Summit Hotels.

KOWLOON SHANGRI-LA, *64 Mody Road, Tel. 2721-2111, Fax 2723-8686. 725 spacious rooms. $2100-$3550. Extra bed $300. Http://www.shangri-la.com.*

This is a beautiful, magnificent-looking hotel with very good standards, but it's not as spectacular as its sister the Island Shangri-La. It has recommended Japanese, Continental and California restaurants. At its superb Napa restaurant, you are serenaded by jazz musicians and get a choice of butter or olive oil on your bread. It has 24-hour room service, a bake shop, 24-hour business center, and executive floors. You can enjoy its small indoor pool, spa, and beauty salon. Rooms have three telephones and voice mail. You can walk six minutes to the Star Ferry or take a ferry directly to Central. It is not as convenient to the MTR but it is within walking distance of the train station.

Moderate

THE KOWLOON HOTEL, *19-21 Nathan Road, Tel. 2369-8698, Fax 2739-9811. E-mail:khh@peninsula.com. Http://www.peninsula.com.hk. 707 rooms. $1500-2650; suites $3600 to Y4000.*

This hotel has a fantastic location. It is right at the MTR, behind its sister Peninsula Hotel, and seven minutes walk from the Star Ferry. It has tiny, functional rooms with plastic sinks. All rooms have fax machines and private fax numbers. The Kowloon lacks the class and quality of its neighbor. It has a pizzeria, a 30-shop arcade, and a fleet of Mercedes. While it has no gym, you can use the facilities at the nearby Salisbury YMCA.

Inexpensive
THE SALISBURY YMCA, *41 Salisbury Road, Tel.2369-2211, Fax 2739-9315. E-mail:sales@ymcahk.org.hk. Http://www.ymcahk.org.hk. 380 rooms. $880-$1270. Suites $1720-$2000. Extra bed $175. Dorm bunk bed $190. No 3% government tax. It too gives 10%-15% discounts to "walk-ins" during low season.* Everybody knows this is the best deal in town. It is next door to The Peninsula Hotel. It has room service, two restaurants of mainly western food, in-room safes, two pools, fitness center, and indoor climbing wall. It provides squash, Laundromat, secretarial and fax services, and piano studios. YMCA membership is not necessary. It first opened in 1924 and is across the street from the Hong Kong Cultural Centre.

See also Chapter 13, *China's Best Places to Stay.*

BOOTH LODGE *11 Wing Sing Lane, at Yau Ma Tei MTR station just north of Tsim Sha Tsui, Tel. 2771-9266, Fax 2385-1140. $620-1200. Extra bed $180. No 3% tax. To reserve space in this 53-room hotel, fax or call with credit card number.*

This hotel close to the Jade and night markets is another great deal, run by the Salvation Army, which does an excellent job. Its medium-sized rooms are spotless, quiet, and offers 12 television channels in English. The staff is friendly and it has a coffee shop and accepts Visa, MasterCard and American Express but not Diners. Alcohol is not allowed.

THE ISLANDS
REGAL AIRPORT HOTEL, *9 Cheong Tat Road, Chek Lap Kok, Lantau Island. It is attached to the airport by a covered bridge. Tel. 2286-8888, Fax 2286-8686. E-mail:rhi@regal-hotels.com. Http://www.regal-hotels.com. $2100-$3200 for rooms, and $6800-$25000 for suites.*

This hotel has in-room safes, pay movie channels, and televisions with games and internet functions. It has non-smoking floors, business center, baby-sitting and travel agent. There's also Chinese and continental restaurants and 24-hour room service. See also Arrivals and Departures above.

Holiday homes have rooms in two or three-story houses and don't take credit cards. Many are in Cheung Chau, Lantau (at Mui Wo) and Lamma Islands. On weekdays, you can get a relatively decent room in one of these places cheaply. Booths with photos are near the ferry exits. Look at the real thing before you commit yourself to staying. A Canadian is charging $350 a night for breakfast and air-conditioned bed on Lamma Island but it is a long walk from the ferry. If you're interested however, telephone Darren Pittman at *2982-8461 or Fax 2982-8424.*

WHERE TO EAT

Hong Kong has a wide cosmopolitan variety of superb restaurants, the best offering in China. Some of the tops are in expensive hotels, others in grubby pigeon holes. Reservations are necessary at popular restaurants, especially for harbor-view tables. The best wine lists are at the top hotels, as are the best high teas.

Generally, restaurants open only for lunch and dinner between 11am-3pm and 6pm-11pm. A few stay open all day. Some are closed on Sunday. Try to get there no later than 11:45am for lunch. Good restaurants are very busy. The top restaurants have dress codes. "Smart casual" generally means no shorts, sandals, collarless shirts and ripped clothing. Rules are less strict for women. Telephone if in doubt. Most accept major credit cards (Visa, American Express, MasterCard and sometimes Diners Club).

DIM SUM & TEA

You must try dim sum at the Luk Yu, Jade Garden, Serenade, or any of the top hotel restaurants. You must have goose at the Yung Kee.

*For traditional British tea, try the **Tiffin Lounge** at the Grand Hyatt 3pm-6pm, the Peninsula, and the **Library** at the Island Shangri-La. Expect to pay (yikes!) about $135.*

Food in Hong Kong is generally more expensive than in North America, sometimes two or three times so. Moderate here means expensive in North America. For a range of prices, you can go cruising in **Lan Kwai Fung** (the trendy upscale hangout for yuppies on Hong Kong Island). Take the MTR to Central, exit on Peddar and go up the hill. It has Californian, Indian, Lebanese, Italian, Tex-Mex, Japanese, German and French food.

On the top end, **Tony Roma's** is great for ribs. It's at *1/F, California Tower, 32 D'Aguilar Street, Tel. 2521-0292.* At the other end, is **Gunga Din's Club**, where you can get chicken *tikka* for $65, *paneer mutter* for $42, prawn *vindaloo* for $75, and *samosas* for $24. Gunga Din's on the lower ground floor at *59 Wyndham Street Central, Tel. 2523-1439.* The neighborhood has even cheaper food too.

Expensive

Among the best are restaurants in the top hotels with dress codes. See hotel listings for **Petrus** for French cuisine and a wine cellar with 10,000 bottles. It's on the 56th floor of the Island Shangri-La; **One Harbour Road** at the Grand Hyatt for Cantonese; **Gaddi's** for Continental in The

Peninsula Hotel; the Kowloon Shangri-La's **Margaux Restaurant** has 450 items on its wine list including 1926 Margaux for $14,500.

Moderate

Tours go to the floating Cantonese restaurants in Aberdeen which are covered in lights and have garish, oriental interiors. Both are novel settings in which to eat; the food is good but not great. The most popular is the **Jumbo Restaurant**. See Aberdeen below.

JADE GARDEN, *Cantonese. 1/F Swire House, 11 Chater Road Central, Tel. 2526-3031. It accepts all credit cards and is open from 10am (Sunday), otherwise 11:30am-11:30pm. The Jade Garden also has branches in Lower G/ F, Jardine House, 1 Connaught Road, Tel. 2524-5098; 1/F, 500 Hennessy Road, Causeway Bay, Tel. 2895-2200, and 1 Hysan Avenue, Causeway Bay, Tel. 2577-9332.*

This is a chain in Central and Causeway Bay. Noodles and rice here cost about $72 and entrees $70-280. Expensive abalone can go up to $520. The Jade Garden has good *dim sum.*

PEKING GARDEN, *Peking cuisine on Hong Kong Island and Kowloon. Try Alexander House basement, Central, Tel. 2526-6456. This is open 10:30am-3pm, 5:30pm-midnight, daily except Chinese New Year's. Eleven other branches are in Pacific Place, Cityplaza, Star House (in Tsim Sha Tsui, Kowloon), Empire Centre, etc. They accept all cards.*

The whole Peking Garden chain is good and cooks demonstrate noodle-making by hand (at 8:30pm), Peking duck carving, and breaking the mud shell of Beggar's Chicken ($330). Popular are dumplings ($22-$90), prawns and chili sauce $180, Peking duck $320, and chicken with walnut in soy bean sauce $98. Try also the onion cakes $24. Reservations are necessary.

Inexpensive

The cheapest places to eat are fast food restaurants like **McDonald's** and Chinese food stalls. Many of these are in the large shopping malls. The **Pacific Place Food Fair** across from Admiralty MTR station in Central is always packed and has stalls that serve Thai, Singapore, Shanghai, Cantonese and American food.

For lower-priced western food, try the **Mall Cafe** in the YMCA (41 Salisbury Road, Tsim Sha Tsui). **Oliver's Super Sandwiches** sells good, deli-style sandwiches (about $21-$39), baked potatoes ($12-$23), soup and salads ($12-$19), breakfasts ($14-$21), and $10 coffee. About 23 Oliver's dot the city in *The Landmark in Central (basement Tel. 2877-6631), Pacific Centre (28 Hankow Road in Tsim Sha Tsui, Tel. 2723-9303), and Ocean Centre Tel. 2735-0068.* **Delifrance** has several restaurants. Get an address list from *1/F, Worldwide House, 19 Des Voeux Road, Tel. 2873-3893*. It offers soups, baguette sandwiches ($23-$38) and rich cheese pasteries.

HONG KONG ISLAND

LUK YU TEA HOUSE, *Cantonese/dimsum. Moderate. 24-26 Stanley Street Central, Tel. 2523-5464, 2523-5463. Open 7am-10pm with dim sum 7am-5:30pm for $25-$55 a plate. Avoid 12:45 noon to 1:45pm when regulars take over. No credit cards.*

This is one of my favorites because all old Hong Kong tea houses used to have surly waiters and spittoons like this. It has no menus in English but public relations man John speaks English. The decor, a reproduction of the original 1920s building, is a lot brighter and cleaner than it originally was. Oh yes, the food is good too. Try the fried milk $120 and sweet and sour pork $100.

JEWISH COMMUNITY CENTRE, *Mediterranean and Kosher. Moderate. One Robinson Place, 70 Robinson Road, Mid-Levels above Central, Tel. 2801-5440. Temporary membership $50.*

The coffee shop at lunch time has a *mezze* platter for $44, *gelfilte* fish for $38, and chicken noodle soup for $65. The Club can deliver food to hotels.

JIMMY'S KITCHEN, *European. Moderate. Basement, South China Building, 1-3 Wyndham Street, Central, Tel. 2526-5293. All cards. Open at noon daily with the last order at 11pm.*

This restaurant has British decor and memorabilia, and hybrid Hong Kong-western food. The same family has operated this place since 1928. Popular are the black pepper steak, roast lamb and beef, and spicy garoupa.

YUNG KEE RESTAURANT, *Cantonese. Moderate. 32-40 Wellington Street Central, Tel. 2522-1624. From Central MTR Street exit, head south uphill along D'Aguilar or Wyndham Streets. Make a right on Wellington. This restaurant is open daily 11am-11:30pm and serves dim sum Monday to Saturday all day. Reservations are recommended especially for lunch. All cards.*

Started over 50 years ago with a small shop and a great recipe for a juicy goose with crispy skin, the Yung Kee now sells about 300 geese a day. It charges $380 for a whole bird, $190 for half. You can also get delicious roast pigeon from $85.

KOWLOON

TANG RESTAURANT, *Sichuan. Moderate. Metropole Hotel, 75 Waterloo Road, Kowloon, Tel. 2761-1711. Open 10:30am-2:30pm; 5:30pm-11pm. All credit cards.*

The personal chef of Deng Xiao Ping comes here regularly as a consultant. *Ma Po dow foo* is $75, half a smoked duck costs $130; chili hot pot is $220, *dan dan* noodles $25; dragon's eye meat bun $25; sauteed chicken with chili and peanuts $80.

SERENADE, *1/F, Hong Kong Cultural Centre, across from the Peninsula Hotel is good for Cantonese food, especially dim sum. Moderate. Tel. 2722-0932.* Its downtown location is convenient.

HONG KONG PUZZLE, *2/F, Harbour Crystal Centre, 100 Granville Road, Tsim Sha Tsui East, Tel. 2721 8282.*

Those who remember pre-1997 Hong Kong, before the new airport, back when rickshaws were a real means of transportation and restaurants were dark and grubby with crabby waiters – these people would probably like this place. It's almost a theme park from that era, currently a work in progress. It's fun and relatively cheap.

LIE YUE MUN

This is a small village beside the Shau Kei Wan Ferry Pier in the New Territories. Take KMB bus 14C from Lam Tin MTR. Shops are full of tanks with all kinds of live seafood (geoducks, parrot fish, crabs, etc). You can have one of the many restaurants cook your choice. It's best to go with a group (see Tours). Or aim for the only HKTA member restaurant.

HOI TIN GARDEN, *at the end of the 200-meter long lane, Tel. 2348-1482.*

Steamed prawns here cost about $200 a catty depending on the season.

THE ISLANDS

Good for seafood are the simple open-air island restaurants on Lamma and Cheung Chow islands near the ferry pier. Make sure the food is thoroughly cooked and piping hot. English is generally not spoken.

SEEING THE SIGHTS

Tours

Hong Kong has more to see than any other Chinese city. The easiest and quickest way is to choose a HKTA tour. These are generally good and save a lot of time. But avoid the night tram tour and the cocktail cruise tour because the guides don't point out much. On the ship, you only get a handful of peanuts and one drink. You might as well just take the public tram and a ferry.

Other tours are good however and many include meals, so you can try a variety of Chinese dishes without worrying about how to order. Tours go to different parts of the New Territories ($325 and $385 for adults). The most popular is **The Land Between** where you might glimpse a People's Liberation Army uniform, Hong Kong's highest mountain, and trees full of birds. From September to mid-June you can go to the **horseraces** ($530). This is a British tradition dating from the 1840s, now a Chinese passion. The clubs have instant replays on their big boards. Guides give lessons on how to gamble and the food is superb. Shatin is a bigger less crowded club, and both it and Happy Valley look great floodlit after dark. Happy Valley is downtown.

You can golf, play tennis or swim at the beautiful **Clearwater Bay Golf and Country Club** on a tour ($430) on Tuesday and Friday mornings, or just golf at the **Jockey Club Kau Sai Chan**, Sai Kung Island, Tel. 2791-3388. For overseas visitors, it's a public course open Monday to Friday except public holidays from 7am-8pm. There's a tour for that too at $430, Wednesdays and Thursdays. If you have more time, it's better to go to the cheaper, larger and less crowded courses in Shenzhen and Zhongshan across the border. The Shangri-La Hotels manage the Xili course in Shenzhen and can make arrangements. Other hotels can also help you. Beautiful **Mission Hills** in Shenzhen has an office in Hong Kong, *Tel. 2851-6396.*

HONG KONG MUST-SEES

You must take the Tram up to the Peak for the view from all sides. Do this preferably at sunset. You must take a tour of Hong Kong harbor even if it is just on a ferry. You must see Aberdeen harbor and eat in a floating restaurant. Do also go to Lantau Island, see the giant buddha and have a vegetarian lunch, and take a tour of the New Territories. If you and your children like aquariums and theme parks, there's Ocean Park. You must see Wong Tai Sin Temple.

One tour goes to the Peak, Stanley Market and Repulse Bay and the Aberdeen Typhoon Shelter. Another tour goes to Ocean Park and Middle Kingdom, both of which you can easily do on your own. One short tour includes the Jade and Bird Markets and exotic Wong Tai Sin Temple. The **Jade Market**, with 400 dealers, is good for those who want to buy but you have to haggle and know stones and prices to get a good deal. Chinese dealers meet here to negociate sales with hidden hand signals early morning, before the tourists arrive. It is open 10am-2:30pm daily at Kansu and Battery Streets near the Yaumatei MTR station in Kowloon.

The **Bird Garden** is tiny and can also be missed. You can see men airing their caged birds in almost every park in the city. Much more exotic markets are in China itself. **Wong Tai Sin Temple** can't be missed. It is unique to Hong Kong, and three million worshippers a year come offering food and incense to this uniquely Taoist god. It has a free herbal medicine, clinic, and over 100 fortune tellers (some of whom speak English). It is right at Wong Tai Sin MTR in Kowloon and is open 7am-5pm. Donations are expected.

Social welfare agencies offer two tours, ideal for visitors who are more interested in meeting people than in seeing places. The **Family Insight Tour** costs $275 and you visit a real family in a government housing estate, and real children at a day-care centre where they learn English. The **Hong Kong Christian Service tour** asks for a donation and has probably improved by now. Its office is at *33 Granville Road, 9/F, in Tsim Sha Tsui, Tel. 2368-7123.*

A one-hour harbor cruise gives you a chance to see and hear that British institution, the **Noon Day Gun**, but you can see this on your own (Causeway Bay MTR stop). Accessible by a tunnel door in the west side of the World Trade Centre on Gloucester Road, the gun is across the road from the Excelsior Hotel.

An especially good tour is to **Lantau Island** to see a fishing village, monastery, and the **Big Buddha**. The vegetarian lunch is delicious and different. See below if you go on your own. There's even a *feng shui* tour and walking tours with taped audio commentary.

Note: some tourist sights are closed for public holidays especially Christmas, New Years Day and Chinese New Year's.

HONG KONG ISLAND – CENTRAL
Li Yuen Streets East & West

Two busy, parallel historic alleys full of shops and street stalls sell clothes, watches, silks, accessories, make-up, umbrellas, underwear, etc. The quality is not great and better in Stanley. However novelty watches are a good buy and actually work. To get here, take the Central MTR exit C-Li Yuen Street to Des Voeux Road. Across the street is World Wide House. Turn left. They're the fourth and fifth alley on your left.

If you continue walking west on Queen's Road Central, you'll find Central Market, the starting point for the free **Central-Midlevels or Hill Escalator**. It is the longest in the world at 800 meters and takes about a half hour. Please note that it runs downhill from 6am-10am and uphill 10:20am-10pm. You will pass **Hollywood Road** and the green and white **Jamia Mosque**. The **Ohel Leal Synagogue**, built in 1902 is at 70 Robinson Road. The escalator ends at Conduit Road. Children should be fascinated. To return to Central, you can catch a taxi, a #3 mini-bus going downhill, or walk down the stairs.

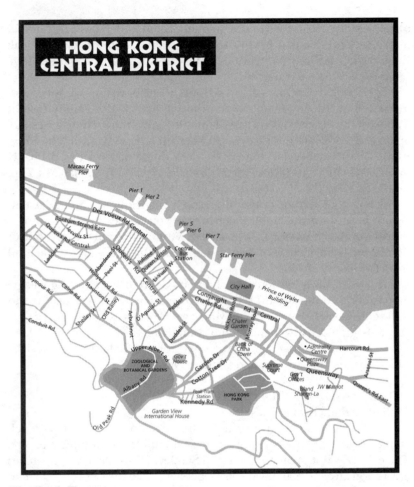

The Peak Tram

You can get a free bus ride from the east side of the Star Ferry Terminal in Central to the lower **Peak Tram Station** on Garden Road. The tram station is across the road from St. John's Cathedral and the Botanical Gardens. Go only if you can see the peak clearly from below. Clouds could obscure your view. Avoid 10-10:30am when all tour groups seem to arrive at once. The tram operates 7am- midnight, every 10-15 minutes and costs $18, or $28 return. For the best view, sit on the right side on the way up or at the very back window. The Peak Tram takes five to eight minutes up to 334 meters above sea level, about 200 meters below the top of Victoria Peak.

The modern, three-story Peak Galleria building beyond the terminal has restaurants and upmarket stores. The best view is from the pavilion to the left as you leave the tram terminal. Harlech and Lugard Roads circle the peak for views of the entire island, the harbor and Kowloon, a very pleasant one hour.

You can return downhill by bus, another beautiful ride. No. 1 minibus connects with the Star Ferry, No. 15 double-decker bus with Exchange Square and No. 15B bus with Causeway Bay. The bus station is down Peak Road from the Peak terminal.

The Peak has several restaurants. A favorite is the **Peak Cafe**, *121 Peak Road, Tel. 2849-7868,* near the tram terminal in a small, charming old building with a patio. It serves delicious, moderately-priced pan-Asian food and is open 10:30am-midnight. The **Cafe Deco**, *118 Peak Road, Tel. 2849-5111* is in the Peak Galleria mall and is more fun than gourmet.

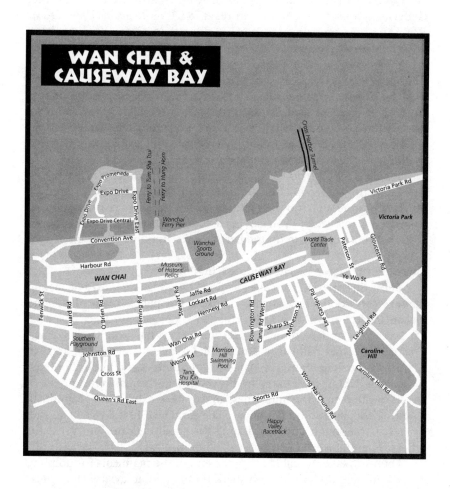

Western

This is full of antique stores, little alleys, ladder streets, and the Man Mo Temple. Take the Hill escalator up to Hollywood Road, and then walk west to the **Man Mo Temple**, about five or six blocks. This is the best temple on Hong Kong island and is dedicated to Man Cheong, the god of literature (with calligraphy brush in hand) and Kwan Kung, the god of war and patron saint of policemen and their enemies, the triads. Kwan Kung was a real third century warrior known in China as Guan Yu (see Luoyang). The inside is very smoky with pewter incense burners, incense spirals, and carved wooden sedan chairs for godly processions. It is open 7am-5pm.

Cat Street is also known as Lascar Row. Nearby are the **Cat Street Galleries**, a collection of antique stores at *38 Lok Ku Road and Upper Lascar Row*. Antiques on sale here can be older than Qinq. You can head downhill from here and end up at the Sheung Wan MTR station.

Aberdeen

This former fishing village with a well-protected harbor, moors fishing boats and pleasure craft. A fresh sea food market operates after 9am all day. You can smell fish everywhere. Look for drying squid, and air-conditioned family junks. 5000 boat people still live in this typhoon shelter; some also have apartments on land.

Take bus No. 70 from Exchange Square near the Star Ferry in Central. Get off at the first stop after the Aberdeen Tunnel and walk about 20 minutes or grab a taxi to the pier (*ma tow*) at the main seawall opposite Aberdeen Center. Here you can get a 20-minute sampan ride for about $50. For a short free trip on the harbor, take Jumbo Restaurant's ferry.

Ocean Park/Water World/Middle Kingdom

These three parks are in one location (*Tel. 2552-0291, 2873-8888*) and they are very good, especially for children. The park is open 10am-6pm. **Ocean Park** admission is $140, child $74. Seniors are free. A special Citybus leaves from Admiralty MTR station every half hour from 8:45am. The price includes admission. No. 6 mini-bus goes from the Star Ferry in Central to the main entrance, daily except Sundays and public holidays.

Ocean Park has two parts. In the lower near the main entrance are a pavilion with free-flying butterflies, an exquisite exhibit of live goldfish, a petting zoo, and an orchid house. The simulator film *Secrets of the Lost Temple* is too rough and frightening for small children but great for others. The English version plays at 3:30pm.

Then you take the cable car to the end of the peninsula for dolphin, whale and high diving shows, a shark tunnel and an aviary. Don't miss Atoll Reef, a three-story salt-water aquarium full of fish, sea turtles, etc.

with different species at different levels. The shows are in an incredibly beautiful setting over the South China Sea. Here are also some amusement park rides including a 27 metre-high ferris wheel.

Water World is a large water park that has a wave pool and water slides that operates May to October. Open daily 10am-5pm, adults $60, children $40, and seniors free. It is attached to Ocean Park.

Middle Kingdom which is also attached to Ocean Park by escalator and has a separate entrance at Tai Shue Wan is a lesson in Chinese history and culture with replicas of famous Chinese temples, palaces, pagodas and street scenes. You can learn to make paper here and have your fortune told – in English. There's also a variety show with acrobats. The only restaurant besides McDonald's is inside. This park is open 10am-6pm, admission $140, children (6-7 yrs) $70.

Repulse Bay & Stanley

From Central, it's a beautiful, 30-minute bus ride to Repulse Bay and another 15 to Stanley, depending on the traffic. Buses 6, 6A, 61, 260, and 973 will take you to Stanley; 61 to only Repulse Bay.

You go to **Repulse Bay** for the scenery. There are changing facilities and lifeguards, but swimming is not advisable. The government says its water quality is good. Look for the posted ecoli levels and decide for yourself. The recent statues of Tin Hau and Kwan Yin are crude. This is a nice place however for a walk along the waterfront to Deep Water Bay and Aberdeen.

Stanley is most famous for its market although the original village is still a dirty, fascinating shanty town. Surrounding these are expensive residential areas. The beach is popular for windsurfing year-round if you don't mind the stench. The British-built Stanley Fort now houses the People's Liberation Army. There is also a large maximum-security prison and a small British graveyard on Stanley Peninsula. The Japanese kept foreign expatriates in an internment camp here during the occupation.

Stanley Market is a popular, pleasant, open-air market with factory over-runs, seconds, silks, and arts and crafts. Go there before you buy anything to check prices. It has more fashionable clothes, larger sizes, and higher prices than other markets but it's cheaper than stores. It is open about 10:00am-5:30pm, depending on the season.

TSIM SHA TSUI

This is shopping heaven, on either side of Nathan Road in **Kowloon**. Here you can find inexpensive clothing, an unbelievable number of camera shops, and good restaurants and bars. By the harbor near the Star Ferry is the huge 600-store Harbour City Mall. Attractions for non-shoppers include Kowloon Park, the Hong Kong Cultural Centre, the

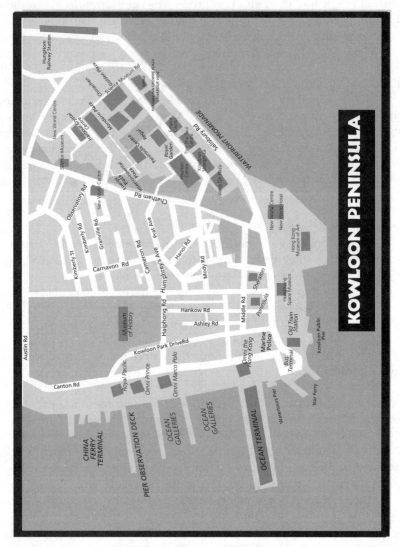

Museum of History, and the Space Museum–all within walking distance of each other. You can get to Tsim Sha Tsui by Star Ferry from Central or Wanchai, and by MTR (Tsim Sha Tsui station).

The Star Ferry is one of the most famous ferry rides in the world, spectacular day or night. It started in 1898. First class is cleaner, more comfortable and has a better view. Second class is more interesting, but with diesel fumes, and is $.30 less. The ferry runs every 5-10 minutes 6:30am-11:30am and takes about eight minutes between Central and Kowloon. It costs $1.70 and $2 for adults. Seniors over 65 ride free.

The **Peninsula Hotel**, the most famous and historic here used to be on the waterfront. Stop here for at least a cup of tea or coffee in its lobby for old world elegance. See Where to Stay above. The **Hong Kong Space Museum**, *2 Science Museum Road, Tsim Sha Tsui, Kowloon, Tel. 2734-2722.* Try a moonwalk at 1/6 gravity or spin in a multi-axis chair in this large, interesting museum with displays, videos and a few hands-on exhibits. Some of its shows are in English. Open 2pm-9:30pm. Closed Mondays. Free on Wednesdays.

The excellent **Hong Kong Museum of History** is in *Kowloon Park, Tel. 2367-2167, 2367-1124.* Photographs, paintings, models, maps and archaeological finds illustrate Hong Kong's history in two barracks buildings from the late 1800s. It is open 10am-6pm Tuesday to Saturday, Sunday 1pm-6pm and closed Mondays and some holidays. $10 for adults. Free on Wednesdays.

The **Hong Kong Science Museum** is on *Science Museum Road at Granville and Chatham Roads in Tsim Sha Tsui East, Tel. 2732-3232.* This unusual pink building with a gray stripe has four floors of 500 mainly hands-on exhibits, a great place for children. It is open 1pm-9pm, Tuesday-Friday, and 10am-9pm Saturday and Sunday. It is closed Monday. Admission is $25 but free on Wednesday.

MONGKOK
Temple Street Night Market
Hong Kong's biggest (about one km long) and best open market for the proletariatis as cheap as it gets. It is open about 6pm daily, is busiest 9pm-11pm, and closes around 1am. Go to Jordan MTR in Kowloon, exit A. Walk west on Jordan two and a half blocks, turn right onto Temple Street.

The first couple of blocks are mainly clothes and food stalls. Temple Street continues slightly to the right for fortune tellers, sidewalk medicine men, and Cantonese street opera, mainly on weekends. Beyond this are more clothes, the Tin Hau temple (closed at night), household goods, mahjong halls and more food stalls. The market ends at Man Ming Lane, so turn right. Yau Ma Tei MTR is only a block or two away.

THE ISLANDS
There are bare hills with great views, no cars, a slower pace, and much to appreciate here. The best to visit of the 235 islands are Lantau and Cheung Chau. HKTA has a $35 guidebook about Cheung Chau with map. Avoid crowds on weekends.

Ferries leave just west of the Star Ferry in Central. They cost between $5-$15. HKTA has ferry schedules. A few ferries run from Peng Chau to Mui Wo (Lantau) to Cheung Chau.

Lantau on your own requires a detailed map and guide book from HKTA. This island with 144 sq km, is about twice the size of Hong Kong, but was not developed because it had little or no drinking water. Lantau strictly limits the number of motor vehicles allowed. It has 70 km of paved hiking trails, and many temples, fishing villages and magnificent views. The beaches are safer here than in more crowded areas, but expatriate residents won't swim even here. The new airport is on the north side. Mui Wo and the big buddha are on the south.

At least 21 ferries leave Hong Kong island every day for Mui Wo (Silvermine Bay) 7am-12:20am midnight for about $17. The trip takes a little over an hour. Hoverferries take 35 minutes. Before you leave Mui Wo, check also the bus schedule back from Taipo or the monastery–unless you want to spend the night on the island. Buses and taxis meet the ferries and the ride to Po Lin Monastery is about 25 minutes.

Access to the buddha is 10am-6pm daily, but you can see it any time from a distance. It is 34 meters high and weighs 250 metric tons. **Po Lin Monastery** was founded in 1905 and is open weekdays and Saturdays from noon to 4 or 5pm. You need to buy a ticket first for vegetarian lunch which is served every half hour. You can sightsee around this impressive temple while you wait. From here you can walk downhill to Taipo Village by paved path in an hour or so, or take a bus.

Cheung Chau. This small island, a former pirate base, is only 2.4 sq km. It has a population of 30,000, many of them commuters. It is home to real fishermen. Cheung Chau has some great but dumpy seafood restaurants, ship building (junks), two beaches, a hotel, walks and bicycles for rent.

To get there, take the hourly ferry from the Outlying Districts Services Pier. The ferry takes one hour and runs from 6:25am-11:30pm. The five daily hoverferries take 35 minutes.

The **Pak Tai Temple** (Temple of Jade Vacuity) is famous because of the colorful Bun Festival, unique to Cheung Chau. Two granite dragons guard the temple and two others decorate the roof. The temple was built in 1783. The Pak Tai god of the sea, now on the main altar, was brought from China in 1777 after fishermen found it in the sea. When the plague hit in the 1800s, villagers carried the statue through the streets. They believe this act stopped the disease. The Bun festival celebrates this event now yearly.

Try the **Baccarat Restaurant**, *9A Pak She Praya Road, Tel. 2981-0668,* a good, open-air Chinese seafood restaurant near the ferry pier. It is open daily 11am-11pm.

NIGHTLIFE & ENTERTAINMENT

You can go on a night cruise tour, or the night races. Read the lists of current sports and cultural events from a HKTA office. *This Week* (an events magazine) is also on HKTA's website. The main **orchestras** are the Hong Kong Philharmonic and the 85-piece Hong Kong Chinese Orchestra. The latter uses traditional Chinese and western instruments. There's live British theatre. A good concierge should be able to help you.

At sunset, take a ferry or watch the lights come on from the Peak. They are both magical. Ride the Hong Kong island **tram** and look in apartment and store windows. Go shopping in Tsim Sha Tsui. Head over to the Space Museum for an **Omnimax** film on the ceiling of the ball-shaped planetarium. It is open until 9pm, but closed Monday, *Tel. 2734-2722.* It's free on Wednesday. There's tennis, squash, bowling, ice-skating or rollerskating. Or just relax in one of Hong Kong's many lounges, pubs and discos.

Recommended are the bars in the top hotels, especially the **Regent's Lobby Lounge** with its great view of the harbor, **J.J.'s** in the Grand Hyatt, or the Peninsula's unusual **Felix** where you can look into the women's washroom from the men's. Bar hop in **Lan Kwai Fong** from about 10pm onwards–see Where to Eat above. Saturday nights are the busiest. Most places are open on public holidays, but telephone ahead to be sure. Most bars take credit cards. The action starts after work at the pubs and after 10 or 11pm at the discos.

Beer usually costs $30-$50, except at happy hour, when drinks are usually half price. Beware of girlie bars, any bars that charges you a fee for conversing with the staff. Generally, these places are rip-offs. You can also get beer at convenience stores and supermarkets.

HONG KONG ISLAND

DELANEY'S, *2/F One Capital Place, 18 Luard Road, Wanchai, Tel. 2804-2880.* All cards. Open Sunday through Thursday 12 noon-2am; Friday and Saturday 12 noon to 3am or the last guest. This lively pub describes itself as a Victorian-style Irish pub. It serves Delaney's ale, its own brew, as well as Guinness, Harp and Caffrey. It also serves a daily roast for $88 to $98, has live Irish music on Wednesdays and Fridays. Reservations for dinner recommended.

KOWLOON

MAD DOGS (British pub) *basement, 32 Nathan Road, Tel. 2301-2222.*
Nice basement bar with friendly British staff. Occasional live music. It only accepts Visa and MasterCard. The happy hour is 5pm-10pm. Live music plays Tuesdays and Sundays. Bangers and mash cost $75; fish and chips $85; British breakfast $79.

BOTTOMS UP, *basement, 14 Hankow Road, Tsim Sha Tsui, Tel. 2721-4509. Open 4:30pm-3:30am, Sundays from 5pm. Happy hour is 4:30pm-8:30pm, two drinks for $66.*

This is the most respectable and popular of the topless bars. You can't miss the sign outside. It is a collage of buttocks. Topless European and Asian women sit inside circular bars and bend low to get drinks. Couples are welcome, but single women aren't. Beer costs $69-$75 and there's no cover charge.

SHOPPING

Prices for many goods are better in North America. Chinese goods are cheaper in China, but the China Products' Stores sell the best of China. They can save you a lot of time. You have to know how much things cost at home before you get a bargain here. Camera film and processing are cheaper here too especially if you pay only for prints that are good.

The best buys are in good-quality clothes, jewelry, watches, pirated CD and software, and crafts. Stores have incredible sales usually just before the Chinese new year and in August, but also whenever tourism is down. For cheaper goods and seconds, look in the street markets like Li Yuen Street above. Prices are good for only Hong Kong-published books, local factory overruns, pearls, jewelry, and eye glass frames. HKTA has a list of sole distributors and authorized dealers so you can be sure you're not getting counterfeits.

Chinese products stores sell not only products from China. They are essentially department stores. They take credit cards and you can usually get a 10% discount. **China Arts & Crafts Stores** have higher quality and prices than China products stores. They sell silk, embroidered table cloths, jewelry, stone carvings, etc. from China. Among these are the **China Arts & Crafts**, *24-28 Queen's Rd (near Pedder Street), Central.* **Yue Hwa Chinese Products**, is at *301-309 Nathan Road, Yau Ma Tei.*

Computers and **cameras** have been cheaper in North America. Clones or copies of computers can be less expensive here, but the Hong Kong government has been cracking down. Besides, you might not be able to import counterfeits into your own country and pirated software may be full of viruses and not compatible with your system. If you want to see what's available try: **Golden Shopping Arcade**, *156 Fuk Wah Street, Shamshuipo, Kowloon.* Take the MTR to Shamshuipo, north of Tsim Sha Tsui, and leave by the Golden Shopping Arcade exit. Walk one block and look for a sign. The arcade is a dirty, crowded, three-story building on the first corner.

Groups of computer shops are also in the **Computer Mall**, *11/12/F, Windsor House, 311 Gloucester Road, Causeway Bay.* Admiralty Centre across from Pacific Place in Central has about 15 small computer shops downstairs. Again, HKTA has the addresses of sole distributors whom you can telephone for reliable outlets. Make sure you buy 110 volts and NTSC videos for North America.

Department Stores might cash travelers cheques at good rates with no service charge. These carry big international name brands like Lanvin and Chanel and have North American prices. Telephone for the branch near you. The main department stores are the middle-priced **Sincere**, *173 Des Voeux Road, Central, Tel. 2544-2688;* cheaper prices; **Shui Hing**, *23-25 Nathan Road, Tsim Sha Tsui, Tel. 2721-1495*. **Lane Crawford** is the best and most expensive. Its main store is at *70 Queen's Road, Central, Tel. 2526-6121.* **Marks & Spencer** is British with branches in Quarry Bay, Excelsior Plaza (Causeway Bay), Pacific Place (Admiralty MTR station) and the Landmark in Central, *Tel. 2869-0976.* It has larger clothing sizes.

In factory outlets you find the best deals on brand-name clothing. HKTA has a list. Among the most convenient are those in the Pedder Building across from the Landmark on Pedder Street in Central (though not all the stores here are factory outlets).

Gems & Jewelry

It is illegal to take out **new elephant ivory**, unless you have an import permit from your own country and an export permit from Hong Kong. Call the Hong Kong Agriculture and Fisheries Department, *Tel. 2733-2283.* If you can prove that you have antique ivory, there should be no problem.

Hong Kong is a great place to buy locally-made **jewelry and carved gems**, especially diamonds, jade, opals, pearls, rubies, sapphires and emeralds, all free of sales taxes. Synthetics and imitations are available but if you buy from a HKTA or Diamond Importers' Association store, you have some protection. Just make sure you get a detailed receipt. For **jewelry and gems**, try *Sunny Tsui, shop no. B, 117A, Basement, Golden Mile Holiday Inn, 46-52 Nathan Road, Kowloon, Tel. 2723-4775.* Open 9:30am-7pm; Sundays 9:30am-5:30pm.

Most **gold** in Hong Kong is 24-carat or 99.9% pure, too soft for jewelry, and with a different color than that used in North America. Some 24-carat necklace clasps are "S" shaped and can be bent sideways to open. You can also buy other gold alloys like 22, 18, 14 and 10 carats.

See Jade in chapter on Shopping before you buy any **jade**. The Jade Market is fun to browse in. See above.

For **porcelain**, the Wah Tung China Limited showroom is *14-17/F, Grand Marine Industrial Building, 3 Yue Fung Street, Shek Pai Wan Road, Tin Wan, Aberdeen.* It has a retail store (higher prices) on Hollywood Road.

EXCURSIONS & DAY TRIPS

To go into other parts of China, you need a **China visa** which you can get through any travel agent, or directly through the Ministry of Foreign Affairs of the People's Republic of China, *Tel.* 2835-3657. The office is in the southwest corner of the **China Resources Building**, *27 Harbour Road, Wanchai* and is open Monday to Friday 9:30am-12:20pm; and 2pm-5:30pm. It takes one working day to process a visa. Travel agents can get visas more quickly at a higher price. Regular single entry visas are $100, double $150, and multible $200 (for three months), considerably less than at a Chinese consulate in North America. Photo service is available. You can get individual visas, especially to Shenzhen, Zhuhai and Haikou on arrival at those cities, but these are not good for the rest of China or for more than 72 hours.

Travel to the rest of China from here is easy and you have lots of choices. There are prepaid day tours including visas to **Shenzhen** and **Zhongshan**. If you have more time there's the rest of China. How about the Silk Road, Tibet, Guilin and Beijing? The main travel agents for China are China Travel Service and China International Travel Service. Other agents buy from these, especially China Travel Service.

PRACTICAL INFORMATION

Your best friend in Hong Kong is a manager or concierge at your hotel, or the Hong Kong Tourist Association (HKTA). Keep picture-identification, like a driver's license, with you at all times. Foreigners are rarely asked for their documents, but it is better to be safe.

Consulates and Trade Commissions: Australia, *Tel. 2827-8881*; **Britain**, *Tel. 2901-3000;* **Canada**, *Tel. 2810-4321, Fax 2810-6736;* **India**, *Tel. 2528-4028;* **New Zealand**, *Tel. 2877-4488*; **Philippines**, *Tel. 2823-8500;* **US**, *Tel. 2523-9011.*

Cyber cafes: the **Pacific Coffee Company** has one computer terminal in each of its 10 branches on which you can play for a quarter hour or so for the price of a muffin. Get a list of addresses from the one in the *1st Class Terminal, Star Ferry Pier, Central, Tel. 2537-1484.*

Emergencies: *Tel. 999* for ambulance, police and fire in extreme emergencies.

Hong Kong Tourist Assocation: Phone the **HKTA** for emergency translations at the HKTA hotline, *Tel. 2807-6177*, 8am-6pm, Monday-Friday, 9am-5pm Saturday, Sunday and holidays. HKTA member stores and restaurants should prominently display its red sailing junk symbol and be listed in HKTA literature. Offices are at the **Star Ferry Concourse**, Tsim Sha Tsui, Kowloon. Open weekdays 8am-6pm, Saturday, Sunday and holidays 9am-5pm; Shop 8, Basement, **Jardine House**, 1 Connaught

Place, Central, Hong Kong Island. Open weekdays 9am-6pm. Saturday 9am-1pm. Closed Sundays. In North America *Tel. 800/282-HKTA.*

The HKTA address is *9/F-11/F, Citicorp Centre, 18 Whitfield Road, North Point, Hong Kong, Tel. 2807-6543, Fax 2806-0303. Http://www.hkta.org.* It also has offices in Los Angeles, *Tel. 310/208-4582,* Chicago *312/329-1828,* New York *212/869-5008* and Toronto *416/366-2389.* Offices are also in other countries like Australia, New Zealand, Beijing, and London. It is non-government, and financed by carefully selected members. Its website in the US is *http://www.hkta.org/usa;* in Canada, its e-mail is *hktayyz@hkta.org.* For its arts festival, *http://www.hk.artsfestival.org.*

Hours: Offices, 9am-5:30 or 6pm, lunch 1pm-2pm. Saturdays 9am-1pm. Closed Sundays; Banks: 9 or 9:30am-4:30pm, Saturday 9 or 9:30am-12:30pm, closed Sundays; Stores: in Central 9, 9:30 or 10am-6 or 7pm. In Causeway Bay and Tsim Sha Tsui 10am-9 or 10pm. Some open past midnight.

Mail: The general post office is next to the Star Ferry in Central and is open weekdays 8am-6pm, Saturdays 8am-2pm, and closed Sundays. There is also a branch at *10 Middle Road in Tsim Sha Tsui* near the Sheraton Hotel.

Medical: Many hotels have doctors on call who charge $850 to $4500 for a house call. Add $200 for middle-of-the-night calls. **Anderson & Partners** have an office in Central. They have been charging $420 for an office consultation, *Tel. 2523-8166.* The **D.L. Clinic** in Kowloon, *Tel. 2721-2111 X 8342* charges $480 for an office consulation. Hong Kong has cheap, public hospitals with emergency rooms and good English-speaking doctors, but you may be in a ward with 20 or more people. **Queen Elizabeth Hospital**, Kowloon, *Tel. 2958-8888;* **Queen Mary Hospital**, *Hong Kong Island, Tel. 2855-4111.*

Money Matters: Hongkong Bank and Guangdong Bank ATMs give out cash for about one US dollar if you have Global Access, ETC, Electron, Visa and Plus System cards. You should be able to access Cirrus cards at Citibanks. American Express has offices here. Many shops, restaurants, and most hotels accept credit cards (Visa, American Express, MasterCard and less so Diners). Credit card fraud is common in Asia, so please be careful. Listen carefully when impressions are made. One or two?

Saving Money: Fly to and from other cities of China out of Shenzhen not Hong Kong. Flights from Hong Kong are more expensive. Look for hotel packages that include airport transfers. Buy food at grocery stores, fast food outlets or markets. The **Park Hotel** in Kowloon has a tea buffet at 3pm-5:30pm with sushi and noodles Monday-Friday for $68; Saturday and Sunday for $78. The **Oasis Bar** in the Renaissance Harbour View Hotel has a weekday Hungry Hour from 5pm-7:30pm with an all-you-can-eat cocktail buffet, for the price of a drink. Use public transport. Take advantage of the free cultural programs at HMS Tamar. Shop at markets. There are also free *tai chi* lessons every Tuesday, Thursday and Sunday at the Middle Road Children's Playground in Tsim Sha Tsui. The HKTA can tell you the time.

Banks, some stores, apartment blocks, restaurants and hotels have free telephones. While hotels might charge a lot for local calls, a public phone is usually nearby which only costs $1. The hour of long distance calls makes no difference to the US, and Canada now. It's cheaper to telephone overseas from Hong Kong than from China.

Unlike mainland China where fines for smoking is a pittance, you might have to pay $5000 if caught in a no-smoking area. But if you are also going to China, wait until you get there to get a haircut or shop for China-made goods. Note: luggage storage at the airport costs $40 per piece for one day, $100 per piece for two days, and $180 for three days. It is **free** if you leave luggage at a hotel.

Telecommunications: Telephone code **852**. A 24-hour Telecom office is at *10 Middle Road, Tsim Sha Tsui,* behind the Sheraton Hotel.

Voltage: 220V. Note that most televisions, videos and VCRs cannot be used in North America. If you buy, make sure your purchases are compatible for North America.

Travel Agents: You can also buy travel tickets at the train station in Hung Hom, directly through an airline office, at the Macau ferry terminal, or Hong Kong China City ferry terminal on Canton Road.

The following travel agencies have been in business a long time. They should not run off with your money. Their English is good:
- **Abercrombie & Kent**, *Tel. 2865-7818, E-mail:akhkg@attmail.com.*
- **American Express**, *Tel. 2732-7327.*
- **Arrow**, *Tel. 2523-7171, E-mail: atahkg@netvigator.com.*
- **China International Travel Service**, *Tel. 2732-5888.*
- **China Travel Service** is at *4/F, CTS House, 78-83 Connaught Road, Central, Tel. 2853-3888, Fax 2541-9777. E-mail:ctsdmd@hkstar.com.* Branches are at *2/F, 77 Queen's Road, Central, Tel. 2525-2284; 1/F, Alpha House, 27-33 Nathan Road, (entrance on Peking Road), Tel. 2721-1331.*
- **Moon Skystar Ltd.** can book the trans-Siberian train and the Silk Road. *Tel. 2723-1376, Fax 2723-6653. E-mail: MonkeyHK@compuserve.com; http://www.monkeyshrine.com.*
- **Thomas Cook**, *Tel. 2853-9888.*
- **Travel Advisers**, *Tel. 2368-5009.*

23. MACAU

Less than an hour south by ferry from Hong Kong is beautiful, little **Macau**, surrounded by Chinese waters on three sides. Settled by the Portuguese in 1557, this, the oldest European settlement on the China coast, is part of China after December 1999, when it becomes a Special Administrative Zone. Pastel-colored Portuguese colonial buildings and seven hills among the high rises, give a Mediterranean feel. But it's been the Las Vegas of the east since the 1840s, a city built on gambling, as well as trade.

Try to spend at least two weekdays here. It's more relaxing and cheaper than Hong Kong, but not on weekends. The food is fantastic.

China gave Portugal land for a colony to keep pirates away. After the handback, China should maintain existing economic and cultural traditions for 50 years. It should continue to use the *pataca* as well as Hong Kong money. Both are accepted at par. Just don't end up with *patacas* which no one accepts in Hong Kong.

The exchange rate is **HK$1=1.03 patacas**; **US$1=7.94 patacas**.

If you go, check with your consulate first about safety. It's had some problems with local triads, the mafia.

ARRIVALS & DEPARTURES

Buses ply between Macau and Gongbei/Zhuhai every 30 minutes 8am-6:30pm. The Macau terminal is next to the Peninsula Hotel. One bus a day arrives from Guangzhou. Contact China Travel Service. A bridge should be completed in 1999 between Zhuhai and Macau, entering at Cotai city between the islands of Coloane and Taipa.

Macau is within commuting distance of the Hong Kong-Macau Ferry Terminal near Hong Kong's Sheung Wan MTR stop. You can get a ferry ticket there at the last minute during the week but not Friday evenings and weekends. Ferries also leave from Hong Kong's Wanchai ten times a day, and from Shekou in China once a day. The Macau-side terminal is near the Floating Casino. The ferry from Hong Kong costs HK$137 and up.

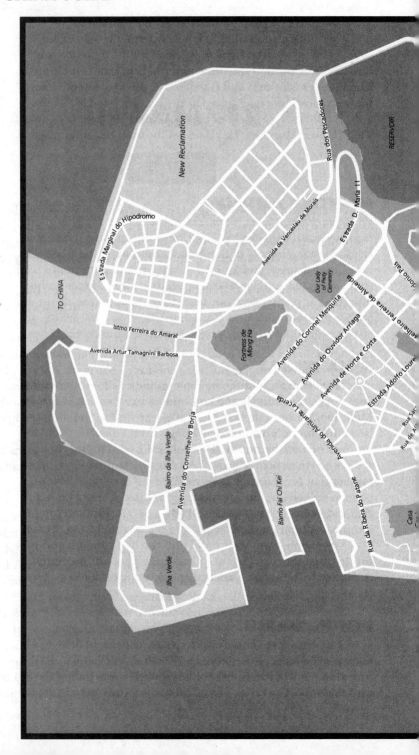

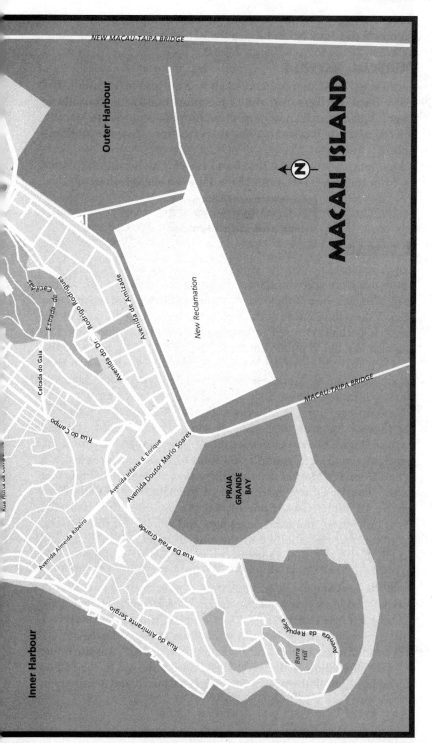

Jetfoils take 45 minutes and are the fastest and most frequent. Telephone in Hong Kong *2859-3333*, in Macau *7907039*.

There are also helicopters from Hong Kong for HK$1205-$1309 at least 26 round trips daily. *Tel. Hong Kong 2559-9800* or *Tel. Macau 727288*. Flights arrive from Bangkok, Kaohsiung, Manila, Pyongyang, and Taipei, and 13 cities in China. The airport is only eight km from downtown.

For those on foot, luggage porters and carts might not be available in the Customs House between Macau and Gongbei. The land border is open from 7am to midnight. You can obtain visas only up to 10pm. The border-crossing is beside the 1573 Barrier Gate in the north part of the city.

You can get your visa if necessary upon arrival, but no visas are required for up to 20 day stays for citizens of Australia, Canada, India, New Zealand, United Kingdom, the U.S., etc.

Macau charges an 80 *patacas* airport departure tax for China, and 130 *patacas* for elsewhere, if passengers are 12 years and older. No tax is charged for those in transit, 24 hours or less.

ORIENTATION

The population is 500,000. The Macau mainland is only 7.5 sq km so getting around is cheap and easy. The whole territory is 21.45 sq km. The island of Taipa with its airport, Hyatt and marine park is joined to the mainland by two long bridges and to the island of Coloane beyond by a causeway. The mainland has the ferry terminal, the downtown and government area, and most of the stores. Coloane has the golf course, Westin Resort and beaches.

GETTING AROUND

AP1 bus service from the airport downtown to the ferry terminal and Barrier Gate costs about six *patacas* and is available 6:15am-1:20am. You can rent an electric self-drive Moke at level one of the ferry terminal, *Tel. 726888 or 726868*. Taxis and public buses are plentiful. Taxis start at 10 *patacas* for the first 1.5 km, and one *pataca* for each subsequent 250 meters. Taxis do however add a surcharge from the airport. Few drivers speak English.

Hotels have shuttle buses. If you catch the Westin Resort bus or the Hyatt bus at the ferry, you can get a quick, free tour out to the islands.

WHERE TO STAY

The **Hyatt Regency** is the closest major hotel to the airport, aside from the four-star **Garden Hotel** at the airport itself. The most romantic and interesting hotel is the **Pousada de São Tiago** but it has fewer services. The famous **Hotel Bela Vista** is no longer available.

Hotel rates go up on weekends and Chinese holidays. Always ask for discounts. Hotels add a 10% service charge and 5% government tax.

POUSADA DE SÃO TIAGO, *Avenida da Republica, Fortaleza de São Tiago da Barra, Tel. 378111, Fax 552170. In North America, Tel. 800/ 44UTELL. 24 rooms. 1380-3500 patacas. Extra bed 330 patacas. Free ferry transfers on request. All cards. You need reservations in summer, New Year's, Christmas, and Grand Prix time.*

This cosy 1981 inn is unique. It was built into the ruins of a 1629 Portuguese fort and its garden. It is full of antique Portuguese leather furniture, short carved wooden beds and chests. It has fancy, old-style telephones, and blue and white Portuguese tiles. It does have a television and mini-bar in each room but with no elevators, you might have to climb three or four levels. It overlooks the harbor, is near the Maritime Museum and good restaurants, and has a tiny outdoor pool, restaurants and bar.

HYATT REGENCY MACAU, *2 Estrada Almirante Marques Esparteiro, Taipa Island, Tel. 831234, Fax 830195. Hong Kong Tel. 2559-0168, Fax 2540-9662. Http://www.hyatt.com. 326 rooms. 1280-1880 patacas for rooms and 3280-16000 patacas for suites. All credit cards. Free shuttle from the ferry terminal and Lisboa Hotel every 30 minutes 10:30am-8pm on weekdays, and to 10pm on weekends.*

A five km drive from the ferry terminal or four-minute three km drive from the airport, this luxury hotel has lots of sports facilities. The heated pool has a swim-up bar. It also has lit tennis and squash courts, gym, and aerobics. It has a program for children 5-12 years old and day care for younger ones. There's 24-hour room service, business center, and small casino.

Its romantic **Flamingo** restaurant is surrounded by tropical greenery and you find cheerful Portuguese ceramics everywhere. The food is unique, the product of a creative chef. Try the baked duck rice or cod. They are delicious. Outside, there's a good view of Macau, and you can rent bicycles or walk to two nearby temples and stores. Almost outside its gate is the Marine Park, *Tel. 973939, Fax 975131.*

WHERE TO EAT

Macanese cuisine is Portuguese with spicy Indian, Malay, African and South American influences. Enjoy it with Portuguese wine. Food in Macau is cheaper than in Hong Kong and jackets aren't required anywhere. However the service is slower, but that's what Macau is all about.

Macanese specialties are African chicken, curried crab, grilled prawns with garlic and chili, cod fish, grilled sardines, *caldo verde* soup (potatoes and sausage) and Brazilian *feijoados* (stews).

A LORCHA, *Macanese/Portuguese moderate. 289 Rua do Almirante Sergio, south near the Maritime museum on the mainland. Tel. 313195. It is open 12:30 noon-3:30pm, and 6pm-11:30pm and closed Tuesdays. It takes MasterCard and Visa.*

You get big portions here. Famous are its charcoal grilled codfish, seafood rice, stuffed squid, roast Portuguese sausage and clams.

FERNANDO'S *Portuguese. Moderate. 9 Hac Sa Beach, on Coloane Island. Tel. 882531. No cards.*

This cute, little place with checkered table cloths is one of Macau's most popular restaurants. It offers big portions and good country cooking. You have to try the delicious house-style clams (*ameijos a casa*) 98 *patacas*, or garlic prawns at 148 *patacas* a catty.

PIZZERIA TOSCANA, *Italian moderate. 1/F, Edificio de Apoio Ao, Grande Premio de Macau sito na Avenida da Amizade. Tel. 726637.*

This unpretentious and casual restaurant is near the ferry terminal to the left beyond the taxi rank. Especially good are its seafood *spaghetti* (58 *patacas*), and its *ravioli di spinaci e ricotta ai quattro formaggi* (60 *patacas*). The staff is friendly and efficient.

EMPEROR COURT, Cantonese moderate. *1/F, New World Emperor Hotel, Rua de Xangai, near the Holiday Inn on the mainland. Tel. 781888, Fax 782287.*

This has good innovative *dim sum* (10-25 *patacas* per plate), sweet and sour pork (50 *patacas*), and jumbo prawns with XO sauce (68 *patacas*). It accepts all cards.

SEEING THE SIGHTS

You can squeeze all of the major sights in one day. If you have two days or more, it is a wonderful place to explore on foot with lots of good hikes. It's even nicer to spend a relaxing week; there's more than what's listed here.

Downtown, you'll find the heart of Macau, along Avenida de Almeida Ribeiro. Here is the senate, its most beautiful church and other historic buildings. The Lisboa and Floating Casinos are nearby in opposite directions along this road. Here you will also find the post office and telecommunications bureau.

Leal Senado is the Royal Senate, currently the Municipal Council. Built in 1784, this yellow and white building is across the street from the main square. The **Largo do Senado** (Senate Square) is actually L-shaped and bordered by restored colonial buildings. The yellow and white building is the **Macau Tourist Office** where you can get free maps and brochures. At the north end of the square is **St. Dominic Church**, built 300 years ago in baroque style and open 10am- 6pm.

Behind the Leal Senado, southwest up the hill on Calcada Tronco Velho is **São Augustino Church** from the early 1800s. Beyond is the **Dom Pedro V Teatro** built in 1872. Then down towards Rua da Praia Grande are more churches and Government House. To the right, the Bela Vista now the Portuguese consul's home is on the hill.

South

It's a long walk from Government House to the **Maritime Museum** past the Bela Vista but do it if you have time and a good map. The museum has lots of real historic boats and some reproductions, a few hands-on displays, fish tanks, and a model of Macau in the 17th century. It offers half-hour cruises of the harbor four times a day. The museum is open 10am-5:30pm daily but not Tuesdays and has a snack bar. It's on *Largo do Pagode da Barra, No.1, Tel. 595481. E-mail: museu@macau.ctm.net.* (If you get an e-mail answer, you're doing better than I did.)

A-Ma Temple (Ma Kok Miu), 400 years old, is the oldest and most famous in Macau. It is across the street from the Maritime Museum. As you enter, spin the ball inside the lion's mouth three times to get rid of bad luck. Three of the temples here are dedicated to A-ma the sea goddess and one to the Buddhist goddess of mercy. It is open dawn to dusk and sometimes has beggars giving you a chance to earn merit. Look for mourners burning paper cars and money for the deceased. The **A Lorcha** restaurant is across the street.

West

It would be best to take a taxi from the A-Ma Temple to Monte Forte where you can check out the museum, and then walk 5-10 minutes down to Macau's most famous attraction, the fascinating facade of St. Paul's/ São Paulo Church. The **Citadel de São Paulo do Monte** on Monte Fort was built by Jesuits in the 1600s. The Jesuits invited the first Spanish governor for dinner. After the meal, the governor kicked his hosts out and took over. The Citadel is open 7am-6pm.

Ruins of São Paulo Church This handsome facade is Macau's most famous landmark and dates from 1602. Italian Jesuits designed it and exiled Japanese Christians helped build it. The facade formerly fronted the Church of the Mother of God also known as St. Paul's. This huge wooden church burned down in a typhoon in 1835.

East

Guia Fortress, Macau's highest point, built in the 1630s, is open 9am-5:30pm. It has the best view of the outer harbor and Taipa. The 1865 **Guia Lighthouse** is the oldest on the China coast. A cable car should help people who don't want to climb.

The **Macau Grand Prix Museum** is in the basement of the Tourism Activities Centre, next to the Forum and the Kingsway Hotel on *Rua Luis Gonzaga Gomes. Tel. 7984108.* The museum is open daily 10am-6pm and has a racing car simulator, and memorabilia from these annual November races. Admission is 10 *patacas*, children under 10 free. For information on the races, contact the Tourist Office.

In the same building is the **Macau Wine Museum** with similiar hours and a 20 *patacas* fee for adults. Children under 10 and seniors are free. *Tel. 7984188.* The museum is charming, centered on wine making in Portugal, and is well worth a visit.

The Islands: Taipa & Coloane

It's fun to rent a car or moke to explore Macau's islands for a couple of hours. Traffic is light apart from rush hours. Taipa Island was once home to pirates, but now makes firecrackers. On the north side of Taipa are the university, the Pou Tai Un Buddhist Temple and the Hyatt Hotel. Further south is the Jockey Club. On Macau's most beautiful street is the **Taipa House Museum** (1920s). You must see this area of former summer homes of wealthy Macanese. The museum is open 9:30am-1pm and 3pm-5:30pm, and closed Monday. Taipa village itself is full of cute little restaurants, shops and bakeries.

Coloane Island still builds junks and fishing boats and has nature trails and Macau's only beaches. Follow the coastal road to pleasant Coloane Village in the southwest corner. The small **Chapel of St. Francis Xavier** here was built in 1928. It houses the arm bone of the famous Jesuit missionary who died in 1552, close to Macau. A 20-meter tall statue of the sea goddess **A-Ma** can be seen on top of 170-meter-high Coloane Peak. Another 20-meter statue extending into the Outer Harbour, is of the **Goddess of Mercy**.

From here head to **Cheoc Van Beach**, Macau's nicest. This small beach has white sand and silty, not dirty, water. It has an outdoor pool and changing rooms. On the other side of the parking lot at **Hac Sa Beach** is **Fernando's** restaurant. See above.

NIGHTLIFE & ENTERTAINMENT

The main entertainment here is **gambling**. Macau has nine casinos with the same games known in the west, but sometimes with minor differences in rules. None of the casinos are as family-oriented or as big as in Las Vegas though the Lisboa and the New Century Hotels bear some similarities. All are open 24 hours with an 18 year old age limit.

The British East India Company held the first horse race on Hac Sa Beach in the 1790s. The **Macau Jockey Club** is on Taipa Island, *Tel.*

631317. The racing season is from September to June, sometimes at night. A free shuttle bus goes from the Lisboa Hotel.

The **Crazy Paris Show** is in the Mona Lisa Hall, Hotel Lisboa, *Tel. 577666.* Fourteen nude and semi-nude European women dance a burlesque-style show. The admission is about 200-250 *patacas.* Shows are 8pm and 9:30pm nightly. Saturday has an extra show at 11pm.

PRACTICAL INFORMATION

Hours: government offices, 9am to 1pm, 2:30pm to 5:45pm Monday-Friday; banks Monday-Friday 9 am-4:30 or 5pm, Saturday 9am to 1pm.

Macau Government Tourist Office, *No. 9, Largo do Senado, Macau, Tel. 315566, Fax 510104. E-mail:promgta@macau.ctm.net. Http:// macau.tourism.gov.mo.* Information Bureau: *Room 307, Yu Yuet Lai Building, 43-55 Wyndham Street, Central, Hong Kong, Tel. 852/2869-7862, Fax 2536-4244.* (A kiosk is in the airport buffer hall); *5757 West Century Boulevard, Suite 660, Los Angeles, CA 90045-6407, Tel. 877/MACAU-00, 310/670-2234, Fax 310/338-0708.*

Telephone code: *853*

24. RECOMMENDED READING

If you know nothing about China, start out with a general history like Brian Catchpole's *A Map History of Modern China,* an easy read (high-school level) with half maps and diagrams. You can graduate from that to *China, Yesterday and Today,* a paperback that you might want to take with you for background. This covers the history of China, its political life, agricultural policy, etc.

Good bedside reading and very informative are the *Wise Man from the West,* about Matteo Ricci's unsuccessful attempts to convert China to Christianity 400 years ago, and *Son of the Revolution,* an autobiography of a young Chinese who grew up on the wrong side of the political fence and married his American teacher. Son of the Revolution is imperative for anyone wanting to get an insider's look at today's system, how the various campaigns since 1949 have affected the kind of people that you will be meeting, and how some Chinese circumvent the rules and stifling bureaucracy.

Sterling Seagrave's *Soong Dynasty* is fascinating, about the Chinese Christian who was educated in America, and whose children controlled China's economy for several decades.

There' also Jung Chang's *Wild Swans,* an excellent story of three generations of women in one family in China and the U.S. And of course Amy Tan's *Joy Luck Club.*

For dynastic history, Raymond Dawson's *Imperial China* is another book to carry along -a good index and lots of juicy gossip about the likes of Tang Empress Wu and her boyfriends. For Beijing, read any biography of the Ming or Qing emperors and that of Empress Dowager Cixi (Tzu Hsi) and her boy friend. For Tibet, read Heinrich Herrar's classic *Seven Years in Tibet* or John Avedon's more recent *In Exile From the Land of Snows,* about the current Dalai Lama's life. Behr's *The Last Emperor* gives more background than the movie.

For British involvement in China, there's George Woodcock's *The British in the Far East,* about the bad, old, but interesting imperialists like Captain Charles 'Chinese' Gordon. For US involvement, there's John Fairbank's *The United States and China.* If you're interested in missionaries, try Pat Barr's *To China with Love* or Alvyn J. Austin's *Saving China-Canadian Missionaries in the Middle Kingdom, 1888-1959.*

For more recent history, Edgar Snow's *Red Star Over China,* not only relates the history of the Long March but has the only autobiography dictated by Mao. Also recommended is Jonathan D. Spence's *The Search for Modern China.* If you are concerned about human rights, get reports from Amnesty International. You probably won't be discussing Tiananmen Square; it's not of interest any more. But if you want some background, do read the Chinese versions obtained from Chinese missions abroad, as well as Western sources like Simmie and Nixon's *Tiananmen Square* or Gargan's *China's Fate.*

For the Cultural Revolution, the classic is Jean Daubier's *A History of the Chinese Cultural Revolution* and Roxanne Witke's *Comrade Chiang Ching,* one of the best books about Chairman Mao's widow. A best-seller in the late 1980s was Nien Cheng's *Life and Death in Shanghai* about the Cultural Revolution.

Among the modern Western novels, a lot of old China flavor is in Pearl S. Buck's *The Good Earth* and *Pavilion of Women.* Or try a Chinese novel. Gu Hua's *A Small Town Called Hibiscus* is very good as a book and movie.

If you're interested in Chinese arts and crafts, I would take along Margaret Medley's *A Handbook of Chinese Art,* Michael Sullivan's *The Arts of China,* or C.A.S. Williams's *Outlines of Chinese Symbolism and Art Motives.* These are all excellent reference books, profusely illustrated, that will help you appreciate the architecture, symbols, mythology, and customs of China. But do keep in mind that Williams's was written before 1949.

The authority on foot binding is Howard S. Levy's *The Lotus Lovers.* You can still find these shoes in antique markets and women with bound feet if you look.

Chinese periodicals can usually be found in bookstores in many Chinatowns. The best-stocked store for China books is **China Books and Periodicals**, *2929 24th Streeet, San Francisco, CA 94110. Http:// www.chinabooks.com.*

Many western periodicals now have their own correspondents in Beijing, and you should keep your eyes open for news reports about China before you go. *China Daily,* Beijing's English language newspaper, is printed also in New York City, San Francisco, and Hong Kong. Hong Kong's *South China Morning Post* has especially good China coverage. See our list of websites early in this book with sites for both. You might also find detailed maps of Chinese cities on the web.

READING LIST

Austin, Alvyn J. *Saving China - Canadian Missionaries in the Middle Kingdom, 1888-1959.* Toronto; University of Toronto Press, 1986.

Barr, Pat. *To China with Love-The Lives and Times of Protestant Missionaries in China, 1860-1900.* New York: Doubleday & Co., Inc., 1973.

Behr, Edward. *The Last Emperor,* Toronto: General Paperbacks, 1987.

Bernstein, Richard, and Munro, Ross H. *The Coming Conflict with China.* New York and Toronto: Alfred A. Knopf, Inc., 1997.

Coonay, Eleanor and Alteri, Daniel. *The Court of the Lion.* New York: Avon Books, 1989.

Coye, Molly Joel, etc., editor. *China, Yesterday and Today.* New York: Bantam Books, 1984.

Dalrymple, William. *In Xanadu, A Quest.* William Collins Sons & Co., London. Toronto, 1989.

Daubier, Jean. *A History of the Chinese Cultural Revolution.* New York, Toronto: Vintage Books, 1974.

Fairbank, John K. *The United States and China.* Cambridge: Harvard University Press, 1983.

Fitzgerald, C.P. *The Tower of Five Glories-A Study of the Min Chia of Ta Li, Yunnan.* West Point, CT: Hyperion Press, 1973.

Gargan, Edward A. *China's Fate-A People's Turbulent Struggle with Reform and Repression, 1980-1990.*

Gu Hua. *A Small Town Called Hibiscus.* Beijing: Panda Books, 1983.

Guisso, R.W.L. and Pagani, Catherine. *The First Emperor of China.* Toronto. Stoddart Publishing, 1989. In the U.S. Birch Lane Press, New York.

Haldane, Charlotte. *The Last Great Empress of China.* New York: Bobbs-Merrill, 1965.

Hopkirk, Peter. *Foreign Devils on the Silk Road.* New York: Oxford University Press, 1989.

Levathes, Louise, *When China Ruled the Seas,* paper back. 1996.

Levy, Howard S. *The Lotus Lovers, The Complete History of the Curious Erotic Custom of Footbinding in China.* Prometheus Books, Buffalo, N.Y. 1992.

Li Nianpei, *Old Tales of China* - a tourist guidebook to better understanding of China's stage, cinema, arts and crafts. Beijing: China Travel and Tourism Press, 1981.

Liang Heng and Shapiro, Judith. *Son of the Revolution.* New York: Vintage Books, 1984.

Lo Kuan-chung. *Three Kingdoms.* Robert Moss, translator and editor. New York: Pantheon, 1976.

McCawley, James D. *The Eater's Guide to Chinese Characters.* Chicago and London: The University of Chicago Press, 1984.

Richardson, Hugh E. *Tibet and Its History,* Boston and London: Shambala, 1984, Random House distributor.

Ryder, G., ed., *Damming the Three Gorges,* Toronto: Probe International, 1990.

Snow, Edgar. *Red Star Over China.* New York: Penguin, 1977 (first published 1937).

Spence, Jonathan. *God's Chinese Son, The Taiping Heavenly Kingdom of Hong Xiuquan.* London: Harper Collins, 1996.

Spence, Jonathan. *To Change China; Western Advisers in China, 1620-1960.* Boston, Toronto: Little, Brown, 1969.

Tsao Hsueh-Chin. *The Dream of the Red Chamber* (Hung Lou Meng), New York: The Universal Library, Grosset & Dunlop, 1973.

Turner-Gottschang, Karen, etc. *China Bound -A Guide to Academic Life and Work in the PRC.* Washington, DC: National Academy Press, 1987.

Van Slyke, Lyman P. *Yangtze: Nature, History and the River.* Reading, MA: Addison-Wesley: 1989.

Walker, Caroline et al. *On Leaving Bai Di Cheng,* the Culture of China's Yangzi Gorges. NC Press, Toronto, 1993.

Warner, Marina. *The Dragon Empress: The Life and Times of Tz'u- Hsi, Empress Dowager of China, 1835-1908.* New York: Macmillan, 1972.

Wu Zuguang. *Peking Opera and Mei Lanfang.* Beijing: New World Press, 1981.

25. CHINESE CHARACTERS

I have listed below as many Chinese characters or pinyin romanization as I could get for the names of restaurants, stores, and tourist attractions. You can communicate by pointing to them so non-English speakers will know where you want to go.

Each city is arranged alphabetically within its region. Within each area itself, I've alphabetized the listings for easy reference.

SOME IMPORTANT AGENCY LISTINGS

CITS 国际旅行社
CTS 中旅社
CAAC 中国民航

REGIONAL & SPECIAL FOOD

BEIJING DISHES (aka Peking or Northern) 北京
- Smoked chicken/duck 熏鸡/鸭
- Crispy duck 香酥鸭
- Peking duck 北京烤鸭
- Sweet-sour fish/pork 糖醋鱼/肉
- Stir-fried pork with bean sprouts (served with pancakes) 京酱肉丝
- Chinese cabbage with black mushrooms 冬菇白菜
- Pan-fried onion cake 葱油饼
- Hot and sour soup 酸辣汤
- Pan-fried dumplings with minced pork 生煎小包子
- Steamed bread rolls 银丝卷
- Assorted meat soup in casserole 什锦砂锅
- Shrimp with popped rice 虾仁锅巴
- Apple/banana fritter 拔丝苹果/香蕉

CANTONESE DISHES (aka Guangdong or Southern) 粤菜
- Deep-fried shrimp toast 炸虾托
- Crisp-skinned roasted goose/pork 烤鹅/烤乳猪
- Steamed chicken with green onion 葱油鸡
- Stir-fried diced fish/filet 松子鱼/炒鱼片
- Shark's fin soup 鱼翅羹
- Steamed live fish 清蒸鱼
- Quick-boiled fresh shrimp 白灼虾
- Stir-fried beef in oyster sauce 蚝油牛肉
- Cantonese stuffed bean curd 酿豆腐
- Sautéed fresh Chinese vegetable 炒新鲜蔬菜
- Assorted meats in winter melon 冬瓜盅
- Bird's nest in coconut milk 椰奶燕窝羹

DIM SUM DISHES 点心
- *Har gau*: smoothly wrapped shrimp dumpling 虾饺
- *Shui mai*: minced pork and shrimp dumpling 烧卖
- *Cha shiu bau*: barbecued pork buns 叉烧包
- *Tsun guen*: deep-fried spring roll with pork, mushrooms, chicken, bamboo shoots, and bean sprouts 春卷
- *Ho yip fan*: steamed fried rice wrapped in lotus leaf 荷叶饭
- *Pai gwat*: steamed pork spareribs 排骨
- *Gai chuk*: steamed chicken in bean curd wrapping 腐竹包鸡
- *Daan tart*: egg custard tart 蛋挞

FUJIAN DISHES 福建菜
- Five spices roll 五香卷
- Fried fish slices 炒鱼片
- Fried pig's kidneys 炒腰片
- Spareribs in sweet-sour sauce 糖醋排骨
- Fish with brown sauce 红烧全鱼
- Buddha Climbs the Wall 佛跳墙
- Shellfish in chicken soup 鸡汤海蚌
- Fried straw mushrooms with pork 草菇肉片
- Fried shrimps in sweet-sour sauce 糖醋虾
- Fried razor clams in sweet-sour sauce 糖醋鲜蚌

SHANDONG DISHES 山东菜
- Abalone with green vegetables on shell 鲍鱼青菜
- Fresh scallops with shell 鲜带壳干贝
- Roast prawns 烤大虾
- Conch with fire 火螺
- Steamed bread 馒头
- Sweet and sour croaker 糖醋黄花鱼
- Three delicacies soup 三鲜汤
- Toffee apples 拔丝苹果

SHANGHAI DISHES 沪菜
- Smoked fish 熏鱼
- Deep-fried shrimp balls 炸虾球
- Vegetarian vegetables 素什锦
- Sautéed fresh bamboo shoots 红烧冬笋
- West Lake fish 西湖醋鱼
- Chicken with cashew nuts 腰果鸡丁
- Scallops with turnip balls 干贝罗卜球
- Won-ton (dumplings) in soup 虾仁馄饨
- Beggar's chicken 叫化鸡
- Sautéed egg plant 红烧茄子
- Lion's head casserole 红烧狮子头
- Sweet sesame dumplings 芝麻汤圆

SICHUAN (SZECHUN) DISHES 川菜
- Smoked duck with camphor and tea flavor (not spicy hot) 樟茶鸭
- Stir-fried chicken with hot pepper 宫爆鸡丁
- Spicy stir-fried prawns 干烧明虾
- Stir-fried shrimp with peas 豌豆烧虾仁
- Stir-fried squid with/without hot pepper 金钓鱿鱼
- Bon-bon chicken 棒棒鸡

- Dry-fried string beans 干煸四季豆
- Steamed spareribs (or pork) coated with rice powder 粉蒸排骨
- Steamed fish with fermented black beans 豆豉鱼
- Ma-po bean curd 麻婆豆腐

SUZHOU DISHES 苏州菜
- Sautéed shrimp meat 清炒虾仁
- Squirrel mandarin fish 松鼠桂鱼
- Stewed turtle 清蒸元鱼
- Stir-fried eel 生炒鳝贝
- Fried crisp duck 香酥肥鸡
- Water-shield soup with floating Mandarin duck 鸳鸯炖菜汤
- Snow-white crab in shell 白雪蟹斗
- Pickled duck 苏州酱鸭

BEIJING 北京
Airport 北京机场
Baita shan (White Dagoba Hill) 白塔山
Baiyunguan (Temple of White Clouds) 白云观
Baohedian (Hall of Preserving Harmony) 保和殿
Beihai (North Sea) Park 北海公园
Beijing Arts and Crafts Co. 北京工艺美术公司
Beijing Department Store 北京百货大楼
Beijing Gu Tianwentai (ancient astronomical observatory) 古天文台
Biyunsi (Temple of Azure Clouds) 白云寺
Capital Museum 首都博物馆
Chairman Mao Memorial Hall 毛主席纪念堂
Chang Ling 长陵
China Art Gallery 中国美术馆
Confucian Temple 孔庙
Cultural Palace of the Nationalities 民族文化宫
Dazhongsi (Temple of Awareness of Life) aka Great Bell Temple 大钟寺
Diamond (Vajra) Throne Pagoda 金钢宝座塔
Ding Ling 定陵
Dragon King Temple 龙王庙
Fangshan Restaurant 仿膳
Fire 火警
Friendship Store 友谊商店
Gu Gong (Imperial Palace) 故宫
Hall of Dispelling Clouds 排云殿
Hall of Five Hundred Arhats 五百罗汉堂
Hall of Jade Ripples 玉栏堂
Jiaotaidian (Hall of Union) 交泰殿

Jingshan (Coal Hill) 景山
Kunninggong (Palace of Earthly Tranquility) 坤宁宫
Liulichang Cultural Street 琉璃厂
Lugouqiao (Reed Valley Bridge) aka Marco Polo Bridge 芦沟桥
Maolong Shop 懋隆商店
Monument to the People's Heroes 人民英雄纪念碑
Museum of the Chinese History 中国历史博物馆
Museum of the Chinese Revolution 中国革命博物馆
Niujie Mosque 牛街清真寺
Overseas Chinese Hotel 华侨饭店
Peking Roast-Duck Restaurant 北京烤鸭店
Police 警察
Qianmen Gate 前门城门
Qianqinggong (Hall of Heavenly Purity) 乾清宫
Quanjude Roast Duck Restaurant 全聚德烤鸭店
Railway Station 火车站
Renshoudian (Hall of Longevity and Benevolence) 仁寿殿
Shisan Ling (Ming Tombs) 十三陵
Sichuan Hotel 四川饭店
Summer Palace 颐和园
Taihedian (Tai Ho Tien; Hall of Supreme Harmony) 太和殿
Tan Zhe Si 潭柘寺
Temple of the Sea of Wisdom 智慧海
Tian'anmen Square 天安门广场
Tiantan (Temple of Heaven) 天坛
Tingliguan (Pavilion for Listening to Orioles) 听鹂馆
Tower of Buddhist Incense 佛香阁
Wangfujing Ave. 王府井
White Dagoba Monastery 白塔寺
Wofo Temple (Temple of Universal Spiritual Awakening) 卧佛寺
Xiangshan (Fragrant Hill) Hotel 香山饭店
Xiangshan (Fragrant Hill) Park 香山公园
Xiequyuan (Garden of Harmonious Interests) 谐趣园
Xinhua Book Store 新华书店
Yonghegong (Lama Temple) 雍和宫
Yuanmingyuan Ruins 圆明园
Zhonghedian (Hall of Complete Harmony) 中和殿
Zhongnanhai 中南海
Zhoukoudian 周口店

Embassies
Australia 澳大利亚大使馆
Britain 英国大使馆

Canada 加拿大大使馆
France 法国大使馆
Japan 日本大使馆
Mongolia 蒙古共和国大使馆
New Zealand 新西兰大使馆
Philippines 菲利宾大使馆
Poland 波兰大使馆
United States 美国大使馆

EAST CHINA

FUZHOU 福州
Baita (White Pagoda) 白塔
Friendship Store 友谊商店
Fujian General Antique Store 省文物总店
Gushan (Drum Hill) 鼓山
Hualin Temple 化林寺
Lingyuan Dong (Spirit Source Cave) 灵源洞
Memorial Hall of Lin Zexu 林则徐祠堂
Qianfo Taota (Thousand-Buddha Pottery Pagoda) 千佛陶塔
Shuiyun Ting (Water and Cloud Pavilion) 水云亭
Wuta (Black Pagoda) 乌塔
Wuyi Mountain 武夷山
Yongquan (Surging Spring) Temple 涌泉寺

HANGZHOU 杭州
Baidi Causeway 白堤
Beigao (North) Peak 北高峰
Cable car 缆车
Feilaifeng (Peak that Flew from Afar) 飞来峰
Gu Shan (Solitary Hill) 孤山
Hangzhou Botanical Garden 杭州植物园
Hangzhou Silk Printing and Dyeing Complex 杭州丝织厂
Hupao (Tiger) Spring 虎跑泉
Huagang Park 花岗公园
Jade Spring 玉泉
Liuhe Ta (Pagoda of Six Harmonies) 六和塔
Longjing (Dragon Well) 龙井
Longjingcun (Dragon Well Village) 龙井村
Meijiawu Tea Garden 梅家坞茶园
Mogan Mountain 莫干山
Pavilion for Storing Imperial Books 御书楼
Pinghu Qiuyue (Autumn Moon on Calm Lake Pavilion) 平湖秋月

Tidal Bore of the Qiantang River 钱塘江观潮
Tomb and Temple of Yue Fei 岳飞庙/岳坟
Wuling Guest House 武陵宾馆
Xihu (West Lake) 西湖
Xiaoyingzhou (Three Pools Mirroring the Moon) 小瀛州（三潭映月）
Yan'an Road 延安路
Yaolin Cave 瑶琳仙洞
Zhang Xiaoquan Scissors Shop 张小泉剪刀店
Zhejiang Hospital 浙江医院

HEFEI (HOFEI) 合肥
Cured Mandarin Fish 腌鲜桂鱼
Fuliji Braised Chicken 符离集烧鸡
Huangshan (Mt. Huangshan) 黄山
Jiuhuashan (Mount Jiuhua) 九华山
Lecturing Rostrum/Archery Training Terrace 教弩台
Ma'anshan (Horse Saddle Mountain) 马鞍山
Stewed Turtle 清炖马蹄
Temple of Lord Bao Zheng 包公祠
Wenzhengshan bamboo shoots and sesame cakes 问政山笋和芝麻糕
Wuhu 芜湖
Xiaoyaojin 逍遥津

HUANGSHAN MOUNTAIN 黄山
Cable car 缆车
Jade Screen Tower 玉屏楼
Lianhua (Lotus) Peak 莲花峰
Tiandu (Heavenly Capital) Peak 天都峰

NANJING 南京
Arts & Crafts Service 工艺美术服务部
Bamboo Garden 竹海
Botanical Garden 植物园
Dasanyuan Restaurant 大三元
Drum Tower 鼓楼
Foreign Languages Book Store 外文书店
Friendship Store 友谊商店
Jiangsu (aka Nanjing) Museum 江苏省博物馆
Linggu (Valley of the Soul) Temple 灵谷寺
Maxiangxing Moslem Restaurant 马祥兴菜馆
Meiyuan Xincun (Plum Blossom Villa) 梅园新村
Ming Palace 明宫遗址
Mochou (Sorrow-Free) Lake Park 莫愁湖

Nanjing City Wall 南京城墙
Nanjing Museum 南京市博物馆
Shanjuan Cave 善卷洞
Shitoucheng (Stone City) 石头城
Sichuan Restaurant 四川饭店
Southern Tang Tombs 南唐二陵
Stone Engravings of the Southern Dynasties 南朝石刻
Taiping Museum 太平天国历史博物馆
Tea Plantation 阳羡茶园
Xiaoling Mausoleum (Ming Tomb) 明陵
Xuzhou 徐州
Xuanwu Lake 玄武湖
Yuhuatai (Rain-Flower) People's Revolutionary Martyr's Memorial Park
Zhanggong Cave 张公洞　　　　　　　　　　雨花台烈士陵园
Zhonghua Gate 中华门
Zhongshan (Sun Yat-sen) Mausoleum 中山陵
Zijinshan (Purple Mountain) aka Bell Mountain 紫金山

NINGBO 宁波
Ayuwang (King Asoka) Temple 育王寺
Baoguo Temple 保国寺
Putuo Mountain 普陀山
Tiantong Temple 天童寺
Tianyige Library 天一阁

QUANZHOU 泉州
Heavenly Princess Palace 天妃宫
Islamic Tombs 圣墓
Old God Rock 老君岩
Overseas Chinese University 华侨大学
Qingjing (Grand Mosque) 清静寺
Tomb of Zheng Chenggong 郑成功墓
Tower of the Two Sisters-in-law 姑嫂塔
Wind-Shaking Rock 风动石

SHANGHAI 上海
Antique Branch of the Friendship Store 友谊商店古玩部
Antique Store 上海古玩商店
Arts and Crafts Store 上海工艺美术商店
Arts and Crafts Trading Corp. 上海工艺美术交易所
Botanical Garden 植物园
Confucian Temple 孔庙
Consulate of Australia 澳大利亚领事馆

Consulate of the United States 美国领事馆
Foreign Languages Book Store 外文书店
Former Residence of Zhou Enlai 周恩来故居
Friendship Store 友谊商店
Hongqiao Airport 虹桥机场
Huangpu Park 黄浦公园
Huangpu River boat trip 黄浦江游船
Industrial Exhibition Hall 工业展览馆
Jade Buddha Temple 玉佛寺
Jiading County 嘉定县
Longhua Pagoda and Temple 龙华塔/寺
Railway Station 火车站
Renmin (People's) Square 人民广场
Shanghai Museum 上海博物馆
Shanghai Tourism Administration 上海旅游局
Shanghai Zoo 上海动物园
Site of the First National Congress of the Communist Party of China
中国共产党第一次全国代表大会会址
Songjiang County 松江县
Square Pagoda 方塔
Statue and tomb of Soong Ching-ling 宋庆龄墓
Tang stone pillar 唐朝石柱
Yuyuan Garden 豫园
Zuibai Chi (Pond for Enjoying Bai's Drunkenness) Garden 醉白池

SHAOXING 绍兴
East Lake 东湖
Jianhu Lake 鉴湖
Lu Xun Memorial Hall 鲁迅纪念馆
Orchid Pavilion 兰亭
No. 2 Hospital 第二医院
Shen's Family Garden 沈园

SUZHOU 苏州
Canglang (Gentle Wave or Surging Wave) Pavilion 沧浪亭
Confucian Temple 孔庙
Hanshan (Cold Mountain) Temple 寒山寺
Huqiu (Tiger Hill) Garden 虎丘
Lingyan (Divine Cliff) Hill 灵岩
Liuyuan (Lingering-in) Garden 留园
Shizilin (Lion Forest) Garden 狮子林
Traveling along the Grand Canal by boat 大运河游船
Twin Pagodas 双塔寺

Wangshi (Fisherman's) Garden 网师园
Xiyuan (West Garden) Temple 西园
Yiyuan (Joyous) Garden 怡园
Zhuozheng (Humble Administrator's) Garden 拙政园

WUXI 无锡
Grand Canal 大运河
Huzhou 湖州
Huishan Clay Figures Factory 惠山泥人厂
Jichang (Entrust One's Happiness) Garden 寄畅园
Jiangyin 江阴
Liyuan Garden 蠡园
Longguang (Dragon Light) Pagoda 龙光塔
Meiyuan (Plum) Garden 梅园
No. 2 Spring under Heaven 天下第二泉
Taihu Lake 太湖
Xihui Park 锡惠公园
Yuantou Zhu (Turtle-Head Islet) 鼋头渚

XIAMEN 厦门
Arts and Crafts Factory 工艺美术厂
Anthropology Museum 人类博物馆
Botanical Garden 万石植物园
Ferry Quay 轮渡码头
Friendship Store 友谊商店
Gulang (Drum Wave) Island 鼓浪屿
International Airport 厦门国际机场
Lacquer Thread Sculpture Factory 漆绒雕厂
Overseas Chinese Museum 华侨博物馆
Railway Station 火车站
South Putuo Temple 南普院
Sunlight Rock 日光岩
Turtle Garden 鳖园
Xiamen Antique Store 厦门文物店
Xiamen No. 1 Hospital 厦门第一医院
Xiamen University 厦门大学
Zheng Chenggong Memorial Hall 郑成功纪念馆

YANGZHOU 扬州
Daming Temple 大明寺
Geyuan Garden 个园
Heyuan Garden 何园
Jian Zhen Memorial Hall 鉴真纪念堂

Shouxi (Slender West) Lake 瘦西湖
Yangzhou Museum 扬州博物馆

ZHANJIANG 湛江
Dashikou 大市口
Jiaoshan Hill 焦山
Jinshan (Golden Hill) 金山
Tongxing Restaurant 同兴楼饭店

NORTH CHINA

BAOTOU 包头
Carpet Factory 包头地毯厂
Kundulun Reservoir 昆都仑水库风景区
Nanhaizi Water Park 南海子水上公园
Tomb of Genghis Khan 成吉思汗陵墓
Wudang Temple 五当召

BEIDAIHE 北戴河
Pigeon's Nest 鹰角石
Temple of Goddess of Mercy 观音祠
Tiger Stone 老虎石

CHENGDE 承德
Anyuan Temple 安远庙
Canglang Islet 沧浪屿
Club Stone 磬锤峰
Friendship Store 友谊商点店
Hall of No Worldly Lust but True Faith aka Nanmu Hall 楠木殿
Imperial Library 文津阁
Imperial Summer Resort 避暑山庄
Jinshan Pavilion 金山亭
Mahayana Hall 大乘之阁
Outer Eight Temples 外八庙
Pule Temple 普乐寺
Puning Temple 普宁寺
Putuo Zongcheng Temple 普陀宗乘之庙
Qing Dynasty-style street 清朝一条街
Xumi Fushou (Longevity and Happiness) Temple 须弥福寿
Yanyu (Misty-Rain) Tower 烟雨楼

DATONG 大同
Brass Products Factory 铜器工厂

Foguang Temple 佛光寺
Friendship Store 友谊商店
Great Wall 长城
Huayan Monastery 华严寺
Nanchan Temple 南禅寺
Nine-Dragon Screen 九龙壁
Sakyamuni Wooden Pagoda at Fogong Temple 佛宫寺释迦塔
Shanhua Monastery 善化寺
Wutai Mountain 五台山

HOHHOT 呼和浩特
Dazhao Temple 大召庙
Great Mosque 清真大寺
Inner Mongolia Museum 内蒙古博物馆
Lingyin Temple 灵隐寺
Tomb of Princess Wang Zhaojun 王昭君坟
White Pagoda 白塔
Wuta (Five-Dagoba) Temple 五塔寺

JINAN 济南
Baotu Spring 豹突泉
Five-Dragon Pool 五龙潭
Heihu (Black Tiger) Spring Park 黑虎泉
Jiuding (Nine-Pagoda) Temple 九鼎寺
Lingyan Temple 灵岩寺
Liubu 柳阜
Pearl Spring 珍珠泉
Shandong Museum 山东博物馆
Simen (Four-Door) Tower 四门塔
Thousand-Buddha Hill 千佛山
Xingguo (Revive the Nation) Temple 兴国寺
Yellow Stone Cliff 黄茅岗
Yilan (Panoramic View) Pavilion 一览亭

QINGDAO 青岛
Antique Store 青岛文物商店
Arts and Crafts Shop 工艺美术商店
Badaguan Area 八大关
Former Residence of Pu Songling 蒲松龄故居
Huiquan No. 1 Bathing Beach 汇泉第一海水浴场
Jimo Hot Spring 即墨温泉
Laoshan Mountains 崂山
Lesser Qingdao Island 小青岛

Lu Xun Park 鲁迅公园
Marine Museum 青岛水族馆
Passenger Quay 客运码头
Pier 栈桥
Qingdao Museum 青岛博物馆
Railway Station 火车站
Shilaoren Beach 石老人海滩
Taiping (Great Peace) Taoist Temple 太平宫
Taiqing Taoist Temple 太清宫
Xiaoyu (Little Fish) Hill 小鱼山
Zhongshan Park 中山公园

QINHUANGDAO 秦皇岛
East Mountain 东山

QUFU 曲阜
Confucian Temple 孔庙
Confucian Mansion 孔府

SHIJIAZHUANG 石家庄
Cangyan Hill 苍岩山
Hebei Exhibition Hall 省展览馆
Longxing Monastery 隆兴寺
North China Revolutionary Martyrs' Cemetery 华北军区烈士陵园
Xibaipo Village 西柏坡
Zhaozhou Anji Bridge 赵州安济桥

TAI'AN 泰安
Daimiao (Temple of the God of Mt. Taishan) 岱庙
Nantian (Southern Celestial) Gate 南天门
Taishan Mountain 泰山
Tiankuang Hall 天贶殿
Tianzhu (Heavenly Pillar) Peak 天柱峰
Tomb of Feng Yuxiang (Feng Yu-hisang) 冯玉祥墓
Zhongtian (Middle Celestial) Gate 中天门

TAIYUAN 太原
Chongshan Monastery 崇善寺
Dingcun Village 丁村
Jinci Temple 晋祠
Pingyao 平遥
Shanxi Museum 山西省博物馆
Shengmu (Sacred Lady) Hall 圣母殿

Yongle Palace 永乐宫

TIANJIN 天津
Ancient Culture Street 古文化街
Dule (Solitary Joy) Temple 独乐寺
Friendship Club 友谊俱乐部
History Museum 天津历史博物馆
Panshan Mountain 盘山
Tianjin Museum of Natural History 自然博物馆
Zhou Enlai Memorial Hall 周恩来纪念馆

YANTAI 烟台
Bathing beach 海水浴场
Dengzhou 登州
Kongtong Isle 空峒岛
Penglai Pavilion 蓬莱阁
Xiguan Village 西关村
Yantai Museum 烟台博物馆
Zhangyu Wine Company 张裕葡萄酒厂

NORTHEAST CHINA

ANSHAN 鞍山
Qianshan Mountain 千山风景区
Tanggangzi Hot Spring Sanatorium 汤岗子温泉

CHANGCHUN 长春
Changchun Film Studio 长春电影制片厂
Chicken with ginseng 人参鸡
Chunyi Hotel 春谊饭店
Friendship Store 友谊商店
Frog oil soup 哈什蚂油汤
Fur Factory 长春市皮毛厂
Houtou (golden orchid monkey head) mushrooms 猴头菇
Jilin Antique Store 吉林省文物店
Nanhu Park 南湖公园
No. 1 Automobile Manufacturing Factory 长春第一汽车制造厂
Songhua Lake 松花湖
Thick deer antler soup 鹿茸羹
Wood Carving Factory 长春木雕工艺厂
Xinlicheng Reservoir 新立城水库

DALIAN 大连
Dalian Museum of Natural History 自然博物馆
Glass Factory 玻璃制品厂
Passenger Quay 客运码头
Railway Station 火车站
Tiger Beach Park 老虎滩公园
White-Cloud Mountain Park 白云山公园

HARBIN 哈尔滨
Ice Sculpture Festival 冰灯游园会
Miniature Railway 儿童铁路
Zhalong Nature Preserve 扎龙自然保护区

JINLIN 吉林
Jilin Exhibition Hall 吉林展览馆
Songhua Lake 松花湖

SHENYANG 沈阳
Beiling, North Tombs (aka Zhaoling) 北陵
Dongling, East Tombs (aka Fuling) 东陵
Imperial palace 沈阳故宫
Laobian Dumpling Restaurant 老边饺子
Qianshan Mountain Park 千山公园
Shenyang Steam Locomotives Museum 沈阳火车博物馆

NORTHWEST CHINA

ANYANG 安阳
Azure-Cloud Palace Temple 碧霞宫和大石佛
Linggu Temple 灵谷寺
Mausoleum of Yuan Shikai 袁林
Red-Flag Canal 红旗渠
Yin Ruins 殷墟
Yue Fei Temple 岳飞庙

DUNHUANG 敦煌
Cangjing (Preserving Buddhist Scriptures) Cave 藏经洞
Carpet Factory 地毯厂
Mingsha (Ringing Sand) Hill 鸣沙山
Mogao Grottoes 莫高窟
White Horse Pagoda 白马塔
Yangguan Pass 阳关
Yumen (Jade Gate) Pass 玉门关

JIAYUGUAN 嘉玉关
Bell and Drum Tower 鼓楼
Jiuquan 酒泉
Jiuquan County Museum 酒泉博物馆
Luminous Jade Cup Factory 玉杯厂
Wei and Jin Tombs 魏晋墓群

KAIFENG 开封
Guild Hall of Three Provinces 山陕甘会馆
Longting (Dragon Pavilion) 龙亭
Pota Pagoda 繁塔
Tie Ta (Iron Pagoda) 铁塔
Xiangguo Temple 相国寺
Yanqing Taoist Temple 延庆观
Yuwang (King Yu) Temple 禹王庙

KASHI 喀什（喀什噶尔）
Abakhojia Tomb 阿巴克和加麻扎
Hanoi 罕诺依
Kongur Mountain 公格尔冰山
Muztagtz Mountain 穆士塔格山
Sanxian (Three Immortals) Buddhist Caves 三仙洞
South Lake 南湖

LANZHOU 兰州
Baita (White Pagoda) park 白塔
Bingling Temple Caves 炳灵寺石窟
Maiji Grottoes 麦积山石窟
Tianshui 天水
Wuquan (Five-Fountain) Hill 五泉山

LUOYANG 洛阳
Arts and Crafts Store 工艺美术商店
Baima (White Horse) Temple 白马寺
Fengxian Temple 奉仙寺
Longmen (Lungmen) Grottoes 龙门石窟
Luoyang Museum 洛阳博物馆
Qiyun (Cloud Touching) Pagoda 齐云塔
Tomb of Lord Guan (Kuan Yu) 关林庙

TURPAN 吐鲁番
Astana Tombs 阿斯塔娜古墓
Flaming Mountains 火焰山

Gaochang 高昌故城
Hui 回族
Imim Minaret 额敏塔
Jiahoe (yarkhoto, Yaerhu)   交河故城
Karez wells 坎儿井
Pazikelik (Baziklic, Bazeklik) Thousand-Buddha Caves 柏孜克里克千佛洞
Uygur (Uighur) 维吾尔族

URUMQI 乌鲁木齐
Baicheng 拜城
Free Market/Bazaar 自由市场
Glacier 冰山
Hongdingshan (Red-topped Hill) Pagoda 红顶山塔
Nanshan Pasture 南山草原
National Minorities Palace 少数民族宫
Tianchi (Heaven) Lake 天池
Tianshan (Heaven) Mountain 天山
Urumqi General Carpet Factory 乌鲁木齐地毯厂
Xinjiang Museum 新疆博物馆

XI'AN 西安
Banpo (Panpo) Museum 半坡博物馆
Binxian County 彬县
Caotang Temple 草堂室
Famen Temple 法门寺
Great Mosque 大清真寺
Greater Wild Goose Pagoda 大雁塔
Horse and Chariot Pit 车马坑
Huxian County 户县
Huaqing Pool 华清池
Huashan Mountain 华山
Lesser Wild Goose Pagoda 小雁塔
Mausoleum of Emperor Qin Shihuang 秦陵
Museum of the Eighth Route Army 八路军西安办事处博物馆
Pits of Terra-cotta Warriors and Horses of the Qin Dynasty 秦俑坑博物馆
Qianling 乾陵
Tomb of Concubine Yang Yuhuan 杨贵妃墓
Ximen (West Gate) 西城门
Zhaoling 昭陵

XINING 西宁
Bird Island 鸟岛
Dongguan Mosque 东关清真寺

Golmud 格尔木市
North Mountain Temple 北禅寺
Qinghai Lake 青海湖
Taer Monastery 塔尔寺

YAN'AN 延安
10,000-Buddha Cave 万佛洞
Baota (Precious Pagoda) 宝塔（延安宝塔）
Former Residence of Chairman Mao 毛主席旧居
Huangling County 黄陵
Yan'an Revolutionary Memorial Hall 延安革命纪念馆

YINCHUAN 银川
Chengtian Monastery Pagoda 承天寺宝塔
Drum and Bell Tower 钟鼓楼
Great Wall 长城
Haibao (Sea Treasure) Pagoda (aka North Pagoda) 海宝塔
Hanyan Canal 汗延古渠
Helan Mountain 贺兰山
Jade Emperor Pavilion 玉皇阁
Mausoleum of the Emperor of the Western Xia Dynasty 西夏王陵
Qingtong Gorge 青铜峡
South Gate Mosque 南关清真寺
Tanglai Canal 唐徕古渠
Tongxin Mosque 同心清真寺
Twin Pagodas at Baizi Pass on Helan Mountain 拜寺口双塔
Xumi Mountain 须弥山
Yinchuan Museum 博物馆
Zhongda Mosque 中大寺

ZHENGZHOU 郑州
Astronomical Observatory 观星台
Dahe Village 大河村
Dengfeng county 登封县
Fawang Temple 法王寺
Gaocheng 告城
Han Tombs at Dahu (Tiger-hunting) Pavilion 打虎亭村汉墓
Huangcheng (Royal City) Mound 皇城岗
Mangshan Mountain 邙山
Mixian County 密县
Qimu Tower 启母阙
Shaolin Temple 少林寺
Shaoshi Tower 少室阙

Songshan Mountain 嵩山
Songyang Academy of Classical Learning 嵩阳书院
Songyue Pagoda 嵩岳寺塔
Talin (Dagobas) 塔林
Taishi Tower 太室阙
Zhongyue (Central Mountain) Temple 中岳庙

TIBET

Drepung Monastery 哲蚌寺
Jokhang Monastery 大昭寺
Norbulingka Park 罗布林卡
Potala Palace 布达拉宫
Sera Monastery 色拉寺
Tashilhunpo (Zhasilhunbu) Monastery 扎什伦布寺

SOUTHWEST

CHENGDU 成都
Arts and Crafts Shop 工艺美术商店
Chengdu Zoo 成都动物园
Cultural park 文化公园
Deer Farm 养鹿厂
Divine Light Monastery 宝光寺
Du Fu's (Tu Fu) Thatched Hut 杜甫草堂
Dujiang Dam Irrigation System 都江堰灌溉系统（灌溉工程）
Erwang (Two Kings) Temple 二王庙
Fulong (Dragon Subduing) Temple 伏龙观
Guanxian County 灌县
Meishan County 梅山县
Qingcheng (Green City) Mountain 青城山
Renmin Road 人民路
Sansu Shrine 三苏祠
Sichuan Museum 四川省博物馆
River-Viewing Pavilion 望江楼
The Institute of Wisdom 文殊院
The Temple of Marquis Wu 武侯祠
Tomb of Liu Bei 刘备墓
Tomb of Wang Jian 王建墓
Wolong Nature Preserve 卧龙自然保护区
Xindu 新都
Yanshikou 盐市口
Zhuge Liang Memorial Hall 诸葛亮殿

CHONGQING 重庆
Arts and Crafts Service 重庆二艺美术服务部
Cable Car 缆车
Chongqing Art Gallery 重庆美术馆
Chongqing Department Store 重庆百货公司
Chongqing Museum of Natural History 重庆自然博物馆
Eling (Goose Neck) Park 鹅岭公园
Friendship Store 友谊商店
Hongyan (Red-Crag) Revolutionary Museum 红岩村革命纪念馆
Sino-American Special Technical Cooperation (Concentration Camp)
中美合作所集中营

DAZU 大足
Baoding Mountain 宝顶山
Greater Buddha Bay 大佛湾
Lesser Buddha Bay 小佛湾
Thousand-armed Goddess of Mercy 千手观音

MT. EMEI 峨眉山
Anshun 安顺
Baoguo Temple 报国寺
Chaiguan Village 柴官村
Dragon Cave 龙宫
Guiyang 贵阳
Huangguoshu Waterfalls 黄果树瀑布
Huangping County 黄平
Jieyin Hall 接引殿
Kaili 凯里
Langde 郎德
Leishan 雷山
Rongjiang 榕江
Taijiang 台江
Tianxing No. 3 Parking Lot 天星三号停车场
Wannian Monastery 万年寺
Whirlpool 漩塘

KUNMING 昆明
Black Dragon Pool 黑龙潭
Butterfly Pool 蝴蝶泉
Daguan pavilion 大观楼
Golden Temple 金殿
Huating Temple 华亭寺

Institute of Nationalities 少数民族学院
Lijiang River 丽江
Longmen (Dragon Gate) 龙门
Qiongzhu (Bamboo) Temple 筇竹寺
Rice Noodles Crossing the Bridge 过桥米线
Sani 撒尼族
Santa (Three-pagoda) Temple 三塔寺
Sanyue (Third-month) Market 三月街
Shibao Mountain 石宝山
Shizhong Mountain 石钟山
Stone Forest of Lunan 路南石林
Taihua Temple 太华寺
Xishan (West Hills) 西山
Yulong (Jade Dragon) Mountain 玉龙山
Yuantong Temple 圆通寺
Yunnan Museum 博物馆
Zheng He Memorial Hall 郑和纪念馆

LESHAN 乐山
Giant Buddha 大佛
Wulong (Black Dragon) Temple 乌龙寺

WUHAN 武汉
Ancient Copper Mine in Tonglushan 铜禄山古铜矿
Antique Store 武汉古玩店
Arts and Crafts Store 工艺美术店
Friendship Store 友谊商店
Guiyang Temple (of Original Purity) 归元禅寺
Hankou (Hankow) 汉口
Hanyang 汉阳
Hongshan Pagoda 洪山宝塔
Hubei Antique Store 湖北古玩店
Hubei Military Government Building 武昌起义军政府旧址（红楼）
Hubei Museum 湖北省博物馆
Lesser East Gate 小东门
No. 1 Hospital, Wuhan Medical College 武汉医学院附一院
No. 2 Hospital, Wuhan Medical College 武汉医学院附二院
Port Passenger Transport Station 武汉港客运站
Uprising Gate 起义门
Wuchang 武昌
Wudang Mountain 武当山
Yellow Crane Tower 黄鹤楼

SOUTH CHINA

CHANGSHA 长沙
Aiwan Pavilion 爱晚亭
Fire 火警
Han Tombs 墓址
Hunan Antique Store 湖南省文物店
Hunan Arts and Crafts Shop 湖南工艺品商店
Hunan Embroidery Factory 湖南省湘绣厂
Hunan Museum 湖南省博物馆
Juzi (Orange) Island 橘子岛
Lushan Temple 麓山寺
Police 警察
Yuelu Academy 岳麓书院
Yuelu Hill 岳麓山
Shaoshan Road Department Store 韶山路百货商店

FOSHAN 佛山
Foshan Museum 祖庙博物馆
Institute of Folk Arts 佛山民间艺术研究社
Shiwan Ceramic Factory 石湾美术陶瓷厂
Silk Weaving and Spinning Mill 丝织厂

GUANGZHOU 广州
Air Australia 澳洲航空公司
Bank of China 中国银行
Banxi (Pan His) Restaurant 泮溪酒家
Beijing Road 北京路
Daxin Ivory Carving Factory 大新象牙工艺厂
Dr. Sun Yat-sen Memorial Hall 中山纪念堂
Foreign Trade Center 外贸中心
Friendship Store 友谊商店
Guangzhou Antique Store 广州文物店
Guangdong Arts and Crafts Service 广东工艺美述服务部
Guangdong Museum 广东省博物馆
Guangdong People's Hospital 广东人民医院
Guangta Smooth Minaret 光塔寺
Guangxiao Temple 光孝寺
Guangzhou Cultural Park 广州文化公园
Guangzhou Jewelry Center 广州市金银首饰总汇
Guangzhou Museum 广州市博物馆
Guangzhou No. 1 People's Hospital 广州第一人民医院
Guangzhou Porcelain and Pottery Shop 广州陶瓷商店

Guangzhou Restaurant 广州酒家
Guangzhou Zoo 广州动物园
Liuhua Park 流花公园
Liurong (Six-Banyan-Tree) Temple 六榕寺
Mausoleum of the Seventy-two Martyrs 黄花岗七十二烈士墓
Nanfang Department Store 南方大厦商店
Nanyuan Restaurant 南园酒家
National Peasant Movement Institute 广州农民运动讲习所
No. 1 Hospital, Zhongshan Medical College 中山医学院第一附属医院
No. 2 Hospital, Zhongshan Medical College 中山医学院第二附属医院
Orchid Garden 兰圃
Painted Porcelain Factory 广州金彩瓷工厂
Passenger Pier for Hong Kong 洲头咀客运码头（往香港）
Qingping Free Market 清平路自由市场
Railway Station 火车站
Shamian (Shamien, Shameen) Island 沙面岛
Shishi (Cathedral of the Sacred Heart) 石室
South China Botanical Garden 华南植物园
Traveling along the Pear River by boat 珠江游船
Xiyuan (West) Garden 西园
Yuexiu Park 越秀公园
Zhen (Chen) Family Temple 陈氏书院（陈家祠）
Zhongshan 5-Road 中山五路

GUILIN 桂林
Cave of Hiding Dragons 龙隐洞
Diecai (Folded Brocade) Hill 叠彩山
Fubo (Whirlpool) Hill 伏波山
Guilin Airport 桂林机场
Ludi (Reed Flute) Cave 芦笛岩
Qixing (Seven-Star) Park 七星岩
Xiangbi (Elephant Trunk) Hill 象鼻山
Yangshuo 阳朔

HAINAN ISLAND 海南岛
Dongshan Mutton 东山羊肉
Five Officials Memorial Temple 五公祠
Haikou 海口
Hele Crab 和乐蟹
Jiaji Duck 加积鸭
Monkey Peninsula 猴岛
Overseas Chinese Farm, Xinglong 兴隆华侨农场
Pearl Farm 珍珠场

Sanya 三亚
The End of the Earth and the Corner of the Sea 天涯海角
Tomb of Hai Rui 海瑞墓
Wenchang Chicken 文昌鸡
Yalong Bay 亚龙湾

JIUJIANG 九江
Causeway between Gantang and Nanmen lakes
甘棠湖和南门湖之间的长堤
Dasheng Pagoda 大胜塔
Yanshui Pavilion 烟水亭

MT. LUSHAN 庐山
Big Heavenly Pond 大天池
Grottoes of the Taoist Immortals 仙人洞
Guling Ridges 牯岭
Hanpokou (the Mouth that Holds Poyang Lake) 含鄱口
Mt. Lushan Botanical Garden 庐山植物园
Pavilion for Viewing the Yangtze 望江亭

NANNING 南宁
Arts and Crafts Service 工艺美术服务部
Foreign Languages Book Store 外文书店
Friendship Store 友谊商店
Guangxi Art College 广西艺术学院
Guangxi Botanical Garden of Medicinal Plants 广西药用植物园
Guangxi Museum 广西博物馆
Institute of Nationalities 广西民族学院
Nanhu (South Lake) Park 南湖公园
Nanning Antique Store 南宁古物店
Yiling Cave 伊岭洞

SHANTOU 汕头
Arts and Crafts Exhibition Hall 工艺展览馆
Chaoyang County 潮阳县
Chaozhou City 潮州市
Embroidery Factory 潮绣厂
Gourd Hill 葫芦山
Han Wengong Temple 韩祠
Jiaoshi Scenic Spot 石风景区
Kaiyuan Temple 开元寺
Lingshan Temple 灵山寺
Maya Bathing Beach 妈屿海滨浴场

Shantou City 汕头市
Wenguang Tower 文广塔
West Lake Park 西湖公园
Zhongshan Park 中山公园

TAISHAN 台山
Feisha Beach 飞沙里
St. Francis Xavier Church 沙勿略墓
Stone Flower Mountain 石花山

ZHAOQING 肇庆
Mateo Ricci Home 利玛窦
Seven-Star Crags 七星岩

ZHONGSHAN 中山
Cuiheng Village 翠亨村
Former Residence of Sun Yat-sen 孙中山故居
Shiqi 石歧
Zhongshan (Chung Shan) Hot Spring Golf Club 中山温泉高尔夫球会

ZHUHAI 珠海
Jiuzhou Islet 九洲岛
Pearl Land Amusement Park 明珠游乐场
Zhuhai International Golf Club 珠海国际高尔夫球场

INDEX

THINGS CHANGE!

Phone numbers, prices, addresses, quality of food, etc, all change. If you come across any new information, we'd appreciate hearing from you. No item is too small! Drop us an e-mail note at: Jopenroad@aol.com, or write us at:

China Guide
Open Road Publishing, P.O. Box 284
Cold Spring Harbor, NY 11724

TRAVEL NOTES

OPEN ROAD PUBLISHING

U.S.A.

National Parks With Kids, $14.95
Utah Guide, $16.95
Colorado Guide, $16.95
Hawaii Guide, $18.95
Arizona Guide, $16.95
Texas Guide, $16.95
New Mexico Guide, $14.95
Disneyworld & Orlando Theme Parks, $13.95
Boston Guide, $13.95
Las Vegas Guide, $13.95
San Francisco Guide, $16.95
California Wine Country Guide, $12.95
America's Cheap Sleeps, $16.95
America's Grand Hotels, $14.95
America's Most Charming Towns &
    Villages, $16.95
Florida Golf Guide, $16.95
Golf Courses of the Southwest, $14.95

MIDDLE EAST/AFRICA

Israel Guide, $17.95
Jerusalem Guide, $13.95
Egypt Guide, $17.95
Kenya Guide, $18.95

UNIQUE TRAVEL

New Year's Eve 1999!, $16.95
The World's Most Intimate Cruises, $16.95
Celebrity Weddings & Honeymoon
    Getaways, $16.95
CDC's Complete Guide to Healthy
    Travel, $14.95

SMART HANDBOOKS

The Smart Runner's Handbook, $9.95
The Smart Home Buyer's
    Handbook, $16.95

CENTRAL AMERICA & CARIBBEAN

Caribbean Guide, $19.95
Caribbean With Kids, $14.95
Central America Guide, $17.95
Costa Rica Guide, $17.95
Belize Guide, $16.95
Honduras & Bay Islands Guide, $16.95
Guatemala Guide, $17.95
Bermuda Guide, $14.95
Bahamas Guide, $13.95
Chile Guide, $18.95

EUROPE

London Guide, $14.95
Rome & Southern Italy Guide, $13.95
Paris Guide, $13.95
Moscow Guide, $15.95
Prague Guide, $14.95
France Guide, $16.95
Portugal Guide, $16.95
Ireland Guide, $17.95
Spain Guide, $18.95
Italy Guide, $19.95
Holland Guide, $15.95
Austria Guide, $15.95
Czech & Slovak Republics Guide, $18.95
Greek Islands Guide, $16.95
Turkey Guide, $18.95

ASIA

Japan Guide, $19.95
Tokyo Guide, $13.95
Tahiti & French Polynesia Guide, $17.95
China Guide, $21.95
Hong Kong & Macau Guide, $13.95
Vietnam Guide, $14.95
Thailand Guide, $17.95
Philippines Guide, $16.95

To order any Open Road book, send us a check or money order for the price of the book(s) plus $3.00 shipping and handling for domestic orders, to:
***Open Road Publishing**, PO Box 284, Cold Spring Harbor, NY 11724*